21st Century Seamanship

WITHERBY Seamanship INTERNATIONAL

Witherby Seamanship International

A Division of Witherby Publishing Group Ltd
4 Dunlop Square, Livingston, Edinburgh, EH54 8SB, Scotland, UK
Tel No: +44(0)1506 463 227 - Fax No: +44(0)1506 468 999
Email: info@emailws.com - Web: www.witherbyseamanship.com

First Edition Published 2015

ISBN: 978-1-85609-632-4

British Library Cataloguing in Publication Data
A catalogue record for this book is available from the British Library.

Printed by The Print Network, Penrith, UK

WITHERBY 1740 275 YEARS 2015

Published by

Witherby Publishing Group Ltd
4 Dunlop Square, Livingston,
Edinburgh, EH54 8SB,
Scotland, UK

Tel No: +44(0)1506 463 227
Fax No: +44(0)1506 468 999

Email: info@emailws.com
Web: www.witherbys.com

Preface

This book has taken ten years to prepare and, as a few have commented, it was probably in the planning long before then, whether I realised it or not.

A career at sea or in a marine-related business requires amassing a terrific volume of knowledge and the art and practice of seamanship is perhaps one of the most encyclopaedic job descriptions there is.

When I went to sea, almost 30 years ago, many would talk of days gone by when no self-respecting Chief Officer would be without his Seamanship Manual, and when I was about 12 or 13, I remember still the day my own father gave me his copy of *'The Boatswain's Manual'*. In recent decades, shipping seems to have moved at a tremendous pace and it left me wondering whether it was possible to capture such a broad scope in a single publication that appeals to the forward thinking seafarer. This is exactly where this book positions itself – a manual for the modern day seafarer in the 21st Century.

This publication takes the traditional values of centuries of good seamanship and blends them with today's reality and it seems appropriate that it is first published in our company's 275th year.

By its very nature, this book is exceptionally broad in its scope and further detailed study of the topics covered in this book is available in the 600+ publications Witherbys has in print today. However, in owning this book, you have shown that you want to know and understand more about your industry, an industry that quietly keeps the world moving, carries over 90% of world trade and is set to almost double in volume over the next 20 years.

I wish you every success in your endeavours and always a safe voyage.

Iain Macneil
Managing Director
Witherby Publishing Group

Foreword

The term 'seamanship' is much misunderstood by those who are not required to practise the art. Seamanship is also hard to define succinctly as the breadth of knowledge, skills and experience the term encompasses take many a lifetime to acquire.

When I arrived aboard my first ship a little over forty years ago, the ships that made up the world's merchant fleets, the technologies employed on board and the regulations that governed the industry, and indeed the seafarers themselves, bore little in common with today. However, despite all the technologies that connect ship and shore and keep communications links open at all times, the fact remains that, once a ship puts to sea, it is primarily dependent upon the actions of the master and crew to safely and efficiently execute the voyage, bringing profit to the owner whilst making sure all aboard return safe and well on completion. All must depend on each other, in a variety of circumstances; the ability to perform the broad range of tasks required safely and efficiently, whilst being fully aware of the associated hazards and mitigating measures, is in the broadest sense 'seamanship'.

The technological advances seen today have led to the launching of more and more specialist ships, all requiring equally specialist knowledge to operate them. There is a danger that the rate of technological advance outpaces the ability of the industry to train competent mariners to operate the increasingly complex ships on which they serve. The need for continued professional development for mariners is inarguable, but this can be difficult to achieve when many ships cannot provide access to the online references enjoyed by most other industries, a problem that has yet to be universally solved. That said, traditional knowledge and skills are still required as it is a stark fact that mooring accidents, lifeboat launching and enclosed space entry continue to kill and injure the unwary, as they have for many decades.

The inclusion in this book of significant incidents in sufficient detail to allow the reader to extract and apply the learning is so valuable as, without doubt, poor decisions and behaviours contribute to far too many accidents at sea. This book provides a solid foundation of knowledge to all those operating, managing and manning today's merchant fleet. I hope that 21st Century Seamanship will be a reference that is ready to hand on every ship and in every shipping company reference library.

David Cotterell
Director, OCIMF
June 2015

David Cotterell joined the Shell Group of companies as a Junior Deck Officer in 1975 and quickly rose in rank to Master within the Shell Fleet. David gained experience in the operation of Crude, Product, LNG, LPG, Chemical, Bulk Carriers and FPSO and FSUs during a seagoing career spanning 18 years. David began his shore career in fleet management in 1993 and has since enjoyed a series of maritime roles in Shell, joining the shipping leadership team in the position of General Manager Maritime Standards and Governance in 2005.

In 2010, David was appointed as the Director of Oil Companies International Marine Forum (OCIMF). Under his strong and diligent leadership, OCIMF is now widely recognised as the foremost authority on the safe and environmentally responsible operation of oil tankers, terminals and offshore support vessels, promoting continuous improvement in standards of design and operation. David is well respected by all stakeholders that he has touched, including the OCIMF membership, Governments, military leaders and a broad spectrum of industry. His professional management style, and deep technical and safety knowledge, is highly regarded across the maritime industry. David retired from Shell in June 2015.

Bibliography – Publications

ABS: Design Against Contact Damage for Offshore Supply Vessels

American Institute of Marine Underwriters Technical Services Committee "On Deck Stowage of Containers"

Australian Safety Transport Bureau Investigation into the Grounding of the Container Ship 'Bunga Teratai Satu'

Australian Safety Transport Bureau Investigation into the Loss of 'Mineral Diamond'

'Best Practice Recommendations Regarding the Use of Nitrogen' by CDI

BP: Statistical Energy Review 2014

Brookes Bell: Carriage of Sulphur

'Bulk Carrier Notes' by Abdul Khalique, published by Witherby Seamanship

'Captains Legal' by Michael Lloyd, published by Witherby Seamanship

'Cargo Notes' by Dhan Swadi, published by Witherby Seamanship

'Checklists - Masters Pocket Book' by Michael Lloyd, published by Witherby Seamanship

'Crude Oil Tanker Basics' by Paul Armitage, published by Witherby Seamanship

DNV, Feb 2008: Bulk Carrier Safety: The Latest IMO Developments

Equasis: Annual Report 2012

EU Council Directive 98/83/EC

Fairplay: Dredging Without a Dredger

Final Report- Research Study on the Sinking Sequence of MV Estonia SSPA Consortium

'FPSO Handbook' by Angus Mather, published by Witherby Seamanship

'Fresh Air in Dark Places' by Olaf Olsen, published by Witherby Seamanship

General Council of British Shipping 'Marine Safety Card No. 1'

Hapag Lloyd Press Release: Grand Alliance Member MISC withdraws from Far East Services - No Impact to Service Structure, 18 May 2009

Horizon Line, on the horizon, Summer 2010 Issue

IACS 'Confined Space Safe Practice'

IACS 'Ship Structure Access Manual' Recommendation No. 90, Oct 2005

'IMPA on Pilotage' by IMPA, published by Witherby Seamanship

'In Command' by Michael Lloyd, published by Witherby Seamanship

International Safety Guide for Oil Tankers and Terminals, 5th Edition (ISGOTT)

'Lifeboat Release Hooks', published by Witherby Seamanship

'Liquefied Gas Handling on Ships and in Terminals' by SIGTTO, published by Witherby Seamanship

'Liquefied Gases Marine Transportation and Storage' by Alain Vaudolon, published by Witherby Seamanship

Lloyd's Register: A Master's Guide to Container Securing

'Lloyd's Register Risk Assessment of Emergency Tow-off Pennant Systems (ETOPS) Onboard Tank Vessels' Information Paper, published by OCIMF, First Edition October 2009

'LNG Operational Practice', published by Witherby Seamanship

'LNG Shipping Knowledge', published by Witherby Seamanship

Maersk News Release: Charlotte Maersk AE11 – Fire onboard

MAIB: Report on the Investigation of the Loss of the Tug Flying Phantom while Towing Red Jasmine on the River Clyde

MAIB: Report on the Investigation of the Structural Failure of MSC Napoli

'Master's Guide to Container Securing', published by the Standard Club

MNTB Training Course 'Entry into Enclosed Spaces'

'Navigation Advanced Mates/Masters' by Nadeem Anwar, published by Witherby Seamanship

'Onboard Safety' by Gary Ritchie, published by Witherby Seamanship

Pennsylvania State University: Containerized Freight Rate Trends 2008

'Pocket Safety Guide - Fire Extinguishers', published by Witherby Seamanship

'Pocket Safety Guide - Lifting Appliances', published by Witherby Seamanship

'Pocket Safety Guide - Manual Handling', published by Witherby Seamanship

'Pocket Safety Guide - Permit to Work', published by Witherby Seamanship

'Response to Marine Oil Spills' by ITOPF, published by Witherby Seamanship

Rolls-Royce 'Steering and Stabilisation'

'Salvage of the Cougar Ace' by Wired.com

SeaNews Turkey: Maersk Sembawang, Biscay

'Shipboard Drills', published by Witherby Seamanship

'Shipboard Safety Officer Notes' by Abdul Khalique, published by Witherby Seamanship

'Shipping Regulations & Guidance', published by Witherby Seamanship

'Ship Squat and Interaction' by Dr CB Barrass, published by Witherby Seamanship

'Ship Stability for Mates/Masters' by Martin Rhodes, published by Witherby Seamanship

'Ship to Ship Transfer Guide 2013' by CDI, ICS, OCIMF and SIGTTO, published by Witherby Seamanship

'Tanker Jetty Safety', published by Witherby Seamanship

'Tanker Safety Training - Liquefied Gases', published by Witherby Seamanship

The Business Times Weekend: 7 Shipping Giants form Super Alliance Against Maersk Line

'The Complete Chief Officer' by Michael Lloyd, published by Witherby Seamanship

'The ECDIS Manual' by ECDIS Ltd, published by Witherby Seamanship

'The Ice Navigation Manual' by House, Lloyd, Toomey & Dickens, published by Witherby Seamanship

The International Safety Management (ISM) Code: A New Level of Uniformity, by Antonio J Rodriguez, Mary Campbell Hubbard, Fowler, Rodriguez, Kingsmill, Flint, Gray & Chalos, LLP New Orleans, Louisiana (http://www.frc-law.com/files/pub_ISM.pdf)

'The Pocket Book of Anchoring' by Michael Lloyd, published by Witherby Seamanship

UK P&I Club - 'Carefully to Carry: Carriage of Forestry Products'

UNCTAD Review of Maritime Transport 2013

USCG Ship's Safety Bulletin January-March 2011

'Validating Safety on Commercial Fishing Vessels' Sponsoring Agency: United States Coast Guard Forrest Dwyer, Michael Mourkas, Heather Sebastian. 2010

Welding in cargo hold sets fire in containership/'Professional Mariner' Aug/Sept 2003

Wilden's Pump User's Guide II (PUG II)

Bibliography – Codes of Practice

A.1045(27), "Recommendation on Pilot Transfer Arrangements" adopted on 30 November 2011

'BLU Code', published by IMO

Code of Safe Working Practices for Merchant Seamen

Health and Safety Executive 'Guidance Note EH-40 Occupational Exposure Limits'

HSC Approved Code of Practice L8 for the Control of Legionella

IMO Resolution A.864(20) 'Recommendations for Entering Enclosed Spaces Aboard Ships'

IMO, SOLAS, Ch XII Reg 12

'IMSBC Code', published by IMO

'International Code for the Construction and Equipment of Ships Carrying Liquefied Gases in Bulk' (IGC Code), published by IMO

IRATA International Code of Practice

ISO 799:2004, Ships and marine technology - Pilot ladders

MCA Marine Guidance Note 397, Guidelines for the Provision of Food and Freshwater

MGN 199, Dangers of Interaction

'The Code of Safe Working Practices for Merchant Seamen (COSWP)', Chapter 17 (Entering Enclosed or Confined Spaces)

UK MCA MGN 423(M) 'Entry into Dangerous Spaces'

UK Merchant Shipping (Emergency Equipment Lockers for RoRo Passenger Ships) Regulations 1988

Water Supply (Water Quality) Regulations 2000

WHO Health and Sanitation Document GDW5 parts 1 and 2

Bibliography – Websites

Amphibia UK Limited:http://www.amphibia.co.uk

Basel Convention: http://www.basel.int/

Countryman & McDaniel, Case of MV *'Ville De Orion'*: http://www.cargolaw.com/2001nightmare_orion.html

Globalsecurity.org, Container Ship Types: http://www.globalsecurity.org/military/systems/ship/container-types.htm

Hollenbach and Friesch, 'Efficient hull forms – What can be gained': http://www.ship-efficiency.org/2007/PDF/HOLLENBACH_FRIESCH.pdf

International Chamber of Shipping, 'Paper FP 54 – Information on Inert Gas': https://www.scribd.com/doc/57495726/ICS-Paper-FP-54-Information-on-Inert-Gas

Marine Accident Investigation Branch, *'Star Princess'* investigation report: https://assets.digital.cabinet-office.gov.uk/media/547c706ae5274a4290000097/Star_Princess.pdf

Maritime & Coastguard Agency Press Office: http://hmcoastguard.blogspot.co.uk

Maritime New Zealand, 'Vessel Stability Guidelines': https://www.maritimenz.govt.nz/Publications-and-forms/Commercial-operations/Shipping-safety/Vessel-Stability-Guidelines-A4.pdf

MCA Merchant Shipping Notices: http://www.gov.uk/government/collections/merchant-shipping-notices-msns

Seafish, 'Fishing Vessel Safety Folder': http://www.seafish.org/media/Publications/SafetyFolder_052007.pdf

The American Society of Safety Engineers: http://www.asse.org

The International Marine Contractors Association, 'Guidance on the Transfer of Personnel to and from Offshore Vessels and Structures': http://www.imca-int.com/documents/core/sel/docs/IMCASEL025.pdf

The International Tanker Owners Pollution Federation, Dispersants: http://www.itopf.com/knowledge-resources/documents-guides/clean-up-techniques/dispersants/

The Standard, 'Standard Safety, July 2010': http://www.standard-club.com/media/23827/StandardSafetyPersonnelTransferJuly2010.pdf

Water Regulations Advisory Scheme: http://www.wras.co.uk

CONTENTS

CHAPTER 1

General Cargo Ship Types

Total World Fleet:

>1,000 GT = 47,601

Source: UNCTAD Review of Maritime Transport 2014

Following an annual growth of 4.1% in 2013, the world fleet reached a total of 1.69 billion Dwt in January 2014. Bulk carriers accounted for 42.9% of the total tonnage, followed by oil tankers (28.5%) and container ships (12.8%). The 2013 annual growth was lower than that observed during any of the previous 10 years and the trend in early 2014 suggests an even lower growth rate for the current year. The slowdown reflects the turning point of the largest historical shipbuilding cycle, which peaked in 2012.

Cargo Ships (Bulk, Container, General, RoRo)

General Cargo >500 GT	= 11,871 ships
Container Ships >500 GT	= 4,878 ships
Bulk Carriers >500 GT	= 10,039 ships
RoRos >500 GT	= 1,422 ships

Source: Equasis: Annual Report 2013

Average age

General Cargo	= 24 years
Container Ships	= 11 years
Bulk Carriers	= 9 years

Source: UNCTAD Review of Maritime Transport 2014

Bulk Carriers

Total Dry Bulk Fleet

10,039 ships

Source: Equasis Annual Report "The World Merchant Fleet in 2013"

Bulk carriers make up 40% of the world's shipping – generally referred to as the bulk fleet.

They range in size from 500 Dwt for a mini bulk carrier to 400,000 Dwt for a valemax VLOC (very large ore carrier). They are used to transport a wide variety of cargoes, including iron ore, grain, coal and cement.

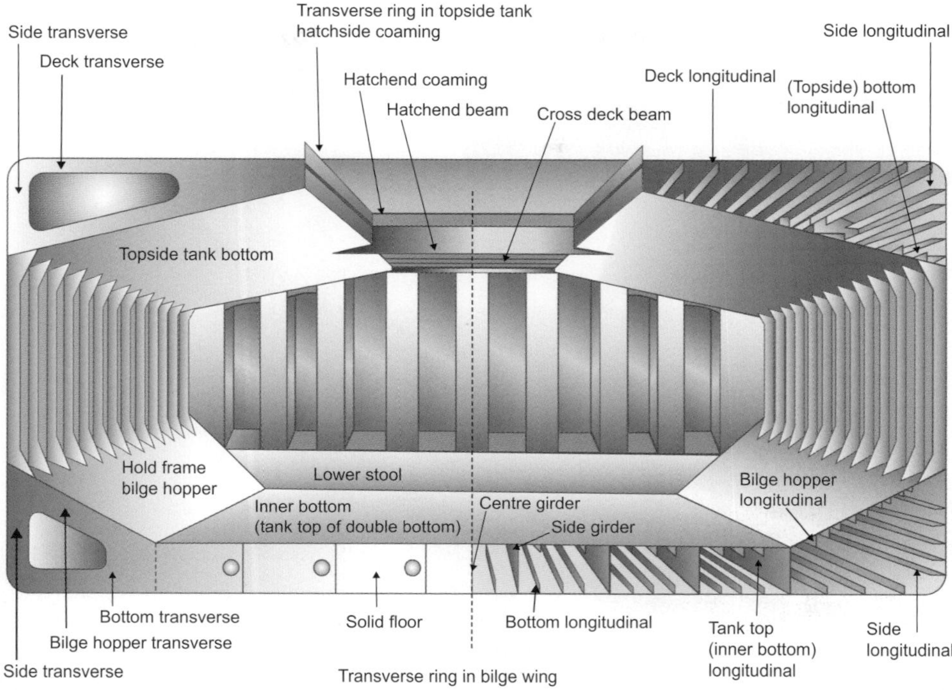

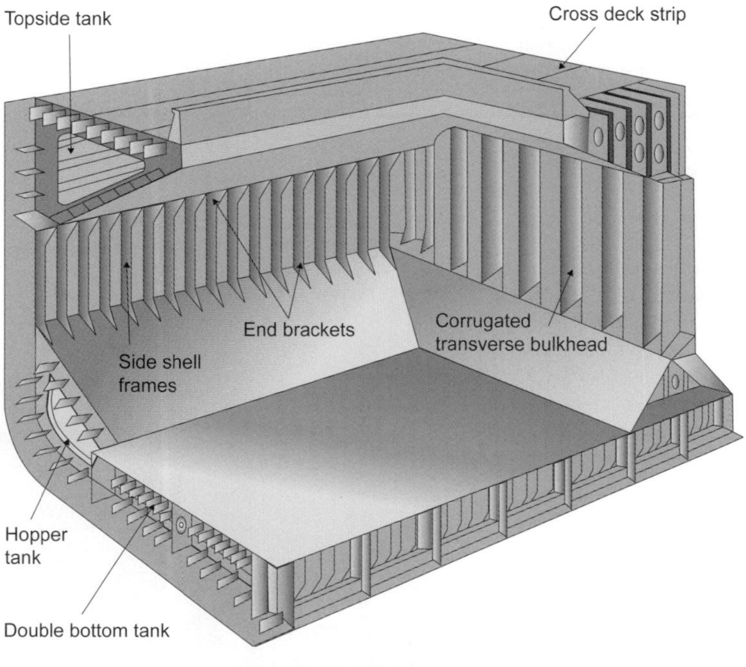

Figure 1.1 - Cross section of a typical Bulk Carrier

Types of Bulk Carriers

Mini Bulk Carriers

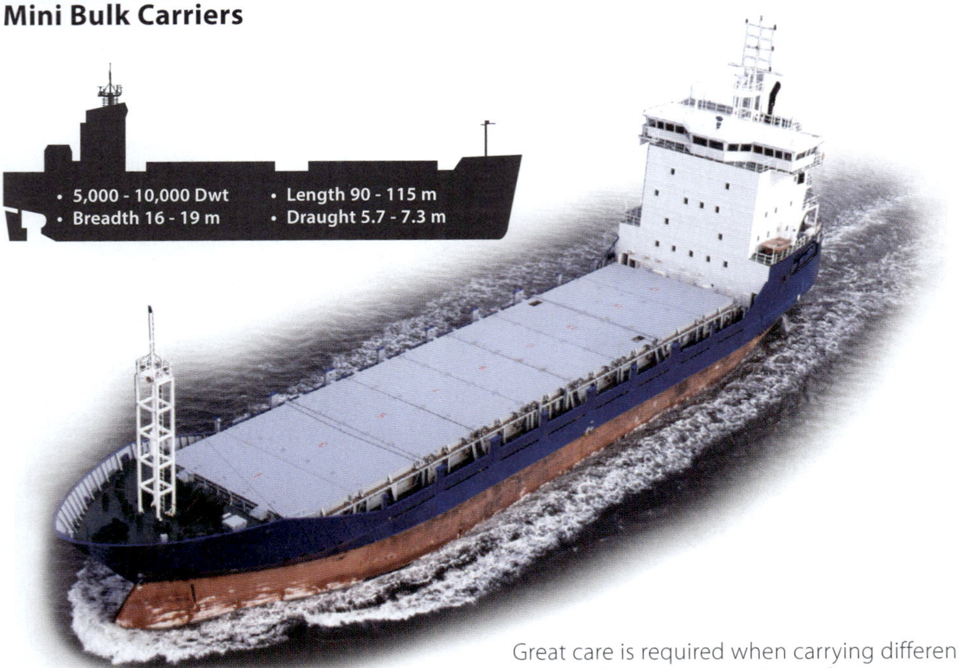

Mini bulk carriers range between 500 and 10,000 tonnes, the smaller generally being single hold. They can be used for many different cargoes and some are equipped with gantry cranes. Many are fitted with moveable bulkheads that give the ships greater flexibility.

Great care is required when carrying different commodities, and in particular finer grain, to avoid leakage around the sides of the bulkhead.

These ships are often poorly manned and this, coupled with the frequent port visits, often leads to severe fatigue problems among the crew.

Handysize

Handysize carriers range between 10,000 and 40,000 Dwt. They generally have five hatches and many are fitted with cranes, which provide the flexibility to load and discharge at berths without such facilities. The smaller vessels can take other cargoes, including containers and deck cargo, as well as bulk. Handysize and Handymax carriers are general purpose vessels and make up approximately 70% of the worldwide bulker fleet.

Handysize Fleet

Vessels (grain and minor bulks) 10,000 - 40,000 Dwt 3,065 vessels.

Source: www.simic.net.cn

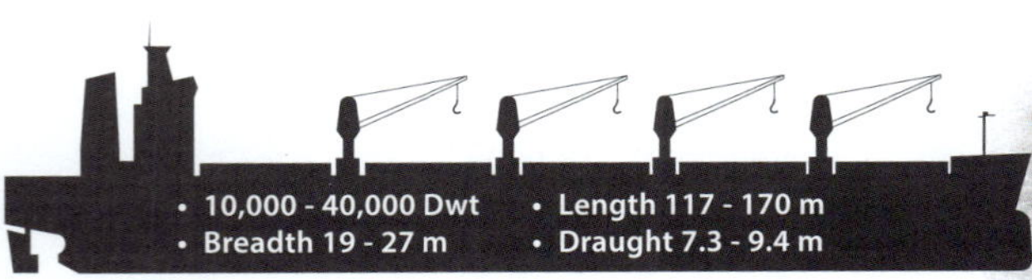

Geared Bulk Carriers

In the Handysize/Handymax range, there is a small percentage of geared Panamax vessels that have cranes, derricks or conveyors that allow them to load or discharge cargo in ports without shore-based equipment.

The fact that these vessels are called bulk carriers can be misleading. They do carry bulk cargoes, but their gantries, hold shapes and hatch top configurations mean they are also capable of carrying containers and a mix of general cargo.

Handymax

(Grain and minor bulks)
40,000 - 60,000 Dwt
2,504 vessels

Source: www.simic.net.cn

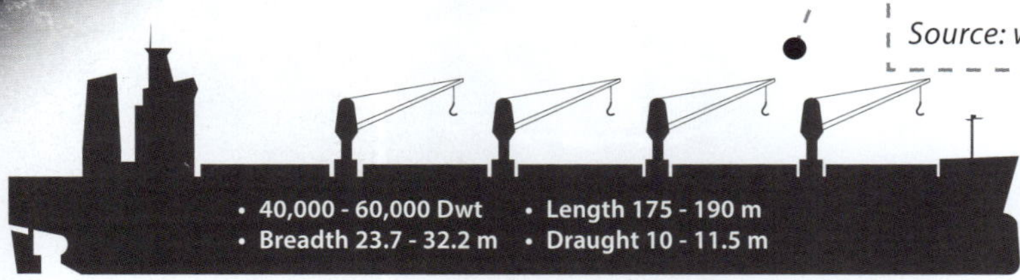

40,000 to 60,000 Dwt ships are referred to as Handymax or Supramax.

Types of Bulk Carriers

Woodchip Carriers

Woodchip carriers are designed to carry woodchips (shredded wood) in bulk. They are usually constructed with six watertight (rather than weathertight) cargo holds to prevent water ingress. This is particularly important as contact with water causes woodchips to expand, which could cause severe structural damage to the ship. Additional security measures are also incorporated to protect the cargo, such as prevention of water penetration through air pipes and ventilation ducts.

Carriage capacities are usually expressed in cubic feet (or metres). For example, a Panamax size woodchip carrier has a capacity of 3.6 million cubic feet (CFT). Some ships are fitted with cargo loading and unloading equipment, including cranes, grab buckets and wings. Conveyor belts on deck are used to pour the chips into cargo holds. As the cargo holds fill, bulldozers are used to compress the cargo. When discharging, the ship's cranes are used together with a grab bucket system running along the bottom of the cargo compartments. The cargo is carried to the forecastle by conveyor, where it is discharged ashore through a single discharging point. However, many ships use conventional grabs to discharge the cargo.

The market for woodchip pellets, driven by EU subsidies and emissions regulations, could result in a 5-10% share of use in coal-fired plants, according to IHS CERA. Across Europe, demand surpassed 5M tonnes in 2010 and was estimated at 7.5M in 2013.

Panamax

Panamax

(Iron ore, coals and grain) 2,066 vessels

Source: www.simic.net.cn

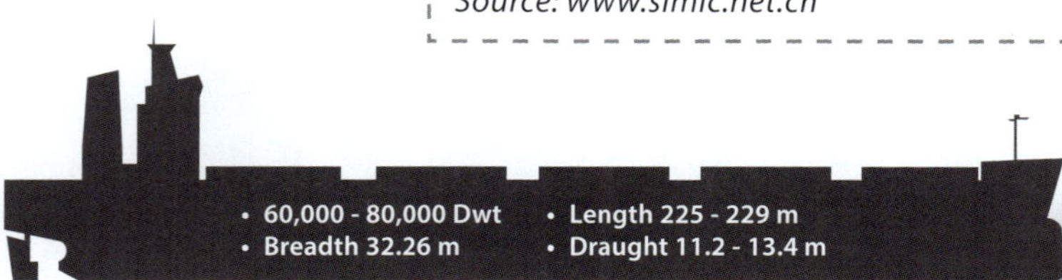

These vessels range from 60,000 Dwt to around 80,000 Dwt. The term 'Panamax' indicates that the vessel has been designed within the size limitations for passage through the Panama Canal.

Capesize

Capesize
(Iron ore and coal) 1,182 vessels
Source: INTERCARGO

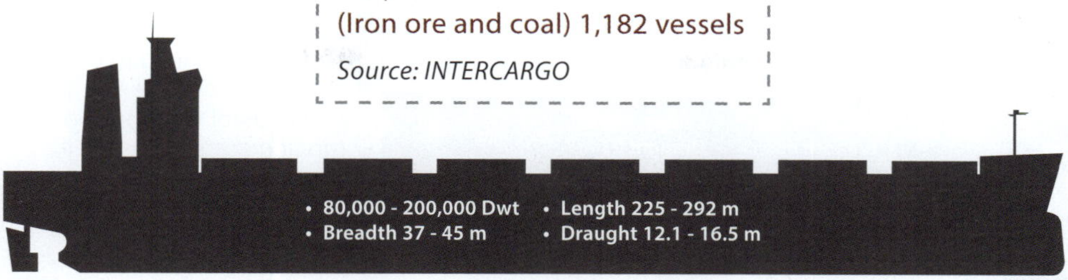

Capesize carriers are too large to pass through the Panama or Suez Canals so are required to make passage around the Capes. Bulk carriers of this size, which are in the range of 80,000 to 200,000 tonnes, tend to carry one specific type of cargo. The vast majority are engaged in carrying iron ore or coal. Specialist knowledge of the dangers of these cargoes is required, as well as a comprehensive knowledge of ship stability and the stresses experienced in a seaway.

Very Large Bulk Carriers

Very large bulk carriers (VLBC) are in the range of 200,000 to 320,000 Dwt. Ultra large bulk carriers (ULBC) are above 320,000 Dwt. These ships have all the problems associated with Capesize carriers and their handling is very specialised, particularly in confined waters and at slow speeds. Predominant cargoes are coal and iron ore.

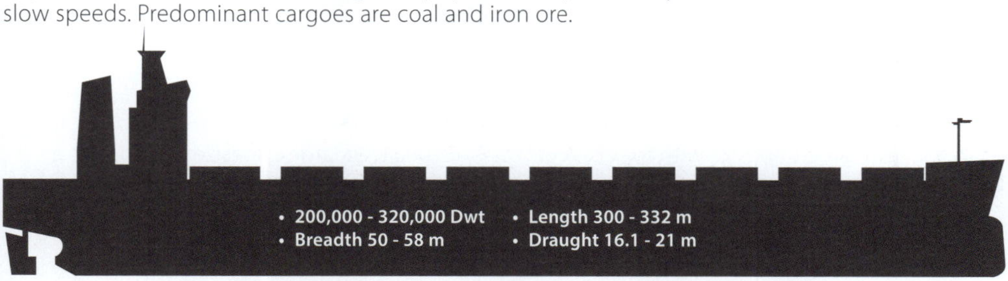

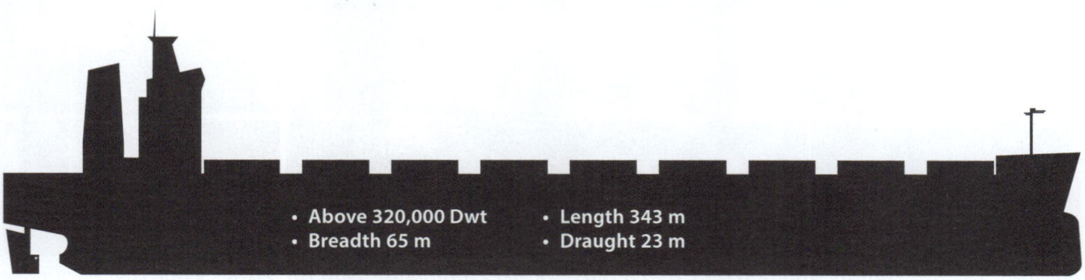

Types of Bulk Carriers

Valemax (VLOC)

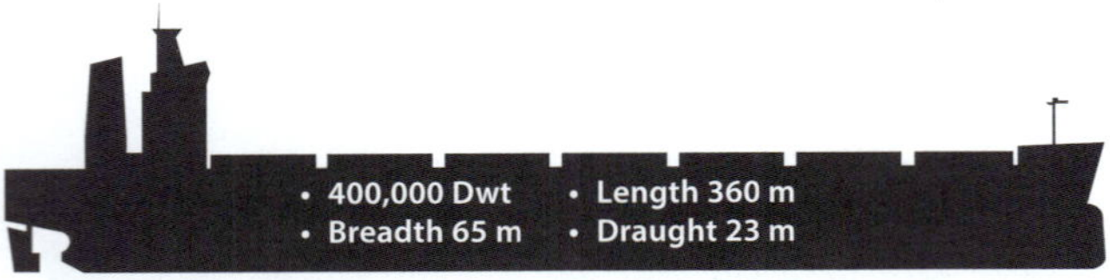

The Valemax very large ore carrier, at 400,000 Dwt, can carry 58,000 tonnes in each cargo hold (which is more than 75% of the total capacity of the Panamax). It has an average loading rate of 13,500 tonnes per hour, delivered to each hold in a single pour.

The term 'Valemax' is derived from Companhia Vale do Rio Doce (one of the world's largest producers of iron ore) which was the first company to order this size of vessel.

Due to their size, Valemax ships are restricted in the ports they can call at, but they typically load at Ponta da Maderia and Tubarao in Brazil and discharge at Rotterdam (Netherlands), Taranto (Italy), Sohar (Oman), Mindano plus two floating Vale stations (Philippines), Kashima, Kmitsu and Oita (Japan) and South Korea.

Operating fully laden, these ships are designed to deliver economies of scale and a reduction of up to 30% in running costs. However, if they have to operate partly loaded, their profitability suffers and there is a likelihood of them running at a loss.

Examples of Port-Specific Bulk Carrier Sub-Classes

Kamsarmax:

~82,000 Dwt Panamax with increased LOA of 229 m

(for Port Kamsar in Equatorial Guinea)

Dunkirkmax:

~175,000 Dwt large Capesize with max LOA of 289 m and max B of 45 m

(for the French port's eastern harbour lock at Dunkirk)

Newcastlemax:

~185,000 Dwt large Capesize with max B of 47 m

(for Newcastle, Australia)

Setouchmax:

~205,000 Dwt large Capesize (VLBC) with a low design draught of 16.10 m and max LOA of 299.9 m

(for ports in Setouch Sea in Japan)

Figure 1.2 - 'Vale Dalian', 400,000 Dwt, delivered May 2012 alongside 'Guo Yan 20' a 75,000 Dwt Panamax bulk carrier

Examples of Port-Specific Bulk Carrier Sub-Classes

Dry-Bulk Trade

General Overview

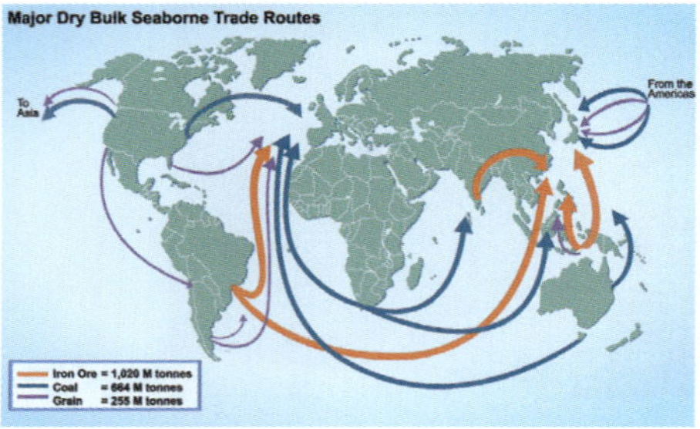

Dry-bulk commodities are the backbone of international seaborne trade, reflecting, in particular, the fast growing demand from emerging developing regions. In 2013, world dry-cargo shipments reached 6.7 billion tons, a 5.5% growth over 2012. The dry-bulks trade increased by 5.6% and accounted for 64.6% of global dry-cargo volumes (Clarkson Research Services, 2014a). Of this total, the five major dry-bulks totalled about 2.9 billion tons while minor dry bulks reached 1.4 billion tons (Clarkson Research Services, 2014a). The five major dry-bulk commodities continued to drive growth in this market segment rising by 6.5% in 2013 as compared with 3.5% in 2012.

Source: UNCTAD Review of Maritime Transport 2014

Grain

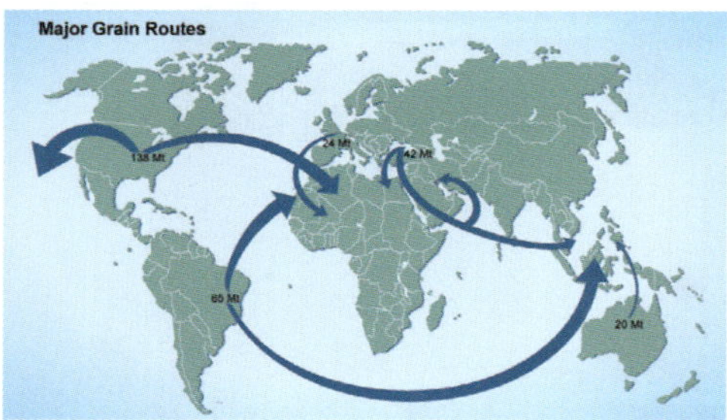

Global grain (including wheat, coarse grain and soybean) shipments increased by 3.2%, taking the total to 384 million tons in 2013 (Clarkson Research Services, 2014a). This growth reflects in particular the more favourable weather conditions in the United States in the case of wheat and the lower prices in the case of coarse grain (Clarkson Research Services, 2014d).

Japan remained the world's largest importer of wheat and coarse grains with a total of 23.9 million tons, followed by China (19.8 million tons).

The United States, the leading world grain exporter with a share of 19% in 2013, expanded its shipments (wheat and coarse grain) by 54.2% in 2013/2014, rebounding from the sharp contraction (minus 31.4%) recorded in the previous year (Clarkson Research Services, 2014a). Wheat export volumes dropped in Argentina and Australia but increased in Canada and the European Union.

Source: UNCTAD Review of Maritime Transport 2014

Coal

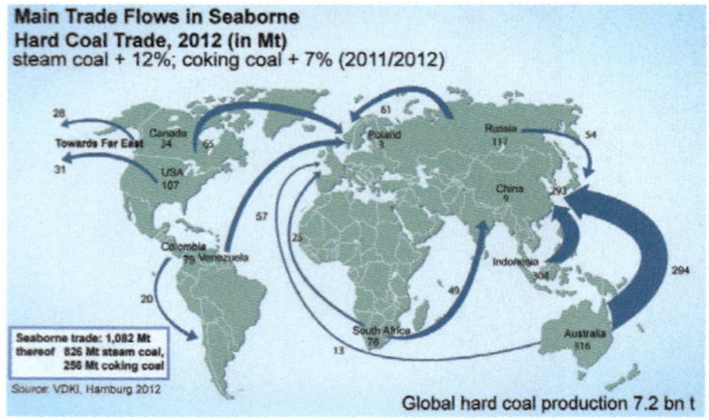

In 2013, the total volume of coal shipments (thermal and coking) increased by 5% to reach 1.18 billion tons. Accounting for nearly 78% of the coal trade, thermal shipments increased by 2.9%, a rate much slower than the 14.6% recorded in 2012. Asian imports are the main contributor to global coal trade with volumes expanding rapidly over recent years. Asia's thermal coal import volumes recorded the fastest growth (5.3%) while import volumes into the European Union contracted by 5.9%. Major importers included China, Germany, India, Japan, Malaysia, the Republic of Korea, Taiwan Province of China and the United Kingdom.

Australia and Indonesia accounted for 64.5% of global shipments in 2013. While Indonesia remained the largest single coal exporter after overtaking Australia in 2010 as Asia's largest coal supplier, world coal shipments increased by 10.2% in 2013 (Clarkson Research Services, 2014a).

Source: UNCTAD Review of Maritime Transport 2014

Iron Ore

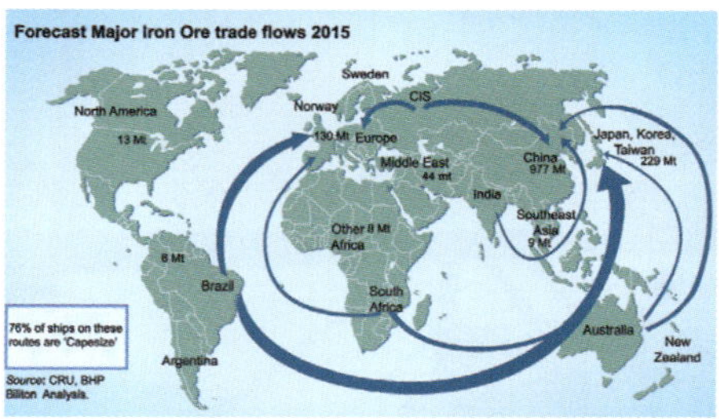

Reflecting continued growth in the steel industry, global iron ore trade increased by a firm 7.1% in 2013 and remained the star performer with volumes doubling between 2004 and 2013. Iron ore shipments totalled nearly 1.2 billion tons in 2013 up from 1.1 billion tons in 2012 and 593 million tons in 2004 (Clarkson Research Services, 2014c). Major iron ore exporters were Australia and Brazil, which together accounted for 75.6% of world iron ore shipments in 2013 (Clarkson Research Services, 2014a). However, other smaller suppliers are increasingly emerging as important markets that can offer promising prospects for shipping, especially in Africa.

China remained the main consumption market for iron ore shipped out of Australia and Brazil in 2013. Driven by large investments in construction and infrastructure, China accounts for over two-thirds of the global iron ore trade.

Source: UNCTAD Review of Maritime Transport 2014

Hazards of Bulk Cargoes

Figure 1.3 - Discharging coal cargo

The main hazards associated with bulk cargoes are:

- Liquefaction
- cargo shift
- structural damage due to improper distribution
- chemical hazards
- other health hazards.

Liquefaction

If the moisture content of certain cargoes is above that of the transportable moisture limit (TML), they may liquefy due to the vibration caused by the ship's movement. This can cause a viscous flow state to develop, resulting in a loss of stability and structural damage as the cargo impacts with the hold. Compaction and vibration may cause the cargo to flow to one side of the ship with a roll one way, but not completely return with a roll the other way. This may cause the ship to progressively reach a dangerous heel and then capsize.

For certain cargoes, shift can also occur below the TML due to rapid moisture migration so they should be trimmed level and loaded as deep as possible. Appendix A of the '*Bulk Cargo (BC) Code*' provides a list of such cargoes.

This moisture content may be due to the nature of the cargo or because it has been stowed in the open, without shelter. Cargoes affected include fine granular types, such as fine coal and concentrates. Precautions for carriage are provided in the BC Code:

- Ships, other than specially constructed ships, should only carry these cargoes if the moisture content does not exceed the TML, as defined in the Code
- cargoes containing liquids should not be stowed in the same cargo space above or adjacent to consignments of cargoes with a tendency to liquefaction
- adequate precautions must be taken to prevent the entry of water into the holds
- while at sea, water should not be used as a cooling medium for such cargoes
- specially fitted cargo ships
  - if the moisture content exceeds the TML then cargo may be carried in ships designed with portable divisions that contain any shift. The divisions should be of sufficient strength and not constructed of wood
- specially constructed cargo ships
  - ships may be specially constructed to carry the cargoes.

Section 8 of the BC Code details test procedures for verifying the moisture content of cargoes:

> *"Half fill a cylindrical can (0.5 to 1 ℓ) with a sample of the material. Strike a hard surface with the can sharply from a height of about 0.2 metres, repeating about 25 times at one or two second intervals. Examine the surface for free moisture or fluid conditions. If apparent then arrangements should be made to have additional laboratory tests conducted before the material is accepted for shipment".*

Prior to loading such cargoes, the master should insist on a certificate, from the shipper or the terminal, detailing the moisture content of a representative sample of the substance. The certificate will form part of the information exchange between the ship and the terminal, as required by the BLU Code and, for UK vessels or vessels at ports in the UK, the SLU Code.

Risk of Cargo Shift

If non-cohesive cargo is stowed incorrectly, it may shift on passage.

The risk of cargoes shifting is determined by their angle of repose.

An angle of repose is:

> *"...the maximum slope angle of non-cohesive, ie free flowing, granular material. It is the angle between the horizontal plane and the cone of such material when at rest on a plane surface".*

Hazards of Bulk Cargoes

Figure 1.4 - Coal piling from a chute shows the 'angle of repose'

Cargoes with an angle of repose of less than 35° are considered to be in danger of shifting. Cargoes with an angle of repose higher than 35° have less likelihood of shifting due to their cohesive nature.

A shipboard test to determine the angle of repose of a granular substance is detailed in Appendix D of the BC Code.

To prevent a shift of cargo, in general all bulk cargoes should be trimmed level and to the boundaries of the holds as far as is possible. At the very least, all cargoes must be trimmed to well below the cargo's angle of repose. Cargoes with a very low angle of repose (below 30°) require special precautions. These cargoes will be similar in nature to grain and the *'International Grain Code (Grain Code)'* must be consulted and followed.

Structural Hazards Due to Improper Distribution

SOLAS Chapter XII, *'Additional Safety Measures for Bulk Carriers'*, sets out the structural strength and damage stability requirements for bulk carriers. It also covers loading instruments, water level detectors and pumping systems.

Structural damage to bulk carriers can occur because of excessive loading rates of high density cargo or due to this type of cargo being dropped into the hold from a height. The BLU Code addresses these concerns and forms part of the ship-shore safety checklist on bulk carriers.

Structural damage to bulk carriers can also occur through improper weight distribution of the cargo. Alternate hold loading, as shown in the following diagram, can cause excessive shearing forces and resultant stresses in the ship's structure.

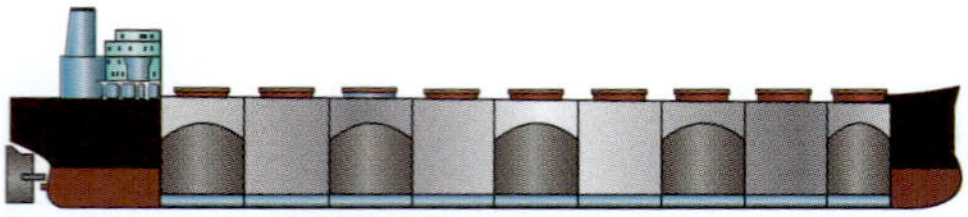

Figure 1.5 - Alternate hold loading

This type of loading should only be permitted if the alternate holds are specially strengthened. The advantage of loading alternate holds is that it raises the centre of gravity and eases racking stresses.

Block hold loading, where cargo is stowed in blocks of two or more adjoining holds, should only be adopted when either such a loading condition is described in the approved loading manual or the approved local loading criteria define the maximum weight limit in each hold or block of holds as a function of the ship's mean draught.

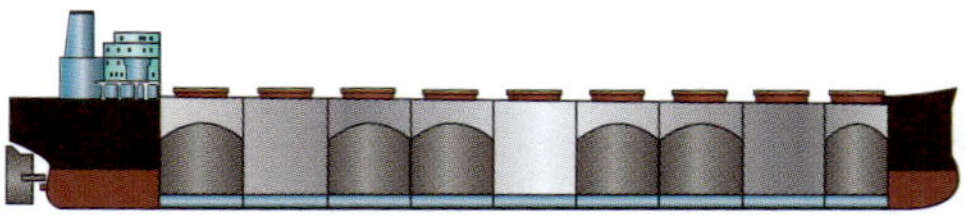

Figure 1.6 - Block hold loading

Uneven distribution of the cargo throughout the vessel's length can cause excessive shearing forces and bending moments. Prior to loading, a cargo plan must be prepared and due allowance made for the rates of ballast discharge. The BLU Code provides a pro-forma loading plan. A loadicator is normally used to ensure that the stresses on the ship do not exceed set limits.

Improper distribution of weight can lead to excessive stability, particularly with high density cargoes such as iron ore. This can create raking stresses on the ship's structure and the resulting heavy rolling can also cause the cargo to shift.

Chemical and Other Health Hazards

Some bulk cargoes are hazardous to human health, listed in Appendix B of the BC Code, because of their toxic or corrosive nature.

Some of these materials are classified as dangerous goods in the '*International Maritime Dangerous Goods Code (IMDG Code)*', and others are materials that may cause hazard when transported in bulk. Such material must be carefully segregated from other materials.

Hazards from such cargoes include the creation of a flammable atmosphere, toxicity, corrosive properties, irritant dust or oxygen depletion.

Prior to loading cargoes that have chemical hazards, it is important to obtain information from the shipper on all known chemical hazards of the cargo and the precautions to be taken on board. Such precautions may include, among other things, wearing proper PPE, atmosphere tests, no smoking regulations, proper cargo venting precautions, protection of machinery from cargo dust, wearing of dust masks and securing all openings to the accommodation.

SI 336 (Carriage of Cargoes) 1999 makes it mandatory for UK-registered vessels to carry atmosphere monitoring equipment on board and to provide training and instructions for its use.

Hold Preparation on Bulk Carriers

Hold Preparation

Figure 1.7 - Preparing a hold after a cargo of coal

For the Master

Before loading a bulk cargo, the master usually has to declare that his ship is ready to load as per the charter party requirements and the charterer's and owner's instructions.

For dry bulk cargoes, there are five levels of hold cleanliness:

Hospital Clean

Hospital clean is the most stringent level, requiring the holds to have 100% intact paint coatings on all surfaces, including the tank top, all ladder rungs and the undersides of hatches.

This standard is a requirement for cargoes such as kaolin/China clay, mineral sands including zircon, barytes, rutile sand, ilmenite, fluorspar, chrome ore and soda ash, rice in bulk and high grades of wood pulp. Generally, this standard of cleanliness will only be met by vessels trading exclusively with such cargoes.

Grain Clean

Grain clean is the most common requirement. The holds must be clean, swept and washed down with fresh water. They should be free from insects, odour, residue of previous cargo, lashing material, loose rust scale and paint flakes, etc. A ship will be required to be grain clean for the majority of bulk and break bulk cargoes, such as all grains, soya meal and soya products, alumina, sulphur, bulk cement, bauxite, concentrates and bulk fertilisers.

Normal Clean

Normal clean means that the holds are swept clean, with no residues of the previous cargo, and washed down. This is requested when the ship is to load a cargo similar to, or compatible with, the previous shipment.

Shovel Clean

Shovel clean means that all previous cargo has been removed using a 'Bobcat' or hand shovels and the hold roughly swept by the stevedores or crew.

Load on Top

Load on top means that the cargo is loaded on top of existing cargo residues. Usually, this means 'grab cleaned'. This standard will commonly be required where a ship is trading continuously with the same commodity and the same grade of that commodity, such as coal.

Hold Preparation on Bulk Carriers

Hold cleaning sequence

The following hold cleaning sequence is generally followed on bulk carriers:

1. Remove all residues of the previous cargo. Sweeping down and collecting cargo residues generally achieves this.
2. Remove any dunnage that is left over in the holds.
3. Holds are then usually washed with seawater and, if required, with a final rinse of fresh water. A fresh water rinse can reduce corrosion and accelerate drying. Special attention should be given to removing residues from areas that can be difficult to reach, such as hatch covers and frames.
4. Bilges and strum boxes are to be properly cleaned and, if necessary, the bilge area is to be disinfected or lime washed. Bilges are then covered with burlap to prevent entry of cargo particles.
5. Hold inspection to be carried out and any damages repaired.
6. Ancillary systems, such as the fixed fire-fighting equipment or ventilation equipment, must be tested.
7. New dunnage should be laid out if required.
8. Hold lighting to be checked.
9. Means of access should be checked for damage and must be free of any hazards.
10. Cargo gear must be checked and rigged for loading or discharge.
11. Hatch covers must be examined for weathertight integrity and, if necessary, the rubber packing renewed.
12. Fumigation is to be carried out if the charterers or cargo owners require it. The IMO publication *'Recommendations on the Safe Use of Pesticides in Ships'* must be referred to.
13. Air pipes, fixtures and fittings must be checked and any repairs carried out.

Bulk Carriers in Port Working Cargo

Carriage of Bulk Grain

Compliance with the Grain Code is a requirement under SOLAS.

The Grain Code normally applies to all ships, regardless of size, engaged in the transport of bulk grain. However, some ships may be exempted from compliance by their flag State due to the sheltered nature of their trade or the specific conditions of the voyage.

Part A contains special requirements and guidance on the stowage of grain and the use of grain fittings.

Part B deals with the calculation of heeling moments and general assumptions.

Part C (which reproduces SOLAS Regulations 8 and 9) states that a master must satisfy the loading port that the ship complies with the requirements of the Grain Code before it can commence loading grain.

According to the Code, the term 'grain' covers the following cargoes:

> ***"...wheat, maize (corn), oats, rye, barley, rice, pulses, seeds and processed forms thereof, whose behaviour is similar to grain in its natural state".***

To prove compliance with the Code, a Document of Authorisation is issued for every ship that satisfies the conditions. This document should accompany or be incorporated into a ship-specific grain loading manual. Both these documents are issued by or approved on behalf of that ship's Flag State Administration. A ship without a Document of Authorisation may be granted an exemption, provided the master can demonstrate compliance with the terms of the Code.

Figure 1.8 - Loading grain into a ship ready for export – silos in background

Bulk Carriers in Port Working Cargo

Figure 1.9 - Loading grain

Figure 1.10 - Loading grain in Portland, Oregon

Contents of the Grain Loading Manual

- Ship's particulars
- light ship displacement
- table of liquid free surface corrections
- capacities and centres of gravity
- curve or table of angle of flooding where less than 40°
- curves or tables of hydrostatic properties, suitable for a range of operating draughts
- approved curves or tables of volumes, vertical centres of volumes and assumed volumetric heeling moments for every compartment
- approved tables or curves of maximum permissible heeling moments for varying displacements and varying vertical centres of gravity
- loading instructions
- a worked example, for the guidance of the master
- loaded departure and arrival conditions for three representative stowage factors.

Stability Requirements

- Vessels should be able to demonstrate by calculations that at all times during the intended voyage the ship will have sufficient intact stability to provide adequate residual dynamic stability after taking into account the adverse heeling effect caused by an assumed shift of grain
- the vessel should demonstrate by calculations that the maximum list will not be greater than 12° after experiencing:
  - a shift of cargo of 15° in every full hold
  - a shift of cargo of 25° in any partly filled compartment
- net residual area between heeling arm curve and righting arm curve up to 40° (or angle of flooding if less than 40°) to be not less than 0.075 metre-radians
- initial metacentric height after free surface correction not to be less than 0.3 metres
- as many compartments as full as possible
- cargo to be trimmed level.

Optional Stability Requirements for Ships without a Document of Authorisation Carrying Partial Cargoes of Bulk Grain

The vessel may load grain if all of the following conditions are met:

- The total weight of grain does not exceed one-third of the ship's deadweight

Bulk Carriers in Port Working Cargo

- filled compartments to be trimmed and fitted with centreline divisions extending the full length and to a maximum depth of 2.4 metres or to be saucered (except in the case of linseed or other such seeds)
- free grain surfaces in partially filled compartments to be trimmed level and secured in accordance with the Code
- the metacentric height (GM) must be 0.30 metres or as determined by the formula in the Code (Section A 9.1.5), whichever is greater
- the master must demonstrate to the Administration that the ship, when loaded, will satisfy the requirements of Section 9 of the Code.

To prevent a shift of cargo causing a heel beyond the permitted limits, the Code specifies methods of securing full and partially full compartments.

Hold Cleaning Requirements

Prior to loading a cargo of grain, all holds must be thoroughly washed, dried and all residues of previous cargoes removed. Surveyors, appointed by shippers, may inspect the hold prior to loading the cargo. Spaces should be closely inspected for insect infestation and fumigated if required. Any fumigation should be carried out in accordance with the IMO publication *'Recommendations on the Safe Use of Pesticides in Ships'* and MGN 284 – *'Recommendations for Ships Carrying Fumigated Bulk Cargoes'.*

Coal

In 2013, the total volume of coal shipments (thermal and coking) increased by 5% to reach 1.18 billion tons. It is mined for export in over 50 countries, and used in over 70 countries to generate electricity. Indonesia is the largest single coal exporter after overtaking Australia in 2010 as the world's largest coal supplier. Other significant coal exporters include the USA, Canada and South Africa. Major coal importing countries include Japan, Korea, the UK, Germany, India and Italy.

The Four Categories of Coal

1. Coal Slurry

This is a mixture of solid coal containing water and is a byproduct of mining. The coal particle size is usually less than 1 mm. It is regarded as a cargo that may liquefy due to its high moisture content.

2. Coal Duff

This is a mixture of coal and water, with the largest coal particles measuring around 7 mm. It is less liable to liquefaction than coal slurry, but does require its moisture content to be monitored.

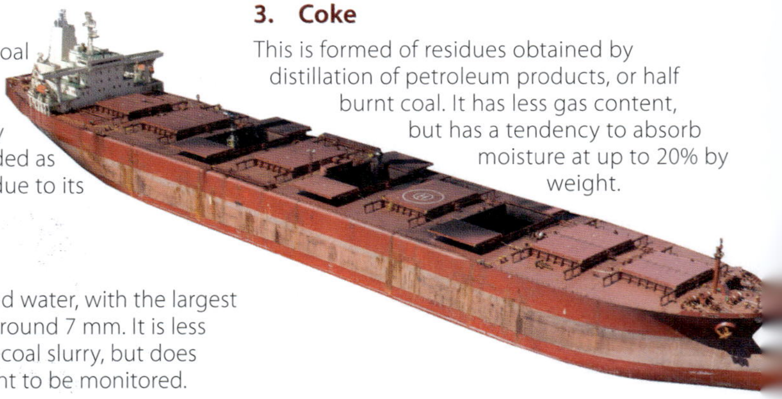

3. Coke

This is formed of residues obtained by distillation of petroleum products, or half burnt coal. It has less gas content, but has a tendency to absorb moisture at up to 20% by weight.

4. Small Coal

This contains particles of coal less than 7 mm in size. It is likely to develop a flow state due to its high moisture content.

Precautions for the Carriage of Coal

General Precautions for the Carriage of Coal

- Bilge wells should be cleaned, residual cargoes removed, suction tested and covered with taped-down, double-wrapped burlap
- hatch top wheels and associated equipment should be greased to ensure that no sparks are caused during opening and closing
- electrical cables, cargo hold lights and any other electrical instruments within cargo holds should be checked for insulation damage to ensure that they are safe for use in an atmosphere containing explosive gases. On bulk carriers, as no lighting is needed, the fuses should be pulled to isolate electricity.

Ships that carry coal should have onboard instruments to measure:

- Methane, oxygen and carbon monoxide levels in cargo holds
- cargo hold temperature (between 0 to 100°C)
- the pH of bilge water.

Installation of instruments and measurement taking should be possible without entering the cargo space.

Loading Cargo

- Extra monitoring should be implemented when coal is loaded in holds adjacent to hot areas, such as heated fuel DB tanks and engine room bulkheads
- the ideal place to monitor the temperature of the load is the centre of the stow. If the temperature is measured from the side, top or corners of the hold, it must be remembered that the temperature at the centre of the cargo will be several degrees higher
- a no smoking policy should be fully implemented on the ship and hot work should not be allowed, particularly near the cargo compartments.

During the Passage

- Except where the shipper provides specific instructions to ventilate the cargo, compartments containing coal should only be ventilated for the first 24 hours after departure from the loading port. There should be regular monitoring of the atmosphere to check the concentration of hazardous elements. Ventilation should only be continued if the amount of methane rises above the acceptable level. Coal should also be ventilated prior to discharge because the build-up of gases could be ignited by a spark from the opening of the hatches
- adjacent stores, mast houses, etc should be monitored on a regular basis for escaped gases
- a higher pH value reading indicates the likelihood of increased corrosion. In such cases the bilges should be kept dry by pumping out any accumulated water. A record of the quantity of bilge water discharged should be kept in the deck logbook to justify any claims of cargo shortage.

Precautions for Coals Emitting Methane

If the shipper has declared that the cargo is liable to emit methane or the methane concentration in the cargo compartment is above 20% of the lower explosive limit (LEL), the following additional precautions should be taken:

- Surface ventilation should be maintained
- hatch covers should not be opened until the accumulated gases have been removed. Hatch covers should then be opened carefully, ensuring no sparks are initiated

Bulk Carriers in Port Working Cargo

- all enclosed spaces, such as store rooms, tunnels and passageways, etc, should be thoroughly monitored for methane
- enclosed hatch covers should be ventilated.

Special Precautions for Self-Heating Coals

If the shipper has declared that the cargo is liable to self-heat, the following additional precautions should be taken:

- If required, the master should seek additional guidance from the shipper on the adequacy of the existing precautions
- if analysis of the atmosphere of the cargo compartment reveals an increased carbon monoxide concentration, it indicates that the coal has ignited:
  - The hatch covers should be closed after loading and additional seals applied
  - surface ventilation should be kept to a minimum
  - if the hold temperature exceeds 55°C or the carbon monoxide concentration rises steadily, expert advice should be sought.

Iron Ore

Iron ore is used for the production of metallic iron in steel making. Although some 45 countries export natural iron ore resources, 7 countries provide 75% of the total exported. The 2 largest exporters are Brazil and Australia, with about 33% of total world exports each. Other exporting countries include Chile, India, South Africa, Canada, Russia and the United States.

Types of Iron Ore

Iron Concentrates

Iron concentrates are produced by either:

The Dry Method

High grade ore is crushed to remove waste material, leaving a low moisture content in the powdered ore. Iron concentrates obtained by the dry method are susceptible to spontaneous combustion because of the air trapped during the crushing process. Due to dampness within the cargo, the sulphur can react with oxygen to produce heat, resulting in spontaneous combustion. Therefore, for concentrates, the holds should be kept closed and ventilation avoided. Concentrates may also emit poisonous/explosive gases, so the cargo spaces should be treated as an enclosed space and appropriate entry procedures followed.

The Wet Method

The crushed rock is washed in water to separate the sulphides. The concentrate has a high moisture content that may liquefy and shift on board ship. The moisture content of these concentrates should, therefore, be checked prior to loading and if it is above the TML, the cargo should be rejected.

Sponge Iron (or Direct Reduced Iron (DRI))

This is produced by heating iron ore at low temperatures, without allowing it to come into contact with air. It is important to allow the piles of sponge iron to be weathered before shipping so that its temperature drops. The sponge iron is separated by magnets so has little moisture content. If it gets damp from contact with air, it is likely to oxidise, and is liable to spontaneously combust and/or emit toxic fumes.

Pig Iron

This is produced by heating the iron ore, which then gives off carbon monoxide. This combines with the iron oxides in the iron ore to produce the metallic iron known as pig iron. Pig iron is obtained in a molten state that can be moulded as required. It contains a comparatively higher quantity of carbon, about 3.5%, and is less pure than sponge iron.

Precautions for the Carriage of Iron Ore

Care should be taken to monitor the temperature of the cargo whether it is in pellet, lump or briquette form. If the temperature exceeds 65°C, it must not be loaded on board unless the shipper's declaration states it has been sufficiently treated for oxidation/corrosion inhibition to avoid any chance of spontaneous combustion should the moisture content increase.

The majority of incidents in which bulk carriers have been lost involve carriage of iron ore:

- Iron ores are heavy cargoes that occupy a small area for a large weight, ie they have a low stowage factor (between 0.24 to 0.80 m^3/tonne). It is therefore important that the tank top has sufficient strength
- trimming of these cargoes is generally required (even though their angle of repose is mostly above 35°) to spread their weight across the entire tank top
- as iron ore is a high density cargo, when loaded on an ordinary bulk carrier (not an ore carrier) it will increase the vessel's GM, making it a 'stiff' ship
- iron ore is commonly loaded with conveyor belts, grabs, chutes and bucket belt unloaders, causing significant quantities of dust during both loading and discharging (enclosed conveyor belt systems generate less dust). The dust may damage ship's machinery as well as the health of personnel
- iron ore is assumed to have a homogeneous moisture content between 0 to 16%. However, if it is kept lying in the open, the moisture content may increase due to absorption from air or rain. If the exact moisture content is unknown, a proper laboratory test may be requested. The master must also ask the shipper to detail the cargo's moisture content and TML.

  2009 saw an increase in incidents attributed to carrying iron ore filings with excessive moisture content, causing sloshing and adverse stability and, in some cases, the rapid loss of the ship. During the monsoon season in the Indian sub-continent, iron ore filings are stored and transported open to the elements. It is worth remembering that the cargo may remain stockpiled before being shipped later in the dry season
- stresses upon the ship, both in port and at sea, should be monitored using an HSMS (hull stress monitoring system) if fitted. The movement of cargo and ballast should be monitored using stress calculating software
- bulk carriers sometimes carry iron ore in alternate holds. This may be at the request of charterers trying to gain the economic advantages of faster turnround and to raise the centre of gravity. To do so, ships must be specially strengthened. SOLAS Chapter XII bans alternate hold loading for single skin ships of 150 metres or more in length, built before 1st July 1999, that carry cargo equal to 90% of the ship's deadweight
- the iron ore standard sampling procedure given in the IMSBC Code should be followed.

It is imperative that the cargo moisture content is tested prior to and monitored during all stages of loading as, once on board, cargo may be extremely difficult to remove. The shipper's test certificate should be presented before loading, be sound and be no more than seven days old. A good indicator during the load is the presence of splatter marks of iron ore filings on the bulkheads. If splatter marks are evident, they should be taken very seriously as an indication that the moisture content is above the TML and the flow moisture point.

If the master is in any doubt, he should contact the owners and the P&I Club correspondent.

Bulk Carriers in Port Working Cargo

Sulphur

Each year, tens of millions of tonnes of sulphur are carried on board ships.

Sulphur is an important feedstock material for the world's chemical industry. Its main source is as a byproduct in hydrocarbon processing (oil and gas). Petroleum and natural gas producing countries are major exporters. Its largest single use is for the production of sulphuric acid, which is used in the production of fertilisers. Sulphur is loaded in granular, pelletised (prilled form), crushed lumps or coarsely grained material.

During the 1970-80s, there were a number of incidents of corrosion damage to cargo holds on board ships after the carriage of sulphur. Research subsequently confirmed that, while dry sulphur does not react with steel, wet sulphur can cause serious damage.

Sulphur is often loaded wet because it is stored in large outdoor piles. In many ports, it is adopted practice to spray the sulphur with fresh water during loading to reduce dust formation.

Protecting a mild steel ship from the corrosive nature of sulphur requires an uninterrupted physical barrier between the steel and the sulphur.

Lime wash is the most commonly used method of protecting the holds against corrosion. Prior to applying lime wash, the cargo holds should be cleaned to 'grain clean' standard.

Lime wash is typically a mixture of 60 to 90 kg of lime (calcium hydroxide) to each 200 litres of water. When the solution is sprayed onto hold structures, the white emulsion needs to completely cover all areas that may be exposed to sulphur or sulphur dust. As the emulsion dries, the lime will react in air to create a layer of white calcium carbonate. This is significantly harder than lime and forms a protective coating. A coat of lime wash must always be given sufficient time to dry and can be expected to last for at least 30 days.

Other Cargo Types Carried on Bulk Carriers

Some bulk carriers do not have upper and lower wing tanks. Instead, they have straight sides to carry square-shaped bundles of forestry products, such as unitised wood pulp, rolled paper or packaged timber cargoes. They can even carry 20 foot containers.

They may have fixed or travelling gantry cranes for loading/unloading. Due to the nature of their cargoes, these vessels may be fitted with dehumidification systems or vacuum equipment for loading/discharging cargoes such as steel slabs/pipes, rolled paper, unitised wood pulp, newsprint, kraft liner board, kraft paper, etc.

Cement

Cement is made from a mixture of elements that are found in natural materials such as limestone, clay, sand and shale. When cement is mixed with water, it can bind sand and gravel into a hard, solid mass called concrete.

Hydraulic cements (eg Portland cement) harden because of hydration or through chemical reactions that occur independently of the mixture's water content. They can harden even underwater or when constantly exposed to wet weather. Non-hydraulic cements (eg lime and gypsum plaster) must be kept dry in order to retain their strength.

Health Effects

Skin Contact

Dry cement powder in contact with mucous membranes can cause severe eye or respiratory irritation.

Contact with wet cement can cause dermatitis. Skin affected by dermatitis feels itchy and sore, and looks red, scaly and cracked.

Wet cement can cause burns. If wet cement becomes trapped against the skin, for example by kneeling in it or if it falls into a boot or glove, a serious burn or ulcer can rapidly develop. These often take months to heal and in extreme cases will need skin grafts or can even lead to amputation. Serious chemical burns to the eyes can also be caused by a splash of cement.

Inhalation of Dust

High levels of dust, which may contain silica, can be produced when cement is handled, for example when emptying or disposing of bags. Exposure to silica can lead to scarring of the lungs. In the short term, exposure to high levels of cement dust irritates the nose and throat, but long term exposure may cause occupational asthma.

Transport of Cement

The transport of cement and related products accounts for approximately 5% of the total volume of dry bulk carrier transportation, and it is growing in volume. While highly profitable, it attracts heavy cleaning and maintenance costs. The main problems are found during the loading and unloading of conventionally built cargo vessels in the areas high above tank top level, which are difficult to reach and clean unless the ship is equipped with suitable working platforms.

Characteristics of Cement

Cement in bulk requires careful handling due to the following characteristics:

- It solidifies when wet
- when manufactured, it is hot and retains the heat
- it may easily stick to non-smooth surfaces
- when contaminated by residues from previous cargoes, it may become useless as a binding agent.

Therefore, when preparing a vessel for cement, it is important to take into consideration that it has a temperature of 110°C on production, is loaded at temperatures of up to 70 to 80°C, and is often exported from cold areas, transported part of the way at low sea temperatures and then unloaded in warm areas with a high air humidity. After loading, cement powder often contracts by as much as 12% once settled in the holds.

These characteristics create perfect conditions for water vapour to condense, solidifying the cement not only on the main deck, but also at the upper parts of the cargo holds.

Bulk Carriers in Port Working Cargo

Loading and Unloading

During loading, it is very important to keep the atmosphere in the cargo holds as dry as possible and it is a good idea to keep the holds closed when not in use. If the climate is warm and humid, the hatches should be closed once discharging has been completed so that a dry atmosphere can build inside the holds.

Figure 1.11 - Plant view

Cleaning

Prior to Loading

- The sides and tank top should be completely dry
- the air in the holds should be dried using dehumidifiers (if on board) for some days prior to loading
- cold water ballast should be avoided in tanks adjacent to holds
- barrier chemicals can be effective when applied prior to loading, but should not be used unless time allows them to dry completely
- all holes/slots on the tank top and bulkheads and all incoming scupper holes should be sealed with tape.

During and After Loading

- If possible, the main deck, hatch covers and incoming tubes should be cleaned using compressed air
- after loading, the main deck, hatch coamings and covers should be swept and cleaned using compressed air
- the same areas should be cleaned using high pressure cleaning equipment (and chemicals, if necessary) after dry cleaning has been completed.

After Discharging

- All cement dust from dry cleaning, and all cargo residues from the tank top and bulkheads, must be collected and removed
- cargo hold bulkheads must be cleaned using compressed air, and hatch coamings and covers should be thoroughly swept
- after dry cleaning, the holds must be cleaned using high-pressure air/water. Chemicals and/or high pressure cleaning pumps should be used whenever necessary
- all areas should be flushed with fresh water
- to avoid packing of the bilge/drain system, portable diaphragm pumps should be used during the cleaning process.

After Cleaning

- All valves in the drain/bilge system must be checked
- the bilge system must be flushed for a minimum of 15 to 30 minutes to avoid cargo residues settling and gradually clogging the system.

Specialised Equipment on Cement Carriers

Cement carriers are fitted with fluidisation systems in the cargo holds, which enable the bulk cargo to flow to a central suction point, ensuring maximum efficiency in discharging cement. Since the vessels are totally enclosed, the operation is environmentally friendly with dust-free operation when discharging pneumatically. The vessels are also able to discharge when it is raining, unlike conventional bulk carriers. The cargo handling equipment can discharge up to 1,000 metric tonnes per hour, subject to the vessel's particulars and the shore facilities.

Mechanical Loading

Mechanical loading uses conveyor belts or screw conveyors to transport the cement to the ship. The shore-based ship loader is connected to a loading point on the ship and the cement is distributed through air slides or screws on deck to different drop points and released into the holds.

Mechanical Unloading

Mechanical unloading uses vertical and horizontal screw conveyors to bring the cement from the holds to deck level, and then feeds boom conveyors for the onward transportation to either shore-based conveyor belts or cement trucks.

Pneumatic Unloading

Pneumatic unloading uses vertical and horizontal screw conveyors to bring the cement from the holds to deck level and into pressure pumps. All pneumatic systems use air pressure to blow the cement through pipelines to the shore terminals.

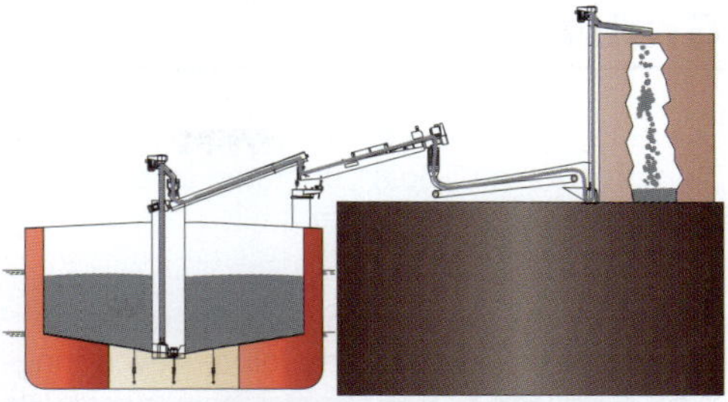

Figure 1.12 - Mechanical discharge from ship to silo

Self-unloading Cement Tankers

Self-unloading cement tankers do not require shore-based ship unloading equipment and have a totally enclosed cargo handling system. They have a fluidised system in the cargo holds but have different loading/unloading technologies and connections to the terminal facilities. The world fleet comprises 245 units between 4,000 and 30,000 Dwt for seaborne cement transportation. There are about 250 units in the <4,000 Dwt range for coastal, lake and river transport (river barges).

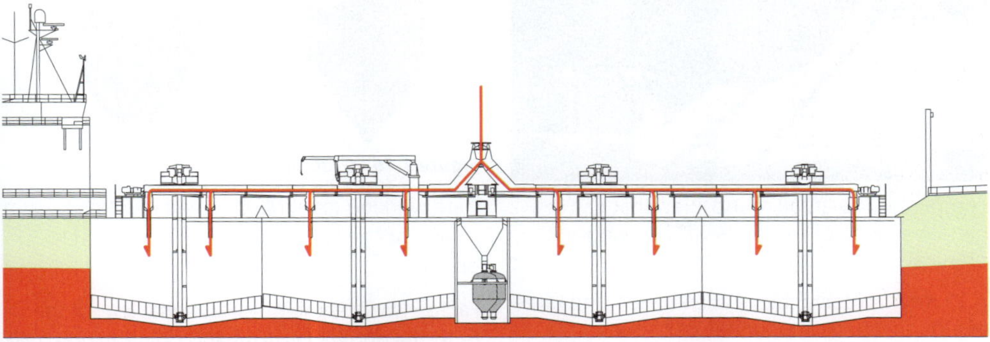

Figure 1.13 - Loading cement into cargo holds

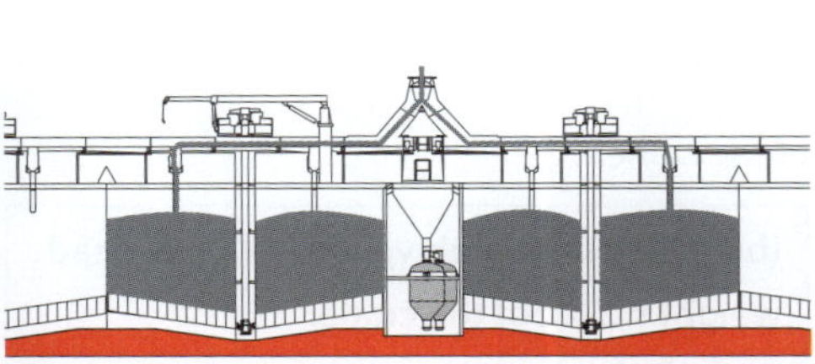

Figure 1.14a - Reclaiming cement from cargo holds (prior to discharge)

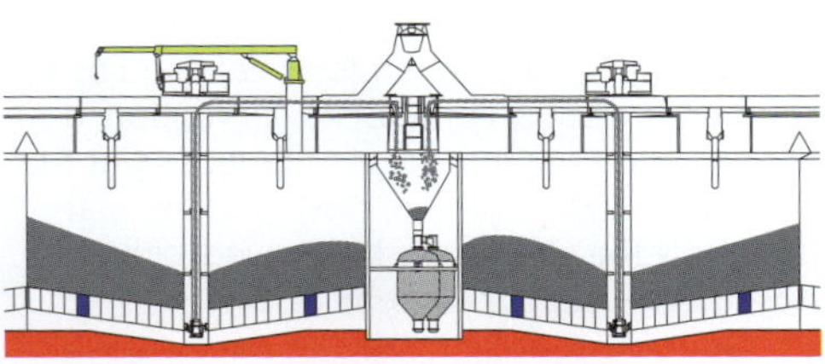

Figure 1.14b - Reclaiming cement from cargo holds

Bulk Carrier Port Equipment

Grabs

The grab mechanism consists of two jaws hinged at the mid-point, operated by either a hydraulic or electric system.

Bulk grabs are suitable for all types of dry bulk cargo. It is impractical to have a different grab for specific products and therefore stevedoring

companies use an 'all round' grab that can handle a range of materials with varying physical characteristics.

A 12 m^3 grab can achieve average loading rates of around 250 to 300 tonnes per hour.

Two drums are wrapped with cable or rope and used to hoist/lower the load vertically. The drums are rotated in opposite directions by two motors, which are referred to as hold and open/close (OC) motors. For hoist/lower motion, both of the motors are moved simultaneously at the same speed. For opening/closing of the grab jaws, only the OC motors are moved, either in hoist (close) or lower (open) mode.

The weight and volume of the grab has to correspond with that of the crane. The SWL

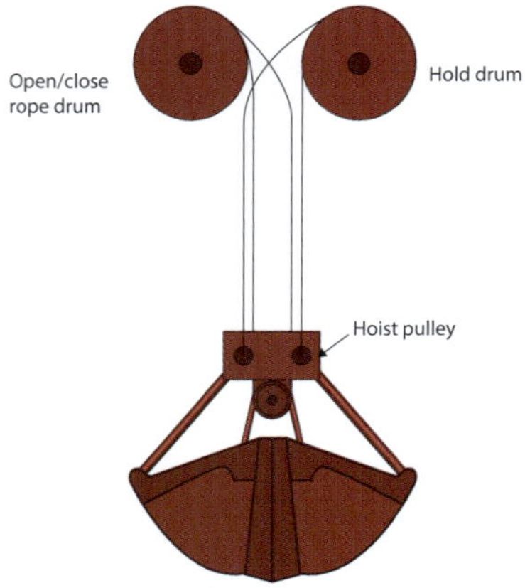

Figure 1.15 - Grab closed

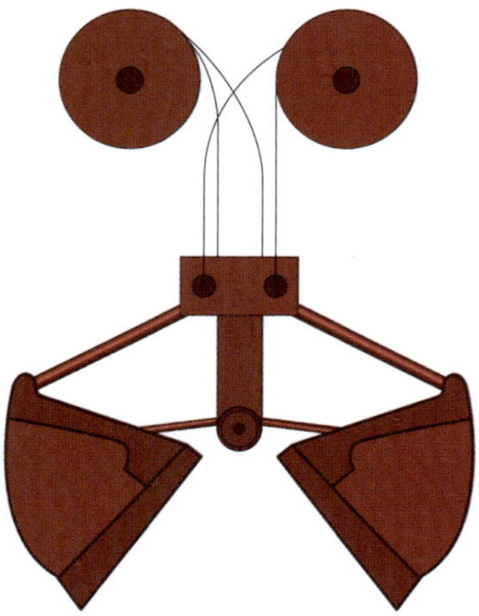

Figure 1.16 - Grab opened

(safe working load) of the crane must be known as well as the type of grab it is permitted to operate.

Factors such as the physical behaviour of the bulk, the angle of repose and how the grab will go through the bulk with its claws, must also be taken into account.

The following formula is used to determine whether the grab and bulk are within the SWL of the crane:

(bulk density × grab volume) + grab dead weight = SWL of the crane.

Figure 1.17 - Grabs working coal

Specialised Grabs

Orange-peel or cactus grabs are used for handling cargoes consisting of large, irregular items, such as scrap metal or certain uncrushed minerals, pig iron, wood chips, crushed car bodies, etc. They are also used extensively in dredging operations.

The orange-peel grab has a capacity of up to 10 cubic metres, allowing 2,000 tonnes of cargo to be loaded onto a ship in 24 hours.

Clamshell Grabs

Clamshell grabs are used mainly for discharge of loose dry bulk cargoes, such as sulphur, soda ash, fertilisers and grains.

The clamshell grab can lift capacities of over 85 tonnes and volumes of over 60 m^3. Most kinds of bulk material can be handled, provided it is not too coarse.

Problems

- Large grab buckets may cause considerable damage if they make contact with the tank top plating
- the internal hold structure and protective coatings in the cargo hold and the adjacent double bottom are vulnerable to damage when cargo is discharged using grabs
- raising or lowering the grab close to the coaming may result in the grab or the grab rope shackles catching on the lips of the hatch cover. This will result in the cover being lifted and dropped heavily, causing major damage to the coaming, the cover and the cover drive mechanism
- if the grab lands heavily, it can puncture the tank top
- the corner of the grab may strike the hopper tank first. This will cause heavy indents or puncture holes in the tank plate
- damage to ladders or coamings can occur, particularly during free digging.

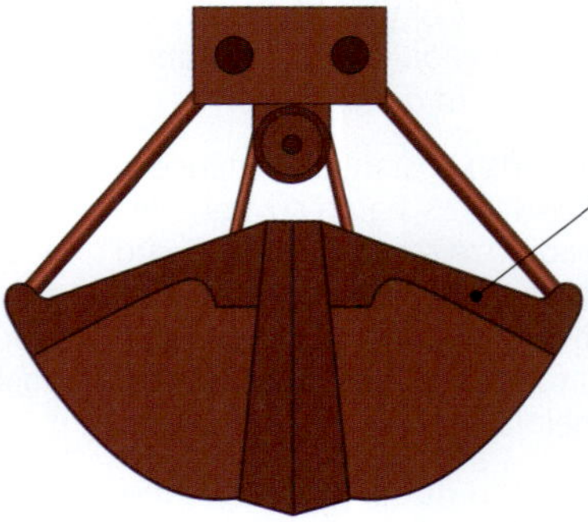

Specifications

Lifting capacity 20 - 85 tonnes SWL

Volume over 60 m^3 (coal)

Bulk goods coal, iron ore, minerals, bauxite, fertiliser, grain, cattle feed, biomass and white bulk

Shell can be open, half closed or closed for environmental-friendly shells

Grab opening in relation to the crane can be longitudinal, transversal and diagonal opening

Disasters and Significant Incidents Involving Bulk Carriers

Bulk carriers are subject to severe stresses, particularly when carrying iron ore, and are known to have a high risk of catastrophic hull failure. Should they founder, this will occur rapidly, leaving crews with little time to issue a distress message or abandon ship. 1990 and 1991 were two atrocious years for bulk carriers, with 27 bulk carrier accidents and significant loss of life. These accidents were all assumed to be caused by hull structural failures.

Disasters and Significant Incidents Involving Bulk Carriers

Larger bulk carriers are more difficult to handle, particularly as most have a single propeller and no thruster units. In a loaded condition, and in extreme weather or at slow speeds approaching ports or anchorages, extreme care is required in their handling.

'Derbyshire'

On 9th/10th September 1980, the *'Derbyshire'* was lost approximately 350 miles Southeast of Japan.

En route to Japan with a cargo of iron ore, the *'Derbyshire'* (previously *'Liverpool Bridge'*) was unable to avoid Typhoon Orchid. The *'Derbyshire's'* last message to her owners was:

> ***"9th September 09:30 GMT; now hove to due to severe tropical storm; estimated time of arrival Kawasaki 14th hopefully".***

No mayday was heard. Six weeks after this last message, one of the *'Derbyshire's'* lifeboats was sighted nearly 700 miles WSW of the search area. The damage to the lifeboat indicated that it had been wrenched with great force from its davits on the ship, suggesting that the sinking occurred very rapidly. All 44 people on board, consisting of 42 crew and two wives, were lost with the vessel.

Cause

The cause of the *'Derbyshire'* sinking was an issue of some contention. She was only 4 years old and initially no investigation was launched as there was no evidence, ie no wreck, to work from.

However, after the loss of two of her sister ships, *'Kowloon Bridge'* and *'Tyne Bridge'*, both suffering structural damage in the region of the engine room bulkhead, investigations revealed that five of the six sister ships, including the *'Derbyshire'*, had been modified in that area.

The modification resulted in a massive longitudinal girder being cut at the bulkhead by frame 65 instead of penetrating the bulkhead to maintain strength. Not only was this girder then much weaker than the continuous massive girder, but it was also out of line with the bulkhead by as much as 35 mm. This discovery, together with mounting pressure for answers from the relatives of those lost on the *'Derbyshire'*, led to the first investigation being launched in 1987. It came to the following conclusion:

> *"The Derbyshire was probably overwhelmed by the forces of nature in Typhoon Orchid, possibly after getting beam on to wind and sea, off Okinawa in darkness on the night of 9/10 September 1980 with the loss of 44 lives. The evidence available does not support any firmer conclusion".*

This was deemed unsatisfactory by the relatives and the search for the wreck of the *'Derbyshire'* intensified. She was finally found in June 1994, broken into approximately 2,000 pieces.

The ROV deployed to survey the wreck ruled out the frame 65 theory. It showed that the tragedy had begun at the ship's bow rather than at frame 65. The photographic evidence showed that the bow was largely intact, which meant it had flooded slowly, allowing it to hold its shape while sinking. By contrast, the other structures of the ship had plunged while full of air, imploding violently under the crushing pressure of deep water.

There is substantial evidence indicating that the *'Derbyshire's'* hatch covers failed due to seawater loading. A reduction in forward freeboard due to trim would increase the frequency and severity of seawater loading on the forward hatch covers and, therefore, the probability of their failure.

With this new information, the investigation into the sinking changed and became focused on how the bow flooded in the first place. This, too, proved to be contentious.

Two out of three government assessors came to the conclusion that the forward bosun's hatch had not been properly secured, implying that crew negligence led to the sinking of the *'Derbyshire'*. The assessors felt that the presence of a mooring rope leading from a hatch and wing nuts that were not fully tightened

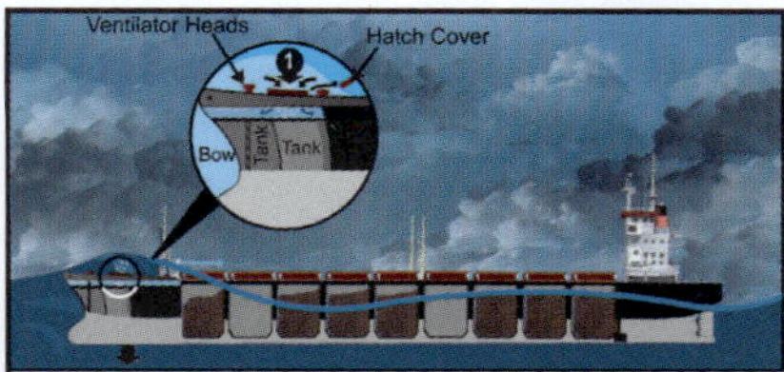

As the *'Derbyshire'* battled with the typhoon, it is believed that the hatch to the bosun's store opened, either because it was improperly secured or due to the force of the seas.

The hatch opening would allow water to flood the bosun's store and forward compartments.

The volume of water across the forecastle allowed water to enter the forepeak ballast tank from the damaged ventilator heads.

It is believed that, over the next 12 hours, with seas repeatedly crashing over the forward part of the ship, these forward compartments filled with water without the bridge noticing the change in trim and the ship sitting heavier.

With the *'Derbyshire'* now trimmed by the bow, this presented more of the deck area to the force of the seas, resulting in No.1 hold filling with 10,000 tonnes of seawater.

With the bow sinking quickly, the remaining cargo holds imploded in a domino effect under the cascading weight of water.

As the *'Derbyshire'* sank, the pressure exerted on the compartments filled with air caused them to implode and fill the remaining spaces with seawater.

supported their conclusion that it was this open hatch that caused the ship to start taking on water.

This conclusion was contested by both family members and some naval experts. The crew on the *'Derbyshire'* were very experienced and well trained and many thought that the idea of them leaving a hatch unsecured when approaching Typhoon Orchid was just too absurd.

The third assessor, Douglas Faulkner, focused on the idea that the *'Derbyshire'* had been the victim of a freak wave, which he scientifically proved were much more frequent than previous mathematical models indicated.

During the reopened formal investigation in April to July of 2000, it was established that the

rope could have been there due to its natural buoyancy and the effects of the water and the wreck over the almost 20 years that it had been submerged. This meant that the theory that the hatches were forced open by heavy wave impact once again seemed most likely.

Disasters and Significant Incidents Involving Bulk Carriers

'Kowloon Bridge'

On 22nd November 1986, the *'Kowloon Bridge'* suffered structural damage and subsequently grounded off the south coast of Ireland.

The *'Kowloon Bridge'* was forced to seek shelter in Bantry Bay to make repairs to deck cracks sustained during heavy weather. Then, after having lost an anchor in a heavy swell, she sailed out of Bantry Bay, only to lose her steerage. She began to drift in continuing heavy seas and, due to the dangerous nature of the situation, the 28 man crew decided to abandon ship and were winched to safety by helicopters in storm force 11 conditions with 9 metre high waves.

Cause

Evidence shows that the *'Kowloon Bridge'* suffered from structural damage in the stern area of frame 65 over a number of years. Reports of cracks in the area and on the main deck dated back to 1982.

The incident also contributed to the initiation of an investigation into the loss of her sister ship, the *'Derbyshire'*, in 1980.

'Mineral Diamond'

On 17th/18th April 1991, the *'Mineral Diamond'* was lost 1,500 miles west of Perth, Australia.

The 10 year old bulk carrier *'Mineral Diamond'*, 141,000 Dwt, sailed with a cargo of iron ore from the Western Australian port of Dampier on 11th April 1991, bound for IJmuiden in the Netherlands via the Cape of Good Hope.

The last message received from the *'Mineral Diamond'* was in the morning of 17th April 1991, reporting that the vessel had reduced speed to 6 knots in force 9 to 10 conditions in position 30° 21'S, 087°48'E. When the ship failed to send her next scheduled AUSREP message, an air and sea search was initiated on 20th April 1991, focusing on an area 1,500 miles west of Perth. When no trace of the ship or survivors was found, the search was abandoned on 24th April. The most probable cause of the loss was sudden and catastrophic structural failure that resulted in the rapid sinking of the ship.

```
RECEIVED AT 09:28 17 APRIL 1991

A/ MINERAL DIAMOND/VRNL//

MRCCAUS AA622349
SEATEX AA0191
MRCCAUS AA62349
48734
TO: SEA SAFETY CANBERRA
FM: MASTER MINERAL DIAMOND
AUSREP/ DR//
A/ MINERAL DIAMOND/VRNL//
B/ 170600Z//
C/ 3021S/08748E//
E/259//
F/ 06.0//
K/ 200600Z/3232S/07500E//
S/ WIND: BF 9/10 DIR:WXS/SWELL
HT:6.0M DIR:VAR/PRES:1006MB//
=RGDS/MASTER
NNNN
SEATEX AA0191
MRCCAUS AA662349
SENT VIA SYDNEY RADIO
```

Figure 1.18 - Last message from the 'Mineral Diamond' received by Australian MRCC Canberra

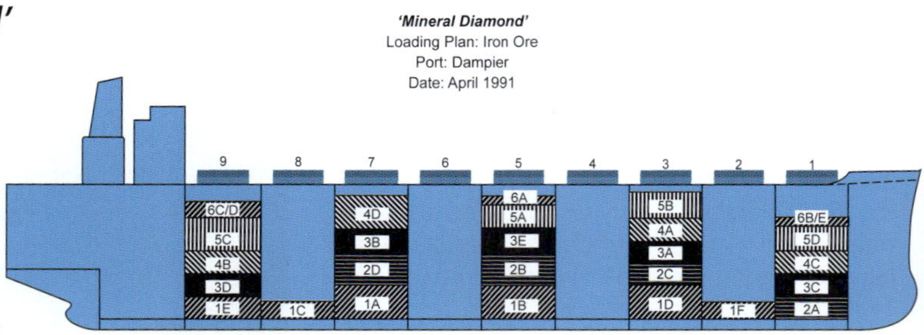

Loading Sequence

1st Run Hold	1st Run Qty	2nd Run Hold	2nd Run Qty	3rd Run Hold	3rd Run Qty	4th Run Hold	4th Run Qty	5th Run Hold	5th Run Qty
7	8,000	1	5,000	3	5,000	3	5,000	3	5,380
5	8,000	5	8,000	7	5,000	9	5,000	5	5,000
8	4,200	3	5,000	1	5,000	1	5,000	9	7,000
3	8,000	7	8,000	9	5,000	7	7,500	1	5,500
9	5,000			5	5,000				
2	3,500								

'Trade Daring'

In November 1994, the *'Trade Daring'* broke her back alongside while loading iron ore.

In November 1994, the 22-year-old, 145,000 Dwt combination carrier *'Trade Daring'* broke her back and sank alongside while loading iron ore at Ponta da Madeira's Pier I in Brazil. The stresses incurred on a ship's hull during loading are substantial and those involved in pouring iron ore at a rate of 16,000 mt/hr into the vessel ultimately resulted in this accident. The port was shut down for more than a month while pumps and cutting tools were used to release the ship, clear the cargo and re-open the pier.

Some months before this incident, another ship that had loaded iron ore in Brazil developed trouble shortly after leaving port. However, the port would not allow her to return as they feared that the ship would sink and block the port. That vessel was subsequently scuttled in the South Atlantic.

In recent years, demands for reduced time in port for ships loading iron ore at Ponta da Madeira have resulted in the loading rate being increased from 16,000 to 20,000 mt/hr.

The *'Trade Daring'*, *'Lassia'* and *'Eurobulker X'* all broke in two while loading or unloading their cargo in port, as a result of incorrect loading or unloading sequences. In response to such occurrences, IACS established a steering committee on bulk carrier safety in 2001 to determine the need for revised design requirements for bulk carriers.

'Pasha Bulker'

On 8th June 2007, the *'Pasha Bulker'* grounded off Newcastle, New South Wales, Australia.

On 7th June 2007, the *'Pasha Bulker'*, 77,000 Dwt and built in 2006, anchored 2.4 miles off the coast of Newcastle, New South Wales, Australia along with 56 other vessels when bad weather hit the area.

At midday on 7th June, *'Pasha Bulker's'* Master paid out more anchor cable following a gale warning. During that evening, 7 ships put to sea. At midnight, the first of the 49 ships remaining in the anchorage started to drag its anchor.

At 06:25 on 8th June, *'Pasha Bulker'* started dragging her anchor in the severe weather. At 07:48 when the ship was underway, there were still 11 ships at anchor. The Master turned the ship away from the coast, now only 1.2 miles away. On its initial east-southeast heading, with the wind and heavy seas fine on the starboard bow, the ship's course made good was in an east-northeasterly direction, parallel to the coast.

At 09:06, the Master of the *'Pasha Bulker'* altered course to put the wind on the port bow in an attempt to make good a southerly course. The alteration was poorly controlled and the ship's heading became southwesterly instead of south-southeasterly as he had intended. With the severe weather now on its port beam, the ship started moving west, towards the coast. The main engine speed was increased to assist the turn to port, into the wind, but this had limited success.

At 09:27, as the ship approached the coast, VTIC offered assistance. The Master declined the

Disasters and Significant Incidents Involving Bulk Carriers

offer and soon after began a turn to starboard. The ship began rapidly closing on Nobbys Beach, now only 8 cables away. The turn was unsuccessful and at 09:46, when grounding was imminent, the Master requested assistance.

At 09:51, *'Pasha Bulker'* grounded on Nobbys Beach. The ship's momentum carried it further onto rock ledges on the beach and its hull was breached, but there was no pollution. The ship was hard aground and the Master requested a crew evacuation. By 13:30, all of the crew had been safely winched off by a rescue helicopter.

At this time, 4 ships still had not cleared the coast, with *'Sea Confidence'* being of most concern. The ship was about 5 cables from the beach and both of its anchors had been let go. At 14:13, authorities ashore directed the Master to accept assistance. A tug was dispatched but was unable to connect a towline in the extreme weather conditions.

Of the other 3 ships, *'Betis'*, at about 3 miles off, was closest to the coast. The windlasses of all 3 ships had failed while they were attempting to weigh anchor. At 16:10, the Master of the *'Betis'* had the anchor cable cut and put to sea. At 20:06, *'Sea Confidence'* also got underway and headed to sea during a lull in the weather, which subsequently deteriorated.

By about midday on 9th June, the last 2 remaining ships had also slipped their anchor cables and put to sea. In the afternoon, salvage personnel boarded the grounded *'Pasha Bulker'* by helicopter.

At 21:38 on 2nd July, *'Pasha Bulker'* was refloated successfully.

On 26th July, after completing temporary repairs in Newcastle, the ship was taken in tow, bound for Vietnam, to undergo permanent repairs.

Safety Designs Incorporated into Bulk Carriers

27 Bulk Carriers Lost in Two Years

1990 and 1991 saw the loss of a total of 27 bulk carriers and the lives of 276 seafarers. These losses were believed to have resulted from catastrophic hull failure. All involved high density cargoes, in most cases iron ore. In 1993, bulk carrier safety was put on the agenda of the IMO's Maritime Safety Committee (MSC). In May 1997, MSC 68 adopted text for a new Chapter XII to SOLAS entitled *'Additional Safety Measures for Bulk Carriers'*.

Water Ingress Alarms for Cargo Holds

The loss of the *'Derbyshire'* showed that hatch cover standards at the time were inadequate. The IMO considered the recommendations of the reopened formal investigation (RFI) into the loss of the *'Derbyshire'* at its Maritime Safety Committee in June 2001 and focused in particular on the recommendation that all masters should be made fully aware of the possible consequences of water entry into forward spaces and any resultant reduction of freeboard.

A particular hazard of bulk carriers is that they can sink very rapidly. For this reason, improved early warning was identified as a means of potentially saving the ship and preventing those upon her from being taken 'unawares'.

It was adopted under SOLAS XII Reg 12 for all bulk carriers from 1 July 2004 that all holds and spaces must be fitted with water level detectors.

"1. Bulk carriers shall be fitted with water level detectors:

1.1.in each cargo hold, giving audible and visual alarms, one when the water level above the inner bottom in any hold reaches a height of 0.5 m and another at a height not less than 15% of the depth of the cargo hold but not more than 2.0 m. On bulk carriers to which regulation 9.2 applies, only the latter alarm need be installed. The water level detectors shall be fitted in the aft end of the cargo holds. For cargo holds which are used for water ballast, an alarm overriding device may be installed. The visual alarms shall clearly discriminate between the two different level detectors in each hold;

1.2.in any ballast tank forward of the collision bulkhead required by regulation II-1/11, giving an audible and visual alarm when the liquid in the tank reaches a level not exceeding 10% of the tank capacity. An alarm overriding device may be installed to be activated when the tank is in use; and

1.3 in any dry or void space other than a chain cable locker, any part of which extends

Safety Designs Incorporated into Bulk Carriers

forward of the foremost cargo hold, giving an audible and visual alarm at a water level of 0.1 m above the deck. Such alarms need not be provided in enclosed spaces the volume of which does not exceed 0.1% of the ship's maximum displacement volume.

2. *The audible and visual alarms specified in paragraph 1 shall be located on the navigation bridge.*
3. *Bulk carriers constructed before 1 July 2004 shall comply with the requirements of this regulation not later than the date of the first annual, intermediate or renewal survey of the ship to be carried out after 1 July 2004."*

Ref: SOLAS Ch XII Reg 12

Alternate Hold Loading Ban for Bulk Carriers

Bulk carriers carrying iron ore are designed to load to their marks by carrying a full cargo in alternate holds (eg cargo holds 1-3-5-7-9) or in block loads (eg cargo holds 1-3-4-6-7-9).

An alternate hold loading plan will reduce the amount of hold cleaning that the ship has to undertake and allows the ship to load and discharge quicker. This method of loading also helps to raise the ship's centre of gravity, making it less 'stiff' and therefore more comfortable for the crew, particularly on ocean voyages. Loading in alternate holds rather than across all holds has been shown to have very little effect on the vessel's rolling period. Loading in alternate holds may require more shifts of the conveyor than loading across all holds.

Structural stress is greater in an alternate hold loading condition than a homogeneous one. In the alternate loading condition, 90-100% of the vessel's hull girder strength is utilised, while homogeneous loading may only utilise 50% of the bending strength and even down to 25% of the shear strength. Therefore, a bulk carrier has substantially more reserve strength when loaded homogeneously.

It was agreed to ban bulk carriers from sailing with any hold empty unless the structural requirements for new ships stated in SOLAS Chapter XII are complied with and the hold frames comply with IACS UR S12 Rev. 2.1 or equivalent.

The ban applies only to the full load condition, which is defined as *"a draught corresponding to 90% of the ship's deadweight at the relevant freeboard"*.

The term 'empty' is defined as *"a hold loaded to less than 10% of the hold's maximum allowable cargo weight"*.

Double Hull Mandated for New Bulk Carriers

New bulk carriers over 150 metres in length are required to be of double hull construction.

Two main advantages of this type of construction are:

- It provides additional protection against side shell failure
- a double hull and smooth inner surfaces have operational advantages.

Studies on bulk receiving terminals have shown that the discharge time for double-hulled bulk carriers is 10 to 25% less than for traditional bulk carriers with exposed frames in the cargo holds when discharging stickier cargoes, such as coke and coal. Importantly, the level of stevedore damage to the hold structure during discharge, particularly the hold frames and frame brackets, was reduced by a factor of six.

The amendments entered into force on 1st July 2006.

Enhanced Survey Programme

This covers the evaluation of hull structure and ship systems in accordance with the IACS Common Structural Rules (CSR) for bulk carriers.

Bulk carrier ESP (Enhanced Survey Programme) is a mandatory Class notation for bulk carriers as defined in SOLAS IX, Reg 1.6 and IACS UR Z11. This Class notation covers the enhanced survey programme according to SOLAS XI-1, Reg 2. The Class notation bulk carrier ESP is assigned following survey reports that verify compliance with the Rules.

It is felt in the industry that this may be the most important safety measure ever imposed on bulk carriers.

The enhanced survey programme was adopted by the IMO Assembly as Resolution 744(18) in 1993.

Container Ships

The carrying capacity of a container ship is determined by her length, breadth and depth, and the number of containers that can be placed abreast on deck and in the holds. Each additional container width requires an increased breadth of 2.8 metres.

Container ship capacity is typically expressed in twenty-foot equivalent units (TEU), corresponding to the number of 20′ x 8′ x 8′6″ containers she can carry. On average, a loaded container weighs about 10 to 12 tonnes, but to allow a margin of safety, a container ship's deadweight is calculated on an average of 12 to 14 tonnes per TEU.

Container ships on global runs, calling at major ports, will have a container capacity that typically exceeds 5,000 TEU. The major port acts as a hub to supply smaller ports around it, and smaller feeder container ships are used for this purpose.

Courtesy of Maersk Line

World Fleet of Container Ships

Container Ships >500 GT = 4,878 ships

TEU Capacity/top 50 operators: 18,429,652

Global containerised trade 2013: 160 million TEUs

Source: UNCTAD Review of Maritime Transport 2014

New container ships are on average 3x the size of those built 20 years ago.

Source: UNCTAD Review of Maritime Transport 2013

Container Ship Sizes

1st Generation (1960s – 1970)

Converted cargo ship

- Length 135 - 200 m
- Draught <9 m
- Max TEU 500 - 800

2nd Generation (1970 – 1980)

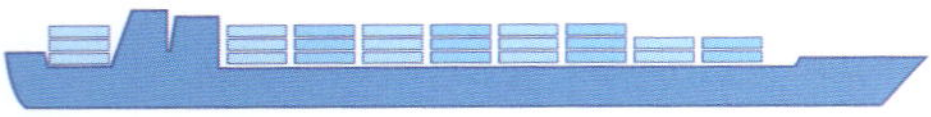

- Length 215 m
- Draught 10 m
- Max TEU 2,600

3rd Generation (1985)

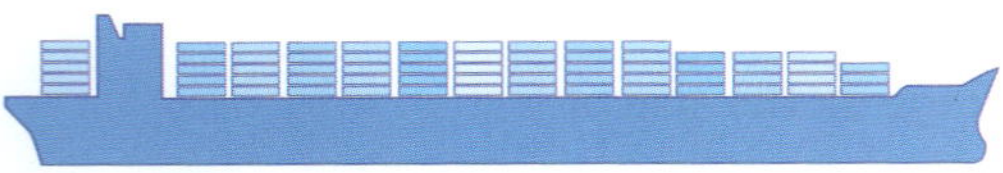

- Length 250 - 290 m
- Draught 11 - 12 m
- Max TEU 3,000 - 4,000

4th Generation (1986 – 2000)

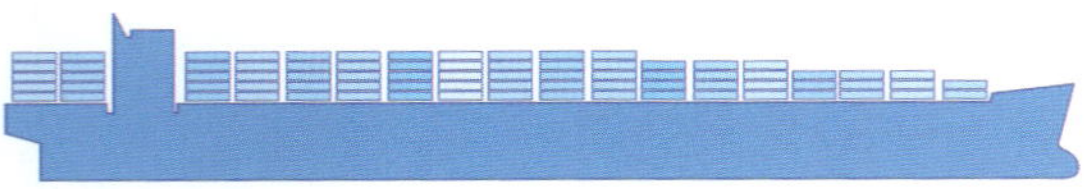

- Length 275 - 305 m
- Draught 11 - 13 m
- Max TEU 4,000 - 5,000

5th Generation (2000 – 2005)

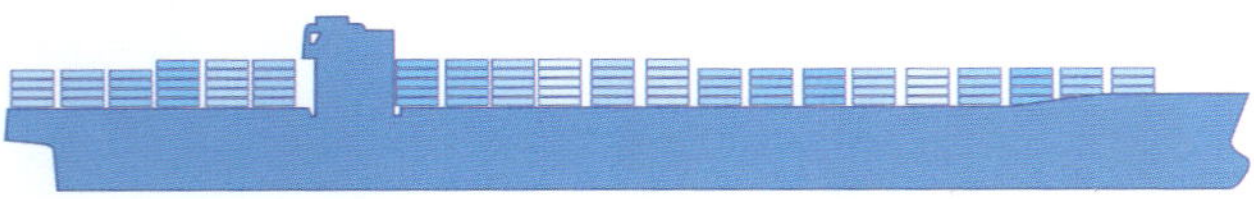

- Length 335 m
- Draught 13 - 14 m
- Max TEU 5,000 - 8,000

6th Generation (2006 –)

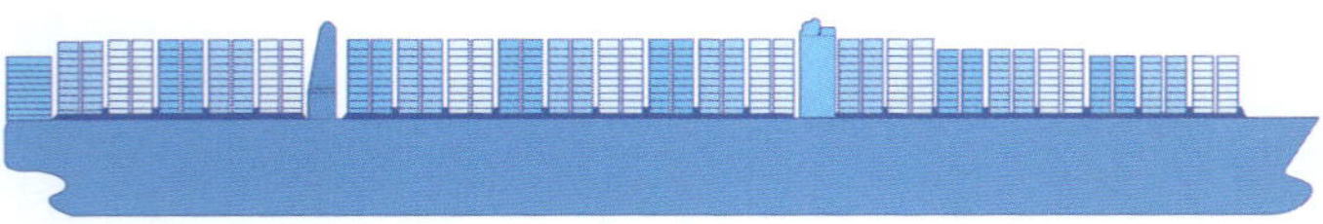

- Length 397 m
- Draught 14 - 15.5 m
- Max TEU 12,000 - 20,000

Small Feeder

Small feeder container vessels are employed for short sea container transportation from a major hub port to outlying ports.

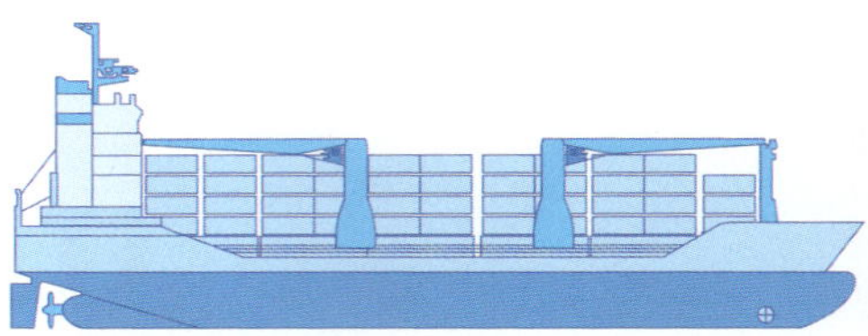

Small feeder

Length: 100 - 140 m
Breadth: 18 - 24 m
Draught: 6.5 - 9.5 m

TEU: <1,000
Typical speed: 15 - 19 knots

Feeder

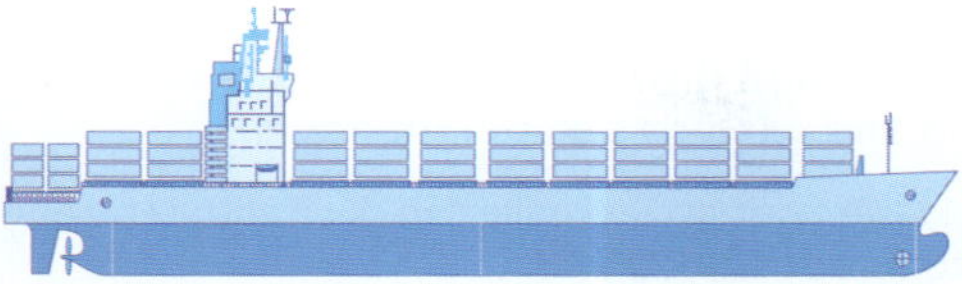

Feeder

Length: 200 - 210 m
Breadth: 23 - 33 m
Draught: 11 - 12 m

TEU: 1,000 - 2,500
Typical speed: 18 - 21 knots

Feeder container vessels are used to supply the very large container ships, particularly in markets where there is a low demand for such large vessels.

Feeder vessels in the range of 400 to 2,500 TEU play a very important role in the container freight market.

Panamax

Panamax

Length: 294 m
Breadth: 32.3 m
Draught: 12 m

TEU: 2,500 - 4,500/5,000
Typical speed: 20 - 24 knots

From the mid 1980s–90s, the maximum container ship size was restricted by the length (294.1 m), breadth (32.3 m) and depth (12.0 m) restrictions of the Panama Canal.

Container Ship Sizes

The Panama Canal

The lock chambers are 305 m long and 33.5 m wide and the largest depth of the canal is 12.5 to 13.7 m. The canal is about 86 km long and passage takes eight hours.

At present the canal has two lanes, but a third lane with an increased lock chamber size opens in 2016 to allow container ships of up to about 12,000 TEU.

Development of Panamax Container Ships

	3rd Generation > 3,000 TEU	10-Abreast ≤4,400 TEU	11-Abreast ≤4,800 TEU	Open-Top Vessel 2,800 TEU	12-Abreast 2,700 TEU
L	= 272.2 m	= 281.0 m	= 282.0 m	= 242.0 m	= 184.0 m
B	= 32.2 m	= 32.2 m	= 32.2 m	= 32.2 m	= 32.2 m
D	= 25.0 m	= 25.0 m	= 21.4 m	= 23.0 m	= 21.2 m
d	= 12.5 m	= 12.5 m	= 13.5 m	= 11.0 m	= 12.8 m

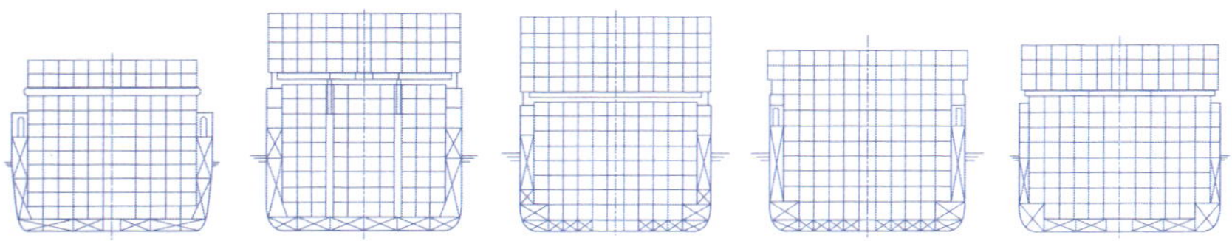

Post-Panamax

Post-Panamax is the name given to a vessel where one or more Panamax dimensions has not been met.

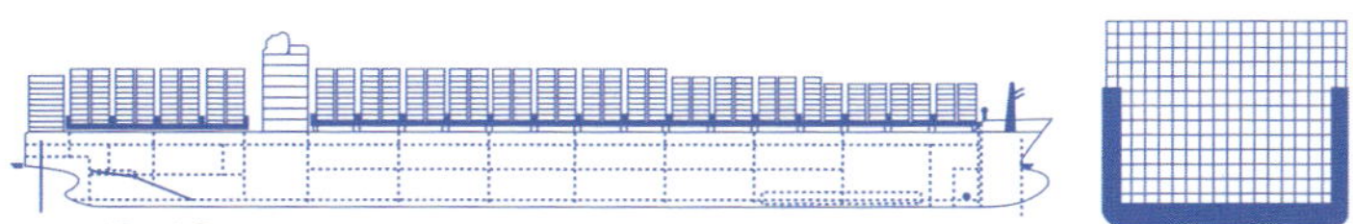

Post-Panamax

Length: 305 - 355 m
Breadth: 43 m
Draught: 12.5 - 13.6 m

TEU: 4,500/5,000 - 10,000
Typical speed: 23 - 25 knots

Courtesy of Maersk Line

A container ship with a TEU capacity of 8,000 exceeds the Panamax breadth requirement by about 13 m. The first container ship with a breadth of more than 32.3 m was built in 1988. In 2004, the global fleet of container ships with a capacity of 8,000 TEU exceeded 100. By 2010, over 30% of the global container fleet, measured by capacity, was classed as Post-Panamax.

'Maersk Kwangyang', built 2007, TEU capacity 6,477

Development of Post-Panamax Container Ships

13-Abreast Max Capacity 4,500 TEU	14-Abreast Max Capacity 4,800 TEU	15-Abreast Max Capacity 7,000 TEU	17-Abreast Max Capacity 8,000 TEU
L = 280.0 m	L = 282.0 m	L = 326.4 m	L = 325.0 m
B = 39.4 m	B = 40.0 m	B = 42.8 m	B = 46.0 m
D = 23.6 m	D = 24.3 m	D = 24.1 m	D = 27.1 m
d = 12.5 m	d = 14.0 m	d = 14.5 m	d = 14.0 m

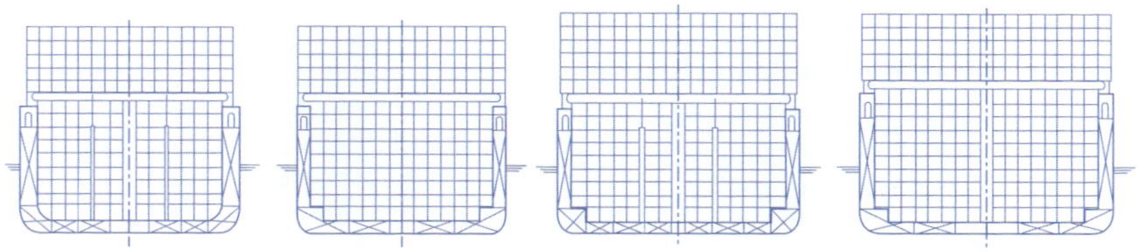

Suezmax/Ultra Large Container Ships (ULCS)

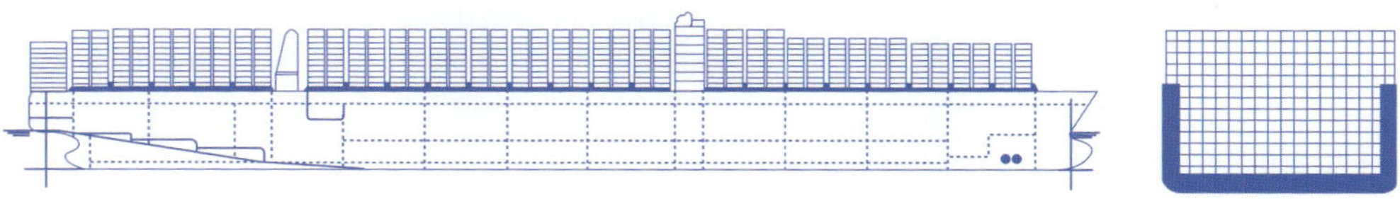

Length: 397 m
Breadth: 56 m
Draught: 15.5 m

TEU: 10,000 - 14,500
Typical speed: 24 - 26 knots

Suezmax or Ultra Large Container Ships (ULCS) carrying up to 14,500 TEU have been regarded as the sixth generation of container ships since their construction began in 2006. These ships, with a breadth of 50 m to 57 m and corresponding maximum draught of 15.5 m, are designed to meet the present Suezmax size. Container ships of this size (10,000 TEU and above) require a twin-engine installation.

'Eugen Maersk'
- ***Built 2008***
- ***397.7 m long***
- ***14,770 TEU***

Courtesy of Maersk Line

Container Ship Sizes

Post-Suezmax (Ultra Large Container Ships)

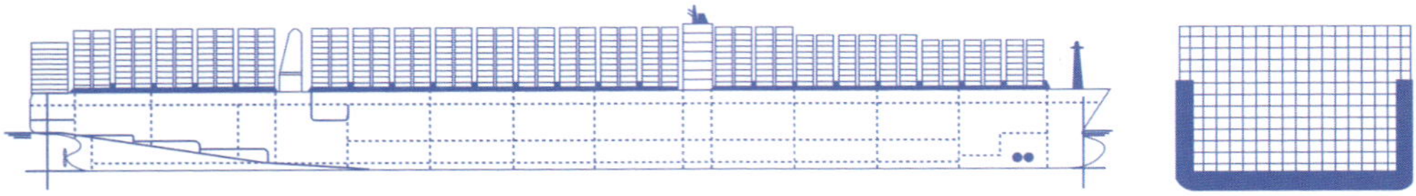

2013 Maersk Triple E Class

- Length: 400 m • TEU: 18,000 • Breadth: 59 m • Typical speed: 25 knots • Draught: 14.5 m

Post-Suezmax (Ultra Large Container Ships)

In 2011, Maersk ordered 10 container ships of 18,000 TEU for US$1.9 billion, with a further 10 vessels to be delivered during 2014 and 2015. Known as the Triple E, this ship is classified as a post-Panamax ship, as its cross-section is too big for the Panama Canal, even following completion of the expansion project in 2016.

The world's first Triple E ship, the *'Mærsk McKinney-Møller',* was launched in February 2013. At 400 m long, 59 m wide and 73 m high and with a capacity of 18,000 TEU, the Triple E is a true giant. The Triple E sets new standards for container ships, with improved economies of scale, from which the Triple E takes its name: Energy, Efficiency and Environmental performance.

Economies of Scale

By moving the bridge forward and the engine rooms further aft, more space is created for stacking containers, increasing the number of container rows from 22 to 23 and increasing overall capacity by 16%.

Energy Efficiency

Improvements to the hull design and a twin propulsion system contribute to overall efficiency. The propulsion system comprises twin super long-stroke engines, operating at a reduced top speed of 23 kts, and the large diameter, four-blade propellers running at a lower rpm improve fuel efficiency.

Recovering waste heat from the engine and exhaust further reduces fuel consumption by an impressive 9%.

Environmental Performance

Triple E container ships will emit 20% less CO_2 than the Maersk E-Class, eg *'Eugen Maersk'* on the previous page, and 50% less than the average container ship operating on the Asia-Europe route.

The Triple E ships will be employed on Europe-Asia trade, where there are 14 ports large enough to accommodate them. In port, an 18,000 TEU vessel serviced by 1 gantry will need 60 days of port stay. Serviced by 16 gantries (8-port side, 8-stbd side), it will need 3.75 days of port stay.

The parameters of Triple E vessels differ little from their predecessor, the Maersk E-Class, but have been adjusted to ensure that they can safely transit the Suez Canal. For example, a ship with a beam of 50 m can transit the Suez Canal up to a draught of 18.9 m, but a ship with a beam of 65 m can only transit up to a draught of 14.5 m. A ship such as the *'Mærsk McKinney-Møller'*, with a beam of 59 m, would be allowed to transit with a 15.95 m draught.

Courtesy of Maersk Line

Figure 1.19 - Triple-E 'Mærsk McKinney-Møller' maiden voyage, July/August 2013

Types of Containers

Standard Containers

ISO 6346 covers the standardisation of containers and establishes the TEU as the base unit.

The standard establishes:

- An identification system for each container through:
  - An owner's code, commonly known as the BIC6 code
  - a letter identifying the type of equipment
  - a serial number
  - a control digit
- a code establishing the measurements and type of container
- a country code
- operating markings.

Twenty-Foot Equivalent Unit (TEU)

Standard containers are also known as general purpose containers. They are closed containers, ie they are closed on all sides. A distinction may be drawn between the following types of standard container:

- Standard containers with doors at one or both end(s)
- standard containers with doors at one or both end(s) and doors over the entire length of one or both sides
- standard containers with doors at one or both end(s) and doors on one or both sides.

Standard containers can vary in dimensions and weight, resulting in a wide range of 'standard' containers.

They are used for all types of general cargo (dry cargo) including those packed in boxes, cartons, cases, sacks, bales, pallets, drums, etc.

Forty-Foot Equivalent Unit (FEU)

High-cube containers are similar in structure to standard containers, but are taller. Standard containers have a maximum height of 2,591 mm (8'6"), while high-cube containers are 2,896 mm (9'6") tall. High-cube containers are usually 40 feet long.

Types of Containers

Open-Top Containers

The walls of open-top containers are generally made of corrugated steel and the floor is made of wood.

They have two distinguishing structural features:

- The roof consists of removable bows and a removable tarpaulin
- the door header may be swivelled out.

These features greatly simplify the process of packing and unpacking the container. In particular, it is very easy to pack and unpack the container from above or through the doors by crane or grab when the roof is open and the door header is swivelled out.

The roof bows of an open-top container support the tarpaulin and contribute to container stability.

Lashing rings, to which the cargo may be secured, are installed in the upper and lower side rails and the corner posts. The lashing rings may take loads of up to 1,000 kg.

Open top containers are primarily used to carry heavy and/or bulky finished products.

Figure 1.20 - Open-top with no cover

Figure 1.21 - Open-top with canvas cover

Flatracks

Flatracks have a high loading capacity floor structure, composed of a steel frame and a softwood floor, and two end walls, which may be either fixed or collapsible. The end walls are stable enough to allow cargo securing to be attached and several flatracks to be stacked on top of one another. Flatracks are available in 20 foot and 40 foot sizes.

A number of lashing rings, to which the cargo may be secured, are installed in the side rails, the corner posts and the floor. The lashing rings may take loads of up to 2,000 kg in the case of 20 foot flatracks or up to 4,000 kg in the case of 40 foot flatracks.

Some 20 foot flatracks have forklift pockets.

Many 40 foot flatracks have gooseneck tunnels at each end, ie a recess in the floor used to centre the container on a gooseneck chassis. The recesses allow the containers to lie lower and therefore to be of taller construction. In addition,

they are sometimes equipped with lashing winches with 2 metric tonne lashing belts.

For transport of certain cargoes, flatracks may be provided with stanchions.

Flatracks are suitable for top or side loading, and are used for items such as heavy machinery, pipes and boats.

Ventilated Containers

Ventilated containers, also known as passive (naturally) ventilated or coffee containers, allow cargo to be ventilated in transit through openings in the top and bottom side rails. The openings do not let in spray. These containers are often used to transport green coffee beans.

The usual size for ventilated containers is 20 feet.

Lashing rings for securing the cargo are installed in the upper and lower side rails and the corner posts. The lashing rings may take loads of up to 1,000 kg.

Refrigerated Containers

Refrigerated containers (reefers) are used to transport goods that need to be kept at a constant temperature above or below freezing point. These are divided into chilled and frozen goods, depending on the transport temperature. Goods principally include fruit, vegetables, meat and dairy products, and temperature sensitive products such as camera film.

High-cube integral units are used to transport large quantities of light goods (eg fruit, flowers).

Chilled meat is sometimes transported hanging, so the ceilings of refrigerated containers are often equipped with hook rails.

Controlled atmosphere refrigerated containers are available for transporting fruit and vegetables that can be stored for a longer period in a controlled or modified atmosphere.

Figure 1.22 - Inside a reefer container

The atmosphere is usually established by flushing the container with nitrogen and CO_2. During transport, the atmosphere is regulated by nitrogen flushing or CO_2 and ethylene scrubbers. Controlled atmosphere containers must be as gastight as possible to prevent penetration of ambient air (oxygen).

Figure 1.23 - Reefer container, showing control panel facing the rear of the cab

Types of Containers

Bulk Containers

Bulk (or bulk cargo) containers are used for transporting bulk cargo, such as grain, feedstuffs and spices.

They have loading hatches in the roof, each approximately 455 mm (1′6″) in diameter. The distance between the hatches (centre to centre) is 1.83 m (6 feet). On the door side, there are two discharge hatches, which are sometimes equipped with short discharge tubes for guiding the bulk cargo. Alternatively, two unloading hatches may be mounted in the doorways.

Bulk containers may also be used for general cargo, and lashing rings are mounted in the top side rails for securing. Some bulk containers are equipped with forklift pockets.

Tank Containers

Tank containers are used for liquid cargoes such as:

- Foodstuffs: fruit juices, spirits, sweet oils
- chemicals: hazardous materials, such as fuels, toxic substances or corrosion protection agents.

Tank containers must be at least 80% full to prevent surging of the contents in transit but must not, as a rule, be over 95% full or there will be insufficient ullage space for thermal expansion.

Tank containers intended for transporting foodstuffs must be labelled 'potable liquids only'.

Some hazardous materials must be transported in tank containers with no inlet or outlet openings below the surface of the liquid.

Tank containers are generally designed for an operating pressure of up to 3 bar (above atmospheric). The test pressure used is 4.5 bar.

Tank containers equipped with insulation or heating may be used for cargo that requires temperature controlled transport. The temperature of the cargo may be precisely controlled using temperature sensors.

Significant Incidents Involving Container Ships

Groundings

'APL Panama'

- **Built 2000**
- **268 m long**
- **52,000 Dwt**
- **4,038 TEU capacity**

On 25th December 2005, *'APL Panama'* grounded in the approaches to Ensenada.

'APL Panama' was on a regularly scheduled trans-Pacific route from Oakland to Mexico, then destined for Japan, Taiwan and China. She grounded as she prepared to enter the port of Ensenada.

The vessel was awaiting the pilot, just a few miles offshore, in a current that was setting her onshore. By the time the Captain became aware of the developing situation it was too late to turn the ship away.

The vessel was pushed onto the beach by the seas and became hemmed in by the build-up of sand, becoming increasingly stuck. The vessel has a light displacement of around 15,000 tonnes and was carrying nearly 30,000 tonnes of cargo at the time.

It took until 10th March 2006 to refloat the vessel. At times, up to seven tugboats were pulling at the ship at full force, delivering a combined capacity of more than 40,000 horsepower, which only pulled the ship a few metres further from the shore. The principle used by the salvage company was to roll the ship from side to side until the sand displaced. Even then, many of the containers had to be removed by crane to make it light enough to refloat.

Significant Incidents Involving Container Ships

Courtesy of MCA

On 18th January 2007, cracks in the hull forced the *'MSC Napoli'* to be deliberately beached.

In the English Channel on 18th January 2007, during what was described at the time as 'the worst storm to hit Britain in almost a decade', the *'MSC Napoli'* suffered engine room flooding due to vertical cracks on either side of the hull.

With the ship's stern starting to settle and the risk of sinking a real possibility, the Captain deliberately beached in Lyme Bay on the south coast of England.

After updating the authorities, the Captain and crew successfully launched their lifeboat in the storm with no accidents.

'MSC Napoli' was carrying 2,318 containers. 103 containers were lost from the ship as she beached: 56 of these came ashore and the remaining 47 are unaccounted for and are presumed sunk. In May 2007, the last of the containers on board were discharged by the Smit Salvage team.

When the ship was refloated in June/July 2007, the damage was found to be more severe than expected. The vessel was broken in two using explosives and towed to Belfast, Northern Ireland, in August 2007, to be scrapped.

Insurers have praised Captain Valentin Velev for his professionalism and seamanship in calmly and correctly assessing the condition of his ship.

'MSC Napoli' – MAIB Recommendations

In April 2008, the UK Marine Accident and Investigation Branch (MAIB) issued its final report into the loss of the *'MSC Napoli'*.

The MAIB investigation identified several factors that contributed to failure of the hull:

- The hull did not have enough buckling strength in way of the engine room
- the applicable Class rules did not specify that the buckling strength calculations continued beyond the amidships area
- there were no safety margins between the hull's design loading and ultimate strength
- the load on the hull probably increased due to the 'whipping effect'. This occurs when the hull impacts with the sea causing the hull girder to vibrate
- the ship was going too fast in the heavy seas.

The MAIB and the International Association of Classification Societies identified 30 container ships that could be affected in the same way. The Classification Society identified 12 ships that required immediate action to be taken.

Conclusions

- Incorrect loading weights of containers continue to be a concern, although this was not the case in this particular incident. The discrepancies of the declared container weights would not have been sufficient to cause the structural failure of the *'MSC Napoli'*
- while it is probable that the wave load effect increased the whipping effect, it is not possible to accurately predict the effect it had on the ship
- the change from longitudinal to transverse hull framing in the engine room possibly caused a weakness in the ship's structure. Regular checks for structural deformation and fatigue cracking should be carried out as part of the ship's inspection
- notification of structural damage, as required by Class Rules, and any repairs or damage that require to be rectified must be understood. Any significant repairs to cracks or structures must be reported by the owner and operator to Class
- while it was thought that the ship was travelling at an appropriate speed for the conditions, a reduction in speed would probably have reduced the risk of the hull failing. Masters should ensure that their vessel is travelling at an appropriate speed in heavy weather conditions
- the master and owner should ensure that all critical machinery is operational before the ship departs
- the owners should ensure that the master and officers understand the increase in bending moments caused by the whipping effect.

The Master was praised for how the ship's personnel safely abandoned the vessel in heavy weather conditions. It was also noted that the Master was very keen on life-saving drills. Owners should encourage masters to make decisions on the basis of safety, knowing that they will be fully supported.

'Ara J'

- **Built 1998**
- **148 m long**
- **16,800 Dwt**
- **1,122 TEU capacity**

On 21st January 2003, welding in the cargo hold started a fire on the *'Ara J'*.

Heat from a welding torch being used for repairs inside the main cargo hold of the *'Ara J'* caused an explosion and subsequent fire while the vessel was berthed in Jacksonville, Florida.

A welder was standing on a container that held Styrofoam packaging material when the container exploded. The welder was thrown off the container by the blast and landed on another worker, breaking his ankle. He was the only person injured.

After hearing the explosion, the foreman of the welding company ran into the cargo hold. Both men became trapped with no way of escaping without passing through flames and smoke. The ship's crew used the vessel's crane to pull the men to safety.

Firefighters were lowered into the cargo hold, where they shifted the containers and successfully extinguished the fire.

The fire caused no major structural damage to the ship, but four or five containers were badly damaged.

USCG photo PA1 Scott Carr

Significant Incidents Involving Container Ships

Fires

'Hyundai Fortune'

- **Built 1996**
- **274 m long**
- **68,000 Dwt**
- **5,551 TEU capacity**

On 21st March 2006, as explosion and fire occurred on board the *'Hyundai Fortune'*.

The *'Hyundai Fortune'* was sailing westbound through the Gulf of Aden when a large explosion occurred aft of the accommodation, catapulting between 60 and 90 containers into the sea.

The explosion started a large fire that spread around the stern of the ship and the accommodation. This resulted in the container stacks in front of the accommodation catching fire. Further explosions resulted as 7 containers carrying fireworks ignited on the stern.

After failing to contain the fire, the 27 crew abandoned ship and were subsequently rescued.

Estimates suggest that at least one third of the containers were damaged by the blaze. Every container aft of the superstructure was either incinerated or lost at sea. The majority of the containers forward of the accommodation were left intact, but all refrigerated containers had spoiled due to loss of power.

The combined cost of the ship and cargo was estimated to be in excess of US$800 million. It was estimated that 10% of the cargo was uninsured.

The hull was towed to Oman where 2,249 containers that were salvageable were offloaded for onward shipment to Europe.

On 23rd March, fire-fighting tugs began to arrive on the scene, but the vessel continued to burn for several days. The engine room was burned and completely flooded, causing the vessel to list.

The blaze completely destroyed the stern area and accommodation block, leaving a massive hole in the hull, astern of the accommodation to the waterline. The hull was sold and the ship is now sailing as the *'MSC Fortunate'*.

There are many theories about the cause of the explosion. These include: a chemical reaction from calcium hypochlorite, which reacts violently when exposed to moisture or heat and has been involved in other explosions on board container ships; the possibility that the 7 containers of fireworks may have spontaneously combusted due to the heat; or that an improperly declared container carrying petroleum-based cleaning fluids exploded because it was stowed near the engine room.

Courtesy of the Defense Visual Information Center

'Charlotte Maersk'

- **Built 2002**
- **347 m long**
- **109,400 Dwt**
- **8,194 TEU capacity**

On 8th July 2010, fire broke out on the foredeck of the *'Charlotte Maersk'*.

After leaving Port Klang in Malaysia, en route to Oman, the *'Charlotte Maersk'* reported a fire on the foredeck at 21:00 LT. The vessel immediately initiated fire-fighting procedures.

The following day, the fire was reported as being contained and under control. The crew and the craft assisting in the fire-fighting continued to cool the area around the fire to prevent it from spreading. Around 150 containers had to be opened and extinguished one at a time.

The fire extinguishing operation progressed by initially cooling one or more containers in a specific area for 4 to 6 hours. Then a thermal camera was used to assess the temperature and determine whether the area could be approached to allow container extinguishing to take place. The temperatures were exceptionally high, in some places around 1,000°C.

There were no reported injuries to the 21 crew members.

Courtesy of Malaysian Maritime Enforcement Agency

'MOL Comfort'

- **Built 2008**
- **316 m long**
- **90,613 Dwt**
- **8,000 TEU capacity**

On 17th June 2013, the *'MOL Comfort'* sank in the Indian Ocean.

The 8,000 TEU *'MOL Comfort'* was a container ship built by Mitsubishi Heavy Industries and owned by the Japanese company Mitsui OSK Lines (MOL). On 17th June 2013, the *'MOL Comfort'* was travelling from Singapore to Saudi Arabia carrying 26 crew members and 4,382 containers. During a period of adverse weather in the Indian Ocean, hull fractures occurred towards the centre of the vessel, causing her to split in two.

Initially, both parts of the ship stayed afloat despite the poor weather. Five tug boats were engaged in the recovery of the ship segments and cargo. All the crew were safely evacuated and no serious injuries were sustained.

It had been hoped that recovery of both halves of the ship would assist in determining what caused the vessel to break in two.

Unfortunately, the aft section sank on 27th June, followed by the bow section on 11th July.

The following factors may have contributed to the incident:

- Poor loading/distribution of containers. Although the number of containers appears to have been evenly distributed, it is difficult to tell how the weight was spread. If the containers towards the ends of the ship were heavier than those in the middle, hogging may have occurred
- basic design and building flaws
- excessive corrosion or wear of the ship. This option seems unlikely as the ship was only five years old at the time of the incident, well within the expected lifetime of a ship of this type. Additionally it had undergone

Courtesy of MRCC Mumbai

Significant Incidents Involving Container Ships

its five-year survey in the month before the incident, at which point any corrosion or wear should have been discovered

- adverse weather conditions
- poor seamanship
- problems with ballast management.

After the incident, MOL ordered inspections of the sister vessels to the *'MOL Comfort'.* These resulted in the hulls being reinforced to approximately twice that required by Class NK. The incident also prompted further discussion on the procedures used for loading containers onto ships.

Loss of Cargo

'Ville D'Orion'

- **261 m long**
- **49,200 Dwt**
- **3,940 TEU capacity**

After encountering force 11 winds for over 12 hours, the *'Ville D'Orion'* arrived in Los Angeles on 24th March 2001 with stacks of containers leaning precariously at its stern. The containers had apparently pulled loose at sea after one of the bottom containers collapsed.

USCG reported that, although 69 containers were damaged in the incident, no containers were lost overboard, no HazMat problems were encountered and no injuries were sustained.

PortPictures

'ITAL Florida'

- **239 m long**
- **49,950 Dwt**
- **3,450 TEU capacity**

On 16th July 2007, the *'ITAL Florida'* met the SW Monsoon in the Arabian Sea. The vessel was hit by 7 to 10 metre high waves on the beam. Several stacks collapsed and three containers were lost overboard.

Courtesy of Tony Tang

'APL China'

On 1st November 1998, the *'APL China'* arrived in the Port of Seattle after encountering Typhoon Babs in the North Pacific. Typhoon Babs was described as a fast-moving storm with 40 to 70 foot swells and high winds, 2,700 miles west of California. The *'APL China'* lost 406 containers and a further 1,000 were damaged. It was the biggest loss since the start of containerisation, reported as exceeding US$100 million. The typhoon resulted in major cargo damage to three other container ships: *'APL President Adams'*, *'MOL Alligator Strength'* and *'Ever Union'*.

ACCLAIM Images

'Horizon Hunter'

On 25th January 2010, the *'Horizon Hunter'* arrived a day late in Honolulu, having encountered a storm with 25-foot seas, 30-foot swells and winds of 50 miles per hour. Six containers were lost at sea with a further 30 damaged.

The damaged containers were wedged in place and had to be removed using heavy lift wires placed on the container spreader of a 100-tonne crane and attached to an appropriate lifting point on the container. This took some time because many of the lift points were too damaged to be used. It took around 36 hours to get the majority of the broken containers off the ship. The vessel then moved to another pier for normal cargo operations and departed for Guam a day later.

Container Damage in Heavy Seas

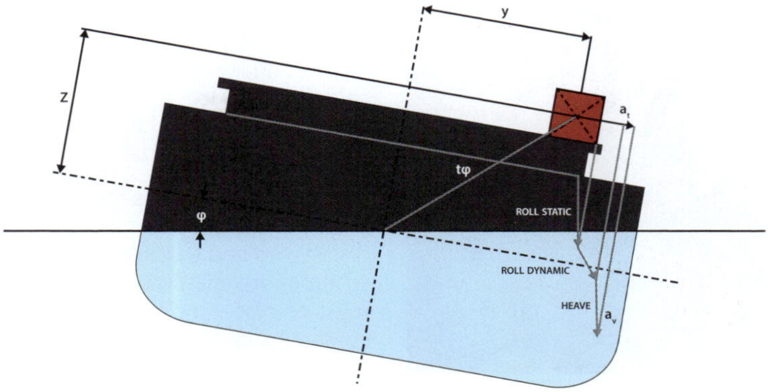

Figure 1.24 - Rolling Condition

Source unknown

Figure 1.25 - Pitching Condition

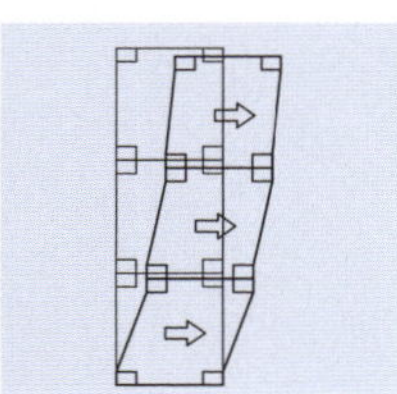

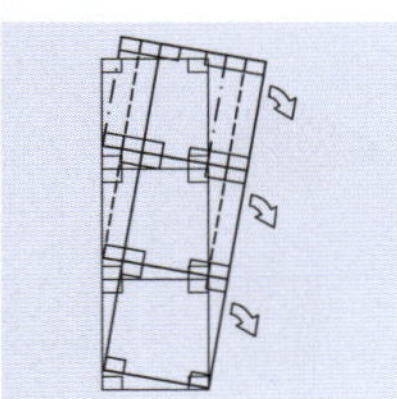

Racking Forces

Racking forces are felt in the container-end and door frame, as a result of the static and dynamic forces parallel to the deck. In the pitching condition, the racking force acts on the container side frames. Effects can be reduced by using diagonal lashing units.

Lifting Forces

Lifting forces can be reduced by using diagonal or vertical lashing units.

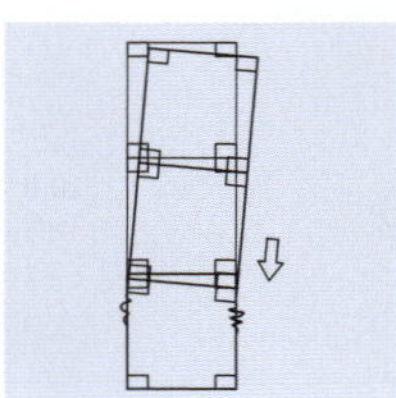

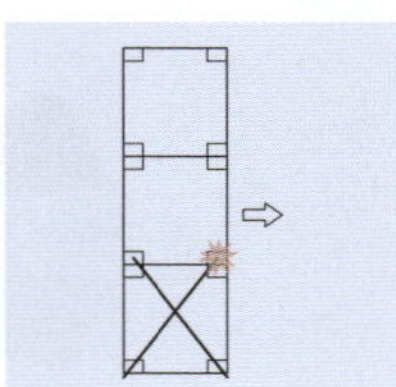

Post Load

Corner post compression cannot be reduced by lashing units, and diagonal lashings may even increase vertical loads. Container weights must be reduced.

Lashing Force

Excessive lashing forces can be reduced by using additional lashing units.

Reproduced with permission from Ship's Equipment Centre, Bremen

Container Stowage

Cargo Securing Manual

Under SOLAS Chapters VI/5.6 and VII/6.6, all cargo vessels of 500 GT or more engaged on international voyages and equipped with cargo securing systems or individual securing arrangements must have a flag State approved Cargo Securing Manual.

Stowage of containers must be carefully planned to ensure that weight is correctly distributed and that securing and lashing schemes are effective. Heavier containers must be placed on the bottom tier and lighter containers on the upper tiers, otherwise the

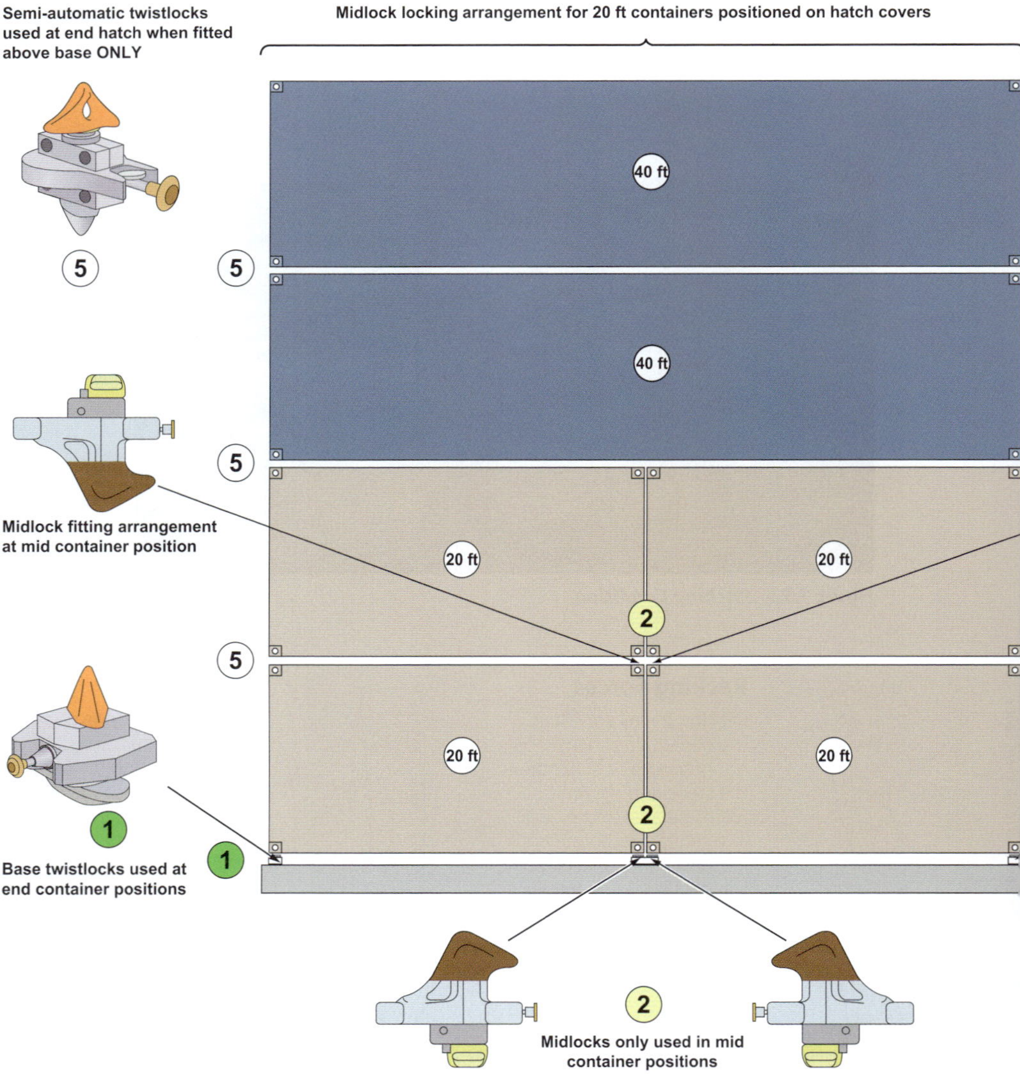

load on the lower tiers may become excessive and the containers will collapse.

There is no agreed definition of what constitutes a heavy or light container, so it often becomes a matter of judgement.

The problem of managing the stow is compounded by carriers that accept cargo while the vessel is already in port and loading. In such cases, the cargo plan becomes obsolete and heavier boxes may end up on top of the stow.

The further a container is placed from midships, the more it will be affected by acceleration forces. Containers stacked on deck near the stern generally have a greater likelihood of loss than those carried forward of the accommodation, so a number of companies have constructed caged arrangements on the poop deck to allow stacking and securing.

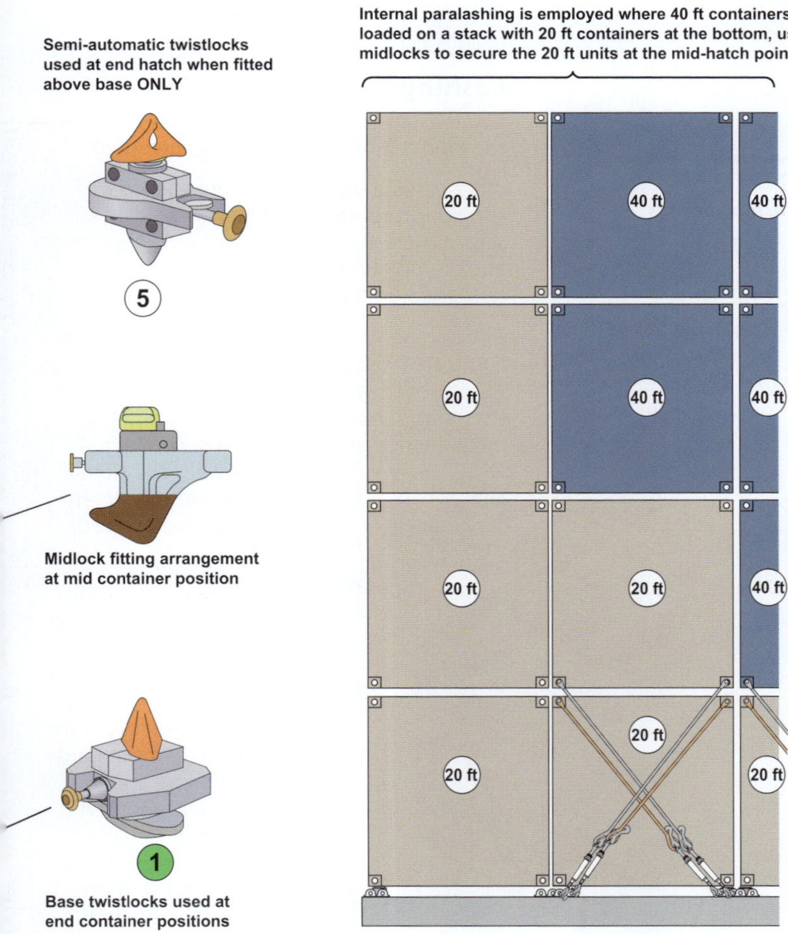

Container Stowage

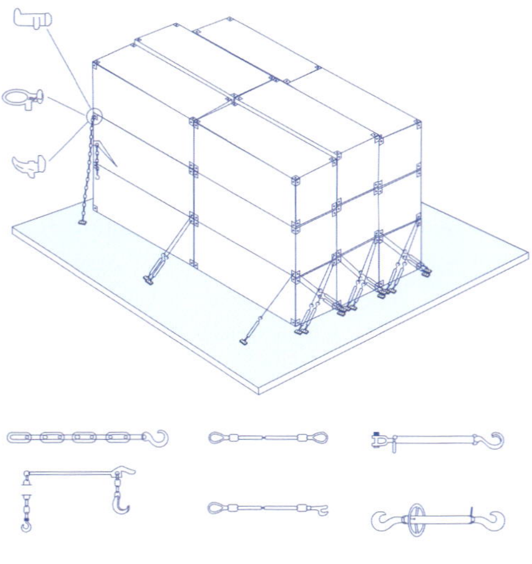

Figure 1.26 - Container lashing fittings

Movement of cargo within the container presents another problem. If cargo is inadequately secured, it can damage the container wall or break through the side during the voyage. If this container is loaded in a lower tier, the damage could cause the stack to collapse. Once this happens, it can create a domino effect in the adjacent rows.

Containers are usually stowed lengthwise as the loading capacity of the side walls is greater than the ends. Also, the stresses in a seaway are usually greater athwartships than in a fore and aft direction. On some conventional ships, containers may be stowed athwartships. Care must be taken to ensure that there is access between containers for checking, lashing and unloading. Containers stowed on deck are exposed to wind stresses as well as the stresses caused by the vessel moving in a seaway. The main principle of container stowage is to ensure a compact stow in all cases.

Lashings

Lashings are used to prevent shifting in both the longitudinal and transverse directions.

All lashings should be separate and each should incorporate a turnbuckle or bottle screw. There should be at least 60% free thread after completion of lashing to allow it to be tightened on passage.

Any lashing system must be approved by the flag State or a designated Classification Society. All approved lashing systems are provided in the cargo securing manual, along with the maintenance procedures. On conventional vessels, additional lashing equipment may also be used.

For under-deck stowage on cellular ships, cell guides are fitted from the tank top to the top of the hold (see Figure 1.30). These guides are the width of a standard container and the boxes are slotted in place. Usually no other lashing is required, perhaps with the exception of stacking cones between container tiers.

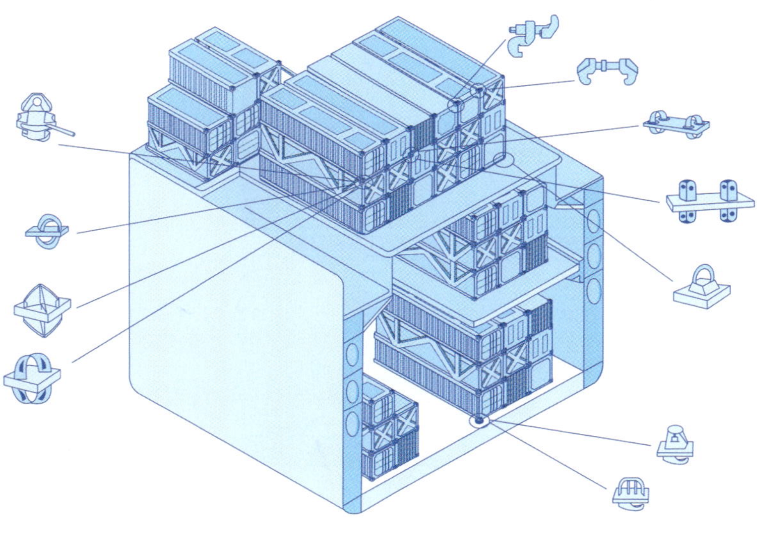

Figure 1.27 - Intermediate fittings

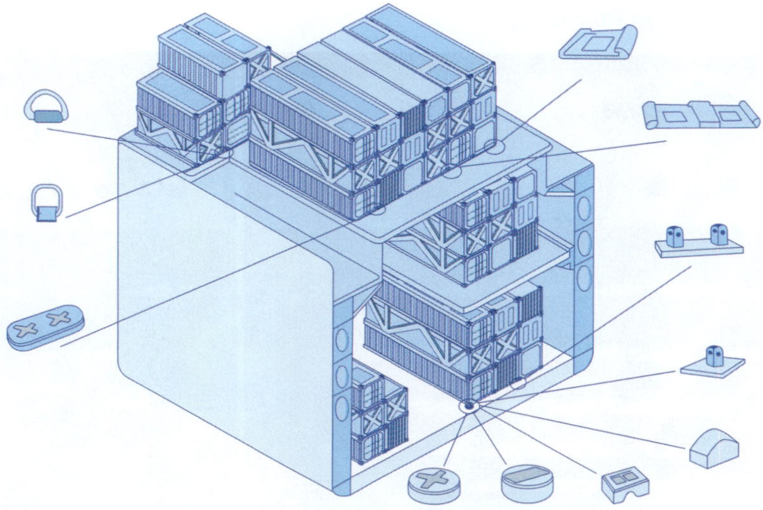

Fittings include: Cone plates, D-rings, deck sockets, dovetail foundations and twistlock foundations.

Figure 1.28 - Bottom foundations

If the lashing fails and a container goes overboard, severe damage may be caused to the ship's structure. Small, apparently insignificant items, such as sounding pipes and air pipes, may be torn out, resulting in flooding of lower compartments.

Crew members have been seriously injured where lashings have parted, and some have lost their lives trying to stabilise shifting cargo.

Always have a good solid stow and a lashing system that anticipates the worst sea conditions that may be experienced.

Securing Mechanisms

A semi-automatic twistlock uses a spring-loaded mechanism to automatically lock the twistlock in place. Containers in the same tier are fitted with intermediate twistlocks that lock them onto the container immediately below. The containers are then held together over the entire width of the ship or the hatch cover using cross lashings tightened by turnbuckles.

To complete the stow, bridge fittings may be fitted on the top row. These are attached to adjoining containers and compact the stow.

Use of bridge fittings is decreasing because the increase in stow height makes it dangerous to manually fit bridge fittings on the top tier.

'The Container Handbook 3' illustrates underdeck lashing of containers on a conventional ship using bridge fittings, stacking cones, twistlocks and chain lashings for the bottom two tiers.

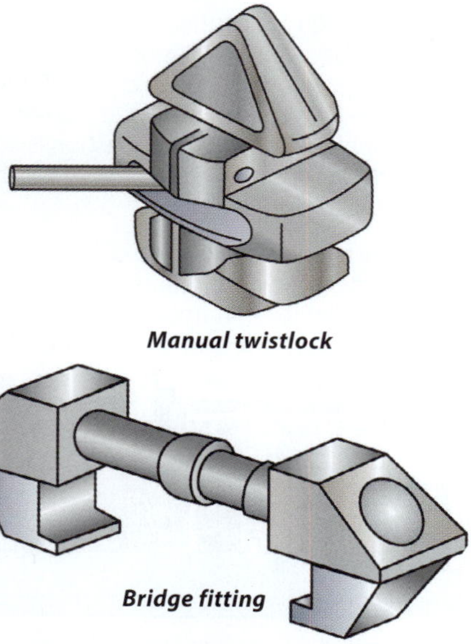

Figure 1.29 - Container securing mechanisms

Container Stowage

Container Stowage Planning

Figure 1.30 - Loading into cell guides

It is vital for the ship to know the location of each individual container during transit. Most ships will stow containers using the 'bay-row-tier' method.

The ship is divided lengthwise into bays, which are numbered from fore to aft. Odd numbered bays are for 20-foot containers and even numbered bays are for 40-foot containers. One 40-foot bay can be divided into two 20-foot bays. For example, if the stowage plan refers to Bay 02 then the container in question is 40-foot in length but if the plan refers to Bay 03, the container is 20-foot in length.

For athwartships stowage, the containers are divided into rows and tiers. The rows are numbered with even numbers from the centre towards the port side and odd numbers from the centre towards the starboard side. If there is an odd number of rows, the centre row is numbered '00'.

Tiers are numbered as follows:

- On deck, the bottom tier is numbered '82', the one above is tier 84 and so on
- underdeck, the bottom tier is tier '02', the one above tier 04 and so on.

The containers are always referred to in the 'bay-row-tier' format. For example, using the container bay plan in Figure 1.32, a 20-foot container stowed underdeck (shaded) will be referred to as Bay 53, Row 12, Tier 12, or 531212. On deck, the shaded container on Bay 54 (40 feet) will be referred to as 540788. The 20-foot box on Bay 55 will be 551184.

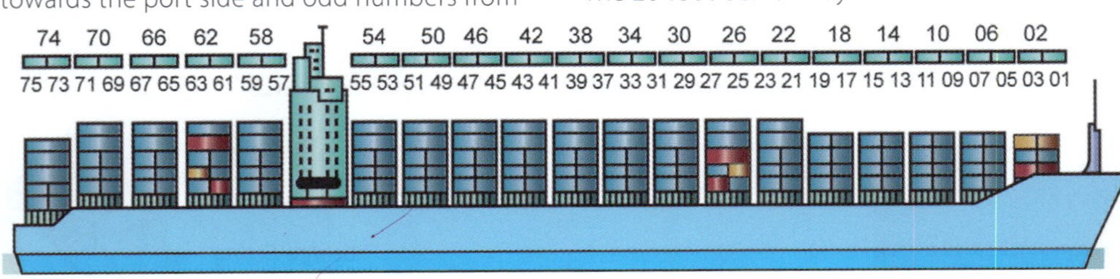

Figure 1.31 - Container ship bay numbers

Bay plans are used to illustrate the containers on a cargo plan. Each bay plan shows the cell and a tier number for each container space and provides space for container codes and weight information. The container codes help to identify the container in that space. The weight information helps the planner distribute the weight of the containers and enter this into the stability computer. Container codes consist of a port code, a container serial number and the container weight.

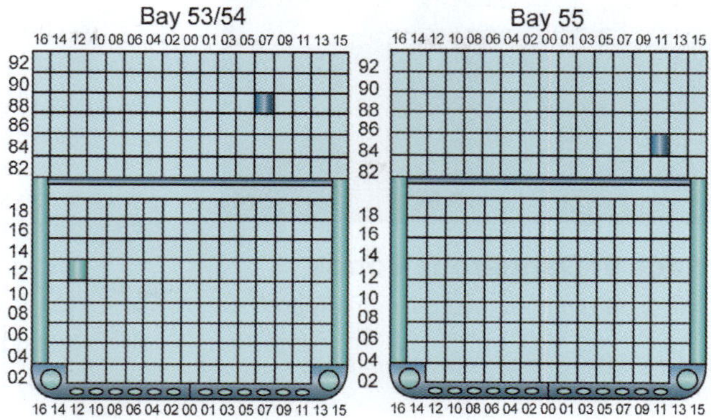

Figure 1.32 - Container bay plan

Duties of the OOW

When loading containers, the OOW must:

- Review and understand the stowage plan
- be aware of special requirements for containers containing dangerous goods, including their stowage, segregation and marking
- ensure reefer containers are placed in their correct slots and their temperatures monitored as per the manifest
- check that any over height or over width cargoes are properly stowed
- check lashings for break bulk cargo stowed on containers
- check that stack limits are not exceeded
- note any physical damage to the containers and evidence of security breach
- check that the door seal is intact
- check for leaks or other evidence of cargo damage
- ensure that the lashing plan is correctly followed
- attend to the ballast to ensure that the ship remains upright and with a reasonable trim by the stern
- check all lashings on completion
- keep proper records
- ensure the ship security plan (SSP) is adhered to.

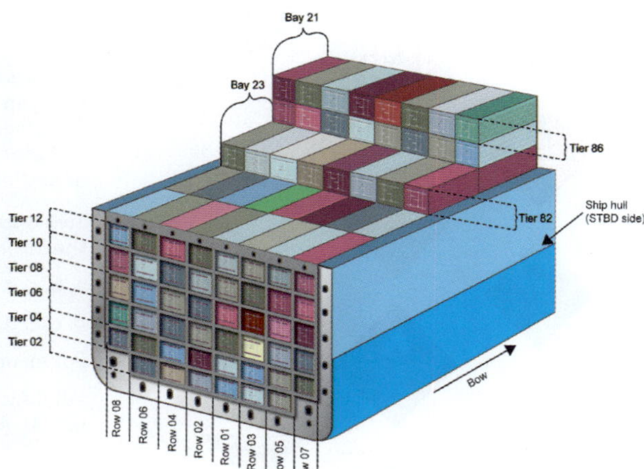

Figure 1.33 - Container identification system

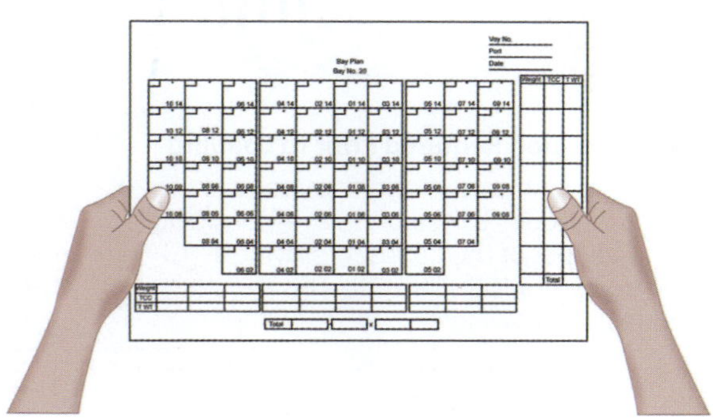

Source 'Cargo Notes'

Dangerous Goods in Containers

Carriage of Dangerous Goods

This section summarises material from UN and IMO sources. Reference should be made to a full copy of the IMDG and any relevant industry-specific publications.

The Classes

Dangerous goods are divided into nine classes based on their associated risks when transported by land, sea or air. This classification is based on UN recommendations that were made in 1957. The class symbols are illustrated below.

Documentation Required Prior to Loading

The regulations governing the carriage of dangerous goods by sea place a responsibility on the shipper of the goods to provide a Dangerous Goods Declaration. This should include the following:

a. The proper shipping name of the material carried.

This is not the trade name but can be the technical name, as long as it accurately describes the goods.

b. The UN Number

This is a 4 digit unique number allocated to all dangerous goods assigned by the United Nations committee of experts (UN List).

c. Hazard class

From 1 to 9.

d. Packing Group (when assigned)

Dangerous substances of Classes 3, 4, 5.1, 6.1 and 8 are assigned to one of three categories (Packaging Groups) according to the degree of danger they present:

- Great danger - Packaging Group I (PGI)
- medium danger - Packaging Group II (PGII)
- minor danger - Packaging Group III (PGIII).

The greater the degree of danger, the more stringent the packaging requirement will be. For other classes, packaging groups may be assigned depending on the degree of severity of any leakage of the substance.

Two options are permitted for the sequence of the information:

a, b, c, d OR

b, c, a, d.

For example:

'Allyl Alcohol, UN1098, 6.1 (3), I' or 'UN1098, 6.1 (3), Allyl Alcohol, I'.

e. Subsidiary Risk

This is an additional risk that may be present in certain goods. For example, a corrosive substance may also be flammable.

f. Marine Pollutant

This classification is included for any substance classified as a marine pollutant under Annex 3 of MARPOL.

g. Number of Packages

Total number of packages to be transported as a unit.

h. Total Quantities

The total volume or mass (in kilograms) is stated for each item of dangerous goods bearing a different Proper Shipping Name. For Class 1 goods, the quantity shall be the net explosive mass.

If the dangerous goods are transported according to the exceptions for dangerous goods packed in limited quantities, the words 'Limited Quantities' shall be included.

i. Flashpoint

If applicable, the flashpoint shall be included for liquid dangerous substances.

j. Any other information required by the IMDG Code or local regulations.

This will include additional information such as the 24 hour emergency contact number required for shipments to the US and additional certificates such as a weathering certificate, etc.

k. Container/vehicle packing certificate.

When dangerous goods are packed or loaded into any container or vehicle, those responsible for packing the container or vehicle shall provide a 'container/vehicle packing certificate' specifying the container/vehicle identification number and certifying that the operation is carried out in accordance with the following conditions:

- The container is clean and dry and fit to receive the goods
- packaging and labelling is carried out as per the IMDG Code
- segregation within the container/vehicle is as per the IMDG Code
- the container is marked and labelled as per the IMDG Code
- a DG note has been received for each dangerous goods consignment loaded in the container/vehicle.

The container/vehicle packing certificate and declaration serves a separate function to the dangerous goods declaration and they are often signed by different people. However, for the sake of convenience, the two declarations are often included in the same document.

Documentation Required on Board the Ship

Dangerous Goods Manifest

Each ship carrying dangerous goods and marine pollutants shall have on board a special list or manifest, setting out the dangerous goods and marine pollutants on board and their locations. Instead of the manifest, a detailed stowage plan, which identifies all dangerous goods by class and sets out their location, may be used.

The dangerous goods declaration is used as a basis for making up the manifest and shall contain at least the information from the DG declaration and, in addition, should contain the stowage position and the total quantity of the dangerous goods or marine pollutants. A copy of the manifest or stowage plan is made available, before departure, to the person designated by the port authority.

Emergency Response Information

Appropriate information shall be immediately available for use in emergency response to accidents and incidents involving dangerous goods in transport. The information may be combined with the Dangerous Goods Manifest or stowage plan and must be immediately accessible in the event of an incident.

The manifest or stowage plan may contain references to the emergency schedules found in column 15 of the dangerous goods list. These will be used, in conjunction with the supplement to the IMDG Code, to decide on a plan of action for emergencies involving dangerous goods or marine pollutants. In place of the above, separate safety data sheets may be provided for each dangerous cargo or marine pollutant carried.

Document of Compliance

Ships of the following descriptions:

- Passenger ships constructed on or after 1st September 1984
- all other ships of 500 tons or over constructed on or after 1st September 1984
- all other ships of under 500 tons constructed on or after 1st February 1992

that are intended for, or that have cargo spaces intended for, the carriage of dangerous goods on international voyages, must carry a document of compliance. The document of compliance will certify that the ship complies with Regulation 54 of Chapter II-2 of the International Convention

Dangerous Goods in Containers

for the Safety of Life at Sea 1974 (SOLAS 1974) and will be limited to five years from the date of issue. The document of compliance is issued by the flag State after a survey. This document is usually in the form of a diagram showing all the spaces on board in which dangerous goods can be loaded. A table then sets out the classes of dangerous goods that the ship is allowed to carry and the spaces in which these classes can be carried. The document also states additional requirements that must be fulfilled prior to carrying the dangerous goods or marine pollutants. This may include additional fire-fighting equipment or ventilation in holds required for certain classes of dangerous goods.

Marking and Labelling

All packaged dangerous goods must be marked and labelled as per the provisions of the IMDG Code. The marking will include an indication of the hazard class and other details such as the subsidiary risks, elevated temperatures, marine pollutants, etc. These markings are required on all four sides of the container and, if the container is bound for an offshore installation, also on the roof.

Marking schemes for limited quantities, as per Amendment 31, require that the outside of the package is marked with a diamond with the UN number in the centre (including the letters 'UN' in front of the number). If there is more than one type of dangerous goods in the package, the diamond must be large enough to contain the UN numbers for all of them. The package does not have to display the class labels required, the marine pollutant mark or the shipping name of the material.

All labels must be affixed in a way that they will still be identifiable on packages that have survived at least three months' immersion in the sea.

IMO Containers

The IMDG Code proposes a more specific treatment for container ships when they carry containers commonly known as 'IMO containers'. These are containers carrying some types of dangerous goods that must be segregated to prevent risks due to incompatibility between cargoes. To accommodate the requirements of the IMDG Code, 'hatchless' container ships are typically built with constructed forward holds for the carriage of IMDG cargoes.

Safety Designs Incorporated into Container Ships

Bow Area

A modern container ship has an elongated, raked bow with reduced flare to minimise the effects of speed loss when the ship is slamming in a seaway.

Containers, particularly those that are in higher stacks stowed forward, can be damaged in bad weather. A wave breaker is constructed on the forecastle to deflect seas that come on deck. A wind deflector may also be located forward of the foremost deck container stack to reduce wind resistance.

Ballasting, Beam and Stability

There are various regional and national regulations concerning ballast water quality, and many regions and countries demand deep water ballast water exchange (BWE) to be carried out before entering port. For example, for countries that have ratified the IMO Ballast Water Convention, BWE at sea is expected by:

- Ships entitled to fly the flag of a Party to the Convention
- ships not entitled to fly the flag of a Party but which operate under the authority of a Party.

Safety Designs Incorporated into Container Ships

There are two methods of BWE:

- Flow through or dilution
- sequential (empty/fill) exchange.

These can be carried out individually or in combination (see Figure 1.34).

There are important operational considerations to be taken into account when carrying out BWE:

- Weather conditions
- avoidance of over and under pressurisation of ballast tanks – ventilation capacity should in general be at least 125% of the maximum flow rate of the water
- minimum/maximum forward and after draughts and trim conditions
- transverse stability and free surface effects on stability, and maintenance of adequate intact stability in accordance with an approved trim and stability booklet
- sloshing loads in tanks that may be slack at any time
- permissible seagoing strength limits of shear forces and bending moments in accordance with an approved loading manual
- torsion stresses and forces
- wave-induced hull vibration
- time to complete the ballast water exchange or an appropriate sequence, taking into account the total volume of ballast water that may have to be pumped in or out
- monitoring and controlling the amount of ballast water
- weather routeing in areas seasonably affected by tropical storms or heavy icing conditions
- documented records of ballasting and/or deballasting
- contingency procedures for situations that may affect the ballast water exchange at sea, including deteriorating weather conditions, pump failure, loss of power, etc.

Reducing the amount of ballast water carried will ease ballasting operations, whether through BWE or the use of a ballast water management system. For example, as container ships have evolved, they have gradually increased in beam width, which increases stability and substantially reduces the requirement to carry extra water weight as ballast. By reducing the amount of ballast water carried, more cargo weight can be carried while retaining the same displacement as in the ballast condition.

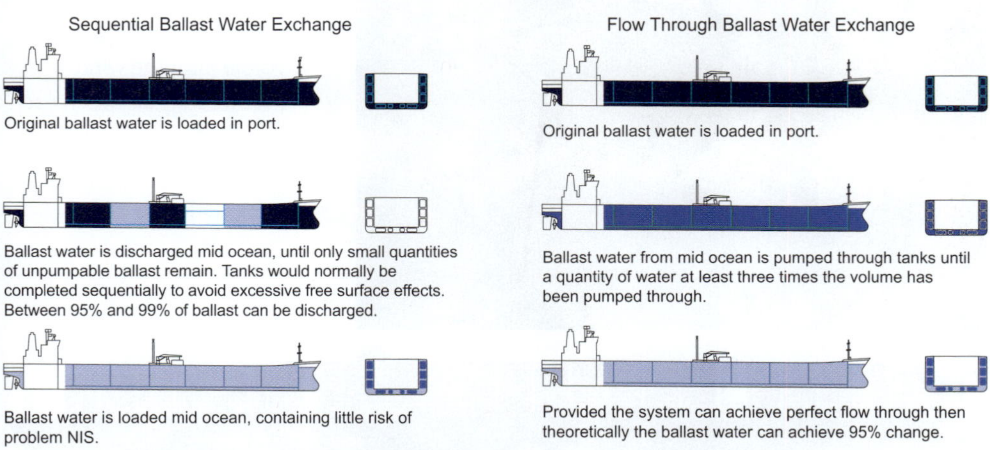

Figure 1.34 - Sequential and flow through BWE

Safety Designs Incorporated into Container Ships

Increasing the beam reduces the ship's rolling period. This is an advantage in container ships that are prone to heavy rolling and vibration, particularly when carrying empty containers.

With a larger beam, improved stability and a reduction in the amount of water ballast necessary, the void space that forms the double hull side has been reduced to typically 1 m width. This in turn allows the container-carrying capacity to be increased.

Hull Monitoring and Decision Support Systems

Following the investigation into the loss of the '*MSC Napoli*', the UK's Maritime Accident Investigation Branch proposed that the industry should develop a system to measure 'whipping'.

Whipping is the juddering vibration that the hull experiences during bow impacts in heavy seas and it may have been a contributory factor in the case of the '*MSC Napoli*'.

These vibrations are not taken into account during the design process of container ships. They are, however, accounted for in hull monitoring systems that show the load on the hull in real time in sea conditions and allow the master and OOW to gauge the effect of any change in these hull stresses after an adjustment to course or speed.

Fire Protection in Cargo Holds

Hatchless cargo holds on container ships cannot be sealed and therefore the use of a CO_2 system, such as would be found in the hold of a cargo ship, is not possible. A water sprinkler system is typically fitted in container ship cargo holds for fire-fighting.

Bridge Visibility

Containers stowed on deck present a particular problem for bridge visibility. The IMO through Assembly Resolution A.708 (17) implemented guidelines for minimum visibility conditions from the bridge.

Field of Vision

- Visible sight of the sea surface from the bridge must not be hidden by more than two ship lengths or 500 metres, whichever is the smaller, on the bow of the ship and 10° at each side, regardless of the loaded or ballast condition of the ship
- any blind spots due to the cargo handling equipment or any other obstruction must not prevent a clear view from the bridge through an arc of more than 10° for each obstruction. The total blind area must not exceed 20°
- the horizontal field of vision from the ship's bridge must extend over an arc of more than 22.5° abaft the beam on both sides of the ship
- from the main conning position, the field of vision must extend at least 60° on either bow
- the ship's side must be visible from the wing
- the structure between each bridge window must be as small as possible and not positioned in front of any work station location.

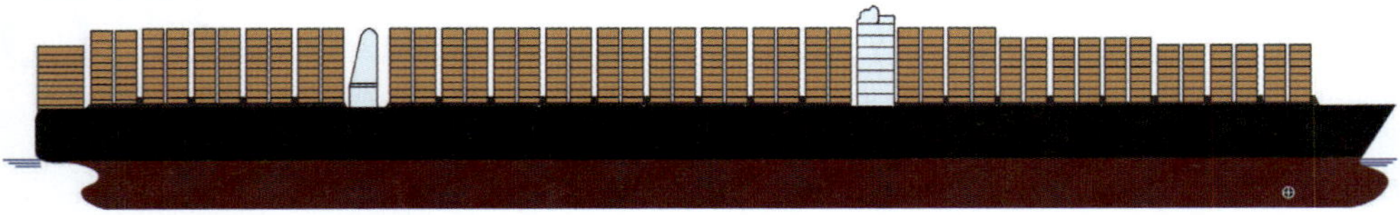

Anti-heeling Systems

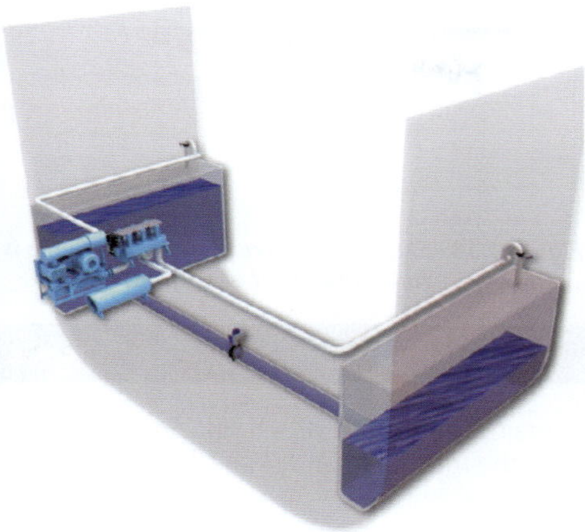

Figure 1.35 - Anti-heeling system

Anti-heeling systems are used to keep ships upright during loading and unloading. They use a constant pneumatic air purge and regulating valve system to force air into the top of one tank while venting the one on the other side. This rapidly transfers water from one side of the vessel to the other, creating a righting moment that compensates for heeling forces.

Systems of up to 5,000 tonnes metres per minute are in operation and can be supplied as either standalone air blower activated, combined with tank stabilisers, pump activated with dedicated heeling pump, or integrated into the ballast system.

Trim control systems can be combined with anti-heeling systems. Unlike anti-heeling systems, these make use of ballast tanks fore and aft to compensate for any trim moments automatically. Alternatively they may be operated by dedicated trim pumps or designed as an integral element within the ballast system.

Parametric Roll Prevention System

Figure 1.36 - Test tank images showing the benefit of a parametric roll prevention system

Parametric roll prevention systems are designed to prevent the build-up of parametric roll in head or following seas. Sea-keeping model tests demonstrate that a system can reduce the risk of parametric disturbance by shifting the critical wave threshold to such high values that the chances of ever encountering such a roll during a vessel's service life become extremely low.

A typical example of a complete ship system will include several pairs of U-shaped tanks and pneumatically-controlled air valves, plus a control unit with pitch and roll sensors. The controller detects the onset of parametric rolling and uses the damping effect of the tanks fluid's oscillations, which is controlled by air valves in accordance with the ship's motion.

Safety Designs Incorporated into Container Ships

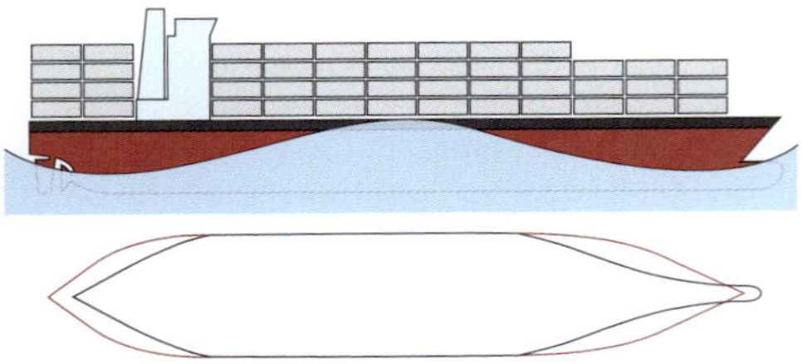

Figure 1.37 - Ship on the wave crest. Waterline is thinner in this condition

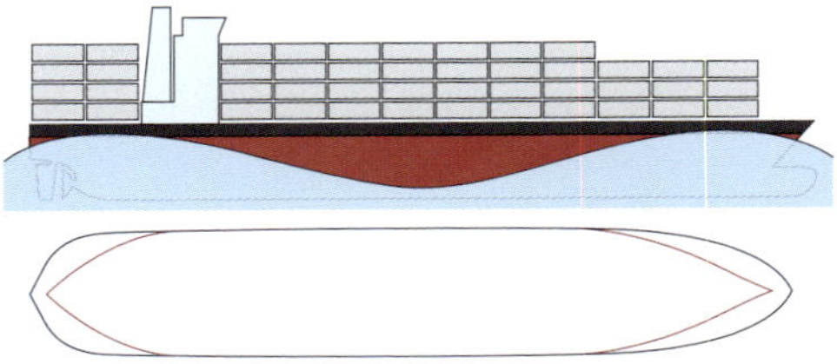

Figure 1.38 - Ship in the wave trough. Waterline is fuller than that of still water

Hatchless Container Ships

Hatchless container ships first appeared in the early 1990s. The first ship, *'Bell Pioneer'*, was built with four holds; three open to the weather and one covered by hatch covers.

Open-Top Container Ships

'Open-top' or 'hatchless' container ships are designed so that one or more of the cargo holds is not fitted with a hatch cover. Almost all of the (about 120) open-top vessels currently in service are of Small Feeder size (500 to 1,000 TEU). However, there are a few Handysize (1,000 to 2,000 TEU) and Subpanamax (2,000 to 3,000 TEU) ships. In a typical design, these vessels have no hatch covers, usually except for holds 1 and 2, which are equipped with hatch covers to allow the carriage of a limited number of dangerous goods containers.
Box type girders are used extensively, which provide considerable strength and rigidity and allow for large open spaces.

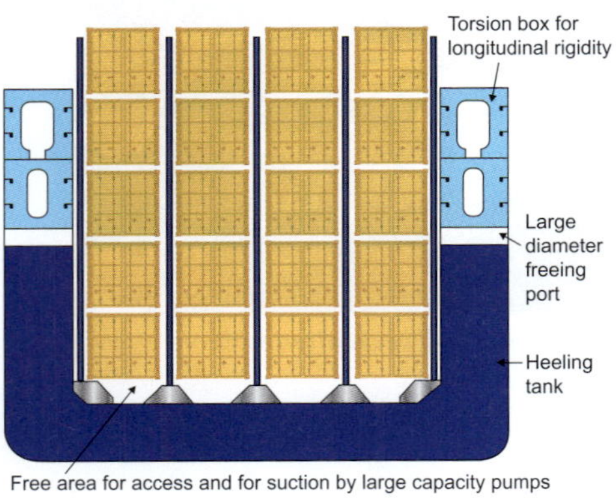

Figure 1.39a - Hatchless container ship

Cargo Access

Cargo holds are accessible through lashing bridges and inclined ladders at both ends of the container bay. These structures can be entered from the main deck and from alleyways next to the hold.

A limited view of containers stowed in the holds is possible from the deck. However, it is not possible to open the doors of a container.

Ventilation

Ventilation must provide at least two air changes per hour, based on the volume of the empty hold. With around 80% of the hold filled with containers, up to ten air changes per hour can be achieved.

Water Ingress

Open ships allow a certain amount of water to enter the holds.

The high-sided structure around the bow provides added protection from green water and, should water enter the holds, it is removed by large stripping pumps. If the pumps fail, water is discharged through freeing ports located at the freeboard deck.

To avoid flooding, open-top ships are equipped with 200 to 300 mm high pedestals on the tank top on which the bottom containers are stowed.

The ships are equipped with at least three independent bilge pumps, each capable of pumping the maximum hourly rate of seawater in seagoing conditions.

- The bilge system for cargo holds is independent of the machinery space bilge system and located outside of the machinery space
- all open cargo holds must be equipped with bilge high level alarms

Hatchless Container Ships

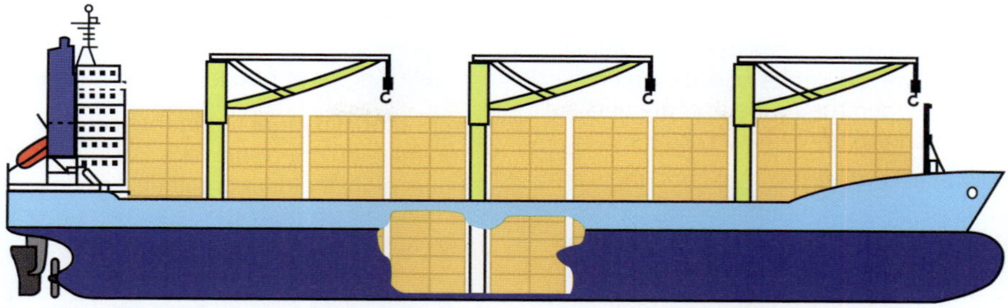

Figure 1.39b - Hatchless container ship

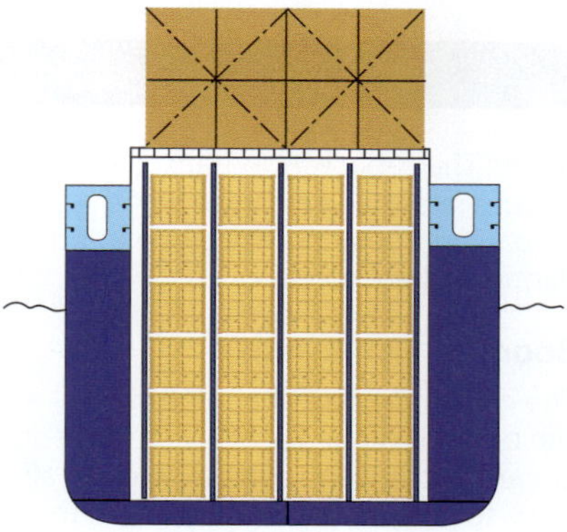

Figure 1.40 - Container ship

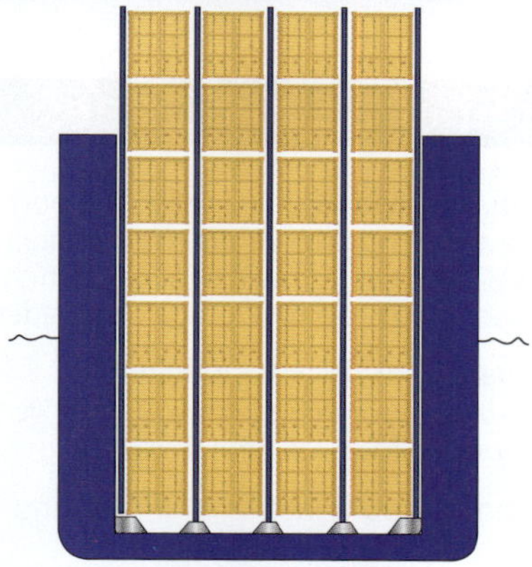

Figure 1.41 - Hatchless container ship

- some open-top container ships use 'rain shelters' (lightweight covers placed on the uppermost containers).

Fire Detection

Open-top container ships are fitted with sample extraction smoke detection systems. Fires are likely to be identified visually by the bridge much earlier as they would see smoke rising from the cargo hold.

Fire Extinguishing

Cargo holds are protected by a fixed water spray system that is capable of spraying water into the cargo hold from deck level downward.

Conventional Versus Open-Top (or Hatchless) Container Ships

Conventional container ships carry approximately 30% of the containers in the hold and the remaining 70% on deck. An open-top hatch ship carries about 80% in the hold, protected by high double sides, and the remaining 20% above the hold level housed in a cell guide system. A conventional short sea container ship would have a freeboard of approximately 2 metres compared with a freeboard of 6.5 metres on an open-top vessel of similar TEU capacity.

Hatchless container ships reveal a fundamental problem in the way in which gross tonnage is measured because the hatchless design was not envisaged when the 1969 tonnage rules were agreed. Consequently, open-top vessels are measured in a way that can make them up to 60 to 70% higher than a conventional ship of similar TEU capacity, because a conventional vessel only measures the under-deck space while on a hatchless vessel all open space from the rail down is calculated and measured.

The advantages claimed for open-top container ships are:

- Removing the hatch covers allows more cargo Dwt to be carried. Furthermore, since the hatch covers were located high in the ship, their removal significantly improves stability
- elimination of the hatch covers removes the need to open and close them, speeding up port turnaround time and reducing cargo operation costs
- the fixed container guides do not terminate at the hatch coaming as in a conventional container ship. Instead, they extend above the deck to the full permissible height of the deck cargo. This provides better

Hatchless Container Ships

securing for the containers stowed above deck and eliminates the need for manually installed lashing cables or rods, which is required when the on-deck containers are stowed on top of the hatch covers

- individual vertical stacks of containers are always accessible independently of the other stacks. On a conventional container ship, containers on deck must be moved to allow a hatch cover to be lifted to give access to a container in a stack below deck
- the maintenance of hatch covers, hatch clamps, coaming gaskets and other hatch securing gear becomes unnecessary.

The potential danger lies in the fact that the containers on open ships are stacked up to 13 tiers high. If older containers are stowed in the lower tier, metal fatigue in the corner posts may cause the whole stack to collapse.

However, the risk of losing containers overboard is greatly reduced due to the cell guides.

Container Gantry Cranes

Containers are loaded/unloaded at the port using container gantries or quayside container cranes (QCCs). These consist of a supporting frame, operation's cabin, boom and spreader.

Gantry cranes normally lift containers individually, but some newer cranes can lift two or even four 20-foot containers at once.

A QCC can cost up to US$10-12 million and takes two years to deliver.

The cost of consumable parts for one QCC crane ranges between US$50,000 and 100,000 per year.

The life of a quayside container crane is easily in excess of 30 years, and could be 40 or more years if the crane structures are properly maintained and protected against corrosion. Fatigue cracks occur as the crane ages, but they can often be repaired.

Supporting Frame

The supporting frame (gantry) is the giant structure of the crane that holds the boom and the spreader. The frame is mounted on rails to enable it to be moved along the quayside.

Operator's Cabin

This is incorporated in the bottom of the boom. The cabin is 80% transparent so that the operator has a clear view of the loading/unloading operation while operating the gantry and the spreader.

Boom

The crane may be either high profile, where the boom is hinged at the waterside of the crane structure and can be raised to allow ships to pass, or low profile, where the boom is retracted into the gantry when not in use.

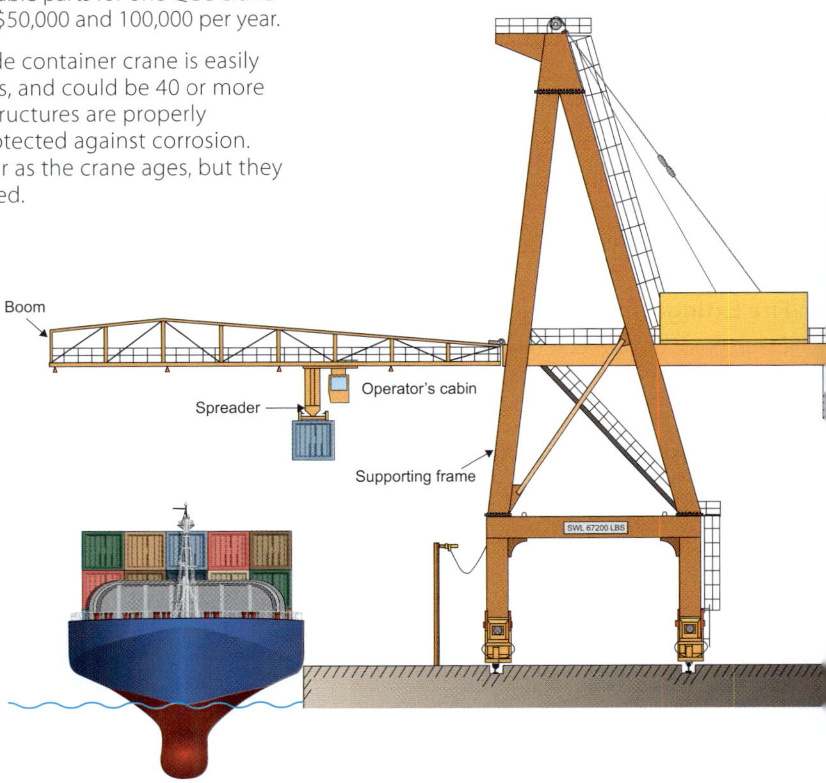

Container Gantry Cranes

Spreader

The spreader is the part of the crane that attaches to and moves the containers. The operator controls movement of the spreader along the boom and operates the hoist. The spreader grips the containers at four locking points using a twistlock arrangement.

Classification of QCCs

QCCs are generally classified by their lifting capacity and the size of container ships they work.

World container port throughput surpassed 600 million TEUs in 2012.

Source: UNCTAD Review of Maritime Transport 2013

Typical Post-Panamax STS Crane

- Doublebox main girder and boom structure
- Capacity: 50-65 ton
- Outreach: 45-55 m
- Hoisting speed: 75/150 m/min
- Trolley speed: 180 m/min
- Gantry speed: 45 m/min

Courtesy of Konecranes Finland Corporation

Typical Panamax STS Crane

- Monobox main girder and boom structure
- Capacity: 40-50 ton
- Outreach: 30-40 m
- Hoisting speed: 60/120 m/min
- Trolley speed: 150 m/min
- Gantry speed: 45 m/min

Courtesy of Konecranes Finland Corporation

Typical Super Post-Panamax STS Crane

- Doublebox main girder and boom structure
- Capacity: 50-65 ton
- Outreach: 60-65 m
- Hoisting speed: 90/180 m/min
- Trolley speed: 210 m/min
- Gantry speed: 45 m/min

Courtesy of Konecranes Finland Corporation

Loading

- Loading is carried out one container at a time as per the cargo plan, keeping ship stability in mind
- normally truck and trailers bring the containers from the storage point to the gantry and the spreader picks up the container and loads it onto the ship
- precision is required to align the container to the hold guides
- stevedores will remove the container lashing and the twist locks.

Unloading

- The spreader is lowered on top of the container, and it locks the four corners by a twist lock mechanism
- the operator lifts the container and uses the transverse motion of the spreader to remove the container from the ship and load it over the truck in the shore platform.

In 2010, there were about 4,900 STS cranes operating around the world. Just over 1,000 were capable of a 22-container reach or more. Half of them were in the Far East.

World Container Trade

World Container Trade

Container Ship Operators

As per 1st May 2014, the largest container-ship operator in terms of container carrying capacity in TEU is MSC, based in Switzerland. It is followe by Maersk Line (Denmark) and CMA-CGM (France). Many of the ships deployed by the operators are in fact not owned by them, but leased from so-called 'charter owners'. In early 2014, it is estimated that about 60% of the order book of new container ships is on account of these charter owners, while the remaining 40% are ordered by the liner operators themselves; historically, the relationship used to be more in the range of 50:5 between operators and charter owners (*Lloyd's List - Daily Briefing, 2014a*).

Larger companies (in terms of total fleet) also tend to operate larger ships. Most of the major carriers have roughly one-third of their fleet (TEU) ir ships of 10,000 TEU or larger, about one-third is in the 5,000 to 9,999 TEU range, and one-third of container carrying capacity is on ships under 4,999 TEU. An exception is UASC, which has mostly larger ships, as it is above all active on the East-West trades. Another exception is Hambur Süd, which mostly operates North-South services and thus deploys relatively smaller ships. Generally, the Trans-Atlantic and Trans-Pacific servic deploy ships between 5,000 and 13,000 TEU, while the Asia-Europe trade also makes use of the 13,000+ TEU ships.

Source: UNCTAD Review of Maritime Transport 2014

Container ships carry an estimated 52% of global seaborne trade in terms of value (World Shipping Council, 2013). Their share of the world fleet has grown almost eightfold since 1980, as goods are increasingly containerised for international transport.

Source: UNCTAD Review of Maritime Transport 2013

The Main Global Container Trading and Shipping Routes

There are three major east-west trade lanes for container shipping:

1) Trans-Pacific

This is the world's busiest container shipping route and also the most unbalanced trade route in the world. At least twice the volume is shipped eastbound, ie Asia-US, as is shipped westbound US-Asia.

Eastbound container ships operate at approximately 80% capacity across most of the year, reaching 90 to 100% each autumn during the peak shipping season. Westbound rates do not always cover the costs of repositioning containers and they often carry commodity-based products such as waste paper and scrap metal.

The total capacity of Asian shipping lines, including Evergreen, Cosco, Hanjin and NYK, now exceeds 30% of the total global capacity.

World Container Trade

2) Europe-Asia

This is the world's second busiest container shipping route and it is continuing to grow as European manufacturers outsource increasing levels of their production to China.

This route is more profitable than the trans-Pacific route, and it absorbed capacity from China-US when the US economy slowed down in 2007.

Container operations on this trade route are dominated by three major alliances, all providing round-trip full container services:

Grand Alliance

Whose partners are: Hapag-Lloyd, NYK and OOCL.

New World Alliance

Whose partners include: Hyundai Merchant Marine, Mitsui OSK Lines and APL (Neptune Orient Lines' container division).

CHKY Alliance

Whose partners include: Cosco, Hanjin/Senator, 'K' Line and Yang Ming.

3) Trans-Atlantic

The trans-Atlantic route also has a significant contrast in volumes, but in this case westbound is stronger than eastbound.

The most common commodities carried westbound from Europe to the US are consumer products. Eastbound, the most common commodities are synthetic resins, organic chemicals, paper and paperboard.

Container operations on this trade route are dominated by the partnership of two large alliances and carriers, namely 'The Grand Alliance/CP Ships partnership' and the 'New World Alliance/Maersk Sealand partnership'.

Three other partnerships offer trans-Atlantic services: Cosco/Hanjin/'K' Line/Yangming, Norasia/Gold Star-Zim/CSCL, and CMA-CGM/P&O Nedlloyd/Contship Container Lines/ Marfret/Hamburg Sud/Hapag-Lloyd.

The route is further serviced by the Mediterranean Shipping Company (MSC), Evergreen, Atlantic Container Line (ACL), Independent Container Line (ICL), Atlanticargo and Star Shipping.

In addition to the east-west shipping routes, two further groups are:

North-South Trades

These routes are carved out around the main centres of production and consumption in Europe, Asia and North America. They link each of the centres with emerging economies in the southern hemisphere.

Direct carriers active on the route include:

- Alianca Navegacao e Logistica Ltda (Brazilian sister company of Hamburg Sud)
- CMA-CGM SA
- CSAV – Compania Sud Americana de Vapores SA
- Grimaldi Naples
- Hamburg Sud
- Hapag-Lloyd Container Linie GmbH
- Libra (owned by CSAV)
- Lykes Lines Ltd LLC (acquired in 1997 by CP Ships)
- Maersk Sealand
- Marfret
- Montemar (acquired in 1999 by CSAV)
- Mediterranean Shipping Company (MSC)
- NYK Line
- P&O Nedlloyd (acquired in 2005 by Maersk)
- Safmarine (acquired in 1999 by Maersk)
- Senator Line GmbH (owned by Hanjin)
- TMM Lines (acquired in 2000 by CP Ships).

None of the three major global alliances operates on these routes. The alliances on this route tend to be informal arrangements that frequently change.

Intra-Regional Trades

These trades operate over shorter distances with smaller ships. The intra-Asia container market, extending to Australia and the Middle East, is the world's largest by volume. It is growing faster than the trans-Pacific or

Europe-Asia routes. The fastest growing intra-Asian exporters are China, Vietnam and South Korea.

The intra-Asia market, like most of the world's container trade, is fuelled by the growth of the Chinese market, which is both a major supplier to and consumer of goods from its Asian neighbours.

Dubai, which serves as a transshipment hub for Asian goods destined for Africa and Central Asia, is also experiencing significant growth.

Top 10 Container Ports

Top 10 Container Ports (in millions of TEUs handled) 2013

Rank	Port	Country	2012	2013	2013/2012
1	Shanghai	China	32.5	33.6	3.3%
2	Singapore	Singapore	31.7	32.6	3.0%
3	Shenzhen	China	22.9	23.3	1.5%
4	Hong Kong	China	23.1	22.3	–3.6%
5	Busan	South Korea	17.0	17.6	3.3%
6	Ningbo	China	16.2	17.3	7.1%
7	Qingdao	China	14.5	15.5	7.0%
8	Guangzhou	China	14.7	15.3	3.8%
9	Dubai	UAE	13.3	13.6	2.3%
10	Tianjin	China	12.3	13.0	5.7%
	Total		**198.3**	**204.1**	**2.9%**

The 20 leading liner companies, 1st January 2014 (Number of ships and total shipboard capacity deployed, in TEUs, ranked by TEU)

Rank	Operator	Vessels	TEU	% 0-4999 TEU	% 5000-9999 TEU	% >= 10000 TEU
1	Mediterranean Shipping Company S.A.	461	2 609 181	27.14	40.42	32.45
2	Maersk Line	456	2 505 935	27.35	47.88	24.77
3	CMA CGM S.A.	348	1 508 007	30.83	34.09	35.08
4	Evergreen Line	229	1 102 245	27.64	53.49	18.87
5	COSCO Container Lines Limited	163	879 696	24.03	42.90	33.07
6	Hapag-Lloyd Aktiengesellschaft	159	762 613	49.34	33.35	17.31
7	China Shipping Container Lines Company Limited	134	750 644	30.40	31.73	37.87
8	Hanjin Shipping Company Limited	115	671 210	30.54	36.95	32.50
9	APL Limited	121	629 479	30.14	44.42	25.45
10	United Arab Shipping Company (S.A.G.)	73	610 294	19.01	15.60	65.39
11	Mitsui O.S.K. Lines Limited	119	607 562	32.26	53.99	13.75
12	Yang Ming Marine Transport Corporation	107	561 172	28.27	46.78	24.95
13	Hamburg Sud	112	539 793	44.48	53.57	1.95
14	Orient Overseas Container Line Limited	98	510 115	27.88	59.18	12.94
15	Nippon Yusen Kabushiki Kaisha	104	488 848	40.45	46.08	13.46
16	Hyundai Merchant Marine Company Limited	64	392 874	20.83	46.44	32.73
17	Kawasaki Kisen Kaisha Limited	72	368 746	34.46	58.01	7.52
18	Pacific International Lines (Private) Limited	137	365 693	86.00	14.00	–
19	Compania Sud Americana de Vapores S.A.	58	320 273	28.94	71.06	–
20	Zim Integrated Shipping Services Limited	71	305 192	63.48	23.34	13.19

Source: UNCTAD secretariat, based on data provided by Lloyd's List Intelligence, available at www.lloydslistintelligence.com.

General Cargo

Merchant ships have always been constructed to reflect the needs of the cargoes to be carried and the trade in which they are employed.

There are still a surprising number of general cargo ships serving ports that retain the infrastructure necessary to handle them. Ships are now generally equipped with cranes, as opposed to derricks, and they require a specialised knowledge of the stowage and handling of a variety of cargoes. Deck cargo will often be a mix of general cargo and containers. Due to the nature of their worldwide employment and longer port stays, general cargo ships can earn extra revenue by carrying a small number of passengers. As they often frequent smaller ports and rivers, an excellent understanding of ship handling will be obtained.

General Cargo Ships

General Cargo >500 GT = 11,871 ships

Source: UNCTAD Review of Maritime Transport 2014

The average age of general cargo ships worldwide is 24.6 years.

General Cargo: Safety Precautions

Dry Cargo Ships

Stowage of Cargo

All crew and shore personnel involved with the opening, closing or removal of hatch covers must be properly instructed in their handling and operation. All stages of opening or closing hatches must be supervised by a responsible person. When hatches are open, the area around the opening should be appropriately illuminated and guard-rails erected.

Procedures for the handling of cargo should be agreed with the berth or terminal operators in advance of loading or unloading.

Loading, stowage and securing of cargo other than bulk cargo should be carried out in accordance with the ship's approved cargo securing manual (see page 91). Cargo securing should be completed before the ship proceeds to sea.

All cargo should be stowed with regard to the order of discharge. When planning the position of cargo and the order of loading and unloading, the effects that these operations will have on access and the safety of personnel should be considered:

- Cargo information, including gross mass of the cargo or cargo units and any special properties detailed on board or in the shipping documents, should be recorded and used in planning
- wherever practical, if more than one port is involved for loading or unloading, cargo should be loaded in layers, rather than in tiers, to avoid the development of high vertical walls of cargo
- care should be taken not to overstow lighter cargoes with heavier cargoes, which may lead to collapse of the stow
- wherever practical, cargo should be stowed to leave safe clearance behind the rungs of hold ladders and safe access as may be necessary
- the need to walk across or climb onto deck cargo, where this may involve an approach to an unprotected edge with risk of falling, should be minimised
- care should be taken to avoid large gaps next to cargo stacked against corrugated bulkheads.

Deck cargo should be kept clear of hatch coamings so it does not obstruct safe access. Access to safety equipment, fire-fighting equipment (particularly fire hydrants) and sounding pipes should also be kept free. Any obstructions in the access way, such as securing points, should be painted white to make them more easily visible. Where cargo is stowed against ship's rails or hatch coamings to such a height that they do not give effective protection to personnel from falling overboard or into the open hold, temporary fencing should be provided.

Suitable safety nets or temporary fencing should be rigged where personnel have to walk or climb across built-up cargo.

When deck cargo is stowed against and above a ship's rails or bulwarks, a wire rope pendant or a chain, extending from the ring bolts or other anchorage on the decks to the full height of the deck cargo, should be provided and used to save personnel having to go overside to attach derrick guys and preventers directly to the anchorages on the deck.

Where beams and hatch covers have to be removed at intermediate ports before surrounding deck cargo is unloaded, an access space at least one metre wide should be left adjacent to any part of the hatch or hatchway that is to be opened. If this is impractical, fencing or lifelines should be used to enable beams and hatch coverings to be removed and replaced in safety.

In the 'tween decks, guidelines should be painted around 'tween deck hatchways at a distance of one metre from the coamings.

Dangerous Goods and Substances

Merchant Shipping Regulations lay down specific requirements for carriage of dangerous substances. The provisions of the IMDG Code, together with those contained in relevant merchant shipping notices, should be complied with. The IMDG Code contains details of classification, documentation, packaging, etc. In particular, it lists and gives details of many dangerous substances.

The general introduction and the introductions to individual classes of the IMDG Code contain many provisions to ensure the safe handling and carriage of dangerous goods, including requirements for electrical equipment and wiring, fire-fighting equipment, ventilation, smoking, repair work, provision and availability of special equipment, etc, some of which are general and others particular to certain classes only. Reference should be made to this information before handling dangerous goods. Where any doubts exist, advice should be sought from a competent authority.

Dangerous substances should only be loaded or unloaded under the supervision of a competent responsible officer. Suitable precautions, such as the provision of special lifting gear, should be taken to prevent damage to receptacles containing dangerous substances.

In compartments containing explosive or flammable cargo all electrical circuits and equipment (including any portable equipment) should meet the recommendations of the IMDG Code. Smoking and naked flames should be prohibited while cargo handling is in progress, except in authorised places, which should be clearly marked.

Emergency response procedures will be under the control of the master and will depend on the circumstances of the incident and the location of the ship.

Personnel required to handle consignments containing dangerous substances should be able to identify dangerous goods from the labelling and placarding. They should be provided with and wear personal protective equipment (including breathing apparatus, where necessary) appropriate to the hazard involved, and should promptly report any leakage or spillage that occurs.

Where there is leakage or escape of dangerous gases or vapours, personnel should leave the danger area and the area should be treated as an enclosed or confined space.

In the event of accidental exposure to dangerous substances, reference should be made to the '*Medical First Aid Guide for Use in Accidents Involving Dangerous Goods (MFAG)*' published by the IMO.

Particular care should be taken when dangerous substances are carried in refrigerated spaces, where any spillage may be absorbed by the insulating material.

Further guidance on the handling and stowage of dangerous goods is contained in the '*Recommendations on the Safe Transport of Dangerous Cargoes and Related Activities in Port Areas*', which is published by the IMO.

Disasters and Significant Incidents Involving General Cargo Ships

'Ice Prince'

13th January 2008

The general cargo vessel *'Ice Prince'* was heading for Alexandria carrying a load of 5,258 tonnes of sawn timber when it suffered total power failure in very rough sea and weather conditions. It put out an emergency call 35 miles southeast of Start Point in the English Channel. The Greek-registered 6,395 tonne ship was already listing 25° when the call was received, at 19:00 by the Brixham Coastguard.

The crew of 20 were stranded on board without power and only navigation lights working off emergency batteries to illuminate their stricken state. The vessel was drifting at nearly 4 knots in heavy seas and a force 7 wind. As other vessels stood by to help, a further call was received indicating that one of the crew needed urgent medical attention. He was airlifted, along with 11 other crew, to Portland while the RNLI Torbay and Salcombe lifeboats took off the remaining 8 crew. All were wearing life jackets and immersion suits, and all survived.

The *'Ice Prince'* began to shed its load into the sea as the list increased to 40°. The French Coastguard tug, *'Abeille Liberté'*, came to stand by the vessel at around midnight but in the darkness its crew were unable to ascertain how much cargo had been lost. Plans to put a line on the *'Ice Prince'* by tug at first light were reported to the Coastguard but by 00:45 the *'Ice Prince'* had already sunk approximately 26 miles off Portland Bill. The crew of the French tug reported that more deck cargo had been lost at sea and that the vessel's stern was on the bottom and its bow out of the water.

The immediate concern was for the recovery of around 2,000 tonnes of untreated sawn timber and for the prevention of pollution from the 313 tonnes of fuel oil she was carrying.

Courtesy of MCA

Safety Designs Incorporated in General Cargo Ships

Hold Fumigation

Fumigants are toxic gases used to eradicate pests that infest ships' cargo. On release, fumigants mix with air and act as either respiratory poisons or suffocants. The fumigant rapidly diffuses from one area to another and through commodities and structures.

The most commonly used fumigants are phosphine and methyl bromide. Others used are carbon dioxide and, more recently, sulfuryl fluoride, which is starting to replace methyl bromide.

The Food and Agriculture Organization (FAO) of the United Nations outlines the following instructions for fumigation procedures:

"The methyl bromide cylinders are placed on the open deck and connected to copper or olyethylene tubing leading into the holds and ending in one or more T-shaped nozzles. At least one 25- or 30-cm (10- or 12-in) circulating fan should be placed as near as possible to the bottom of each hold and, when the gas is released, the fans should be operated for 30 minutes in order to prevent stratification and to aid distribution of the gas. Fans are also useful in hastening aeration after fumigation. The penetration of methyl bromide is outstanding and the gas will escape unless adequate precautions are taken for sealing.

Many modern ships have steel rolling hatch covers, called "McGregor type", which require no extra sealing for methyl bromide fumigation.

Safety Designs Incorporated in General Cargo Ships

Source: MAIB Fumigated Cargo

These covers are lowered into place off their dollies onto a rubber gasket and the full weight is sufficient for a good seal. If the dollies are warped after rough use the side bolts may be used to pull them down into place."

Methyl bromide penetrates well into cracks, crevices and spaces under boards where grain and other foods accumulate, and where the insect populations multiply and spread through the cargo and other parts of the ship.

Safety Measures

Masters loading cargoes that require fumigation must ensure:

- The vessel can safely load the planned cargo. Special care should be taken to ensure fumigant gases cannot enter the vessel's accommodation
- ship's staff responsible for the loading and carriage of cargoes requiring fumigation are fully aware of the risks
- the vessel is equipped with appropriate safety and gas monitoring equipment
- before commencing any fumigation, a thorough safety briefing should be given by the suppliers of the fumigant
- a regime of sampling is established at the earliest opportunity, and then throughout the voyage, to detect the presence of fumigant in accommodation spaces and working areas.

Cargo Bilge Systems

Cargo ships have hatches that are open to the weather during cargo loading and discharge and they may carry cargoes that themselves release moisture during the voyage. These ships are therefore fitted with bilge pumps so that any cargo hold or watertight compartment can be pumped out when the ship has a list of up to 5° and is on an even keel.

Hazards of Working the General Cargoes

Hold Ventilation

Ships may be fitted with natural or forced ventilation systems. These are used to:

- Prevent cargo or ship sweat
- remove any odour or taint of previous cargoes
- reduce the build-up of dangerous gases
- supply fresh air to 'live' cargoes
- remove heat that is given off by certain cargoes.

When the system is used to prevent ship or cargo sweat, continuous monitoring of the hold atmosphere must be carried out.

Hygroscopic Products

Hygroscopic products are mainly of plant origin and have natural moisture content. They may retain, absorb or release water vapour. Excessive amounts of inherent moisture may lead to significant self-heating and 'moisture migration' within the cargo, resulting in caking,

Hazards of Working the General Cargoes

Figure 1.42 - Forward hold vents on a general cargo vessel

Ship Sweat

Ship sweat occurs when the air within a cargo hold is cooled beneath its dewpoint. This usually occurs when a ship loads in a warm climate and proceeds to a colder climate. As the sea and air temperatures cool, the steelwork may eventually cool beneath the dewpoint of the warm moist air in the hold, causing condensation (sweat) to form on internal steel surfaces of the cargo hold. The condensation may run down the bulkheads to the bottom of the hold.

Sweat may also drip onto the cargo from above having formed on the under-deck structure and the underside of the hatch covers. Where possible, cargo should be covered with waterproof coverings to protect it from the sweat dripping from above.

mildew or rot. Examples of hygroscopic products include grain, rice, flour, sugar, cotton, tobacco, cocoa, coffee and tea.

Non-Hygroscopic Products

Non-hygroscopic products have no water content. However, certain commodities (eg steel) may be damaged if stowed in a moist environment. Others may be damaged if packaged using a hygroscopic material (eg wood, paper).

Cargo Sweat

Cargo sweat is condensation that forms on exposed surfaces of the cargo if large amounts of warm, moist air are introduced into a hold containing substantially colder cargo. This usually occurs when the voyage is from a colder to a warmer place and the outside air has a dewpoint above the temperature of the cargo. To prevent cargo sweat forming, all ventilation should be restricted until the temperature of the cargo is above the dewpoint temperature of the outside air.

To prevent ship sweat, holds should be surface ventilated as long as the dewpoint of the outside air is lower than the temperature of the air inside.

If the dewpoint of both the outside and the hold air can be determined:

- Ventilate if the dewpoint of the air inside the hold is higher than the dewpoint of the air outside the hold
- do not ventilate if the dewpoint of the air inside the hold is lower than the dewpoint of the air outside the hold.

In general terms, hygroscopic cargoes need to be monitored more carefully than non-hygroscopic cargoes. Ventilation is rarely required if only non-hygroscopic cargoes are carried. As far as possible, hygroscopic and non-hygroscopic cargoes should not be stowed together because of the differing ventilation requirements.

Accurate records and logs must be maintained to defend against cargo claims.

Specific Issues with General Cargoes

Tainting

Tainting occurs when cargo is contaminated either by direct contact with another cargo or foreign matter, or by its odour.

A comparatively minor off-flavour or odour can cause commercial damage to high-value cargoes.

Coffee beans

Coffee beans are extremely sensitive to foreign odours. The specific intrinsic odour of an individual coffee variety may even taint other varieties. For example, Brazilian 'Minas' coffee has a sharp, carbolic odour and 'Rio' coffee has an iodoform-like odour. These 'hard' coffee varieties may odour taint 'softer' varieties.

Cotton

Cotton is sensitive to unpleasant or pungent odours. Odour taint may be caused by, among other things, kerosene, diesel fuels, fish oil, fish meal, stabilised meal and naphthalene.

Tobacco

Tobacco has a slight, pleasant odour and can taint other products.

Cocoa beans

Cocoa beans have a strong odour that may taint, for example, raw coffee, so they should not be stowed together.

Tea

Tea is extremely odour sensitive so many freight contracts contain a special tea clause stipulating that certain goods that could impair the aroma of tea must not be stowed in the same compartment. Such products include sugar, safflower, rhubarb, rubber, rapeseed, hides, turmeric or cassia.

Rice

Rice, and particularly brown rice, is highly odour sensitive. It must not be stowed near fleeces or wool, as tainting by the fatty odour will occur.

Salt

Salt is sensitive to unpleasant or pungent odours.

It must not be loaded in holds or containers that were previously used to transport living animals or other odour tainting goods.

To prevent spoilage of salt, it must not be stored with sugar, hides, tobacco, fish products or other goods with an intense odour.

Cars

Odour tainting of the upholstery can occur due to adjacent cargo areas handling goods with a strong odour such as fish meal.

Specific Issues with General Cargoes

Spontaneous Combustion

Spontaneous combustion occurs when a material increases in temperature without drawing heat from its surroundings. This happens when the surface area exposed to the air is minimal (such as a scrunched up oily rag). Dissipation of the heat cannot take place and the temperature of the material increases until it bursts into flames.

Smouldering and heated material suddenly exposed to air can also start a fire or trigger an explosion.

For spontaneous ignition to take place there must be sufficient oxygen available for the reaction to occur, but not so much draught that the heat is carried away as quickly as it is generated.

Cargoes at risk of spontaneous combustion include cotton, flax, hemp, coconut fibre and jute.

Fire-fighting Guidance

The best fire-fighting medium is injected CO_2. Hatches should be cooled from the outside with water sprays and not opened up until fire-fighting tugs arrive or port is reached.

It is very difficult to extinguish a fire in these fibrous cargoes because of the excess oxygen in the fibres. Oxidation maintains the fire from the inside. When fighting a fire, steel straps should not be broken, nor should the bales be opened, since relieving the compression increases the oxygen supply and makes it impossible to fight the fire effectively. Smouldering fires inside bales often last for weeks.

Water must not be used for fire-fighting because the swelling capacity of many of the fibres will result in a 20 to 45% increase in volume and may cause damage to the cargo hold, cell guides or container walls.

Prevention

The most common and practical advice to avoid spontaneous combustion is to have good housekeeping practices. Bins for oily rags should be provided and kept covered so that oxygen is not available for oxidation.

Cotton

Flax

Hemp

Coconut fibre

Jute

Common Cargo Types and their Characteristics

Cocoa

Cocoa beans are the dried seeds of the cocoa pod, the fruit of the cocoa tree, which is grown in equatorial regions. The inner nib of the cocoa bean is used to produce cocoa butter, cocoa liqueur, cocoa powder and cocoa cake. The beans are used mostly in the food and cosmetic industries. Cocoa is grown principally in West Africa, Central and South America and Asia with the Ivory Coast producing almost 40% of the world market. Although cocoa is largely produced in developing countries, it is mostly consumed in industrialised nations, with the USA being the largest importer.

Packaging/Transport

Cocoa is packaged in jute bags, but this is an ideal environment for harbouring infestation. Cargo fumigation is usually carried out before shipment and the ship should obtain a fumigation certificate before the cargo is loaded. The residue of the fumigation powder is hazardous to humans.

Cocoa beans are at risk of cargo sweat due to the variation in temperature between the loading and unloading locations. The cargo hold should be well ventilated and covers should be placed over the bags of beans to provide protection from dripping condensation within the hold. Containers should be lined with kraft paper or rattan to absorb excess moisture and to prevent the possibility of mould damage.

General

Cocoa should be unloaded swiftly on arrival at the port to avoid further condensation developing due to the change in temperature.

Coffee Beans

Coffee beans are the seeds of the coffee shrub, which grows in a tropical climate. The green coffee beans are removed from their husk, with each coffee cherry producing two coffee beans.

Coffee is loaded from a wide range of countries in Africa, Asia and South America, with Brazil being the world leader in coffee production, followed by Vietnam, Indonesia and Colombia.

Packaging/Transport

Coffee is usually packaged in new jute or sisal bags. As with cocoa, the risk of infestation in the cargo hold is high and fumigation needs to take place prior to shipment. A fumigation certificate should be obtained before loading. The residue of the fumigation powder is hazardous to humans. Coffee may also be infested with mice, rats and cockroaches.

General

About 95% of coffee is transported in one of two types of container:

- Standard containers – when standard containers are used, extra care should be taken with ventilation to avoid cargo sweat. Containers should be stowed below deck to avoid extreme temperature swings during the voyage. Packing paper can be used to line the container and protect the cargo
- Ventilated containers – these containers have ventilation openings along their entire length, but the ventilation must come from an external source to maintain a constant air supply. They should be stowed below deck to avoid extreme temperature changes and the possibility of seawater spray contamination.

Common Cargo Types and their Characteristics

Logs

Lumber is loaded either dry from the quayside or lighters or directly from the water. When lifted from the water, the lumber is known as rafted logs.

The volume of each stow is the combined volume of logs and the voids between them, which are filled with air or water during transportation. Timber cargo changes its physical properties (moisture content, density, looseness, etc) but, to a certain degree, retains its quality, so it is possible to transport it on weather decks. When exposed to ship's motions and vibration, the logs become compacted and transfer the load to all the ship structures enclosing them.

Logs are prone to decomposition while en route. The process of decomposition results in a depletion of oxygen in the surrounding area. When this occurs in a ship's hold, a dangerously low O_2 atmosphere is created. This is a significant but hidden danger of carrying logs.

Stevedores have died from asphyxiation due to an oxygen depleted atmosphere within the hold. The three main factors involved are mould on the logs, the humidity in the hold and lack of ventilation throughout the voyage. It is important to be aware of the dangers and to ensure that the holds are opened for as long as possible before commencing cargo operations. This is particularly important in humid climates where the risk will be greatly increased.

Log Driving and Rafting

Log driving is a method of transporting individual logs downstream to sawmills or to await loading onto a ship. Log rafting involves tying the logs together to form a raft prior to floating them to a terminal where they are loaded on board by cranes.

Depending on weight and length, roundwood logs are shipped individually or in bundles. Individual logs may weigh up to 15 metric tonnes. Roundwood logs carried in the holds do not need to be secured. However, ships carrying logs must have an accepted plan for roundwood deck cargo loading, lashing and securing.

Cargo lashings are usually attached to securing points on the deck edges on either side of the ship. The lashings are taken up and over the deck cargo stow to tensioning devices located close to the centreline.

Carriage of Roundwood Logs

All lashings should be checked daily while on passage and tightened if necessary. This is particularly important for fabric lashings, which have a greater tendency to stretch than steel wire rope. This routine is often not conducted in heavy weather, as an inspection of the timber stow is considered too dangerous. As a vessel rolls and pitches in heavy weather, accelerations are imparted to the stow, and the lashings are subjected to the highest loads. When lashings are stretched, their effectiveness is reduced and the risk of a shift is far more likely. The vessel should slow her speed and heave to if necessary to allow the crew to carry out this inspection safely.

Cargo Shift

If a timber deck cargo does shift, the lashings will tighten and, providing they don't break, will eventually arrest the shift. A shift may result in an angle of list, which can be reduced by adding ballast water to the high side. However, a vessel should not be ballasted upright, because the lashings at this stage are doing very little to prevent a shift the other way. If a shift the other way occurs, the weight of the ballast water will increase the list, possibly to dangerous proportions on that side.

Upright Supports and Hog Wires

The tendency for the deck cargo to slide will be reduced if uprights secured with hog wires are fitted to restrict transverse movement. The weight of the cargo will help to hold the hog wires in place, and this arrangement will provide a rigid box structure. If steel upright supports, with suitable sockets along the sides of the vessel, are provided, the use of hog wires may be unnecessary, providing the uprights and sockets are of substantial construction.

Courtesy of Neil Doyle

Carriage of Sawn Timber

Timber is sawn wood or lumber, cants, logs, poles, pulpwood and all other types of timber in loose or packaged form.

Stowage Considerations

The 'Code of Safe Practice for Ships Carrying Timber Deck Cargoes' recommends the following to be checked prior to loading timber on the weather deck:

- *Hatch covers, and other openings to spaces below that area, should be securely closed and battened down*
- *air pipes and ventilators should be efficiently protected and check valves or similar devices should be examined to ascertain their effectiveness against the entry of water*
- *accumulations of ice and snow on such areas should be removed*
- *all deck lashings, uprights, etc should be in position before loading. This will be necessary should a pre-loading examination of securing equipment be required in the loading port*
- *ensure that access to all areas of the ship regularly used in the necessary working of the ship is not impeded.*

During loading, timber deck cargo should be kept free of any accumulations of ice and snow. On completion of loading, but before sailing, a thorough inspection of the ship should be carried out. Soundings should also be taken to verify that no structural damage has occurred, causing ingress of water.

The height of timber cargo should be restricted to ensure that:

- *Adequate visibility is assured*
- *a safe margin of stability is maintained at all stages of the voyage*
- *cargo does not overhang the ship sides*

Carriage of Roundwood Logs

- *the weight of the timber deck cargo does not exceed the designed maximum permissible load on the weather deck and hatches.*

For ships that use timber load lines, the cargo should be stowed so as to extend:

- *Over the entire available length of the well or wells between superstructures and as close as practicable to end bulkheads*
- *at least to the after end of the aftermost hatchway in the case where there is no limiting superstructure at the aft end*

- *athwartships as close as possible to the ship sides, after making due allowance for obstructions such as guard-rails, bulwark stays, uprights, pilot boarding access, etc. This is provided that any area of broken stowage so created at the side of the ship does not exceed a mean of 4% of the breadth*
- *to at least the standard height of a superstructure other than a raised quarterdeck*
- *to meet the requirements of the approved stability manual.*

The basic principle is that there should be a solid stow during all stages of the loading process. This can only be achieved by the constant supervision of responsible officers.

Securing

Every lashing should pass over the timber deck cargo and be shackled to independent eye plates that are adequate for the intended purpose, and then efficiently attached to the deck stringer plate or other strengthened points. They should be installed in such a manner as to be, as far as is practicable, in contact with the timber deck cargo throughout its full height.

All lashings and components used for securing should:

- *Possess a breaking strength of not less than 133 kN*
- *after initial stressing, show an elongation of not more than 5% at 80% of their breaking strength*

Source: 'Code of Safe Practice for Ships Carrying Timber Deck Cargoes', 1991

- *show no permanent deformation after having been subjected to a proof load of not less than 40% of their original breaking strength.*

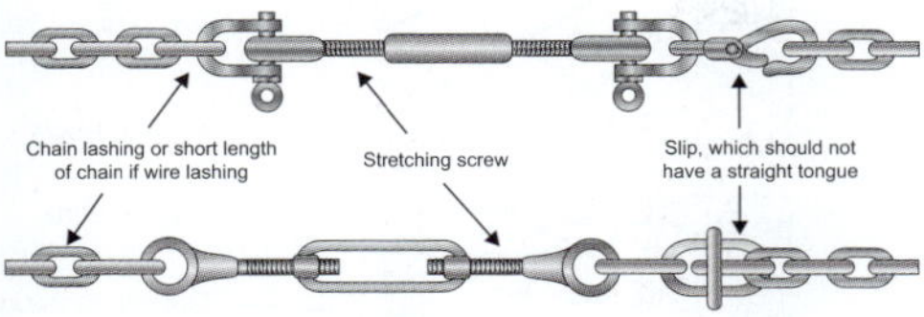

Figure 1.43 - Example of securing lashings

Every lashing should be provided with a tightening device or system so placed to safely and efficiently operate when required.

After completion of lashing, there should be at least half the threaded length of screw available for tightening during the voyage. The spacing of the lashings should be such that the two lashings at each end of each length of continuous deck stow are positioned as close as is practicable to the extreme end of the timber deck cargo.

Timber uprights should be fitted when required by the nature, height or type of timber carried. When fitted, uprights should be:

- *Of adequate strength*
- *fitted at intervals not exceeding 3 m*
- *secured adequately to the deck.*

Lashings should be spaced depending on the height of the cargo:

- *For a height of 4 m and below, the spacing should be 3 m*
- *for heights of above 4 m, the spacing should be 1.5 m.*

Rounded angle pieces of suitable material and design should be used along the upper outboard edge of the stow to bear the stress of the lashings.

If the timber deck cargo is stowed over the hatches and higher, it should, in addition to being secured by the lashings recommended, be in a system of athwartship lashings (hog lashings) joining each port and starboard pair of uprights near the top of the stow and at other levels appropriate for the height of the stow.

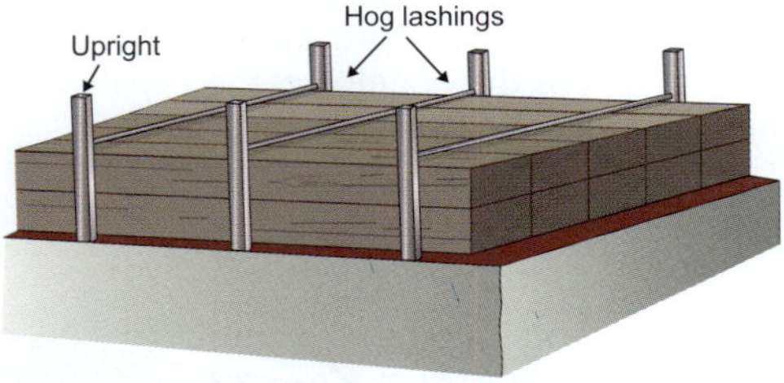

Figure 1.44 - Timber deck cargo secured by hog lashings

Courtesy of MAIB

Figure 1.45 - Timber deck cargo showing wire lashings and turnbuckles

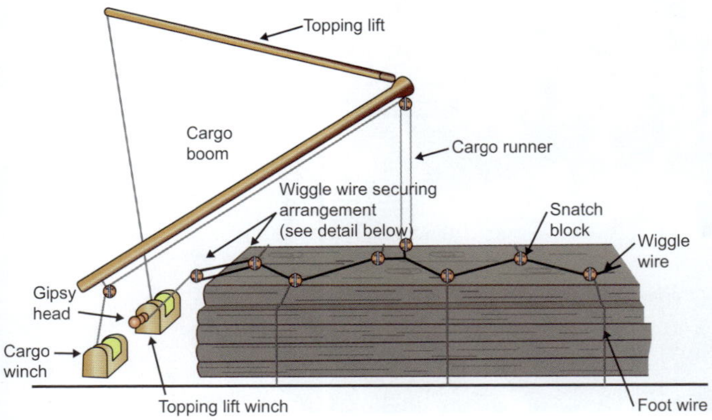

Figure 1.46 - Lashing system to tighten the stow

A lashing system to tighten the stow, where a dual continuous wire rope (wiggle wire) is passed from side to side over the cargo and held continuously through a series of snatch blocks, can also be used. The dual continuous wire rope should be led to a winch or other tensioning device to facilitate further tightening. This can also be used as a quick release mechanism in order to jettison the cargo in case of an emergency.

Source: 'Code of Safe Practice for Ships Carrying Timber Deck Cargoes', 1991

Carriage of Roundwood Logs

All lashings and securing devices must be tested and certified. A record must be maintained of all certificates, testing and inspection dates.

Lashing plans must be provided to the ship and these must be available for inspection.

On completion of lashing, a walkway or other means of access that does not endanger the lives of crew members must be provided to other areas of the ship.

Prior to and immediately after sailing, all lashings must be examined and tightened as necessary as the vibration of the ship may have caused them to loosen. Records of all checks and adjustments to lashings must be maintained in the ship's logbook.

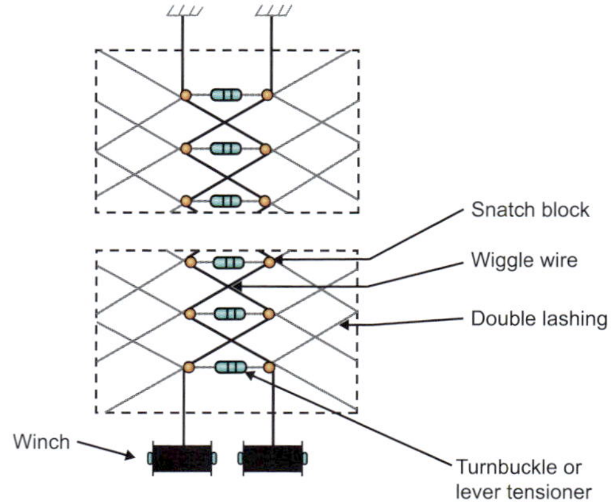

Figure 1.47 - Wiggle wire securing arrangement

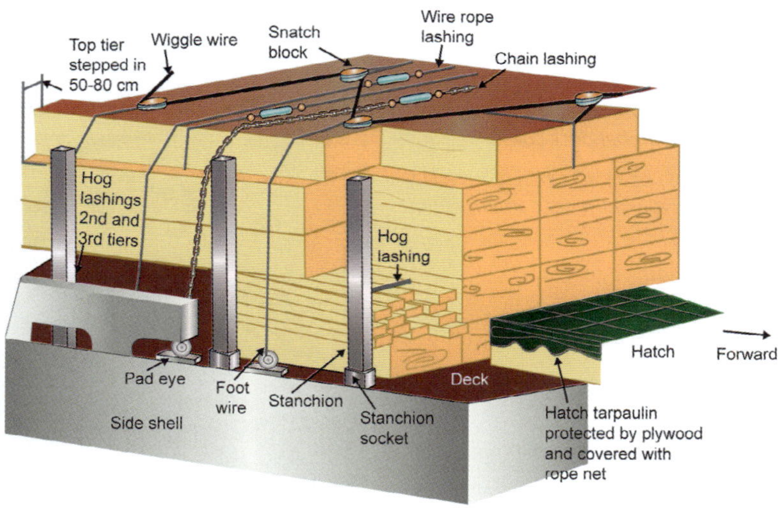

Figure 1.48 - Typical lashing system for deck cargo

Figure 1.49 - Cargo shift

Other General Cargoes

Cotton

Cotton belongs to the category of fibres/fibrous materials, which are classified as follows:

Plant Hairs

- Cotton seed-hairs
- Kapok tree fruit hairs

Kapok Fruit

Stalk Fibres (soft fibres)

- Flax, ramie (fine spinnable fibres)
- Hemp, jute, kenaf

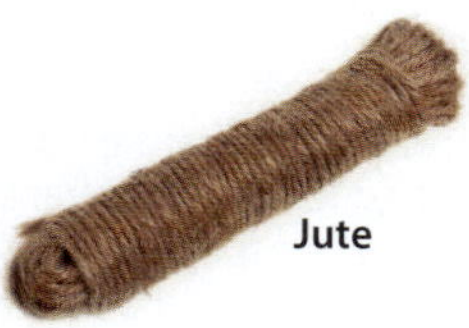

Jute

Leaf Fibres (hard fibres)

- Sisal, manila hemp, palm fibres

Sisal

Bast

- Linden, raffia palm, willow

Willow

Packing/Transport

Cotton is usually shipped in largely square bales that are compressed to various degrees. Bales weigh between 100 and 330 kg, depending on the country of origin. The bales are tied firmly with steel straps or wire. Strapping is essential to maintain compression of the bales during transport as this reduces the risk of spontaneous combustion. Bursting or chafing of the steel straps and wires may lead to sparking and external ignition. The bales are wrapped in jute or plastic fabric, or sometimes in plastic films that are perforated to regulate bale moisture content.

Each bale of cotton or vegetable fibres must be covered with bagging on at least three quarters of its surface, including both ends. Any poorly compressed bale or any bale with bindings should not be transported.

- Each bale of wet cotton must be stowed separately from any bales of dry cotton or vegetable fibres in a 'tween deck space, and not overstowed. Any bale of cotton or vegetable fibres saturated with water should not be transported by ship
- bales of cotton or vegetable fibres showing contact with oil or grease should not be accepted for transportation
- cotton or vegetable fibres must be stowed in a hold or compartment that meets the following requirements:
  - All traces of cargo debris, oil or residue in the hold or compartment must be removed
  - each ventilation cowl serving the hold or compartment must be fitted with a spark screen
  - when a bulkhead of the hold or compartment is common with a source of heat, a wooden bulkhead must be erected between the bulkhead and any cotton or vegetable fibres
  - each hold or compartment must be equipped with a carbon dioxide or overhead water sprinkler system or other approved fixed extinguishing system
- naked lights or any item likely to produce sparks are not permitted on the vessel during loading or unloading of cotton or vegetable fibres
- upon completion of stowage, each opening must be completely closed
- at least one fire hose must be connected while cotton or vegetable fibres are being loaded or unloaded
- smoking is not permitted on a vessel during the loading or unloading of cotton or vegetable fibres except in designated smoking areas.

Scrap Metal

Scrap Metal

The term 'scrap metal' covers a range of ferrous metals that are generally intended for recycling. These include borings, shavings, turnings, cuttings, iron swarf and steel swarf. Scrap metal has an inherent danger in that it can heat spontaneously, leading to fire. This is due to its high surface area compared to its mass, making oxidation easy. Scrap metal is classified in the IMO *'Code of Safe Practice for Solid Bulk Cargoes'* as materials liable to self-heating and spontaneous ignition.

Vibration and movement of the vessel can cause friction and heating, and many owners are reluctant to ship scrap metal because of the damage it can do to holds.

Any dry bulk carrier is suitable to carry scrap iron/steel. It may also be carried in freight containers.

Borings, shavings and turnings are frequently contaminated with oils that have been used in the cutting process. Oily rags and other combustible matter may also be found among the loads, further increasing the risk of spontaneous combustion. The oxidation process can be accelerated if the materials are wet or damp.

Loading of Scrap Metal

The following precautions should be taken when handling scrap metal:

- Cargo should be loaded, segregated, stowed and carried in accordance with the latest edition of the IMO *'Code of Safe Practice for Solid Bulk Cargoes'* (BC Code)

- prior to loading, the temperature of the material should not exceed 55°C. Any wooden material should be removed from the cargo hold before loading commences
- the surface temperature of the cargo should be taken prior to, during and after loading and daily during the voyage.

  Temperature readings during the voyage should be taken in such a way that entry into the cargo space is not required. If entry is unavoidable, or alternatively, if entry is required for this purpose, sufficient breathing apparatus, additional to that required by the safety equipment regulations, should be provided.

  If the surface temperature exceeds 90°C during loading, further loading should cease and should not recommence until the temperature has fallen below 85°C. The ship should not depart unless the temperature is below 65°C and has shown a steady or downward trend in temperature for at least eight hours. During loading and transport, the bilge of each cargo space in which the material is stowed should be as dry as practicable
- during loading, the scrap metal should be compacted in the cargo space with a bulldozer or other means as this will help to remove air from the stow. After loading, the material should be trimmed to eliminate peaks and further compacted. While at sea, any rise in surface temperature of the material indicates a self-heating reaction problem. If the temperature rises to 80°C, a potential fire is developing and the ship should make for the nearest port, cargo that was wet before loading is more likely to heat in transit

Water should not be used at sea as this may compromise the vessel's stability. Early application of an inert gas to a smouldering fire may be effective. In port, copious quantities of water may be used but due consideration should be given to stability

- scrap metal must not be allowed to come into contact with seawater.

The requirements for entry into cargo spaces are very important. Many lives have been lost by officers and crew members entering a hold to inspect a heating problem without taking adequate precautions for confined space entry.

Scrap Metal Carried in Containers

Containers that are declared as carrying a single type of metal waste must not be allowed to be contaminated by other metals.

The inside of a container must be free from acid, alkalis or other substances liable to react with cargo to form a hazardous atmosphere.

Any container for sea transport should be packed and secured to ensure even distribution of weight across the unit and to prevent movement of material.

Case Study

In one incident, temperatures in excess of 500°C were recorded 6 feet below the surface of the cargo. Temperatures of this order may cause structural damage to the steelwork of the carrying vessel. Flames are frequently seen in cargoes of metal turnings, usually the result of ignition of the cutting oils, rags, timber and other combustible materials mixed with the turnings. Spontaneous heating of metal turnings has caused several major casualties.

In the incident mentioned above, the vessel was moved from port to port in attempts to agree discharge. After weeks of delay all the holds were eventually flooded to reduce the heat for safe discharge of cargo. Following discharge of the turnings the vessel loaded a cargo of conventional scrap. Rough weather was encountered, during the subsequent voyage. Cracks developed in the shell plating, the holds flooded and the vessel, along with 29 lives, was lost.

Aluminium Ingots

Aluminium ingots are non-hazardous but they react with acids or alkalis and may generate flammable gas. They should be stored away from strong alkalis, halogens, oxidising agents, halogenated hydrocarbons and any fire or explosion risks, eg ammonium nitrate.

Contact must be prevented with all strong acids including hydrochloric acid, sulphuric acid, nitric acid and strong alkalis, eg potassium hydroxide and sodium hydroxide.

Scrap Metal

Steel Cargoes

There are many types of steel cargoes and they are categorised as follows.

Category A - Packed or wrapped

- Special quality wire rods in coil form, for example pre-stressing wire, tyre cord and high tensile wire rods. This type of wire rod is usually wrapped in strong waterproofed reinforced material
- cold rolled steel sheeting in coils and packages
- coated steel in coils and packages, for example galvanised, aluminised and paint-coated
- tin plate in steel boxes - also shipped in coils on wooden skids. These products are usually wrapped in plastic-coated kraft paper, with an outer layer of steel sheet wrapper. The bundles are then secured with flat metal strapping bands.

Figure 1.50 - Cold rolled steel

Category B - Not packed or wrapped

- Structural steels; beams, angles, flats, channels, reinforcing bars, squares and rounds. Usually shipped in 20 or 40 feet (6 metre and 12 metre) bundles, secured by wire bands or strapping bands
- single flat steel plates and bundles of steel plates secured with strapping bands
- hot rolled steel sheeting in coils and bundles, secured with metal strapping bands
- steel slabs, billets, blooms and mild steel hot rolled wire rods
- scrap: ferrous metal, borings, shavings, turnings, cuttings, iron swarf or steel swarf.

Guidelines for Steel Cargoes

Proper and efficient stowage is essential to avoid shifting, chafing and crushing damage. The guidelines for particular cargoes should be observed, and the following rules complied with:

1. Never go to sea with the top horizontal tier of a steel cargo not fully completed. If the tier cannot be completed, it should not be loaded, as securing with wires to the ship's sides and tomming with timber cannot be considered as proper precautions against shifting. In certain circumstances, this rule may not apply to steel coil cargoes.
2. Steel products should never be permitted to rest against the ship's structure in stow. Dunnage should always be used to prevent this occurring.
3. Underdeck steel cargoes should not be secured to component parts of the vessel's structure, with the exception of wire rod cargoes in certain circumstances (for example, half hatch stowage).

Figure 1.51 - Bundles of steel rods

Paper Reels

Regardless of their size or the type of packaging, all reels of paper are susceptible to damage by wetting or bad handling. Bad handling typically results in the breaking of bands or puncturing and contamination of the paper reel.

Reels of paper should be stored on flat surfaces and covered with paper. Blocks of reels must be protected from damage on all the exposed sides. The most appropriate type of storage is a box-shaped compartment. If reels are to be stored in compartments that are not box shaped, or if they are to be stored with other break bulk items, the surface where the reels are stored should be horizontal, level and stable. The block must be correctly secured on all sides. This might be by fitting a fence, made from gratings, plywood and timber, around the open faces of the block stowage and using wire, webbing or fibre rope as lashing around the block that is attached to either the bulkhead or the ship's side structure.

The lashings must not touch the reels and the fencing must only cause the minimum amount of chafing or rubbing. Additional soft packing may be used to prevent this.

The ship should be watertight and, if the ventilation system is used, ventilators should be closed whenever bad weather is imminent or encountered. Paper should not be ventilated if it is loaded in a port with low ambient temperature for transit to an area of higher ambient temperature.

Major uses of paper are newsprint and the manufacture of corrugated fibre board. Newsprint reels are used on high speed printing presses, where any interruption in the printing process, due to fault in the paper, will result in a substantial financial loss. Ships should take particular care to ensure that only sound reels are accepted. Newsprint reels are generally additionally wrapped with a further waterproof barrier.

Scrap Metal

Heavy Lift Cargoes

Heavy lift cargoes are units too large to fit in a container. They fall into three main types:

- Industrial cargoes, such as a refining column or a container crane
- offshore structures, including jack-up rigs, semi-submersible rigs and other offshore equipment

- small ships or dredgers, ferries or yachts and small cargo ships. It is sometimes safer and less expensive to move a vessel of this type and size by heavy lift ship than to take it under its own power.

Heavy Lift Ships

Heavy lift ships can be divided into three main groups:

- Powerful tug barge systems that allow large structures to be floated around the world
- semi-submersible heavy lift ships that can be ballasted down to allow the heavy load to be floated onto the deck on a pontoon, after which the vessel deballasts to its normal freeboard
- larger cargo ships equipped with heavy lift cranes that can pick up many small to medium-sized heavy lift cargoes.

Heavy lift ships are usually less than 15,000 Dwt and are fitted with two or more heavy cranes capable of working together. Cranes are often situated on the side of the vessel, allowing the cargo space to be unobstructed. The ships have anti-heeling ballast tanks and strengthened hatch covers to allow heavy cargo to be loaded on deck. Some have RoRo access and strengthened ramps so that cargo can be rolled on.

Preparation and Planning

A heavy lift operation must always be carried out with great care and a risk assessment is essential before a heavy lift takes place. The most critical stage is when the weight has just left the ground, as it acts as if it has been placed on top of the lifting gear and this causes a rise in the ship's centre of gravity. Initial stability must be adequate to avoid a situation where the ship's centre of gravity rises above its transverse metacentre, causing a capsizing lever to form. Avoidance of slack tanks will minimise a free surface effect further raising the centre of gravity. The lifting hook must be exactly above the load to avoid the load dragging on the ground and swinging, causing excessive strain on the gear.

Clear communication is essential for the execution of any heavy lift. Clarification on key stages should be sought early in the process. These include:

- Collection and delivery locations as well as installation details or the specific area for the cargo to be set down
- distribution and strength of support points
- acceptable anchoring points and confirmation that welding is permitted or required

- any cradles required and responsibility for design and supply
- what secondary steelwork, if any, is to be installed for the transportation and what is shipped loose.

Precautions

When loading or discharging heavy lifts, deck officers should be aware of the following precautions and procedures:

- The stability of the vessel should be adequate and the maximum angle of heel should be acceptable. All free surface effects (FSE) should be eliminated by either 'pressing up' or 'emptying' tanks
- if a conventional jumbo derrick is employed the rigging plan should be referred to with regard to the positioning of 'preventer backstays' to support any mast structure
- a careful check on the condition of the derrick and associated gear should be made before commencing the lift. Particular attention should be paid to the SWL of shackles, blocks and wires
- it should be ensured that all the ship's moorings are taut and that men are standing by to tend as necessary. Fenders should be pre-rigged and the gangway lifted clear of the quayside
- all cargo winches affecting the load should be placed in 'double gear'
- the deck area where the load is to be landed should be clear of obstructions, and heavy bearers laid to accept and spread the deck weight
- the ship's deck capacity plans should be checked to ensure that the deck space is capable of supporting the load
- the winch drivers and controller should be seen to be competent, and all non-essential personnel should be clear of the lifting area
- any ship's side rails in the way of the load should be lowered or removed and any barges secured to the ship's side should be cast off
- steadying lines should be secured to the load itself and to the collar of the floating block if fitted
- all relevant heads of departments should be notified before commencing the lift
- designated lifting points should be used to take the weight slowly. An inspection all around the deck should be made once the load clears and before allowing the lift to continue.

Cargo Securing Manual

SOLAS Chapters VI and VII require a cargo securing manual (CSM) to be on board all types of ships, other than solid and liquid bulk, engaged in the carriage of cargoes.

Cargo units and cargo transport units must be loaded, stowed and secured throughout the voyage in accordance with this manual.

Chapter 1 contains general statements dealing with the requirement to practise good seamanship and the requirement to maintain all securing devices to a good standard.

Chapter 2 provides details of the specifications of fixed and portable securing devices and their maintenance schemes. Plans or sketches can be used to illustrate the type, location and total number of securing devices on board.

Chapter 3 provides handling and safety instructions and an evaluation of the forces acting on the cargo transport units using tables and diagrams of those forces acting on the cargo in relation to the metacentric height.

Chapter 4 contains handling, safety, stowage and securing instructions for containers and other standardised cargoes. It illustrates allowable stowage patterns, evaluation of forces acting on cargo transport units and principles of stowage and securing both on deck and under deck. Stowage and securing plans must be available illustrating, among other things, stowage patterns, the maximum stack weight limitations and permitted stack heights.

It contains further information on the nominal increase of forces or accelerations with an increase of initial stability. Recommendations should be given for reducing the risk of cargo losses from deck stowage by restrictions to stack masses or stack heights where high initial stability cannot be avoided.

RoRos and Car Carriers

The RoRo design resulted from the Second World War requirement for landing craft to land vehicles directly onto the beachheads.

RoRo

World fleet

RoRos >500 GT = 1,422 ships

Source: UNCTAD Review of Maritime Transport 2014

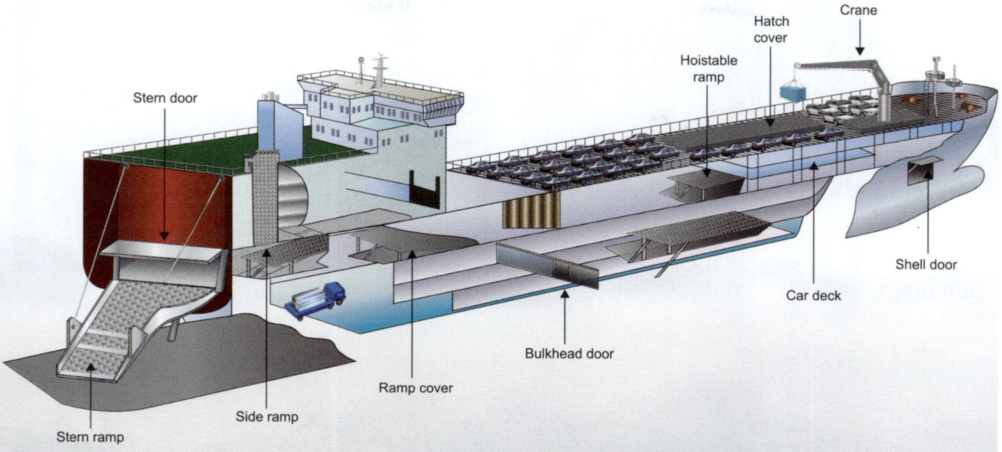
Crane
Hatch cover
Hoistable ramp
Stern door
Shell door
Car deck
Bulkhead door
Ramp cover
Side ramp
Stern ramp

RoRos and Car Carriers

Courtesy of USCG

The RoRo finally came into its own in the late 1960s and early 1970s, with the large increase in imported cars. The first pure car carrying vessel was built in 1973.

Figure 1.52 - Car carrier schematic operating cargo

The majority of RoRo cargo traffic (apart from cars) is carried on large ferries, mostly in the form of container trucks.

RoRo: Safety Precautions

RoRos

General

The movement, stowage and securing of vehicles on vehicle decks and ramps should be supervised by a responsible ship's officer assisted by at least one competent person.

Smoking and naked flames should not be permitted on any vehicle decks. Conspicuous 'No Smoking' or 'No Smoking/Naked Lights' signs should be displayed.

On passenger ferries, passengers and drivers should not be permitted to remain on vehicle decks without the express authority of a responsible ship's officer. The period prior to disembarkation when passengers and drivers are requested to return to their vehicles should be kept to a minimum.

Ventilation

Vehicle decks should have adequate ventilation at all times.

On passenger vessels, ventilation fans in closed RoRo spaces must normally be run continuously whenever vehicles are on board. An increased number of air changes may be required when vehicles are being loaded or unloaded, or where flammable gases or liquids are stowed in a closed RoRo space.

To reduce the accumulation of fumes, drivers should be instructed to stop their engines as soon as practicable after embarking and to avoid starting up prior to departure until instructed to do so. During loading and discharging, ventilation may be improved by keeping both bow and stern doors open, provided there is adequate freeboard at these openings. When there is doubt about the freshness of the atmosphere, it should be tested to confirm the oxygen level is at or greater than 20.8% and that dangerous levels of carbon monoxide are not building up.

Disasters and Significant Incidents Involving RoRos and Car Carriers

'Herald of Free Enterprise'

Date: 6th March 1987
Location: Departing Zeebrugge
Ship type: RoRo car and passenger ferry
Date built: 1980
Flag: British
Incident: Capsize
Fatalities: 193

Incident

In the early evening of 6th March 1987, the *'Herald of Free Enterprise'*, which was carrying around 460 passengers, 80 crew members and 131 vehicles capsized as it departed the Belgian port of Zeebrugge en route to the UK. It capsized about 90 seconds after leaving the harbour, ending up on its side and half submerged in shallow water only 100 yards from the shore. Only a turn to starboard in her last moments prevented the ship from sinking entirely in much deeper water. The disaster resulted in the deaths of 193 people.

Disasters and Significant Incidents Involving RoRos and Car Carriers

Cause

The *'Herald of Free Enterprise'* had two main vehicle decks. At Dover and Calais, double–deck ramps connected to the ferry, allowing simultaneous vehicle access to both decks. However, at Zeebrugge there was only a single level access ramp that did not allow simultaneous deck loading. This single ramp could not quite reach the upper vehicle deck and so water ballast had to be pumped into tanks in the bow of the *'Herald'* to allow loading.

The *'Herald'* had a new design of clamshell doors that opened and closed horizontally. This design made it impossible for the ship's Master to see from the bridge whether the doors were opened or closed. Before releasing her moorings, it was normal practice for the Assistant Bosun to close the doors, with the First Officer remaining on deck to ensure this had happened before returning to the bridge.

On the evening of the incident, to keep on schedule, the First Officer returned to the bridge before the ship dropped her moorings, leaving the closing of the doors under the responsibility of the Assistant Bosun. However, the Assistant Bosun had taken a short break after cleaning the car deck upon arrival at Zeebrugge. He had returned to his cabin and was still asleep when the ship dropped its moorings at 18:27. The Captain assumed that the doors had been closed.

As the ship increased her speed, a bow wave began to build up under her prow. At 15 knots, the bow was down three feet lower than normal and water began to break over the main car deck through the open doors at a rate of 200 tonnes per minute. The resulting free surface effect of a few centimetres of water across the expanse of a car deck caused the ship to lose stability.

Within seconds, the ship began to list 30° to port. The ship briefly righted herself before listing to port once more, this time capsizing with large quantities of seawater pouring into the ship.

The entire event took place in less than a minute. There had been no chance to launch any of the ship's lifeboats. The water quickly reached the ship's electrical systems, destroying both main and emergency power and leaving the ship in darkness.

Repercussions

Escape from the vessel was extremely difficult due to the lack of illumination, extreme list and the limited number of apertures that would allow escape. Many involved in the incident also experienced great difficulty in attempting to don lifejackets.

The *'Herald of Free Enterprise'* resulted in amendments in both design and the use of technology (see page 185).

'Cougar Ace'

Courtesy of USCG

Date: 23rd July 2006
Location: 230 miles south of Alaska's Aleutian Islands
Date built: 1993
Flag: Singapore
Incident: Loss of stability during ballast transfer
Fatalities: 1 (member of the salvage team)

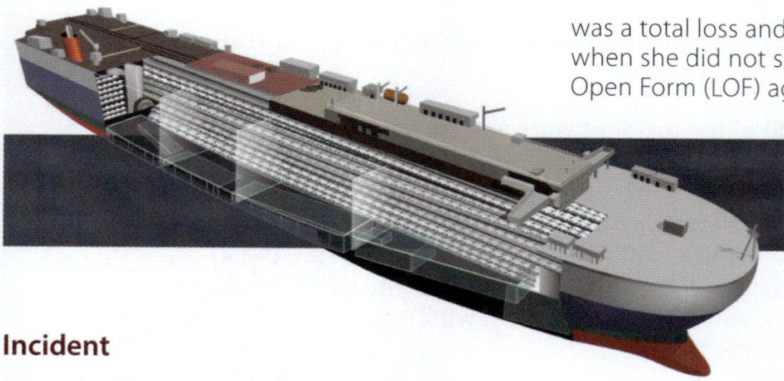

Incident

On 23rd July 2006, the *'Cougar Ace'*, a 55,000 tonne car carrier with a maximum car carrying capacity of 5,542 CEUs across 14 decks, was sailing between Japan and the USA with a cargo of 4,703 cars with an estimated value of US$103 million. At a location about 230 miles south of Alaska's Aleutian Islands, the crew were conducting a mid-ocean ballast water exchange before the ship entered US territorial waters.

As the ship went through the process of emptying and recharging the ballast tanks with seawater, the crew became aware of the vessel rolling. As a large swell wave hit, she failed to return from a roll and continued to list further and further to port.

The ship's starboard ballast tanks failed to refill properly, placing the ship at a point of negative stability (-ve GM). The ship was tipped over by the action of the swells, and rolled to an angle of loll, ie the point at which the increasing ship's water plane area had returned the ship to a state of positive stability. This increase in water plane area did not occur until the ship had listed over to approximately 60°, with the propeller clear of the water and the rudder resting hard to port in the air.

The crew were rescued by the USCG and the Air National Guard.

During the first 24 hours after the incident, Mitsui, the ship's owners, thought that the ship was a total loss and would go down. However, when she did not sink they signed a Lloyd's Open Form (LOF) agreement with the salvage company Titan.

Titan hired a vessel geared for salvage ops and proceeded to the site of the *'Cougar Ace'*.

Titan's 3D Naval Architect began building an approximate model of the ship based on photographs and diagrams supplied by the owners. The team input measurements and soundings taken on board into a 3D modelling program, to allow them to simulate how the ship would respond as the ballast water was moved to restore her to an upright and stable condition.

Inside the ship, the salvage team found hundreds of cars on the cargo decks, tilted on their side, each secured to the deck by four nylon webbing straps.

The salvage team determined that a wedge of water in the car decks weighing 1,026 tonnes would have to be pumped overboard and then the high-side ballast tanks filled with 160.9 tonnes of ballast water to bring the ship back to an even keel. However, the computer model showed that any more weight than that could easily roll the *'Cougar Ace'* over on her starboard side with the potential risk of such a sharp movement causing the car lashings to snap. A pile-up of cars on the starboard side could easily have capsized the ship, resulting in her sinking.

The *'Cougar Ace'* was now 140 miles from the coast, with the weather forecast to deteriorate. The salvage team connected a towline to the *'Cougar Ace'* to halt its rate of drift.

Building swell, combined with the ship's roll, brought the vessel perilously close to submerging her vents and possibly sinking. The *'Sea Victory'*, a 150 foot tug, arrived and passed a line to the *'Cougar Ace'*.

Titan believed that the ship could easily flop over when the operation to right her began so, to reduce this risk, the largest of the port side ballast tanks was filled to counterbalance any rapid roll. The three stages to right the ship are shown on the next page.

Disasters and Significant Incidents Involving RoRos and Car Carriers

The 'Cougar Ace' incident highlighted the dangers when attempting a ballast water exchange at sea.

The regulations at the time of the incident were as follows:

Ballast Water Exchange Standard – D-1

- **Ships performing ballast water exchange shall do so with an efficiency of 95% volumetric exchange of ballast water**
- **for ships exchanging ballast water by the pumping through method, pumping through three times the volume of each ballast water tank shall be considered to meet the standard described.**

Pumping through less than three times the volume may be accepted provided the ship can demonstrate that at least 95% volumetric exchange is met.

This incident demonstrated that, without a properly prepared BWE plan, ships are presented with a serious risk of losing stability during ballast transfers, due in part to increased free surface effect causing a reduction in the ship's dynamic stability, which can lead to an angle of loll developing and the likelihood of capsize.

New BWE/BWM rules stipulate that, after a vessel's first renewal survey following the date of entry into force of the convention, no ship (constructed before entry into force) shall conduct BWE as the only means of BWM.

The Stages to Right the Ship

1. Large salvage pumps were positioned on the 9th deck to pump the flood water overboard.
2. The water level in No. 5 port ballast tank (red) was checked to ensure there was adequate counterbalance before starting to fill the starboard ballast tank (yellow).
3. The fifth starboard tank was filled with 160.9 tonnes of seawater to bring the ship fully upright.

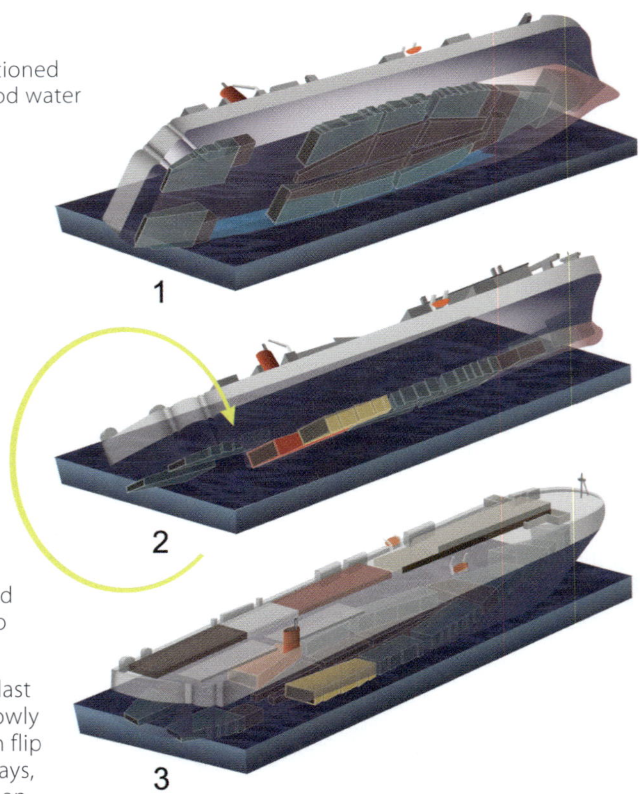

As the water level in No. 5 port ballast tank decreased to 20%, the ship slowly started to lift. There was no sudden flip from the ship. Over the next two days, the ship was gradually returned to an upright position, with the owners taking the ship back a few days later.

Safety Designs and Innovations Incorporated into RoRos and Car Carriers

Active Tank Stabilisation Systems

Unlike passive stabilising tanks, systems such as the Rolls-Royce controlled system react immediately to any change in roll motion. These systems use a U-shaped system, half-filled with water, and side tanks that are connected by a water cross duct. Air cross duct(s) with integrated stabiliser valves are incorporated for air exchange between side tanks.

Controlled tank systems are designed to give 40 to 50% lower roll on average. They are also effective at low speed or when stationary.

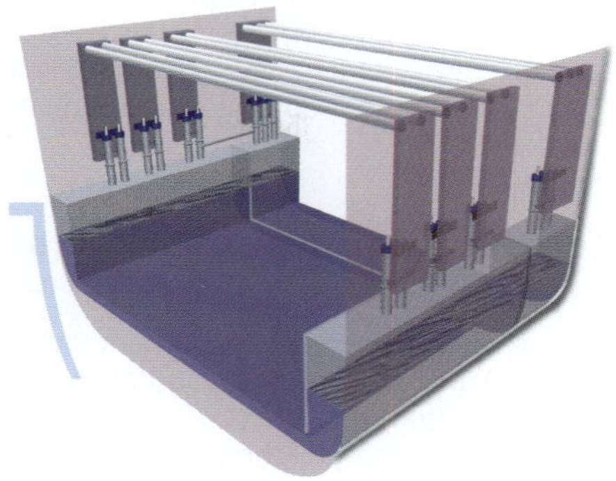

Reproduced with permission from Rolls-Royce

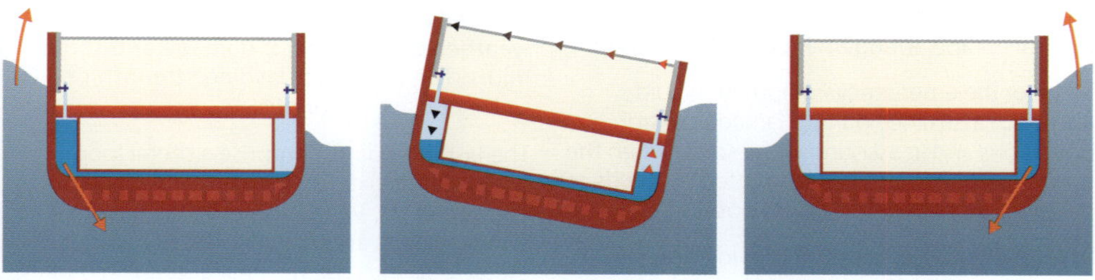

Indicator Lights to Confirm RoRo Visor is Closed

Shortly after the *'Herald of Free Enterprise'* disaster in 1987, the UK approached the IMO with a request that a series of emergency measures be considered for adoption.

In April 1988, the IMO adopted a new package of amendments, including a regulation that required the fitting of indicator lights on the navigating bridge. The indicators warn the bridge if any doors that might lead to a flooding risk are left open. Another new regulation required monitoring of special category and RoRo spaces to detect undue movement of vehicles in adverse weather, fire, the presence of water or unauthorised access by passengers while the ship is underway.

A later amendment added a new regulation requiring cargo loading doors to be locked before the ship proceeds on any voyage and to remain closed until the ship is at its next berth.

Damage Stability

Further amendments were adopted in October 1988 relating to the stability of passenger ships in a damaged condition. The amendment applied to ships built after 29th April 1990 and stipulated that the maximum angle of heel after flooding but before equalisation should not exceed 15°.

Lightweight Survey Every Five Years

When the *'Herald of Free Enterprise'* was examined after sinking, her centre of gravity was found to be much higher than the ship had calculated. This was due to the addition of new facilities, such as hairdressing salons and shops, on the upper decks. This prompted a further amendment requiring

Safety Designs and Innovations Incorporated into RoRos and Car Carriers

that a lightweight survey must be carried out for passenger ships, to verify any changes in lightweight displacement and the longitudinal centre of gravity, at periods not exceeding five years.

Emergency Equipment Lockers for RoRos

The provision of emergency equipment lockers was a recommendation of the Court of Formal Investigation into the loss of the *'Herald of Free Enterprise'*. The purpose of the equipment is to provide means in unusual circumstances, eg when a ship is at a very large angle of heel, to assist passengers and crew to escape from enclosed spaces within the ship when the normal escape arrangements cannot be used.

Some of the emergency equipment would also be of assistance during damage control operations and in assisting with escape when the normal escape routes are obstructed by debris or by doors jammed in the closed position.

At least one locker must be provided on each side of the ship. Where only one locker is provided on each side, it should be large enough to contain the equipment listed below. Where more than one locker is provided on each side, each locker should contain at least sufficient equipment to deal with escape from one side opening, eg hand lamp/torch, two adult lifting strops and a hand-powered lifting arrangement with associated rope.

Emergency Equipment Lockers

Emergency equipment should be of good quality. The following minimum scale of equipment is specified for the purpose of the Regulations and should be provided on each side of the ship and stowed in one or more lockers:

- **Fireman's axe (long handled) × 1**
- **Fireman's axe (short handled) × 1**
- **Pin maul (7 lb) × 1**
- **Crowbar × 1**
- **Hand lamp/torch × 4**
- **Padded lifting strop (adult) × 6**
- **Padded lifting strop (child) × 2**
- **Hand-powered lifting arrangement × 3**
- **Lightweight rigid collapsible ladder at least 3 metres long × 1**
- **Lightweight rope ladder (equal in length to beam of ship or 10 metres, whichever is less) × 1**
- **First Aid Kit × 1**
- **Blankets (sealed in plastic bags) or thermal protective aids × 6**
- **Waterproof jackets and trousers × 4 sets**

Reference: UK Merchant Shipping (Emergency Equipment Lockers for RoRo Passenger Ships) Regulations 1988

Lashing Points

Many heavy vehicles are not fitted with secure lashing points or, if they are, they are often placed too low, which means the vehicle cannot be properly secured. This has resulted in vehicles moving during rough weather, causing major damage and serious injury. The minimum lashing strength needs to be at least 10 tonnes.

The lashing points comprise a metal loop permanently fixed to the vehicle's chassis. The size of the vehicle determines how many lashing points are required. The hole inside the metal loop must be no smaller than 80 mm in diameter.

Carriage of Vehicles

Safety

Ship's crew are at risk of accidental injury during the loading and unloading of vehicles and it is important that:

- Crew and shore staff are kept away from moving vehicles
- access to the vehicle decks is prevented during loading and unloading
- personnel on the vehicle decks involved in the cargo operation are fully aware of the dangers and are wearing high visibility clothing
- experienced drivers are used.

Vehicle Protection for Transport

Courtesy of Tvabutzku

New vehicles are externally protected in plastic film with foam cushioning blocks on areas that may be knocked, such as bumpers or car doors. Within the vehicle, display screens are protected with plastic film with coverings often provided for the steering wheel and the driver's seat.

Loading of Vehicles

The fuel tank typically contains no more than 3 litres of fuel, being sufficient for the vehicle to be driven on and off the ship during transport.

Damage to vehicles can occur during loading and unloading due to collisions between vehicles or with the ship's structure. Excess speed is often a contributory factor.

Another cause of damage is when a vehicle presented to load or unload has no fuel or a flat battery and, to prevent delay to the loading operation, the vehicle is 'shunted' into position using another vehicle which is cushioned with rubber tyres.

During loading or unloading of motor vehicles, it should be ensured that:

- The angle of all ramps on the ship are at no more than 12° so that the underneath of the vehicle or any spoilers avoid damage
- for trucks, the angle of the ramps should be between 6 to 7° so that the top of the truck avoids the risk of damage
- the windows on the vehicle provide a clear and unobstructed view
- right-hand or left-hand drive vehicles are stowed such that, once the vehicle is parked in position, the driver can get out on the unobstructed side
- the fuel tank contains the appropriate quantity of fuel (ie no more than 3 litres)
- the vehicle's battery is functional and, if it is disconnected for the voyage, it has been reconnected prior to unloading.

General Guidance on Securing Vehicles

All vehicles are fitted with some form of suspension (leaf/coil spring or air suspension), which means that they can vibrate and move with the motion of the ship. Sufficient space must be allowed between individual vehicles to prevent them contacting one another due to the vessel's motion. The spacing to the front should be no less than 30 cm and to the sides no less than 10 cm.

Only wheel chocks matching the correct wheel diameter should be used.

Carriage of Vehicles

Hooks should be correctly tensioned and not strained to the point of bending the hook. Any tensioning belts should not be twisted.

The vehicle's parking brake must be applied for both manual and automatic cars.

On a manual car, the gearbox should be left in 1st gear. On an automatic car, the gear selector must be in park. In all cases, the steering lock must be engaged.

Lashing Vehicles

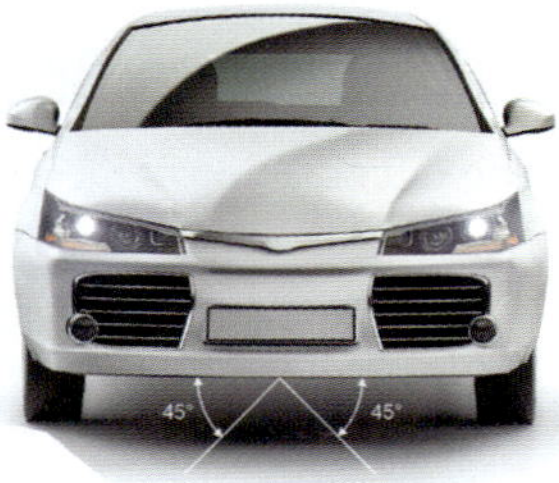

- Lashing operations must be carried out at the same time as the loading operation and must be done by a separate gang
- the lashing gang should move their equipment between parked vehicles below spoiler level and they should neither lean against the vehicle nor use its bumpers or vehicle body as a support when standing up
- the lashing gang must wear work clothes without metal fastenings or zips
- the lashing gang should aim to achieve an angle of 45° measured horizontally from the bumper and an angle of 30° measured vertically from the bumper
- lashings must be regularly inspected and tightened when necessary during the voyage.

Further guidance can be obtained from 'MGN 418 Roll-on/roll-off ships stowage and securing of vehicles': http://tinyurl.com/pxukvwk

CHAPTER 2

Tankers

Oil Tankers

Developments in the world economy have shaped the tanker trade in 2013. Other defining factors included the high oil price levels (average oil prices exceeded US$100 per barrel for a third consecutive year), demographics, geopolitical uncertainties, technology and energy efficiency gains, and also changes in supply and demand with traditional consumer markets such as the United States emerging as large suppliers and potentially large exporters of crude oil. In 2013, less crude oil volumes were imported into the United States and more refined oil products were exported from its ports. Developing economies, in particular China and India, are emerging as large crude oil importers, including with the view to the current and planned expansion of their refinery capacities. This in turn may further shift tanker trade patterns, with Asia becoming an important oil products supplier.

Source: UNCTAD Review of Maritime Transport 2014

Total World Tanker Fleet

Supply Crude Tankers, Product Tankers, Chemical/Oil Tankers and Pure Chemical Tankers

Oil and Chemical Tankers >500 GT = 10,224

Source: UNCTAD Review of Maritime Transport 2014

Oil Tankers

Crude and Product Tankers

Tankers vary substantially in size and capacity, but their general appearance is always the same. Increases in size, however, eventually limit operations through draught restrictions and available dry dock capacity.

Oil tankers constructed before 1993[1] did not have double bottoms or double shells and the cargo tank area extended over the length of the hull to the ship side and bottom. Two continuous longitudinal bulkheads extended throughout the length of the cargo space, dividing this into three tanks across the ship and, at the same time, providing longitudinal strength for the ship. Machinery spaces and accommodation were all positioned aft of the cargo space, with no accommodation extending into the cargo area. Doors into the accommodation were not permitted to face the cargo area and all windows were fixed to reduce the possibility of vapours entering the accommodation. The main pump room was positioned aft of the tank space and immediately forward of the engine room. No cargo was permitted to be pumped through the machinery space.

Forward of the cargo tanks the space was used to house ballast, stores, spare bunkers, equipment, etc. Aft of the cargo space were the fuel bunkers, fresh water and machinery space. Each cargo tank was oil tight and a small ullage and inspection hatch was required. Each tank had a vent pipe fitted with a valve, which ensured that the pressure in the tank remained close to atmospheric pressure. This provided a ready means of protecting the tanks against over or under pressure.

Classes of Crude Oil Tanker

Tankers are used to transport crude oil and petroleum products and range in size from small coastal tankers, primarily used for products, to larger VLCCs used for crude.

Panamax Tankers

Panamax
Fleet of 378 (basis 308 LR1 product and 70 crude)
Source: Lloyd's List, 2014

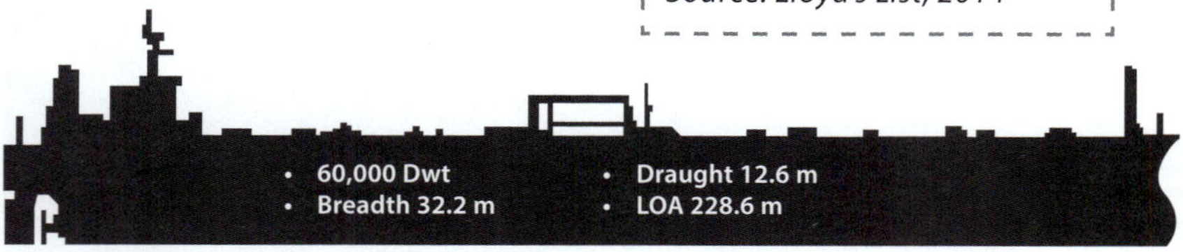

Ships in the 55,000 to 75,000 Dwt size range meet the dimensions of the maximum size of tanker that can transit the Panama Canal. The constraints of the canal locks dictate a maximum length of 274.3 metres and maximum breadth of 32.3 metres. Panamax tankers are mostly found in North America, importing crude and fuel oil.

[1] These tankers were not built to the requirements of OPA 90 or the previous MARPOL Annex I Regulation 13g (now 20), the text of which stipulated the requirements for double hull tankers.

Aframax Tankers

Aframax
Fleet of 723
Source: Lloyd's List, 2014

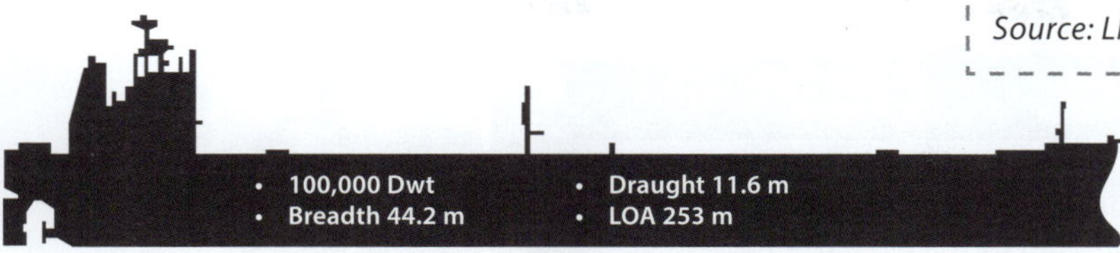

Aframax tankers are employed on a wide variety of short and medium-haul crude oil voyages. They range from 75,000 to 120,000 Dwt. The biggest tanker that can be accommodated fully laden in US ports is 100,000 Dwt, and this is only at a limited number of ports. Aframax ships are the largest size defined by the average freight rate assessment (AFRA) scheme. The AFRA scheme, overseen by the London Tanker Brokers' Panel, uses a classification system to standardise contract terms, establish shipping costs and determine the ability of ships to travel into ports or through certain straits and channels.

117,000 Dwt Stena Ice-Aframaxes, built to navigate the Baltic Sea first year ice

Courtesy of Stena Bulk

Suezmax Tankers

Suezmax
Fleet of 485
Source: Lloyd's List, 2014

Note: The size of Suezmax vessels is increasing from an average of 141,774 Dwt for those still trading that were built before 1990 to an average of 154,536 Dwt for those built since 1998.

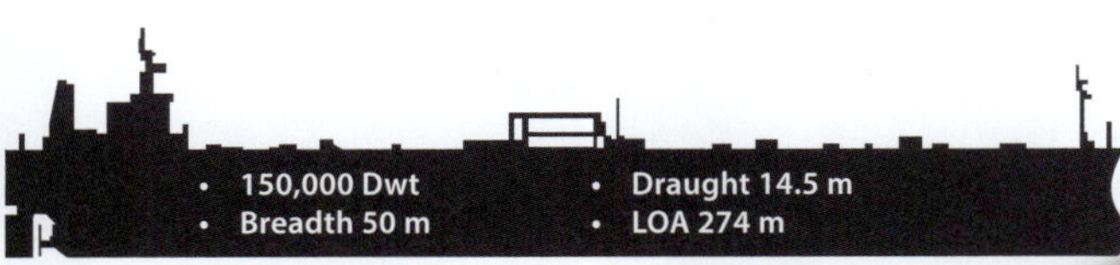

156,000 Dwt

Suezmax tankers are in the 120,000 to 200,000 Dwt size range and are capable of lifting one million barrel cargoes. They are the largest tankers that can transit the Suez Canal fully laden.

Oil Tankers

Very Large Crude Carriers (VLCCs)

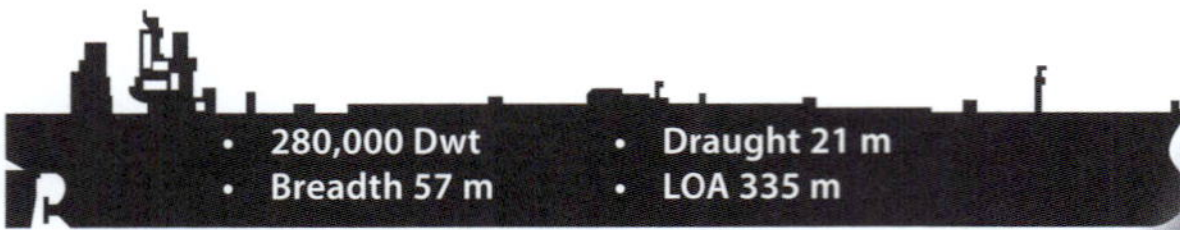

VLCCs are tankers in the 200,000 to 320,000 Dwt size range. Construction of ships of this size was prompted by the rapid growth in global oil consumption during the 1960s and, in 1967, closure of the Suez Canal, which necessitated voyages around the Cape of Good Hope. VLCCs remain the most effective way of transporting large volumes of oil over relatively long distances.

Ultra Large Crude Carriers (ULCCs)

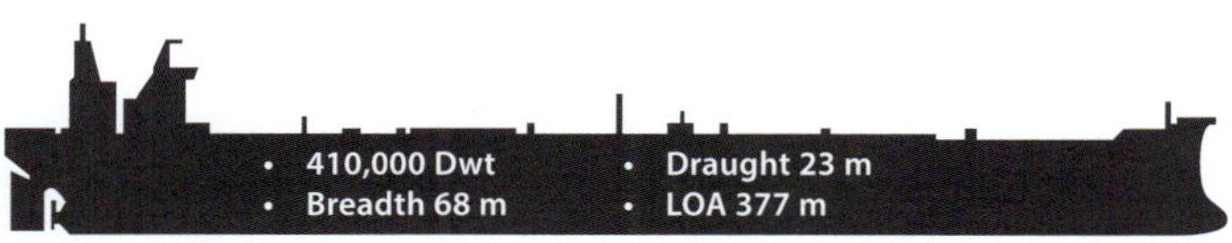

These tankers are in excess of 320,000 Dwt.

Most ships of this type were built in the mid to late 1970s and were delivered at the point when oil prices increased and demand collapsed. Due to their limitation to serving only a few deepwater ports, ULCCs failed to achieve their full potential and there are now fewer than 40 of them remaining.

The *'Jahre Viking'*, at 565,000 Dwt, was the longest ship ever built and held the record for the greatest deadweight tonnage. She was built in 1979 and consisted of 17 sets of port, centre and starboard cargo tanks. She was subsequently lengthened after sustaining damage during a missile attack during the Iran/Iraq war in 1988.

As the increased phase-out of single hull vessels took effect, she spent time in storage off Qatar as the *'Knock Nevis'* and was scrapped in Alang, India in March 2010.

VLCC & ULCC
Fleet of 631
Source: Lloyd's List

'Jahre Viking'/'Knock Nevis' key particulars

Length:	458 m
Beam:	69 m
Draught:	26.4 m
Deadweight:	565,000 mt
Speed:	13.6 kn

Figure 2.1 - 'Jahre Viking'/'Knock Nevis'

Disasters and Significant Incidents Involving Oil Tankers

'Amoco Cadiz'

Date:	16th March 1978
Location:	Portsall, Brittany, France
Ship type:	Oil tanker
Date built:	1974
Flag:	Liberian
Type of pollutant:	Iranian and Arabian light crude oil
Quantity transported:	227,000 tonnes
Quantity spilled:	227,000 tonnes
Reason:	Steering failure/ grounding

Figure 2.2 - The 'Amoco Cadiz'

Incident

Following steering gear failure, the '*Amoco Cadiz*' ran aground off the coast of Brittany on 16th March 1978. Over a period of two weeks, during rough conditions, the entire cargo of 223,000 tonnes of Iranian and Arabian light crude oil and 4,000 tonnes of bunker fuel was released into the sea. The volume of the pollutant increased fivefold as the weather formed an oil and water emulsion known as 'mousse' which, by the end of April, had contaminated 320 km of the Brittany coastline. The incident had a huge impact on the marine life in the area.

Cause

Initially, the rudder stuck in the hard-a-port position, causing the ship to veer to the north. The Master became concerned about obstructing the approach to the west-going traffic lane and so stopped the engine and transmitted radio warnings that the ship was not under command. He requested other vessels to keep clear but made no request for outside assistance. Once the vessel lost her original momentum, she began to drift under the influence of the wind and tidal stream. This, combined with some confusion in establishing a Lloyd's Open Form to deal with the costs of a tug, were the main contributing factors that led to the grounding.

Impact

Approximately 30% of the oil spilled from the '*Amoco Cadiz*' evaporated and 14% dissolved in the seawater. It is estimated that only 28% of the oil washed up on the French shoreline.

The removal of bulk free oil trapped against the shore using skimmers proved difficult because of the amount of seaweed and debris mixed with it. Removing the oil by vacuum trucks and agricultural vacuum units proved much more successful, and a large amount was simply removed by hand.

A fortnight after the accident, millions of dead molluscs and sea urchins washed ashore. Echinoderm and small crustacean populations almost completely disappeared from some areas, although populations of many species had recovered within a year.

Nearly 20,000 dead birds were recovered. Oyster cultivation in the estuaries was seriously affected, with an estimated 9,000 tonnes destroyed as a result of contamination and to safeguard market confidence.

Repercussions

The grounding resulted in a 14-year lawsuit between the French State and the parent company, Amoco International Oil Company.

The French State and thousands of individuals belonging to various associations together claimed a total of over 152 million Euros (1978 value).

As a result of this disaster, the French government set up measures to reduce the risks of accidents and to ensure better response resources.

A new marine pollution response plan was established off the coast of Brittany and a new traffic separation scheme was set up that aimed to ensure that vessels transporting hazardous materials were kept 30 nautical miles off the coast. A powerful deep-sea tug was placed on permanent standby to assist vessels using the shipping lanes, and a specialised technical centre was created to ensure continuous technical surveillance.

Disasters and Significant Incidents Involving Oil Tankers

The French Government also introduced stricter regulations concerning laden tankers approaching the French coastline. Radio reports now have to be made to the French marine authorities and the areas in which laden tankers can operate are restricted. To ensure that laden tankers pass further offshore, the French Government also insisted that the IMO reconfigure and move some of the traffic separation schemes in the vicinity of the French coastline further seaward.

'Torrey Canyon'

Date:	18th March 1967
Location:	Isles of Scilly
Ship type:	Oil tanker
Date built:	1959
Flag:	Liberian
Type of pollutant:	Crude oil
Quantity transported:	121,000 tonnes
Quantity lost:	121,000 tonnes
Reason:	Grounding

Getty Images

Figure 2.3 - The 'Torrey Canyon'

Incident

On 18th March 1967, the *'Torrey Canyon'* ran aground on Seven Stones Reef at the western entrance to the English Channel due to navigation error and subsequent technical and human failures. Attempts were made to refloat the ship but when an explosion in the engine room killed a crew member, it was decided to abandon the vessel. On 26th March, heavy seas caused the vessel to split in two.

The entire cargo of approximately 121,000 tonnes of crude oil was released into the sea. Various attempts were made to disperse the oil including the use of chalk and chemical detergents. When these proved unsuccessful, the decision was made to bomb the wreck to start fires that would consume the remaining oil. The RAF and the Royal Navy dropped 62,000 lbs of bombs, 5,200 gallons of petrol, 11 rockets and large quantities of napalm onto the ship over a two day period. Despite direct hits and intense flames, the wreck failed to sink and only minimal amounts of oil were burned off. The mission was called off when particularly high spring tides put out the flames.

Cause

Strong currents during the night of 17th March meant that the *'Torrey Canyon'* was pushed northeast while on autopilot. The Master then decided to proceed through the gap between the Isles of Scilly and the Seven Stones with only a small scale chart of the area. Navigational adjustments made to avoid fishing nets brought the vessel very close to the reef, which was obscured from view by a high tide.

When a navigational error made by an inexperienced junior officer was realised, the vessel was already among the submerged rocks of the Seven Stones and failed to respond to alterations and adjustments. The crew, including the Master, became confused and it was eventually discovered that the autopilot had inadvertently been knocked into the disengage position. It was re-engaged only as the *'Torrey Canyon'* hit Pollard's Rock at full speed.

Impact

The pollution resulting from the *'Torrey Canyon'* was not just caused by the loss of the entire crude oil cargo but also by the chemical dispersants and detergents used by the authorities. The chemicals dropped onto the wreck in the attempted bombing also contributed to the environmental impact.

Oil

The oil spill formed into three distinct slicks that affected large areas of the Cornish coastline, the Channel Islands and parts of Brittany.

An estimated 25,000 birds died as a direct result of the *'Torrey Canyon'* spill. Thousands of oiled birds were picked up from beaches for treatment but the survival rate was only 1% due to ingestion of oil, pneumonia and improper handling and cleaning.

Manual methods were used for the removal of oil on many of the sandy beaches, although the complex nature of the coastline made it impossible for a complete clean-up. Approximately 4,000 tonnes of oil and oil emulsions were removed from the foreshores of Guernsey and 4,200 tonnes from French beaches.

Dispersants and Detergents

In an attempt to minimise the impact of the oil, the seashores were sprayed with detergents that were acutely toxic to many marine mammals and plants. The toxins also killed off many shore species, such as limpets, and the shore ecosystems took years to recover.

Repercussions

Claims were made by the British and French Governments against the owners of the vessel. Four months after the oil spill, the British Government was only able to serve its writ against the owners by arresting the *'Torrey Canyon's'* sister ship, the *'Lake Palourde'*, when she put in for provisions at Singapore.

The *'Torrey Canyon'* incident set in motion the chain of events that eventually led to the adoption of MARPOL, as well as a host of conventions in the field of liability and compensation.

The IMO Assembly convened an international conference in 1973 to adopt a completely new convention. This also served to transform the Sub-Committee on Oil Pollution into the Marine Environment Protection Committee (MEPC). The MEPC was eventually given the same standing as the Maritime Safety Committee, with a remit to deal with all matters relating to marine pollution.

One of the main issues raised by the *'Torrey Canyon'* incident was the question of who was to be held responsible for the damage caused by oil pollution and how to determine the liability and level of compensation. In 1969, a conference convened by the IMO adopted a new convention, placing responsibility firmly with the shipowner.

'Marpessa', 'Mactra' and 'Kong Haakon VII' - Three explosions in one month in 1969

Figure 2.4 - 'Mactra'

The *'Marpessa'* was 100 miles north-northwest of Dakar and cleaning her tanks in accordance with established procedures at the time. Two crew members were killed in the blast and many others were injured. The explosion obliterated all the deck lines and it proved impossible to fight the fire. As a result of the fire and/or initial explosion, the engine room, pump room and No. 5 tanks became flooded. The *'Marpessa'* sank slowly over several days and become the largest single shipping loss, up to that time, on 15th December 1969.

'Mactra'

On 29th December 1969, the *'Mactra'*, en route from Le Havre to the Persian Gulf, exploded off the coast of Mozambique when the crew were washing the cargo tanks. The *'Mactra'* had five port, centre and starboard cargo tanks, and the explosion occurred in No. 4 centre. The explosion blew out the bulkheads into numbers 3 and 5, leaving a void space 400 feet long and 50 feet wide into which the deck fell. An officer and an AB were killed in the explosion and a further six crew were injured. The vessel did not take on any water and, after anchoring off Beira, subsequently reached the safety of Durban harbour.

Disasters and Significant Incidents Involving Oil Tankers

'Kong Haakon VII'

On 30th December 1969, *'Kong Haakon VII'* was en route from Finnart (Glasgow) to the Persian Gulf when an explosion and resulting fire occurred in her No. 3 and 4 tanks during tank cleaning operations, about 180 miles off Monrovia. The explosion caused the deck to be blown upwards, but fortunately none of the crew were injured. The Master and crew abandoned ship and then reboarded after the fire had died down, allowing the tanker to proceed at slow speed to Monrovia.

Conclusions

These three explosions led to a tanker industry investigation. It concluded that static electricity created by the tank cleaning jet of water was the likely source of ignition of the gas-in-air mixture that had been left in the tank after the cargo had been discharged. In essence, these massive tanks could create their own 'weather conditions' during washing, the equivalent of a thunderstorm in a tank.

Physicist Edward Pierce reported on this 'storm theory' to the 1970 conference on lightning and static electricity held in San Diego. He had experimented over the previous four years on the build-up of static in his bathroom during showering. During the first five minutes of a shower, he observed, the electrical field in his bathroom steadily built up in intensity. The effect was too small to present any danger, but that might not be the case in a cargo tank on an oil tanker. There, Pierce calculated, the electrical charge could easily exceed 10,000 volts per metre after about 45 minutes of washing.

This research resulted in the requirement for inerting and the washing of tanks with crude oil (ie Crude Oil Washing).

'Betelgeuse'

Date:	8th January 1979
Location:	Bantry Bay, Ireland
Ship type:	Oil tanker
Date built:	1968
Flag:	French
Type of pollutant:	Mixed Arabian crude oil
Quantity transported:	114,000 tonnes
Quantity lost:	40,000 tonnes
Reason:	Explosion/structural failure
Fatalities:	50

Press Association

Figure 2.5 - The 'Betelgeuse'

Incident

The tanker *'Betelgeuse'* exploded while unloading its cargo at Whiddy Island terminal, Bantry Bay, Ireland. All 41 crew members, an officer's wife and eight terminal workers died in the explosion.

Cause

The *'Betelgeuse'* was in an appalling condition. An inspection nine months before the explosion had revealed 37 cracks in her crude cargo tanks, and a major oil leak had been reported to the ship's owners only a week before the disaster. The ship also lacked an inert gas system and had no effective disposal method for the treatment of dangerous vapours during ballasting operations.

The ballasting procedures were incorrect for the conditions in the bay at the time of the incident. Calculations based on the load ballast conditions of the ship showed that the longitudinal structural members near the deck of No. 4 ballast tanks would have buckled under the strain. This buckling caused structural failure between the vapour spaces of No. 3 wing tanks, containing light crude, and the No. 4 ballast tanks, allowing vapour to enter and an explosive mixture to develop. The resulting impact between buckling steel plates could have generated the sparks that ignited the gas mixture.

A muffled explosion occurred in tanks very near the centre of the ship. This broke the back of the ship just aft of No. 3 tanks and caused a release of light crude from No. 3 wing tanks. A fire started amidships but, as crude oil spread, the fire soon engulfed the whole ship. The lack of a passageway from the jetty to the shore contributed to the high number of fatalities.

After the fire had been extinguished, the heat and fumes continued to prevent emergency crews from commencing the operation to pump off the remaining oil until two weeks after the explosion.

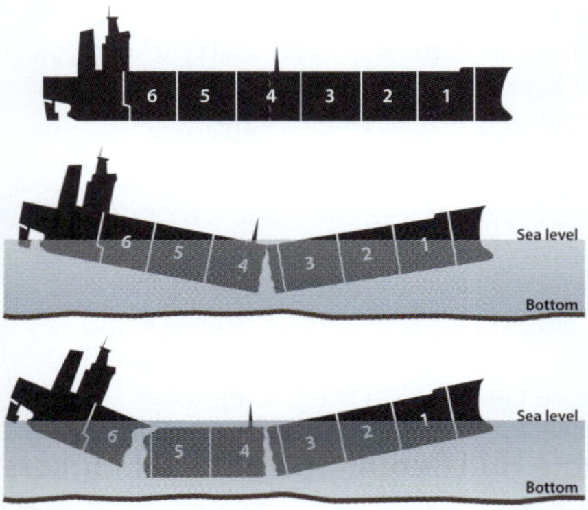

Figure 2.6

Oil spill booms were deployed to attempt to contain the oil and 35 tonnes of dispersants were sprayed on 12 consecutive days by aeroplane. This prevented the oil from reaching the shoreline. However, the local fishing and shellfish industry was seriously affected as was the local seabird population.

Conclusions

The reports of the official investigation identified three main contributory factors:

1. The poor condition of the *'Betelgeuse'* for which its operator, Total SA, was to blame. The 11-year-old vessel had been worked hard and was at the end of its service life.
2. Incorrect cargo discharge planning resulted in the buoyancy of the hull becoming uneven and therefore strained. Lack of crew training or wilful malpractice were possible explanations and Total was held largely to blame for this.
3. There was no adequate fire-fighting or rescue system either on the vessel or on the jetty and Gulf and Total were held jointly to blame for this.

It was determined that an improper discharge operation had caused the vessel to break her back and rupture several empty ballast tanks. Vapour from the ruptured tanks had escaped into the vessel and exploded in a fireball. However, the tribunal's findings were never accepted by Total.

The tribunal strongly advocated the introduction and use of inert gas to displace air in spaces above the tanks and to replace discharged cargo, and the close supervision of structural stresses during discharging and ballasting operations.

'Exxon Valdez'

Date:	24th March 1989
Location:	Prince William Sound, Alaska
Ship type:	Oil tanker
Date built:	1986
Flag:	American
Type of pollutant:	Crude oil
Quantity transported:	180,000 tonnes
Quantity spilled:	38,500 tonnes
Reason:	Grounding

Incident

The pilot disembarked the *'Exxon Valdez'* at 23:24 on 23rd March. The presence of ice in the southwest bound traffic lane meant the vessel had to move into the northeast bound lane (see Figure 2.8). The ship then hit Bligh Reef at 00:04 on 24th March, severely holing her forepeak tank and starboard tanks 1, 3 and 5. She also tore through centre tanks 1, 2, 3 and 4. The resulting oil spill had a significant impact on the surrounding environment.

Figure 2.7 - The 'Exxon Valdez'

Disasters and Significant Incidents Involving Oil Tankers

The majority of the oil was spilled within the first eight hours after the ship's grounding. For the three days after the spill, conditions were calm and the oil generally formed a slick heading southwest. However, on 26th March, a storm generated winds of over 70 mph in Prince William Sound and weathered much of the oil, causing it to cover a much larger area, and changing it into mousse. Mousse does not burn and is very difficult to remove from the sea surface or from the shoreline.

Cause

The probable cause of the grounding was the failure of the Third Officer to properly manoeuvre the vessel and closely monitor the vessel's progress because of fatigue and excessive workload.

Other contributing factors were established to have been:

- The failure of the Master to provide a proper navigational watch because of his impairment from alcohol
- the failure of the Exxon Shipping Company to provide sufficient crew for the '*Exxon Valdez*'
- the lack of an effective vessel traffic service because of inadequate equipment and manning levels
- the lack of effective and appropriate pilot and escort services.

Impact

The distribution of the oil along the shoreline was sporadic in terms of coverage and varied in depth both on the surface and within the beach substrate.

By the summer of 1989, 790 miles of shoreline within Prince William Sound and 2,400 miles in the Kenai Peninsula was found to be oiled. The spill killed an estimated 250,000 seabirds, 2,800 sea otters, 300 harbour seals, 250 bald eagles and up to 22 killer whales.

After an initial lack of urgency in the immediate response, the clean-up operation then proceeded on a massive scale. A variety of methods were used to deal with the oil, including skimming, both manual and mechanical retrieval, and hot water and high pressure cleaning on the shorelines.

Double Hull Requirement for Oil Tankers

The '*Exxon Valdez*' disaster resulted in the 'double hull' amendment of 6th March 1992 being voted in for all tankers built after 6th July 1996 (MARPOL Convention, rule 13F).

Emergency tow packages, similar to those employed in Prince William Sound, are now required on all tankers.

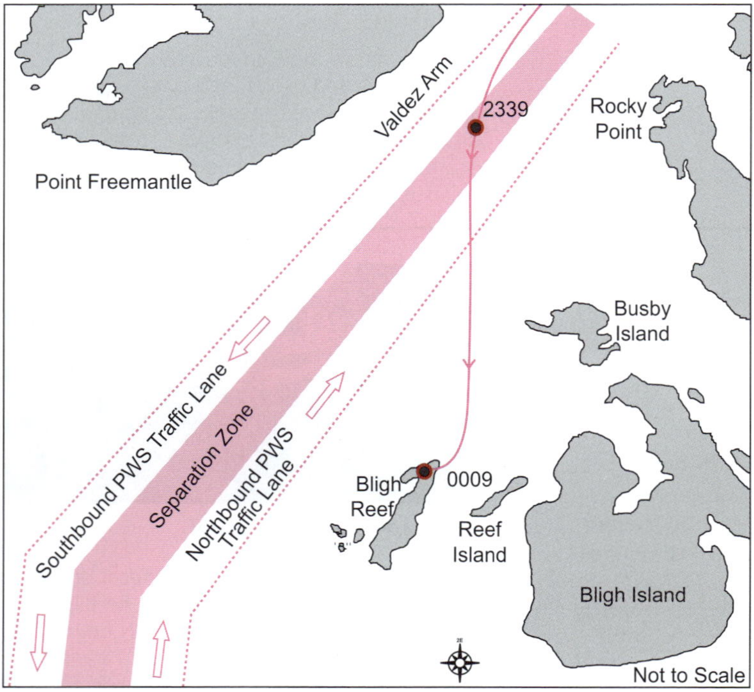

Figure 2.8 - Track of the 'Exxon Valdez' on the 23rd and 24th March 1989

'Kirki'

Date: 20th July 1991
Location: ~55 miles off Cervantes, Australia
Ship type: Oil tanker
Date built: 1969
Flag: Greek
Type of pollutant: Crude oil
Quantity transported: 82,660 tonnes
Quantity lost: 17,700 tonnes
Reason: Structural failure

Courtesy of AMSA

Figure 2.9 - The 'Kirki'

Incident

In rough seas and strong winds, the *'Kirki'* experienced problems with her forepeak ballast tank and found that, instead of being empty, it was filled to sea level. The weather conditions deteriorated and, at 03:00 on 21st July, the bow of the *'Kirki'* sheared off completely. A fire, fuelled by the cargo of crude oil, increased the rupture in the forward bulkheads and the oil began to leak into the sea. The 37 crew members were all safely evacuated by helicopter. The ship was towed further out to an area west-northwest of Dampier where the remaining 64,300 tonnes of crude were transferred to the tanker *'Flying Chipper'*.

Cause

The incident was attributed to the structural failure of the forepeak. A sample of plate taken from a position adjacent to the main fracture line at the bow was examined and found to be in a severely corroded state with up to 90% of the plate thickness lost in some areas. Such severe loss of thickness should have been picked up during previous inspections.

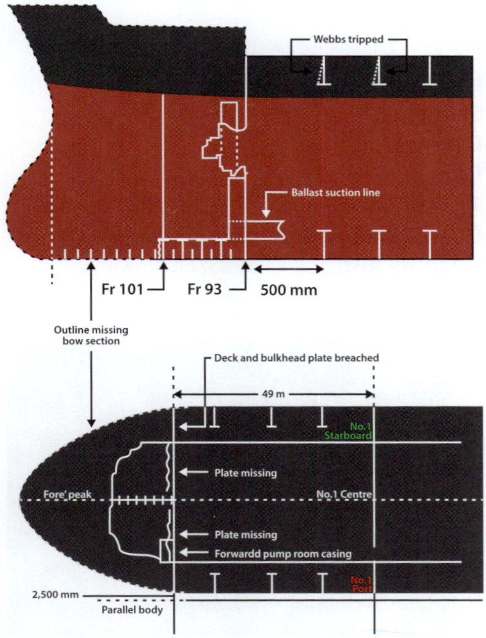

Figure 2.10 - Outline missing bow section

However, reports showed that the *'Kirki'* had in the past used painted canvas over patches to hide the poor condition of the steel.

It is not possible to be precise about the cause of the structural failure forward of the bow area. Ultimately, it was either a loss of bow plating or the action of seawater, which had flooded the forepeak and put great strain on the area of frame 93, leading to an overload on the structure. Either one or a combination of these factors led to excessive stress on an area of the ship's structure already weakened by corrosion and the effects of repair work.

Impact

Although it was the largest single oil spill in Australian waters, the environmental impact of the incident was minimal. Fortunately, the weather conditions and the presence of the Leeuwin Current moved the oil away from the coast and the vast majority dissipated naturally.

Repercussions

The *'Kirki'* incident highlighted the need for an overhaul of AMSA, the Australian Maritime Safety Agency, and their spill response arrangements. The 1993 review made a total of 30 recommendations for policy, administration and operation, all of which were implemented by 1995.

Disasters and Significant Incidents Involving Oil Tankers

'Braer'

Date:	5th January 1993
Location:	Garths Ness, Shetland
Ship type:	Oil tanker
Date built:	1975
Flag:	Liberia
Type of pollutant:	Crude oil
Quantity transported:	85,000 tonnes
Quantity lost:	85,000 tonnes
Reason:	Engine failure

Courtesy of MAIB

Figure 2.11 - The 'Braer'

Incident

The *'Braer'* suffered engine failure and, despite the best efforts of crew and volunteers, as well as various attempts to attach a tow to a tug, it drifted into rocks and grounded. The vessel completely broke apart on 12th January. The entire cargo of crude oil was released into the sea with adverse effects on the local wildlife and the industries dependent on it.

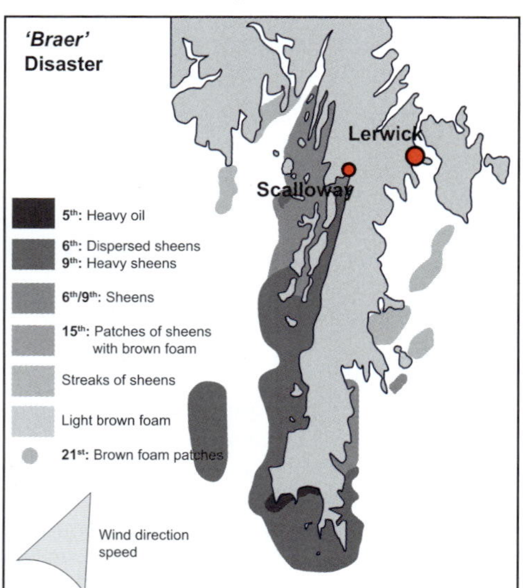

Cause

After routine adjustments, the auxiliary boiler that provided steam to pre-heat the oil for the engine could not be relit. The decision was made to continue to run the *'Braer'* on diesel. Unfortunately, seawater had contaminated the diesel fuel supply after loose piping on deck had rolled in the bad weather and struck the diesel vents, completely sheaving them and allowing water into the diesel tanks. The engines stopped, quickly followed by failure of the generator. The radio equipment was run on emergency power but the navigational equipment and radar were not.

Confusion between the Master and the coastguard delayed tugs getting to the *'Braer'*. However, tugs could not attach a line and all on board were evacuated. A short time later the ship grounded on the rocks at Garths Ness.

Impact

Fortunately, the type of oil the *'Braer'* was carrying was light and easily biodegradable. This, combined with the severe weather conditions in the weeks after the grounding, meant that the majority of the oil dispersed naturally by wave action and evaporation. The oil spill did, however, have an impact on the bird colonies of the Shetland Islands. A total of 1,542 dead birds were found, but a much larger number will have been lost in the sea and not accounted for.

Tides spread the oil underwater around the Shetland Islands' 900 miles of coastline, and fisherman found oil in their catch at points where it was not predicted to be. According to the fishermen, the fishing grounds were still depleted in 1996 and the shellfish extracted were still affected by oil.

The landscape of the Shetland Islands meant that a great deal of work was required to ensure that oil did not spread into lochs and dams. Sand booms and earth dykes were put across estuaries to halt the oil's progress, which proved to be quite successful.

Repercussions

Following a report into the incident, several recommendations were made for the IMO to consider:

- The Marine Directorate of the Department of Transport should, through the IMO, seek the revision and strengthening of STCW and stress the need for practical experience, training and a thorough assessment of competence in seamanship

- the ISM Code should be implemented by the shore management of shipping companies
- the Marine Directorate of the Department of Transport should, through the IMO, ensure that the revision of Resolution A535(13) (Provision of Emergency Towing Equipment for Tankers) incorporates provisions for safe access to the anchors from the after superstructure of tankers
- the Marine Directorate of the Department of Transport should ensure that HM Coastguard, on receipt of a request for towage assistance from any vessel carrying petroleum or dangerous cargo, relay the request immediately by all means of communication. This action should be taken regardless of whether or not the vessel has declared an urgency situation
- delegation of powers to a senior officer of the Department of Transport located in the area of the incident, when local knowledge might result in a faster response to the emergency.

'Prestige'

Date:	13th November 2002
Location:	Near Cape Finisterre
Ship type:	Tanker
Date built:	1976
Flag:	Bahamas
Type of pollutant:	Heavy fuel oil
Quantity transported:	78,000 tonnes
Quantity lost:	64,000 tonnes
Reason:	Structural damage

Getty Images

Figure 2.12 - The 'Prestige'

Incident

During a storm off northwest Spain, one of the *'Prestige's'* cargo tanks ruptured. The Master was concerned that the ship might sink but he was refused permission to seek refuge by the Spanish, French and Portuguese authorities. Soon the damage to the ship increased and it is reported that a 40 foot section of the hull broke off, releasing a substantial quantity of oil.

On 19th November 2002, the ship broke in half, releasing more oil into the sea.

Cause

A Spanish investigation came to the conclusion that the *'Prestige's'* hull was always likely to have failed. Previous intensive investigations on her two sister ships, the *'Alexandros'* and the *'Centaur'*, showed that both ships were likely to fail at holds 61 and 75. They had both been scrapped by 2002. Concerns were expressed over the *'Prestige's'* continued use. The stormy conditions are most likely to have exacerbated a pre-existing structural weakness and placed such a strain on the structure that it could not cope.

The breaking of the hull was avoidable; it occurred while the ship was being moved away from the Spanish coastline. The damage to the middle of the ship meant it could not cope with the increasing wavelength of the seas. The pressure this placed on the badly damaged hull caused it to break apart.

Impact

The oil from the *'Prestige'* polluted the seabed and contaminated large stretches of the coastlines of Spain, Portugal and France. The worst affected area was Galicia, which is a very important ecological region, supporting coral reefs, many species of sharks and birds, and a fishing industry. The heavy coastal pollution forced the region's government to suspend offshore fishing for six months, which had a massive economic impact on the area. In Galicia, 41,600 people depended directly on fishing, practically all of whom were affected by the oil spill.

Disasters and Significant Incidents Involving Oil Tankers

The volume of fish caught in Galicia accounted for 40% of the total Spanish catch, which made Galicia the foremost fishing region in the whole of Europe. The imposed fishing ban during the winter months caused a massive loss of income.

Repercussions

On 14th December 2002, the Spanish Government approved a legislative decree by which single hull oil tankers carrying heavy fuel oil are banned from entering Spanish ports, anchorages and maritime terminals under Spanish sovereignty.

Following the *'Erika'* oil spill, the European Commission had already identified two main needs: to quicken the phase-out of single hull oil tankers and to tighten up traffic control in European waters. The *'Prestige'* spill confirmed the need for these measures and led to determined action on implementation and vessel inspection.

In May 2003, a new protocol was adopted to improve the international regime for compensation of victims of oil pollution from oil tankers, creating a supplementary compensation fund. As a result, the total amount available for compensation for each incident in the member states of the supplementary fund is 750 million SDR (special drawing rights).

The IMO approved modification of the Finisterre maritime traffic scheme. It now has four traffic lanes (where there were two), using the two most distant for dangerous goods vessels. As a result of the separation, a new radar-AIS system has had to be installed on the Galician coast, to control the passage of vessels at 42 miles offshore.

'Sea Empress'

Date:	15th February 1996
Location:	Milford Haven
Ship type:	Tanker
Date built:	1993
Flag:	Liberian
Type of pollutant:	Forties light crude oil
Quantity transported:	130,000 tonnes
Quantity lost:	72,000 tonnes
Reason:	Grounding

BARRY BATCHELOR/AFP/Getty Image

Figure 2.13 - The 'Sea Empress'

Incident

The tanker *'Sea Empress'* ran aground on rocks when attempting to enter the Haven through the west channel, puncturing her starboard hull. Tugs were sent to refloat her but she detached and grounded several times, each occasion opening new sections of hull and releasing more oil. Almost a week after the initial incident, and after spilling around 72,000 tonnes of oil, she was eventually pulled free.

Cause

The incident is largely blamed on pilot error when the vessel was pushed off course by the current on entering the Haven, which initiated the whole chain of events.

However, lack of appropriate tugs in the area and a general lack of knowledge of local currents also played a part.

Impact

Estimates suggest that a total of 200 km of coastline were affected with a substantial impact on a 100 km stretch. 25,000 tonnes of waste were created by the clean-up operation.

The *'Empress'* was one of the worst spills for birds in northern European waters. Around 7,000 damaged or dead birds were found and over 25 species were affected.

Repercussions

Localised changes made include:

- Changes to pilot training and other requirements specifically relating to Milford Haven Port Authority
- tidal surveys and the development of computer models to enhance knowledge and understanding of tides in the area.

IMO legislation changes included:

- All tankers are now required to have an emergency towing point
- the presence and availability of four emergency towing vessels around the UK (Fair Isles, Stornaway, Falmouth and Dover) throughout the year (this was subsequently removed as part of the Conservative Government's austerity measures in 2010)
- the reassessment of National Contingency Plans and the roles of stakeholders in an emergency situation
- a number of scientific studies covering species recovery rates and the effects of hydrocarbons on the environment and marine and coastal wildlife.

'Erika'

Date:	12th December 1999
Location:	40 miles off Pointe de Penmarc'h, southern Brittany
Ship type:	Tanker
Date built:	1975
Flag:	Maltese
Type of pollutant:	Heavy fuel oil
Quantity transported:	31,000 tonnes
Quantity spilled:	19,500 tonnes
Reason:	Structural damage

MARINE NATIONALE/AFP/Getty Images

Figure 2.14 - The 'Erika'

Incident

On 11th December 1999, the *'Erika'* encountered extremely bad weather and developed a serious starboard list. Despite attempts to manage it, the list worsened and, as the weather deteriorated, cracks appeared along the main deck. During an attempt by tugs to move the *'Erika'* away from the French coastline, the hull broke into two pieces, releasing large amounts of fuel into the sea.

Cause

The weather conditions were poor, with the *'Erika'* having to deal with 60 mph winds and 20 foot waves. Such conditions placed the ship's structure under great strain and the condition of the ship, in terms of corrosion, cracking and quality of repairs, meant that the structure failed. Other possible factors included local failure, vulnerabilities in the design and a failure to deal with the evident corrosion and to sufficiently monitor repairs.

Impact

The *'Erika'* was carrying a cargo of heavy fuel oil that had a specific gravity quite similar to seawater. It was of a highly viscous, non-volatile, insoluble nature and could not be dispersed by chemicals.

The oil spill is estimated to have killed up to 300,000 seabirds. The 44,000 that were actually found dead is the largest number recorded for any oil spill in the western European seas.

Repercussions

On 21st March 2000, the European Commission adopted a first series of proposals, known as the 'Erika I package'. The Erika I package provided an immediate response to certain shortcomings highlighted by the *'Erika'* incident, including increased Port State controls, monitoring Class Society activities and speeding up the timetable for eliminating single hulls.

Port State Control

PSC is a defensive measure against sub-standard vessels. The flag States that do not ensure their vessels meet with internationally required standards will be refused entry into EU ports. Following the *'Erika'* incident, procedures for inspections were simplified and more vessels were subjected to thorough investigations.

Disasters and Significant Incidents Involving Oil Tankers

Classification Societies

Prior to the *'Erika'* amendments, it was discovered that the Societies, which have classified more than 90% of ships, did not undertake subsequent performance checks. The EC issued a directive regarding assessment of the procedures and activities of Classification Societies. If standards are not met, the EU may withdraw approval for the Classification Society to operate in European waters.

Single Hull Phase-Out

After the incident, Europe accelerated the phase-out of single hull tankers in line with the United States' Oil Pollution Act (OPA) 90. According to the regulations adopted following the *'Erika'* incident, Category 1 and 2 tankers were allowed to continue after 2005 and 2010 only if they passed a condition assessment survey (CAS).

On 5th April 2005, the existing Regulation 13G was revised and a new Regulation 13H added on the prevention of oil pollution to include oil tankers carrying heavy grade oil as cargo. Amendments made to the CAS scheme were also adopted.

The CAS amendments require more stringent and transparent verification of the reported structural condition, documentation and survey procedures of single hull vessels aged 15 years and older. CAS is conducted during the Enhanced Survey Programme.

Under the revised Regulation 13G of MARPOL Annex 1, the final phase-out dates were brought forward as follows:

- Category 1 tankers (pre-MARPOL tankers) - from 2007 to 2005
- Category 2 and 3 tankers (MARPOL and smaller tankers) - from 2015 to 2010.

Other Changes

The directive increased the powers of intervention of Member States, and imposed the carriage on board ships in Community waters of Automatic Identification Systems (AIS) as well as Voyage Data Recorders (VDR). It also made it compulsory for each Member State to have ports of refuge for vessels in distress.

Ballast Terms used on Oil Tankers

It used to be normal practice for tankers to discharge dirty ballast water (oil mixed with seawater) into the ocean, but this is now illegal.

In the past, as oil tankers discharged their cargo, they pumped seawater into the cargo oil tanks to provide ballast for the return trip. When the ship arrived at the loading port, this oily ballast was discharged into the port (with the oil interface being measured carefully and any oil on top being returned to the 'slop' tanks) and crude oil was loaded into the cargo tanks. Today, all tankers have segregated ballast tanks, ie they have tanks that are only used for ballast.

Clean Ballast

Clean ballast is ballast contained in a cargo tank that has previously contained oil, which has been cleaned to ensure no visible trace of oil would be present on the water if discharged.

"Clean ballast means the ballast in a tank which, since oil was last carried therein, has been so cleaned that effluent therefrom if it were discharged from a ship which is stationary into clean calm water on a clear day would not produce visible traces of oil on the surface of the water or on adjoining shorelines or cause a sludge or emulsion to be deposited beneath the surface of the water or upon adjoining shorelines. If the ballast is discharged through an oil discharge monitoring and control system approved by the Administration, evidence based on such a system to the effect that the oil content of the effluent did not exceed 15 parts per million shall be determinative that the ballast was clean, notwithstanding the presence of visible traces".

IMO, MARPOL

Dedicated Clean Ballast

This is ballast water carried in dedicated clean ballast tanks (CBT) that at no time carry

Ballast Terms used on Oil Tankers

oil cargo. The tanks are identified on the ship's International Oil Pollution Prevention Certificate (IOPPC) and are subject to the detailed operational procedures specified in the CBT operation manual.

Dirty Ballast

This is ballast water that is contaminated or is carried in tanks that have been contaminated by oil.

> *"Water that is put into a tank which has been crude oil washed but not water rinsed shall be regarded as dirty ballast".*
>
> *IMO, Crude Oil Washing Systems*

Segregated Ballast

This is ballast water completely separated from the cargo and fuel systems with permanently dedicated tanks, lines and pumps.

> *"Segregated ballast means the ballast water introduced into a tank which is completely separated from the cargo oil and oil fuel system and which is permanently allocated to the carriage of ballast or to the carriage of ballast or cargoes other than oil or noxious liquid substances as variously defined in the Annexes of the present Convention".*
>
> *IMO, MARPOL*

Figure 2.15 - Dedicated clean ballast discharged in port

Slops

Slops are dirty ballast residues and tank washings, either from machine water washing, crude oil washing (COW) or both, retained in a slop tank. Residues are decanted and then the clean water discharge is controlled through an oil discharge monitoring and control system. The remaining cargo residues are retained on board pending discharge ashore.

> *"Slop tank means a tank specifically designated for the collection of tank drainings, tank washings and other oily mixtures".*
>
> *IMO, MARPOL*

Measures to Reduce Pollution

Vapour Emission Control Systems

Approved vapour emission control systems are required on tankers if they are to comply with MARPOL Annex VI Regulation 15 regarding control of emission of volatile organic compounds (VOC) when loading, discharging or ballasting in port. The systems are required to connect and be compatible with vapour emission control systems (VECS) provided at designated ports and terminals. This enables closed loading and discharge operations to be conducted that prevent any discharge to the atmosphere.

Onboard vapour control systems are used to return tank vapour that is displaced from tanks when the cargo is loaded. Vapour balancing is when the vapour is returned to the shore tank that the cargo has been discharged from. Vapour processing is when the vapour is discharged directly to the facility for processing.

The system comprises:

- A dedicated manifold connection that must meet the criteria recommended by OCIMF
- pressure vacuum (P/V) valves set at an appropriate relief level that allows discharge of vapours at 125% of the maximum load rate
- drains at the lowest point to collect and remove condensate from the vapour
- gauging systems (fixed or portable) to monitor closed loading
- alarm systems that warn of high levels in the cargo tanks to prevent cargo entering the vapour system.

Prior to arrival at ports equipped with VECS, appropriate preparations are required in accordance with the ship's VOC management plan manual. These include:

- Confirmation of vapour manifold size connection requirements
- required cargo transfer rate and limitations
- testing of associated alarms, gauging equipment and P/V valves
- IGS operation tested and appropriately set up/blanked
- inert gas O_2 and H_2S content below 8% and 10 ppm respectively.

Shipboard vapour emission collection systems and port VECS should comply with the IMO MSC/Circular. 585 and be certificated by the USCG in accordance with US CFR 46 part 39 if trading in the USA.

Figure 2.16 - Vapour manifold (product tanker)

Double Hull Design

MARPOL Annex I Regulation 18 requires crude oil tankers of 20,000 Dwt or above and product tankers of 30,000 Dwt or above, delivered after 1st June 1982, to be fitted with segregated ballast tanks (SBT).

Before 1989, oil tankers were constructed with a single hull. In 1989, in response to the '*Exxon Valdez*' incident, the USA created the Oil Pollution Act 1990 (OPA 90) that required all tankers to have double hulls if they called at US ports.

After further studies in 1992, the Marine Environmental Protection Committee (MEPC) adopted amendments to MARPOL Annex I requiring double hulls or alternative designs for tankers delivered on or after 6th July 1996. A timetable was created that would eventually see the scrapping or conversion of all single hull tankers by 2015.

In 1999, the '*Erika*' incident accelerated the phase-out dates to 2010, subject to criteria such as age, ballast segregation and deadweight.

Tanker Category	Brought forward from
Category 1 (pre-MARPOL tankers)	2007 to 2005
Category 2 20,000 Dwt and above carrying crude oil, fuel oil, heavy diesel oil or lubricating oil as cargo 30,000 Dwt and above carrying other oils, which do comply with the protectively located SBT requirements (MARPOL tankers) **Category 3** 5,000 Dwt and above but less than Category 2	2015 to 2010

Although double hulls provide additional protection against pollution, there are operational and stability conditions that need to be considered.

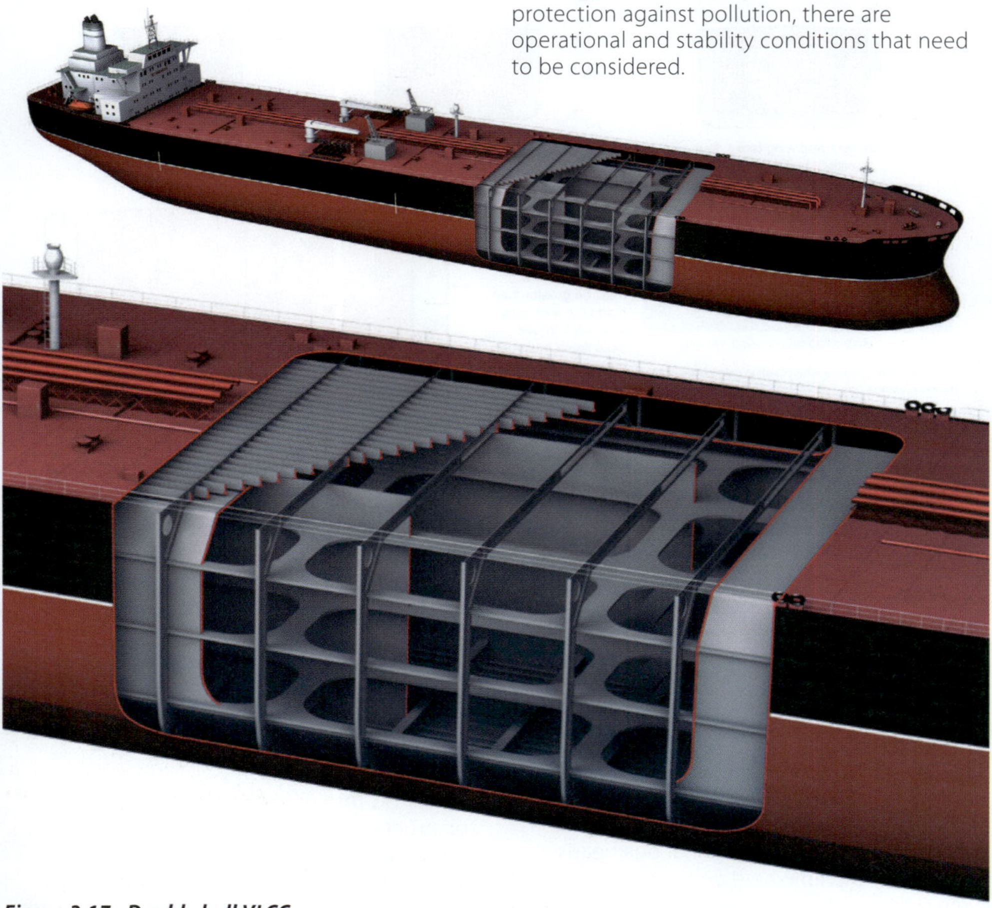

Figure 2.17 - Double hull VLCC

Measures to Reduce Pollution

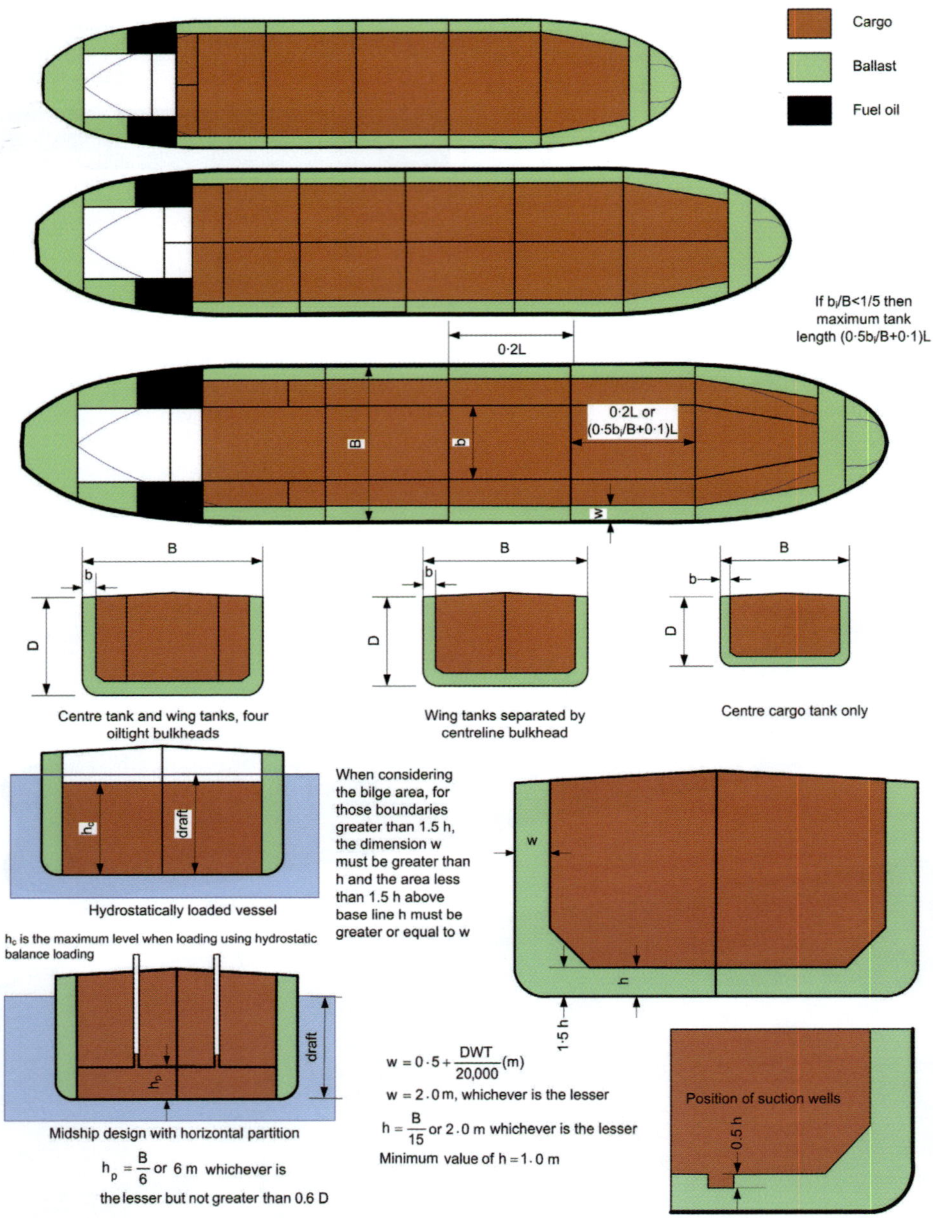

Reproduced from 'Crude Oil Tanker Basics'

Figure 2.18 - Double hull SBT and alternative arrangements for tankers

Stability

The original single hull tanker, which was normally transversely divided into three tanks, proved a very stable and structurally sound design. Having two longitudinal bulkheads ensured that, even where one or more tanks were slack, the free surface effect (FSE) was still insufficient to reduce the metacentric height (GM) to unacceptable levels.

Double bottom oil tankers are often constructed with a single central cargo tank without any transverse division. This is partly as a result of the additional strengthening provided by the double hull, which incorporates ballast wing and double bottom tanks. The effect of this is to:

- Greatly increase the FSE when tanks are slack, loading or discharging. This problem is exacerbated when cargo operations are undertaken at sea, eg ship to ship (STS). Where there is no longitudinal division, the effect of cargo sloshing within the tank can cause internal structural damage and increase tank pressure. Similar effects are created when ballasting the double bottom if it is not divided, and it is of particular concern if an undivided U-shaped ballast tank is employed on smaller tankers. The FSE must also be accounted for when complying with the ballast water management requirements
- increase the height of the transverse centre of gravity, consequently reducing the GM and the righting lever (GZ).

Corrosion

Double hulls on SBT tankers are prone to corrosion due to the large area of steelwork within the ballast tanks and the (normally) exclusive carriage of salt water.

It can be more difficult to inspect and monitor the performance of tank coatings because of the complex cellular construction. SOLAS Chapter XI requires enhanced survey of ships, including ultrasonic thickness measurement.

To reduce the increased effect of thermal barrier induced corrosion, caused by the introduction of double hulls in oil tankers, the 87th session of the IMO Maritime Safety Committee (MSC) set new SOLAS construction regulations. The regulations require approved corrosion protection of the bottom and under-decks of cargo tanks on crude oil tankers and crude oil/ product tankers that are either contracted for building after 1st July 2013, the keel is laid after 1st January 2014 or are delivered after 1st January 2016.

The regulations require either:

- Protective coatings that meet the Cargo Oil Tank Corrosion Prevention Standards (MSC.291.87) that have a target life of 15 years where the coating remains in good condition, or
- use of corrosion resistant steels that will maintain the structural integrity for 25 years.

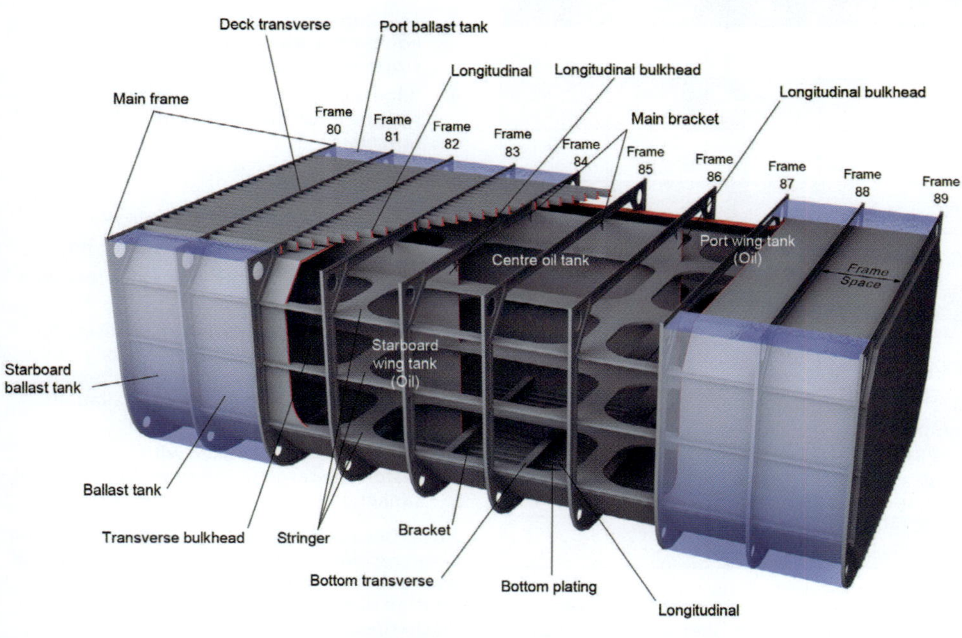

Figure 2.19 - Segregated ballast double hull tanker cutaway (expanded detail view of Figure 2.17)

Permissible Discharges of Oil from Tankers

Discharge of oil from ships includes the discharge of bilge water from machinery spaces (engine room and cargo pump rooms), fuel oil sludge, and ballast water that may contain oil, such as heavy weather ballast that has been carried in a cargo tank or tank washing residues.

In a sea area with Special Area status under MARPOL Annex I (see the table below), the discharge of oil, oily sludge and oil-contaminated residues from tank washing, or oil-contaminated ballast water is forbidden. In such areas, oily waste must be retained on board in the ship's slop tank until it can be discharged to a reception facility in port.

To reduce the need to wash ships' cargo tanks and dispose of volumes of water washings at sea, oil tankers >20,000 Dwt and product carriers >30,000 Dwt must have segregated ballast tanks (SBT).

All oil tankers and larger merchant vessels must be fitted with monitoring equipment for the discharge of oily water.

Special Areas	Adopted	Date of Entry into Force	In Effect From
Annex I: Oil			
Mediterranean Sea	2 Nov 1973	2 Oct 1983	2 Oct 1983
Baltic Sea	2 Nov 1973	2 Oct 1983	2 Oct 1983
Black Sea	2 Nov 1973	2 Oct 1983	2 Oct 1983
Red Sea	2 Nov 1973	2 Oct 1983	*
"Gulfs" area	2 Nov 1973	2 Oct 1983	1 Aug 2008
Gulf of Aden	1 Dec 1987	1 Apr 1989	*
Antarctic area	16 Nov 1990	17 Mar 1992	17 Mar 1992
North West European Waters	25 Sept 1997	1 Feb 1999	1 Aug 1999
Oman area of the Arabian Sea	15 Oct 2004	1 Jan 2007	*
Southern South African waters	13 Oct 2006	1 Mar 2008	1 Aug 2008

* The Special Area requirements for these areas have not taken effect because of lack of notifications from MARPOL Parties whose coastlines border the relevant special areas on the existence of adequate reception facilities (regulations 38.6 of MARPOL Annex I and 5(4) of MARPOL Annex V).

Control of discharge of oil from tank areas including cargo pump room, for oil tankers of all sizes:

Outside special areas, more than 50 nautical miles from the nearest land, any discharge is prohibited, except clean or segregated ballast, or when:

- The tanker is proceeding en route
- the instantaneous rate of discharge of oil does not exceed 30 litres/nautical mile
- the quantity of oil discharged into the sea does not exceed:
  - 1/15,000 for existing tankers
  - 1/30,000 for new tankers

  of the total quantity of the cargo which was carried on the previous voyage, and
- the tanker has in operation a monitoring and control system for the discharge of oil, and stop tank arrangements as required by MARPOL Regulation 15.

Oil tankers of all sizes plus other ships of 400 GT and above

Control of discharge of oil from machinery spaces

Within special areas

Any discharge is prohibited, except when:

1. The ship is proceeding en route, and
2. The oil content of the effluent without dilution does not exceed 15 ppm, and
3. The ship has in operation oil filtering equipment with automatic 15 ppm stopping device, and
4. Bilge water is not mixed with oil cargo residue or cargo pump room bilges (on oil tankers).

Outside special areas

Any discharge is prohibited, except when:

1. The ship is proceeding en route, and
2. The oil content of the effluent is less than 15 ppm, and
3. The ship has in operation an oil discharge monitoring and control system, oily-water separating or filtering equipment, oil filtering system or other installation required by Regulation 16, and
4. Bilge water is not mixed with oil cargo residue or cargo pump room bilges (on oil tankers).

Note: Oily mixtures that are not mixed with oil cargo residue or cargo pump room bilges, and where the oil content of the effluent without dilution does not exceed 15 ppm, may be discharged outside special areas without any additional restrictions.

Safety Designs and Innovations Incorporated in Today's Oil Tankers

Inert Gas

Inert gas (IG) is a mixture of gases that do not contain sufficient oxygen to support combustion of hydrocarbons. It is used as a safety system in oil tanker cargo tanks.

Before the 1960s, it was believed that the high volume of hydrocarbons within tank atmospheres produced too rich an environment to burn and would prevent combustion. Unfortunately this was not always the case and there were a series of incidents, including three VLCC non-inerted tank cleaning explosions in December 1969, that changed the view of the industry:

'Marpessa'	12th Dec 1969	off Dakar
'Mactra'	29th Dec 1969	off Mozambique
'Kong Haakon VII'	30th Dec 1969	off Liberia.

See pages 111-112 for more details on these three incidents.

The primary danger is from the build-up and consequent discharge of static electricity during water and crude oil washing (COW). Introducing inert gas to the tanks, which removes the oxygen side of the fire triangle, ensures combustion cannot be supported. Figure 2.20 shows the oxygen/hydrocarbon mixtures required for combustion of atmosphere in a crude oil cargo tank. This flammable mixture is also known as the flammable or explosive envelope.

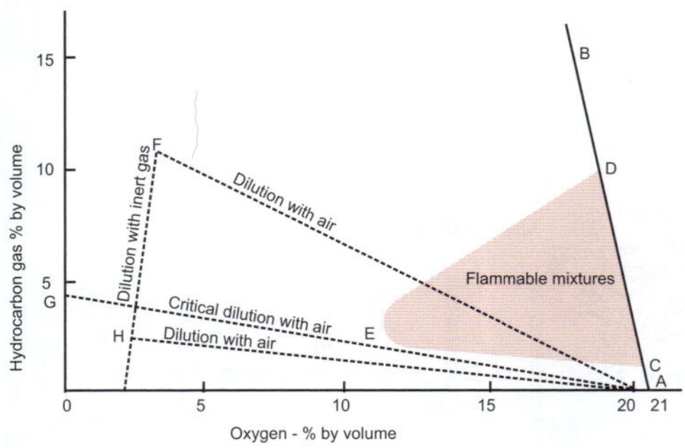

Figure 2.20 - Flammable range diagram

Oxygen content below 'E' is considered inert and unable to support combustion. SOLAS requires that the oxygen content in the tank remains below 8% and the IG supply below 5%.

Hydrocarbon content below 'C', the lower explosive limit (LEL), is considered too lean to burn. Hydrocarbon content above 'D', the upper explosive limit (UEL), is considered too rich to burn.

As a result of the accidents, SOLAS 1974 required that all new tankers over 30,000 Dwt ordered from 1979 were fitted with inert gas systems. The existing regulatory requirements are outlined in the IMO's Inert Gas Systems manual.

Inert Gas Requirements from 2016

In 2014, IMO approved amendments to SOLAS and the Fire Safety Systems Code to mandate the use of inert gas on new oil tankers of below 20,000 Dwt and new chemical tankers. The amendments provide for a revised lower size limit of 8,000 Dwt and allow for vessels of less than 20,000 Dwt to use shore-supplied inert gas rather than install an inert gas system where appropriate.

The regulations will enter into force on 1st January 2016.

Inert gas on oil tankers is normally produced by the following methods:

- Inert gas generators
- flue exhaust gas systems.

Inert Gas Generators

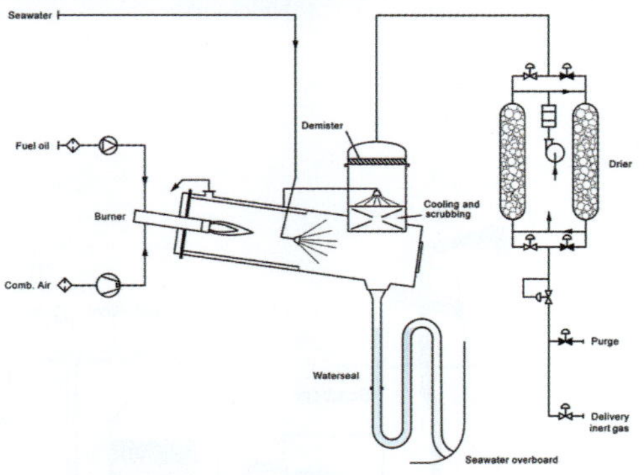

Figure 2.21 - Inert gas generator

On smaller tankers, IG generators can be used to produce sufficient gas, generally up to 15,000 m³/hour, to inert the required cargo spaces. However, on most crude oil tankers, IG generators are used for topping-up to increase the pressure of small ullage spaces or to complete the final stages of a discharge. Topping-up generators are likely to produce IG at a rate of around 500 m³/hour so will not

Safety Designs and Innovations Incorporated in Today's Oil Tankers

be able to maintain pressure during bulk cargo discharges.

The percentage of oxygen and other substances will vary a little, but typical composition of gases from IG generators is:

Carbon dioxide (CO_2)	15%
Oxygen (O_2)	0.5 - 3%
Nitrogen (N_2)	82 - 85%
Carbon monoxide (CO)	30 ppm max
Hydrogen (H)	100 ppm max
Sulphur dioxide (SO_2)	50 ppm max.

Flue Gas Systems

The most common method of producing IG on board oil tankers is using flue gas systems, which take the exhaust gas from the boiler and produce sufficient IG to meet 125% of the cargo discharge rate.

Flue gas is hot, acidic and contaminated exhaust gas produced by the ship's boilers that cannot be directly blown into the tank without being cooled and cleaned of impurities.

The system is normally controlled from within the cargo control room and has a series of alarms and measurement systems for pressure, temperature and oxygen content.

A flue gas system has the following components:

Scrubber

Using seawater spray, the scrubber (or scrubbing tower) cools the gas from between 300°C and 450°C to 3° above the seawater temperature. The exhaust gas is simultaneously cleaned, reducing sulphur dioxide by 90% and solid particles by 95%.

Fans

There are usually at least two IG fans or blowers with a capacity rated at 125% of the collective cargo pump capacity.

Deck Seal

The deck seal (or deck water seal) uses water to prevent any return flow of gas or cargo vapour.

Non-return Valve

This is a mechanical valve that provides a secondary means of preventing any backflow of IG.

P/V Breaker

This is a liquid-based system that prevents excessive pressure or vacuum within the system. The liquid normally consists of water and glycol to prevent freezing in low temperatures.

Figure 2.23 - P/V breaker

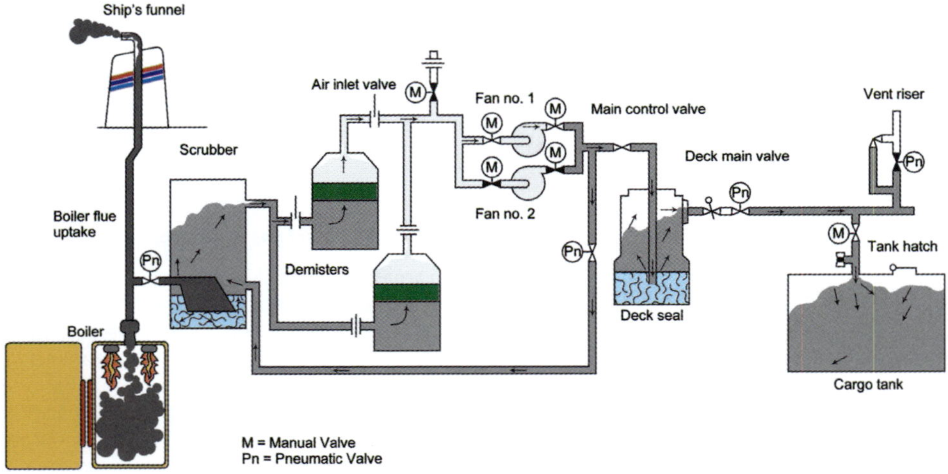

Figure 2.22 - Flue gas IGS

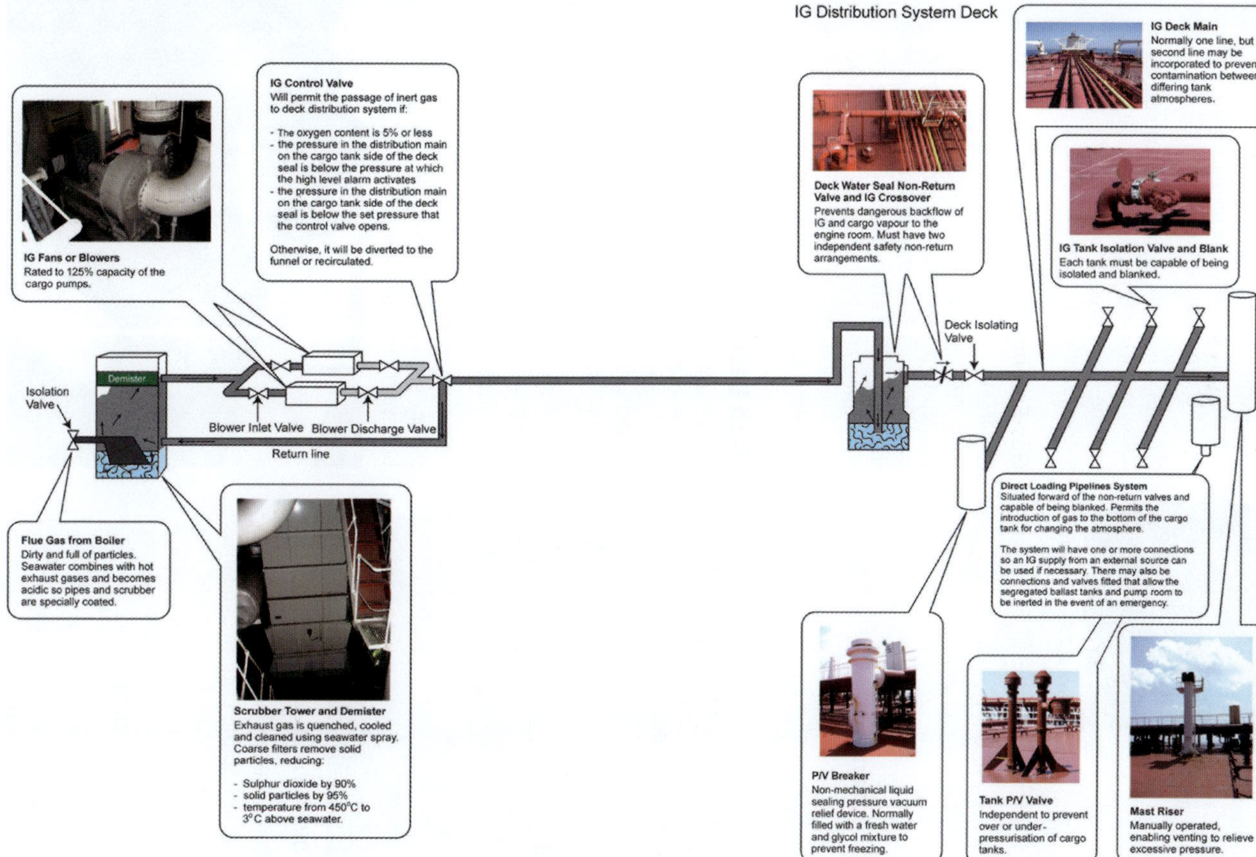

Figure 2.24 - Inert gas system (flue gas)

When inerting, a pressure of 1,200 mmWG is normally the maximum allowable with a working pressure of 650 to 700 mm being a typical value. Accurate pressure gauges such as manometers should be used to monitor the operation. If flue gases from the engine room are used, suitable scrubbing equipment should be installed, mainly to remove the SO_2, cool the inerted vapour and remove soot particulates.

Safety Designs and Innovations Incorporated in Today's Oil Tankers

P/V Valves

These are mechanical valves independently fitted to individual tanks that prevent over/under pressurisation.

Figure 2.25 - P/V valve

Mast Riser

This is a manually operated venting structure used to relieve excess pressure by venting to the atmosphere. The use of the mast riser is restricted in many ports where the vapour collection system is prescribed.

Gas Replacement

Inerting

Inerting a cargo tank can be achieved by either dilution or displacement.

Dilution involves the direct introduction of inert gas into the cargo tank at a high flow rate so that it mixes and dilutes throughout the entire content.

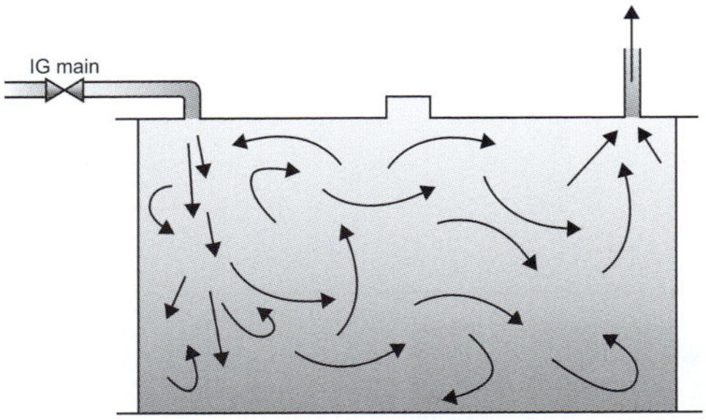

Figure 2.26 - Dilution method

Displacement is achieved by a slower rate of introduction of IG into the bottom of a tank. IG is heavier than air and creates a lower and denser level with a stable horizontal interface. As the IG content increases, the lighter gas is pushed up and vented from the top.

Purging

Purging is the reduction of hydrocarbon content through the introduction of IG. This prevents the atmosphere within a tank entering the flammable range during the gas-freeing process when oxygen is introduced.

Purging can be difficult by the displacement method as IG is slightly lighter than hydrocarbon gas. However, where a tank has been crude oil washed, the hydrocarbons that would otherwise concentrate at lower levels are more likely to be distributed evenly throughout the atmosphere and the displacement method may become more effective.

Purging is normally considered complete when there is less than 2% hydrocarbons by volume. This reduces further as the tanks are subsequently gas-freed.

Gas-Freeing

Gas-freeing is the process of introducing oxygen using the dilution method into a purged tank using fresh air, either from portable deck fans or mechanical fans within the system. The atmosphere should be monitored and it should not be considered gas-free until steady readings of 21% oxygen and 1% LEL (LFL) are achieved.

High Level Alarm Systems

To prevent overspill, cargo tanks require a visible and audible independent high level alarm system that provides notification when capacity reaches 95%. The alarm indication should be provided in the:

- Cargo control room (CCR)
- engine control room (ECR)
- bridge.

If the system does not have a self-testing facility, each individual high level alarm must be tested prior to loading.

Figure 2.27 - High level alarm

Continuous Fishplate

Tankers are fitted with a continuous deck edge fishplate, enclosing the main deck area from bow to stern, to contain any cargo or bunker oil spills on deck (see Figure 2.28). If there is a single main deck level around the vessel, a transverse fishplate should be fitted aft of the last cargo tank to prevent the flow of cargo around the poop/accommodation deck area.

There will be a way of draining any spilled oil from the deck area into a slop tank.

Gas Measurement and Detection

SOLAS CH II-2/4 requires that all oil tankers are fitted with equipment that can measure both oxygen concentrations and flammable vapour concentrations on board. This is in addition to requirements for the carriage of at least one portable instrument capable of measuring flammable vapour concentrations.

Oil tankers greater than 20,000 Dwt, constructed on or after 1st January 2012, that do not have a constant inerting system for ballast and void spaces adjacent to cargo tanks are required by SOLAS CH II-2/4 to be provided with a fixed hydrocarbon gas detection system in such spaces. Audible and visual alarms are required in the CCR, ECR and bridge.

Slop Dump (Emergency Drain) Valve

Figure 2.28 - Fishplate and slop dump valve (emergency drain)

The slop dump (emergency drain) valve arrangements are generally provided on the port and starboard side of the aftermost portion of the tank deck area. Positioned immediately before the transverse fishplate, they connect directly to the port and starboard slop tanks.

Before opening the valves, it is important that the correct draining procedures are followed. This will involve isolating the slop tank from the IG system and depressurising the tank before opening. Crew training is important to ensure that spilled oil does not get blown overboard. The valves should be tested every three months.

Spill Preparedness

Every oil tanker should have a Shipboard Oil Pollution Emergency Plan (SOPEP) which sets out the action to be taken in the event of a spill and the spill response equipment that must be distributed evenly throughout the vessel.

Oil dispersant should never be used without the authorisation of the coastal State.

As a minimum, the following equipment should be expected:

- Absorbent pellets
- non-sparking hand scoops, shovels and buckets
- suitable containers for recovered cargo
- emulsifiers for deck cleaning
- suitable protective clothing
- non-sparking portable compressed air diaphragm pumps with hoses in good operating condition (eg Wilden pumps)
- containment booms
- chemical detergents for dispersal.

Any location on deck where an oil spill is likely to occur must be fitted with an oil spill tray (save-all). Areas include:

- Bunker manifolds
- vents for bunker tanks
- cargo manifolds
- service and storage oil tank vents.

Scuppers must always be plugged in port and during all cargo, ballast and bunker handling operations, except when clearing rainwater.

Figure 2.29 - Wilden pump rigged aft of the transverse fishplate

Tank Cleaning

Tank cleaning can be defined as 'any operation performed upon a cargo tank for the purpose of improving its physical condition by the removal of residues of previous contents'.

The main reason for cleaning a ship's tank is to prepare it for carriage of the next cargo so that the cargo will meet its specification when discharged. Many products, particularly chemicals and several 'white' products, can withstand very little contamination before going off specification, causing it to be downgraded or rejected. For example, it takes very little motor spirit residue to lower the flashpoint of kerosene to a point where it cannot be sold and must be re-refined.

Other reasons for tank cleaning include:

- A tanker scheduled to undergo repairs or drydocking will, in most cases, have to present herself at the repair yard with all cargo tanks clean and gas-free
- a tanker engaged in black oil trades, particularly crude oil, may experience a build-up of heavy sediments in the cargo tanks that affects carrying capacity and pumping performance. The vessel will take whatever opportunity is available to crude oil wash its tanks as a sediment control measure.

Ships must not tank wash or gas-free within a port without the agreement of both the jetty operator and the port authority.

Where is Tank Cleaning Conducted?

Tank cleaning (other than crude oil washing) should always take place at sea as the gas-freeing associated with it, along with its consequent risk of vapour build-up, can be better controlled on a ship under way. It is also better for the terminal if an incoming ship is already cleaned and ready for loading as it reduces jetty occupancy time.

However, there are many occasions when tank cleaning will take place alongside. For example, a ship may be reloading after discharge (particularly a chemical tanker) and require washing for product quality, the terminal inspector might have rejected pre-washed tanks and requested additional cleaning, or the ship might be taking advantage of the terminal's slop facilities.

A large proportion of major accidents on tankers have taken place during tank cleaning operations and, while many improvements have been made in equipment, if a ship fails to follow the given procedures, a risk still exists.

Equipment

There is a wide range of mechanical tank cleaning devices but they all fall into two categories; fixed and portable. Both operate on the same basic principle of directing a high pressure fluid jet onto the structure of the tank, dislodging residues which then fall to the bottom. Fluid residue can then be pumped away but solids will remain in the tank and will have to be removed manually if necessary.

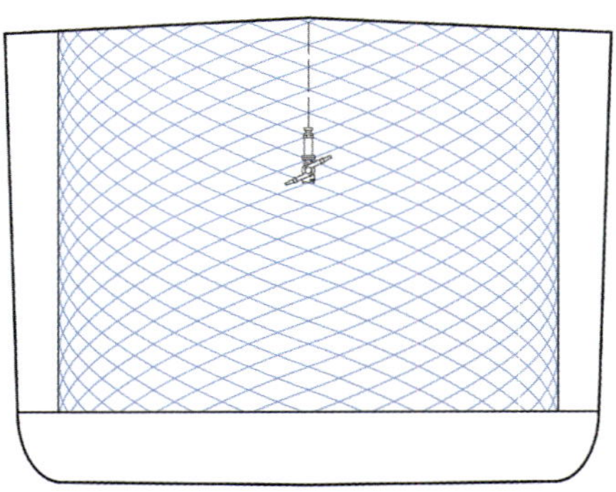

Figure 2.30 - Washing Cycle Pattern for a 360° Free Rotating Washing Machine

A portable machine consists of a pair of nozzles and a turbine-driven gearbox. The whole assembly is secured to the end of a high pressure water hose, lowered into position in the tank through a deck access plate, and the water turned on. The water pressure drives the turbine and gearbox, causing the nozzles to rotate both vertically and horizontally, directing the jets onto the structure of the tank. Each type of machine is designed to operate at an optimum pressure, somewhere in the range of 6 to 10 bar, with a maximum throughput of approximately 25 tonnes/hour.

The advantages of a portable machine are that it can be set into the position desired, moved as necessary and it uses less fluid. Disadvantages are its inability to throw a worthwhile jet more than 8 metres, the labour intensity of its use and the time it takes.

A fixed tank cleaning machine often uses the same 'portable' machine, but it is mounted permanently in the cargo tank with fixed pipework. The most common fixed machine consists of a single large nozzle mounted below the deck and driven by a gearbox arrangement, which is usually mounted on the deck itself. Modern installations can be programmed to operate either between preset vertical arcs or to a direct spot in the tank.

The main advantage is that the use of fixed pipework provides much higher pressure and throughputs (about 150 tonnes/hour).

Disadvantages include cost and an increased safety hazard through the build-up of static electricity.

Crude Oil Washing (COW)

Crude oil washing (COW) is an internationally accepted method of minimising oil pollution risks. It is governed by regulations laid down in Annex I, Regulation 13B of the 1978 protocol to the 1973 Marine Pollution Convention (MARPOL 73/78) which requires that the cargo tanks of crude oil tankers are washed using crude oil washing.

Prior to the use of COW, cargo tanks were washed with seawater while on passage to the next loading port. The mixture of oil residue and seawater that resulted from this operation was allowed to settle in the tanker's slop tanks, where the oil and water would naturally separate, the oil floating to the surface and the clean water below. After this settlement period (generally at least 24 hours), the water below the oil cap in the slop tank would be removed, initially by decanting by gravity and then slowly pumping the water overboard into the sea.

The idea of washing tanks by spraying them with cargo at high pressure (8 to 10 kg/cm^2) originated as part of the 'over-rich' philosophy of cleaning large tankers. By spraying crude oil, the light ends vaporised and increased the hydrocarbon content of the tank atmosphere to a level significantly above the upper flammable limit, in theory leaving a non-inerted tank completely safe to wash with high capacity equipment. However, a series of serious accidents in the late 1960s and early 1970s showed that using inert gas was safer, making the installation and use of inert gas plants a mandatory factor for tank cleaning.

Solvent Action

Using crude oil as the cleaning medium utilises the solvent action of the lighter hydrocarbon components in the oil. This washes down any clingage on the internal surfaces of the tank's structure and removes sediment on the tank bottom. The solvents break down the heavier deposits in the tank, which are introduced in the cargo being discharged ashore.

By using oil rather than water, a significant reduction in cargo tank corrosion is achieved. It is also more environmentally friendly than using water.

Typical Voyage

Passing cargo oil through the tank cleaning system and back into the cargo tank being discharged scours the tank structure and puts the crude oil solids back into suspension in the cargo. The result is an increased cargo outturn. A typical VLCC, with a full cargo of Middle East crude, could have 1,000 to 1,500 tonnes of oil remaining on board after discharge (pre-COW), some of which is clingage to the steelwork but most of which comprises heavy sediments on horizontal surfaces. If 'ROB' (remaining on board) was water washed back into a slop tank on board, decanted out and retained as part of the next cargo, a procedure known as 'Load on Top', on the next voyage the ship could lift proportionately less cargo.

If that same ship is fully crude oil washed, the ROB can be reduced to as little as 200 tonnes with an average crude. The 1,000 tonnes of additional oil that can be pumped ashore has a significant value to the receiver.

Disadvantages of Crude Oil Washing

Full crude oil washing of a VLCC extends the cargo discharging time because a portion of the cargo is being circulated. This only applies

Tank Cleaning

if the cargo discharge rate is unrestricted by the shore. As many VLCCs can reach shore throughput maxima, they can crude oil wash without extending turnaround time.

As far as the ship is concerned, the operation increases the workload at a time when staff are already under pressure and, as close supervision is required, it demands a constant responsible deck watch. It is not unknown for shipping companies to provide additional 'flying squad' staff to assist the crew when a major washing operation, such as pre drydock, is proposed.

The Washing Operation

The conduct of the operation must be mutually agreeable to both ship and shore. Adequate qualified staff must be available to conduct and supervise the operation.

Two important prerequisites for COW are:

- The ship must be fitted with an inert gas system that is in use during washing, producing sufficient good quality inert gas to maintain a positive pressure within the cargo tanks
- the ship must be fitted with a system of fixed tank cleaning machines and permanent pipework as only fixed systems can be used.

The inert gas requirement is a safety measure. When crude oil is being ejected from a tank cleaning machine nozzle at 8 to 10 bar, a large amount of vapour will be produced until the tank atmosphere becomes gas saturated, so there is a high possibility of the atmosphere passing through its flammable range.

Dry and Wet Crudes

The crude oil used for COW must be 'clean and dry'. This means that crude with a water content must never be used. If the ship's slop tank is to be used as the source of washing fluid, it is essential that any load on top residues are discharged and the tank refilled from the bulk cargo. This is a safety precaution. Nearly all crude oil contains solids in suspension, which serve to effectively dissipate any static electricity generated by the oil as it passes through the pipework. Any water in the crude will tend to retain the static charge and increase the risk of spark generation.

Crudes Unsuitable for Washing

The following crudes are unsuitable for COW:

- Crudes that are viscous or waxy as they will lead to a high amount of cargo remaining on board
- crudes that are particularly volatile as they will result in excessive gas creation.

It is common for terminals to ban COW on ships where the presence of H_2S in the cargo tanks is over 200 ppm.

Washing Cycles

A crude oil tank is washed in two stages; a top wash and then a bottom wash.

A top wash is usually started when approximately two-thirds of the tank have been discharged. The nozzle of the machine is set to 30° elevation and washed to 150° elevation and down again.

When the top wash has been completed, the machines are stopped and are re-programmed to wash the bottom of the tank. When the discharge of the tank has been completed, the bottom wash can commence. The nozzle elevation is set to +30° to -30°, making four or five passes sweeping across the tank bottom.

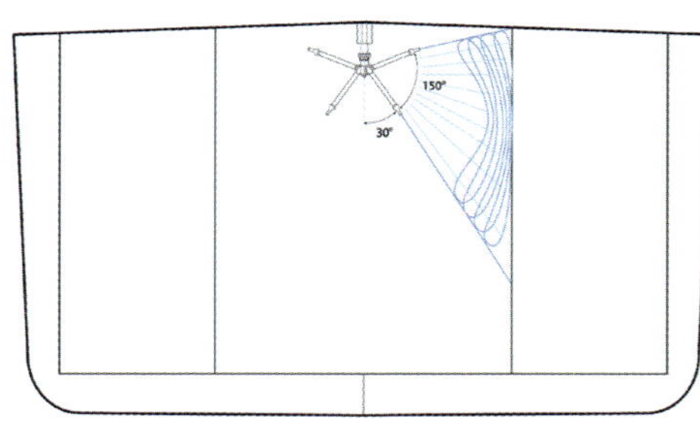

Figure 2.31 - Top wash from +30° to +150°

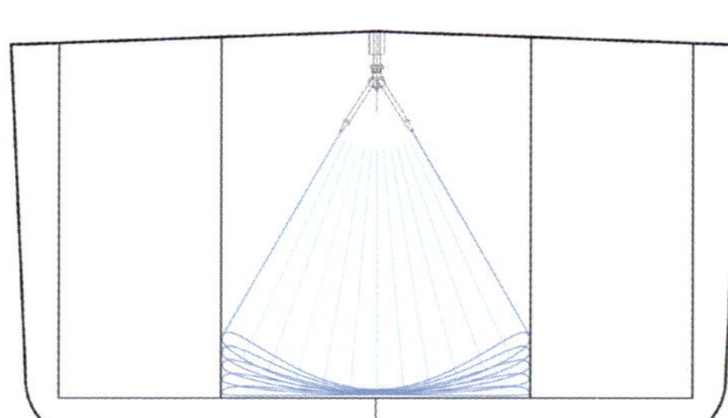

Figure 2.32 - Bottom wash from -30° to +30°

Frequently, ships will leave 20 to 30 cm of fluid in the bottom of the tank to assist in agitation and break-up of sediments. The number of bottom sweeps required will depend on the condition of the tank and the complexity of its structure. The final step is to turn off the COW machines and drain as much fluid from the cargo tank as possible. The removal of the crude washings is done using cargo eductors and should leave only a few small puddles of oil along with a few traces of sediment in the blind corners.

Vapour Generation During COW

Difficulty can arise during crude oil washing if the ship is discharging at a reduced rate or discharging has been stopped or suspended. The vapour generated by the washing can increase pressure within the tank to a point where relief valves lift and vapour escapes to the atmosphere. This is not necessarily dangerous but is undesirable and may even be prohibited by the local authority. To avoid this, in a reduced discharge situation, the ship should be able to control the inert gas pressure to maintain a stable pressure. When no discharging is taking place, considerable washing time can be gained by starting at a low positive tank pressure. These methods mean that the atmosphere becomes heavily over-rich but, because it is inert, no danger results.

Water Washing

Although COW is a very efficient and effective cleaning method, some residues will remain on board. Subsequent cargo requirements may, and tank entry preparations will, require the cargo spaces to be water washed to remove the remaining residues.

Water washing uses seawater and employs the COW machines.

The cargo residues/water mixture is pumped into a slop tank where it is left to settle. The cargo will separate on top of the water and the water can then be discharged through the oil discharge monitoring and control systems in accordance with MARPOL Annex I.

The details of discharges, along with any cargo/ballast operations or incidents, must be recorded in the Oil Record Book Part II - Cargo/ballast operations, which is likely to be inspected frequently by many parties, including Port States.

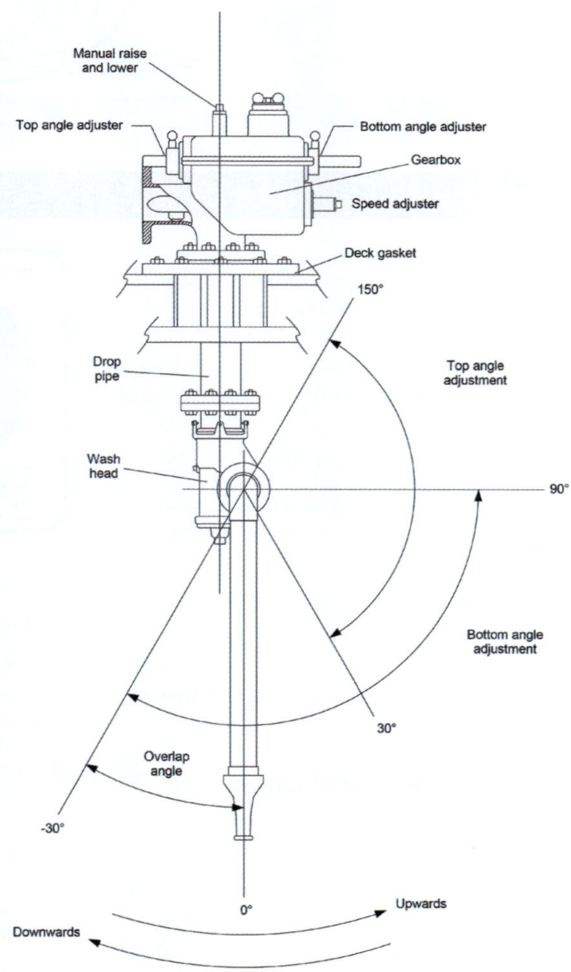

Figure 2.33 - Fixed COW machine

Global Crude Oil Market

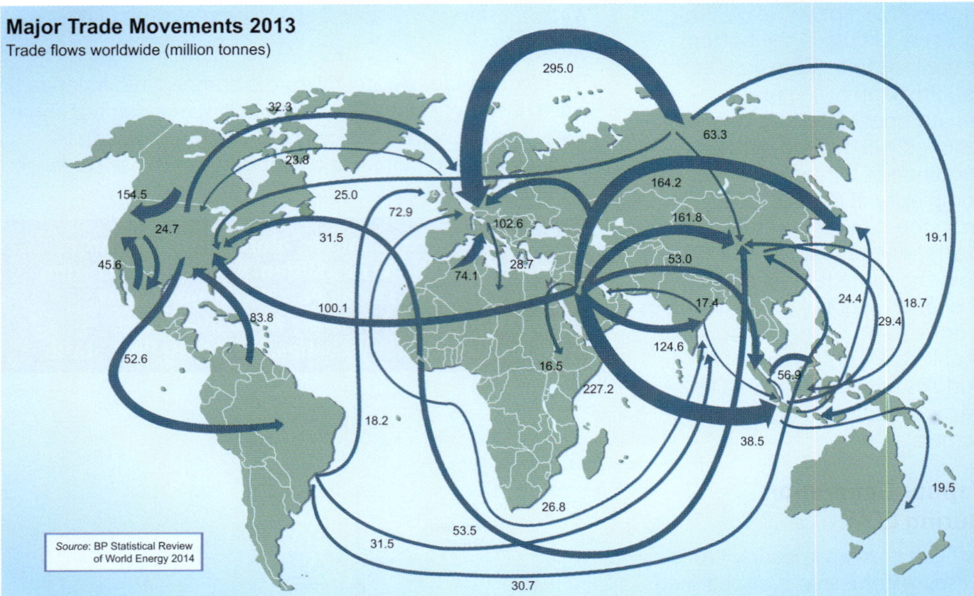

Supply and Demand of Oil

Demand for oil is largely driven by the global economy through population growth, social and economic development, and local 'affluence' factors such as increasing vehicle ownership.

Generally, where supply exceeds demand, the price of oil will reduce and where demand exceeds supply, the price will increase.

OPEC countries hold over 80% of the world oil reserves with the countries in the Middle East accounting for more than 65% of OPEC reserves and retaining more than half of the global volume of petroleum and oil supplies.

The OPEC member countries are:

- Algeria
- Angola
- Ecuador
- Iran
- Iraq
- Kuwait
- Libya
- Nigeria
- Qatar
- Saudi Arabia
- United Arab Emirates
- Venezuela.

Supply and Demand of Tankers

Increasing available tonnage for transportation influences the supply/demand balance between available cargo and available ships. As available ship numbers increase, competition for cargo increases and freight rates inevitably drop.

Regulatory changes can influence the supply and demand balance. The phasing out of single hull

OPEC share of world crude oil reserves, 2013

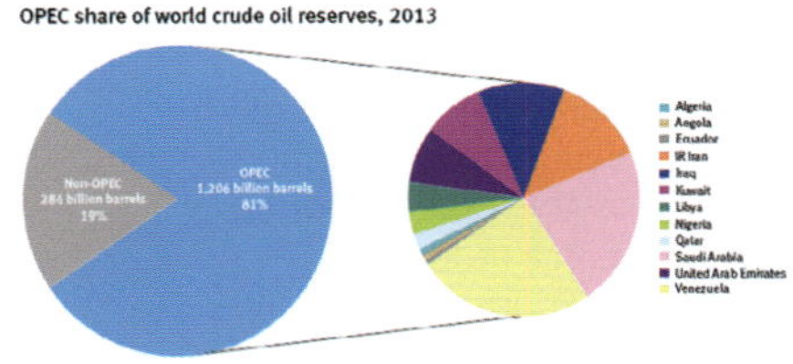

OPEC proven crude oil reserves, at end of 2013 *(billion barrels, OPEC share)*

Venezuela	298.4	24.7%	Iraq	144.2	12.0%	Libya	48.4	4.0%	Algeria	12.2	1.0%
Saudi Arabia	265.8	22.0%	Kuwait	101.5	8.4%	Nigeria	37.1	3.1%	Angola	9.0	0.7%
IR Iran	157.8	13.1%	UAE	97.8	8.1%	Qatar	25.1	2.1%	Ecuador	8.8	0.7%

Source: OPEC Annual Statistical Bulletin 2014.

tankers reduces the number of ships available and the introduction of EEDI and SEEMP will make new compliant ships more attractive to reputable charterers making them more marketable.

Similarly, emission control areas (ECA) may reduce available tonnage from certain trades, eg in EU waters where they do not have the capability of meeting the SOx and NOx regulations that entered into force in 2012 and 2015.

The price of bunkers, combined with the prevailing market condition and environmental perceptions, can lead to slow steaming. Slow steaming reduces excess tanker capacity by extending their period on-hire, helping to reduce the tanker supply.

Crude Oil

Crude oil, compiled of hydrocarbons and other compounds, is usually black, brown or yellowish in colour. It is formed naturally from the fossils of animals and plants. The viscosity and relative weight of crude oil varies and it can be light or heavy, sticky or non-sticky.

Crude oils that contain appreciable quantities of hydrogen sulphide or other reactive sulphur compounds are called 'sour'. Those with less sulphur are called 'sweet'.

API of Crude Oil

The American Petroleum Institute (API) is the trade association that represents all aspects of America's oil and natural gas industry.

The American Petroleum Institute gravity, or API gravity, is a measure of how heavy or light petroleum liquid is compared to water. If its API gravity is greater than 10, it is lighter and floats on water; if less than 10, it is heavier and sinks. API gravity is measured in degrees using a hydrometer. The API scale was designed so that most values would fall between 10 and 70 API gravity degrees.

Crude Oil Classification

Crude oil is classified as light, medium or heavy, according to its measured API gravity.

Light crude oil is defined as having API gravity higher than 31.1°API (less than 870 kg/m^3)

Medium oil is defined as having API gravity between 22.3°API and 31.1°API (870 to 920 kg/m^3)

Heavy oil is defined as having API gravity below 22.3°API (920 to 1,000 kg/m^3)

Extra heavy oil is defined as having API gravity below 10.0°API (greater than 1,000 kg/m^3). An example of extra heavy oil is bitumen.

Sour Crude

Sour crude has a hydrogen sulphide level greater than 1%. It also contains carbon dioxide. It is usually processed into heavy oil, such as diesel, instead of gasoline to reduce processing costs. Venezuela is the world's major producer.

Sweet Crude

Sweet crude contains less than 0.5% sulphur, and contains trace amounts of hydrogen sulphide and carbon dioxide. It is commonly used for processing into gasoline.

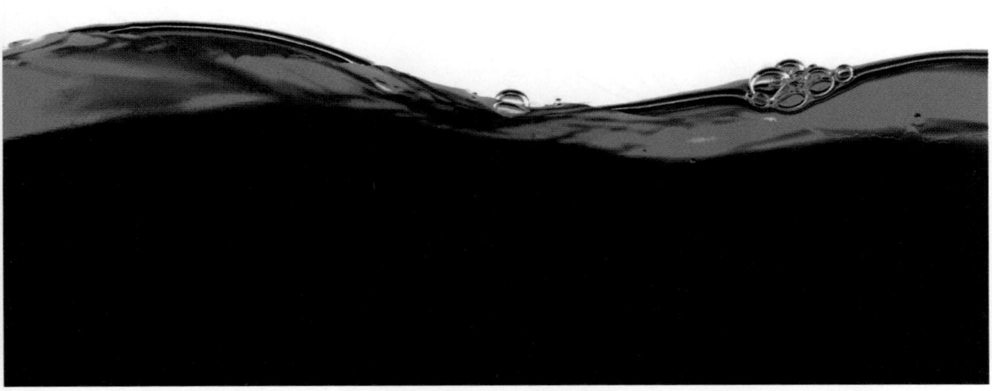

Major SPM/SBM Deepwater Ports

A single-point mooring (SPM) or single-buoy mooring (SBM) is the term used for a crude oil loading (or discharge) buoy. They are typically located in deep water, a safe distance offshore and with substantial manoeuvring room for VLCCs. They offer substantial savings over the cost of building a marine port.

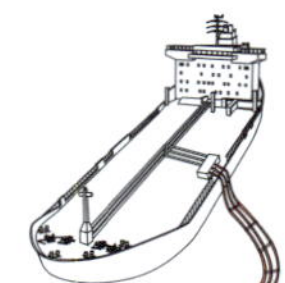
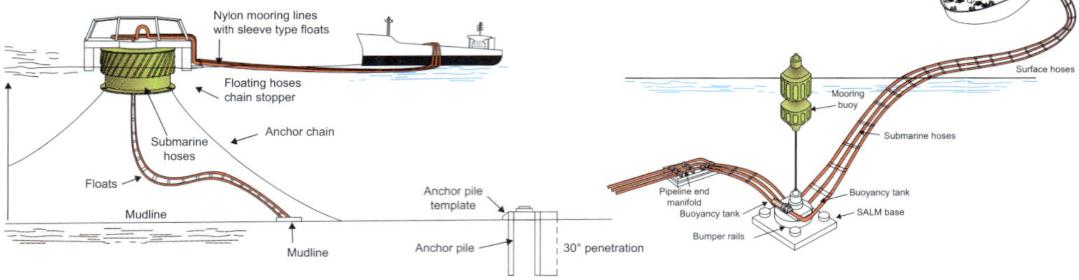

Figure 2.34 - Connection to SPM/SBM

While there are a substantial number of offshore mooring buoys located around the world to allow for the safe and efficient loading of crude oil to/from VLCCs, there are a small number of strategic ports that are key to the world's supply of crude oil that use SPMs or SBMs.

Ju'aymah Oil Terminal

The Ju'aymah crude oil loading terminal in Saudi Arabia is the world's largest and busiest SPM facility. Ju'aymah is designed for topping off VLCCs that have part loaded at the Ras Tanura Sea Island, or for completing the full load of VLCCs that are advised to come straight to Ju'aymah.

Ju'aymah Oil Terminal		
Berth	**Maximum depth**	**Maximum vessel size**
SPM No. 31	32.1 m	500,000 Dwt
SPM No. 32	33.8 m	500,000 Dwt
SPM No. 33	34.0 m	500,000 Dwt
SPM No. 34	35.0 m	750,000 Dwt
SPM No. 35	32.0 m	750,000 Dwt
SPM No. 36	32.2 m	450,000 Dwt

The Ju'aymah terminal consists of a group of 6 single-point mooring berths: 4 x Catenary Anchor Line Mooring (CALM) and 2 x Single Anchor Line Mooring (SALM).

The SPMs are located between 7 to 10 miles offshore where the water depth exceeds 32 metres. Crude oil loading rates of up to 130,000 barrels per hour are attainable at each SPM buoy.

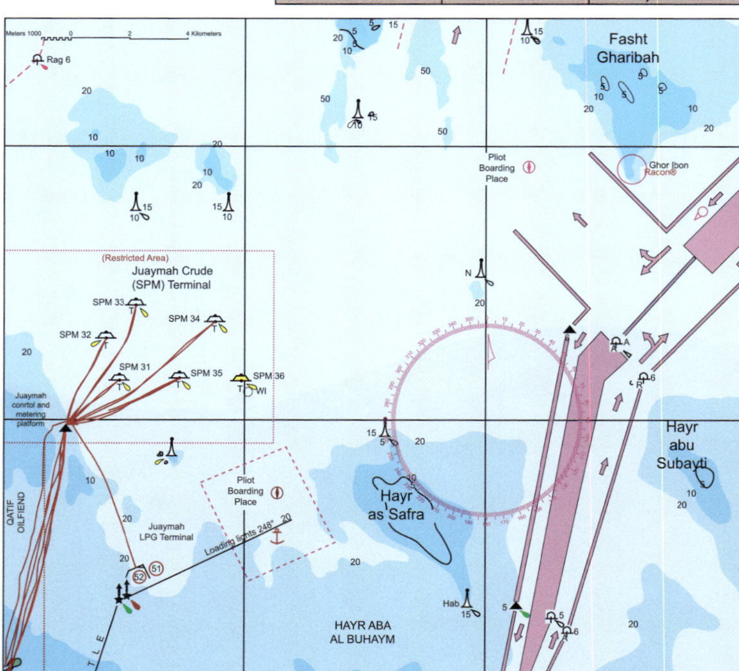

Ain Sukhna

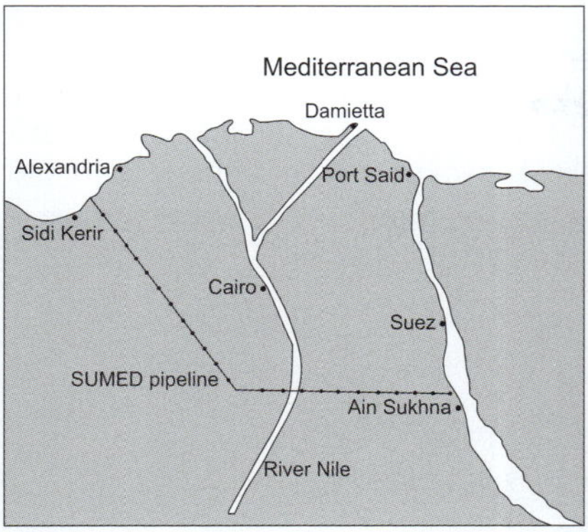

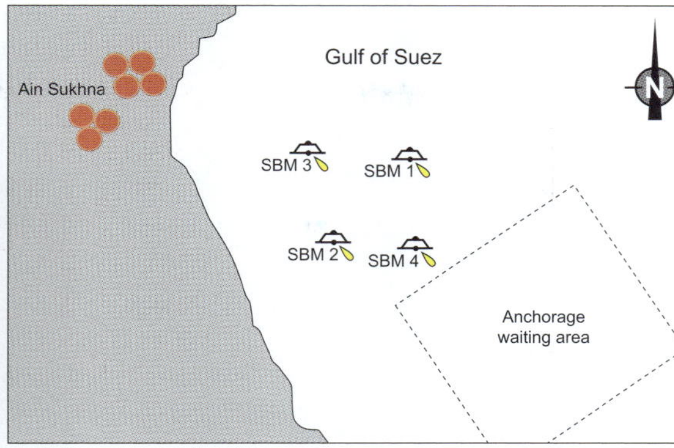

Ain Sukhna onshore terminal in the Gulf of Suez consists of 16 floating roof storage tanks of 120,000 m^3 (1 million barrels) capacity each with a total crude oil capacity of 1.62 million m^3 (16 million barrels). It has 4 SBMs which can be used simultaneously for the discharge of crude oil.

Ain Sukhna connects to the SUMED (Suez-Mediterranean) pipeline, which transfers oil to the port of Sidi Kerir, offshore Alexandria in the Mediterranean Sea.

The SUMED pipeline project was started after the extended closure of the Suez Canal in June 1967. Agreement to construct the pipeline was reached in 1973 between Egypt, Saudi Arabia, UAE, Kuwait and Qatar, and the pipeline was opened in 1977.

The SUMED pipeline is 320 kilometres (200 miles) long. It consists of 2 parallel lines of 42 inches (1,070 mm) diameter. Its capacity is 2.5 million barrels per day.

The SUMED pipeline has offered VLCC and ULCC charters the option of discharging part of their cargo at Ain Sukhna to reduce their draught to 66 feet (20 metres) and reload that parcel of cargo on the Mediterranean side after safely transiting the Suez Canal. The other alternative is for the tanker to discharge fully at Ain Sukhna and return to the Persian Gulf, a journey of 8 days, to load the next cargo.

Berth	Maximum vessel size
SBM 1	250,000 Dwt
SBM 2	250,000 Dwt
SBM 3	350,000 Dwt
SBM 4	500,000 Dwt

Sidi Kerir

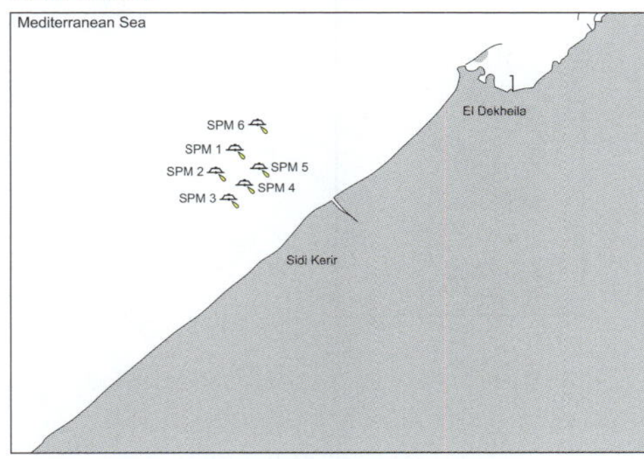

Sidi Kerir Sea Terminal is situated about 27 km west of Alexandria (see also Ain Sukhna for details of SUMED pipeline).

The terminal consists of 15 floating roof storage tanks with a capacity of 103,000 m^3 (863,000 barrels) each and 15 floating roof storage tanks with a capacity of 117,000 m^3 (981,000 barrels). This gives a total capacity of 3.3 million m^3 (27.6 million barrels).

Berth	Maximum vessel size
SBM 1	350,000 Dwt (400,000 with SUMED's approval)
SBM 2	350,000 Dwt (400,000 with SUMED's approval)
SBM 3	250,000 Dwt
SBM 4	250,000 Dwt
SBM 5	250,000 Dwt
SBM 6	350,000 Dwt (400,000 with SUMED's approval)

Major SPM/SBM Deepwater Ports

Louisiana Offshore Oil Port (LOOP)

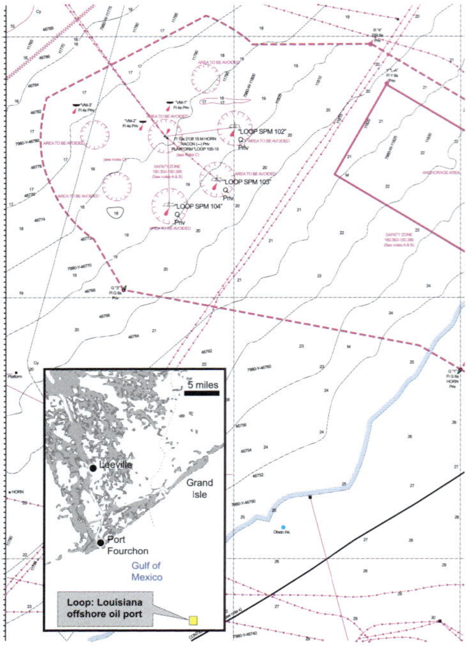

LOOP is America's only deepwater port for laden VLCCs and ULCCs. It opened in 1981, having cost US$770 million to build.

Tankers offload via one of three SPMs, each of which was constructed to accommodate tankers of up to 700,000 Dwt.

LOOP is located 18 miles south of Grand Isle off the coast of Louisiana, and the oil that is received is pumped to LOOP's onshore facilities, Fourchon Booster Station and on to Clovelly Dome Storage Terminal, which are located just on-shore in Fourchon, LA and 25 miles inland near Galliano, LA.

The Clovelly Dome Storage Terminal is used to store crude oil in one of eight natural underground salt caverns with a total capacity of 40 million barrels of crude. The LOCAP pipeline (throughput capacity of 1.7 to 2.4 million barrels per day), operated by LOOP, connects Clovelly to St James, LA 54 miles to the north. From here the crude oil can be pumped in measured batches to other pipeline systems, to reach refineries throughout the Midwest and as far north as Canada.

Multi Buoy Mooring (MBM)

MBMs are used in areas that typically experience fairly benign weather conditions. An MBM is far more cost effective to build than an SBM. A disadvantage of some MBMs is that the tanker has to moor using both her port and

Figure 2.35 - Tanker berthed to a Multi Buoy Mooring (MBM)

starboard anchors, before she secures to the mooring buoys amidships, on either quarter and directly astern.

The MBM shown below is referred to as an All Buoy Mooring (ABM). The tanker does not need to use her anchors but moors to buoys from her port and starboard bows.

You can identify the loading hose, held in position by the crane, on the port side amidships.

Chemical Tankers

Chemical tankers are more complicated than other types of liquid-carrying tankers, as they usually have more tanks, valves, pumps, blanks and lines. They may have several different kinds of cargo on board at the same time, ranging from bulk liquid chemicals and solvents to animal oils or petroleum products. There are three main types of chemical tanker:

- Type 1 - for the most hazardous cargoes (offering the highest level of protection)
- Type 2 - intermediate protection
- Type 3 - the lowest form of protection for the least harmful chemicals.

Fleet figures for IMO Type 2 and 3 chemical tankers consist of more than 1,100 ships operated by approximately 50 chemical and product tanker operators.

Chemical Tankers

Pure chemical tankers: 732

Source: Lloyd's 2014

Chemical tankers have seen a trend towards larger vessels, providing economies of scale. The share of ships above 36,000 Dwt has increased from 23% in 2005 to 28% in 2013, while the share of those vessels below 10,000 Dwt fell from 47% in 2005 to 40% in 2013.

Source: IHS Fairplay 2013

Chemical Tankers

Chemical Tanker Types

Type 1
Specialised Chemical Tankers

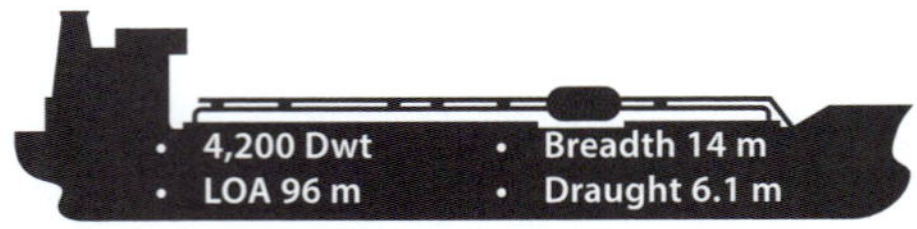

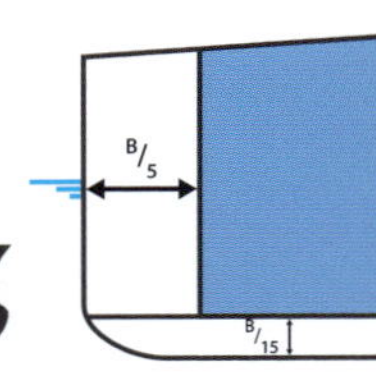

Specialised chemical carriers are designed to carry products referred to in Chapter 17 of the IBC Code. Products in this category have the potential to cause severe environmental and safety hazards and the highest level of preventative measures are required to stop an escape of cargo. The design principle is that the cargo-carrying compartments are located at a minimum distance from the hull of the ship. This guards against potential release caused by collision or grounding.

The regulations for Type 1 vessels state that the cargo tanks should be located at a distance of not less than the breadth of the ship divided by 5 or 11.5 m, whichever is less; B/15 or 6 m from the moulded bottom plating, whichever is less; and in no case less than 760 mm.

These vessels are smaller than Type 2 and 3 vessels and are often dedicated to single cargo trading. The tanks will either be coated or stainless steel, depending on the type of cargo, and they may not exceed 1,250 m^3 capacity.

Type 2
Complex Parcel Chemical Tankers

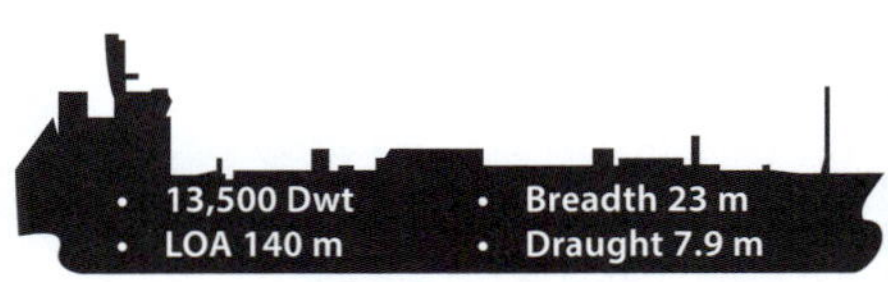

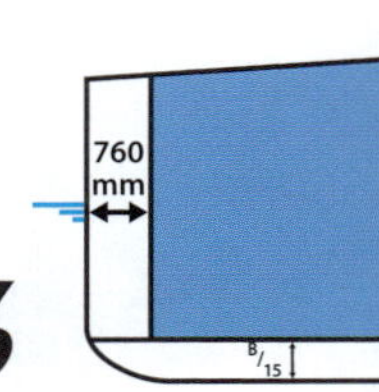

Complex parcel chemical tankers are designed for the carriage of IBC Code Chapter 17 products that have the potential to cause moderately severe environmental and safety hazards. Preventative measures are required to stop an escape of the cargo.

The regulations for Type 2 vessels state that the cargo tanks should be located at a distance of not less than 760 mm from the side shell plating and B/15 or 6 m from the moulded bottom plating.

These ships can be up to 40,000 Dwt and may have as many as 54 cargo tanks, each with its own individual pump and pipeline.

The tanks are usually constructed of stainless steel, which provides maximum flexibility on cargo selection. The temperature and other specifications of the compartments can be regulated according to the specific requirements of the liquid being transported. Typically, these tankers carry a number of high value 'just in time' cargoes in small amounts where nitrogen is used as an inert gas. The maximum tank size is 3,000 m^3.

Type 3
Product/Chemical Tankers

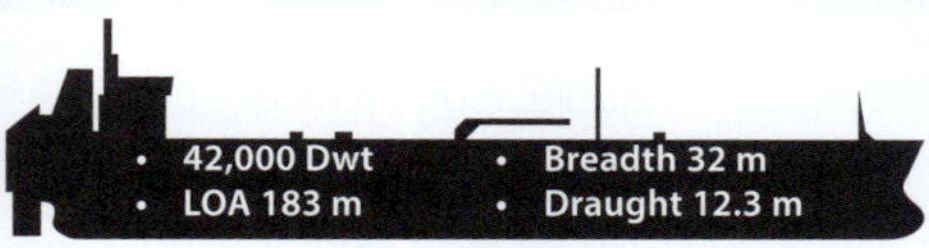

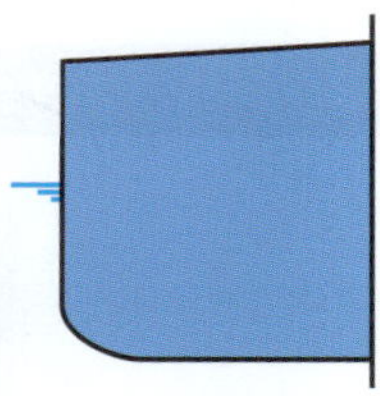

Product or chemical tankers are designed for the carriage of IBC Code Chapter 17 products with sufficiently severe environmental and safety hazard potential to cause some concern. They require a moderate degree of containment to increase survival capability in a damaged condition. There are no restrictions on the location of cargo tanks in a Type 3 ship.

Type 3 tankers are of a similar size to Type 2 but have fewer cargo tanks. The pump and pipeline arrangements are unlikely to be as complex and so are less flexible. The tanks are likely to be constructed of coated steel, rather than stainless steel, and can carry petroleum products such as gasoil, naphtha and gasoline.

General Notes

- High specific gravity (SG) cargoes increase loading stresses
- high relief valve settings increase internal pressure
- cargoes carried at high temperatures produce high thermal stress within the structure
- the danger of corrosion created by many of the chemicals requires that most tanks are either coated with a suitable lining or constructed of stainless steel

Chemical Tankers

- double bottoms are necessary for Type 1 and Type 2 tanks but not Type 3
- gauging of tanks may be open, restricted or closed, depending on the nature of the chemical being carried
- tank venting may be open or controlled depending on the cargo being carried. Where controlled venting is necessary, pressure vacuum relief valves are fitted to each tank. These may come to common vent headers, depending on the compatibility of the cargoes. Masts with controlled venting arrangements must be at least 10 metres from air intakes, openings to accommodation spaces, etc and should be at least 4 metres above the weather deck
- most tanks are 'integral'. This means they form part of the ship's hull, and so are subject to the same stresses as the hull.

Some cargoes, because of their nature, need to be carried in independent tanks. These are installed within the hull but are not an integral part of the ship's structure.

Figure 2.36 - Chemical terminal, Barcelona

Disasters and Significant Incidents Involving Chemical Tankers

'NCC Mekka'

Mid-afternoon on 4th June 2004, while en route from Santos to Aratu (Brazil), the 37,000 Dwt chemical tanker '*NCC Mekka*' sustained a low pressure explosion in tank 1CS while in the process of tank cleaning. This tank had previously carried paraffinic solvent. This was followed by another explosion in the adjacent tank 1CP, which was fully loaded with ethanol. The deck was fractured in several places and the escaping ethanol caught fire, spreading all the way aft to the deck house.

The crew extinguished the fire 30 minutes later using the vessel's foam monitors and managed to bring the vessel to the Rio de Janeiro roadstead. The Bosun and one seaman died following the incident.

Water ballast and ethanol were co-mingled and, following emergency consultations with the company, the Master decided to perform an emergency discharge (ethanol and water ballast) into the sea.

Causes

Water-driven rotary tank-washing machines were being used to wash tanks that had contained paraffin solvent which, from a product data sheet subsequently provided by the shipper, was found to have a flashpoint of minus 40°C. Prior to the explosion, the tanks had been subjected to a half-hour cold seawater wash, followed by a two-hour hot seawater wash at about 60°C. Around 200 litres of detergent had then been added to the tank via the closed sampling inlet of a Butterworth hatch. Two to three cubic metres of fresh water was added via the cargo line system and a three-hour washing programme commenced using the fresh water/detergent at ambient temperature. This fresh water/detergent wash was in progress at the time of the explosion.

Investigators considered various sources of ignition, including mechanical friction from the cleaning machines and/or the deepwell pump, an electrical short-circuit in tank monitoring systems and structural damage. All these were excluded based on information available and examinations carried out after the explosion.

The conclusion was that there must have been a charged atmosphere in tank 1CS and that a static discharge had taken place inside the tank. What led to the discharge was not clear, but it was suggested that a static charge could have been created from the detergent-loaded water wash.

Although the vessel was fitted with an oil-burning inert gas generator, the cargo tanks were not inerted at the time of the incident. At the maritime inquiry, the Chief Mate stated that the IG system on board (which was based

Disasters and Significant Incidents Involving Chemical Tankers

on oil combustion) was unacceptable to the charterers due to low purity. However, no explanation was given as to why nitrogen was not used for inerting or why, in the absence of an inerting medium, the cargo was not rejected.

'Sunny Jewel'

On 14th December 2004, the vessel *'Sunny Jewel'* discharged a cargo of reformate. This cargo, which is a dangerous and flammable liquid, is used as a base material in the production of gasoline. On 15th December while on a ballast voyage, the vessel sustained an explosion in her cargo length area. The flames, which started in one of her cargo tanks during tank cleaning operations, spread to adjoining tanks, igniting flammable gases inside. This resulted in almost all of the deck plating being blown off and the side shell plating being holed, resulting in tank flooding. The Bosun and two other crew members, who were on deck at the time of the explosion, were lost. Eventually, the fire was brought under control but the vessel sustained a serious list and subsequently foundered. Pollution was also recorded as a result of fuel oil spillage from her tanks.

Causes

1. Although not definite, it is assumed that the steam nozzle used in the tank cleaning may have created a static electrical discharge in an explosive atmosphere.
2. The gas-freeing period lasted only an hour and a half, resulting in a lack of air changes inside the cargo tanks.
3. Subsequent gas testing was only planned to be conducted through the oil-tight hatch in the aft part of each tank, rather than in other locations such as the middle or forward sections of the tank.
4. While the time to draw an atmosphere sample into the gas detector (with a pipe length of 20 metres) is calculated as 34 seconds, the Chief Officer only allowed 15 seconds (which corresponds to a 1 metres sampling pipe).
5. The vessel was not fitted with an IG system.

'Bow Mariner'

At 18:05 on 28th February 2004, the chemical tanker *'Bow Mariner'* caught fire and exploded while the crew were engaged in cleaning residual MTBE from cargo tank No. 8 stbd. The

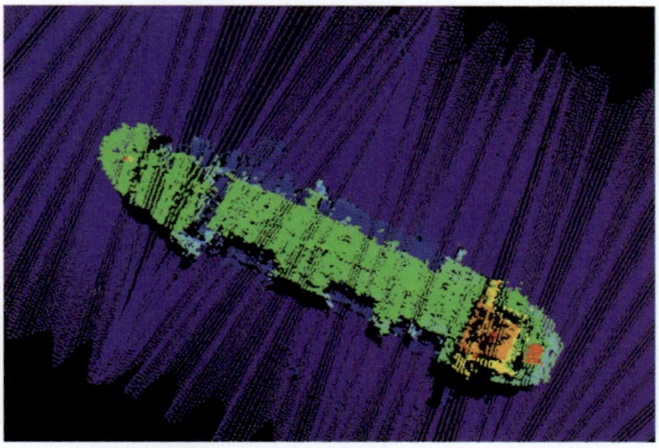

Figure 2.37 - Multi-beam sonar image taken by the NOAA ship 'Rude' on 4th March 2004, of the sunken tanker 'Bow Mariner'

ship sank by the bow at 19:37 about 45 miles east of Virginia, USA. Of the 27 crew members on board, six abandoned ship into an inflatable raft and were rescued by USCG. An unknown number of other crew members abandoned ship into the water. USCG and other vessels recovered three of these crewmen; one was already deceased and the other two died before reaching hospital. The remaining 18 crew were missing, presumed dead.

Causes

1. The cause was the ignition of a fuel/air mixture that was within its flammable limits, leading to a fire on deck.
2. The ignition source could not be determined. Sources that could not be ruled out include electrostatic discharge, mechanical sparks caused by metal-to-metal contact, faulty electrical equipment, hot soot or particles from the funnel, or sparks from changing the batteries of portable electrical equipment in a hazardous location.
3. Opening the 22 cargo tanks that previously held MTBE exposed the crew to toxic fumes, permitted flammable vapours that were heavier than air to accumulate on deck and diluted the fuel-rich atmosphere in the cargo tanks with oxygen, bringing them into the flammable range.
4. The fire was followed by two significant explosions that occurred less than two minutes apart. Each of these explosions was actually a series of rapid explosions, as each of the empty tanks exploded within seconds of one another.
5. The explosions caused catastrophic damage, leading to immediate flooding of nearly the

Disasters and Significant Incidents Involving Chemical Tankers

entire cargo block. The ship sank within an hour and 32 minutes of the first explosion.

6. The cargo tanks were not inerted during the previous discharge of MTBE, as required by the vessel's safety, quality and environmental management system (SQEMS). The tanks were not required to be inerted by US law or international conventions because the vessel was constructed before 1st July 1986. If the tanks had remained closed, the explosions would not have occurred.
7. The entry of the Bosun into the cargo tanks wearing an SCBA was dangerous and ill-advised, but did not violate the manager's confined space entry policy in effect on the date of the incident. (The policy has since been revised to prohibit entry under the same circumstances.)
8. The failure of the Master to properly organise a response to the explosions contributed to the high loss of life. He abandoned ship without sending a distress signal, without attempting to contact a nearby ship, without conducting a proper muster or search for injured crewmen and without attempting to launch primary life-saving appliances.
9. The Master and the Chief Engineer abandoned ship within 10 minutes of the first explosion, leaving behind crew members they knew to be alive. Their premature action exposed the crewmen who entered the water with them to the cold water far earlier than necessary and contributed to the high loss of life.
10. The actions of the Third Officer, making his first trip as a licensed officer, were commendable and helped save his own life and the lives of five others.
11. The lack of immersion suits contributed to the high loss of life.
12. The failure of the Master to conduct regular and effective fire and boat drills contributed to the high loss of life.
13. There is evidence that the operators and senior officers failed to follow proper relief and indoctrination/familiarisation training for critical crew members.
14. There is evidence of a lack of cohesiveness between the three senior officers, who shared the same nationality, and the other officers and crew, who shared a different nationality, but it could not be determined whether this contributed to the extent of the incident.

'P. Harmony'

On 15th January 2001, after discharging gasoline, the '*P. Harmony*' was making an 11-hour passage to port where the next cargo was to be loaded. Following the instructions of the charter, the crew started tank cleaning operations by fitting a water-driven fan to ventilate the tank, with ducting extending to the lower portion of the tank.

Due to the cold weather, the water in the pipes was freezing, making the operation of the fans difficult. After completing the ventilation of the tank immediately forward of the slop tanks and considering it to be gas-free, 2 crew members entered the tank to remove residual oil. There was an explosion that tore away bulkheads to adjoining tanks, one of which contained A-1 jet fuel and kerosene slops that ignited.

The hull was breached in way of the tanks and the engine room and the ship flooded rapidly, developing a starboard list and then sinking. The crew escaped by jumping into the sea and 7 were recovered by passing ships. Of a crew of 16, 7 survived, 3 bodies were recovered and 6 were lost.

Causes

The source of ignition was not identified. However, there was a high probability it was either due to a discharge of static electricity from winter clothing, or from the ventilation ducting, or from an ordinary metal paint can that was used to carry tools coming into contact with metal and causing a spark. While it is normal procedure not to enter tanks until gas concentrations are below danger levels, it could not be determined whether the officer in charge of the operation followed these procedures properly. The crew was under pressure to complete the tank cleaning operation due to the short voyage time to the load port. Given the equipment available and the prevailing weather conditions, there was insufficient time to ventilate and clean all the tanks as requested. Later examination of the cargo to be loaded in the next port disputed the need to actually clean the tanks.

Chemical Cargoes

Seaborne chemical trade can be divided into three main product segments:

- Organic chemicals
- inorganic chemicals
- vegetable oils and animal fats.

In 2011, trade figures were:

Organic substances	93.3 million tonnes
Inorganics (phosphoric acid, sulphuric acid and caustic soda)	21.1 million tonnes
Vegetable/animal oils & fats	52.7 million tonnes
Other cargoes (including lube oils and potable alcohols)	17.2 million tonnes

Organic Chemicals

Organic chemicals form the core chemical group and account for approximately 49% of chemical commodities carried by sea.

An organic chemical, also referred to as an organic compound, is constructed of molecules that possess carbon-based atoms.

Organic compounds are generally categorised as being either natural or synthetic, although sub-classifications also exist. Natural organic compounds are derived from living organisms, ie plants or animals. Examples include methanol, xylene, ethylene glycol, styrene, benzene, ethanol, toluene and acetic acid.

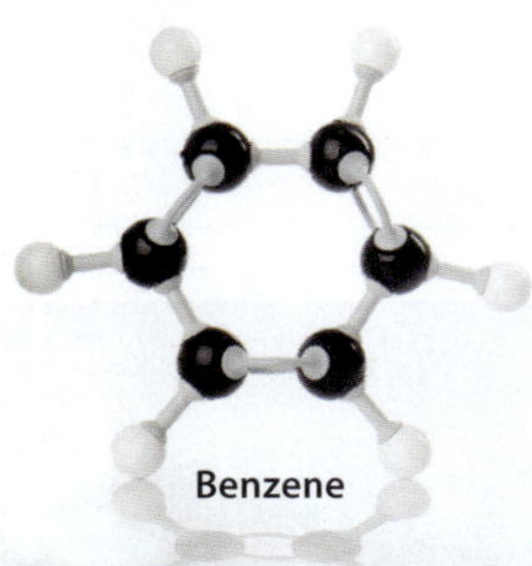
Benzene

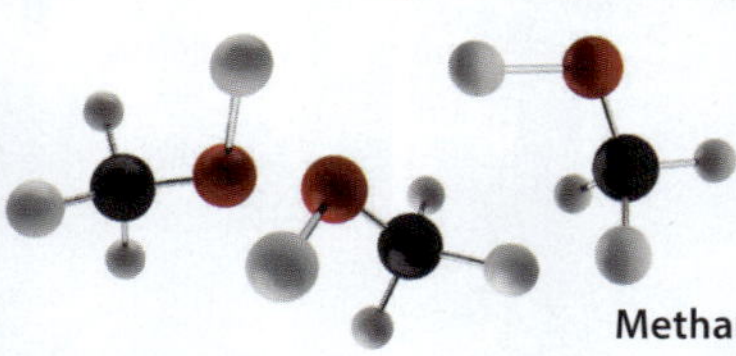
Methanol

Inorganic Chemicals

Inorganic chemicals are chemicals of mineral origin. They are derived from sources other than petroleum products and do not necessarily have carbon structures. The most significant inorganic chemicals are phosphoric acid, sulphuric acid and caustic soda, which are used as inputs in industrial and manufacturing processes.

Vegetable Oils and Animal Fats

Growth in this segment has outpaced that in organic and inorganic chemical trades. China and India are key contributors to this growth, particularly due to increased consumption of palm oil and soybean oil. In addition, estimates for consumption by the European Union have been revised upwards, boosted by the increased use of bio-fuels in the energy sector.

Included in this category are:

- Cottonseed oil
- peanut oil
- hemp oil
- kapok seed oi
- coconut oil
- linseed oil
- olive oil
- palm oil
- rapeseed oil
- castor oil
- mustard oil
- sesame oil
- soy oil
- sunflower oil.

Ethylene

Ethylene is used as a feedstock in the production of plastics, fibres and other organic chemicals that are ultimately used in the packaging, transportation and construction industries. Around 55 to 60% of ethylene consumed worldwide is used in the manufacture of plastic and polythene packaging.

About 50% of ethylene produced worldwide is obtained from naphtha, particularly in Europe and countries without indigenous natural gas (Japan, Korea and Taiwan). About 28% is produced from ethane.

In recent years, growth in ethylene consumption in China and India has been driven by local demand, while the Middle East is emerging as an ethylene production hub due to the low cost of the necessary feedstocks, such as ethane, propane and condensate.

Ethylene is often used as a benchmark for the performance of the petrochemical industry and an early indicator of slow-downs and pick-ups in the global economy.

Top Importers of Ethylene in 2012

Country	Value (million US$)	World share %
World	75,046.3	100.0
China	12,750.4	17.0
Germany	4,418.6	5.9
USA	3,945.1	5.3
Belgium	3,365.6	4.5
Italy	2,779.0	3.7
France	2,430.4	3.2
Vietnam	2,391.8	3.2
Turkey	2,304.8	3.1
United Kingdom	2,203.2	2.9
Singapore	2,186.2	2.9
India	2,166.8	2.9
Mexico	1,994.5	2.7
Spain	1,414.8	1.9
Russia Federation	1,414.0	1.9
Canada	1,340.9	1.8

Source: UN Comtrade

Top Exporters of Ethylene in 2012

Country	Value (million US$)	World share %
World	69,385.1	100.0
Saudi Arabia	7,712.2	11.1
USA	7,540.7	10.9
Belgium	6,259.2	9.0
Singapore	4,282.6	6.2
Germany	3,920.2	5.6
Canada	3,854.6	5.6
Republic of Korea	3,729.5	5.4
Thailand	3,525.6	5.1
Netherlands	3,479.2	5.0
France	2,466.8	3.6
Qatar	2,357.0	3.4
Iran	1,517.9	2.2
Brazil	1,395.0	2.0
Spain	1,180.5	1.7
Japan	1,178.2	1.7

Source: UN Comtrade

Ethylene being used in industry to create polythene

MARPOL Annex II

MARPOL Annex II Regulations for the control of pollution by noxious liquid substances in bulk categorises substances posing a threat of harm to the marine environment. Chemicals pose the greatest threat and have the most severe controls placed on their shipment and discharge into the sea.

The revised MARPOL Annex II was adopted by resolution MEPC.118(52) in October 2004.

The categories are:

Category X Noxious liquid substances which, if discharged into the sea from tank cleaning or deballasting operations, are deemed to present a major hazard to either marine resources or human health and, therefore, justify the prohibition of the discharge into the marine environment.

Category Y Noxious liquid substances which, if discharged into the sea from tank cleaning or deballasting operations, are deemed to present a hazard to either marine resources or human health or cause harm to amenities or other legitimate uses of the sea and, therefore, justify a limitation on the quality and quantity of the discharge into the marine environment.

Category Z Noxious liquid substances which, if discharged into the sea from tank cleaning or deballasting operations, are deemed to present a minor hazard to either marine resources or human health and, therefore, justify less stringent restrictions on the quality and quantity of the discharge into the marine environment.

Other Substances Substances which have been evaluated and found to fall outside Categories X, Y or Z because they are considered to present no harm to marine resources, human health, amenities or other legitimate uses of the sea when discharged into the sea from tank cleaning of deballasting operations. The discharge of bilge or ballast water or other residues or mixtures containing these substances is not subject to any discharge requirements of MARPOL Annex II.

Vegetable Oils

The vegetable oils listed in Chapter 17 of the IBC Code are regulated as pollution category Y and ship Type 2.

However, via Regulation 4.1.3 of the revised MARPOL Annex II, an Administration 'may' allow the carriage of these substances in a ship Type 3 if the ship complies with all the requirements for a ship Type 3, as identified in the IBC Code, except for cargo tank location.

This new Regulation was proposed to alleviate any potential tonnage shortage in the vegetable oil trade resulting from the re-categorisation of many vegetable oils in the revised Annex II.

Note: MEPC.148(54) *'Guidelines for the transport of vegetable oils in deep tanks or in independent tanks specially designed for the carriage of such vegetable oils on board dry cargo ships'* allows general dry cargo ships that were certified to carry vegetable oil in bulk before 1st January 2007 to continue to carry these vegetable oils on specific trades.

Onboard Equipment

Chemical tankers present a number of hazards to personal health and the environment, including toxicity, corrosivity, flammability and reactivity. Many of the cargoes are classified as marine pollutants.

Corrosive liquids, such as hydrochloric acid, sodium hypochlorite and sulphuric acid, present specific transport problems as a result of their aggressive nature. Traditional stainless steel tanks cannot be used for these liquids and rubber lining is an expensive process, with limited durability and adverse effects on the structure of the tank if the liner fails.

Handling large numbers of cargoes with different chemical and physical properties on a single voyage presents a substantial workload for the crew. To minimise port turnaround times and to streamline cargo handling operations, chemical parcel tankers are equipped with highly automated cargo control and monitoring systems.

Main Engines

Before 2001, chemical parcel tankers, in common with most other tankers, used slow-speed diesel engines connected to a cast (fixed pitch) propeller. By 2002, chemical parcel tankers were being built with diesel-electric propulsion systems with four medium-speed diesel engines driving an electric motor. In such a configuration, the diesel-electric propulsion system provides four times the redundancy of conventional main engines and energy efficiency savings when in port. Other benefits include reduced vessel emissions, less noise and vibration than slow-speed diesels and the ability to fit an electrically-powered bow thruster for increased manoeuvrability.

Cargo Tanks

Parcel tankers typically have stainless steel cargo tanks throughout to ensure the vessel can carry a wide range of cargoes. On older chemical tankers, stainless steel was often used only for centre tanks, with the wing tanks being coated. The absence of internal stiffeners and framing inside the tank reduces cargo loss, speeds operations and facilitates cleaning.

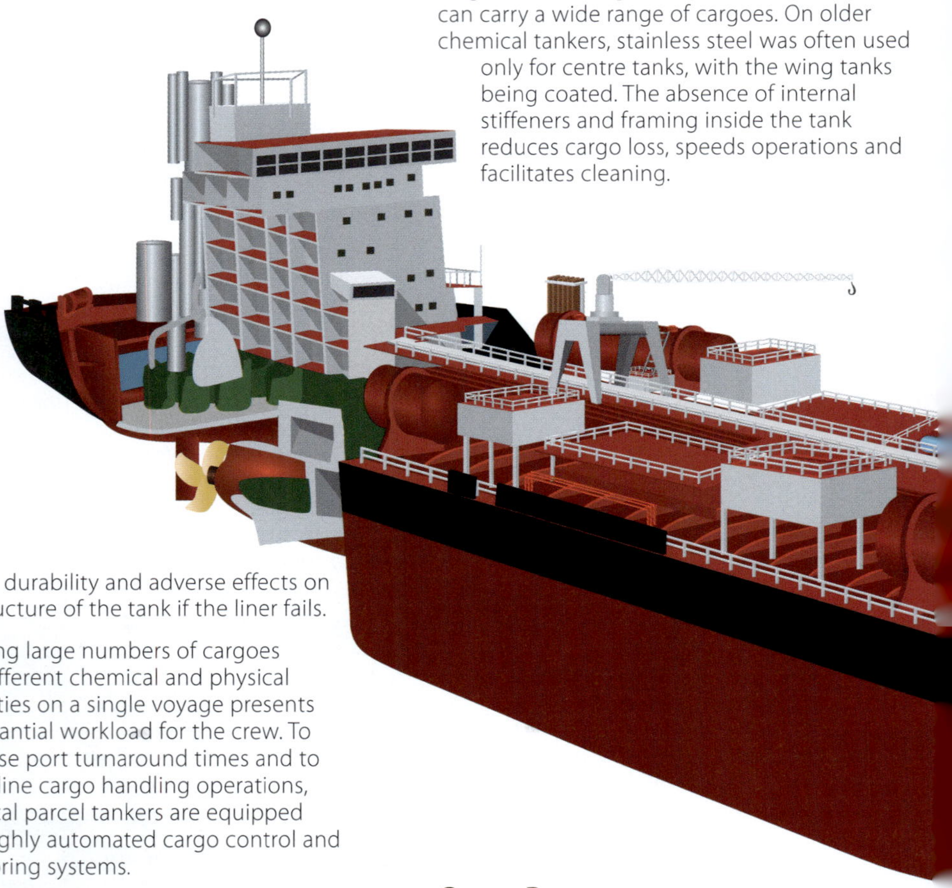

Cargo Pumps

Each tank is equipped with its own stainless steel deepwell cargo pump. The single pump, line and manifold crossover for each tank ensures that each tank can carry a different cargo in a fully segregated manner. Pumps are positioned to the aft of each tank in suction wells and either to port or starboard to allow optimal cargo outturn.

Nitrogen Generator

A dedicated nitrogen generator provides a high-purity product for use in blanketing and purging cargoes, reducing atmospheric pollution and increasing the level of cargo care.

Cargo Heating

Cargo can be heated using hot water, steam, thermal oil or a combination of these. Cargo cooling systems can also be provided to permit the carriage of semi-gaseous chemicals.

Vapour Emission Control System (VECS)

A fully automatic vapour emission control system prevents atmospheric pollution during cargo loading and discharge.

Inert Gas Systems

IMO approved amendments to SOLAS and the Fire Safety Systems Code in May 2014 to mandate the use of inert gas on new oil tankers of below 20,000 Dwt and new chemical tankers. The amendments provide for a revised lower size limit of 8,000 Dwt and allow for vessels of less than 20,000 Dwt to use shore-supplied inert gas rather than install an inert gas system. There is also a provision for chemical tankers to have the option of dispensing with the inerting of tanks prior to loading, provided that inert gas is applied for the discharge and thereafter throughout the tank cleaning phases.

The regulations will enter into force on 1st January 2016.

Ship/Shore Connection

A chemical tanker will often have a single dedicated line from the pump in each tank to the manifold area, which is the connection between the ship and the shore. While the shore may be fitted with hard arms, often cargo hoses will be used. Cargo hoses must comply with the requirements of the IBC Code. The hoses must be checked before each use and both the hoses and jointing gaskets at all flanges must be suitable for the product to be transferred. During use, care must be taken to ensure that the hoses are correctly supported and are not subject to any bending beyond the radius of curvature as recommended by the manufacturer.

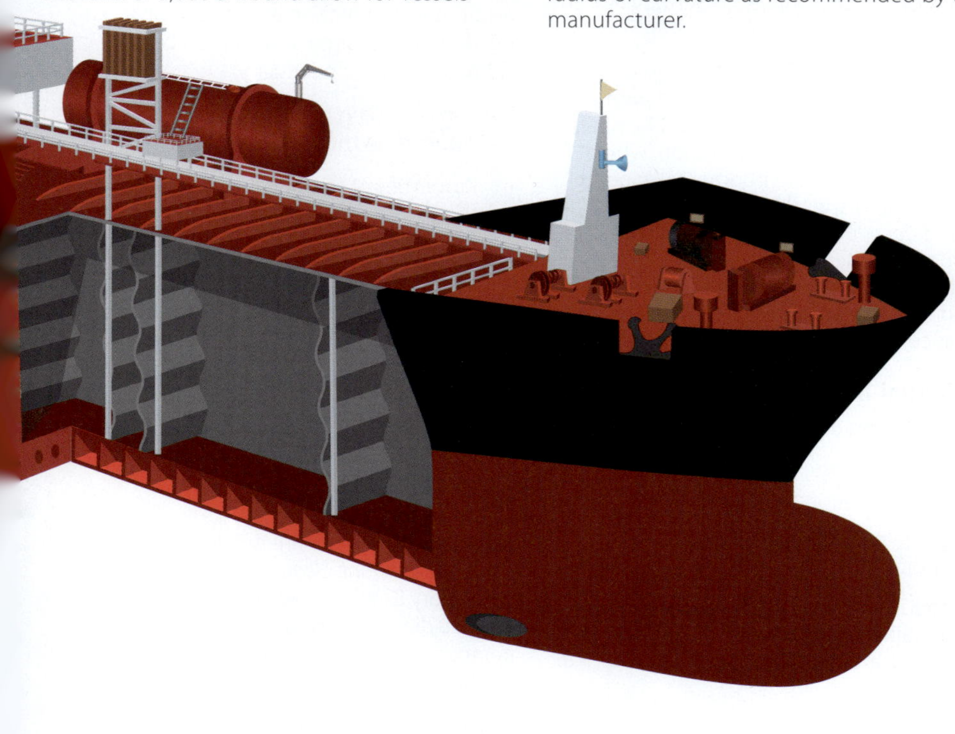

Chemical Tank Cleaning

Before tank cleaning commences, as much cargo as possible must be removed. Items to consider include:

- The ship's trim and list
- viscous cargoes may be stripped to a single tank and from there be pumped ashore using a small bore stripping line of around 50 mm
- cargo temperature may need to be kept sufficiently high to allow cargo to drain from remote corners of the tanks, particularly in cold climates
- waxy deposits under the heating coils can sometimes be melted out by filling the coils with water and then applying heat.

Tank cleaning, together with gas-freeing, is probably the most hazardous operation routinely undertaken on a chemical tanker.

It is therefore of the utmost importance that all operations connected with tank cleaning and gas-freeing are carried out according to the approved procedures and arrangements for the ship.

All ships certified to carry noxious liquid substances in bulk must be provided with a Procedures and Arrangements (P&A) Manual, approved by the Flag Administration, which addresses the marine environmental aspects of removal and disposal of residues from cargo tanks, and describes how to perform these operations. The Manual should be adhered to in all respects, including the performance of mandatory pre-wash requirements in accordance with MARPOL 73/78 Annex II.

P&A Manual-Index of Sections

1. Main features of MARPOL 73/78, Annex II.
2. Description of the ship's equipment and arrangements.
3. Cargo unloading procedures and tank stripping.
4. Procedures relating to the cleaning of cargo tanks, the discharge of residues, ballasting and deballasting.

Table 1 – List of noxious liquid substances allowed to be carried

Table 2 – Cargo tank information

Addendum A: Flow diagram

Addendum B: Pre-wash procedures

Addendum C: Ventilation procedures

Addendum D: Determination of permitted residue discharge rates for Category B substances (if necessary)

Additional information and operational instructions required or accepted by the Administration (if necessary).

The tank cleaning methods that can be applied will depend on the:

- Properties of the previous substance and the substance to be loaded
- vessel's technical equipment
- availability of chemical additives
- tank coating and its condition
- ambient temperature
- seawater temperature
- weather conditions
- available time
- crew's experience.

The leading independent publication on this subject is the *'Tank Cleaning Guide'*, published by Laboratory Dr Verwey, Rotterdam. This publication lists 390 different substances, each with the appropriate symbols of the various tank cleaning methods to be applied.

The standard of cleanliness varies depending on the previous cargo and the requirements for the next cargo.

Tank washing and cleaning operations on board chemical tankers mainly require water washing, with chemical cleaning additives only being required for a small number of cargoes.

The most important decision when tank cleaning is which of the following are to be used:

- Cleaning agent
- water and cleaning agent
- ventilation
- water only
  - with fresh or seawater
  - with hot or cold water.

The wrong decision may lead to serious consequences and severe financial losses. A few substances, toluene-di-isocyanate (TDI) for example, will react with water and form insoluble sediments.

The tank material and coating resistance must be considered before the application of any cleaning agent.

Stainless Steel

Stainless steel can corrode as a result of contamination on the steel surface. Corrosion resistance may be improved through the use of pickling. This is an acid treatment applied to the surface of stainless steel to remove contaminants and assist the formation of a continuous passive chromium oxide film. Pickling will not remove grease or oil, which may require removal using detergent or alkaline before pickling.

Zinc Silicate

Corrosion resistance may also be improved by applying a zinc silicate epoxy coating. This provides cathodic protection similar to galvanising.

Epoxy coatings offer a good level of protection against a range of cargoes. They are usually resistant to some weak acids and strong alkalies and do not absorb oil-like substances. After transporting aggressive cargoes, the coated tank has to be ventilated until the cargo has been desorbed (released) from the coating film, which can take several days.

Cleaning agents with a pH value beyond the bounds of 6.5 to 9.0 are not acceptable for applying to zinc silicate coated tanks (eg caustic soda NaOH pH =14.

Cleaning agents may be applied in various ways:

- Portable washing with the cleaning agent solution
- direct application of the cleaning agent
- injection of the cleaning agent into washing water
- lift method
- steaming with a cleaning agent
- others, as per the manufacturers' instructions.

Steaming

Steaming is one of the best methods of cleaning non-flammable substances or cargoes liable to taint from the tank, as the steam can reach every corner and under each stringer. Examples of sensitive cargoes are glycols, glycerin, vegetable and animal oils and molasses. Steaming for 45 to 60 minutes is usually sufficient to freshen the tank and associated lines. The steam can be applied through a line from the manifold or directly into the tank cleaning hatch. The pump in the tank being steamed must be started to discharge any condensed water. On completion, the tank lids may either be opened to allow the steam to clear leaving the inside hot and dry, or left closed to allow the steam to condense onto the surface of the tank leaving it wet. This will give the best cleaning for chlorides but the vessel will need more time for tank drying.

Chemical Tank Cleaning

Note: Steaming 'sweats out' cargo from pores, etc. Cargo piping may also have to be steamed out. Epoxy coatings should not be heated above 60 to 80°C.

Steaming with a Cleaning Agent

This method yields good results but can be hazardous. For example, steaming with toluene is restricted because of the risk of explosion.

Tank cleaning agents may be corrosive, skin sensitive or toxic and when heated may give off irritating fumes. Personnel handling them must be familiar with the MSDS (Material Safety Data Sheet) and wear the appropriate personal protective equipment (PPE).

Fixed Tank Washing Machines

Fixed tank washing machines in a chemical cargo tank allow an inert atmosphere to be maintained during the washing operation and allows the washing to be conducted in a closed system that prevents the release of noxious vapours.

Manual Cleaning

The most expensive and least safe method of tank cleaning is manual cleaning. Wherever possible, manual involvement should be reduced to inspection and final drying up of washing water. The following safeguards should be applied:

- Manually cleaning a tank necessitates tank entry to scrape the tank surfaces and wipe clean the tank interior. The person entering the tank must be wearing a full hazard suit
- a high-pressure jet will typically be used to clean the tank bulkheads. Safety gear should be worn, which can include a harness and rope attachment
- no one should enter any cargo tank unless express permission has been received from the responsible officer and all appropriate precautions taken
- an entry permit should be issued
- personnel should be aware that the introduction of a solvent into the tank might also generate additional risks, such as toxicity or flammability
- all slops must be disposed of in accordance with the ship's P&A Manual.

Cleaning by Ventilation

Substances suitable for ventilation are clearly identified in the 'list of noxious liquid substances allowed to be carried' in the P&A Manual. Substances with a vapour pressure greater than 5 x 103 Pa at 20°C may simply be removed from a cargo tank by ventilation.

The safety hazards relating to cargo flammability and toxicity should be considered before ventilation of noxious liquid substance residues from a tank. The ventilation procedures in the P&A manual must be strictly followed and the precautions listed in the ICS Tanker Safety Guide (Chemicals) adhered to.

Port authorities are likely to have further regulations on cargo tank ventilation and a request for written agreement should be made before any procedure commences.

Draining

Once gas-free, any remaining water must be discharged from all cleaned cargo tanks and lines. Filters and pumps (where applicable) must also be drained. Filters must be opened, cleaned and prepared for inspection. All end valves of the cargo lines must be closed and the cargo line filled with compressed air. The cargo line is then blown through each end valve to purge the water from the cargo line into the tank. All cargo valves should then be opened to aid ventilation of the lines.

Drying

Drying the tank is only a concern in wet weather conditions, when the humidity is very high. The tank will be absolutely dry at a dewpoint of minus 40°C or below, a condition that can be reached if the tank is blown with an appropriate gas, such as nitrogen. The easiest way to dry the tank and reduce humidity is to dry the air before introducing it to the tank. Alternatively, to evaporate water from the surfaces the tank's heating coils (if fitted) can be used to raise the temperature in the tank while ventilating the tank with a portable ventilator.

Hydrocarbon Test

Methanol is generally agreed to be one of the most demanding cargoes with respect to tank cleaning and 'wall wash' testing. The

Figure 2.38 - Entering a chemical tanker for cleaning

ultimate requirement is for a tank to be left with zero water and as near as possible zero hydrocarbons. Chloride salt contamination is tested using silver-nitrate solution, described under 'Chloride Test' below. Non-contaminated methanol will dissolve clearly in water so the test for hydrocarbons is developed on the principle that methanol contaminated with hydrocarbons, when mixed together with water, will create a milky, cloudy liquid that is, in part, a solution but that shows as a colloidal emulsion. This discolouration is measured by a laboratory, giving readings in NTU (nephelometricturbity units). A demanding exporter may require as little as 0.5 NTU before accepting the tank for methanol cargo loading.

Figure 2.39 - Tank heating coils

Chloride Test

The principle of the test is that chloride salts, when mixed with a silver nitrate solution, give a milky, cloudy effect.

The procedure is as follows:

- Distilled water is rinsed onto the tested surface of the tank or equipment and is collected into a Nessler tube (a narrow glass cylinder used for colour comparison in samples)
- the solution is filtered using a funnel with filter paper placed on the top of another Nessler tube
- the tube is filled to exactly 100 ml with distilled water
- 5 drops of silver nitrate solution are added
- the contents are thoroughly mixed
- the mixture in the tube is compared with another Nessler tube, filled with 99 ml of water, 1 ml of standard chloride solution (1 mg chloride per 1 ml) and 5 drops of the silver nitrate solution.

The tank must be re-washed and tested again if the sample shows as cloudy or not completely clear.

Chemical Tank Cleaning

Cargo Tank Vapour Return Systems

For many of the noxious liquid substances (NLS) carried on a chemical tanker, it is not permissible to vent the vapours from the cargo tanks, lines and connections to atmosphere. Such cargoes are normally classed as 'toxic products' and are subject to closed loading conditions.

The same restriction applies when inerting the cargo lines, tanks and connections with nitrogen from onshore, such as for the carriage of acetic acid. If no vapour return line is fitted, the inerting nitrogen would have to be vented to the atmosphere, and this loss represents a huge cost to the terminal. Some toxic cargoes have a Threshold Limit Value (TLV) that is so low that any release to the atmosphere is hazardous to personnel in the surrounding area. For these cargoes the crew must wear protective suits on deck and, while working cargo, access to and from the ship is suspended. The MSDS for the cargo will indicate all hazards and precautions.

Figure 2.39 shows the requirements for vapour return line manifolds. The important feature that ensures a cargo line cannot be connected is the 'stud' that is set at '12 o'clock' on the flange of the manifold and reducer. This must never be removed and must be replaced if damaged. The shore vapour return arm or hose will have a hole in the 12 O'clock position to accommodate the stud.

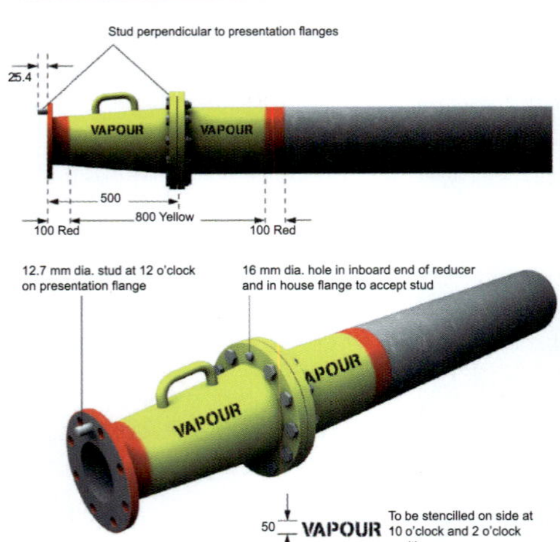

Figure 2.40 - Vapour manifold flanges

The vapour return line is a line running from the cargo tank back to the cargo manifold area. Each vapour return line will have its own separate manifold, which must be specially marked. This ensures that there is no mistake when connecting the loading line to the vapour return line.

The IBC Code lays down the requirements for ships returning the most toxic chemical vapours to shore.

It is important that there is a balanced safe pressure between the ship and shore. The tank must evacuate the vapours at a speed fast enough to ensure positive pressure is maintained below the set opening pressure of any pressure relief valve in the tank venting system.

IMO guidelines recommend that tank pressure should be less than 80% of the relief valve setting. It is very important that, at the pre-cargo operations meeting with the shore terminal staff, agreement is reached on the liquid loading rate and the expected pressure at the vapour connection. Plans for how these will be controlled must be in place.

At no point must liquid be allowed to enter the vapour line as it will reduce the cross-sectional area of the pipeline and reduce its ability to allow the maximum vapour to flow. The knock-on effect would be a build-up of pressure in the cargo tank.

Figure 2.41 - Manifold arrangement on a chemical tanker

Heated Cargo

Substances that have not reached the required discharge temperature may be identified as 'solidifying substances' or 'high viscosity' substances.

- Cargoes with a melting point of less than 15°C must be discharged with a temperature of at least 5°C above melting point. For example, benzene, with a melting point of 4.5°C, should be discharged with a temperature of at least 9.5°C to avoid the prewash requirements
- cargoes with a melting point equal to or greater than 15°C must be discharged with a temperature of at least 10°C above their melting point. For example, phenol, with a melting point of 40.9°C, should be discharged with a temperature of at least 50.9°C to avoid solidification or be classed as 'solidifying'.

If relevant, the viscosity at 20°C and the melting point will be stated on a certificate of quality. The temperature at which the viscosity will be reduced to acceptable limits will also be stated, eg 25 mPa or 60 mPa, as appropriate.

Heating instructions must be strictly followed to avoid waxing, sedimenting, stratifying, crystallising, separating or anything else that may damage quality. The cargo temperature must be measured at least twice a day, in the morning and evening. The measured temperature must be recorded in a heating log. Any deviation without an immediately apparent reason must be analysed and an attempt to solve the situation made. The engine room should advise whether there is any boiler water loss or increased water consumption as this may indicate a leakage from the heating coils. Traces of cargo in the return condensate indicates leakage in the heating coils.

While cargo heating, condensate return water should be periodically drained onto the deck to inspect the cargo traces for heating coil damage. If damage is suspected, the appropriate heating section should be blanked off. Special attention must be given to tanks with a slow rising temperature.

Nitrogen Blanket Cargo

Nitrogen has been in use for many years on chemical tankers to reduce the oxygen content in empty tank spaces when carrying certain chemicals that can be adversely affected by oxygen. This is done either for safety reasons, such as to prevent a flammable atmosphere from developing, for cargo quality reasons, or for other reasons such as padding (or blanketing) with nitrogen during transit.

A permanent nitrogen overpressure must be maintained (this may be about 70 mb). Tank pressures have to be checked and recorded daily in the pressure control log. Any loss of nitrogen in the tank should be refilled from the vessel's reserve of nitrogen. The use of nitrogen padding must be strictly controlled in accordance with the cargo requirements and/or inhibitor certificate as applicable.

Pumps

The two types of pumps used on chemical tankers are positive displacement pumps and kinetic or centrifugal pumps.

Displacement Pumps

Displacement pumps function by displacement of the liquid inside the pump. Examples include the piston pump and the screw pump. A pipeline system equipped with displacement pumps must have a safety valve and a bypass line to protect the discharge line. Piston pumps and screw pumps have excellent suction properties, but any deterioration of the cargo pipework will cause a reduction in the discharge rate.

Displacement pumps are allocated to groups of tanks, normally one pump per group. The suction and discharge valves of a positive displacement pump must always be open

Chemical Tank Cleaning

before starting the pump and must remain open until it is stopped. Activation of the over-speed trip of these pumps must be avoided and particular care and attention must be taken when the cargo level in the tank is reduced to the final 0.5 m of liquid. At this point, the pump's speed should be reduced.

Submerged Deepwell Pumps

Submerged pumps are used when an individual pump is required in each cargo tank. Cargo enters the eye of the impeller and is thrown out by centrifugal force.

These pumps will be either hydraulically operated or electrically powered. A good example of a submerged pump is the Marflex deepwell pump, shown in Figure 2.41, which is driven by an electric motor. It has an oil lubricated shaft that runs in a separate support pipe. The service life of an oil lubricated shaft is estimated at more than 10,000 running hours, based on the service life of the bearings and the motor, and this is deemed sufficient for the 20 to 25 year life expectancy of a chemical tanker.

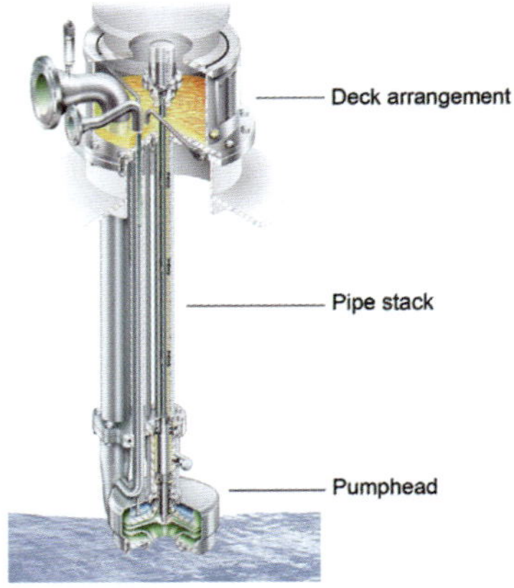

Reproduced with permission from Marflex BV

Figure 2.42 - Submerged pump

Stripping

Stripping of cargo tanks should be performed in accordance with the guidance in the vessel's P&A Manual and with regard to any manufacturers' instructions. During tank stripping and line clearing, the ship's list and trim must be maintained within the guidance in the P&A Manual.

If the pump is left unattended as the cargo level approaches the bottom of the cargo tank, the pump will periodically lose suction through insufficient cargo flow (this is known as cavitation).

The pump's speed should be reduced and, in this way, the discharge capacity will stabilise. The cargo pump will steadily continue to strip the cargo tank. Stripping can be transferred into a single ship's cargo tank prior to discharging ashore, resulting in a quick and efficient strip.

When the cargo tank is empty, the cargo stripping valve should be opened and the main cargo valve closed. The remaining cargo in the main cargo pipe is purged, by means of inert gas or compressed air, via the stripping pipe into the cargo line on deck. During the purging/stripping procedure, the pump should be kept running (the impeller acts as a dynamic foot valve) until the cargo pipe has been purged empty. This procedure will guarantee the minimum amount of cargo remaining in the pump well.

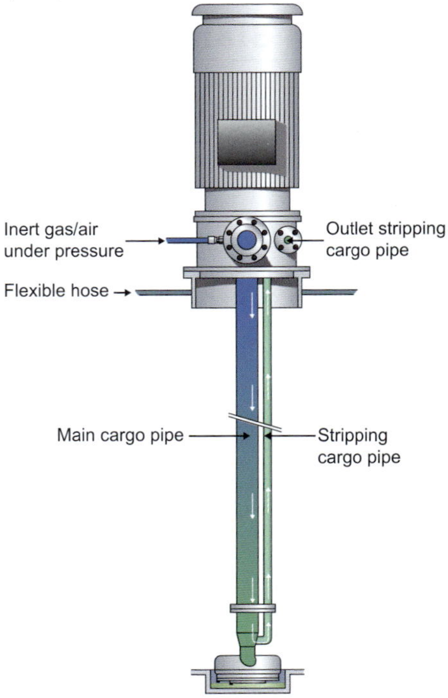

Reproduced with permission from Marflex BV

Figure 2.43 - Deepwell pump

As an example, typical figures from the Marflex range of pumps quote 12 litres of remaining liquid from a 100 m^3/hr pump to 50 litres of remaining liquid from a 2,000 m^3/hr pump.

After purging the cargo pump and the pressure line up to the discharge valve, the remaining cargo line must be emptied. The compressed air or inert gas should now be admitted into the cargo line. The pressure medium will expand and push the remaining cargo through the stripping connection, close to the cargo pump barrier to the manifold connection. The manifold connection is normally located outboard of the manifold barrier and is provided with ball valves.

Prohibition of Discharges into the Sea from Chemical Tankers

Regulation 13 of Annex II of MARPOL 73/78 (Annex II) prohibits the discharge into the sea of Noxious Liquid Substances (NLS) of Categories X, Y or Z or of ballast water, tank washings or other residues or mixtures containing such substances, except in compliance with specified conditions including procedures and arrangements based upon standards developed by the IMO.

Exceptions

Annex II prohibits the discharge into the sea of any effluent-containing substances, except when the discharge is made under conditions that are specifically detailed for each Category.

Examples of the conditions and parameters that will be detailed include:

- The maximum quantity of substances per tank which may be discharged into the sea
- the speed of the ship during the discharge
- the minimum distance from the nearest land during discharge
- the minimum depth of water at sea during discharge
- the need to effect the discharge below the waterline.

Procedures and Arrangements Manual

Annex II requires that each ship that is certified for the carriage of NLS in bulk shall be provided with a 'Procedures and Arrangements Manual'.

This Manual must be written in accordance with Annex II, Appendix 4 and concerns the marine environmental aspects of the cleaning of cargo tanks and the discharge of residues and mixtures from such activities. The Manual is not a safety guide and reference must be made to other publications specifically to evaluate safety hazards.

The purpose of the Manual is to identify the arrangements and equipment required for compliance with Annex II and to assist the ship's officers with all operational procedures with respect to cargo handling, tank cleaning, slops handling, residue discharging, ballasting and deballasting, which must be followed, to ensure compliance.

In addition, this Manual, together with the ship's Cargo Record Book and the International Certificate of Fitness for the Carriage of Dangerous Chemicals in Bulk, will be used by Administrations for control purposes in order to ensure full compliance with the requirements of Annex II by the ship.

The master must ensure that no discharges into the sea of cargo residues or residue/water mixtures containing Category X, Y or Z substances takes place, unless such discharges are made in full compliance with the operational procedures contained in this Manual.

Gas Carriers

World LPG

Fleet 1,282 LPG Carriers with 226 on order

Source: Clarksons.com (April 2015)

LPG cargoes carried by ship (70 million tonnes in 2014). Ammonia cargoes carried by ship (15.9 million tonnes in 2014)

Source: Clarksons.com (April 2015)

World LNG

Fleet 426 LNG Carriers in service at the beginning of 2015, with 159 on order

Source: LNG World Shipping (April 2015)

LNG cargoes carried by ship in 2014 = 239.2 million tons imported (representing a 1% increase vs. 2013)

Source: GIIGNL 'The LNG Industry in 2014'

Gas Carrier Types

Liquefied Gas Carriers (LPG and LNG)

The fleet of liquefied gas carriers in service in 2014 consists of approximately 1,650 gas carriers, of which around 1,100 are LPG carriers, with 400 LNG carriers and approximately 150 ethylene carriers making up the balance.

Gas carriers are divided into two main groups:

- Liquefied Petroleum Gas (LPG) carriers, which are designed to carry mainly butane, propane, butadiene, propylene and vinyl chloride monomer (VCM) and are able to carry anhydrous ammonia
- Liquefied Natural Gas (LNG) carriers, which are designed to carry liquefied natural gas (which is mostly methane).

Gas carriers are classed in three types based on hazard potential:

- Type 1G, designed to carry the most hazardous cargoes
- Type 2G and 2PG, designed to carry cargoes with a lesser degree of hazard
- Type 3G, designed to carry cargoes of the least hazardous nature.

Most gases, including LNG, are carried in category 2G or 2PG carriers.

Tank types used

Type 'A': Constructed of plain surfaces (prismatic tanks)

Type 'B': Spheres

Type 'C': Cylindrical pressure vessels

(Note: These tanks are used where appropriate, regardless of gas carrier type.)

Classes of LPG Gas Carrier

Fully Pressurised

These ships have a cargo capacity of 3,500 m³. They carry the cargo in spherical or cylindrical steel tanks, designed to withstand 17 bar G. No means of temperature control is necessary for the gases carried.

The tanks are generally Type C cylindrical and no secondary barrier is required. A double bottom is constructed for ballast water. The hold space around the cargo tanks does not need to be inerted but sufficient inerting material must be carried and available for use.

Fully Pressurised

Fleet of 545 vessels (100 – 10,000 m³)

Source: LPG World Shipping

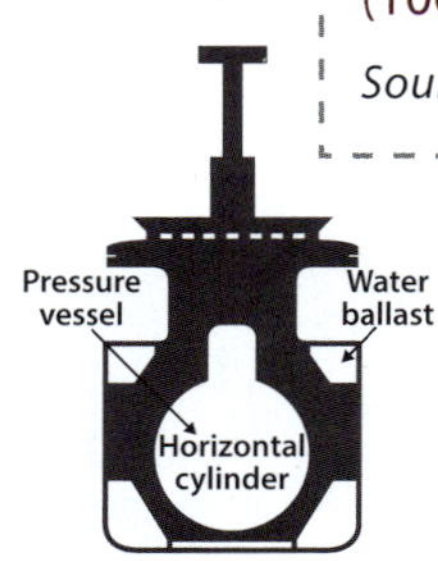

Semi-Pressurised/Fully Refrigerated

These vessels are fitted with a refrigeration plant and are designed for high pressure cargo tanks (pressure vessels), although not as high as required for fully pressurised carriage.

The ships are larger than the fully pressurised ships and are generally between 3,000 and 15,000 m³.

The ships are designed to minus 48°C, making them suitable for the carriage of butane, butadiene, VCM, ammonia, propane and propylene.

The reliquefaction plant usually has substantial capacity and, if required, cargo can be loaded as a gas and then reliquefied on board.

The inner hull volume is used more efficiently than on the fully pressurised vessels and the number of tanks varies from two to six.

A double bottom is constructed for ballast water and the hold space around the cargo tanks does not need to be inerted. However, sufficient material must still be carried and available for use.

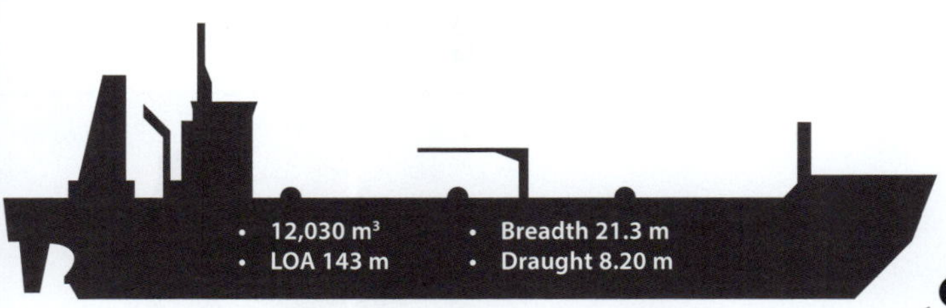

Midship type section

Semi-Pressurised/Fully Refrigerated (Semi-Ref) Gas Carriers

Fleet of 311 vessels with 40 on order

This includes 128 liquefied ethylene gas carriers (LEGCs) and a further 30 are on order.

Source: LPG World Shipping

Gas Carrier Types

Fully Refrigerated

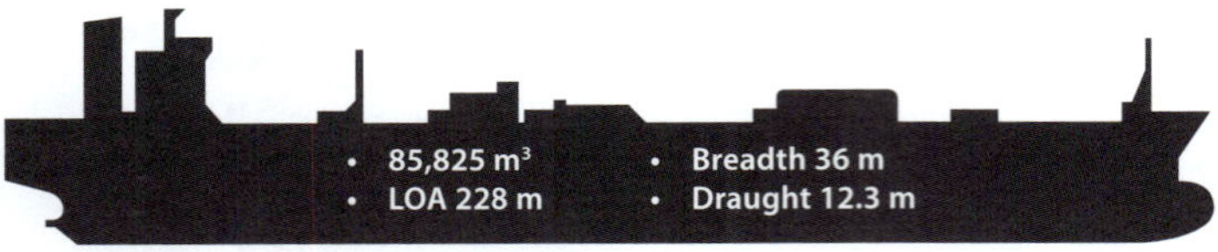

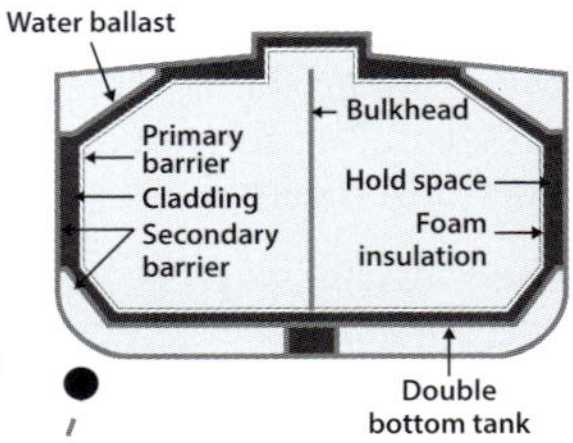

These ships are designed to carry cargoes at almost atmospheric pressure to a temperature of minus 48°C, making them suitable for the carriage of butane, butadiene, VCM, ammonia, propane and propylene.

The ships typically range from 15,000 m^3 to 85,000 m^3, with three common sizes for LPG/ammonia trades of 30,000 m^3, 52,000 m^3 and 80,000 m^3.

The tanks extend to nearly the full width of the ship, with ballast in the double bottom and upper hopper or wing tanks. These tanks normally have a centreline bulkhead fitted with two equalising valves. Caution is necessary as the tanks carry a large free surface area and if the vessel has problems with ballast or levelling the cargo during loading they can quickly list over to 2 or 3°.

When carrying flammable cargoes, the hold space is inerted.

Fully Refrigerated LPG Carriers

Fleet of 253

Very large gas carriers (VLGCs) (75,000 – 85,000 m^3)

Fleet of 149 with 79* on order.

Large gas carriers (LGCs) (52,000 m^3)

Fleet of 20

Mid and handy-size gas carriers (MGCs) (15,000 – 30,000 m^3)

Fleet of 84

Main Source: LPG World Shipping

*Other Sources: *LPG Forecaster report published by shipping consultancy Drewry August 2014*

Classes of LNG Carrier

LNG is liquefied by refrigeration to minus 162°C. This process is carried out ashore before the cargo is loaded onto the ship, which is fully insulated.

LNG carriers range from 80,000 to 200,000 m^3.

As with all gas carriers, where the liquid is carried in tanks that are not pressure vessels, a secondary barrier may be necessary. A secondary barrier is a containment outside of the primary tank that can, in the event of an emergency, contain the cargo for a period of 15 days.

There are two main types of LNG ship:

- Spherical Type 'B' tanks/Kvaerner Moss Rosenberg, which require only a partial secondary barrier
- membrane systems such as Gaz Transport and Technigaz (known as GTT (Gaz Transport Technigaz) since the companies merged). This system has a primary and secondary barrier and an insulation layer.

Membrane (Gaz Transport or Technigaz)

There are two membrane systems in use. In both cases the insulation is fitted directly into the inner hull and the primary barrier consists of a thin metal membrane less than one millimetre thick. The Gaz Transport system uses two such membranes constructed of 'Invar' (36% nickel-iron low expansion alloy). One acts as the primary barrier and the other the secondary barrier and they are separated by plywood boxes of perlite insulation. Similar boxes are fitted between the secondary barrier and the inner hull. Loading is transmitted through the insulation to the ship structure. No centreline division is possible in this type of tank. The other system, developed by Technigaz, has a stainless steel membrane as the primary barrier while the secondary barrier is included in the insulation, which consists of load-bearing balsa and mineral woods.

Figure 2.44 - Cross-section of LNG carrier of the Gaz Transport style

Q-Max and Q-Flex

Q-Max (Qatar-max)

Capacity:	266,000 m^3
Length:	345 metres
Draught:	12 metres
Average speed in knots:	19.5 kts

Q-Max is a membrane type of LNG carrier. 'Q' stands for Qatar and 'Max' denotes that it is the maximum size of ship able to dock at the LNG

Gas Carrier Types

terminals in Qatar. Ships of this type are the largest LNG carriers in the world.

Since 2005, a total of 14 Q-Max vessels have been built.

The first trip by a Q-Max tanker was completed in January 2009, when the tanker delivered 266,000 m^3 of LNG to the Port of Bilbao BBG Terminal, Spain.

- These LNG carriers are powered by electronically controlled slow-speed diesel engines rather than steam propulsion as found on older LNG carriers
- they are fitted with dual propeller and rudders (giving 100% redundancy)
- they are fitted with an onboard reliquefaction plant that cools boil-off gas (BOG) and converts it back to liquid for return to the tanks.

Q-Flex

Capacity:	210,000 to 216,000 m^3
Length:	315 metres
Draught:	12 metres
Average speed in knots:	19.5 kts

The first Q-Flex LNG carrier was delivered by Hyundai Heavy Industries in late 2007. In total, 31 Q-Flex LNG Carriers have been constructed.

Spherical Tanks (Moss Rosenberg)

Spherical tanks are generally produced in aluminium or 9% nickel steel. The sphere is welded to a steel skirt connected to the hull and is then free to expand and contract as necessary. Insulation is fitted to the outside shell of the sphere but no secondary barrier is considered necessary across the upper part. However, below the sphere, an aluminium drip tray, together with splash plates, provides secondary protection for the hull.

- Anti-roll and anti-collision chocks must be fitted in way of each self-supporting tank
- pipe access to tanks is via the dome on top of the tank
- refrigeration plant is fitted to reliquefy cargo boil-off for returning to tanks on LPG carriers

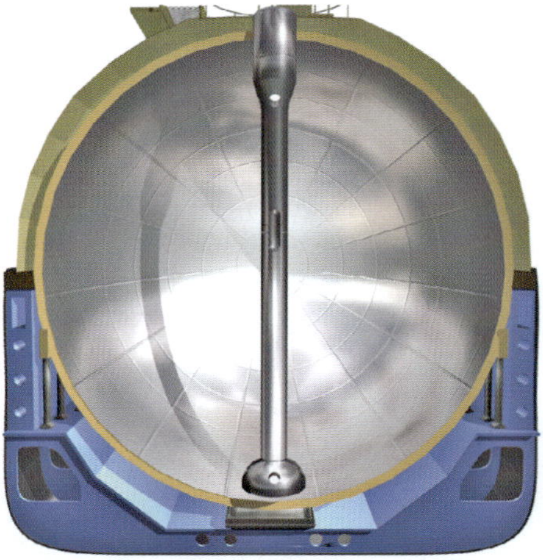

Figure 2.45 - Cross-section of Moss Rosenberg style LNG carrier

- boil-off from LNG carriers is generally used to drive the main machinery of the ship (steam turbine)
- deepwell or submerged pumps are fitted to each tank
- thermocouples are fitted throughout the tanks and the surrounding area to monitor temperatures during cool down and in service.

Significant Incidents Involving Liquefied Gas Carriers

LNG sea transportation has an exemplary safety record and in 50 years and over 76,000 cargoes there has not been a major incident or disaster. There was one notable accident involving an LNG carrier in June 1979 when the '*El Paso Kayser*' ran aground at a speed of 19 knots, loaded with 99,500 m^3 of LNG. The ship suffered heavy damage over the whole length of her bottom and some flooding of ballast compartments. However, the cargo containment system was not breached and no LNG was spilled.

The LPG sector, which currently has about three times as many ships as the LNG sector, has a similar record with no notable losses.

LPG/C '*SCF Tomsk*'

October 2007

The Liberian gas carrier *SCF 'Tomsk'* had completed offloading LPG at the Coastal Petroleum Dominicana, SA facility, San Pedro de Macoris in the Dominican Republic, when the vessel broke loose from its single buoy mooring (SBM) and grounded on a reef during Tropical Storm Noel.

The vessel, still laden with approximately 5,000 tonnes of LPG, sustained serious bottom damage that caused a breach of several ballast tanks. The salvage company Titan blew down the damaged ballast tanks, transferred the cargo internally to another cargo tank, and deballasted the vessel.

Once refloated, the *SCF 'Tomsk'* was manoeuvered back to the SBM where the remaining cargo was safely discharged and the vessel redelivered to her owners. All 23 crew members were reported safe and no products on board the ship leaked into the sea.

Figure 2.46 - SCF 'Tomsk'

Products Carried on LPG Carriers

Vinyl Chloride Monomer

Product Overview

Vinyl chloride monomer (VCM) is a colourless gas with a sickly sweet odour. It is extremely flammable at room temperature, sparingly soluble in water and soluble in alcohol. Its vapours can travel considerable distances and, as they are heavier than air, tend to collect in low lying areas. The vapours may cause flash fires so all sources of ignition should be removed.

VCM is often stored as a liquid under refrigeration with a density of 0.91 gm/cc.

Physical and Chemical Properties

Chemical formula:	C_2H_3Cl
Melting point:	–153.7°C
Boiling point:	–13.9°C
Vapour density:	2.2
Specific gravity:	0.910
Flashpoint:	–77.8°C

Uses

Nearly all VCM is converted into PVC or vinyl copolymers. PVC is among the largest volume plastic produced around the world. Examples of PVC usage include piping, cable insulation, window frames, vehicle interiors and telephones. It has many packaging uses including shrink wrap, jar lids and can linings.

Hazards

- VCM is a hazardous material and must be handled carefully and properly. Between loads, the vessel must be dried, then purged with nitrogen. VCM in a gaseous form must be controlled carefully under refrigeration
- VCM is an extremely flammable vapour and liquid that produces toxic smoke. In the event of a fire, emergency personnel and fire-fighters should wear positive-pressure self-contained breathing apparatus (SCBA) and protective fire-fighting clothing
- only a few minutes of exposure to concentrations of over 1,000 ppm may cause serious central nervous system effects, such as dizziness, drowsiness, disorientation, tingling, numbness or a burning sensation in the hands and feet, impaired vision, nausea, headache, difficulty in breathing, cardiac arrhythmias, unconsciousness or even death
- prolonged or repeated exposure by inhalation causes damage to the lungs and kidneys and has been known to cause cancer, particularly liver cancer
- personal protective equipment such as breathing apparatus, protective clothing and gloves should be worn in accordance with national regulations and company standards.

Inhibitor

Care should be taken to ensure that VCM does not polymerise during the voyage. For a voyage of extended duration, it might be necessary to add an inhibitor.

Butadiene

Product Overview

Butadiene is a highly reactive, colourless gas or pressurised liquid with a mild, aromatic odour. It is extremely flammable and may form peroxides with air, leading to explosive decomposition. It is sensitive to heat, shock or heating above 27°C and is incompatible with strong oxidising agents, such as copper and copper alloys.

Physical and Chemical Properties

Chemical formula:	C_4H_6
Melting point:	–113°C
Boiling point:	–4.5°C
Critical temperature:	152°C
Critical pressure:	43.22 bar
Flashpoint:	–108°C

Uses

- Butadiene is used as a feedstock in the manufacturing of synthetic elastomers, predominantly styrene-butadiene rubber (SBR) and polybutadiene
- styrene butadiene rubber is used in adhesives, sealants, coatings and rubber articles, such as shoe soles
- butadiene can be polymerised to polybutadiene rubber (BR). The main use for BR is tyre products but it is also used as an impact modifier of polymers, such as high impact polystyrene (HIPS)
- butadiene is one of the components used in the manufacture of acrylonitrile-butadiene-styrene (ABS), which is the largest-volume engineering thermoplastic resin.

Hazards

Butadiene can enter the body through inhalation or absorption through the skin. It may affect the nervous system, is a suspected human carcinogen, and may cause genetic damage, birth defects or impair fertility.

PPE must be worn when connecting/disconnecting hard arms or working with butadiene cargo. This should include self-contained breathing apparatus and a protective rubber suit or equivalent.

Propylene

Product Overview

Propylene is a colourless, low-boiling, volatile gas with a sweetish odour. It is highly flammable and therefore all sources of heat and ignition should be removed. As the vapours are heavier than air, they may accumulate in confined spaces, particularly at or below ground level.

Propylene can form an explosive mixture with air and may react violently with oxidants.

The transportation of propylene by ship in the US must meet the requirements of 49 CFR 176 and 46 CFR.

Physical and Chemical Properties

Chemical formula:	C_3H_6
Melting point:	–185°C
Boiling point:	–47.7°C
Critical temperature:	92.4°C

Uses

Propylene is a chemical that is used in the production of a wide variety of chemical and plastic products. Commercial propylene is used to produce polypropylene, acrylonitrile, oxo chemicals, propylene oxide, cumene, isopropyl alcohol, acrylic acid and other chemicals used in the manufacture of many chemicals and plastics. Examples include:

- Propylene glycols for paints, household detergents and automotive brake fluids
- polypropylene fibres for indoor/outdoor carpeting
- polyurethane systems for rigid foam insulation and flexible foam seat cushions
- moulded automotive trim parts.

Polypropylene is one of the most versatile bulk polymers due to a combination of good mechanical and chemical properties that make it suitable for a wide range of uses.

Hazards

- Propylene is not irritating to the skin or eyes in its gaseous state. However, in high concentrations, it may cause asphyxiation and death
- propylene is an extremely flammable material and should only be handled with adequate ventilation.

Propane

Product Overview

Propane is a stable, colourless, odourless gas to which an odourant is added so that any leakage can be easily detected. It is non-toxic and presents no threat to soil, surface water or groundwater.

At one and a half times the weight of air, propane will settle into low areas and poses a risk of fire and explosion in enclosed areas.

Propane is normally shipped in its compressed liquid form at minus 42°C. In this form, propane is half the weight of water. One unit of liquid propane will expand to a volume 270 times larger as it changes state to a gas.

Propane has a high octane rating and excellent properties for spark-ignited internal combustion engines.

Physical and Chemical Properties

Chemical formula:	C_3H_8
Boiling point:	–44.5°C
Melting point:	–188°C
Flashpoint:	–104°C
Auto-ignition temperature:	468°C

Uses

Propane is used for heating livestock facilities and commercial green houses, and for crop drying. It is also used in homes for air conditioning, heating water, cooking and refrigerating foods, drying clothes, lighting, and fueling fireplaces.

Metal workers use propane tanks to fuel cutting torches, soldering, vulcanising and other processes that need a ready heat source.

Products Carried on LPG Carriers

Portable propane heaters provide a convenient source of heat. They are used to heat asphalt for highway construction and repairs and to dry concrete, plaster and fuel pitch.

Propane is a valuable feedstock for the chemical industry. About 45% of propane consumption is as a raw material for making plastic bags, nylon and other products.

Hazards

- Propane is a highly flammable liquid gas under pressure
- it can form explosive mixtures with air
- contact with escaping liquefied gas may cause frostbite on the skin. Contact with the eyes may cause permanent damage or blindness
- at air concentrations of below 1,000 ppm, propane is virtually non-toxic. However, high concentrations can cause asphyxiation.

Ammonia

Product Overview

Anhydrous ammonia is a clear, colourless gas at standard temperature and pressure conditions. It has a very pungent odour, which is its main safety feature as it can be detected by smell before it becomes a health hazard. A concentration of more than 5,000 ppm will disable a person, meaning escape is impossible and resulting in suffocation.

This gas is lighter than air and, although not readily ignited, explosions of ammonia in confined spaces have been reported. Vapour clouds can be controlled using a water fog.

Emergency personnel responding to a release of ammonia must take extreme caution and protect themselves against inhalation of the gases and mist.

Anhydrous ammonia is a liquid when compressed or cooled. It is stored under pressure to prevent vaporisation so a large volume can be made available for use. One cubic foot of anhydrous ammonia in a liquid state produces 855 cubic feet of ammonia gas. The cylinders must be regarded as pressure vessels at all times.

Physical and Chemical Properties

Chemical formula: NH_3
Boiling point: −33.5°C
Melting point: 77.7°C

Uses

- Ammonia is the most widely used compound in the fertiliser industry. It is the starting material for the production of a number of nitrogenous fertilisers, such as ammonium phosphates, ammonium sulfate, ammonium nitrate and liquid fertiliser solutions
- ammonia is used in certain alkalies such as soda ash, dyes, pharmaceuticals, vitamins, cosmetics and synthetic textile fibres
- it is used in several areas of water and waste water treatment, such as pH control, in conjunction with chlorine to produce potable water and as an oxygen scavenger in boiler water treatment
- ammonia is widely used as a refrigerant in the food, beverage, petrochemical and cold storage industries
- it is used as a corrosion inhibitor in refineries.

Hazards

- All cylinders are portable gas containers and must be regarded as pressure vessels at all times

17.5 million tonnes of ammonia was shipped by sea in 2011 with the main ammonia exports coming from Ukraine, the Middle East, North Africa and the Caribbean/South America.

- although ammonia is not considered a poison, even small concentrations in the air can be extremely irritating to the eyes, throat and airways
- inhalation of high concentrations produces violent coughing as a result of an alkaline, caustic action. If rapid escape is not possible, severe lung irritation, pulmonary oedema and death can result
- ammonia penetrates the eyes rapidly, causing anything from mild irritation to destruction of the eye. Exposure to high gas concentrations can lead to temporary blindness and severe eye damage. Direct contact with liquid ammonia will produce serious eye burns
- contact with liquid anhydrous ammonia produces skin burns on contact. Alkalis such as ammonia cause liquidisation of human tissue, and therefore ammonia burns keep spreading until the chemical is diluted
- swallowing of the liquid results in severe corrosive action of the mouth, throat and stomach
- because of its high alkaline properties, high concentrations of ammonia can cause damage to flora and aquatic fauna.

Prevention of Cargo Leaks

- The most important task on board LPG and ammonia carriers is to prevent leaks of cargo in the form of a liquid or gas
- although the leak of cargo does not cause sea pollution, it poses the risk of fire and explosion as it spreads to a large area
- if a large amount of cargo is involved in the leak, it may cause serious secondary accidents that are not only confined to the vessel, but which may also affect the environment, such as the brittle fracture by excessive cooling of the vessel hull.

Safety Designs and Innovations Incorporated into Liquefied Gas Carriers

- **Liquefied gas carriers are constructed with a double hull that provides protection for cargo in the event of a collision or grounding and from radiant heat**
- **cargo tanks are located away from the hull**
- **gas detectors and safety alarms are situated between the steel hulls and continuously monitor for cargo leaks**
- **the cargo-system safety features include an extensive instrumentation package that safely shuts down the system if it starts to operate outside of predetermined parameters**
- **ships have gas and fire detection systems and nitrogen purging**
- **should fire occur on a ship, two 100% safety relief valves are designed to release the ensuing boil-off to the atmosphere without overpressurising the tank.**

Water Drench Systems

Work carried out by several organisations, including the Health and Safety Executive, established that the application of 9.8 litres per square metre per minute of water is sufficient to protect a vessel from the effects of a pool fire or the radiant heat from a nearby fire.

Safety Designs and Innovations Incorporated into Liquefied Gas Carriers

In the event of a fire, water drench systems are activated either automatically or manually. These systems consume large amounts of water, eg a 23 metre diameter Moss type (spherical tank) would require approximately 310,000 litres of water per hour to protect it.

Water drench systems require regular maintenance to ensure that piping is in good condition and that nozzles are not blocked.

Innovations on LNG Carriers

Reliquefaction

In 2006, the cost of an LNG reliquefaction plant was reported to be around US$30 million.

The tanks of an LNG carrier enable a cargo of liquefied natural gas to be kept in a liquid state at minus 161.5°C. However, there will be some warming up during transportation and gas will naturally evaporate from the cargo. This is used in the boiler to produce some of the steam that is required for a steam-turbine propulsion plant. The boil-off gas could also be reliquefied and returned to the cargo tanks as a liquid. This makes it possible to deliver the full amount of loaded LNG to the discharge port, which can be more profitable than using it as ship's bunkers.

Diesel propulsion systems offer better fuel economy than steam turbines.

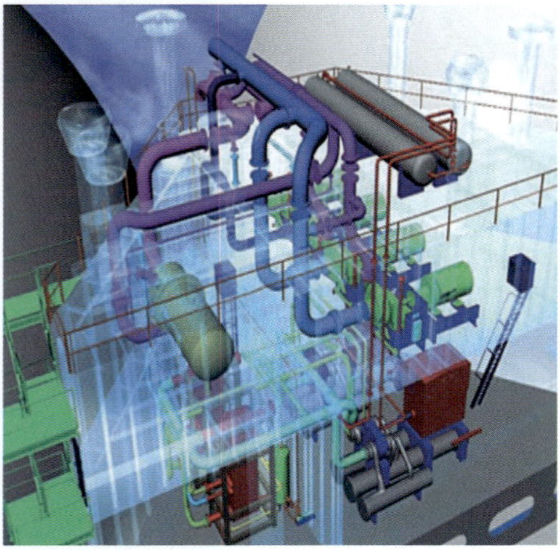

Reproduced with permission from Moss Maritime as

Figure 2.47 - Moss RS Reliquefaction Concept

Reliquefaction systems allow the installation of more efficient propulsion systems on LNG carriers. The efficiency of diesel engines is up to 50%, compared with approximately 30% for a steam turbine plant.

This higher efficiency results in lower energy consumption and lower operating costs. The potential economic advantage of diesel engine propulsion is reported as saving US$2 to 5 million per year for an LNG carrier, depending on the size and trade of the ship.

Use of a reliquefaction plant could have the following economic benefits:

- An increase in the cargo quantity actually delivered
- reduced heel required on ballast voyage
- savings in total fuel consumption
- permits more economical freight contracts
- allows tanks and lines to be pre-cooled prior to the load port with comparatively small heel retention.

The IGC Code requires a system with 100% redundancy.

The flow diagram in Figure 2.47, which is for a conceptual reliquefaction plant, shows the following:

- Boil-off gas is removed from the cargo tanks by means of two conventional low-duty (LD) compressors operating in series (the LD compressor capacity is adjusted automatically in accordance with the boil-off rate)
- the boil-off gas is cooled and condensed to LNG in a cryogenic heat exchanger or 'cold box' (the cryogenic temperature inside the cold box is produced by means of a nitrogen compression-expansion cycle)

This is a closed loop refrigeration cycle using N_2 as the refrigerant gas.

- non-condensibles, mainly N_2, are removed in a separator vessel and vented to atmosphere
- from the separator, the LNG is forced or pumped back to the cargo tanks.

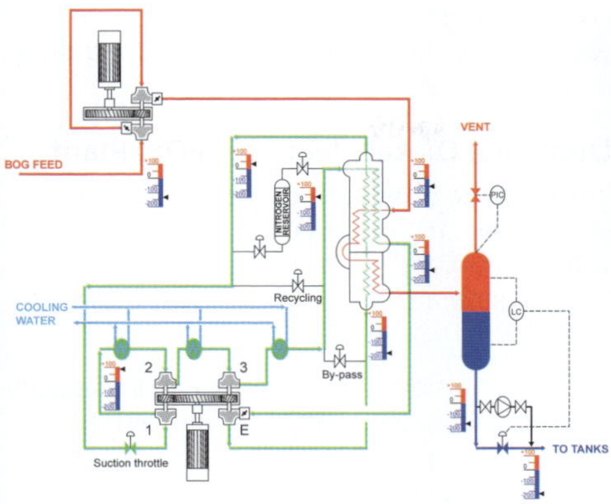

Figure 2.48 - LNG reliquefaction system process

LNG Gas Combustion Unit (GCU)

A gas combustion unit provides an environmentally-friendly solution for excess boil-off gas combustion on new LNG carriers. Such ships fitted with a marine diesel engine and using a reliquefaction plant to manage the boil-off gas (BOG) would be able to dispose of the BOG via the GCU if the reliquefaction plant was unavailable.

The GCU can handle small volumes of waste gas from the reliquefaction plant during normal operations and can be used to dispose of gas from the ship's cargo tanks when they are being warmed up.

Either of the LD compressors can individually feed the gas combustion unit. The unit comprises a gas burner, usually of the 'swirl' type, and a specially designed combustion chamber. The unit is generally sited in the ship's funnel and operation is usually fully automatic and integrated with the ship's control system.

Typical capacity range is from 0.5 up to 7.5 tonnes/hr methane.

Figure 2.49 - Gas combustion unit

Exmar

Figure 2.50 - World's first LNG regasification vessel (LNG RV)

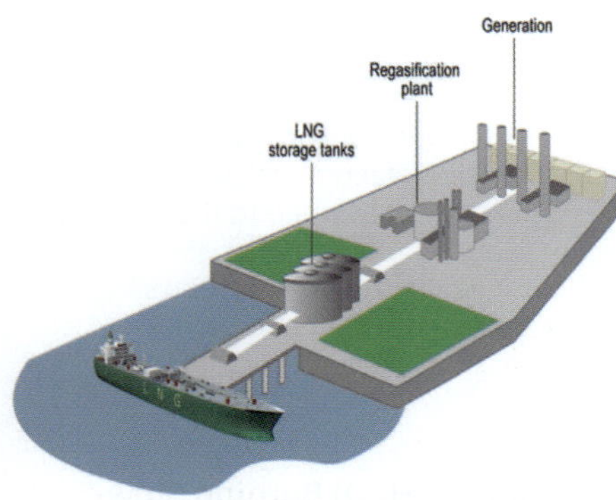

Figure 2.51 - Schematic of a typical land-based LNG receiving terminal

LNG Regasification

With the continued growth in the demand for LNG around the world, many LNG receiving terminals are still in the planning or construction stage.

A land-based or offshore LNG receiving terminal will typically take five to seven years to construct, from the initial feasibility study to the first cargo. This has provided an opportunity for the LNG regasification vessel (LNG RV).

A typical LNG RV is 138,000 m^3 and has a regasification capacity of 500 mmscfd. For the first ships of this type, which entered into service in 2005, the cost for the regasification plant was an additional US$30 million over the build cost.

LNG Propulsion

Traditional Steam Turbine Plant

A steam propulsion plant is flexible in that it will operate on HFO, BOG or both. The main turbine typically produces 30,000 to 40,000 SHP for a single fixed-pitch propeller and electrical power is derived from a 6 MW turbo-alternator plant. However, with the excellent performance history of alternatives to steam propulsion systems, many LNG carriers built since 2004 have chosen diesel propulsion alternatives for their ships. The increased cost of marine bunkers may have contributed to that decision.

Other factors include advances in technology to make the reliquefaction of LNG viable; allowing BOG to be returned to the cargo; the reducing availability of steam engineers; and the inherent limit that steam turbines impose on the practical size of an LNG carrier.

The alternative propulsion systems to steam are:

Heavy Fuel Oil (HFO) Burning Slow-Speed Diesel Propulsion

An HFO-burning slow-speed diesel ship utilises a reliquefaction plant to control BOG and return it to the cargo tanks. Propulsion, electrical power and auxiliary machinery are more like that found in other modern merchant ships, driving twin screws, with shafts fitted with clutches and brakes. This makes recruiting and training of engineers easier.

Dual-Fuel Diesel Electric (DFDE) Plant

With a single screw, the diesel-electric option involves electric motors of around 11.7 MW, with power supplied by four compact dual-fuelled generator sets with a 32 MW total capacity.

DFDE propulsion systems require high capacity electric switch gear, frequency converters, and electric motors. Long-term maintenance requirements of the many cylinders for the four-stroke engine should be taken into consideration.

DFDE can burn gas, HFO or MDO – combinations being possible with more than one set in use.

Gas Turbine Propulsion System

This system has been promoted as a good option for LNG carrier use due to the quality of gas fuel readily available on board. The system has yet to be applied for LNG carrier propulsion, probably due to the unfamiliarity of the system. Gas turbines are widely used for electric generation from the recovered gas from the wells on FPSOs, using large turbines in the 6 to 36 MW range.

Courtesy of Teekay

Figure 2.52 - Main turbine on an LNG carrier

Propulsion systems that do not burn BOG for steam propulsion must have a gas combustion unit (GCU) for the disposal of surplus BOG in various operational conditions, such as arrival port, departure port, excessive BOG after cargo loading, canal transit, and any other scenarios where the build-up of BOG will present a problem.

Liquefied Gas Trade

LNG Trade

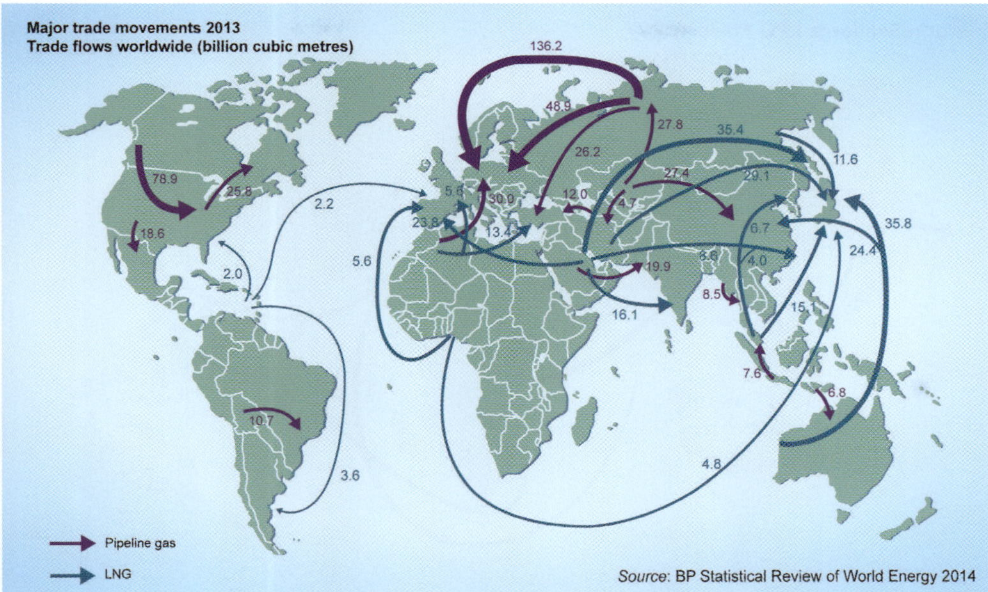

Figure 2.53 - 'British Trader', the first LNG tanker to discharge at the LNG Gate Terminal in Rotterdam, when it opened in June 2011

Liquefied Gas Trade

LPG Trade

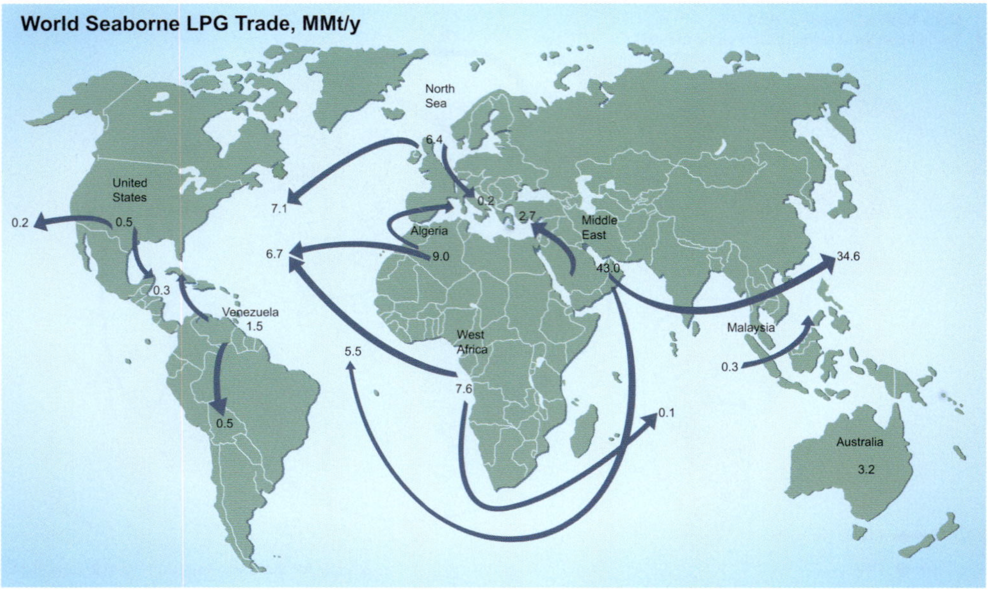

Almost half the world fleet of LPG carriers are of the fully pressurised type

CHAPTER 3

Other Ship Types

Ferries

Ferries vary significantly in size, from those operating in inland waters and harbours to large seagoing passenger and vehicle carriers.

Ferries are always early adopters of the latest navigation systems, particularly in waters such as the English Channel where they operate in extremely high density traffic and require exceptionally high levels of vigilance from their bridge officers.

The vulnerability of ferries to quick capsize, owing to the large free surface area of the vehicle decks, has been highlighted in recent years as a result of a number of serious accidents.

This type of ship is highly manoeuvrable and often operates in surprisingly difficult weather conditions, with the larger vessels suffering from problems of windage due to the exposure of their upper superstructure.

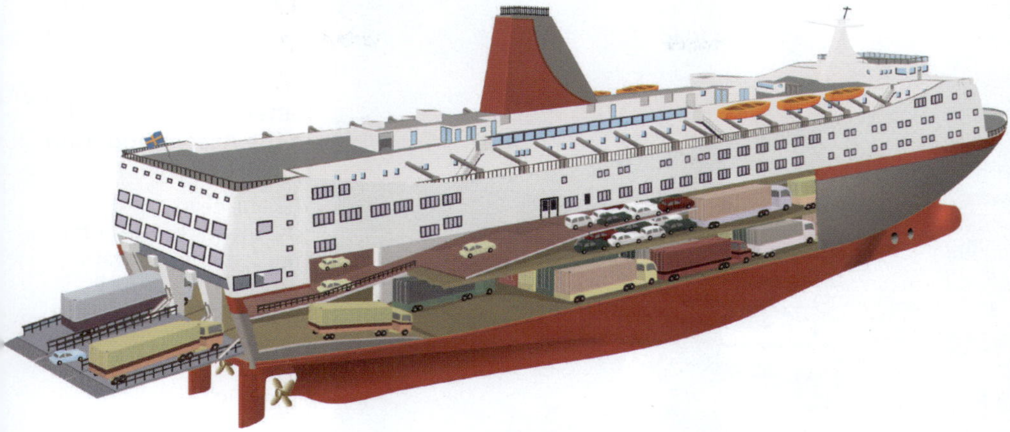

Passenger Ships

Fleet of 6,597

Source: MARISEC

Disasters and Significant Incidents Involving Ferries

'Scandinavian Star'

Getty Images

The *'Scandinavian Star'* had just been taken over by new owners and was switching trade from one-day cruises in the Caribbean to a ferry service from Norway to Fredrikshavn in the north of Denmark. This change of use required considerable ship modifications and these works were not complete when the ship sailed on her first trip from Oslo. The Portuguese crew were unfamiliar with the ship and had not been given emergency training.

The emergency equipment and systems on board were not up-to-date and there was a lack of fire doors, missing sprinkler heads, lifeboats in a poor state of repair, deficiencies in the alarm system and poor technical arrangements of escape ways.

During its first trip from Oslo to Fredrikshavn, on the night of 7th April 1990, two fires broke out in the passenger accommodation. The first fire, which started in a pile of bedclothes, was extinguished quickly. However, the second fire, which almost certainly started with a naked flame, escalated and killed 158 of the 482 on board. It is believed that both fires were started deliberately.

Shortly after starting, at around 02:00 flames and toxic smoke spread rapidly through the cabin sections on decks 4 and 5 and then further upwards throughout the ship. At 02:24 Mayday was signalled from the vessel and, at 03:20 the Captain gave the order to abandon ship. It is estimated that the majority of the people who perished were already dead by 02:45.

Factors Influencing the Development of the Fire

Panel Materials Used in the Accommodation Construction

The bulkhead panels and suspended ceilings in the corridors and stairways consisted of a core of non-combustible material surfaced with laminated plastic. This laminated plastic had high flame spread characteristics and accounted for the rapid spread of the fire, particularly since it formed an uninterrupted surface covering walls and ceiling in all corridors and stairways.

If the surfaces of the suspended ceilings had been made of non-combustible material, this would have created an obstacle to the flashover in the corridor, which could have restricted the spread of fire.

During the early, intense phase of the fire, a large amount of grey-black smoke was produced by the burning laminated plastic, which considerably reduced visibility along the escape routes. When ignited, laminated plastic produces large amounts of carbon monoxide and hydrogen cyanide.

Fire Doors

The fire doors between the various fire zones were kept open by means of magnetic catches. If the bridge was alerted to the presence of fire by one of the manual fire alarms in a corridor, the OOW was supposed to close the fire doors in the zone where the alarm signal was coming from.

Most of the fire doors were eventually closed, although the exact time this occurred is uncertain. However, some of the fire doors in the areas affected by fire and smoke remained open during the entire incident.

Ventilation System

The ventilation on board was based on overpressure in all living and public spaces and underpressure (suction) on the car deck.

In the early phase of the fire, it was primarily the pressure distribution in the ship created by the ventilation system that determined the direction of the fire. Flames and smoke were drawn towards areas of low pressure.

At the start of the fire, a sliding door from a stairway on the port side to the car deck was open. A suction effect caused the fire to spread rapidly from the stairway on the starboard side across the corridor and down the stairway towards the source of the suction.

The normal practice when a fire is discovered is to turn off the ventilation system and close the ventilation ducts by means of fire dampers to subdue the fire and prevent it from spreading through ducts. The ventilation system on the *'Scandinavian Star'* may not have been stopped until 02:30. While it was functioning, there was an overpressure in the cabins, preventing smoke from seeping in.

Evaluation of the Conduct of the Crew

The actions of the crew during the fire shows a lack of coordination and leadership at all stages, from the initial discovery of the first fire to the final evacuation of the ship. The operational command failed to function as laid down in the emergency plan and the senior officers did not mobilise their emergency groups. This meant that, for the majority of the time, the crew acted as individuals and not as a coordinated unit.

The fire doors on deck 3 could not be closed automatically and required a button to be pressed at the side of the doors. Because these doors were open, fire was able to spread along the length of the ship, into the stairwells and to other decks. No serious attempts were made to contain or extinguish the fire and no attempt was made to mobilise the fire-fighting group.

During the evacuation of the ship, the crew succeeded in disembarking those who had reached the boat decks into the lifeboats. However, the alarm only rang for a short period of time and there was no coordinated effort to wake passengers who were asleep in their cabins. Here too, there was no overall leadership and the crew failed to function as a unit.

The fact that the crew did not, at any time, act in cooperation was not simply due to the lack of leadership during the emergency itself. A large proportion of the crew were Portuguese and spoke little English. They had a poor knowledge of the ship and the emergency plan. Despite the fact that the majority of the crew were new to the ship, no fire or abandon ship drills had been carried out.

Impact at the IMO

The 1992-1996 Fire Safety Amendments: SOLAS 74/II-1

The *'Scandinavian Star'* incident raised a number of issues relating to fire protection and evacuation.

In December 1992, the IMO adopted a comprehensive set of fire safety amendments, applicable to both new and existing passenger ships. The amendments required the installation of the latest fire safety features applicable to any modern hotel, such as automatic sprinkler and smoke detection systems. They also required the upgrading of fire safety bulkheads to non-combustible materials and improved methods for assisting escaping persons, such as the use of low location lighting.

The International Safety Management Code (ISM Code)

Originally, the IMO confined itself to regulating the technical side of the industry. However, after the disasters involving the *'Herald of Free Enterprise'*, the *'Scandinavian Star'* and the *'Estonia'*, they began to focus on matters such as management, operations, human behaviour and the human factor in maritime casualties.

The IMO Assembly adopted The International Safety Management Code (ISM Code) in 1993. The Code was later adopted in May 1994 as a new Chapter IX in the 1974 SOLAS Convention. See Chapter 22.

'Estonia'

The *'Estonia'*, built in 1980, sank in the Baltic Sea on 28th September 1994, claiming 852 lives.

Disasters and Significant Incidents Involving Ferries

The Disaster

The RoRo passenger ferry '*Estonia*' departed from Tallinn (Estonia) on 27th September 1994 at 19:15 for Stockholm, with 989 persons on board, 803 of whom were passengers.

When the '*Estonia*' left Tallinn, the wind was southerly and about 15 knots, with good visibility and rain showers. By midnight, as the '*Estonia*' left sheltered waters, the wind had veered to southwesterly and was 30 to 35 knots in seas of 3 to 4 metres, causing the passengers to become sick. Shortly afterwards the fin stabilisers were extended.

During his scheduled rounds of the car deck, at around 01:00, a seaman heard a metallic bang from the bow area as the vessel hit a heavy wave. The seaman informed the two officers on navigational watch and was ordered to try to find out what had caused the bang. The seaman did so by waiting at the ramp, listening and checking the indicator lamps for the visor and ramp locking devices. He reported that everything seemed to be normal. Further reports of unusual noise, starting at about 01:05, were made by many passengers and some crew members who were resting.

At about 01:15, the bow visor separated from the bow and tilted over the stem. The ramp was pulled fully open, allowing large amounts of water to enter the car deck. Very rapidly, the ship took on a heavy starboard list. She was turned to port and slowed down.

Passengers started to rush up the staircases and panic ensued. Many passengers were trapped in their cabins and had no chance of getting out in time. Lifejackets were distributed to passengers who managed to reach the boat deck and they either jumped or were washed into the sea. Some managed to climb into liferafts, which had been released from the vessel, but no lifeboats could be launched due to the heavy list. At about 01:20, a weak female voice called "Häire, häire, laeval on häire," the Estonian words for "Alarm, alarm, there is alarm on the ship", over the public address system.

A Mayday call from the '*Estonia*' was made at 01:22, but it did not follow international formats. This was followed by a call to the '*Silja Europa*' but the power failed before the '*Estonia*' could state her position. At about 01:24, all four main engines stopped. The main generators stopped and the emergency generator started automatically, supplying power to essential equipment and to limited lights in public areas and on deck. The ship was now drifting, lying across the seas. The list to starboard increased and water started to enter the accommodation decks. Flooding of the accommodation continued with considerable speed and the starboard side of the ship was submerged by about 01:30. During the final stage of flooding, the list was more than 90°. The ship sank rapidly, stern first, and disappeared from the radar screens of ships in the area at about 01:50.

About one hour after the '*Estonia*' sank, four passenger ferries arrived on the scene of the accident, with the first rescue helicopters arriving at 03:05. During the night and early morning, helicopters and assisting ships rescued 138 people.

What Caused the Accident?

- The accident was the result of the failure of the bow visor attachments under wave impact loads
- the bow visor attachments were not designed to withstand even the rather moderate wave conditions at the time of the accident
- the Classification Society, Bureau Veritas, had no detailed rules for the design of visor locking devices and hinges
- the Finnish Administration did not make any hull surveys because the ship was classed under the rules of an approved Classification Society.

Why Did the '*Estonia*' Capsize and Sink?

- The forward car ramp was forced open when the bow visor attachments failed
- there was no collision bulkhead extension in proper position according to SOLAS
- the full length open car deck on this type of RoRo ferry makes them extremely sensitive to the free surface effects of water ingress
- the officers did not reduce speed or change course when the first indications were given of something being wrong at the bow or the forward part of the car deck
- the bow visor could not be seen from the conning position and the indicator lamps for the locked visor did not detect failure of the locking devices
- the ship was turned towards the waves when it started to heel over.

Safety Designs and Innovations Incorporated in Ferries (and Passenger Ships)

Improvements to Ferries Following the *'Herald of Free Enterprise'* Disaster

Shortly after the *'Herald of Free Enterprise'* disaster in 1987 (see page 95), the UK approached the IMO with a request that a number of emergency measures be considered for adoption. The first of these amendments to SOLAS were adopted in April 1988, including:

- A new regulation requiring indicators on the navigation bridge for all doors which, if left open, could lead to major flooding of a special category space or a RoRo cargo space
- means of detecting and monitoring water leakage into such a space
- means of monitoring special category and RoRo spaces to detect undue movement of vehicles in adverse weather, fire, the presence of water or unauthorised access by passengers while the ship is at sea
- the provision of supplementary emergency lighting for RoRo passenger ships.

These amendments entered into force in October 1989, 18 months after adoption, the minimum time period allowed under SOLAS.

SOLAS 90 Damage Stability

Further amendments were adopted in October 1988 and entered into force in April 1990. These are known as the 'SOLAS 90' standard, and relate to the stability of passenger ships in the damaged condition. They apply to ships built after 29th April 1990. Work on developing this standard began following the loss of the *'European Gateway'*, which capsized following a collision with another ship in 1982, and ended up lying on her side in relatively shallow water with the loss of five lives.

The amendments require:

- The maximum angle of heel after flooding but before equalisation shall not exceed 15°
- masters must be supplied with data necessary to maintain sufficient intact stability, including information showing the influence of various trims, taking into account operational limits
- cargo loading doors must be locked before the ship proceeds on any voyage and must remain closed until the ship is at its next berth
- a lightweight survey must be carried out on passenger ships to verify any changes in lightweight displacement and the longitudinal centre of gravity, at periods not exceeding five years.

SOLAS Amendments 1989-1992

Further amendments to SOLAS were adopted in April 1989 and entered into force on 1st February 1992. The most important dealt with openings in watertight bulkheads in passenger ships. From 1st February 1992, new ships have had to be equipped with power-operated sliding doors, except in specific cases. These doors must be capable of being closed from a console on the bridge in not more than 60 seconds. All watertight doors must be kept closed except in exceptional circumstances.

In May 1990, new amendments relating to the subdivision and damage stability of cargo ships (including freight-only RoRo ships) were adopted. These apply to ships of 100 metres or more in length built after 1st February 1992 and are based on the so-called 'probabilistic' concept of survival.

A series of amendments relating to safe stowage and securing of cargoes were adopted in May 1991, with a revised SOLAS Chapter VI 'Carriage of Cargoes' entering into force on 1st January 1994. The new chapter referred to the 'Code of Safe Practice for Cargo Stowage and Securing', which includes a number of annexes dealing with 'problem' cargoes such as wheel-based cargoes.

Safety Designs and Innovations Incorporated in Ferries (and Passenger Ships)

A/Amax

The April 1992 amendments to SOLAS included a slightly modified SOLAS 90 standard for existing RoRo passenger ships. This was phased in between 1st October 1994 and 1st October 2005 and was based on the value of a ratio known as A/Amax, determined in accordance with a calculation procedure developed by the IMO's Maritime Safety Council, to assess the survivability characteristics of existing RoRo passenger ships. A/Amax is a simplified probabilistic approach that can be used to assess the survivability standard of one ferry against another. It assumes a number of simplifications and is a rough guide that allows all countries to make relatively quick calculations on a representative number of ferries. It is not a survivability standard as such, but it enables a hierarchy of vessels to be established.

The Stockholm Agreement

In 1993, Denmark, Finland, Norway, Sweden and the United Kingdom adopted the 'Stockholm Agreement' concerning specific stability requirements for RoRo passenger ships undertaking regular scheduled international voyages between or from designated ports in Northwest Europe and the Baltic Sea. This meant that existing ferries operating on most of these routes would have to meet the requirements of SOLAS 1990.

Fire Safety Standards for Existing and New Passenger Ships

Important fire safety measures for existing passenger ships carrying more than 36 passengers were adopted in April 1992, influenced by the '*Scandinavian Star*' incident.

Further fire safety standards for new passenger ships, built on or after 1st October 1994, were adopted in December 1992.

Wave-Piercer Catamarans

The traditional catamaran is a fast, stable, two-hulled boat, but on choppy seas it gives a rough ride. In 1984, ship designer Phil Hercus successfully combined the strength and speed of the catamaran with a wave-piercing hull design called SWATH (Small Waterplane Area Twin Hull), a design that had been used to stabilise oil platforms. These new-style catamarans ride steadily above the water while their hulls plough through the waves. Constant development of the wave-piercer design has led to larger vessels with increased speed, capacity and reliability. 96 metre long catamaran ferries now operate, carrying up to 950 people and 300 cars at average speeds in excess of 40 knots. Cargo configuration is flexible and uses mezzanine ramps to adjust the arrangement of cars and trucks.

Cruise Ships

The passenger ship of the past has evolved into the cruise ship of today, although these are increasingly being superseded by the new style of high-rise 'Hotel Ship'. This type of vessel is vulnerable to the effects of bad weather at sea, particularly storm conditions, and will go to great lengths to avoid it.

Cruise ships are highly manoeuvrable vessels with advanced propulsion systems and use the latest navigation and communications facilities on board.

Evolution of the Passenger Liner/Cruise Ship Over the Last 100 Years

'Titanic'

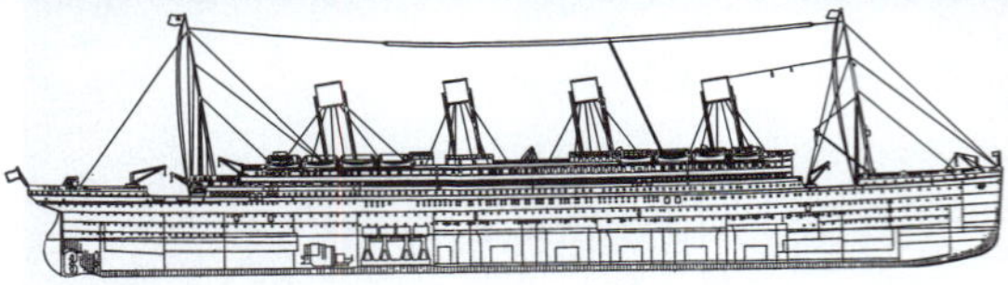

Statistics		LOA	269 m	(882 ft)
Launched	1911	Breadth	28 m	(92 ft)
No. of Passengers	2,453	Draught	10.5 m	(34 ft)
No. of Crew	1,094	GT	46,328	

'Norway'

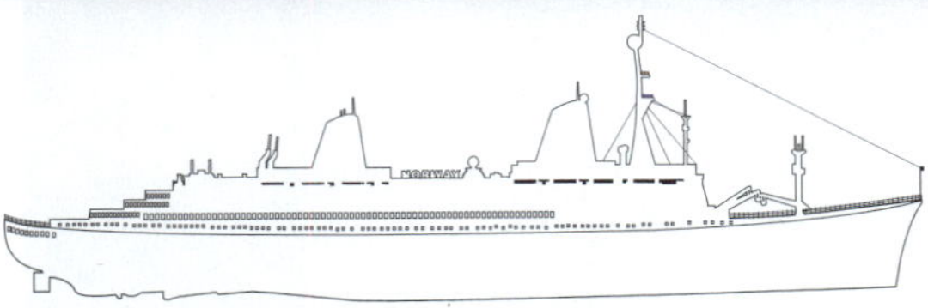

Statistics		LOA	316 m	(1,035 f
Launched	1960	Breadth	34 m	(110 ft)
No. of Passengers	2,565	Draught	10.8 m	(34 ft)
No. of Crew	875	GT	76,049	

'Queen Elizabeth 2'

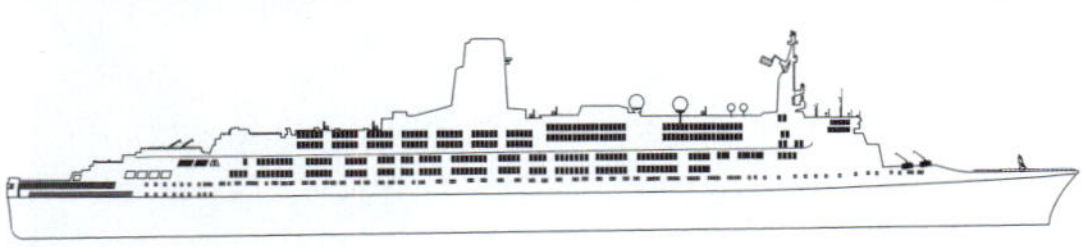

Statistics		LOA	294 m	(963 ft
Launched	1968	Breadth	32 m	(105 ft
No. of Passengers	1,892	Draught	9.8 m	(32 ft)
No. of Crew	1,040	GT	70,327	

'Queen Mary 2'

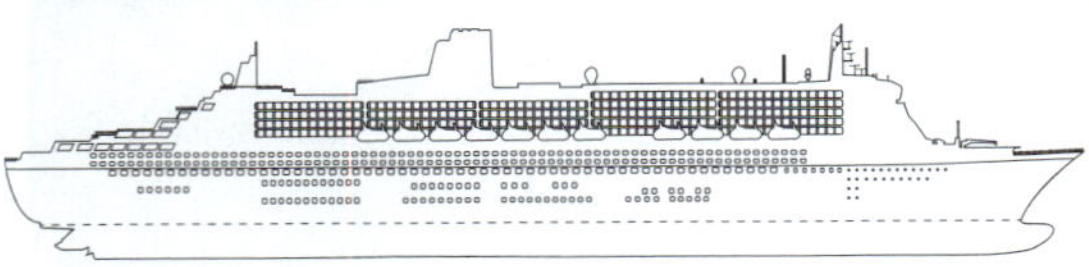

Statistics		LOA	345 m	(1,132
Launched	2003	Breadth	41 m	(135 ft
No. of Passengers	3,056	Draught	10 m	(33 ft)
No. of Crew	1,253	GT	151,400	

'Allure of the Seas'

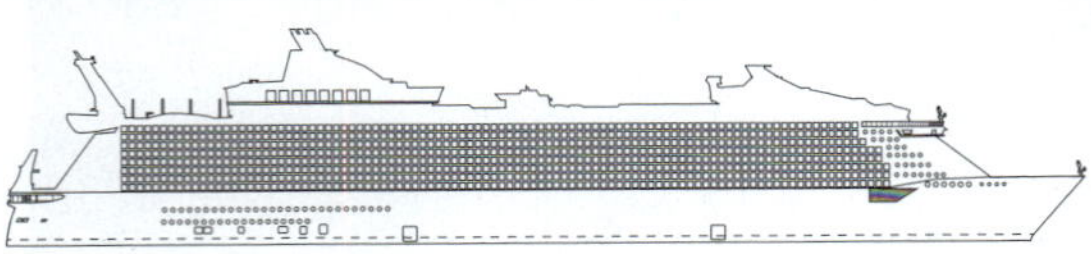

Statistics		LOA	360 m	(1,181
Launched	2010	Breadth	60 m	(198 f
No. of Passengers	6,300	Draught	9.3 m	(31 ft)
No. of Crew	2,165	GT	225,282	

Disasters and Significant Incidents Involving Cruise Ships

'Norwegian Dream' and 'Ever Decent'

On 24th August 1999, the Panamanian-registered container vessel *'Ever Decent'* collided with the Norwegian Cruise Line ship *'Norwegian Dream'* and caught fire, in the English Channel, 17 miles off the Kent coast.

At the time of the incident, weather conditions were good. The container ship was heading on a southeasterly course, bound for Zeebrugge, across one of the English Channel's shipping lanes while the *'Norwegian Dream'* was heading southwest for Dover. Approximately five minutes before the collision, the *'Ever Decent'* radioed the *'Norwegian Dream'* proposing a course alteration to starboard as they were on a collision course. However, the OOW on the Norwegian Dream was distracted and failed to respond. Other than making the VHF call, the *'Ever Decent'* took no collision avoidance action. 24 people on board the cruise ship, including a number of crew members, were hurt when the vessels collided.

The *'Norwegian Dream'* continued to sail to Dover, despite the large gash in her bow and the three containers that had fallen from the *'Ever Decent'* onto her deck. The crew of the *'Ever Decent'* remained on board to continue fire-fighting efforts while the Captain guided his ship and its cargo of flammable chemicals into shallow water, where he was able to bring the vessel to an almost upright position, from a 40° list, with water ballast. However, during this operation, the ship lost several containers into the sea.

'Sally Albatross'

The *'Sally Albatross'*, a 25,000 GT passenger ferry, constructed in 1992 from the burnt-out shell of an earlier cruise ferry, was grounded off Helsinki on 4th March 1994.

The vessel approached Helsinki with over 1,100 passengers and 158 crew on board. Conditions were poor at the time, with severe winds, ice and a temperature of minus 5°C. The crew and the OOW were unfamiliar with the ship's new automatic chart system, for which they had received little training, and so the ship was off course.

At 14:45, the vessel struck a rock, piercing the double skin and flooding the engine room. A Mayday call was issued as the ship tried to refloat under her own power, and an evacuation of the passengers commenced through the stern and onto other vessels. The ship trimmed and reached a 25° heel. A few hours later the vessel was towed further onto the rocks to prevent her sinking.

The *'Sally Albatross'* was eventually refloated on 18th April and towed into port.

Courtesy of Crociere UK

Disasters and Significant Incidents Involving Cruise Ships

'Star Princess'

On 23rd March 2006, a fire broke out on board the cruise ship *'Star Princess'*. The vessel was en route from Grand Cayman to Jamaica with 2,690 passengers and 1,123 crew members on board. One passenger died and 13 others were treated for smoke inhalation.

The fire broke out at around 03:00 on an external balcony on the vessel's port side, later thought to have been started from a discarded cigarette. The fire spread rapidly along neighbouring balconies and then onto those of the upper decks, assisted by strong winds. The fire also spread into the staterooms, but was contained by each room's fixed fire-smothering system, lower combustibility contents and thermal boundaries. At 03:20, the passengers were instructed to go to their muster stations, but dense smoke had entered staterooms and hallways, hampering their evacuation.

The crew fought the fire with water hoses from adjacent balconies and internal alleyways and, at 04:36, the Captain informed the passengers that the fire had been extinguished. The *'Star Princess'* resumed passage into Montego Bay under her own power where the passengers were disembarked.

Courtesy of Roberts

'Carnival Splendor'

On 8th November 2010, the cruise ship *'Carnival Splendor'* was on the second day of a 7 day cruise from Long Beach, California to the Mexican Riviera when a fire broke out in the engine room, cutting all electrical power to the ship and leaving it drifting 55 miles off the Pacific coast.

The fire started in one of the ship's 6 diesel generators after an internal malfunction and took around 3 hours to extinguish. All cruise ships are built with extra power supplies so if one fails another takes over. However, the *'Carnival Splendor'* was left with only auxiliary power as the fire had burned too many electrical connections to enable the ship's engineers to restart full power. None of the 3,299 passengers or 1,167 crew was hurt but they were left low on food supplies and without air conditioning, hot water, or mobile phone or internet service. US Navy helicopters dropped supplies of food and water to the stricken vessel.

Tugs were dispatched to tow the *'Carnival Splendor'* to San Diego, where it finally docked 2 days after the fire.

'Costa Classica' and 'Lowlands Longevity'

In the early hours on 18th October 2010, the cruise ship *'Costa Classica'* suffered extensive structural damage in a collision with the 86,000 tonne bulk carrier *'Lowlands Longevity'* at the entry to the Yangtze River in China.

Both vessels had been travelling in the same direction near the deep-water channel of the Yangtze River. It is reported that, as a result of a power failure on the *'Costa Classica'*, the bridge lost the ability to command the vessel.

Most of the 1,300 passengers were asleep when the order was given to put on lifejackets and assemble at muster stations, as plans were put into action for an emergency evacuation. Several passengers were injured and 3 were later transferred to hospital for treatment.

The collision caused a 60 ft long and 4 ft high gash into the passenger cabins along the starboard side of the *'Costa Classica'*. The vessel docked a few hours after the incident and, following 96 hours in emergency drydock for repairs, resumed her voyage.

Figure 3.1 - The atrium and galleria on board the MV 'Paradise'

Tugs

Tugs vary in size, from the larger ocean-going type to the more familiar harbour tug. Considerable ship handling skills are required on these vessels when towing, particularly in the confined waterways of a harbour or river. The main dangers present on tugs are breaking of the towline and capsize, known as 'girting'.

Tugs

A tug can deal with:

- The forces interacting between the tug and the vessel to be assisted at slow and high speeds
- the two principal forces acting on the tug while berthing, ie the propeller thrust and the towline force.

The aim is to minimise the danger of capsizing under all operating conditions.

Tugs and the Safety of Tankers

Tugs provide assistance in the following areas:

Escorting

This is carried out from the tanker's arrival position off the port, at speeds of 7 to about 12 knots.

Offshore berthing

This includes assistance in mooring and hose handling operations at offshore terminals with single point mooring (SPM) or single buoy mooring (SBM).

Fire-fighting and standby duties

This includes provision of a rapid response to cover fire-fighting and emergency towing within the port area.

Escorting Tankers

Tankers may need a tug escort in high traffic tanker routes and in narrow or dangerous waters. The basics of ship handling continue to apply, but the key areas for the tug are available speed, towline force and available time.

Tanker escorting is comparatively new and its need was proposed after a number of serious tanker accidents. The case for escorting is based on a risk analysis of possible and likely accidents and their severity. The primary benefit provided by an escort or safety vessel is immediate assistance to the vessel, achieved by connecting the tug to the tanker. The best connection position is at the stern of the tanker. However, in certain cases, such as fire or explosion, connection to the stern of the vessel may be hampered and the alternative is to make fast at the bow of the tanker.

While under escort, a tanker must maintain a speed that allows the tug to provide efficient assistance in the event of loss of control, taking into consideration the inertia forces of the tanker. The tanker's speed must be sufficient to allow control of the vessel in the prevailing conditions.

An escort vessel should:

- Be able to quickly and safely make fast at the stern of a tanker at escorting speed
- under normal circumstances, follow the tanker with as little interference to the behaviour of the tanker as possible
- be able to immediately exert an effective braking force
- be able to immediately apply active steering forces that exceed the tanker's own capabilities under the prevailing conditions
- be able to make fast at the bow of a tanker safely and at high speed, taking into consideration the existing pressure conditions in this area
- be able to immediately fight any fire on board the tanker while moving
- be able to take immediate appropriate action to prevent any oil spill spreading.

Offshore Berthing

At offshore terminals with single point/buoy mooring (SPM or SBM), oil is handled by floating hoses. Tugs are used to connect the hose lines to the tanker and, as these are easily kinked or squeezed, control must be extremely sensitive and precise.

Fire-fighting and Standby Duties

The modern tug is an ideal fire-fighting vessel because a vast amount of power can be diverted from the main engines to the fire-fighting pumps without rendering the engines either ineffective or incapable of keeping the vessel under control. In the case of escort vessels, effective fire-fighting could even begin while the tanker is still on passage or while reducing her speed.

At many loading and discharge berths it is common to have the tug acting on standby duties. This allows it to be quickly deployed for fire-fighting or emergency duties. In the event of oil pollution, the tug can be used to position skimmer arms, operate skimmer vessels without self-propulsion or arrange oil spill booms.

Types of Tugs

Conventional Tugs

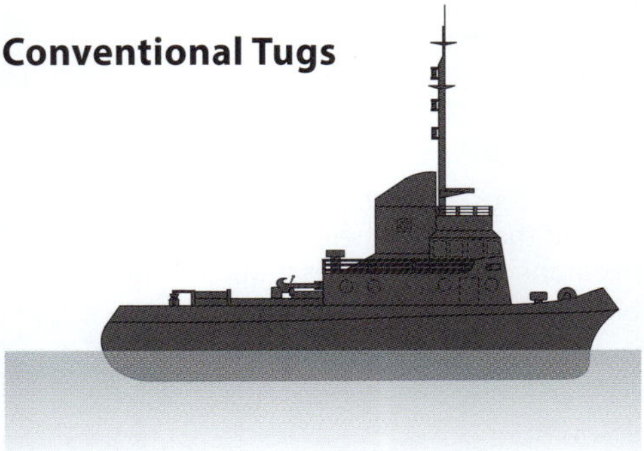

Conventional tugs are operated in many parts of the world and are recognisable by the following features:

- Its propulsion unit is generally a single-screw propeller and a standard rudder. This is similar to the configuration on many merchant ships today, although more recently they may have been replaced by a controllable pitch propeller
- the location of the towing hook, which is generally fixed amidships, tends to limit the tug's manoeuvrability and leaves it at risk of capsizing (or girting) if it gets into an awkward position, particularly if the vessel she is connected to is turning. The risk of capsize to the tug is the same, regardless of whether she is connected to the bow or the stern.

Tractor Tugs

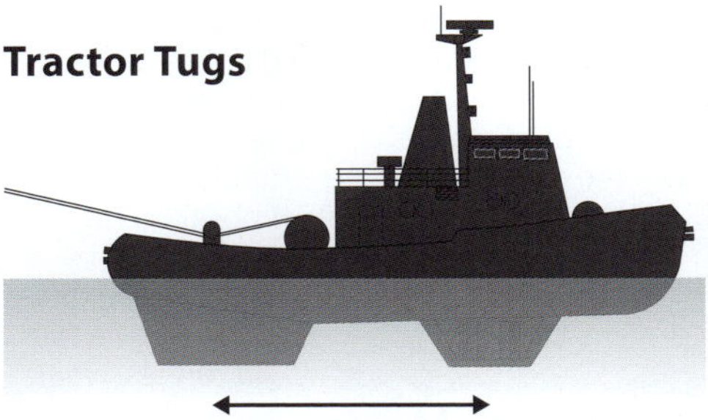

LEVEL EFFECT BETWEEN TOWING POINT AND PROPULSION UNIT

A tractor tug uses multi-directional propulsion units that consist of controllable pitch rotating blades located below the conning position in the wheelhouse. A leading manufacturer of this type of propulsion unit is Voith Schneider and, in the hands of a skilled tug master, they offer a high degree of manoeuvrability. The towline is operated from a winch drum, which the tug master can operate remotely from the wheelhouse, to increase or decrease the length of towline as required.

Tugs

Azimuth Stern Drive Tug

LEVEL EFFECT BETWEEN TOWING POINT AND PROPULSION UNIT

This type of tug combines the benefits of both conventional tugs and tractor tugs. The main propulsion units are located aft, like a conventional tug, but these units are two rotating azimuth systems, similar to those in use on a tractor tug. The towing position can be located either amidships, like a conventional tug, or forward. When secured to the forward winch, this tug can push or pull (tow). When pulling, the tug gains a huge lever effect from the distance that the propulsion units are from the forward winch position. Tugs are generally rated by 'bollard pull', the force produced by a tug, in tonnes, when pulling against a static bollard.

Salvage Tugs

This type of tug requires the highest levels of seamanship. Every emergency at sea is different, and the masters of these boats have to make decisions very quickly on scene and the crews have to be multi-skilled, often in hazardous conditions. Apart from their towing ability, these tugs have to provide high level fire-fighting and damage control.

Salvage tugs are stationed at key points around the world where they are best positioned to assist ships requiring their services urgently.

Safety on Tugs

Watertight Integrity

The watertight integrity of the tug should be maintained at all times. When a tug is engaged on any towage operation, all watertight openings should be securely fastened.

All watertight openings should be marked with a sign stating that they are to remain closed during towage operations. Any such openings used while moving about the tug during a towage operation should be re-secured immediately after use.

Testing and Inspection of Towing Equipment

Towing hooks and alarm bells, if fitted, should be inspected daily.

The emergency release mechanisms on towing hooks and winches should be tested, both locally and, where fitted, remotely, at frequent intervals to ensure correct operation.

All towing equipment in use should be inspected for damage before undertaking and after completing a tow.

Connecting and Disconnecting the Towing Gear

Before commencing a tow, the master should determine the towing gear suitable for the operation and instruct the crew accordingly.

When receiving heavy lines, the tug crew should be aware of the risk of injury through being struck by a 'monkey's fist' or other weighted object attached to the line. They should stand clear and, where possible, indicate the area that the heaving line is to be thrown to.

When connecting to a tow, the crew on deck should ensure that the towing gear is clear of any obstructions, is able to run freely and is released from the tug in a controlled manner.

During disconnection, the crew on deck should be aware of the risk of injury if the towing gear is released from the tow in an uncontrolled manner and they should avoid standing directly below. They should also be aware that any towing gear that has been released and is still outboard may 'foul' on the tug's propeller(s), steelworks or fendering, causing it to become tight unexpectedly.

Use of Bridle/Gob Rope During Towing Operations

A suitable bridle/gob rope should be used where it is identified, through the position of the tug in assisting the tow or the nature of the operation, that the towline is likely to reach such an angle to the fore and aft line of the tug that a 'girting' situation may arise.

Crew Safety During Towing Operations

Once the towing gear is connected, the deck crew should indicate this to the master, clear the area and, if required to remain on deck, stand in a safe position. If the crew are required to attend the towing gear during a towing operation, the length of time exposed should be kept to a minimum.

During towage operations, the towing gear, equipment and personnel should be continuously monitored and any change in circumstances immediately relayed to the master. This is particularly important on tugs where the master has a restricted view of the towing gear or personnel.

Safety on Tugs

During all towing operations where a tug is made fast to the tow, the crew should be aware that the tow may have to be released in an emergency situation, and that this may occur without warning.

Communications

Prior to undertaking the tow, relevant information should be exchanged and an effective means of communication established. Secondary/ alternative means of communication, where possible, should also be agreed.

Internal communications are equally important and the tug master should ensure that the crew are aware of the intended operation, including any special circumstances or instructions, and that an effective means of communication is established between the master and crew during the towing operation.

Interaction

Interaction and its effects on the tug and its handling are well known and appreciated in port/harbour towage. Masters and crew are reminded that these effects increase with speed. MGN 199(M) provides guidance on the effects of interaction.

In areas where interaction exists, and when manoeuvring alongside a tow, the master should be aware of the possibility of underwater obstructions, such as bulbous bows, stabiliser fins, etc, and areas of the ship's sides, that are to be avoided such as pilot doors. The use of bow thrusters by the vessel being towed may present a hazard to the tug.

When in close proximity to or coming alongside a tow, the crew should be aware of interaction and the effect it may have on the tug. This may take the form of sudden movement or contact and may result in loss of balance or movement of equipment and other objects.

Source 'Code of Safe Working Practices for Merchant Seamen'

Disasters and Significant Incidents Involving Tugs

'Flying Phantom'

Getty Images

The most common risk and the cause of most tug-related disasters is 'girting', where a vessel experiences athwartship forces from its towline that can lead to a capsizing or foundering. In some circumstances, however, girting forces may be used as part of normal or standard operating procedures.

The risk of girting increases as the distance between the tug and the barge is reduced, which is often done to improve manoeuvrability. Often, when the towline is shortened, the vertical angle of the towline will increase, rendering the tow pins ineffective.

On 19th December 2007, the tug *'Flying Phantom'* was girted and sank, while acting as a bow tug. She was assisting the bulk carrier *'Red Jasmine'* during a transit of the River Clyde in thick fog. Three of the tug's four crew were lost; only the mate managed to escape from the tug's wheelhouse and was subsequently rescued.

After the *'Flying Phantom's'* towline had parted during the capsize, the Pilot on board *'Red Jasmine'* completed the transit to the berth safely, with only a stern tug to assist him.

The investigation identified a number of factors that contributed to the accident, including:

- The emergency release system for the towing winch on board the *'Flying Phantom'* had operated, but not quickly enough to prevent the tug from capsizing
- there were no defined operational limits or procedures for the tug operators when assisting/towing in restricted visibility
- the routine observed by the tug's crew prior to towing or entering fog was ineffective, resulting in the watertight engine room door being left open and the crew not being used in the most effective manner once the fog was encountered
- the port risk assessment was poor, and the few control measures that had been put in place after a previous similar serious accident in thick fog proved ineffective
- the lack of an accepted international industry standard for tug towline emergency release systems.

Lloyd's Register was recommended to take forward a proposal to the International Association of Classification Societies (IACS) to develop a standard for tug towline winch emergency release systems. Svitzer Marine Ltd was recommended to derive suitable limits and necessary guidelines for operating in restricted visibility. Finally, the British Tugowners Association (BTA) were recommended to highlight to its members the importance of tug crews' emergency preparedness.

Source 'MAIB'

'North Arm Venture'

On 19th July 2009, the *'North Arm Venture'*, a 1970s tug with four crew on board, was towing the barge *'North Arm Express'*, loaded with fuel and deck cargo, from Toba Inlet to Sechelt Inlet in Skookumchuck Narrows, British Colombia.

The tug Master increased power to half ahead to proceed into the ebb current on the approach to the narrows. The barge experienced a sheer to starboard and, even though the Master altered his course to port, the barge did not follow through the turn and continued on its course. The *'North Arm Express'* overtook the tug and, pulled starboard

Figure 3.2 - 'North Arm Venture' girting on her starboard side

Disasters and Significant Incidents Involving Tugs

by the force from the towline, the tug girted on its starboard side and quickly capsized, within a few minutes of the original incident. The four crew members on board were rescued, two suffering minor injuries.

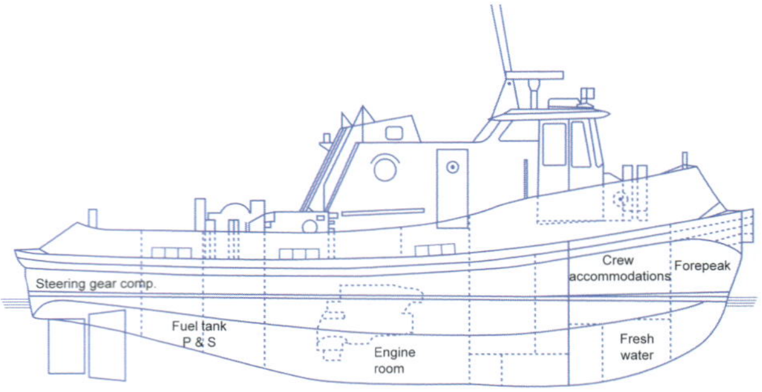

Figure 3.3 - Layout of the 'North Arm Venture'

In the absence of procedures or guidelines, the tug Master lacked important information that could have helped him decide how to respond to the girting situation. Three options were available to the Master once it became apparent that the barge was not responding and that the tug was at risk of girting:

1. Abort the towline (completely or in part).
2. Attempt to regain control.
3. Allow the tug to be towed stern first by the barge.

The Master chose what he thought would be the lower risk option, which was to try to regain control rather than abort the tow. The consequences were, in fact, far more severe and costly than if he had opted to abort.

One crew member who was asleep was thrown from his berth, landing on the deck head. However, he was able to escape via the forward open escape hatch, which had been left open to circulate fresh air. He was then assisted onto a barge by a local kayaker, who had paddled out after watching the event from shore.

Closure of Watertight Doors and Hatches

Due to warm temperatures, the crew occasionally left some of the tug's watertight closures open, to allow fresh air to circulate. At the time of the incident, several of these were not secured for sea, including the vessel's port side main deck watertight door, two engine room skylight hatches, the master's porthole and the forward escape hatch located in the forecastle's deckhead.

'Ijsselstroom'

The tug *'Ijsselstroom'* had been employed to assist construction of the new breakwater and berth at the port of Peterhead, Aberdeenshire. On 14th June 2009, a Swedish cargo barge, *'Tak Boa 1'*, arrived with a full load of rocks. The *'Ijsselstroom's'* Master deployed the tug's towline over her stern with the intention of maintaining position and heading in relation to the barge using differential ahead power on her two engines. No bridle wire was rigged and, as the lead tug increased speed, the Master was not able to control the *'Ijsselstroom's'* yawing motion. Within five minutes, the tug had sheered to starboard, girted and capsized.

The investigation noted several contributory factors including:

- Reliance by Van Wijngaarden Marine Services (owners and operators of the tug) on their masters' individual knowledge of a port rather than a more strategic staff training programme
- operational errors made by the Master and crew
- the Pilot of *'Tak Boa 1'* had not followed the necessary risk assessment required by the port nor had he discussed entry with the Master of the *'Ijsselstroom'*
- the *'Tak Boa 1's'* Master was not aware of the tug's operational limitations or towing methods.

Safety Designs and Innovations Incorporated in Today's Tugs

Carrousel Towing Design

The Carrousel system allows the towline to rotate freely 360° around the tug, improving manoeuvrability, tug response time and the safety of the tug in the most extreme braking pull situations. The Carrousel consists of a large rotating ring with a hydraulic winch that is fitted on the raised main deck level. It can be placed immediately above the centre of lateral resistance to maximise the towline forces and minimise the need for steering propulsion on the tug. The dynamic bollard pull of the tug will be around 160 tonnes. The direction of pull can be changed easily from bow to stern or vice versa to alleviate the risk of capsizing. The design manufacturers claim that capsizing as a result of towline force is statistically no longer feasible for a Carrousel tug as it offers more stability and an increase in hydrodynamic forces.

Tug Winch Design

The tug market has focused on two main areas of concern:

- Peak loads
- slack wires.

This led to the development of self-tensioning winches. The latest winches are designed to address the risks during peak and slack loads by responding as follows:

- When the load is higher than a preset value, the winch will automatically pay out the wire with high speed (100 m/min)
- when the load is too low, the winch will prevent the wire becoming too slack and pick up the slack.

These features are designed to prevent breaking of the towing wire.

Dredgers

Dredgers are commonly seen in harbours, rivers and fairways. There are many different types of craft that can be placed under the general heading of 'dredgers', including:

- Maintenance or clearance dredgers
- capital dredgers
- suction dredgers.

Dredgers

Maintenance or Clearance Dredgers

This category includes the traditional bucket dredgers seen in and around ports and harbour areas throughout the world. The purpose of these craft is to maintain the depth of water where there is a problem of silting up or shoaling. Many of these vessels used to be owned by a local harbour board, who would employ them under the direction of the port hydrographer. However, due to rising costs, this type of work is now commonly carried out by suction dredgers, hired in for specific dredging tasks.

Capital Dredging

This form of dredging is designed to enlarge existing channels, ports, marinas and boat harbour areas or to create new ones. It can also include dredging for civil engineering projects, to create trenches for pipes, cables or immersed tube tunnels, or to remove material unsuitable for foundations. There are a number of ways of achieving this including:

- Mechanical, using towed ploughs or chains and buckets
- hydraulic, using underwater high pressure fluid jets.

Suction Dredgers

Modern suction dredgers are highly specialised vessels designed to be capable of self-loading and self-discharge. Suction dredgers employed in harbour maintenance and port construction are usually built with an enclosed cargo hold, while those employed to extract marine aggregates will have an open cargo tank. Typically, these vessels will be of just under 100 metres LOA with a beam of around 16 metres and a cargo hold capacity of around 2,400 cubic metres.

Suction dredgers are designed for maximum carrying capacity and the hull form closely resembles that of a small bulk carrier or tanker, with a block coefficient of greater than 0.8. The design is such that when operating in port areas with depth restrictions they are on an even keel. When observed in open waters at maximum speed, the combination of high block coefficient and dynamic squat heel the vessel forward and they are very noticeably trimmed 'down by the head'.

Cargo is loaded from the seabed using a dredge pipe that is launched over the side. The end of the pipe, called the 'draghead', is either lowered onto the seabed or hovered just off the bottom. A large pump is used to pump the harvested material into the ship. Some vessels use an in line pump that is placed within the pipe construction and is lowered overboard with it. This arrangement gives an increase in pump efficiency and enables cargo to be loaded at a higher rate and loading operations to be carried out to a greater depth.

Prior to commencing loading, the cargo hold will be partially or fully loaded with seawater ballast. During the loading operation the material is pumped into the hold in suspension and, as the solid ballast fills up the tank, the ballast water overflows from the hold spillways that are sited at the upper level of the cargo tank. After completion of loading, there is still a considerable volume of water within the saturated ballast in the tank. This method of loading means that for long periods of time the

Figure 3.4 - Sand suction ship, Rotterdam

Figure 3.5 - Dredging machine boring head

vessel is subject to very large free surface effects. This is compensated for in the ship design with the engine room, cargo pump room and shipside tanks, including associated void spaces, providing a good level of reserve buoyancy.

After completion of loading, suction dredgers will carry out self-discharge. The method of discharge will depend on the type of operation that they are engaged in at the time.

Material obtained when maintaining the depth of a channel is normally silt and does not usually have any commercial sale value. Vessels engaged in clearance work take the loaded spoil to a designated area away from shipping channels. Usually the vessel will pump it out, but it may use bottom dump valves or a split hopper type vessel. Here, the bottom of the cargo tank will split in half by use of hydraulic rams, to enable the spoil to fall clear.

For marine civil engineering projects, one method of very rapidly obtaining material for reclamation sites is to use marine-dredged aggregates. This type of capital dredging involves vessels loading from an area where an increase in depth is required and delivering it to the construction site. The aggregate is then pumped out and dispersed.

Marine aggregate suction dredgers are usually owned by companies with interests in the manufacture of concrete. The vessels load the aggregate from licensed dredging areas, transport it to a delivery yard, often on estuary tidal berths, and then self-discharge it to a processing plant. Most marine dredged aggregate used for building material is dry discharged using the vessel's own equipment, such as drag wire buckets or a rotating wheel with buckets attached. The material is loaded onto an onboard conveyor belt system and then to the shore. Some vessels pump the material in suspension into large holding and settling tanks. However, due to the large volumes of water required, the difficulties of recycling this waste water and possible problems with contamination, it is no longer a popular solution.

Safety Designs and Innovations Incorporated in Dredgers

Flexible Spud Carrier

Strong winds and high waves can create problems for cutter suction dredgers. The waves can exert enormous pressure on the spud that holds the dredger to the seabed, straining or even breaking it. Very heavy seas can force the dredger to stop working and to take shelter in a harbour.

A flexible spud carrier can help to solve this problem by moving with the flow of the waves and handling the forces exerted on the spud. This allows the dredger to work longer in heavy seas.

How it Works

The cutter suction dredger *'D'Artagnan'* is one of the first dredgers equipped with a spud carrier system that has been made more flexible by the introduction of crossed wires. The movement of the ship results in rotation of the spud carrier, stretching the wires and generating forces in the opposite direction to the rotation of the spud carrier. The system includes hydraulic cylinders to regulate the forces in the wires so the spud carrier bends to the waves in a controlled way, preventing overloading of the spud.

Development of New Construction Materials

Dredgers are relatively heavy ships, which limits their payload and efficiency. Investigations are being conducted into the application of lightweight materials, such as sandwich panels, for non-critical parts of the construction.

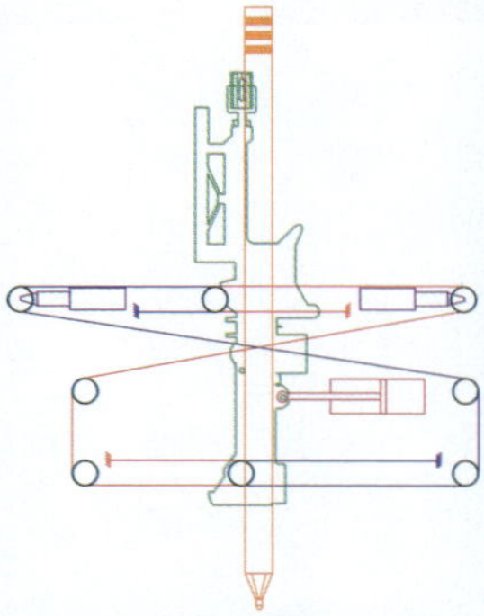

Figure 3.6 - Sketch of longitudinal buffering system on board 'D' Artagnan

Reproduced with permission from IHC Dredgers

Offshore Support Vessels (OSVs)

There are over 7,000 work boats in the offshore support sector. They support offshore locations from initial installation and commissioning to the transport of equipment, stores and provisions, the addition of new wellheads and tiebacks to the installation, and standby/guarding duties.

OSVs date back to the 1950s in the Gulf of Mexico, where oil exploration first moved offshore. The initial vessels were surplus World War II vessels and fishing boats that were used to supply offshore rigs with cement, mud, spare parts, crews, fuel and food. In 1955, the first purpose-built OSV was constructed, featuring a forward wheelhouse and a long flat afterdeck, typical of the design that is still used today.

The offshore sector remains one of the fastest growing in shipping, with new designs and larger ships constantly adding to the existing fleet. As there is a need for the oil industry to venture into deeper waters, and as older ships are replaced, newer, larger ships of increasing technical complexity are being designed and constructed. The work in support of the oil industry, which must be carried out in all weathers, requires ships with good sea-keeping ability that are handled by officers with a very high standard of seamanship.

World Offshore Fleet

Offshore vessels >500 GT = 5,073

Offshore vessels <500 GT = 2,367

Source: Equasis - 'The world merchant fleet in 2013'

OSV Ship Types

Anchor Handling Tow Supply (AHTS) Vessels

These vessels are designed to lay down and pick up the many anchors holding the platforms and related installations in position, as well as to tow the platforms to new locations. They are also able to carry supplies to the platforms.

Supply Ship

These ships supply larger offshore locations. Before the advent of dynamic positioning (DP), they would Mediterranean moor to the platforms, keeping the vessel from contact with the rig. In bad weather they would try to maintain position using engines and thrusters for as long as possible to allow the rig crane to 'snatch' loads off the deck. This type of cargo receiving is still carried out in calmer waters. By using DP, larger vessels can maintain their position alongside the platform in quite strong weather, only breaking away when the weather becomes too rough. They carry water and cement in special tanks and this bulk cargo is pumped up to the platforms by hose. Quite a number of the larger type are equipped with towing wires and winches as well as rescue craft, enabling them to have a multi-purpose role.

Emergency Response and Rescue Vessels (ERRV)

Commonly referred to as 'standby ships', ERRVs are primarily employed for the safety of those working at fixed locations offshore. Many of them are converted from older supply and fishing vessels, but newer, purpose-built vessels are now appearing. They are equipped for rescue and medical support and act as a place of refuge for survivors. They have secondary roles as guard ships and pollution control. As they are on station and may have to launch their boats in severe weather conditions, excellent ship and boat handling skills are required in addition to high standards of seamanship.

Dive Support Vessel (DSV)

The prime purpose of this type of OSV is to support diving operations on the seabed. The ships have:

- A dynamic positioning (DP) system to maintain the ship's position over the dive site
- a saturation diving system - this provides a mixture of helium and oxygen to eliminate the narcotic effect of pressurised nitrogen and enables divers to work for extended periods of time underwater, decompressing only at the end of their duties
- a diving bell, which transports the divers between the saturation chamber and the undersea workplace
- a moon pool, through which the bell is lowered. This usually has a support structure to support the diving bell through turbulent waters near the surface.

It is quite common for these vessels to support a remotely operated vehicle (ROV) in addition to heavy lift facilities.

Ships Serving Offshore Oil and Gas Installations

General Safety

Ships serving offshore oil and gas installations are often expected to operate in adverse weather conditions. Cargo operations should not be undertaken, except in an emergency, if there is any danger of the crew being injured by water on deck or by shifting cargo. For the avoidance of doubt, an emergency does not mean when an installation is short of water, food or drilling equipment.

The master of the vessel has the final responsibility for ensuring that any operation is carried out with proper regard to the safety of all those on board and that measures are taken to minimise risk.

The offshore installation manager (OIM) controls the entry of all vessels into the 500 metre zone around the installation and can modify or terminate any support vessel activity that they regard as hazardous to the installation or persons on it.

The crane driver may also terminate a cargo operation on safety grounds.

Where a vessel has open stern and deck gangway doors and a low freeboard, particular care should be taken against loss of watertight integrity by ensuring that scuttles, deadlights, hatches and ventilators are securely closed. Freeing ports should be kept clear and unobstructed to ensure the rapid drainage of water trapped on the deck.

While work is being carried out on the deck, the ship's heading and speed should be adjusted to provide as safe a working platform as possible. A lookout should be kept to give warning of imminent oncoming, quartering or following seas, or the operation suspended until the risk of shipping seas is over.

At all times when work is being carried out on the deck, there should be an efficient means of communication between bridge, crane and crew. This should be by a handheld radio on an uncluttered working frequency, backed up by a tannoy system.

During hours of darkness, sufficient lighting should be provided at access ways and at any work location.

Lighting should not dazzle the navigational watch or interfere with prescribed navigation lights.

If working on deck cannot be avoided during bad weather, lifelines should be rigged. Decks should be kept free from ice, slush and any substance or loose material likely to cause slips or falls.

Crew working in cold and wet conditions should wear waterproof garments over warm clothing. The need to avoid undue exhaustion and hands and limbs becoming numbed should be taken into account when making arrangements for relief at suitable intervals.

If it is necessary for crew to work in an exposed position, they should, where practical, wear a safety harness and lifeline, and one of the approved types of self-inflating buoyancy aids

Ships Serving Offshore Oil and Gas Installations

which would not unduly hamper or impede working movements.

Safety helmets and high visibility garments should be worn during work on deck.

Further advice and guidance on Offshore Support Vessel operations may be found in the UKOOA/ Chamber of Shipping publication *'Guidelines for the Safe Management and Operation of Offshore Support Vessels'*.

Carriage of Cargo on Deck

The master is responsible for ensuring that a competent person has checked that deck cargoes are safely secured before the vessel proceeds on passage. Areas on the deck that are not to be used for cargo stowage should be clearly marked or otherwise indicated.

To aid unloading at sea, independent cargo units should be individually lashed. Where it is not practical to lash individual pieces of cargo, then groups of lifts intended for the same delivery location should be secured together. Lashings should be able to be easily released and maintained.

All lashings should be checked at least once during each watch while at sea.

Where fitted, pipe posts should be used to restrain the movement of tubular cargo.

Discarded rope and damaged or unserviceable equipment and cargo should not be jettisoned at sea but retained for disposal ashore.

Lifting, Hauling and Towing Gear

All mixed and running gear should be carefully maintained and regularly inspected. More frequent inspections should be made where gear has had hard use or is exposed to sea and weather.

In all operations that may impose large loads or shock strains upon the gear, precautions should be taken against sudden failure that may cause injury to personnel. As far as possible, the system should ensure that the weakest element is at a point where failure is likely to cause least danger.

While gear is under load, personnel essential for the operation should stay in protected positions whenever possible. Anyone not engaged in the operations should keep clear of the working area.

Preparation for Cargo Handling

It is important to plan cargo handling in advance, both at the shore terminal and offshore. The objective of pre-planning is the safe and practical restraint of cargo carried on the deck of offshore support vessels so that personnel, the ship and the cargo may be reasonably protected at all stages of carriage and during cargo operations offshore.

The master and the offshore liaison manager or their representatives must liaise prior to unloading or backloading of cargo.

The order should be pre-planned to avoid, wherever possible, the 'slotting-in' of containers and the necessity for any person to climb on top of the cargo.

Before loading, the master should ensure he is provided with details of any unusual items of cargo, including dangerous goods, cargoes requiring special sea-fastening arrangements or heavy lifts.

Approaching the Installation and Cargo Handling

The master should pre-plan his approach to the installation with the vessel set up prior to the final approach to take account of the prevailing wind and tide, etc.

In the event that it is necessary to drop anchor, personnel should never stand forward of the windlass when letting go anchors at the installation. This is particularly important in vessels of this type because of the length of the chain and the loads imposed. Care should be taken when stowing the anchor cable in the locker.

In bad weather and under certain conditions of trim, considerable amounts of water may be shipped over the after-deck when the vessel is approaching an installation stern-on under power. Personnel should be alert to this possibility and remain in positions of shelter and safety until it is safe to proceed onto the deck.

Life-saving equipment, including a lifebuoy, boathook and heaving line, should be readily available at a suitable position on the stern and other points of particular danger when mooring and while cargo handling is in progress.

The transfer of cargo at sea is a difficult operation at any time and the risks are greatly increased when heavy or bulk items are being handled from a combined deck space in a seaway.

The master has the authority to decide the sequence of cargo discharge to and backloading from the installation.

When cargo is being unloaded at the installation, the lashings of each individual item or cargo should not be released until the item is about to be lifted as there are grave risks if all cargo lashings are removed before loading operations are begun. Once unlashed, cargo should be secured against movement as much as possible until lifted.

Personnel should be at all times alert to the danger of being hit or crushed should items of cargo swing during a lift or become dislodged through sudden movement of the ship. For this reason, all personnel should seek positions of safety during the lifting and lowering of cargo. If, in some circumstances, cargo hooks have to be held until the strain is taken, as when pipes are to be unloaded, crew members engaged in the operation should immediately move to a safe position before the actual lift is started.

Lifts should hoist the load well off the deck and swing it clear of the ship as quickly as possible.

If any backloading has to take place from the installation during off-loading of cargo from the vessel, care should be taken to ensure that the cargo taken on board is immediately secured against movement until it can be properly stowed.

It is essential that an efficient means of communication, preferably by radio link, is established by the installation crane operator and the working deck officer, who should at all times be in visual contact with each other.

Dive Support Operations

Once installations are fixed in position, deck space is often at a premium and maintaining a dive team and equipment for comparatively few operations may not be viable. Instead, the installation will employ a dive support vessel (DSV) as required. This may be a purpose-built DSV or an offshore/fishing vessel that has been modified for diving operations.

Converted vessels often have very limited operational capability due to the equipment they carry and the weather conditions they face.

During diving operations, DSVs maintain their position using dynamic positioning and employ systems used for saturation diving. Saturation diving utilises a mixture of helium and oxygen breathing gas to counter the narcotic effect of nitrogen experienced by divers working in deep water.

A high risk to saturation divers is decompression sickness (also known as the bends), caused by a reduction in ambient pressure that results in the formation of bubbles of inert gases within body tissues or blood vessels. The bubbles can damage the tissues or block blood vessels and may be fatal. To avoid this divers remain in compression chambers for the duration of their work to minimise the number of decompressions they are exposed to. These chambers are kept at pressure on the surface or maintained underwater. The process of decompression

Getty Image

Courtesy of US Dept of Defense

Figure 3.7 - Diving bell used to transport divers from saturation living quarters on the surface.

is very gradual and controlled. For very deep saturation dives a mixture of hydrogen, helium and air is used.

DSVs are among the most technologically advanced merchant ships, often with two main engines, controllable pitch propellers, and azimuth and stern thrusters to enable a high degree of manoeuvrability on station. The propulsion systems are directly linked to the ship's multiple DP systems (eg fan beam, acoustic, GPS and/or taut wire).

Remotely operated vehicles (ROV) are increasingly used, which reduces the need (and hazards) for many saturations dives.

Modern DSVs are likely to have ROV capability with large cranes and control rooms, helicopter landing decks and computerised dive control and monitoring systems.

Figure 3.8 - Remotely Operated Vehicle being prepared for deployment

Standby Vessels

Standby vessels (SBVs), also known as Emergency Response and Rescue Vessels (ERRVs), provide a number of functions to support offshore installations, although the primary role is that of emergency cover to save lives.

Installations in the UK are governed by the offshore installations (Prevention of Fire and Explosion, and Emergency Response) Regulations 1995 (PFEER), with guidance from Oil & Gas UK (formerly UKOOA). These require and make recommendations for the capability to rescue persons who have fallen overboard, cover in the event of evacuation, on-scene coordination (OSC), reserve radio duties and enforcement of installation policy.

Many of the original SBVs were converted fishing boats or other vessels. Fishing boats, although now less used, provide a stable platform from which to launch and recover fast rescue craft (FRC) and recover casualties from the water, due to the relatively deep hull. On many modern SBVs, stabilising tanks that reduce the roll period are fitted, often consisting of flume tanks. Flume tanks reduce the rate at which ballast moves athwartships when the ship rolls, due to their shape or due to baffle plates within the tank. They ensure additional weight remains on the higher side to reduce the speed and extent of rolling. These tanks are often fitted high on the ship, so they can significantly reduce the ship's GM and stability, particularly when bunkers and fuel are consumed from lower tanks during the voyage. They are sometimes mistakenly and misleadingly referred to as stability tanks.

Reproduced from Ship Stability for Mates and Masters

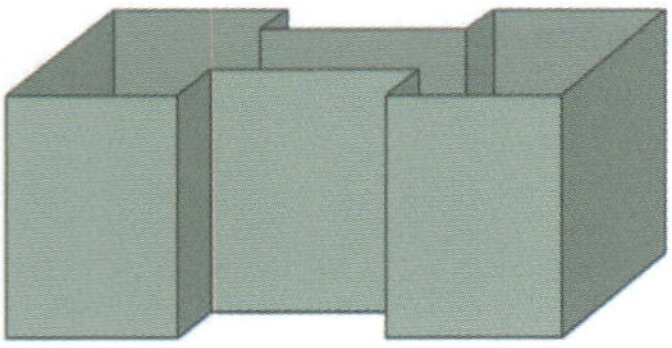

Figure 3.9 - Flume tank seen from aft

SBVs must be highly manoeuvrable and they often have twin controllable pitch propellers (CPPs), tunnel thrusters, azimuth thrusters or other similar systems. As with offshore support vessels, the manoeuvring controls can be transferred to the back of the bridge to enable a clear view during operations.

SBVs carry FRCs to enable quick response for casualty recovery from the sea. They are fitted with either outboard engines (petrol or diesel) or a single inboard diesel motor that drives a jet propulsion unit. Jet propulsion driven FRCs are very manoeuvrable, sit deeper in the water due to their extra weight and do not have propeller blades that risk injuring a casualty during recovery. Some flag States require propellers to be fitted with guards.

Daughter craft are often carried on SBVs. They are similar to large FRCs with enclosed cabins and can be launched from the SBV to provide cover for nearby installations and to help recover casualties. They also have navigation equipment and carry additional medical equipment. They increase the flexibility of the SBV, provide extra weather protection for the crew but are limited by the weather when launching and recovering from the SBV.

SBVs use climbing nets or powered recovery systems to retrieve casualties from the sea.

Climbing nets hang from the ship's side and require casualties to be able to pull themselves out of the water, which may not always be possible, especially in cold or adverse conditions.

The most common powered system is the Dacon Scoop, which is a large stiff framed net attached from the ship's side to an extendable crane that is lowered into the water. Other systems are used including powered rescue nets that swing outboard. The after end is lowered into the sea and casualties are lifted clear as the SBV moves astern.

From Standby Vessels – Masters Pocket Book Series

Figure 3.10 - Dacon Scoop

SBVs may also use rescue baskets, which are lightweight buoyant cages that can be lowered into the sea for casualties to climb into and then recovered using a crane.

SBVs are fitted with fire monitors for fighting fires on installations and protective spray systems that cover the external deck areas on the SBV itself.

Dedicated areas are provided on board for survivor recovery, reception, decontamination, medical treatment and sanitary areas. The medical equipment includes defibrillators and survival packs.

Traditional SBVs will normally remain on station for around one month, with crew changeovers taking place when a relief boat covers the installation for a few days to allow the SBV to return to port for provisions and fuel. Occasionally crew will be transferred between vessels, generally by FRC. Transfers to the installation normally only occur in emergency situations.

While on station the crew will frequently carry out training drills, when the weather permits, to ensure they can meet response times and safely complete their role. As a result the crew are generally very proficient in casualty recovery techniques including launching, recovering and handling FRCs.

Additional Duties

In addition to emergency cover, SBVs are tasked as guard vessels to prevent unauthorised ships entering the 500 metre prohibited zone around installations. Many ships will be contacted by the SBV when in transit through offshore oil exploration and exploitation areas. Part of the reason for contacting ships and fishing vessels early is that it alerts the installation to potential dangers.

Some SBVs conduct towing and other operations with tankers, normally in connection with FPSOs. The role may involve assisting with ropes and hoses and, occasionally, emergency towing drills. Such ships are commonly older anchor handlers, although some purpose-built SBVs have towing capability.

Pollution control systems such as booms and chemical dispersants are carried, but there is not normally any spill suction or containment system for on board storage.

A number of ships will fulfil some supply boat roles in carrying deck or liquid bulk cargoes to or between installations.

From Standby Vessels – Masters Pocket Book Series

Figure 3.11 - Caledonian Vanguard - Jigsaw

Jigsaw

Launched in 2006, BP's Jigsaw project uses three 94 metre Regional Support Vessels (RSVs) stationed in specific regions to provide cover for nine platforms (previously covered by six SBVs) and a fourth RSV for backup/relief. In addition, two Super Puma helicopters provide dedicated cover.

The RSVs each carry two 18.8 metre autonomous recovery and rescue craft (ARRC), which provide cover for installation overside work, although launch and recovery are limited by sea conditions. Similarly, helicopters are restricted in their operations by weather and, more significantly, poor visibility.

Disasters and Significant Incidents Involving OSVs

With the exception of the capsizing of the anchor handling tug supply (AHTS) vessel '*Bourbon Dolphin*', there have been relatively few major incidents involving offshore support vessels. Considering the demanding conditions that these vessels routinely operate in, this suggests an inherently stable design.

The construction of platform supply vessels (PSVs) and anchor handling tugs (AHTs) is such that they have a comparatively large beam for their length, small draught, large buoyant superstructure and high bow forward, but have a low freeboard aft. This provides the ship with a naturally high GM and righting lever in normal and working conditions. However, once the deck edge is immersed, a significant reduction in GZ occurs at early angles of heel. An excessive stern trim has a similar effect due to immersion.

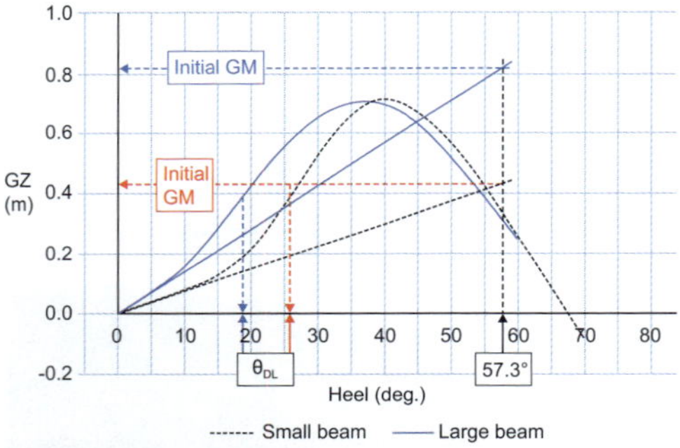

Figure 3.12 - GZ curves

The following factors can affect stability:

- Simultaneously loading and discharging bulk liquids and solid deck cargo at sea
- the effect of wind and swell on dynamic stability
- when ballasting is undertaken at sea, the full tank FSE needs to be applied as soon the operation is commenced

- water can be trapped in deck cargo pipes and allowance should be applied in accordance with the IMO Code on Intact Stability
- some ships have stabiliser tanks that are used to reduce the roll amplitude but also reduce the metacentric height (GM).

During cargo operations, it is recommended that cargo with a higher centre of gravity (deck cargo) is discharged first and cargo with a lower centre of gravity (bulk liquids, barites, etc) is loaded first. Operational requirements, including installation priorities and available storage space, may complicate this, but the stability of the vessel must take priority. Similar

Courtesy of Ebbe Holsting

stability problems are likely to be experienced during anchor handling operations due to the weight of equipment being handled and the resultant forces exerted on the vessel.

AHTS vessels have complicated construction requirements as, in addition to cargo carrying flexibility, they require high capacity thrusters, engines and winches to provide the necessary bollard pull involved in rig moving operations. The effect of an anchor chain under tension and its angle of attack (the direction at which the forces act on the vessel) will dynamically affect stability.

All such factors, ie bulk liquids and their FSE, any cargo weight (eg retrieved wire on the winch drum), cable tension, shipped water, propulsion equipment, environmental forces and buoyancy, combine to form dynamic and changing effects on the ship's righting lever. It is essential that the ship's capabilities, requirements and limitations are fully understood by the ship builders, operators, masters and officers to ensure the safety of the vessel. In the case of the

'*Bourbon Dolphin*', several of these factors were not fully understood or communicated and culminated in disaster.

'*Bourbon Dolphin*'

The '*Bourbon Dolphin*' was an AHTS vessel that capsized on 12th April 2007 while performing anchor handling duties for a drilling rig in the North Sea off the coast of Shetland. The ship was involved in moving the drilling rig '*Transocean Rather*' in depths of 1,100 m. The rig had 8 anchors with mooring lines 3,500 m long, constructed of chain and wire sections.

While laying the final anchor, after all the chain had been run out, the vessel began to drift east and requested assistance. The '*Highland Valour*' tried unsuccessfully to secure the chain. When drifting towards another anchor mooring, the '*Bourbon Dolphin*' tried to manoeuvre west at the same time as the chain shifted from the inner starboard towing pin to the outer port towing pin, creating a serious list to port. The starboard engine stopped, the vessel initially righted, then listed again and rolled over to her port side.

Eight lives were lost in the accident including that of the Master and his 14-year-old son. This accident forced a re-evaluation of the design and operation of AHTS vessels. It highlighted weaknesses in the ship design and failures in the safety systems of the ship operator and the rig. The Norwegian Minister of Justice and Police implemented a special inquiry commission to investigate the causes of the accident and to recommend countermeasures to prevent such occurrences in the future. Some of the main findings of the commission are set out below:

The '*Bourbon Dolphin*' was of a new design and was a relatively compact ship combining the functions of a PSV and an AHT. However,

- Critical stability issues were not clearly communicated to the company by the builder
- under certain loaded conditions, the ship had insufficient stability in relation to lateral forces
- the anchor handling capability provided by the builder was unrealistic
- the pulling power of the winch was over dimensioned in relation to the vessel's stability capacity.

She was a new design for the company, who:

- Should have undertaken greater critical assessment of her ability and characteristics at the building or operational stages
- failed to provide ship-specific operational procedures within the SMS for anchor handling operations. There was also a lack of risk assessment
- failed to account for a material reduction in bollard pull when thrusters were used
- did not stipulate sufficient requirements for crew qualifications; there was a lack of experience within the crew
- did not provide the Master with sufficient time or overlap with the outgoing Master to familiarise himself with the ship before taking command.

During the incident, a number of critical factors were identified:

- The roll reduction tank was most likely in use, reducing the metacentric height

Courtesy of Ebbe Holsting

Disasters and Significant Incidents Involving OSVs

- the chain was lying against the outer starboard towing pin as the inner starboard pin was depressed, causing a shift in the angle of the cable
- lack of communication and coordination together with human error were demonstrated on the rig and the ship during the operation
- weather and current conditions adversely affected the vessel's residual stability while listed
- the vessel's stability characteristics were insufficient for the conditions and the operation being attempted
- the vessel's current load condition
- an unfavourable heading in relation to external dynamic forces
- changed point of attack from the weight of chain aft (depressing of the towing pin)
- reduced manoeuvrability due to blackout of the starboard engines
- a lack of understanding concerning the chain emergency release, which should have been activated earlier.

In common with other ships that have forward wheelhouses and operate in harsh sea areas, offshore vessels have experienced instances where bridge windows have been smashed and the bridge has been swamped by heavy seas. This danger can be reduced by careful adjustment of speed and heading, irrespective of any external commercial or operational pressures.

Safety Designs and Innovations Incorporated in Offshore Support Vessels

Diesel Electrical Propulsion

Electric motors are compact and this allows them to be fitted into the confined space available on an OSV. The positive effect on propulsion makes it a cost effective option, suitable for straight shaft or azimuth propeller drives. A diesel electric drive eliminates the need for a long intermediate propeller shaft. The conventional main engine arrangement is replaced by alternator engines. This arrangement can be located out of the space below deck, to allow more cargo carrying capacity. If a high voltage system (6.6 Kv) is needed, a larger switchboard, generators and transformers with specially designed air conditioned compartments will be required. High voltage systems require less bulky equipment and cabling and offer greater efficiency.

Electric Podded Propulsion System (Azipod)

The requirement for offshore support vessels capable of operating in ice is increasing and the azipod is the leading propulsion system for ice-going and ice-breaking vessels. An azipod is unique, having a short, gearless shaft transmission from motor to propeller, full torque in all directions and high manoeuvrability and redundancy features which prove extremely advantageous in ice operations.

Voith Schneider Propulsion (VSP)

The Voith Schneider propulsion system has a reputation for reliability, even if only one propulsion system is available, as it offers a built-in level of redundancy. Tests demonstrate that the Voith Schneider propeller allows effective roll stabilisation, both when sailing and while the vessel is stationary. VSP offers a fast and precise control of thrust level which results in a high degree of manoeuvrability – a crucial requirement of offshore support vessels.

Anchor Handling in Deep Water

Anchor handling tugs require increasingly powerful main engines to tow drilling rigs and perform anchor handling operations. This is particularly important with the increase in deep water exploration. Heavier anchoring gear is required to move larger drilling rigs, to handle

Safety Designs and Innovations Incorporated in Offshore Support Vessels

their anchors, chain and mooring lines and to meet the demands of the new generation of deepwater rigs and platforms.

An anchor handler may well have a main engine power that exceeds 25,000 hp and exerts a bollard pull exceeding 300 T. The anchors managed by these vessels require winches exceeding 600 T brake capacity and rig chain locker capacities that approach 1,000 m^3. The vessels themselves may have a beam that is greater than 25 m and rollers in excess of 4 m diameter. Dynamic positioning has, therefore, become a standard requirement.

Dynamic Positioning - Basic Principles

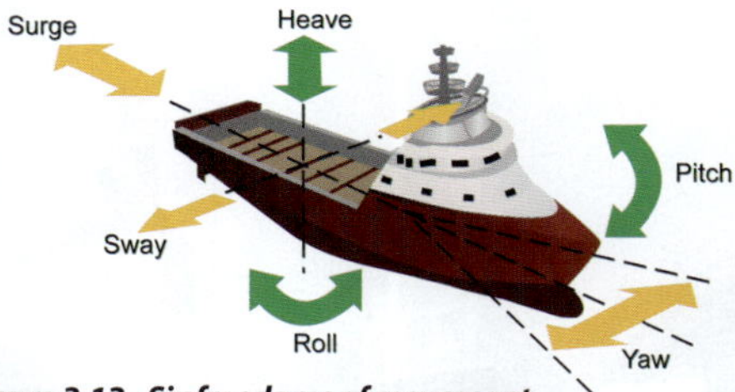

Figure 3.13 - Six freedoms of movement

A ship experiences a number of forces from wind, waves, swell and current and its response to these forces, in terms of change in position, heading, speed, roll and pitch, can be measured. A dynamic positioning system computes the forces that the thrusters must produce to control the vessel's motion in three degrees of freedom - surge, sway and yaw - in the horizontal plane.

Dynamic positioning (DP) is a system controlled by computers that maintains a vessel's position and heading on station, through integrated operation of the vessel's own propellers and bow and stern thrusters. Offshore vessels that operate in close proximity to offshore installations or require accuracy and position keeping ability will often be fitted with DP.

There are three classes of DP:

- DP 1 has no redundancy. Loss of station keeping ability may occur in the event of a single fault.
- DP 2 has built-in redundancy so that no single fault in the DP system will result in system failure.

  Loss of station keeping ability should not occur should a single fault occur to an active component or system, ie generators, thrusters, switchboards, etc.
- DP 3 requires duplication of the DP controls, power supply, bilge drainage, vessel stability and fire equipment, such that, even in the event of an emergency or disaster on board, the DP remains fully operational.

  Loss of station keeping ability should not occur from any single failure including a completely burnt fire subdivision or flooded watertight compartment.

For further information on Dynamic Positioning, refer to page 256.

Rules to Improve Design to Prevent Contact Damage to Side Structures

Contact damage to the side structures of an offshore supply vessel (OSV) might include local denting of plating between stiffeners, permanent deformation in side frames, buckling of deck beams and local buckling in web frames and decks. When an OSV comes alongside a pier or an offshore installation, it may come into contact with structures that may expose its side to very large local loads, resulting in contact damage.

Traditionally, contact damage was rarely addressed in structural design codes, or was treated in a rather simplistic manner. However, in the recent formulation of IACS common scantlings rules, design formulae are included that provide guidance on the design of side shell plating against a possible contact event.

Improvements in Noise Levels on Board for Crew Comfort

Work on board ship in an offshore environment is demanding. During construction, particular attention is given to reducing potential vibration and noise levels within the ship, to improve the comfort of the crew. There is an optional Comfort Class notation, which addresses a higher level of crew comfort on board.

These rules incorporate ISO Standard 6954-1984 '*Mechanical vibration and shock – Guidelines for the overall evaluation of vibration in merchant ships*', as well the IMO Noise Code, Resolution A.468(XII), '*Code on Noise Levels on Board Ships*'. According to this notation, the noise is measured on a scale of 1 to 3 with 1 being the highest level.

Floating Production, Storage and

There are numerous small oil fields around the world that have never been put into production because the costs involved in developing the field and laying pipelines far exceed the value of the recoverable oil reserves. Due to the relatively cheap charter costs of an FPSO, these small, more marginal fields can now be exploited. The success of the FPSO has led to them being used for the exploitation of deepwater oil fields.

FPSOs have tended to be converted oil tankers primarily for the production of oil, but there are a few in service for the storage of gas. Since the late 1990s, there has been an increase in the number of purpose-built units.

Offloading (FPSOs)

Number of FPSOs worldwide: 186

Source: FPSO.com 2014

Conversion

Conversion is relatively inexpensive and takes less time than building a new unit. It involves the installation of an oil and gas process plant, gas turbine power generation, a revolving turret/mooring system to allow the FPSO to weathervane, a helicopter landing deck and an offloading facility.

Disadvantages of Converting

The main disadvantage of a converted FPSO is that the design and equipment installed are constrained by the capabilities, size and stability characteristics of the tanker. The tankers being converted have usually been operational for a number of years, so fatigue and increasing maintenance costs of an elderly ship determine the lifespan of viable operation as an FPSO.

A purpose-built unit is more expensive than a converted unit but has fewer design limitations.

Types of FPSO

There are many different types of FPSO operating around the world. The two main designs are:

1. Discharge/Export to Offloading/Shuttle Tanker

The FPSO stores the crude in her tanks until nearly full. A shuttle tanker is then connected and the crude is discharged for transportation to a discharge port.

Advantages

The main advantage for this type of operation is that the FPSO can operate on marginal fields where it is too expensive to lay a pipeline system. The shuttle tanker can be instructed to discharge the crude at any port that enables the oil company to obtain the best price for the oil on the spot market.

Disadvantages

Using shuttle tankers is weather dependent. In bad weather, the shuttle tanker may not be able to connect to the FPSO's offloading hose and, depending on the remaining space available in the storage tanks, production may have to stop. The charter cost of the shuttle tanker has to be met out of the operational cost of the FPSO, reducing profits.

2. Discharge/Export to Pipeline

The oil is processed on board the FPSO and is then exported via a fixed pipeline to a receiving oil refinery or storage terminal. Fixed pipeline FPSOs operate on larger oil fields where it is financially viable to lay the pipeline.

Advantages

When using a fixed pipeline system, the FPSO does not rely on exporting to a shuttle tanker and so has no charter cost for the tanker and is not weather dependent. Production is continuous as long as the receiving refinery is operational and has sufficient space in its storage tanks.

Disadvantages

If the receiving refinery is shut down for a prolonged period of time, eg for maintenance, or the pipeline becomes unavailable, the FPSO would have to produce to storage. A shuttle tanker may have to be chartered on the spot market, which is far more expensive than having one on permanent charter. A spot charter shuttle tanker may not be available, which would mean that production would have to stop.

FPSO Operations and Characteristics

An FPSO is used for producing oil from an oil field. Well fluids brought on board the FPSO rise from the oil wells by natural reservoir pressure, which is controlled by choke valves at the wellheads. The well fluids are passed through a number of separation vessels, which act like weirs, for the separation of water and gas from the oil. The oil then passes through a filter system, which removes silt and sand. Chemicals are injected into the oil to help reduce the build-up of wax and hydrocarbon condensates and it is then exported by pipeline or stored in the cargo tanks.

Storage

The produced oil is stored in the ship's cargo tanks for later offloading to a shuttle tanker. Most FPSOs have storage capacity for approximately 10 to 14 days' production. Stored oil is discharged to the shuttle tanker using an offloading hose and the FPSO's main cargo pumps. The volume of oil exported is metered on the FPSO and measured on the shuttle tanker.

Shuttle Tanker

Shuttle tankers are the most commonly used method of transporting oil from the FPSO to the discharge port. Shuttle tanker(s) serving an FPSO are typically on a 7 to 10 day round trip schedule, which gives a small amount of leeway for any delays due to bad weather. Careful scheduling is essential to avoid the field operator having to shut down the oil processing plant should the tanks become full.

Gas

Gas that is separated from the oil on board is used as fuel for the gas turbine generator or reinjected into the oil field so that reservoir pressure can be maintained. Any remaining gas is flared off. Waste heat produced by the turbines is used to make steam for the operation of utilities such as steam-driven pumps, accommodation temperature control and as a heat transfer medium for liquids and gases requiring a temperature increase.

Pipeline Export

Some FPSOs are linked into a pipeline system. This enables them to export the oil directly from the process system without first storing it in the ship's cargo tanks. The separated gas may also be exported by pipeline. The cargo tanks are still occasionally used for oil storage when problems arise at the oil receiving station, such as maintenance shutdowns, emergencies, etc. The oil in the tanks is generally exported utilising the ship's cargo pumps.

Relocation

Once the field life or charter has come to an end, the FPSO may be moved to another field. If the building costs have already been covered from the first oil field worked, the future profits for the owner may be very good.

Refitting

Between charters, an FPSO may be taken to a shipyard for refitting. The cost of this compared to refitting a conventional fixed platform is significantly lower.

Decommissioning

The decommissioning costs of an FPSO at the end of its working life are a fraction of those of a fixed conventional platform. An FPSO can be sailed or towed to a ship-breaking yard for dismantling while a fixed platform has to be dismantled on site. The FPSO's owner will receive payment for scrap from the ship breakers for the vessel.

Pipe and Cable Laying Ships

Pipe Laying Ships

Pipe laying has been conducted in depths in excess of 2,500 metres and this is set to increase as ever deeper exploration is required.

A dynamic positioning system is essential on pipe laying vessels to maintain course and speed during the pipe laying operations.

The '*Solitaire*' is the world's largest pipe laying vessel at 300 metres long and 96,000 Dwt. She was originally built as a bulk carrier in 1972 and was subsequently converted into a pipe laying vessel at the Swan Hunter Shipyard in the UK. The vessel has been operational since 1998, can accommodate up to 420 crew and has a pipe capacity of 22,000 tonnes, meaning she is less reliant on offshore pipe supply.

In 2007, the '*Solitaire*' set the record for ultra-deep water pipeline by laying pipe to a depth of 2,775 metres. She is capable of laying more than 9 km of the heaviest pipe per day.

Cable Laying Ships

Despite the sharp increase in satellite communications, it is still necessary to lay fibre optic cables and this, along with the maintenance of existing cables will ensure the continued need for cable ships. In 2009, it was reported that across the Atlantic alone there were over 50 cable breaks to locate and repair.

Submersible craft (ROVs) can operate from cable ships to repair breaks in shallow waters, but in deeper waters the cable must be grapple and each end brought to the surface for repair.

Figure 3.14 - Cable laying vessel 'Asean Explorer'

Figure 3.15 - Cable laying ship, Sognefjord, Norway

Figure 3.16 - Pipe laying vessel the 'Solitaire'

Seismic Survey Ships

Seismic survey activity across the world has increased and will continue to do so as new technologies allow exploration for oil to be carried out in deeper and more hostile environments.

Seismic survey ships, carrying increasingly sophisticated and expensive equipment, are now encountered in deeper waters and subzero environments.

12.6t
H
21

Seismic Survey Ships

Courtesy of CGG

A seismic survey records and compiles data about the profile of the seabed and the earth's crust by using high energy, low frequency sound waves that penetrate the sea floor. The results show where hydrocarbons are likely to be found, providing data that can be interpreted to show rock formations, etc. Seismic surveys may also be carried out in mature field areas to assess geological problems encountered during production. Due to their lack of manoeuvrability and cargo field of operation, seismic vessels may pose a hazard to supply and standby vessels tending to the rig or traffic passing in the vicinity.

Vessels are chartered on either a daily rate or by the amount of area they cover. Daily rates for a large seismic survey vessel conducting 3D or 4D data acquisitions can be between US$300,000 to 400,000 per day.

The Vessels

Seismic survey ships are specialist vessels that can be up to 90 metres in length and can travel at speeds of up to 9 knots. They have a crew of between 30 and 70 people, made up of mariners, engineers and specialist survey staff.

The vessels cannot operate when waves are higher than about 3 metres.

The Operation

The data is acquired by the transmission of an acoustic signal from underwater equipment, commonly referred to as 'guns', towed astern of the vessel. The guns transmit the signal to the seabed at predetermined intervals and the returning signal is received by seismic cables or 'streamers'. The returning signals have bounced off formations in the earth's crust and this data is used, either on board or ashore, to produce a 2, 3 or 4 dimensional profile of the survey area's seabed.

A vessel may tow up to 10 streamers, each 100 metres apart, at lengths extending up to 5 nautical miles, which are usually 6 to 12 metres below the surface. Positioned along the streamers are a series of hydrophones and hydroplanes, known as 'birds', which are fitted with wings to control the depth of the streamer. The end of the streamer is illuminated by a 'tailbuoy', a float that is conspicuously coloured and at night may also exhibit a flashing white light, usually the International Signal Code 'uniform'. They can also be detected by radar.

As the streamers must be kept horizontally spread apart, 2 'barovanes' are towed either side of the vessel by spread ropes. A barovane is a tubular float, approximately 4 metres in length, with vanes vertically attached below. As the barovane is towed through the water, hydrostatics acting on the vanes pull them away from the vessel to the required spread distance.

For the streamers to spread apart there must be a continuous water flow over the vanes. Seismic ships are, therefore, unable to stop and must maintain an operational speed of between 4 and 6 knots. If the ship loses

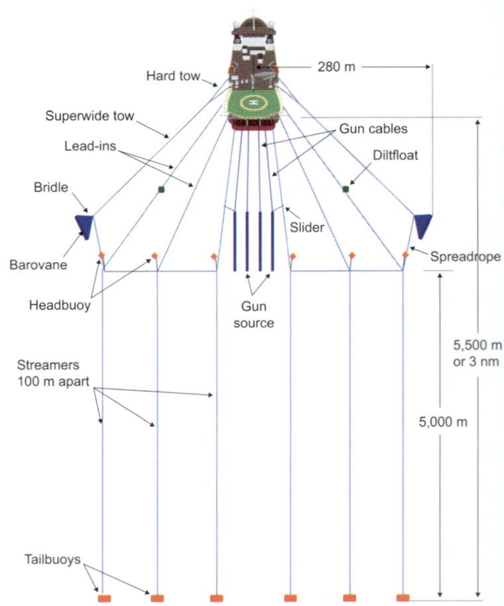

Figure 3.17 - Seismic array line diagram

propulsion, the effect on the streamers can be catastrophic, with the potential loss of highly expensive equipment and production time.

Information Gathering

The survey ship must inform all relevant authorities prior to starting a prospect. Information is then broadcast as a navigation warning via Sat C, NAVTEX, Ts & Ps, etc. The information will include:

- The vessel's name
- coordinates of the prospect boundary areas
- length of streamers, etc.

Securite safety navigation broadcasts are also made on VHF channel 16 by the OOWs on board the survey ship or the guard vessel(s) if in attendance. The use of automated identification systems (AIS) and integrated bridge systems has made the task of guiding vessels clear of seismic gear more straightforward. A display showing the extent and position of the streamers in relation to a plotted target when approaching the survey area makes it possible for the OOW to guide safely clear while selecting the best possible route rather than deviating too far from the intended track.

Once the vessel is safely past and clear of the operation, the survey ship should inform it that they are now clear and that it is safe to resume their original track.

What to Expect

When approaching a survey area, the following can be expected:

- **Vessels carrying out seismic survey operations will be engaged in towing and will be severely restricted in their ability to manoeuvre due to the nature of their work. COLREGs should be adhered to**
- **a safe passing distance should always be given to the survey ship and her gear. Securite messages regularly broadcast from the survey ship will inform all shipping within the vicinity of the passing distances required. As a guide, this would normally be two to three miles ahead or either side of the survey ship and its gear, and two to three miles astern of the tailbuoys marking the end of the streamers. These distances are likely to vary, depending on the proximity of any other navigational hazards and the feather angle on the streamer cables**
- **it is common to see guard vessels in convoy with a survey ship. Their job is to mark the extremities of the operation and to 'chase away' any vessels not maintaining a safe distance from the operation. A vessel that is not keeping a sufficient distance can expect to be closely approached by the guard vessel. White flares will be fired into the air to attract attention, the guard vessel whistle used and light signals flashed with an Aldis lamp. Once the identity of the vessel that is straying into the area has been established, it will be contacted by VHF radio and a request made for clearance**
- **the survey vessel often launches its workboat to conduct repairs to the seismic equipment. These small boats are usually fitted with radar reflectors and are conspicuously coloured. They are not normally seen in open water, but instead stay close to the streamers and the survey ship**
- **a survey can last for several months and the survey vessel will rarely go into port, meaning that all replenishment and crew changes are carried out at sea. The guard vessels can also act as supply vessels, going alongside for stores and fuel transfers or ahead of the survey ship to conduct over the bow re-fuelling in tandem. During this operation, the supply and survey ship are connected by a distance line and a fuel hose and are to be regarded as one composite unit**
- **most seismic survey ships have helicopter landing decks and there may be an increased amount of helicopter operations in the survey area. This is largely due to the prolonged periods between port calls and the necessity for crew changes and supplies.**

Research Ships

There are several different types of research vessels, including oceanographic, ice and hydrographic.

A research vessel is specially designed to conduct often various research roles at sea. Certain roles can only be conducted by specific hull types, eg research in ice, where the hull is ice strengthened.

Some of these roles can be combined into a single vessel, but others require a dedicated vessel. Due to the demanding nature of the work, research vessels are often constructed around an icebreaker hull, allowing them to operate in polar waters.

US Coast Guard photo by Petty Officer Patrick Kelley

Oceanographic research vessels conduct climatological research on both the water and the air in addition to surveying the seabed. These vessels normally carry divers and Remotely Operated Vehicles (ROVs). An example of an oceanographic research vessel is NOAAS Ronald H Brown (shown below right).

Polar research vessels are built with an ice-strengthened hull, particularly for use in the Antarctic. These vessels are often built with substantial cargo carrying capacity for the carriage of stores to Antarctic research bases. An example of a USCG Polar Research Vessel is shown below.

Hydrographic survey vessels are designed to conduct surveys of the physical features of the ocean and coastal areas for the production of nautical charts. These vessels can also conduct seismic surveys and the geological data that is captured can be used by geologists looking for rock types that are likely to contain oil beneath the seabed.

The '*Ronald H Brown*' (above), owned by the United States of America's National Oceanic and Atmospheric Administration, is a state-of-the-art oceanographic and atmospheric research platform and is the largest vessel in the NOAA fleet.

In the Arctic Ocean, US Coast Guard Cutter '*Healy*' (left) is taking part in a multi-year, multi-agency Arctic survey that will help define the Arctic continental shelf.

Drill Ships

A drill ship is a vessel that has been modified to accommodate a drilling platform, derrick, drilling equipment and a 'moon pool', a hole extending through the hull into the water through which the drilling equipment is deployed.

Drill ships are principally used for exploratory deepwater drilling for new oil or gas wells. While on station, they are kept in position by either a system of anchors or the ship's propulsion (dynamic positioning system).

Some drill ships are capable of drilling in depths greater than 2,500 metres. They are also used for well maintenance, installing subsea trees or well completion work, for example casing and tubing installation. The cost of a modern drill ship is >US$900 million.

In 2009, there were around 40 drill ships in service and by 2013 that number had increased to 105, with a further 18 units scheduled for delivery in 2014 and 2015.

he speed of growth indicates the level of activity and interest in this sector riven by the need to provide units that can operate in deep water and for peration in remote areas of the world, particularly those with 'Polar Class' otations that can operate in the Arctic and similar harsh environments.

ompanies investing in this sector are drawn by the attractive and stable day ıtes and the speed with which a drill ship can be moved from one drilling site ɔ another. Drill ships boast the longest contracts among the three main mobile ffshore rig types and the average length of contract for each rig is just over years.

ɔurce: ABS (ABS is the largest Classification Society in the offshore drilling sector.)

Drill Ships

Drill Ship Equipment

The procedure for drilling a well is generally the same whether the vessel employed is fixed or floating. The major differences occur in the selection of equipment used to occupy the space between the seabed and the drill floor. On a floating vessel, this equipment must include a motion, or heave compensation, system that will accommodate vessel movement relative to the seabed.

Figure 3.18 - The riser and slip joint exiting the moon pool of a deepwater drill ship exploring for oil and gas

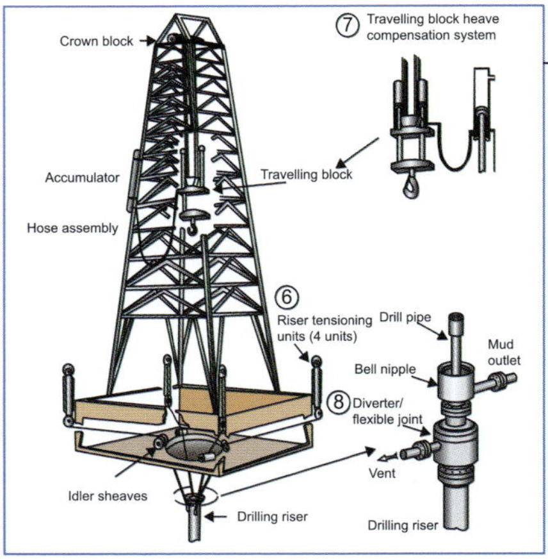

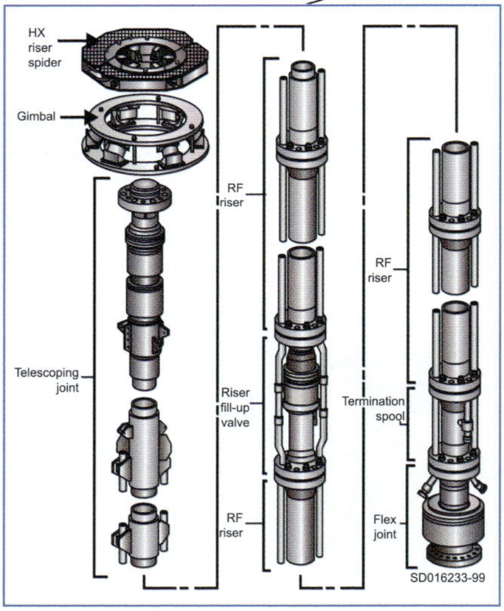

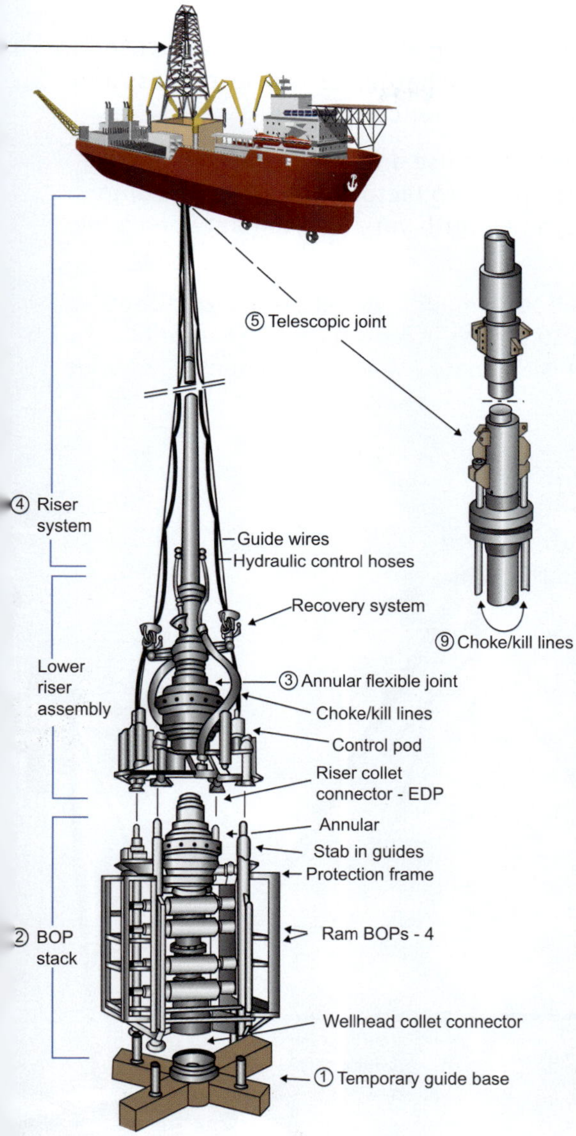

1 **Temporary guide base**
After installation of a guide base on the seabed, drilling operations may proceed. Wires extending from the drill ship to the guide base assist in the location of the drill string and wellhead equipment.

2 **BOP (blowout preventer) stack**
This is mounted on the seabed and ensures that, in the event of an emergency necessitating suspension of the drilling programme and departure of the vessel, the well may be left in a secure condition.

3 **Annular flexible joint (Marine riser flexible joint)**
A flexible ball joint located between the emergency disconnect package (EDP) and the marine riser can tolerate a certain amount of lateral movement of the drill ship relative to the wellhead. A second ball joint is attached to the top of the riser, frequently incorporated within the diverter.

4 **Riser system (Marine drilling riser)**
The length of steel pipe extending from the BOP stack to the drill ship is referred to as the marine drilling riser. It provides a return passage for the drilling mud. The riser incorporates a telescopic joint, the top half of which is attached to a tensioning system.

5 **Telescopic joint**
The telescopic joint permits relative vertical movement between the stationary lower section of drilling riser, which is attached to the seabed, and the upper section of the drilling riser, which is connected to the drilling derrick.

6 **Riser tensioning units**
The riser tensioning system, or heave compensation system, is designed to keep the drilling riser in tension and to minimise the effects of hull movement. It can accommodate up to 15 metres (50 feet) of vertical wave-induced motion or heave.

7 **Travelling block heave compensation system**
The travelling block is fitted with a heave compensation system that is similar to, if somewhat less sophisticated than, that employed to tension the riser.

8 **Diverter**
The diverter sits on top of the drilling riser and provides a way of controlling an influx of hydrocarbons into the well bore during the early stages of drilling.

9 **Choke and kill lines**
Subsea choke and kill line connections are arranged slightly differently to those on a surface well as they are manifolded to permit pressure release, or the pumping in of drilling mud, through either connection.

Fishing Vessels

Fishing vessels differ from other ships trading at sea in that they are used to hunt, locate, catch, load (and sometimes discharge), as well as process and conserve their cargo (fish) at sea, in all weather conditions.

There is huge variation in fishing vessels in use around the world, ranging from 2 metre long skiffs or dug-out canoes to factory trawlers exceeding 130 metres in length, with their voyage length varying from between a few hours to over a year.

The world fishing fleet consists of about 4 million vessels, of which about two-thirds are undecked, less than 10 metres in length and often not fitted with means of mechanical propulsion. It is estimated that Asia accounts for about 80% of these undecked vessels.

The average size of decked vessels is between 10 to 15 metres in length and about 20 GT. Vessels that are larger than 24 metres in length and greater than 100 GT represent about 1% of the world fishing fleet with China having about 50% (25,600) of such vessels.

Source: Food and Agriculture Organization of the United Nations

Fishing Vessels

Fish Factory Ship

Fish factory ships, also known as fish processing vessels, originate from the large ships used for whaling. Today the term refers to any ship that is equipped to process catches for various uses. A factory ship is usually the main ship in a fleet that sails from its home port to catch, prepare and store various types of fish for market. A fish factory ship that only has processing ability and is only used as a mother ship is generally referred to as a klondiker.

Figure 3.19 - Polish factory trawler

Trawler

Modern trawlers are usually decked vessels with the wheelhouse and accommodation being forward, midship or aft. They usually have motorised winches, electronic navigation and sonar systems. Fishing equipment will vary depending on the size of the vessel and the technology it uses. The design features will also vary, particularly as in some maritime jurisdictions vessel inspections are not compulsory for smaller commercial fishing vessels.

Figure 3.21 - Trawler

This fishing method involves pulling a trawl through the water behind one or more vessels. Trawls are large cone-shaped fishing nets that are either dragged along the bottom of the sea or in mid water. Most nets have doors on either side of the opening so that it can be held open. Some nets that are used for fishing on the bottom will have a chain attached so that the net can be kept close to the bottom of the sea bed.

Trawling gear varies according to local tradition, bottom conditions and the size of the trawling boats, which can range in power from 30 hp to a large factory trawler of 10,000 hp.

Figure 3.20 - Vessel with trawl net

Large winches are used to pull the net back up and, as it is lifted on board, the net is rolled onto a power drum. The end of the net (also known as the bag or cod end) traps the fish and is usually pulled onto the vessel using a slanting stern ramp.

The largest trawlers can be up to 600 feet long. Towing the net for two hours often yields enormous catches, including large quantities of unwanted types of fish (by-catch). The catch will be kept refrigerated and may be processed on board into fillets or minced fish for the fresh and frozen market.

Pair Trawling

This is where two vessels tow a single trawl. The trawl is opened horizontally by maintaining a distance when towing.

Figure 3.22 - Pair Trawlers

The trawlers are able to work in both mid and bottom water trawls. As each vessel deals with one warp, only one winch is required, although most pair trawlers have two winches.

Purse Seining

Figure 3.24 - Combined Trawler/Purse Seiner

Some smaller fishing vessels are specifically designed for purse seining. Larger trawlers that are equipped with purse seines are known as combined trawler/purse seiners.

A purse seine is a long line of netting that is held in position by a series of floats at the top of the net and a weighted line (lead line) along the bottom. A series of metal rings (purse rings) are attached to the lead line, through which the purse line passes. The seine is drawn around a shoal of fish and then closed (pursed) at the bottom by pulling on the purse line.

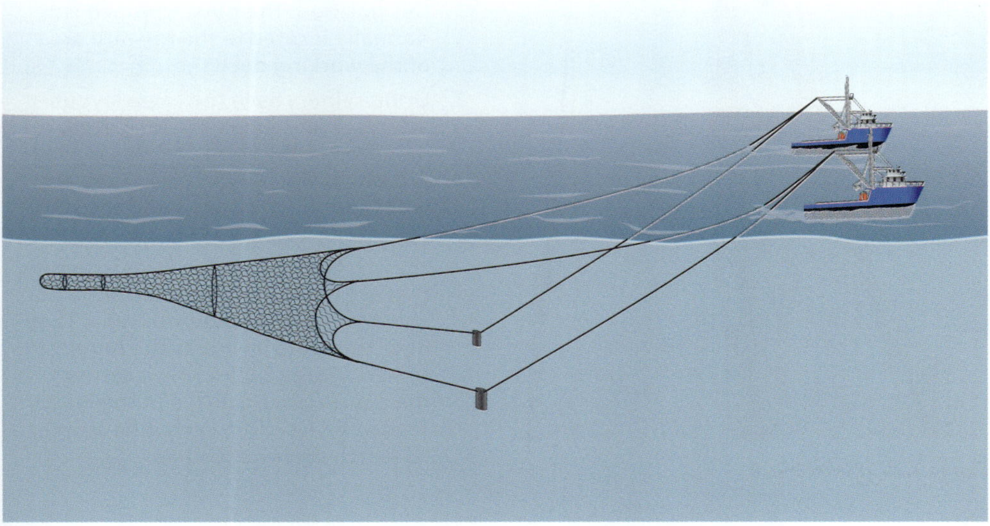

Figure 3.23 - Pair Trawlers

Fishing Vessels

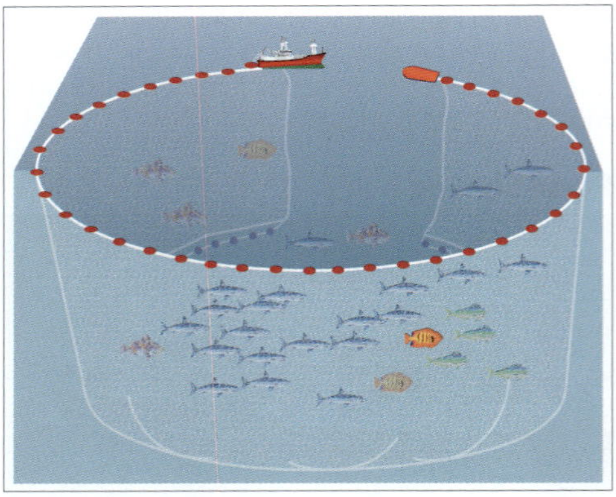

Figure 3.25 - Purse seining

The power block/sheave block located at the aft end of the purse seiner is used to pull on the purse line and to haul in the nets.

Purse seines are mostly used to catch large and small pelagic species that are found in shoals, eg mackerel, herring, sardines, certain tuna types (schooling) and whiting.

Figure 3.26 - Power block

Figure 3.27 - American seiner

There are various types of purse seiners:

1. **American seiners have their wheelhouse forward and are most commonly found on both coasts of North America. The net is stowed at the stern and is passed over the stern. The power block is typically attached to a boom on a mast located aft of the wheelhouse.**
2. **European seiners have their wheelhouse located aft. The net is stowed in a net bin at the stern, and is passed over the stern from this position. The pursing winch is normally located in the forward area of the working deck.**
3. **Drum seiners have the same layout as American seiners except a drum is mounted in the stern and this is used instead of the power block. They are mainly found in Canada and the USA.**
4. **Tuna purse seiners are large purse seiners, typically >45 metres in length, that are equipped to handle large and heavy purse seines for tuna. They have the same layout as the American seiner. A large boom which carries the power block is fitted at the mast. These vessels often carry a helicopter to search for tuna schools.**

Beam Trawlers

Beam trawlers use robust outrigger booms to tow a beam trawl on either side of the vessel. Beam trawling is used when fishing for flatfish and shrimp, particularly in the North Sea. Beam trawlers are medium sized high-powered vessels, towing at speeds of up to 8 knots.

Figure 3.28 - A Dutch beam trawler

Figure 3.29 - Longliners in Larnaca, Cyprus

Figure 3.30 - Baiting a longline

Longliner

Longlines consist of a main line up to a mile long with thousands of branch lines (also known as leaders, snoods or gangions). Each branch line has a baited hook at the end. The line may be laid along the seabed or set to hang near the surface. The lines may be anchored at the end of each set and will have a buoy or flag on the surface indicating its position. Longline vessels usually set several lines at once for a 24 hour soak. The lines are retrieved using a power winch and side roller. Typically longliners are large vessels of 50 to 100 feet long with a weather cover on the stern to protect the crew. When not in use, the longlines are coiled and stacked on deck in tubs. Most of these vessels can pack 20 to 40 tonnes of iced product before returning to port. The vessels are easily identified by their distinctive weather covers and also by the number of buoys and flags that are tied along the rails when they are not fishing.

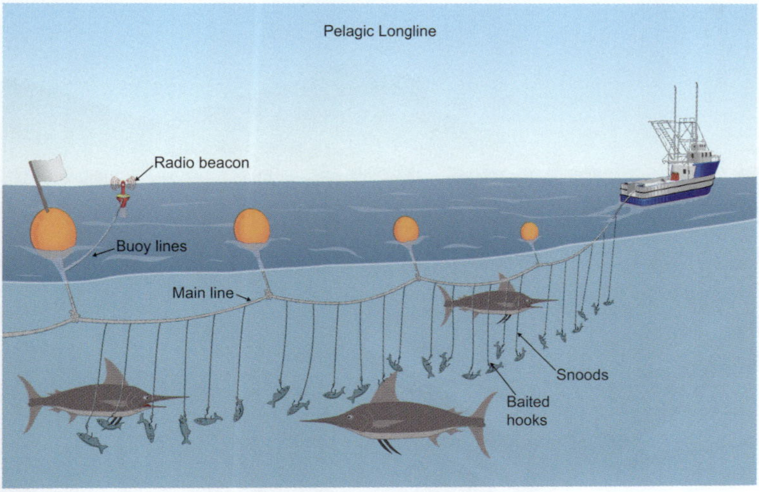

Figure 3.31 - Longline fishing

Fishing Vessels

Dredge Fishing

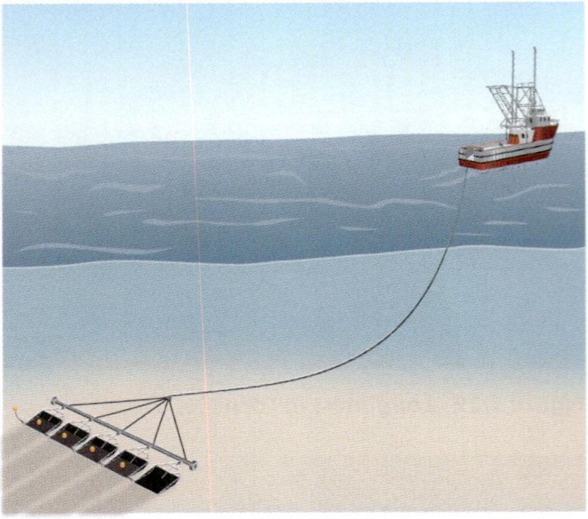

Figure 3.32 - Dredge fishing

Dredge fishing is similar to trawl fishing but these vessels aim to catch bivalve molluscs such as oysters, clams and scallops from the seabed. Dredging involves dragging a heavy frame with an attached mesh bag along the sea floor to catch species living on or in the mud or sand.

Crabbers and Lobster Boats

These boats use pots/frames covered with fishing net to catch crab, shrimp and lobster. The pots themselves are baited inside with fresh fish and are all connected on strings of 10 to 30 pots connected by a line to a surface buoy. The pots can be set anywhere from just off the shoreline to waters up to 100 metres deep, ie the continental shelf.

Figure 3.33 - Inkwell or Devon-Type Pots

There are various shapes and sizes of crab boats, ranging from aluminium skiffs with outboard motors to seagoing vessels of 30 metres or more. It is difficult for a casual observer to identify a crabber unless the decks are stacked with pots.

Figure 3.34 - Lobster boat in Capetown

Risks Relating to Fishing

The risk of an accident in the fishing sector is much greater than in other sectors, with each type of fishing vessel having its own unique dangers.

Overloading Leading to Capsize

Fishing vessels are often overloaded, typically by:

- Taking on too much fish in their hold. The added weight reduces the freeboard of the fishing vessel. As the decking level gets nearer to the water, the range of stability decreases, as does the strength of the righting lever
- taking on too much fish on deck. This lifts the centre of gravity dangerously, which limits the range of stability and brings the vessel much closer to a capsize condition, ie the vessel will capsize earlier and at a lower angle of roll.

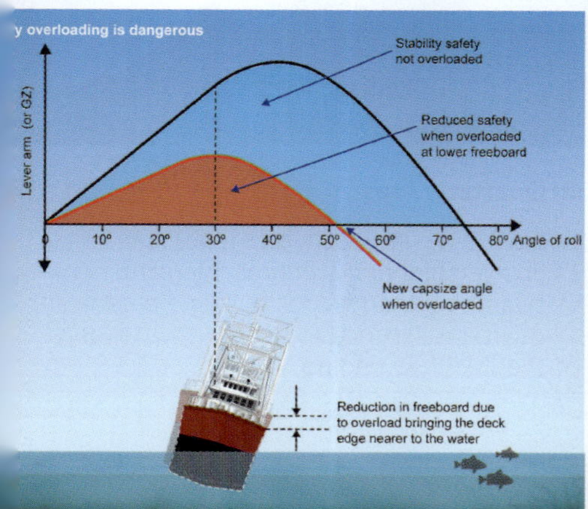

Figure 3.35 - Why overloading is dangerous

Trawling, Dredging and Towing

The act of towing a trawl has an impact on the fishing vessel's stability as there is a reduction in the vessel's freeboard from the lever action of the tow and the weight of the load.

If the vessel is trawling in a rough or heavy sea, the combined effect may be dangerous. A heavy roll when towing may also cause the vessel to turn and roll to the tension of the lines.

Figure 3.36 - Stability when towing, dredging or trawling

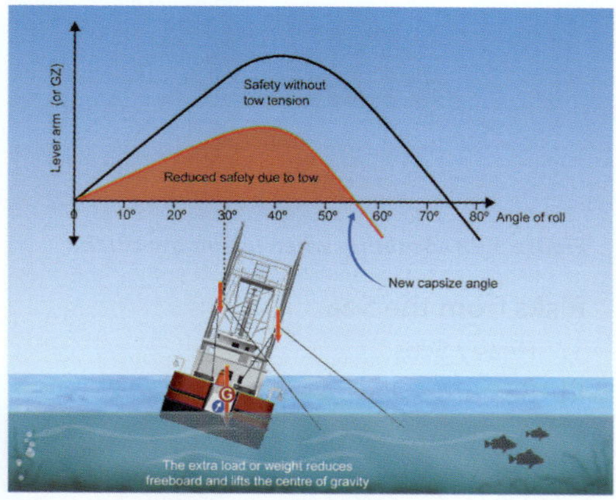

Figure 3.37 - The extra load or weight reduces freeboard and lifts the centre of gravity

Courtesy of USCG

Heaving the Catch on Board

The weight of the catch will act through the highest block or pulley that is lifting it and will result in a shift of the centre of gravity.

Fishing Vessels

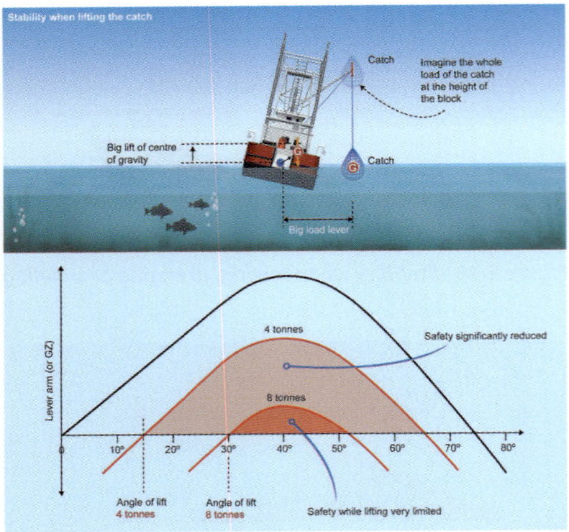

Figure 3.38 - Stability when lifting the catch

Risks from the Sea

1. Heavy Seas

(i) Beam-on seas

In beam-on seas, there is a high risk of a fishing vessel rolling heavily and, if the vessel is overloaded or engaged in an activity that is temporarily reducing her range of stability while fishing, large rolls can easily lead to capsize.

The large forces from heavy seas that are breaking are very dangerous for fishing vessels, especially if they are already overloaded. The risk to the fish that is already on board is high and all items need to be safely secured.

(ii) Following seas

When running with a following sea, great care is required to avoid broaching. Running in the same direction as the sea will make steering very difficult. Each passing wave slows and then accelerates the vessel and each surge of the vessel potentially pushes the vessel off course and makes it very hard to steer. The danger from being swamped and capsizing is extreme.

(iii) Quarterly seas

For fishing vessels, quarterly seas present an even higher risk of broaching and swamping than following seas. Here the aft quarter is exposed to breaking waves and the risk of swamping.

2. Swamping of the deck and free surface effects

Waves coming on deck (green water) are a major stability hazard for fishing vessels due to the added weight and the free surface effect.

Figure 3.39 - Free surface effect

The combined effect of these hazards causes a dramatic loss of stability. The added water weight raises the vessel's centre of gravity and this results in a reduction in the vessel's freeboard. As the water shifts, it will rapidly attempt to roll the vessel.

The free surface effect can be easily seen by rocking a partially filled bottle of water and feeling the strain it exerts as the wedge of water builds up at the extremity of the bottle. This should clearly demonstrate why there is a need for freeing ports on the deck to quickly remove any surface water.

General safety guidelines for fishermen:

- **Never wear rings or watches on deck**
- **never stand in the line of ropes under tension**
- **never wrap ropes around your hand**
- **never stand below derricks/cranes carrying loads**
- **use light reflectors on external clothing**
- **avoid running turns on winch drums**
- **practise safety drills**
- **wear personal protective clothing.**

Figure 3.40 - Why free water tries to roll the vessel over

Disasters and Significant Incidents Involving Fishing Vessels

Scallop dredger 'Solway Harvester'

On the evening of 11th January 2000, the 19.43 metre Scottish scallop dredger *'Solway Harvester'* was reported as missing.

The investigation found that the bilge alarm was not functioning before the accident. Without this, it is likely that those on board were unaware she was taking water into the fish hold until, probably, a few minutes before the accident. It also found that the bilge pumping arrangements were not working as intended.

Courtesy of MAIB

Figure 3.41 - 'Solway Harvester'

Following an extensive search, the wreck of the *'Solway Harvester'* was found in a depth of 35 metres, 11 miles southeast of the Isle of Man. All of her 7 crew had drowned. Subsequent events included an underwater survey, the recovery of the bodies by the Isle of Man authorities and, eventually, the salvage of the vessel. MAIB inspectors carried out extensive interviews, a very detailed examination of the wreck and a range of model tests. All the evidence indicated that the *'Solway Harvester'* began to take water into her fish hold through open ice scuttles while she was making way during the late afternoon of 11th January 2000. She was, at that time, heading for shelter in the lee of the Isle of Man. It was a foul night and a strong southwesterly wind was blowing. She stopped and, with the way off her, came beam to sea and started to roll heavily. The floodwater in the fish hold reduced her stability to such an extent that she became vulnerable to a capsize. The heavy rolling in large waves caused her cargo of bagged scallops and loose gear to shift. This, together with the reduced stability, caused her to capsize at about 17:45.

The *'Solway Harvester'* lost her stability due to the weight of 6 to 9 tonnes of water in her fish room, a shift in weight on board, the failure of watertight integrity and the effects of heavy rolling. A capsize was inevitable.

Source: ***MAIB***

Courtesy of MAIB

Figure 3.42 - 'Solway Harvester' following salvage

CHAPTER 4

Offshore

Offshore Supply Vessels – Stability Considerations

Special attention should be given to the loading, discharging, trim and stability of offshore supply vessels for the following reasons:

- Both solid and liquid cargoes have to be loaded and discharged, often simultaneously, at sea
- there is a risk of entrapment of water in a deck cargo of pipes
- these vessels have a low freeboard in way of the cargo deck area aft but a large buoyant superstructure at the forward end
- when heeled beyond the angle of after deck edge immersion, severe loss of stability in terms of righting levers can occur as a result of the tendency of the vessel to trim further by the stern
- these vessels often have stabiliser tanks.

All these factors must be considered during compilation of the stability information for the vessel. Such information must include additional notes for the guidance of the master of any supply vessel.

Loading/Discharging Cargoes at Sea

A supply vessel is called upon to perform complex cargo operations while at sea. This will include loading and discharging cargoes, both solid and liquid cargoes often simultaneously, in addition to having to deal with personnel transfers. It is essential that all on board maintain a high level of awareness to ensure safety of the crew and stability of the vessel.

The following points should be considered:

- Any trim limitation and minimum freeboard at the stern should be maintained. Ballasting should be carried out to counteract the effects of loading and discharging cargo
- cargo should always be discharged uppermost first, ie discharge deck cargo prior to discharging from cargo tanks lower down in the vessel
- when liquid cargo is to be discharged, as soon as pumping commences a full free surface of the tanks being pumped out should be allowed for

- when a tank is to be ballasted at sea to counteract the removal of cargo from the vessel, it should be noted that:
  - the tank should be assumed to have a full free surface as soon as ballasting commences, and
  - the free surface will adversely affect the stability of the vessel before any benefit can be assumed from the weight of ballast water taken on board.

Before ballasting commences, it is important to unload a sufficient quantity of the highest deck cargo to lower the centre of gravity of the vessel.

Allowances for Entrapment of Water in Pipe Cargoes

When pipes or casings are carried on deck, an allowance must be made for the volume of entrapped water regardless of whether or not the pipes have wooden plugs. The *Code on Intact Stability for all Ships (IMO)* details the allowances that should be made as follows:

(Regulation 4.5.8.4) *Where pipes are carried on deck, a quantity of trapped water equal to a certain percentage of the net volume of the pipe deck cargo should be assumed in and around the pipes. The net volume should be taken as the internal volume of the pipes, plus the volume between the pipes. This percentage should be 30 if the freeboard amidships is equal to or less than 0.015 L and 10 if the freeboard amidships is equal to or greater than 0.03 L. For intermediate values of the freeboard amidships the percentage may be obtained by linear interpolation. In assessing the quantity of trapped water, the Administration may take into account positive or negative sheer aft, actual trim and area of operation.*

Instructions as to what allowance should be applied and how it should be applied must be included in the guidance notes for the master in the stability data book. It should be emphasised that the mass of this water is additional to the cargo deadweight permitted by the appropriate load line mark.

Freeboard Limitation Aft

Excessive stern trim will always result in severely reduced freeboard aft, and the position of deck cargo and tank contents should be arranged to minimise stern trim. Regulation 4.5.5.2 of the *Code on Intact Stability for all Ships (IMO)* states:

A minimum freeboard at the stern of at least 0.005 L should be maintained in all operating conditions.

A statement as to the *maximum permissible trim* and the *minimum freeboard at the stern in mm* should be included in the guidance notes for the master in the stability data book.

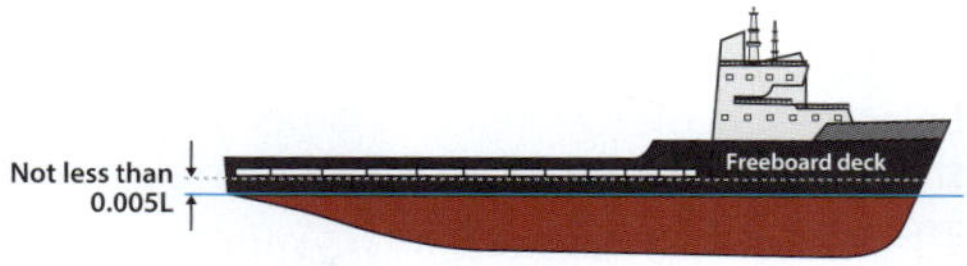

Figure 4.1 - Freeboard aft

The Effect of Stern Trim and Reserve Forward Buoyancy on Stability

Supply vessels are characterised by a broad beam and shallow draught. The broad beam makes these vessels initially very stable but the low freeboard aft causes the deck edge to be submerged at small angles of heel. Beyond the angle of deck edge immersion, any benefit of the broad beam is soon lost. All superstructure is in the forward quarter of the vessel leaving the after three-quarters available for cargo. This arrangement causes problems with respect to reserve buoyancy distribution when the ship is heeled.

The Effect of Stern Trim

A ship trimmed by the stern will have less overall stability than when on an even keel. Admittedly, the GM and the stability at small angles of heel may be greater in the trimmed condition due to the greater water plane area increasing BM and the slightly greater KB, both leading to an improved KM initially.

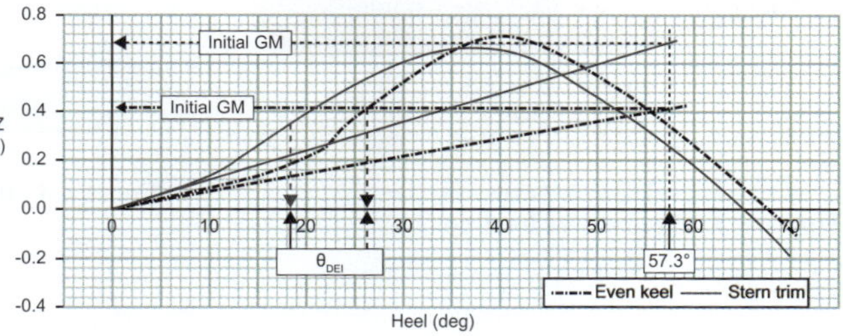

Figure 4.2 - GZ curves for even keel and trimmed conditions

Offshore Supply Vessels – Stability Considerations

However, the premature angle of heel at which the aft deck edge becomes immersed in the trimmed condition will result in an earlier deterioration of the GZ curve. The GZ curves for even keel and trimmed conditions are illustrated in Figure 4.2.

When a supply boat is heeled beyond the angle of deck edge immersion aft sufficiently to cause the forward superstructure to displace water, the effects can be quite dramatic as the ship will both trim by the stern and suffer a loss of stability even if the ship is on an even keel when upright. This is explained as follows:

Consider a typical supply boat on an even keel being progressively heeled to larger angles as shown in Figures 4.3 to 4.5.

- represents the vessel's intact water plane area
- represents the vessel's intact underwater volume providing buoyancy force upthrust, and
- represents water shipped on deck after the aft deck has become immersed.

In the upright condition, the ship is on an even keel. F is the longitudinal centre of flotation (located at the geometric centre of the water plane area) and is the point in the ship's length about which it will trim.

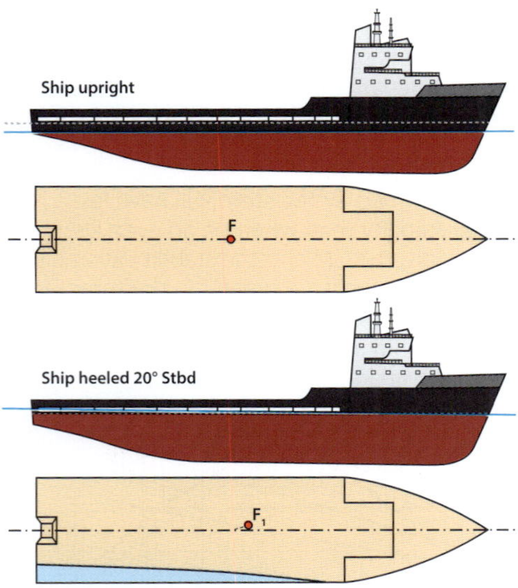

Figure 4.3 - Progressive heeling (1)

At 20° heel to starboard, the aft deck has become immersed, evidenced by the water on deck on the low side. Water plane area aft on the low side has been lost causing F to move forward. This is akin to moving the pivot point on a see-saw, as shown in Figure 4.4. The ship starts to trim by the stern.

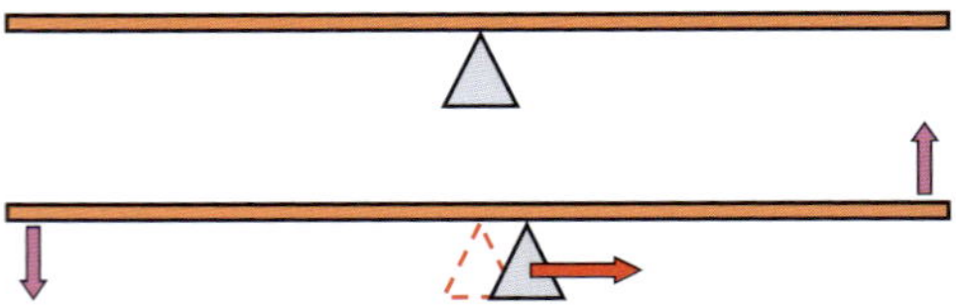

Figure 4.4 - Movement of the pivot point

The ship is now heeled progressively further.

At 30° heel the reserve buoyancy of the forward superstructure takes effect, volume of buoyancy being transferred from the high side aft where it is not being used to the low side forward on the heeled side. This causes the LCB to move forward creating a stern trimming couple. This, accompanied by the continuing forward movement of the centre of flotation, causes the ship to trim significantly further by the stern as it continues to heel.

At 45° heel, stern trim has increased causing the situation to become dangerous, whereby the after deck is becoming awash to such an extent that the angle of progressive flooding may soon be reached.

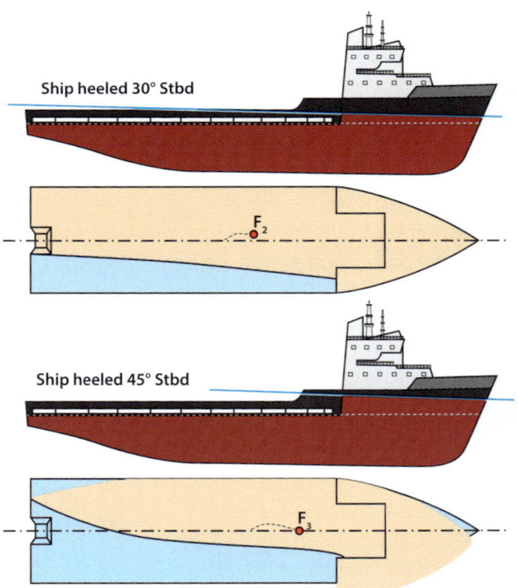

Figure 4.5 - Progressive heeling (2)

The effects on the ship being heeled to large angles of heel can have serious consequences with respect to reducing the angle of heel at which progressive downflooding takes place.

What are the effects of such ship behaviour on the curve of statical stability?

As the ship trims by the stern, it loses buoyancy at the superstructure on the low side and gains buoyancy in way of the main hull on the high side. Figure 4.6 illustrates the loss of buoyancy forward due to the lift of the bow and gain of buoyancy aft due to sinkage. This redistribution of buoyancy (from forward low side to aft high side) results in a shift of the centre of buoyancy towards the high side, ie to a position B_1, closer to the centreline than B (Figure 4.6). Thus, righting lever (GZ) is reduced.

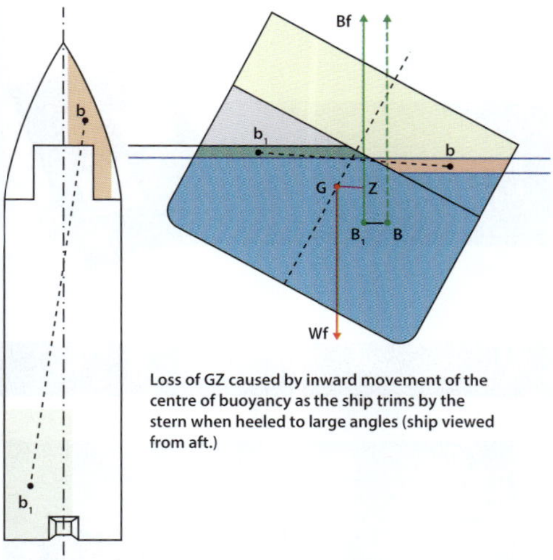

Figure 4.6 - Movement of centre of buoyancy

'Fixed Trim' and 'Free to Trim' Basis KN Values

The KN values supplied for most ships are for an assumed condition of trim (usually even keel) and are calculated on a 'fixed trim' basis. This means that any inward movement of the centre of buoyancy as the ship is heeled to large angles as depicted in Figure 4.7 is ignored. If KN values for a supply vessel are calculated on a 'fixed trim' basis, this means that the values of GZ calculated for angles of heel where the reserve buoyancy of the forward superstructure takes effect will be greater than their actual value; the stability of the ship will be overestimated.

For supply vessels, it is preferable that the KN values of the ship are derived on a 'free to trim' basis. This means that the KN values are reduced to take account of the effect of the vessel trimming by the stern as it is heeled to larger angles where the reserve buoyancy of the forward superstructure takes effect, causing the reduction in GZ values.

When determining GZ values for such vessels, always check the KN data. It should indicate the condition of trim assumed and whether the values are for an assumed 'fixed trim' or 'free to trim' basis. Remember that:

The problems described are generally only relevant to vessels with large forward superstructures and low freeboards aft. On most cargo vessels that operate with only a small stern trim, any such effects will generally be insignificant.

Intact Stability Criteria for Supply Vessels

Due to the hull form of supply vessels, this alternative stability criteria may be substituted for the criteria laid down in regulation 3.1.2 of the *Code on Intact Stability for all Ships covered by IMO Instruments (IMO)* (for UK ships, regulation 8.15 in *Load Line – Instructions for the Guidance of Surveyors (MCA)* allows the use of this alternative criteria).

- *The area under the curve of righting levers (GZ curve) should not be less than 0.070 metre-radian up to an angle of 15° when the maximum righting lever (GZ) occurs at 15° and 0.055 metre-radian up to an angle of 30°*

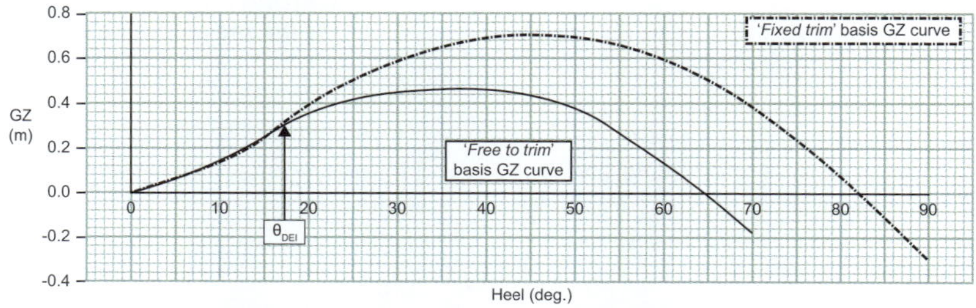

Figure 4.7 - 'Fixed trim' KN data will give greater GZ values than the ship will actually have when heeled beyond the angle of deck edge immersion – stability will be overestimated!

Offshore Supply Vessels – Stability Considerations

when the maximum righting lever (GZ) occurs at 30° or above. Where the maximum righting lever (GZ) occurs at angles of between 15° and 30°, the corresponding area under the righting lever curve should be:

$$0.055 + 0.001(30^\circ - \theta_{max}) \text{ metre-radian}$$

(θ_{max} is the angle of heel at which maximum GZ occurs)

- *The area under the righting lever curve (GZ curve) between the angles of heel of 30° and 40°, or between 30° and the angle at which progressive downflooding takes place (θ_f), if this angle is less than 40°, should be not less than 0.03 metre-radian.*
- *The righting lever (GZ) should be at least 0.20 m at an angle of heel equal to or greater than 30°.*
- *The maximum righting lever (GZ) should occur at an angle of heel not less than 15°.*
- *The initial transverse metacentric height (GM) should not be less than 0.15 m.*

Stabiliser Tanks

Most supply vessels are fitted with stabiliser tanks for the purpose of reducing roll amplitude during cargo load and discharge operations at sea. It is essential that they are filled to the correct level to provide optimum roll restriction. Guidance notes on the use of such tanks should be provided in the ship's stability data book. It must be recognised that the large free surface moments that these tanks cause will significantly reduce the ship's stability and must always be allowed for.

Extracted from Ship Stability Mates/Masters

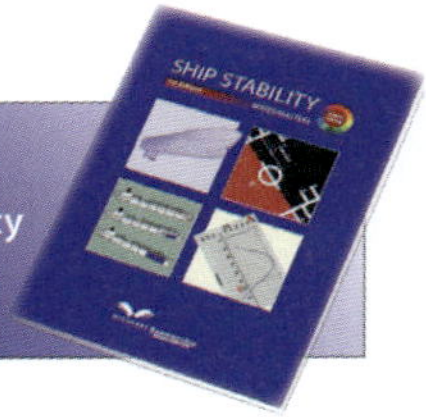

Remotely Operated Vehicles

US DOD Imagery

Remotely operated vehicles (ROV) are unmanned mini submarines operated from a ship or offshore unit. They were developed by the military and first used in the offshore industry in the 1970s. They may be used as an alternative to deep-sea divers for inspection, testing, surveys, maintenance and scientific purposes, including oceanography, fishing, mineral exploitation, etc. Modern ROVs are capable of installing and maintaining wellheads without saturation divers, allowing exploitation of deeper natural reserves.

US DOD Imagery

Figure 4.8 - 15th October 2001 - An ROV operated by Japan Marine Science and Technology Center (JAMSTEC) searches the deepwater site following the lift and move of the 'Ehime Maru'

ROVs vary in construction but will normally have:

- Buoyancy tanks to control depth and trim
- a frame to provide structure and protection against impact
- electric power packs
- lighting
- video camera

Remotely Operated Vehicles

- cased sensitive equipment
- directional control thrusters.

A tool sled may be fitted along with various sensors and/or articulated manipulators or crab claws, cutting equipment, sampling equipment, temperature sensors and other specialist equipment including sonar and magnetometers.

ROVs are linked to the surface vessel by a control cable known as the tether or umbilical. This may incorporate the ROV power supply.

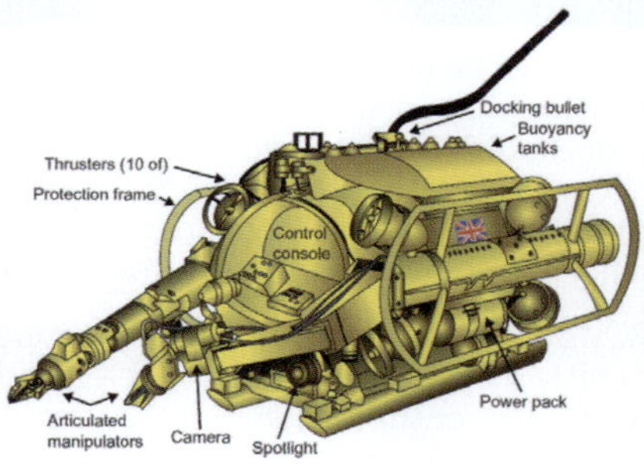

Reproduced from Offshore Engineering 3rd Edition

ROVs are normally classified by size, weight, power and capability:

- Micro – often less than 3 kg and useful for small areas inaccessible to divers
- mini – typically less than 15 kg, fulfilling similar roles to the micro
- general work – usually around 5 hp, used for light survey work often with manipulators, can typically operate to depths of 1,000 m
- light work – usually around 50 hp, with two or more manipulators, working depths of up to 2,000 m
- heavy work – often up to 220 hp, with a minimum of two manipulators and working depth of around 3,500 m
- trenching/burial – up to 500 hp but occasionally higher, able to work in depths of up to 6,000 m. Some are used to lay cables from a mounted sled.

Both micro and mini ROVs can be used from small boats primarily for inspection purposes and are sometimes referred to as *eyeball class*.

Launching procedures can vary from manhandling in small boats to large purpose-built winch systems that can handle units up to 2 tonnes. Some ROVs, particularly those used for very deep work, may be operated via a submersible garage.

ROVs may be deployed directly from a crane or from a tether management system (garage or cage).

US DOD Imagery

US DOD Imagery

Remotely Operated Vehicles

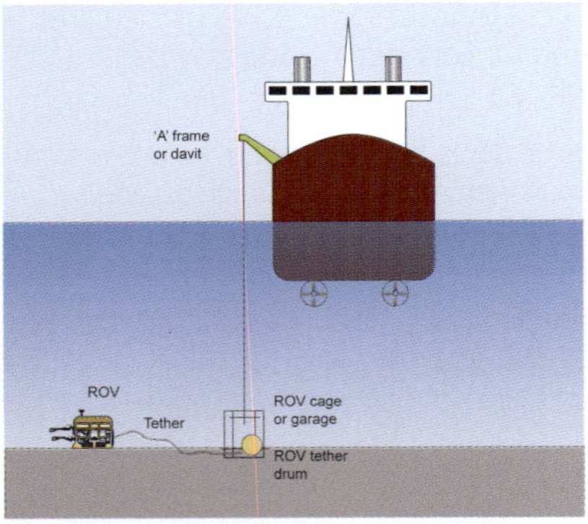

Figure 4.9 - ROV tether management system

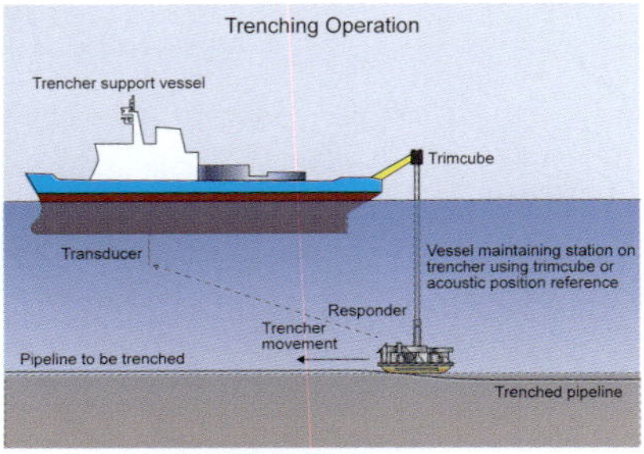

Figure 4.10 - Trenching operation

US DOD Imagery

Care must be taken when deploying an ROV to avoid entanglement with the thrusters or propellers. Some ships' dynamic positioning (DP) systems have a *follow sub* or *follow target* mode that allows the ROV to become the reference point (using acoustic transponders).

ROV operators may be known by a number of titles, including mechanical or electrical technicians or supervisors, but they are commonly referred to as ROV pilots.

Dynamic Positioning

Introduction

Certain DP operations will require the vessel to remain in one position and direction irrespective of the weather or sea conditions. Offshore operations that require this level of control include diving, underwater cable laying, drilling, mine sweeping and surveying.

Integrated control systems that help vessels maintain their position by continuously reacting to the conditions acting on the ship are called Dynamic Positioning Systems (DP system).

A DP system computes the position error by continually measuring the present position against the intended position. Based on these findings, the DP system can determine what thruster action is required to move the vessel as close as possible to the intended position.

Dynamic Positioning Overview

Dynamic positioning (DP) allows a computer system that is integrated with the ship's propellers and thrusters to control and maintain the vessel's position and heading, based on inputs received from sources such as DGPS, wind sensors, motion sensors and gyro compasses. A variety of further sub-functions may be available, such as track-follow or weathervane modes, but controlling position and heading are the most important.

The DP computer program contains a mathematical model of the vessel including information pertaining to the wind and current drag of the vessel and location of the thrusters. This knowledge, combined with sensor information, allows the computer to calculate the required steering angle and thruster output for each thruster. This allows operations to take place at sea where mooring or anchoring is not feasible due to, for example, deep water, congestion on the sea bottom (pipelines, templates), etc.

Dynamic positioning can be either absolute, where the position is locked to a fixed point over the bottom, or relative to a moving object like another ship or an underwater vehicle. The vessel can also be positioned at a favourable

Dynamic Positioning

angle towards the wind, waves and current; this is called weathervaning.

Dynamic positioning is utilised by much of the offshore oil industry and there are currently more than 1,000 DP ships.

The Six Freedoms of Vessel Movement

All vessels have six freedoms of movement: roll, pitch, yaw, surge, sway and heave.

DP deals with the automatic control of surge, sway and yaw. Surge and sway are the main factors affecting the vessel's position, whereas yaw relates to the vessel's heading.

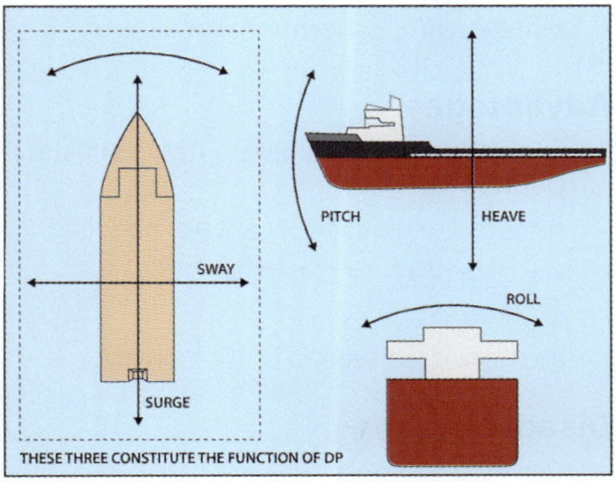

Figure 4.11 - The six freedoms of vessel movement

Setpoint values prescribed by the DP operator determine the position setpoint that relates to surge and sway, and the heading setpoint that relates to yaw.

The vessel must be able to control its position and heading within acceptable limits when faced with a variety of external forces. If these forces are measured directly, the control computers can apply immediate compensation.

Some examples of this are:

- Compensation for wind forces, where a continuous measurement is available from wind sensors
- plough cable tension in a cable laying vessel, where forces are generated that could disturb station keeping. Sensors connected to the cable tensioners allow direct feedback of these external forces to the DP control system and compensation to be ordered from the thruster before any departure from the intended track develops.

Some DP vessels, eg dredgers, pipe lay barges and cable laying vessels, have a requirement to follow a predetermined track. Others need to be able to weathervane about a specified spot. Other vessels follow a moving target, such as a submersible vehicle (ROV) or a seabed vehicle. In these cases the vessel's position reference is the vehicle rather than a designated fixed location.

Dynamic Positioning Modes

- **Follow target mode:** enables the vessel to automatically follow a moving target and keeps the vessel within a position window relative to the target
- **Joystick:** allows the operator to control the vessel manually using a joystick for position and heading control
- **Joystick high-speed:** allows the operator to manoeuvre the vessel manually at normal cruising/manoeuvring speeds
- **Auto heading:** automatically maintains the required heading
- **Auto position:** automatically maintains the required position and heading
- **Mixed joystick/auto:** allows the operator to select automatic control of either one or two of the surge, sway and yaw axes
- **Follow target:** allows vessels to automatically follow a moving target
- **Anchor assist:** provides thruster assistance when operating within a mooring pattern
- **Autopilot:** allows the vessel to steer automatically on a predefined course
- **ROT pilot:** allows the operator to manoeuvre the vessel using Rate Of Turn control
- **Auto track:** The auto track modes (low-speed, move-up and high-speed) make the vessel follow a specific track that is described by a set of waypoints. All auto track modes are for marine operations only and not navigation purposes
- **Track line:** enables the vessel to follow a constant Course Over Ground (COG). It is for marine operations only and not for navigation purposes.

Dynamic Positioning

DP Equipment Class

IMO DP equipment classes are as follows:

- **DP Equipment Class 1 (DP1):** loss of position may occur if there is a single fault, ie there is no redundancy in the system.
- **DP Equipment Class 2 (DP2):** loss of position should not occur from a single fault of an active component or system, including a single inadvertent human action. DP2 vessels have dual control computers and sufficient thrusters so that the vessel will retain its position even if half of them are lost.
- **DP Equipment Class 3 (DP3):** loss of position should not occur from any single fault of an active component or system, any single failure of a static component, any single inadvertent act, fire in any one fire sub-division or flooding of any one watertight compartment. Drill ships are a good example of a DP 3 vessel. A control room equipped with an additional control station is stationed separate from the main bridge. This means that, if there is a flood or fire that affects the main bridge, control can be transferred to the auxiliary station and position keeping should not be compromised.

DP Class Requirements

The following activities may be conducted by DP vessels:

- Drilling
- diver support
- pipe laying
- cable laying and repair
- accommodation or 'flotel' services
- hydrographic survey
- salvage
- dredging
- rockdumping (pipeline protection)
- subsea installation
- lifting (topsides and subsea)
- well stimulation and workover
- platform supply

- shuttle tanker offtake
- floating production (with or without storage)
- heavy lift cargo transport
- passenger cruises
- mine countermeasures
- oceanographical research
- seabed mining.

DP is also used in

- Rocket launch platform positioning
- repair/maintenance support to military vessels
- ship to ship transfer and
- manoeuvring conventional vessels.

Advantages

- Excellent manoeuvrability – easy to change position
- no tugs are required for anchor handling
- water depth is not an issue
- quick to set up
- an obstructed seabed is not an issue.

Disadvantages

- Complex system
- expensive to install
- high fuel costs
- if the system fails or there is a blackout, it is possible to run off position
- thrusters may cause underwater hazards for divers and ROVs
- more maintenance is required.

Slinging for Offshore Operations

These are general guidelines, the majority of which are pertinent to all types of slings whether constructed from wire rope, grade 8 chain or man-made fibres. The most important thing to remember is that man-made fibre slings are not to be used as the primary lifting gear for lifts to and from vessels, offshore installations, etc, where dynamic loading occurs.

All slings when not in use should be stored in a warm dry atmosphere either coiled or hanging on purpose-built racks. Wire rope and chain slings should be lubricated periodically to prevent corrosion.

The most common lifting operation between a shore base and an offshore installation is the handling of tubulars such as drill pipe and casing. The slings should be positioned so that they are a quarter of the tubular length in from each end. This keeps hogging and sagging to a minimum.

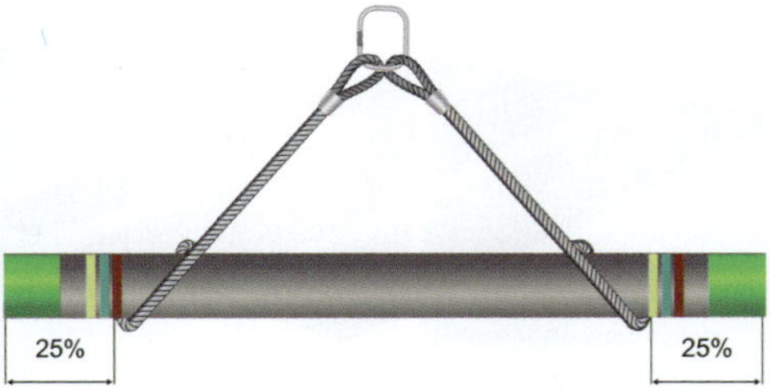

Figure 4.12 - Slinging of tubulars

Each sling should be double wrapped and choked, locked in with a wire rope grip, and secured with a tie-wrap, making sure that the ropes don't cross over on the underside of the bundle. This stops the bundle from coming slack when it is landed.

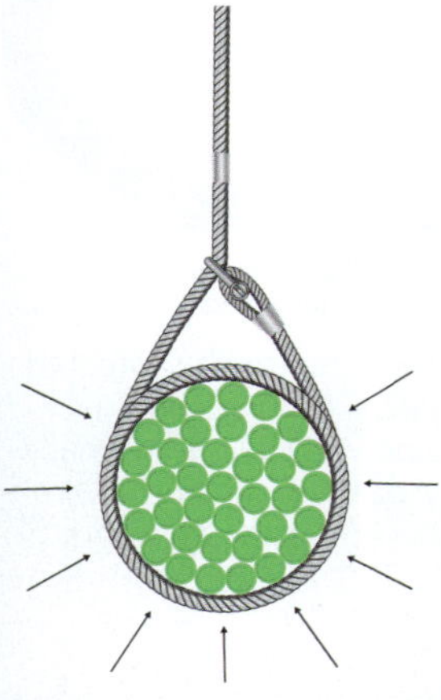

Figure 4.13 This hitch compresses the load and prevents it from slipping the sling

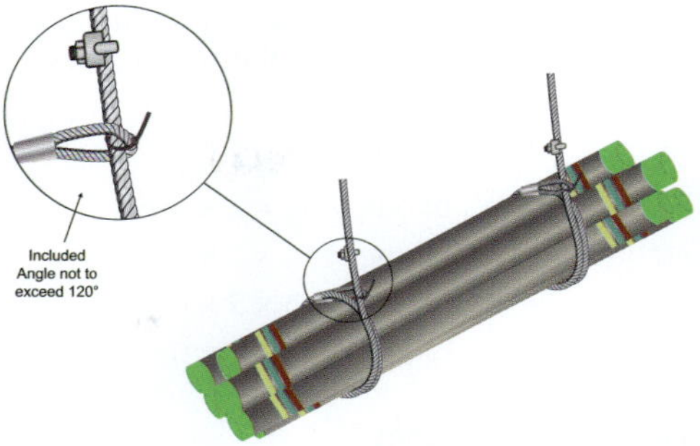

Figure 4.14 - Din 1142 type wire rope grips are preferred for lifting tubulars

Only tubulars of the same diameter should be lifted together in a bundle. If the sizes are mixed, the smaller ones will slide out if the bundle gets jarred or tilted (the same applies to bundles of materials with different cross-sections).

Because the slings will be in choke hitch and operating at an angle, each sling must be rated at the total weight of the bundle. For example, two six tonne slings will be needed for a six tonne lift.

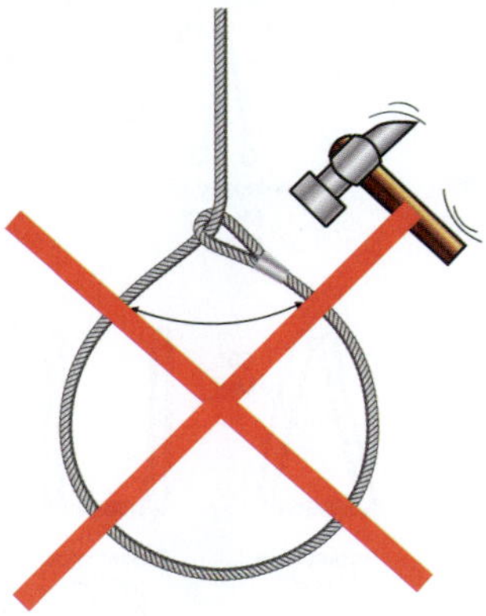

A hammer should never be used to tighten the choke hitch. This will increase the effective sling angle and weaken the sling.

When lifting more than one bundle or pipe at a time, each pair of slings must be kept the same length to avoid problems when the load is being unhooked, especially on a moving supply vessel.

Multi-leg slings

Multi-leg slings are rated at a certain tonnage from 0° to 90° and this SWL should not be exceeded even if the angle is less than 90°. When using slings in pairs however, you must

Slinging for Offshore Operations

be aware of the increased loadings in the slings when lifting at an angle. For this reason, they are derated as follows:

0°	=	SWL of one sling × 2
30°	=	SWL of one sling × 2 × 0.966
60°	=	SWL of one sling × 2 × 0.866
90°	=	SWL of one sling × 2 × 0.707
120°	=	SWL of one sling × 2 × 0.5

Mode Factor (M)

Slings vary in capacity depending on the mode or configuration.

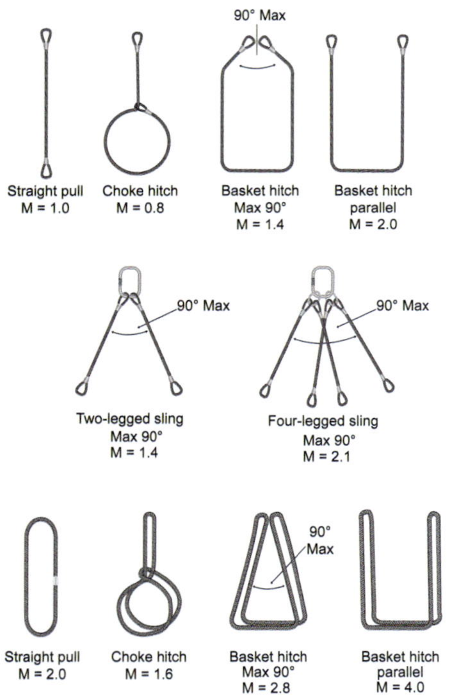

When landing a load, timber packing should be used to prevent the slings being crushed by the weight of the load.

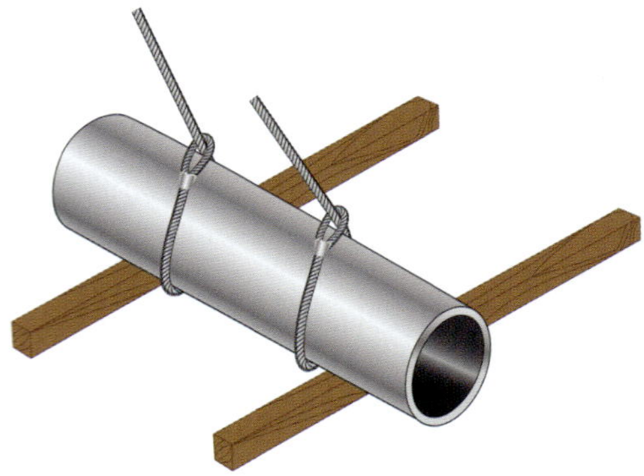

Slings should not be wrapped around sharp edges such as 'I' beams or bundles of sheet steel as this will severely weaken the sling and possibly lead to sling failure. If the situation can not be avoided, suitable packing (such as timber joined by webbing) should be used to protect the slings.

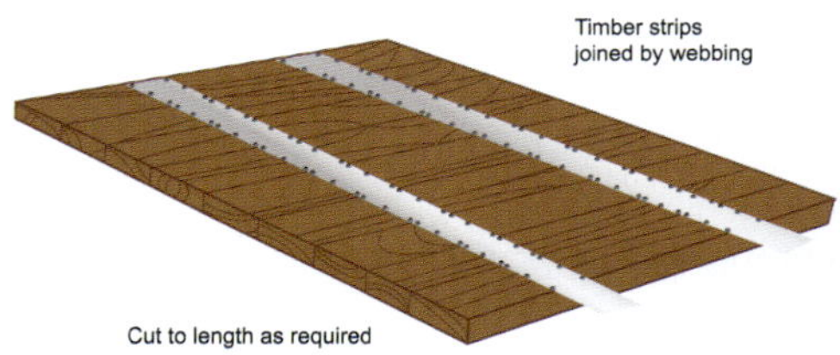

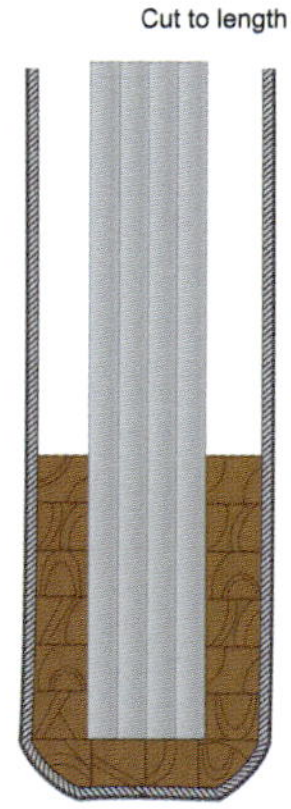

Typical application lifting sheet steel

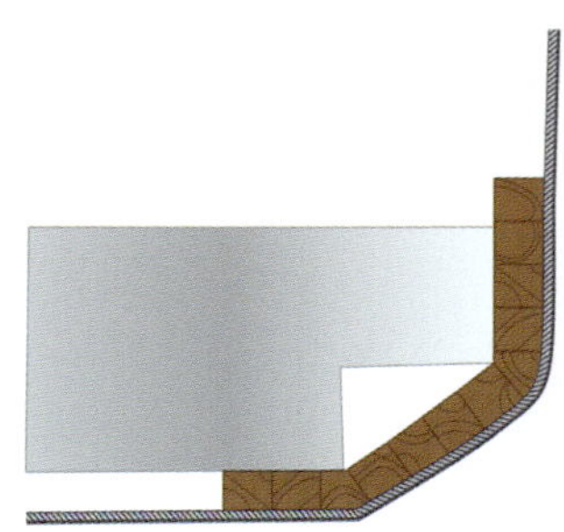

Packing round sharp corners

Sometimes the load will need to be protected from the slings (eg special coatings on structural steel and pipework). This is normally achieved by placing PVC tubing over the wire rope when the sling is being manufactured.

Positioning of Loads

The positioning of loads on a vessel is very important and can make the difference between whether or not they can be offloaded at their destination, especially if the weather conditions are marginal for lifting operations.

This is more critical for heavier loads but even lighter loads positioned in the middle of the vessel can cause problems if the vessel cannot manoeuvre close enough to the installation. For that reason, cargo must be prioritised and positioned on the vessel accordingly.

If the vessel is shared between installations or operating companies, which is often the case, the positioning of cargo will be affected by the order in which it will be taken off. However, there are other considerations such as each individual crane's ability to handle loads.

A crane's lifting capacity decreases as the radius increases and therefore heavier loads or priority containers (food for example) should always be placed towards the side of the vessel that will be alongside the installation. This is to allow the vessel to maintain an acceptable distance from the installation when manoeuvring the load to within the crane's working radius for that particular load.

The positioning of standard containers and open top containers next to each other does not usually present problems, but consideration is required when placing other types of loads together on the vessel. The aim is to prevent any load snagging against another load when being lifted. A typical example of poor vessel loading would be the positioning of bundles of tubulars in close proximity to fuel or oil tanks. There is the possibility that the tubulars could get tangled up in the tank protection frame or even pierce the tank should the bundle swing.

Figure 4.15 - Tubulars (capped) for shipping offshore. The capping prevents the retention of seawater within the tube when encountering heavy weather.

The preparation of a deck plan for the supply vessel can save a lot of time by reducing the amount of double handling. It will also lessen the risk of injury to personnel and damage to equipment.

Pre-Slung Containers for Offshore Use

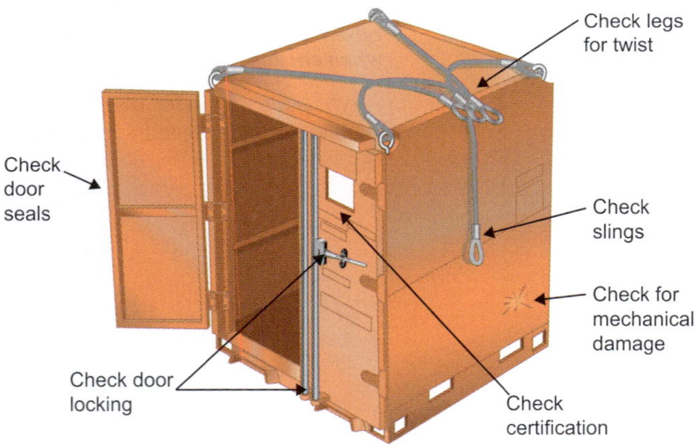

Pre-Shipping Checklist

1. Check structure and general condition of CTU.
2. Check condition of door locks and seals.
3. Check capacity of the CTU and ensure it is not overloaded.
4. Check certification date and make sure there is at least one month's certification remaining.
5. Ensure correct hazard labels are affixed if applicable.
6. Ensure old hazard labels are removed.
7. Check that heavier cargo is at the bottom.
8. Make sure there are no sharp items next to soft-skinned drums.
9. Ensure there is adequate packing between the items of freight.
10. Check the cargo is lashed down or wedged in place.
11. In open top units, check drainage holes are clear.
12. Check door safety nets are fitted where possible.
13. Ensure there are no loose items on the roof of the CTU.
14. Check condition of slings and shackles.
15. Check the weight is as manifested.

Heli-Fuel Tanks

Pre-Shipping Checklist

1. Check structure and general condition of tank.
2. Check condition of protection frame.
3. Check certification date and make sure there is at least one month's certification remaining.
4. Ensure correct hazard labels are affixed if applicable.
5. Ensure old hazard labels are removed.
6. Check that valves are locked shut and there are no leaks.
7. Ensure there are no loose items on the roof of the tank.
8. Check all bolt-on covers are secure.
9. Check condition of slings and shackles.
10. Check gross weight of the tank and ensure it is not overloaded.

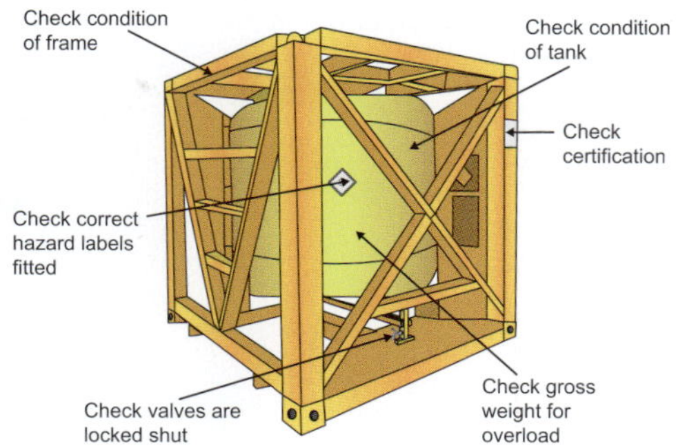

Cargo Transport Units

The majority of cargo is shipped in either containers or 'open tops'. These are commonly known as Cargo Carrying Units (CCUs) but are officially called Cargo Transport Units (CTUs). There are standards governing the design, manufacture, testing and periodic examination of these units. Compliance with the standards should guarantee their quality and integrity. The certification data is prominently displayed on a plate on the CTU and confirms the latest date of proof load test, visual examination and NDT. Depending on the applicable regulations or standards, the visual inspection can be valid for between 6 and 14 months. Local regulations specify the length of time between inspections.

Before using a CTU it is important to ensure that it is in certification by checking the data plate.

The following abbreviations are used on data plates:

T = Test (Load Tested)
V = Visual (Examined Only)
VN = Visual and Non-Destructive Tested

Apart from statutory examinations by independent inspectors, the user should also check the containers for any obvious damage or excessive corrosion. It is not sufficient just to check the data plate.

DATA PLATE

Owner's Name:

Container Identification:	1234
Tare weight	1.2 tonnes
SWL/Payload	3.8 tonnes
Maximum Gross Weight	5 tonnes

Date of last test/examination

30/09/13 T	
20/03/13 V	
10/09/13 VN	

As with all other lifting equipment, CTUs and their lifting slings must be visually examined by the user prior to loading or using.

To avoid certification problems on the units' return trip, they should not be sent on a voyage or offshore unless they have a full month of certification remaining.

Every CTU should be marked with three weights:

1. Tare weight = the weight of the empty unit.
2. SWL/Capacity = the weight of load it can carry.
3. Gross weight = the summation of the tare and SWL.

Cargo Transport Units

Berglok Chain Slings

This is a non-welded chain sling for offshore container lifting. Instead of welded links the Offshore Berglok chain coupler is used to connect to the master link as an end link.

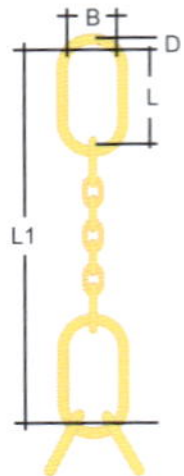

Offshore master link – Type OMTR
Connection to chain with BL-OFFS

Code	Max. load tonnes max. 45°	S.F.	For chain size mm	L	B	D	L1
OMTR-10-8	3.4	8.0	10	270	140	26	1,000
OMTR-13-8	5.7	8.0	13	270	140	32	1,000
OMTR-16-8	10.0	6.8	16	270	140	36	1,000
OMTR-19-8	17.5	5.5	19	300	180	45	1,200

Note: Max angle measured from vertical line - S.F. = Safety Factor.

4-Legged Berglok chain sling fifth leg – Type OSBF-4L

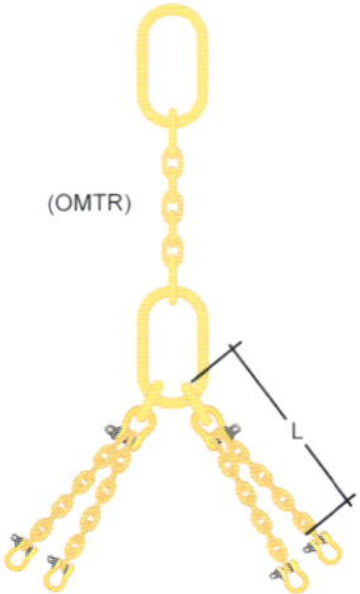

Code	Max. load tonnes max. 45°	S.F.	For chain size mm	Use with shackle
OSBF-4L-10	3.4	8.0	10	BS-10 OFFS
OSBF-4L-13	5.7	8.0	13	BS-13 OFFS
OSBF-4L-16	10.0	6.8	16	BS-16 OFFS
OSBF-4L-19	17.5	5.5	19	BS-19 OFFS

Note:
1. Max angle measured from vertical line - S.F. = Safety Factor.
2. L = Length to suit your requirements, ie container size.

Sea Fastening

Sea fastening is the tying down and securing of cargo to prevent it moving around the vessel's deck in bad weather. All cargo should be restrained in the three directions of movement, ie forward to aft, port to starboard and against upward movement.

For the majority of containers positioned along the side of the vessel, it is common practice to use winches on the deck to secure them.

Most vessels have eyeplates or rings sunk into the decks to which various types of lashing equipment can be attached. The most popular and easy to use are polyester cargo ratchet lashings. For heavier duty restraint, loadbinders are used with chain and rigging screws.

Support stools are normally secured to the deck for shipping large pipes. The pipes are lashed down onto them for stability during transit.

Larger loads may have transportation frames to support the load and to spread the load over the strong points of the vessel's deck.

WARNING

Securing a load by welding directly to the vessel deck is to be avoided at all costs due to the danger of some of the welds still being intact as the lift takes place.

If any special sea fastening arrangements have been made, it is vitally important that the supply vessel crew are instructed as to the removal procedure once the load has arrived at the destination.

Depending on the complexity of the project, procedural documents, job packs or even specialised personnel may have to be on board to assist with the offloading.

If the load is of a substantial height, ladders may be required to allow the deck crew access to hook up the rigging when offloading.

Sea Fastening

Duty	Breaking Strain
Standard	5,000 kg
Heavy	10,000 kg

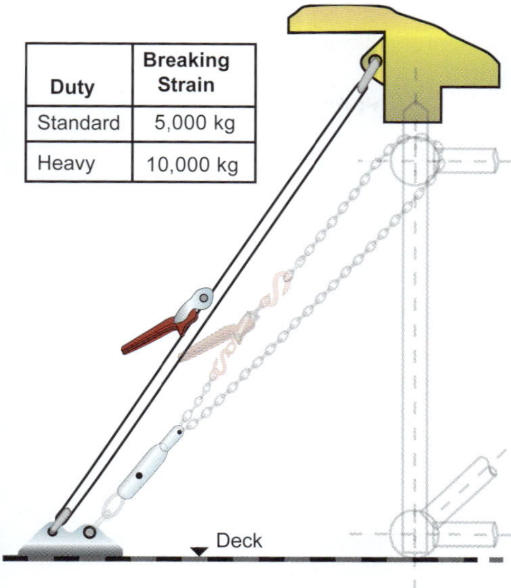

Cargo Restraint Assembly

Duty		Breaking Strain
Std	10 mm dia.	7,360 kg
Hvy	13 mm dia.	11,800 kg
X Hvy	16 mm dia.	16,800 kg

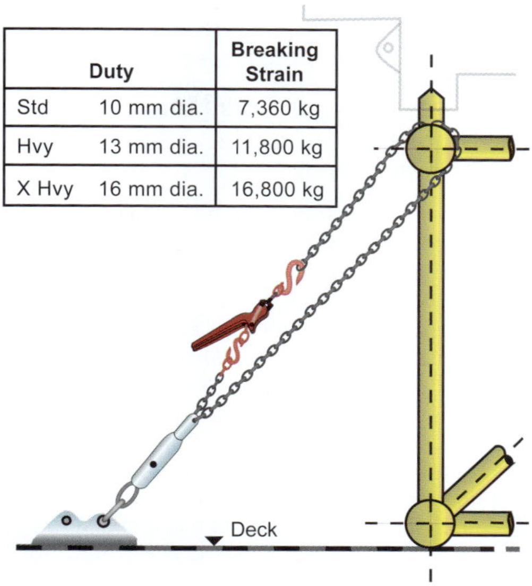

Load Binder, Chain and Turnbuckle

Note: Hold down capacity = one-third of breaking strain

Adverse Weather

In adverse weather, the first and most important task is to evaluate the priority of cargo against the chances of it being damaged in transit. There is no point in shipping it out if it arrives at the destination damaged and possibly unusable; it will only get sent back at great cost to all concerned. It would be more efficient to ship it a few days late as opposed to shipping it on time, then having to wait weeks to have it repaired.

If the cargo is essential and has to be shipped, consideration must be given to packaging it more securely due to the possibility of it shifting within the CTU in transit and becoming a hazard at the other end when it is opened.

In severe weather conditions, there is the added possibility of the cargo breaking loose on deck, which can be very hazardous to the deck crew when they try to resecure it on a pitching and heaving deck. There is a huge risk of them being trapped and crushed between loads or the load and the side of the vessel.

Additional or stronger sea lashings may be used to compensate for rough weather.

Crane Operations

The most common restriction to crane operations is bad weather, specifically high winds which can blow the load out of the safe operating radius, possibly resulting in an overload situation.

The maximum wind speed allowable is dependent on the crane design and specifications. The limit set by the manufacturer may be reduced at the discretion of the crane operator, who has the final say as to whether or

Adverse Weather

not a lift takes place. However, extreme caution should be exercised when carrying out lifting operations in wind speeds exceeding 40 knots. Materials that have a large 'sail area' or that are light in weight, eg steel plate, scaffold board bundles, tubulars, etc, should not be lifted in high or gusting winds.

In an offshore environment, the sea state must also be considered. If a supply vessel is pitching up and down in a heavy swell, snatching of the load will take place, and this increases the dynamic loading on the crane. Even if the crane is multi-reeved and has the capacity to lift the load, it must be remembered that the more the line parts, the slower the hoisting speed, eg if it is on four falls, it will only lift at a quarter of the speed. This is particularly important when working supply vessels as the load should be lifted quickly enough to avoid it re-impacting on the deck as the vessel rises on the following wave. Lloyd's Register of Shipping recommend minimum hoisting speeds (hook speeds) to prevent this situation:

Beaufort Force	Minimum speed allowable
2	0.2 metres per second
4	0.33 metres per second
6	0.46 metres per second
8	0.64 metres per second

The crane operator should enter the sea state data on the safe load indicator system prior to carrying out any lifts. The crane operator is responsible for confirming weather conditions on a regular basis and updating the safe load indicator accordingly.

In bad weather conditions, each lift must be judged on the requirement for making the lift. Consultation between the deck foreman, crane operator and vessel master must take place before the lift is carried out.

Carriage of Bulk Cargoes on Offshore Support Vessels

Offshore support vessels such as supply boats and anchor handlers do not just carry deck cargo but also carry dry and liquid bulk cargoes which are transferred by hose to/from the shore/installation. Common dry cargoes include cement and barites. Liquid cargoes include potable water, diesel, brine and oil-based mud. Some offshore vessels are capable of carrying chemicals such as methanol.

Water is carried for a number of reasons, including potable water for consumption on the installation and water for operational purposes such as mixing drill water with cement powder. The main difference between transporting potable and drill water is the tanks that they are carried in; potable water cannot be carried in drill water tanks. Other than stability, the main concern with carrying large volumes of water is the typically low shore pressure and time required to load it.

Mud (oil-based or water-based) is principally used as a drilling fluid to provide a hydrostatic head and to help recover the drilling slurry. Originally comprised of barite and diesel, it is now a high value blend of chemicals which should be loaded with care. It is important that the particles are kept in suspension while the mud is in the tanks. This is commonly achieved by recirculating the fluid using a pump. Some tanks are fitted with agitators that rotate and keep the mud in motion.

Residues will be left on board after discharge because of the composition of the mud. The volume will depend on any obstacles and the internal structures within the tank. The greater the volume of suspended particles (barite), the greater the specific gravity and the increase in residues. When new mud is to be loaded, cleaning requirements must be established, as different compounds may not be compatible. Some ships will have mud tank cleaning systems on board, but contractors will more

Carriage of Bulk Cargoes on Offshore Support Vessels

frequently be employed to clean the tanks and dispose of the residues. However, the ship must ensure the tank is acceptable to receive the next cargo.

Some chemical additives in mud may present contact or ingestion hazards so the crew must wear appropriate PPE when handling hoses (eg gloves, safety goggles/face mask, overalls, safety footwear, etc). The safety data sheets provided with the cargo should be consulted and retained for reference.

Brine cargoes are chemical compositions used in drilling, often in place of mud. They have similar characteristics to mud but are generally more valuable and are more prone to contamination from other cargoes or water. Safety precautions are also similar to mud, but some brines pose greater risks. Of particular note are brines containing zinc bromide and calcium bromide which are very hazardous to health, pollutant, present a significant fire hazard and are very corrosive.

Due to the nature and high value of mud and brine cargoes, independent surveyors may be employed by operators to oversee loading.

Dry bulk cargoes are often carried in hopper tanks with the discharge point located at the bottom of the tank. To load and discharge the cargo, it is necessary to pressurise the air in the tank. Before discharging to the installation, air is normally blown to ensure the line is clear and to check for leaks. Once confirmed ready and the tank is appropriately pressurised, the valves can be opened for discharge. It is important to maintain a sufficient balance of pressure that will keep the cargo moving without over pressurising (as this reduces the volume moved). As the cargo passes through the hoses, they may be seen to jump or move on deck – particularly in older systems and when the discharge starts.

Operation manuals for equipment and the ship's safety management system (SMS) will set out procedures for operations. Great care must be taken to avoid pollution, and pollution prevention equipment must be in place in case of spills. Any incident should be reported and recorded appropriately.

Offshore support vessels fitted with the necessary infrastructure may carry bulk liquid chemicals. Typically methanol (and mono-ethylene glycol (MEG)) is used offshore as a hydrate inhibitor, to prevent the formation of hydrates, water molecules that attach to other molecules, which can block gas lines.

Methanol is a colourless, flammable toxic liquid with a flashpoint around 12°C, lower than diesel but higher than petrol. The main hazards are associated with ingestion or poisoning through contact with clothes soaked in methanol. Signs of poisoning include drunkenness, headaches, nausea, blurred vision, avoiding sunlight and either impaired breathing or unconsciousness. Inhalation in high concentrations, eg 50,000 ppm, can be fatal; lower concentrations may cause narcosis. Asphyxia/anoxia is a risk due to the oxygen deficiency in tank atmospheres.

The flames from burning methanol may be invisible, but the heat will be apparent. The IMDG Code advises fighting the fire from as great a distance as possible using copious quantities of water. This will also help cool the tanks as water may not be the most effective extinguishing agent. Alcohol-resistant foam is much more effective.

Methanol tanks should have an inerted cofferdam and some form of inerting medium (typically nitrogen) capable of inerting to less than 3% O_2. The nitrogen will be supplied from either bottles or a generator. When involved in methanol operations, PPE should include solvent-resistant gloves and face, respiratory and body protection.

Another chemical less frequently carried is glycol and, while more stable, the hazardous data sheets should be consulted prior to operations and carriage.

The ship's INLS certification will list cargoes that are permitted for carriage and provide appropriate guidance.

Carriage of Bulk Cargoes on Offshore Support Vessels

Hose connection manifolds are normally located at the after end of the cargo deck, with many supply ships also having manifolds port and starboard of midships. Hoses are normally colour coded:

- Black – mud
- red – brine
- brown - fuel
- green – drill water
- blue – potable water
- yellow – cement
- orange – barite.

Hose connections are usually either the lugged-screw 'Weco' type for water, mud and dry bulks, or the self-sealing Avery-Hardoll type for fuel, brine and chemicals.

Figure 4.16 - Weco type hose connector

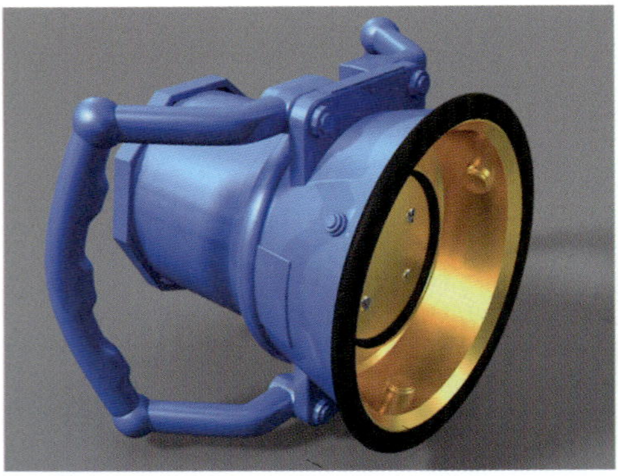

Figure 4.17 - Avery-Hardoll type hose connector

When loading, carrying and discharging bulk cargoes, attention must be paid to the stability of the ship. This must include consideration of the free surface effect and the dynamic forces experienced while conducting such operations at sea.

MGN 283 provides guidance for the back loading of bulk liquids from offshore installations, with reference to certification, testing and reporting requirements. The master should confirm the following before commencing operations:

- *the contaminated cargo has been sampled in accordance with guidance given in the good practice guidelines, such that the sampling should be set up to detect the worst case situation;*
- *the flashpoint of the contaminated cargo exceeds 60°C;*
- *there is no trace of Hydrogen Sulphide (H_2S) in the product mass;*
- *the tanks into which the contaminated cargo is to be loaded should not contain or have contained a previous contaminated cargo and only minimal residual cargo of oil-based or water-based mud should be present in the tank;*
- *the Appendix II Analysis Form attached to the MGN should be completed, signed and given to the master before back loading commences.*

CHAPTER 5

Machinery and Equipment

Main Engine Overview

Most marine engines use fuel oil or diesel oil and can be divided into two main types:

- Large, slow-running direct drive engines with a limited number of cylinders
- medium to high-speed engines driving through reduction gears.

Slow-Speed Engines

Slow-speed engines run at between 40 to 120 rpm. A slow piston speed, fewer working parts and low rates of wear make them very efficient, economical and reliable.

Most large, slow-speed, direct drive marine diesel engines operate on the two-stroke cycle.

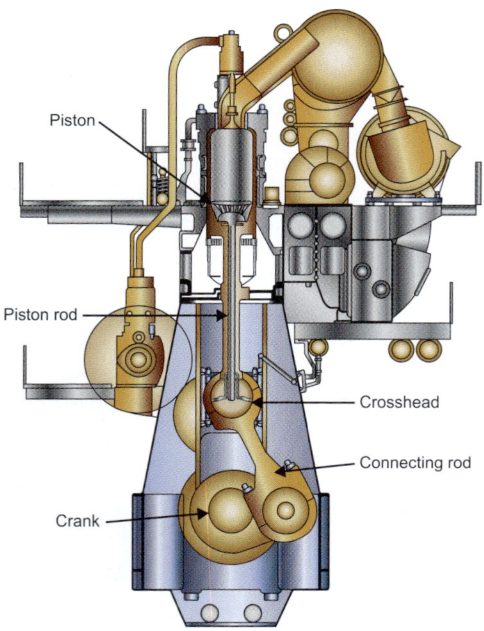

Figure 5.1 - Slow speed (two-stroke)

Medium and High-Speed Engines

The majority of medium and high-speed diesel engines are designed to operate on a four-stroke cycle and they tend to be much smaller and less powerful than slow-speed engines.

Medium speed generally refers to between 400 and 1,000 rpm, and high speed in excess of 1,000 rpm. Consequently, these engines require gearing reduction to decrease the drive speed before being connected to the tail shaft and the ship's propellers.

The power/weight and power/size ratios make these engines particularly attractive where engine room size is constrained. They are commonly found on ferries and coastal vessels. Long-stroke versions are also produced to give greater fuel economy while running on heavy fuel oil.

The majority of medium and high-speed diesel engines for main or auxiliary drives operate on the four-stroke cycle, which takes place during four consecutive strokes, or two complete revolutions, of the engine.

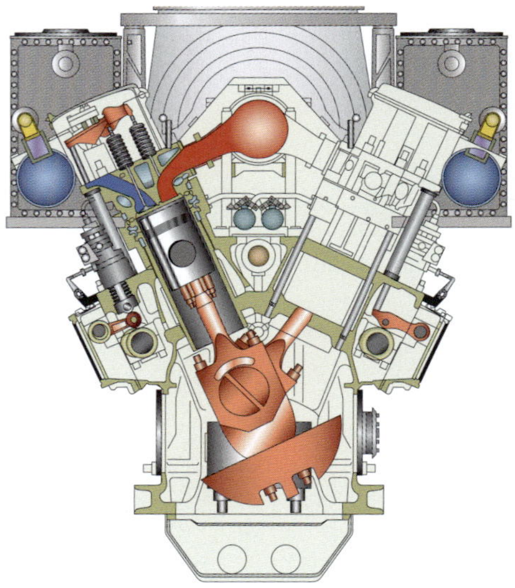

Figure 5.2 - Medium-high speed vee engine (four-stroke)

Diesel Engine Operation

In a diesel engine, the cycle consists of four operations within the cylinder:

1. Compression of a charge of air.
2. Injection of fuel which then ignites.
3. Expansion of the hot gases formed during combustion.
4. Expulsion of the used gas to exhaust.

The cylinder is then recharged with air and the cycle is repeated.

Diesel engines can be designed to complete this cycle once during each revolution, termed the two-stroke cycle, or alternatively it can take two engine revolutions to complete the cycle, the four-stroke cycle. An engine can only operate on the cycle for which it was designed.

Gas and Dual-Fuel Engines

Due to the rising cost of traditional fuel and increasing environmental legislation, there is growing interest in the use of natural gas as a marine fuel.

A number of different engines are being produced but the two main types are dual fuel, which can burn gas or liquid fuel, and single gas fuel, which are exclusively gas burning.

In some engines, the changeover between diesel and gas fuel can be completed automatically and instantly, from a backup fuel system, in the event of a break in supply.

Dual engines can work on the same principle as diesel, ie induction, compression, expansion and exhaust. When the engine is burning diesel only, the engine uses a conventional diesel combustion process. However, when burning gas, the engines use lean-burn, where the volume of gas in the gas/air mix is much smaller than that associated with liquid fuels.

Single Gas Fuel

Most large LNG tankers are equipped with steam turbine power plants that allow them to use boil-off gas as a fuel, although engine manufacturers are now producing dedicated gas-burning reciprocating piston-based engines.

Fuel Systems

Most marine diesel engines are configured to operate on heavy fuel oil (HFO). However, vessels operating in Emission Control Areas (ECAs) are required to burn fuel with a lower sulphur content than normal HFO. Low sulphur heavy fuel oil is available, but some vessel operators also use distillate (diesel) fuel as a compliance option. In effect, this means that many ships need two fuel supply systems – one for operations outside ECAs where HFO may be used, and one for ECA compliant fuel.

Starting

To start main engines, or engines such as diesel generators, it is necessary to use a system that delivers sufficient torque to 'turn them over'. These engines are typically fitted with an air-start system that uses the energy stored in an appropriately sized compressed air pressure vessel. These systems include starting-air receivers and compressors.

Smaller plant, including emergency generators, may use electric starter motors similar to the starter motors found in cars.

Figure 5.3 - Starting-air receiver

Starting-air receivers are used to store compressed air for the starting and manoeuvring of main engines, starting auxiliary engines, and supplying pneumatic control and other auxiliary air pressure systems.

Figure 5.4 - Starting-air compressors

Starting-air compressors recharge the starting-air receivers and deliver compressed air for other users on board. At least two air compressors must be fitted, each of which is capable of supplying all demands.

Machinery and Equipment

Automatic Oil-Water Separator

Figure 5.5 - Oil-water separator

The suction mode automatic oily-water separator is claimed to reduce effluent level to 2 ppm of oil in the mixture or less. To achieve this low level, the separator incorporates concentric cylindrical oil coalescing cartridges through which the oil-water mixture is drawn by a positive displacement pump. In the normal mode, a controller constantly monitors the oil-water interface level and the overboard discharge. If the effluent exceeds a set limit, the process is stopped and an alarm given.

Sewage and Sludge

Figure 5.6 - Sewage plant

On 1st August 2010, amendments to MARPOL Annex IV (Sewage) entered into force for existing ships. The original legislation entered into force on 1st August 2005 for new ships of 400 GT or over on international voyages.

Under these regulations, ships are prohibited from discharging sewage unless one of the following criteria is met:

- Uncomminuted or non-disinfected sewage can only be discharged at a distance >12 nautical miles from land
- comminuted and disinfected sewage can be discharged at a distance >3 nautical miles from land
- a certified sewage treatment plant is in operation.

Retention Systems (Holding Tank)

The main advantage of this system is simplicity in operation and virtually no maintenance. They must comply with present regulations, have sufficient storage capacity and have a visual indicator of the contents.

With some retention systems, the sewage is first passed through a comminutor, which macerates the solids, giving greater surface area. The mix is then passed into a chlorine contact tank where it must remain for at least 20 minutes before discharge overboard.

Biological Treatment Plants

These systems use fresh air and aerobic bacteria to decompose the sewage.

Raw sewage passes through a comminutor into the collection compartment. When the level in this compartment rises sufficiently, overflow of the liquid takes place into the treatment/aeration compartment where the sewage is broken down by aerobic activation. Fluid in this compartment is continuously agitated by air, which supplies the necessary oxygen for purification.

The effluent is then pumped to the settlement compartment where the sludge settles out leaving treated effluent, which passes over a weir into the chlorination compartment before discharge overboard.

With the extended aeration system, it can take 5 to 14 days before the plant is fully operational because of the prolonged aeration of sewage necessary to produce the bacteria that carry out the purifying process. Therefore, the plant should be kept operational at all times. It should be noted that oil or grease entering the system kill useful bacteria.

Chemical Treatment Plants

These are recirculation systems in which the sewage is macerated, chemically treated, then allowed to settle. The clear, sterilised, filtered liquid is returned to the sanitary system for further use and the solids are periodically discharged to a sullage tank or incinerator.

Shell and Tube Type Heat Exchanger (Stack)

Figure 5.7 - Shell/tube exchanger

A tube stack is made up of stress-relieved aluminium brass tubes expanded into naval brass tube plates. One plate is fixed and the other is free to allow for expansion of the stack. Brass circular baffles give radial flow to the fluid and support to the tube stack.

Plate Heat Exchanger

A plate heat exchanger consists of a variable number of gaskets and titanium (stainless steel or aluminium brass) plates, clamped together between a closing pressure plate and a frame. The surface of the plates is corrugated to give strength and additional heat transfer surface. The most recent development is to use a criss-cross pattern. This gives additional support, allows pressure to be increased and plate thickness to be reduced.

Gaskets are usually nitrile rubber bonded to the plate and arranged so that, in the event of failure, the two fluids cannot mix.

Figure 5.8 - Shell/tube exchanger plate heat exchanger

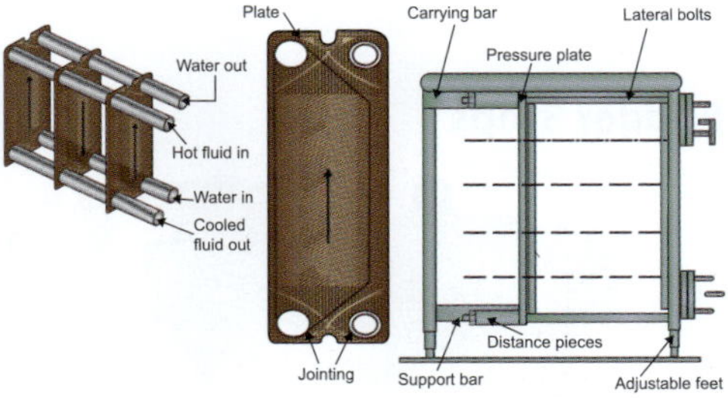

Figure 5.9 - Titanium plate heat exchanger

Machinery and Equipment

Steering Gear

Figure 5.10 - Steering gear

Steering gear is required to:

(a) Operate continuously

(b) move the rudder rapidly to any position in response to an order from the bridge during manoeuvring, and hold it in the required position

(c) have arrangements for relieving abnormal stress and returning the rudder to its required position

(d) maintain the ship on course regardless of wind and waves and sea.

Rudder Stops

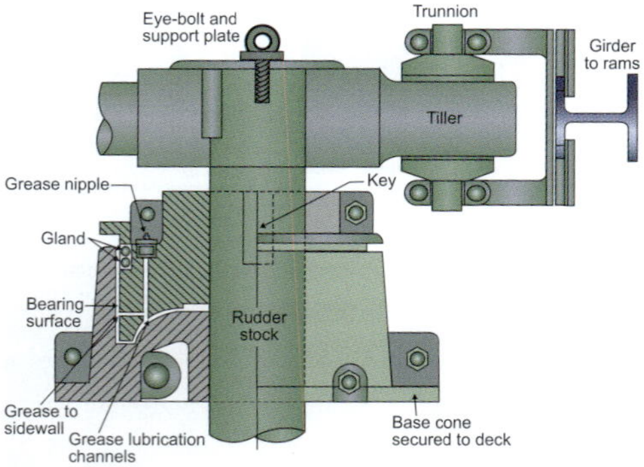

Figure 5.11 - Rudder stop

External rudder stops are fitted to limit the rudder's movement to, say, 39° each way from the mid-position. There are also stops in the steering gear set to limit the angle to which the rudder can be moved by the gear. These are set to typically 37° each way from the mid-position. The latter are necessary to prevent the rudder being forced against the outside stops. The outside stops prevent unlimited rudder movement, which could arise from damage, causing the rudder to become disconnected and possibly contact with the propeller. Limits on the telemotor are set at 35° each way from the mid-position. Lifting of the rudder in bad weather is prevented by jumping steps.

Ram Type Hydraulic Steering Gear

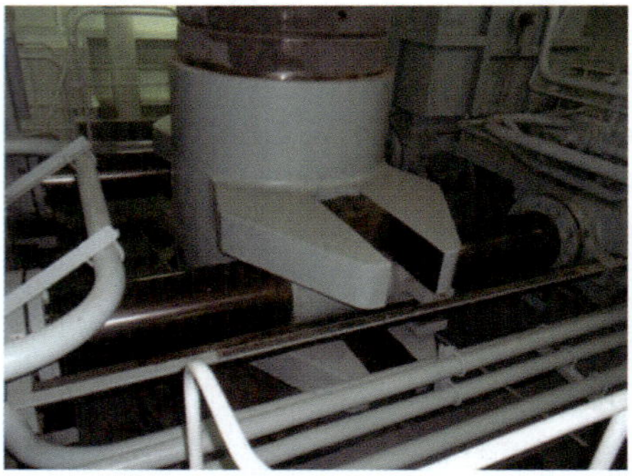

Figure 5.12 - Hydraulic 'four ram steering gear'

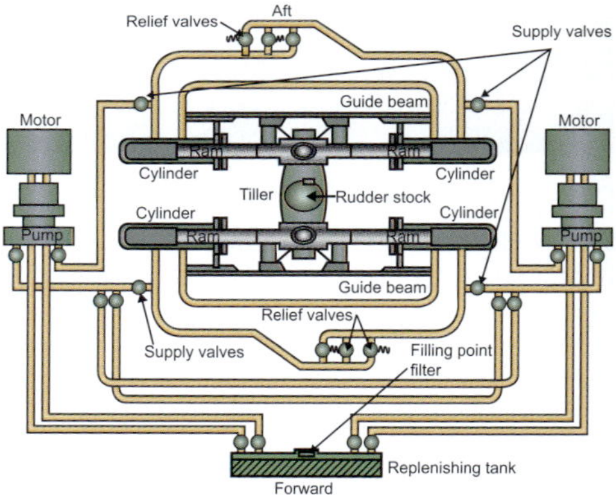

Figure 5.13 - Hydraulic 'four ram steering gear'

Operation of Four Ram Gear

The pipe arrangement of the four ram system shows the connections from two pumps to four rams. Because of the non-reverse lock arrangements, one pump can be stopped with the valves left open. All four rams work together but, in the event of damage, either pair of rams can be isolated from the pressure pumps and allowed to idle with the bypass open. The remaining pair of rams then operates as a two ram gear. The bypasses are in parallel with the relief valves.

In an emergency, the rudder can be locked by closing the supply valves. The relief valves between the pipes connecting the opposing rams are designed to lift if pressure in the system rises to

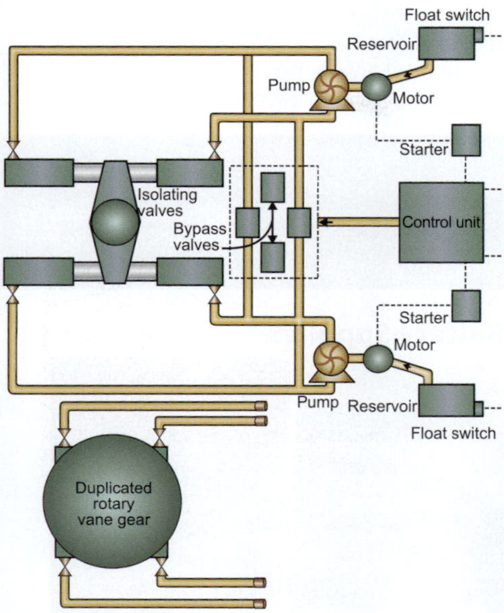

Figure 5.14 - Isolating a pair of rams

about 10% above normal. This will occur due either to the rudder being hit by a heavy sea or from direct loading. Bypassing of oil from one side of the system to the other through the relief valves permits the rams to move and abnormal stress on the rudder stock is thereby avoided. The hunting gear will cause the rudder movement to be corrected by putting the pump on stroke.

The four ram gear consists of two pairs of rams, each pair being capable of supplying 50% of the torque required. For normal full ahead running, they are operated together to provide 100% torque, with one pump and motor power unit in use. The system operates in the same way as other four ram arrangements, but duplication of the hydraulic pipework as well as pump and motor power units gives an additional safeguard with complete hydraulic system redundancy.

Shaft Bearings

Introduction

Main propulsion shafting is supported by bearings which maintain the shafting in proper alignment. These bearings divide themselves into two groups; bearings inside the hull watertight boundary and bearings outside the hull watertight boundary.

The requirements imposed upon main shaft bearings are severe. The bearings are required to operate at speeds ranging from 0.1 rpm, when on turning gear, to 100 or more rpm, in either direction of rotation. Unlike some applications, the bearing loads do not vary with rpm but are essentially constant at all speeds. Reliability is heavily emphasised in the design of bearings because they have no redundancy and a single bearing failure may incapacitate the propulsion system.

In addition to radial bearings which support the main shafting, there is a main thrust bearing located inside the ship which transmits the propeller thrust from the shafting to the hull structure.

Shaft Support Bearings

Figure 5.15 - Shaft support bearing

Bearings located inside the ship's watertight boundary are called line shaft bearings, but they are sometimes referred to as steady or spring bearings. Almost without exception, these bearings are ruggedly constructed and oil-lubricated. Except in special cases, the bearings are self-lubricated by rings or disks arranged in such a manner that lubrication is effected by the rotation of the shaft.

Bearing housings are split horizontally at the shaft centreline. The bottom half of the bearing must be very robust since it carries the vertical shaft load and any side load that exists.

Ship Side Valves

Figure 5.16 - Ship side valve

Machinery and Equipment

Ship side valves control the flow of seawater into the pipe systems for uses such as circulating the condensers, coolers and potable water maker and filling the ballast tanks. Inlet valves are submerged below the light load line, and water enters on the underside of the valve (so that it will not cease to operate even if the spindle is broken). The entrance to these valves is covered with an externally mounted ship's side grid to prevent debris being sucked in. In rivers and shallow waters, sand may be drawn into the main injection valve, which is often placed above the bilge keel, and a higher ship's side valve (or seachest) is often provided and used in shallow waters.

Ship side valves are required to allow flow in only one direction. To prevent flow in the opposite direction, non-return valves are fitted in the piping system.

Emergency Generator

The power rating of an emergency generator is determined by the size and type of ship. On some small vessels, a few kW will suffice for emergency lighting, but large and more sophisticated ships, such as LNG and LPG carriers and cruise liners, may require hundreds of kW for emergency lighting, re-starting of the main engine auxiliaries and to power fire-fighting equipment. An emergency generator is hooked up to its own emergency switchboard and both are usually located beside one another in a room well above the waterline, eg on or above the boat deck. In normal operation, the emergency switchboard is supplied from the main switchboard by a cable called the 'bus-tie'. It is not normally possible to synchronise the emergency and main generators. Special interlocks in the control circuits of the circuit breakers, at each end of the bus-tie, prevent parallel running.

Figure 5.17 - Emergency generator

Starting of the emergency generator prime mover is often automatic. The run-up is initiated by an electrical relay which monitors the normal mains power supply.

Correct functioning of the autostart equipment is vital to the production of emergency power. Regular, weekly testing of the emergency generator should include simulation of the loss of normal power.

Battery Supplies

Figure 5.18 - Emergency batteries

A properly maintained emergency battery will immediately supply electrical power when required. This feature makes the ship's emergency batteries a vital component in the provision of power to essential and emergency systems on board.

Essential power supplies, eg for GMDSS equipment, telephone systems, fire detection, general alarm circuits, etc, are often supplied from two sets of batteries worked on a regular charge/discharge cycle.

Emergency battery supplies, eg for emergency generator start-up and emergency lighting, are used in a standby role to give power when the main supply fails. Ships' batteries are usually rated at a nominal voltage of 24V dc.

Battery maintenance includes keeping the cell tops clean and dry, checking the tightness of terminal nuts and applying a smear of petroleum jelly to such connections to prevent corrosion. Care must be taken when checking batteries (such as when using a hydrometer to check the batteries' specific gravity). Protective rubber gloves and eye goggles must be worn when handling electrolyte. Insulated spanners should be available for use on cell connections to prevent inadvertent short-circuiting of battery terminals.

For all rechargeable batteries, it is essential to replace water lost during gassing and by normal evaporation with the addition of distilled water to the correct level above the plates. Exposure of the cell plates to air will rapidly reduce the life of the battery.

Diesel Engines

Engine Types

Marine diesel engines can be divided into two main types; large, slow-running direct drive engines with limited numbers of cylinders, and medium to high-speed engines driving through reduction gears. Cylinder sizes do not necessarily distinguish engine types; slow speed engines are available with cylinder bores down to 260 mm, while medium-speed engines are produced with bores up to 620 mm.

Slow-Speed Engines (55 to 150 rpm)

Large, slow-speed, direct drive main engines operate exclusively on two-stroke cycles. Slow piston speed and fewer working parts make them very economical in lube oil consumption and give low rates of wear and remarkable reliability.

Medium and High-Speed Engines (400 to 1,000 rpm)

Most of these engines are designed to operate on a four-stroke cycle. They are much smaller than equivalent slow-speed engines, but require gearing reduction to reduce the drive speed before they are connected to the tail shaft and the ship's propellers.

Their power/weight and power/size ratios make these engine types particularly attractive where engine room size is constrained. Long-stroke versions are produced to give greater fuel economy while running on heavy fuel oil.

Medium and high-speed engines may be constructed in either 'in-line' or 'Vee' configurations. As the name implies, Vee engines are constructed with two banks of cylinders arranged at an angle using a common crankcase and bedplate with considerable saving in size and weight. Twice as many cylinders can be accommodated in a given length, although the width of the engine is increased (see diagram on page 295 c.a. 1309).

The Work Done Diagram

In the original patent by Rudolf Diesel, the diesel engine operated on the diesel cycle in which heat was added at constant pressure. This was achieved by the blast injection principle (fuel injection). Nowadays the term is used to describe any reciprocating engine in which the heat induced by compressing air in the cylinders ignites a finely atomised spray of fuel, ie fuel injection.

This means that the theoretical cycle on which the modern diesel engine works is better represented by the dual or mixed cycle, illustrated below. The area of the diagram, to a suitable scale, represents the work done by the piston during one cycle.

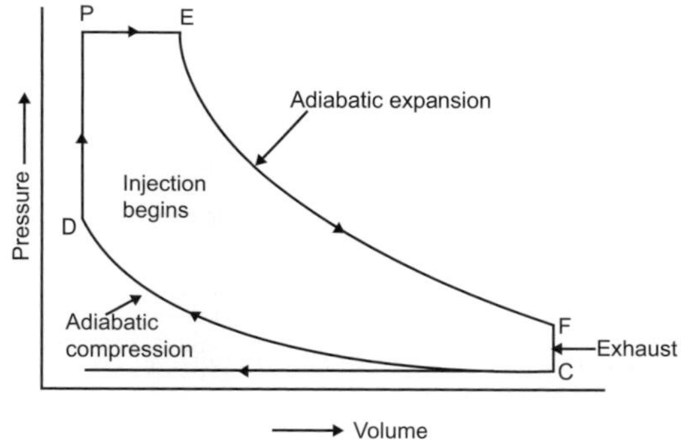

Figure 5.19 - Dual or mixed diesel engine cycle

Starting from point C, the air is compressed adiabatically to point D. Fuel injection begins at D, and heat is added to the cycle partly at constant volume, as shown by vertical line DP, and partly at constant pressure, as shown by horizontal line PE. At point E, expansion begins. This proceeds adiabatically to point F when the heat is rejected to exhaust at constant volume as shown by vertical line FC.

The ideal efficiency of this cycle is about 55 to 60%, ie approximately 40 to 45% of the heat supplied is lost to the exhaust.

For a four-stroke engine, the exhaust and suction strokes are shown by the horizontal line at C, and this has no effect on the cycle.

Engine Cycles

The term 'cycle' refers to one complete sequence of operations required to produce power in an engine. This cycle of operations is continuously repeated while the engine is running. For a diesel engine, it consists of four operations within the cylinder:

Machinery and Equipment

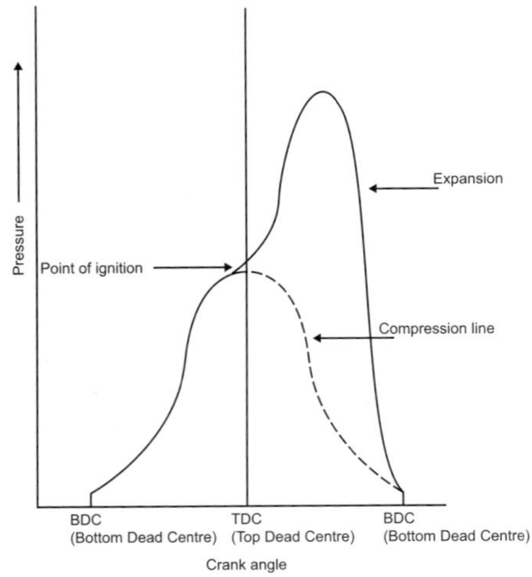

Figure 5.20 - Engine cycle

1. Compression of a charge of air.
2. Injection of fuel which then ignites.
3. Expansion of the hot gases formed during combustion.
4. Expulsion of the used gas to exhaust.

The cylinder is then recharged with air and the cycle is repeated.

Diesel engines can be designed to complete this cycle once during each revolution, ie the two-stroke cycle, or they can take two engine revolutions to complete the cycle, ie the four-stroke cycle. An engine can only operate on the cycle for which it was designed.

Engine stroke is measured as the full distance through which the piston moves between each end of its travel. Therefore, it must move through two complete strokes (one up and one down) during each revolution of the engine.

Engine timing refers to the relative time or position of the crank at which each operation during the cycle is commenced and is completed. It is measured as the angle through which the crank has been rotated from a datum position such as top or bottom dead centre (TDC or BDC).

Two-stroke cycle. Practically all large, slow-speed, direct drive marine diesel engines operate on the two-stroke cycle. As its name implies, a two-stroke cycle takes place in two consecutive strokes of the engine piston, or one revolution of the crankshaft. Therefore, each stage of the cycle is repeated during every revolution of the engine. The two strokes of the cycle may be termed compression stroke and power (or expansion) stroke. Operations take place in a fixed order and must occur when the piston reaches a corresponding position in its stroke. These positions are displayed as volumes on an indicator diagram which corresponds to the pressure within the cylinder. It is convenient to express them in terms of angles of crank position measured from top dead centre (TDS) or bottom dead centre (BDC) and they may be shown as a circle on a timing diagram.

Actual timing may differ between engines due to construction and design differences such as ratio of connecting rod length/crank length, stroke/bore ratio, engine speed, engine rating, etc.

Position

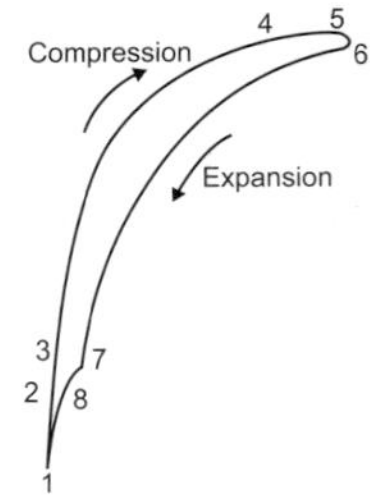

Figure 5.21 - Engine stroke

1 represents bottom of stroke (BDC). Position 5 represents top of stroke (TDC).

1-2 Completion of scavenge. Air is entering the cylinder, expelling exhaust gas and recharging it for the next combustion. Scavenge and exhaust are open.

2-3 Post-scavenge. Scavenge ports have closed and some air within the cylinder may lead to exhaust. In some engines, 2 and 3 are made to coincide to eliminate leakage of air.

3-4 Compression. Exhaust has now closed and the air trapped within the cylinder is compressed by the upstroke of the piston to raise its temperature sufficiently to ignite the fuel.

4-5-6 Fuel injection takes place and combustion occurs causing a rapid rise in pressure. The period for which this continues depends upon the fuel pump setting and the power to be produced.

6-7 Expansion. Combustion completed, the hot gases expand, forcing the piston downwards and converting the heat energy from combustion into work on the piston.

7-8 Exhaust blowdown. Exhaust has opened, allowing gas to pass to exhaust manifold, and pressure drops rapidly in the cylinder.

8-1 Scavenge. Scavenge ports have opened and air enters to expel the remaining exhaust gas. 1-etc Scavenging then continues for the next cycle.

Four-stroke cycle. The majority of medium and high-speed diesel engines for main or auxiliary use operate on the four-stroke cycle, which takes place during four consecutive strokes, or two complete revolutions, of the engine.

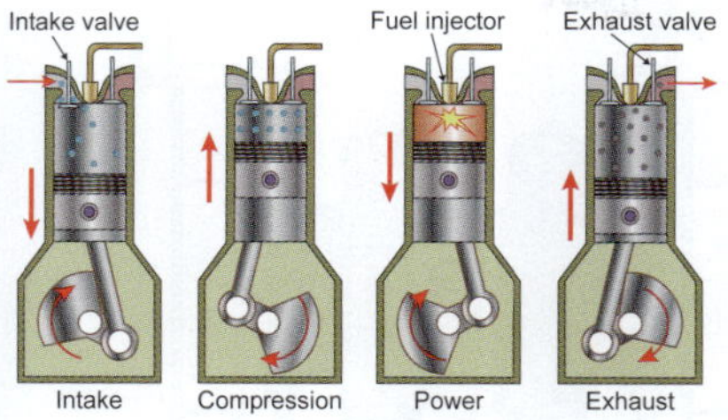

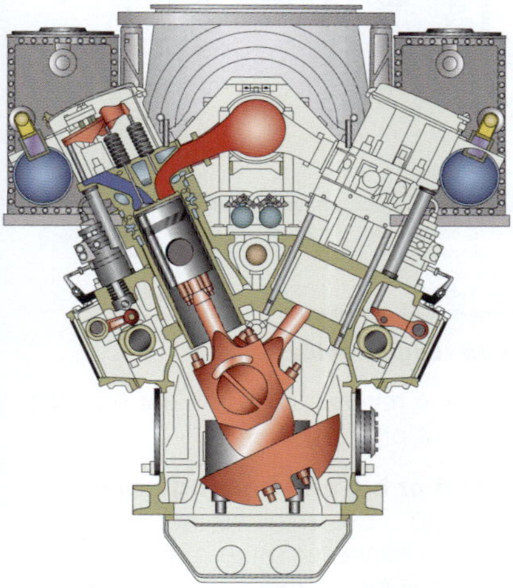

Figure 5.22 - Medium-high speed Vee engine (four-stroke)

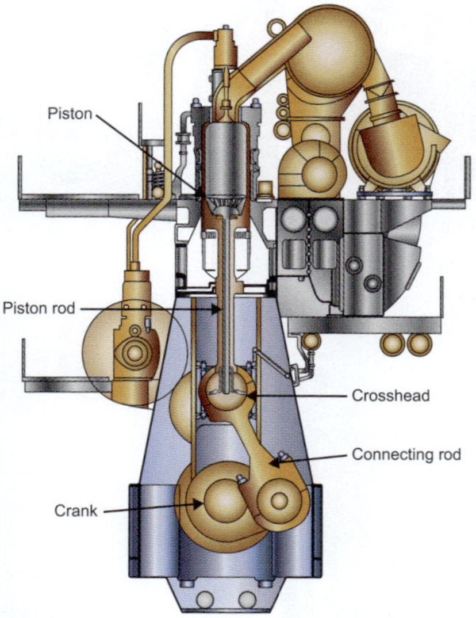

Figure 5.23 - Slow speed (two-stroke)

The Crankshaft

A crankshaft consists of a number of cranks, which are rotated by piston forces transmitted through the connecting rods and bottom end bearings. In-line engines have one crank for each cylinder. Every crank is made up of two crank webs joined by a common crankpin to which the bottom end bearing is fitted. Each web is also connected to a journal to form part of a continuous shaft. A main bearing will support the shaft at each journal. One end of the shaft will be flanged to transmit the engine power and the other end is termed 'free'. Gear or chain drive wheels are added to drive camshafts and other mechanisms if they need to be synchronised with the crankshaft movement. Crankshafts of direct drive engines may incorporate a thrust bearing.

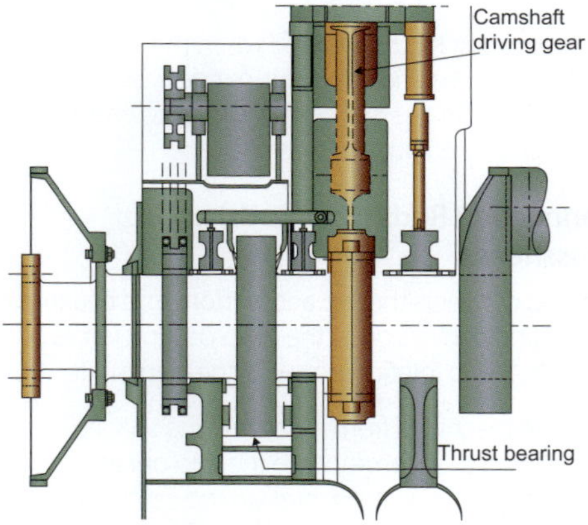

Figure 5.24 - Crankshaft

The crankshaft receives and transmits the full working power of the engine and is subjected to fluctuating bending, torsional and shear stresses.

Main bearings are fitted to support the crankshaft at each journal. They support the weight of all working parts. They must be secure, accurately bored and aligned to prevent any distortion in the shaft. Each bearing is loaded by its adjacent units and wear rates may not be equal. This must be checked and recorded regularly. These checks are known as crank deflections.

Turning Gear

Turning gear is used to turn or rotate the engine when it is not being used (such as in port or at anchor). It can also be engaged to lock the engine in a given position as required for maintenance.

Machinery and Equipment

The gear usually consists of a reversible, electric motor drive which can be engaged to rotate the engine flywheel through a set of gears. The motor is of limited power and it is necessary to open all cylinder indicator cocks to relieve compression while turning the engine. The electric load on the motor should be monitored while turning as an excessive load may give warning of an obstruction in the engine or propeller system.

The turning gear must be engaged before working within the engine. If personnel are required to enter the engine, a permit to work must be raised (confined space entry-machinery). Appropriate isolations must be put in place, eg blocking devices applied, or electric fuses removed to prevent inadvertent movement of the engine.

The gear must be disengaged when the engine is prepared for sea and safety cut-out devices may be incorporated in the manoeuvring gear to ensure this has been carried out.

Connecting Rods (Con-Rods) and Crossheads

This rod connects the top and bottom end bearings, permitting conversion of the reciprocating forces on the piston into rotating power in the crankshaft.

Rods are machined from a steel forging shaped at each end to accommodate the appropriate bearings. A hole is bored through the centre of the rod to allow passage of lubricating oil between the bearings – downward in crosshead engines but upward in trunk piston engines.

The length of the rod is as short as the specification permits, as this determines the overall height of the engine.

Engine guides are vertical sliding bearings fitted to crosshead engines to maintain alignment of the crosshead during the length of the engine stroke. Guide bars are secured to the frames adjacent to the unit. Guide slippers (or shoes) are attached to the ends of the crosshead.

The crosshead or top end bearing transmits the full gas load from the piston to the connecting rod and crankshaft. The load fluctuates throughout the engine cycle. The two-stroke cycle causes an almost continuous downward force, tending to squeeze the oil film from the underside bearing surfaces.

Movement of the bearing is limited by the small angle through which the connecting rod articulates and reverses direction during each engine revolution.

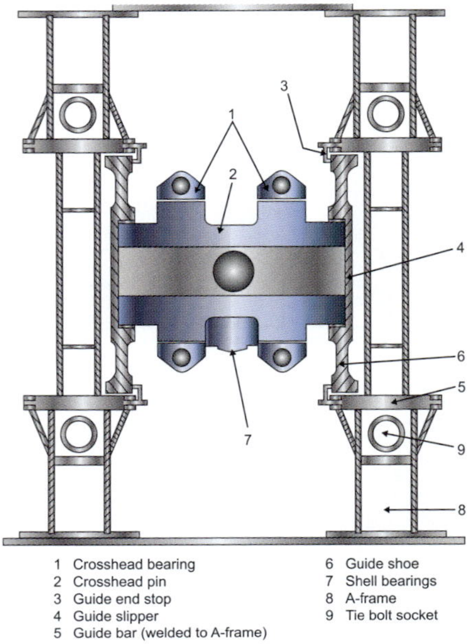

Figure 5.25 - Engine guides

Bottom end or big end bearings transmit loads similar to those in the connecting rod (or crosshead). However, there is the benefit of a continuous sliding movement between

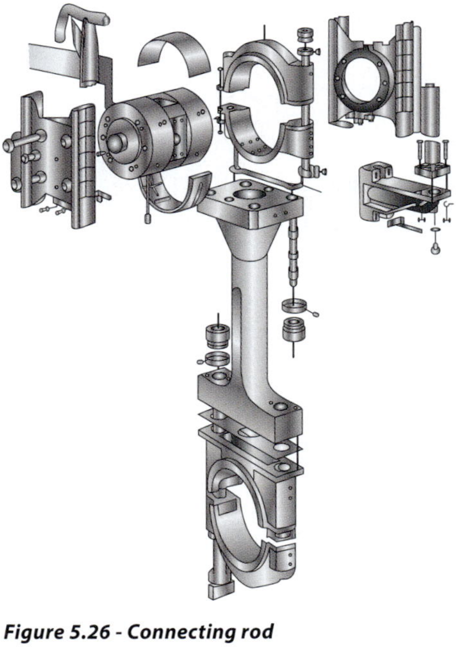

Figure 5.26 - Connecting rod

the crank pin and bearing surfaces which establishes continuous oil lubrication.

Some designs have the bottom end bearing as a separate unit, bolted to the connecting rod. This allows the piston and rod to be extracted (or pulled) for overhaul without disturbing the bearing.

Vee-type engines have the connecting rods from two cylinders connected to each throw of the crankshaft.

Pistons

Pistons require construction properties similar to those of cylinder liners. The piston crown must be able to withstand a high gas load and be able to transmit the force from this to the piston rod. It must have a long fatigue life to be able to tolerate the fluctuating mechanical and thermal stresses (ie the surface of the piston is exposed to very hot combustion gases followed rapidly by cool scavenge air during each engine cycle).

Large two-stroke engine pistons are subject to rigorous conditions due to the large-bore cylinders and heavy fuels. The piston crown must be supported against bending while allowing cooling of its underside. The shape is concave to give an efficient combustion space.

Figure 5.27 - Pistons

Cooling of pistons is necessary to remove excess heat from combustion and to limit thermal stressing. It also controls thermal expansion to maintain correct clearances between piston and liner and between ring grooves and rings. Cooling is achieved by circulating a coolant (oil or fresh water) through internal passages within the piston.

Piston cooling and cylinder jacket cooling must be continued for a period after the engine is stopped to allow a gradual reduction in temperature and reduce thermal stress.

Cylinder Liner

Cylinder liners are designed to give an extensive working life that allows long intervals between each overhaul. They must possess low wear rates and friction losses from the sliding motion of the piston rings under fluctuating pressure and temperature.

Figure 5.28 - Cylinder liner

In large two-stroke engine liners, scavenge air ports will be formed near the lower end.

All scavenge air port edges are designed to direct the flow and reduce ring snagging. Cylinder liners in four-stroke engines require no ports and are of simpler design.

To remove excess heat, reduce thermal stress and maintain a surface temperature at which an oil lubrication film can be retained, liners require an external cooling system. This is often referred to as jacket cooling and is carried out by circulating fresh water between the outer surface of the liner and the cylinder jacket or sleeve in which it is supported.

Cylinder liners require adequate lubrication to reduce piston ring and liner friction and wear. The oil film also acts as a gas seal between the liner and the rings and as a corrosion inhibitor.

Ideally lubricators should be timed to inject oil between the piston rings as they pass.

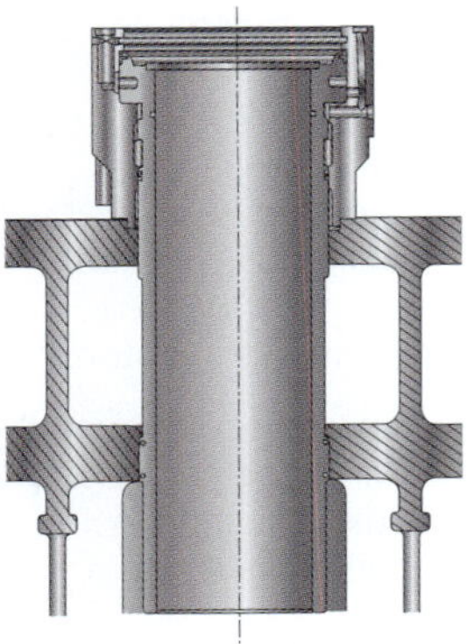

Figure 5.29 - Cylinder liner for MAN - B&W four-stroke engine

The majority of cylinder lubrication will be achieved by oil splashing from the crankcase into the open lower end of the liner. To avoid uneven or excessive lubrication, an oil scraper or control rings fitted to the piston skirt spread oil around the circumference and return excess to the crankcase.

Operation of an engine with insufficient cylinder lubrication will result in high wear rates to the liner and piston rings. Corrosion of the liner may increase when burning heavy fuel. Loss of oil seal to the piston rings will cause blowpast of hot gases, causing local overheating, rapid breakdown of surfaces and possibly piston seizure.

Excessive lubrication will cause carbon deposits. These may cause the piston rings to stick in the grooves, allowing possible breakage or blowpast. There will be fouling of the exhaust system including the turbocharger and contamination of scavenge spaces.

Cylinder Head (Cylinder Cover)

Figure 5.30 - Cylinder cover/cylinder head

The cylinder head is the top part of the combustion space and needs to be of sufficient strength to withstand the gas load at maximum pressure. The cover is positioned on the top of the cylinder liner flange and is secured to the cylinder block by a number of cover studs and nuts. These are tightened hydraulically to maintain a gastight seal.

Fitted to the cylinder head of a large two-stroke engine will be a central exhaust valve and cage, two or three fuel injectors, a starting-air valve, relief valve and indicator connection. Medium-speed four-stroke engines generally have two exhaust valves and two air inlet valves per cylinder, one centrally placed fuel injector, and an air-start, pressure relief and indicator valves.

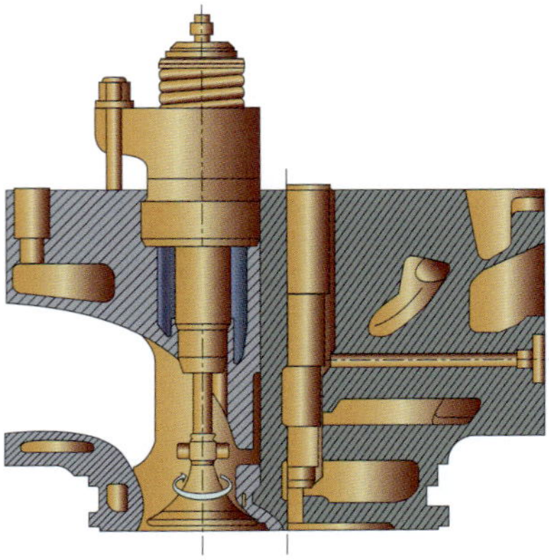

Figure 5.31 - Schematic of cylinder head

Camshafts and Valve Gear

The camshaft operates the valves and fuel pumps which control the engine cycle. Each valve or pump is actuated by a cam follower which rises or falls as the cam rotates beneath it. The profile or shape of each cam is designed to give the correct timing, speed and height of lift to its corresponding follower.

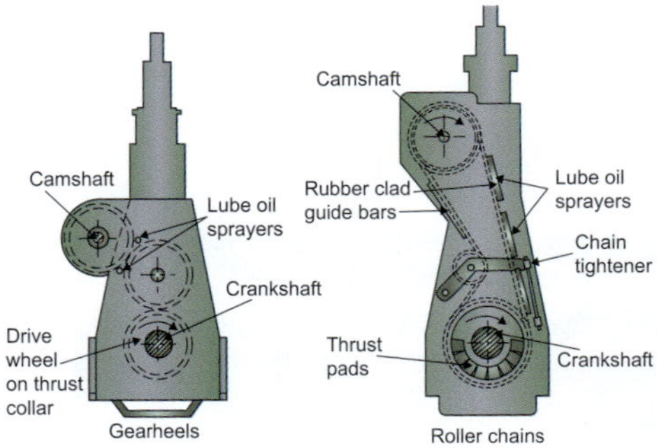

Figure 5.32 - Camshaft arrangement for a large two-stroke engine

- Camshaft rotation must be accurately synchronised with the crankshaft and this timing must be checked periodically and after any adjustments or repairs have been carried out

- vee-type engines will require a separate camshaft for each bank of cylinders
- four-stroke engines require inlet valve, exhaust valve and fuel pump cams for each cylinder, and since this cycle is completed in two engine revolutions, the camshaft rotates at half engine speed
- two-stroke engine camshafts rotate at full engine speed. They have fewer cams since they do not require air inlet valves. Loop or cross scavenge engines do not need exhaust valve cams.

So that they remain aligned with engine timing, camshafts are driven from the crankshaft. Camshaft bearings are supported from the engine structure in a position convenient to the operating mechanisms that the shaft is to control.

Two forms of camshaft drive are in use on board ship:

1. A train of gear wheels arranged in positions and sizes to give appropriate speeds and directions as required (typically used in most medium-speed engines).
2. A series of sprocket wheels connected by a roller chain.

The chain should be renewed when its stretch/ extension approaches 2%. The life of a camshaft drive should be limited to 15 years, regardless of wear.

Adjustment is usually limited to the length of two chain links and when this has been fully taken up the chain must be shortened by removing two links. To carry this out, two adjacent pin links are removed with their common roller link. The ends of the chain are then brought together and joined by riveting a new pin link.

On no account should an old pin link be riveted a second time.

After tensioning adjustment, the timing of the camshaft must be checked. If it is incorrect, the camshaft flange is slackened and adjusted to synchronise the cam timings with the crankshaft position. This may be checked either by putting one engine unit on top centre position or from corresponding marks on the flywheel. After repositioning the camshaft, the flange is tightened. When in use, the chain is lubricated by means of oil sprayers which direct a continuous stream of lubrication oil into the chain bearings. This oil will lubricate and cool the bearings and will cushion fluctuating forces.

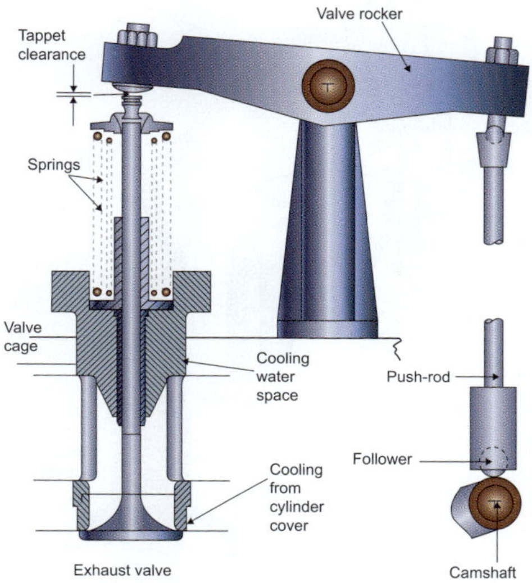

Figure 5.33 - Tappet clearance on exhaust valve

Tappet clearances are necessary to allow for thermal expansion of the valve spindle length at working temperature and to ensure that positive closing of the valve continues as it 'beds in' or 'seats' during use. Clearances should normally be set while the engine is cold and the cam follower is off the cam peak.

Excessive tappet clearances will cause the valve to open late and close early in the cycle. It will also cause noise and reduce its maximum lift, which will eventually result in damage due to the impact of working surfaces. Insufficient clearance will cause the valve to open early and close late, with increased maximum lift.

Hydraulically-operated exhaust valves are now fitted to most large two-stroke engines, where the push-rod, rocker lever and tappet are all replaced by a hydraulic system. The exhaust cam follower raises the piston of a single acting, high pressure oil actuating pump. As the piston is raised, it delivers oil at high pressure through a reinforced pipe to a hydraulic piston attached to the top of the valve spindle, forcing the valve to open. When the cam peak has passed, a helical return spring forces the follower down onto the cam profile,

Machinery and Equipment

lowering the actuating piston and releasing the hydraulic oil pressure. This allows the valve spring to force the valve closed, returning oil from its hydraulic cylinder.

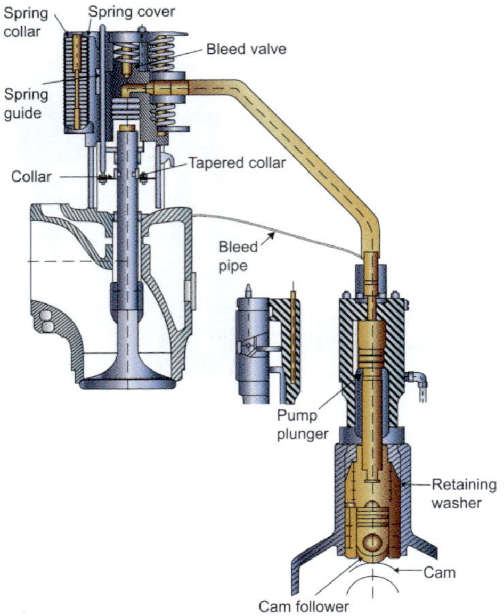

Figure 5.34 - Hydraulically-operated exhaust valve

Turbocharge Systems

Figure 5.35 - Diesel engine turbocharger

Engines are turbocharged to increase the power output and efficiency. The efficiency of a turbocharger system is improved by fitting a charge air cooler after the compressor. This cools the air at a constant pressure before supplying it for compression in the engine cylinders. The mass of air per cycle can now be increased and the quantity of fuel injected can be raised to give a corresponding increase in engine output and thermal efficiency. The turbine drives a directly coupled air compressor, which draws air from the atmosphere and compresses it. The air is then cooled in a change air cooler before being supplied to the engine through scavenge ports.

The turbocharger is 'free running' and at any engine speed the exhaust gas energy must cause the turbine to run at a stable speed so the compressor will supply the correct mass of air to the engine. It is then said to be 'matched' to that engine.

Two stage turbocharging is currently only used in high-speed four-stroke engines. Two turbochargers are fitted in series, each acting as one stage of the charge air compressor. They are matched to avoid surge at all speeds.

Fuel Systems

Diesel engines are configured to operate on heavy fuel oil. They will also require low sulphur fuel oil for use when operating in Emission Control Areas (ECAs) and diesel for use when manoeuvring in port.

Fuel Injection

Figure 5.36 - Fuel injectors on diesel engine

The fuel injection system is designed to deliver the correct amount of fuel oil at exactly the right time to assist the combustion process.

Fuel Oil Tanks

Fuel oil bunker needs to be treated on board before it is delivered to the engine. First it is transferred from the storage tank to a settling tank where it is heated to help the separation and settlement of any water and sludge, so that this can be drained off. After settling, the fuel oil can be passed through the fuel oil purifiers to the fuel oil daily tank.

There are usually two daily tanks, used alternately, one in use while the other is being recharged.

For a large engine, there will typically be two purifiers (of adequate capacity) in use, operating in series. The first purifier removes water, solubles, sludge, etc while the second acts as a clarifier to remove solids. The purifier must be fitted with the correct disc to match the oil density.

En route to the engine, the oil first passes to the primary pump which raises the pressure to about 4 bar. The booster pump receives oil from the primary discharge, raising its pressure to between 10 and 12 bar and delivering it through the heater, viscosity regulator and fine filter to the main engine fuel pumps.

The fuel oil heater reduces the oil's viscosity, which assists efficient combustion. The temperature required will depend on the oil quality, but should not exceed 150°C. The stainless steel mesh filter removes particles larger than 50 microns.

Fuel Injectors

A fuel injector consists of a body, a nozzle and a needle valve. High pressure fuel travels down through the body to the nozzle, where it enters a space surrounding the needle valve. The needle valve is kept closed by an intermediate spindle and spring in the injector body. The injector opening pressure can be set by adjusting a compression nut that acts on the spring.

The needle valve will open when the fuel pressure acting on the needle valve applies sufficient force to overcome the load on the spring. The fuel oil is then forced out through a series of small holes that are sized and arranged to atomise all of the fuel oil, such that it will then readily burn.

Figure 5.37 - Fuel injector

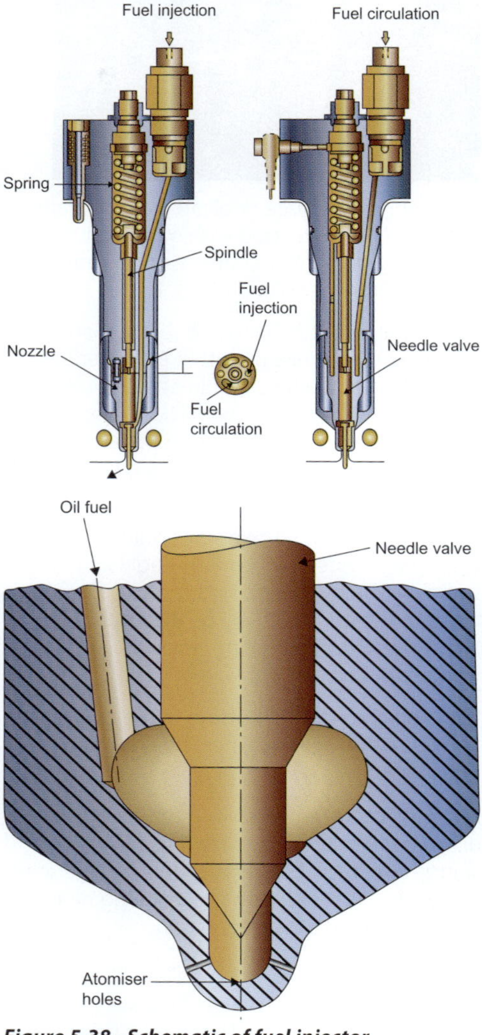

Figure 5.38 - Schematic of fuel injector

Engine fuel systems are designed for normal working conditions. If an engine is run for prolonged periods at a reduced speed, combustion will not be as efficient and may lead to fouling and wear. When prolonged periods at a reduced speed are expected, such as during 'slow-speed' steaming, a set of reduced-speed injectors may be fitted which have a reduced orifice area to ensure optimum atomisation rates. Fuel pump timing will also need to be adjusted.

Machinery and Equipment

Lubrication

Large engines require dedicated oil circulating systems. These are fitted with motor-driven circulating oil pumps, coarse suction strainers, fine discharge filters and oil coolers.

Each component is fitted in duplicate, one set being used while the other is on standby. Fine filters should be capable of being cleaned without interruption of the oil flow. Mesh size will depend on the bearing materials and clearances. In most large engines, it is 50 microns.

Lubricating oil pressure pumps draw oil from the main engine drain tank through suction strainers. The oil then passes through fine filters to the engine. It will be distributed to all bearings, piston cooling, sprayers, exhaust valve actuators, control systems, etc.

Used oil drains to the bottom of the crankcase and passes through strainers by gravity to the drain tank.

A bypass centrifuge system is fitted to purify oil from the drain tank to remove water, sludge and insolubles. This should be operated continuously at sea, with the oil being heated to 70 to 90°C to assist separation.

Full Flow Filters

Full flow filters, ie filters with a capacity large enough to cope with the full rate of oil circulation, are usually restricted in their fineness of filtration. There are, however, fine filters available which filter down to 10 microns particle size, using 'disposable' filter elements of special quality felt.

Fine Filters

Fine filters, operating on the bypass principle, are widely used, particularly for smaller engines. They are capable or removing solids down to a size of 1 to 2 microns.

Figure 5.39 - Fine oil filter

Centrifugal Separators

On marine diesel engines, the centrifuge is much more widely used for bypass (or batch) filtration. An efficient centrifuge, used as a purifier, ie with both clean oil and water discharges, can operate satisfactorily with continuous water contamination of the oil exceeding 10%.

Centrifuges

Figure 5.40 - Purifier

As lubricating oil passes through a diesel engine, it becomes contaminated by wear particles, combustion products and water. Filtration of lubrication and fuel oils removes unwanted particles such as cotton threads, paint chippings, small pieces of metal, etc, which could cause damage to pumps and engines. Filtration does not separate water from the oils and a centrifuge will be required for this purpose.

The basic type of oil centrifuge in use on board ship consists of a large diameter bowl fitted with discs.

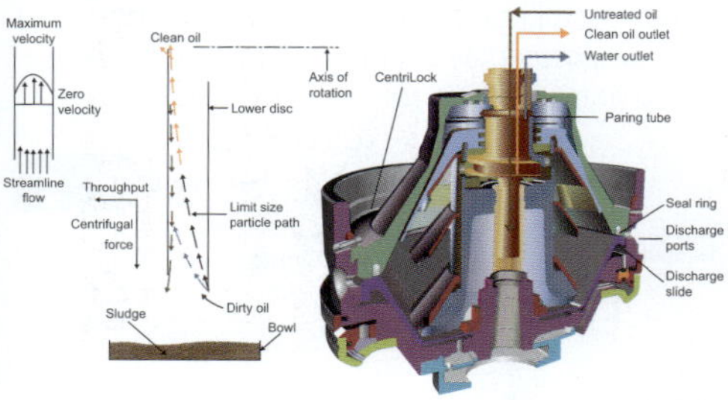

Figure 5.41 - Action of particles in a disc-type centrifuge

If the flow of oil is streamlined between two plates in parallel, the velocity of the oil varies from zero, where it is in contact with the plate, to its maximum velocity value at the mid-point between the plates. The flow of oil between two discs in a centrifuge is radially drawn inwards and upwards to the clean oil outlet. Any particles in the oil will be thrown radially outward by centrifugal force. The magnitude of the force depends on the size of the particle, the speed squared and the radius at which the particle is located.

Bowl-Type Centrifuge

Figure 5.42 - Bowl of a centrifuge

The bowl of a centrifuge is made of stainless steel and may be up to 60 cm in diameter. In operation, it rotates at between 5,000 and 8,000 rpm. The centrifuge is brought up to operating speed and then fresh water is introduced to form a water seal. The dirty oil that is to be purified is then pumped in through the distributor channel.

Separation of the oil, water and sludge occurs between the discs, with the water and sludge being thrown radially outwards along the under surface of the discs for discharge at A. The purified oil moves radially inwards and upwards and is discharged at B.

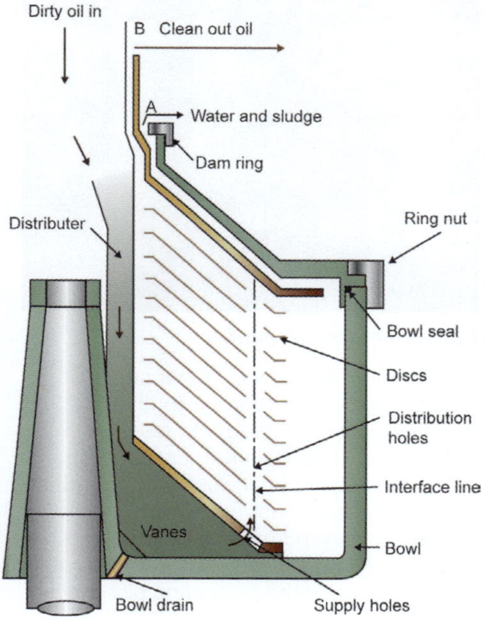

Figure 5.43 - Disc-type centrifuge

Centrifugal Purification of Lubricating Oils

Lube oil purifiers are typically designed to operate on a continuous bypass system, where oil is continuously taken from the engine sump (or drain tank) by a purifier feed pump and passed through a heater before entering the purifier. After purification, it is discharged from the purifier and enters the suction inlet of the main lubricating pump.

The system layout may vary slightly depending on the engine arrangement etc, but undoubtedly the best arrangement for the continuous bypass purification of lubricating oil is to take oil for the purifier from a point in the lubrication plant where the oil has passed through the engine, had time to settle, and therefore should be at its dirtiest.

Machinery and Equipment

Figure 5.44 - Lube oil purifier

The optimum liquid throughput rate of a purifier is approximately one-third of the maximum purifier throughput rate. The purifier should have sufficient capacity to accommodate the total volume of lubricating oil in the system about twice every 24 hours. (**Note:** The maximum purifier throughput rate is only used in the event of substantial water contamination of the lubricating oil system).

Starting and Manoeuvring Safety

Starting-Air

There are a number of methods of starting a diesel engine. These include manual, electrical and mechanical devices. The techniques used on a specific engine are determined by its size, design and function. In main engines, or smaller engines such as a diesel generator, the three methods are unable to deliver the substantial torque necessary to turn over such large engines. These engines are typically fitted with an air-start system that uses the energy stored in a appropriately sized compressed air pressure vessel. For a direct drive reversible engine, the air-start system must be capable of starting the engine either ahead or astern.

Each cylinder needs to be fitted with an air-start valve, which will be fitted with a 'distributor', the function of which is to ensure that air is introduced into the appropriate cylinder at the correct time while starting from any position of rest.

The start-air is introduced into the cylinder just before Top Dead Centre (TDC), as this allows the start-air to accumulate, ready to force down the piston once it is over TDC. With the first unit pressurised, the engine may be brought up to the 'fuel initiation' speed.

Starting-Air System

The next two diagrams show a typical start-air system for a large two-stroke engine, where clean, dry, compressed air at starting pressure (30 bar) is stored and supplied from the air receivers.

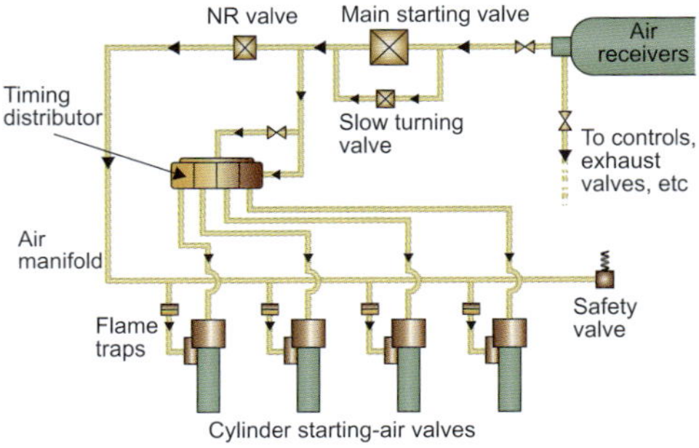

Figure 5.45 - Starting-air system

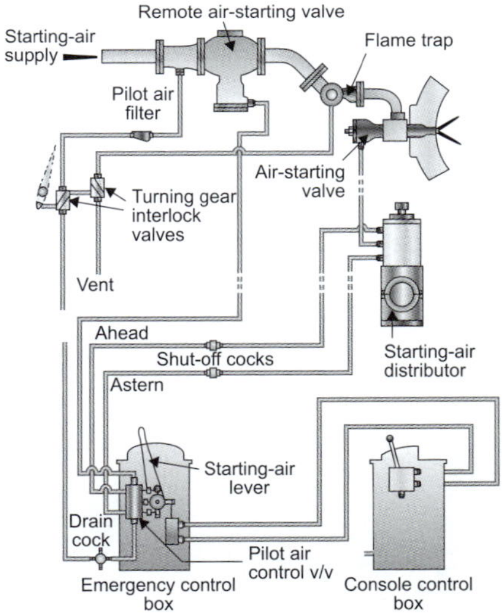

Figure 5.46 - Starting-air system

Starting-air is shut off from the engine as soon as the engine starting speed has been reached, at which time fuel is introduced and the engine speed increased.

Figure 5.47 - Starting-air receiver

Starting-Air Receivers are required to store compressed air for starting and manoeuvring main engines, for starting auxiliary engines, and to supply pneumatic control systems and other auxiliary air pressure systems.

> Two starting-air receivers are fitted and their total capacity must be able to deliver at least 12 starts for reversible engines and 6 starts for non-reversible engines before recharging is required.

Starting-Air Compressors recharge the starting-air receivers and deliver compressed air for other uses on board. It is a requirement that at least two air compressors are fitted, each of which is capable of supplying all demands.

Figure 5.48 - Starting-air compressors

Direct Reversing Engines

A ship's means of propulsion must be capable of operating astern, either by means of reversing the propeller or by altering propeller pitch (ie a controllable pitch propeller).

To operate astern, all the stages in the engine cycle may require re-timing. The start-air will be required to initially turn the engine in the reverse direction and the distributor will need to supply compressed air to the appropriate cylinders in the correct order. Re-timing can also be carried out by adjusting the position of the distributor cam with respect to the main camshaft.

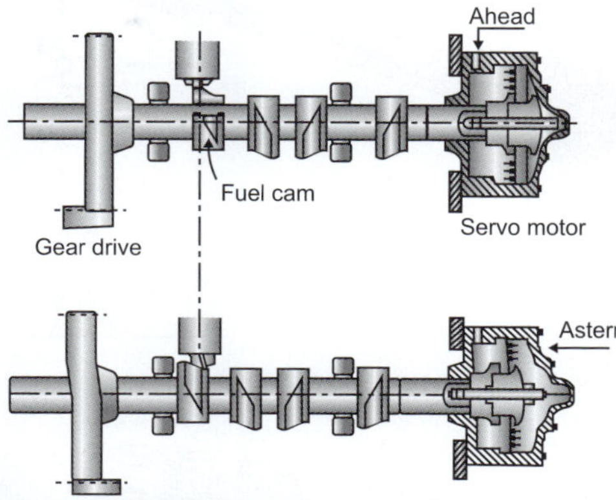

Figure 5.49 - Engine timing/starting-air arrangement

Coupling, Clutches and Gearboxes

If the shaft speed of a medium-speed diesel engine is too high, a gearbox arrangement will need to be fitted. There is often a clutch fitted, to disengage the engine from the gearbox, and the connection between the engine and the gearbox is often flexible to dampen vibrations.

Gearboxes

The gearbox used to reduce a medium-speed engine drive to a speed suitable for propeller revolutions will be single reduction of a reduction ratio that is typically in the region of 2:1 to 4:1.

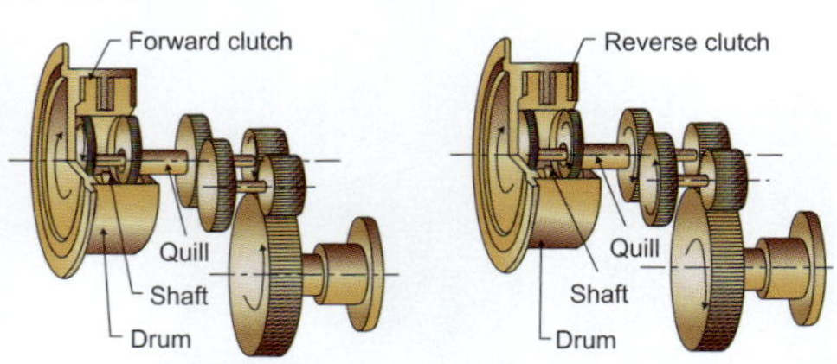

Controllable Pitch Propellers (CPP)

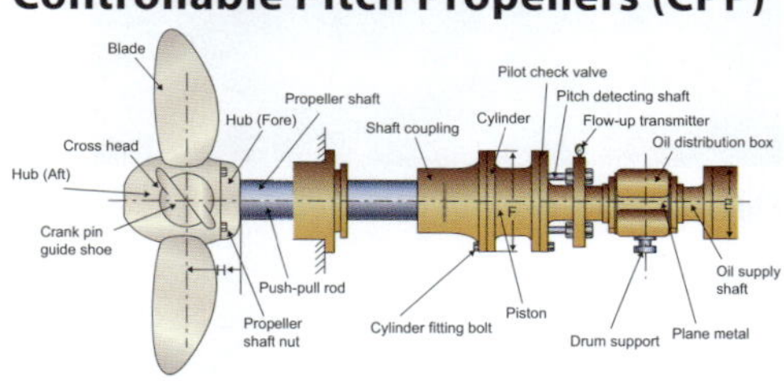

Machinery and Equipment

The CPP arrangement is typically found on medium-speed diesel engines and, in these installations, speed is reduced through a unidirectional gearbox.

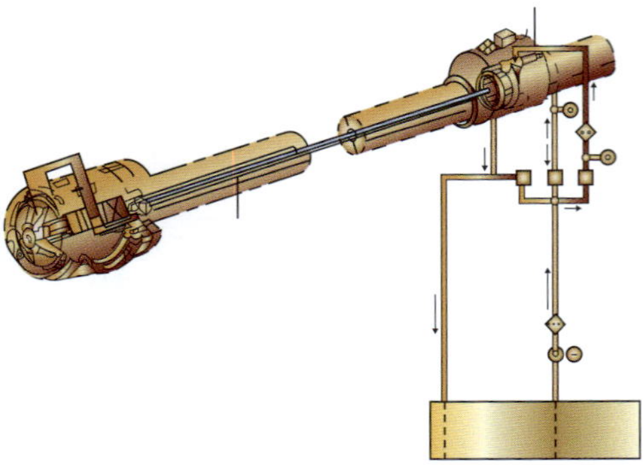

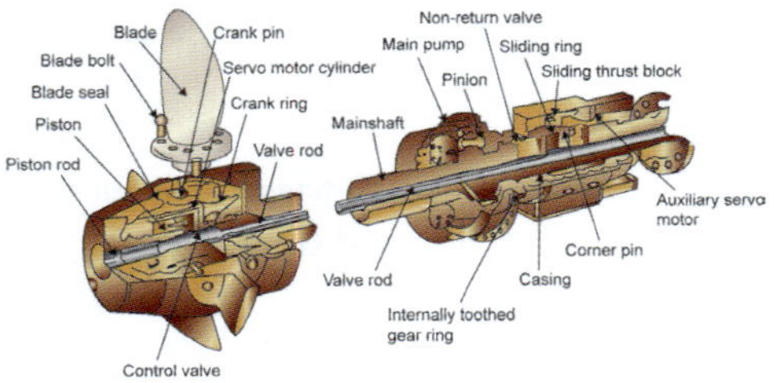

Governors

Figure 5.50 - Governor on a diesel engine

A governor facilitates speed regulation by regulating the fuel supply. It is able to control the load and load share, and to regulate rates of acceleration. A governor is typically configured for the particular engine for which it is to be used.

Crankcase Explosions

A crankcase explosion will result in substantial damage to the main engine. It is important therefore that all engineers understand the circumstances that could lead to an explosion. Appropriate preventative measures must be in place and must be monitored appropriately.

Key facts regarding crankcase explosions:

- An explosion can occur in any confined space where oil is present, such as a chain case, gear case or crankcase of a diesel engine (or air compressor)
- the force of an explosion is determined by the available volume of explosive vapours. It is this factor that makes large sized, slow-speed main engine explosions so catastrophic
- crankcase explosions are typically initiated by a hot spot or overheated component in the area of the crankcase, such as overheating of bearings, piston rod glands or timing chain, or sparks from piston blowpast
- under normal operating conditions, the atmosphere in the crankcase will be saturated with globules of oil created by the lubricating oil splashing onto moving surfaces. However, this mixture will not readily burn or explode
- engine size does not affect the likelihood of explosion. They are just as likely in a lifeboat engine as in a large slow-speed diesel engine.

All known sources of crankcase explosions can be removed through proper maintenance, correct lubrication and cleanliness.

How a crankcase explosion typically occurs:

1. The atmosphere in a crankcase consists of large oil droplets (100 to 300 mm in diameter) throughout the available volume in the crankcase. (These droplets are so large that they will not ignite explosively.)
2. A hot spot (minimum temperature of 360°C) will vaporise these globules.
3. The gaseous vapour that is created will rise to the cooler upper parts of the crankcase,

where it will condense into an oil mist. This oil mist will now comprise of droplets of oil of approximately 2 to 10 mm in diameter.

4. If subsequently ignited by a hot spot or spark (or if it rises above its auto-ignition temperature of 370°C), this oil mist can cause a heavy explosion.

The earlier that the generation of oil mist can be detected, the less chance there is of an explosion occurring, provided that the appropriate procedures are then followed.

Crankcase Oil Mist Detector

Oil mist detection is monitored by a crankcase mist detector, which initiates visual and audible alarms in the event of an oil mist forming.

Crankcase explosion relief valves (or crankcase explosion doors) must be installed to open automatically at mid-range pressures, allowing the pressure to be released and preventing pressure build-up. The valves close instantly when the pressure drops, preventing the ingress of air and eliminating the possibility of a major explosion.

The pressure relief valves, in common with all relief valves on tankers, are fitted with wire gauze to prevent emission of flames.

Figure 5.51 - Crankcase oil mist detector

Should oil temperatures continue to rise to the point of slowing or stopping the engine, the best course of action is to increase the flow of lubricating oil when it is safe to do so and if possible.

Once stopped, it is prudent to operate the engine turning gear, with indicator cocks open to prevent seizure of overheated parts.

The crankcase should never be opened until it has been given time to cool. All crew should be warned to avoid the area around the crankcase explosion relief valves.

The diagram below shows a 'Graviner' type oil mist detector which will continuously monitor the atmosphere from within the crankcase space of a diesel engine. An oil mist detector will detect the presence of oil mist at concentrations below the level at which an explosion would occur, thus raising the alarm in sufficient time to reduce or stop the engine and prevent an explosion, or substantial damage, occurring.

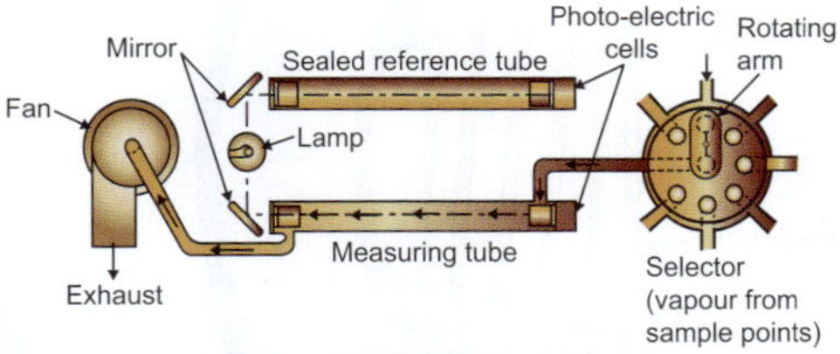

Figure 5.52 - 'Graviner' type oil mist detector

The oil mist detector consists of two parallel tubes with a photo-electric cell at one end and a lamp at the other. The photo-electric cell emits an electric current which varies depending on the brightness of the light that reaches it.

One tube is the reference tube and the other is the measuring tube. The reference tube is sealed and contains clean air. It is used as a reference for measuring the level of oil mist in the measuring tube. A sample of the atmosphere in the crankcase is drawn into the measuring tube. If the light in the measuring tube is obscured before it reaches the cell, this indicates that oil mist is present in the sample and the alarm will be raised.

Crankcase Relief Valves (Crankcase Explosion Doors)

A crankcase explosion relief valve consists of a light spring-loaded non-return disc valve.

Machinery and Equipment

The disc is of aluminium alloy which reduces its mass and the inertia to be overcome when opening or closing valves rapidly.

Figure 5.53 - Crankcase relief valve

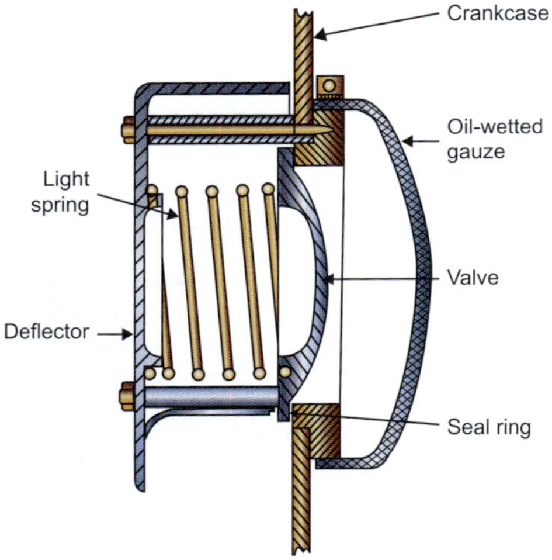

Figure 5.54 - Crankcase explosion relief valve

When the relief valve is 'sat', it must make a gas and oil tight seal. A non-stick oil and heat-resisting rubber ring is fitted to the disc face.

Crankcase doors require little maintenance but should be tested periodically by hand and the gauze cleaned.

Scavenge Fires

A scavenge fire is usually caused by the ignition of unburned fuel oil and carbon deposits that have been blown from the engine cylinder into the scavenge spaces. Unburned fuel oil (or cylinder lubricating oil) will be due to incorrect combustion caused by a faulty fuel injector, faulty fuel pump timing, insufficient scavenge air, partially choked exhaust, low compression, or afterburning caused when operating an overloaded engine. The oil will enter the scavenge space due to worn or defective piston rings/cylinder liner, or through incorrectly timed or excessive cylinder lubrication. It can be ignited by hot gases and burning particles from blow past of piston rings.

A scavenge fire will manifest itself as a drop in power and irregular running of the engine. There will be a rise in the exhaust and jacket temperatures local to the fire area and a high local temperature in the scavenge trunk. There will also be surging of the turbocharger, sparks and smoke emitted from the scavenge drains and a smell of smoke/hot paint. Scavenge fires are often a precursor to a crankcase explosion as they introduce heat into the crankcase. This is one reason why the fire should be extinguished as soon as is reasonably possible.

When a scavenge fire occurs, the engineer should:

- Raise the alarm
- reduce speed (when safe to do so)
- shut off the supply of fuel
- call the chief engineer
- increase the cylinder lubrication oil to the affected unit to prevent it seizing.

In many cases, once these actions are completed, a minor fire should soon burn out and conditions return to normal.

Units that have been affected by fire should be operated on reduced power until the scavenge space can be inspected and the cylinder and piston overhauled.

In the event of the fire continuing to burn, the engineer should:

- Stop the engine
- maintain normal cooling
- engage turning gear to prevent seizure
- introduce CO_2 as a fire extinguishing medium into the scavenge trunk. This will rapidly extinguish the fire, but the doors must not be opened until sufficient time has been allowed for cooling as any hot spots could cause re-ignition.

After the space has cooled down, the scavenge trunking and scavenge ports should be cleaned and the cylinder liner, water seals, piston, piston rings, piston rod and gland inspected.

To prevent scavenge fires:

- Adhere to the applicable maintenance guidelines

- inspect scavenge trunking areas as part of a planned maintenance program. Remove any build-up of contaminating deposits, keeping an appropriate record
- blow through scavenge drains regularly and record any oil observed.

Engine Room Safety Systems

Auto Start-up Function

A number of machinery systems (including the electrical generators) are fitted with a duplicate or standby unit which will automatically start should the machinery system stop working. The standby unit must fulfil the role of the unit that has stopped and initiate an alarm to indicate the failure of the original running unit.

Reduction of Power

Power reduction protection temporarily reduces machinery output power if there are very high temperatures, low pressures or excessive load.

Typical triggers on a main engine are:

- High scavenge air temperature
- high oil mist level in the crankcase
- low piston cooling pressure or flow
- high piston cooling outlet temperature
- low cylinder cooling pressure or flow
- high cylinder cooling temperature
- high exhaust gas temperature on a cylinder, or high exhaust gas temperature deviation from average exhaust temperature.

Machinery Shutdown

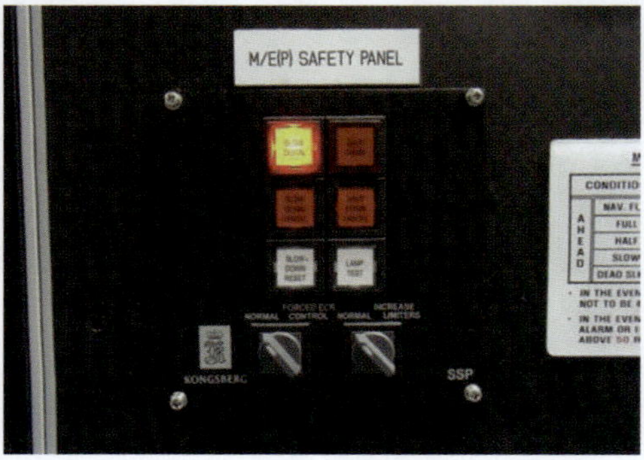

Figure 5.55 - Main engine slowdown alarm

The various machinery shutdown systems protect the machinery by isolating the fuel or power supply, thus stopping the machinery.

In certain cases, if no remedial action is taken after a specific period of time, a complete engine shutdown is initiated.

Bilge Level Detection System

A bilge alarm system warns when the level in the machinery space bilges reaches a specific level (this level will be before the bilge actually overflows onto the tank top).

Overflow of machinery space bilge may be hazardous because:

1. It may present a fire hazard, particularly if there is oil in the bilge water.
2. There is added free surface effect across the tank top, which will reduce stability of the vessel.
3. Splashing may damage electrical motors.

Ships >2,000 GT must be fitted with two independent bilge alarm systems. A number of ships are fitted with automatic pumping of machinery bilges.

Fire Detection Alarm Systems

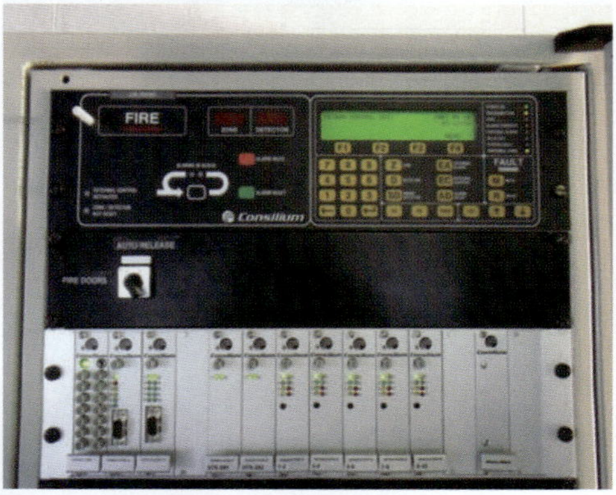

Figure 5.56 - Fire detection panel

The engine room fire detection and alarm system must not be located in such a position that fire in the engine room would render it inoperative. Typically, it is located on the bridge or emergency HQ. The alarm system will give local audio and visual alarms, and indicate the space where the fire has been detected.

If the warning alarm located on the panel is not acknowledged within a specific time, it will initiate the main fire alarm signal throughout the vessel.

Machinery and Equipment

Individual fire zones should be capable of being temporarily isolated, and the status of each zone must be displayed on the panel. Should a detector head be inadvertently switched off, the alarm system must reactivate that detector head automatically after a period of time, typically 30 minutes.

The fire alarm detection system must also be self-monitoring and any power or system failure should raise a separate alarm with a different tone to that of the main fire alarm.

Auxiliary Boilers

Figure 5.57 - Two cylindrical auxiliary boilers

Aside from boilers that are used for main propulsion systems on steam turbine vessels (such as LNG carriers), auxiliary boilers found on motor ships are of a more simple and robust construction typically consisting of two drums with an integrated furnace. These auxiliary boilers may deliver saturated steam for use on board.

As these boilers may be used infrequently and the condensate return may include particulate matter and/or oil from the steam consumers, the boilers may not always reach the desired quality standard for steam and internal deposits may lead to tube failure. It is important that proper maintenance of filters and steam systems is conducted to reduce these risks.

Potable Water Maker

A number of methods are used to create potable water from seawater, including ion-exchange and electro-dialysis, but the most commonly used (and cost effective) marine system is evaporation.

In an evaporator system, heat is used to boil the seawater. The steam/vapour leaves the various solids that are contained in seawater in the evaporator (as brine).

As these dissolved solids build up in the brine, they are deposited as scale and reduce the efficiency of the heat transfer process. The scale deposits can often be removed from the heating surfaces by thermal shock when the evaporator is operating, and by mechanical or chemical means when it is shut down.

The fresh water created can be used as feed water for the boilers or for domestic purposes. If it is to be used as potable water, the vapour must pass through a distillation plant and be sterilised (typically using a silver steriliser or UV) prior to use.

Figure 5.58 - Potable water evaporator

Marine Diesel Engine Components

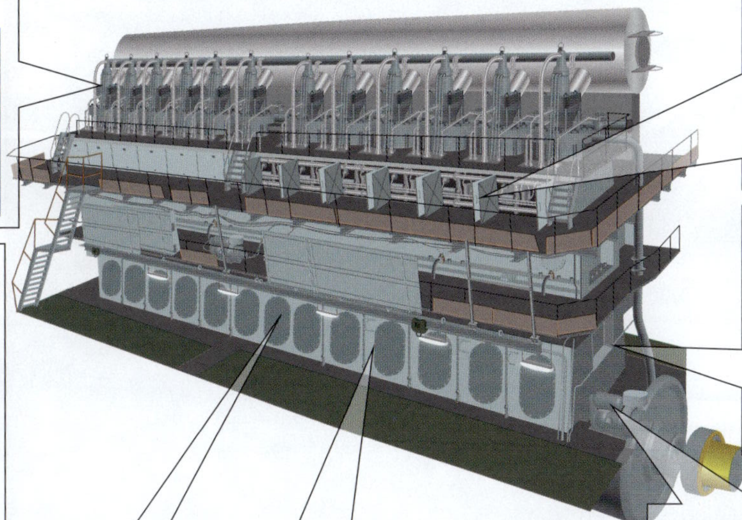

This is positioned on the top of the cylinder liner flange and secured to the cylinder block.
Fitted to the cylinder head of a large two-stroke engine will be a central exhaust valve and cage, two or three fuel injectors, a starting-air valve, relief valve and indicator connection.
Medium-speed four-stroke engines generally have two exhaust valves and two air inlet valves per cylinder, one centrally placed fuel injector, and an air-start, pressure relief and indicator valves.

Turbocharge Systems

Turbochargers operate by using a turbine to drive a directly coupled air compressor, which draws air from the atmosphere. The air is then cooled before being supplied to the engine through scavenge ports.
Engines are turbocharged to increase the power output and efficiency.

Crankshaft

The crankshaft consists of a number of cranks, which are rotated by piston forces transmitted through the connecting rods and bottom end bearings. In-line engines have one crank for each cylinder.
Each crank consists of two crank webs joined by a common crankpin to which the bottom end bearing is fitted.
Each web is also connected to a journal to form part of a continuous shaft. A main bearing will support the shaft at each journal.
Gear or chain drive wheels are added to drive camshafts and other mechanisms if they need to be synchronised with the crankshaft movement.

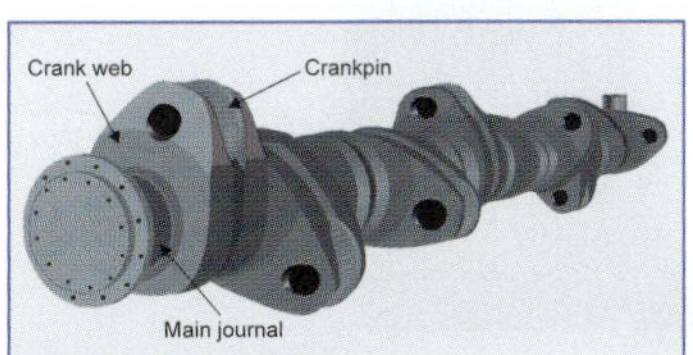

Cylinder Liner

Cylinder liners are designed to give an extensive working life and allow long intervals between each overhaul. They must possess low wear rates and friction losses from the sliding motion of the piston rings under fluctuating pressure and temperature.
To remove excess heat, reduce thermal stress and maintain a surface temperature at which an oil lubrication film can be retained, liners require an external cooling system. This is often referred to as jacket cooling and is carried out by circulating fresh water between the outer surface of the liner and the cylinder jacket or sleeve in which it is supported.
Cylinder liners require adequate lubrication to reduce piston ring and liner friction and wear. The oil film also acts as a gas seal between liner and rings and as a corrosion inhibitor.

Pistons

The piston crown must be able to withstand a high gas load and be able to transmit the force from this to the piston rod.
Large two-stroke engine pistons are subject to rigorous conditions due to the large-bore cylinders and heavy fuels. The piston crown must be supported against bending while allowing cooling of its underside. The shape is concave to give an efficient combustion space.
Cooling of pistons is necessary to remove excess heat from combustion and to limit thermal stressing. It also controls thermal expansion to maintain correct clearances between piston and liner and between ring grooves and rings. Cooling is achieved by circulating a coolant (oil or fresh water) through internal passages within the piston.
Piston cooling and cylinder jacket cooling must be continued for a period after the engine is stopped to allow a gradual reduction in temperature and reduce thermal stress.

Connecting Rods (Con-Rods) and Crossheads

This rod connects the top and bottom end bearings, enabling conversion of the reciprocating forces on the piston into rotating power in the crankshaft.
The crosshead or top end bearing transmits the full gas load from the piston to the connecting rod and crankshaft.
Some designs have the bottom end bearing as a separate unit, bolted to the connecting rod. This allows the piston and rod to be extracted (or pulled) for overhaul without disturbing the bearing.
Vee-type engines have the connecting rods from two cylinders connected to each throw of the crankshaft (termed side by side).

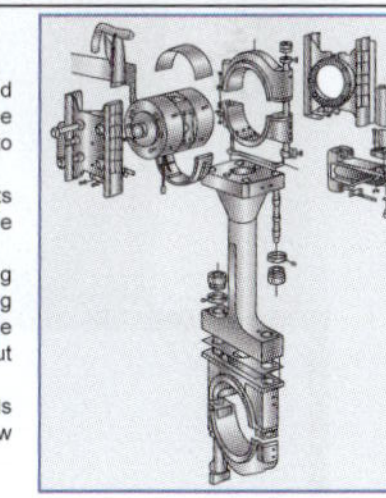

Camshafts and Valve Gear

A camshaft operates the valves and fuel pumps which control the engine cycle. Each valve or pump is actuated by a cam follower which rises or falls as the cam rotates beneath it. The profile or shape of each cam is designed to give the correct timing, speed and height of lift to its corresponding follower.

- Camshaft rotation must be accurately synchronised with the crankshaft.
- Vee-type engines will require a separate camshaft for each bank of cylinders.
- Four-stroke engines require inlet valve, exhaust valve and fuel pump cams for each cylinder, and since this cycle is completed in two engine revolutions, the camshaft rotates at half engine speed.
- Two-stroke engine camshafts rotate at full engine speed. They have fewer cams since they do not require air inlet valves, and loop or cross scavenge engines do not need exhaust valve cams.

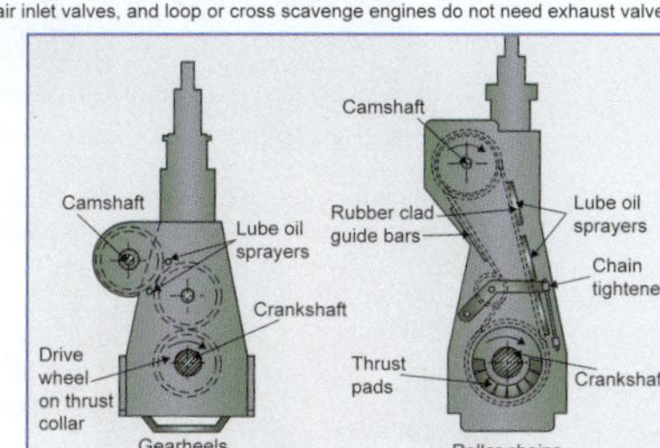

Machinery Breakdowns

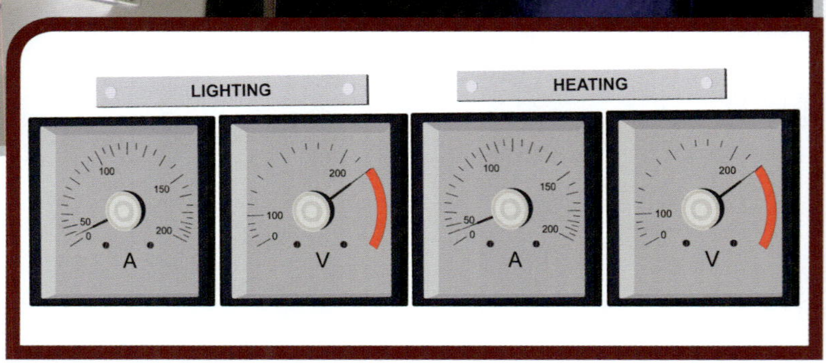

Machinery breakdown, particularly in busy waterways, can often lead to collision or grounding. All too often, machinery fails during manoeuvring or berthing.

General Reasons for Machinery Breakdown

- Equipment not fit for marine environment
- water ingress (oil, fuel, machinery, etc)
- marine organisms in systems (heat exchangers, pipes, valves, filters, seachests, etc)
- not maintained properly (ill-defined procedures, design flaws)
- operator mistakes:
  - fatigue (fewer crew, more work)
  - complicated user-interface.

Typical Machinery Breakdown

Machinery breakdowns fall into five main groups, with P&I clubs reporting that claims for damage in each of these groups typically cost US$500,000 each.

Claims Type	Percentage of Claims 2005-09
Main engine	45
Steering gear	6
Auxiliary engine	22
Boilers	6
Propulsion	18
Other	3

Table 5.1 - Machinery damage claims in a 5 year period (Source: Swedish Club)

Main Engine Damage

The table below shows the eight most common main engine failure types.

Claims Type	Percentage of Claims 2005-09
Turbocharger	41
Cylinder, cylinder liner	19
Crankshaft, crank bearing	9
Bearing, main bearing	5
Frame, bedplate, entablature	5
Gear wheels	2
Camshaft	2
Piston	2
Multiple parts	15

Table 5.2 - Types of main engine claim in a 5-year period (Source: Swedish Club)

General Recommendations to Prevent Main Engine Damage

- The crew should be well trained and familiar with the engine
- ensure that the planned maintenance system is up to date
- only use spare machinery parts from reliable suppliers
- ensure that filters and purifiers for lubricating oil operate correctly. Sample should be analysed as per manufacturers recommendations
- ensure that fuel oil is in accordance with the engine manufacturer's specifications
- monitor engine performance over a period
- adhere to manufacturer's instructions
- take measures to reduce the risk of engine room fires, particularly regarding:
  - the cleanliness of the engine room
  - the condition of pipes and fittings
  - the insulation/lagging of hot surfaces
  - the operation of quick-closing valves, fire dampers, etc.

Assessment of Findings from Marine Insurers

- Medium-speed engines need extra care. These engines are over-represented in the damage statistics, more or less independent of the make
- do not trust new engines just because they are new. Statistics show that new engines have teething troubles
- for low speed engines, the causes of turbocharger, cylinder liner and journal/bearing damage should be given priority
- for medium-speed engines, the causes of damage to the crankshaft/connecting rod,

Machinery Breakdowns

journal/bearing, piston/piston rod and turbocharger should be highest on the agenda.

Turbochargers

Turbocharger failures make up the majority of main engine damage.

Damage to turbochargers (whether connected to the main engine or to an auxiliary engine) has a significant impact on the vessel's ability to trade. Damage to a turbocharger will lead to a significant reduction in speed while at sea and costly repairs.

Major Contributors to Turbocharger Breakdowns

- Overdue maintenance. Bearings, compressor wheels and turbine blades have service life limitations. Compressor wheels, for example, can have a 50,000 to 100,000 work hours life depending on their use. (This is equivalent to 7.5 to 15 years of use.) Due to operational and financial constraints, overhauls are occasionally postponed until drydocking rather than undertaken while the ship is in service

  Obvious signals such as surging at full load or rising exhaust gas temperatures often indicate that an inspection/service is required
- non-manufacturer parts being used in place of original manufacturer's parts. Due to the harsh service environment of a turbocharger, inferior quality parts, often with slight discrepancies in material, design and dimensions, can easily lead to damage
- maintenance not performed by the manufacturer. Maintenance or servicing undertaken by the crew, shipyard or other personnel not qualified by the manufacturer can cause major problems. The smallest service oversight can easily lead to a complete turbocharger shutdown
- missing service letters. Particularly when there is a change of ownership of a vessel, the service letters and logbooks for the turbocharger, as well as for other critical pieces of machinery and equipment, can be missing. This break in information does not allow the new owners or ship managers the opportunity to assess the maintenance and service needs of the turbochargers
- change of use. Turbochargers specified for slow steaming may need components to be replaced for full speed steaming. If this is disregarded, operational problems and/or reduced lifecycle of the rotating parts of the turbocharger due to elevated speed may result
- upstream maintenance resulting in damage to the turbocharger. In many cases, damage to turbochargers occurs when maintenance has been conducted on other machinery or systems upstream of the turbocharger. Since the turbocharger is downstream of most other engine machinery, any foreign objects, loose parts, forgotten equipment or incorrectly reassembled machinery may eventually move downstream and damage the turbocharger. Such items include loose bolts, injection nozzle fragments, compensator bellow bits, welding electrode stumps, wrenches and screwdrivers, rags or any other foreign objects. Due to the extreme service speed of a turbocharger, even minute particles may damage vital parts and lead to severe damage.

Steering Gear Failure

The steering gear is one of the most important items of equipment and it should be tested before arrival at and departure from any port, in accordance with the following checklist.

Steering Gear Test Checklist

To be carried out not more than six hours before arrival and at least two hours before departure

1. In port, OOW check rudder clear.
2. Test main and secondary communications, bridge to steering flat.
3. Check oil level on bridge telemotor at the steering stand, if applicable.
4. With each steering motor separately and then together:
   - Normal steering operation from bridge
   - non-follow-up (NFU) operation from bridge
   - operating bridge wing consoles P&S, if applicable.

5. Test steering gear power failure (audible and visual) alarm.
6. Check autopilot fully operational. Align autopilot heading indicator with ship's head and engage autopilot. Now turn autopilot to port and starboard. The rudder must follow.
7. Synchronise the gyro repeater in steering flat, if applicable.
8. Visual inspection of steering gear and connecting linkage, confirmed okay by duty engineer.
9. Test gyro off-course alarm (audible and visual). With auto-pilot still engaged, move the autopilot heading marker. Off-course alarm must activate.
10. Test any other off-course alarm(s) if fitted.
11. Check illumination of all rudder indicator read-outs.

Auxiliary Engines/Generators

The auxiliary diesel engines provide onboard electricity. They are referred to as auxiliary to identify them from the main diesel engines, which are used for propulsion of the ship. Auxiliary engines are typically four-stroke diesel engines.

Problems with Auxiliary Engines

1. The engine does not start

The following are typical reasons for auxiliary engines not starting:

- The air receiver pressure is too low. Once the pressure of the air receiver is restored, you will be able to start the compressors
- if the air receiver pressure is satisfactory, check the starting-air valve on the air bottle and all the valves in the line
- check for leakage in the starting-air piping
- the individual air-starting valves on the cylinder heads might be stuck or sticky
- the air distributor may be faulty and not allowing air into the cylinders. Try rotating the engine with the turning gear and restart.

2. The engine turns on air but does not run on fuel

Failure to start could be due to one of the following:

- Fuel does not reach the fuel injection pump because there is air in the system
- the fuel oil filters are choked
- the fuel line valve is not open
- the trips have been not reset after the last time the engine was stopped
- fuel oil service tank is at a low level. Beware that the other generators are also going to stop
- there is water in the line
- the fuel valves are faulty and not giving proper atomisation or are choked
- the fuel pump timing is wrong
- leaking fuel injection pipes
- seized plungers of the fuel pumps
- fuel rack linkage stuck in position
- seized delivery valves or broken plunger springs in injection pump
- the engine is cold.

3. The safety valve lifts during starting

The safety valve lifts when there is uncontrolled combustion inside the cylinder, which may be due to the following:

- Defective fuel oil valves
- incorrect fuel pump timings
- the safety valve is opening early. This may be caused by a broken spring or a loosened nut
- engine is over cooled
- fuel linkage problems or fuel rack stuck in maximum position
- dripping fuel injectors.

4. Hunting of the engine

This may be due to the following:

- The tachometer may be out of order.
- the fuel line may need to be purged of air, particularly fuel filter has been changed and the engineers have forgotten to purge the air and prime the system

- the engine is cold and there is uneven combustion. This can be caused by forgetting to put the engine on pre-heating after stopping in the last time
- the governor is faulty. The governor oil is supposed to be removed and spaces flushed with clean kerosene before filling up with oil again. Sometimes sludge adheres to the pilot valves, which causes hunting
- some fuel injectors are sticking and firing intermittently. This might happen in engines that are run on heavy fuel oil. These engines are supposed to be changed over to diesel oil for approximately 30 minutes before stopping, to flush the pipelines.

Maintenance of Marine Diesel Engines

A marine diesel engine must be maintained in accordance with the advice of the manufacturer and the requirements of Class and the company's SMS.

Daily Checks on the Engine

The following daily checks should be made by all watchkeeping engineers in their duty hours:

- Check the fuel level in the service tank and drain the service and settling tank of any water
- check the lube oil level in the sump of the engine
- check the governor lube oil levels
- check the lubrication of the rocker arms (if running)
- check lube oil pressure, water pressure, exhaust temperatures, cooling water temperature, lube oil inlet temperature, etc (if running)
- drain the condensate from the scavenge manifold and the air coolers
- lubricate the fuel racks, linkages and fuel pump rack operating gear.

250 Hours Routine

When an engine has run for 250 hours, the generators must be changed over, the engine stopped and the following cleaned:

- Lube oil filters
- fuel oil filters
- turbocharger air filters.

1,000 Hours Routine

The 1,000 hours routine is little more exhaustive and includes inspection of the injection system and the running gears. The following are typically undertaken:

- Inspect the crankcase
- remove the fuel injectors and pressure test them. Adjust the pressure as necessary
- change the turbocharger blower and turbine side oil
- check the tappet clearances
- record the performance of the engine.

2,000 Hours Routine

The crankshaft alignment must be checked and the graph plotted. It must be cross checked with the original figures. It is very important that the engines are maintained within the limits of the initial alignment to ensure satisfactory performance of the engine and the alternator bearings. Misalignment can be caused by hogging and sagging of the ship during loading and discharging cycles. It is the duty of the operational engineers to check for crankshaft deflection at regular intervals and to monitor alignment of the engines.

4,000 Hours Routine

The checks at 4,000 hours are known as half decarbonisation and include the following:

- Removed, overhaul and remove carbon from all cylinder heads
- inspect, lap and test the exhaust and inlet valves
- overhaul the starting-air valves
- renew all gaskets and 'o' rings
- clean the cooling water spaces of the cylinder heads
- clean the top of the piston and the cylinder liner and inspect for signs of abnormal combustion
- renew the lube oil if required as per the analysis reports.

8,000 Hours Routine

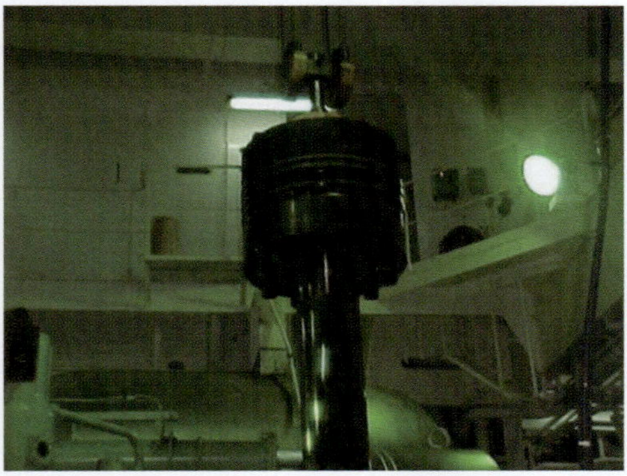

Figure 5.59 - Withdrawal of piston

The 8,000 hours routine is called decarbonisation and includes the following:

- Remove cylinder heads and overhaul
- withdraw pistons, clean and inspect
- change the piston rings and, depending on wear, inspect the shell bearings
- clean exhaust piping and silencer
- inspect big end bearings
- overhaul turbocharger and renew the ball bearings.

25,000 Hours Routine

Renew the connecting rod bolts.

Boilers

Common failures associated with boilers are pitting, erosion, stress corrosion cracking, hydrogen damage, vibration damage, stress rupture, corrosion fatigue, caustic gouging, distortion, thermal fatigue, acid dewpoint corrosion, over temperature, fatigue, maintenance damage, material flaws and/or welding flaws.

Improper operation and defective maintenance/water treatment are also common causes for boiler failures. Tube rupture and corrosion are frequent problems with steam boilers.

Repairs in Marine Boilers

Typical onboard repairs include plugging of leaking tubes and replacing leaking manhole joints. Major repairs like the renewal of damaged tubes and furnace rebuilding must be carried out in dry dock.

Propulsion Damage

Propulsion damage in this context includes damage to the propeller, propeller shaft, bearings etc.

Propellers

The main factors that detract from optimum propeller condition are fouling, cavitation and physical damage. Any distortion from the true shape can cause an imbalance and hence vibration, which in turn causes increased cavitation, loss of thrust, drive shaft damage, wear on the numerous bearings, and increased fuel consumption due to decreased efficiency.

Damage Repairs

Propellers can easily be damaged if they strike a buoy, floating debris or ice. The damage is usually to the tip, which can become bent or even have large chunks taken out of it. Physical damage of this nature is what most commonly causes vibration. The solution in this case is to trim the blades equally to remove the damage, achieve a proper balance and reduce excessive cavitation. However, poor trimming can make the problem worse and there have been cases where inaccurate trimming has resulted in propellers being damaged beyond repair.

Main Propulsion Shaft

Propulsion shaft failures occur with an alarming level of frequency in all machinery failures.

Permanent damage may result if the shaft bends, for example due to hull deflection or if the bearings are out of alignment. Repair will be costly and the ship will be out of service for several weeks.

Suitable monitoring of shaft alignment using the proper tools is essential for identifying abnormal behaviour of the shaft line, ie excessive wearing of intermediate bearings, accelerated stern bearing clearance growth, bearings foundation structure or weld cracks or shaft vibrations that were not detected previously during ship operation.

CHAPTER 6

Pilotage

Pilotage

Pilotage is a joint task carried out by a team that includes the pilot, the ship's master and his crew, mooring gangs and boatmen and, where applicable, tugs and their crews.

The aim of pilotage is to safely navigate a vessel into and out of port, to limit the possibilities of damage to property and ships, and to reduce the risk of marine pollution and damage to the environment.

Who is the Pilot?

Maritime pilotage services are established throughout the world to provide properly qualified and experienced local pilots.

All marine pilots are vastly experienced but their backgrounds may be very varied; they may be master mariners who have previously themselves commanded merchant vessels or they may have been trained 'on the job' through an apprenticeship scheme.

Pilotage services are organised in many different ways. They may be state controlled through legislation or they may be locally organised, as in the United Kingdom, by Competent Harbour Authorities.

Pilots may be employed by government departments or by harbour authorities or may be self-employed.

IMO Resolution A.960 lays down 'Recommendations on training and certification and operational procedures for maritime pilots (other than deep-sea pilots).'

Within its preface, it contains the following note:

Estuary navigation, manoeuvring in confined waters ports or canals, demands great nautical skill. Merchant vessels with ever larger dimensions have to be safely guided through narrow waterways, often in heavy traffic.

The pilot acts as the partner of the captain coping with this demanding role, which requires long experience as well as specific knowledge of the vessel and the estuary.

Within a very short period of the time pilots have to acquaint themselves with the characteristics and manoeuvring of an unfamiliar vessel, while taking weather conditions, currents and tides into account, before setting course and giving instructions to sail.

Much of the impetus for Resolution A.960 and for other pilotage-related input at the IMO originates from the International Maritime Pilot's Association (IMPA). IMPA attends IMO sessions as the acknowledged experts on matters relating to pilotage. Since its formation in 1971, IMPA has represented pilots from around the world and has contributed greatly to navigational safety, security and environmental concerns of international shipping.

Responsibility

The following two examples from the UK Pilotage Act and the Canadian Pilotage Act firmly fix responsibility for any damage or loss that occurs while a ship is under pilotage with the owner or master. There are only a few exceptions, such as the Panama Canal, where a particular local ruling will apply.

> *"The fact that a ship is being navigated in an area and in circumstances in which pilotage is compulsory for it shall not affect any liability of the owner or master of the ship for any loss or damage caused by the ship or by the manner in which it is navigated".*

UK Pilotage Act

> *"Nothing in this Act exempts the owner or master of any ship from liability for any damage or loss occasioned by the ship to any person or property on the ground that*
>
> *(a) the ship was under the conduct of a licensed pilot; or*
>
> *(b) the damage or loss was occasioned by the fault, neglect, want of skill or wilful and wrongful act of a licensed pilot."*

Canadian Pilotage Act

Who is in Charge?

Whenever a pilot boards a vessel as a representative of his service, he acts as a servant of the vessel. He alone remains responsible to the service provider for the act of pilotage.

No-one other than the ship's master should interfere with the conduct of the pilotage.

Breakdowns in communication on the bridge play a major part in accidents in pilotage waters. The pilotage of a ship requires teamwork but someone has to be in charge. While the pilot is on board, he works for the master, even if only on a temporary basis. If the pilot is given navigational control of the ship, he effectively becomes the leader of the bridge team, with the master working within that framework in a support role while retaining overall command of the vessel. If the master is familiar with the port and chooses to retain control as well as command, the pilot will act as an advisor, although the Port State or the port may have regulations in force regarding this.

In the UK, the Merchant Shipping Act of 1894 defines the word 'Pilot' as:

> *"A person not belonging to a ship who has the conduct thereof."*

In 1971, a judge determined that a pilot can only act in such a capacity when he personally has conduct of the ship, ie the control and handling of the ship. If the master supersedes him for any reason and continues the passage, the pilot ceases to be a pilot. This would effectively mean that a ship in a compulsory pilotage area is proceeding without a pilot, which would contravene the Pilotage Act as follows:

> *"If the master of a ship navigates the ship in an area and in circumstances in which pilotage is compulsory for it by virtue of a pilotage direction without notifying the competent harbour authority which gave the direction that he proposes to do so, he shall be guilty of an offence and liable on summary conviction to a fine not exceeding level 2 on the standard scale."*

Passage Plan

The need to prepare and follow passage plans is now well established on board vessels. This need is detailed in IMO Resolution A.983(21) and is a requirement of a vessel's SMS under ISM clause 7 regarding shipboard operations. The general principles of passage planning are also contained within chapter VIII/2 of the STCW convention.

It is important that the plan is dynamic to allow for the movement of other vessels. Any constraints or restrictions due to pilot boarding must be incorporated.

Passage plans must make allowance for the fact that, before approaching the pilot boarding ground, the vessel may need to adjust her course and speed to ensure that the best possible lee can be achieved. There is also a requirement in many safety management systems to test emergency systems and engines at the end of sea passage before picking up an inward pilot.

Although the pilot will bring on board his own specialised knowledge and a specifically tailored passage plan, the vessel must have prepared its own passage plan which it continually monitors until it is adapted following the master/pilot information exchange.

The Pilot Boarding Ground

One very important consideration in the passage plan is the location of the pilot boarding ground.

The boarding ground should be located just far enough out to sea to ensure that the ship has room to manoeuvre in safe waters for her draught, there is some shelter for boarding and disembarking and it is accessible to all types of pilot boat. The approach to the boarding ground must always be treated as an area of high risk and prepared for accordingly.

Pilot boats often operate in areas where the available sea room may be compromised due to shallow water or sandbanks. There may also be heavy levels of traffic movement.

Pilotage

Times of pilot rendezvous can be provided either by the pilotage service or a local VTS. Some larger ports have two boarding grounds, one for good weather and another for rough weather.

Weather

A weather assessment should always be made before approaching a boarding ground. If the pilot station has closed due to bad weather, the approach will have to be delayed to await their advice. Even if a port is open in poor weather conditions, this does not exempt the ship from making a proper weather assessment or mean that an approach should be considered as safe. As the pilot boat approaches the ship, the pilot may request that a further more effective lee be made.

Handling the Ship for Pilot Transfer by Boat

Prior to arrival at the pilot boarding ground, the vessel should have placed her engines on standby and astern movement of the engines should have been tested. The pilot station or the pilot boat will notify the vessel of the required boarding speed. When manoeuvring the vessel in close proximity to other ships or small craft, hand steering must always be used. Where a requested lee is not possible, the pilot boat must be advised so that boarding can be postponed until the ship can approach a safer area. If forming a lee still does not provide a suitably calm area for the pilot boat to approach, taking a turn out of the ship should be considered. If the ship is brought short round and then returned to the original course, the seas inside the diameter of the turn can be temporarily calmed.

Regulations require that an officer is in charge of the deck when the pilot boards and disembarks. A crew member must be ready with a lifebuoy and to assist as required.

If there are no remote engine or helm controls on the bridge wing, an officer/helmsman must be present to operate the controls as required.

Boarding Vessels

Most pilot boardings take place from some sort of pilot boat, such as a fast launch.

In some locations pilot transfer may be by helicopter, either by winch or by landing on a designated helipad on the deck.

Pilot Ladder and Access Equipment

Ladders

Pilot ladders must be regularly inspected as they are usually stowed on deck with only a canvas cover. The steps must all be horizontal and equally spaced, and any associated lashings and seizing must be inspected for damage. The deck fastenings and shackles must also be checked.

Pilot ladder inspection is included specifically within PSC inspections. The specifications for a pilot ladder are set out in the IMO publication *'Procedures for Port State Control 2011'*, Appendix 6:

> *10.3 During the inspection the PSCO should also ensure that the pilot transfer arrangements comply with SOLAS regulation V/23 and the unified interpretation of SOLAS regulation V/23 (MSC.1/circ.1375).*
>
> *The specifications for a pilot ladder, as stated by the International Maritime Pilots' Association, are as follows:*
>
> - *The side ropes must consist of two uncovered ropes, not less than 18 mm in diameter, be continuous with no joints, splices or shackles beyond the top step and made of Manila or other material of equivalent strength, durability and grip*
> - *the steps should be made of hardwood or other material of equivalent strength, stiffness and durability. They should have an efficient non-slip surface and the four lowest may be of rubber or other material of sufficient strength and stiffness as the other fitted steps*
> - *the steps should be not less than 400 mm between the side ropes, 115 mm in width*

and 25 mm in depth, excluding any non-slip coatings or grooving. They should be equally spaced not less than 300 mm or more than 380 mm apart and be secured in such a way that each step remains horizontal

- *ladders with more than five steps should have spreader steps not less than 1.8 metres long at intervals that will stop the ladder from twisting. The lowest spreader should be at the fifth step from the bottom and the interval between each spreader should not exceed nine steps*
- *ships with a freeboard of more than 9 metres, if no side door is available, must use a combination ladder.*

A combination ladder combines the vessel's accommodation ladder and the pilot ladder.

When the pilot ladder is used with an accommodation ladder:

- *The length of the accommodation ladder must be such that the angle of the ladder slope does not exceed 55°*
- *the lower platform of the accommodation ladder must be horizontal when in position and ready for use. The treads and steps of the ladder must provide a safe foothold at the operative angle*

- *the accommodation ladder and platform should have rigid stanchions and handrails on both sides. However, if hand ropes are used, they must be tight and properly secured*
- *the pilot ladder must be rigged immediately adjacent to the accommodation ladder and the upper part of the ladder must extend to at least 2 metres above the lower platform of the accommodation ladder.*

Access to the Deck of the ship from the pilot ladder:

- *If through a gate, then adequate handholds should be in place*
- *if over a bulwark or rails, the ladder on the inboard side should be securely attached to prevent the ladder from turning. Two handhold stanchions should be fitted on either side at the position of embarking on or off the pilot ladder.*

These should be not less than 0.7 metres and not more than 0.8 metres apart. Each stanchion should be not less than 32 mm in diameter and should extend not less than 1.5 metres above the top of the bulwarks. These stanchions should not be attached to the bulwark ladder.

Ships with a freeboard of more than 9 metres, must use a combination ladder if no side door is available.

Other Pilot Boarding Equipment

Manropes

Manropes tend to be neglected as many ports do not require their use. However, they are part of the pilotage equipment and must be taken out and inspected with the same frequency as the ladders.

Illumination

Any illumination provided at night must be shone from aft of the ladder to illuminate both the ladder and the sea area where the pilot boat comes alongside. This ensures that the boat crew and the pilot will not be blinded.

The pilot boat may come alongside ahead of the ladder and then slip back alongside the ship, or come alongside before the ladder

Pilotage

and ride up to it, depending on which part of the boat is used for pilot boarding and disembarking. Therefore, the side of the ship in the way of the ladder must also be illuminated. The area from the head of the pilot ladder to the accommodation must be well lit and free from obstructions.

Lifebuoy

As the pilot boat approaches, a crew member should be standing by about 20 metres along the deck ready with the lifebuoy so that he can throw it over the side should the pilot fall. If the lifebuoy is properly positioned, the pilot will be carried down to it by the speed of the ship through the water. As it is difficult to hold onto a lifebuoy being towed through the water, it should not be secured to the ship but instead regarded as buoyancy aid and to assist with location.

Heaving Line

Many pilots carry a case or electronic equipment that has to be hoisted on board. A heaving line should always be ready to be sent down to the boat if required.

IMO Assembly Resolution A.1045(27) 'Recommendation on Pilot Transfer Arrangements'

The IMO Assembly adopted Resolution A.1045(27), 'Recommendation on Pilot Transfer Arrangements' on 30 November 2011, and this revoked Resolution A.889(21).

While covering the items detailed in SOLAS Ch V Reg 23, which entered into force on 1st July 2012, the following additions were made to Resolution A.1045(27).

Paragraph 6 makes provision for the *'Safe Approach of the Pilot Boat'* as follows:

> *"Where rubbing bands or other constructional features might prevent the safe approach of a pilot boat, these should be cut back to provide at least 6 metres of unobstructed ship's side. Specialized offshore ships less than 90 m or other similar ships less than 90 m for which a 6 m gap in the rubbing bands would not be practicable, as determined by the Administration, do not have to comply with this requirement. In this case, other appropriate measures should be taken to ensure that persons are able to embark and disembark safely".*

Paragraph 7 makes provision for the *'Installation of Pilot Ladder Winch Reels'* as follows:

> ***"7.1 Point of access***
>
> *7.1.1 When a pilot ladder winch reel is provided it should be situated at a position*

which will ensure persons embarking on, or disembarking from, the ship between the pilot ladder and the point of access to the ship, have safe, convenient and unobstructed access to or egress from the ship.

7.1.2 The point of access to or egress from the ship may be by a ship's side opening, an accommodation ladder when a combination arrangement is provided, or a single section of pilot ladder.

7.1.3 The access position and adjacent area should be clear of obstructions, including the pilot ladder winch reel, for distances as follows:

.1 a distance of 915 mm in width measured longitudinally;

.2 a distance of 915 mm in depth, measured from the ship's side plating inwards; and

.3 a distance of 2,200 mm in height, measured vertically from the access deck.

7.2 Physical positioning of pilot ladder winch reels

7.2.1 Pilot ladder winch reels are generally fitted on the ship's upper (main) deck or at a ship's side opening which may include side doors, gangway locations or bunkering points. Winch reels fitted on the upper deck may result in very long pilot ladders.

7.2.2 Pilot ladder winch reels which are fitted on a ship's upper deck for the purpose of providing a pilot ladder which services a ship side opening below the upper deck or, alternatively, an accommodation ladder when a combination arrangement is provided should:

.1 be situated at a location on the upper deck from which the pilot ladder is able to be suspended vertically, in a straight line, to a point adjacent to the ship side opening access point or the lower platform of the accommodation ladder;

.2 be situated at a location which provides a safe, convenient and unobstructed passage for any person embarking on, or disembarking from, the ship between the pilot ladder and the place of access on the ship;

.3 be situated so that safe and convenient access is provided between the pilot ladder and the ship's side opening by means of a platform which should extend outboard from the ship's side for a minimum distance of 750 mm, with a longitudinal length of a minimum of 750 mm.

The platform should be securely guarded by handrails;

.4 safely secure the pilot ladder and manropes to the ship's side at a point on the ship's side at a distance of 1,500 mm above the platform access point to the ship side opening or the lower platform of the accommodation ladder;

and

.5 if a combination arrangement is provided, have the accommodation ladder secured to the ship's side at or close to the lower platform so as to ensure that the accommodation ladder rests firmly against the ship's side.

7.2.3 Pilot ladder winch reels fitted inside a ship's side opening should:

.1 be situated at a position which provides a safe, convenient and unobstructed passage for any person embarking on, or disembarking from, the ship between the pilot ladder and the place of access on the ship;

.2 be situated at a position which provides an unobstructed clear area with a minimum length of 915 mm and minimum width of 915 mm and minimum vertical height of 2,200 mm;

and

.3 if situated at a position which necessitates a section of the pilot ladder to be partially secured in a horizontal position on the deck so as to provide a clear access as described above, then allowance should be made so that this section of the pilot ladder may be covered with a rigid platform for a minimum distance of 915 mm measured horizontally from the ship's side inwards.

Pilotage

7.3 Handrails and handgrips

Handrails and handgrips should be provided in accordance with section 5 to assist the pilot to safely transfer between the pilot ladder and the ship, except as noted in paragraph 7.2.2.3 for arrangements with platforms extending outboard. The horizontal distance between the handrails and/or the handgrips should be not less than 0.7 m or more than 0.8 m apart.

7.4 Securing of the pilot ladder

Where the pilot ladder is stowed on a pilot ladder winch reel which is located either within the ship's side opening or on the upper deck:

.1 the pilot ladder winch reel should not be relied upon to support the pilot ladder when the pilot ladder is in use;

.2 the pilot ladder should be secured to a strong point, independent of the pilot ladder winch reel; and

.3 the pilot ladder should be secured at deck level inside the ship side opening or, when located on the ship's upper deck, at a distance of not less than 915 mm measured horizontally from the ship's side inwards.

7.5 Mechanical securing of pilot ladder winch reel

7.5.1 All pilot ladder winch reels should have means of preventing the winch reel from being accidentally operated as a result of mechanical failure or human error.

7.5.2 Pilot ladder winch reels may be manually operated or, alternatively, powered by either electrical, hydraulic or pneumatic means.

7.5.3 Manually operated pilot ladder winch reels should be provided with a brake or other suitable arrangements to control the lowering of the pilot ladder and to lock the winch reel in position once the pilot ladder is lowered into position.

7.5.4 Electrical, hydraulic or pneumatically driven pilot ladder winch reels should be fitted with safety devices which are capable of cutting off the power supply to the winch reel and thus locking the winch reel in position.

7.5.5 Powered winch reels should have clearly marked control levers or handles which may be locked in a neutral position.

7.5.6 A mechanical device or locking pin should also be utilized to lock powered winch reels".

Changes to the 'Pilot Transfer Arrangements' from 1st July 2012

SOLAS Ch V Reg 23 on 'Pilot Transfer Arrangements' was completely replaced on 1st July 2012 with a new text as detailed in the SOLAS Amendments 2010 and 2011 (Resolution MSC.308(88) refers).

The main changes to SOLAS Ch V Reg 23 are as follows:

- *Newbuilds - Equipment and arrangements for pilot transfer which are installed on or after 1 July 2012 shall comply with the requirements of this regulation [Reg 23 para 1.2 refers]*
- *Existing ships - Except as provided otherwise, equipment and arrangements for pilot transfer which are provided on ships before 1 July 2012 shall at least comply with the requirements of SOLAS Ch V Reg 17 or 23, as applicable, of the SOLAS Convention in force prior to that date. [Reg 23 para 1.3 refers]*
- *With respect to ships constructed before 1 January 1994, the requirement that shipside doors used for pilot transfer shall not open outwards shall apply not later than the first survey on or after 1 July 2012. [Reg 23 para 1.5 and 5 refers]*
- *A pilot ladder shall be certified by the manufacturer as complying with this regulation or with an international standard acceptable to the Organization. [Reg 23 para 2.3 and ISO 799:2004, 'Ships and marine technology - Pilot ladders refers']*
- *All pilot ladders used for pilot transfer shall be clearly identified with tags or other permanent marking so as to enable identification of each appliance for the purposes of survey, inspection and record keeping. A record shall be kept on the ship as to the date the identified ladder is placed into service and any repairs effected. [Reg 23 para 2.4 refers]*
- *Mechanical pilot hoists shall not be used. [Reg 23 para 6 refers]*
- *Two man-ropes to be provided of not less than 28 mm and not more than 32 mm in diameter [Reg 23 para 7.1 refers].*

Reference:

ISO 799:2004, Ships and marine technology - Pilot ladders A.1045(27), 'Recommendation on Pilot Transfer Arrangements', adopted on 30th November 2011.

MSC.308(88)
http://shippingregs.org/52.re

Recent Regulation Changes in SOLAS for Pilot Boarding

Securing the Pilot Accommodation Ladder to the Ship's Side

When a combination (pilot accommodation) ladder is used, means should be provided to securely fix the lower platform of the accommodation ladder portion to the ship's side.

Reason

The accommodation ladder can easily swing out of control with small movements of a large vessel, making the passage between the pilot ladder and the accommodation ladder hazardous.

Mechanical Pilot Hoist

The use of mechanical hoists is now forbidden.

Prohibition of Outward Opening Ship Side Doors used for Pilot Transfer

The use of outward opening ship side doors used for pilot transfer should be prohibited on all ships. Currently, such doors are prohibited only on ships built after January 1994.

Reason

Outward opening ship side doors are an unreasonable hazard to pilot safety, and present a serious danger to approaching pilot boats.

Diameter of Manropes

There are currently no requirements for the maximum diameter of manropes. Manropes should be of 28 to 32 mm diameter so that pilots can grip the ropes safely.

Reason

Grip tests have been conducted by groups of pilots, with the conclusion that a minimum diameter of 28 mm and a maximum of 32 mm would be safest for use during pilot transfer.

Rigging and Use of Manropes

The regulations should clearly specify the method of fixing the rope end to the ring plate (for manropes only) fixed on the deck. The manropes should be ready for use when the pilot disembarks, or pending a request from a pilot approaching to board.

Source: *IMO RESOLUTION A.889(21)*

Exchange of Information

Each pilot engagement should begin with an exchange of relevant information between the master and the pilot.

It is imperative that the master, the bridge team and the pilot understand that they share responsibility for good communication. They must be fully aware of their roles within the safe passage of the vessel.

The information exchange normally starts well before arrival at the pilot station. Initial contacts may be made through the vessel's agent and may involve:

- Port/berth of destination
- ETA at the pilot station so that berth, pilot and tug availability can be arranged
- draught of the vessel

Pilotage

- number of persons on board
- any IMO dangerous goods carried
- any known defects that may impact on the vessel's status.

Information from the Bridge Team

When the pilot has arrived on the bridge and been given the pilot card, a full brief of the current bridge state must be provided. This should include:

The handling characteristics of the ship:

- Whether right-hand or left-hand propellers, variable pitch, etc
- the thrusters and expected power
- the rudder response
- the capabilities of the helmsmen
- the engine response times and maximum standby rpm
- confirmation that all the navigation gear and steering was checked before entering the port waters
- the master's own assessment of the handling of the ship.

The Bridge:

- Any immediate shipping or hazard in the vicinity of the ship
- the current speed and course
- the draught and, if entering fresh water, the calculated fresh water draught
- calculated squat
- the air draught if applicable
- introduction of the OOW
- the gyro error and confirmation that all gyro repeaters, including the radars, have been synchronised
- the location of the VHF sets
- the main ARPA radar and its range. The pilot may be unfamiliar with the radar controls but they can be adjusted by the OOW during the passage to his requirements
- the echo sounder or Doppler system and the range scale required
- the location and status of ECDIS or any other electronic charting system
- the pilot should be advised of any defects whatsoever that may interfere with the conduct of the ship.

Information from the Pilot

Once the master and the bridge team have briefed the pilot on the current state of the bridge operations and the position of the ship, the pilot will provide information which may include:

- The port's passage plan and the intended route. This may be supplemented by reference to a port chartlet or it may be referenced to the vessel's charts
- the intended berth, the ETA for the berth, the predicted tide for arrival time, the anticipated UKC and what allowances have been made in calculating this
- the length of berth available for the ship, clear of obstructions such as cranes, loaders, dischargers and barges
- type of fendering provided at the berth and any locks that have to be passed through
- whether the vessel is going through mud or thick weed. The engine room should be warned so that they can oversee their cooling system and change over from lower to upper intakes
- anticipated port movements and any possible restrictions that may occur

- the weather forecast
- tidal predictions for the passage and minimum UKC at critical points
- tug requirement, including number and bollard pull
- tug rendezvous position and times and how and where they will be secured or stationed
- VHF channels to be monitored
- if applicable, the time of arrival at pilot to pilot transfer locations and the ladder arrangements required.

This information from the pilot is sometimes provided through an MPX card (Master/Pilot Exchange of Information). Both the pilot card and the MPX card can help to ensure that essential items are not overlooked.

Although the pilot has valuable local knowledge, it is vital that the master assesses the overall situation regarding draught, the weather, tug availability, the size of ship and the movement of other shipping and, should any doubts exist, these must be dealt with before pilotage commences.

Even with a mandatory pilot on board, it is imperative that the bridge team continues to perform their navigational watch duties, including monitoring the progress of the vessel and the conduct of the pilot.

Helmsmen

At some ports, dedicated local helmsmen board the vessel. Some pilots may prefer to use an autopilot rather than a helmsman for the majority of the transit, but there may be a company SMS guideline that prohibits this. Any changeover must be carried out well before entering confined waters where hand steering is required.

Speed

In many ports, ship speed is governed by strict regulation. While the pilot is aware of these regulations, it is the responsibility of the ship to comply. The speed limit may vary with different draught and hull considerations and, where strict speed restrictions are imposed, it is likely that the vessel's speed will be monitored. If limits are exceeded, the master will be liable to a fine.

Engines

Pilots often operate modern main engine and bowthrust controls themselves, after being shown the system and advised of any critical rpm. For more complicated systems, incorporating azimuth thrusters around the hull, it may be preferable for an officer more familiar with the system to keep control.

There may be times when the pilot will require full rpm to be set and he should be advised if notice is required for any reduction. The engine room should be kept up to date with the progress of the pilotage passage at all times.

Figure 6.1 - A ship can still roll quite heavily just before entering the port

The OOW

The OOW will be familiar with the master's position and the procedures for taking over the con, but he must be clear about what happens when the pilot arrives on the bridge. This is particularly important if the master is not on the bridge for all of the pilotage passage. The OOW should be identified to the pilot as it is essential that the pilot knows who is in the bridge team.

Pilotage

Standing Orders Under Pilotage

The master's standing orders must include a section on what is expected of the OOW when the ship is under pilotage, an example of which is shown below.

1. *When the pilot is on the bridge, he is to be treated with all the courtesies as for the rank of Captain. The pilot is responsible to me for the direction of the ship. His presence on the bridge does not relieve the OOW of any of his responsibilities for the safe navigation of the ship and he will continue with this, continually ascertaining the position of the ship and advising the pilot of any navigation or shipping hazards he feels might endanger the ship or interfere with the passage.*
2. *Should the pilot at any time give an order that does not directly concern the navigation of the ship, or have any complaint regarding any aspect of the ship, I am to be immediately informed.*
3. *You are to advise the pilot of any defect of any equipment appertaining to the safe navigation of the vessel.*
4. *The pilot must be advised of any pending change in watch personnel on the bridge and the time of these changes coordinated with him.*
5. *If at any time you are concerned as to the actions of the pilot, you are to advise the pilot of the same and inform me immediately.*
6. *Because of the pilot's presence and mine, you must not assume that we have noticed something that is not correct. You must, at all times, assume that we have not noticed and you are to advise us of your concerns.*

If the helmsman does not understand the pilot, it is essential that the OOW acts as interpreter as required.

Anchor Party

Prior to entering inland waters, and normally before the pilot embarkation position, the anchors will be cleared away and ready for letting go. On short pilotage passages, it is normal to go to anchor stations at the start of the inward passage unless the ship is entering in bad weather and it is hazardous for crew to be sent forward, in which case the anchor party will have to wait for more sheltered waters. On a prolonged pilotage, the manning of the ship will dictate formation of the anchor party.

For safety, with the ship so close to land, the anchor party should always be in position. However, the manning levels on board, together with the corresponding fatigue, will have to be considered. Any officer or rating who has spent several hours standing on the forecastle cannot be expected to carry out a watch on arrival and, apart from being unreasonable, may contravene the hours of work regulations.

Discussions with the pilot will determine where he requires the anchor party to be on their station. If the visibility closes in then, regardless of the manning, the anchors should be ready for letting go at any time.

At some ports and for river or canal transits, irrespective of anchor party requirements, there may be a requirement for a forecastle lookout with communication links to the bridge to be posted.

The Mooring Arrangements

Unless stipulated by the port, the number of mooring lines used is decided by the ship. The pilot may advise on the state of the berth, any strong currents, the distance of ships passing and what shelter is available. It is essential that the pilot is made aware of the number of crew available for putting out the mooring lines and, from the experience of the master, the time this will take. The pilot will then decide what rotation of lines should be run out and how to keep the vessel alongside during this operation.

Master on the Bridge or Not

Whether the master remains on the bridge with the pilot for all or part of the passage will depend on a number of factors, most importantly his trust of the pilot. After the initial meeting and monitoring of the progress of the pilotage, if doubts arise about the pilot's abilities or condition, the master cannot leave the bridge. A decision may have to be made whether to continue in pilotage mode, request that the pilot be relieved or take over the pilotage which, if in an unknown port, may be very difficult and also against port regulations. If it is felt that the ship cannot continue with the existing pilot, the ship must be stopped or slowed down in a safe area while the matter is being dealt with by the pilotage authority. As this may cause considerable delay to the berthing of the vessel, logbook entries should be made regarding the circumstances, and a statement of fact and note of protest may have to be made. Equally, if the pilot is not satisfied with a member of the bridge team, that person must be immediately replaced without any discussion and the matter can be resolved when the ship is safely alongside. As long as the pilot is the leader of the bridge team, his request must be complied with. The master should be on the bridge at all times during any difficult navigational area or when the pilot requests his presence. On prolonged passages, there may be occasions when the master can leave the bridge with the agreement of the pilot, provided that he is within immediate call if required.

Pilotage Exemptions

In some areas, pilotage exemption certificates are issued to masters or mates who can prove their ability based on familiarity with the port. Some authorities demand a formal examination and others may only require a visit to the harbour or pilotage office.

However, in difficult conditions, the master must feel free to ask for extra assistance, including the employment of a pilot if required.

Non-Compulsory Pilotage Areas

These vary from fairly large open areas, such as the English Channel, Malacca Strait and the Inland Sea in Japan, to narrow channels such as the Dardanelles. Where pilotage is offered, there is a reason for this and, if the master has no experience of the area or there are difficult weather conditions, pilotage is likely to be highly beneficial.

These pilots are often referred to as deep-sea pilots and, when considering their use, the following should be considered:

- The familiarity of the bridge team with the area to be transited
- the proliferation of navigational hazards, such as oil/gas installations and offshore renewable energy installations
- the available depth of water in relation to draught, under keel clearance and the vessel's intended route
- the port rotation schedule and the possible fatigue mitigation that employment of a deep-sea pilot might enable
- the possibility of adverse weather conditions and/or poor visibility.

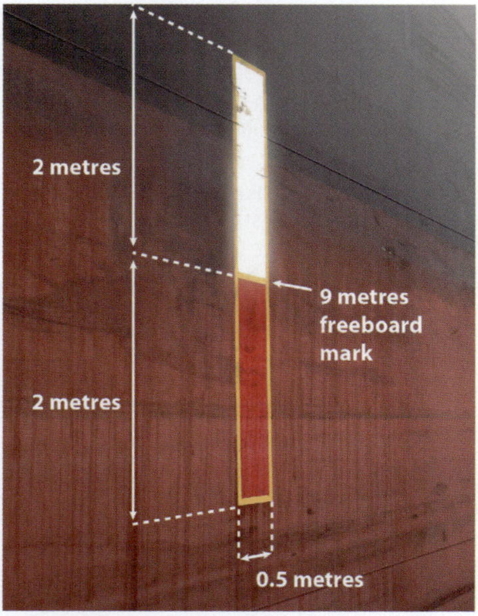

Figure 6.2 - This image shows the recommended 9 metre red/white freeboard mark. When the red section is visible above the waterline, this means that the freeboard exceeds 9 metres and a combination arrangement should be used.

Pilotage

What Pilots Want to Know About the Ship's Engines and Machinery Plant

Main Engine

- On boarding, test the engines astern before proceeding.
- What is the percentage output when going astern?
  Some engine types, eg steam turbine, will only deliver about 40% of the ahead power when going astern.
- Number of starts available.
  Class requires that a ship has sufficient compressed air-start storage capacity for the starting-air on the main engine to allow for 12 starts of the engine, ie 6 ahead and 6 astern.
- How long does it take for the compressors to recharge the air-start system?
  When recharging the air-start system, two compressors should be used, rather than just one on duty and one on standby, to ensure that the air-start system is recharged as fast as possible, particularly when manoeuvring in close confines such as when berthing or entering locks when a number of engine movements will be required in a short period of time.
- On new ships that are fitted with computer-controlled engines, it must be possible to disconnect the ship out of computer control as this hampers the ability for the pilot to increase rpm in many cases until load is out of a certain range.
  Pilots are very wary of engines that are computer controlled!

Steering Gear

- Time to move the rudder from 35° to port to 35° to stbd.
  This should be less than 28 seconds.
- Are 2 x steering motors running?
- Are the rudder and rpm indicators running?
- Is the ship fitted with an 'active rudder', such as a 'Becker' rudder?

Electrical Power

- Preference is that 2 x generators are running and that each generator can take the hotel load.
- DO NOT use shaft generators with the pilot on board.

Thrusters

- Number of thrusters and any limitations.
- If fitted with a stern thruster, can you actually use the stern thruster when going astern?
  This is not possible on many ships.

Propellers

- On ships fitted with CPP, which is the fail-safe direction in the event of loss of hydraulic power?
  Many ships on losing hydraulic power 'fail-to-closed', but some 'fail-to-open', ie on losing hydraulic power the blades will adopt the full pitch position.

REQUIRED BOARDING ARRANGEMENTS FOR PILOT

In accordance with SOLAS V/23 & IMO Resolution A.1045(27)

INTERNATIONAL MARITIME PILOTS' ASSOCIATION
H.Q.S. "Wellington" Temple Stairs, Victoria Embankment, London WC2R 2PN Tel: +44 (0)20 7240 3973 Fax: +44 (0)20 7210 3518 Email: office@impahq.org
This document and all IMO Pilot-related documents are available for download at: http://www.impahq.org

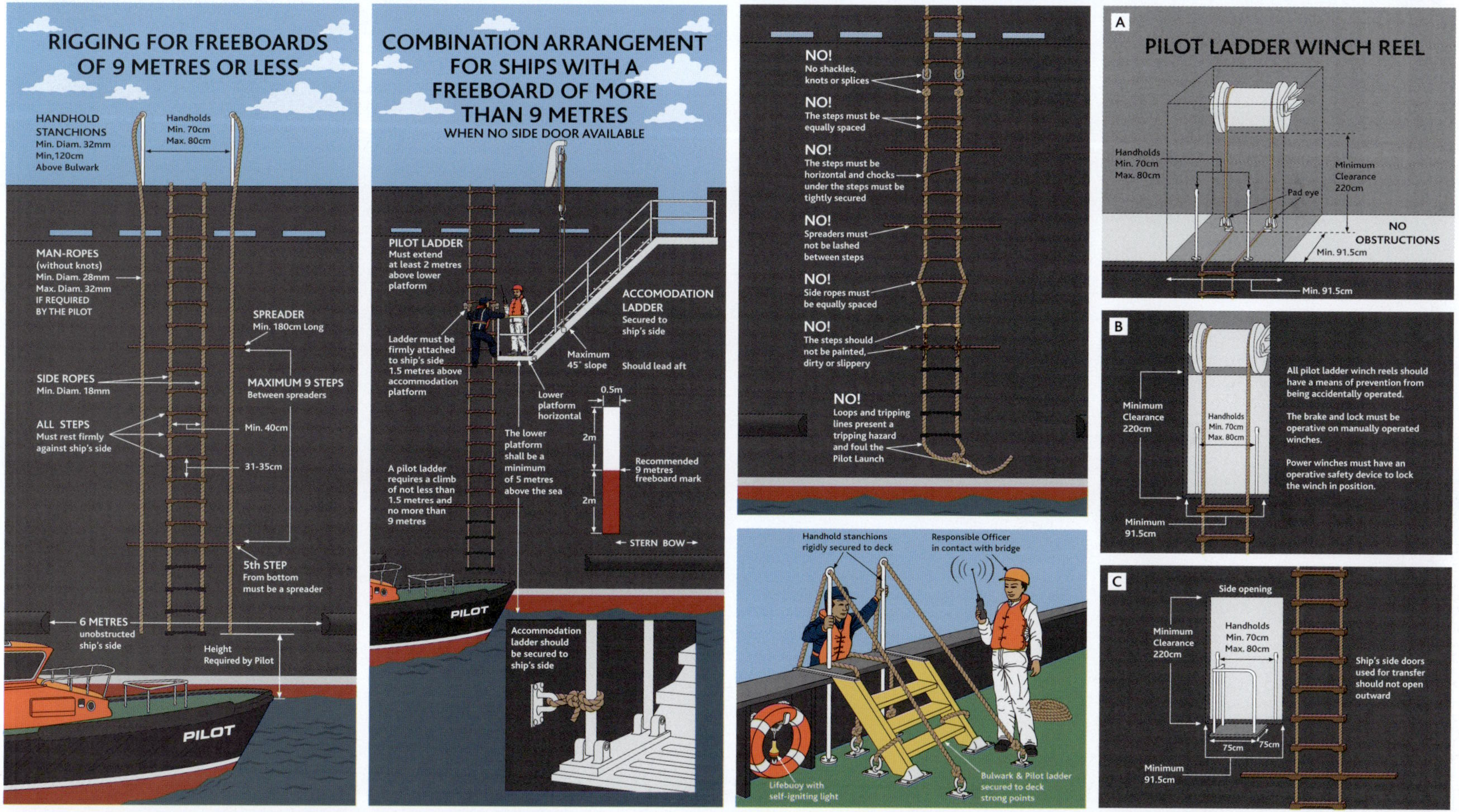

CHAPTER 7

Ship Handling

Ship Manoeuvres

The type of propulsion equipment fitted to a vessel has a huge bearing on its manoeuvrability. Equipment can vary from a single propeller to more sophisticated configurations that include bow thrusters and azipods.

Ship Propulsion

Propellers

The blades of a propeller are angled so that their rotation around the shaft creates forward movement. The angle of the blade, coupled with the rotation, creates 'pitch'. Pitch is the theoretical forward movement of the propeller in one rotation of the propeller. However, some forward movement will be lost. This is called slip and can be calculated where the pitch is known.

$$\text{Theoretical distance} = \text{Revolutions} \times \text{pitch}$$

$$\text{Propeller slip\%} = \frac{\text{theoretical speed or distance moved} - \text{actual speed or distance moved}}{\text{theoretical speed or distance moved}} \times 100$$

Due to the introduction of the EEDI (Energy Efficiency Design Index) and the increasing need to reduce operating costs, propeller efficiency is becoming more important. The efficiency measures a propeller's effectiveness in converting the mechanical power to propulsion, based on the thrust measurement and shaft power (torque × rotational speed), ie:

$$\text{Propeller efficiency} = \frac{\text{thrust force} \times \text{ship speed}}{\text{shaft power}}$$

Transverse Thrust

When a propeller rotates, its blades cause the water to move in an astern direction. As the water moves past the propeller, it creates a force on the propeller known as transverse thrust (or 'paddlewheel effect'), which causes a forward or astern running propeller to move the stern to starboard or port.

If the propeller is right-handed (ie it rotates clockwise while moving ahead), transverse thrust is directed to starboard when making headway, and to port when making sternway. This is reversed for a left-handed propeller.

Generally, transverse thrust is small when making headway and much larger when moving astern.

Masters should have an understanding of the extent to which transverse thrust will affect a particular vessel.

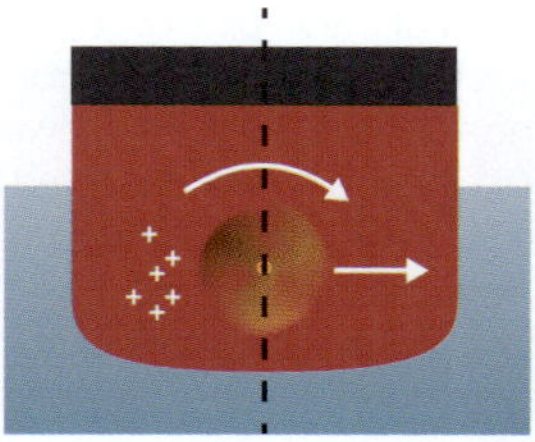

AHEAD
Higher pressure on the port side transverse thrust causes small swing to port 'hardly noticeable'

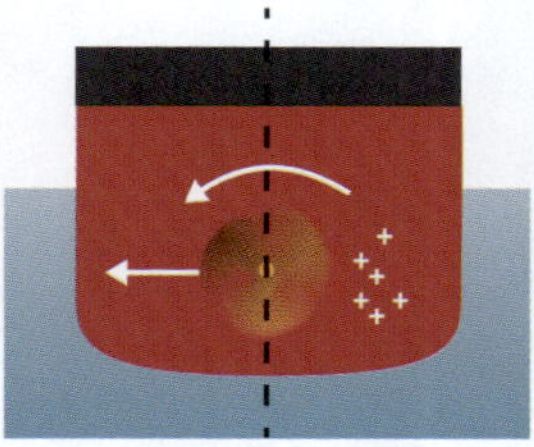

ASTERN
Higher pressure on the starboard side much more significant transverse thrust causes swing starboard

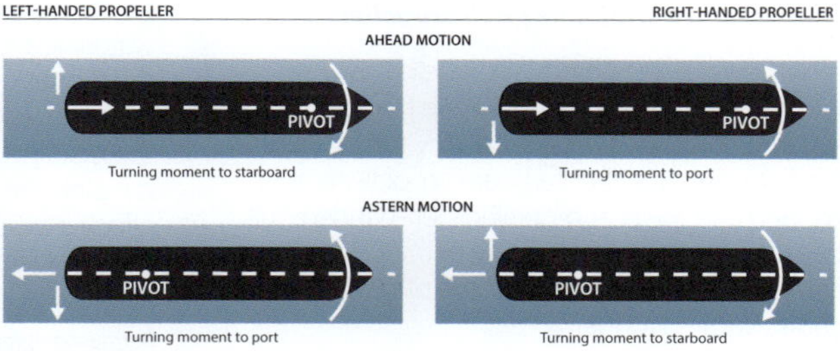

Swing due to transverse thrust of a right-hand propeller in ahead and astern motion:

AHEAD ASTERN

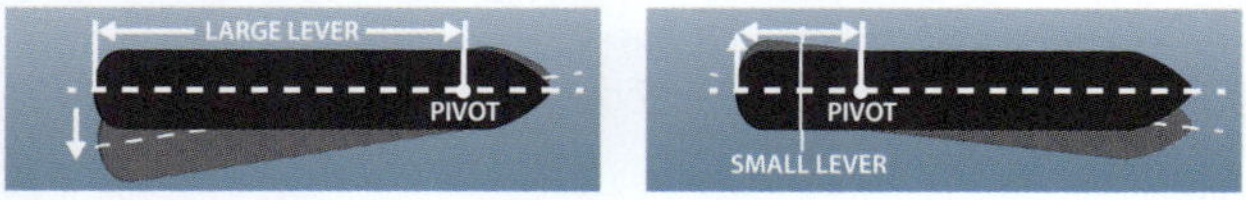

As the water flow around a ship's hull changes, so does transverse thrust. The difference is most noticeable in shallow water. For example, a ship that turns to starboard in deep water may well turn to port in shallow water. Also, the magnitude of the force will change and, by implication, there will be a range of water depths for which the bias may be difficult to predict, particularly when a ship is stopping in water of reducing depth.

Ship Manoeuvres

Transverse thrust is often used to help bring the ship's stern alongside during berthing. When a propeller is put astern on a ship moving forward at speed, the initial effect of transverse thrust is slight. However, as the ship's forward motion decreases, the effect of transverse thrust increases.

Twin Propellers (twin screw)

Figure 7.1 - PSV Contra-rotating out-turning controllable pitch propellers

A twin-screw vessel has two propellers, one on each side of the centreline, that are manoeuvred by separate throttle controls. Generally the propellers are out-turning, ie the starboard propeller is right-handed and the port propeller is left-handed. This balances the sidewise pressure of the propellers and makes it possible to keep the ship on a straight course with no rudder.

Twin screws are used on ships that require high manoeuvrability, such as offshore ships, ferries and passenger ships. It is common for the propellers of such ships to be fitted with variable pitch blades. The speed and direction of controllable pitch propellers (CPP) can be quickly adjusted, without adjustment to the engine or shaft rotation.

By varying the pitch between the propellers, the ship's heading can be adjusted without the use of the rudders, greatly enhancing manoeuvrability when moving astern and at very slow speeds where little water flow passes the rudder.

Bow Thrusters

Bow thrusters increase manoeuvrability by enabling a vessel to create sideways thrust both to port and starboard. This is particularly beneficial when close manoeuvring is required, such as when berthing, and can reduce the need for tug assistance. There are two types of bow thruster - tunnel thrusters and azimuth thrusters.

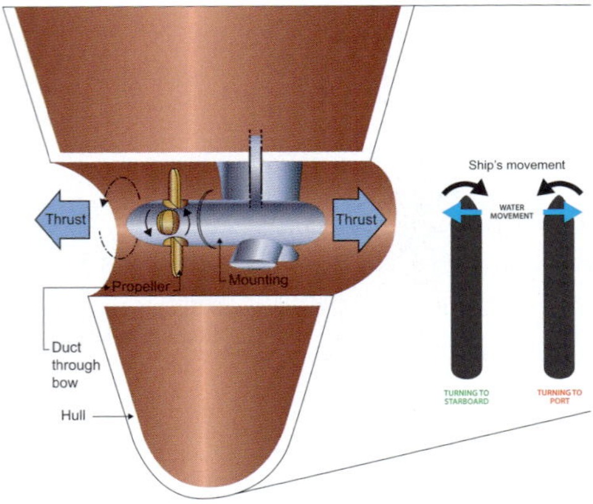

Figure 7.2 - Bow thruster

Tunnel Thrusters

A tunnel thruster is a hydraulically or electrically powered thrust unit mounted in an athwartship tunnel built into the bow of the ship below the waterline. During operation, water is forced through the tunnel, generating sideways thrust. The power unit is an auxiliary machine, ie it is not connected to the main power system of the ship. The thrust unit is mainly controlled from the bridge and is most effective when used when the ship is stationary. Some vessels may have more than one bow thruster and may also have one or more stern thrusters.

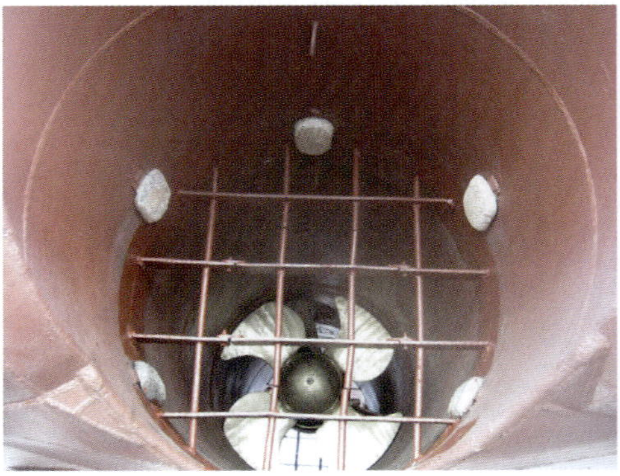

Figure 7.3 - DSV Tunnel bow thruster with protective grating

Tunnel thrusters increase the vessel's resistance to forward motion through the water, but this can be mitigated through proper fairing aft of the tunnel aperture. It is important to ensure that the tunnel remains below the waterline at all times. If not, thruster performance will be impaired and damage may be sustained to the thrust unit and the hull around it. Ship operators should take care to prevent fouling of the tunnel and thruster, either through the use of a protective grate or by cleaning.

Azimuth Thrusters

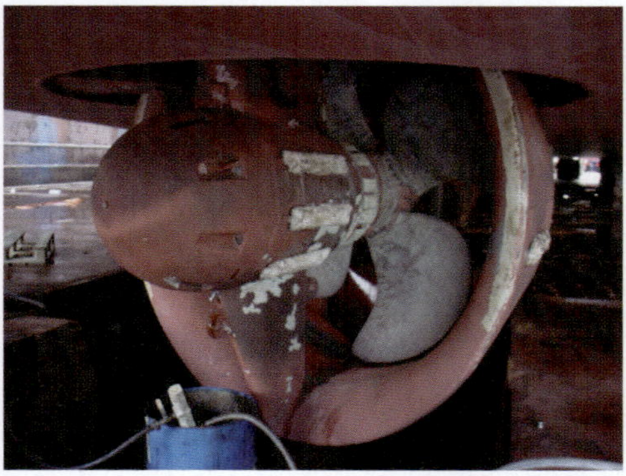

Figure 7.4 - Azimuth thruster from an AHTS being overhauled during dry dock

Azimuth thrusters consist of a thruster mounted on a frame that can be rotated through 360° and retracted into the hull when not in use. They are frequently independent of the main propulsion system and are relatively powerful units, in some cases being capable of independently propelling the ship forward at speeds in excess of 6 knots.

Figure 7.5 - Thruster mark on hull

The presence of a bow thruster is indicated by a white cross symbol marked over the position of each thruster on each side of the vessel, above the waterline.

Many offshore vessels are required to maintain position with a fixed heading while carrying out operations at sea. In such circumstances, it is normal for the ship's head to be maintained by linking the compass heading to the propulsion system and for the athwartship and fore and aft movement to be controlled by the operator using a joystick or by a dynamic positioning (DP) system.

Azipods

An azipod combines vessel propulsion and steering, thereby replacing traditional propellers, drive shafts and rudders.

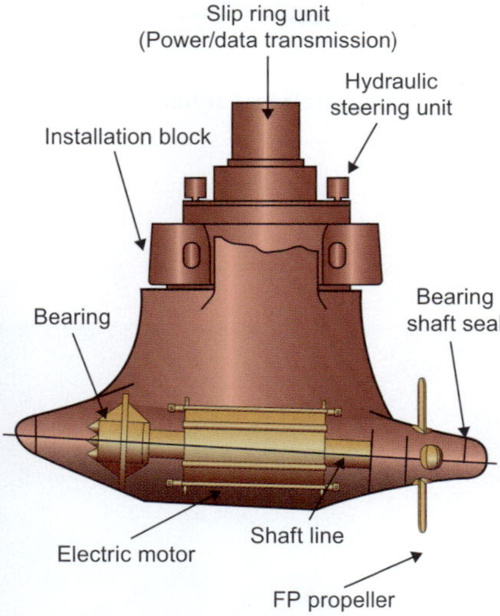

Figure 7.6 - Schematic of azipod

Azipods are suspended beneath the waterline at the aft end of the ship, mounted on a short propeller shaft perpendicular to the centreline of the ship's hull.

An azipod's propeller is fixed pitch, but the shaft can be rotated to any position in 360° to change the direction of the ship's movement or to keep her on course. Azipods are capable of moving the ship bodily in any direction. The position and speed of the azipods are controlled from the bridge and each azipod can be operated independently of the other.

Azipods provide excellent control at slow manoeuvring speeds and also reduce ships' turning circles when underway at service speed.

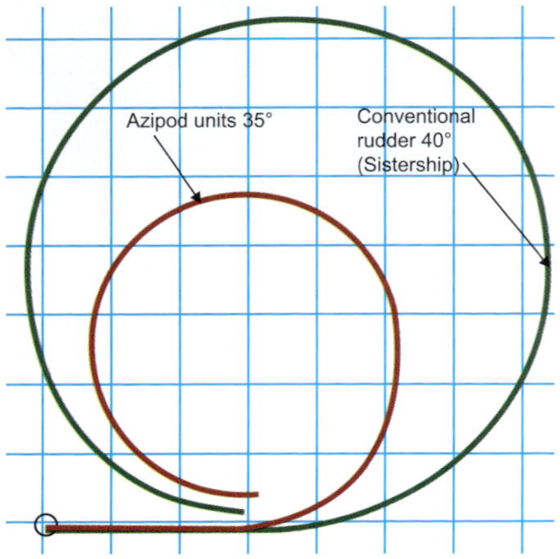

Figure 7.7 - Turning circle test at full speed

Ship Manoeuvres

Turning Short Round

When single-screw vessels must be turned in restricted waters, the ship will normally be positioned to the port side of the channel, harbour or waterway.

To start the swing, the engine speed is set at half or, if required, full ahead and the rudder placed hard to starboard. The ship will then move ahead, swinging the stern to port and, therefore, the head to starboard. The engines are then stopped and put astern and the rudder placed amidships. Using transverse thrust, the ship's stern will continue swinging to port. The rudder is again placed to starboard and the engines put ahead. This procedure is repeated until the vessel is on the desired heading.

In strong winds, it is wise to turn in such a way that the tendency to back into the wind can be used to increase the turn. If the wind works against the turn, dropping an anchor may be necessary to maintain control and safely execute the turn.

Berthing a single right-hand screw vessel to port (with no wind or tide)

A right-hand screw vessel is best suited to berthing port side to as the stern cants to port due to transverse thrust when the engine is put astern. At the final stage of the approach, the engine going astern stops the vessel and at the same time swings the stern in towards the berth.

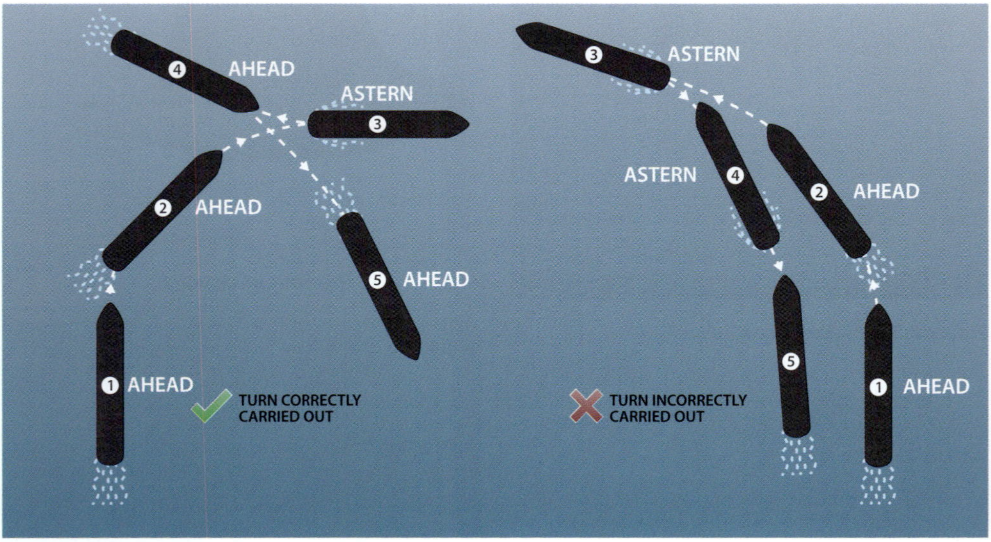

Figure 7.8 - Turning in restricted waters (single screw)

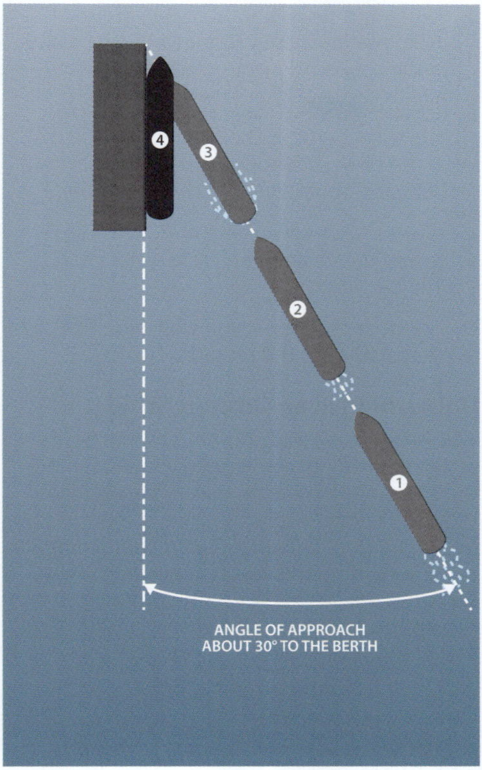

Figure 7.9 - Berthing a single right-hand screw vessel, port side to

1. Minimal speed for steerage. Approach at a moderate angle, approximately 30° to the berth.
2. Maintain a slow controlled speed. Steer to maintain course. Stop engines just before the berth.
3. Put engines astern, rudder to starboard and the stern will swing to port.
4. Stop engines, rudder amidships.

Berthing a single right-hand screw vessel to starboard (with no wind or tide)

In general, the approach has to be much slower and at a finer angle to the berth than for a port side alongside berthing. Astern propulsion to slow down or stop the vessel should be avoided as transverse thrust will cause the vessel to sheer to starboard and she may strike the berth. If for some reason astern propulsion is unavoidable, it is possible to reduce transverse thrust by swinging the vessel slightly to port before putting the engine astern.

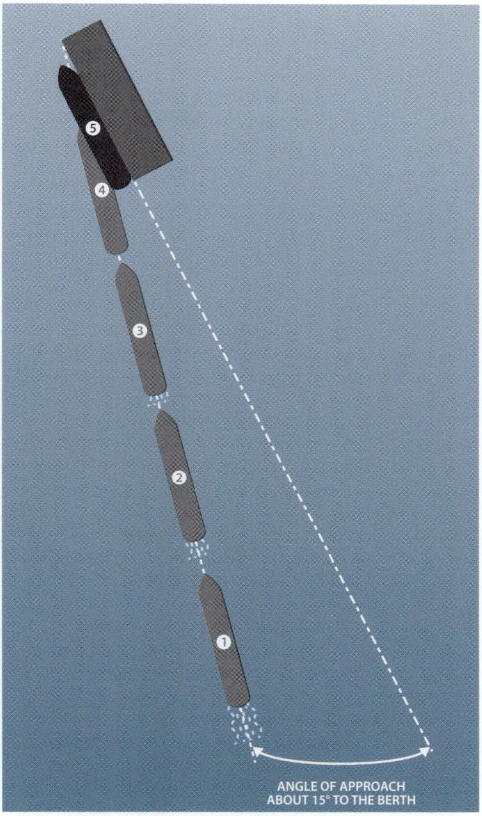

Figure 7.10 - Berthing a single right-hand screw vessel, starboard side to

1. Reduce speed or stop engines. Approach at a minimal angle, approximately 15° to the berth.
2. Maintain minimal speed for steerage.
3. Vessel almost stationary. Put rudder to port, brief kick ahead on engines to swing the stern in towards the berth.
4. Stop engines, rudder amidships.

Coming Alongside

With a right-handed propeller, it will generally be easier to come alongside port side to. When a bow line is secured and the engines are given a kick ahead or astern, the stern will swing alongside.

Unberthing (no wind or tide)

The most convenient option is to take the ship stern out first, but there are a few considerations. When the engine is put astern, transverse

Ship Manoeuvres

thrust brings the stern back towards the berth. Therefore, the first movement should be to get the stern away from the berth, which also causes the bow to come into contact with the berth at a point further forward. Depending on the shape of the bow, additional fenders forward may be required to prevent possible damage.

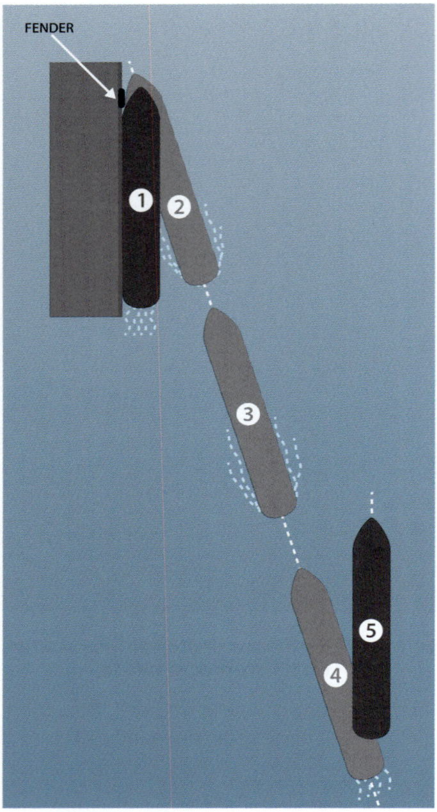

Figure 7.11 - Unberthing a single right-hand screw vessel from a berth

1. Full port rudder, brief kick ahead (to swing the stern away from the berth).
2. When the stern is at a suitable distance from the berth, put rudder amidships and engine astern. Pay out the head line.
3. Ensure the stern stays at a safe distance from the berth as the ship comes astern. If the stern is coming close to the berth, repeat steps (1) and (2). Let go the head line.
4. When the vessel is at a safe distance from the berth, stop engines.
5. Starboard rudder, engines ahead. Turn the vessel to steer the required course.

Unberthing in an Onshore Wind

While a wind blowing the ship off the berth will assist unberthing, an onshore wind (blowing the ship onto the berth) makes the operation more difficult, particularly when using the method just described. Use of a spring line may assist in holding the vessel in position while swinging the stern out. This helps prevent potential damage caused by the vessel's movement along the berth.

If an onshore wind is anticipated prior to berthing, the vessel can use the offshore anchor, ie the starboard anchor if moored port side, to enable far greater control when unberthing.

Picking up a Mooring Buoy

The effects of transverse thrust need to be considered when picking up a mooring buoy, eg SPM operations. When making the approach, the buoy should be kept marginally on the starboard bow because, when the engines are put astern to stop the ship, the bow will tend to swing to starboard, bringing the buoy immediately under the ship's bow.

Use of Anchors when Berthing

Use of Anchors when Berthing

Anchors are commonly used in berthing a ship either as part of a predetermined mooring pattern, such as an open moor or Mediterranean moor, or to assist a ship in the approach or departure from a berth. A ship with limited power or propulsion systems can lay an anchor from the outboard side when approaching a berth with an onshore wind. This not only enables the rate of approach to be controlled when berthing, but provides the means to unberth the ship into relatively strong winds.

Dredging Anchors

The term dredging anchors refers to the practice of paying out sufficient scope for

Use of Anchors when Berthing

the anchor to make contact with the seabed but not enough that it can dig in. Before considering such a manoeuvre, it may be necessary to obtain permission from the port authorities. The nature of the seabed must be assessed.

A bow anchor can be dredged from a ship going forward or astern so that the ship's pivot point moves to the position of the hawse pipe. To overcome the anchor's drag, the main engines are used, giving good steering at low speed. When going forward, corrective action will be needed to prevent the bow from swinging to port or starboard.

If the anchor digs in, it could cause the ship to stop and necessitate breaking the anchor out again. Digging in can also damage the ship, anchor or windlass. It is, therefore, important to use as little cable as possible; typically the length of cable should be between one and a half and two times the depth of the water.

Local knowledge regarding the nature and condition of the seabed is important to avoid dredging in an area where the bottom is foul or where unacceptable damage to the seabed may occur.

The operation can take one of two forms:

A) Using the cable to act as a spring effect, turning the aft part of the vessel in towards the berth (the pivot point acting well forward), or

B) Positioning the vessel up tide, ahead of the berth, and allowing the tide effects to move the vessel astern, deliberately dragging the anchor backwards, allowing the ship to fall back towards the berth (the rudder action being used to cause the vessel to draw to a position parallel alongside).

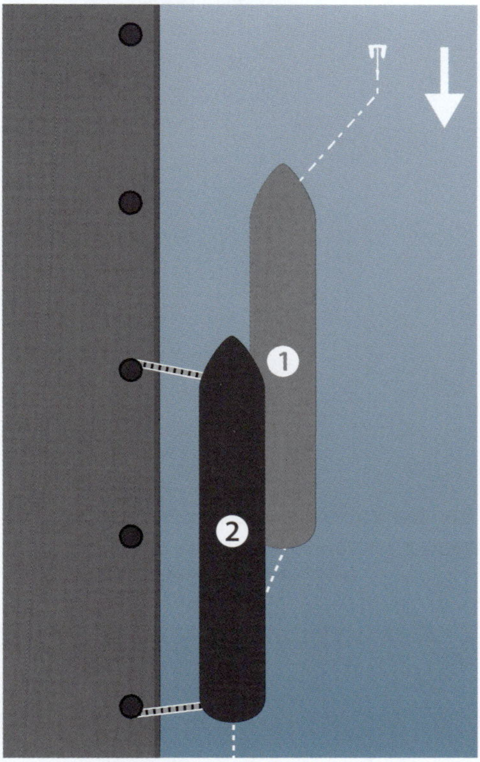

Figure 7.13 - Turning the ship using the anchor (snubbing round)

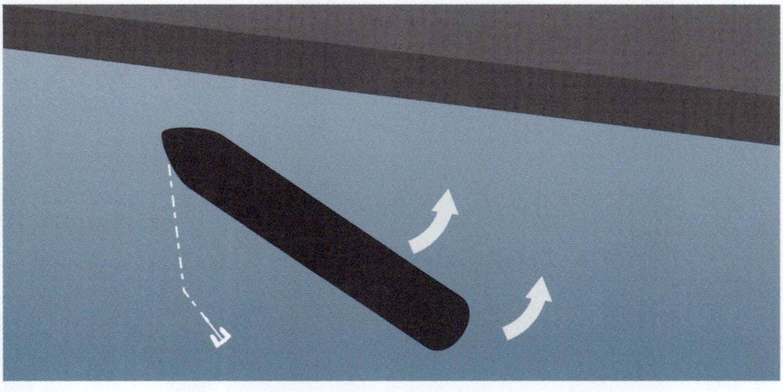

Figure 7.12 - By dredging an anchor from an up-tide position with a flow stream past the rudder, the helm can be applied to generate a parallel closing movement towards the berth

A ship may be turned without tug assistance by using the anchor and kicking ahead with the engines (snubbing round). This moves the pivot point forward and reduces the radius of the turn. The manoeuvre should be conducted at slow speed, using short bursts of propulsion, with the rudder on the same side as the anchor was lowered.

Use of Anchors when Berthing

Figure 7.14 - Turning the ship on the anchor (ship's position every 60 seconds)

Open Moor

An open moor is when a vessel is anchored with both anchors leading ahead. It is used when a single anchor would not provide sufficient weight to hold the vessel, eg in very strong tide or wind conditions.

1. Approach the anchorage with wind or current on one bow.
2. Weather anchor or upstream anchor is let go on the run (1).
3. The headway is continued and cable is laid up to one third of the final length of the cable.
4. The second anchor is let go.
5. The first anchor is held at the gypsy.
6. The vessel brings-to on her weather cable. It gradually grows taut to windward.
7. The bow develops a rapid swing into the stream or wind.
8. Both the anchors are veered.
9. Finally the anchors are at one point on each bow.

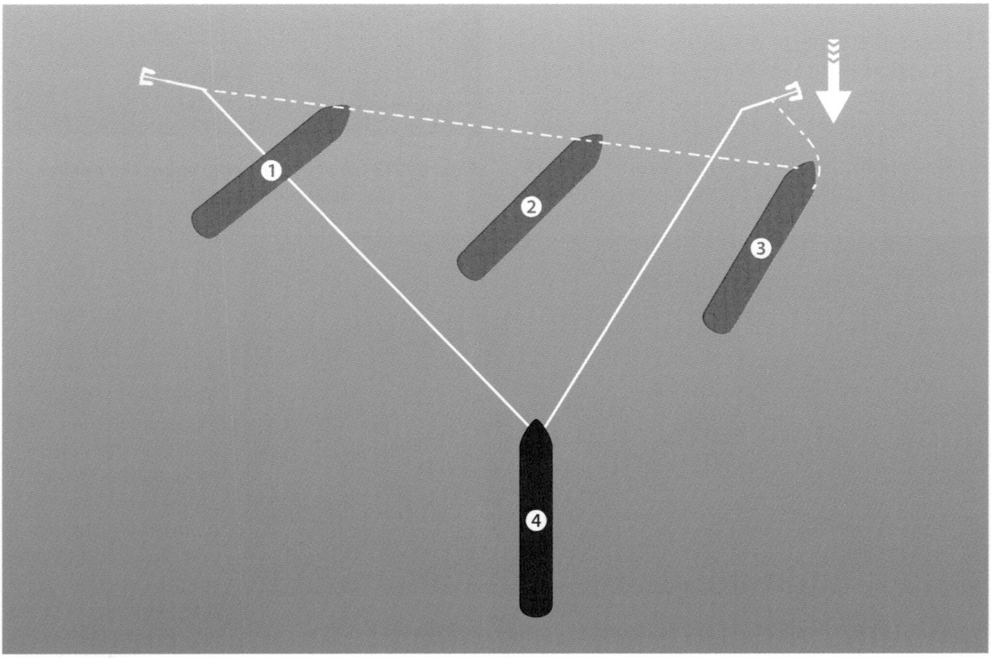

Figure 7.15 - Open moor

Lightering Operations (Ship to Ship Transfer)

STS Operation, image from 'Crude Oil Tanker Basics' by Paul Armitage

General

Lightering operations, also known as ship to ship (STS) operations, are conducted at sea and involve the transfer of liquid cargoes. The most common cargoes transferred in this way are crude oils, but LPG and LNG cargoes are also transferred in this manner. The industry terminology used for the vessel discharging the cargo is the Ship To Be Lightered (STBL), and the vessel loading is the Service Ship (SS).

Lightering operations often take place because the tanker (typically a VLCC or ULCC), is too large for the discharge port. It is a very common operation in areas such as the USA or China as their coastal areas have limited water depth, but they are countries with high oil import requirements.

The operations (mooring, loading and unmooring) can take place when the STBL is underway or at anchor. The ships are most commonly moored alongside one another but sometimes may adopt a tandem lightering formation with the SS moored astern of the STBL. This type of operation is found in areas including Oman and Australia.

Figure 7.16 - VLCC tandem lightering off NW Australia (HJ Schaefer)

Lightering Operations (Ship to Ship Transfer)

Manoeuvring

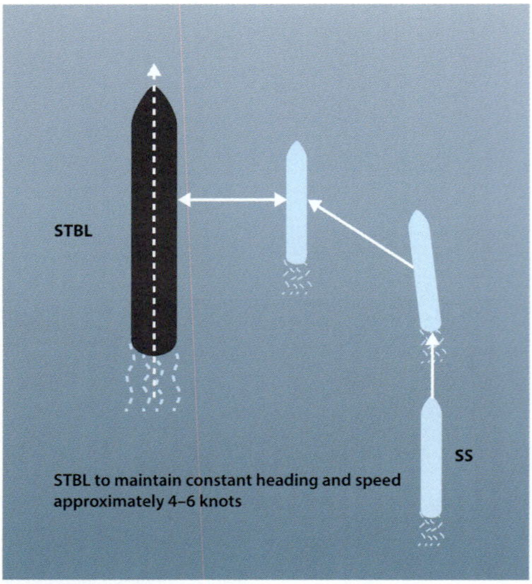

Figure 7.17 - Approach of Service Ship (SS) to Ship To Be Lightered (STBL)

If mooring is to be completed while underway, the process will typically proceed as follows:

1. The STBL will maintain a steady course at slow speed, 4 to 6 knots. The sea and wind is generally kept on the port bow of the STBL.
2. The SS would normally approach on a near parallel course and match the speed of the STBL. It is recommended that the SS moors port side alongside the STBL.
3. Speed adjustments should be kept small (typically in the 5 rpm range).
4. An approach angle should not be excessive, and an angle in the region of 4 to 6° is considered suitable as the ships begin to close in.
5. When the vessels make contact, they should be as near as possible to parallel.

Interaction

The effects of interaction between the ships as they close in should not be underestimated. The speeds of the ships should be kept to the minimum at which they can be safely controlled to minimise these effects.

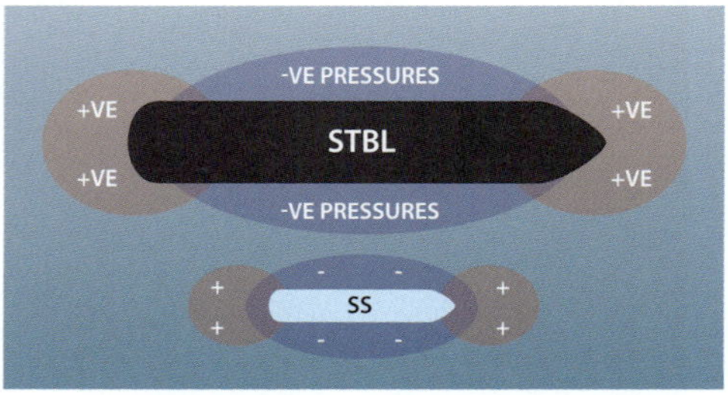

Figure 7.19 - Positive and negative pressure areas

Ships can be thought of as creating areas of positive pressure around the bow and stern and negative pressure along the main body of the ship when making way through the water. The effects of these areas, where similar repel

Figure 7.18 - The angle of approach between the SS and the STBL should be within 4 to 6°

and dissimilar attract, increase as the distance between them reduces and proportionately to the square of the ship's speed.

If the vessels are too close, when the bow of the SS approaches the stern of the STBL, the two positive pressure bulbs will repel and require additional helm to correct steering. Similar problems will be experienced as the ships draw level and the distance begins to close, so speed must be kept to a practicable minimum to maintain control. A close watch should be kept for any turbulence in the water between the ships at this time and during the subsequent operations. The crew should be made aware of such dangers.

Full communication should be kept between the two ships and any change to the engines or heading on the STBL should be relayed to the SS in advance.

Lines should be made fast as agreed in the mooring plan. Thereafter, the manoeuvring of the combined ships would normally be controlled by the STBL, during which the SS would have the helm amidships and engines stopped.

If the cargo transfer is to continue underway, the speed through the water must be minimal on a steady course. If going to anchor, the offside anchor should be used.

If it is decided that the ships are to be allowed to drift, the rolling of both ships should be watched closely, with a particular emphasis on deteriorating weather conditions. If necessary, the engines should be run and the ships' heads brought slowly to a suitable heading.

When lightering occurs between two ships and one is at anchor, common in areas with limited searoom, similar considerations should be taken in respect of sea and weather conditions. Rolling or yawing of the anchored ship must be considered when approaching and a steeper approach angle may be required. It is not unusual for a tug to be employed to help keep the ship on a steady heading.

Mooring Preparations

All moorings should meet the recommendations specified in Mooring Equipment Guidelines and STS Transfer Guide. Moorings should be arranged and of sufficient length that they permit sufficient movement for weather conditions and freeboard change. However, they must not allow excessive movement between the two ships.

While standard ship mooring design is intended for vessels berthed alongside in ports or terminals, standard tanker rigging configurations will generally suffice for lightering operations.

STS Transfer Guide

It is normal practice for the SS, undertaking the manoeuvring, to use her lines to moor. Additional lines from the STBL may be used depending on the prevailing weather and sea conditions.

Consideration should be given to the differences in freeboard height between the vessels throughout the operation, ie the STBL freeboard increases and the SS decreases during the operation. The greater the vertical component of the angle made by the lines, the lower its resistance to horizontal forces.

Heaving lines and strong messenger lines should be made ready in preparation for the intended operation.

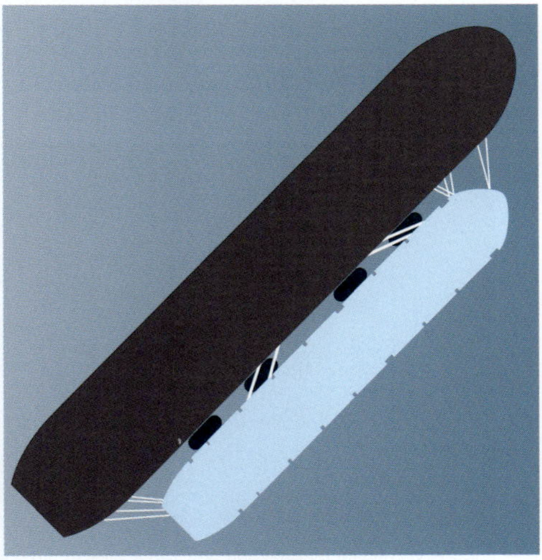

Figure 7.20 - Typical STS mooring arrangement

The STS Transfer Guide recommends that rope tails of at least 11 metres are fitted to wire ropes, with a breaking strain 25% greater. These add elasticity, are easier to handle and can be cut in an emergency.

Mooring lines should not be of excessive or uneven tension.

Lightering Operations (Ship to Ship Transfer)

Cargo Transfer

A number of factors specific to lightering operations should be considered:

- Weather conditions and parameters for continued operation
- limitations imposed by the cargo equipment, such as hose length/structure, ship piping, venting, inert gas production capacity, etc
- ballasting operations, including freeboard differences, free surface moments, BWM and local restrictions.

Unmooring

Potential hazards during unmooring include unpredictable weather and tidal factors, yawing and the lack of physical resistance provided by the STBL. These considerations are of particular concern for ships at anchor and the use of tugs should be considered. In some conditions, the STBL may be required to weigh anchor and complete the unmooring operation while underway.

Manoeuvring is normally achieved by singling up the lines fore and aft, letting go the forward lines and using the helm and engines to swing the bow out before letting go the aft lines and moving ahead. Care must be taken, particularly aft, that the ships do not come into contact, risking damage to either ship. Where there is significant difference in freeboard, damage could be sustained to the rudder or propellers. Suitable secondary fendering aft of the parallel body may provide some protection.

Crew must be made fully aware of the dangers when mooring and unmooring during lightering operations. Sudden or unexpected weight may come on the mooring lines due to environmental factors or unexpected ship movements.

Fenders

Where mooring lines are intended to keep the vessels close together, the fenders serve to both maintain a safe separation and provide protection.

Fenders may be stowed in special cradles on board dedicated ships or may be provided by an STS provider. Fenders must meet the construction and operating specifications indicated in the STS Transfer Guide.

While it is simpler to secure the fenders to the STBL for the duration of the lightering operation, they are likely to be more effective when rigged on each manoeuvring vessel. The exact configuration should be agreed between the ship masters and/or the overall person in charge.

Primary fenders will normally be rigged along the parallel body to provide maximum protection when alongside. Secondary fenders fore and aft provide protection during mooring/unmooring.

Dedicated Lightering Ship

A dedicated lightering ship is a ship designed to perform multiple STS operations. These ships are usually fitted with adequate primary and secondary fenders, which upon completion of an STS transfer are capable of being lifted and stowed in onboard cradles. They are usually fitted with their own hoses and are generally capable of performing STS operations without external assistance such as support craft.

Figure 7.21 - When the vessels make contact, they should be as near as possible to parallel

Discharging Ship and Receiving Ship

The Ship To Be Lightered (STBL) may also be known as the Discharging Ship and the vessel loading is the Service Ship (SS) and may also be known as the Receiving Ship or Lightering Ship.

- OCIMF, ICS, SIGTTO and CDI guidance:
  - Ship to Ship Transfer Guide (2013 Edition).

As the operations are conducted at sea, there will probably be limited port service assistance.

Figure 7.22 - Yokohama type mooring fenders used in STS operations

Regulations and Guidance

In addition to complying with organisational requirements including SMS, lightering is controlled by international regulations and guidance and, where the transfer occurs within port limits, territorial waters or some EEZs, national requirements. Such regulations and guidance will include:

- UNCLOS
- IMO Conventions and Codes:
  - SOLAS
  - MARPOL
  - STCW
- Flag State Control
- Port State Control
- national and international agreements (eg EU)
- OCIMF guidance:
  - ISGOTT
  - Mooring Equipment Guidelines (MEG 3)
  - Ship to Ship Service Provider Management

The operation should be under the advisory control of one person, either the STS superintendent (or mooring master) or one of the two ships' masters. However, it should be remembered that at no time does either master relinquish authority for the command of their vessel or the operations that take place on board.

It is recommended that an STS superintendent, normally employed through an STS service provider, is employed where masters of the ships involved are unfamiliar with the operations.

It is recommended that safety drills are conducted before the operation and procedures for mooring failure, fire, pollution, damage, etc should be considered. Normal tanker cargo operational safety considerations should be implemented and the STS transfer guide should be closely examined before any transfer activity is planned.

Lightering Operations (Ship to Ship Transfer)

Courtesy of Fendercare Ltd

Figure 7.23 - The Service Ship (SS) in the light condition approaches the fully laden Ship To Be Lightered (STBL)

References

Ship to Ship Service Provider Management – OCIMF, First Edition 2011

STS Transfer Guide (CDI, ICS, OCIMF, SIGTTO, 2013 Edition)

CHAPTER 8

Anchorwork

Anchorwork

Anchors on Merchant Vessels

Admiralty Stockless/Bower

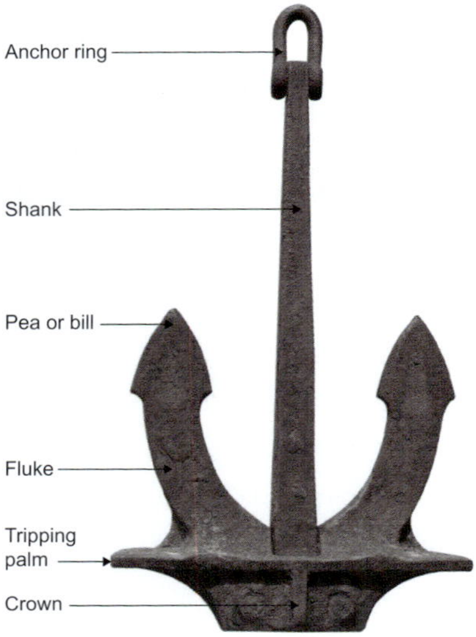

Figure 8.1 - The admiralty stockless/bower anchor

This is the most universally used anchor for large commercial ships. It is designed to dig into the bottom when the cable is pulled horizontally, and to easily lift out of the ground when the cable is pulled vertically.

The admiralty stockless/bower anchor is the most universally used anchor for large commercial ships. It is designed to dig into the bottom when the cable is pulled horizontally and to easily lift out of the ground when the cable is pulled vertically.

The anchor's hold depends on the horizontal pull exerted by the chain lying on the bottom, so it is essential that sufficient chain is run out to allow this.

This anchor has a holding power of up to 7 to 8 times the weight applied.

Admiralty Cast 14 (AC14)

These anchors are becoming increasingly common, particularly on larger vessels. For an anchor design to be approved as a High Holding Power (HHP) anchor, it must be tested at sea to show that it has at least twice the holding power of a standard stockless anchor of the same mass. The HHP anchor shown in Figure 8.3 has approximately 2.5 times the holding power of the standard stockless anchor. The diagram shows how the flukes have developed in size compared to the standard stockless anchor. The flukes dig into the bottom ground, so their increased size provides increased holding power.

Super High Holding Power (SHHP), anchors are regarded as having 4 times the holding power of an ordinary stockless anchor.

Figure 8.2 - The admiralty stockless/bower anchor on the seabed

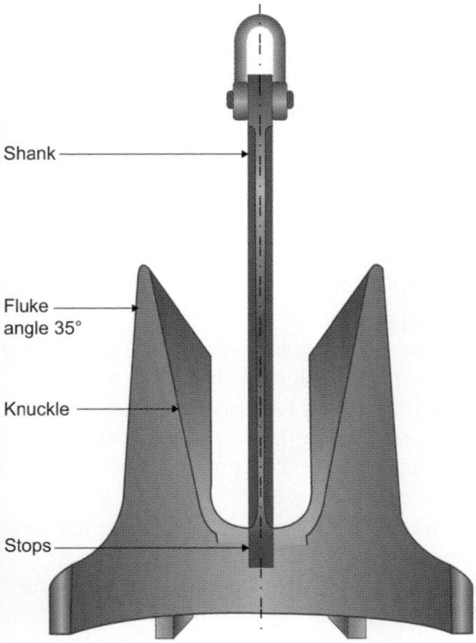

Figure 8.3 - High holding power anchor (HHP)

Remember that, in poor holding ground, the holding power of anchors is significantly reduced.

Anchor Design

The following statements from the International Association of Classification Societies (IACS) are very important:

> *"The anchoring equipment (approved) is required for temporary mooring of a vessel within a harbour or sheltered area, while waiting for a berth, tide, etc.*
>
> *The equipment is therefore not designed to hold a ship off fully exposed coasts in rough weather or to stop a ship which is moving or drifting. In this condition, the loads on the anchoring equipment increase to such a degree that its components may be damaged or lost owing to the high energy generated, particularly in large vessels."*
>
> *"The anchoring equipment presently required herewith is designed to hold a ship in good holding ground in conditions such as to avoid dragging of the anchor. In poor holding ground, the holding of the anchors will be significantly reduced."*

The requirements for anchor weights and chain sizes are standardised and depend on the equipment number assigned to the vessel.

Anchor and Chain Damage and Loss

In 1982, a review of large vessels and anchor and chain holding power found that, on paper, the chain was more reliable than the anchor. It was also found that, as ships became bigger, the degree of chain reliability over the anchors improved. A conclusion of the study was that the apparent improved chain reliability came from the fact that the larger the ships became, the more windlass brakes were slipping and anchors not holding.

Nearly 3% of lost anchors resulted from the stoppers being improperly closed and the vibrations on the ship's forecastle causing the guillotine or compression bars to work upwards, eventually becoming ineffective in holding the chain.

Heavy seas can damage anchors in the hawse pipe, impacting on the anchor crown and driving the anchor further inboard. This causes very high bending moments on the shanks and flukes, with the constant jarring causing pins to loosen.

Some designs rely on the two flukes and the shank providing a three point support system, the shank being drawn up into the hawse pipe like a wedge to stop it from rattling in the hawse pipe. There have been cases where tugs have had to be hired to free the anchors from the hawse pipe.

The shanks for HHP anchors can sometimes bend sideways when the effects of wind and tide swing the ship and she tries to drag the anchor round with her.

The Holding Power of Anchors

It is very difficult to accurately define holding power because of the number of factors affecting it, including:

- Type of anchor
- ground composition
- draught of vessel
- depth of water
- wind
- wave action
- current

Anchorwork

- deadweight of the vessel
- wind area.

The anchor is designed to dig into the seabed, and the size and shape of the flukes will determine how effectively the anchor digs into the various types of ground. Three forces come into play when the anchor is digging, as shown in Figure 8.4.

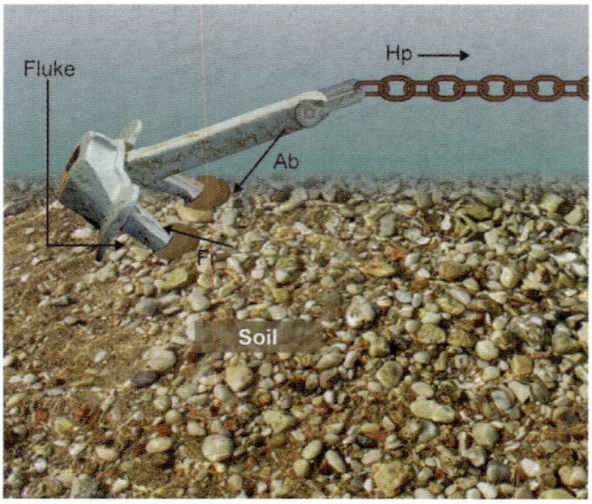

Figure 8.4 - Forces involved for a digging anchor

The holding pull (Hp) which is applied through the anchor rode (ie chain or cable).

The fluke friction (Fr) which is the friction against the surface of the flukes exerted by the bottom soil.

Anchor breakout (Ab) which is the force required to break the anchor out from against the wedge of bottom soil around the flukes.

Another factor is the angle of scope of the rode to the main anchor shackle. The scope is the ratio of length of cable to the depth, measured from the seabed to the windlass.

Choosing the Anchor Position

When deciding the position to anchor, the following must be taken into account:

1. *Depth of water*
   Both the tidal rise and fall and the expected swell must be considered. While the holding power of the anchor and cable will be greater in shallower water, the ride of the ship will be better in deeper water. There is also a greater danger of touching ground with the swell in shallow water.
2. *Clear ground*
   Foul areas in which a ship cannot anchor will be seen from the chart. However, care must also be taken in ports that have a high incidence of ships parting their cables, often leaving their anchors and cables on the seabed. Ports on the east African coast within the Agulhas current are particularly badly affected. The current can run at 6 knots and if this is not taken into account the sudden weight of the ship when anchoring can lead to loss of equipment.
3. *Holding ground*
   The two components of the anchor holding power in the ground are the breakout strength and the frictional resistance, which both depend on the bottom soil composition. The bottom soil is often a mix and the holding power of the soil will be the weakest link in the anchoring equation.

   Forming a definitive list of bottom soil and its holding power is difficult because of the variation in composition. For example, clay should provide a good holding ground but this will not be the case if it is soft.

Figure 8.5 - Scope angle

The Chain

Figure 8.6 - Anchor cable

All chain cable is subject to a proof load test and a breaking load test, with additional mechanical tests carried out when required.

Table 8.1 shows the relationship between chain strengths, the size of ship and the anchor weights required. For example, a 25,000 Dwt ship must have a stockless anchor of 6.45 tonnes and a chain length of 605 metres, with a chain breaking load of 263 tons.

If this were scaled up, it would mean that a 250,000 Dwt ship would require an anchor of 64.5 tonnes and a chain length of 6,050 metres!

Therefore, as ships become larger and heavier, the old rules on sizes and weights of anchors and how they are to be placed can no longer be used. Because of this, far more care must be taken when anchoring and when taking the decision of whether or not to anchor.

Shackles and Joining Gear

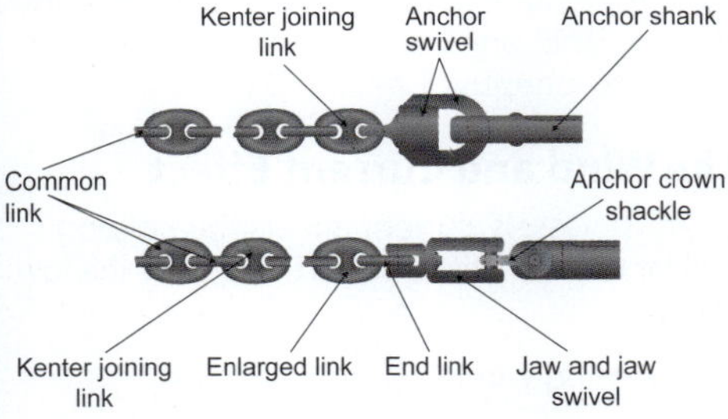

Figure 8.7 - The different types of joining arrangements for anchors

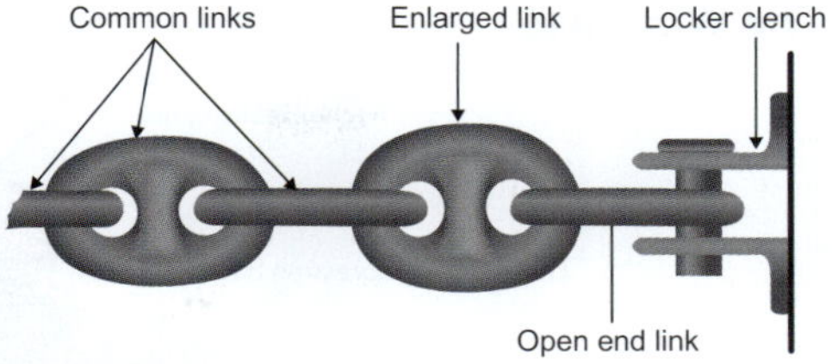

Figure 8.8 - Securing arrangements

Figure 8.8 shows a typical securing arrangement at the bitter end in the chain locker.

Figure 8.9 illustrates a Kenter lugless shackle showing it (a) fitted and (b) broken, with the pin withdrawn.

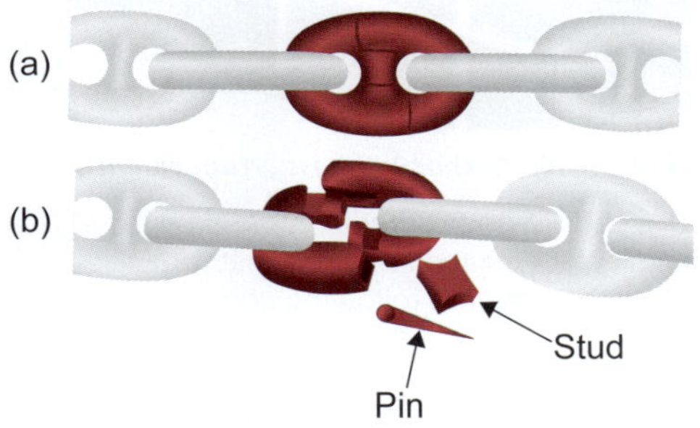

Figure 8.9 - Kenter shackle

Weight				Studlink chain			Chain breaking load	
Ship Dwt	Equip No. (EN)	(kg) Stockless	(kg) HHP	Length (m)	Diam GR2 (mm)	Diam GR3 (mm)	GR2 Tonne	GR3 Tonne
25,000	2080-2330	6,450	4,837	605	70	300	263	300
50,000	2870-3040	8,700	6,525	632.5	84	407	368	407
100,000	4000-4200	12,300	9,225	687.5	97	561	477	561
250,000	6100-6500	18,800	14,100	742.5	120	812	694	812
500,000	9400-10000	29,900	22,425	770	152	1,165	1,030	1,165

Table 8.1 - Chain strengths and breaking loads

Anchorwork

The Windlass

Figure 8.10 - Anchor windlass arrangement

The performance criteria required by Lloyd's Register for a windlass show that it must operate under the following conditions:

- A steady pull for 20 minutes
- a peak pull for 2 minutes
- a heaving speed
- a brake proof load
- a design that will not collapse under a load equivalent to the breaking load of the cable.

The equation used to determine the pulling power is:

The continuous pulling power (Z)Kg
= Constant x (the chain diam mm)^2

The constant is based on the chain grade. For grade 2 and 3, it is 4.25.

This could be worrying for the master of a very large vessel. For example, assume the following conditions, which would not be considered excessive:

- Wind force 6
- current 3 knots
- anchor depth 100 metres
- lifting rate 9 metres/min.

On a vessel of 250,000 Dwt fitted with grade 2 cable of 120 mm:

$$Z = 4.25 \times 1{,}202 \text{ Kg} = 61.2 \text{ tons}$$

If the vessel was fitted with an HHP anchor, such as the AC14, with a weight of 16 tons, and knowing that the cable weighs 0.6008 tons per fathom, this vessel could only lift a maximum of 5 shackles of cable in a vertical lift. Therefore, the ship would be limited to anchoring in a depth of 137 metres.

However, this is purely academic as the length of chain required to be carried on ships, under the IACS rules, is 742 metres. Therefore, based on a recommended ratio of cable to depth of 6 to 10 times, the maximum effective anchoring depth, in this example, is limited to a depth of 74 to 123 metres.

The Wind and Current Effect

On most vessels, current affects the holding pull far more than wind, particularly in shallow waters.

In increasing wind/current:

- To safely hold the ship in position, both anchors must be used
- to safely anchor with both anchors, the draught/depth ratio must be at least 2
- the larger the ship, the greater the effect of current over wind.

Under IACS rules, the holding pull required for anchors is as follows:

Vessel Dwt	Max holding power both SS anchors	Max holding power both HHP anchors
50,000	60 tons	130 tons
100,000	90 tons	190 tons
150,000	110 tons	230 tons
200,000	130 tons	270 tons
250,000	150 tons	315 tons
300,000	170 tons	350 tons

Table 8.2 - Holding pull comparisons

A number of conclusions can be drawn from analysis of Table 8.2:

- In deteriorating weather conditions, vessels of the sizes listed cannot remain safely at anchor if they are only equipped with standard anchors
- if trying to anchor in deeper water, the wave conditions would be worse so this chart would be of little help
- vessels equipped with HHP anchors can remain provided that both anchors are deployed.

The effect of tide or current is least when the ship is head on to the flow, so the weight on the cable is least when in this position. Any ship left with the helm amidships will yaw around this position. When the ship yaws, the current effect moves off the bow and the weight on the anchor is considerably increased, depending on the degree of the current off the bow. If the ship is yawing, it is better to have a constant yaw to one side than have the anchor pulled from side to side. To achieve this, a slight amount of wheel can be applied to give the vessel a sheer to one side.

If the current is strong, there will be a considerable increase in pulling power from the current as well as from the sheer of the vessel. Under these conditions, the helm should be manned and the ship steered to keep the bow into the current.

On large vessels, it is preferable that this is done at the first sign of yawing, rather than allowing any further weight on the anchor. If there is any further increase in wind, consideration should be given to heaving anchor and riding the weather out at sea.

For further data on the holding power of anchors, see the OCIMF publication *'Anchoring Systems and Procedures for Large Tankers'*.

Anchorages

Regardless of the type of anchorage, whether designated on the chart or by port instruction, when an accident occurs all ports place the responsibility with the ship. The master is responsible for the navigation of the ship and he should not attempt to anchor if there is any doubt that the anchorage is safe.

If the ship is required to wait a few hours for a berth and it has seaway, it may be preferable to drift or slowly cruise in the area rather than anchoring. This is less acceptable if the waiting time is longer or if the ship has to navigate an extended passage back to a safe area.

Figure 8.11 - Singapore eastern anchorage

Anchorage often becomes compulsory because many ports will not accept a ship as having 'arrived', for notice of readiness purposes, until it has anchored in a defined port area anchorage.

Manoeuvrability

Another problem in anchorage areas is the limitation of manoeuvrability available to the larger ships. In the worst case, a loaded VLCC or VLBC, when making a final approach, may have the engine stopped a mile away from the selected position, with a speed of four knots or less. When light, especially if deballasted ready for loading, manoeuvrability will be severely hampered by wind and current.

Figure 8.12 - Manoeuvrability in an anchorage can be a problem, particularly when the ship is in the ballast condition

At up to three cables away from the anchor position, and with the engines about to come astern, under no circumstances is the vessel able to manoeuvre within the context of the existing rules, even though the ship is still required to comply with the international regulations.

Anchorage Types

The anchorage itself, and the way in which it is defined and controlled, is of prime importance, particularly with the intense pressures of pollution and environmental controls.

Anchorages can be divided into three basic types:

Open anchorage	An undefined anchorage in open waters
Defined anchorage	An anchorage in open waters with defined limits
Confined anchorage	An anchorage confined on more than one side by natural or man-made hazards.

The type of port control is often misstated, with many ports claiming to have traffic control when their service is traffic advisory.

Positioning

In anchorages without defined anchor positions, a problem that often arises is ships anchoring too close together. The distance a ship will anchor away from other vessels depends on the prevailing or expected weather conditions, exposure of the anchorage, size of ship, holding ground and, occasionally, engine maintenance requirements.

A safe distance for a coastal vessel will be too close for a VLCC. Where a VLCC or VLBC has anchored at a distance of seven cables away from other vessels, a coastal ship will often come in and anchor between the two. To the small ship this will appear safe, but not to the large. The large vessel can protest the position of the other vessel but, if the smaller ship refuses to move, the larger ship has a duty to move on the principle that it perceives the danger. Carried to an extreme conclusion, in a busy unrestricted anchorage, the larger ship could be on the move all day or even have to move out of the anchorage altogether if there is no other safe position in which to anchor.

Responsibilities in Anchorages

In open anchorages, where ships can anchor where they choose and the only restrictions are those imposed by draught and depth, it is reasonable for the port to have no responsibility. Defined and confined anchorages are a different matter.

The port states the limits of a defined anchorage, having taken into account the number of ships that can be expected to anchor at the same time and the variations of size and manoeuvrability of those ships. By defining an anchorage, a port states that ships must anchor within their given limits, so it has an obligation to provide a safe anchor position. If this is not available, the port must advise the ship to anchor outside of the port limits, but still accept that the ship has arrived for notice of readiness purposes.

Approach to the Anchorage

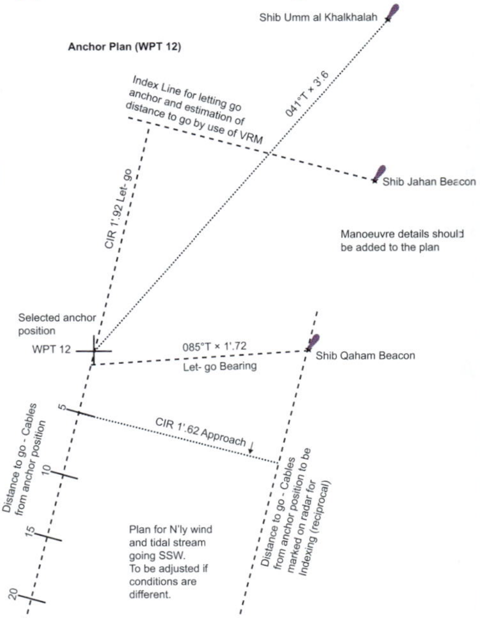

Figure 8.13 - Prepare your anchor plan in advance

Before making any approach to an anchorage, the master and the navigating officer should have studied the approach and drawn up an anchorage plan.

As the vessel gets closer, the lie of other ships in the anchorage will become apparent and this should generally be the direction of approach. The ship should be able to maintain a steady course over the last mile, while reducing speed. When the anchor is let go, the ship will fall back, with the ship's head in the same direction that the other vessels are lying. It is not essential that this direction is followed, and it might well be that there are reasons why this cannot be done, but it is the preferred direction for anchoring.

Port control should be asked about expected movements that may take place during the approach, not only in the anchorage but also to and from the port. If any ship is heaving anchor in the area that has been chosen, it is better to wait until her anchor is up and she is under way.

The lie of the cables of the anchored vessels will provide a good indication of the current. There are certain ports that are notorious for having strong running currents, particularly on the East African Coast.

If the area is particularly susceptible to strong winds, a sheltered anchorage is preferable, bearing in mind that means the ship is closer to land.

The expected time in the anchorage will influence the decision on location and the amount of cable paid out. If the stay is expected to be prolonged, it is preferable to have more room around the ship, so more cable can be walked out.

Type of Seabed in Chart Notation

Notation	Composition	Suggested Holding Ability
S	Sand	Average
M	Mud	Average to Good
Cy, Cl	Clay	Average to Good
G	Gravel	Poor
Co	Coral	Poor* (see separate section in RH column)
Cb	Cobbles	Poor
Sn	Shingle	Poor
P	Pebbles	Poor
St	Stones	Poor
Rk, Rky	Rock, Rocky	Very Poor
Ch	Chalk	Poor
Sh	Shells	Poor
Wd	Weed	Poor to Average
S/M	Two layers (shown here: sand over mud)	Average to Good

Note that lower case letters are used for these qualifying terms:

s	small	when added to shingle, gravel and pebbles, change to average
f	fine	as above
m	medium	
c	coarse	
h	hard	when added to sand, mud or clay, change to good
sm	small	
bk	broken	
v	volcanic	

- *Coral
  Anchoring on coral is prohibited in the coastal areas of many countries as the physical damage from anchors can be severe and slow to recover. Anchor damage is generally proportional to the size of the ship because of the weight of the anchor and the length of the anchor chain. Areas where anchoring is prohibited are marked on charts as 'specially designated marine reserves'. The IMO amendments to the General Provisions on Ships' Routeing (Resolution A.572(14) Section 2.1.14) define a No Anchoring Area as:

  A routeing measure comprising an area within defined limits where anchoring is hazardous or could result in unacceptable damage to the marine environment. Anchoring in a no anchoring area should be avoided by all ships or certain classes of ships, ***except in case of immediate danger to the ship or the persons on board.***

Methods of Anchoring and Mooring

Anchoring to a Single Anchor

Figure 8.14 shows a ship making a final approach in line with the other vessels anchored.

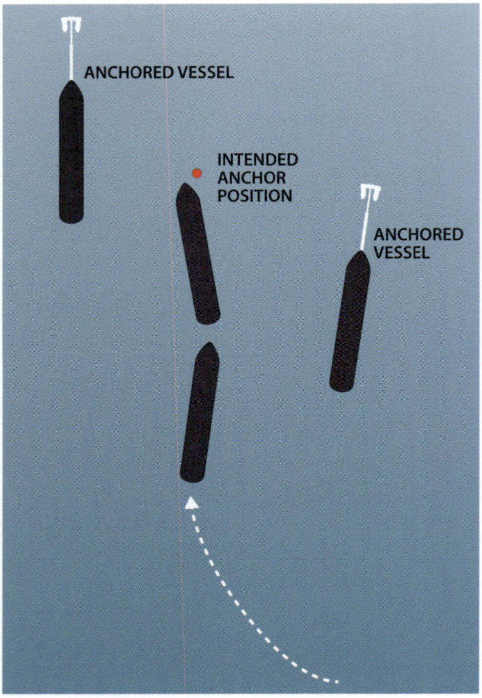

Figure 8.14 - The standard single anchoring method

When the ship starts to come astern just before the chosen position, depending on whether the propeller is right or left-handed, the bow will fall off; even with variable pitch there will be some effect from this. This should be allowed for on the final course prior to coming astern. When the ship is stopped, she can let go or walk back, depending on the depth of water and the current.

On very large vessels, the ship should be stopped when letting go the anchor, and then very gradually allowed to fall astern, walking back or releasing the cable in a controlled manner until the required amount is let out. The GPS can be used to indicate when the ship is stopped and falling back. However, as this often flickers between ahead and astern at very slow speeds, the old rule of thumb should be used that, when the surge from the astern movement of the propeller reaches two-thirds the length of the ship, let go or walk back the anchor. This works well provided that there is little or no current running. If there is current, a simple bearing marker of a close fixed object will provide the same indication. To calculate how many cables are needed, the angle of scope must be considered, unless the vessel is only on a short stay before getting under way and it is good weather. With the increasing size of modern ships, and bearing in mind the angle of scope, a minimum of 6 to 7 times the depth of water should be paid out. For very large vessels, this should be increased to 8 to 10 times the depth.

Because the ship is anchoring against the direction of pull on the cable, there is no need to have the ship going astern under power as the natural force of the combined wind and current will bring the ship astern. However, if the cable is not bringing up, a short astern movement will rectify the problem.

The holding power of the anchor, apart from when influenced by weather and current, varies with the amount of cable that is put out. The longer the cable, the more horizontal the pul on the anchor. For this reason, a ship with a long catenary will ride more easily in deep water than a ship with the same scope of cable in shallow water. If the weather conditions are expected to worsen, it is far better to walk out a few shackles rather than be faced with doing so when the anchor drags. The cable should be walked back as this will avoid any unnecessary sudden weight coming on the cable, which could start the anchor from the dug-in position.

Which Anchor?

Ships often work on the alternate system, meaning that whichever anchor was used last time the other will be used next time. This is suitable for clement weather ports in the tropics and in summer in areas where the weather conditions are known to be good. However, the old rule of port anchor in the northern hemisphere and starboard anchor in the southern should be followed.

If Figure 8.15 is studied, it can be seen that in (1) the vessel is lying to the port anchor with the wind from the west.

In (2) the wind increases. The ship lets go the starboard anchor and pays out more chain on the port anchor to ensure that the starboard anchor has enough scope of chain to hold.

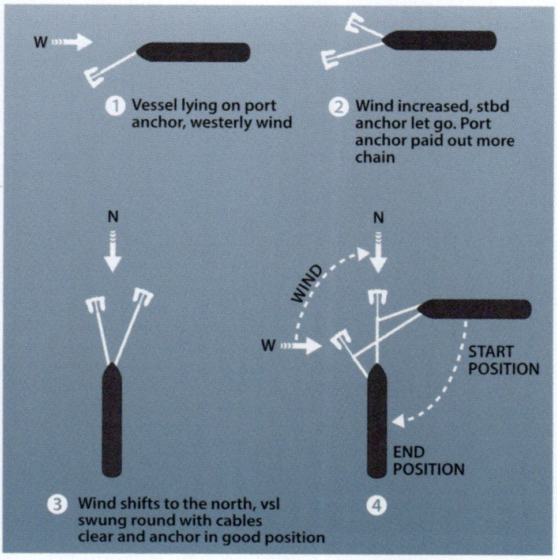

Figure 8.15 - Anchoring in the northern hemisphere

In (3) the wind, as is normal in the northern hemisphere, veers to the right, ie from westerly to northerly. The ship shifts round with both cables clear and the anchors still set in a good position.

The end position illustrates the movement of the ship with the cables clear. If the ship had anchored with the starboard anchor first, the shift of wind and the subsequent swing of the ship would have crossed the cables.

The opposite applies in the southern hemisphere.

Using Both Anchors

Under normal circumstances, one anchor in a seaway should be sufficient. If the weather worsens, more chain should be laid out before letting go a second anchor. This is because one anchor with a long scope of chain provides better holding than two anchors with a short scope. If after this action the vessel is dragging, it is questionable whether the ship should remain at anchor.

As illustrated in Figure 8.15, the wind will generally follow set patterns of movement in the northern or southern hemisphere and, if the correct anchor order is followed, there should be no problem. If the wind should back, the ship will swing the wrong way. However, if this happens, it is likely that, with the change of the wind to southerly, the wind force will have decreased and the ship will be able to reduce to one anchor again. If this has not occurred, the ship can steam up to the starboard anchor using the engines, heave it up and then, when the ship has swung to the wind, let it go again.

The main benefit of using two anchors in normal conditions is that the swing of the vessel is limited. The use of two anchors in a running or standing moor, with one ahead and the other astern, will initially take more room.

If using both anchors in an open moor, in preparation for expected high winds, they should be laid out perpendicular to the expected direction of the wind. The angle between the anchors is critical as too little will not keep the vessel's head to wind, and too much will not provide the increased holding strength. The aim should be to achieve an angle of between 60° and 90° (for maximum holding and swing reduction).

Figure 8.16 shows the anchors laid out with 6 shackles on each cable and a 90° angle between the anchors. This is achieved as follows:

1. The vessel will be anchored normally with the port anchor.
2. When the ship has brought up, walk back the anchor to 9 shackles (Position 1).

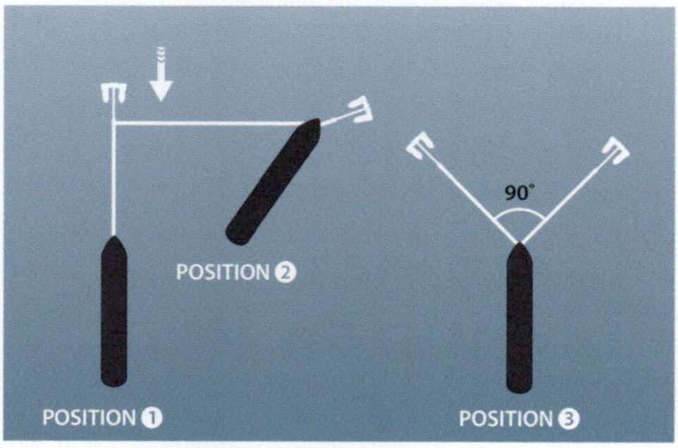

Figure 8.16 - Lying two anchors

3. Hold on the port anchor, angle the ship to approximately 60° to starboard and slowly steam ahead.
4. When the ship is abeam the post anchor's position, ie when the port cable is at 90° to the ship, let go the starboard anchor (Position 2).
5. With the engines now stopped and the wheel amidships, the port anchor can be heaved in to 6 shackles and the starboard anchor let out to 6 shackles.

Methods of Anchoring and Mooring

6. The ship, when brought up to the new position, will now have 6 shackles out on each anchor and an angle of 90° between them (Position 3).

The advantage of choosing 90° as the initial angle is that it allows for error either way without compromising the holding power or swing, allowing further cable to be let out if required and reducing the angle to 60° without compromising the holding power of the anchors.

The Anchor Watch

The following are suggestions for anchor watch standing orders:

- On anchoring, the swing circle around the anchor position should be drawn on the chart. The position of the vessel within the swing circle should be monitored frequently, both by radar and visually. The position should be fixed by land-based points
- anchor signals should be properly displayed
- the distance from other vessels in the vicinity should be watched. Should there be any sign of your vessel or other vessels dragging in the anchorage, call the master, put the engines on immediate notice, call the anchor party and contact the other vessel/s and advise them of the situation
- changes in weather, wind direction and swell should be reported to the master, especially if the ship begins to yaw
- all ship movements should be watched and port VHF channels monitored for weather warning, ship movement information and pilots
- small boats should be watched closely and warned off if they come too close
- gangways or ladders, if lowered, should be hoisted when not in use
- at night, all deck lights should be switched on and in working order. If any ship should commence anchoring in a position that is considered too close, call the other vessel and advise them of your concern. If the other ship persists in anchoring in such a position, this should be logged and the master called
- flags should be properly displayed.

Standing Moor

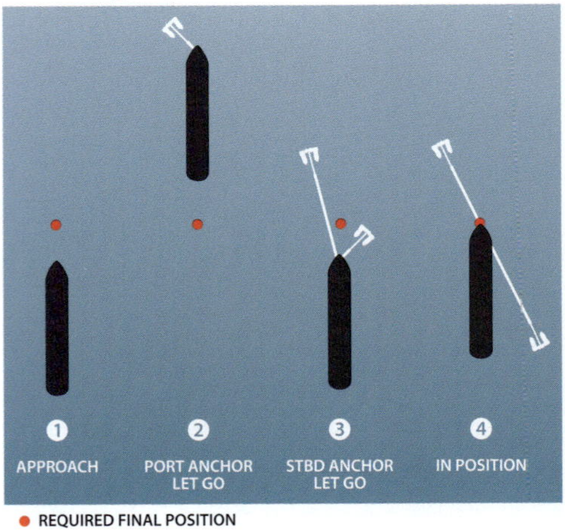

Figure 8.17 - Standing moor

In the standing moor, shown in Figure 8.17, the ship must steam ahead of the selected position (1). As an example, the intention here is to finish the manoeuvre with 5 shackles on each cable. The ship is stopped a distance of 4 shackles ahead of the position and the port anchor is let go (2). The cable is then paid out 10 shackles as the ship falls back on the current. When 10 shackles are paid out on the port anchor, the starboard anchor is let go (3). The port anchor is put in gear and heaved in to 5 shackles while paying out the cable of the starboard anchor to 5 shackles. The manoeuvre is completed with 5 shackles on each cable (4). If the current is particularly strong and the ship has difficulty in heaving in the port cable, this is easily overcome by using the engines, while taking care not to overrun the cable.

Running Moor

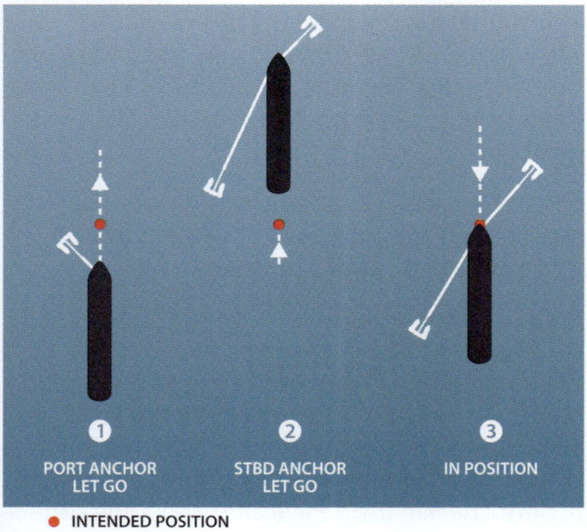

Figure 8.18 - Running moor

This example assumes that the completed moor will have 5 cables out on each cable. The approach to the intended position is made as before, but 4 cables before reaching the position, the port anchor is let go, with the ship slowly steaming ahead (1).

The port anchor is paid out, while the ship continues over the intended final position, until 10 shackles are paid out on the port anchor. The port anchor is then held and the starboard anchor is let go with the ship stopped (2).

The ship is now allowed to set back, paying out the starboard anchor to 5 shackles while heaving in the port cable to 5 shackles. With 5 shackles out on each cable, the ship is moored in position (3).

All navigational rivers are tidal for part of their passage and it is in these tidal parts that moorings are used. As the tide changes, the ship will swing. It is important to ensure that the ship swings in the same way on one turn of the tide and in the opposite way on the next, keeping a clear hawse. To achieve this, just as the tide is finishing give the vessel a cant with the helm so that the new tide will always swing the vessel round on the same side as both the anchors. If the ship is close to the bank of the river, when the ship swings cant the stern out from the bank into the deeper water. This will ensure that the change of tide will catch the vessel on the quarter, swinging the ship away from the bank.

In the further reaches of a river that are beyond tidal reach, there is only the current heading downstream to deal with, so a single anchor holding is used. However, as the river narrows and becomes shallower, the current becomes stronger and the bottom often gives way to a mix of mud and rock. More ships drag anchor in the upper reaches of rivers than anywhere else and considerable care must be exercised. The engines should be on instant readiness at all times and a constant anchor watch kept. If the strain on the cable is considered excessive, even after letting out more cable, the engine should be used to ease the strain.

Berthing Using Anchors

Anchors can also be used in combination with mooring lines to secure the ship to jetties, structures and other vessels.

The Mediterranean Moor

This type of mooring was often used in the Mediterranean for smaller vessels and it is still used in many ports to enable a larger number of pleasure craft to have access to the jetty. It is designed for situations where there is little or no current and weather conditions are generally benign.

On a single-screw vessel, the approach (if possible) should be made directly head on to the position in which the ship will eventually be secured (see Figure 8.20). At a distance of approximately twice the ship's length, the starboard anchor is let go and, when on the bottom, let out a little to hold the weight on the brake (1). The headway on the ship will snub the cable, causing the vessel to come round (2). If necessary, the wheel can be put hard over and the engines used to keep the vessel coming round. Once the ship is round, with the engine put astern the ship will back towards the berth, letting out cable as it becomes tight. It is important that some tension remains on the cable as this acts as a brake when the ship is close to the berth (3). If some tension is kept when the engine is stopped, the ship will instantly start to come ahead (4).

Methods of Anchoring and Mooring

Figure 8.19 - Mediterranean moor

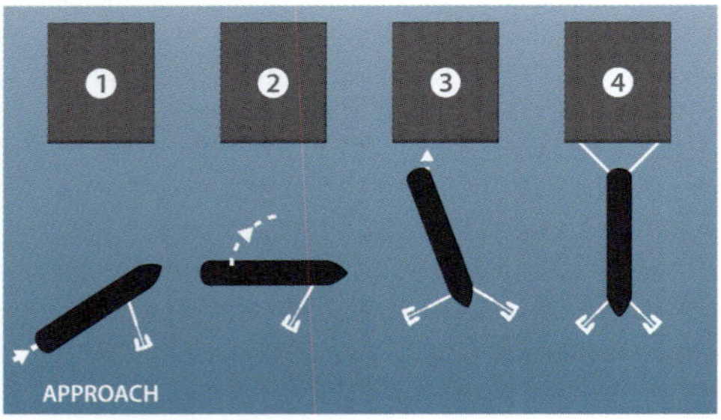

Figure 8.20 - Mediterranean moor

If required, two anchors can be used. The better method is to approach parallel to the intended berthing position, then make a running moor with the calculated distance between the anchors placing the ship with equal lengths of cable opposite the berthing position. With engines and helm, swing the ship and back into the berth. If the ship has twin screws, the swinging is made easier by splitting the engines. With the bow thrust added, the ship can be turned before letting go the anchor/s.

The Baltic Moor

This method is thought to have originated in the Baltic when securing to very old and fragile timber berths. The idea is to come alongside without putting any of the ship's weight on the berth.

Since this type of mooring was introduced, the size of ships has increased considerably and this mooring is now rarely used.

A Baltic moor requires a mooring rope or wire of at least the same length as the ship. The offshore anchor is prepared by leading a good stern mooring line forward to the bow and then, by sending a person overside, shackling the mooring line to the anchor just above the anchor shackle (using a light seizing line). The mooring line must be secured lightly outboard of the ship along the length.

Figure 8.21 - Baltic moor

The ship approaches the intended position on a parallel course at a distance that will allow a good scope on the anchor (see Figure 8.21). When the ship is dead centre of the intended position, let go the starboard anchor (1). As the anchor drops, the seizing line retaining the mooring rope will break, allowing the mooring rope to enter the water with the anchor.

Once the anchor is on the bottom, with the mooring rope on the windlass barrel being paid out, the ship moves ahead, letting out the cable until the ship is off the intended final position (2).

Breast lines are then sent away fore and aft and the ship is heaved towards the berth. At the same time, the anchor should be put in gear and the cable and the after-mooring line paid out as required. Keep a light tension on both, stopping and starting the heaving to keep the ship parallel with the berth. Once the ship is at the required distance off, springs and further lines can be sent away (3).

The distance and angle can be adjusted for the tide with the after windlass and, if necessary, with the anchor cable.

Manoeuvring with Anchors

Considerable care must be taken in any manoeuvre that is likely to put severe weight on the cable, and therefore the pulling power of the anchor, and no dependency should be placed on the anchor holding. Particularly on very large vessels, the anchor is not designed for anything other than holding the ship temporarily in position while waiting for a pilot or berth.

There are still a considerable number of ships with single propellers and no thrusters. The larger the ships are, the more they need to use their anchors during berthing. During berthing, an anchor is used in two ways. One is planned use, which is often required by the pilot or master, and the other is emergency use, again often on the pilot's orders but occasionally to deal with an emergency perceived by the master.

Emergency use is always unexpected, and therefore the anchor must be ready at all times when manoeuvring, with the personnel standing by. Tugs frequently part their lines during berthing, particularly if the ship is approaching the berth too fast. In an emergency, the anchor can be used as a breaking effect, to hold the bow steady or to pull the bow off in the direction of the cable lead. When coming full astern, the anchor stops the ship's head from falling off and assists in stopping the ship. It is essential that the officer in charge on the forecastle ensures that it is clear before dropping the anchor, particularly where tugs are present.

Figure 8.22 - Check it is clear to drop the anchor!

Masters must have an understanding of how to use their anchors in a seamanlike manner and must not assume to rely on a pilot. In some ports, pilots are not provided, occasionally pilots go on strike, and some pilots board and quickly lose the confidence of the master.

Anchors to Assist Berthing – Example 1

Figure 8.23 demonstrates use of the anchor for an assisted berthing, where tug availability is poor or tug power is low and where the berth is restricted. The timber and pulp berths of the west coast of British Colombia are typical of this type and it is normal to use anchor work for 50,000 Dwt vessels.

The aim is not to stop the vessel with the anchor, but to use it as a brake for the bow when the power is taken off the vessel. The ship makes a normal approach with the course and speed determined by the current. Once in a position parallel to the berth, about half a ship's length to the final position, the starboard anchor is let go to a short stay (Position 1).

Using the helm and engine, the ship is manoeuvred alongside, veering out the cable as required (Position 2). Once secured, the cable can be slacked down. The advantage of leaving the cable down is that, when the ship has to depart, the cable can assist the vessel in backing out of the berth.

Methods of Anchoring and Mooring

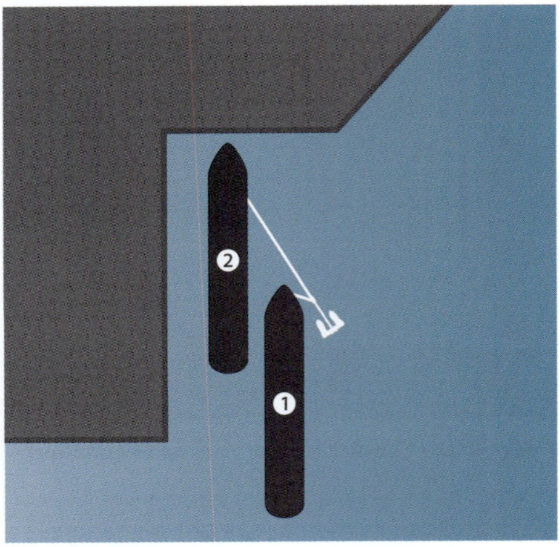

Figure 8.23 - Using the anchor for assisted berthing

Anchors to Assist Berthing – Example 2

Figure 8.24 assumes the ship is single screw with no thrusters. The ship makes an approach with the head lined up on the end of the berth (1).

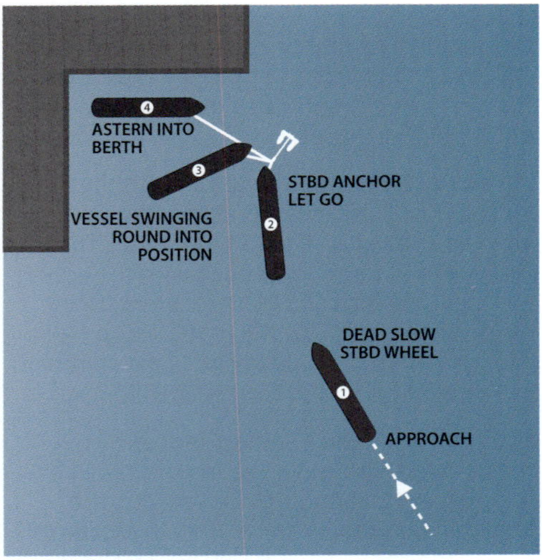

Figure 8.24 - Berthing with a single screw

Just before the anchor position, the ship puts the wheel to starboard and comes astern on the engine. This has the effect of turning the ship to starboard as it lets go the starboard anchor. It also stops the vessel from continuing ahead and dragging the anchor out of position (2).

By use of the helm and engine, the turn of the ship can be continued until the ship is turned into the berth (3).

With the ship now turned, the anchor can be let out as the ship comes astern and used as a brake to bring it up in position (4).

When the ship is secured, it may not be possible to heave the anchor up, but this is not a problem as the anchor will assist in the unberthing of the ship. Meanwhile, the cable should be walked back into the water to avoid danger to small craft in the area.

If too much weight is placed on the anchor, it is immediately dragged out of position. The whole operation, which is highly weather dependent, must be carried out very slowly, taking time to use the engines ahead and then stopping as soon as the ship starts to come round. When weight comes off the anchor coming ahead again, gradually bring the ship round.

Large Vessels

The most important factors to consider when anchoring a large ship are:

- When anchoring a very large vessel, the ship should be stopped over the ground and the anchor walked back. If possible, the vessel should be left to gradually come astern from the anchor position and the cable paid out as this occurs. In this way, when the required scope of cable is paid out, the anchor can be held without any sudden pulling on the anchor
- careful consideration must be given to the current in any intended anchorage, particularly for a deep draught vessel. This is because of the severe effect the current will have on the pulling power of the anchor
- the ratio of depth to draught should, if possible, be at least 2 to 1
- the ratio of scope of cable to depth should be at least 6 to 1, and preferably 8 to 1
- in the case of open anchorages, in conditions where wave motion might be experienced or where the vessel is expected to remain at anchor for a prolonged period, 2 anchors should be used with a 60° to 90° angle between them
- when any very large vessel is anchored in poor wind or current conditions or near to

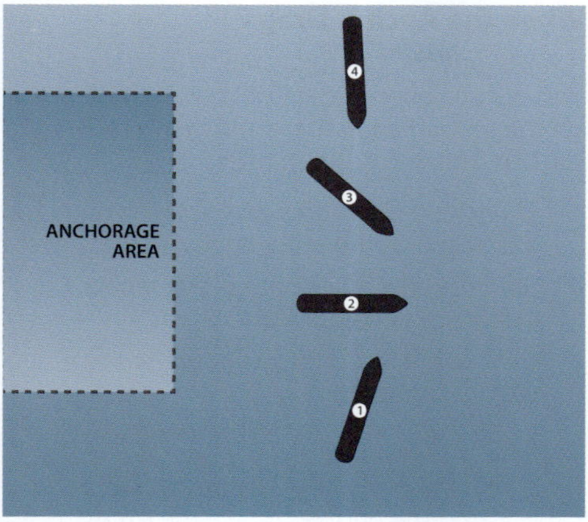

Figure 8.25 - Turning to the current of an anchorage

other vessels or land, the engines must be on immediate notice

- there must be a strict anchor watch kept, especially on the position of the vessel. If any change in current or wind is experienced, the ship should be put on standby until it has settled into the new condition
- when making any decision to anchor, consideration must be given to the anchorage and the ground. If there are other ships in close proximity or the ship is near land or shoals, these must also be part of the consideration. If you have any concern at all about the anchorage or the weather, you should not anchor
- whenever anchors are used for manoeuvring, the anchor should be thought of as a drag, not a brake. **No berth or anchorage should be approached with the idea that the anchor can be let go and that this will stop the ship**. The intention is to drag the anchor and use the dragging effect to slow or turn the bow. When using the anchors in such a manoeuvre, the position should be approached very slowly and, if possible, the vessel should be stopped at the point from which it is intended to start the manoeuvre. The anchor can then be walked back the required scope, which should be short enough to allow the dragging. Only then should the engines and helm be used
- if a very large ship is approaching an anchorage with the current, and there is a good reason why the ship either cannot delay for the current to change or make the approach from the other direction, under no circumstances should the anchor be used to snub the ship round.

When a ship needs to turn while approaching an anchorage with the current astern, she should approach parallel to the anchorage before putting the engines astern (see Figure 8.25). If the ship has a right-handed propeller, the bow will begin to cant. The ship will now either check her advance and stop in the water or slow and cant heavily to starboard (1). When the way is off the ship (2), stop the engines and put the wheel hard over to starboard. Give a full ahead burst of the engines. With the wheel hard over, this is not going to provide much advance to the ship, but it will bring it round quickly (3) into a position against the current from which it can continue to come round until the course is reversed (4) and it can make her way into the anchorage. During this manoeuvre, if the ship is still under the influence of the current and is caught beam on (2), the 'up current' anchor can be let go and used to drag while the bow comes round towards the current.

In an emergency, the anchors might have to be used.

Two examples of such emergencies are:

1. In Rotterdam with a 200,000 Dwt vessel. While approaching the berth, which was

Hanging off an Anchor

at the end of a cut with a sea wall dead ahead, a position was reached where the engines should have been stopped to allow the ship to slowly take off speed before coming astern and to take on the forward tug. The speed at this time was approximately 4 knots. The engines failed to come astern. There was no time to walk back the anchors so, after ordering the tug to keep clear, the port anchor was let go from the pipe and held at 1 shackle on deck and then the starboard anchor let go in the same way. Both anchors dragged along the bottom and eventually, together with the after tug, stopped the vessel at about 60 feet from the sea wall.

2. In a more 'planned' emergency, with a 300,000 Dwt ship. A steam chest had blown in the engine room so there was only one engine and very little stern power. It was essential to anchor for repairs and the only place was Las Palmas, which has only a very narrow ledge, just off the breakwater, where a ship can anchor. It is not intended for 300,000 Dwt ships. The ledge was approached with the starboard anchor (chosen as that would pull the bow away from the breakwater) walked back to 5 shackles. The engine was stopped about 1.5 miles away and the ship drifted in. The anchor was put on the break and the port anchor walked back to one shackle. On arriving at the face of the bank, as it rose up, the anchor touched bottom and began to drag, slowing the ship as it got closer in. As the ship slowed, more chain was paid out on the starboard anchor until the vessel was stopped, and then the port anchor was let go. The cables were adjusted until the vessel was moored with two anchors, which was necessary to limit swing because of the close proximity of other ships crowding onto the ledge.

A trailing anchor can assist a ship while drifting by slowing down the rate of drift, but ensure that no more cable is put out than the windlass can retrieve.

When the Anchor Drags

It is not uncommon for a ship to drag anchor. This occurs when the anchor fails to dig in on the seabed and slips, causing the cable to slacken. This can happen because:

- The speed of the ship astern is too great for the anchor to hold on a poor ground
- the ground is so poor that the anchor cannot dig in properly
- the current/wind is too strong for the weight of the ship
- insufficient anchor chain has been laid out.

Dragging can be rectified by paying out more cable, using the engine to take the excess speed of the ship, or taking up the anchor and moving to a better holding ground. If there are strong winds, waiting until they ease might be the better option.

The worst scenario is when the anchor drags after the engines have been rung off and put on notice, especially in the vicinity of land, vessels or other dangers.

The main engine will obviously be required as soon as possible. However, if it cannot be immediately used and the situation requires prompt action, two options available are to pay out more cable or to let go the second anchor. In both cases, sufficient cable should be paid out so that there is a good chance of the weight of the extra cable causing the shank of the anchors to lie on the seabed, taking the pulling power horizontally on the anchor and causing the flukes to dig in and hold. If the situation is critical, this is not the time to worry about the two anchors becoming entangled.

If you are dragging down onto other vessels, they must be immediately warned of the situation, by VHF and sound signals, in the hope that they might be able to use their engines and wheel, even if anchored, to manoeuvre out of the way. At the same time, you will have some steerage way on your ship and this should be used to best advantage to steer your ship to avoid collision. If you have time, give the course and speed of your dragging to the other vessels so that they can calculate their degree of danger and take action.

Once you have use of your engines, if the situation is critical it is better to safeguard your ship than your anchors. If you have to use power while your anchors are dragging and there is insufficient time to heave them up, ensure the forecastle is clear and then steam your ship out of danger. Hopefully, if the anchors dragged into that situation they will drag out again, but if they do not then it is better to lose your anchors and cable than to endanger your ship.

Ships of the past would have been able to slip their anchors and would have had an anchor buoy bent on ready for such emergency. As anchor buoys are no longer in general use, if there is time when the anchor is lost it would be helpful to note the position on the GPS.

There are still ports in the world that require ships to moor to harbour moorings/buoys using their anchor cables. The sheer size of the cables on very large ships usually precludes this, but on average size ships it may be possible.

It is important to have plenty of warning of this requirement, particularly if the ship has never carried out the action or if it has been a long time since it last did so.

It is important to check that all of the equipment for the operation is on board:

- The wire pennant for hanging off the anchor
- chain hooks
- punch for removing the pin from the joining shackle
- lead pellets for resealing the pin after use
- senhouse slip
- sledge hammer
- overside ladder
- safety harness
- blow torch.

The operation is a simple task if you have the tools. Clear the anchor from the hawse pipe so that the broken cable end can run down it and, with a shackle on the end, be shackled to a buoy.

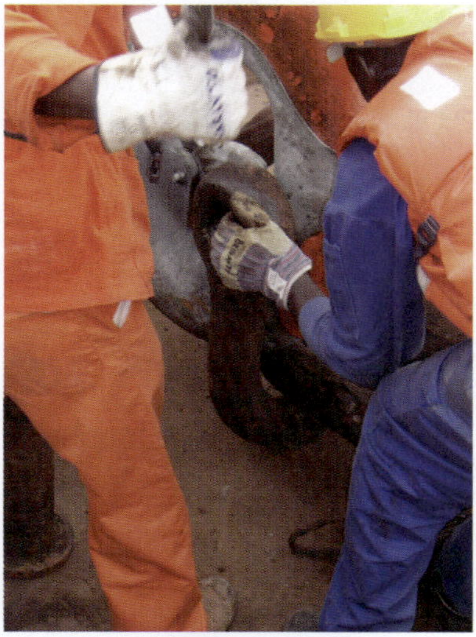

Figure 8.26 - Breaking the anchor cable

First, walk back the anchor until it is just clear of the hawse pipe. Prepare the hanging off pennant by seizing up one eye to compress it enough to go through the anchor ring.

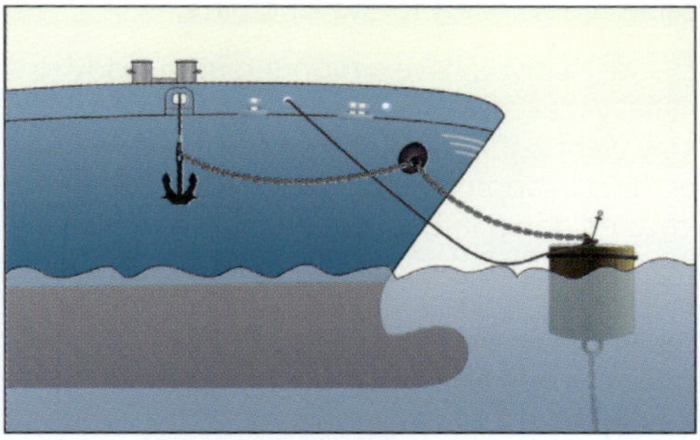

Figure 8.27 - Breaking the cable with the anchor hung off and the ship on the buoy

Put the ladder over, with one person (with a harness on) over the side, and lead one end of the hanging off pennant through the anchor ring. Secure a line to this and heave inboard, putting one eye of the pennant over the after bollard and the other on the senhouse slip, which will be secured to the bollard. Site it so that when the anchor is hanging vertically it will be well clear of the hawse pipe.

Pay out the anchor until its weight is taken by the pennant. The anchor should now be hanging directly below the fairlead for the bollard. Pay out the cable until the first joining shackle appears. Using the chain hooks, pull

Hanging off an Anchor

the chain clear onto the deck alongside the cable run. Secure the anchor end of the cable with a lashing, making sure that it is pulled to one side of the hawse pipe. This ensures that when it is broken it will not slide down the pipe.

Using the sledge hammer and punch, break the shackle. If it is stiff, try using the blow torch to heat it up. If the cable has been properly maintained during dry dockings, it should have been broken within the last few years, so it will come eventually.

If the anchor cable has not been maintained, you might have to call for burning gear to cut it off.

Once this is done, move the anchor end of the cable to one side and prepare the mooring end of the cable. Some ports want the shackle bent on, and others want it lowered down on a line. Again, you should find this out beforehand. Either way, they will want a long pennant of rope on the end to hold it to the buoy while the shackle is being secured. The mooring cable is now ready for walking back.

Ensure that you have a mooring rope ready to initially make fast to the buoy. Again, the port may want a shackle and a pennant on the end of this. On approach to the buoy, this will be lowered down into a boat and taken to it. Once the rope is fastened, you will heave on it and pull the buoy under the walked back anchor cable. Holding the ship in this position, the cable is made fast. The mooring rope can then be slacked off, but keep this fast as it is required for letting go.

When you are ready to let go, heave on the mooring rope until the buoy is in position for letting go of the cable. When the cable is let go, make sure that you get your shackle back. You are now in a position to slip the buoy. Heave up the cable until it is on deck and reconnect with the joining shackle, plugging the end with a new lead pellet. Once joined, take up the cable on the windlass until the weight of the anchor is taken up and it is heaved into a position just below the hawse pipe. This ensures that when you let the slip go the anchor will not swing, possibly damaging the hull. When you are ready, using the sledge hammer and keeping all crew away, clear the retaining ring from the senhouse slip and pull the end of the pennant free of the anchor, using the winch if necessary.

Ground Tackle Maintenance

The following precautions should be taken to ensure the anchor functions correctly:

- When heaving up the anchor, make sure that it is washed down properly, freeing the ground soil and debris from around the flukes and fluke swivel areas. If this is left, the debris can quickly build up and solidify, reducing the fluke angle and the efficiency of the anchor
- cleaning the anchor reduces the build-up of mud in the chain locker and helps keep the suctions free
- if the anchor cable has not been washed down properly, the mud can dry on the cable and when next let go this mud can fly off and cause injury to crew in the vicinity
- if the ship is of the size and trade where breaking the anchor for buoy moorings might occur, it is wise to break the joining shackle at periodic intervals to ensure that it is not seized
- occasionally, and particularly after an anchorage when strain might have been put on the anchor, have the anchor walked out and viewed from the jetty, looking for any sign of a bent shank or flukes. Check the main pin on the D anchor joining shackle. See that the split pin is in position and replace it if it is worn or missing.

Anchor Markings

Wire markings are used to assist with recognition of the number of shackles.

The marking should be as follows:

At 15 fathoms	One turn of wire on the first stud from each side of the joining shackle.
At 30 fathoms	Two turns of wire on the second stud from each side of the joining shackle.
At 45 fathoms	Three turns of wire on the third stud from each side of the joining shackle.

A similar pattern continues for further shackles.

Ensure that the cables are marked in clear white paint and that they are repainted regularly, ie each joining shackle is painted red with the number of shackles painted in white above and below the red joining shackle. This is still the best way of knowing how many shackles are out on your cables.

Regular greasing of the windlass and removal of old grease, especially from the brake spindle, ensures that the brake can be fully screwed up. This should be carried out frequently, particularly on heavy bulk cargo vessels where the build-up of debris can mix with the grease and form a hard substance that prevents the brakes from being properly applied.

Check the compression bar/guillotine bar for wear, particularly at the sides, as any wear might allow the bar to slide up from the chain.

Have the chain stoppers greased regularly and ensure that they can be fully tightened.

Check that the hawse pipe covers and the spurling pipe covers fit properly and, if cement or foam is used for the spurling pipe, that this is effective in stopping water ingress. Make sure that old cement and foam is removed.

Ensure that your stock of groundwork equipment is adequate for the tasks expected. The spare joining shackles, D rings and links should all be kept well greased and the spile pins ready. The wire strop for hanging off the anchor should have the same safe working load capacity as the anchor and the senhouse slip should be in good condition.

In dry dock it is essential that:

- Both anchors and cables are walked back out of the chain lockers and ranged along the dock bottom. All the shackles should be opened up and inspected, replacing where necessary
- the outboard length is changed with the inboard length
- the chain locker is inspected, the bitter end connection checked, the chain locker cleaned and coated and drains cleaned out
- prior to the cables being taken back, they are all freshly marked.

Heaving Anchor

An anchor requires little maintenance and may often be forgotten, but the possibility of damage cannot be ignored. Strain on the windlass should be avoided as far as possible. There are a number of rules to follow when heaving anchor:

- Prior to heaving anchor, check for other movements of ships in the area
- plan your departure from the anchorage
- ensure that the anchor party is adequate for the task and is wearing safety equipment
- ensure that it is clear to heave the anchor. Small boats have been known to secure to cables while fishing and people have been known to climb the cables
- test communication before commencing heaving. Ensure that water is on for washing down and that paint is ready for marking the cable
- have the bridge constantly advised about the amount of cable and the direction of the cable and weight. As an example, 5 shackles, 3 points on the port bow, moderate weight (note: windlasses are designed for vertical lifts not heaving a weighted and leading anchor cable)
- if the windlass takes strain or the cable report is of heavy weight, use the engines and take the weight off the cable. If a strong current is flowing, weight should be taken off from commencement of heaving. However, be careful not to let the ship fall back suddenly, jolting the cable
- on the report up and down, do not assume that the anchor is now about to come clear of the bottom. While it is most probable, it is not certain
- on the report 'anchor aweigh', ensure that the anchor signals are immediately taken down and, if it is at night, the navigation lights are displayed. While the anchor is aweigh but has not yet been sighted, you

Hanging off an Anchor

should not attempt to get under way. If the ship is moving into shallower waters and is under way with the anchor still being heaved, there is a chance that if it moves into the shallows the anchor will catch again on the seabed. If the ship has speed at that time, severe damage can occur, especially to the windlass.

Once the anchor is sighted and clear, the ship is free to navigate. If the report is not clear, it must be ascertained what the fouling is and whether it is attached to the bottom. If this is not immediately apparent, it would be prudent to make the other anchor ready in case the ship has to re-anchor. If it is suspected that the fouling is caused by communications or electric cables, under no circumstances should any attempt be made to pull free. The harbour authorities should be immediately advised of the situation and, if necessary, the other anchor walked back to hold the ship's position and ensure that no further strain is put on the equipment.

When the anchor is up and stowed, if still navigating in coastal waters keep the anchor on the brake with the compression bars or device screwed tight. If heading for deep sea, have the anchors secured, the hawse and spurling covers on and the spurling pipe cemented or foamed.

When choosing your anchor position, ensure that, if the anchor does drag and you have to heave up and leave the anchorage, you have sea room to cope.

Below are some the extracts from an enquiry into a ship dragging its anchor, resulting in considerable damage to itself and another vessel.

The Master and watchkeeping deck officers did not appreciate that the ship had dragged anchor from its original position, indicating that the combination of the depth of water, holding ground and ship's freeboard combined to make the anchorage insecure and alert them to the increased risk of dragging anchor in deteriorating weather.

The Master and watchkeeping deck officers did not detect the early signs of dragging and increased the risk of an accident by not reacting sufficiently early to the dragging of the ship's anchor.

The need to monitor the ship's position from a consistent set of reference marks was not fully appreciated by the Master and officers.

The limitations of the anchors was not fully appreciated.

Inadequate communications between the two ships meant that the Master was unaware that the anchor could not be recovered before the collision occurred.

The Master was preoccupied with the recovery of the anchor and did not drive the ship ahead, either dragging the anchor or releasing the bitter end and allowing it to pay out, while the opportunity existed.

The Master undertook no contingency planning regarding recovery of the anchor, nor did he think through his intended action or make any realistic assessment of how long it would take to recover the anchor.

The position relative to the most imminent danger was not monitored while trying to weigh anchor.

Always remember that you do not have to anchor. If you have any concern about anchoring, the weather, the position, or the traffic in the anchorage, then wait. As long as you are in communication with the port and they can advise you when you are required to approach for pilot boarding, there is no problem.

Figure 8.28 - Fouled anchor

Securing Anchor for Sea

Once the ship clears port limits/fairway buoy, the anchor should be secured. This will ensure that, with any rolling or pitching, the anchor will not run out on its own. The bow stoppers should be laid across and the cable secured using devil's claws between the windlass and the bow stopper.

The spurling pipe should be sealed to prevent the entry of seawater into the chain locker. This is done by fitting steel covers and then pouring cement over them.

Prior to the next port, the cement must be broken away and the devil's claws removed. The bow stoppers are only removed when the ship enters narrow water, generally around the area of the fairway buoy.

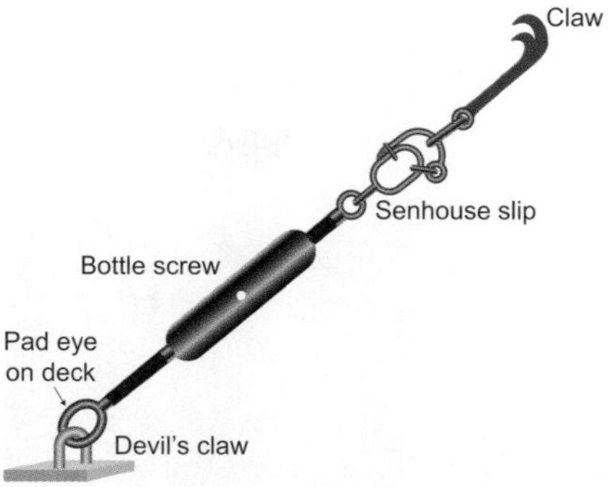

Fouled Anchor and Fouled Hawse

Fouled Anchors

If the anchor gets caught on an underwater obstruction, it is described as a ***fouled anchor***.

The anchor can become fouled either around its own cable or by fouling another obstruction.

This is why the anchor is reported as 'all clear' once it is entirely sighted clear of any obstruction.

Difference Between a 'Fouled Anchor' and a 'Fouled Hawse'

A fouled anchor is an anchor fouled by an obstruction such as a discarded mooring wire or by its own anchor cable turned around the fluke of the anchor.

A fouled hawse is where a ship is moored with two anchors and the anchor cables have become entwined, usually caused by a change in the wind or tidal direction, causing the vessel to swing round and cross the cables.

Clearing of a Fouled Anchor (Slipping an Anchor)

Where an anchor is fouled, it may be possible to work it loose by:

1. Slowly moving ahead until the cable leads astern, bringing the cable in until it is taut and then moving further ahead.
2. Steaming the ship in a circle with the cable taut.
3. Putting the engines astern.

If it is suspected that the anchor has fouled on a submarine power cable or pipeline, shore authorities should be notified. Retrieval of the anchor should not be attempted as it could cause damage to the submarine equipment. The Australian Notice to Mariners advises that in the event of any vessel fouling a pipeline, *"the anchor or gear should be slipped and abandoned without attempting to get it clear. Any excessive force applied to a pipeline could result in a rupture and, in the case of a gas pipeline, the consequential sudden release of gas at high pressure – somewhat like an explosion – could cause serious damage or loss of the vessel."*

Where it is necessary to release the cable, the anchor may be slipped. Slipping the anchor involves attaching a marker buoy by rope to the cable, preferably after leading it back up the hawse pipe adjacent to the cable link being released. The rope should be of a length sufficient for the depth of water. The cable can be released from the bitter end, but is normally broken between the brake and the compressor at a Kenter joining shackle. Before releasing, the cable should be up-and-down with all weight off.

When releasing the compressor bar, all personnel should be clear and the position logged.

The Bitter End

Where there is a need to quickly release an anchor, this can be achieved by removing the pin at the 'bitter end'. The bitter end normally consists of a steel box attached to the chain locker. Inside the box is an 'L' shaped pin that is passed through the final link of the anchor chain.

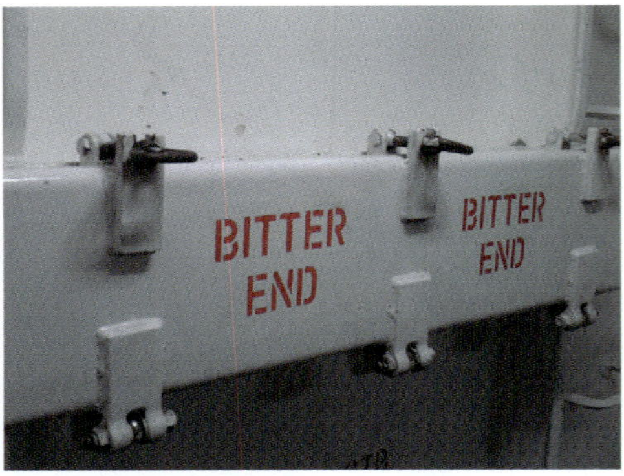

Removal of the pin should be straightforward requiring little physical effort and the final release of the cable should be achievable with a sledge hammer. The UK P&I Club produced a bulletin that advised of inspections of new ships where bitter ends were drilled and fitted with a split pin.

Clearing a Foul Hawse

There are four methods of clearing a foul hawse:

1. If the foul is a single turn, this can be cleared using the engines and proceeding in the opposite direction during the change of tide.
2. A tug can be connected to the stern of the vessel, which will rotate own vessel until the turns are removed.
3. Where a flat-top barge is available, break the sleeping cable, lower the riding cable onto the barge and work on the deck of the barge to clear the foul.
4. If method i) is not feasible, and methods ii) and iii) are unavailable, with a competent crew a foul hawse can be released as follows.

Items required to clear a foul hawse

- Natural fibre rope suitable for lashing
- three good wires, for use as a preventer wire, easing wire and a wire messenger
- equipment to open the Kenter shackle
- sharp knife or hacksaw and a long rod or pole.

Procedure to clear a foul hawse

1. You must plan to complete this operation within 6 hours, ie the time available between changes in tide. Therefore you must prepare as much as you can prior to your time window commencing.
2. Clearing the foul hawse should commence once the ship has turned on the tide.
3. Heave the riding cable such that the foul is clear of the water.
4. Lash both cables together using the natural fibre rope immediately above the foul.
5. Rig a preventer wire from a fairlead on the starboard side, passing this through the sleeping cable after the lashing.
6. Heave on the preventer wire and secure it to a set of mooring bitts (this will prevent the sleeping cable being lost).
7. The preventer wire should be rigged such that it may be slipped once the foul is cleared.
8. Walk back the sleeping cable until the next joining shackle appears on deck.
9. Rig an easing wire on the shackle outboard of the Kenter joining shackle and take the weight of the easing wire on the drum end.
10. Break open the Kenter shackle (the weight of the sleeping cable is now held on the easing wire).
11. Rig the wire messenger from the port side windlass drum.
12. Take a half turnaround the riding cable with the wire messenger in the opposite direction to the foul and pass the end of the wire messenger up through the hawse pipe of the sleeping cable and secure it to the end of the sleeping cable.
13. While easing back on the easing wire from the starboard windlass, pick up the slack on the wire messenger on the port windlass, thus removing half a turn from the fouled cable at a time.
14. This procedure is repeated, removing half a turn at a time until the foul is cleared.
15. When the foul is cleared, heave up on the easing wire while paying out on the messenger wire until the end of the sleeping cable is retrieved and can be re-joined.

Fouled Anchor and Fouled Hawse

16. Once the Kenter shackle is secured and the cable is rejoined, the temporary easing wire and the wire messenger can be removed, and the preventer wire can be slipped and cleared.

17. The natural rope lashing that is holding both cables together can be cut using a sharp knife or hacksaw on a rod. Alternatively, on ships not carrying hazardous cargoes, the lashings could be soaked in flammable liquid and then set on fire. Once the natural rope has burnt, if necessary you can heave on both cables to finally released them.

18. Both anchors are now clear and may be retrieved..

Case Studies

Heavy Weather Grounding

In May 2007, the one-year-old bulk carrier '*Pasha Bulker*', 76,000 Dwt, grounded off Newcastle, Australia.

The vessel was in light ballast condition and ready to load coal, and was anchored 2.5 miles offshore, south of the Newcastle harbour entrance. The Master anchored with nine shackles in 35 metres of water in a designated anchorage where more than 50 vessels were also at anchor.

The vessel was scheduled to berth in three weeks' time. After two weeks of good weather, the wind strength increased from the southeast. The Master, on receiving a gale warning, paid out an additional shackle of cable. During that evening, a number of vessels left the anchorage and put to sea due to the worsening weather. A few hours later, the first of the remaining vessels started to drag anchor. The local Vessel Traffic Information Centre advised the vessels that were dragging anchor and, within 24 hours, more vessels had also put to sea. 41 ships remained at anchor, enduring 40 knot winds and eight-metre high seas.

Early the following morning, the '*Pasha Bulker*' began dragging her anchor and the anchor was weighed. However, with the rapid rate of drift caused by the ship dragging its anchor, the vessel closed to only 1.2 miles from the shore. The Master attempted to turn the vessel away from the coast, but with such strong winds and the substantial windage area due to the ship being in the ballast condition, the vessel was driven onto the beach, grounding onto the rocky shoreline and breaching the hull. At the time of the grounding, the average wind speed was recorded as approximately 40 knots.

The windlasses of three vessels in a similar situation all failed when attempting to weigh anchor, with one vessel cutting its cable when under considerable tension, and the other two managing to slip their cables. These vessels were fortunately able to pull away from the coast.

Two weeks later, the '*Pasha Bulker*' was refloated and later towed to a repair yard.

In the Standard Club's publication 'Standard Safety' 2008, the ballast condition of a ship was identified as a potential problem, with reference to the '*Pasha Bulker*', ie:

Often a contributing factor in anchoring incidents is the fact that the vessel is in ballast condition. On any size of vessel, when the vessel is in ballast condition, there is an appreciable increase in windage area. Apart from the additional forces imposed on the cable, the vessel will probably behave differently at anchor to when it is loaded. The Pasha Bulker AMSB Report grounding noted that the vessel had 22,000 tonnes of ballast on board, which was sufficient for good weather; however, the fore and aft peak ballast tanks were empty. The ballast was

Case Studies

not sufficient to fully immerse the propeller, giving a mean draught of only 6.0 metres. In the heavy weather ballast condition, the vessel would have had a draught of 8.50 metres. This is significant to reduce forward slamming in heavy weather, increasing propeller immersion and, importantly, reducing windage. This could have made the vessel more manoeuvrable, and, in heavy weather, prevented potential slamming.

Lower wind forces on a ship due to reduced windage at deeper heavy weather ballast conditions can significantly improve the control of the vessel. When vessels are in ballast, the master should consider taking maximum ballast with the onset of heavy weather, even if this means the vessel is no longer load ready.

Gas Pipeline Rupture

On 13th December 2008, the container ship '*APL Sydney*', dragged her anchor, snagging and then rupturing a submarine gas pipeline in Port Phillip, Australia.

At 14:28 on 13th December, '*APL Sydney's*' anchor was let go in Melbourne's Outer Anchorage, about 0.5 nm upwind of the pipeline, and shortly afterwards the Pilot left the ship.

The Australian Transport Safety Bureau investigation found the ship's anchor had been let go too close to the pipeline in gale force winds and insufficient anchor cable was deployed. The anchor then dragged towards the pipeline and snagged it.

The Pilot reboarded '*APL Sydney*' at 16:03. After first considering release of the anchor, at 16:15 he concluded the anchor was south of the pipeline and decided to drag it clear. The Master accepted his plan and at 16:20 the ship's main engine was started. At 16:21, the gas pipeline ruptured. There were no injuries and the pipeline was isolated.

Too Close to Shore - Total Loss

A well-found reefer vessel at anchor waiting for orders, in ballast condition close to the Spanish coast, dragged anchor in poor weather, with the wind gusting to 50 knots, and ended aground on rocks and was declared a total constructive loss. Even with local knowledge, the vessel anchored only 6 cables from the shore on the Pilot's instructions in a designated anchorage. There was less than one hour from the time the OOW confirmed that the anchor was dragging to the vessel being aground. The Master had taken the precaution of having the main engine on immediate notice and on bridge control two hours before the vessel started to drag. However, due to the fact that the vessel was in ballast, the rate that the vessel dragged its anchor and the close proximity of the shore allowed no time to react and redeem the situation. In this incident, the windlass hydraulics failed when trying to raise the anchor and the vessel grounded on rocks.

Submarine Gas Pipeline Damaged by Anchor

A container vessel arrived in a port and anchored in the designated waiting area under pilotage. When the Pilot disembarked, the wind speed was observed to be 35 knots, gusting to 48 knots. A submarine gas pipeline was 0.6 nm downwind.

Summary of Significant Events

12:00 Sea Pilot boarded at designated outer pilot station.

14:28 The ship's starboard anchor was let go on a heading of 108° with a 35-knot gale blowing from 200°. (The heading was chosen to create a lee for the sea Pilot to disembark safely, and the drift rate increased substantially under this beam wind situation until the ship became wind-rode at about 14:55.

Evidence suggests that the ship was never 'brought up' to five shackles and was continuously dragging anchor and drifting in a NE direction.)

14:36 Sea Pilot disembarked.

15:01 The Master concluded that the anchor was not holding and requested permission from harbour control to move the vessel. He was instructed to maintain position and await the Pilot.

15:27 Harbour control gave permission to move the vessel. The Master used ahead engine power to relieve stress on the anchor and commenced shortening cable.

15:48 Starboard anchor windlass disabled with two shackles still out.

15:49 Ship's starboard anchor presumed to have snagged the pipeline.

16:03 Sea Pilot reboarded the vessel.

16:11 On Pilot's advice, decision made to slip the anchor cable from deck.

16:20 On Pilot's advice, new decision made to attempt to dredge the anchor clear by using the engine.

16:21 Submarine gas pipeline ruptured.

16:27 Vessel manoeuvred clear and anchor no longer fouling the ruptured pipeline.

16:34 Emergency shutdown valves of gas pipeline operated.

20:11 Permission received from pipeline operator to use gas cutting equipment subject to safe gas detector readings.

21:00 Decision made to gas-cut the cable at the hawse pipe.

21:53 Starboard anchor cable successfully cut at hawse pipe lip and anchor with about 2 shackles of chain abandoned.

00:48 Vessel anchored in southern part of outer anchorage using 8 shackles on port anchor.

Findings Arising from the Investigation

1. The rupture was the result of attempting to dredge the anchor instead of slipping it.
2. The anchor had been let go too close to the pipeline in the poor weather conditions.
3. There were deficiencies in the port's risk management with respect to the pipeline and anchorage boundaries and its shipping control procedures.
4. There were deficiencies in the ship's safety management system with respect to passage planning, the Master's authority, crew familiarisation and the working language.
5. There were deficiencies in the pilotage company's procedures for anchoring and mobile telephone use.
6. The windlass failed at a critical time due to excessive loading in the system.

CHAPTER 9

Tugs and Towing

Tugs and Towing

Most large vessels will use tugs during berthing and unberthing operations in port.

If tugs are employed, they normally arrive on scene at the same time as the berthing pilot or as the ship makes its final approach. It is essential that the crew are at their stations to make the tugs fast. The bridge requires sufficient warning of this from the pilot to ensure crew are in place, particularly at night. Working lights will have to be used on deck during the hours of darkness, with the exception of those shining towards the bridge.

The following is a standard clause from a tug hire contract.

"The expression 'while towing' shall cover the period commencing when the tug ... is in position to receive orders direct from the hirer's vessel to commence pushing, holding, moving, escorting, or guiding the vessel or to pick up ropes or lines, or when the tow rope has been passed to or by the tug ... whichever is the sooner, and ending when the final orders from the Hirer's vessel to cease ... and the vessel is safely clear of the vessel."

Figure 9.1 - Tugs will normally arrive to meet the ship at the same time as the pilot boards

Towlines

It is becoming increasingly common for tugs to use their own lines as a result of problems, including strength and quality, that have been experienced when using ships' lines.

It is important to ensure that the tug's line is put on the correct bitt. The safe working load of bitts is often not clearly defined and this can pose a danger to the crew.

High modulus rope enables vessels and tugs to provide towlines of similar or greater strength to traditional towlines. It has the added advantage that it weighs only a fraction of equally strong steel wire and synthetic ropes and is far easier for the reduced crews of today to handle.

In addition, this type of rope has low elongation, which results in low energy storage in the rope. This considerably increases the safety of those engaged in towing operations as the backlash in the event of a breakage will be far less.

Courtesy of Voith, AG Heidenheim

Figure 9.2 - A Boxer escort tug with a Voith Schneider propeller in action

Tug Position and Pushing Points

Tug position varies between locations. For example, in the USA, the majority of tugs 'strap' themselves alongside during manoeuvring, while some ports use tugs on long leads. While this reduces the likelihood of breaking the towline and allows the tug to escape from a dangerous position, it does hamper the tug's ability to quickly respond to different pull directions.

As tugs have become more powerful, side shell reinforcement is now fitted to the hull of larger ships. These tug push points will be located in way of existing transverse structure and will be clearly marked. Tugs can dent a ship's hull, and older ships will often show the typical indentations on the shoulders and the quarters caused by impact from tugs.

Tug Types

Conventional

Conventional tugs normally have a traditional stern-based propulsion system, ie:

- Single or twin propeller
- fixed or CPP
- possibly a shroud (or Kort) nozzle that directs and increases thrust.

This type of tug is often powerful and has good sea keeping qualities, but they can be difficult to manoeuvre and slow to react to manoeuvring changes. Traditionally, they have winches fitted just aft of the accommodation structure and many incorporate gob ropes aft to minimise the risk of girting.

Tractor (Voith Schneider)

Tractor tugs frequently incorporate two multi-directional propulsion units, situated approximately one-third of the length from the bow, commonly either the Voith Schneider or Schottel systems.

The Voith Schneider system incorporates vertical blades that rotate individually and in a circle to provide thrust in the required direction. A large skeg is normally fitted on the centreline on the underside of the hull aft of the units to provide improved directional control and protection against grounding.

The Schottel system uses two Azimuth propulsion units in the same position as the Voith Schneider system.

By having the propulsion units further forward, tractor tugs enable the towing point to be situated further aft, allowing a better turning moment and greatly reducing the risk of girting.

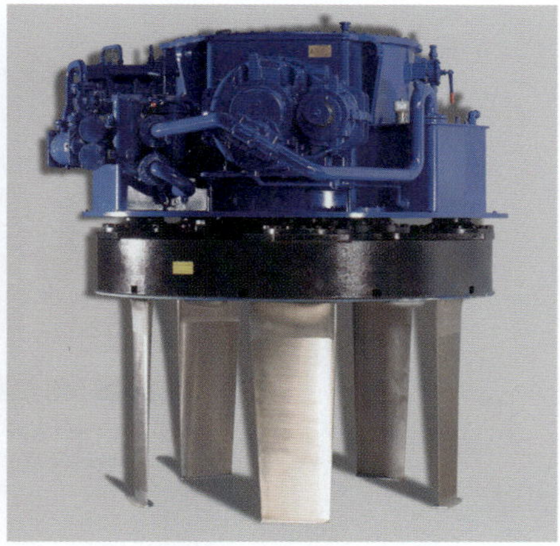

Courtesy of Voith AG, Heidenheim

Figure 9.3 - The Voith Schneider system

Advantages of tractor tugs include excellent manoeuvrability, full power thrust in any direction, simple controls and rapid changes in directional control. However, they are more expensive than conventional systems, have a lower bollard pull and are less effective when steaming. Their draught is considerably increased and additional crew training may be required.

Further Information

View Voith Schneider animation

http://tinyurl.com/d2xq9tw

Azimuth Stern Drive (ASD)

Azimuth stern drive (or Z drive) tugs use similar propulsion units to those described for the Schottel system in tractor tugs, but are positioned at the stern, provide improved handling when underway and good bollard pull and manoeuvrability. They have a smaller draught than tractor tugs, as they are normally placed under the flare of the stern, and perform very well when towlines are led from the bow. However, they are not as manoeuvrable as tractor tugs, remain susceptible to girting, may require additional training for handling and are more expensive than conventional propulsion systems.

Working Tugs Forward

Conventional

When ships move forward through the water, the area surrounding the bow forward of the pivot point experiences positive pressure while the main body of the hull creates an area of suction (negative pressure). Consequently, tugs working at the side of the hull will tend to be drawn towards the ship while those at the bow will be pushed away (repelled). The magnitudes of the forces are affected by hull shape and draught and are increased by:

- Increasing speed
- shallower water
- reducing the distance between the vessels.

When tugs are operating around the bow, the pilot, master and tug master must be fully aware of these effects and the vessels' limitations.

Where a conventional tug works directly ahead when escorting a ship, the normal practice is

to run the towline from the stern. To reduce the likelihood of girting, a gob rope is used to move the pivot point aft in line with the propulsion unit. If not, the pivot point will remain ahead of the thrust position and, when the tug alters course, this will create a lever that acts to increase the alteration. If the tug is in close proximity to the bow when underway, positive pressure may make this worse, preventing corrective helm having an effect and bringing the tug beam-on to the ship, risking capsize or collision. Consequently, the speed of the ship must be kept within safe limits.

When the tug is working alongside the ship's shoulder, the effects of positive pressure remain and serve to push the tug away from the ship. The effect on the tug will depend on its position in relation to the bow:

- If forward of the shoulder/slightly ahead of the bow, it is likely to push the stern away, with the potential to sheer across the path of the ship
- if aft of the shoulder, the potential exists for the bow to be pushed away and the stern to be pulled towards the hull.

In both cases, the pressures can be controlled by a reduction in speed and maintaining a safe distance when underway.

Tractor

Tractor tugs generally use their aft towing point, leading the towline directly astern, as this provides the greatest pull and control. Alternatively, they may be used to push against the shoulder of the ship. When positioned off the bow and made fast forward with the ship moving through the water, it is important that the speed of the ship is slow enough to ensure there is no risk of girting.

Tractor tugs with a forward towing winch fitted may lead the towline from the bow. This is most likely when pulling the ship off the berth to enable the tug's bow to push and check the ship's athwartship movement.

In some areas, tractor tugs commonly make fast alongside the ship's shoulder. Working in such close proximity requires care due to interaction, heeling effects and backwash when using the thrusters to port and starboard.

ASD

These tugs are very effective when pushing alongside, using their bows against the quarters of the ship in the same manner as when employed forward or when directly astern of the ship. The tugs will often approach from directly astern to avoid the propeller wash. The lack of a skeg means the hull shape loses some effect.

Working Tugs Aft

Conventional

The stern area of the ship, particularly aft of the propeller, has similar positive pressure effects as that of the bow which, when combined with the dangers represented when working close to the propeller, makes tug manoeuvring difficult. Where a tug is approaching a ship underway from the quarter, the positive pressures can cause the bow to sheer away from the ship so additional power and helm may be required to compensate.

The dangers of potential low pressures around the stern, the potential for a tug to sheer towards the ship and the dangers associated with the ship sheer astern have been well documented.

When working in close proximity to the propeller, it is safest for it to be stopped but, in the case of CPPs, this may not be possible. Where the propeller is still turning, additional care must be taken to avoid the effects of interaction, propeller wash and the danger of towline propeller entanglement.

Tractor

Tractor tugs are sometimes used alongside the stern quarter to provide port and starboard movement at very slow speeds where the rudder becomes ineffective. The further aft that the tug is positioned, the more effective it becomes as a result of the increased distance from the pivot point of the ship. This method may be more appropriate for 'dead ship' manoeuvring alongside a berth with a number of tugs.

Tractor tugs may be employed astern of the ship, using their aft towing points to control the ship's movements, when in a narrow channel and when escorting. To do this, they move astern through the water (at slow speeds) and control movement by moving outward of the ship to port and starboard as required.

This is particularly effective as the tug can use its weight and hull shape (including the skeg) combined with the thrusters to good effect in controlling direction and speed. It is sometimes known as indirect towing.

ASD

When towing directly ahead from the stern tow point, ASDs act in a similar manner to conventional tugs and therefore have the same risks. However, if towing from the tug's bow, the full effect of the stern thrust units is achieved over the full radius of the ship's bow with minimal risk of girting. Care must be taken when the tug is moving/escorting stern first in this manner if there is any likelihood of stern squat.

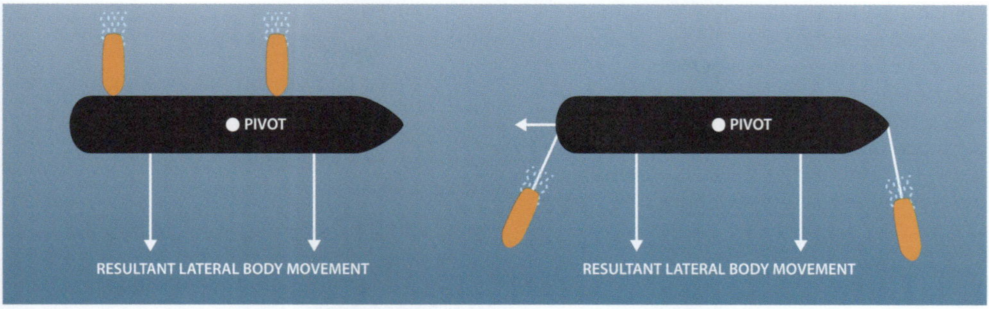

Figure 9.4 - The effect of tugs when a ship is stopped

ASD tugs are effective when pushing against (and pulling via a towline at) the shoulders and along the body of the ship due to the position of the stern thrusters. As these are away from the ship, they are less affected by backwash and the tug's angle can be easily adjusted while keeping the tug bow in position.

When a ship is stationary in the water, with negligible wind and in water deep enough for squat to be discounted, the pivot point will normally lie at the longitudinal centre of gravity (LCG). Consequently, the effect of tugs fore and aft will be roughly equal.

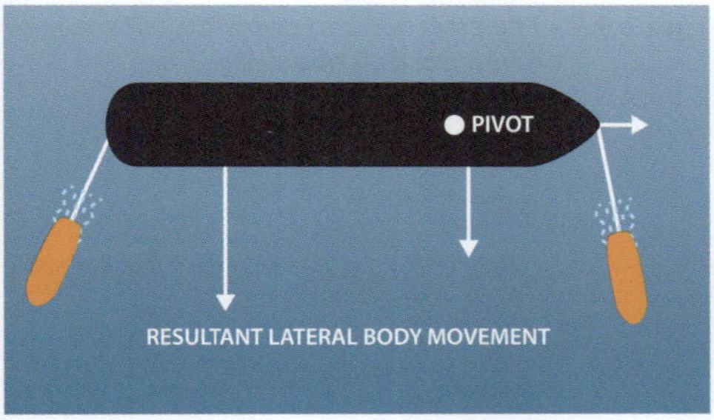

Figure 9.5 - The effect of tugs pulling when making headway

When a ship is making headway, the pivot point will move forward, roughly a quarter of the length from the bow. Therefore, the turning effect (moment) of tugs astern will be greater than those forward.

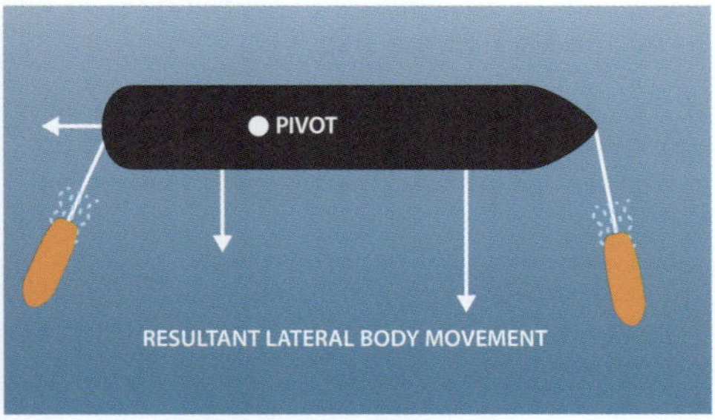

Figure 9.6 - The effect of tugs pulling when making sternway

When moving astern, the opposite holds true, ie the pivot point lies approximately a quarter of the length from the stern and forward tugs have greater effect.

Working Alongside/Pushing

Working with a tug alongside is common practice for tractor and ASD tugs or where a number of tugs are involved in the operation. This can be very effective, but the effects of interaction between the tug and the ship must be appreciated due to both the suction effect as the tug approaches the ship underway and the wave effect as their positions close in on one another.

The effect that the force exerted from a tug has on the ship will depend on its position in relation to the pivot point of the ship and whether the ship is stationary, making headway or moving astern.

Figure 9.7 shows the effect of the tug pushing alongside when making headway. When moving ahead, the pivot point is forward so any force exerted directly abreast of it will result in lateral bodily movement of the ship. The further from the pivot point the tug exerts a lateral force, the greater the turning effect will be on the stern of the ship.

When moving astern, the ship's pivot point also moves towards the stern so the forces will act in a similar manner, ie the further forward the tug exerts a force (pushes or pulls), the greater the turning effect on the bow.

A hip tow is another form of towing alongside and normally comprises three lines (bow, stern and spring) to provide a more rigid connection and may be more common when moving unpowered vessels or barges.

It should always be remembered that the forces exerted by the ship and the tug must be fully assessed and adjusted for wind and tidal conditions.

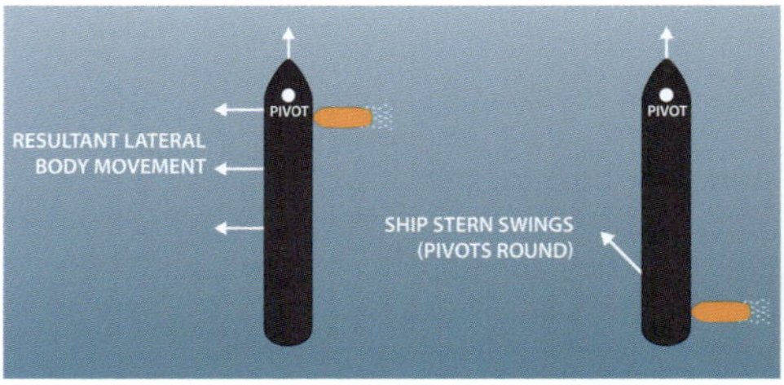

Figure 9.7 - The effect of a tug pushing alongside when making headway

Routine Berthing with Tugs

In determining the number of tugs that are to be used when berthing, the following factors should be considered:

- The port requirements, including those relating to ship types
- the size and windage area of the ship
- the manoeuvring capabilities of the ship, including:
  - Propeller(s)
  - rudder type
  - thrusters
- the strength and direction of current or tide
- the strength and direction of the prevailing wind
- the UKC.

The position of the tugs when manoeuvring is critical to the way the ship's movement is controlled and, particularly when several tugs are involved, they will be more effective when the ship is stopped. This also reduces interaction effects and improves safety.

While smaller ships (up to around 120 m) may use a single tug forward in lieu of a bow thruster, Figure 9.8 illustrates the approach of a small ship with a single right-hand propeller and no thrusters into a head current using a tug astern.

In this example, the ship is berthing port side with a current on the bow. The ship approaches the berth at a relatively steep angle and a tug is employed to help stop the ship. The forward spring is used to drive against when using the engines to stem the tide and the helm is used to bring the ship alongside. If necessary, the offshore anchor can be deployed. Where no current is involved, the tug is used aft to aid and control the effects of transverse thrust that swings to port when the engines are put astern. Where a ship is berthing starboard side to with no tide, the tug becomes even more valuable.

On larger ships, typically over 150 m and particularly in busy ports, several tugs are commonly used to help keep the ship parallel with the berth during mooring operations.

In Figure 9.9, the ship uses the main engines to bring the ship into a position parallel with the intended berth. A tug is again made fast astern to prevent the ship moving too far ahead when stemming the current. A further two tugs make fast on the offshore side, pushing the ship alongside and checking her lateral speed to keep her parallel.

Routine Berthing with Tugs

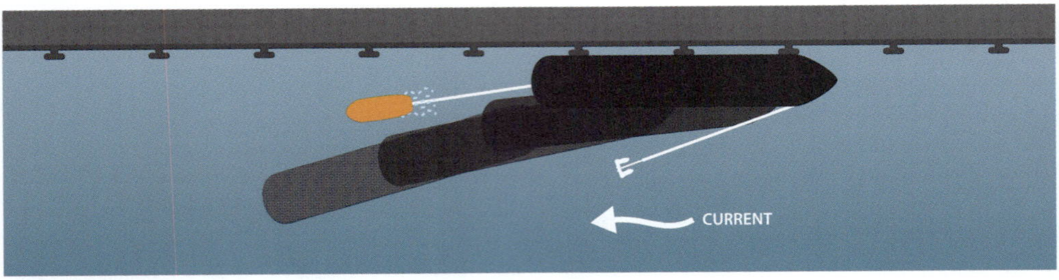

Figure 9.8 - Mooring a small ship alongside

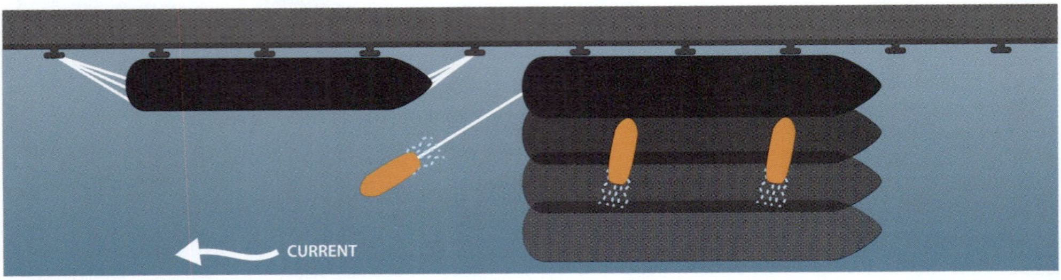

Figure 9.9 - Mooring a large ship alongside

Which Side to Make Fast to?

The side that individual tugs make fast to will depend on:

- The purpose of the tow, eg berthing, escorting, anchoring
- the type of tug
- the extent of manoeuvring involved
- the direction of the turns
- whether underway or stationary
- the number of tugs involved in the operation.

Where a large turn is made while making headway, a tug would normally be most effective by pulling on the side being turned in to. Where there is no headway, making fast the tug on the starboard bow of a ship with a right-handed propeller will make best use of the transverse thrust effect from the ship's propeller.

Entering a Dock (with Tug Assistance)

Tugs are frequently used to assist ships entering docks, and a typical sequence is shown in Figure 9.10. The ship is turned to bring the head into the current or tidal stream and makes fast alongside the dock. While using the ship's mooring lines to control the manoeuvre, the tug assists by either making fast on the outer quarter to pull the stern forward and then round the knuckle (protected by fenders), or may position on the shore side quarter to push the vessel. A second tug may, depending on the circumstances, make fast forward to assist in controlling the ship's bow.

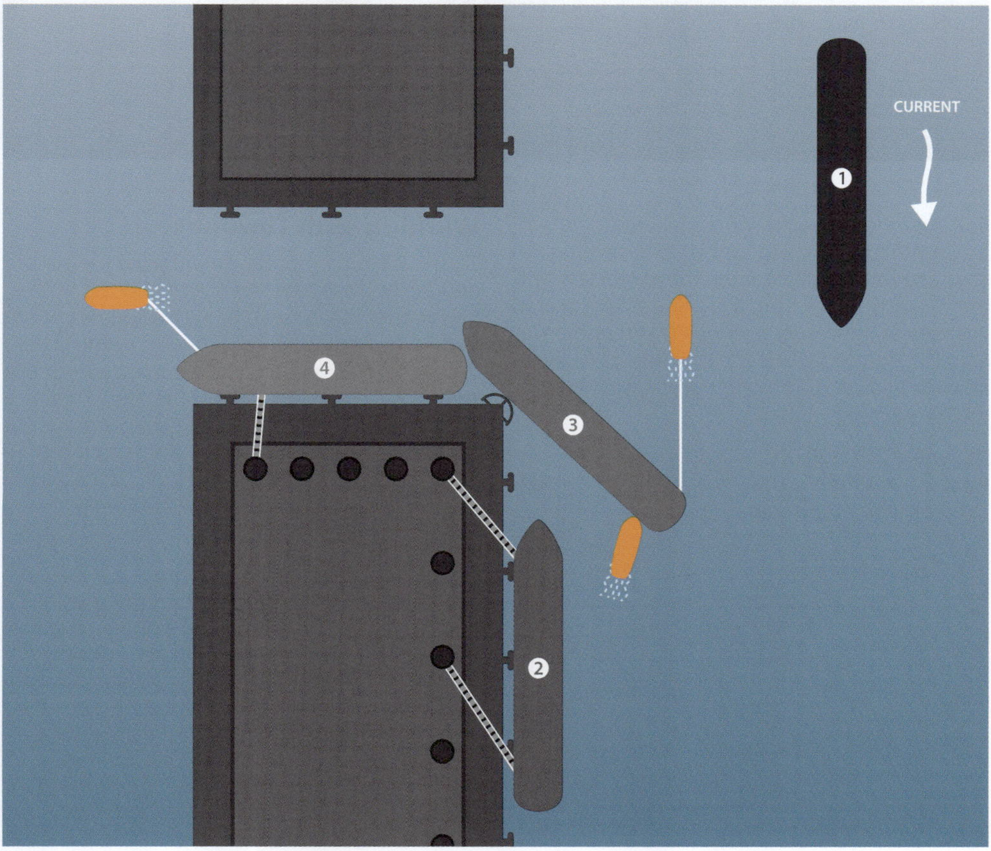

Figure 9.10 - Entering a dock with tug assistance

Routine Berthing with Tugs

Emergency Response Manoeuvres

Tugs used in emergency manoeuvres, eg controlling disabled tankers or providing steerage for ships with inoperative rudders, will either apply forces from a towline astern or, if it is a conventional tug, may push from either the stern or alongside. This provides forces to the ship for braking, turning or compensating for a malfunctioning rudder.

All tankers over 20,000 Dwt are required to have an emergency towing arrangement fitted at either end of the ship.

Working with Towlines

Towlines are commonly provided by the tugs and are normally at least 6 inch hawsers, lead from either the forward or aft towing bitts. Care should be exercised as the quality of the lines cannot be guaranteed and the stresses that can suddenly be exerted are considerable. There are no guarantees that the breaking strength of the line will meet Class recommendations (ie 4 times that of the bollard pull). Ships and tugs are likely to pitch and roll at different times, meaning large strains can quickly come on and may cause the line to break.

Similarly, it must be ensured that the towline is placed on the correct bitt and not one that has been constructed for lighter loads – this may not be immediately evident to the deck crew working the lines. It should always be possible to quickly and safely cast off a towline.

Bow to Bow Collision Case Study

On 13th April 2005, at around 02:10, the UK-registered tug *'Thorngarth'* was assisting the Liberian-registered chemical tanker *'Stolt Aspiration'* when the two vessels collided, as *'Thorngarth'* was attempting to recover her position ahead of *'Stolt Aspiration'*. *'Thorngarth'* was holed below the waterline and sustained significant structural damage. The tug's engineer suffered a broken arm. *'Stolt Aspiration'* suffered only minor damage to its bow and there were no other injuries or pollution.

'Stolt Aspiration' was approaching Alfred Lock, the entrance to the Birkenhead Docks on the River Mersey. To assist the vessel in passing through the locks, a Pilot was on board and the services of two tugs were utilised, *'Thorngarth'* acting as the bow tug with *'Ashgarth'* assisting aft. The weather was overcast with rain showers but, at the time of the accident, visibility was moderate, with light winds.

Both tugs were designed to tow over the bow and the standard approach for the bow tug is to meet the ship 'bow to bow'. The tug passes her gear up to the ship's forecastle and then quickly reverses away from the bow of the ship to take the weight of the towing gear, towing stern first.

While carrying out this manoeuvre, *'Thorngarth'* initially positioned herself correctly, right ahead of *'Stolt Aspiration'*, and passed her messenger line up to the forward mooring party. The tug then started to move away from the ship and began to turn slightly to one side. The turning effect was countered and the tug closed in on the port bow of the ship, regaining its position ahead of the ship by increasing engine power.

Once more ahead of the ship, the tug started to turn and this was again countered as the tug approached the starboard bow of the ship. While attempting to recover from this position and move ahead of the ship, the tug ended up across the bow of *'Stolt Aspiration'*, which then struck *'Thorngarth'* on its starboard side.

The accident was caused by the tug Master's lack of familiarity with his vessel and lack of training in the particular manoeuvre he was required to perform. This was one of a number of similar incidents involving tugs in a four month period that was attributable to a lack of tug master training and familiarisation. This prompted the MAIB to issue Safety Bulletin 02/2005, highlighting the need for an assessment of the 'tug to task' allocation before each towing operation, and ensuring that tug masters are fully trained.

Figure 9.11 - Movement of 'Thorngarth' ahead of 'Stolt Aspiration' (not to scale)

Girting

Girting (or girthing) is the capsizing/overturning effect on a towing vessel caused by an external force experienced abeam. This is typically caused by a towline attached to a towed ship.

The effect of this force can cause the tug to heel significantly and, if sufficient, can cause the vessel to capsize. The likelihood of capsizing is increased where water is able to flood though unsecured openings at deck level when heeled beyond the angle of deck edge immersion (DEI). The DEI on tugs and offshore vessels is typically less than those expected on more traditionally-shaped ships and, once it has been exceeded, it acts to reduce the ship's GM and righting lever.

The resultant force is comprised of vertical and horizontal components which create a heeling lever. Girting can be caused by the towing vessel moving too quickly through the water or

Gob Rope

Tractor tugs with towlines that run from the stern are less prone to girting than tugs with more central tow points. Tugs often use 'gob ropes' so that the towline runs from the stern to help avoid girting.

Figure 9.12 - Gob Rope

turning too sharply away from the tug. This is most likely to occur when towing alongside or from a sudden movement by the towed vessel, resulting in a force sufficient to overturn the tug.

This phenomenon is not exclusive to traditional tugboats and can occur in offshore anchor handling vessels (AHVs) and trawlers.

In reality, AHVs are at greater risk as any sudden force is likely to be exerted from a lower angle and will act to immediately pull the ship downward, heeling the vessel and exceeding the DEI. The lower relative aft freeboard of an AHV will have a serious detrimental effect on the GM as the stern trim increases and the stern is eventually submerged. This effect of stern trim (free to trim) is discussed in Chapter 4.

On a traditional tug, it is more likely that the strain will come from an angle above the tug, which will initially pull the tug towards the towed vessel, rather than creating an instant heeling force. It is the water resistance from the tug when being pulled through the water that will cause the heeling effect.

Figure 9.13 - Tug and AHV showing resultant girting forces

The tension in the towline creates an upward component of force on the tug similar to discharging a 'high' weight, resulting in an effect similar to lowering the KG (height above the metacentre). On the AHV, the downward force from tension in an anchor cable acts in the same way as a weight being added outboard of the centreline, creating a heeling moment.

The capsize of the AHTS vessel '*Bourbon Dolphin*' (see page 219) was partly attributed to these forces, when the anchor chain slipped from the inner starboard towing pin to the outer port towing pin (while turning).

Girting

Girting Forward

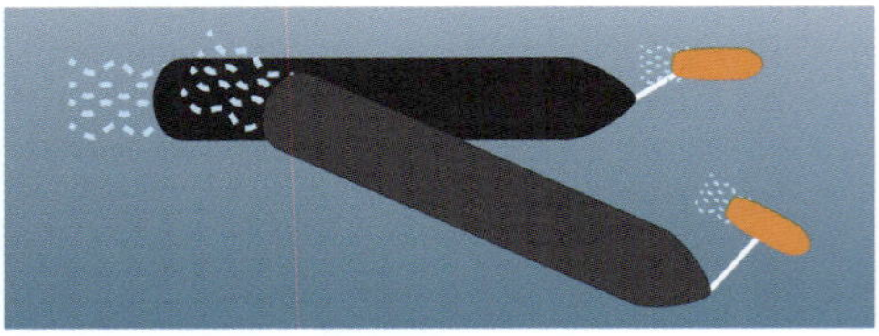

Figure 9.14 - Girting forward

Where a tug is made fast to the forward end of a ship underway, the situation remains relatively safe while both vessels are proceeding on parallel courses and at slow speeds. However, if the ship:

- Alters course, the tug may be pulled out of position and be dragged on its beam (Figure 9.14)
- increases speed, the tug may be pulled on to its beam and the weight will cause it to veer towards the ship
- is too close to the tug and the tug alters course away from the ship too sharply, a similar situation could result.

In each case, because the tug is dragged transversely, unless the towline is released or breaks, there is a serious risk that the tug may capsize.

Girting Aft

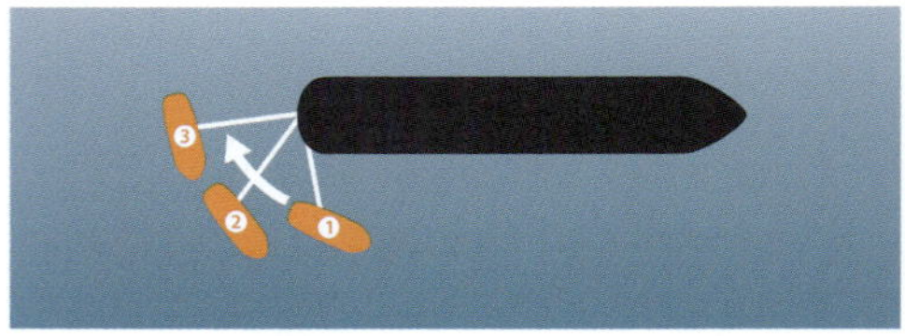

Figure 9.15 - Girting aft

Where a tug is made fast astern of a ship, the risk is often greater than when forward, particularly where the towline is not made fast to the front of the tug. An increase in the speed of the ship (or even the rpm of the propeller) can increase the tension on the line and cause the tug to swing astern. Where the tug cannot respond in time, there is a danger that she may end up being dragged beam-on and rapidly capsize with insufficient time to release the line.

Bollard Pull

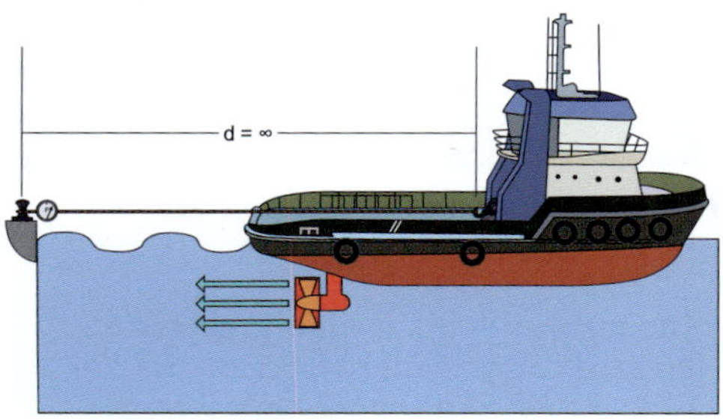

Bollard pull is the pulling capacity of a towing vessel at zero speed. The break horsepower of an engine does not give an accurate value of the pulling ability of the towing vessel. By calculating the bollard pull, the actual force the vessel can exert when towing is known, and this acts as a measure of the towing vessel's usefulness. The thrust of force developed is the bollard pull and is expressed in tonnes.

To calculate bollard pull, a towline is attached to a fixed point (the bollard) via a strain gauge or dynamometer and maximum power applied. Ideally bollard pull is calculated and certified by a Classification Society when the tug is built, or after a major engine overhaul. In general, two surveyors are needed when conducting the test, one ashore and the other in the engine room.

After the bollard pull test, a certificate stating the calculated bollard pull will be issued. There is no mandated requirement for renewal of the bollard pull test certificate, but a depreciation of bollard pull of 1% per year after the certificate's issue should give a realistic estimation of the current bollard pull.

Static Towing

Static towing, also known as pull-back or hold-back towing, is the procedure where tugs are used to provide an additional safeguard for tankers that are not fitted with dynamic positioning (DP), when loading cargo at offshore locations such as an F(P)SO or SBM/SPM.

The pull-back or hold-back tug is generally attached by a long towline to the stern of the non-DP tanker and picks up the weight, to assist the non-DP tanker in keeping a steady distance away from the mooring point. Keeping a steady weight on the towline from the stern of the non-DP tanker to the pull-back or hold-back tug, known as 'static towing', removes the need for the tanker to be constantly engaged in astern movements to avoid contact with the mooring point. All offshore loading facilities to which a tanker is connected by hawser require a means to prevent the tanker riding up and making contact with, and causing damage to, the mooring point.

Offshore loading, by its very nature, is exposed to the weather conditions and challenges for the operators range from:

- Strong currents or swell conditions
- strong winds, squalls or hurricanes/typhoons
- storms, which are graded by their expected severity, ie 1-year, 10-year or 100-year events.

As part of its 'Safety Case Assessment' the mooring point will have undergone a number of risk assessments to determine the safe parameters during which various tanker types can remain connected to the mooring.

Although each mooring point is typically designed to allow the offloading tanker, or offloading tanker and F(P)SO, to weathervane around a fixed mooring point, it is easy for the offloading tanker to drift towards the mooring point, whether that be an SBM/SPM buoy or F(P)SO to which it is connected, particularly when swell and wind are acting in opposing directions.

Courtesy of TitusEapen – Public Relations Department of BPCL-Kochi Refinery

Figure 9.16 - Tanker loading from an SPM, with a pull-back tug connected astern, engaged in static towing

Fatal accident while engaged in static towing

On 26th May 2013, the tug 'Jacson 4' capsized when it encountered heavy ocean swells, while engaged in static towing off the coast of Nigeria. Eleven out of twelve crew on the tugboat died in this incident. The twelfth crew member, the cook, was rescued after spending nearly three days in a small air pocket in the capsized vessel, approximately 30 m under water. It is unclear exactly what happened in this incident, but reports suggest that the tanker broke free from the SPM, ie the mooring hawser parted and the actions of the tanker resulted in the girting of the tug. The tug had open hatches and portholes which allowed it to rapidly capsize and sink.

Static Towing

Recap on 'Girting'

Girting occurs when a towline exerts a heeling force on the tug sufficient to overpower the tug's righting lever and cause it to capsize. This can happen very quickly and is the most common reason for tugs to capsize. With little or no prior warning, there is often no time to release towing gear, even using quick release mechanisms.

Usual causes are the ship under tow either turning quickly away from the tug or having a straight line speed too fast for the tug to cope with.

If a tug is attached to the stern of a larger vessel, a heeling moment can be experienced if the direction of tow and the centreline of the tug become misaligned. Drag forces on the underwater section of the tug's hull add to the forces experienced and can cause the maximum bollard pull of the tug to be exceeded, leading to girting.

For further information on girting, refer to page 378.

Static towing

Many terminals have found that, to manage the tanker on the SPM, it is advantageous to make use of a tug while the tanker is made fast. Static towing usually involves towing right astern at low power for a continuous period, and is particularly useful in tidal or varying current or wind conditions. Static towing helps to maintain a steady, low mooring load on the hawser and avoids peak loads, yo-yoing and riding up to the SPM.

Towing over the bow of the tug rather than stern reduces risks and improves tug sea keeping capabilities. In rough seas, a long towline may be necessary. Communication with the Tug Master should be established to ensure that the relative position of the tanker with respect to the SPM is effectively managed.

Reference: OCIMF 'Single Point Mooring Maintenance and Operations Guide', Third Edition 2015

Recommendations relating to the prevention of girting include:

- Inclusion of set-up and use of quick release towing in the Safety Management System (SMS)
- Checks to ensure that all watertight doors, hatches, manholes, ports and windows on the weather deck are closed and secured to prevent flooding if the deck becomes immersed
- Watertight doors and hatches should be regularly maintained and easily identifiable, eg painted in a different colour or marked 'to remain closed during towing'
- Tugs should, where possible, not be operated at maximum power, to allow some reserve for use in the case of emergencies
- Maximum speed for operations should be established with all parties
- Any modifications to towing equipment should be checked by the tug's Classification Society prior to use
- Pre-towing checklists should be available and used in all operations
- If any steering problems are encountered on the tug, speed should be reduced and, where necessary, the towline should be released.

Source: West of England P&I Club

Figure 9.17 - Non-DP Tanker loading from an FPSO, with a pull-back tug connected astern, engaged in static towing

CHAPTER 10

Mooring Operation and Safety

Mooring Safety

During mooring and unmooring operations a sufficient number of personnel should always be available at each end of the vessel to ensure a safe operation.

A responsible officer should be in charge of each of the mooring parties and a suitable means of communication between the responsible officers and the bridge team should be established. If this involves use of portable radios, the ship should be clearly identified by name to prevent misinterpretation. All personnel involved in mooring operations should wear suitable protective clothing.

Vessels' heaving lines should be constructed with a 'monkey's fist' at one end. To avoid personal injury, the 'fist' should be made only with rope and should not contain added weighting material.

Areas where mooring operations are to be undertaken should be clutter free as far as possible. Decks should have anti-slip surfaces provided by fixed treads or anti-slip paint coating, and the whole working area should be adequately lit for operations undertaken during periods of darkness.

All equipment used in mooring operations should be regularly inspected for defects, and any defects found corrected as soon as possible. Particular attention should be paid to the risk of oil leaks from winches. The surfaces of fairleads, bollards, bitts and drum ends should be clean and in good condition. Rollers and fairleads should turn smoothly and a visual check should be made to ensure that they have not been weakened by corrosion.

Mooring ropes, wires and stoppers should be in good condition, Ropes should be frequently inspected for external wear and tear between strands. Wires should be regularly treated with suitable lubricants and inspected for deterioration internally and broken strands externally. Splices in ropes and wires should be inspected regularly to check they are intact. Where wire rope is joined to fibre rope, a thimble or other device should be inserted in the eye of the fibre rope. Both wire and fibre rope should have the same direction of lay.

Ropes and wires that are stowed on reels should not be used directly from stowage, but should be run off and flaked out on deck in a clear and safe manner, ensuring sufficient slack to cover all contingencies. If there is doubt about the amount required, the complete reel should be run off.

It is often difficult to achieve an ideal mooring layout, but ship's equipment can be employed to the best advantage if the following general principles are applied:

- Breast lines provide the bulk of athwartships restraint
- backsprings provide the largest proportion of the longitudinal restraint
- very short lengths of line should be avoided where possible, as such lines will take a greater proportion of the total load when movement of the ship occurs.

Careful thought should be given to the layout of moorings, so that the leads are most appropriate without creating sharp angles, and ropes and wires are not fed through the same leads or bollards. Pre-planning of such operations is recommended and a risk assessment of the operation should be completed, particularly in cases where the ship is having to use an unusual or non-standard mooring arrangement.

Personnel should never stand in a bight of rope or wire. Operation of winches should be undertaken by competent personnel to ensure that excessive loads do not arise on moorings.

Where moorings are to be heaved on a drum end, one person should be stationed at the drum end, backed up by a second person backing and coiling down the slack. In most circumstances, three turns on the drum end are sufficient to undertake a successful operation. A wire on a drum end should never be used as a check wire.

A wire should never be led across a fibre rope on a bollard. Wires and ropes should be kept in separate fairleads or bollards.

When stoppering off moorings, the following principles apply:

- Natural fibre rope should be stoppered with natural fibre
- man-made fibre rope should be stoppered with man-made fibre stopper (but not polyamide)
- the West Country method (double and reverse stoppering) is preferable for ropes
- wire moorings should be stoppered with a chain, using two half hitches in the form of a cow hitch, suitably spaced with the tail backed up against the lay of wire, to ensure that the chain neither jams nor opens up the lay of the wire.

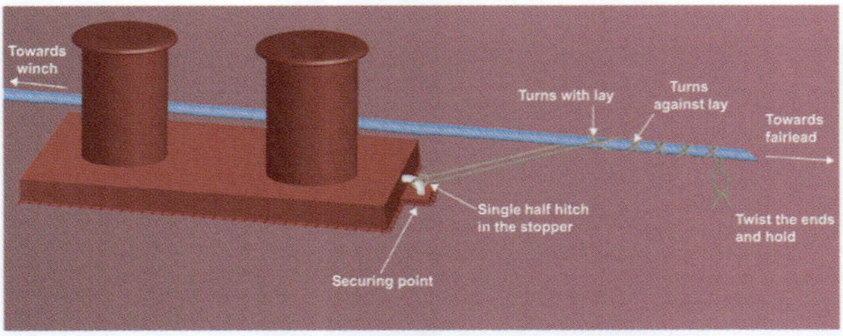

Figure 10.1 - Applying a rope stopper to a mooring rope

Mooring Safety

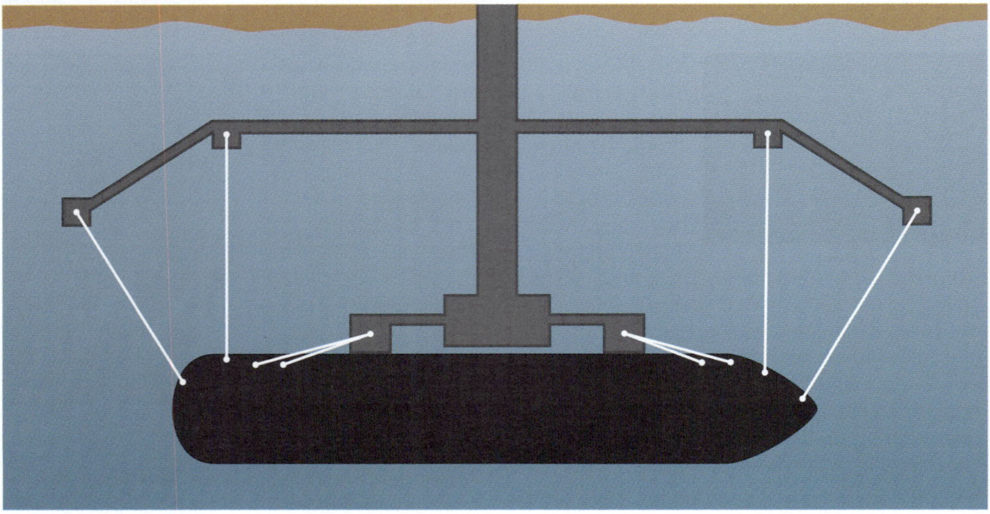

Mooring Lines

Mooring lines are designed to match the mooring strength requirements of the ship but, if they should snap, they have such substantial stored energy that they will snap back with a strength of force that can sever limbs or even cut someone in half!

General Mooring Considerations

Longitudinal mooring loads: These are the forces that act longitudinally on the ship. They are resisted by the spring lines and to an extent by the head lines and stern lines.

Lateral mooring loads: These are the forces that act athwartships on the ship. They are resisted by the breast lines and to an extent by the head lines and stern lines.

The main load on a ship's moorings is typically the lateral load. Therefore, there are generally more head, stern, and breast lines than spring lines.

Whenever possible, mixing of wire and rope mooring lines should be avoided. Where combination mooring lines are used, they should be restricted to head lines and stern lines.

Wire moorings with synthetic tails should be regarded as synthetic mooring lines.

If the ship cannot deploy lines of the same construction, the following considerations should be taken into account:

- Where possible, lines used in a particular service (ie springs, breast lines, etc) should be of the same length, construction and breaking strain
- any two mooring lines leading to the same mooring hook/bollard ashore must be of the same construction
- where possible, no more than two mooring lines should be attached to a shore mooring hook/bollard.

The total length of a mooring line should not be less than 30 metres/100 feet, to allow for changes in tide and ballast conditions and to provide sufficient elasticity.

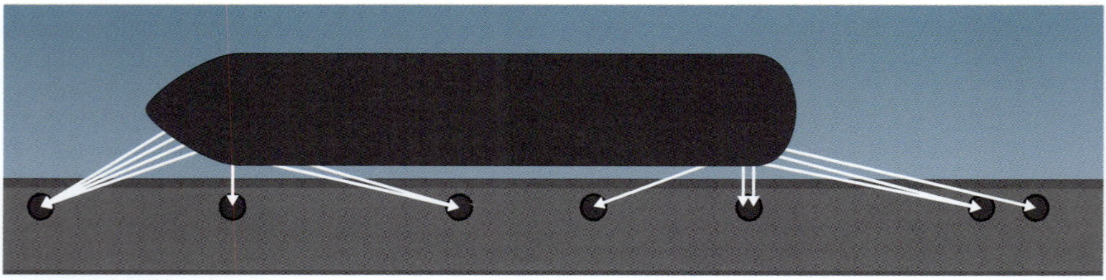

Figure 10.2 - Mooring loads

Head Lines and Stern Lines

Head lines are often the first lines sent ashore from the ship.

The head line fixes the ship to a point and then a tug (or the tide) is used to bring the ship alongside.

Head lines and stern lines are led well ahead and astern to reduce the fore and aft motion of the ship.

Bow and stern lines provide a level of both lateral and longitudinal restraint.

Stern lines are generally sent after the head lines.

When mooring alongside, the head lines and the forward springs create a pulling arm while the stern lines and back springs form the other pulling arm.

Head lines and forward springs prevent the ship from creeping astern on the berth. Stern lines and back springs prevent the ship from creeping forward on the berth.

Head and stern lines are generally not required for safe mooring provided shore mooring points are suitably designed and arranged. This means that a vessel can be moored most efficiently within its own length.

Mooring Safety

Breast Lines

Head lines and spring lines are often the only lines that are required to hold a ship in position and alongside but, on certain berths, it will be necessary to send out breast lines to hold the ship alongside. If the breast line is not positioned at 90° to the ship, the breast line's effectiveness diminishes.

On berths where there is a large rise and fall of the tide and a short lead for breast lines, their effectiveness is reduced due to their need for constant monitoring and readjustment.

To be effective, the vertical angle of a breast line between the ship and the mooring point and the horizontal should not exceed 25 to 30° in all stages of the tide and the ship's ballast condition.

The steeper the orientation of a line, the less effective it is in resisting horizontal loads. As an example, a line orientated at a vertical angle of 45° is only 75% as effective in restraining the ship as a line orientated at a 20° vertical angle.

Similarly, the larger the horizontal angle between the parallel side of the ship and the line, the less effective the line is in resisting a longitudinal force.

Breast lines should be run out from a position as far forward or as far aft as possible.

In some circumstances, the master or pilot may instruct that breast lines are not to be run until the vessel is alongside and in position.

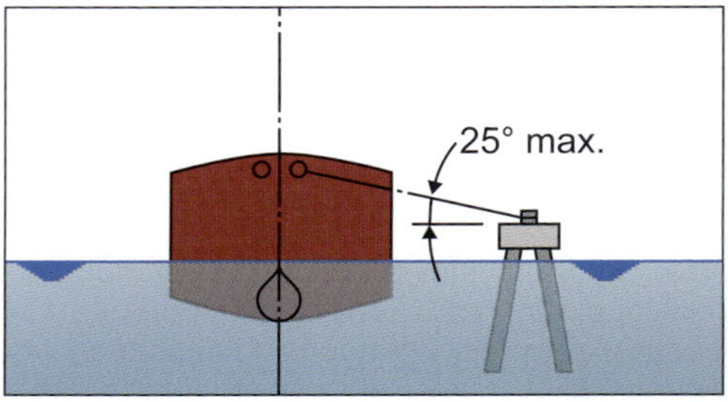

Spring Lines

Spring lines are the second lines to be sent ashore. Their function is to prevent the ship from surging forward and to hold the ship's fore and aft position on the berth.

Head lines and forward springs prevent the ship from creeping astern on the berth. Stern lines and backsprings prevent the ship from creeping forward on the berth.

Spring lines are run at a shallow angle to the fore of the berth, typically between 5 to 10°.

Note: Where two spring lines are led in opposite directions from the bow or stern, they function the same way as breast lines.

Mooring Safety

Difference in the Function of Spring and Breast Lines

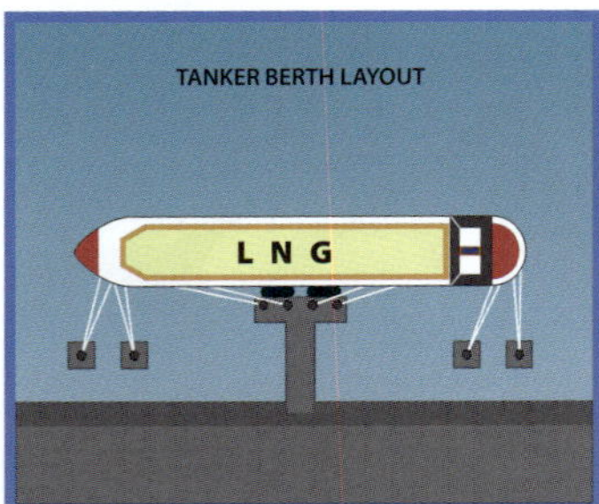

It is important to understand the difference between the role of spring lines and breast lines. Spring lines restrain the ship in the fore and aft directions. Breast lines restrain in only one direction, ie holding the ship on the berth. Breast lines remain under strain throughout the period alongside the berth. Only the fore or aft springs will be under strain at any time, depending on the direction of tide or current.

For this reason the method of line-tending differs between spring and breast lines.

Soft and Stiff Mooring Lines

Wire mooring lines are 'stiff' moorings which allow relatively little movement of the moored vessel under load. This is an advantage on certain ship types where cargo operations require minimal vessel motion alongside. However, wire lines are more difficult to tend than synthetic mooring lines and respond poorly to conditions that change quickly.

Moorings that utilise synthetic lines (ie nylon, polypropylene, or polyester) are 'soft' moorings which allow movement of the moored vessel under load. Synthetic lines are easier to handle than wire lines. Also, any increase in loading due to conditions that change quickly can be accommodated with synthetic lines unlike wire mooring lines.

Wire moorings fitted with 10 to 15 metres of synthetic rope tails are easier to handle than wire lines alone. Furthermore, these tails give added elasticity to wire lines, which may provide for a more favourable response to dynamic loads.

Load on the Mooring Pattern

The overall mooring pattern affects the load distribution on the respective lines. The effectiveness of a mooring line is influenced by its slope (ie the vertical angle formed by the angle where the mooring line meets the mooring point ashore and the horizontal line at the mooring point).

The steeper the angle of the mooring line, the less effective it is in resisting horizontal loads. The following guidelines can be used to help maximise the load capability of a specific mooring arrangement.

Line Lead Angle

- Mooring lines, both fore and aft, should be arranged as symmetrically as possible about the midpoint to ensure even load distribution
- breast lines should be positioned perpendicular to the ship's fore and aft centreline
- line lead is best if the angle is as shallow as possible, and preferably no more than 45°
    a) a 45° line angle equates to a 70% efficiency for breasting force (perpendicular to berth)
    b) a 30° line angle equates to an 87% efficiency for breasting force
- spring lines should be led at as shallow an angle as possible to the ship's fore and aft line
- the slope of all mooring lines should be kept as small as possible.

Balancing the Mooring Load

- Achieving a balanced load in all mooring lines is the most important factor in stability of the mooring pattern
- a 15 metre line will stretch half as much as a 30 metre line under the same load. As the total stretch of a line varies with its length, the shorter lines will assume greater loads and will quickly become overloaded during conditions that apply rapid loads on the mooring, such as changes in weather or tide
- do not mix lines of different materials and construction
- if using short and long mooring lines in the same direction, the shorter lines will be absorbing most of the load.

Safety Considerations when Handling Mooring Ropes and Wires

Mooring ropes are made of synthetic material and have a lot of inherent elasticity. When 4 to 6 turns are on the drum end, they may slip and sustain friction heat damage.

Always hold ropes being heaved from the underside with the palm facing upwards. If the rope jumps, the hand will then be out of the way.

Do not pass ropes and wires from the same lead.

Mooring Safety

Typical Mooring Arrangements

Suggested Arrangement for Vessels less than 10,000 tons Dwt:
Forward - 3 spring lines, 2 breast lines
Aft - 3 spring lines, 2 breast lines

Suggested Arrangement for Vessels less than 20,000 tons Dwt:
Forward - 3 spring lines, 2 breast lines, 2 head lines
Aft - 3 spring lines, 2 breast lines, 2 stern lines

Suggested Arrangement for Vessels less than 30,000 tons Dwt:
Forward - 3 spring lines, 3 breast lines, 2 head lines
Aft - 3 spring lines, 3 breast lines, 2 stern lines

Suggested Arrangement for Vessels 30,000 tons Dwt and greater:
Forward - 3 spring lines, 3 breast lines, 3 head lines
Aft - 3 spring lines, 3 breast lines, 3 stern lines

Wire Moorings for Large Tankers

The following are the minimum wire mooring line requirements for all tankers over 75,000 tons deadweight.

Vessel's Size Tonnes Kdwt	Minimum Wires Required	No. of Wires Recommended
75 – 160	8	12
161 – 250	10	12
251 – 300	12	14
301 – 350	12	16
351 – and above	14	16

Types of Mooring Lines

Synthetic fibre lines are manufactured from polypropylene, nylon, etc. They offer a high load/diameter ratio, are relatively light and are easier to maintain. Their lifetime is relatively long.

Steel wires are stiff, have high load/diameter ratios and low elongation. Their lifetime is long.

Combi-lines are a combination of steel wires with synthetic tails. The tails should not be longer than 15 m. Because of the synthetic tails, these lines offer excellent shock absorption. They are frequently used for the mooring of large tankers.

If tails are used on wire mooring lines, the same size and type of tail should be used on all lines run out in the same service. Synthetic tails are often used on the ends of wire mooring lines to permit easier handling and to increase line elasticity. The addition of a 10 m nylon tail, for instance, increases line elasticity of a 45 m long wire line 5 to 6 fold.

Types of Mooring Lines used for Various Ship Types

- Coasters, which operate on domestic or short sea routes, are typically less than 10,000 Dwt, and are generally moored with polypropylene lines
- general cargo ships, from 5,000 to 10,000 Dwt, are typically moored with polypropylene lines. Larger cargo ships are generally equipped with nylon lines and/or steel wires
- large tankers are generally moored with steel wires and steel wires with nylon tails
- bulk carriers typically use synthetic lines with steel spring lines
- container ships are generally moored with steel spring lines and with polypropylene mooring lines.

Mooring to Buoys (General)

Where mooring to buoys is undertaken from a ship's launch or boat, personnel engaged in the operation should wear lifejackets. A lifebuoy with a lifeline attached should be readily available in the boat.

Means should be provided to enable a person who has fallen into the water to climb back on board the launch or boat. If a boarding ladder with flexible sides is used, it should be weighted so that the lower rungs remain below the surface of the water.

Where mooring to buoys is undertaken from the ship, a lifebuoy with attached line of sufficient length should be available for immediate use.

When slip wires are used for mooring to buoys or dolphins, the eyes of the wires should never be put over the bitts, as at the time of unmooring it may not be possible to release the load sufficiently to lift the eye clear. To prevent accidental slippage of the wire eye(s) over the bitts or other obstruction, the eyes should be seized, partially closing the eye.

Split Drums

Introduction

Split mooring drums are normally only used for wire mooring ropes, which are found on larger ship types. The brake holding capacity for a split drum winch is always calculated based on the first layer on the tension drum. If more than one layer is wound onto the drum, a substantial loss of brake holding power will result.

The following diagrams show the correct direction of feed for a mooring winch and a typical arrangement of a split mooring winch drum.

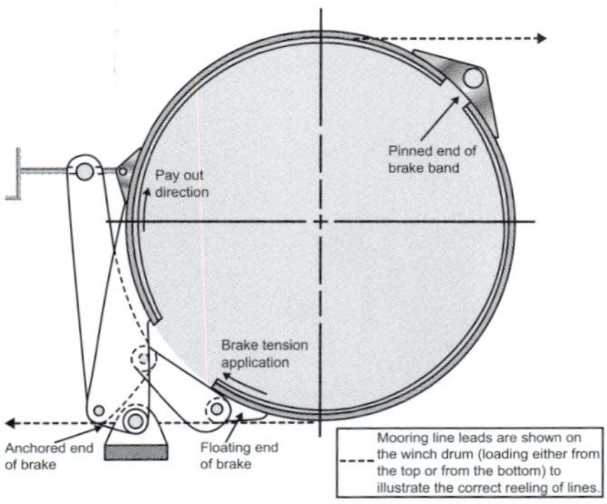

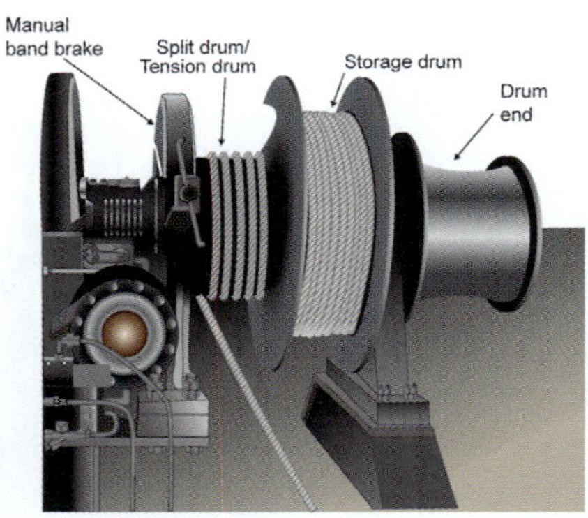

Split Drum

The split drum or tension drum is a drum that is separated from the main storage drum by a notch in the drum flange between the split drum and the storage drum.

For effective operation, the split drum operates with only one row of mooring wire (typically 5x turns) on the split drum and will provide a constant, high brake holding power.

Operation

The mooring wire from the split drum is sent ashore, paying out from the storage drum.

Once the line is made fast, the line is heaved in on the storage drum until it comes near taut. It is then immediately slacked out, until between 3 and 4 rotations of the main storage drum are made, leaving the split or notch in the drum flange at either the 5 o'clock or 7 o'clock position (depending on P or S side alongside). Then the winch is stopped with the mooring wire slack. At this point, an AB with a robust open hook approaches about 1 metre down from the drum flange, and pulls the mooring wire to guide it into the split or notch in the drum flange. At this point, the mooring wire is brought up light and should leave about 5 turns on the split drum.

Figure 10.3 - Pulling hook for mooring wires

The maximum tension for the highest loaded line during the mooring operation should be less than the holding load for the winch. The approximate mooring winch size for variable ship sizes is seen from Table 10.1 below.

Number of winches	Nominal size (tonnes)	Drum load kN	Holding load kN	Design rope dia mm	Min breaking strength of rope kN	Approximate ship size range. Tons deadweight	
						Conventional ships. Tankers, bulk carriers etc	Special ships with large wind area. Container, Ro-Ro, Passenger etc
4	12	120	310	26	378	8,000	5,000
4	16	160	470	32	573	15,000	8,000
6	16	160	470	32	572	25,000	12,000
6	20	200	590	36	725	35,000	20,000
6	25	250	730	40	895	50,000	30,000
6	32	315	880	44	1,080	65,000	45,000
6	40	400	1,050	48	1,290	80,000	60,000
6	50	500	1,280	51	1,590	110,000	85,000
6	64	640	1,560	57	1,980	150,000	120,000
6	80	800	1,940	64	2,420	210,000	
6	100	1,000	2,430	77	3,400	300,000	

Table 10.1- ISO Mooring winch size and approximate ship size

Correct Layering

Split drum winches minimise crushing damage and are normally only used with wires. The brake holding capacity for these winches is always quoted for only a single layer of wire on the tension drum.

The number of layers of line on the drum affects the brake holding power.

The force at which the brake will slip will vary, depending on the number of layers of wire left on the drum. The more layers of wire on the drum, the greater the reduction of brake holding power, ie with only 4 turns on the split drum, the brake holding power required is 20% less than that required for one turn on the split drum.

On split drum winches, the number of layers of wire on the split drum should never result in a second layer of wire on the drum, as this would crush the wire beneath in the first layer.

A split drum winch should always keep a minimum of 8 wraps of wire rope on the main storage drum at all times. This is to ensure that the connecting point of the rope to the winch does not experience any load.

A correctly set up split drum will have only around 4 or 5 turns on the smaller drum and the remainder of the rope on the larger drum.

The mooring line must be reeled on the winch drum in the correct direction, and winch drums should be marked to indicate the correct reeling direction. Winches fitted with a disc brake are not subject to this problem. Brake bands are designed for the mooring line to pull directly against the fixed end of the brake band, tending to tighten the floating end of the brake. Reeling in the wrong direction can reduce the brake holding power by up to 50%.

Figure 10.4 - Split drum winch

Brakes must be tightened appropriately to achieve the designed holding capacity. The use of hydraulic brake applicators or a torque wrench showing the degree of torque applied is desirable. *(Ref: ISGOTT Section 3.5.5)*

Oil, moisture or rust on brake linings can reduce the brake holding power by up to 75%.

Brake holding power should be tested annually, or after excessive loading has been experienced. Brakes should have a brake holding power of about 60 to 80% of the breaking load of the mooring wire or rope, permitting slippage before the wire or rope breaks.

Mooring Line Failure (Case Studies)

Snap Back Fractures Leg

21st March 2004

At 10:30, a RoRo cargo vessel was mooring on her usual berth in London, stemming a strong flood tide, with an offshore wind of about 25 knots, with occasional stronger gusts. The Master was holding the vessel alongside using the main engine and two forward bow thrusters, while the crew fore and aft passed the lines ashore. The crew forward struggled to get a heaving line ashore, but managed to get two head lines ashore. Then, a sudden strong gust of wind caught the vessel, causing a lot of weight to come onto the two head lines. The Bosun ordered the A/B on each winch to slacken back. However, while the A/B on the port winch heard the order and slackened his rope, the A/B on the starboard winch did not hear the order due to the wind noise. The rope on his winch parted with such force that it struck the Bosun, fracturing his right leg.

Fatal Accident in Snap Back Zone

7th August 2007

At 22:14, a ferry was unberthing from her normal berth in Dublin in calm conditions. While letting go aft, the winch operator on the stern line heaved in instead of slacking back. The stern line parted and snapped back, striking the Second Officer, who was

Mooring Line Failure (Case Studies)

stood in the snap-back zone near the fairlead. Both his legs were broken and the left leg was almost severed. The recoil of the line ashore also dislocated a shore linesman's shoulder and elbow. The Second Officer was evacuated to hospital, where his left leg had to be amputated. He remained in a critical condition and died 6 days later. Analysis of the mooring line after the accident showed it had deteriorated due to exposure to UV radiation from sunlight, reducing its breaking load from 60 to 35 tonnes.

Bollard Pulled Out of Quay

22nd February 2008

Divers attended a large ferry to remove mooring lines that had fouled the bow thrusters while berthing in Newcastle. The divers boarded at 10:12 and requested the bow thrusters and engines be isolated, but no formal checklist was completed. At around 13:30, the wind increased to >40 knots. This caused the vessel's mix of polyamide/polypropylene mooring lines to stretch. The mooring load now became concentrated on the forward breast lines and at 13:34 the shore bollard was pulled out of the quay. The remaining forward mooring ropes parted as the bow swung to port. At this time, the diving supervisor instructed the diver in the water to swim ashore. The diver surfaced, entangled in the trailing mooring ropes. The starboard anchor was released to check the ferry's movement, just missing the diver. However, the ferry's swing was not checked and the mooring lines aft parted. The port anchor was also let go but contact with an oil rig under repair across the dock could not be avoided. The ferry landed heavily on the opposite berth and was out of service for 10 days for repairs.

Snap Back Causes Fatality

6th July 2008

A cruise ship was moored alongside in Alaska at high tide, with an ebbing tide and a 25 knot wind gusting to 35. Four hours after berthing, the Chief Officer went out to check the moorings, which had been checked one hour before. During the check, a synthetic line snapped back, striking the officer on the head and neck. He later died. It is believed that slackened lines, caused by an outgoing tide and strong winds, created powerful surges and heavy strains on the nylon mooring lines which caused them to part. In addition, the mooring lines, which were led at a severe angle to the shore, were chafing as they passed through the fairlead.

Parted Mooring Line Causes Fatality

23rd August 2009

At about 11:30, a dumb steel lighter was berthing in Hong Kong with the assistance of a tugboat. A crew member from the lighter, who was ashore waiting to catch the mooring ropes, was hit by the snapping of parted mooring rope from the bow of a vessel on the adjacent berth. He later died in hospital.

Mooring Wire Parting

27th January 2011

A vessel was moored at Richmond Long Wharf in calm seas with no swell. At 18:35, the deck watch reported that one of the stern lines was lying slack in the water with the rope tail left on the bitts ashore. The parted line was examined and it was found that the wire had parted at the eye. The tail rope and Tonsberg shackle were found to be in good order. The weather was calm and there was no undue strain on the wire eye. This suggested closer examination of the ship's planned maintenance. It was discovered that, while high pressure greasing was applied to the wire, it was not applied to the eye of the wire due to its awkward nature. After this incident, the company changed its maintenance policy regarding mooring wires, such that all mooring wire eyes are cropped and renewed at every drydocking.

Fatal Crush Injury from Mooring Line

In 2006, a 15,000 Dwt vessel ship was unmooring and had singled up to one head line and back spring forward with a tug fast on the starboard quarter. The bridge requested *'let go everything forward'*. It was confirmed as let go but not clear. As the ship moved off the berth, an AB who was standing in the bight of the spring line suffered a fatal crush injury as the line immediately tightened when it snagged on an underwater obstruction on the jetty. The line moved up to his waist and he was dragged around the mooring bitts and to the ship's side fairlead.

CHAPTER 11

Waterways, River Transits and Canals

Transit of a Narrow Channel

Ship Handling and Squat

Ship handling in a narrow channel requires a full appreciation of the available searoom, excellent situational awareness and a good working relationship between all members of the bridge team.

As a deep draught ship transits a shallow channel, it experiences squat (ie sinkage). The hull compresses water under the hull, forcing a faster flow towards the stern. The ship creates a low pressure zone under its hull, creating squat. The faster a ship moves, the deeper it sinks.

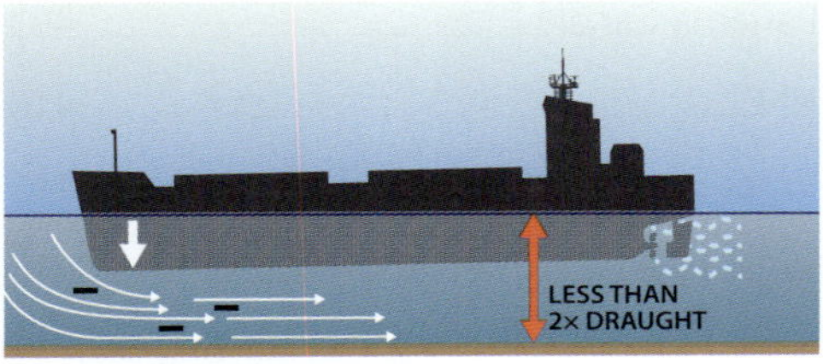

Figure 11.1 - Squat in shallow water

Bank Effect

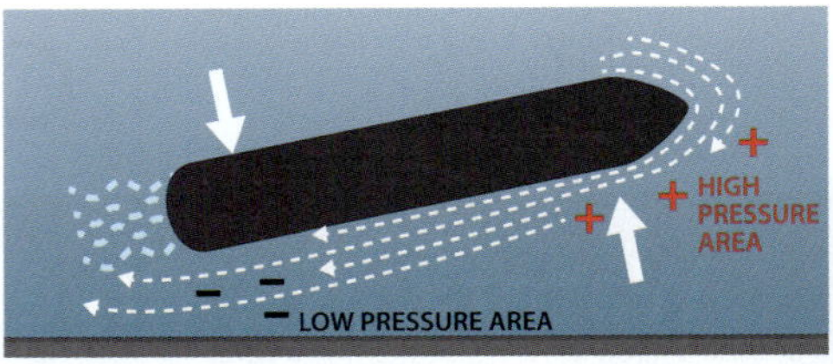

Figure 11.2 - Bank effect

The hull compresses water against the banks, creating a low pressure area that draws the stern of the ship towards the bank. The bow wave at the front of the ship tends to push the bow away from the bank, towards the centre of the channel.

Keeping the ship in the middle of the channel ensures the forces acting on the ship balance and assist in maintaining the course, but other traffic, local rules and the Collision Regulations often prevent this.

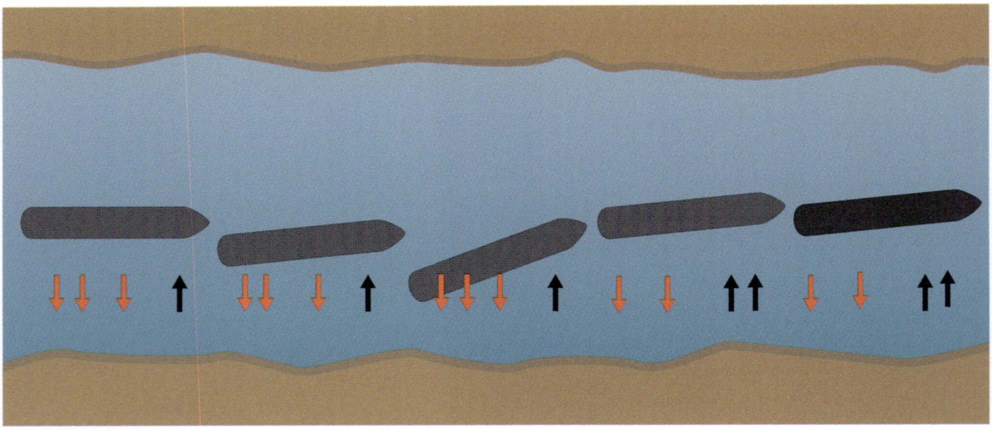

Figure 11.3 - Bank effect

Interaction between Vessels

Ships that pass one another in narrow channels experience interaction due to their close proximity. When passing, the relative speed between the two vessels will determine the effect experienced. The MCA Marine Guidance Note 199, 'Dangers of Interaction', provides the following guidance:

When vessels intend to pass in a narrow channel, whether on the same or opposing courses, it is important that the passing is carried out at a low speed. The speed should be sufficient to maintain control adequately but below maximum for the depth of water so that, in an emergency, extra power is available to aid the rudder if necessary. If a reduction in speed is required, it should be made in good time before the effects of interaction are felt. A low speed will lessen the increase in draught due to squat as well as the sinkage and change of trim caused by interaction itself. Depending on the dimensions of both the vessel and the channel,

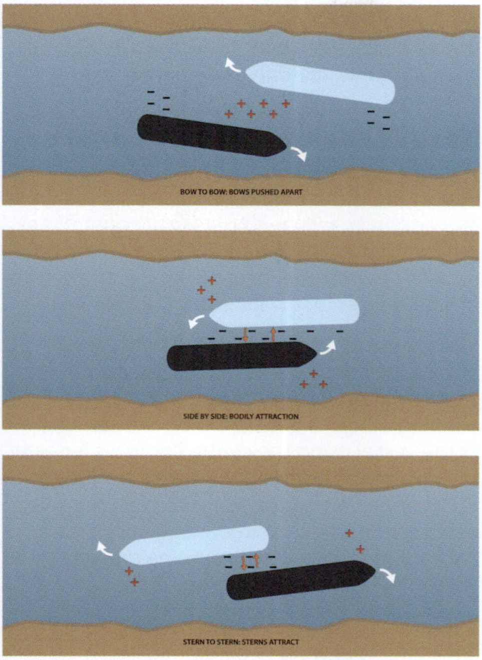

Figure 11.4 Ships meeting

speed may have to be restricted. When vessels are approaching each other at this limiting speed, interaction effects will be magnified, and therefore a further reduction in speed may be necessary. Those in charge of handling of small vessels should appreciate that more action may be required on their part when passing large vessels which may be severely limited in the action they can take in a narrow channel. Regardless of the relative size of the vessels, an overtaking vessel should only commence an overtaking manoeuvre after the vessel to be overtaken has agreed to the manoeuvre.

MGN 199, Dangers of Interaction
http://tinyurl.com/qyx7zes

Overtaking

Overtaking in a narrow channel must be done with great care. After the ship to be overtaken has agreed to be passed, she should provide as much room on the proposed side as navigational circumstances permit and slow as much as steerageway considerations permit to reduce the time required to complete the manoeuvre. The overtaking vessel should pass at moderate speed, minimising the time alongside and giving the overtaken ship as much space as possible. Some attraction between the ships should be anticipated. The closer the passage and the higher the speed, the greater will be the effect.

The reason the collision regulations require agreement from the ship being passed is that the ship being overtaken is most likely to encounter a problem during the manoeuvre. No ship should agree to being passed until they are comfortable with the conditions. It is always worth considering the merits of having the overtaking ship wait for more room for passing, or perhaps not passing at all.

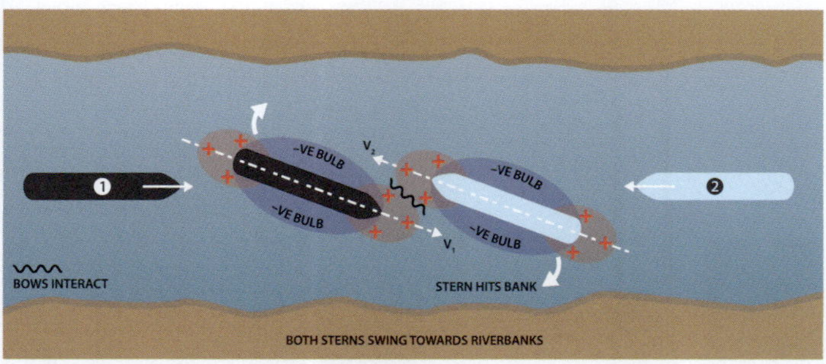

Figure 11.5 - Interaction in narrow channel

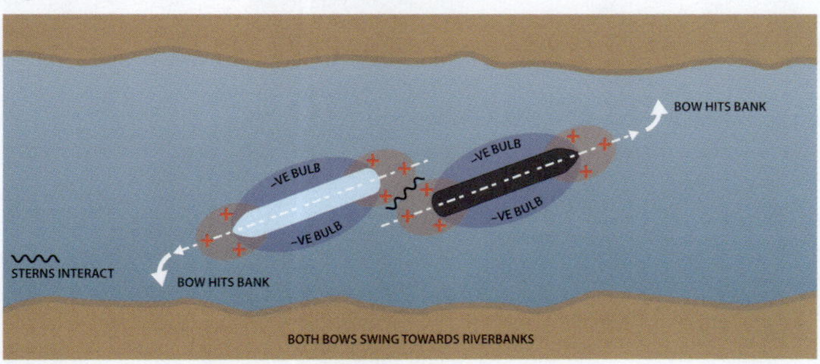

Figure 11.6 - Interaction in narrow channel

Transit of a Narrow Channel

Making Alterations

When navigating narrow channels, it is vital that the effects of forces acting on the ship are understood and the ship handler knows when to apply the correct amount of rudder, how to adjust steering and effectively con the vessel.

When altering course, it is essential to know when to start the turn and the amount of rudder required. Applying a small amount of rudder a little early is easier to correct than waiting until the last second then applying full rudder. If the turn is made too early, it is generally better to reduce the amount of helm than to stop the turn completely.

If the turn is made late and it is unlikely the turn can be tightened by helm alone, it may be necessary to use the engines. Provided the ship is not already at full ahead, a single-screw ship may increase the rate of turn by giving the engines a kick ahead to increase the water flow past the rudder. Alternatively, a twin-screw ship may be able to reverse the engines on the inboard side to significantly tighten the turn.

By proceeding along the channel at a reduced speed, the option of briefly increasing engines is retained to improve rudder responsiveness with little or no increase in speed. Similarly, when proceeding at slow speeds, typically less than 7 knots, ships with bow thrusters can take advantage of their effects where necessary.

Navigationally Restricted Areas

Where it is necessary to pass through very narrow areas of a channel, the ship's heading and approach will need to take account of any prevailing wind or current. Where there is no current or wind, the ideal position is the centre of, and on a course parallel to, the channel.

Making use of a transit, leading lights and/or parallel indexing techniques assists in maintaining the correct approach. If the conning officer is positioned on the centreline of the vessel using the centre compass repeater, the apparent movement of the extremities of the channel (eg bridge spans) can be observed moving to port and starboard against their backgrounds. If they appear to be moving aft at an even rate, the ship is in the centre and will pass midway between the points.

If the effects of wind or current are setting the ship off track, the heading must be corrected. A potential problem of this is the effective increased width of the ship relative to the channel. It is essential that any increased width is accounted for when making the approach and it would be sensible to stay slightly up-current or up-wind of the centre.

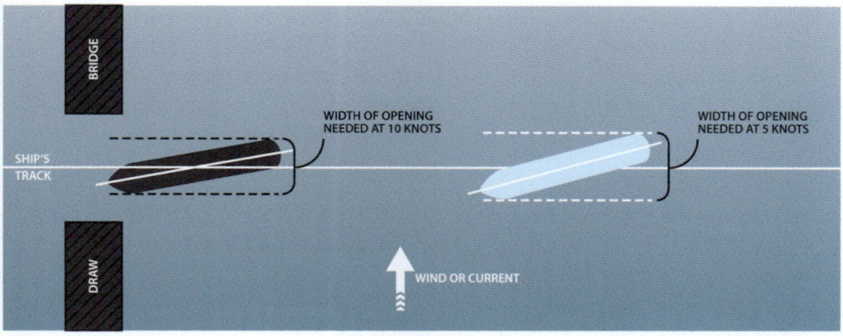

Figure 11.7 - Cross channel set in a narrow channel

Current in Narrow Channels

It is common to experience current in a narrow channel. In some areas, the currents may be very strong with restrictions being imposed on ships transiting particular passages. Areas such as the Kanmon Kaikyo that joins the Japan Inland Sea to the Korea Strait can experience currents in excess of 9 knots. Local regulations impose restrictions on the number and size of ships that can pass at specific times of day, with consideration given to tidal and weather conditions.

Figure 11.8 - Kanmonkyo Bridge, Kanmon Kaikyo, Japan

Currents are normally either tidal or produced by rivers and they generally follow the direction of the channel. Currents flowing towards the ship, known as head currents, are safer as the flow of water assists steerage and slows the ship's speed over the ground.

Currents flowing with the ship are known as stern, fair or flowing currents. Fair currents affect the ship's responsiveness and make the deployment of an anchor in an emergency extremely difficult and dangerous as the ship will swing round with the current. Remaining within the centre of the channel will help carry the ship within the current, but speed will need to be monitored carefully to minimise speed over the ground without loss of helm.

Planning and Preparations

It is important that a ship is properly prepared for navigating in narrow channels, with allowances made for realistic UKC, the effects of squat and interaction with other ships or the channel.

Planning should include:

- Ensuring a safe speed
- identifying alteration points
- identifying reporting requirements
- establishing primary and secondary position fixing/monitoring requirements
- determining tidal changes and requirements
- contingency planning.

When navigating in restricted channel areas, all appropriate navigational aids should be used, including visual means, radar and the echo sounder. Communications with other vessels should be kept to a minimum, ensuring any agreements are fully understood and actions carefully monitored.

Narrow channels and fairways may fall within a traffic separation scheme (TSS) or vessel traffic service (VTS) with additional requirements, and vessels may be required to maintain a listening watch on an appropriate VHF channel in addition to the ship's AIS transmissions.

International Collision Regulations Rule No. 9 (COLREGs)

(a) *A vessel proceeding along the course of a narrow channel or fairway shall keep as near to the outer limit of the channel or fairway which lies on her starboard side as is safe and practicable.*

(b) *A vessel of less than 20 metres in length or a sailing vessel shall not impede the passage of a vessel which can safely navigate only within a narrow channel or fairway.*

Transit of a Narrow Channel

(c) A vessel engaged in fishing shall not impede the passage of any other vessel navigating within a narrow channel or fairway.

(d) A vessel shall not cross a narrow channel or fairway if such crossing impedes the passage of a vessel which can safely navigate only within such channel or fairway. The latter vessel may use the sound signal prescribed in Rule 34(d) if in doubt as to the intention of the crossing vessel.

(e) (i) In a narrow channel or fairway when overtaking can take place only if the vessel to be overtaken has to take action to permit safe passing, the vessel intending to overtake shall indicate her intention by sounding the appropriate signal prescribed in Rule 34(c)(i). The vessel to be overtaken shall, if in agreement, sound the appropriate signal prescribed in Rule 34(c)(ii) and take steps to permit safe passing. If in doubt she may sound the signals prescribed in Rule 34(d).

(ii) This Rule does not relieve the overtaking vessel of her obligation under Rule 13.

(f) A vessel nearing a bend or an area of narrow channel or fairway where other vessels may be obscured by an intervening obstruction shall navigate with particular alertness and caution and shall sound the appropriate signal prescribed in Rule 34(e).

(g) Any vessel shall, if the circumstances of the case admit, avoid anchoring in a narrow channel.

Locks

A lock is used to transfer a vessel up or down between water levels. Locks are commonly used to maintain a constant water level in docks that would otherwise be tidal, or for canals to overcome variations in topographical height.

Locks are operated as follows.

The water in the lock is lowered to the lowest level by opening a valve in the lower gate.

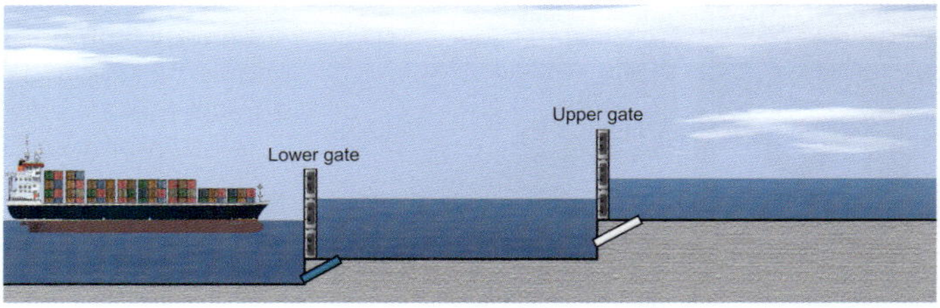

Once the water levels have equalised, the lock gates can be opened and the vessel can enter the lock. The lower gate and valve can then be closed and the valve in the upper gate opened.

This allows water to flow from the upper level into the lock. When the water levels have equalised, the gates can be opened and the vessel can proceed.

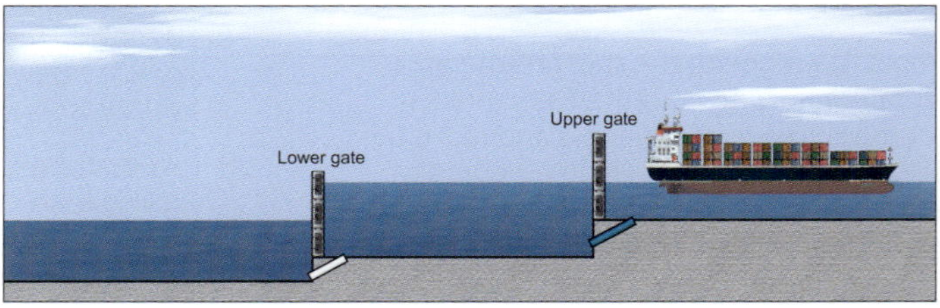

Locks

Figure 11.9 - Container ship transiting locks in Panama during a tropical downpour

Tugs may be used to align the ship for entry and she may be held steady in the lock using mooring lines secured to the shore. In the Panama Canal, mules (locomotives) are used to manoeuvre the ship while in the locks.

Lock Gates

There are various types of lock gates, but the mitre-type is most commonly used. This consists of two gates, normally constructed of steel, that meet at an angle, with the apex directed upstream, to ensure the water pressure acts to keep the doors closed. This angle also prevents the gates being opened until the levels on either side of the gate have equalised.

Figure 11.10 - Mitre gates, Panama Canal

Smaller canals may have a single gate that also opens upstream but works on similar principles.

Figure 11.11 - Sliding gates, Kiel Canal

Panama Canal

Panama Canal Expansion

On 15th August 1914, the first official transit of the Panama Canal was made by *SS 'Ancon'*, the canal having taken 9 years to construct.

The build-up to the construction was the first occasion when the US flexed its might beyond its own borders. Panama, having gained independence from Spain in 1821, was now part of Colombia and, rather than negotiate with Bogota, US President Theodore Roosevelt chose to incite a nationalist insurrection and gave support to the Panamanian rebels fighting for independence. The Republic of Panama

Panama Canal

was born in 1903, though a slender '*Canal Zone*' was handed over to America in perpetuity.

President Roosevelt tasked William Taft (his eventual successor as president) to oversee the project. Learning from the French attempt that lasted over eight years from 1881, during which time more than 20,000 workers died (mostly due to yellow fever and malaria), Taft backed a lock-canal system and, with excellent wages on offer, there was no shortage of construction workers.

After 9 years' work and a further 5,609 deaths, the canal opened, in what was regarded as mankind's greatest achievement until the moon landings.

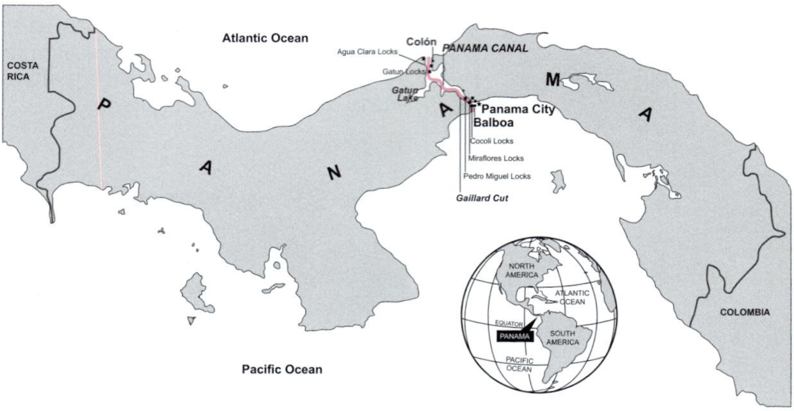

Construction Works 1903-1914

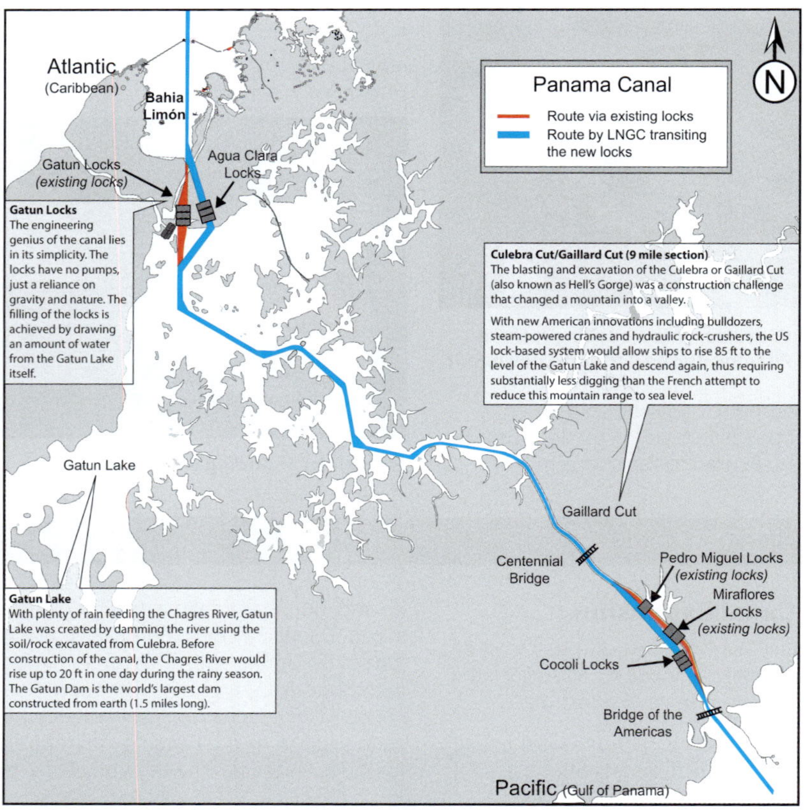

Existing Canal – Southbound Transit

Ship enters the Gatun locks on the Atlantic side. Each of the three chambers raises the ship by an average of 28 ft, lifting the ship by approximately 88 ft to the level of the Gatun Lake. It takes around 20 minutes to raise or lower the ship in each lock, typically taking 2 hours to transit the locks.

Typically, 2 to 3 locomotives (mules) will make fast on either side of the ship, using wires supplied from the locomotives. Each locomotive has the equivalent of 40 tonnes bollard pull.

After clearing the three locks at Gatun, the ship has a 24 mile transit of the Gatun Lake.

Next the ship has a 9 mile transit through the Culebra/Gaillard Cut.

The ship has to drop 28 ft from the Gatun Lake to the level of the Miraflores Lake, with a short 2 mile transit to the locks at Miraflores.

The ship has two chambers to pass through at Miraflores before she enters the Pacific Ocean.

Panama Canal

The 2007-2015 Expansion Project

With the tailing off of the Cold War, America agreed to hand over control of the canal to Panama, on 31st December 1999.

The Panama Canal Authority (ACP) estimated that the canal would reach its maximum sustainable capacity between 2009 and 2012. The only long-term solution to alleviate the congestion problems was determined to be the expansion of the canal through a third set of locks. The Panamanian President formally proposed the project on 24th April 2006, and a national referendum approved the proposal by a 76.8% majority on 22nd October 2006.

The project began on 3rd September 2007, with the third set of locks scheduled to open in early 2016.

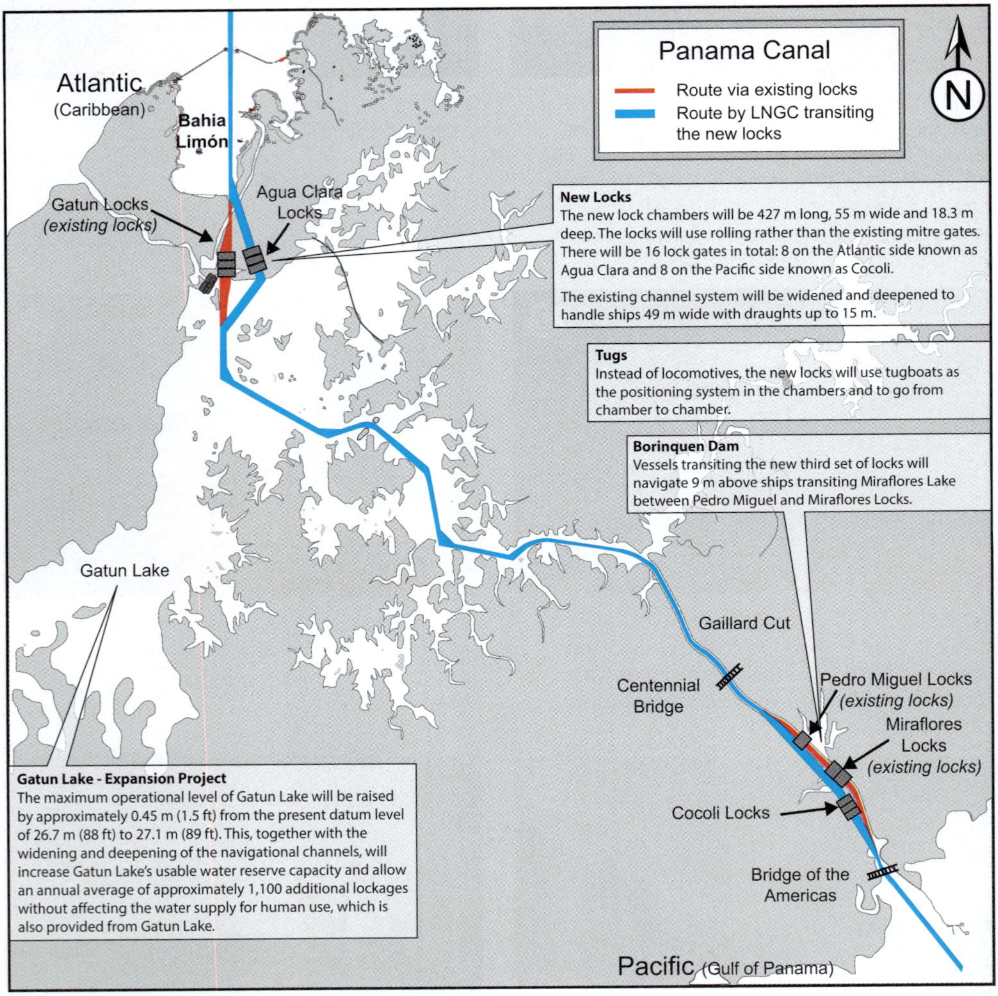

Courtesy of ACP

Panama Canal

Dimensions of the Existing and the New Locks

Maximum size of vessels (Panamax) in existing locks: 4,400 TEU

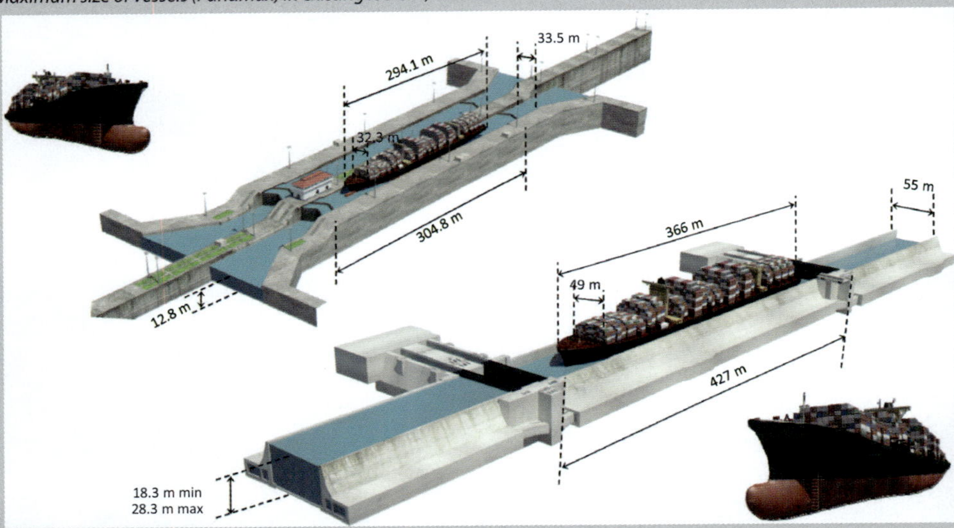

Maximum size of vessels (New Panamax) in new locks: 13,000 to 14,000 TEU

Max Dimensions: Existing Locks

	Lock Dimensions
Breadth	33.53 m (110 ft)
Length	320 m (1,050 ft)
Depth	12.56 m (41.2 ft)
	Max Ship Dimensions
Max Beam	32.30 m (106 ft)
Max Length	294.13 m (965 ft)
Max Draught	12.04 m (39 ft 06 in)

Max Dimensions: New Locks

	Lock Dimensions
Breadth	55 m (180 ft)
Length	427 m (1,400 ft)
Depth	18.3 m (60 ft)
	Max Ship Dimensions
Max Beam	49 m (160 ft)
Max Length	366 m (1,200 ft)
Max Draught	15.2 m (50 ft)

Panama Canal Cost

Original 1905-1914 = $335 million
(Adjusted for inflation, this would equal $33.7 billion today.)

2007-2014 Canal expansion
$5.2 billion, the largest cost items being the construction of the two new locks estimated at US$1.11 billion and US$1.03 billion each.

Panama Canal in Numbers

The maximum capacity of the existing canal is 37 to 42 ship transits per day.

14,000 vessels pass through the existing canal every year, and approximately 70% are headed to the US.

Once a vessel enters the first set of locks on either side of the canal, the transit time averages 9 hours.

Length of Canal - approximately 50 miles
Length of Culebra Cut - 9 miles
Length of Canal on Gatun Lake - 24 miles
Area of Gatun Lake - 64 square miles
Elevation of Gatun Lake - 85 feet above sea level
Amount of water used by one ship going through Canal - 52 million gallons (234,000 m^3)
Height of tide on Atlantic side = 3 ft
Height of tide on Pacific side = 15 to 18 ft

Panama Canal in US$

Each ship transiting the canal earns Panama approximately $50,000 on average, which, in total, makes Panama more than $1.3 billion a year (2011 figures).

The transit fee for a 2014 Panamax container ship carrying 4,500 containers is $450,000.

Container ships are billed $82 per full container, $74 for an empty one.

Cruise ships pay a surcharge of $134 per bed.

NY Times 2013

The Canal reports that last year the operating expenses of the Panama Canal were $6.5 bn, on a revenue of $8.9 bn, leaving a profit of $2.4 bn.

The ACP expects its annual transfers to the state to triple between 2005 and 2015 and perhaps to rise eightfold, to over $4 bn, by 2025.

What Next?

Nicaragua

A Chinese telecom billionaire is eyeing another route for a Central American canal - through Nicaragua.

The canal he envisages would be three times as long as the Panama Canal, would be able to handle VLCCs, and would cost $60 billion.

In July 2014, the government endorsed the route for a 173-mile potentially sea-level (and therefore lock-free) canal connecting the Pacific to the Atlantic using the Brito River, Lake Nicaragua and rivers on the Atlantic side.

Nicaragua has granted a 50-year renewable concession to the Chinese to build the canal, but this route has many sceptics.

Suez

There are ongoing works to convert the original Suez Canal into a two-lane marine highway. The ambitious Egyptian plan came in a surprise announcement by Egypt's president in August 2014.

Panama

In August 2014, the state-owned China Harbour Engineering Company said they were exploring the idea of investing in a fourth set of locks on the Panama Canal to further increase capacity.

UKC

Underkeel Clearance (UKC) refers to the distance between the keel of a vessel and the sea floor.

UKC is estimated from some or all of the following factors:

- The vessel's manoeuvring characteristics
- accuracy in the assessed vessel's draught including influence of water density and hogging or sagging
- the vessel's squat and/or settlement (related to vessel's speed)
- increase in draught due to vessel's trim
- increase in draught due to vessel's roll
- increase in draught due to vessel's pitch
- increase in draught due to vessel's heave
- accuracy in the predicted or measured tide height or mean sea level
- accuracy in the declared charted depth
- allowance for possible siltation since last survey.

UKC Allowances

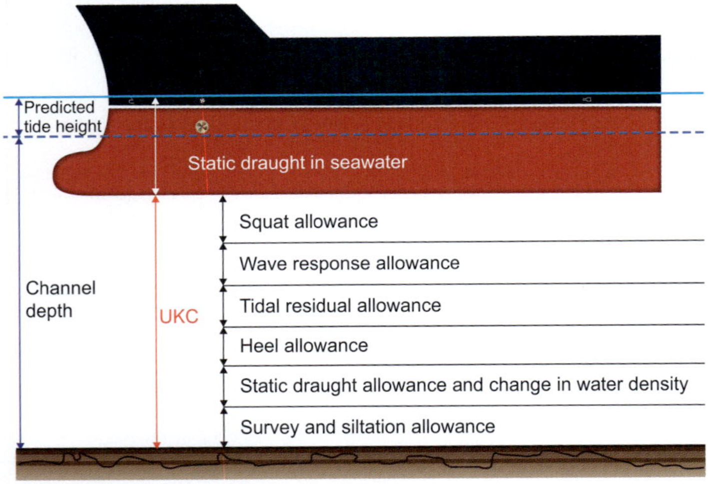

Figure 11.12 - Factor allowances associated with a Gross UKC Calculation

Wave Response Allowance

In channels subject to wave action, ships will experience heave, roll and pitch motions which combine to produce vertical displacements of the hull. The magnitude of these dynamic and irregular displacements at each point of the vessel's transit depends on many factors, including:

- Directional wave spectrum (describing wave energy distribution as a function of frequency and direction)
- ship dimensions, hull shape and stability data
- ship speed
- water depth/draught ratio.

Squat Allowance

Squat is a combination of bodily sinkage and change in trim of a vessel while sailing. The major factors affecting squat are ship form and initial trim, vessel speed through the water, vessel acceleration and deceleration, depth/draught ratio, channel width and depth of cut, abrupt depth changes, changes in fluid density, and passing and overtaking vessels.

Changes in Water Level other than Tidal

In addition to the change in water level due to predicted astronomical and seasonal effects, water levels are also affected by meteorological changes in wind speed and direction and in barometric pressure. These changes in water level represent the difference between measured and predicted water levels and are known as the tidal residuals. In certain circumstances, this difference can be substantial (of the order of 40 cm or greater).

Changes in Water Density

Changes in water density have the same effect as a change in water level in terms of draught and the resulting UKC. It is important to identify where these changes occur and by how much the density has changed.

Survey Allowance

Safety factors may include allowances such as hydrographic survey tolerance, saltation allowance and draught tolerances.

Heel Allowance

Heel causes the bilge corner to come closer to the seabed, and it must be allowed for when calculating nett UKC. During the transit, both turning and wind cause the ship to heel. Heel effects are small for bulk carriers, but significant for container ships.

A container ship with level static trim may have significant heel due to wind and turning in calm water, so the maximum dynamic draught may occur at the bilge corner.

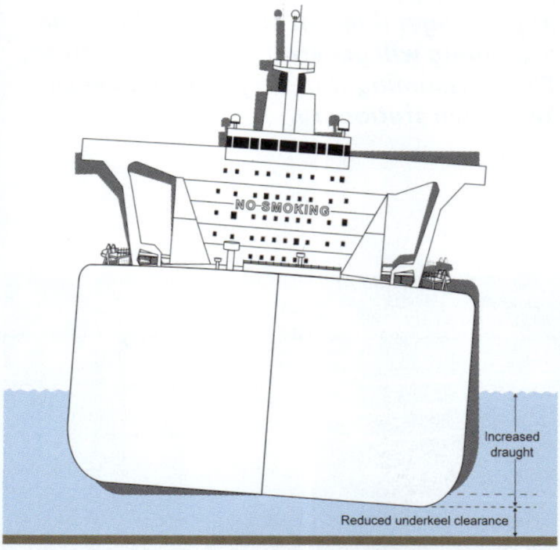

Increased draught due to heel

A ship with a 20 m draught and 58 m beam will have an increased draught at the following angles of heel:

Heel Angle	Draught
0.5°	20.25 m
1°	20.50 m
1.5°	20.75 m
2°	21.00 m

This reduced underkeel clearance is based on the following formula (for a box-shaped vessel):

Heeled draught = (½ beam × sinθ) + (upright draught × cosθ)

Figure 11.13 - Heel allowance

Minimum UKC Allowances

UKC allowances are as follows:

- Ocean passages - 20% of the deepest draught
- fairways - 15% of the deepest draught
- inside ports (A) - 10% of the deepest draught (see Note A)
- inside ports (B) - master's discretion (see Note B)
- canals - as per local navigation rules.

Note A

Inside ports (A) *refers to vessels over 50,000 tonnes summer deadweight. As a matter of principle, 10% UKC should be maintained. However, in cases where voyage orders from charterers specify a draught or cargo nomination that will result in a lesser UKC, and if there are reasonable local regulations, rules or recommendations by relevant authorities which endorse such voyage orders/nominations, the Master may use his discretion in deciding whether or not to comply with such voyage orders and/or nominations.*

In such cases the following conditions should be confirmed with the relevant authorities or terminals, as the case may be, and complied with:

(A) The Master must obtain the latest sounding chart/information for the berth, including the nature of the sea bottom, directly from the local authorities or terminals well before arrival/lightering. Should this not be possible, the Master should request guidance from the Owners/Charterers.

However the vessel must berth at discharge ports and unberth at load ports only at the time of high water.

(B) At discharge ports, commence cargo operations well before low water.

(C) The vessel must vacate the berth if in any doubt about the risk of grounding.

(D) The terminal and charterer's agent should be kept fully informed of the situation and must be prepared to assist in berth vacation if required.

(E) The Master must inform his Owners of any anticipated reduced UKC at the earliest opportunity.

Note B

Inside ports (B) *refers to vessels less than 50,000 tonnes summer deadweight. Where the vessel is required, by operational considerations, to reduce UKC below 10%, the Master must take full account of the factors listed above which govern determination of a safe UKC.*

Source: INTERTANKO Recommendation

What Exactly is Ship Squat?

Ship squat is the loss in UKC as a ship moves forward after being at rest. Squat is made up of two components: mean bodily sinkage and trim ratio forward of aft.

When a ship proceeds, she pushes water ahead of her. In order not to leave a 'hole' in the water, this volume of water must return down the sides and under the bottom of the ship. See the streamlines in Figures 11.14 and 11.15.

The streamlines of return flow are speeded up under the ship. This causes a drop in pressure, resulting in the ship dropping vertically in the water. See Figures 11.19, 11.20 and 11.21. Note the different contours of the various bows.

As well as dropping vertically, the ship generally trims forward or aft. See Figures 11.20 and 11.21. If the ship is on an even keel when static, the trimming effect depends on the ship type and the C_b. See Figure 11.19.

The overall decrease in the static UKC, forward or aft, is called ship squat. It is not the difference between the draughts when stationary and the draughts when the ship is moving ahead.

If the ship moves forward at too great a speed when she is in shallow water, say where the static even keel UKC is 1.0 to 1.5 metres, then grounding due to excessive squat could occur at the bow or at the stern.

For full-form ships, such as VLCCs or Capesize OBOs, grounding will generally occur at the bow. For fine-form vessels, such as passenger liners or container ships, the grounding will generally occur at the stern. This is assuming that they are on an even keel when stationary.

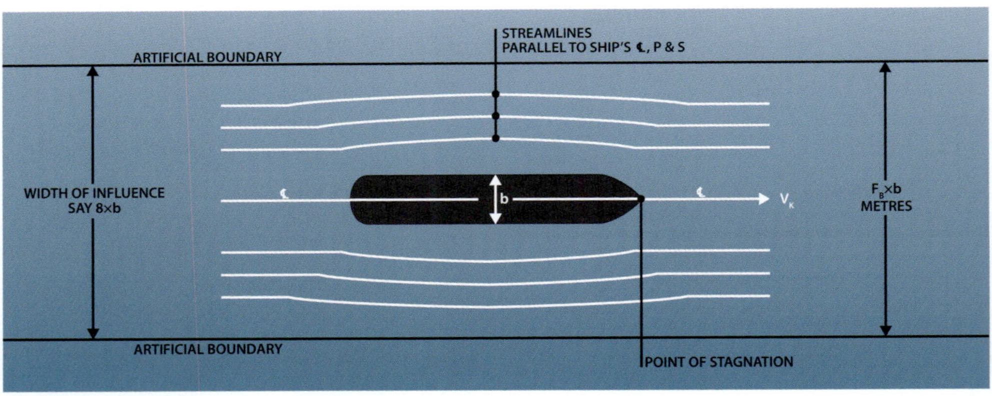

Figure 11.14 - Streamline flow around a moving vessel in open water. Vessel is of full-form contours. Lots of parallel body

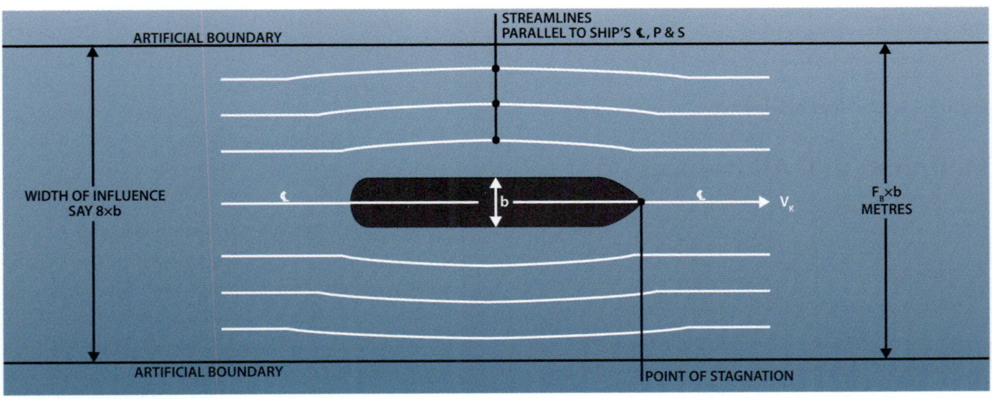

Figure 11.15 - Streamline flow around a moving vessel in open water. Vessel is of fine-form contours. No parallel body

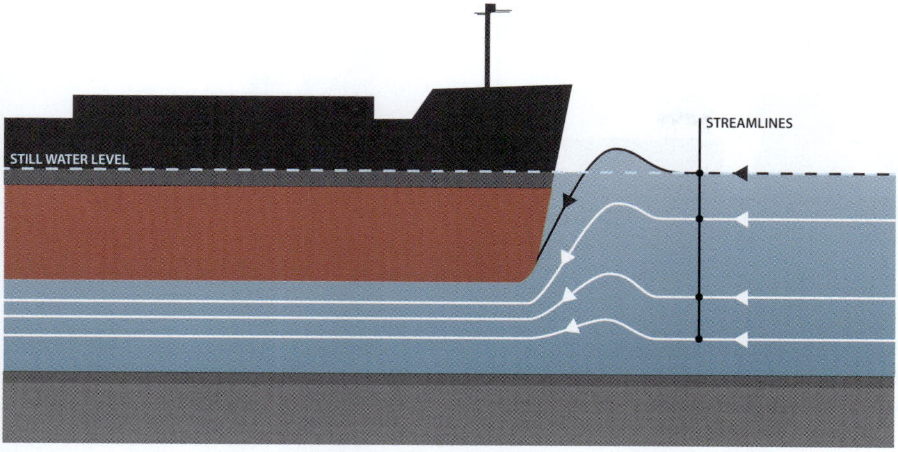

Figure 11.16 - Streamline flow around a soft-nosed bow

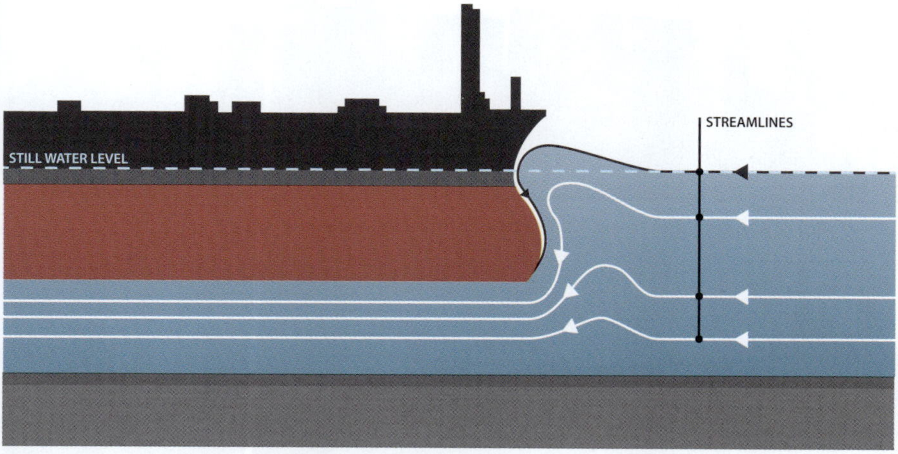

Figure 11.17 - Streamline flow around a bulbous bow

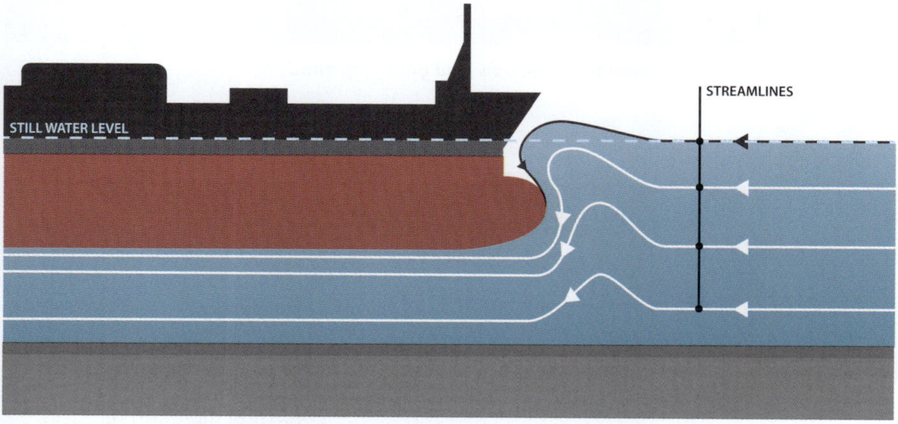

Figure 11.18 - Streamline flow around a ram-bow or cylindrical bow

What Exactly is Ship Squat?

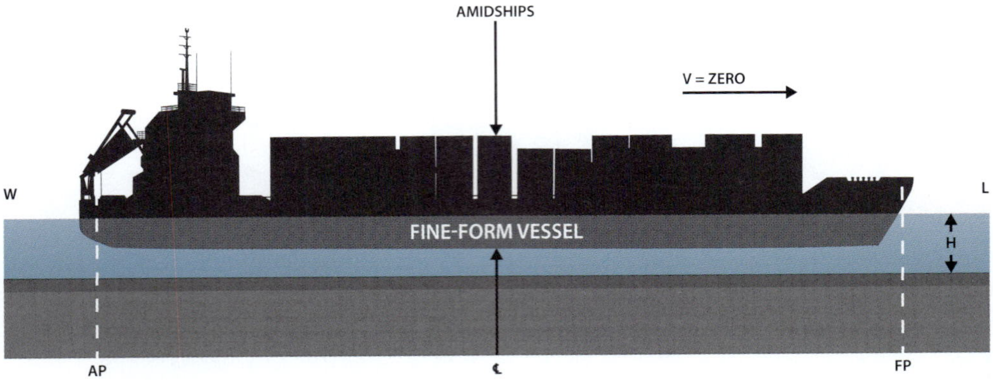

Figure 11.19 - Ship is stationary with small underkeel clearance (UKC). Ship is on an even keel

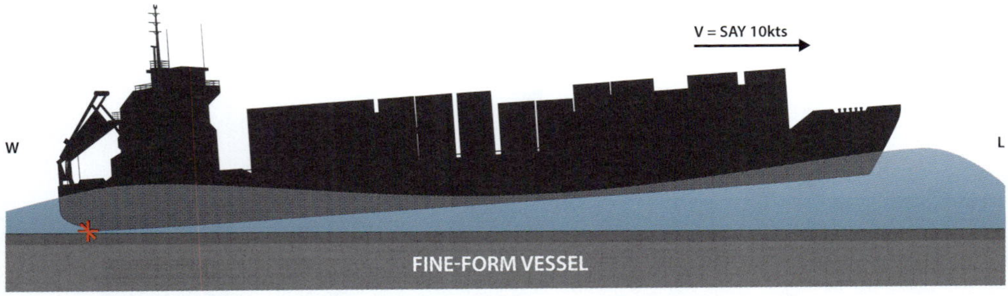

Figure 11.20 - A ship grounding due to excessive speed producing excessive squat

Figure 11.21 - Ship at speed, now trimming by the bow and going aground

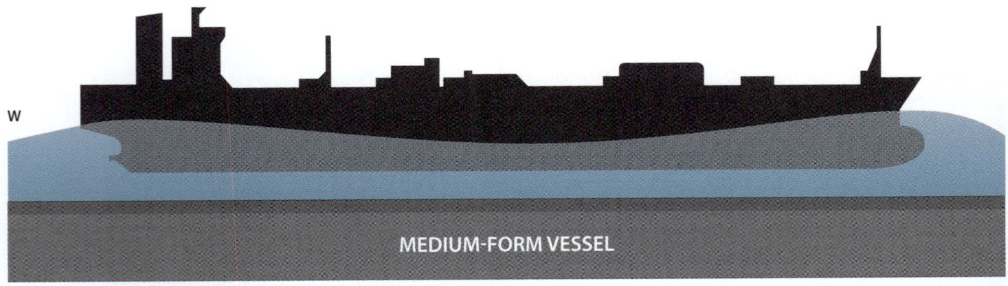

Figure 11.22 - Ship at forward speed. No trimming effects. Grounding can occur at stern, amidships and at the bow

What Exactly is Interaction?

Interaction is the resultant effect of positive and negative forces around the ship's hull when meeting another ship or obstruction.

Note: As ships have increased in size (especially in breadth moulded), it has become more important to consider interaction.

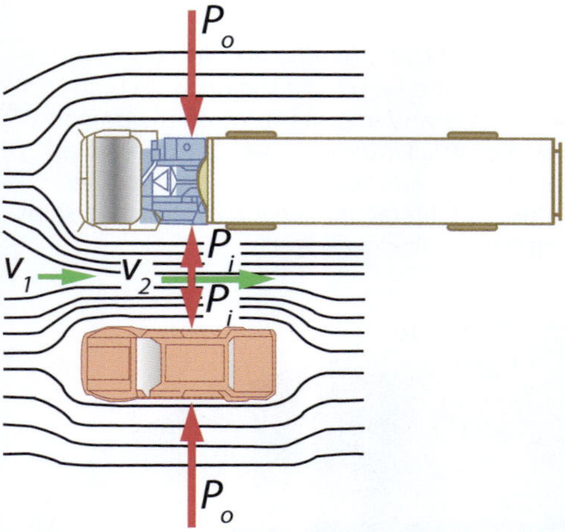

Figure 11.23a - Car passing a lorry

Another way of thinking of this phenomenon is to compare it to driving along a motorway, particularly in windy weather.

If you are in a small car overtaking a lorry, you may feel as you approach the lorry that the car is being pushed away. Once you are parallel with the lorry, you may feel that you are being sucked into it, with the sensation of being pushed away as you pass the driver's cab.

These are all similar to the interaction effects that a smaller ship would experience when overtaking or passing a larger ship in close proximity.

In February 1998, the UK Maritime and Coastguard Agency (MCA) issued a Marine Guidance Note 'Dangers of Interaction', alerting owners, masters, pilots and tug masters on this topic.

Interaction can cause one or more of the following:

- If two ships are passing or overtaking in a river, the squats of both vessels could be doubled when both amidships are directly in line
- when they are directly in line, each ship will develop an angle of heel and the smaller ship will be drawn bodily towards the larger vessel. See Figures 11.23(a) and 11.23(b)
- both ships could lose steerage efficiency and alter course without a change in rudder helm

V_1 and V_2 are ship speeds

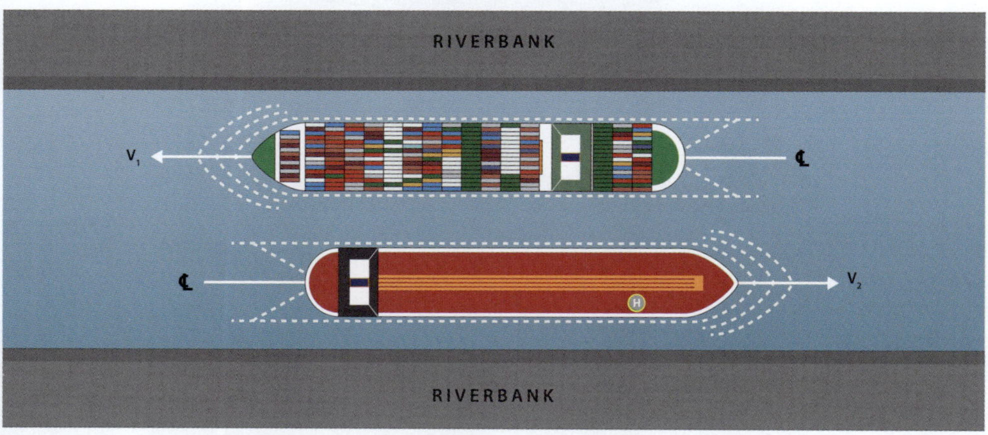

Figure 11.23b - Oil tanker passing container ship

What Exactly is Interaction?

- the smaller ship may suddenly veer off course and head into the adjacent riverbank
- the smaller ship could veer into the side of the larger ship or, worse still, be drawn across the bows of the larger vessel, bowled over and capsized.

These effects of interaction are caused by the pressure bulbs that exist around the hull form of a moving ship-model or a moving ship. Figure 11.24 shows these pressure bulbs in plan view. Figure 11.25 shows them in profile view.

As soon as a vessel moves from rest, hydrodynamics produce positive and negative pressure bulbs as illustrated. For ships with a greater parallel body, such as an oil tanker, these negative bulbs will be comparatively longer in length. When the ship is stationary in water of zero current speed, these bulbs disappear.

In Figure 11.24, note the elliptical domain that encloses the vessel and the pressure bulbs. This domain is very important. When the domain of one vessel interfaces with the domain of another, interaction effects will occur. The effects of interaction are increased when ships operate in shallow waters.

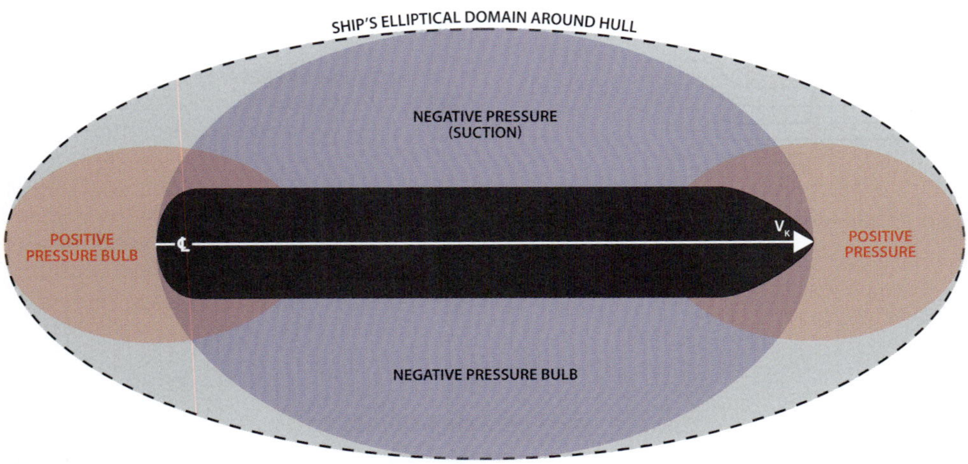

Figure 11.24 - Pressure distribution around ship's hull

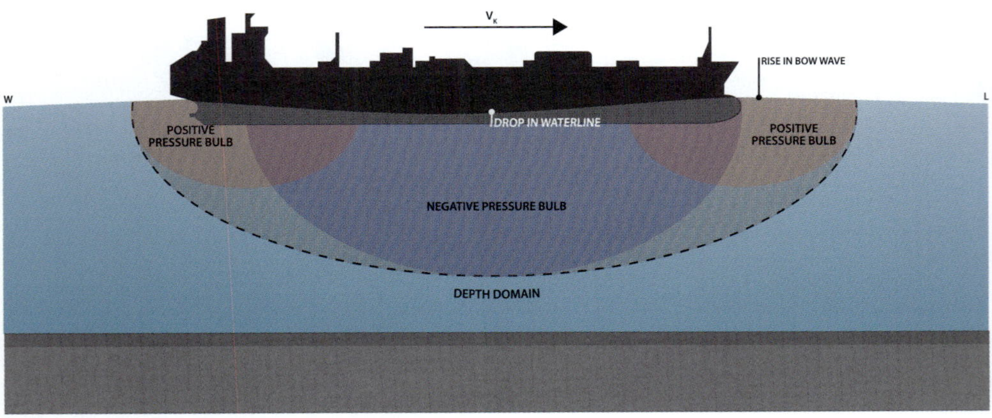

Figure 11.25 - Pressure distribution around ship's profile

Ship to Ship Interaction

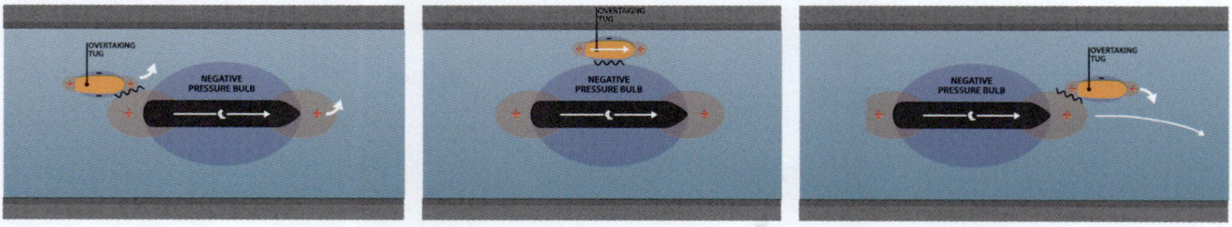

Figure 11.26 (a), (b) & (c) - Ship to ship interaction in a narrow river during an overtaking manoeuvre

Figures 11.26(a), 11.26(b) and 11.26(c) show a tug overtaking a large ship in a narrow river. Three cases have been considered:

Case 1: The tug has just come up to the aft port quarter of the ship. The domains have come into contact and interaction occurs. The positive bulb of the ship reacts with the positive bulb of the tug. Both vessels veer to port side. Rate of turn is greater on the tug. There is a definite possibility of the tug veering off into the adjacent riverbank, as shown in Figure 11.26(a).

Case 2: The tug is in danger of being drawn bodily towards the ship because the negative pressure (suction) bulbs have interfaced. See Figure 11.26(b). The bigger the differences between the two deadweights of these ships, the greater will be this transverse attraction. Each ship develops an angle of heel. There is a danger of the ship losing a bilge keel or of fracture of the bilge strakes occurring. This transverse squat results in increased loss of clearance at forward speed. Figure 11.23b shows this happening with the tanker and the container ship.

Case 3: The tug is positioned at the ship's forward port quarter. See Figure 11.26(c). The domains have come in contact via the positive pressure bulbs. Both vessels veer to the starboard side. The rate of turn is greater on the tug. There is great danger of the tug being drawn across the path of the ship's heading and bowled over.

Note how, in these three cases, it is the smaller vessel that ends up being the casualty.

Cases 4 and 5: Figures 11.27 and 11.28 provide further examples of ship to ship interaction effects in a narrow river. In Figure 11.27, there is the possibility of a stern making collision with a nearby riverbank. In the second situation, there is the possibility of a bow making contact with a nearby riverbank.

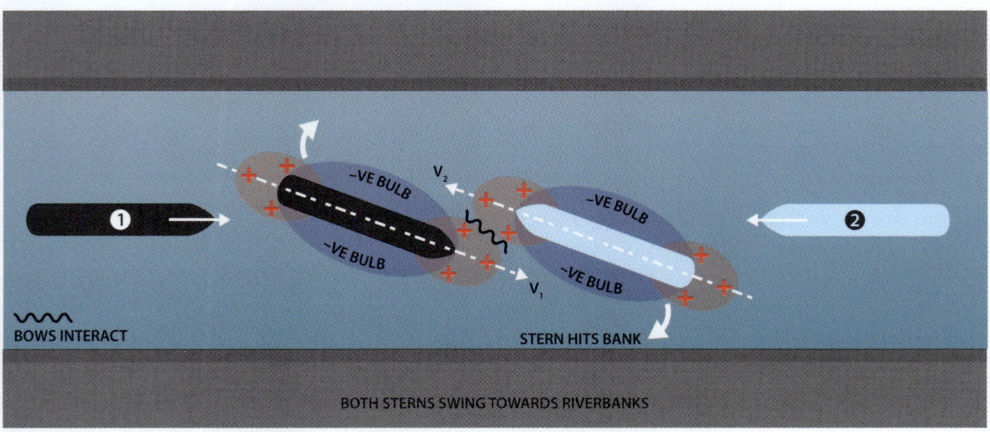

Figure 11.27 - The 'approach' situation

What Exactly is Interaction?

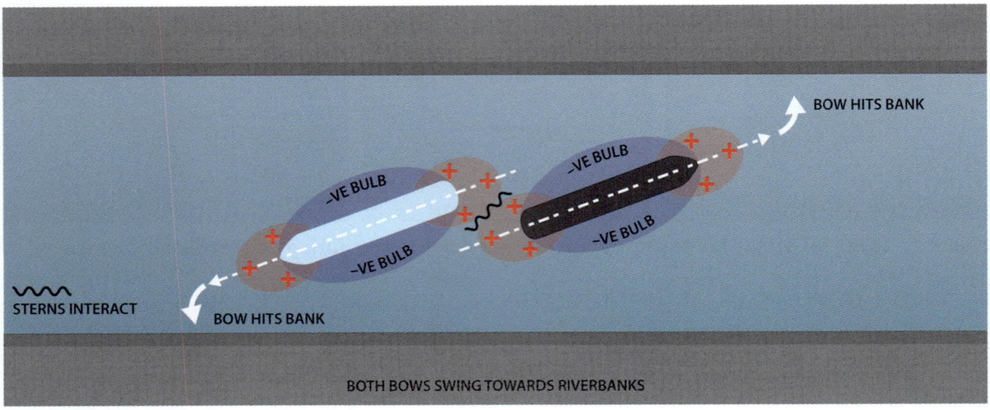

Figure 11.28 - The 'leaving' situation

Methods for Reducing the Effects of Interaction

Refer to Figures 11.26 to 11.27.

Both ships should reduce speed and then, if safe, increase speed after the meeting crossing manoeuvre time slot has passed. Resist the temptation to go for the order 'increase revs'. This is because the forces involved with interaction vary as the speed is squared. Consequently, doubling the speed quadruples the interaction forces and moments. Dangers of an accident occurring greatly increase.

Halving the ship speed would quarter these interaction forces and moments. However, too much reduction in speed produces a loss of steerage because rudder effectiveness is decreased. This effect is even more pronounced in shallow waters.

Keep the distance between the vessels as large as possible, bearing in mind the remaining gaps between each shipside and the riverbank.

Prevent the vessels from entering another ship's domain, by crossing in wider parts of the river, for example.

Cross in deeper parts of the river rather than in shallow waters, bearing in mind the increases in squat.

Make use of rudder helm. In Case 1, starboard rudder helm could be requested to counteract loss of steerage. In Case 3, port rudder helm would counteract loss of steerage.

Ship to Shore Interaction

Figures 11.29 and 11.30 show ship to shore interaction effects. Figure 11.29 shows the forward positive pressure bulb being used as a pivot to bring a ship alongside a riverbank.

Figure 11.30 shows how the positive and negative pressure bulbs have caused the ship to come alongside and then to veer away from the jetty. Interaction could, in this case, cause the stern to swing and collide with the wall of the jetty.

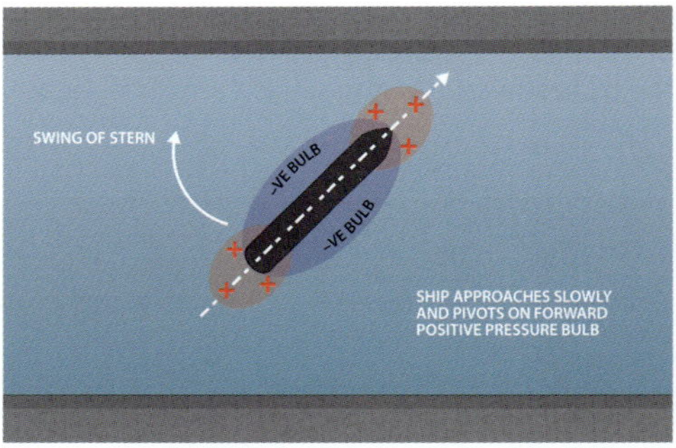

Figure 11.29 - Ship to bank interaction

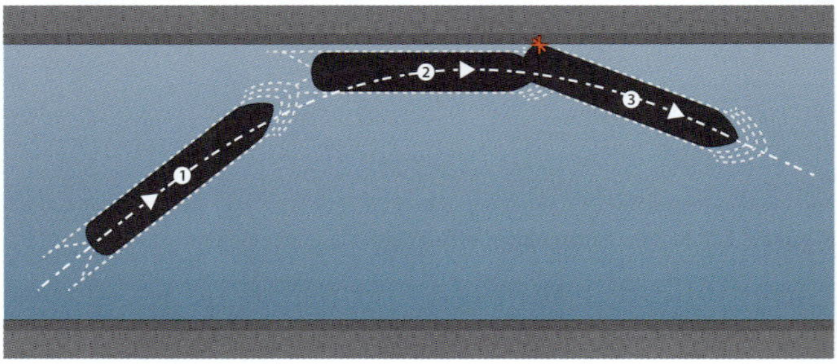

Figure 11.30 - Ship to bank interaction

CHAPTER 12

Preparing a Ship for Ice

Preparing a Ship for Ice

Courtesy of Michael Lloyd

Figure 12.1 - Weather setting in, ice accretion starting

There are many considerations that must be taken into account when preparing a ship for ice, ranging from the deck and engine preparation to the hull integrity, navigation, accommodation and experience of the crew. The ice environment is so far removed from the environment of normal blue water shipping that adaptation by the crew to the conditions, as well as to changes to the ship, is essential.

A ship in transit must ensure that all its needs for fuel, provisions and spares are met before entry into an area such as the Canadian Arctic.

Only limited and costly opportunities exist for restoring or obtaining spare parts and fuel is almost impossible to obtain. Arrangements may be possible for advance fuel orders, but the bridge team must prepare the ship to be totally self-contained unless specific deliveries are planned well in advance.

Emergency response is greatly affected by the area's remoteness. There are no salvage tugs waiting for calls for assistance and few helicopters within range to take injured crew or passengers to modern medical facilities. There are no commercial pollution response ships or equipment in areas such as the Canadian Arctic, although all Coast Guard ships carry rudimentary oil spill response equipment, some of which is pre-positioned. In the Arctic, the Coast Guard takes the place of the pollution response companies that mariners are familiar with on the Pacific and Atlantic coasts. Although there may be up to six Coast Guard ships operating in the Northwest Passage area for most of the navigation season, it should not be assumed that one is within immediate response range unless the transiting ship is already accompanied by an icebreaker. Almost all of the icebreakers are equipped with helicopters and all carry a medical professional (to nurse level at least) as well as the usual rescue specialists.

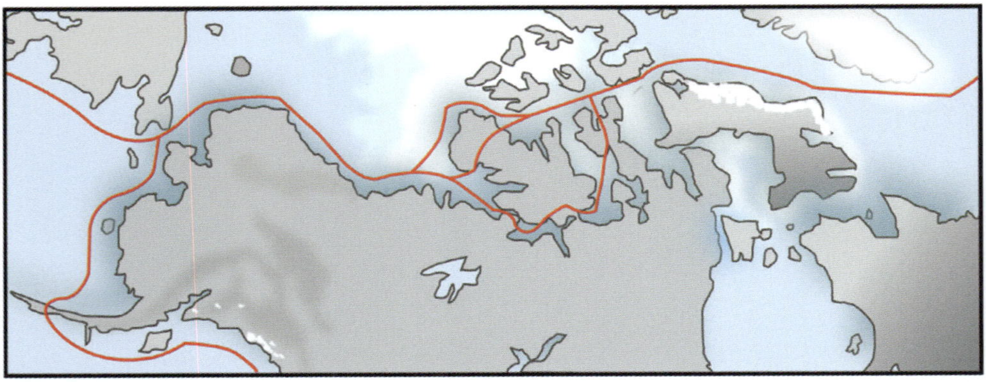

Figure 12.2 - The route of the Northwest Passage

Any ship hoping to successfully navigate through ice concentrations should be suitably constructed and equipped. Operational features such as engines, steering gear and navigation equipment are essential elements for carrying out the voyage.

Engines

These must be reliable and responsive to bridge orders. Manoeuvring speeds, inclusive of astern movements, must be anticipated if the ship is proceeding through pack ice. Filters to sea suctions must undergo regular inspections by watchkeepers and any dangers of overheating must be countered by effective watchkeeping duties. Access to suction strainers to allow easy removal and cleaning will be useful for ships operating within the ice environment. Purifiers and fuel injection elements must be well maintained to ensure continuous and reliable operation of main engines.

Steering Gear

This must be capable of quick and effective response. Emergency and auxiliary steering systems should be tested before entering ice infested regions.

Navigation Equipment

All instruments should be operationally tested before entering ice limits. Any defects should be corrected, if possible, and inexperienced officers should have onboard training on new or unfamiliar equipment. The master's standing orders for ice sightings, movement in ice and expected navigation duties should be in line with the available bridge equipment. Bridge wing searchlights should be kept clean and operational for anticipated use.

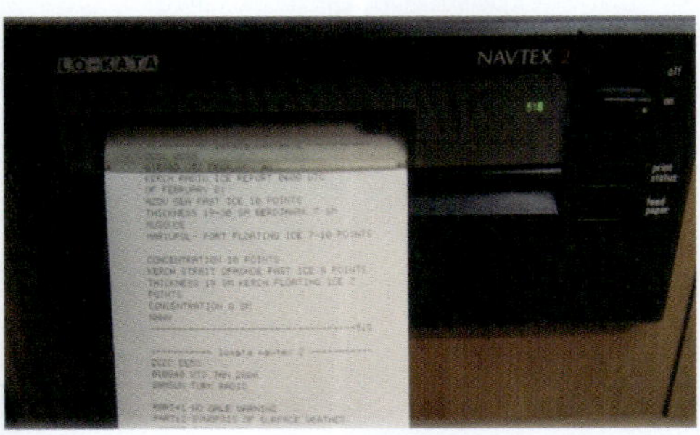

Wikipedia

Figure 12.3 - A NAVTEX receiver prints an incoming message

Communications

These systems, both internal and external, should be without defect, and backup systems should be tested periodically to ensure reliability. VTS and local communication procedures should be incorporated into the passage plan. Full use should be made of NAVTEX and ice reports relevant to the ship's progress.

Ice Strengthening

Where a ship has limited ice strengthening, additional provision should be considered.

Ballast and Trim

Source unknown

Figure 12.4 - Insufficient ballast

The ship should be ballasted as deeply as possible, keeping in mind the requirement to allow for freezing of the ballast tanks if they are unheated. The normal practice is to fill to only 90% to allow for expansion of the ballast water during freezing. The ballast tanks will remain unfrozen in relatively cold conditions because of the free water effect and constant movement of the water. However, ice can form on the steelwork in the ballast tanks and to the sounding pipes, air pipes and valves to these tanks. If prolonged navigation in ice is expected then some form of heating should be provided to the ballast tanks above the waterline. If the ballast tanks do not have heating, circulating the ballast water will keep the water moving and prevent it from freezing. Any ice that forms in ballast tanks will equate to a deadfreight value.

Preparing a Ship for Ice

To allow for expansion, do not fill ballast tanks to more than 90%.

There is a real possibility of ballast water freezing, particularly in tanks that are positioned close to the ship's side. Freezing tanks can cause expansion and subsequent cracking or distortion to the tank structure. Because of the wind chill effect, ballast tanks above the waterline will be at greater risk than those tanks below.

Ice will form in seawater (with a density of 1,025) at minus 1.8°C (28.8°F).

The trim should provide the best handling ability while keeping the propeller as deep as possible to avoid ice damage to the tips of the blades. Should a ship steer best on an even keel, it is essential that the propeller is at least some distance below the waterline, allowing for the thickness of ice that may be encountered. If the ship is in ballast and has the capability of ballasting the holds, this should be considered if the ship's stability can safely allow it.

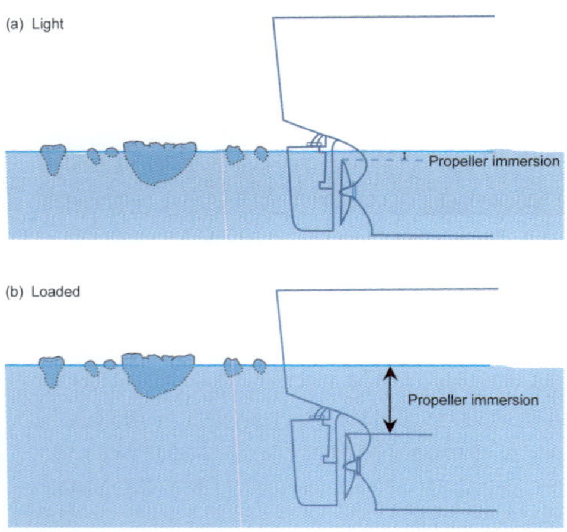

Figure 12.5 - The importance of ship's draught and waterline in ice

Damage to rudders, propellers or pod propulsion units is usually caused by heavy surface ice formations. If the propeller can be submerged below levels of surface ice, it tends to have less ice contact and so suffers less damage. Exposure of rudder couplings, Azipods and propeller blades at surface level increases the possibility of contact with surface ice, resulting in damaged propeller blades and jammed steering units. Ducted propellers or ducted Azipods are more likely to accumulate ice formations than conventional, open designed propellers.

Courtesy of Aker Arctic

Figure 12.6 - Twin Azipods

Freshwater Tanks and Fire Lines

Freshwater tanks, such as those in the lifeboats, should be no more than 75% full and all exposed waterlines, both salt and freshwater, should be drained down.

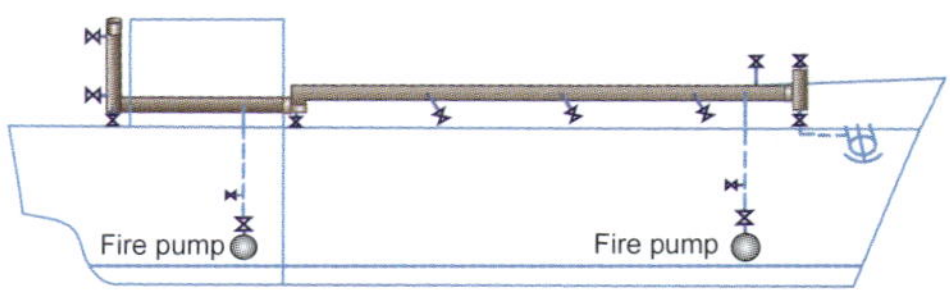

Figure 12.7 - Fire line

The fire line must be drained completely before arrival in cold weather areas and all exposed valves left cracked open. If this is not carried out, moisture within the valve can freeze and make it impossible to open. After use in cold conditions, it is important to drain the fire line quickly. To achieve rapid draining (less than 10 minutes) the following valves should be opened fully:

- Lowest valve on the main deck
- upper exposed bridge deck valves
- upper exposed forecastle valves.

The airflow from the upper valves will accelerate the speed of drainage. Once the line is drained, all exposed valves must be left cracked open, except for the:

- Valve for washing anchors. This avoids ice accumulation in the anchor hawse pipe and an accidental drop in pressure if a fire occurs
- isolating valves in the forecastle.

Main Engine

The main engine on ships operating in very low temperatures (minus 30°C or less) will be exposed to operational conditions and events not normally occurring on conventional trade routes.

Diesel Engines

Ships fitted with diesel engines, either as the prime mover or for electrical generation, may experience occasions when the diesel engine will not fire because of the low temperature of the combustion air/fuel mixture, preventing auto-ignition when compressed in the engine cylinders.

Ships fitted with diesel engines that switch to marine diesel oil (MDO) for manoeuvring would have to carry sufficient MDO bunkers for prolonged operation in ice conditions. There have been numerous accounts of ships running out of MDO when operating for longer than anticipated in ice.

Diesel Electric Propulsion

Due to the problems of conventional diesel engines operating at very low temperatures, increased numbers of ice-operating vessels are electing to be fitted with four-stroke diesel-electric propulsion systems.

The four-stroke arrangement has advantages over two-stroke arrangements in heavy ice as the four-stroke engine can provide 100% torque at low rev/min.

Shaft Seals

Shaft seals are frequently damaged.

Sea Inlets

There is a type of ice (frazil) that does not receive much attention even though it can cause great difficulties. Suspended ice crystals, usually less than half a millimetre in length, can be found in the upper few metres of water exposed to sub-zero temperatures. The crystals themselves are usually very low in salinity, but they carry high concentrations of ions that alter the bulk electrical and chemical behaviour of the water on their surfaces. The crystals are widespread, as they are a transient stage in the formation of a sea ice crust, and in areas of open water they can have an important impact because, under the right conditions, they can bring about rapid solidification. Ships in Arctic waters can encounter problems at water intakes and in pumps when the agitation of suspended ice crystals leads to rapid consolidation.

If ice or slush enters the sea inlet chests, the flow of seawater to the engine cooling system can be obstructed. This problem is encountered by the majority of ships entering ice-covered waters and may result in overheating of the prime movers and a loss of propulsion power, creating a 'dead in the water' scenario. Deep draughted vessels are less affected by these conditions.

Ships that operate in ice must prevent the engine cooling system from becoming blocked.

There are several design features that can prevent the build-up of ice in these circumstances.

The systems in Figures 12.8 and 12.9 provide possible solutions to preventing the sea inlet becoming blocked by ice.

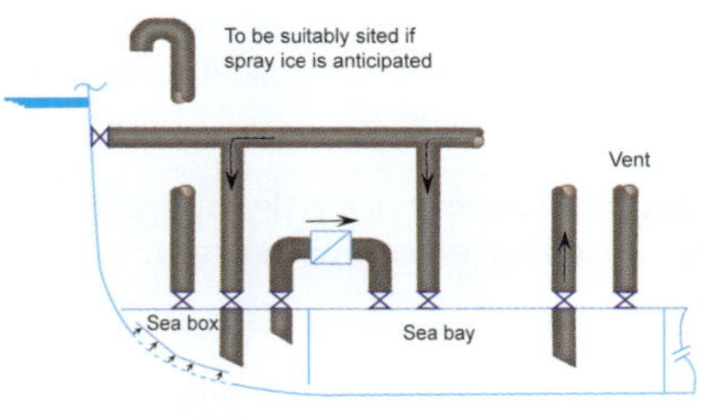

Image based on data in 'Winter Navigation on the River and Gulf of St Lawrence', Transport Canada, 2005

Figure 12.8 - IMO suggested circulation system arrangement

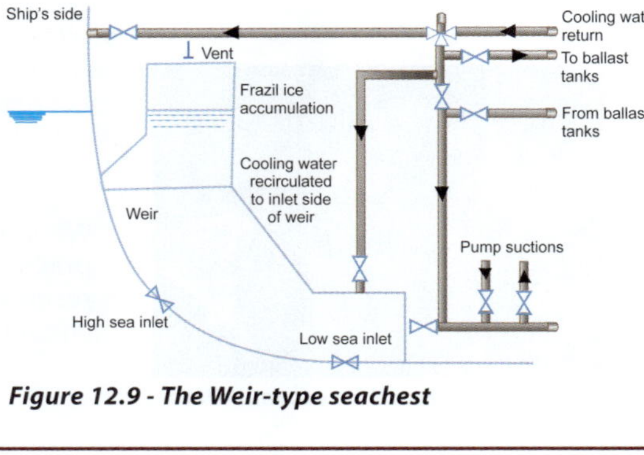

Image based on data in 'Winter Navigation on the River and Gulf of St Lawrence', Transport Canada, 2005

Figure 12.9 - The Weir-type seachest

Preparing a Ship for Ice

To limit ice ingress under both arrangements:

- Water coming into the sea strainer must be kept above 20°C
- keep high sea suction closed
- low sea suction may need to be slowed
- discharge overboard should be almost closed to obtain positive recirculation.

To avoid ice accumulation in the strainers, it is important to reduce the quantity of seawater being pumped into the cooling system. This can be achieved in a number of ways:

- Reduce the rate of flow through the seawater pump discharge valve
- use a lower capacity pump instead of the main seawater pump
- reduce the flow of cooling water to all other cooling systems in the engine room
- if the ship does not have direct steam injection into the seachests, a steam hose can be run. However, the use of steam alone is not enough to melt ice, even under light ice conditions.

It is advisable to use only one seachest at a time. Monitoring seawater pressure at the inlet is the best check for the presence of ice in the circuit. Fluctuations and, eventually, a significant pressure drop will indicate that it is time to clean the strainer.

Cleaning the strainer is a risky operation and must be carried out with great caution.

Engine room personnel must use alternate seachests and isolate the one about to be cleaned. Take care that inlet and outlet valves are completely shut and tight before removing the strainer cover as ice may remain on the inlet and outlet valve seats. If this is the case, repeat opening and closing of valves until the ice clears out. After opening the strainers, open the sea inlet valve slightly to flush out any remaining ice. A large quantity of ice and water can easily accumulate in engine room bilges. Following this operation, replace the strainer cover.

It may be necessary to repeat this operation a number of times. To reduce downtime at each strainer, each location should be equipped with the necessary tools and accessories.

Do not use a seawater strainer without its perforated plate properly installed inside. This plate acts like a filter, preventing large chunks of ice entering the circulating system.

Sometimes ballast water can be stored and used on a temporary basis for cooling or back-flushing. On ice class ships, a ballast system may allow interconnection with the engine room seawater cooling system, by gravity or otherwise, through use of the after-peak or wing ballast tanks. For double bottom tanks, a ballast pump is necessary. In both situations, sea suction valves must be closed to avoid loss of water. A careful study of cooling water and ballast diagrams will reveal the options available.

On ballast tanks, the air pipe vent can be removed to prevent the ball sticking. If this is not practical, a manhole may be opened. In these circumstances, someone must be assigned to continuously stand by at the tank with a radio and communication should be maintained with the officer at the ballast console.

Fuel, Water and Provisions

Ensure that there are ample reserves of all these essentials. If a ship becomes fast in the ice, it may be some time before an icebreaker can reach it. In St Petersburg in 2004, over 40 ships were icebound in a particularly hard freeze. If this had occurred in a remote area, it might have been a long time before assistance arrived.

Whenever working in ice, it is best practice that a minimum of 10 days of reserves of fuel, water and provisions should be kept.

TP 14335 - 'Winter Navigation on the River and Gulf of St Lawrence', Transport Canada, January 2005. Reproduced with the permission of the Minister of Public Works and Government Services Canada, 2008

Figure 12.10 - Frazil ice accumulation

Searchlights

To enable the ship to continue under way at night, good searchlights are essential. They must be mounted to provide a bright beam of light at least 90 metres (approximately 100 yards) ahead of the ship.

It is preferable to have two lights with a remote control that allows the beam to be directed out on each side of the ship. If this is not available, it is prudent to stop the ship at night when encountering heavy ice.

Courtesy of Woods Hole Oceanographic Institution (Photographer Chris Linder)

Figure 12.11 - Powerful searchlights from the USCG icebreaker 'Healy' in the Arctic

Deck Protection

TP 14335 - 'Winter Navigation on the River and Gulf of St Lawrence', Transport Canada, January 2005. Reproduced with the permission of the Minister of Public Works and Government Services Canada, 2008

Figure 12.12 - Inaccessible decks due to build-up of ice

Covers

Courtesy of Michael Lloyd

Figure 12.13 - Freezing-up of hatches

Covers that are positioned over exposed deck equipment achieve two goals. They prevent water from getting on and into the equipment and freezing, and also allow the ice to be removed easily. PVC or plastic is a better fabric to use than canvas. Avoid material made from natural fibres for painters, embarkation ladders, ropes or protective tarps as natural fibres absorb moisture and lose their flexibility and durability under cold weather conditions.

Steam pipes on deck, as used for steam windlasses, should be kept lagged and the condition of the lagging should be monitored for deterioration. In extreme temperatures, it is considered normal practice to keep the steam-powered machinery ticking over to prevent pipes from icing.

Courtesy of Michael Lloyd

Figure 12.14 - Unexpected ice formation

Covers should be considered for the following equipment:

- Open boats
- winches and windlasses
- pilot ladders
- sounding pipes
- filling pipes
- ventilators
- hatch accesses
- machinery control areas.

Scuppers

Clear the scuppers of ice and insert rubber hose piping into them. When the pipes are frozen, the rubber tubing can be removed to reveal ice-free scuppers, enabling water on the decks to drain away.

Preparing a Ship for Ice

Low Temperature Grease

This grease should be used on exposed moving parts, such as windlasses, winches, door hinges, davits and cranes. Its use prevents water from entering the moving parts and freezing. It should not be applied where oils are used as this will clog the machinery. Check with any maintenance manuals for advice before using these greases. If the radar scanners are kept running all the time, there should not be a problem with them, so even alongside they should be left in operation.

Hydraulic Tanks and Lines

If there is no heating system in operation for the hydraulic tanks, these may be filled with oil suitable for cold weather conditions. Any exposed piping should be insulated. Portable heaters are ineffective at keeping deck equipment ice-free, although they are often used in deck houses containing machinery, particularly on ships that do not enter ice-covered waters on a regular basis.

Ice Accretion and Stability

Courtesy of NOAA

Figure 12.15 - The 'Miller Freeman' iced up

When a ship is preparing for ice conditions, its stability must always be considered. Any reduction of water from a full ballast tank will present a free surface effect. This will make a considerable difference to the overall stability of the ship.

Ice accretion is the process where a layer of ice builds up on solid objects exposed to freezing precipitation, sea spray, super-cooled fog or cloud droplets.

Figure 12.16 - High sea icing

A ship that trades in a geographic area where ice may form must be provided with stability information that indicates the effect of ice formation on exposed hull areas, including both the ship's superstructure and deck cargo. There are two levels of ice allowance that depend on the geographic area of operation:

- A full icing allowance
- a half icing allowance.

The full icing allowance is based on the assumption that all exposed horizontal surfaces will carry an ice weight of 30 kg/m^2 and all vertical surfaces will carry a weight of 15 kg/m^2.

Figure 12.17 - Ice accretion

A very severe case of ice accretion occurred when a 120 metre ship left a European port with a 0.2 metre trim by the stern, reaching the Quebec City port with a trim by the bow of approximately 4 metres. The ship was directionally unstable.

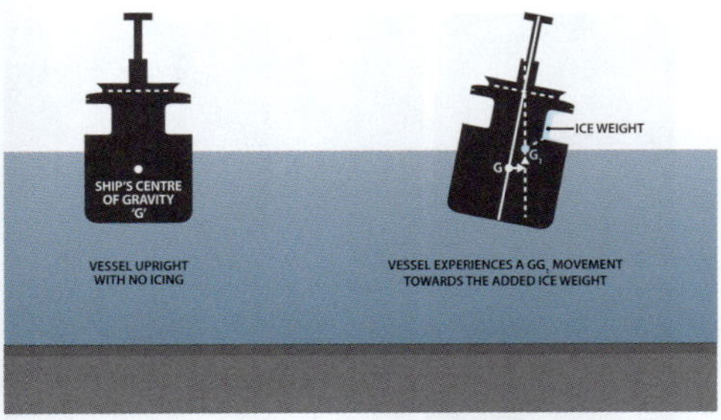

Figure 12.18 - Movement of 'G' aboard a ship with asymmetric icing

The position of the ship's centre of gravity is calculated with regard to the heights of the ice-covered surfaces. An additional percentage increase should be included to account for ice forming on cranes, derricks, rigging etc. The master must obtain a figure that accounts for ice weight on board the ship and add this to the ship's displacement. Asymmetric icing, where only one side or part of the ship acquires a degree of icing, can occur. This can lead to the ship generating a list angle and may leave it vulnerable to external forces, such as wind and wave action.

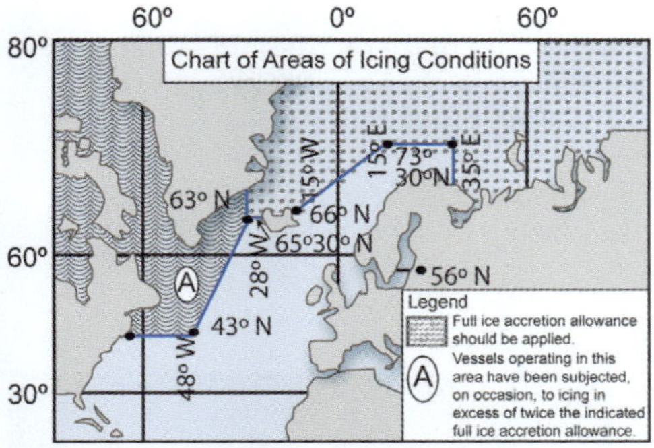

Figure 12.19 - Chart of areas of icing conditions in the North Atlantic

Full icing allowance must be made for ships in the following eastern North Atlantic regions (see Figure 12.19):

- The area north of latitude 65°30'N, between longitude 28°W and the west coast of Iceland
- north of the north coast of Iceland
- north of the rhumb line running from latitude 66°N, longitude 15°W to latitude 73°30'N longitude 15°E, north of latitude 73°30'N between longitude 15°E and 35°E, and east of longitude 35°E
- north of latitude 56°N in the Baltic Sea.

Full icing allowance must be made for ships in the following western North Atlantic region, including Baffin Bay and Davis Strait (see Figure 12.19):

- The area north of latitude 43°N, bounded in the west by the North American coast and the east by the rhumb line running from latitude 43°N, longitude 48°W to latitude 63°N, longitude 28°W and then along longitude 28°W.

All sea areas north of the North American Continent and west of the North Atlantic areas defined above are subject to the full icing allowance.

North Pacific regions requiring full icing allowance during the icing season include:

- The Sea of Okhotsk
- the Gulf of Tartary
- the Bering Sea.

In addition, all areas in the southern hemisphere south of latitude 60°S have a stipulation for a full icing allowance.

Preparing a Ship for Ice

A build-up of ice on the ship's forecastle will cause a change of trim by the head and the propeller to rise.

The amount of ice accretion is influenced by many factors:

- Wind force
- air temperature

Courtesy Canadian Coast Guard

Figure 12.20 - Sea spray that will freeze on contact with the ship

- ship's course
- ship's speed
- wave height
- temperature of the sea surface.

Seawater spray will freeze on contact with the ship when the air temperature is less than minus 6°C and the sea temperature is less than minus 1°C. During the winter months, these values are regularly exceeded in the Pacific, Atlantic and Baltic areas. In the Baltic and Great Lakes, which has brackish to fresh water, icing will occur when the temperature is only just below 0°C. Icing can also take place at higher water temperatures if the air temperature is below 0°C. In this case, the air cools down the water breaking over the ship and ice is formed when the water comes into contact with the cold surfaces on board.

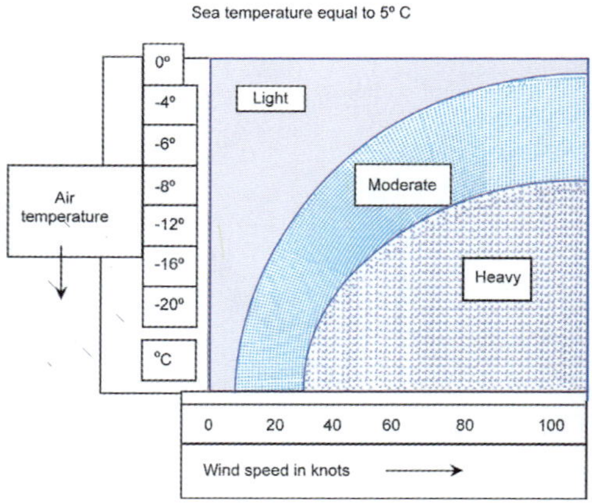

Figure 12.22 - The rate of ice accumulation and build-up

Ice accretion becomes a consideration in strong winds where the air temperature is minus 2°C or lower.

Courtesy of Michael Lloyd

Figure 12.23 - Ice accretion after one night of bad seas

TP 14335 - 'Winter Navigation on the River and Gulf of St Lawrence', Transport Canada, 2005. Reproduced with the permission of the Minister of Public Works and Government Services Canada, 2008

Figure 12.21 - Severe ice accretion in bow area

One centimetre of ice can create an added surface weight of approximately 20 kg/m^2. The rate of icing is estimated at:

- Light icing <0.7 cm/hour
- heavy icing >2 cm/hour.

Courtesy of Michael Lloyd

Figure 12.24 - 'Northern Venture' coming alongside in ice

If a ship encounters the appropriate environmental conditions, there can be a build-up of ice on the deck, with the bulk of the ice being forward and on the windward side. The tonnage of this ice can vary, but on a large ship it is easily possible to accumulate 300 tons of ice in a 24 hour period. As the layer of ice grows, a displacement in weight takes place. This displacement reduces the stability of the ship. Some ships are more prone to the effects of ice accretion than others:

- Container ships
- LNG carriers of the Gaz Transport/Technigaz design
- high-sided car carriers
- ships with deck cargo.

The accretion rate can, dependent on the weather, be lessened by either altering course or reducing speed or through a combination of both. In severe storms however, even with the ship hove to, the rate of ice accretion will quickly increase.

Considerations in Ice for Specific Ship Types

Container Ships

Container ship trade has grown substantially in recent years, with ships commonly carrying more than 9,000 teu (20-foot equivalent units) with many of these units above deck, generating very high sided ships. This configuration increases the windage area of the ship and exposes a massive area that is susceptible to ice accretion, causing instability.

There are several other ice accretion dangers associated with container ships:

- Falling ice from stack heights can cause injury to personnel at deck level
- excessive weight through ice/snow accumulation can affect load lines and cause the ship to submerge her Plimsoll marks
- frozen and iced lashings can become strained under the additional weight, making them difficult to adjust or release.

Many container ships operate with heavy pontoon hatch covers designed to accept deck loading, which themselves create heavy loads. It is not unusual for hatch pontoon lids to become frozen down in situ on top of the hatch coamings and become difficult to remove. It can also be difficult to open hydraulic hatch covers in extreme

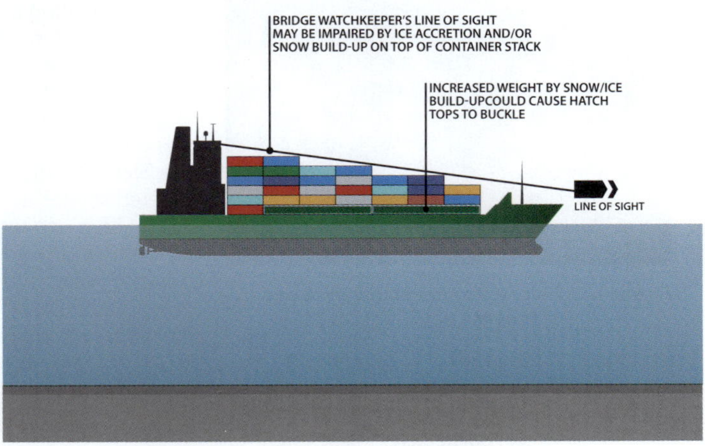

Figure 12.25 - Dangers of ice accretion on container ships

Preparing a Ship for Ice

cold climates, because the hydraulic fluid in reservoirs and pump lines becomes cold and more viscous.

Ships such as those carrying timber cargoes may also be affected in a similar manner. Although these cargoes are not generally as exposed as containers, they have the disadvantage that the cargo can absorb water in heavy seas, with ice and snow increasing the instability.

Tankers

Shiptalk

Figure 12.26 - Ice accretion on the deck of a tanker

Shiptalk

Figure 12.27 - Ice accretion on the deck of a tanker

When tankers are fully loaded, they tend to lie low in the water, with limited freeboard, and so are prone to taking considerable sea spray. Accumulation of ice, particularly in the fore end of the vessel, is an increased likelihood. This will clog hawse pipes and spurling pipes on the forward mooring deck and disrupt the anchor equipment. Deck scuppers may become blocked and not shed water from the fore end.

Tank systems fitted with air pipes and pressure vacuum valves may become covered in ice and cease to function effectively. General deck equipment, including access doorways to pump rooms and store rooms, may be directly affected by freezing conditions, making their operation difficult.

Tanker Operations

Tanker operations tend to involve specialist facilities such as the single point mooring buoys that can be found in the southeast area of the Barents Sea. These are strong enough to accommodate vessels of between 40,000 to 70,000 tons, permitting offshore loading to take place, supported by ice resistant strengthened foundations.

Shiptalk

Figure 12.28 - Single point mooring (SPM)

Other facilities include man-made islands for accommodating offshore oil/gas recovery and pipeline forwarding systems. With all the operations, the emphasis is on safety and protection of the environment against oil spills and pollution. The largest tanker currently working, with the highest ice classification, is the *'Stena Arctica'* (Ice Class 1A Super), which entered service under the Swedish flag in 2005. She is engaged between the Russian port of Primorsk and the southern Finnish port of Porvoo. The ship is a crude oil carrier of 117,000 deadweight tons, measuring 250 metres overall length, with a beam of 44 metres and designed to navigate in difficult ice conditions of up to 1 metre thick.

Expansion and development of oil production in the Arctic Ocean regions has led to a need for floating storage and offloading units in several locations. An example is stationed off the port of Murmansk. This site receives deliveries from the Prirazlomnoye oil field (Barents Sea), employs bow loading techniques, and forwards deliveries to overseas markets.

Courtesy of Stena Bulk

Figure 12.29 - 'Stena Arctica', Finnish-Swedish Ice Class 1A Super (117,000 Dwt tanker)

Courtesy of Patrick Toomey

Figure 12.30 - M/T 'Lunni' at Rea Point, Melville Island, Canadian High Arctic

Tanker operations typically involve anchoring with stern lines to the shore but in some instances the bow is placed directly on the beach, particularly in heavy ice conditions.

LNG Carriers

LNG carriers have deck features, such as spherical tanks, that can cause high ice loads to build up on deck. Both the spherical tanks and membrane containment systems have large deck surfaces with a marked angle of inclination. Ice accumulation can become hazardous if either the weight of the ice exceeds deck design loads or the ice falls onto the flat deck with considerable impact force. The deck can be strengthened to withstand these ice loads. However, a relatively economical solution is to fit obstructions onto the inclined surfaces to limit ice build-up.

Courtesy of Sakhalin Energy

Figure 12.31 - The ice-strengthened LNG carrier 'Grand Elena'

The essential deck machinery of an LNG carrier must be accessible at all times, regardless of the build-up of ice. Steam or thermal oil tracing and heating will be used for critical deck machinery.

It is vital to take into consideration the maximum temperature of the steam or heating medium within the cargo area and to the auto-ignition temperature of the cargo that is carried.

Boil-Off Gas (BOG)

LNG is at minus 162°C and the cargo that boils off is used to fuel the boilers on ships fitted with steam turbines. On more recent ship types, the BOG is used in dual-fuelled diesel engines.

This BOG passes through a vapour blower and heater before passing along a double walled line to the machinery spaces. The line is double walled to maintain a supply of nitrogen around the fuel supply line, but typically it is not insulated. Therefore, it will be necessary to consider the effect of temperature drop for the BOG supplied to machinery spaces.

Relief Valves

The low temperature that can mean ice accumulates on relief valves will require careful consideration during normal operation and cargo loading. Such systems may need heat tracing lines to be fitted to maintain functionality.

Emergency Shutdown System (ESDS)

Control of the valves at the manifold and cargo tank domes is critical on LNG carriers. These should be checked carefully, by referring to the manufacturers' manual and by testing, to ensure they operate in the relevant conditions.

Preparing a Ship for Ice

Trace Heating Caution

When applying local heat, such as by a heat tracing line, to cargo (LNG) related valves or equipment to ensure its continued functionality in an Arctic environment, there is the possibility of creating a vapour trap that could impair the operation of the valves or equipment.

Where such measures are retro-fitted, a suitable temperature controller should be fitted to ensure that keeping the equipment ice-free does not result in direct heat transfer into the LNG being loaded.

Sloshing

Gaz Transport Technigaz believe that *"sloshing generated in the cargo tank by ramming should be negligible compared to the one due to continuous open seas excitation"*, Pascal Le Balc'h (GTT) Arctic Shipping 2006.

Handling LNG Carriers in Ice

An LNG carrier following the broken channel left by an icebreaker may experience problems because of its larger beam, resulting in a very high risk of impact collision damage.

Bulk Carriers

Courtesy of Laurentian Pilotage Authority

Figure 12.32 - Bulk carriers passing one another in the St Lawrence seaway

Bulk carriers are large ships, usually with a broad beam construction. In the majority of builds, they have a wide open deck space with sliding hatch covers.

The large open deck areas lead to extensive snow cover when operating inside high latitudes and cold climates, affecting the ship's stability. Should the snow build up, it often freezes and turns to ice, making uncomfortable and dangerous working conditions for deck personnel.

Courtesy of DJ House

Figure 12.33 - Sliding hatch tops on the deck of a bulk carrier covered by ice

Hatch top covers are likely to be side-sliding, using hydraulic pumping systems, so tend to need time to warm through in low temperatures. Mechanical movement or movement by hydraulic control, with hatch covers often in excess of 40 tons, is often affected by ice accretion or heavy snow build-up. Many chief officers tend to keep pumps running well before needed to overcome anticipated delays.

Cruise Passenger Ships

Courtesy DJ House

Figure 12.34 - The 'Star Princess' navigating in the confined area of Glacier Bay, Alaska

The most recent development of shipping in ice is the growth of the cruise ship industry, which is involved in ice tourism in both the Arctic and Antarctic regions. With the increased building programme in Class 1 Passenger Ships (but not ice strengthened) many more specialist routes have become extremely popular, such as:

- Antarctica
- inside the Arctic Circle regions
- the Baltic
- Alaska.

These areas are only visited in the summer months when icing is not a problem.

Cruise Ships in Ice-Covered Waters

Shiptalk

Figure 12.35 - Cruise ship

The entry of increasing numbers of cruise ships into polar regions has raised many concerns. Many of these ships are not ice-strengthened and do not have ice experienced captains, officers or crew. In the past, small cruise ships, most of which were ice-strengthened and had at least a few officers with ice experience, were the traditional way for tourists to enter polar regions. Now, far larger cruise ships, with thousands of passengers, are already cruising these regions and many more are planned.

An example is the cruise of the *'Golden Princess'* into Antarctic waters with 2,425 passengers. A spokesperson for the company said that ice strengthening was not necessary as they were only cruising in summer months when there were not many icebergs. As the Master of the *'Titanic'* found out, and more recently the Master of the MV *'Explorer'* (which was ice strengthened), it only takes one.

If we look at the recent accident record of cruise ships in ice regions, shown in Table 12.1, it hardly gives confidence. A factor that must also be considered, particularly when seeing the number of groundings recorded, is the fact that the charting of these regions can be very poor, with some of the charts dating back to the early part of the 19th century. More deficiencies in this charting are being revealed as more areas are opened to navigation, so navigators must exercise the utmost caution when using them.

The secretariat of the Antarctic and Southern Ocean Coalition (ASOC) has already expressed its concern over the cruise industry's ice incursions and believes that there is an urgent need for the Antarctic treaty consultative parties to establish sensible operating rules

Date of Incident	Ship	Consequences
July 1997	*'Hanseatic'*	Hapag-Lloyd's *'Hanseatic'* ran aground off the north coast of Norway's Spitsbergen Island with 226 passengers and crew on board. There were no injuries.
July 2003	*'Mona Lisa'*	The *'Mona Lisa'* grounded on rocks in the Barents Sea. 690 passengers were evacuated.
November 2006	MV *'Lyubov Orlova'*	MV *'Lyubov Orlova',* with 150 passengers on board, grounded on Deception Island in Antarctica. Ship towed off and passengers disembarked at Ushuaia.
January 2007	MV *'Nordkapp'*	The MV *'Nordkapp'* ran aground off Deception Island in Antarctica. All 371 passengers and crew were safely evacuated. 700 litres of diesel were spilt with consequential environmental damage.
August 2007	MV *'Aleksei Maryshev'*	MV *'Aleksei Maryshev'* was struck by ice falling from a calving glacier. Many passengers were injured.
November 2007	MV *'Explorer'*	The MV *'Explorer'* sank after striking ice off the South Shetland Islands in the Arctic Ocean. 154 passengers and crew were rescued. 180,000 litres of diesel were on board.
December 2007	MV *'Fram'*	MV *'Fram',* with 318 passengers on board, struck a glacial iceberg in the Antarctic. Damage to the ship was sustained but there were no casualties.
July 2008	*'Spirit of Glacier Bay'*	Ran aground near the Glacier Bay National Park.

Table 12.1 - A list of some recent cruise ship accidents in ice regions

Preparing a Ship for Ice

before a catastrophe occurs. Among other steps, the ASOC wish:

- A ban on ships exceeding a certain size
- a limit on the number of passengers
- a limit on the fuel on board each ship
- mandatory ice strengthening requirements
- elimination of heavy fuel oil (HFO) south of 60°S.

The Antarctic Treaty was signed in 1959, with the prime aim of preventing military and commercial incursions into the area. Its members meet each year and adopt recommendations, but there is no one to enforce them. This leaves the Antarctic open to unrestricted tourism.

The cruise industry regulates itself through the International Association of Antarctica Tourism Operators (IAATO) and the Association of Arctic Expedition Cruise Operators (AECO). These associations provide guidelines, such as limits to the number of passengers landing in sensitive areas and restricting the proximity to wildlife and icebergs. Unfortunately, these are only guidelines and some companies have refused to join, continuing to disregard the associations' recommendations.

Courtesy of DJ House

Figure 12.36 - The 'Star Princess'

Mr Jim Barnes, the Executive Director of ASOC, has said that, under the environmental protocol of the Antarctic Treaty, the whole of Antarctica is a reserve that is supposed to be dedicated to science and the protection of the wilderness and the environment.

It must be noted that cruise ships tend to sail closer to ice formations than would be the case for merchant ships.

Similar concerns have been expressed for the Arctic regions. The number of cruise ship passengers in Greenland has more than doubled since 2003, while Svalbard in the Norwegian Arctic has seen steady growth. In comparison to the 1980s, when there was an average of less than 1,000 tourists per year, cruise ships brought 37,552 tourists during the 2007 season. For this reason, the Norwegian government plans to restrict cruise traffic around Svalbard and prohibit cruise ships from using heavy fuel oil.

Fishing Vessels

Courtesy of Craig Taylor

Figure 12.37 - Deep-sea fishing trawler 'Shetland Challenger'

The fishing industry uses a mixture of builds including wood, fibreglass and steel hulls. Overall, the wood and composite hulls are more susceptible to contact damage from surface obstructions such as ice. They are also considerably lighter, which leaves their stability questionable if they encounter ice accretion on high rigging. Smaller ships are far more vulnerable to ice build-up than the larger commercial ships. Ice accumulation rates can often be reduced by changing course and running before the wind. However, disastrous capsize examples have been noted in the North Atlantic waters, where boats have been faced with a southerly gale and run northward before the wind into higher latitudes and colder climes.

Many of the older design fishing boats have been phased out or converted to other uses. The more modern designs tend to be fitted with fewer deck obstructions that can retain slack water. The obvious dangers of ice accretion are well known but, coupled with landing a heavy trawl from the water, they could well cause serious stability problems.

Courtesy of Canadian Coast Guard

Figure 12.38 - The F/V 'Cape Richards' trapped in ice during the Newfoundland 2007 ice jam

De-Icing

Courtesy of Canadian Coast Guard

Figure 12.39 - Iced deck fixtures

Salt and Sand

Whatever quantity of salt and sand you think is necessary, order more. It is cheap and very, very useful.

Store both salt and sand ready for use:

- Forward
- aft
- on the bridge.

De-Icing Tools

Shiptalk

Figure 12.40 - Ice build-up on deck

Steam lances are effective in light ice conditions and close to 0°C temperatures. However, in heavy ice conditions, the steam can freeze as it leaves the lance, making the problem worse. Shovels are essential for removing newly fallen snow before it freezes on top of the old. It must be ensured that there is a path along the deck for personnel to move around. When it is necessary for the crew to remove ice accretion, the ship should be turned to provide as much protection from adverse weather as possible. It is unlikely that personnel will be able to work for longer than 20 minutes at any one time so a strict rota of work must be employed.

Ice can be knocked off using wooden mallets, pickaxes and crowbars, but these must be used with care due to the damage that can be done to the fabric of the ship. Extreme temperatures can cause brittle fractures in cast steel structures when they are struck by hammers. The equipment should be stowed in an enclosed space, such as the forecastle or aft store, to be readily available for use.

Reproduced with the permission of the Minister of Public Works and Government Services, 2008

Figure 12.41 - The crew of the HMCS 'Frederiction'

Preparing a Ship for Ice

Courtesy of Canadian Coast Guard

Figure 12.42 - Crew removing ice accretion with mallets

Ice falling from a mast stay or shrouds can easily penetrate thin steel plating. When ice on upper structures is being cleared, some form of cushioning, such as wooden cargo pallets or cushioned canvas sheeting, should be positioned to cover lower decks. Much of this ice can be shaken off by hand or knocked off with mallets.

When working on deck in the ice, care must be taken to avoid ice falling accidentally from the rigging and masts. It is recommended that safety helmets are worn.

If the ship does not have heated bridge windows or a blown hot air system, there must be a good supply of de-icing spray available. If there are replicated bridge wing controls, de-icing spray can be used to keep the controls free of ice. Antifreeze must also be used in all the lifeboat engine cooling systems.

The alternative to engaging the crew in ice removal is to compensate for the additional upper weight. This can be achieved following a stability assessment taking account of the ship's icing allowance by adding ballast water, below the ship's centre of gravity (G) position, to the lower part of the ship. This is only possible where tank space is available to be filled. Alternatively, a combination of compensation and clearance will further enhance the safety of the ship.

Compensating for the added weight of ice alone, by adding ballast to lower tanks, may not be adequate to retain the positive stability of the ship. Where ballasting is carried out, additional free surface effects may be incurred during the ballast operation.

TP 14335 - 'Winter Navigation on the River and Gulf of St Lawrence,' Transport Canada, 2005. Reproduced with the permission of the Minister of Public Works and Government Services Canada, 2008

Figure 12.43 - Forward mast area guy wires draped in ice

Safety

When dealing with safety in ice, the issues of equipment, training and personnel must be considered a priority. External safety equipment will be severely affected by ice and, although this will cause considerable difficulties, it must be ready for use. Although the IMO Guidelines quoted in this section are for Arctic ice-covered waters, other ice-covered waters such as the Baltic and the St Lawrence Seaway also need such guidelines because of the equally difficult ice conditions prevailing.

The lowest temperature for Quebec in January is recorded at minus 37°C, without any additions for wind chill factor.

In cold conditions, cargo cranes can become more hazardous to operate as they commonly exhibit sluggish hydraulic control and slippery brakes. Fatal accidents have occurred because of these problems.

Lifeboats and Survival Craft

In the unfortunate event that a ship is involved in a major incident and it becomes necessary to take a secondary line of defence, ie abandon ship into the survival craft, the greatest threat to life for personnel is the cold. The extreme low temperatures of the high latitudes will also affect the operations of the survival craft.

Survival experts have always envisaged that the ship is the best lifeboat but, when its integrity is unsustainable, it must be abandoned.

It must be expected that lifeboats and their launching systems (davits) will develop ice accretion. This will affect the davits and lead to boats being locked into their stowed positions. Poor shipkeeping by not removing ice formations promptly could, at the very least, delay launching or cause mishap during the launch. If wire falls, sheaves and release mechanisms are frozen, the launch could be more difficult or may be thwarted altogether. Throughout the ship's time in ice conditions, the lifeboats, rescue craft, liferafts and launching equipment must be regularly cleared of any ice build-up. When carrying this out, it is essential that the equipment is not damaged and wooden mallets should be stored close by.

All moving parts of the lifeboat/liferaft davits must be greased, including all the cables. It is recommended that enclosed lifeboat access door hinges and retaining brackets are also greased. Petroleum jelly (vaseline) should be put on the plastiglass helmsman's view window and any other windows. Scrapers and de-frosting sprays should not be used on these windows as, if they are plastic, this can cause damage.

Figure 12.44 - Passengers and crew in liferafts after evacuation from the stricken cruise ship MV 'Explorer', Antarctic Ocean, 2007

TP 14335 - 'Winter Navigation on the River and Gulf of St Lawrence', Transport Canada, 2005. Reproduced with the permission of the Minister of Public Works and Government Services Canada, 2008

Figure 12.45 - Access to forecastle and forward liferaft is severely hampered by the presence of ice

Courtesy of DJ House

Figure 12.46 - Totally enclosed free-fall lifeboat, seen in fine weather conditions, stowed on its trackways at the aft of the dry cargo ship 'Scandi Spirit'

All safety equipment must be covered, preferably with an artificial material (ie not canvas) to limit moisture absorption.

Free-fall launching trackways need to be clear of ice formations to function correctly. Ice accretion is a major obstruction to launching devices and must be cleared well beforehand. It must not be allowed to increase on or around survival craft.

Preparing a Ship for Ice

It must be realised that lifeboats and liferafts covered in ice and snow will take much longer to release than if the build-up is removed regularly.

Courtesy of DJ House

Figure 12.47 - A partially enclosed lifeboat stowed on the ferry 'Barfleur'

In high latitudes, launching into clear water may be problematic because of heavy ice floes concentrated at surface level below the launch positions. For this reason, and also to avoid damage, it would be more prudent to launch free-fall lifeboats by lowering them with the recovery davit, rather than by the free-fall method. If the ship is beset by ice, lowering of the lifeboats will not serve any purpose except to provide shelter to those who have left the ship. Liferafts could also be used in this way. If there is water or thin ice around the ship then the boats can be used, but care must be taken not to rub against any ice that may be present.

There is little experience of boat work or abandon ship procedures in ice. Few ships exercise these procedures because of the extensive preparations necessary in ice conditions. However, with enclosed boats and the davits properly greased, these exercises are both feasible and necessary. Should the ship be severely damaged, these boats will be the mechanism for the crew to evacuate the ship.

The IMO Guidelines for Ships Operating in Arctic Ice-Covered Waters state:

Rescue boat drills should be conducted as follows:

As far as is reasonable and practicable, rescue boats should be launched each month as part of the evacuation drill, with their assigned crew on board, and manoeuvred in the water with due consideration of the dangers of launching into Arctic ice-covered waters if applicable.

If rescue boats launching drills are carried out with the ship making headway, such drills should be practised in sheltered waters only and under the supervision of an officer experienced in such drills.

In an exercise in severe weather in northern Canada, it was found that the boats could be prepared for launching within 13 minutes. The main difficulties were found to be the crew working in bulky winter clothing, slippery decks and ice on railings and other superstructure areas that were not greased or protected.

In ice, liferafts are not to be used unless there is no alternative. Ice can severely damage rafts through either:

- Piercing the rubber
- rubbing the abrasive ice surface against the raft and generating friction, weakening the fabric and eventually leading to a puncture.

A recommended practice in heavy ice cover, where boats cannot be launched, is to lower the liferaft containers onto the ice, carry them to a safe ice floe and inflate them on the ice for shelter.

Lifeboat Engines

The International Life-Saving Appliances (LSA) Code states the following:

No engine shall be used for any lifeboat if its fuel has a flashpoint of 43°C or less (closed-cup test).

The engine starting systems and starting aids shall start the engine at an ambient temperature of minus 15°C within 2 minutes of commencing the start procedure.

Rescue Boats

It is normal practice to start lifeboat engines prior to the boat taking to the water. Boat engines are expected to be able to start in conditions where fuel, lubricating oil and cooling fluid (if any) are at minus 15°C. Should operating conditions be colder than this, engines may not start or function correctly.

Propellers, although usually manufactured in bronze alloys, may exhibit brittle fractures in extreme cold conditions. Coxswains should take care to ensure that rotating propellers do not come into contact with heavy ice floes, causing broken blades. Some propellers are fitted with ducting that provides a limited amount of protection from damage through contact with the ice.

The boats can operate at up to 6 knots, but this will depend on the judgement of the coxswain, the surface ice type and its concentration. Fuel is limited to operating at 6 knots for a 24 hour period.

Figure 12.48 - Rescue boat in ice

Lifeboat Survival Equipment

Lifeboat Compass

Under normal climatic conditions, lifeboat compasses are expected to perform as any other magnetic compass. However, when operating near the poles, the angle of variation could be considerable and render the compass heading unreliable.

Water Tanks

Liferafts tend to have tinned freshwater units. The drinking water contained in lifeboats is often in bulk tanks, which are known to experience freezing when the ship is in extreme low temperatures and can crack with the expansion of the frozen water. To avoid damaged tanks, chief officers normally drain a third of the water if the ship experiences freezing conditions. While this reduces the amount of water available in an abandonment situation, the alternative would be no water at all. In the event that additional water is required by personnel in lifeboats, old ice or snow, which contains less salt than new, should be used as a water source.

Boarding Ladders

Rope ladders with wooden rungs are common to most lifeboats and provide a way of boarding for anyone in the water. They are usually fitted with gunwale hooks to secure the ladder to the boat's side. The rungs are made of wood for two reasons:

- They float outwards toward anyone in the water
- the wood would not 'burn' (freeze) a survivor's hands, as metal might in cold climates.

The last rung is often made in a non-ferrous metal that causes it to lie below the surface, weighting the end of the ladder down slightly and making it easier for a casualty to climb up.

Fire-fighting

Fire is a considerable danger. This is heightened in the accommodation areas by the extra heaters and the load put on the electrical fuse boards and wiring. With the fire main drained down, reliance is on extinguishers for the initial fire-fighting, so prevention is essential.

Watchmen should check the accommodation areas at least every hour.

Fire-fighting outside the accommodation is even more of a problem when the fire main system is drained down. Further inspections at night are usually not feasible with the prevailing weather conditions found in ice waters. For this reason, any heaters used should be placed securely so that they cannot

Preparing a Ship for Ice

move and the area they are secured to must be free of materials that could cause fire. Materials must also be kept away from the bulkheads.

The IMO Guidelines for Ships Operating in Arctic Ice-Covered Waters state:

Fire drill scenarios should vary each week so that emergency conditions are simulated for different ship compartments, with appropriate emphasis on those changes to standard procedure made necessary by operations in Arctic ice-covered waters and low temperatures.

Each fire drill should include elements required by the SOLAS Convention plus additional elements made necessary by operation in an Arctic environment.

Finally, as the ship will be reliant on fire extinguishers for fire-fighting, a plentiful supply of spare extinguishers should be carried and placed in suitable areas of the ship to increase the fire-fighting potential. When the fire main is brought into use for a fire or exercise, it is essential that, after any use, it is drained again. This must be carried out within 10 minutes of completion.

Damage Control

The IMO Guidelines for Ships Operating in Arctic Ice-Covered Waters state:

All ships navigating in Arctic ice-covered waters should be adequately equipped and their crews properly trained to provide effective damage control and minor hull repair.

Damage control equipment should, in accordance with the above, be sufficient to enable a ship, as far as practicable, to make temporary repairs to a minor hull breach or to take precautionary measures to prevent escalation of damage or flooding, so that the ship may proceed to a location where more substantial repairs can be affected.

General Safety

Figure 12.49 - Considerable levels of ice build-up on a ship in the Bering Sea

Even normal work is severely affected by ice. Unless fitted with heating arrangements to walkways, using salt and sand is the only way in which the walkways used for essential crew movement can be kept clear and non-slip. On the bridge wings, if there are bare metal decks, wooden duck boards should be placed down and a supply of sand and salt kept on the bridge for use.

Should it be necessary to have a crew member working over or near the side, a lifeline must be used. However, should he fall into the sea the chances of getting him back will be remote and, even if he could be recovered, the extreme cold of the water will limit chances of survival.

When working with ice clearing tools, the risk of accident is increased by the winter conditions. With extreme cold, an accidental laceration can occur without the person realising until blood is seen or, as bleeding also slows in the cold weather, until the person enters into the warmth of the accommodation and takes off his protective clothing.

When gasoline is very cold, it can cause severe skin burns and so it must never be allowed to come into contact with the skin. The skin should also be prevented from coming into contract with metal objects.

In addition to the personal survival kit (detailed below) there is provision for a group survival kit for voyages that might prevent the lowering and operation of survival craft. That could include any ship operating in high concentrations of ice, as on many occasions the boats cannot be lowered into water because of the ice coverage and thickness.

The IMO recommended personal survival kit for ships that are expected to meet weather conditions where the average daily temperature is below 0°C:

Head protection	1 piece
Neck and face protection	1 piece
Hand protection (gloves)	1 pair
Feet protection (socks)	1 pair
Insulated suit	1 piece
Immersion suit	1 piece
Thermal underwear	1 set
Hand warmers	240 hour duration
Sunglasses	1 pair
Survival candle	1 piece
Matches	2 boxes
Drinking mug	1 piece
Whistle	1 piece
Penknife	1 piece
Handbook (Arctic survival)	1 piece
Carrying bag	1 piece

Preparing a Ship for Ice

Checklist for the Deck Department

The following represents a list of items to be checked prior to entering ice or carrying out ice operations:

General

- ☑ Check the inventory of cold weather gear on board and replenish any deficiencies
- ☑ if the ship is not fitted with double glazing, perspex or cling film placed over windows can help insulate the accommodation
- ☑ examine towing fittings on forecastle and ensure that a suitable messenger is available to pick up a bridle or towline
- ☑ ensure regular monitoring of the water level in all spaces and compartments. This could be as frequently as hourly in areas of heavy ice concentrations. This should also be instigated after a strong ice impact
- ☑ searchlights fitted and tested
- ☑ pilot ladders should not be lowered too early as ice can accumulate from spray
- ☑ ship's hydraulic systems are filled with a fluid suitable for cold weather operations. Ships fitted with tunnel thrusters should not use these as they are liable to damage from ingested ice, resulting in damaged blades.

Deck Service Lines

Isolate and drain the following lines, leaving the drains open:

- ☑ Fire mains. Valves must be left cracked open
- ☑ general service line and fresh water line to all deck outside taps
- ☑ deck air line
- ☑ chain locker eductor
- ☑ anchor wash lines
- ☑ winch cooling lines
- ☑ all external taps
- ☑ drain bridge window wash systems unless antifreeze has been added
- ☑ be alert for the formation of ice at any overboard discharges.

Whistles

- ☑ Drain main and forward whistles and close drain cocks.

Safety Gear

- ☑ Stow forward liferaft and LSA gear
- ☑ stow deck foam and water fire extinguishers in heated areas
- ☑ stow lifebuoys.

Lifeboats

- ☑ Drain freshwater tanks
- ☑ ensure portable freshwater tanks are full and located in a warm room nearby
- ☑ fit lifeboat drain plugs

Consider the addition of:

- ☑ sets of sub-zero temperature insulated clothing (S, M and L sizes) including jackets with hood, trousers, gloves and boots that can be worn beneath immersion suits
- ☑ sets of thermal underwear and socks
- ☑ sets of face masks and goggles
- ☑ sleeping bags (down filled)
- ☑ Arctic type igloo shaped survival tents
- ☑ additional high energy food supplies, such as chocolate bars.

Grease

Grease should be applied liberally to all the moving parts on the decks including:

- ☑ Windlasses
- ☑ mooring winches
- ☑ cargo winches
- ☑ engaging clutches
- ☑ pins
- ☑ operating handles
- ☑ brake clamping bolt threads

- ☑ all nipple points
- ☑ sounding pipe cap threads
- ☑ hatch dogs
- ☑ davits
- ☑ cranes.

Note: A little antifreeze is effective when mixed into the grease.

Halyards and Stays

- ☑ If halyards are left up, they should be slacked down.

Protection

- ☑ Covers off all searchlights
- ☑ covers on hatch control boxes
- ☑ covers on all fire hydrants
- ☑ covers on all fire hose boxes
- ☑ covers on all mooring lines on drums, leaving lashings clear before making fast to enable release
- ☑ covers on bunkering sounding pipes
- ☑ grease and burlap (hessian) hatch drive motors and gypsies.

Heaters

The following heaters should be switched on:

- ☑ Forecastle fan and space heaters
- ☑ winch hydraulic header tank and hatch hydraulic heaters
- ☑ anti-condensation heaters on hydraulic systems
- ☑ winch, hatch pump and exhaust fan motor heaters
- ☑ any deck house space heaters
- ☑ fire pump and davit heaters
- ☑ space heaters in emergency headquarters.

Additional Items for Tankers

- ☑ Decontamination showers and eyewash stations should be accessible to crew in all weather conditions
- ☑ drain foam lines
- ☑ cargo heating coils either to be empty or steam to be circulated
- ☑ aftpeak tank to be heated, if ballasted
- ☑ pressure vacuum (P/V) breaker to have the correct amount of antifreeze (glycol)
- ☑ steam to be opened to deck water seal and cargo oil pump separators
- ☑ crude oil wash (COW) lines and COW machine stand pipes to be drained
- ☑ P/V valves to be operated to ensure free movement
- ☑ insulate lines from cold with a trace-heating system. Care should be taken that thermostats are functional and have enough power to run through cables to provide effective trace heating.

Tankers – Cargo Heating Systems

If cargo heating system is not required:

- ☑ Drain/blow through inlet/exhaust lines to remove all presence of water.

If cargo heating is required:

- ☑ Introduce steam to the cargo heating system before encountering freezing temperatures
- ☑ consider fitting a small diameter line (jumper line) between the supply and return manifolds on the forward tanks to prevent freezing of the exhaust returns
- ☑ test all steam and exhaust valves for tightness so as to prevent leakage into 'dry lines'
- ☑ maintain heating until ship reaches warmer climates
- ☑ blow through all coils/lines with air immediately after turning off the steam.

Additional Items for Gas Carriers

- ☑ Drain both deck water spray/sprinkler lines and safety relief valve drains
- ☑ drain both safety relief valves and vent masts
- ☑ cargo heaters and cargo condenser freshwater cooling systems to be kept on continuous circulation. Suitable antifreeze is to be added
- ☑ emergency eye wash and decontamination shower lines and tanks to be drained

Preparing a Ship for Ice

- ☑ each ship should attach and post a pipeline drawing of the number and location of the drains and indicate which drains are to be blanked and drained. The same should be clearly marked at their location
- ☑ isolation valves of lines to be posted and clearly marked at their location
- ☑ if space heaters are not provided, cluster-lights may be safely rigged close to the machinery and electrical panels, and kept on.

Note for Dry Cargo Ships

Ships regularly trading in ice should carry a long-handled blow torch fired by propane and a sufficient stock of cylinders should be maintained on board.

Figure 12.50 - Tanker alongside in Vladivostock

Checklist for the Engine Department

The engine room should not be left unattended in ice-covered waters.

General

- ☑ Ensure there is sufficient fuel and freshwater for at least 7 days extended manoeuvring when approaching Canadian waters
- ☑ can trace heating lines be utilised?
- ☑ are combustion air preheating systems operational for diesel engine jacket water heaters and other systems as applicable?
- ☑ compartment space heater switched on
- ☑ change over to ballast seawater recirculating tank (if fitted)
- ☑ oil tank heaters on (keep steam valve cracked open to prevent bursting of pipe)
- ☑ keep all steam tracing lines active
- ☑ heat up diesel oil settling and service tank to 30°C
- ☑ clean diesel oil filters daily to prevent wax accumulation
- ☑ lube oil and heavy oil purifiers should be run continuously
- ☑ keep sterntube cooling water tank slack (after peak)
- ☑ oily-water separator to be drained of all water if exposed
- ☑ regular check of the stern glands to determine whether water is passing through.

Domestic/Sanitary System

- ☑ Monitor domestic freshwater pumps since continuous running is an indication of ruptured piping
- ☑ watch the freshwater tank levels
- ☑ crack the steam on freshwater tank coils
- ☑ circulate fresh water continuously to eliminate any possibility of freezing
- ☑ maintain a small flow of water through the sanitary system and soil drains
- ☑ if the ambient space temperature falls below 5°C (41°F), apply heating to the sanitary holding tank and the overboard line. If time permits, purge air or steam through all wash water outlets that do not drain to a level well below the waterline. If necessary, either add a small amount of antifreeze (environmentally safe) or salt to unused drain traps and toilets, or insert rubber hoses for easy future removal.

Ventilation

- ☑ Reduce ventilation and/or provide shields to avoid any direct cold airflow against control and gauging equipment and also small diameter piping systems
- ☑ with a diesel-driven ship, closing dampers and reducing the ventilation will not create a higher than normal vacuum to build-up inside engine room spaces

Recirculation of air in the engine room should be avoided as this will result in a build-up of aromatic hydrocarbons and noxious gases.

- ☑ close funnel flaps as required
- ☑ stop engine room vent fans and/or close distribution flaps, as conditions dictate
- ☑ leave the funnel skylights open to maintain funnel circulation (ensure funnel temperature is kept above freezing)
- ☑ use engine room fan heaters as required.

Auxiliary Boiler

- ☑ Run on backup if steam demand makes it necessary.

Main Engine Seawater System

- ☑ Maintain seawater temperature at inverter (45°F or 7.2°C)
- ☑ activate seawater recirculation system by recirculating to low seachest and/or pump suction, as required
- ☑ monitor suction and discharge pressures of seawater pumps and carry out steam injection if any signs of ice formation are noticed in seachest. This is determined by

Preparing a Ship for Ice

pressure/flow fluctuations. Steam injection hoses to be kept ready. Open steam to seachests and the overboard discharge valve, if required.

Hydraulic Pump Rooms

- ☑ Ship's hydraulic systems should be filled with fluid intended for cold weather operation
- ☑ space heater switched on
- ☑ oil tank heater switched on
- ☑ compartment vent closed or a shield must be used
- ☑ 70% isopropyl alcohol should be used to remove moisture in hydraulic oil and assist the movement of the controls.

Steering Gear Flat Compartment

- ☑ Space heater switched on
- ☑ if no space heater is available, run hydraulic pumps continuously and use oil suitable for low temperatures
- ☑ oil tank heater switched on
- ☑ compartment vent closed or a shield must be used.

All Under-Deck Passages and Duct Keel

- ☑ Space heater switched on
- ☑ compartment vent should be closed or a shield must be used.

Bow Thruster Room

- ☑ Space heater switched on
- ☑ oil tank heater switched on
- ☑ close compartment vent or a shield must be used.

Emergency Generator Room

- ☑ Fuel: use winter grade oil

SOLAS II-1, Regulation 44 states:

Emergency generating sets shall be capable of being readily started in their cold condition at a temperature of 0°C. If this is impracticable, or if lower temperatures are likely to be encountered, provision acceptable to the Administration shall be made for the maintenance of heating arrangements, to ensure ready starting of the generating sets.

- ☑ add antifreeze (suitable to minus 40°C) to generator and compressor
- ☑ close the external vents
- ☑ any fresh water lines to be blanked off
- ☑ radiator vents must be open for recirculation
- ☑ space heater switched on.

Double Bottom Tanks

- ☑ Transfer maximum heavy fuel oil up to the wing tanks
- ☑ isolate unused heating coils and blow through with air or leave steam on and ensure returns maintained warm
- ☑ turn on bilge tank heating coil, unless tank is empty.

Fire Main

- ☑ Put the pump suction on a low seachest
- ☑ drain the fire main down to sea level
- ☑ leave the fire pump suction and discharge valves open.

Deck Air

- ☑ Isolate deck service air at the engine room valve and drain the line
- ☑ ensure that air supply to control air and whistle is moisture free.

Sea Inlets

- ☑ Reduce quantity of seawater pumped into cooling system to reduce blockage by ice
- ☑ monitor pressure of seawater at inlet and clean strainer as necessary.

Extracted from the Ice Navigation Manual

The International Code for Ships Operating in Polar Waters (The Polar Code)

Background

New routes are becoming accessible in Arctic and Antarctic regions, such as the Northern Sea Route and the Northwest Passage, both of which offer significant reductions in journey length between major shipping destinations. With increased traffic through these sensitive areas, experts believed it was important to establish a comprehensive integrated framework of mandatory regulations to protect the region and to ensure the safety of seafarers working in these harsh conditions.

In the last few decades, there have been many pieces of guidance and regulation issued that relate to shipping in polar regions, including regulations under MARPOL, SOLAS, STCW and the United Nations Convention on the Law of the Sea (UNCLOS). In 2002, an MSC Circular (no. 1056) on 'Guidelines for ships operating in Arctic ice-covered waters' was issued and, following requests that these be extended to Antarctic waters, an IMO Assembly Resolution (A.1024(26)) was passed in 2009 providing 'Guidelines for ships operating in polar waters'. Other IMO guidelines relating to voyages in polar regions cover planning for operations in areas remote from SAR facilities, cold water survival, waste disposal restrictions and training recommendations.

The aim of the Polar Code is *"to provide for safe ship operation and the protection of the polar environment by addressing risks present in polar waters and not adequately mitigated by other instruments"*. Containing provisions relating to both safety concerns and environmental protection, it will be mandatory under SOLAS and MARPOL and will enter into force on 1st January 2017.

Structure of the Polar Code

The Polar code is split into two main sections. Part I covers safety measures and Part II covers pollution prevention measures. Each of these sections is then further divided into Parts A and B, with Part A containing mandatory points and Part B containing further information and additional guidance (recommendations).

Part I-A: Safety measures (mandatory)

This section includes:

- Polar Water Operational Manual (PWOM)
- ship structure
- stability and subdivision
- watertight and weathertight integrity
- machinery installations
- fire safety/protection
- life-saving appliances and arrangements
- safety of navigation
- communication
- voyage planning
- manning and training.

Note: Part I-B provides additional guidance on the above topics.

Part II-A: Pollution prevention measures (mandatory)

This section includes prevention of pollution by:

- Oil
- noxious liquid substances in bulk
- harmful substances carried by sea in packaged form
- sewage from ships
- garbage from ships.

Note: Part II-B includes further guidance on the above topics and guidance from other sources, including recommendations related to ballast water management and anti-fouling systems.

The key points of the Polar Code have been summarised in an infographic released by the IMO and available in six languages on their website at: http://tinyurl.com/d9c9Lr2

Ship Categorisation

As part of the Polar Code, ships operating in polar waters will be placed in one of three categories (A, B or C) according to the amount and severity of ice in which they are designed to operate.

The International Code for Ships Operating in Polar Waters (The Polar Code

Ships must be classified for operations in the ice conditions expected on voyages they intend to undertake. It is important to note that ice levels vary both throughout the year and between years, so ships that are suitable for a particular route on one voyage may not be suitable for voyages made on the same route at different times.

Ship categories as defined in the Polar Code

Category A	• Designed for operation in at least medium first-year ice which may include old ice inclusions • PC 1 to 5* or equivalent
Category B	• A ship not included in category A, designed for operation in at least thin first-year ice which may include old ice inclusions • PC 6 and 7* or equivalent
Category C	• Designed to operate in open water or in ice conditions less severe than those in categories A and B

*Polar Class designation as defined in the IACS Unified Requirements for Polar Class Ships.

Who will be affected by the Polar Code?

The Polar Code affects ships intending to operate in the defined polar regions of both the Arctic and Antarctic. Ships will be required to have a Polar Ship Certificate and a Polar Water Operational Manual (PWOM) on board prior to entering polar waters. These will be ship-specific documents drawn up based on operational assessment of ship capabilities and must provide guidance on risk-based procedures to be followed in both normal operations and in emergency situations. The PWOM structural requirements will be applicable to new ships built on or after the entry into force date of 1st January 2017.

Polar waters are defined in:

- SOLAS – Regulations XIV/1.2 and XIV/1.3
- MARPOL
  - Annex I – Regulation 11.46.2
  - Annex II – Regulation 10.21.2
  - Annex IV – Regulation 7.17.3
  - Annex V – Regulation 3.13.2

The extent of polar waters defined in the above regulations is shown on the following maps.

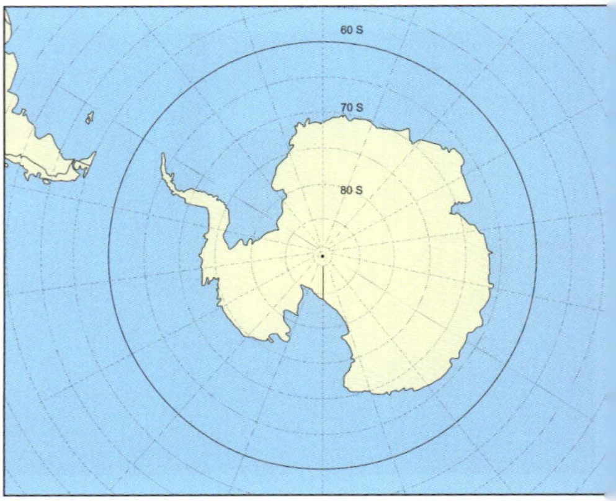

Maximum extent of Antarctic area application (from MSC.385(94) – the Polar Code)

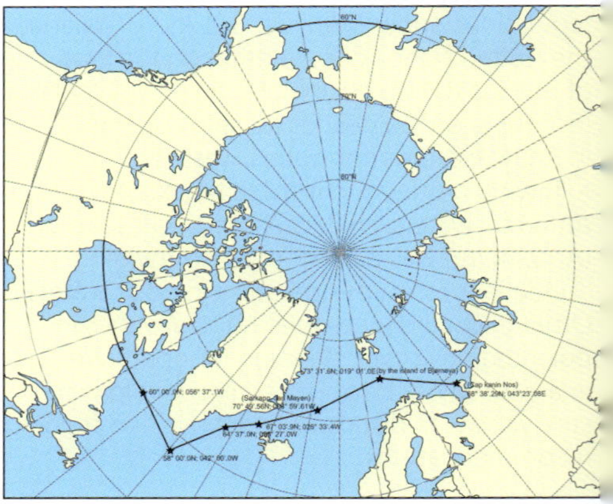

Maximum extent of Arctic waters application (from MSC.385(94) – the Polar Code)

CHAPTER 13

Non-Standard Operations

Helicopter Emergency Landing Areas

Recommendation on Emergency Helicopter Landing Areas

Definitions

'Helicopter landing area' means an area on a ship designed for emergency and occasional landing of a helicopter.

'Diameter (D)' means the overall length of the helicopter with the rotors turning. The maximum value of D will depend on the type and size of the helicopter. This should be agreed by the Administration taking into account the particulars of the ship and its area of operation.

Positioning of Landing Area

Helicopter landing areas should be located on an upper deck. The landing areas consist of an outer manoeuvring zone and a clear zone. It is important that, whenever possible, the clear zone is close to the ship's side.

The first requirement is to identify a location where there is clear access to the operating area and to the exit from it to the ship's side.

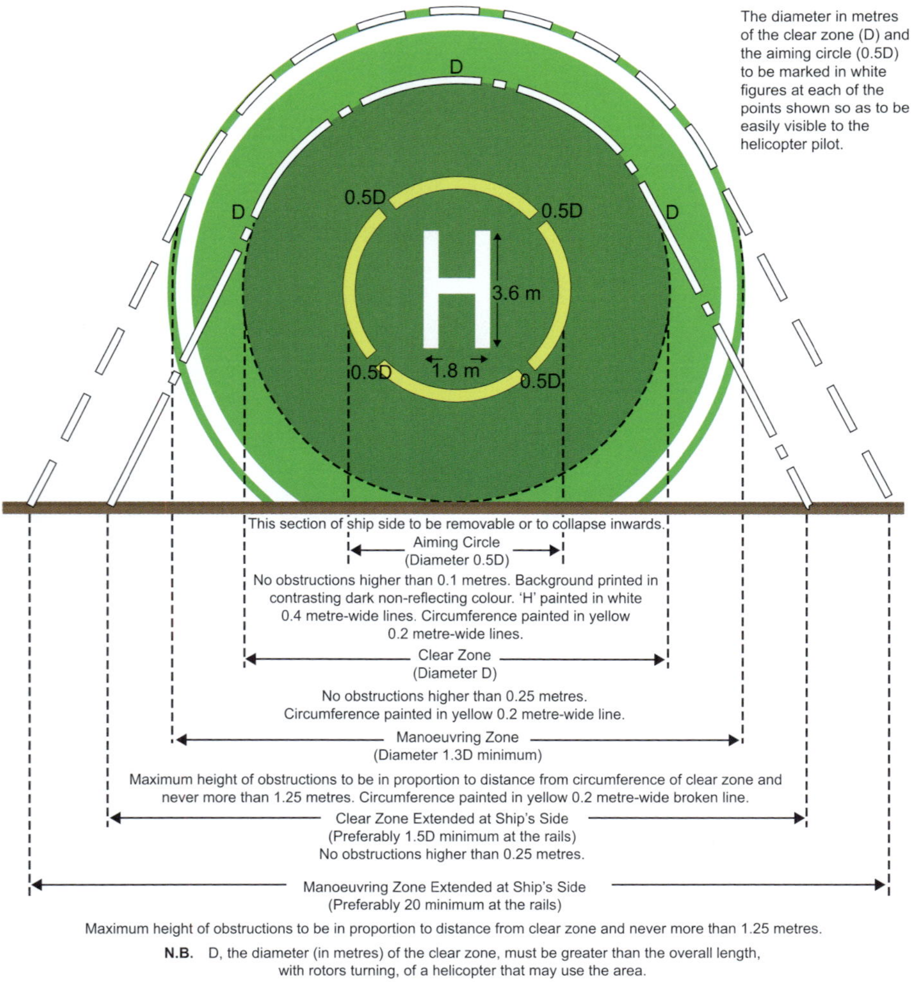

Source: MSN 1737 'Helicopter Operations at Sea'

Figure 13.1 - Landing area at ship's side

Once that location has been identified, the second requirement is to establish the best position within the area for the manoeuvring zone that will give the largest clear zone.

Details of Landing Area

Landing Area at Ship's Side

Landing areas should be as large as possible and set out to provide safe access for helicopters from the ship's side. Due account must be taken of possible helicopter slippage and wind and ship movement. Where the boundary of the clear zone is close to or in line with the ship's side, and where the height of fixed obstructions so permits, helicopter safety will be improved by extending the clear and manoeuvring zones to the ship's side symmetrically, thereby widening the approach to the landing area (see Figure 13.1). This extended landing area at the ship's side is therefore the preferred operating area.

Landing Area without Unobstructed Access from Ship's Side

Where it is not possible to provide an operating area with clear access from the ship's side, the landing area should be set out as shown in Figure 13.2 and, if practicable, placed on the ship's centreline.

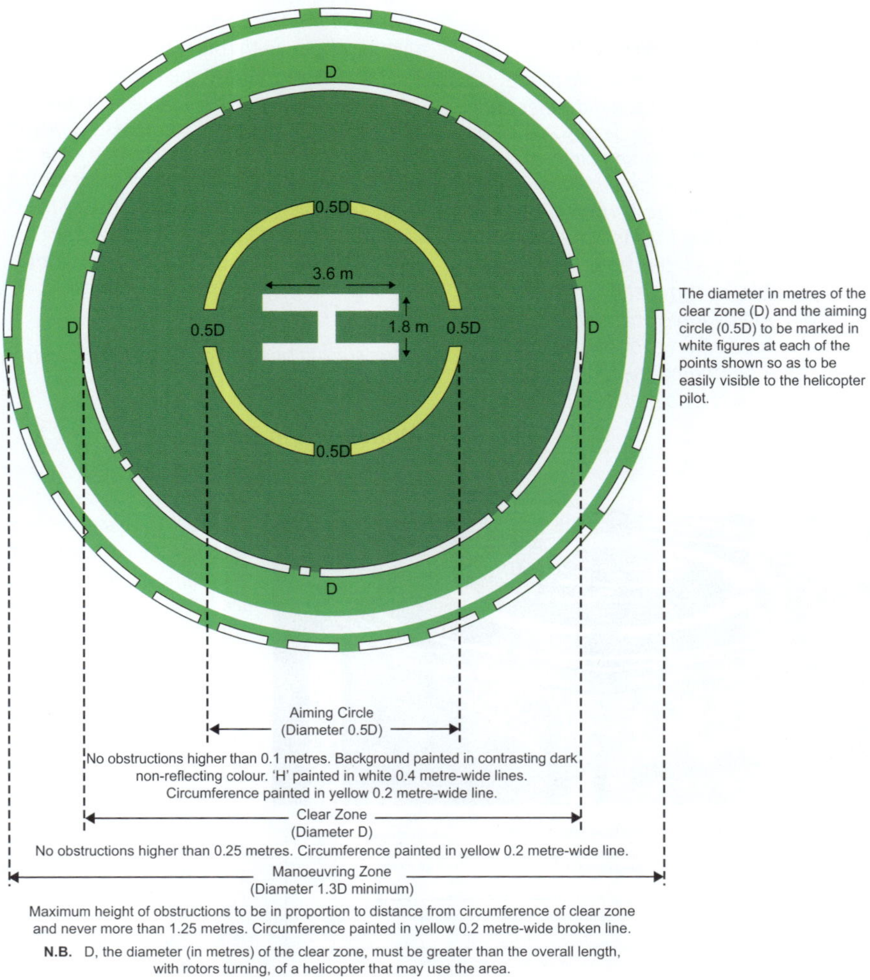

Source: MSN 1737 'Helicopter Operations at Sea'

Figure 13.2 - Landing area without unobstructed access from ship's side

Helicopter Emergency Landing Areas

Dimensions of landing area

In establishing a landing area, it is essential to ensure a safe correlation between:

- *The dimensions of the aiming circle, clear zone and manoeuvring zone and the maximum permitted height of obstructions in these zones, and*
- *the sizes of helicopters expected to use the facility.*

In particular, the clear zone of the landing area should be as large as practicable. Its diameter (D) should be not less than the overall length of a helicopter (with its rotors turning) that may use it. Other dimensions of the landing area should be in proportion to the diameter of the clear zone, as illustrated in Figures 13.1 and 13.2.

Aiming Circle (Touch Down Zone)

The aiming circle is an area concentric to the centre of the clear zone and has a diameter half that of the clear zone itself. A circle of some 10 m diameter is required for the aiming circle of a landing area suitable for the large helicopters in normal marine use. The circle should accommodate with safety the landing gear of helicopters for which it is intended and should therefore, if possible, be completely obstruction-free. If there are unavoidable obstructions, they should have rounded edges capable of being traversed without damaging the landing gear of a helicopter and should be no higher than 0.1 m.

The aiming circle should be completely covered with a matt anti-slip surface painted in a dark non-reflecting colour which contrasts with the other deck surfaces. Its circumference should be marked with a yellow line 0.2 m wide, with the diameter in metres of the aiming circle clearly indicated in white figures at four points in the circumference line as shown in Figures 13.1 and 13.2.

The letter 'H' should be painted at the centre of the aiming circle in 0.4 m wide white lines forming a letter of dimensions 3.6 × 1.8 m.

Clear Zone

The diameter of the clear zone will depend on the available landing area. The clear zone should however be as large as practicable, recognising that its diameter (D) must be greater than the overall length, with rotors turning, of a helicopter able to use the landing area. Where the landing area is at the ship's side, safe helicopter access will be enhanced by widening, where possible, the boundaries of the obstacle-free clear zone at the ship's side to a dimension of at least 1.5D (see Figure 13.1). The circumference of the clear zone should be marked by a yellow line 0.2 m wide, with the diameter (D) in metres indicated in white figures at points in the circumference line as shown in Figures 13.1 and 13.2.

There should be no fixed obstructions in the clear zone higher than 0.25 m.

Manoeuvring Zone

The manoeuvring zone of the landing area extends the area in which a helicopter may manoeuvre with safety by enlarging, to a diameter of at least 1.3D, the area over which the rotors of the helicopter may overhang without danger from high obstructions. When the landing area is at the ship's side, safe helicopter access will be enhanced by widening, where possible, the boundaries of the obstruction-free manoeuvring zone at the ship's side to a dimension of at least 2D (see Figure 13.1).

If it is impossible to remove all obstructions from the manoeuvring zone, a

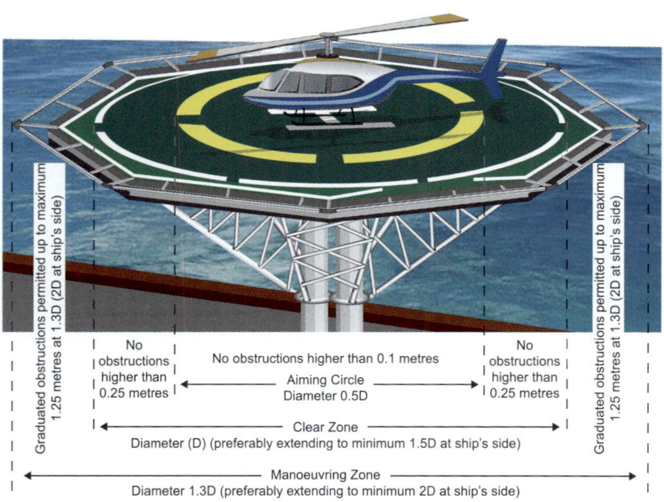

Source: MSN 1737 'Helicopter Operations at Sea'

Figure 13.3 - Landing area - permitted height of obstructions (elevation)

graduated increase in the permitted height of obstructions, from 0.25 m at the circumference of the clear zone to a maximum of 1.25 m at the circumference of the manoeuvring zone, is acceptable. However, such height above 0.25 m should not exceed a ratio of 1:2 in relation to the horizontal distance of the obstruction from the edge of the clear zone (see Figure 13.3). So, for example, an obstruction of 1 m in height (0.75 m more than the maximum obstruction height in the clear zone) should be at least 1.5 m outside the circumference of the clear zone. All obstructions in the manoeuvring zone should be clearly marked in contrasting colours.

To assist the helicopter pilot in his positioning, the circumference of the manoeuvring zone should be indicated by a broken yellow line of 0.2 m width (see Figures 13.1 and 13.2).

Use of Landing Areas for other Purposes

It is considered that helicopter landing areas may be used for other purposes in normal circumstances, but it should be possible to clear this area readily as required.

Night Operations: Lighting

The following general remarks apply in all cases:

- *Lighting should be arranged so as to illuminate the operating area and should not be directed towards the helicopter, and*
- *a wind pennant or flag should be illuminated.*

Fire-Fighting Appliances and Rescue Equipment

Where helicopters land or conduct winching operations on an occasional or emergency basis on ships with helicopter landing areas, equipment fitted in accordance with Chapter II-2 of SOLAS 74, as amended, may be used. This equipment should be made readily available in close proximity to the landing or winching areas during helicopter operations, and should include the following:

- *At least two dry powder extinguishers having a total capacity of not less than 45 kg*
- *carbon dioxide extinguishers of a total capacity of not less than 18 kg or equivalent*
- *a suitable foam application system consisting of monitors or foam-making branch pipes capable of delivering foam to all parts of the helicopter landing area*
- *at least two nozzles of an approved dual-purpose type (jet/spray) and hoses of sufficient length to reach any part of the helicopter landing area*
- *two sets of fireman's outfits*
- *in addition, at least the following equipment:*
  - *adjustable wrench*
  - *blanket, (fire resistant)*
  - *cutters, bolt 60 cm*
  - *hook, grab or salving*
  - *hacksaw, heavy duty complete with 6 spare blades*
  - *ladder*
  - *life line 5 mm diameter x 15 m in length*
  - *pliers, side cutting*
  - *set of assorted screwdrivers*
  - *harness knife complete with sheath.*

Source: MSN 1737 'Helicopter Operations at Sea'

High Line System

A high line system is suitable for transfer of persons and dry goods up to a nominal lifting capacity of about 300 kg. As no special winches are used, the transfer capacity is limited.

The system contains the following key items:

- Manila high line as support line for the traveller block, to be operated manually on board the supplying ship
- release hook of the support line at the counter point on the receiving ship
- traveller block running on the support line for a chair to transfer one/two persons or rigged litter for the transfer of a casualty or for light cargo, like mail, etc
- manila line for hauling out to be operated manually on board the receiving ship
- manila line for hauling in to be operated manually on board the supplying ship.

Courtesy of US Navy

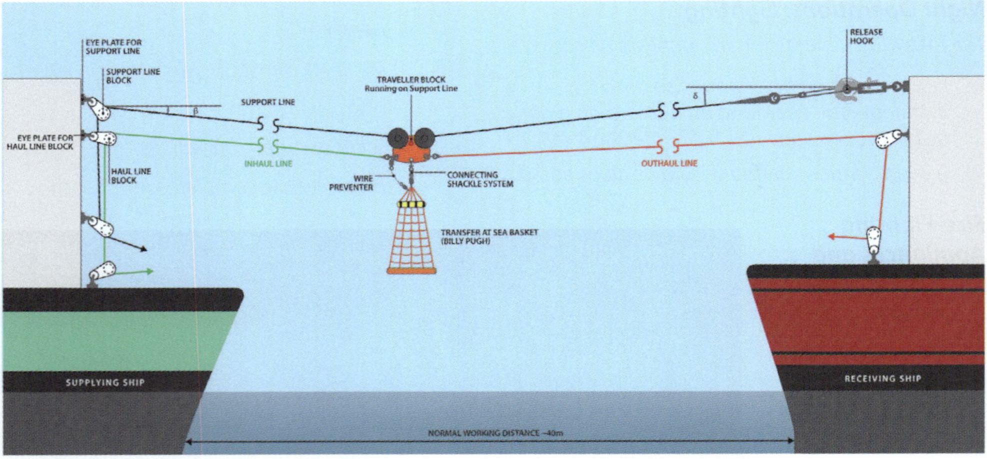

Figure 13.4 - High line system

Personnel Basket Transfer

Subject to local regulations and company and charterers' procedures, basket transfers by personnel basket to or from vessels can be undertaken using a number of different devices. The three main devices used are:

1. **Billy Pugh** – the oldest design of personnel transfer basket, in which personnel are transferred while holding on to the outside of the lifted structure.

2. **Esvagt** – a rigid-framed construction with buoyancy ring and fenders, in which personnel stand inside the basket.

Personnel Basket Transfer

3. Personnel transfer capsule – a rigid-framed device with buoyancy panels, in which personnel sit strapped in bucket seats.

Personnel baskets should be thoroughly examined before use to ensure all parts are in safe working order.

The following additional factors should be taken into consideration:

- The suitability of the vessel(s) to maintain station
- the likely route of the basket during transfer and differences in freeboard between the vessels or offshore structures involved
- wind speed, vessel movement and limitations of the crane.

It should be ensured that:

- The crane operator is competent for man-riding operations
- the crane is fully operational and certified for man-riding operations
- the transfer basket is visually inspected before starting the transfer. It should be marked with its safe working load and there must be a valid certificate of test and/or inspection
- communications are established between banksmen, crane and vessel
- environmental and vessel motion conditions are suitable
- crane operator and banksmen have good visibility of the pick-up, transfer and landing area.

The crane, including wire ropes, rigging, shackles, safety slings and hooks, must be of an appropriate type and certified for personnel transfer and adhere to any local or national legislation.

The transfer basket should be correctly rigged onto the crane prior to transfer and the crane hook pennant should be of sufficient length to keep the hook well clear of the personnel being transferred.

Tag lines attached beneath the basket to control the swing when raising and lowering should be carefully monitored to prevent any risk of them becoming snagged.

Dangers of Personnel Transfer in an Offshore Environment

- Poor communication between ships, on deck or with the person being transferred, and language difficulties
- insufficient or inexperienced crew or untrained crane operator
- pendulum effect, where the basket starts to swing and injuries can occur
- back and neck injuries occurring when the basket is landed heavily on deck – particularly in poor weather
- poor crane performance
- crane failure - wires, blocks, hooks, hydraulics, brakes
- weather (wind, visibility, temperature) or sea state
- ability of ship to remain on station or movement of other ship
- night-time transfers, lighting
- crane driver not being able to see the lift when over the side
- not using the appropriate transfer equipment/basket
- not wearing the appropriate clothing and/or life-saving appliances.

Transfer Stores OPL (Off Port Limit)

Ships transiting the waterways but not wishing to come off charter or leave international waters can take advantage of the significant off port limit (OPL) operations undertaken by local companies. These services include receiving stores, spares, provisions and even a change of crew while still offshore, thus avoiding the time and expense of putting in to port. Tugs and other vessels can bring the required stores and personnel out from shore and effect a transfer while the ship is still on the high seas.

Examples of areas where such transfers are conducted include:

- Las Palmas
- Nigeria
- UAE
- Oman
- Port Elizabeth
- Port of Durban
- Klang
- Singapore.

Within an OPL, you can usually arrange the following services for your vessel:

- Cash to master
- provisions
- personnel transfer
- crew changes
- ship stores
- ship spare parts
- medical supplies and medical personnel
- garbage disposal.

Procedures for Vessel to Vessel Transfer Using a Small Boat

Vessel to vessel transfer using a small boat can be challenging, particularly for inexperienced personnel. The masters of both vessels should consider the weather and sea state when assessing whether it is safe to allow close approach and transfer, even when making a lee. The operation should be carried out in good visibility and during daylight hours. Crew should be standing by and available for launching from one of the vessels to assist those being transferred. An experienced person should supervise the moment of transfer and maintain communications with the bridge.

The following additional points should be taken into consideration:

- Before the boat comes alongside, adequate communication lines must be open between both bridges and clearance obtained from both masters before the transfer commences
- surfaces for the transfer areas on the vessels should be non-slip and cleared of all loose items and obstructions
- many texts state that a Jacob's ladder should be used, but, due to the risks involved, it is common practice at sea to use the same arrangements as for the boarding of a pilot
- lifelines with a lifebuoy (and light) should be available
- transfers should take place on the opposite side of the vessel's man overboard boat in case this is required to be launched
- following a briefing on the procedure, one person at a time should be transferred, wearing an inflatable lifejacket, proper footwear, appropriate clothing and, if necessary, (in harsh environments) an immersion suit. Luggage should be transferred separately
- personnel should board using both hands and a handrail or support should be provided. Where necessary, there should be access in or through bulwarks using movable gates. Transfer points must be cleared quickly.

Procedures for Vessel to Vessel Transfer Using a Small Boat

The skipper of the small boat employed for the transfer should ensure that:

- The boat is sound, fully operational, equipped for the number of persons to be transferred and complies with applicable regulations for the area of operation
- emergency equipment (water, radio, flares, torch, man overboard equipment, etc) is available on board
- a lifebelt and heaving line are available for use from either station at the transfer point
- when the boat comes alongside a vessel or offshore structure, relative movement is taken into consideration
- the position of fenders on vessels and units is taken into account, together with any likely action of the water surging up between the boat and the vessel or structure when in close proximity.

Towing in Ice

A request by a ship to be towed may be directed through agents, shipowners, by the ship's master or made to a port authority, the port director, harbour master, or to the officer commanding the icebreaker itself. To avoid fees for salvage, any fees or costs involved should be ascertained before the towing operation is commenced. A written agreement between the interested parties is preferred whenever possible.

Once the request has been agreed, the type of towing arrangement must be considered.

It is not recommended that commercial ships tow one another unless specially fitted for close coupled towing.

Towing with a Long Lead

The type of towline should be established and attention should be paid to the dangers associated with hawsers close to propellers, particularly when towing from a stern position. It is preferable to secure the tow during the hours of daylight, but in polar regions this may not be possible. The leads for the line should be well parcelled and protected against chafing and the length of the towline should be adjustable.

Long tows are not advisable for icebreakers as the channel they form can quickly clog with ice and increase the resistance of the towed vessel. Therefore, tows in ice are short and possibly even close coupled as a composite unit. Another reason for keeping the towed length to a minimum is to prevent rapid wear of the cable resulting from too many layers on the winch drum. There should be no more than four or five layers on the drum to prevent the outer layer being depressed into the lower windings on the drum during towing operations.

Prior to the operation, prevailing weather conditions, communications between the two ships and the navigation signals should be considered. Detailed records, including times and positions, should be maintained throughout with appropriate entries made in the ship's logbook. A report should also be made to the owners and agents of the towed ship.

The icebreaker should be notified of areas on the towed vessel that might prove capable of accepting the towline, such as a usable strong point, chafing chain or stopper arrangement. Other information to be provided includes details on fairleads, insurance wire, diameter of bitts and the size of any towing bracket fitted.

Source unknown

Figure 13.5 - The 'Shirase' towing 'Aurora Australis'

Towing in Ice

The towed vessel should make every effort to keep the towline taut despite variations in the speed of the icebreaker caused by the ice.

While under tow, the route of the ship must be a safe passage with adequate UKC throughout. The navigation should be such that the passage plan is charted (under tow) and the agreed route will not present additional hazards to the well-being of the ship.

Courtesy of the Finnish Maritime Administration.

Figure 13.6 - Towing with a short lead

All modern icebreakers are fitted with special towing devices or towing winches and some are specifically constructed for the task. Any ship requesting icebreaker assistance should expect to be involved in towing and have towing gear rigged continually and ready for immediate use. Where towing operations are to be undertaken, these can be with either a short or long stay towline. The speed of any towing operation will be at the discretion and order of the master of the icebreaker.

Large tankers are fitted with emergency towing brackets which, if towing becomes necessary, can make the operation much more practical. The width of many tankers' beam can be problematic and may make the employment of a single icebreaker ineffective. Therefore, two icebreakers would be used, one to open up a wide enough passage in the ice to allow reasonably unobstructed movement while the other tows.

Towing with a Short Lead

In compact heavy or hummocked ice, the icebreaker pulls the ship to be assisted close to its stern.

This type of towing configuration is necessary in thick ice because an icebreaker does not open a clear channel for ships to pass through. The path made by the icebreaker creates a jumbled brash of ice and pressure from both sides of the pack causes this to close in only a couple of metres behind the icebreaker or towed vessel.

The icebreaker's steering is impaired because of the weight of the ship following, and course alterations must be carried out in loose ice.

Anchors are hung out from or pulled clear of the hawse pipe to allow the tow sling of the icebreaker to pass through the anchor hawse pipes.

While towing in heavy ice, it is advantageous to use a towing bridle that would spread the load onto more than one set of bitts.

Close Coupled Towing

In thick ice, when the icebreaker has gone ahead, there may be many large pieces of broken ice in the channel. In such circumstances, particularly in the Baltic, the icebreaker will tow the ship by pulling it into a small docking 'V' at its stern (a notch). The icebreaker will hand over two or four bridles, which are to be fastened to the towing bollards. The ship being towed has its bow flush against the stern of the icebreaker. This is called 'close coupled towing'. The advantage of this system is that the ship being towed is directly behind the icebreaker and so has a far better chance of passing through any ice. In addition, the icebreaker can benefit from the extra mass that the towed ship can give when clearing particularly difficult ice areas. An additional benefit from close coupled towing is that the risk of collision has been removed.

Courtesy of DJ House

Figure 13.7 - Icebreaker in a close towing operation in the Baltic Sea

Courtesy of Patrick Toomey

Figure 13.8 - Connecting snatch block between towing line and bridle

istock

Figure 13.9 - Icebreaker stern showing the docking 'V' to facilitate towing

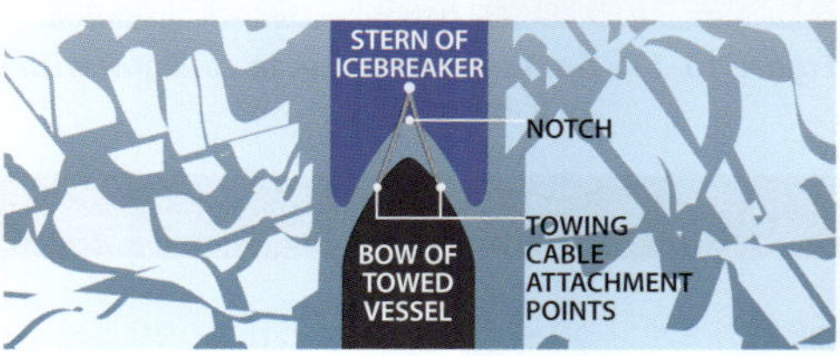

Close coupled towing requires considerable skill:

- The ship should be prepared to make fast or cast off the towing cable at any time (the bridle is designed to part before the towline, and therefore the foredeck is a dangerous place to be)
- for bulbous bowed ships, the distance between the topside of the bulb and the icebreaker hull must be at least 2 metres (see diagram below)

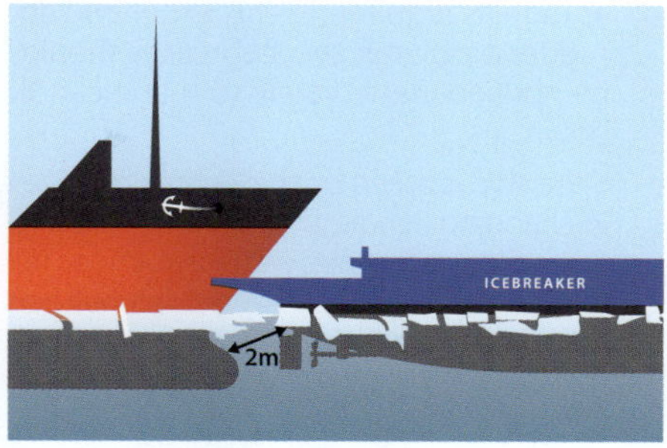

- where anchors are attached on the outside of the ship, and so may come into contact with the icebreaker's towing notch, the anchors must be catted, ie moved astern (see below), or placed onto the deck before the towing operation begins
- during a towing operation, the towed ship is steered manually and must be ready for immediate manoeuvring.

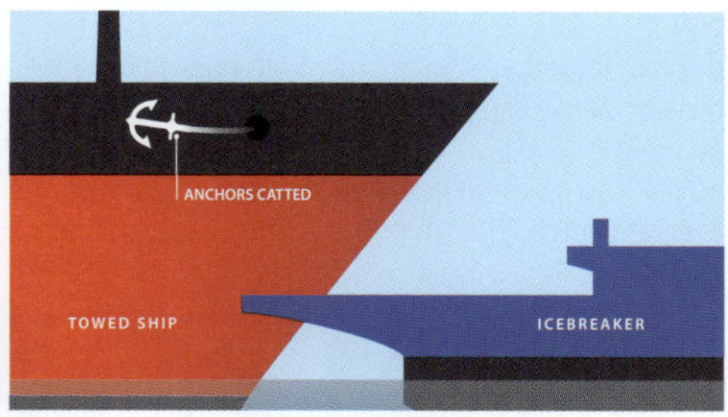

Courtesy of Patrick Toomey

Figure 13.10 - Anchors lifted on deck in preparation for close coupled towing

The hull of the towed ship acts as an active rudder for the icebreaker. When proceeding straight ahead, the ship should be kept in a straight line with the icebreaker's masts.

Towing in Ice

- The towed ship's propulsion machinery should only be used as instructed by the icebreaker
- if the ship cannot keep the engine output as high as required, or it is experiencing rudder problems, the icebreaker should be notified immediately so that it can slow down
- if the ship is asked by the icebreaker to assist in changing course, the helm has to be turned in accordance with instructions from the icebreaker as the towed ship's hull acts as the rudder for the whole towing combination.

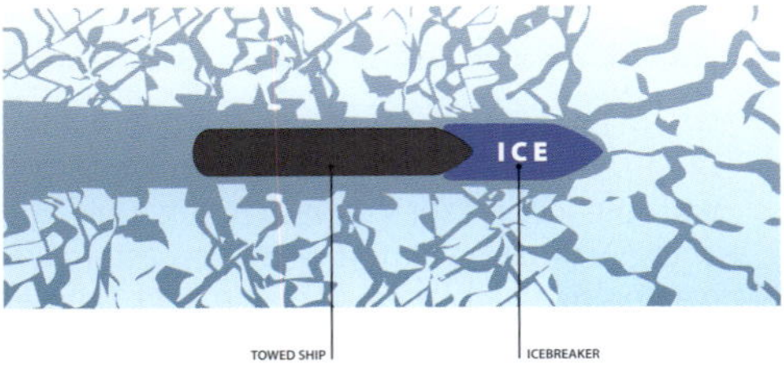

Should the icebreaker have to come astern while carrying out close coupled towing, the towed ship must come astern, bringing the icebreaker with it. Before doing this, it will be necessary for the towed ship to go at least half ahead for some time to allow the propeller wash to clear any ice away from the area astern. The towed ship must advise the icebreaker when the ice is clear and then both vessels can come astern. Jack-knifing may occur, which, if allowed to become excessive, will part the bridle. When jack-knifing does occur, the icebreaker will immediately apply ahead power to straighten up the ship. If insufficient stern movement has been achieved for the next ram, the manoeuvre must be repeated. If the towed ship is wider than the icebreaker, she may experience damage on the shoulders.

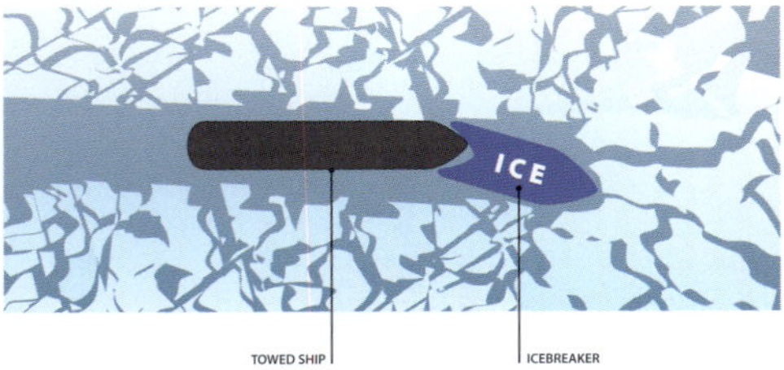

The bow of the ship pictured in Figure 13.11 was damaged after collision with an icebreaker's towing fork when the breaker came to a sudden halt in heavy ice in the Bothnian Bay. The damaged area was located on the forepeak, 2 metres above the waterline, and was 2 metres wide and 5 metres deep. The icebreaker's towing fork was also damaged.

Incidents and Accidents in Winter Navigation in the Baltic Sea, winter 2002-2003, Reproduced courtesy of the Finnish Maritime Administration

Figure 13.11 - Damaged bow due to collision with an icebreaker

Towing Ship to Ship

Situations could arise where a tow is carried out by a conventional ship as no tugs are available. However, this is an exceptionally dangerous procedure.

It is a SOLAS requirement for the master to assist those in distress, provided that the crew of the rescuing vessel are not imperiled themselves. The case for towing ship to ship could arise if, due to the prevailing weather conditions or other hazards, it is not possible for either the crew in distress to abandon their own ship or the rescuing vessel to remove them.

Towing ship to ship could be carried out for salvage. In such a case, due to the risks to the towing vessel, it is essential that the operator's consent is obtained before committing to such an enterprise.

CHAPTER 14

Stood by New Builds

Stood by New Builds

Standing by a new build involves an officer monitoring and observing the construction of a new vessel by the shipyard. The length of time spent standing by a new build has been gradually reducing over the years as both shipyards and the shipowners commissioning the ship wish to reduce the production costs involved with having an officer standing by on the construction and fitting out project.

Standing by a new build can require different levels of scrutiny. An in-depth supervision could involve monitoring the build from when the hull is laid up to sea trials. Standing by does not restrict the officer's duties to the yard in which the ship is predominantly being constructed, and the process could require visiting the premises of any subcontractors employed by the ship builder.

The role is important not just in terms of ensuring the build quality for the reassurance of the owner. An officer standing by may have to liaise between the builder, class society representative and any other interested regulatory body to ensure that any necessary requirements are complied with and certification granted appropriately.

The officer stood by plays an important role in formulating the final building specification and design. It is important that the ship design is intuitive and conducive to good ship and seafaring practice, eg there is no equipment obstructing the line of sight from the bridge windows.

Shipyard Safety for Deck Officers

Methods of shipbuilding and the shipyards themselves can be hazardous with obscure dangers waiting to strike any worker at any time. Even the most experienced are susceptible to danger if they lose their concentration. Therefore, a principal objective for any shipyard owner or manager is to establish a sound health and safety culture and practice. Workers should not have to learn safety rules simply because an accident has occurred.

If a deck officer is being seconded to a shipyard but is unfamiliar with shipyard operations, he must be provided with sufficient training prior to deployment. This must include training in enclosed space entry and emergency rescue procedures. He must also be aware of the dangers associated with metal plate, pipes, gas, cranes, and high voltage current and equipment. These dangers may be mitigated through job safety analysis, risk assessment, training and personal protection.

Stood by New Builds

A shipyard deck officer can be a valuable asset to any company during repairs or shipbuilding projects. They can help to control progress of the work with the best interests of the company in mind, and by building good relationships with project supervisors can ensure that the construction or repair is planned and implemented safely.

The shipyard's safety checks and briefings conducted at the beginning of the day before commencing operations are a priority.

Conclusion

Modern shipyards are vast and highly technical. They are the world's leading providers of engineering, design and construction in ship building and need to be able to meet the needs for the most up-to-date high-tech designs within the maritime industrial sector.

High levels of health and safety must be maintained across their operations and due regard given to ensuring their activities are environmentally sustainable and delivered within budget.

To integrate all these complicated processes and objectives the deck officer should be prepared to deal with meetings, authorisation responsibilities and communications with different levels of management throughout the project.

CHAPTER 15

Paints and Coatings

Paints and Coatings

Costs

Paint and coating costs vary widely. The cost of repairing non-performing coating systems in service can be high and disproportionate to those of a new build.

The cost of coatings and their application may typically represent:

- 0 to 5% of total ship cost at construction – commercial ships
- 0 to 15% of total ship cost at construction – chemical tankers
- 5 to 15% of annual maintenance costs for commercial ships
- up to 50% of drydocking costs – for large ships.

(Safinah Ltd)

There is an extensive range of ships' paint and coatings available and advanced products continue to be developed. Products used must be of the highest quality to ensure the coating provides the protection required for as long as possible and can cope with the differing weather conditions a ship will experience.

Adhesion

For the bonding between organic coatings and surfaces to be secure, it is important that there is no other matter between the surface and the paint. Any contamination will lead to an eventual breakdown of the bond in that area so it is essential that the surface is correctly prepared before painting.

A rough surface profile provides a greater surface area, resulting in a better bond. Zinc particles in both the primer and the topcoatings adhere well to the steel and, in the primer, act as a sacrificial anode layer of paint, assisting in the protection of the steel surface.

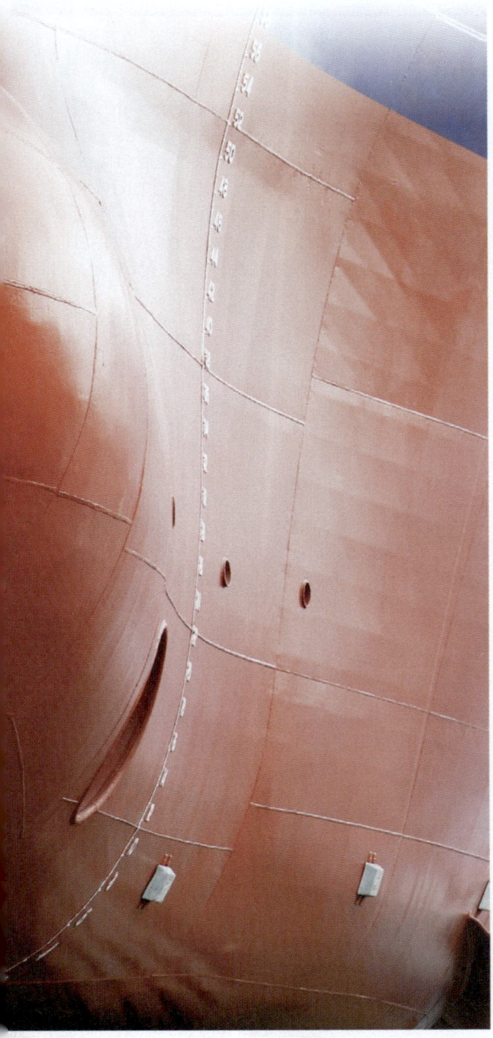

Paint

The primary purpose of paint is to seal the pores on wood and steel to decrease decay and inhibit the formation of rust. Paint smoothes out the surfaces and makes them washable and the introduction of colour gives a pleasant appearance to the overall finish.

Protective Clothing

The following protective clothing is essential when working with paint:

- Long-sleeved gloves
- cotton overalls
- disposable overall with a hood (these should be replaced daily)
- safety goggles
- hard hat.

When using spray paint, the best practice is to wear a full face mask. If only goggles are worn, a barrier cream should be applied to any exposed skin areas. Any rash that develops should be thoroughly cleaned and an anti-inflammatory cream applied to the affected area.

If paint gets into the eyes, they should be flushed with water or an eye solution for at least 10 minutes. If the eyes continue to give pain, medical treatment must be sought. A respiratory mask should be worn to protect against inhalation of paint particles.

Gloves and cotton overalls should be replaced if there is any paint breakthrough. The fabric sweatband inside the hard hat should be washed regularly. Masks should be cleaned daily and the filters renewed.

Paint Requirements

The metal parts of a ship are subject to differing environments. The bottom of the ship is rarely dry, the middle sections of the hull constantly change from wet to dry in seawater and the topsides are frequently subject to a variety of temperatures, wind and weather. Each area requires different preparation and the paint selected must have properties suited to the particular area to which it is being applied.

Bottom Paints

These are anti-corrosive and anti-fouling paints that are normally applied in drydock by shore personnel. It is important that they are applied correctly, with the anti-corrosive being applied first.

Anti-corrosive

It is essential that this coating is properly applied and covers the entire bottom, as anti-fouling paint can cause pitting if it comes into direct contact with the steel.

Anti-fouling

Anti-fouling paints are used to protect the underwater surface of the hull from corrosion and to reduce the drag caused by the build-up of marine organisms.

In 2001, the IMO approved a treaty to ban organotins from anti-fouling paints by January 2008. Before then, many anti-fouling paints contained tributyltin (TBT) or similar compounds, which are toxic and have adverse effects on the environment. Without anti-fouling paint on the hull, a biofilm forms that can add up to 20% drag and increase barnacle coverage by over 60%, adversely affecting fuel consumption and greenhouse gas emissions.

To replace the traditional anti-fouling coatings, the paint industry now produces non-toxic foul release coatings, which fall into two categories:

- Ablative hydrophilic polymer films: these form a sacrificial coating that attracts rather than repels water. The film requires a constant flow of water across its surface, which acts like a polish, keeping it smooth and free of any growth
- low free surface energy coatings: these give a non-stick or non-adhesive coating that again uses water flow to help prevent any growth on the surface.

Hull

The most important function of painting is to prevent corrosion. However, it is essential that the hull paint not only provides the best anti-corrosion protection but also provides a smooth surface, particularly on and below the waterline, as this can reduce frictional resistance by approximately 60% for the average vessel.

Surface friction of the hull is caused by:

- Marine growth
- paint roughness
- weld beads
- buckling or indentation.

Increasingly, hull coatings using silicone are being developed to achieve a reduction in friction. Experiments have been carried out using coatings based on silicone dioxide, which is chemically engineered to repel water. This, combined with an air delivery system at the bow, is intended to form a thin layer of air between the water and the underwater hull surface that will reduce the friction to 30% for the average ship, half of the present figure.

Primers

Primers are rust inhibitors that are applied as base coats onto prepared bare steel. They seal the pores of the steel and provide a smooth surface for the topcoats. At least two coats of primer are normally used before applying the topcoats. On aluminium and galvanised steel, only zinc chromate primers should be used.

Paint Types

Paint types can be divided by their drying properties. These are:

- Chemical curing paints - consisting of two components that are mixed together, causing a chemical reaction between the base and the hardener
- oxidative paints - the drying process is initiated by the chemical reaction between the oil in the paint and the oxygen in the air
- physically drying paint - the drying process is caused by the evaporation of the solvents in the paint.

Paint Coating Type	Advantages	Disadvantages
Alkyd Paints These are made up from alcohol and acid and are more suitable for exposure to mild environments.	• Easy to apply (one pack product) • good adhesion and penetration • good finish and colour.	• Limited resistance to solvents and chemicals • poor resistance to extreme humidity • limited film thickness • limited water resistance.
Vinyl Paints These are physically drying paints used for a wide variety of purposes in the marine environment. The term 'vinyl' covers many different types of manufacture of these paints and compatibility can be an issue between the different brands.	• Easy to use (one pack product) • good water resistance • quick drying • can be applied in a wide differential of temperatures.	• Can be a compatibility issue between various brands • poor resistance to strong solvents.
Chlorinated Rubber Paints These are physically drying paints widely used in the marine environment.	• Not temperature dependent • easy to recoat • good water resistance • good chemical resistance.	• Poor solvent resistance • can give off chlorine with age • low heat resistance.
Epoxy Coatings These are very versatile coatings that tend to be made for specific applications with good adhesion to steel. Solvent-free epoxy coatings are made for use in water tanks.	• Good water resistance • good adhesion • good chemical resistance • tough surface.	• Temperature limitations on application • care has to be taken in applying (two pack product) • poor resistance to sunlight (topcoat may be required for decorative purposes).
Mastic Epoxy Coatings These are made from a blend of resins depending on the manufacturer and are among the most versatile of all marine coatings.	• More user friendly and cheaper than epoxy coatings • very good water resistance • thick coats.	• Chalking in sunlight (additional topcoat may be required for decorative purposes) • different paints are required for different areas of the ship.
Polyurethane Coatings These are chemically curing paints that are excellent for use as topcoats on epoxy coatings and for painting plastics and wood.	• Good all round weather resistance • excellent decorative appearance • good solvent resistance • good all-purpose paint • can be worked in temperatures down to 0°C.	• Two component (but can be one) • can cause skin irritation.
Zinc Coatings Inorganic zinc coatings are used in the marine industry as primers which also provide cathodic protection.	• Cathodic protection • good solvent and chemical resistance • good recoatability.	• Two pack paint • humidity required for curing.

Surface Preparation

Surface preparation is often a compromise between what should be done and what is possible with the small number of crew and limited time available on the majority of ships. Unfortunately, if surface preparation is not carried out correctly, the painting that follows will be more for cosmetic appearance than for the protection for which it is primarily intended.

The surface being painted must be clear of all rust, dirt, oil, grease or salt and be completely dry or the paint cannot adhere properly or fill all the pores of the steel. There are a number of cleaning solutions for the preparation of surfaces, but care must be taken that very strong cleaning agents are not used on existing paintwork as they tend to burn or soften the existing coating. Thinners are commonly used to remove grease and oil but, if these are used, the surface must be washed clean afterwards.

Whichever method is used to prepare metal for painting, it is essential that time is allowed for an initial coat of primer to be applied and to dry.

Solvents and Cleaners

Common solvents, such as paraffin or white spirit, can be used to remove grease but they leave an oily residue. There are various commercial cleaners that can be water rinsed and these can be used provided they are compatible with the existing paint.

Hand Tools

Wire brushes and scrapers are good for cleaning out pitted surfaces, welding areas, light rust and paintwork where power tools cannot be used. Chipping hammers must be used with care as they can dent the steelwork and form high and low areas. The paint will follow these contours, leaving thinner paint on the high area, which will wear off more quickly than in the thicker area and spots of rust may develop.

As hand preparation will not leave a clean substrate, the coating can be expected to break down within two years.

Chains

Using a length of small steel chain, with a rope at each end held by a crew member and with a turn around the rail, can still be the most effective way of removing paint and scale from a rail. If all the paint or scale is not removed, a scraper can be used to remove the residue.

Water Washing

If paint is to be applied on top of paint, water washing with a high pressure fresh water hose may be acceptable to remove any salt residue adhering to fine cracks in the paint. If this is not done properly, the newly applied paint will blister and crack.

Power Tools

Power tools improve steel preparation provided they are properly used. Care must be taken that the surface of the metal is not polished as this will reduce the roughness required to 'key' the paint.

Portable Grinder

This can be used with a grinding wheel and a variety of rotary brushes, enabling different rust conditions to be dealt with by the same tool. A portable grinder can also scale in difficult areas.

Power Chisels and Hammers

These can also be used but precautions against denting must be taken.

Needle Guns

Needle guns will not dent the metal and can work in small areas that tend to be missed by the larger tools. The guns are either air driven or electric and can be of different sizes. Varying needle sizes can be used, depending on the size of area and the condition of the scale or paint being removed.

Deck Hammers and Flails

For large deck spaces, deck hammers or flail tools, often referred to as 'deck lawnmowers', are a very quick and effective way to clear badly deteriorated decks of scale and old coatings.

Blast Cleaning

Water

Effective water jet blasting is dependent on the nozzle design, water pressure and the amount of water generated. While it can be useful for removing loose paint and rust, it will not remove hardened paint, mill scale or 'black' rust, nor will it provide the surface profile required for coating adhesion. Relatively good surfaces without rust, prepared in this way, can be expected to last up to five years, but on the average older surface, this reduces to less than two years. Water blasting, even with ultra-high pressure blasting equipment, should be regarded more as cleaning than as rust removal.

Grit

Grit is the most effective way of removing rust, scale and old paint. Prior to blasting, it should be ensured that the surface is free from grease. Rough edges, such as welding seams, should be ground down as the paint runs away from any sharp edges leaving a thinner coating. Weld spatter is a regular cause of coating breakdown.

The surface obtained during blasting is dependent on the grade and type of abrasive used, the air pressure and the skill of the operators. Sand, slag, mineral grit and steel shot can be used to achieve varying degrees of roughness.

Care must be taken not to over-recycle abrasives as some are less effective than others when reused. After grit blasting, surface dust must be removed. Compressed air is normally used on the open decks, but industrial vacuum cleaners should be used in tanks.

Sandblasting

Silica sand is most commonly used for sandblasting, but the residue forms silica dust, which can cause lung disease. As a result, the use of silicone sandblasting is strictly controlled in many countries and regulations are in force regarding ventilation, PPE and air supply.

Spot Blasting

Before spot blasting takes place, the area to be blasted should be marked out. The coating of the area around this will inevitably be damaged by scattering blast particles and must be treated and recoated as necessary.

Slurry Blasting

Slurry blasting uses a mix of water and abrasive particles. There is no dust residue from this type of blasting but the bare metal will rust very quickly without primer applied.

Preparation of Galvanised Steel

Degreasing most galvanised surfaces requires some effort, but it needs to be undertaken to ensure that the surface is clean, dry and grease free.

Heavy blast cleaning of galvanised steel should be avoided. However, if the steel is corroded and a rougher surface is required, a light blasting is acceptable. Once completed, the dust should be immediately blown off the surface.

Hand or power tools can be used with the exception of chipping hammers.

Preparation of Aluminium

Light blasting can assist paint adhesion to the surface, but any form of grit containing iron or copper should not be used as it will contaminate the aluminium surface. However, the use of aluminium oxide is permissible. Care must be taken when using hand tools that the surface of the aluminium is not scratched. Commercial paint remover and wooden or plastic scrapers can be used to remove old paint coatings.

Before painting, a coat of etch primer should be applied to provide a key for further paint coats. The colour should change from pale yellow to green/brown, indicating successful etching, and, if this does not occur, the adhesion of further coats will be poor. If there is no colour change, the surface should be scraped clean, treated with an aluminium pre-treatment solution and the acid etch primer then reapplied.

Surface Preparation

Preparation of Fibreglass

Glass reinforced plastic (GRP) is a polyester resin strengthened with glass fibre. A mould is made, into which a wax release agent is applied, followed by a polyester gel coat and then strengthened by applying a laminate of polyester resin weave. Over time, the gel-coated surface is affected by ultraviolet degradation and normal wear and tear, which causes the cosmetic appearance to deteriorate.

As a gel coat cannot be reapplied on the ship, paint can be applied. This is particularly important on lifeboats, where it is necessary to keep a good colour to the luminous orange.

Prior to painting, the surface must be thoroughly cleaned and degreased. A light hand or power tool sanding should assist with surface adhesion of the paint coat.

Preparation of Wood

Bare wood must be sanded, after which any flaws or indentations can be filled with an all-purpose filler or wood filler. This is followed by a primer that is intended to soak into the grain and take some of the porosity out of the wood. If the wood is not clean, washing down with sugar soap prior to priming will degrease it. If there are any knots in the timber, they should be treated with knotting solution.

For previously painted surfaces, there is no need to remove all the paint if it is not flaking and is in a stable condition. The surface should be cleaned with sugar soap, sanded down with a fine paper to give a key for the new paint, then undercoated to give a better finish and to stop the paint from 'dragging' on the surface.

Painting

The key to successful painting is preparation. While the material to be painted must be prepared properly, so must the area around it. Spindles should be greased to keep the paint off. Paint must not be allowed to spill onto rubber seals as it hardens and degrades the rubber and prevents proper sealing. Windows and ports should have sealing tape or grease applied.

Tools, such as brushes, rollers, stages and masking tape, should all be laid out ready for use. It is essential that the weather is checked prior to starting the work.

The lines on the stages and bosun's chairs should be checked and the wood outreaches should be padded where they come into contact with the paintwork to avoid scraping it.

Rollers are good for large smooth areas but they are often reused for all surfaces, which results in areas being missed or splattered with the wrong paint. The paint tool kit for the day should always include a mix of brushes and rollers.

It is important to check the use-by date of the paint before application. If it has gone beyond the shelf life, the paint will have deteriorated.

Painting Defects

The following chart lists some of the problems that occur when paint is not applied properly or has aged.

Spray Painting

The standard air spray requires a compressed air pressure of between 40 and 70 psi to atomise the paint, with an air temperature between 5°C and 21°C. Hot spray methods, using a conventional air spray but with additional equipment for heating the paint, use less paint as there is reduced 'bounce back' off the surface (overspray).

Preparation

It is essential that all surfaces not intended to be painted are covered and that masking tape is used to seal this covering down. Certain areas cannot be sprayed and must be painted by hand after the spraying is completed.

Ensure that the spray gun is completely clean, particularly at the nozzle, and that the paint is strained through cheesecloth before being put into the container.

Painting

Defect	Cause	Recommendation
Sound paintwork faded but adhering	Normal wear and exposure to elements.	Remove oil/grease marks. Clean the surface. Remove any loose paint.
Paintwork heavily crusted with previous paint	Previous touch-ups carried out without proper preparation.	Remove oil/grease marks. Clean the surface. Remove crusts of old paint to sound surface. Dust down.
Paintwork flaking and poor adhesion	Painted over moist surface. Painted over contaminated surface. Too short an interval between coats.	Remove oil/grease marks. Clean the surface. Remove flaking paint down to sound surface by chipping or wire brushing. Dust down.
Paintwork with limited areas of blistering/corrosion	Painted over moist surface. Using equipment containing water, eg brushes/rollers stored in water. Using finishing coats over bare steel. Poor initial surface treatment.	Remove oil/grease marks. Clean the surface. Scrape blisters and remove any corrosion. Wash to remove any fluid from blisters.
Areas of corrosion and heavy rust	Maintenance neglected over a period of time or carried out with no preparation of surfaces.	Remove oil/grease marks. Chip to remove heavy rust. Remove remainder of corrosion. Grit blast/power discing where possible or hand brushing if these means are not available. This method is not suitable for extensive areas of rust.
Paint surface cracking or crocodiling	Soft coat of primer or undercoat overcoated with a hard finish coat. Too short an interval between coats. Paint unsuited to its use.	Remove oil/grease marks. Chip or scrape to remove cracked paint to reveal sound paint or bare steel. Wipe/dust down.
Brush marks on surface	Using over-strong brush strokes. Paint too thick when applied. Undercoat with poor flow.	Clean down surface as necessary. Lightly abrade marked areas with wire brush or emery block.
Bubbling on the surface	Application by brush or roller carried out too vigorously and paint 'worked' too much. Freshly painted surface exposed to strong sunlight.	Clean down surface as necessary. Lightly abrade area to remove the bubbles by light power discing or hand scraping.
Cissing (withdrawal of paint in spots)	Surface contaminated by grease, etc. Previous coat is not compatible with topcoat (check that correct paint has been applied).	Remove the cissed paint wherever possible. Thoroughly degrease exposed surface by light power discing or hand scraping.
Sagging	Excessively thick coats applied. Spray gun unskilfully used. Application over high gloss. Too much thinner.	Remove areas of sagging to reveal sound coatings beneath. Fresh coats may be removed by hand scraping, other coats by power discing.
Wrinkling	Paint applied too thickly. Fresh paint exposed to direct sunlight.	Remove areas of wrinkling to reveal sound coating beneath. Wipe/dust down surface. Light power discing/hand scraping.

Painting

The manufacturer's instructions for nozzle width and pressure should be followed for the type of paint being used.

Ensure that the correct PPE is used.

Check for wind. Any wind across the painting area will completely disrupt the spray and the coating applied.

Cleaning

On completion or when changing paint type, it is essential that the gun is completely cleaned before reuse. Always use the same material that was used to thin the paint to clean the gun and spray the thinner through the gun until it comes out clear. The container should then be wiped clean with a rag dampened in the same thinner. The most common part for blockage is the nozzle where paint has dried, so disassemble the air cap and nozzle and wipe them clean, making sure all air passages are clear of paint.

Spray Painting Defects

'Orange Peel'

The surface finish resembles orange peel. This may be caused by the use of improper thinners, insufficient atomisation, holding the gun too far away from or too close to the surface, an improper mixture of materials or low humidity. This can be dealt with by sanding, to level the surface of the paint, once it is thoroughly cured.

Peeling

This is almost always due to not cleaning the surface properly or incompatibility of paint films. Before any spraying is attempted, the surface must be absolutely clean.

Sags or Runs

These are caused by the paint being too thick or drying too slowly. Again, sanding can be undertaken when the paint is cured.

Pinholes

These may be caused by water or excessive thinner in the paint. Small bubbles form that break on drying, leaving tiny holes.

Blushing
This resembles a powdering of the applied coating. The paint will appear to be blotchy, milky or cloudy and this is very common in lacquer paints or other paint systems. The cellulose material in the lacquer separates from its solvent and returns to its original powder form. Water usually causes this and it can occur because of surface moisture or excessive humidity. When blushing occurs, it cannot be corrected by sanding and the entire area must be cleaned off and repainted.

Paint Safety and PPE

Safety Precautions for the Paint Locker

Most paint presents a safety hazard both to the ship and to the health of those working with it.

Oils of organic origin dry by oxidation, producing heat that, if it cannot escape, can increase to an ignition temperature and spontaneously combust, resulting in fire. It is essential that all paint, thinners and associated materials are kept in sealed containers.

Mineral spirits evaporate rather than oxidise. While not leading to spontaneous combustion, the gases given off can be hazardous to health or cause an explosion. Therefore, it is important to ventilate the area.

If there is canvas or other material on the deck of the paint locker to protect the deck, it must be taken up at the end of the day, removed and dried out. Leaving it in the locker could cause spontaneous combustion.

Linseed oil, turpentine and fish oils are of organic origin and can form serious fire hazards when left on rags. Used rags should be kept in a metal container and disposed of once work has finished each day. The rags should not be left in the locker overnight.

Personal Safety

The main hazard of paint is that it contains solvents and active ingredients that can wet and remove the natural fat from the skin and cause a skin rash. Damage to the lungs and the nervous system can be caused by these solvents and paint particles. Dry paint, such

Paint Safety and PPE

as on work clothing or overspray dust, can also cause irritation, particularly when in contact with sweaty skin.

All paints and coatings come with the manufacturer's recommended safety procedures and instructions for use. These will include the surface preparation required, the drying time, equipment and any other pertinent requirements.

An MSDS for the product is also provided, along with instructions regarding the ventilation requirements and any particular protective measures to be taken. It is important to read and follow all the recommendations and instructions on the sheet.

Protection while Blasting

Special protective clothing must be worn during blasting operations.

During the application of the abrasive, pressure can drop within the hose lines. This often causes surges that can throw operators off staging or scaffolding, so safety harnesses must be worn at all times.

Precautions while Spraying

During spray painting, the crew should take the following basic precautions:

- If painting in well-ventilated spaces or outside, a dust cartridge respirator can filter out particles of paint effectively, provided the cartridge is replaced at regular intervals
- if ventilation is poor, it is essential that a proper air-fed hood and masking system is used
- under no circumstances should rags or cloths be tied over the mouth and nose. These do not filter the paint properly and can become impregnated with paint particles, allowing paint to enter the mouth
- when working with any form of paint spray, anyone not engaged in the spraying should be kept out of the area. Those working with the spray should always be upwind of the area being sprayed. If working in a confined area close to other work areas, the area should be screened.

Dry spray also causes health problems and should be removed from the area, on completion, by brushing or hosing down.

CHAPTER 16

Drydock

Planning

Some months before the drydocking, a list of everything requiring attention should be prepared, even if at that stage it is uncertain where the drydocking will take place. This list should detail even the most basic requirements, such as gangways, phone lines, shore power and sewage lines. Many operators will specify how the drydocking list is to be prepared but, if not, it is suggested that the list is divided into the following basic sections:

- Services
- hull
- safety items
- deck
- catering department
- surveys
- electronics
- crew work
- supplementary repairs
- stores and spares.

Services

Fire Mains Connection

This must be made as soon as the ship loses water for the ship's fire main service.

Freshwater

Even if the ship has a sufficient supply from the freshwater tanks and these are not being opened up for cleaning, they will have to be replenished to the amount on board at the docking time for stability purposes. This also applies to various other ballast tanks that may have to be filled.

Sewage Lines

The location of the drydock will determine the necessary requirements.

Shore Power

Shore power should be requested, even if it is not considered essential by the ship.

Gangways

Two should be requested so that, if crane work is taking place in way of one gangway, the other can be used.

Shore Workers' Facilities

Depending on the size of ship, various facilities may be required such as an office, changing areas, sanitary facilities and even a basic canteen. If the ship cannot provide these, or does not want shore workers using crew facilities, the dock must be required to provide them for their own staff. Many drydocks will have portable toilets and cabins that can be lifted onto the deck for these purposes.

Security

The operators or the shipyard may require a gangway watch to be kept, which the ship may not be able to provide, particularly if it is maintaining its own watch system and checking on hot work areas and enclosed spaces. In this case, a shore watch service should be requested.

Cranes

It may seem strange to request cranes in a drydock but many have to hire these by the hour and they must be pre-arranged, particularly for ships' stores and spares. Rarely in a drydock can the ship's own storing cranes or even cargo cranes reach the dockside.

Transport

Increasingly, drydocks are becoming more safety conscious and there may be restrictions on crew movement in the dock area. If this is the case, some form of transport between the gates and the ship may have to be organised.

Waste Removal

This usually consists of placing skips on board at intervals during the drydock. Often the yard will do this for the removal of their own waste and the ship can utilise them for the ship's waste, but otherwise skips will have to be organised. Waste oils or chemicals will require separate disposal facilities.

Preparation

Hull

If records have been properly maintained, the shell expansion plan should have a record of all dents sustained since the ship was built and notes as to what work has been carried out at previous drydocks. Many plans are now computerised and are therefore much easier to record, but the plan is still needed to identify the frame numbers where there are indentations.

Indentations that have occurred since the last drydock must be listed with their frame numbers and the approximate depth of the indentation. If possible, after outside inspection, the indentations should also be inspected from inside the hull for any cracking of the frames. Listed alongside the indentation should be any extract of the log entry that corresponds to it or which could be associated with it, such as tugs landing heavily or the ship landing heavily alongside.

Although it is impossible to view the bottom of the ship, any incidents involving grounding either on passage or while alongside should also be recorded in the list to assist Class and P&I in the drydock.

Draught, Freeboard and Tug Markings

These should be listed for repainting along with other markings such as pilot recommended metre freeboard mark, thruster warnings, bulbous bow, etc.

Seachest Covers and Gratings

Some operators require the ship to list these for removal, cleaning out and coating.

Hull Painting

As ships become larger and drydock less frequently, hull blasting and coating is now usually undertaken by the technical department ashore. On small ships and in small companies, however, the ship may still be required to list these items on their initial drydock list.

Safety Items

It is recommended that all safety items are either highlighted and given a separate coding, such as S1, S2, etc, or are placed under a completely separate heading of 'Safety'. This ensures that the technical department ashore is aware of these items and also enables the ship to send a copy of this separate list to the Safety Department.

A copy of the initial safety list should be retained by the ship. If items are removed from this list by the operators and subsequently there is an accident or incident involving the items removed, the list can be presented to the appropriate bodies or investigation. The safety officer ashore should obtain the original list with the initials of the person who removed these items.

Items to include on the Safety List

Gangways

The drydocking allows the gangways to be lifted off their platforms and the platform examined for any damage. The platform can be scaled and cleaned as required and then coated before the gangway is replaced. The underside of the head of the gangway should also be examined before being replaced.

Galley Uptakes

Over a period of time, these uptakes become coated with grease from the galley stoves. This grease can, when heated, drip down onto the stoves and cause a fire hazard. It is important that the drydocking includes steam cleaning of these uptakes.

Lifeboats

As with gangways, the drydock provides the opportunity to land the lifeboats and have the davits properly examined and maintained by either shore labour or ship's staff. While the boats are ashore they can also be checked over and painted if required.

Safety Barriers

During the drydock, manholes will be opened for work inside the tanks and it is unlikely that the ship will have sufficient safety barriers to put up around them. A sufficient number should be requested, even if it is normal shipyard practice to provide them.

Preparation

Shore Gangway Lighting

Quite often in drydock, the shore gangway lighting, including at the head and foot of the gangways, is inadequate. By specifying this as a requirement, the attention of the drydock is drawn to this important safety item.

Tank and Hold Ladders

A number of these, particularly on older vessels, will be corroded, broken or bent. These must be examined, cropped and repaired as required.

Pollution Barrier

If the ship is going to a layby berth to prepare the draught and trim before docking, there will be considerable pumping taking place, probably into the hours of darkness, as well as shore workers on board in the engine room who are not familiar with the various controls. It is a wise precaution to have a pollution boom put around the ship while pumping and transferring tanks during this period.

Deck

Assuming that the items previously listed havAssuming that the items previously listed have been placed on a separate safety list, the remaining standard items for the deck department are:

Plugs

It is common practice to remove the plugs from the tanks on the bottom. Depending on the size of the ship, these plugs can be handed over to the chief officer for safe keeping or kept in a dock office with a list given to the chief officer.

While alongside layby berths or in drydock, it is important that the crew still look after the tidiness of the vessel and look for potential safety hazards

Anchors

Anchor maintenance is often neglected but drydock is the ideal place to carry it out. Both anchors and cables should be walked back out of the chain lockers and ranged along the dock bottom. All the shackles should be opened up and inspected, replacing where necessary. The outboard length should be changed with the inboard length. The anchor's markings should be renewed before replacing the chain in the lockers.

Chain Lockers

While the chain is out of the lockers, the chain lockers should be inspected, cleaned out, coated and the drains cleaned.

Halyards

On many ships, the halyards are placed high on a single main mast on the monkey island, which is often difficult and dangerous to work on, particularly at sea. It is recommended that all the main mast halyards are put down for replacement, taking advantage of the availability of a drydock crane for this task.

Scupper Plugs

When work on the hull begins, plugs will be required for all main deck scuppers to avoid interference with the coating and painting. If the ship does not have them, they will have to be provided by the dockyard.

Catering Department

On many ships, there is no officer in charge of this department and it is left to the deck department to oversee the day-to-day running and repairs. As this department is often undermanned, it is important that as much as possible is done by yard labour during the ship's stay.

Provided steam cleaning of the uptakes has been included in the safety list, standard items should include:

Deck Protection

This consists of supplying and laying craft paper or similar over all the accommodation deck surfaces. All cabin and office spaces that may be used by shore personnel, such as the master's and the chief engineer's quarters, should also be covered.

Fumigation

If there is any insect infestation, such as cockroaches, the drydocking provides the opportunity to have the galley and other infested areas fumigated by shore companies.

Oven Cleaning

All too often during the normal running of the ship, it is difficult to ensure that this task is done properly and the drydock provides the opportunity for this to be carried out.

Accommodation Maintenance

The accommodation, particularly with long intervals between drydocks, always requires some degree of repair, eg painting woodwork, recovering furniture, replacing flooring or dry cleaning curtains.

Provisions and Dry Stores

Extra provisions and cleaning materials may have to be ordered to cope with consumption during the drydock. If the ship is run on a budgetary system, this list should be sent to the office for approval and costing into the drydock account, rather than coming out of the ship's budget.

Surveys

An efficient ship will maintain its own list of surveys and due dates regardless of records kept by the shore departments. This enables the ship to plan the surveys and request them to fit in with the ship's programme.

The drydock always presents the best opportunity to complete many of these surveys, particularly as Class will be available in the port. A list of the surveys required should be sent, together with any additional work, repair or maintenance of equipment associated with that survey requiring completion prior to the survey taking place.

Electronics

The electronics list will include items from both the engine and deck departments unless the items are included within those departments' own drydock specifications. Electro-technical officers are increasingly found on board ships and, if one is on board, it will be his responsibility to ensure completion of the electronics list.

Much of the bridge and engine room electronic equipment is not designed to be maintained by the ship's staff and, in these cases, arrangements should be made for maintenance companies to attend, in accordance with the manufacturer's instructions.

Crew Work

The ship's management knows best what work is required to be carried out by the crew in the drydock repair period. It is better at the planning stage to at least outline the work required to be done rather than have other work imposed.

However, once the ship has docked, there is often a considerably greater amount of work required to be carried out by the crew and this means that the original tasks given to them are often not completed.

When making out the drydock work list, it is important that items are only scheduled for the attention of the ship's crew if there is no doubt they will be able to complete them. For all other items, shore labour should be requested.

Supplementary Repairs

The later any additional items are submitted to the office, the more problematic they become, particularly when they are regarded as non-essential. If the final drydock list has been prepared and the costing and budget completed, there is a good chance that, unless essential, additional items will not be included. This is why it is imperative that, after the preliminary list has been completed and sent, any further items that become apparent are immediately sent without waiting for more to accumulate.

Stores and Spares

Alongside the various items listed, if stores or spares are required for the repair, these should be listed as well as the part numbers if known. Additional paint and cleaning materials should also be considered.

Final Preparation

It is essential that, prior to the drydock, a meeting is held to organise the management of the ship during the drydock period. While a number of the functions of normal shipboard management can continue, there are additional duties to be delegated. On arrival at the yard, whether to a layby berth for drydock preparation or direct to the dock, a considerable number of requests will be made to the ship's management and the more that can be done to prepare for these before arrival, the easier the management function will be.

The drydock specification should now be with the ship so a schedule of work for the ship's staff can be reviewed. An example of the special notes to the repair yard included in these specifications is shown below.

Special Notes to Repairers

This specification shall not be released to third parties without the owner's prior permission in writing.

1. **When submitting repair bills, the owner's code numbers should be stated for each individual item.**
2. **No additional or extra work beyond that specified is to be put in hand, unless specially ordered by the attending superintendent, who must be informed of time and price prior to commencement of work.**
3. **Full credit to be allowed for all time in the specification that is not carried out.**
4. **All sizes given in the specification are given in good faith but are not guaranteed. The contractor is to take his own measurements and, where it has not been possible to provide exact dimensions for various items, unit tariff price is to be applied, in which case the unit price should be given if not specified in the shipyard's tariff.**
5. **An outline planning repair schedule is to be submitted before commencement of work.**
6. **All readings, wear downs, calibrations, etc to be recorded with adequate copies supplied to ship's staff and owner's superintendent immediately as taken and a complete set submitted at the end of repair period with cost included in tender.**
7. **The contractor is to supply all tools, equipment, material, etc that may be required to carry out the work and to be fully responsible for all such equipment with cost included in tender.**
8. **All equipment that has been installed, repaired or overhauled by the contractor to be tested to the satisfaction of the superintendent and the ship's chief engineer/chief officer.**
9. **No extension of time will be allowed for extra work carried out unless initially agreed that this work cannot be carried out in docking period.**
10. **All machinery and pipes, etc to be reassembled with new joints, bolts/studs, and packing and locking washers/locking pins with costs included in tender as standard tariff.**
11. **Facilities to be provided, if required, for onloading ship's store/spares. Quote price for craneage on an hourly basis.**
12. **Temporary telephone service to be provided on board for communication purposes. Quote price for connection/disconnection and daily charge, if any.**
13. **For painting in drydock, scupper chute to be fitted in hull discharge openings. Quote price for each fitted/removed including staging.**
14. **All repair items subject to cancellation by attending superintendent.**
15. **A work done list is to be compiled and submitted to the attending superintendent for signature for work completed prior to the superintendent's departure from yard.**

Shipboard Management

Regardless of who is attending the drydock from the operating office or their position in the company, the master is in command of the ship and is responsible for all activities and persons on the ship. It is very easy in the drydock for shipboard management to descend into crisis or disappear altogether without strict control.

In spite of the number of visitors, workmen and activities going on, the ship must continue to function as a disciplined unit and continue

to provide amenities for those on board.
A shipboard office will be required for meetings and visiting surveyors and superintendents, and if possible a space should be designated and prepared before arrival. The ship's plans can be placed ready for use and desk space is always an advantage.

Plastic cups, coffee makers and boilers can be ordered and readied for use. It considerably reduces the workload on the catering staff if everyone makes their own tea or coffee. An officer of the day system should be established with a central office containing the gangway noticeboard, which directs everyone visiting the ship. Provided this officer has direct communications with the senior officers and the superintendent, he will know where to locate everyone on board and can also deal with the various domestic problems that will certainly occur.

Ship Condition

Once the drydock has been nominated, the ship will receive information regarding the stipulated drydock draught and trim condition. On a large ship, this can be difficult to achieve prior to docking as the condition will prohibit functional manoeuvrability. The ship will therefore be required to berth at a layby berth while this condition is achieved. Any tanks required to be opened up for inspection may interfere with the ballasting.

Safety

The ship's safety officer plays an important role in the drydock. If the officer is a head of department with many other responsibilities, it may be necessary to appoint a deputy officer to take over the day-to-day tasks in the dock.

Prior to docking, a fire emergency procedure must be decided, including the alarms that will be broadcast throughout the ship, particularly on the decks.

At this stage, the ship's safety requirements regarding 'no go' areas for shore personnel, smoking, hot work, enclosed spaces, guarding of openings in the deck and any other general requirements particular to the ship should be itemised and a copy of the ship's safety policy, together with the name of the safety officer and any deputy designated as the drydock safety officer, sent ahead to the dock office.

It is also useful to request a meeting with the dock safety officer as soon as possible on arrival to discuss liaison between the ship and the dockyard.

While the normal safety functions of the ship carry on, there will be additional personnel on board carrying out the various repairs throughout the day and night, many of which will require some degree of watch. It is common for the dock to provide fire watch, but the responsibility still remains with the ship to arrange these watches and to integrate them with the ship's own fire watch system.

The ship should prepare a precise schedule for enclosed space entry. This must involve a request for entry, a risk assessment, a certificate of air quality and ventilation, authorisation by the responsible senior officer and provision of the appropriate rescue and standby personnel. Again, this should be sent ahead of the ship's arrival to the drydock. Advance notification of the ship's safety arrangements to the dock does not interfere with any liaison or amendments that can be made after discussions with the drydock management. It does, however, prepare the dock for the ship's requirements and give them sufficient warning to prepare labour for the arrival. A hot work board should be prepared to allow easy reference to and recording of the state of all hot work being undertaken on board.

Drills

Prior to arrival, a pollution drill and a fire drill, based on the drydock situation of the ship, should be held, particularly if any new signal or muster point has been designated for the ship's stay.

Shipboard Routine

The normal shipboard routine in port may be disrupted during the stay. Galleys, laundries, heads and showers, heating and air conditioning may be shut down and cabins may have to be evacuated for shore workers.

As the drydock repair list is known by the ship before entry, some preparations and alternative arrangements may be put in place to assist with shipboard management when these events occur.

Preparation

Ship's Staff

If work is continuing around the clock, sleep can be a problem for those on board, particularly the watchkeepers. This is an important issue and should be remembered when scheduling crew working hours.

Drydocking for many ships is the only period during a voyage when the crew have time to get off the ship and relax. Transport can be arranged in many yards to assist with this.

The ship may also have additional personnel on board who have arranged to join the ship during the docking period. Their presence must be borne in mind, particularly if there are children involved, and special arrangements may have to be put in place regarding their safety.

Pollution

The ship's pollution equipment must be checked before arrival and any additional stores ordered as required. The ship must be guided by the pollution requirements and controls of the dockyard but must ensure that everything that can be done on board is done and that the shipboard pollution plan is followed.

Catering

The catering department can be put under considerable strain during drydock. Apart from trying to keep the ship's accommodation in some form of orderliness, meal times will often be extended to cope with the various visitors on board. The scheduling of ship's staff mealtimes and the mess rooms to be used can be decided before arrival. It is important that all heads of department and officers of the day are aware that any extra meals required must be advised to the chief steward or cook as soon as possible in order that food may be prepared. In addition, if any work is scheduled for the galley, mess rooms or food storage areas, the catering department must be advised as soon as possible.

The shore may provide protective coverings for the alleyways and working cabins which will certainly help to keep the areas clean. However, as these are often flimsy in nature, they may have to be replaced during an extended drydocking period.

It is also wise to include laundry and dry cleaning in the services required on arrival and some of these items can be readied to be landed on arrival.

Security

The ship's security officer should familiarise himself with the dockyard's security policy and ensure that the ship's security procedures conform to this. If gangway security is required but is not provided by the dockyard, the ship may have to hire private security for this purpose . Whoever provides security, a list of persons on board must be maintained. The dockyard and the ship should both keep a record of staff movements.

Drydocking Calculations

Sequence of Events During Drydocking

Figures 16.1 to 16.3 illustrate what happens as the ship enters the dry dock and the water is pumped out of the dock.

1. The ship enters the dry dock with a small trim by the stern and is floated into position.
2. The gates are closed and water is pumped out of the dock until the ship touches the blocks aft. Once the ship touches the blocks aft, this denotes the start of the critical period (it is now that the ship will start to experience a loss of stability).
3. As more water is pumped out of the dock, the true mean draught will start to reduce as the ship experiences more and more support at the stern. The upthrust afforded by the blocks at the stern is termed the 'P force', and this continues to increase as the buoyancy force reduces. Throughout the docking process, the ship will displace a progressively lessening volume of water as the true mean draught reduces and the P force increases to provide more support

Drydocking Calculations

for the ship (in effect, the P force takes over supporting the ship and the role of the buoyancy force in supporting the ship reduces). At this stage, the aft draught will be reducing at a greater rate than the rate at which the forward draught is increasing, and the ship will be trimming by the head as the overall true mean draught reduces. The loss of stability will also be increasing as the P force increases.

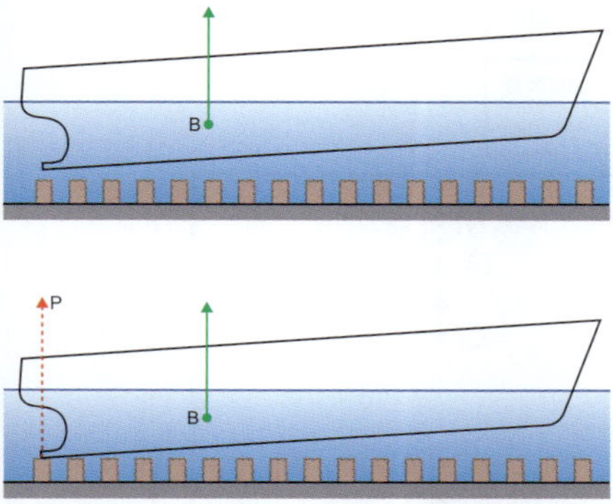

1. ***Ship enters dock with a small trim by the stern.***
2. ***Water is pumped out of the dock until the ship touches the blocks aft.***

Figure 16.1

4. Eventually the ship will come to rest on the blocks along its entire length. This critical instant denotes the end of the critical period since, for a flat bottomed ship, the problem of stability loss is no longer of concern.

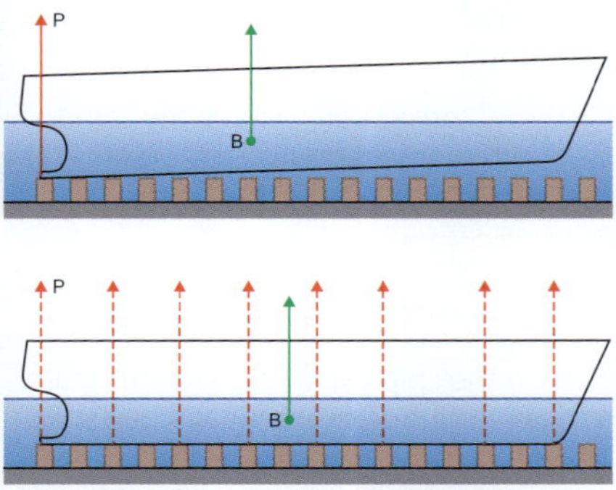

3. ***During the critical period, P force increases as the effect of the Bf reduces – overall TMD reduces as the ship trims by the head.***
4. ***On touching the blocks fore and aft, the draughts start to reduce uniformly fore and aft.***

Figure 16.2

5. After settling on the blocks fore and aft, water continues to be pumped from the dock and the draught reduces at the same rate fore and aft. The upthrust P becomes uniformly distributed along the ship's length and continues to increase as the effective buoyancy force reduces.
6. When the dock becomes nearly empty and the ship is fully dry, the upthrust P will be equal to the ship's displacement, having now replaced all the upthrust afforded by the buoyancy force.

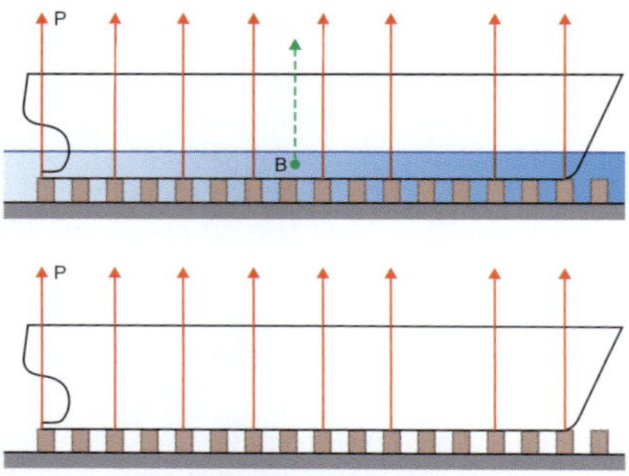

5. ***On touching the blocks fore and aft (critical instant), draughts reduce uniformly and P force becomes distributed along the ship's length.***
6. ***Once the ship is dry, the P force has completely taken over from the buoyancy force.***

Figure 16.3

Calculating the P Force

Calculation of P Force at any Stage During Drydocking

Throughout the drydocking procedure, the true mean draught reduces as it would if the ship were rising out of the water due to weights being discharged.

Consider the formula:

$$\text{Rise (cms)} = \frac{\text{w (t)}}{\text{TPC}}$$

The P force may be considered to have the same effect on true mean draught as if a weight had actually been discharged. Therefore: Reduction in TMD (cms) =

$$\frac{\text{P force (t)}}{\text{TPC}}$$

or:

$$\text{P force (t)} = \text{Reduction in TMD (cms)} \times \text{TPC}$$

This formula may be used to calculate the upthrust at the blocks at any stage in the docking

Drydocking Calculations

process since the true mean draught is always reducing as water is taken out of the dock.

Calculation of P Force During the Critical Period when Drydocking

In the period between the ship touching the blocks aft (start of the critical period) and touching the blocks forward and aft (the critical instant), the ship undergoes a change of trim.

The change of trim at any stage during the critical period may be considered to be the same as the change of trim that would have occurred had a weight 'w' been discharged from a position at the aft perpendicular equivalent to the upthrust P in tonnes (if it is assumed that the ship is on the blocks aft at the aft perpendicular).

Consider the formula: $\text{COT (cms)} = \dfrac{w \times d}{\text{MCTC}}$

If the force P is considered to have the same effect as a weight discharged at the aft perpendicular, then:

$$\text{COT (cms)} = \frac{P \times d}{\text{MCTC}}$$

or:

$$P = \frac{\text{COT (cms)} \times \text{MCTC}}{\text{Dist LCF foap}}$$

This can be used to calculate the P force during the critical period only.

Loss of Stability when Drydocking

Loss of stability commences as soon as the ship touches the blocks aft and continues to worsen as the value of the P force increases. The maximum loss of GM of concern occurs the instant immediately prior to the ship settling on the blocks forward and aft – this time being termed the critical instant. Once the ship is flat on the blocks, it will be in a safe condition as the risk of heeling over as a result of becoming unstable will have passed (most ships having a substantial area of flat bottom). For ships that have a relatively small percentage of flat bottom area, additional measures must be taken such as using side shores to support the ship in the upright condition when in the dry dock.

Either of two methods of calculation of the loss of GM may be used.

Loss of GM as a Result of a Rise in G (Increase in KG)

Consider the upward movement of G that would occur if a weight 'w' is discharged from a position at the keel (Kg = 0 m). When discharging a weight, the centre of gravity of the ship, G, will move directly away from the centre of gravity of the discharged weight to G_V as shown in Figure 16.4.

GGv will be equal to the loss of GM where:

$$GG_V = \frac{w \times d}{W - w}$$

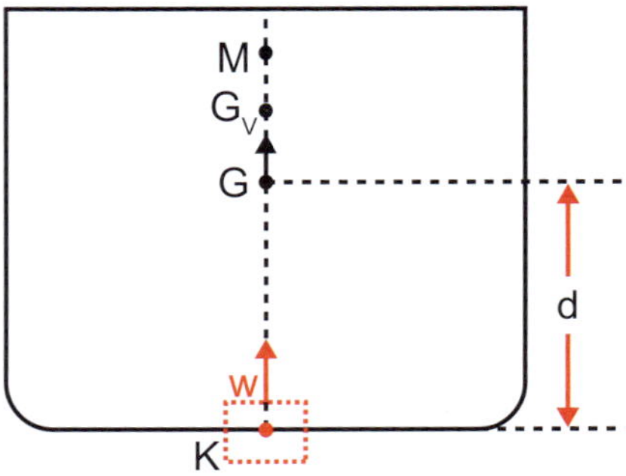

Figure 16.4

'd' is the distance between the centre of gravity of the ship (G) and the centre of gravity of the discharged weight which was at the keel 'K'. Therefore, distance 'd' is the initial KG of the ship.

(It should be noted also that KM changes as a result of a reduction in the ship's draught.)

If the P force is considered to have the same effect as discharging an equivalent weight from the keel then:

$$\text{Loss of GM} = \frac{P \times KG}{W - P}$$

The effect on the ship's stability is made clearer if the available righting moment at a particular angle of heel is considered. Figure 16.5 shows a ship during the critical period where it has taken the blocks at the aft end only. During docking, the ship becomes heeled to a small angle of inclination by an external force such as the wind.

The forces acting are as follows:

Wf is the total weight force acting downwards through the centre of gravity at G;

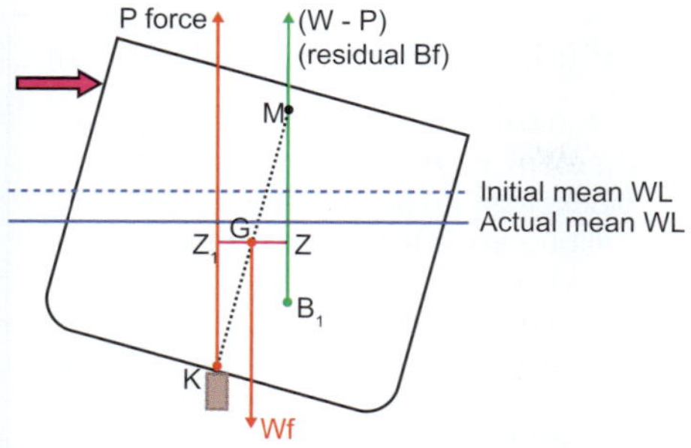

Figure 16.5

(W – P) is the remaining, or residual, buoyancy force acting upwards through the geometric centre of the underwater volume at B_1;

P is the upthrust of the blocks exerted at the keel aft.

(W – P) × GZ   represents a righting moment;

P × GZ_1 represents a capsizing moment.

Therefore, the available righting moment is given by:

Available righting moment
= [(W – P) × GZ] – (P × GZ_1)

It is essential that the righting moment afforded by the upward acting (remaining) buoyancy force remains greater than the capsizing moment afforded by the upthrust of the P force acting at the keel at all times prior to the ship touching the blocks forward and aft. If the ship should become unstable during the critical period, it will lurch off the blocks to one side resulting in structural damage to the ship, movement of the blocks and great embarrassment!

It is for this reason that the loss of GM is calculated for the critical instant (when the ship touches the blocks forward and aft) to ensure that adequate stability is maintained prior to the ship taking the blocks overall.

Loss of GM as a Result of a Fall in M (Decrease in KM)

Consider Figure 16.6 which illustrates the ship heeled by an external force such as the wind during the critical period where the ship has taken the blocks at the aft end only.

The total weight force of the ship acts downwards through G. Counteracting this are the two upward forces; the P force acting upwards at the keel and the residual buoyancy force (W – P) acting upwards through the centre of buoyancy (B_1). The resultant of the two upward acting forces acts through the new metacentre (M_1) such that:

$$P \times x = (W - P) \times y \quad (1)$$

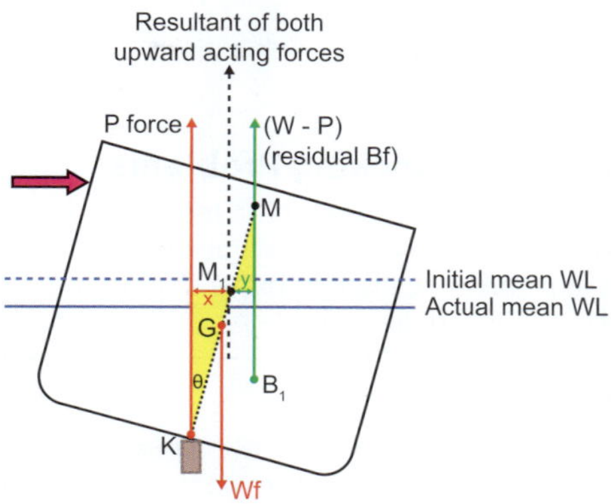

Figure 16.6

MM_1 represents the resulting fall of the transverse metacentre (or loss of GM).

Consider the two similar triangles:

$$\text{Sin}\,\theta = \frac{y}{MM_1}$$

Therefore: $y = \text{Sin}\,\theta \times MM_1 \quad (2)$

Also: $\text{Sin}\,\theta = \frac{x}{KM_1}$

Therefore: $x = \text{Sin}\,\theta \times KM_1 \quad (3)$

Combining formulae 1, 2 and 3 above gives:

$$(W - P) \times \text{Sin}\,\theta \times MM_1 = P \times \text{Sin}\,\theta \times KM_1$$

Divide both sides by Sin θ:
$(W - P) \times MM_1 = P \times KM_1$

Expanding this gives:

$$(W \times MM_1) - (P \times MM_1) = P \times KM_1$$

$$\therefore \quad (W \times MM_1) = (P \times KM_1) + (P \times MM_1)$$

$$\therefore \quad (W \times MM_1) = P \times (KM_1 + MM_1)$$

$$\therefore \quad (W \times MM_1) = P \times \text{Initial KM}$$

$$\therefore \quad MM_1 = \frac{P + \text{Initial KM}}{W}$$

i.e. $\boxed{\text{Loss of GM} = \frac{P \times KM}{W}}$

Drydocking Calculations

Note: In this formula, the KM value is that which corresponds to the true mean draught for the instant that the loss of GM is being calculated and not that for the initial true mean draught that the ship has prior to docking. It is found by entering the hydrostatic data with a displacement value that corresponds to that given by (W – P).

W in this formula is the ship's initial displacement.

Typical Drydocking Problems

In the following example, both methods of calculating the loss of GM will be used. An explanation is included to prove that both methods are equally valid.

Example 1

Prior to entering dry dock, MV *'Almar'* has draughts F 4.86 m, A 5.24 m and an effective KG of 9.16 m.

Calculate:

a) The GM when the ship takes the blocks forward and aft (at the critical instant);

b) the draughts at the same instant.

Solution (a)

1. Calculate initial TMD.

   AMD = 5.05 m

   Enter data with AMD and obtain LCF position.

$$\text{LCF} = 86.32 + (\text{-}0.02 \times \frac{0.05}{0.1}) = 86.31\text{m foap}$$

   Use this to calculate the TMD.

$$\text{TMD} = \text{dA} - \left(\frac{(\text{dA} - \text{dF})}{\text{LBP}} \times \text{LCF foap}\right)$$

$$\text{TMD} = 5.24 - \left(\frac{0.38}{167.87} \times 86.31\right)$$

$$\text{TMD} = \mathbf{5.045\,m}$$

2. Enter data with TMD 5.045 m.

$$\text{Displacement} = 15{,}120 + (320 \times \frac{0.045}{0.1}) = 15{,}264\,\text{t}$$

   MCTC = 312 t–m LCF = 86.31 m foap

3. Calculate the P force at the critical instant.

   The initial trim of the ship is 38 cms by the stern. When the ship touches the blocks forward and aft, the effective trim will be zero, ie the ship will be on an even keel. The ship will have therefore experienced a change of trim of 38 cms by the head – as if a weight equal to the P force had been discharged from the aft perpendicular.

$$\text{P} = \frac{\text{COT (cms)} \times \text{MCTC}}{\text{Dist LCF foap}}$$

$$\text{P} = \frac{38 \times 312}{86.31} = 137.4 \text{ tonnes (138 tonnes)}$$

4. Enter data with the effective displacement (W – P) at the critical instant to obtain KM.

   Effective displacement =
   W – P = 15264 – 138 = 15,126 tonnes

$$\text{KM} = 10.70 + (\text{-}0.10 \times \frac{6}{320}) = 10.698\,\text{m}$$

5. Calculate the loss of GM (both methods used).

   Method 1

$$\text{Loss of GM} = \frac{\text{P} \times \text{KG}}{\text{W} - \text{P}}$$

$$\text{Loss of GM} = \frac{138 \times 9.16}{(15{,}264 - 138)} = \mathbf{0.084\,m}$$

   Method 2

$$\text{Loss of GM} = \frac{\text{P} \times \text{KM}}{\text{W}}$$

$$\text{Loss of GM} = \frac{138 \times 10.698}{15{,}264} = \mathbf{0.097\,m}$$

6. Calculate the GM at the critical instant.

   Method 1

KM at critical instant	10.698
KG	9.160
Initial GM	1.538
Loss of GM	0.084
GM at critical instant	**1.454**

Method 2

KM at critical instant	10.698
KG	9.160
Initial GM	1.538
Loss of GM	0.097
GM at critical instant	**1.441**

Both answers are different but both are valid since a true measure of a ship's stability is its righting moment value at any given angle of heel.

Within small angles of heel, the righting moment is given by:

Righting moment (t–m)
= Displacement × GM × Sin θ

By Method 1

At the critical instant, the effective displacement = W – P = 15,126 tonnes since the P force acts as a weight being discharged from the keel.

RM = Displacement × GM × Sin θ

RM = 15,126 × 1.454 × Sin θ
= **21,993 Sin θ t–m**

By Method 2

By considering the loss of GM as a result of the fall of the metacentre:

RM = Displacement × GM × Sin θ

RM = 15,264 × 1.441 × Sin θ
= **21,995 Sin θ t–m**

(The slight difference arises due to rounding up of values in the calculation.)

Solution (b)

At the critical instant, the ship will be on an even keel. The draught at the same instant may be calculated by one of two methods.

Method 1

The initial TMD has already been calculated as being 5.045 m.

Entering the data with this, obtain the TPC value.

$$TPC = 31.96 + (0.04 \times \frac{0.045}{0.1}) = 31.98\ t$$

$$\text{Reduction in TMD (cms)} = \frac{\text{P force (t)}}{\text{TPC}}$$

$$\text{Reduction in TMD} = \frac{138}{31.98} = 4.3\ \text{cms}$$

∴ Draught at critical instant
= 5.045 – 0.043 = **5.002 m (Ans)**

Method 2

If the effective displacement at the critical instant is (W – P)

Effective displacement = W – P = 15,264 – 138 = 15,126 tonnes

Enter the data with this displacement value to obtain the TMD at the critical instant.

$$TMD = 5.00 + (0.1 \times \frac{6}{320}) = 5.002\ m$$

Therefore, the draught at the critical instant = **5.002 m (Ans)**

(Clearly method 2 is much easier!)

During the docking operation, it is essential that the 'critical instant' draught is determined as both draughts forward and aft will be constantly being read. As the ship's draught approaches that as calculated for the critical instant, also evidenced by the fact that the ship will be in a near even keel condition at that time, the rate at which the water is pumped out of the dock will be slowed down to allow final adjustment of the ship's fore and aft alignment prior to the ship taking the blocks overall. Once on the blocks, the rate of pumping will be increased again.

Practical Considerations During Drydocking

The major considerations that should be borne in mind are:

- That the P force is kept to an acceptable level, and
- that the ship maintains an acceptable positive GM during the critical period.

The Requirement to Limit the P Force

During the critical period prior to taking the blocks fully forward and aft, the P force will be acting at a single point on the stern frame of the ship. The stern frame is specially strengthened to accept the forces exerted on it during drydocking but there will be a

Drydocking Calculations

maximum limit that must not be exceeded. If the P force becomes too great, structural damage will occur. It is usual to have acceptable near-light conditions of loading for drydocking specified in the ship's stability data book. If an actual P force value is not quoted, it may be approximated from the recommended condition(s) given by rearranging the drydocking formulae and calculating it. Under normal circumstances, the ship's Classification Society will investigate any proposed drydocking condition and verify that it is appropriate. Under exceptional circumstances, a ship may be drydocked in a part-loaded condition but this will only ever be done after taking Classification Society advice. It would often be more prudent to discharge any cargo on board prior to entering drydock.

An obvious method to limit the P force during the critical period is to keep the initial trim by the stern small. Consider the formula for calculating the P force during the critical period:

$$P = \frac{\text{COT (cms)} \times \text{MCTC}}{\text{Dist LCF foap}}$$

It is clear from the above that P force is directly proportional to the change of trim that the ship will undergo. Limiting the trim will therefore limit the maximum loads that will be experienced by the stern frame. The greater the displacement of a given ship, the more important will be the need to limit the docking trim.

Limiting the Loss of GM

Consideration of the formulae will indicate that the greater the trim of the ship when docking, the greater will be the loss of GM.

$$P = \frac{\text{COT (cms)} \times \text{MCTC}}{\text{Dist LCF foap}}$$

$$\text{Loss of GM} = \frac{P \times KG}{W - P} \quad \text{or:} \quad \text{Loss of GM} = \frac{P \times KM}{W}$$

Clearly, the greater the trim, the greater the P force; the greater the P force, the greater the loss of GM.

Alternatively, the ship should drydock with a greater effective GM that will ensure that stability is maintained. Improving the ship's initial GM will be achieved by:

- Lowering the effective KG by lowering weights within the vessel, discharging weights from high up or taking on an acceptable amount of ballast in double bottom tanks, or
- minimising free surface effects by topping up slack tanks wherever possible.

Example 2

MV *'Almar'* about to drydock requires a minimum GM of 0.3 m at the time the ship takes the blocks forward and aft. Current draughts are F 6.89 m and A 8.47 m. KG is 8.86 m.

Calculate the maximum permissible trim by the stern on entering the drydock.

Solution

1. Calculate initial TMD.

   AMD = 7.68 m

   Enter data with AMD and obtain LCF position.

$$\text{LCF} = 85.01 + \left(-0.09 \times \frac{0.08}{0.1}\right) = 84.94 \text{ m foap}$$

Use this to calculate the TMD.

$$\text{TMD} = dA - \left(\frac{(dA - dF)}{\text{LBP}} \times \text{LCF foap}\right)$$

$$\text{TMD} = 8.47 - \left(\frac{1.58}{167.87} \times 84.94\right)$$

$$\text{TMD} = \mathbf{7.671\,m}$$

2. Enter data with TMD 7.671 m.

$$\text{Displacement} = 23{,}580 + \left(340 \times \frac{0.071}{0.1}\right) = 23{,}821\text{t}$$

$$\text{MCTC} = 347 + \left(2 \times \frac{0.071}{0.1}\right) = 348 \text{ t-m}$$

$$\text{LCF} = 85.01 + \left(-0.09 \times \frac{0.071}{0.1}\right) = 84.95 \text{ m foap}$$

$$\text{KM} = 9.37 + \left(-0.01 \times \frac{0.071}{0.1}\right) = 9.363 \text{ m}$$

We must assume that KM remains constant in this case.

3. Calculate the allowed loss of GM.

KM	9.363
KG	8.860
Initial GM	0.503
Minimum critical GM	0.300
GM at critical instant	**0.203**

4. Calculate the maximum allowed P force and hence the maximum initial trim.

Method 1

$$\text{Loss of GM} = \frac{P \times KG}{W - P} \qquad 0.203 = \frac{P \times 8.860}{(23{,}821 - P)}$$

$\therefore$ 0.203(23,821 – P) = 8.860P

$\therefore$ 4,834.663 – 0.203P = 8.860P

$\therefore$ 4,834.663 = 8.860P + 0.203P

$\therefore$ 4,834.663 = 9.063P

$\therefore$ P = 534 tonnes

$$P = \frac{COT \times MCTC}{d} \qquad 534 = \frac{COT \times 348}{84.95}$$

$$COT = \frac{534 \times 84.95}{348} = \textbf{130 cms (Ans)}$$

To ensure that a GM of 0.3 m is maintained at the critical instant, the trim of the ship must not exceed 1.30 m by the stern.

Method 2

$$\text{Loss of GM} = \frac{P \times KM}{W} \qquad 0.203 = \frac{P \times 9.363}{23{,}821}$$

$$P = \frac{0.203 \times 23{,}821}{9.363} \qquad \therefore\ P = 516 \text{ tonnes}$$

$$P = \frac{COT \times MCTC}{d} \qquad 516 = \frac{COT \times 348}{84.95}$$

$$COT = \frac{516 \times 84.95}{348} = \textbf{126 cms (Ans)}$$

For further information on ship stability, refer to 'Ship Stability Mates/Masters'.

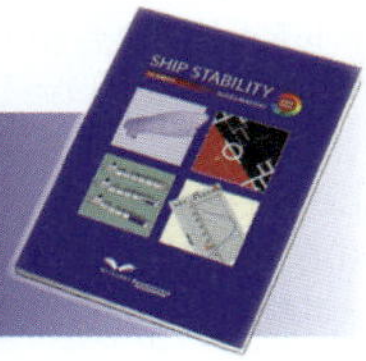

The Layby Berth

The majority of ships intending to drydock will initially berth alongside a layby berth for dock entry preparation to achieve the final draught and trim required. The dockyard manager will have the docking plan of the ship to ensure that the blocks can be properly positioned. The tank content and the blocks must be arranged so that the weight of the ship is positioned to place the least stress on the hull. A variety of bottom thrusters are now available and considerable care must be taken that the correct position of these is taken into account.

Figure 16.7 - Aligning the blocks

The Layby Berth

Ships Docking for Damage Repair

Ships docking for damage repair may not be able to conform to the trim requirement of the docking plan or the dock. It must be remembered that the plan is based on a ship being in the light condition required for a normal drydocking. Should the ship have any list or cargo on board, this docking plan cannot be relied upon.

In this case, the best action may be to discharge any cargo before docking to ease potential stresses as much as possible.

Tanks

Some of the tanks that are necessary for ballasting may be required to be emptied in the drydock for repair or maintenance. If it is essential that such tanks are filled for berthing, they will then be emptied in the dock. This is not unusual, with drydocks often cutting holes in the hull rather than waiting for the water to drain through the smaller plug holes. Once the calculations have been made, the relevant shore department and the drydock should be advised which tanks require emptying. Small ships that will be berthing directly on arrival should also be aware of this problem as it will be essential that sufficient ballast is kept in the vessel for manoeuvrability, particularly if entering without tug assistance.

The calculated time to prepare the ship for docking should also be advised to all interested parties.

Pollution

If a boom has been provided for use during tank pumping, this should be checked for placement before pumping commences. If there is no boom, a strict watch must be kept overside for any sign of pollution in the water. If there is any residue of oil in the water, as often happens near to repair yards, this must be noted in the logbook and should be brought to the attention of the yard.

Supply Lines

If the ship is to be put into the drydocking condition at a layby berth, it will be on shore power at this berth and then a 'dead ship' move will be made to the drydock. Prior to departure, these lines must all be disconnected and a check made that this has been done.

Internal Security

Many drydocks are notorious for the theft of ship's property and it is essential that, just prior to entry, all loose gear and equipment is stowed away and store rooms locked. It is recommended that access to the accommodation is controlled through certain doors and the remainder are kept locked. All ship's personnel must be reminded to keep their cabins locked at all times when not present and, depending on the yard security, it may be wise to lock the door at night when sleeping. The bridge must be cleared of all equipment that is not essential to the docking and anything left out must be stowed away immediately when docking is completed.

If toilets are allocated for shore workers' use or if there is a deck toilet available, these must be clearly marked. If not, the yard must be reminded to supply a chemical toilet on the deck.

Deck Equipment

All loose gear that could fall overside if the ship lists must be stowed away. Cranes, gantries and derricks should be secured down in a stowed position and all overside fittings stowed inboard. All lifebuoys, lifelines and items such as SARTs should be stowed away and the lifeboats, if enclosed, should be locked or the equipment removed.

Weather

Once at the layby berth, various shore power lines and cables will be attached and work will commence on many of the scheduled items. If the ship's engines are disabled, it is essential that a careful watch is kept on the weather as the ship is now in a very vulnerable position, with a very light ballast condition and no engines. On the approach of bad weather, additional lines and shore tugs may be required to hold position.

In the Dock

Figure 16.8 - Graving dock

There are two basic forms of drydock, the most common of which is the graving dock, a permanent purpose-built dock on land with a base lower than sea level. The ship enters and, after the caissons are closed, the water is pumped out and the ship comes to rest on blocks that are pre-positioned for each particular ship according to the ship's docking plan. More than one ship may be docked at the same time if the dock is large.

The second type of dock is the floating dock which uses floodable buoyancy tanks to lower the whole structure down to allow the ship to float in. Pumping out the tanks raises the structure up to enable the docked ship and dock working area to clear the water.

Docks are often in sections, allowing for shortening or lengthening as required. Bow and stern sections can be added for moving the docks to different ports. Smaller vessels can also be accommodated on slips with a cradle arrangement on rails, onto which the ship is eased and then the cradle winched up onto the shore work area which can be enclosed.

The reason a ship enters drydock, unless it is for unscheduled repairs, is to examine and maintain the ship's underwater hull and the associated inlets, rudder and propeller areas. The length of time between drydockings is decided by the operators in accordance with Classification Society requirements. With the continuing improvement in coatings over the last few decades, this interval has been extended by many companies. The problem associated with any extension is that many other repairs requiring specialist shore labour and equipment are also delayed, often interfering with the efficient operation of the ship.

Figure 16.9 - Floating dock

In the Dock

The Drydock

Figure 16.10 - Blocks aligned - dock ready for flooding

Entry into drydock is controlled by the docking master, who is essentially a pilot, employed by the dockyard, specialising in berthing ships in the dock. Even though the vessel is a 'dead ship' for manoeuvring purposes, responsibility remains with the master.

Tugs will be used to manoeuvre the ship and it is essential that they are made fast in plenty of time to allow them to position the ship before entry. The normal approach is directly head in, with the bow centred on the middle of the head of the dock. However, if the wind is strong, particularly if it is a few points on the bow, the ship may head towards the wind. Either a tug may be positioned by the knuckle to push the ship off while turning into the dock or the knuckle may be used to land on and turn the ship into the dock. Smaller vessels can be warped round if the layby berth is next to the dock. Any approach must be discussed with the docking master and approved by the ship's master before the docking commences.

Shore personnel are often placed on board for handling the lines. Initially the ship's lines may be used and then changed over to shore lines. In such cases, the ship's movement is usually controlled by the tugs until the ship's and dock's lines can be made fast, when the shore winches then take over positioning the ship as required for landing on the blocks.

Figure 16.11 - Entry into the dock

Once the ship is centred and the lines are fast, the water level can be lowered. The time of landing on the blocks should be recorded. All the ship's lines should be stowed away below to prevent any damage or loss. As soon as the shore gangways are set in place, the securing and lighting arrangements should be implemented. The lighting can be enhanced by the ship's floodlighting if required or if no shore lighting is available.

Hull Inspection

When the dock is pumped clear of water, the initial hull inspection can take place. On large ships this can take some time as the area to be covered is considerable. Several passes will be required, working inwards from the outside, from bow to stern. Good beam torches will be required as well as spray cans of luminous paint.

The Four Primary Areas of Inspection

Damage to the Bottom of the Ship

Damage will be in the form of indentations or rippling, often caused by grounding. When damaged areas are found, they should be marked with spray paint and numbered so that they can easily be identified and referred to. The bilge keel is often found to be damaged or even missing in parts. These are tack welded to the hull to avoid damage to the hull plating.

Fouling and Coating Breakdown

Fouling of the bottom will depend on a number of factors such as the ship being anchored for long periods of time in warm waters, the length of time between dockings, the type of coating and any grounding incidents that, while not damaging the hull, may have scraped away the anti-fouling coating, exposing the hull to fouling. The paint representatives will attend the docking to supervise the preparation and application of new coatings and to analyse any breakdown.

Figure 16.12 - Examples of hull fouling

Intakes and Grilles

Scaffolding will have to be rigged to remove the grilles on the various outlets in the hull and to check the insides and any associated propellers. On occasion, these grilles are damaged or even missing.

In the Dock

Figure 16.13 - Example of seachest before/after

Rudder and Propeller

Scaffolding will need to be rigged to properly check the stern glands, rudder and propeller. This initial inspection will show whether there is any damage in these areas.

Figure 16.14 - Checks of the stern gland and propeller

Morning Meetings

Depending on the operators, the ship is, at this stage, often in the hands of the attending superintendents, assisted by the ship's staff. The normal procedure usually involves a meeting each morning between the superintendents, ship's staff and the various representatives of the dock departments concerned. On major dockings, it is quite normal to have dedicated superintendents in attendance for the steelwork and the paint and often a controller for the accounting. Representatives of private companies, such as those supplying the coatings or making hatch repairs, could also be in attendance.

The following plans and information should be available:

- The drydock plan
- the general arrangement plan
- the shell expansion plan
- the ship's stability information
- the ship's general particulars
- the crew list
- certificate and survey list
- the tank arrangements.

At least 20 working copies of the drydock specification should be prepared to allow those concerned to carry them around and make notes as required.

Although the repairs are the responsibility of the superintendents and the dockyard, the safety and routine of the ship are not. These must be maintained at all times by the ship.

The Anchors

Often in a drydocking, anchor maintenance is the responsibility of the ship although the anchors and chain could be surveyed by the attending Class surveyor. Once the anchors and chain have been lowered into the drydock bottom and the chain ranged, the anchor should be examined for any sign of a bent shank or flukes. The main pin on the D anchor joining shackle should also be checked and the split pin sighted in position. If this is worn or missing, it should be renewed. The main pin on the joining shackle can be spot welded to prevent loss. It is suggested that, unless otherwise arranged, the first and second shackle after the short link should be swapped to the bitter end.

Figure 16.15 - Anchors ranged out in dock

Before taking the chains back on board, they should be marked with wire and canvas and painted. Wire markings are useful to assist in knowing the number of shackles paid out, particularly when the painted marks have been obscured by mud or in darkness. The marking should be as follows:

- At 15 fathoms: one turn of wire on the first stud from each side of the joining shackle
- at 30 fathoms: two turns of wire on the second stud from each side of the joining shackle
- at 45 fathoms: three turns of wire on the third stud from each side of the joining shackle followed by a similar pattern for further shackles.

The shackles should be painted white. The anchors can also be painted.

In the Dock

Figure 16.16 - Freshly painted anchor chain

While the chains are out, the chain locker can be cleaned out. On large vessels, there may be up to 2 tonnes of mud and a tonne of water to clear out. The eductor system should be blown through with compressed air to check it is clear and the eductor valves opened up to renew the jointing and gland packing. While the chains are off the windlasses, the opportunity must be taken to check the windlass for any wear or damage. The brake linkages should be opened up on all windlasses and winches and the brake linings renewed where required. The spurling pipes should be free of old cement or foam and the covers should fit snugly. The compression bars should be checked for any wear, particularly at the sides, which might enable the bar to slide up from the chain. If necessary, this can be built up.

The Hatches

Depending on the age or condition of the ship, the hatch tops may be lifted off and taken ashore for spot blasting and/or repair. Whether or not this is done, the opportunity must be taken to examine and repair the coamings and rubbers as required. A water test should be carried out on any tops being replaced.

The Gangways

While the gangways are lifted for examination of the platforms, the opportunity should be taken to scale, clean, paint and grease them before replacing, not forgetting the underside of the gangway head.

Lifeboats and Davits

While the lifeboats are off the davits and ashore, the boat hulls can be inspected thoroughly for any damage and repainted if the colour has dulled. In addition, if the perspex view ports for the coxswain have deteriorated, these should be replaced. The hooks must also be carefully examined.

The davits will also be free for inspection and maintenance. The wires should be reeled off the barrels and inspected for damage. If the wires are being replaced at the end of their five-year cycle, new grease should be applied as they are spooled onto the winch barrels, paying particular attention to the wire going on first as this part tends to dry out as regular greasing often does not reach the bottom layers of the wire.

The skates should be checked for corrosion and new ones ordered if necessary. The release gear, davit switches and sheaves should all be cleaned and lubricated and the winch controls and braking arrangement inspected.

The trackway rollers and trackway should be cleaned of old grease, inspected for any damage and re-greased, ensuring that the rollers are turning freely. All the bottle screws should be opened up and greased, particularly at the heads. The cradle arms should be checked for any damage or distortion.

When the boats are replaced and the ship is alongside the layby berth, the boats should be lowered to the embarkation deck for test purposes.

The Hull

Before any work can start on the hull, scupper chutes must be fitted to all the hull discharge openings and the deck scuppers plugged.

Figure 16.17 - Hold cleaning preparation

Any indentations found on the ship's underwater area must be marked on the shell expansion plan with the depth of the indentation. If any repairs are made, these must also be recorded. The hull is normally blasted with a high pressure water jet to remove any fouling and then finished with a fresh water washdown prior to coating. Badly corroded areas can be spot blasted as required. If this is done, it is important that the stern seal area and permanent anodes are covered before blasting.

Painting of the hull is a strictly controlled process, generally under the supervision of the attending paint representatives and the operator's superintendents.

Figure 16.18 - Wet and dry scraping of the hull

An example of a drydock hull preparation and painting specification is shown below.

Owner's No. Item

D20 Notes for Painting

A. Drydock paints to be supplied by owner – actual quantity of paints consumed to be recorded and submitted to attending superintendent before completion of drydocking. (Original coating: Chugoku Marine Paint)

B. All exterior hull and bottom must be thoroughly rinsed with high pressure fresh water after being washed down by seawater high pressure jet.

C. Following area calculated for reference only:

- Topside 4,700 m^2
- vertical side 9,000 m^2
- flat bottom 13,600 m^2.

D2 Disc-sander or sandblast to be decided on spot by owner's attending superintendent (cover up stern seal area before commencement of blasting)

(Allow for 800 m^2 sand blasting)

Quote unit price/m^2

Disc-sander

Sand-blast:	S.A. 2
Grit-blast:	S.A. 2.0
Grit-blast:	S.A. 2.5

D24 Bottom keel to deep load line to apply two touch-up coats of A/C. (Existing Chugoku paint: Epicon Marine HB-AL)

A/C film thickness/coat 100μ

(Assume T/U area 600 m^2 × 2 coats)

D25 Flat bottom to deep load line to apply two full coats of A/F

(Existing Chugoku Paint: AF Seaflo SP)

A/F film thickness/coat 60μ

D27 Topside to apply two touch-up A/C, then one full coat of topside black (Existing Chugoku Paint: Epicon Marine Topside)

Topside film thickness/coat 40μ

(Assume T/U area 300 m^2 × 2 coats).

In the Dock

Seachests

The seachest grids should be removed, cleaned out and coated with anti-corrosive and anti-fouling coatings. It is quite possible that the zinc anodes in the seachests will need replacing.

A list of all bottom plugs removed and holes cut must be given to the chief officer unless the plugs are labelled and kept by the ship ready for replacement. If the ship's crew are replacing these, the gaskets must be renewed.

Figure 16.19 - Seachest grid

All bottom plugs must be carefully labelled after removal

Stern Area

If a duct is fitted around the propeller, it should be examined and air pressure tested for cracking or leaking due to the stresses and vibration caused by the cavitation force in this area. Nitrogen gas is often used to charge the duct area on completion.

It is common to require the tail end shafts to be drawn and the bearing wear measured. The forward and aft stern seal rings will be renewed and the liner inspected.

Figure 16.20 - Stern inspection

It is common to require the tail end shafts to be drawn and the bearing wear measured. The fore and aft stern seal rings should be renewed and the liner inspected.

The propeller should be examined for damage, blade distortion or tip corrosion and cracking. Depending on the operator's policy, the propeller may be polished. It is claimed that a power saving of up to 10% can be achieved following effective propeller cleaning and polishing.

The rudder should also be examined for any damage or wear. The rudder carrier/pintles clearances should be checked and compared to the previous readings. The rudder gland packing should be checked and renewed as required.

Valves

Any sea valves specified will be opened up, inspected, overhauled and repainted internally. The glands will be repacked and the valves closed up. These valves include the ship's side valves, scupper overboard valves and storm valves. Inside the engine room, various salt water valves will also be overhauled.

Engineering

The engineering department will be heavily involved in opening up various machinery for attending surveyors. This could include the main and auxiliary boilers, air conditioning and generator condensers and the many sea valves and pumps.

In addition, the following tanks may be required for opening, cleaning and surveying:

- Fuel oil service and settling tank
- diesel oil service and settling tank
- main engine sump tank
- auxiliary cooling freshwater expansion tank
- main engine freshwater expansion tank
- cascade tank
- oil sludge service tank
- sewage tank.

Figure 16.21 - Sea valve

Safety

While in the dock, the ship's safety officer or the officer designated to act as the drydock safety officer must be authorised to act with the master's authority over any incident or procedure that is against safety regulations or the safety interests of the ship.

In the Yard

It is essential that a meeting is held between the ship's safety officer and the dock safety manager so that all safety efforts can be coordinated. It also allows the ship to state its onboard safety policy.

It may be necessary to arrange a stowage area for PPE that the ship's crew may have to wear during transit through the dock area to the entrance gate when proceeding ashore. There may also be dock 'no go' areas that have to be identified to the crew on board.

While in the dockyard, the safety of ship's personnel must be taken into account. The yard may have regulations regarding walking areas, out of bounds workshop areas and traffic control, particularly if ship's staff are using cars or other means of transport. The

yard will generally have their own first aid post and instant communication with the local emergency services so, should there be any emergency on board, one call to the yard office will initiate the emergency response of the service required.

Hot Work and Enclosed Spaces

If a status board has been prepared, this can be used to record each day's hot work areas and enclosed spaces to be entered. It is essential that, prior to any hot work

Safety

being approved, the area and any adjacent compartments are checked by the safety officer for any combustible materials or gases. If the drydock is not providing fire prevention equipment, this must be the ship's responsibility. Only after all these precautions have been taken and the risk assessment completed can the safety officer give his approval for the work to take place.

Yards are usually well prepared as regards hot work and enclosed spaces entry. For hot work, they will provide their own watchman service and have a fire extinguisher standing by. The hot work list should be given to the ship each morning at the daily meeting before the start of work and this should be placed prominently on a status board in the ship's office, stating the start and completion times and who has signed the work off. On completion of hot work, the ship's safety officer must again check the work area and adjacent compartments to ensure that all is well.

The same must apply for entry into enclosed spaces. A list must be kept of any tank lids that are off, when ventilation was started and completed and that oxygen tests have been completed and the space verified as safe. It is also important to ensure that the open tank accesses are guarded properly by a guard-rail and notice.

Even if watchmen are provided by the yard, it is essential that the ship has a watchman on duty through the night. Apart from the normal checks, he must also check the hot work areas that were worked on during the day and, of course, monitor any night work that is going on.

Figure 16.22 - Hatch repairs in dock

Security

If the yard is a secure area, gangway security, while still having to be considered, can be assumed to have been taken care of by the yard. The ship's security officer will have to make contact with the yard security and coordinate with them regarding their policies.

Yard security may affect the ship's personnel going ashore. The gate will require an up-to-date crew list and the ship's company may have to have ship identification. If not provided by the company or the yard, identity cards showing the name of the ship, name of the crew member and rank or rating should be made and put in plastic holders that can be clipped to work clothing or shore gear.

To prevent theft on board, any shore personnel found in the accommodation areas should be challenged and, if they have no reason to be there, they must be reported to the repair manager. If the ship has been prepared properly, all stores lockers will be secured and portable deck equipment locked away. This should include outboard engines, if present on any rescue boat.

The fire equipment cannot be stowed away as it will be required quickly in the event of a fire. However, nozzles, particularly brass ones, should at least be removed to the ship's office where they can be easily accessed if required. If the position of any such equipment is changed, all on board must be advised of the new stowage position.

Fire Control

A new temporary fire muster list, based on what is required between the yard and the ship, may be necessary. In the event of fire, many yards will require everyone not directly concerned with the fire to evacuate the ship and be accounted for in an area away from the immediate scene of operations.

If the present alarm system is reliant on internal alarm bells, these may not be heard by personnel working on the decks or on the hull in the dock. The ship's whistle can be the most effective means of alerting those on board of an emergency, provided all personnel are made aware of its significance.

It is unlikely that the number and position of ship's crew on board at any one time will be known, and therefore the ship's sea fire emergency stations cannot be relied upon. In this case, a plan will be required to use whatever crew are on board to best advantage or, if they are not required, to ensure that they leave the ship and are accounted for.

It is also unlikely that there will be a complete list of the shore personnel on board or, even if they are on a security gangway checklist, that there will be time to check them. This will have to be the responsibility of their supervisors, who should notify the officer in charge if anyone is missing and their workplace.

To determine what crew are available in an emergency, it will be necessary to assemble them all in one area, preferably near the gangway, where those not required can be immediately sent ashore. An officer should be stationed at the gangway with the ship's fire plan to meet the shore fire-fighting teams and escort them to the area of the fire or to the officer controlling the incident. This officer must be in communication with the fire party.

Before finalising any dock fire plan, it must be discussed with the dock safety and fire officer to coordinate the fire effort. As the dockyard team will have more experience, it is better that the ship fits in with the dock requirement, provided that it does not compromise the safety of those on board.

Pollution

Very strict pollution controls are required. Generally, no pumping of tanks will be allowed while in the dock, but if it is unavoidable strict controls must be in place. It is essential that pollution equipment is at hand, ready for use. The dock will have an emergency number to call in the event of pollution.

On the decks, scupper plugs must be in place, not necessarily for pollution prevention, but also to stop any fouling of the cleaned and coated hull or those working below.

Crew Welfare

For many ships, the drydock is a time when, after work, the crew have a rare chance to go ashore and relax. The yard may have a transportation system for crew or allow the shore workers' transport systems to be used. If families are on board, it is always good to have a day off the ship for sightseeing as living on board a ship in dock is not very pleasant for anyone, particularly those not concerned with the repairs. If the ship has been several days in dock, Customs will usually visit for a bond issue, if requested.

If required, the floor covering can be renewed from time to time during the docking period, as it deteriorates quickly. Just because the ship is in drydock does not mean that the accommodation can be allowed to become dirty.

If, for maintenance reasons, heating cannot be provided on board, many yards can provide safe accommodation heaters.

Figure 16.23 - Managing crew rotation for shore leave is important in drydock

Final Checks

Completion

Throughout the docking period, a variety of work will be completed and require a completion signature. Officers assigned to inspect completed work should note the completion and inspection date on their drydock specification, which can then be transferred to that of the senior superintendent attending. This will also give the officers the opportunity to ensure that all bare metal areas are painted on completion of the repair. At the same time, work not done to a satisfactory standard should be notified to the superintendent as soon as possible in order that it can be dealt with. Items not completed satisfactorily should also be advised to the master who has to sign, together with the chief engineer, that all items on the specification list and any supplementary list have been completed to his satisfaction.

Prior to unberthing, the ship must be in the same condition of stability as when entering. All the tanks have to be adjusted to the same quantities as on arrival and this includes the freshwater tanks. If a large quantity of mud has been removed from tanks, the same amount of water can be used to balance this.

If the ship is going back to a layby berth to ballast and prepare for sea, most of these checks can be carried out there, particularly if the ship is, like entry, a 'dead ship'. If the ship is to proceed directly to sea, all checks must be completed before departure from the dock.

It must be remembered that the ship, at this stage, is not in a seaworthy condition, particularly for manoeuvring purposes and it is strongly advised that, when the dock is flooded, the ship remains there until she is properly ballasted. If the draught will not allow this, a standby berth for this purpose should be requested.

Figure 16.24 - Final checks on the layby berth

Final Hull Check

Are all plugs returned and sealed?

It must be ensured that all the plugs are back in place, any openings cut in the hull are welded tight again and that all the markings, such as draught, tug positions, thruster warnings, etc, have been painted in correctly. Once checked, permission to flood or partly flood can be given. It is the practice in some yards to partly flood so the ship is still on the blocks but not afloat and can be sounded around. If there is any water ingress, the water can be pumped out again without having to reposition the ship. Either way, the ship must be sounded when in the dock.

Before the vessel floats, the riggers must be standing by to take up on the lines, and the crew ready to make the tugs fast. The gangways must also be removed.

Theoretically, the ship will float at exactly the same draught as when entering, but owing to the often indeterminably small amounts of weight deducted and added, this is rarely the case. However, by ensuring that all tanks are at the same quantities, the draught will be very close.

With all shore supply lines disconnected, the ship can be eased out of the dock, controlled by the tugs and the shore windlasses, and returned to the layby berth for final preparations for departure. Final ballasting to seagoing condition can take place at this berth.

When main engine power is restored, engine trials can begin. The area around the ship, particularly under the stern, must be checked first to ensure it is safe to proceed. It is essential that extra lines are put out for these trials as they can be prolonged and full power may also be required. It is suggested that during the trials all hands are called to stations fore and aft and that the bridge is manned as for sea. Regardless of the engineering requirements, should the engine power begin to cause concern, the engines should be stopped and the ship allowed to settle at the berth before recommencing or running out additional lines.

If the windlass has been opened or the brake liner renewed, the anchors should be lowered to water level, then taken out of gear and let go from the brake for test purposes.

All the scuppers should be unblocked if there is no bunkering or this has been completed. All the rubbish and residue from the docking still on the decks should be placed into skips and transferred ashore.

When seawater has been restored, the main fire line should be tested.

It should be ensured that all the new survey certificates, or the temporary ones, are on board ready for the next port.

Leaving the Dock

When the ship sails from the drydock yard, there will be a number of additional persons on board, including personnel from the dockyard, the Classification Society, the operating office and manufacturers' representatives. In addition, there could be a compass adjuster unless the ship's master will be responsible for this.

If the harbour pilot is to remain on board for the trials, he will direct the ship to the most appropriate location. Alternatively, before he disembarks, he should be asked for advice.

The trial area should be away from the harbour approaches, free of traffic, including fishing boats, and suitable for the ship to anchor if required. For compass adjusting, a fixed point ashore will be required for bearings.

Finally, when all are satisfied that the trials have been completed successfully and the new deviation card is handed over, the ship can return towards the harbour where the shore personnel can be disembarked.

Figure 16.25 - Off for sea trials

CHAPTER 17

Lay-up of Ships

Lay-up of Ships

Figure 17.1 - Maersk container ships laid-up in Loch Striven, Scotland 2010

Courtesy of Olaf Olsen

It is important that ships are laid-up in a technically correctly manner or it might be difficult to reactivate them successfully. This also ensures less likelihood of damage being caused to the ship either by being laid-up incorrectly, during lay-up or on reactivation.

It is important that the shipowner coordinates any lay-up with local and national authorities, as they must agree for the ship to be laid-up in their waters.

What is Lay-up?

The terms 'lay-up' or 'laid-up' refer to a ship that is temporarily taken out of service. This often occurs during an economic downturn, when there are too many ships for the number of available cargoes, as it can be more economical for the shipowner to lay-up than to continue trading and lose money.

Laying-up a ship is completely different to taking it out of service for drydocking, repairs or when waiting for either cargo or orders to be delivered. Lay-ups reduce daily operating costs while maintaining the ship's safety and security, protecting both the ship and the environment. A ship is classified as being laid-up if there is no cargo on board, it is not being used as a storage facility and the only crew left are for safety and security purposes, the majority having been signed off after preparation for lay-up.

A shipowner will consider a number of factors when deciding to lay-up a ship, including:

- The length of the anticipated period of lay-up
- the necessity to reduce running costs
- the age of the ship and its value.

Costs and Reasons for a Lay-up

The costs for lay-up can be divided into daily and initial. Daily costs are only incurred once the ship has actually been laid-up and finish when it is taken out of lay-up. Initial costs are incurred in preparation for lay-up proportional to the amount of time spent in lay-up. The longer this period of time, the higher the costs will be.

The decision to lay-up freight ships is not based on the immediate market but on the market of the future and likely freight rates when cargo is required to be transported. The decision to lay-up should be taken when the freight rate for a charter is less than the average variable costs minus the lay-up costs for the same amount of time as the potential charter. Ships are generally laid-up when the market rates have become unprofitable.

The ship manager is primarily responsible for planning, preparing and developing procedures for a smooth lay-up and will produce the operations plan to ensure that the crew have recorded any deficiencies or faults accurately.

Types of Lay-up

Seasonal (Winter)

Vessels may also be laid-up due to severe cold weather conditions, commonly known as 'winter lay-up'. Areas of the world where this can occur are:

- Great Lakes, North America
- North Sea, UK
- Northern UK
- Port of Montreal, Canada
- Thunder Bay Port, Canada
- Sturgeon Bay, Wisconsin, USA
- Port of Toledo, Oregon, USA
- Port of Duluth-Superior, Minnesota, USA
- Chicago, USA.

Strategically Planned

Ship operators in the oil trade will often lay-up fully laden tankers when oil prices are low to benefit when they increase.

Hot

Hot lay-up is suitable for vessels that are to be out of service for a limited number of weeks only, eg three months. Reactivation of the vessel takes 24 hours. There must be a small number of crew on board to maintain a full-time fire, leakage, mooring and security watch. The minimum amount of machinery is kept running, ensuring that electrical and electronic systems are kept in good order by a crew who are familiar with the vessel. Onboard inspections can be carried out easily as access is good and lighting is available. Berths for short term lay-up are relatively easy to find.

Warm

Warm lay-up is suitable for ships that are to be out of service for 12 months. Reactivation will take about a week. The ship's manning will be reduced below the trading limit and this must be agreed with the flag State, Classification Society, insurers and local authorities. Most vessels will only receive a temporary permit allowing them to be in this condition in port. There may be local restrictions on operations carried out on board, and these must be fully clarified before the ship is laid-up.

Cold

Cold lay-up is suitable for vessels that are likely to be laid-up for an extended period of time, eg five years. Reactivation will take about three weeks. Onboard manning levels are usually in line with emergency requirements for fire, flood, mooring and security watches. Cold lay-ups tend to be in remote locations, making access to the vessel more difficult. On reactivation, it may be necessary for the vessel to go to drydock before returning to trading, but this will depend on the amount of marine growth on the hull.

Preparation for cold lay-up should include the following:

- Preparations for cold lay-up must be documented accurately, as any changes may be significant when the ship is reactivated. It is important that the critical equipment manufacturers are contacted to ensure that the appropriate precautions are taken
- cold lay-ups require detailed checks to be carried out, including the hull, engine room, the ship's electrical and electronic systems and the contents of the galley and sick bay
- it is important that the hull is protected from fire and flood and that security measures are in place. Cooling salt water systems must be drained and ventilated by blown air until they are dry to prevent rust or other types of corrosion
- glass windows and portholes must be fitted with blanks
- it is important that there is only one point of external access and all others should be secured from the inside
- funnels should be covered at the top and protected from the weather
- anchors must have marker buoys attached
- bilge level and alarm systems should be arranged so that they operate both audibly and visually
- the external electrical power supply should be provided by a deck gen-set or by shore power. Rotation machinery, shafts and gearboxes should be regularly turned over,

Lay-up of Ships

as well as having perspex covers so that they can be inspected for any signs of moisture and corrosion. The steam plant (including boilers) must be either dry purged with N_2 or wet laid-up

- all onboard emergency starter batteries must be removed or at least disconnected
- all electrical systems should be checked and tested regularly.

Long Term

Long term lay-up is used for vessels that are to be laid-up for longer than five years. Reactivation will take about three months. The preparations for this type of lay-up are comprehensive and any necessary repair work carried out when the vessel is reactivated is likely to be extensive and unpredictable, eg the alarm system may require replacement if it is outdated. Several vessels may be laid-up side by side to minimise supervision costs.

Lay-up Preparation

- General information – any equipment that is government controlled must be included on an inventory
- phase-down of crew – a full crew is kept on board until the day after lay-up, when the number of crew should be reduced as necessary. Only security personnel should stay on the vessel during lay-up
- general crew tasks – any unused spaces should be cleaned out and locked up and an inventory should be made of any moveable items. All keys must be tagged and stored in the master's office
- master's responsibilities – overseeing the transition from operations to lay-up, organising the ship's records, documents and logs, signing off the crew and final voyage accounts, meeting with the department heads to review any problems that may have been encountered on the vessel's last voyage and submitting a report to the port engineer
- chief engineer – supervising preparation of the ship's machinery and systems for lay-up, organising and completing all engineering records, documents and logs, preparing all machinery for lay-up, storing spare parts and submitting repair lists to the port engineer.

Concerns During Lay-up

Concerns have been raised about how lay-ups are actually managed as a result of several ships being badly damaged, or even written off in some cases, while they were laid-up.

It is very important that insurance underwriters agree to the location of the lay-up and the associated arrangements, including supervision and marine surveys.

Some of the most common hazards experienced by ships during lay-up are:

- Sinking
- collision danger to other shipping
- breaking adrift, which may result in a collision or the ship becoming grounded
- fire or explosion on board
- hull degradation
- machinery degradation
- crew safety issues

- pollution
- damage to the environment
- security problems. Ships in lay-up can be an easy target for pirates
- vandalism, which can result in damage to expensive pieces of equipment
- deterioration and moisture, which are catalysts for corrosion and can cause severe damage to the steel structure as well as to the onboard computers and navigational equipment. Moisture can also cause mould and may damage materials and pose health risks to the crew when the ship is reactivated.

In 2011, during a period of severe financial downturn, 130 vessels were laid-up outside the port of Singapore and the rate of new builds coming from China and Korea slowed considerably. Vessels laying idle can also have a negative bearing on freight rates and bank finance.

Microbial Infections On Board during Lay-up

A frequent problem during lay-up is microbial growth in the fuel and oil system.

If hydrocarbons are stored in a closed system for a long period of time, it is likely that there will be microbiological growth. Even a small amount of water combined with optimum temperatures (approximately 30 to 40°C) will provide excellent conditions for bacteria to grow.

Microbial growth (biomass) and corrosion (biocorrosion) may result in:

- Steel and metal surfaces corroding
- sludge formation
- water contaminants emulsifying
- toxic gas (H_2S) developing
- deterioration of oil products
- a reduction in lubrication properties.

The worst case scenario will require the entire system to be emptied cleaned, and any corrosion damage repaired.

Microorganisms can live and multiply in distillate fuels, lubricating oils and hydraulic oils, particularly if water settles at the bottom of a tank during lay-up. Water in lubricating oil, as a result of condensation or a leak, provides excellent conditions for bacteria to grow.

Oil systems should be tested regularly for microbial growth. The regularity of these tests will depend on temperature, oil type, water concentration and whether or not a biocide treatment has been used.

Lay-up of Ships

Distillate fuel tanks should have samples taken from the bottom drain, or as close as possible to it, as the concentration of microorganisms is highest there. Once the tests have been completed, using the dip slide method, any treatment necessary should be carried out immediately.

The sampling method used depends on how and from where samples are to be taken. Contaminated water may be in dead legs from where it is impossible to get samples, while those taken from the top may not have any bacteria present. Therefore, consideration should be given to using spread sampling devices.

Microbial growth can be prevented by carrying out regular checks, draining the water frequently and taking the correct actions to combat contamination from the start of lay-up.

Maintenance During Lay-up

During lay-up, steel should be maintained and the machinery systems kept in near operating conditions. The main way of achieving this is to preserve the internal spaces using dehumidification units, which remove the moisture that can cause major damage to the control rooms, resulting in short-outs on restart. The moisture is removed by either heating the air, moving it through desiccant towers or by moving it past refrigerant coils.

Dehumidification units are expensive to hire and carry additional costs for the temporary ducting and wiring that must be installed. This ducting may make it difficult to carry out any repair work as access to some areas will be reduced. The cost of removing this equipment once the vessel is reactivated must also be taken into account and is often the main reason why owners do not use this system for short term lay-ups. However, it is not unusual for short term lay-ups to last longer than anticipated and, as a result, the ship may suffer from the lack of dehumidification and start to deteriorate and corrode as soon as it is secured. If the machinery spaces are not dehumidified, even during a short term lay-up, expensive repairs may have to be carried out.

Dehumidified air is the only type of atmospheric corrosion control that can be used in areas where personnel may enter. In spaces that are not accessible, corrosion can be controlled by displacing the oxygen rich atmosphere with an oxygen depleted one.

Tankers, LPG carriers and LNG carriers are usually fitted with primary inert gas plants that produce a combination of carbon dioxide and nitrogen. Cargo tanks that are piped into these systems can be inerted using this oxygen-depleted gas, meaning that any corrosion will be halted. In conventional tankers, this process is not guaranteed to dry the cargo tank as residual cargo or condensation may be present. For example, conventional tankers tend to use flue gas from the main engine as the feed to an IG plant, which cleans the gas before it enters the cargo tanks. Sulphur and other stack products may still be present in the gas and, when these are combined with moisture, they may produce an acid that could attack the tanks. It is important that any products of inert gas are identified and that the tanks are completely dry before the vessel is laid-up. LPG and LNG carriers are fitted with inert gas generators that use diesel oil, creating cleaner and dryer products. Inerting ballast tanks or ullage spaces over ballast water should only be carried out when strict procedures are followed, including:

- Ballast tanks must be sealed and air tight
- warning signs should be placed on all access plates
- any surrounding enclosed areas must be monitored
- tank vents must be sealed.

The gas that is produced must be checked to ensure that an acid will not form when it comes into contact with the sea or any moisture in the tanks.

Most LNG carriers use nitrogen for inerting cargo tank barrier spaces. Dry nitrogen can be circulated through boiler tubes, steam piping, turbine and gear cases, which removes moisture and provides an inert, dry and non-corrosive atmosphere for lay-up.

Construction that Improves Lay-up

Towing Fittings

Towing fittings, made up of deck-mounted towing pads and radius chocks, are required on tankers for emergency towing. Fittings that have pendants to the water provide additional safety for ships in lay-up in the event that they are blown off dock or lose their anchor gear while at anchor. The fittings allow ships to be easily towed from lay-up, so they do not have to be crewed.

Stern Anchor

A single wildcat, aft windlass and centreline hawse pipe with chain and anchor provide good flexibility for lay-up. When the stern is brought close to shore, the stern anchor can be slipped and the anchor chain taken ashore, which is useful during lay-up in a location such as a fjord, as the stern chain can be tensioned. Anchorages in restricted waterways may also use stern anchors as they reduce ship swinging and surging.

House Deck Drains

These drains are continually blocked by falling paint, debris or dirt and clearing the drain strainers and pipes can take a considerable length of time. Using larger drains, with easily removable inlet screens and no horizontal runs, including sloped horizontal runs, minimises this problem. Using external drains made of glass reinforced plastic (GRP), or a similar non-corrosive material, and carrying out sufficient cleanouts to allow direct access to all straight piping runs is beneficial for maintenance.

Stack Cover and Access to the Top of the Stack

Boilers in lay-up may not have been cleaned, depending on the length of time the vessel was in service after the last cleanout and how long it is to be laid-up. Rainwater can enter the boiler through the stack, soaking the floor and combining with the residues of burnt fuel oil to cause corrosion that may completely destroy the floor tubes. Tarpaulins over the stack frequently fail during rainstorms, so more permanent stack covers are recommended.

Flag State Requirements

Owners should notify their flag State when a vessel is to be laid-up or taken out of service for a prolonged period of time. Most flag States require official notification, including the date and location of the lay-up, so that this information can be registered.

Flag State requirements vary from a simple notification to a detailed document about the lay-up. For example, Hong Kong requires a copy of the lay-up survey report confirming that the ship is to be maintained while it is laid-up.

Lay-up of Ships

Liberia requires the ship's operators to submit a lay-up plan that includes the procedures to be used, the proposed manning level and the emergency response information for a short term lay-up. It is important that the flag State is consulted and the relevant requirements are checked before lay-up.

Safe Manning

This is the responsibility of the flag State. For cold lay-ups, there should, as a minimum, be watches organised for fire, leakage, mooring and security and the owner should receive guidance from the vessel's flag State, insurer and local port authorities to agree the final manning levels on board.

The following may be considered as sufficient manning for a hot lay-up when a ship is required to get underway in an emergency or if the port authorities require it:

- The master, one deck officer, three deck crew
- a chief engineer and two engineering crew
- sufficient crew to maintain all safety functions, eg prevention of explosions.

CHAPTER 18

Heavy Weather

Heavy Weather

carriers have become broader and broader as the block coefficient has increased, until many ships resemble large powered barges. This has turned the cut into the sea into a smash.

Both the fine and broad bow types can give problems when running at speed into seas. The fine bow cuts into the sea and, instead of rising, can try to cut through the wave, leading to green seas over the bow and very wet decks forward. The ship with the broad bow will thump into the wave, pushing the seas aside with the flare, and the bow will rise and fall heavily. The finer the bow, the more speed you can achieve, but you really do not want to bury your nose into the seas. The trim of the ship can assist considerably with the pitching. Trimming by the bow will push your bow further down into the sea while too much trim by the stern will make it more difficult to keep your head into the sea. The answer to heading into the sea in heavy weather is to have the ship slightly trimmed by the stern and not push your ship too hard. Every ship performs differently and you will soon know how your ship is dealing with the weather. Your schedule is not as important as the care of your ship and so you should consider a reduction in speed if your ship is pounding hard or has green seas over the bow.

There are types of ships, such as bulk carriers and tankers, that can accept water on deck as a matter of course and there are other ships that wish to avoid this. The amount of water the ship takes on her decks depends on the amount of pitch or roll, coupled with the stability, freeboard and the speed. A ship's roll varies with the degree of stability, with a stiff ship rolling more quickly than a tender ship and a light ship pitching more than a laden one.

If we look at a situation where the ship is heading into the sea, the water the ship takes on deck will vary with the distance between the waves, which is known as the period of encounter. A ship heading into a sea with a short period of encounter will pitch less and take less water on deck than a ship heading into a sea with a long period of encounter that tends to bury the head into the oncoming wave, causing water over the bow. The same applies to a beam sea, so if the period of roll is less than the period of encounter, again you will ship less seas. If the period of roll is more than the period of encounter, as the ship rolls she will come against the next wave and the clash of this against the hull will cause water on the decks.

Heading into the Sea

Ship's bows are designed to point into the sea, which is why they tend to be sharper than the stern. The problem is that many modern cargo

Running Before the Sea

Whenever I discuss this with others, someone inevitably raises the subject of pooping. Yes, this is possible and must always be considered, but the prospect of broaching is far more dangerous.

I have read advice about putting the sea on the quarter to avoid pooping but it is my experience that, unless you have ample power up your sleeve, this is not a good idea. In a low power vessel, and most of us drive around in vessels that are low in power in relation to the size of the ship, in really bad weather it is too easy to broach your ship. If you are running before the sea and your ship is steering well, set your speed to just below that of the approaching waves and keep the seas directly astern. A surprising number of ships can do this without too many problems. Should you experience difficulty with the steering or you take excessive water over your stern, and this is causing or could cause damage, rather than trying to adjust the seas to a different direction, come round and head into the sea. This should be done sooner rather than later.

Turning the Ship

It is particularly important to study the pattern of the waves if you want to turn your ship to put the sea on your stern. To put the sea on your stern, watch the waves form then, after a particularly large wave, wait for a few more and turn. Run your engines up to full speed and hard-over the wheel, preferably without too much initial headway on the ship.

To put your head to the sea after running with the sea astern, again watch the seas carefully. Wait until you see the waves rising and then, as the large wave approaches, put the wheel over with engines full ahead before it gets to you. I recommend that you have a little speed on the ship for this manoeuvre as ships are more reluctant to steer with the sea astern. By the time the ship has the sea on the beam, it should be on the decline again.

Heaving To

There is nothing wrong with doing this if you consider that the weather conditions are such that you are taking too much water on board, that you are pitching and rolling too violently or that damage to the ship might be the result of pressing on. In normal seas in storms, it is speed not the sea that causes most damage, both to the ship and to the cargo. Containers stacked high on the forward hatches, timber lashed high on the decks and shifting cargoes below must all be cared for as well. Advice is given to heave to with seas off the bow and, in one publication I read, it recommended allowing up to 45 degrees off! Certainly not something I would try in a low powered vessel. What you are looking for is enough power on the engine to maintain steerage way and to avoid falling off the seas. The wind will generally be in the same direction as the seas and you can see this from the appearance of the sea.

When hove to and in extreme weather, I believe that the best place for the sea is directly on the bow unless you have a high powered vessel and you wish to try to ease the pitch, in which case you can try the ship with the wind slightly off the bow, but not much more than 10 degrees.

If you fall off the wind, you have two choices to get back. The first is to increase power with the wheel amidships to build up a little speed, then put the wheel hardover. Depending on the power available to you, this might work. The other way is to accept that you cannot claw back and put the wheel over the opposite way, increase to full power and take the ship right round.

Should you not be able to get back with the wind ahead, you have two alternatives provided you have the sea room. The first is that you accept that you cannot get back so you stop your engine. The ship will then find its own angle to the seas and wind and will drift. You will experience severe rolling but you will have no speed and that will help with the seas. If you do this, the rule of thumb to use for your drift is around 2 knots. Add another knot for a safety margin and you will see from the proximity of land whether this course of action is safe to carry out. If you cannot or if the rolling is too severe for your ship, you will have to come about and put the ship on a course with the wind astern or on the quarter, steering the best course to take you clear of land or other shipping and on which your ship is best steered on. If you have the seas on your stern or quarter, try to have only enough power to make you just a little faster than the advancing waves.

A great deal of advice has been written on handling ships. Inevitably, the way to handle your ship will depend on the ship as well as the conditions at the time, as each ship acts in a different way. However, it is surprising what a ship can do and survive provided she is not forced against the sea. Apart from the circumstance of rogue waves, I personally feel that many of the ships that are at sea are lost as a result of poor ship handling.

Extract from 'In Command' by Captain Michael Lloyd

Heavy Weather

Extreme Weather at Sea

Extreme weather at sea can occur suddenly in many parts of the world and when it is encountered it is not always possible to get out of the way.

The actions that can be taken are limited by the ship type, engine power, the force of the weather and the proximity of land or dangers such as other ships.

Figure 18.1 - MV 'Suilven' off New Zealand

Figure 18.2 - In May 1974, the Norwegian tanker 'Wilstar' was hit by a freak wave off the east coast of South Africa's Natal Province

Figure 18.3 - Cruise liner, Antarctic Ocean

Preparations for Heavy Weather

- Apply additional lashings where appropriate
- temporarily move equipment to avoid loss
- daily monitoring of weather forecasts
- early adjustment of course and/or speed to avoid the worst weather conditions
- early notification of heavy weather and instruction for the crew to prepare
- check securing arrangements for deterioration and replace or double up as required
- press-up or empty ballast tanks to reduce the effects of free surface
- check bilge alarms and pumps
- check scuppers are clear and that no obvious material on deck can subsequently block them
- secure forward compartments, bosun's/forecastle store, paint lockers, etc
- if the ship is rolling heavily and/or the propeller is coming out of the water or heavy slamming occurs, the ship's speed should be reduced further
- adjust course and/or speed if green water is being shipped on deck
- over-reliance on the ship's autopilot may be dangerous in heavy weather.

Study of incidents suggests that there is an increase in damage during the hours of darkness, as the OOW is not able to estimate wave height correctly.

Damage Sustained in Heavy Weather

'Maersk Newport'

The *'Maersk Newport'* sailed from Le Havre, France for Algeciras in Spain, just after midnight on 10th November 2008, in force 4 to 5 winds. Overnight, the weather deteriorated and by the next afternoon it had further increased to force 8 to 9 with rough seas. At around 13:00, the bow thruster room bilge alarm sounded and a number of holes were found in the bow thruster room's port side shell plating, through which water was pouring. The port anchor chain lashing was found to have released and the anchor had fallen, against the windlass brake tension, into the water. As the ship continued to pitch in the heavy seas, the anchor had impacted against the hull, causing the damage. It was later found that five adjacent compartments had also flooded.

Despite the forecast poor weather conditions, no specific heavy weather checks had been carried out. By the time they became necessary, it was too dangerous for the crew to go onto the deck, so the anchor securing arrangements were not checked. The port anchor chain lashing arrangement failed because neither it, nor the windlass brake, had been sufficiently tightened and the hawse pipe cover was not fitted.

The vessel continued her passage and arrived in Algeciras on 13th November to work her cargo and carry out the necessary repairs.

'FR8 Venture'

On 11th November 2006, while outbound from Scapa Flow in the Orkney Islands, Scotland and transiting the Pentland Firth, the 74,065 Dwt Singaporean-registered tanker, *'FR8 Venture',* shipped two large waves over her bow. This resulted in the deaths of two able seamen and serious injuries to an ordinary seaman, all of whom were working on the forward mooring deck. The waves also caused minor damage to the ship. The circumstances were as follows.

After carrying out a ship to ship transfer of crude oil, the *'FR8 Venture'* weighed anchor from Scapa Flow. The wind was west to west-northwest and near gale force, with waves of about 4 to 5 m high. The ship's freeboard was about 6.6 m and spray was being shipped on deck. The tidal stream was flowing generally in the same direction as the wind.

After securing the port anchor, the Bosun, the two ABs and an OS began stowing three loose mooring lines down into the forward storeroom. The Bosun instructed the OS to place a securing wire through the starboard anchor cable and, just as the OS turned towards the cable, a large wave was shipped over the bow. The ship pitched into the following trough and then a second larger wave was shipped on board. The two ABs were swept aft, towards and under the flying bridge while the OS was swept aft and hit a protection plate for the forward liferaft. The Bosun managed to cling on to the storeroom door when the first wave was shipped, then on to the ladder rungs of the foremast as the second wave swept over the foredeck.

The subsequent investigation identified the following safety issues:

- The two large waves that were shipped over the bow should have been expected in the prevailing weather conditions
- the Master should have delayed the sailing so that the ship could be secured for sea in sheltered waters
- having decided to leave the shelter of Scapa Flow before the foredecks were secured for sea, the Master's assessment of when the crew should have been clear of the foredeck of the ship allowed little margin for error

Damage Sustained in Heavy Weather

- the crew should have been forward earlier, leaving the stowing of the after ropes until the fore part of the vessel had been secured
- a risk assessment would have prompted the need for precautionary measures, such as considering the option of turning the ship away from the weather, when safe and practicable to do so, to secure the anchors.

MV *'OOCL America'*

The 66,047 GT, Hong Kong-registered container vessel MV *'OOCL America'*, built in 1995, sustained heavy weather damage on 31st January 2000 during a voyage from Long Beach, California to Kaohsiung, Taiwan. The vessel encountered severe weather in the Pacific Ocean and lost an estimated 350 containers overboard. The 217 that remained on board were crushed or bent out of usable condition.

'Shin Kakogawa Maru'

On 10th June 1994, the 124,292 Dwt *'Shin Kakogawa Maru',* built in 1981, was on passage from Port Dampier, Australia to Gijon in Spain when she sustained a 6 m long crack in the shell plate during bad weather off Richards Bay, South Africa. The crew were disembarked by helicopter on 13th June as the ship was very low in the water, with cargo holds 1 and 2 flooded and structural damage in cargo hold 7. The vessel was later towed to the Bay of Nacala in Mozambique for temporary repairs.

Ship Movement in Heavy Weather

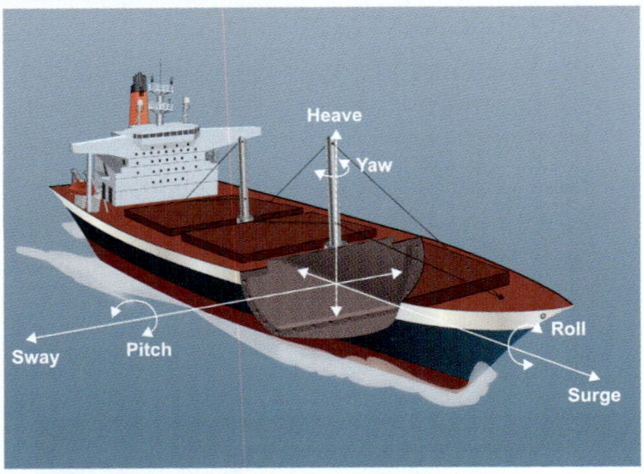

Figure 18.4 - Freedoms of motion

There are six types of motion experienced by a vessel. Three are rotational (roll, pitch and yaw) and three are linear (sway, surge and heave).

At sea, the wind, waves and swell cause the ship to move. The stronger the wind and the greater the height of the sea and swell, the more the ship will move.

Container Vessels – Bow Flare Impact in Heavy Weather

Container vessels tend to have considerable bow flare to allow for deck stowage of as many containers as possible.

Numerous cases have been recorded where the bow or stern area has been overloaded and is unable to endure the heavy impact load from the waves, with the structure often suffering considerable damage. OOWs must be aware that the ship's structure may be overloaded in heavy weather and, due to containers stacked on deck, it may not be possible to see whether green water is being shipped on deck.

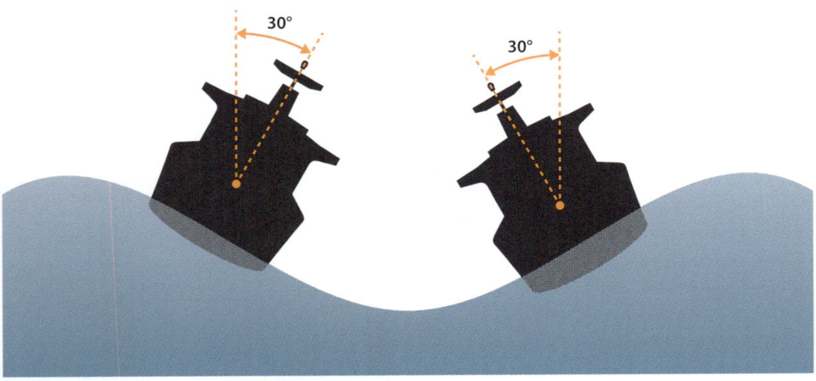

(a) Rolling 30° to port and starboard, and swaying to port and starboard, as each wave passes

Ship Movement in Heavy Weather

(b) Pitching to 10° bow up and surging astern, and pitching to 10° bow down while surging ahead, as each wave passes

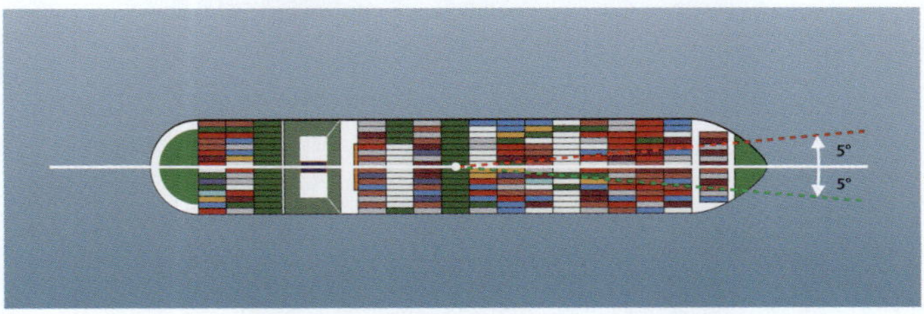

(c) Yawing 5° port and 5° starboard as each wave passes

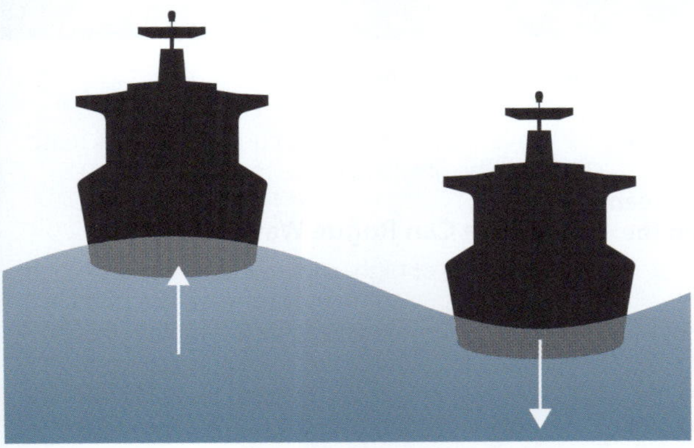

(d) Heaving up and down as each wave passes

Figure 18.5 (a-d) - Movement of a ship in a seaway

Parametric Rolling

Special attention should be paid when a vessel experiences rolling in following or stern quartering seas. This phenomenon, known as parametric rolling, may in rare cases lead to the vessel capsizing. The usual precaution is to turn the vessel into the seas and reduce speed.

Areas Prone to Damage

- Deck fittings
- LSA equipment on deck, liferafts and lifebuoys (forward liferaft in particular)
- plastic boxes, such as those for fire hoses and immersion suits
- manifold drip trays and save-alls.

The vessel's motion depends on the direction of approach of the wind and waves relative to its heading:

- If the wind and swell are from ahead, the ship will pitch and surge but will roll only a little
- if the ship is experiencing a strong wind on the beam, with associated high beam swell conditions, it will roll and sway heavily but will not pitch very much.

A ship will, to a certain extent, experience all six motions at the same time. The motions that are typically felt most by the ship's crew and the cargo are roll, pitch and heave.

The three linear movements affect all parts of the ship equally, regardless of location, while the effect of the three rotational movements increases with distance from the ship's longitudinal centre of gravity (LCG).

Freak Waves (Source: SKULD Beacon)

Rogue Waves

Figure 18.6 - The most dangerous rogue waves do not follow any known model

Rogue waves, also known as freak, monster, extreme or hundred-year waves, are exceptionally large and spontaneous ocean surface waves that are a threat to even the largest ships and ocean liners.

What Causes Rogue Waves?

A huge number of variables influence the formation of this type of wave, including the depth of the water, tidal forces, wind blowing across the water, physical objects such as islands that reflect waves, and interaction with other waves and ocean currents. The term 'fetch' describes the unobstructed distance of ocean over which the wind can blow on the water and the faster the wind is and the longer it blows, more fetch and bigger waves are created.

The textbook rogue wave is one that is double the significant wave height, ie the height of the highest one-third of the waves. Scientists are not completely sure why they become so large but one theory is that ocean currents cause waves to 'pile up' when they run into currents head on. Powerful storms can create significant wave heights of 12 to 15 metres and, when these large waves run into a strong current, it can increase wave heights and cause the waves to break.

Where Can Rogue Waves Occur?

The areas of highest predictable risk are where a strong current runs counter to the primary direction of the waves, for example the area near Cape Agulhas off the southern tip of Africa where storm waves moving up from the south crash into the current. Mathematical predictions suggest rogue waves here could reach 60 metres in height and this area has the largest number of recorded rogue waves and ship casualties to date, with 20 ships reporting rogue wave strikes since 1990. Other areas that have a particular tendency to be exposed to rogue waves are the seas off Norway, the Gulf Stream, the Kuroshio Current, the Nantucket Shoals and Cape Horn. The Gulf Stream, which runs up the east coast of the United States, is another potential rogue wave source.

Satellite research indicates that rogue waves can also occur in high seas in areas that are not affected by known currents or geographical formations and this unpredictability makes 'random' rogue waves more problematic. It is thought that some waves 'steal' energy from neighbouring waves to grow large and unstable, usually characterised by 'holes in the sea' and steep 'breaking' waves. Instead of breaking on sand, however, rogue waves at sea can break on a vessel that has just fallen into the wave's 'hole' or trough.

Not all rogue waves occur in strong ocean currents. Scientists believe some waves may be caused by randomly occurring wave reinforcement. Whenever 2 waves interact, their wave height is added together, for example a 5 metre wave passing over a 10 metre wave results in a briefly occurring 15 metre wave. Occasionally, several waves may come together at just the right moment and create one huge wave in relatively calm seas. If 10 waves that are only 2 metres high come together, they will result in a 20 metre wave. This fits descriptions of rogue waves that seem to appear out of nowhere and disappear after just a few minutes.

How Strong are They?

A 12 metre wave has the force of about 6 MT/m^2 but a breaking rogue wave has a tremendous force, around 100 MT/m^2. Modern day vessels are designed to withstand only 15 MT/m^2, so it is understandable why some ships do not survive encounters with rogue waves.

What can Mariners do?

On 27th April 1985, the tanker '*Taganrogsky Zaliv*', from the former Soviet Union, encountered a rogue wave, as a result of which a seaman was killed and washed overboard. According to the description by the ship's crew, the unusual wave looked like a deep hole in the sea that appeared so suddenly in front of the ship that it was impossible to take any precautionary measures to avoid sliding down into the deep wave trough.

Mariners should be aware of areas already known to have a higher risk of rogue waves and that the following sea conditions may create them:

- Low pressure systems
- wind blowing in one direction for more than 12 hours
- waves travelling at the same speed as a moving weather system
- waves going against a strong current
- fast waves catching a set of slower moving waves and merging.

The most dangerous rogue waves are those that cannot be predicted and do not emerge out of a known set of factors likely to create them. In many of the cases in which a vessel has survived a rogue wave encounter, the wave was spotted just in time for the vessel to take at least some action to limit the wave's destructive effect.

Courtesy of SKULD Beacon 2005

Case Studies

'Louis Majesty'
6th March 2010/Mediterranean

The cruise ship *'Louis Majesty'*, en route from Barcelona to Genoa with 1,350 passengers and 580 crew on board, was badly damaged after being hit by a 10 metre high rogue wave. Two people were killed and 14 others were injured.

'Norwegian Dawn'
16th April 2005/North Atlantic

A rogue wave, estimated to be more than 21 metres high, hit the cruise ship '*Norwegian Dawn*,' after it ran into heavy seas in an overnight storm off Florida while on passage to New York. According to a Norwegian Cruise Line spokesperson, the sea seemed to have calmed down when the wave appeared out of thin air at daybreak. The vessel's experienced Captain said he had never seen anything like it.

'Queen Elizabeth II'
11th September 1995/North Atlantic

The cruise liner '*Queen Elizabeth II*' encountered a 29-metre rogue wave that Captain Ronald Warwick described as *"a great wall of water – it looked as if we were going into the White Cliffs of Dover."*

'Stolt Surf'
20th October 1977/Pacific

The chemical tanker '*Stolt Surf*' encountered a hurricane-like storm and huge waves while voyaging across the Pacific from Singapore to Portland, Oregon. Photographer Karsten Peterson of Denmark was on board and provided an eyewitness account. *"When the big waves came crashing towards us, we had to look* UP *in order to see the top of the waves! And that was from the bridge deck, which is already 22 metres above sea level".*

Freak Waves (Source: SKULD Beacon)

'World Glory'
13th June 1968/South Africa

The tanker *'World Glory'*, carrying 49,000 tonnes of crude oil, encountered an abnormally large wave 105 km east of Durban. The ship broke in half and sank within four hours.

'Esso Languedoc'
1980/South Africa

This rare photo of a rogue wave was taken by first mate Philippe Lijour on board the supertanker *'Esso Languedoc'*, during a storm off Durban. The mast seen starboard in the photo stands 25 metres above mean sea level. The wave approached the ship from behind before breaking over the deck, causing only minor damage. The mean wave height at the time was between 5 to 10 metres.

Bow Damage in Heavy Weather

'Kirki' Oil Spill

On 21st July 1991, the Greek tanker *'Kirki'* lost its bow off the coast of Western Australia.

The ship, operated by a Greek crew of 37, was on charter to BP Australia Ltd and was carrying a full cargo of 82,650 tonnes of Murban light crude from Jebel Dhanna to BP's refinery at Kwinana, Western Australia. In addition to cargo, the vessel also had on board approximately 1,800 tonnes of heavy fuel oil bunkers, 200 tonnes of gas oil, 100 tonnes of marine diesel and 35 tonnes of lubricating oil.

During the latter part of the voyage, the vessel encountered rough seas and heavy swell with predominantly west to southwesterly weather. Problems were first noticed at about 22:00 Western Standard Time (WST) on Saturday 20th July when it was found that the forepeak ballast tank had filled with seawater, causing the vessel to trim by the head. The vessel was about 55 nautical miles northwest of Lancelin. At about 20:00 WST, the ship was noticed to be down by the head. Speed was reduced and course altered to 090T to bring the weather on the beam and ease the effect at the bow. Efforts to pump out the tank were unsuccessful and it was found that serious structural damage had occurred to the ship's forward hull section. At the time of the incident, the wind was westerly 35 knots and a gale warning was current.

At 03:00 WST on Sunday 21st July, the damaged bow section broke off causing the collision bulkhead to fracture and expose the No. 1 cargo tanks to the sea. Cargo oil was spilled and subsequently fire broke out from the bow, probably as a result of arcing from exposed electrical cables. At this time, the *'Kirki'* was 24 nautical miles southwest of the West Australian fishing village of Cervantes, 245 km north of Perth. The weather was severe, with force 8 winds from the west/southwest, rough seas and heavy swells. During the ensuing hours, fire broke out from the forward area a further five times, each time being extinguished by the sea.

Conclusions

The inspector concluded:

- The flooding of the forepeak tank on the evening of 20th July was due either to a failure in the ship's shell plating forward of frame 93, or the shearing of the forepeak ballast pipeline at the shell plating on the port side
- it is not possible to be precise about the cause of the structural failure forward of

Bow Damage in Heavy Weather

frame 93 (the bow). It was either due to the action of seawater, which had flooded the fore-peak, impinging heavily in the area of frame 93, which led to an overload on the structure, or to a loss of bow plating. Either one or a combination of these factors led to excessive stress on an area of the ship's structure already weakened by corrosion and the effects of repair work

- the source of the ignition causing the original fire was either sparks caused by the mechanical action of the tearing of the steel work, or the arcing of broken electrical cables forward
- the subsequent five fires were caused either by static electrical discharges or by the arcing of broken electrical cables
- there is no evidence that the loading operation at Jebel Dhanna contributed in any way to the incident
- any stress to the ship's hull caused by maintaining propeller revolutions at 95 rpm through the gales of 4th to 6th July and in the sea conditions of 18th to 20th July was to an area already weakened structurally. It would have been prudent to reduce the revolutions in such weather.

VLCC *'Tochal'*

The VLCC *'Tochal'*, while rounding the Cape of Good Hope fully laden, was hit by heavy seas that resulted in her entire lower bow section forward of the collision bulkhead falling away. This was how she looked before loose steel was cut away.

'World Horizon'

The *'World Horizon'* lost most of her bow in heavy weather off the Cape of Good Hope. Here she lies waiting for temporary repairs before sailing from Cape Town.

Source: http://web.uct.ac.za/depts/shiplaw/capstorm.htm

Structural Damage to the Bow Area

'Atlas Pride'

In September 1991, the *'Atlas Pride'* suffered substantial damage to her bow and the complete loss of her forepeak, when she met a freak wave off South Africa.

The vessel proceeded safely, but with a heavy forward trim, to a port of safe refuge for survey and repairs.

Extent of Damage

The following damage was noted:

- The forward compartment access dog house had its watertight door torn off and washed overboard, resulting in flooding of the entire forward space from the keel and up to the main deck
- the stores hatch cover was torn open, breaking the dogs, and was formed around the hatch coaming by water pressure
- the ventilator at the base of the forward mast was damaged beyond repair
- two small goose neck ventilators in the forward area were damaged by distortion
- the starboard ballast tank vent head received minor damage
- below the deck, inside the stores area, all machinery and equipment were flooded. The paint locker fire door was badly distorted and torn off its hinges
- the emergency fire pump diesel engine was damaged including its wiring harness, starting batteries, and various other accessories.

Synchronous Rolling

When a ship is in heavy seas, she may experience:

- Synchronous rolling motion
- parametric rolling motion
- reduction of intact stability caused by surf-riding on the wave crest amidships.

Scenario	Occurrence		Effect
	Direction	Periods/Encounter	
1. Synchronous rolling motion	All directions	Natural rolling period of a ship coincides with the wave encounter period	Heavy oscillations with high amplitude
2. Parametric rolling motion	Head and stem wave conditions	Wave encounter period is approximately equal to half of the natural roll period of the ship	Heavy oscillations with high amplitude
3. Reduction of stability caused by riding on the wave crest amidships	Following and quartering seas	Wave length larger than 0.8 × Lpp and significant wave height is larger than 0.04 × Lpp	Large roll angle and capsizing

Table 18.1 - Effects and occurrence of these ship motion scenarios

Synchronous Rolling

Synchronous rolling occurs when the natural rolling period of the ship coincides with the wave encounter period, resulting in large rolling motions of the ship. This may happen when the stability of the ship causes a shorter natural roll period or when sailing in high quartering or beam seas.

The wave encounter period is the time in seconds in which the ship meets the waves.

For beam seas, the encounter period is equal to the wave period. For head waves, the encounter period is shorter than the wave period. For following seas, the encounter period is normally larger than the wave period.

Depending on the effectiveness of damping mechanisms on the vessel, such as bilge keels and active stabiliser fins, the roll angle can quickly resonate to angles of 50° or more. This is most likely to occur in high quartering and beam seas.

Dangers associated with synchronous rolling include:

- The vessel rolls to dangerously large angles of heel
- sometimes angle of heel increases beyond the point from which it can recover and the vessel may capsize
- cargo lashings can part on container and RoRo vessels
- parting of lashings can result in structural damage
- cargo shift can occur, resulting in loss of stability due to heavy list and possible capsize
- structural damage can occur with high density cargo
- injury to personnel.

The best way of reducing synchronous rolling is to alter the vessel's course. Ships are constructed with means to dampen rolling and these typically include the installation of bilge keels. However, if more control is required, anti-roll tanks and fins are used.

CHAPTER 19

Participating in SAR

Participating in SAR

Effective search and rescue operations require coordination between the various organisations and units concerned, including aircraft, ships and shore-based life-saving facilities.

A Brief Description of SAR Operations

Department of Defense photo by US Air Force Tech Sgt Michael R Holzworth/Released

When the SAR organisation becomes aware of an actual or potential emergency, the information collected and the initial action taken are often critical to a successful operation.

It must be assumed that in each incident there are survivors in need of assistance, whose chances of survival are reduced by the passage of time. The success of a SAR operation depends on the speed with which it is planned and carried out.

Information must be gathered and evaluated to determine the nature of the distress, the appropriate emergency phase and the action to be taken. Prompt receipt of all available information by the Regional Control Centre (RCC) is necessary to ensure an immediate decision on the best course of action and a timely mobilisation of SAR facilities to ensure that:

- Anyone in distress is located, supported and rescued in the shortest possible time
- any contribution survivors may be able to make towards their own rescue is used while they are still capable of doing so.

Experience has shown that, following an accident, the chances for survival of injured persons decrease by as much as 80% during the first 24 hours, and those for uninjured persons diminish rapidly after the first three days. Uninjured persons who may appear able-bodied and capable of rational thought are often unable to accomplish simple tasks and

are known to have hindered, delayed or even prevented their own rescue.

Timing of a SAR Mission

The order of events in a SAR incident are as follows:

1. The RCC is made aware of a marine distress.
2. The RCC gathers information on the distress incident and uses its authority to task vessels.
3. The vessel or vessels to be tasked are contacted.

SAR Communications

Standard VHF communications procedures are followed for any SAR incident, including marine information broadcasts. For Maydays and Mayday relays, vessels are required to maintain a continuous radio watch on channel 16 or any frequencies allotted by the controlling authority during a search.

Communications with the RCC can be conducted either by satellite, mobile phone or by radio.

It is good practice to log all incoming and outgoing radio transmissions. Writing down messages before they are sent ensures that all information is transmitted correctly.

Initial Action by Assisting Vessels

The following immediate action should be taken by any ship receiving a distress message:

- Acknowledge receipt of the message
- gather the following information from the vessel in distress if possible:
  - position of vessel
  - distressed vessel's identity, call sign and name
  - number of persons on board

- nature of the distress
- type of assistance required
- number of victims, if any
- distressed vessel's course and speed
- type of vessel and cargo carried
- any other pertinent information that may facilitate the rescue

- vessels should maintain communications with the vessel in distress while attempting to advise the RCC of the situation
- the following information should be communicated to the distressed craft:
  - own vessel's identity, call sign and name
  - own vessel's position
  - own vessel's speed and estimated time of arrival (ETA) to distressed vessel's position
  - distressed vessel's true bearing and distance from ship.

Proceeding to the Area of Distress

- Establish communications between vessels proceeding to the same area of distress
- maintain active tracking, radar and AIS on vessels in the general vicinity
- estimate the ETAs of other assisting vessels to the distress site
- assess the distress situation in order to prepare for the rescue operation on scene.

On Board Preparation

A vessel on its way to assist a vessel in distress should have the following equipment ready for possible use:

Life-saving and Rescue Equipment

- Lifeboat
- inflatable liferaft
- lifejackets
- survival suits for the crew
- lifebuoys
- portable VHF radios for communication with the ship and boats deployed
- line-throwing apparatus
- buoyant lifelines
- boat hooks
- hatchets
- rescue baskets

- pilot ladders
- scrambling nets
- supplies and survival equipment, as required
- fire-fighting equipment
- cameras.

Signalling Equipment

- Searchlights
- torches
- flares.

Medical Equipment

- Stretchers
- blankets
- medical supplies and medicines
- clothing
- food.

Miscellaneous Equipment

- If fitted, a gantry crane for hoisting on each side of ship with a cargo net for recovery of survivors
- a line running from bow to stern at the water's edge on both sides for boats and life craft to secure alongside
- on the lowest weather deck, pilot ladders and manropes to assist survivors boarding the vessel
- the vessel's lifeboats ready for use as a boarding station
- floodlights set in appropriate locations, if recovery is to be at night.

En route to the Scene

- To ensure that all necessary equipment is assembled, consider the following:
  - the weather (are warm clothes required?)
  - the expected duration of the rescue (is extra food and water necessary?)
  - the kind of incident (is any special equipment needed?)
- brief the crew:
  - prepare short-term strategies
  - define priorities
  - assign tasks
  - prepare the equipment that will be needed
  - make the hospital ready.

Rescue and OSC

Survival Craft: Methods of Attracting Attention

- Activate an EPIRB (Emergency Position-Indicating Radio Beacon)
- use of pyrotechnics:
  - (a) Volume of orange coloured smoke. Buoyant canister or handheld. Normally two per boat/liferaft
  - (b) handheld red flare, operated at arm's length and held well overside. Normally six per boat. Mainly used to attract aircraft
  - (c) rocket parachute flare. Hand operated to show a red star shell at about 300 metres. Used mainly to attract surface craft. Normally four per boat/liferaft
- the transmission of SOS by any available means, eg by use of a torch or by the emergency radio
- the raising and lowering of the arms, an international distress signal for use at close range only. More effective if used in conjunction with another signal
- a square flag with a ball or anything resembling a ball above or below it. This is an international signal of distress
- burning rags or oil from a container such as a bucket or other improvised holder. Oil giving off black smoke forms a focal point for air and surface craft
- the continuous sounding of a whistle, a gun or other explosive signal. International signal of distress over short range
- use of the daylight signalling mirror (heliograph) to reflect the rays of the sun. Limited in range to about 5 miles to attract attention
- international orange canopy or upper structure of a boat, fitted with retro-reflective tape for detection by searchlights
- SART – Search and Rescue Transponder provides 12 digit radar signature up to 5 miles. AIS SART with prefix 970 may also be used.

Flares

Rocket Parachute Flares

Figure 19.1 - Rocket parachute flare

Four of these flares are carried in each lifeboat and liferaft, with a further 12 on the bridge. When operated, they eject a red flare on a parachute at 300 metres (1,000 feet) that burns for 40 seconds at 30,000 candela.

To operate:

1. Hold signal firmly by ribbed handle. Unscrew RED bottom cap. Do not point at people or property.
2. Hold rocket vertically above head pointing away from body.
3. Ensure hands remain clear of top. To fire - pull red ball sharply down.

Handheld Flares

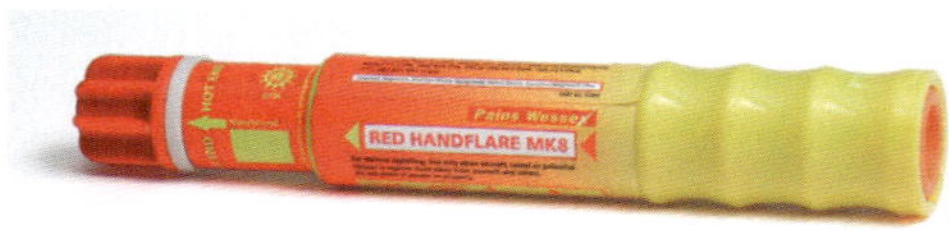

Figure 19.2 - Handheld flare

Six handheld flares are carried in each lifeboat and liferaft. When operated, they release a hot red flame for 60 seconds at 15,000 candela.

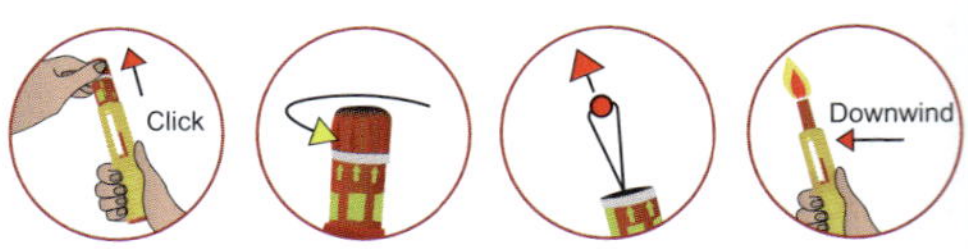

To operate:

1. Pull out red end until telescopic tube is fully extended and engaged.

2. Unscrew red end cap and point away.
3. Pull ball out sharply to fire.
4. Hold at arm's length. Point downwind. End plug ejects after 2 seconds' delay.

Smokefloats

Figure 19.3 - Smokefloats

Two smokefloats are carried in each lifeboat and liferaft. When activated, they produce dense orange smoke for a minimum of 3 minutes. They provide effective position marking during rescue operations and can be used to indicate wind direction.

To operate:

1. Remove plastic cap. Point away from body.
2. Pull ring firmly away from canister. Ensure hand remains clear of hot end.
3. Throw canister overboard immediately. Smoke will be emitted after a 2 second delay.

MOB Smokefloat

These are fitted to the lifebuoys on either bridge wing. In addition to a light that far exceeds SOLAS requirements regarding light output and duration, they also provide 15 minutes of dense orange smoke.

Figure 19.4 - Man Overboard (MOB) smokefloat

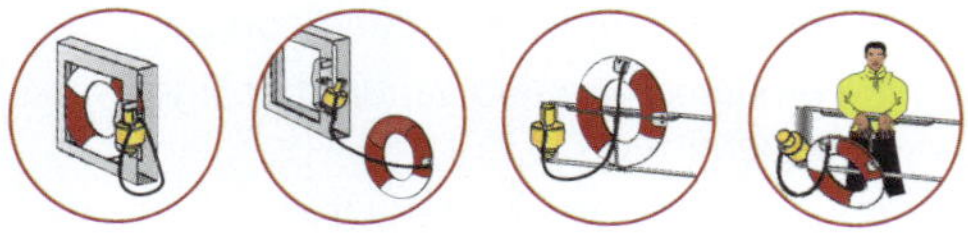

To operate:

1. MOB smokefloat and lifebuoy mounted on bridge wing in ready to fire position.
2. Release locking pin and lifebuoy falls, automatically deploying MOB smokefloat.
3. Alternatively, manually throw lifebuoy overboard.

Requirements for Survival Craft Emergency Position-Indicating Radio Beacons (EPIRBs)

SOLAS requires that all ships constructed after 1st July 1986 are equipped with two manually activated emergency position-indicating radio beacons that comply with the regulations, one stowed on either side of the ship. Their stowage should be such that they can be deployed in any of the survival craft rapidly, with the exception of the liferafts required by Regulation 26.1.4.

Figure 19.5 - An emergency position-indicating radio beacon (EPIRB)

Rescue and OSC

An EPIRB must:

- Be of a highly visible colour, so designed that they can be used by an unskilled person. Their construction should be such that they may be easily tested and their batteries shall not require replacement at intervals of less than 12 months, taking into account testing arrangements
- be watertight, and capable of floating and being dropped into the water without damage from a height of at least 20 metres
- be capable of manual activation and de-activation only
- be portable, lightweight and compact
- be provided with indication that signals are being emitted
- derive their energy supply from a battery forming an integral part of the device and having sufficient capacity to operate the apparatus for a period of 48 hours. The transmission may be intermittent. Determination of the duty cycle should take into account the probability of homing being properly carried out, the need to avoid congestion on the frequencies and the need to comply with the requirements of the International Civil Aviation Organization (ICAO)
- be tested and if necessary have their source of energy replaced at intervals not exceeding 12 months.

EPIRB Case Studies

USCG Rescues eight after Freighter Runs Aground
4th September 2008

A Coast Guard aircrew rescued eight crew members from the motor vessel *'Anais'*, which ran aground near South Caicos Island, Turks and Caicos Islands.

The Coast Guard Command Center in Miami received a radio beacon (EPIRB) alert indicating the *'Anais'* was in distress. Search and rescue coordinators determined the vessel had run aground but the crew was not in immediate danger and did not need to be removed. Adverse weather conditions associated with Tropical Storm Hanna prevented search and rescue teams from removing the crew at the time.

Search and rescue coordinators monitored the crew on board the *'Anais'* regularly until a helicopter crew from Coast Guard Air Station Clearwater could safely transport the eight men from the *'Anais'* to Amberges Cay, Turks and Caicos Islands.

Round the World Yacht Crew Rescued
18th January 2008

Rescue Coordination Centre New Zealand (RCCNZ) facilitated the rescue response after its equivalent in France called at 13:20 (NZDT) to report it had picked up a signal from the French trimaran *'Groupama III'* from its 406 MHz EPIRB.

RCCNZ Mission Coordinator Keith Allen said the incident highlighted the value of people carrying a 406 MHz EPIRB, which had greatly assisted in the rescue:

> *"Because the 406 MHz variety EPIRB is able to be detected by satellite within minutes, it gives rescuers an accurate position very quickly, which greatly speeds up any emergency response. The fact that the beacon was also registered with up-to-date ownership details meant that rescue agencies knew straight away who was in trouble and were able to make contact with them."*

The yacht had overturned 80 nautical miles east of Dunedin shortly after 13:00. All ten crew members were winched to safety by three rescue helicopters. All of the crew were uninjured and were dressed in survival gear when they were picked up from the yacht's hull.

Capsize of Catamaran
11th April 2007

The Cospas-Sarsat system detected a 406 MHz distress signal about 175 nautical miles southwest of Tampa, Florida. The EPIRB automatically activated when the 35 foot catamaran S/V *'Paradox'* hit a squall and capsized. The USCG launched an aircraft to the scene and the crew located the vessel with two persons clinging to the hull. Air Station Clearwater then launched a helicopter to the scene. The crew of the helicopter hoisted the two people on board and transported them to a hospital in the lower Florida Keys.

Helicopter Crash
19th January 2005

The Indian Mission Control Centre (INMCC) detected a distress signal from a Cospas-Sarsat EPIRB on board a crashed helicopter belonging to Hindustan Ink near Daman (20 24.2N 072 54.4E). Both the pilots were rescued and had only minor injuries.

Voyage Data Recorder (VDR)

Figure 19.6 - Voyage data recorder. This is a protective storage unit that is either in a retrievable fixed unit or float free unit

A data recording system is required for all merchant vessels by SOLAS amendments under IMO Res.A.861(20).

The VDR collects data from a number of sensors on board the ship and stores the information in an externally mounted protective storage unit. The protective storage unit is tamper-proof and designed to withstand the extreme shock, impact, pressure and heat that could be associated with a marine incident.

The last 12 hours of stored data in the protected unit can be recovered and examined by the authorities or the ship's owners to assist in investigating a marine loss.

There is also a Simplified Voyage Data Recorder (S-VDR), which is defined under IMO Performance Standard MSC.163(78) as a lower cost VDR for use by smaller ships, where only basic ship's data is recorded.

Voyage Data

The information recorded in the unit(s) may include the following:

- Position, date and time
- speed
- gyro heading
- radar* - as displayed or AIS data if no off-the-shelf converter is available for the radar video
- audio from the bridge, including bridge wings
- VHF radio communications
- echo sounder* - depth underkeel
- main alarms* - all IMO mandatory alarms
- hull openings* - status of hull doors as indicated on the bridge
- watertight and fire doors* - status as indicated on the bridge
- hull stress* - accelerations and hull stresses
- rudder* - order and feedback response
- engine/propeller* - order and feedback response
- thrusters* - status, direction, amount of thrust % or rpm
- anemometer and weather vane* - wind speed and direction.

Data marked with * may not be recorded in an S-VDR.

Search and Rescue Transponder (SART)

Figure 19.7 - SART

SOLAS requires that a Global Maritime Distress Safety System (GMDSS) on board has one or more SARTs.

These devices may be either a radar-SART (search and rescue transponder) or an AIS-SART (AIS search and rescue transmitter).

The radar-SART assists in the location of a survival craft or ship in distress by creating a series of dots in the direction of the vessel in distress as viewed on another ship's radar display.

A SART will only respond to a 9 GHz X-band (3 cm wavelength) radar. It will not be seen on S-band (10 cm) or other radar.

Rescue and OSC

Surface Vessel/Aircraft Radio Communications Frequencies

- 2182 kHz: Designated search and rescue (SAR) aircraft are required to carry this frequency. It is an international distress frequency for radio-telephony. Silence periods operate for three minutes on the hour and on the half hour to allow the reception of distress calls
- 156.8 MHz: The VHF maritime distress frequency (channel 16). Designated SAR aircraft should have this additional frequency to enable communications to the distressed vessel and other participating SAR units
- 3023 and 5680 kHz: HF radio-telephony frequencies for SAR on-scene use. Carried by designated SAR aircraft and the majority of civil aircraft. May also be employed by coast radio stations and shipboard operators
- 121.5 and 243 MHz: The international aeronautical distress frequencies carried by all aircraft engaged in designated SAR duty. Designated SAR and civilian aircraft are recommended to guard 121.5 MHz frequency subject to cockpit duties permitting. Aeronautical survival craft radio equipment operates on 121.5 and/or 243 MHz. Emergency position-indicating radio beacons also operate on these frequencies
- 123.1 MHz: An aeronautical on-scene frequency which may be used by both aircraft and surface vessels as a common VHF frequency for search and rescue operations.

If communication difficulties arise between ships and aircraft while engaged in search and rescue activity, information may also be relayed through the rescue co-ordination centre (RCC).

Surface-to-air Visual Signals

Recommended signals as issued by the UK Department for Transport, Life-Saving Signals Card, SOLAS No. 2, are given in Table 19.1.

Message/meaning	ICAO visual symbol
Require assistance	V
Require medical assistance	X
No or negative	N
Yes or affirmative	Y
Proceeding in this direction	↑

Table 19.1 - Surface-to-air visual symbols to be displayed on the deck or on the ground

Aircraft reply signals are shown in Figure 19.8.

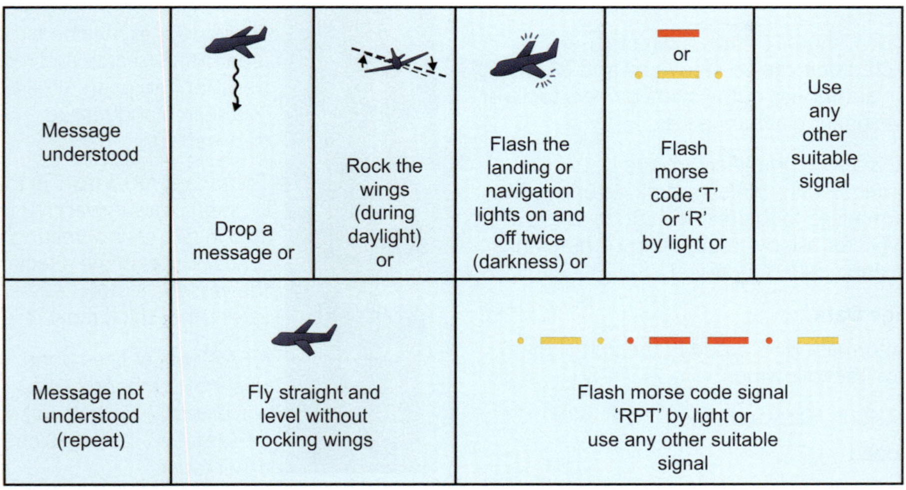

Figure 19.8 - Reply signals made by an aircraft

Air-to-surface Visual Signals

Signals given by aircraft employed in search and rescue operations to direct ships towards another aircraft, ship or person in distress are shown in Figure 19.9.

Response signals by surface vessels towards an aircraft engaged in search and rescue operations are shown in Figure 19.10.

Procedures			Signification
 1. Circle the vessel at least once.	 2. Cross the vessel's projected course close ahead at a low altitude while rocking the wings (see note).	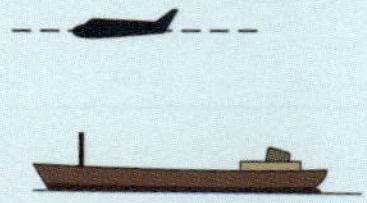 3. Head in the direction in which the vessel is to be directed.	The aircraft is directing a vessel towards an aircraft or vessel in distress. Repetition of signals shall have the same meaning.
 4. Cross the vessel's wake close astern at low altitude while rocking the wings (see note). NOTE: Opening and closing the throttle or changing the propeller pitch may also be practised as an alternative means of attracting attention to the rocking of the wings.			The assistance of the vessel is no longer required.

Figure 19.9 - Air-to-surface visual signals

Rescue and OSC

Procedures			Signification
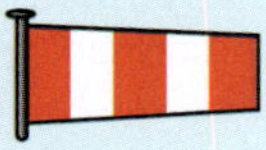 Hoist code and answering pendant close up: or	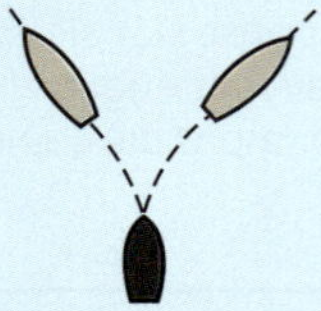 Change the heading to the required direction: or	Flash morse code 'T' by signalling lamp	Acknowledges receipt of aircraft's signal
 Hoist international flag 'N' (November) or		Flash morse code signal 'N' by signal lamp	Indicates inability to comply

Figure 19.10 - Response signals by surface vessel towards an aircraft engaged in search and rescue operations

Equipment Droppable by Aircraft

The type of droppable container or package varies according to the circumstances of the survivors and their requirements. For marine incidents, the containers must be buoyant and may be dropped free-fall or by parachute.

Containers are colour coded as follows:

- Food and water - Blue
- blankets and protective clothing - Yellow
- medical supplies and first aid equipment - Red
- miscellaneous equipment - Black.

In addition, liferafts in a ready packed condition are kept available for use in the event of:

- Survival craft being damaged during launch or survival craft not being capable of being launched
- survival craft being overcrowded
- survivors being in the water
- survival craft becoming unserviceable.

Developing the Search Area

Where multiple search units are employed to search select areas, each area should be allocated geographic coordinates. This will reduce the possibility of overlap and time wasting and assist reporting to eliminate specific sea areas.

Once the search area(s) has been established and an appropriate pattern confirmed, the track space for the unit or units engaged must be established. This must be selected to provide adequate safe separation between searching units while at the same time taking into account the following:

- The target size and definition
- the state of visibility on scene
- the sea state inside the designated search area
- the quality of the radar target likely to be presented
- height of eye of lookouts
- speed of vessel(s) engaged in search operations
- number of search units engaged
- available daylight remaining
- masters' experience
- recommendations from MRCC
- height above sea level (for aircraft).

Additional influencing factors include:

- Night searches can be ongoing with effective searchlight coverage
- length of search period may be restricted by the endurance of the vessels engaged
- whether the target can make itself more prominent.

Pattern and track space should be selected with reference to 'IAMSAR Volume III' and with respect to the circumstances prevailing at the incident.

IAMSAR Search Patterns

Many different types of search patterns are available to SAR units and, in conjunction with the OSC, an appropriate pattern to suit the conditions should be put into operation. Most of the following examples are suitable for either air or surface units. In all cases, the navigator of the search craft will play a key role.

The majority of searches take place within defined limits, depending on the target's capability and endurance. Individual search units are usually designated a specific area and the navigator will need to plot the extreme boundaries before instigation of the pattern.

The type of pattern and track space employed should reflect the nature and size of the target and take into account the prevailing weather conditions, particularly the state of visibility. Where more search units are employed, the accuracy is generally increased and/or the area of coverage is increased.

Expanding Square Search Pattern

The expanding square search pattern can be employed by either surface vessels or aircraft search units. Where more than one aircraft is involved, they fly at different heights and on headings 45° off the original.

The ship begins at the probable location of the target and expands outward in concentric squares. Accurate navigation is required to monitor the ship's position towards course alteration points. All course alterations are 90°.

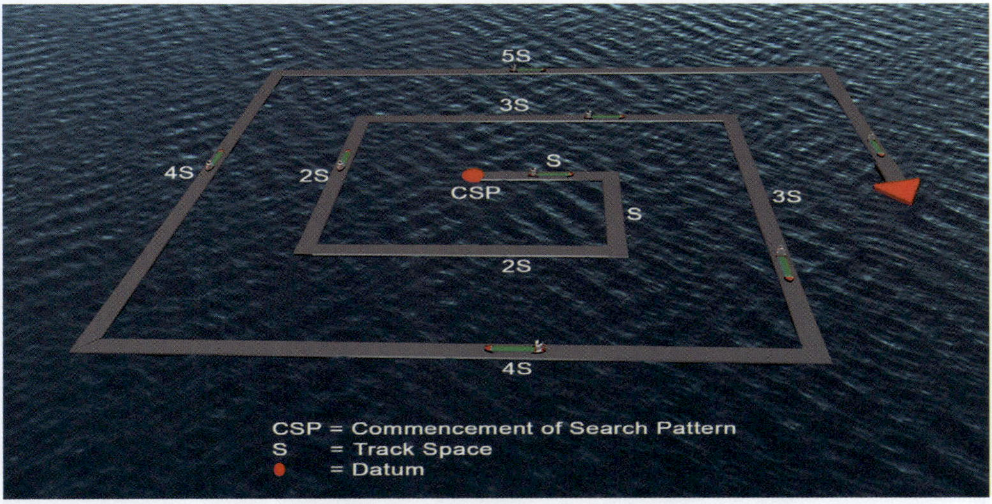

Figure 19.11 - Expanding square search pattern – one ship

The track spacing will vary depending on visibility and sea conditions relative to the type of target.

Sector Search Pattern

The sector search pattern is employed when the position of the target is known with reasonable accuracy and the search is over a small area, as in man overboard or where the casualty has been sighted and then lost.

A suitable marker, ie a smoke float or beacon, is used for reference and is dropped at the most likely position of the target. All turns are 120° to starboard. This pattern gives a very high probability of detection close to datum and quickly spreads the search over the probable area.

Upon completion of the first search, the pattern should be reorientated 30° to the right and searched again as shown by the dashed line in Figure 19.12.

Rescue and OSC

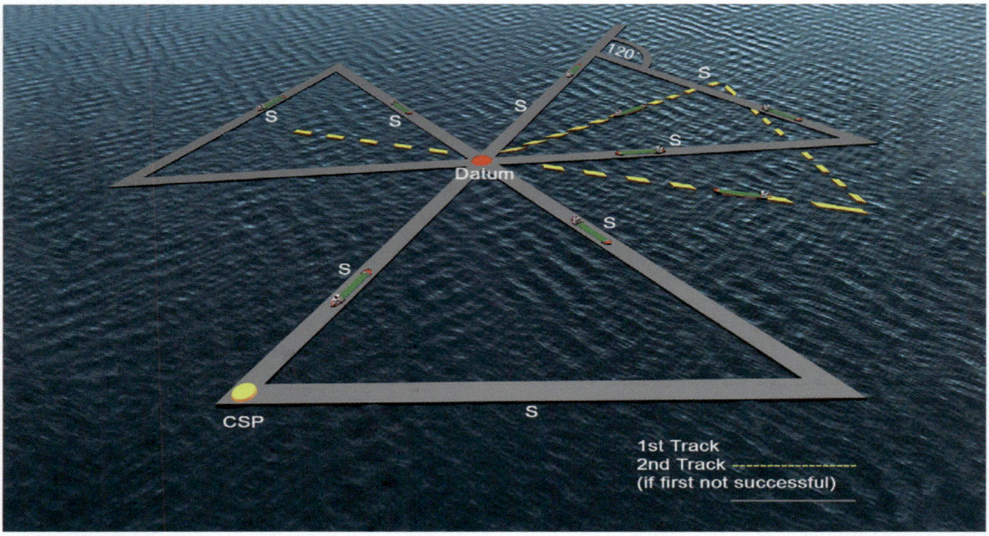

Figure 19.12 - Sector search – one ship. 'S' represents track space (distance or time variable) and CSP represents commencement of search pattern

Parallel Search Pattern

This is used when the search area is large or where only the approximate location is known.

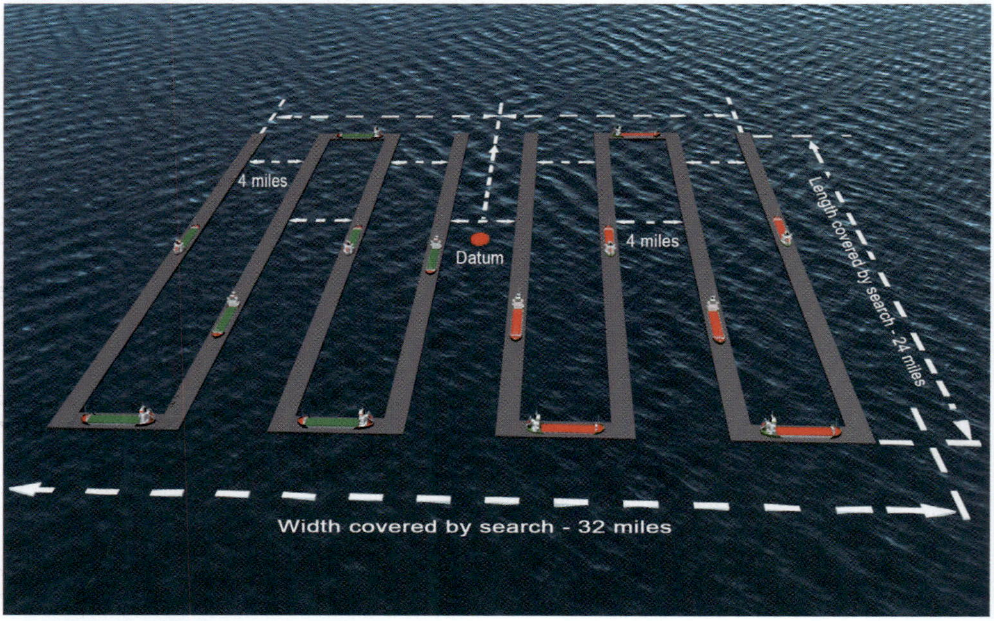

Figure 19.13 - Parallel search – two ships

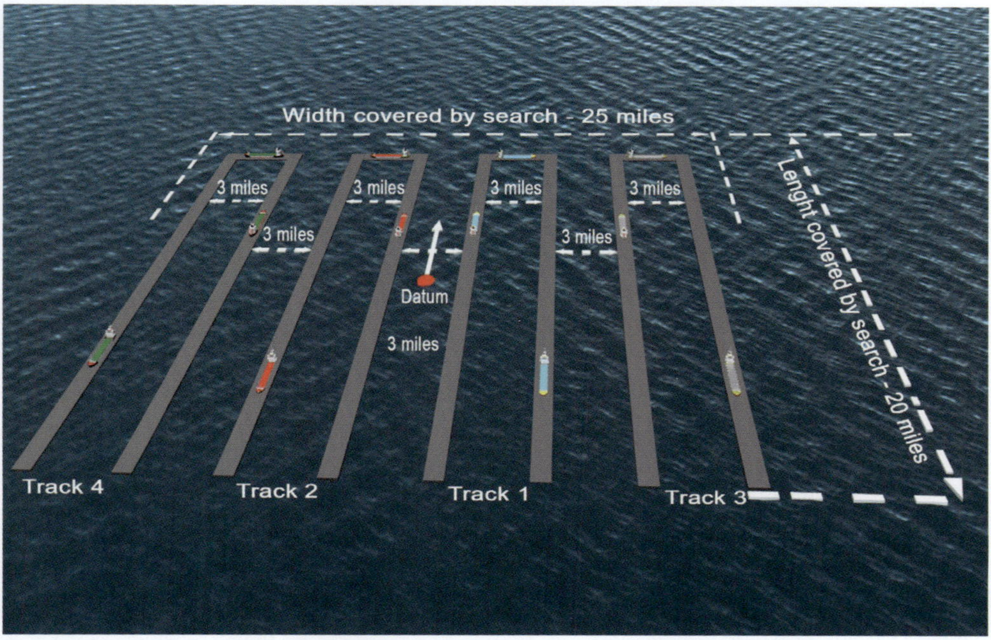

Figure 19.14 - Parallel search – four ships

*Arrow from Datum indicates the direction of drift.

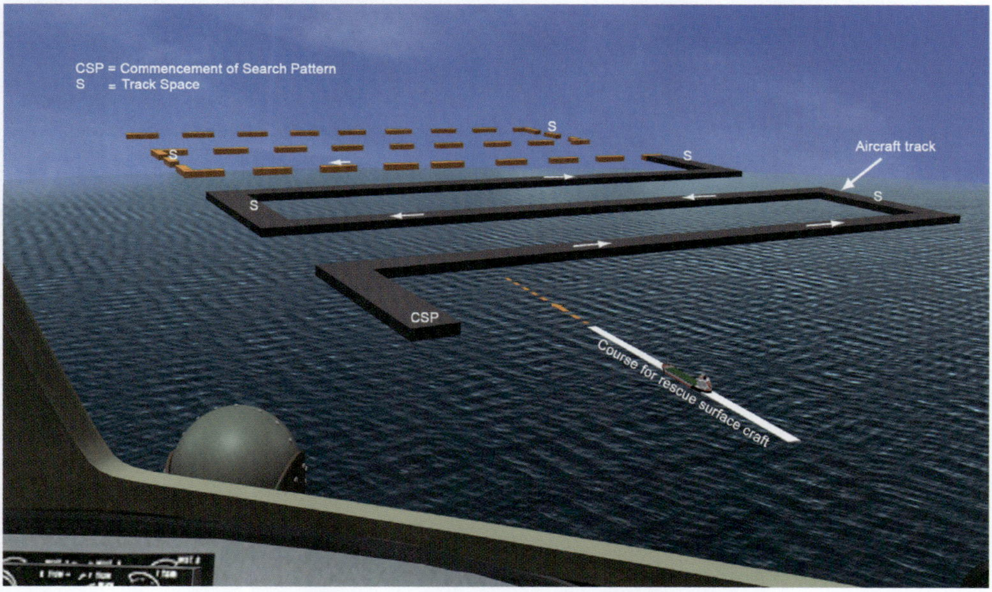

Figure 19.15 - Coordinated creeping line search – one ship and one aircraft

Rescue and OSC

Coordinated Creeping Line Search

This search combines the use of both aircraft and surface unit(s). The surface unit proceeds along the major axis of the search area while the air unit(s) plan their advance to match the ship's movement.

Fixed wing aircraft (other than seaplanes) can only locate, and effective communications are required to effect recovery by the surface units.

Greater accuracy is achieved with increased unit numbers. Aircraft tend to fly at a height that permits visible detection.

Search Units

High-sided vessels pose difficulties for casualties and vessels with a lower freeboard and good manoeuvrability are generally better suited to effect recovery operations.

Many ECDIS units are capable of generating search and rescue patterns in accordance with recognised SAR search schemes. Some example screen shots are shown here:

Courtesy of ECDIS Ltd

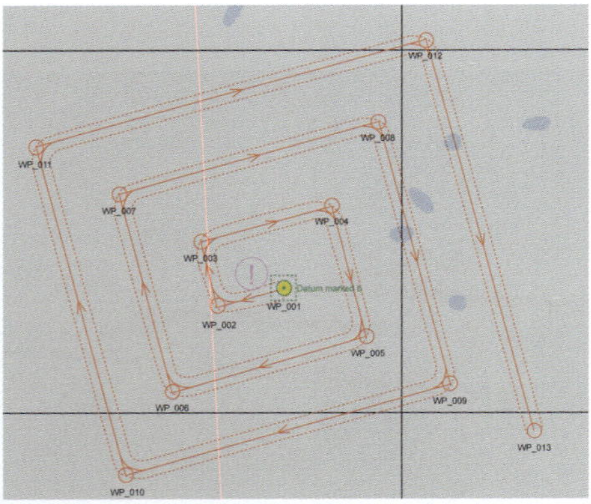

Figure 19.16 - ECDIS screen shot: Expanding square search

Courtesy of ECDIS Ltd

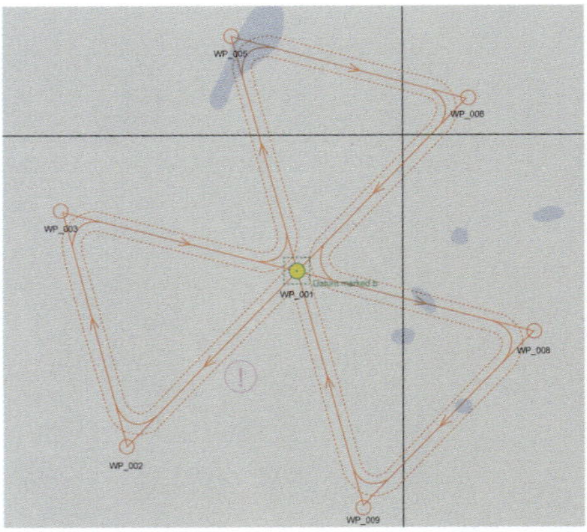

Figure 19.17 - ECDIS screen shot: Sector search

Courtesy of ECDIS Ltd

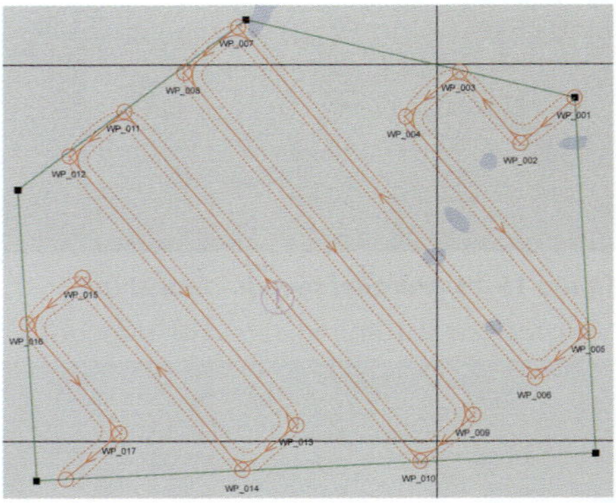

Figure 19.18 - ECDIS screen shot: Parallel search

Typically, the ECDIS unit will calculate and make the appropriate corrections for set and drift to the SAR pattern.

CHAPTER 20

Oil Spills/Pollution

Oil Spills

Recovery of Heavy Oils

The success of a clean-up operation following a heavy oil spill depends on the quantity spilt, the location, the physical characteristics of the product, the weather conditions and the speed of response.

Oil products exhibit a wide range of physical and chemical properties, the most significant for spill response being density, viscosity, pour point and volatility.

Relative Density/Specific Gravity

Most heavy fuel oils will float in seawater, but those with higher specific gravity may float lower in the water and disperse less readily than others. In calm seas, skimming is an effective clean-up method for floating oil.

Viscosity

Viscosity is directly related to temperature and, in cold environments, viscous products become more difficult to skim, pump and clean from equipment. High viscosity products are resistant to dispersion, enabling them to travel considerable distances at sea, causing widespread contamination.

Pour Point

The pour point is the temperature at which oils begin to solidify and lose their flow characteristics.

Some products will rapidly solidify (or semi-solidify) if spilt into the sea and, although this prevents the product spreading, it makes clean-up extremely difficult.

Volatility

As the volatile elements evaporate, the remaining product will become heavier and increasingly viscous. The rate of evaporation depends on the rate of spread and the surface area of the slick, ambient temperature, wind speed and water turbulence.

Weathering Processes

When oil is exposed to the environment following a spill, it will undergo changes over time in a process known as 'weathering'. Most weathering processes will assist breakdown and assimilation of a spill, eg dispersion, dissolution, sedimentation and biodegradation. Others can promote its persistence, eg emulsification.

The fate of an oil spill is determined by a combination of the weathering processes and by the characteristics of the oil itself. Spreading, evaporation, dispersion, dissolution and emulsification occur in the early stages following a spill. Oxidation, sedimentation and biodegradation occur in the later stages.

Spreading

The rate of surface spread depends on the quantity spilt, density, viscosity and surface tension. High viscosity products will initially take the form of a coherent slick, before gradually breaking down into fragments. Light oils, with low viscosity, spread much more rapidly and may spread out very thinly over a large area. This presents the main obstacle to effective recovery.

A surface slick will drift according to the current and wind speed. As a slick drifts, it will tend to become thinner and more easily fragmented.

Dispersion

The combined forces of wind, waves and current can cause spills to fragment and disperse over a huge area. Initially, the oil will form narrow bands or 'windrows' parallel to the wind direction. Over time, droplets of oil will mix into the upper layers of the water column where turbulence causes them to disperse, promoting dissolution, sedimentation and biodegradation. Dispersion occurs most rapidly where oil is light and of low viscosity and in rough seas.

Emulsification

In rough seas, many crudes and heavy oils will take up water droplets and form water/oil emulsions, which may be up to four times the volume of the initial spill. Due to a higher viscosity, emulsions are much more resistant to dispersion and weathering, particularly at lower temperatures and can persist for many months, or even years.

Evaporation

Lighter fractions of oil compounds will evaporate readily. Petrol, kerosene and diesel may evaporate completely in a matter of days, leaving behind a viscous heavy oil residue. The rate of evaporation is dependent on the ambient temperature, wind speed and sea conditions.

Dissolution

Dissolution plays only a small part in the weathering process and tends to occur when the product is already finely dispersed in the water column. Heavy components of crude oil are virtually insoluble in seawater, whereas light compounds, such as benzene and toluene, are slightly soluble.

Oxidation/Tar Ball Formation

Some products react with oxygen leading to the formation of soluble products or persistent tars. This process is promoted by sunlight, but is very slow and has only a minor effect on the overall weathering process. Oxidation of emulsions or thick layers of very viscous oils can cause the formation of highly persistent tar balls which may wash ashore.

Sedimentation/Sinking

Very few oils have a specific gravity high enough to sink in seawater. Most remain afloat and may sink only after attaching to sediment particles. If attached to very fine sediment, oil may remain suspended in the water column in the form of flocculates, which over time will be widely dispersed.

Biodegradation

A range of marine microorganisms are able to break down oil compounds and this process is one of the main ways in which small traces of a spill are eventually removed. The rate of biodegradation depends on the characteristics of the oil, ambient temperature, climatic conditions, availability of oxygen and nutrients, and whether the oil is at sea or on the shore. Where oil droplets are formed, by dispersion for example, the rate of biodegradation can be increased.

Oil Slick Movement

Computer-based oil spill trajectory models are widely used in predicting how a spill might behave and whether it is likely to reach the shore.

The movement of some spills can also be calculated manually from wind and current data, as shown here. The influence of 3% of the wind speed combined with 100% of the tide/current speed results in movement of the oil from A to B.

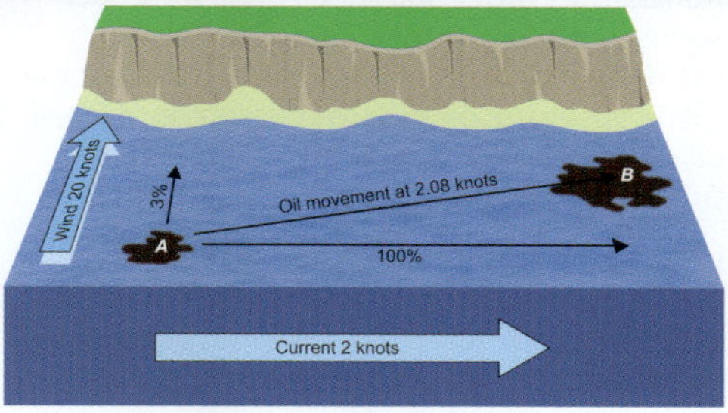

Figure 20.1 - Calculating oil slick movement

Aerial Reconnaissance

Reconnaissance flights play a vital role in establishing the location and extent of oil spills, and are critical to an effective response. The information gathered can also be used to monitor any changes in the nature of the oil, for example emulsification, and in verifying modelling predictions of its movement and fate at sea. Data from aerial surveys are also used to facilitate the deployment and control of clean-up operations at sea as well as the protection of coastlines and preparing the on-shore clean-up response.

Courtesy of US Coast Guard

Figure 20.2 - Oil spill in Bayou Dupont, New Orleans September 2011

Aerial Reconnaissance

Aerial reconnaissance can use visual and/or remote sensing. Both methods rely on the skill of highly experienced observers to provide accurate interpretation of the results.

Visual Surveys

Visual surveys provide a simple method of assessing the location and extent of the spill and, by incorporating geo-referenced observations, the movement can also be tracked. A high degree of skill is required to exclude other influences, such as cloud shadow, sediment or floating seaweed. It is also possible to quantify the oil by assessing changes in the visual appearance of the surface of the sea and comparing against colour comparison scales. However, this can be very difficult in rough seas or with emulsions or very heavy fuel oils.

Remote Sensors

A range of sophisticated remote sensors can be used to locate and measure oil spills by detecting changes to the colour, roughness, temperature and reflectance of the surface of the sea. Side-looking airborne radar (SLAR) provides long range detection of oil pollution, while infra-red and ultraviolet line scanners and microwave radiometers can be used to provide details of the thickness of the oil. Laser-fluoro line scanning sensors can identify the oil type and provide data on thickness.

Use of Dispersants

The Use of Chemical Dispersants to Treat Oil Spills

When used appropriately, chemical dispersants can be an effective response to an oil spill. Chemical dispersants work by rapidly transferring larger quantities of oil from the surface into the water column, accelerating the natural process of dispersion. Wave energy then causes the oil slick to break up into small oil droplets which are quickly diluted and subsequently biodegraded.

In common with other response techniques, the decision to use dispersants must be given careful consideration and take into account oil characteristics, sea and weather conditions, and environmental sensitivities.

Dispersant Composition

Chemical dispersants are designed to enhance natural dispersion by reducing the surface tension at the oil/water interface, making it easier for waves to create small oil droplets. Modern chemical dispersants are a blend of surfactants (surface active agents) in a solvent. The solvent has two functions: it reduces the viscosity of the surfactant which enables it to be sprayed and it promotes the penetration of the surfactant into the oil slick.

Mechanism of Dispersion

Following an oil spill, some of the oil will disperse naturally into the water column. The extent to which this occurs depends on the type of oil spilt and the mixing energy of wind and waves. Just as with oils with a lower viscosity, light and medium crude oils are more amenable to natural dispersion so they respond better to the application of dispersants. The use of dispersants is not effective with viscous heavy oils, oils with a pour point close to ambient temperature or emulsified oils.

Natural dispersion takes place when the mixing energy provided by the waves and wind is sufficient to overcome surface tension at the oil/water interface and break the oil slick into droplets of variable sizes. Severe storm conditions in Shetland, UK, at the time of the grounding of the MV *'Braer'* caused virtually all of the 84,000 tonne cargo of Gulfaks North Sea crude oil to be dispersed naturally and resulted in minimal shoreline impact.

Source: ITOPF http://tinyurl.com/pd2sdo5

Figure 20.3 - Natural dispersion of spilled oil during the MV 'Braer' grounding, Shetland Islands, UK, 1993

Oil Spill Containment Valve to Slop Tank

Oil Spill Containment Valve to Slop Tank

Figure 20.4 - Spill valve

Following a spill on deck, the bulk of the accumulated oil can be transferred to cargo tanks using drains or portable pumps.

Crude oil tankers often have drains or spill valves, allowing drainage to go directly into the designated cargo tanks against positive tank pressure. An example is shown in Figure 20.5. They should be opened with care. If the drain valve deck opening is near the side of the vessel, the level in the tank may be above the deck opening because of the camber. If the tank pressure is high enough, the initial release of trapped vapour, caused by sudden opening of the drain valve, may cause some of the accumulated oil to be blown overboard. Therefore, the drain valve and valves must initially be opened slowly to release any gas pressure.

As part of the oil spillage response plan, portable air-driven pumps with air and oil discharge hoses must be available to allow the transfer of accumulated oil to cargo oil tanks. These pumps must be ready to be quickly deployed anywhere on deck.

The use of clean water during oil spill drills in loaded and ballast conditions will identify where the air and oil discharge hoses should be connected. It is helpful to indicate clearly the air and oil discharge connections that are to be used for dealing with an oil spill.

Accumulated oil should be transferred under closed conditions through fixed connections with valves fitted to each tank. It might be possible to utilise the portable UTI gauge connections that, in some cases, are designed to be quickly converted for transferring oil if there is a spill.

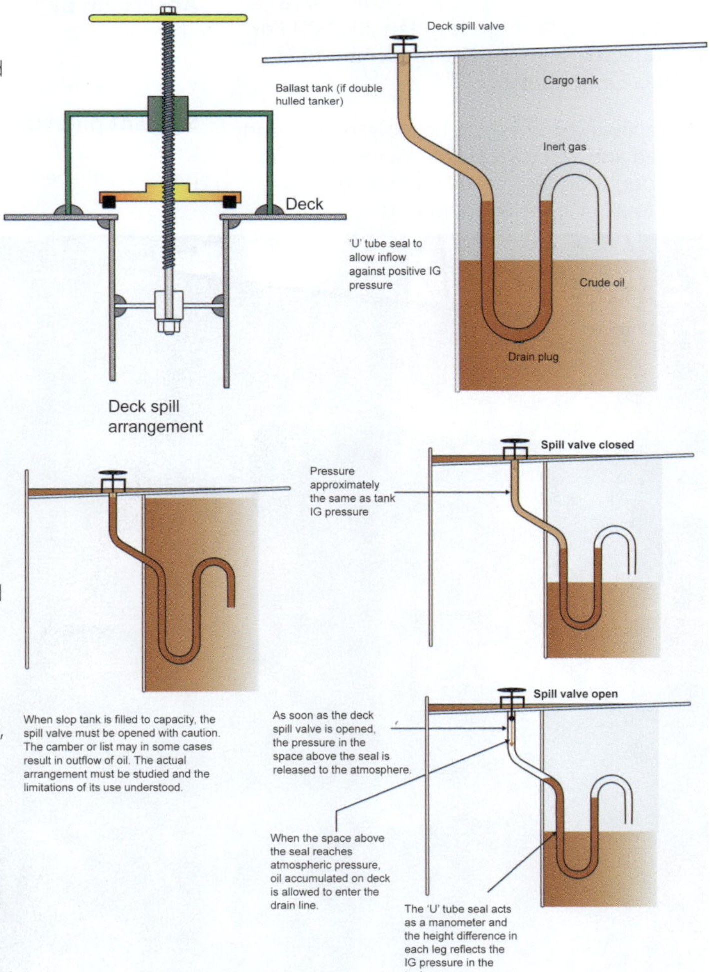

Figure 20.5 - Deck spill valve arrangement

Reproduced from 'Crude Oil Tanker Basics'

Oil Spill Containment Valve to Slop Tank

Ignition of flammable vapour is a serious risk, so portable pumps must be suitably earthed or grounded before use and before being removed or any hose connections replaced. Fire-fighting equipment and a fire-fighting party should be standing by with protective equipment and self-contained breathing apparatus.

When an oil spill occurs, its movement across the deck must be carefully monitored. It may be difficult to judge the flow of oil in the case of viscous crudes. Directing operations from the bridge or bridge wings, where a view of the whole deck is possible, may provide a better idea of the oil's movement and a more effective deployment of oil transfer resources.

Sand bags and oil booms, if available, can be placed in positions that divert the flow of oil to areas where facilities for transfer or recovery are available.

When only residual oil remains, it may be appropriate to consolidate it by pumping it into portable containers or manifold save-alls for transfer to suitable cargo tanks. Absorbent pads, pillows or granules can be used to remove residual oil from the deck.

SOPEP Locker

MARPOL 73/78 requires all ships of 400 GT and above to carry a Shipboard Oil Pollution Emergency Plan (SOPEP).For oil tankers, the tonnage requirement is 150 GT and above.

The following items must be stowed in a clearly marked and easily accessible locker and are to be brought on deck ready for immediate use prior to all oil transfer operations.

The SOPEP locker must contain:

Absorbent pads and rolls
These low cost sorbents are used for cleaning spills on land and water and are ideal for a variety of environmental applications.

Sorbent pillows
Used to absorb large amounts of fluid where a pad is insufficient.

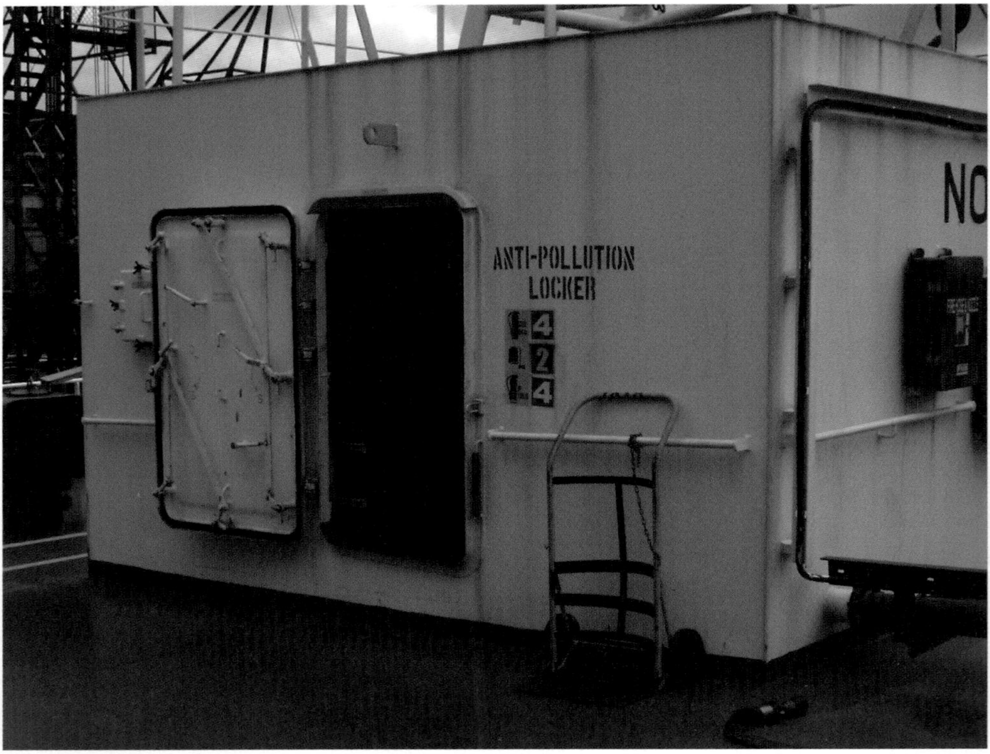

SOPEP Locker

Absorbent granules
Used for the clean-up of oil and chemical spills.

Saw dust
Used to absorb oil spills.

Oil booms
Used to contain and absorb spills on or off water.

Containment booms
Used to surround and contain oil or sewage spills.

Drain seals
Used to form a tight seal to block out liquids.

Conical plugs
Ideal for blocking circular drains before a spill or as soon as one occurs.

Spill dams
Contain and divert spills before contamination takes place.

Brooms/bristle brush
Used to scrub the oil to emulsify it.

Mops
Used to clean the contaminated area.

Trash buckets
Used to collect and transport the recovered oil to the disposal site.

Oil spill dispersants
Used to disperse the oil into the water column before it approaches an oil-sensitive site.

Scoops and shovels
Used to collect the spilled oil. Must be plastic or non-spark.

Sand buckets
Used to absorb the oil.

PPE
Appropriate personal protective equipment, hand scrubs, chemical resistant gloves, rubber boots, eye protection, etc.

SOPEP Locker

Specific Requirements for the USA

Shipboard Oil Spill Control Equipment must meet the requirements under OPA '90, USCG 33 CFR Part 155 - Discharge Removal Equipment for Vessels Carrying Oil, and the California Oil Spill Contingency Regulations CA 1644.

OPA '90 requires oil tankers operating in US territorial waters to have oil discharge removal equipment on board for on-deck oil spills.

Vessels with an overall length of 400 feet or less must be able to contain and remove on-deck oil spills of at least 7 barrels (294 gallons or 1,111 litres). Vessels with an overall length of 400 feet or greater must be able to contain and remove on-deck oil spills of at least 12 barrels (504 gallons or 1,905 litres).

CHAPTER 21

Practical Aspects of Salvage

Practical Aspects of Salvage

Source: MAIB Report on the grounding of 'Maersk Kendal'

Salvage companies are appointed to salvage vessels (that are not owned by them) following a shipwreck, grounding or other misfortune.

The insurers of the ship will offer salvors a percentage of the value of the ship and its cargo if they can save it. The rewards are potentially immense, but salvage carries the risks of huge financial loss and physical danger to the salvors. If the salvage effort is ultimately unsuccessful, the salvors receive nothing.

The aims of salvage include:

- To make the vessel seaworthy again (this may require repairs in drydock)
- to clear a shipping route, channel or TSS for safe navigation
- prevention of pollution and protection of the marine environment
- to salve the vessel or its cargo for its resale value or for scrap.

Any salvage operation has to be assessed for dangers and planned accordingly.

Salvage Surveys

The initial appraisal or salvage survey gathers information about the marine casualty, the incident and the surrounding area to allow a salvage plan to be formulated.

The Salvage Plan

The purpose of a salvage plan is to:

- Detail the work required
- highlight what equipment and resources are available
- project manage salvage activities
- detail key dates and times
- identify the distinct stages of the salvage operation.

The level of detail in the salvage plan will depend on the circumstances of the casualty and the difficulty of the salvage operation.

Few tugboats are fully dedicated to salvage work and for most of the time salvage tugs will be employed on general towing contracts (barges, platforms, etc).

Salvage tugs are fitted with specialised equipment, such as:

- Extensive towing equipment and additional towlines/cables, allowing towing from both bow and stern and at irregular angles
- additional cranes
- substantial portable pumping capacity
- fire-fighting equipment
- equipment that provides versatility for the salvors, including:
  - welding equipment
  - compressed air tools
  - oxy-acetylene cutting gear (gas axe)
  - diving equipment
  - steel for repairs.

Floating Cranes

Floating cranes are used extensively during salvage to:

- Offload cargo
- position salvage gear
- lift sunken wrecks

- lift sections of wrecks that have been cut up in situ
- incline stranded ships to reduce damage to the seabed (eg coral reefs)
- prevent unstable sunken ships from capsizing during salvage operations.

Lightering

Lightering is the process of offloading cargo from the casualty to a receiving vessel to enable the casualty to be refloated once the necessary reduction in draught is achieved.

Pumping

When a ship sinks in shallow water, pumping out flooded spaces is the most straight forward method of recovering buoyancy. The salvors may also pump in compressed air to remove floodwater and to regain buoyancy.

However, a ship raised with compressed air may refloat very quickly. The salvor will not have total control and there may be limited time to react to any problems.

Tugs

Tugs may be used by salvors to assist a ship where she is:

- Drifting without power onto a lee shore
- lightly grounded on a muddy or sandy bottom, where removal of cargo is not required.

Salvage Methods

Methods of salvage range from simple hole patching and pumping out flooded spaces to cutting up the wreck into sections for removal.

Ships that are driven/impacted aground/beached above the low water level, where the predicted tide alone will not allow the vessel to float off, will need to be salvaged by the patching of external holes in the ship's hull and pumping out flooded compartments.

Vessels that ground leaving the superstructure below the mean low water level require a more substantial salvage effort to raise them. Divers must make the entire vessel watertight before it can be lifted by pumping out flooded spaces, attaching lifting devices from surface cranes, or by a combination of these techniques.

Unsalvageable vessels are left in place, sectioned and removed, or flattened with demolitions.

Righting Capsized Ships

Ships tend to capsize when they sink and come to rest at a severe angle. This makes salvage a more challenging operation as the ship will usually need to be righted before refloating. There are four methods of handling a capsized ship:

- Refloating the ship onto her side and then moving her to another location
- rotating the ship until she is completely upside down and then refloating the upside down ship
- righting the ship in place, then refloating her
- cutting up the ship into sections or demolishing as required in situ.

A combination of methods may be used to right a capsized ship:

- Restoring buoyancy by pumping out flooded spaces
- adding rotational ballast to the high side
- applying a dynamic pull to the high side of the ship, along with a mechanical lift on the low side.

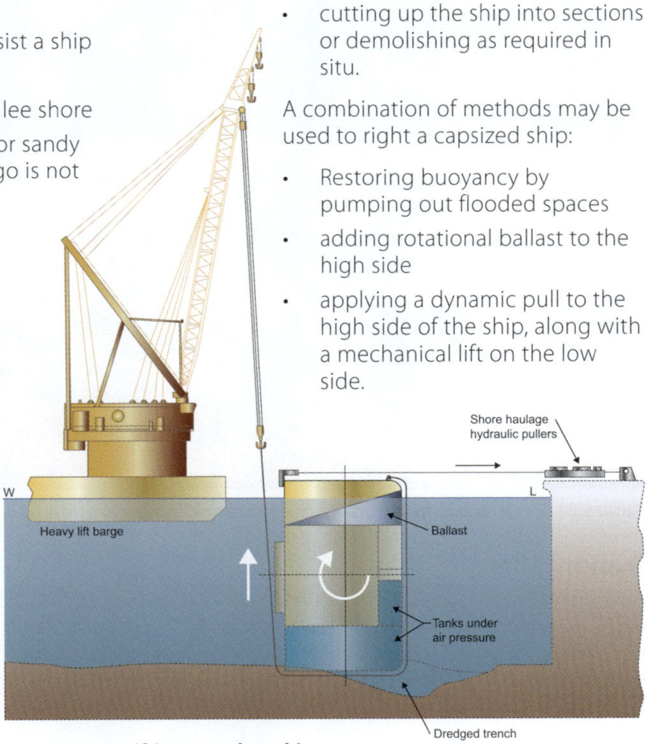

Figure 21.1 - Lifting a sunken ship

Practical Aspects of Salvage

Offshore Operations

A ship that is capsized and sunk a considerable distance offshore is more challenging to salve. These challenges are rarely insurmountable, but can add greatly to the cost and duration of the operations, eg delays due to severe weather.

Lifting

A sunken ship may be raised by:

- Buoyant lifts
- tidal lifts
- mechanical lifts.

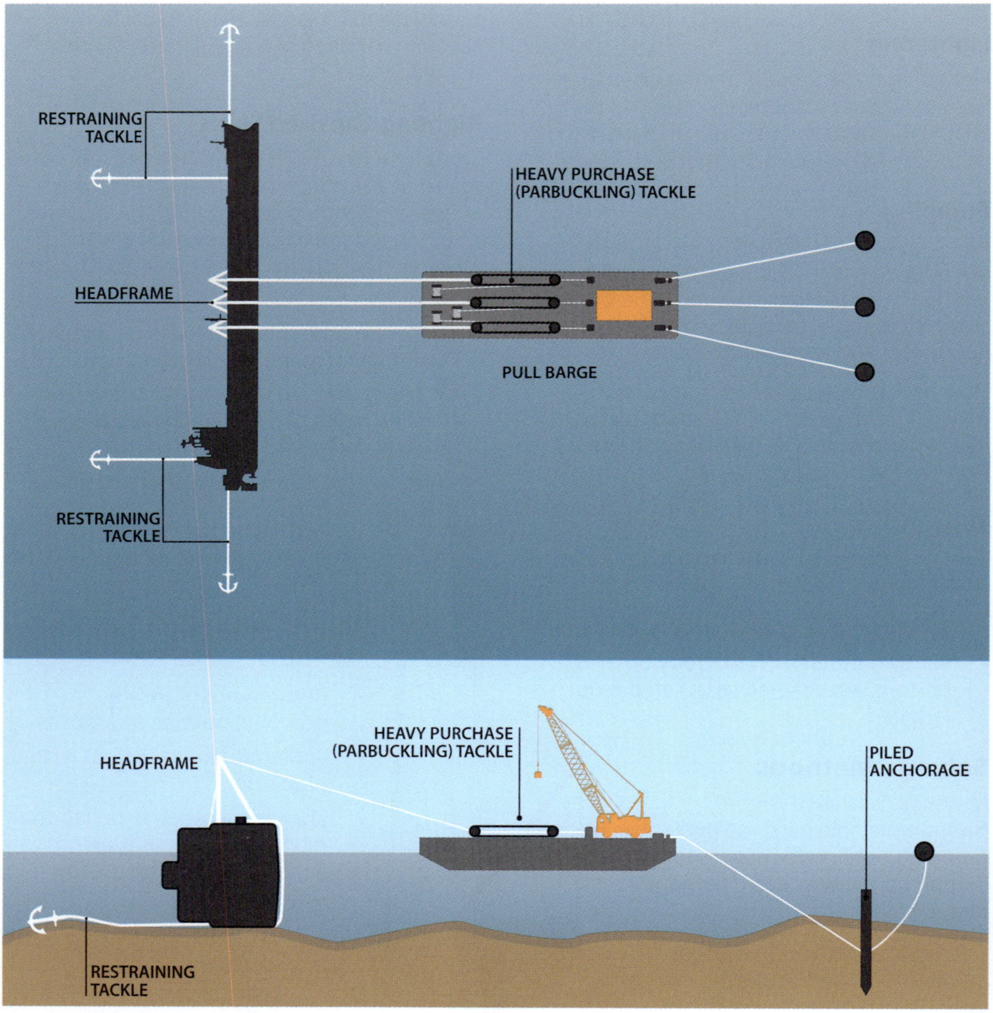

Figure 21.2 - Offshore heavy purchase (parbuckling) operation

Buoyant Lifts

Buoyant lifts are made by rigging lift devices externally and securing them by wire rope or chain passed under or attached to the sunken ship. When the lift device is blown with compressed air, it provides a lift equal to its internal volume less its weight.

Collapsible, inflatable lift bags (variable-volume devices) and rigid steel pontoons (fixed-volume devices) are the only buoyant lift devices that have been consistently successful in salvage.

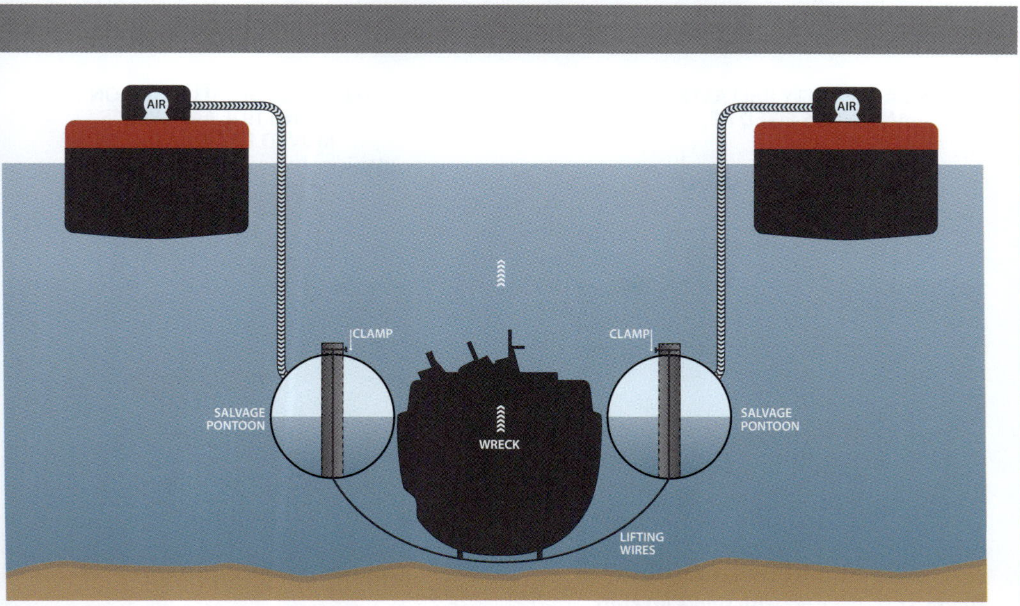

Figure 21.3 - Buoyant lift

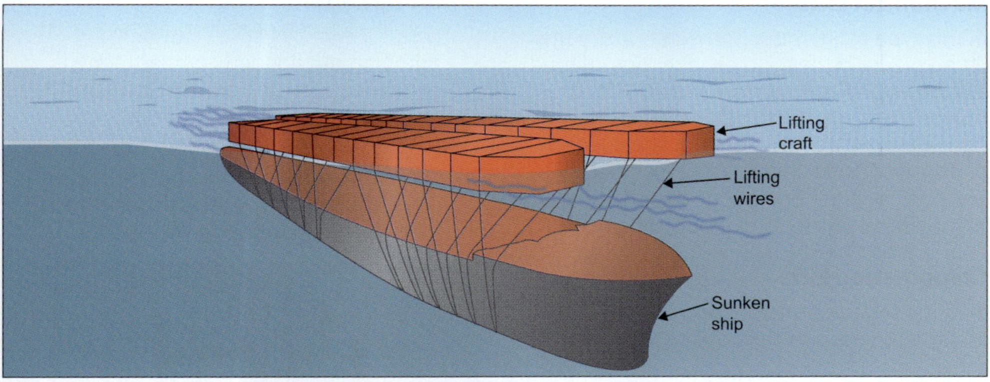

Figure 21.4 - Lift craft supporting sunken ship in wire cradle

Tidal Lifts

Tidal lifts are made using lifting barges that obtain their lift from the rise of the tide. This type of lift is most effective in areas with a substantial tidal range. The lift barges are moored above or beside the sunken ship and a network of heavy wire ropes is passed under the ship. The lift barges are ballasted to their deepest safe working draught at low water and the lift wires are hauled tight and stopped off. As the tide rises, the barges' buoyancy lifts the sunken ship; further lift is obtained by deballasting the barge. When the sunken ship has been lifted, it is moved into shallow water, still supported by the lift barge, and the process repeated.

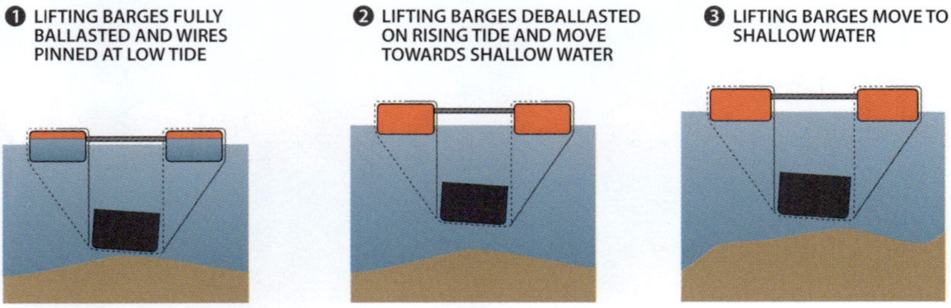

Figure 21.5 - Tidal lift sequence

Practical Aspects of Salvage

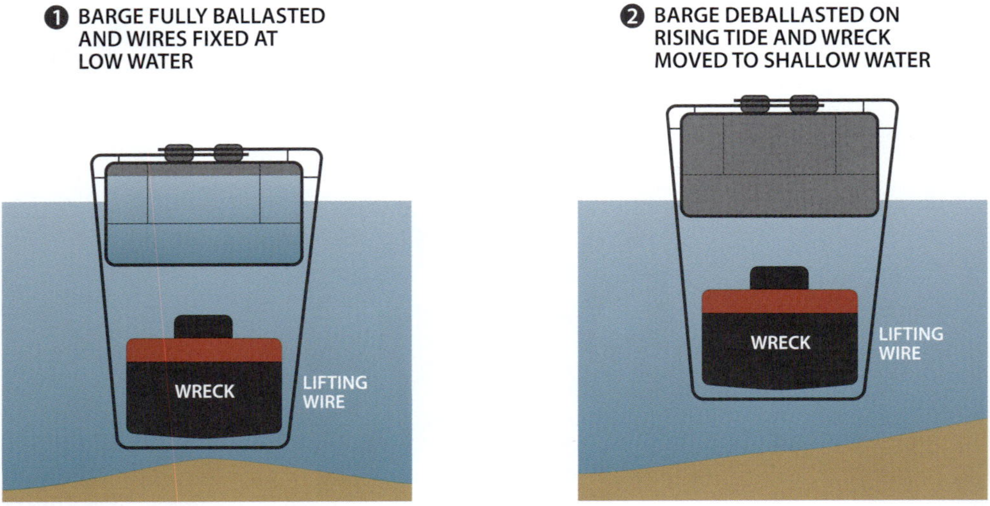

Figure 21.6 - Belly lift with single lift craft

Mechanical Lifts

In this type of lift, the salvage units apply their lifting power by heaving on wire ropes rigged around the hull of the sunken ship. Lifting power is obtained from vertical lift tackles rigged from A-frames, cranes or sheer legs, or from horizontal tackles rigged on deck. Mechanical lifting operations are independent of the tide or any form of induced buoyancy.

Combination Lifts

In many salvage situations, a combination of lifting methods may be required, eg:

- Compressed air buoyancy in several compartments, combined with several pairs of barges to provide buoyant lift, and bow lift craft at each end providing mechanical lift
- pumping out flooded compartments combined with one or more pairs of side lifting barges providing tidal lift
- a combination of compressed air in some compartments, pumping out others, with derricks providing a stabilising mechanical lift at each end of the sunken vessel.

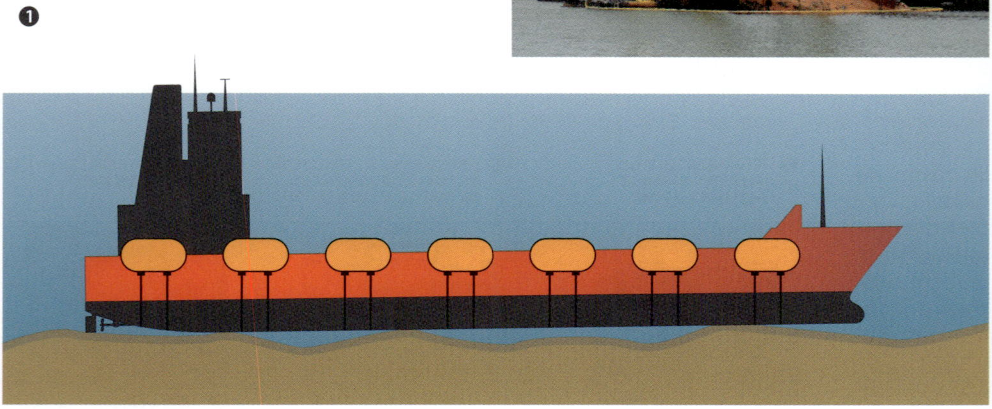

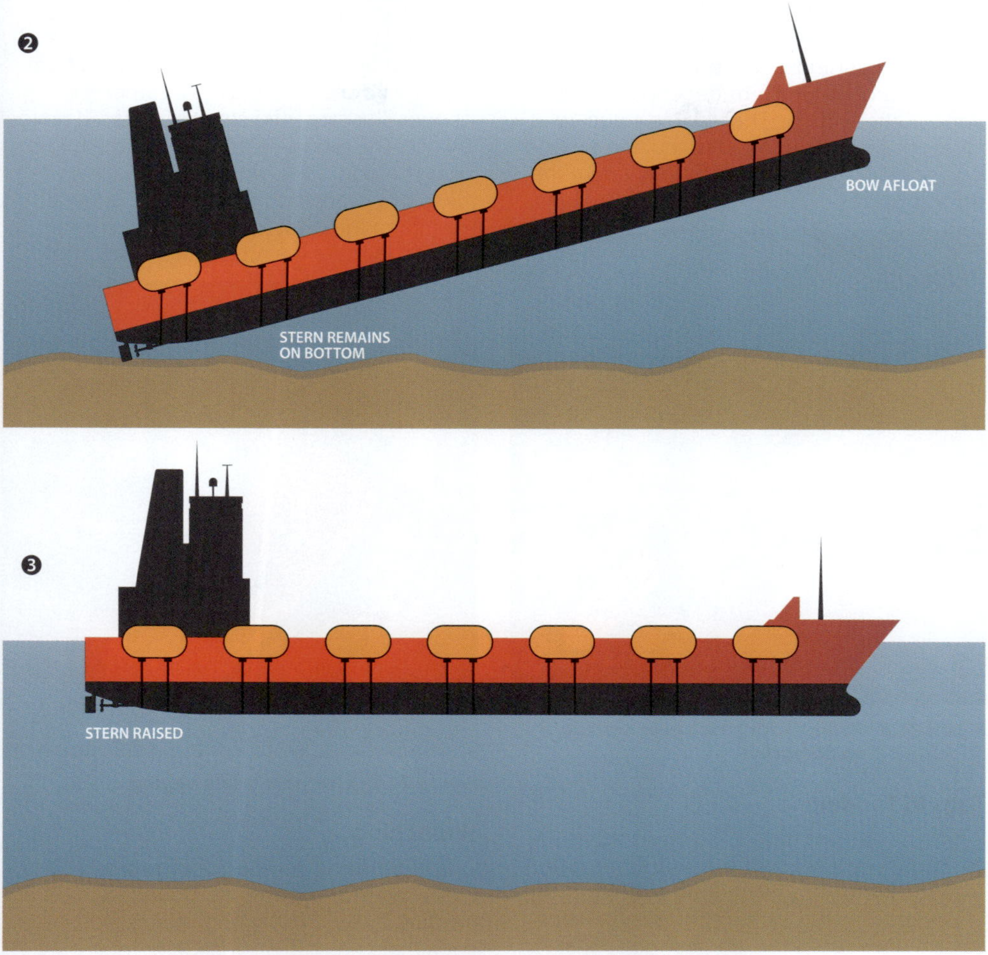

Figure 21.7 - Flotation pontoons raising a ship that has sunk in shallow water

Salvage Ships and Tugs

Salvage ships and tugs should only approach a grounded ship after surrounding depths have been verified by a hydrographic survey. Anchors should be ready for letting go at all times.

Safe approach can be made by anchoring to seaward of the stranded ship and backing towards it while veering anchor chain. The anchor holds the bow into the sea and holds the ship in position if propulsion is lost.

Tugs must be positioned to:

- Achieve the most effective pull
- avoid fouling any salvage equipment that is led out from the shore.

To achieve the most effective pull, tugs usually pull independently from the seaward end of the grounded ship. Tugs can also pull both ends to wrench the ship's stern into the sea.

To prevent fouling of towlines and tugs, the towlines of all tugs should be approximately the same length. Fenders should be rigged on each salvage ship or tug to absorb energy and prevent damage should the tugs drift together.

Practical Aspects of Salvage

All towlines should be significantly longer than the beach gear ground legs leading from the stranding. The distance between the towlines and ground legs depends on the slope of the seafloor. The towline catenary must not be deep enough to foul the ground legs. Short distances are sufficient where the slope is great.

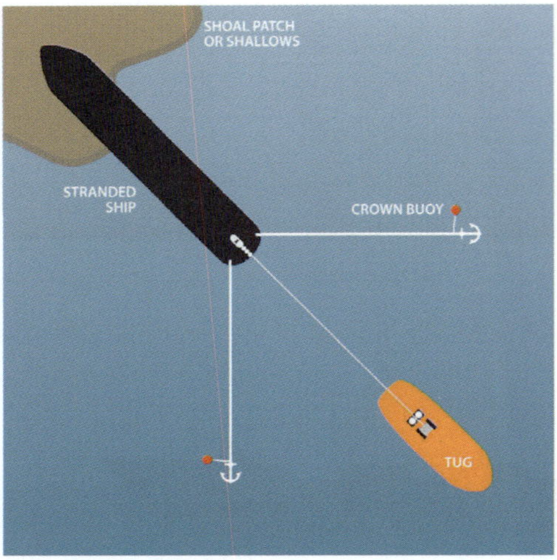

Figure 21.8 - Pulling with beach gear and tug combination

Tugs in Tandem

When the inboard tug has no bow thruster, or the bow thruster cannot hold her head in the seas and currents, a second tug may be rigged in tandem. The tug in the lead position helps control the head of the inboard tug so that its pull is directed in the desired direction.

Whenever tugs are rigged in tandem, their overall manoeuvrability is reduced. If the lead tug loses propulsion, the seas and wind may cause it to drag the other tug aground. Towlines should be rigged with pelican hooks, and cutting equipment should be at hand. Anchors on both tugs should be ready for letting go.

When tugs pull in tandem, the total bollard pull of both tugs is transmitted to the stranded ship through the inboard tug's towline. The total bollard pull must not exceed the breaking strength of this line and, if possible, should not exceed the safe working load (SWL).

To keep the inboard tug on a particular heading, the lead tug will usually use her bow thruster to control her head. If she has no bow thruster, or the bow thruster is not powerful enough, she may rig a Liverpool bridle. The Liverpool bridle consists of a line rigged from the forward shoulder bitts to a carpenter stopper. The carpenter stopper is placed on the towline. The towline is slacked and the bridle takes the load. The Liverpool bridle allows the tug to head into the winds and current by shifting the pivot point of the tug further forward to make the rudder more effective.

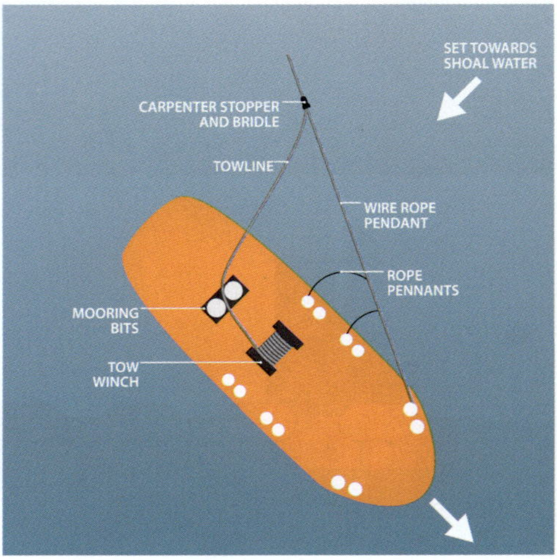

Figure 21.9 - Liverpool bridle rigging

Wrenching

One of the principal uses for tugs in salvage is to wrench or change the grounded ship's heading by pulling her from side to side. Wrenching helps break friction or rotates the stranding to the heading for refloating. To wrench, tugs swing in an arc while pulling. Grounded ships are wrenched more quickly by tugs than by beach gear. Tugs for wrenching should be positioned so that the arc through which they swing is centred about the planned refloating path.

If there is sufficient room, wrenching tugs should swing through an arc of at least 60°. When more than one tug is wrenching, the swing should be coordinated so that they pull in the same direction. When the stranded ship begins to move, the tugs should stop swinging and steady on the course that gives maximum pull along the refloating path.

Tugs and beach gear may be used together to wrench the stranding. The tug normally pulls against the seaward end of the ship. The beach gear wrenching legs can be rigged from both sides of the ship's grounded end. If the ship is bow on the beach, as the tug swings the stern in one direction, the purchases heave the bow in the opposite direction.

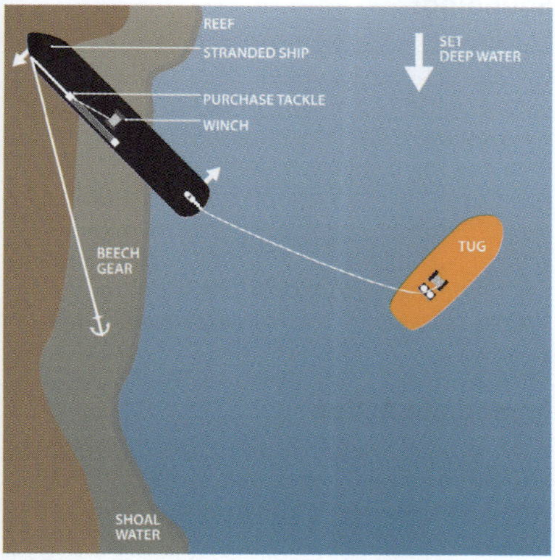

Figure 21.10 - Wrenching with a tug and purchase combination

Ground Removal

Removal of the ground under a ship allows the ship to sink deeper into the water and recover some of the buoyancy lost on grounding. It will sometimes be necessary to remove ground to seaward of the ship to form a channel to deep water. The effectiveness of ground removal depends on the nature of the seafloor under the ship. If the ship is embedded into the rocks, these must be removed to allow the ship to move.

Scouring

Scouring is the use of currents to remove ground from around a ship. Currents may be produced by the propeller wash of tugs alongside, the ship's propeller wash, or jetting pumps. Breakwaters, or groins, may be built perpendicular to the beach to set up currents that will prevent ground build-up around the ship or will scour away the ground.

Dredging

Dredging is used to move large quantities of soft seafloor material from around and under a casualty and to dig channels to deep water. Methods include digging trenches alongside the casualty, constructing a pond into which to refloat the casualty, or digging channels to deeper water.

Wrecking

The condition of a sunken or stranded ship may be so poor that it can be classified only as a 'wreck' that cannot be returned to service. Where wrecks are a navigational or environmental hazard or an obstruction to port operations, salvors must remove them.

Sometimes it may be possible to refloat a section of the wreck, leaving salvors to dismantle some or all of the remainder. Dismantling is called wrecking in place.

Salvage of a Stranded Ship

By the time salvage vessels arrive to assist a stranded ship, immediate decisions are required to mitigate the situation and to ensure a successful salvage operation. These decisions are often made in the face of adverse weather conditions and must be based on the best and most accurate information available.

While stranded, the ship is often subject to loads not normally encountered by a ship at sea. In addition, the grounding event often results in significant damage to the hull. Therefore, understanding current and potential loads on the ship is important in determining a safe salvage plan.

To prevent movement of the ship into a more precarious position, the ship may be stabilised using anchors or by flooding down. The basic steps to free a stranded ship are:

- Reduce the ground reaction of the ship
- push or pull the ship into deeper water
- increase the depth of water around the stranded ship, or
- a combination of the above.

Action on Board When the Ship is Aground

Assessment of Situation

Prompt refloating of a grounded ship will reduce stresses on the hull and exposure to the effects of rising and falling tides and changing weather. Oil will be less likely to leak from a ruptured tank when the ship is afloat. However, if the ship is badly damaged, refloating may be

Practical Aspects of Salvage

inadvisable due to the risk of further damage, increased pollution and possible loss of the ship.

The master should obtain information about the following:

- Tides
- currents
- weather, including wind, state of sea and swell
- any forecast changes in the weather
- nature of the bottom
- depth of water around the ship
- the calculated buoyancy needed to refloat
- draught and trim after refloating
- condition of the ship, including stresses on the hull.

Assessment of Damage

The extent of damage sustained as a result of grounding will depend on the nature of the bottom, the speed at the moment the ship grounded, the construction of the ship, etc.

An assessment of the extent of the damage should be made to properly assess the possibility of refloating. The assessment should include a visual inspection, together with sounding of cargo tanks and other compartments, and examination of empty spaces, etc. Great care should be taken when opening ullage plugs, sighting ports, tank cleaning plates, etc due to the loss of buoyancy that may result. Particular attention should be paid to the spindles of valves in pipelines near the bottom of the ship. Where the valves have become seized or where the extended spindles have come up through the deck, this often indicates the severity of the bottom damage.

Soundings

Soundings should be taken around the ship to determine as accurately as possible the extent of the grounding. If the sea is too rough for accurate sounding, it may be possible to measure the distance from the seabed to the main deck. By marking this on a longitudinal section from the general arrangement drawings, the location and extent of grounding can be determined. If possible, soundings should be taken of the route selected to reach clear water.

Immediate Action

If the ship is structurally intact, an immediate attempt may be made to refloat her, with or without assistance. The master should consider use of the ship's engines, tugs and ground tackle, as well as the possibility that further damage may be caused to the ship.

If the ship has structural damage, refloating carries greater risk but may still be the best course of action. However, if there are signs of excessive hogging or sagging or of undulations in the sides of the hull, more careful consideration is required before attempting to refloat the ship. In these circumstances, lightening of the ship may reduce the risk of further damage and of pollution.

It should also be assessed whether the conditions are favourable for refloating, eg

Figure 21.11 - Two tugs attempting to salvage 'BSLE Sunrise', Valencia, Spain (September 2012)

rising tide, wind and currents in a direction away from the stranded position with no rocks that could damage the hull.

Before attempting to refloat (using the ship's engines), the ship should change from the low cooling water intakes to the high intakes. If the ship is hard aground, continuous running of the engines astern is unlikely to produce any positive result. It may cause silt to build up or damage the engines to the extent that they cannot be used later when refloating may have a higher chance of success.

If the ship is aground on a lee shore or is working in a seaway, consideration should be given to counter-flooding to prevent her from going further aground or sustaining damage. When on a lee shore, lightening should only take place under controlled conditions when the ship can be held against wind and current.

Recovering Buoyancy

If a ship has taken on a considerable amount of water, a critical part of the salvage operation will be recovering buoyancy. This will involve restoring the watertight envelope, eg by patching damage to the hull, and then refloating using one or a combination of the following:

- Pumping out flooded spaces
- blowing out flooded spaces with compressed air
- combined sealing off/patching with both pumping and blowing with compressed air
- inducing buoyancy with special flotation materials placed inside the hull.

Pumps

Pumps provide a quick, easy and controllable method of recovering buoyancy.

Before commencing pumping, the salvors will need to calculate the combination of pumps that will be required, in relation to the volume of water to be removed, the individual capacity of the pumps and the timescale. It may also be necessary to pump out cargo, bunkers, ballast, etc.

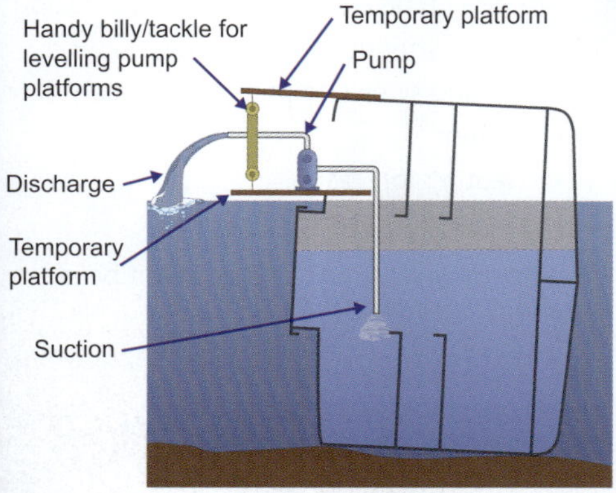

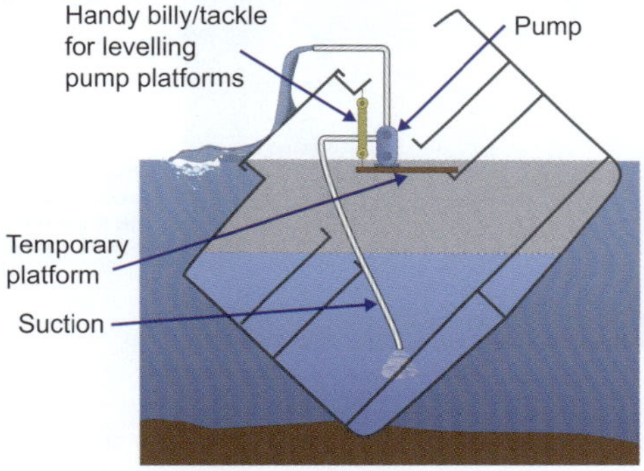

Figure 21.12 - Pump levelling platforms

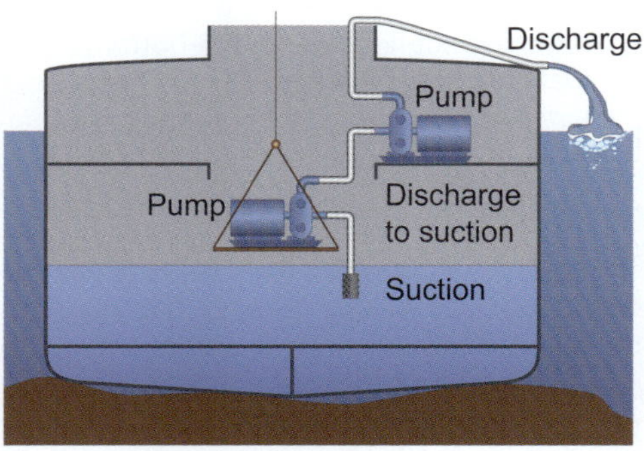

Figure 21.13 - Pumping in series

Water Removal Using Compressed Air

Pumping compressed air into a compartment provides efficient removal of floodwater, but this method is harder to control than a water pumping operation. In particular, serious structural damage may result if the compartment is overpressurised. Compressed air will also cause a ship to refloat more rapidly, lessening control of the salvors and reducing the time available to react to any difficulties.

Recovering Buoyancy

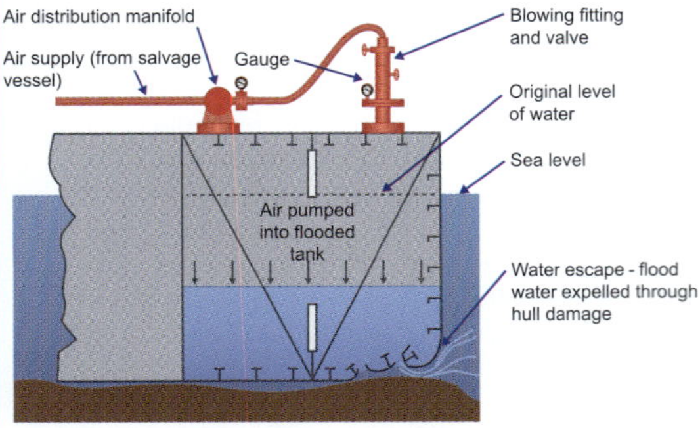

Dewatering through hull damage

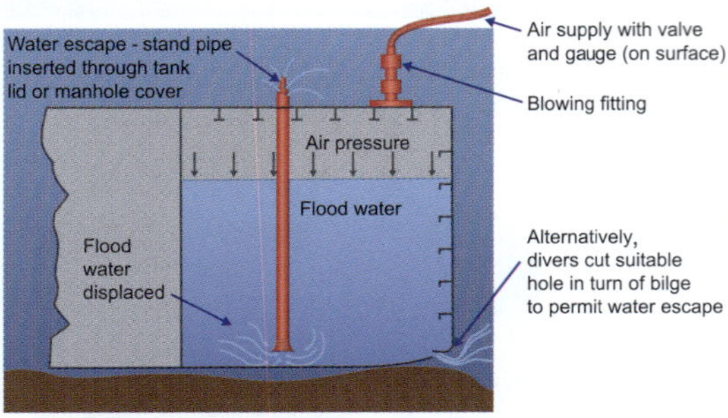

Dewatering a closed compartment

This method of salvage is particularly suitable for:

- Pumping out flooded spaces in ships that have bottom damage
- pumping out flooded double-bottom tanks that are open to the sea
- refloating ships sunk on their side or upside down
- pumping out stranded and beached ships.

The amount of buoyancy that can be recovered depends on the volume of water that can be removed without air leaking from the compartment. For example, if the ship has sustained damage along her bottom, almost all the buoyancy can be recovered. The higher up the damage, the less recoverable buoyancy. In such cases, the salvors may need to carry out extensive preparatory work to ensure the space to be pumped out is completely airtight, as compressed air will rapidly escape through any gaps.

Induced Buoyancy

If a hull is very badly damaged and cannot be made watertight, buoyancy may be recovered by placing buoyant objects or a large buoyant mass inside the hull, eg lift bags etc. This method can be very time consuming and labour intensive as the objects must be placed and secured with care to prevent them floating out of the compartment.

Stress and Stability

If the ship is damaged or the cargo has shifted, the ship's crew will have no means readily available to determine what impact the salvage operation would have on ship stresses and stability. The following information should be sent to the ship's managers as soon as possible:

i. Loading condition:
   - cargo/ballast (weights and distribution)
   - fuel
   - draught

ii. Damage:
   - location and extent

iii. Condition of the ship:
   - extent to which aground (soundings around the vessel)
   - draught forward, amidships (port and starboard) and aft
   - cargo and fuel - loss or change in amount or distribution
   - action already taken - pressurisation of tanks, internal transfer of cargo, jettison of cargo, bunkers or ballast, etc

iv. Local conditions:
   - tide - range and whether rising or falling
   - wind - strength and direction
   - sea and swell - height and direction
   - current
   - weather forecast
   - nature of bottom.

Any additional information that might be of use should also be included.

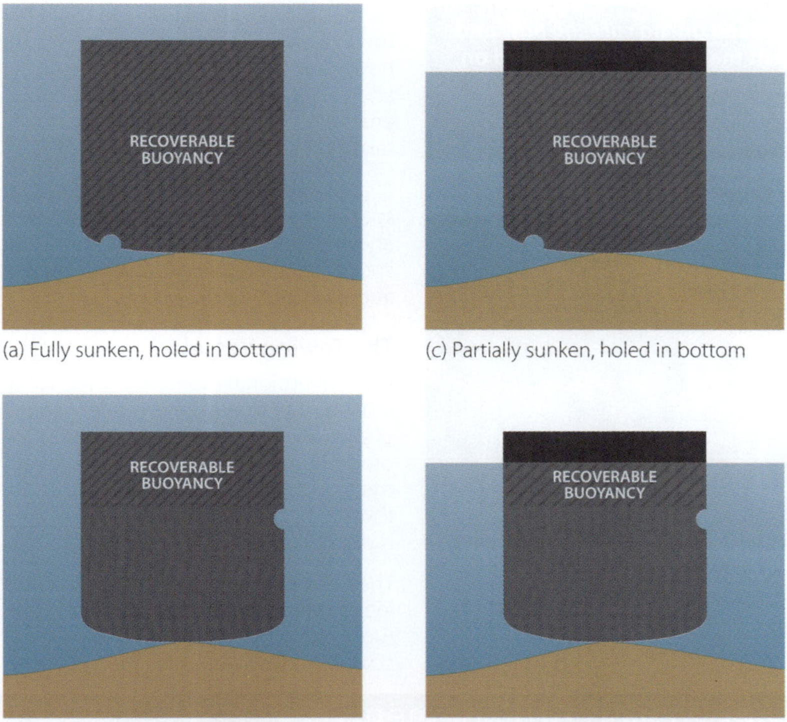

(a) Fully sunken, holed in bottom

(c) Partially sunken, holed in bottom

(b) Fully sunken, holed in side

(d) Partially sunken, holed in side

Figure 21.14 - Recoverable buoyancy

Emergency Towing

Towage or Salvage?

In a towage contract, the vessel requiring the tow should be in a normal condition with no abnormal risk, apart from the day-to-day hazards experienced at sea. However, in a salvage situation, the vessel requiring assistance is usually at some risk. This means that a towage contract is for the purpose of offering a towing service, while the salvage contract is to save a vessel in danger.

If the vessel is drifting towards land, whether due to wind or current, a Safety or Urgency message should be sent to alert the local authorities. If there is time, the situation should be discussed with the vessel's operators but **it remains the master's duty to safeguard the lives of those on board.**

Remuneration

A towage contract will be based on a fixed fee or charter or daily charter rate to cover the distance required to a port of refuge.

Emergency Towing

Salvage is based on *'no cure, no pay'* and any payment made does not depend on a contract and can be awarded even if the master of the salvaged vessel has declined assistance.

The Towed Ship

In a salvage situation, the towed ship will generally be a 'dead ship', will have little time to prepare and will often have little specialist equipment for such a tow.

As the salvage vessel (salvage tug) arrives, the tow master will normally indicate to the ship how he wishes the towage to be undertaken and will approach the ship close enough to enable lines to be passed for the towline to be taken on board.

A specialist salvage vessel will carry not just specialist equipment but specialist personnel and, weather and conditions permitting, specialists such as a salvage master, engineers and divers.

The Towing Vessel

If a conventional tug is employed for the tow, it has a duty to ensure the safety and success of the tow. This includes making up the tow properly, inspecting the towline, ensuring that the towline is an appropriate length for the towage to be undertaken and ensuring the tow is displaying the proper lights.

The crew of the tug must keep a proper lookout (from the towed vessel as well as the tug, if the scope of the towing hawser or the size of the tow warrants it).

Emergency Towing Arrangements

Figure 21.15 - Emergency towing arrangement

Emergency Towing Arrangements

In 1983, the IMO made it compulsory for new tankers over 20,000 GT to be fitted with emergency towing fitments. Subsequent amendments make it a requirement that all tankers over 20,000 GT are fitted with emergency towing fitments fore and aft.

Fittings usually consist of an anchor point known as a 'Smit bracket' to which is secured a chafing chain led through a ship's lead. This permits a tug to take the vessel in tow in the event that the vessel starts to founder. The ship's crew, prior to abandoning the vessel, should deploy the chafing chains through the fairleads, so that they can be easily reached by the salvage tugs.

Different arrangements are current within the industry and some vessels are fitted with a towline that can be quickly secured to the chafing chain. The carriage of the vessel's own towing spring provides a certain amount of flexibility, which would permit any vessel to take up the tow, not just a designated tug.

IMO Resolution MSC.35(63), which covers the installation of emergency towing arrangements on tankers, was passed after the loss of the *'Braer'* in 1993.

IMO resolution MSC.35 (63) which covers the installation of emergency towing arrangements on tankers was passed after the loss of the *'Braer'* in 1993.

Figure 21.16 - Smit towing bracket

Emergency Towing Arrangements on Tankers

Reference: SOLAS Chapter II-1, Regulation 3-4

Emergency towing arrangements shall be fitted at both ends on board every tanker of not less than 20,000 tonnes deadweight.

Figure 21.17 - Strong point leading to Panama chock

Emergency Towing Arrangements

Emergency towing arrangements for tankers required by 1st January 1999.

By 1st January 1999, all tankers (including oil tankers, chemical tankers and gas carriers) of not less than 20,000 tonnes deadweight must have an emergency towing arrangement fitted at both ends.

The requirement, in Chapter II-1 of SOLAS, came into force for new ships from 1st January 1996. Ships built before 1st January 1996 had to have the emergency towing arrangement fitted at the first scheduled drydocking after 1st January 1996 but not later than 1st January 1999.

On 1st July 2002, a number of amendments to the Safety of Life at Sea (SOLAS) Convention entered into force which impact tankers.

The regulation on emergency towing arrangements for tankers has been expanded to include more detailed technical requirements, in particular the ability to rapidly deploy towing arrangements, and provisions for adequate strength during bad weather conditions.

Characteristics of Disabled Ships

A disabled ship will drift, influenced by the effects of wind, waves, tide and current. The combined effect of these forces can result in a drift force that can be considerable.

The effect of wind force is directly proportional to the exposed freeboard area of the vessel. The rate of drift is directly proportional to any increase in wind speed. If there is no wind, the vessel will drift with the current.

The combined force of wind and waves may cause the vessel to turn and change its heading. The angle of deviation from the intended course is termed 'leeway'.

In general, a drifting ship will be most stable when it is approximately beam on to the wind and waves. Therefore, most ships will drift broadside to. The effect of drift will be determined by the ship's resistance to motion (ie drag). A larger ship will offer greater resistance. A ship's displacement will affect the actual drift and leeway, with drift speed varying depending on whether the vessel is laden or in ballast.

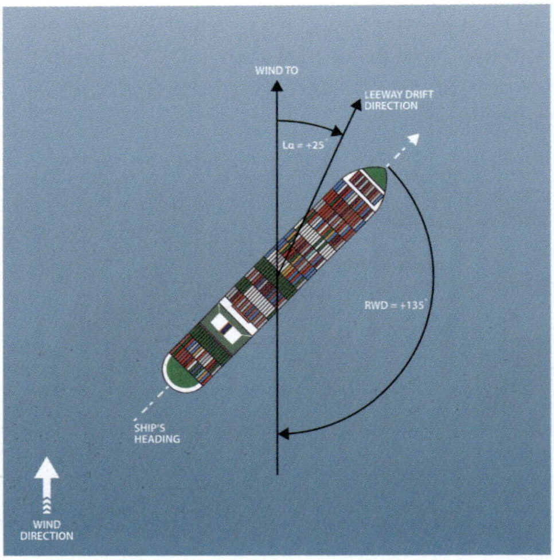

Figure 21.18 - Relationship between wind direction and leeway direction

Sea and Surface Currents

Sea and surface current effects are directly proportional to the underwater area of the vessel and the speed of the current.

Tidal Currents

The force of tidal currents is in proportion to a vessel's underwater surface area and speed.

Characteristics of Disabled Ships

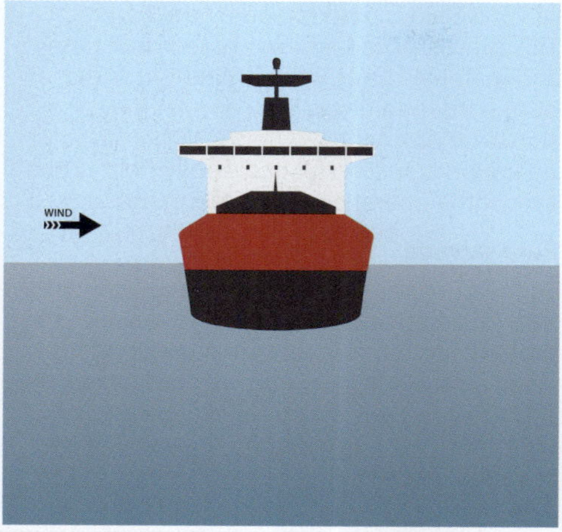

Figure 21.19 - Wind effect is directly proportional to freeboard area

Figure 21.20 - Effect of wind and current is indirectly proportional to displacement

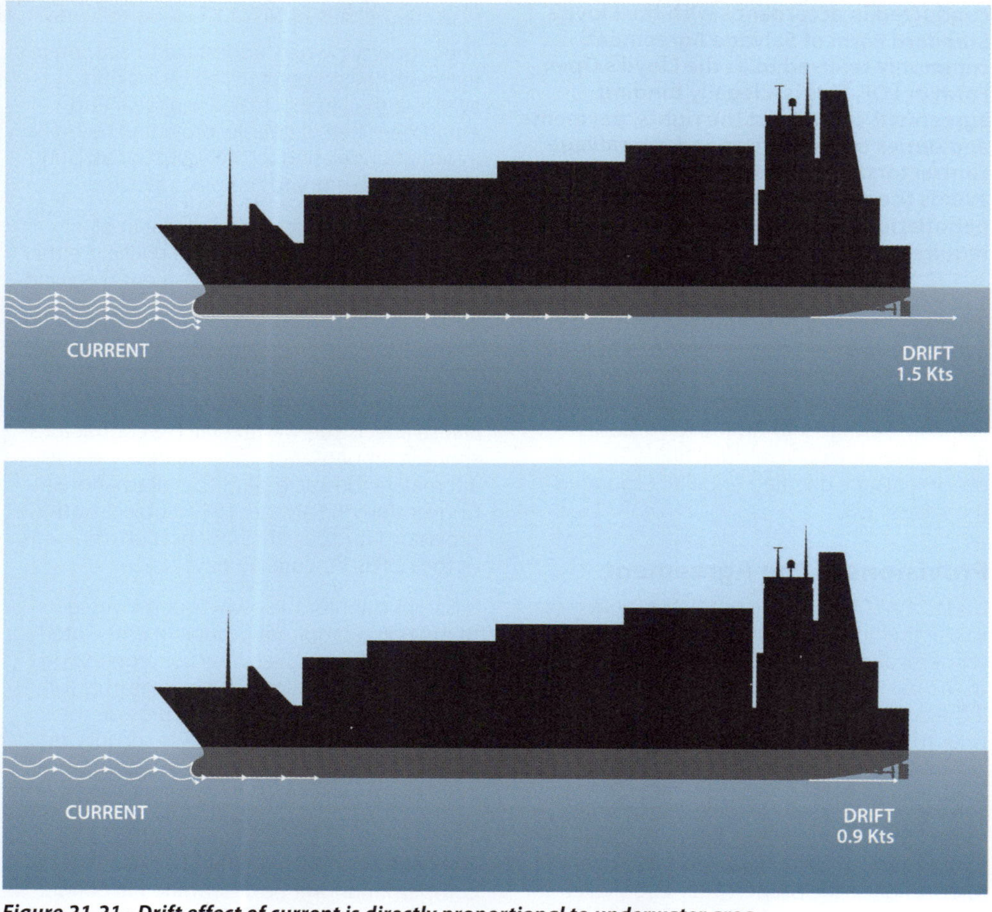

Figure 21.21 - Drift effect of current is directly proportional to underwater area

Legal Aspects of Salvage

Salvage is a commercial undertaking and the commitment entered into with the master is to provide whatever assistance might be needed until a problem encountered by the ship is brought under control and the ship is taken to a safe place.

There are two main types of salvage agreement:

- **Contract salvage**
- **pure salvage.**

Contract salvage

The owner of the ship (or asset) and salvor enter into a contract prior to commencement of salvage operations and the amount that the salvor is paid is determined by the contract. This can be a fixed amount based on a 'time and materials' basis, or any other terms that both parties agree to. The contract may also state that payment is only due if the salvage operation is successful or that payment is due even if the operation is not successful.

Pure salvage

There is no contract between the owner of the ship (or asset) and the salvor. The salvor of the property under pure salvage must bring his claim for salvage in a court that has jurisdiction, and the court will award salvage based on the 'merit' of the service and the value of the salvaged property.

Lloyd's Open Form (LOF)

A marine salvage operation will usually be conducted in accordance with the Lloyd's Standard Form of Salvage Agreement, commonly referred to as the Lloyd's Open Form or LOF. This is a legally binding agreement setting out the rights, payments and duties of the owners and the salvage contractors. Use of a standard agreement avoids the need for time-consuming negotiations when a ship is in distress and requires urgent assistance.

The LOF is very short and provides the basic details of the salvage operation, such as the parties, property to be salvaged, location, etc. More detailed information is contained in separate reference documents - the Lloyd's Standard Salvage and Arbitration Clauses (LSSA) and Lloyd's Procedural Rules. These documents are deemed to be incorporated in the agreement.

Provisions of the Agreement

Under the LOF, salvage contractors undertake to use their best endeavours to salve the property and to prevent or minimise damage to the environment throughout the operation. If the contractors render any salvage services prior to the date of the agreement, these services will still be covered by the agreement.

Salvage will generally involve transporting the property to a place of safety as specified in the LOF. Complete performance is deemed to occur once the property has been taken to the place of safety and is in a safe condition, ie it can be left unattended and requires no ongoing salvage services.

The property owners undertake to cooperate fully with the contractors, eg by making available the vessel's machinery gear and equipment free of charge, providing technical information relating to the vessel, or assisting with gaining entry to the place of safety.

If during the operation the prospect of a satisfactory outcome becomes unlikely, either party may terminate the agreement by giving reasonable prior written notice to the other.

The LOF will also indicate whether or not the SCOPIC (Special Compensation P&I Club) Clause is incorporated into the agreement. This clause affects the way in which a contractor's special compensation is calculated and is an alternative to Article 14 of the International Convention on Salvage, 1989. Subject to these provisions for special compensation, the basis of the LOF is 'no cure, no pay'.

It is important for the owners of the vessel to provide prompt notification of entry into the agreement to the owners of property on board. Following successful salvage, this will enable the property owners to provide the salvage contractors with salvage security, in accordance with Clause 4 of the LSSA Clauses. This obligation is separate to the provision of General Average security.

The contractor's remuneration and/or special compensation will be determined in London in accordance with the LSSA Clauses and Lloyd's Procedural Rules.

Port of Refuge

Definitions

A 'port of refuge' is a shelter for a ship in a damaged condition that represents a danger to life, health and/or the environment.

The IMO defines it as a place where a ship in need of assistance can take action to enable it to stabilise its condition and reduce the hazards to navigation and to protect human life and the environment.

EU Directive 2002/59/EC defines it as a port, part of a port or another protective berth or anchorage or any other sheltered area identified by a Member State for accommodating ships in distress.

The IMO uses the term 'place' of refuge rather than 'port' due to the often less than ideal factors of having a casualty alongside in port. The use of the word port was considered too narrow and restrictive.

A place of refuge may be a constructed harbour, port, natural embayment, potential grounding site or offshore waters.

A ship's master faced with a maritime casualty, *force majeure* or some other operational situation may seek a place of refuge.

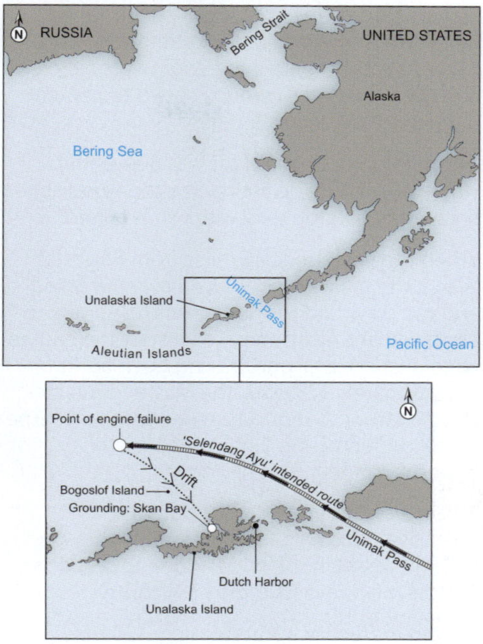

Case Study: *'Selendang Ayu'*

On 8th December 2004, the Malaysian-flagged bulk carrier *'Selendang Ayu'*, en route westbound from Seattle to China, ran aground on the north shore of Unalaska Island.

Port of Refuge

Early in the voyage, the vessel encountered head seas and winds ranging from force 7 to 11. The vessel experienced engine problems and the crew had to reduce speed to prevent damaging the engines.

Transit through Unimak Pass was uneventful. However, once in the Bering Sea, the vessel again encountered rough seas, with winds at force 6.

When the vessel was 46 miles from Bogoslof Island, the main engine's No. 3 cylinder failed and the crew had to shut down the engine to effect repairs. All attempts to restart the engine were unsuccessful and, having been adrift for approximately 12 hours, the Master contacted Dutch Harbor to request towing assistance. The vessel drifted within 3 miles clear to the east of Bogoslof Island.

Three vessels came to assist but, despite extensive efforts, it was impossible to tow or halt the vessel in the wind and sea conditions. The crew was evacuated by helicopter.

Having drifted for approximately 100 miles, the vessel ran aground on Unalaska Island and broke in two. As the final crew members were being airlifted, a huge wave hit the bow of the vessel and engulfed the helicopter, with the loss of six lives.

The grounding resulted in the spillage of 336,000 gallons of fuel oil and diesel fuel, and a clean-up operation lasting nearly four years.

International Law or Guidance Related to Place of Refuge

There was no specific international law or guidance relating to places of refuge until the creation and adoption of IMO Resolution A.949(23) in December 2003.

Before then, seafarers relied on the continued historical good faith between mariners and port authorities when a place of refuge was necessary.

The *'Torrey Canyon'* incident led to the creation of the Intervention Convention 1969, which gave coastal States legal authority to reject a ship that presented an environmental threat.

The 'United Nations Convention on the Law of the Sea' (UNCLOS) does not directly address places of refuge, but some of the Articles of UNCLOS have some applicability when considering places of refuge:

Article 18 – Meaning of Passage

2. Passage shall be continuous and expeditious. However, passage includes stopping and anchoring, but only in so far as the same are incidental to ordinary navigation or are rendered necessary by force majeure or distress or for the purpose of rendering assistance to persons, ships or aircraft in danger or distress.

Article 195 – Duty not to Transfer Damage or Hazards or Transform One Type of Pollution into Another

In taking measures to prevent, reduce and control pollution of the marine environment, States shall act so as not to transfer, directly or indirectly, damage or hazards from one area to another or transform one type of pollution into another.

Article 221 – Measures to Avoid Pollution Arising from Maritime Casualties

1. Nothing in this Part shall prejudice the right of States, pursuant to international law, both customary and conventional, to take and enforce measures beyond the territorial sea proportionate to the actual or threatened damage to protect their coastline or related interests, including fishing, from pollution or threat of pollution following upon a maritime casualty or acts relating to such a casualty, which may reasonably be expected to result in major harmful consequences.

2. For the purposes of this article, "maritime casualty" means a collision of vessels, stranding or other incident of navigation, or other occurrence on board a vessel or external to it resulting in material damage or imminent threat of material damage to a vessel or cargo.

Both Articles 17 and 18 of UNCLOS imply that coastal and port States have the right to impose preconditions on a ship in distress in return for granting it the right to enter their territorial waters to find a Place of Refuge.

In response to the *'Erika'* incident of 1999, the European Union adopted EU Directive 2002/59/EC, on 27th June 2002, *'establishing a Community vessel traffic monitoring and information system'*. Article 20 of the Directive deals with places of refuge:

Article 20 – Places of Refuge
Member States, having consulted the parties concerned, shall draw up, taking into account relevant guidelines by IMO, plans to accommodate, in the waters under their jurisdiction, ships in distress. Such plans shall contain the necessary arrangements and procedures taking into account operational and environmental constraints, to ensure that ships in distress may immediately go to a place of refuge subject to authorisation by the competent authority. Where the Member State considers it necessary and feasible, the plans must contain arrangements for the provision of adequate means and facilities for assistance, salvage and pollution response.

There has been debate over whether places of refuge should be openly declared or undisclosed. Some member nations fear that, if places of refuge are made public, nearby communities might protest the decision or substandard ships could take advantage of the information.

IMO Resolution A.949(23) – Guidelines on places of refuge for ships in need of assistance, adopted on 5th December 2003, was developed for the intended use when a ship is in need of assistance but the safety of life is not involved.

IMO Resolution A.950(23) – Maritime Assistance Services (MAS), adopted on 5th December 2003, provides the structure and guidelines for Member States in creating Maritime Assistance Services as recommended in Resolution A.949(23).

The development of Resolution A.949(23) is in the hope that the need for a ship seeking a port of refuge to then require the assistance detailed in the SAR Convention will be reduced or negated completely. The aim is to successfully get the vessel to a suitable place of refuge before the situation escalates.

Problems for Coastal State Authorities

When determining whether to grant a place of refuge to a ship, a coastal State must determine:

- The risk to the shore and coast by allowing refuge
- the possibility of legal action by those affected by any pollution
- financial responsibility for any required clean-up operations
- the increased risk to life and the environment if refuge is refused
- whether an environmental disaster will occur further offshore where it will be harder to manage.

Case Studies

MV *'Erika'*, 1999

On 8th December 1999, the Maltese-flagged oil tanker *'Erika'* sailed from Dunkirk, France with an intended destination of Livorno, Italy, with a cargo of approximately 31,000 tonnes of fuel oil. Soon after sailing, the ship encountered a force 9 gale.

At approximately 12:30 on 11th December 1999, a substantial starboard list developed.

Two hours later, the Master sent a distress alert to MRCC Etel. MRCC Etel acknowledged the distress alert and requested the *'Erika'* to confirm this or to indicate that she was safe.

At 16:06, the Master called the company office in Ravenna. The Master told them that, despite some noticeable cracks, the situation seemed to be under control. Due to the ship's condition, they advised the Master that he should head to the safest place of refuge. It was agreed that this would be Donges.

On checking the cargo and ballast tanks, the Master found the segregated No. 2 starboard ballast tank, which should have been empty, contained both seawater and fuel oil with the ullage equal to the sea level. Cracks and buckling were noticed on the deck in the way of this tank.

At 22:27 the *'Erika''s* Master sent a telex to MRCC Etel, copied to the ship's agent at Donges, giving details of the situation, and also making clear that the ship had developed cracks on the main deck.

At 05:10 on 12th December 1999, the Master sounded the general alarm and all crew mustered on the boat deck.

At 08:00 a French naval rescue helicopter arrived and the least experienced crew members were taken off first.

Port of Refuge

At around 08:08 when the *'Erika'* was in the Bay of Biscay, approximately 45 miles off the French coast, she suffered complete structural failure and broke in two, spilling a substantial part of her cargo.

According to the ship's agent, the Harbour Master of St Nazaire had refused permission for the vessel to enter the port of Donges. It appears the Master was not aware of this and, when the ship started to break in two, she was still on course to that port. It can, therefore, be argued that the refusal to enter Donges did not alter the course of events and was not relevant to the loss of the *'Erika'*.

MV *'Prestige'*, 2002

In November 2002, the MV *'Prestige'*, a Greek-owned, Bahamian-flagged tanker, sank off the coast of Spain, causing serious oil pollution.

The *'Prestige'* began leaking oil on 13th November 2002, while carrying 76,972 tonnes of heavy fuel oil, 50 km from the coast of Galicia, Spain. The Master requested a place of refuge from the Spanish authorities but was denied and the authorities ordered that the vessel be towed towards the Northeast Atlantic.

On 15th November, the Master stopped *'Prestige'*''s engine, fearing excessive vibrational forces they may cause. After noticing a 30-metre crack in the hull, further requests were made for a place of refuge, but again the Spanish authorities refused, ordering that the vessel be towed westerly.

The *'Prestige'* broke in two and sank in international waters on 19th November 2002. Approximately 70,000 tonnes of oil escaped from the vessel. It is generally believed that the vessel and the cargo could have been saved if the vessel had been allowed a place of refuge. This is evidenced by the fact that the ship stayed afloat for six days after the initial cracking began.

There is also a belief that bringing the *'Prestige'* into a secluded bay on the coast as a place of refuge, where any pollution could have been directly controlled and more easily managed, would have been a better solution rather than the widespread pollution that resulted from the ship's breakup at sea.

M/T *'Magnitude'*, 2002

Six days after the *'Prestige'* sank, the *'Magnitude'*, with 90,000 tonnes of HFO on board, was awaiting entry to Milford Haven to discharge. At daybreak, the crew found themselves in the centre of an oil slick, which was issuing from a visible crack in the side of the vessel.

While cargo was transferred from the tanks near the crack, contact was made with the Milford Haven Harbour Master, who held a meeting with his local environment group to explain the situation. It was agreed that, despite the risk of pollution from the vessel, bringing the vessel into the port presented the least risk of pollution to the greater environment.

The vessel was brought into the port, boomed and discharged successfully, with little or no pollution.

Should a Place (or Port) of Refuge be Sought?

Under What Circumstances?

- **The ship is damaged to such an extent that it is unsafe to continue the voyage**
- **in such cases, the vessel should deviate to the nearest safe port (ie a port of refuge)**
- **it is a justifiable deviation**
- **the ship is repaired as necessary at the port and the voyage may be resumed once the ship becomes seaworthy.**

Issues for the Master

The following must be considered when deciding upon a port of refuge:

- **Can the port be reached safely? (sufficient fuel, extent of damage)**
- **are the port authorities friendly/ hostile?**
- **can the vessel enter port and remain there safely?**
- **are suitable repair facilities available at the port?**
- **can cargo be discharged ashore if necessary?**
- **are there suitable crew repatriation facilities?**
- **can ship's spares/stores be imported easily?**
- **is the port free of war or civil unrest?**
- **are the required charts on board?**

When deciding upon a port of refuge, the owners and the ship's insurers should be consulted.

After Deciding on a POR

- Inform the owner, charterer and agent at original destination and give them the reason for entering POR
- consult the underwriter
- consider State requirements at POR
- inform agent at POR
- inform port authorities
- contact P&I Club at POR.

While Deviating to a POR

Inform the owner:

- Date, time, position and nature of incident
- ROB of D/O, FO and FW on board
- current situation on board
- weather: current and predicted
- master's intention to deviate
- name of POR
- ETA at POR
- assistance required.

Inform Agents at POR

- Name and port of registry
- official number, IMO number
- ship's particulars (GT, NT, LOA, LBP, draught)
- reasons for entering
- expected time of arrival
- amount of cargo and distribution
- details of assistance required.

Upon Arrival

- Obtain a pilot
- enter the ship in the customary manner
- obtain pratique.

After Entry

- Issue note of protest, reserving the right to extend
- inform the owner and charterer of the ship's safe arrival
- inform the underwriter in accordance with tender clause
- inform the P&I agent and underwriter's surveyor
- if the cargo is to be discharged, inform GA adjuster and qualified independent cargo surveyor to be present before breaking bulk (opening/closing of hatches)
- arrange damage survey by Class. If no Class surveyors are available, make arrangement with other Classification Society surveyor to have damage surveyed
- after receiving the surveyor's report/ recommendation, call for tenders with advice from underwriter representative. In tender, include the statement "lowest or any tender not necessarily accepted"
- arrange repairs under the supervision of surveyor/underwriter's surveyor
- after repair, arrange for a survey. Once satisfied, the surveyor will issue an interim certificate. If he is not employed by a Class Society, he will issue a certificate of seaworthiness
- a proper record is to be kept commencing from the time of deviation to the port of refuge. Copies to be sent to the owner for P&I claims
- issue more protests, giving full details of damage and repairs. Copies to be dispatched to the owner
- the ship can be cleared to resume voyage.

Salvage Case Studies

'Marco Polo'

24th October – 20th November 2009

On Saturday 24th October 2009, the passenger ferry *'Marco Polo'* grounded en route to Split, carrying around 100 passengers and crew on board.

On the same day, the owners signed an LOF contract with SMIT's local partner, towage and salvage company Jadranski Pomorski Servis (JPS). When it became obvious that a refloating could not be done with tugs only, SMIT Salvage mobilised a salvage team on 28th October to draw up and execute the salvage plan and subsequently the challenging operation started.

The operation entailed installation of additional strong points on the aft deck and skid beams in the bulbous bow to minimise the friction coefficient in combination with lifting bags. The bottom section of the bulb was separated from the vessel by cutting and additional support was installed inside of the bulb to facilitate the full use of the skid beams while pulling the *'Marco Polo'* off with three JPS tugs.

The vessel was successfully refloated on 20th November and was subsequently towed to Mali Losinj for redelivery to her owners.

'Eco Africa'

12th October – 16th December 2009

On 12th October 2009, while the 150,000 Dwt MT *'Eco Africa'* was discharging her cargo of crude oil at a terminal in the Gulf of Suez, a fire broke out in the engine room. SMIT Salvage was contracted by the owners to render assistance under an LOF contract. A specialised salvage team was immediately mobilised from Rotterdam and simultaneously fire-fighting equipment was mobilised as well. An AHTS supported by two local tugs was utilised for boundary cooling of the *'Eco Africa'*. After being towed to the outer anchorage, the fire was extinguished. Subsequently, water was pumped out of the engine room into one of the vessel's cargo tanks and, after preservation treatment of the engines, she was safely redelivered to her owners.

'Golden 168'

24th – 25th December 2008

On 24th December 2008, a Chinese general cargo vessel, *'Golden 168'*, suffered a severe engine room fire that immobilised the main engine. The vessel was drifting 250 nautical miles northeast of East London, South Africa and was experiencing extremely adverse weather conditions with swells peaking at 12 metre heights.

The vessel was in ballast, lying beam onto the swell, and was rolling up to 45° each way. The heavy rolling resulted in the aft crane breaking out of its cradle and smashing into the bridge structure.

The *'Smit Amandla'* was on salvage station in East London and was immediately mobilised. An LOF was agreed with the owners, with the assistance of SMIT Salvage Office, Singapore.

In light of the Master's concern regarding the safety of his vessel and crew, the *'Smit Amandla'* steamed at full speed to minimise the time that the *'Golden 168'* was subjected to adverse weather conditions. The tug arrived on the morning of 25th December and, despite the extremely adverse weather conditions, was able to make fast and commence with the tow to Durban.

On arrival in the Port of Durban, a salvage master and crew were flown out to the casualty by helicopter and the tow was handed over to another SMIT vessel, the *'Pentow Service'*. The *'Golden 168'* was then towed into Durban where she was redelivered to her owners.

'Sibulk Innovation'

24th April – 5th May 2008

The bulk carrier *'Sibulk Innovation'*, fully laden with bauxite, was en route from India to China, when she collided with another tanker off Singapore and suffered ruptures in cargo holds Nos. 2 and 3 and topside tanks Nos. 2 (P) and 3 (P). Both cargo holds flooded quickly and the vessel was severely down by the head. Following emergency procedures, the Master dropped anchor and awaited assistance. SMIT Salvage in Singapore was contracted to render immediate assistance. Work/accommodation barge *'Ibis'* and the *'Smit Luzon'* were mobilised. After the initial dive inspection, and with the extent of damage known, the salvage team commenced with underwater patching of the ruptured cargo holds and topside tanks. De-watering operations commenced after patching was completed and, with continuous pumping for about two days, the cargo holds were pumped dry. The vessel subsequently shifted to another anchorage, under its own power, and was redelivered to her owners on the 5th May.

'Fedra'

10th October 2008 – mid-January 2009

As a result of a very severe storm, the 64,000 Dwt bulk carrier *'Fedra'* was driven ashore at Europa Point, Gibraltar. Within hours, she broke at the No. 6 cargo hold, separating her bow from her stern. A Titan Salvage team was in Gibraltar, removing the wreckage of the *'New Flame'*. The team mobilised to the *'Fedra'* and took a leading role in saving the lives of the crew by lifting them from the wreck to the land utilising a mobile crane. Within a few days, the team determined that the bow could possibly be refloated but the stern was destroyed. Titan removed the fuel oil, refloated the bow and removed the accommodation from the stern before the winter storms could destroy them. Over the next few weeks, the fuel was removed, but efforts to remove the bow and accommodation were slowed by political problems concerning disposal. These problems were resolved just prior to the year's end and the contract was successfully completed by mid-January 2009.

'APL Panama'

25th December 2005 – 12th March 2006

This was one of the largest refloatings of a laden container ship ever undertaken. The *'APL Panama'*, a 52,267 Dwt ship with a capacity of 4,038 TEU, ran aground on 25th December 2005 on the beach in Ensenada, Mexico. Operating under an LOF, Titan safely redelivered the ship to its owner on 12th March. During the project, Titan mobilised several salvage teams and specialised salvage gear from various depots in the United States and overseas. Included in the mobilisation were 20 truckloads of salvage gear, five 300 ton hydraulic pullers, seven tugboats with a combined bollard pull of 500 tons, a flat-deck barge upon which the pullers were mounted, three crawler stick cranes of varying sizes, a SkyCrane helicopter and a dredge. Titan safely removed all fuel from the ship, along with more than 1,200 containers, and then removed large quantities of sand from around the vessel in order to refloat it.

Salvage of Cargo from the War-Damaged *'Gaz Fountain'*

The LPG carrier *'Gaz Fountain',* had loaded propane and butane at Ras Tanura and sailed on 11th October 1984 for Fujairah.

During the morning of 12th October, when in the mid Persian Gulf, she was stalked by an Iranian aircraft that subsequently attacked her with guided air-to-ground armour-piercing rockets. Three rockets are reported to have hit the vessel.

The crew operated the cargo emergency shutdown system, stopped the ship's engines and abandoned ship in the lifeboats. They were rescued soon after and without injury.

Before leaving the ship, the crew closed doors between the lower accommodation and the engine room, with considerable benefit.

Courtesy of Capt J A Carter, presented at GASTECH 1985

Figure 21.22 - 'Gaz Fountain' being lightered, November 1984

Salvage of Cargo from the War-Damaged *'Gaz Fountain'*

Damage Sustained

One rocket exploded on deck above No. 2 tank near the centreline. The deck was breached in two places into the void space but fortunately No. 2 tank did not rupture. Some of the top insulation wrapping was stripped off the tank, and the cofferdam bulkhead immediately forward of the space was holed.

The main explosive blast from this missile appears to have gone upwards and outwards above the deck.

All service pipework and electric cabling carried on the overhead walkway, above the blast, was blown upwards. Much of the piping was ruptured or badly bent and the electric cabling destroyed. Escaping gas from the ruptured pipework caught fire.

The other two rockets hit the deck in the vicinity of No. 3 tank, port side aft. One apparently exploded above the deck and did little obvious damage except for rupturing the pipework on the deck liquid N_2 tank, which was empty. The other penetrated the deck at an oblique angle and travelled 5 m forward in the containment space above the cargo tank before detonating. The resultant explosion lifted the deck some 40 cm over an area of about 2 m × 2 m. However, it also blew inwards and opened up the tank roof over an area of about 3 m × 2 m.

This tank was full of butane which, during its initial and continued release, established a large fire on deck above the entry hole.

It is believed that some of the nearby accommodation windows were shattered by the rocket explosions. These openings into the accommodation probably led to the start of multiple fires in the accommodation block. The accommodation and lower accommodation spaces were completely gutted before the fire burned itself out.

The closed doors from the accommodation into the engine room significantly contributed to the prevention of fire spreading into the engine room.

All electric cabling on deck and in the accommodation was burnt out.

The Selco Salvage tug *'Salvanguard'* arrived late on 13th October 1984.

Salvage Response

'Salvanguard' approached the casualty operating her mast water/foam cannons. It was reported that, after intensive water cooling of the main fire areas (over Nos. 2 and 3 tanks), it was possible to extinguish the gas fires with powerful water jets.

The vessel was then taken in tow towards Dubai. This was to:

- Remove the casualty from an area of possible further aerial attacks
- prevent gas build-up on and around the vessel now that the fires were extinguished
- prevent the risk of the vessel grounding or becoming a hazard to other shipping
- reduce the logistical problems of supplying the full expert salvage team and materials for repairs.

While the vessel was under tow off Dubai, the first priority was to resecure the vessel's gastight integrity. Temporary patches were made up to cover the deck holes, small shrapnel holes being plugged with wood bungs. The main damaged deck area over No. 3 tank, through which gas was continuously escaping, was covered with a soft foam rubber slab, timber boarding, canvas and sandbags. No attempt was made to seal the hole in the cargo tank itself. This temporary patch was then reinforced with a large cement box.

When the basic gastight integrity of the casualty was restored, she was anchored about 15 miles off Dubai. At that time, some six days after the attack, sufficient intact piping remained to set up safe manual venting for No. 1 tank. The damaged venting pipework above No. 2 cargo tank was replaced with cryogenic steel piping and a flexible hose was fitted to No. 3 cargo tank and led up a mast clear of the deck.

Ruptured pipework was isolated or sealed before it could be dismantled.

As the casualty's own pumps might be usable, consideration was then given to renewal of burned out electric cabling.

Over 3 km of wiring and cabling were replaced.

The services of MV *'Ribagorca'* were obtained, and she arrived for the transshipment on 15th November 1984.

Only the starboard pump in each tank was to be used. The main reasons for this were:

- The vessel was already listed to starboard with no guarantee it could be safely corrected
- the damage to No. 3 tank was on the port side. Any debris would, hopefully, have been confined in the port side by the centreline bulkhead and there would obviously be less risk of entraining debris into the starboard pump
- during the initial stages of discharge, care and planning was necessary to ensure cargo in No. 3 did not spill out through the hole damage
- by maintaining a starboard list, the maximum amount of cargo could be drained from the port side of the tank via the bulkhead levelling valve to the pump.

All air in the newly repaired pipelines was displaced to atmosphere by purging with bottled nitrogen and the three pumps were successfully tested on 27th October together with a pressure test of the repaired cargo pipelines.

Cargo and Discharge Considerations

The main problem associated with the cargo itself was in assessing quantities due to the lack of suitable information and the impossibility of obtaining correct cargo temperatures.

Initial cargo calculations indicated an overall loss due to the attack and subsequent venting of about 350 tonnes in the first 10 days.

Several alternative discharge plans were drawn up to accommodate different sizes of potential lightering ships.

Due to the damage, several constraints were placed on possible discharge sequences:

- Propane and butane parcels needed segregation. Additionally, the two butane parcels required segregation because of the risk that the butane in No. 3 was contaminated by the explosions
- the limits of list and trim permissible before the level of No. 3 tank was reduced to well below the damage hole
- to achieve maximum outturn when draining tanks, a good trim was desirable. 3 to 4 m was reported as normal. However, as only the starboard pump was to be used and maximum cargo had to be drained from port to starboard through the bulkhead levelling valve, the optimum trim to achieve this was calculated as 1 m
- during cargo discharge, it would be necessary to take on ballast to control the trim and stress on the vessel. To prevent the risk of free ballast water movement through the ruptured upper bulkheads of ballast tanks, ballast levels could only be brought to a minimum ullage of 5 m. This limited the total ballast weights that could be taken on board.

Discharging two cargo grades through two hoses simultaneously to speed up the discharge was considered. This possibility was discarded for two reasons:

- Maintenance of a relatively low tank pressure in No. 3 during the discharge was necessary to prevent leakage around the repairs
- to ensure adequate, safe tank pressures for discharge, the free venting of tanks would have to be stopped or reduced prior to the operation.

The fixing of MV *'Ribagorca'* as the lightering vessel imposed one further constraint on the discharge plan. Her minus 50°C rated tanks were insufficient to lift all the propane on *'Gaz Fountain'*, being a few hundred cubic metres short. Blending as much propane into the butane in *'Gaz Fountain''*s No. 2 tank during the discharge was agreed on a time basis. Such operation then required pre-checking to ensure the mixed temperature did not end up below the rated minus 5°C temperature of *'Ribagorca''s* butane tanks.

The discharge plan adopted, and which proved entirely successful for the operation, was:

1. Part discharge No. 3 to ensure cargo was well below the damage hole.
2. Effect transfer of propane from No. 1 into the butane at No. 2.
3. Discharge all No. 2 tank.

Salvage of Cargo from the War-Damaged *'Gaz Fountain'*

4. Part discharge further quantity from No. 3 tank to maintain trim.
5. Discharge all propane from No. 1 tank.
6. Complete discharge of butane from No. 3 tank.

To ensure hull stresses remained within acceptable limits, the discharge plan was forwarded to Kockums, who had made the original loading computer for the ship, and found acceptable.

On 15th November 1984, just over one month after the *'Gaz Fountain'* was attacked, the *'Ribagorca'* arrived to take off her cargo.

Discharge followed the plan described and was completed without any disruption at 05:15 on 20th November. Allowing for stoppages to change grades and for draining, an overall pumping rate of 211 tonnes per hour was achieved.

A total *of* 17, 204.2 tonnes of propane and butane was received by *'Ribagorca'.* Compared to *'Gaz Fountain''s* original loading figures, this indicated an overall loss of about 1,200 tonnes.

It was not possible to completely discharge all the propane due to limitations on board *'Ribagorca'.* However, over 100 tonnes was mixed with the butane on board *'Gaz Fountain'* over a seven hour period and the little pumpable liquid that remained was eventually discharged overboard in a controlled manner at the start of gas freeing operations.

All operations, including the extended gas freeing of the insulation around No. 3 cargo tank, were completed on 12th December and the ship was handed back to her owners.

Salvage of *'Tricolor'*

The 1987-built *'Tricolor'* was lost following a collision with the container ship *'Kariba'* on 14th December 2002, some 20 miles off the coast of Dunkirk. The Norwegian-flagged *'Tricolor'* was en route to Southampton from Antwerp, laden with nearly 3,000 luxury cars. There were also some 2,000 tonnes of bunkers on board. The *'Tricolor'* suffered damage so severe that she went down in less than half an hour. All crew members were evacuated to safety.

The ship came to rest on her port side, lying just under the surface of the water, at a position within one of the world's busiest shipping lanes. Her location and the winter weather conditions proved to be major challenges. On 16th December, the general cargo vessel *'Nicola'* grounded on the wreck. The *'Nicola'* was refloated by two tugs, but two subsequent collisions occurred with different vessels.

The wreck removal was performed by Combinatie Berging Tricolor - a consortium of salvors headed up by SMIT Salvage. It includes Scaldis Salvage & Marine Contractors, URS Salvage & Marine Contractors and Multraship Salvage.

The first phase of the salvage response – the recovery of the *'Tricolor's'* bunkers – was completed over a two-month period. SMIT deployed 'hot-tap' subsea pollutant recovery technology for the task. Fuel oil was pumped from the *'Tricolor'* by a ship to ship transfer and stored on board the sheerlegs *'Asian Hercules II'* in two dedicated reception tanks. Subsequently, recovered oil was transferred to the diving support vessel *'Normand Flower'*.

Over 1,600 tonnes of fuel oil was recovered, despite prolonged periods of severe weather (winds up to force nine and swells up to five metres). Around 5% of the vessel's bunkers remained within the hull and were recovered during the wreck removal.

As a precaution against collision with the wreck during the pump-out, five Cardinal buoys were placed around the site (one fitted with a Racon). Several guard vessels also patrolled the area of the wreck, while regular information was broadcasted on VHF.

The plan to remove the 15,536 Dwt wreck required the hull to be cut into nine sections. Two sheerlegs worked in tandem to lift the large sections onto the *'Giant 4'* barge, for transportation to a disposal facility at Zeebrugge, Belgium.

Salvage of 'Tricolor'

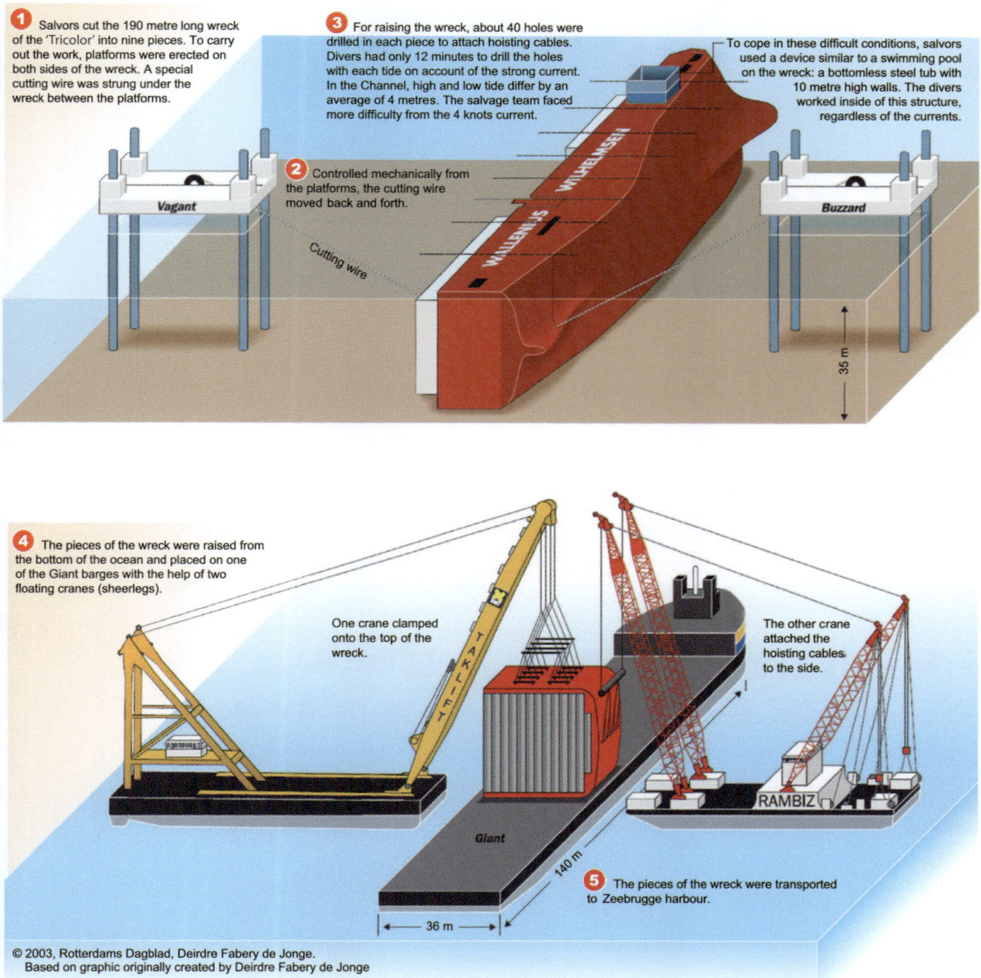

Figure 21.23 - Salvage of the 'Tricolor'

CHAPTER 22

Main Codes and Conventions

AFS Convention

Anti-Fouling on Ships Convention

International Convention on the Control of Harmful Anti-fouling Systems on Ships (AFS Convention)

"Anti-fouling system" means a coating, paint, surface treatment, surface, or device that is used on a ship to control or prevent attachment of unwanted organisms.

The International Convention on the Control of Harmful Anti-fouling Systems on Ships (AFS Convention), which entered into force on 17th September 2008, prohibits ships from applying or re-applying organotin compounds, such as TBT, which act as biocides in their anti-fouling systems. Ships must either not carry this type of compound on their hulls, external parts or surface, or must apply a coating that forms a barrier to prevent leaching from the underlying non-compliant anti-fouling systems. The Convention also establishes a mechanism to prevent the potential future use of other harmful substances in anti-fouling systems.

Article 10 of the AFS Convention prescribes that ships shall be surveyed and certified in accordance with the regulations of Annex 4 of the Convention: surveys of ships shall be carried out by officers duly authorised by the Administration or as provided in Regulation 3(1), taking into account guidelines for surveys developed by the Organization.

As it relates to marine pollutants, the AFS Convention was, and subsequent amendments will be, developed and adopted through the Marine Environment Protection Committee (MEPC) of IMO.

2010 Guidelines for Survey and Certification of Anti-fouling Systems on Ships

The 2010 Guidelines for Survey and Certification of Anti-fouling systems on Ships were adopted on 1st October 2010 as Resolution MEPC.195(61). They revoke the previous Guidelines, MEPC.102(48), adopted in 2002.

The stated aim of the Guidelines is to assist the Administrations and recognised organisations in the uniform application of the provisions of the AFS Convention and assist companies, shipbuilders, manufacturers of anti-fouling systems, as well as other interested parties to understand the process of the surveys and issuance and endorsement of the certificates.

The Guidelines provide the procedures for a survey to ensure that a ship's anti-fouling system complies with the AFS Convention and those necessary for issuance and endorsement of an International Anti-fouling System Certificate (IAFS).

The Guidelines apply to surveys of ships of 400 GT and above engaged in international voyages, excluding fixed or floating platforms, FSUs and FPSOs.

A ship will be issued with an International Anti-fouling Certificate after successful completion of the survey. Subsequent surveys are required when the anti-fouling systems are changed or replaced.

The sole purpose of the survey activities described in these Guidelines is to verify compliance with the provisions of the Convention. Consequently, such surveys do not relate to any aspect not regulated by the Convention even if such aspects relate to the performance of an anti-fouling system on the hull of a ship, including the quality of workmanship during the application process.

For practical reasons, application of paint to the hull can only be completed in a drydock, so it should be inspected, verified and registered in the ship's logbook.

2011 Guidelines for Inspection of Anti-fouling Systems on Ships

Guidelines for Inspection of Anti-fouling Systems on Ships were developed to be consistent with the survey guidelines for anti-fouling systems adopted at MEPC 61. The Guidelines were adopted on 15th July 2011 as Resolution MEPC.208(62) and apply to ships of 400 GT and above engaged in international voyages.

The Guidelines set out the initial documentation checks to be made by Port State Control Officers (PSCOs) together with the more detailed inspections where clear grounds exist that the requirements are not being met.

Ships can be detained or dismissed from a port where certification is missing or invalid, the ship admits non-compliance or sampling proves non-compliance. Where such action is taken, the flag State will be advised, as will the Recognised Organisation that has issued a relevant certificate.

General Requirements for Surveys

A survey is required:

- Before the ship is put into service and the International Anti-fouling System Certificate required under Regulation 2 or 3 of Annex 4 to the Convention is issued for the first time
- whenever an anti-fouling system is changed or replaced.

A major conversion affecting the anti-fouling system of a ship may be considered as a new building as determined by the Administration.

Repairs affecting approximately 25% or more of the anti-fouling system should be considered as a change or replacement of the anti-fouling system.

A non-compliant anti-fouling system controlled under Annex 1 of the Convention that undergoes repair must be repaired or replaced with a compliant anti-fouling system.

Conduct of Surveys

Initial Surveys (Surveys in Accordance with Regulation 1(1)(a) of Annex 4 to the Convention)

- The initial survey should verify compliance with the Convention
- as part of the survey, it should be verified that the anti-fouling system complies with the Convention
- checks or tests must not affect the integrity, structure or operation of the anti-fouling system.

AFS Convention

Surveys when the Anti-fouling Systems are Changed or Replaced (Surveys in Accordance with Regulation 1(1)(b) of Annex 4 to the Convention)

.2 *If the existing anti-fouling system is declared not to be controlled under annex 1 of the Convention, without being documented by an International Anti-fouling System Certificate, a verification should be carried out to confirm that the anti-fouling system complies with the requirements of the Convention. This verification may be based on sampling and/or testing and/or reliable documentation, as deemed necessary based on experience gained and the existing circumstances. Documentation for verification could, e.g., be MSDSs, or similar, a declaration of compliance from the anti-fouling system manufacturer, invoices from the shipyard and/or the anti-fouling system manufacturer.*

Surveys of Existing Ships Requesting only an International Anti-fouling System Certificate

.1 *If the existing anti-fouling system is declared not to be controlled under annex 1 of the Convention, a verification should be carried out to confirm that the anti-fouling system complies with the requirements of the Convention.*

Appendix II – Guidance for Surveys under the International Convention on the Control of Harmful Anti-fouling Systems on Ships

- Ensure anti-fouling and/or sealer to be applied complies with the Convention
- verify that the same anti-fouling/sealer is being applied as was declared
- confirm that non-compliant anti-fouling has been removed or a sealer applied
- confirm that there is a completed Declaration on Anti-fouling Systems
- surveys when anti-fouling is changed or replaced: endorsement of the Record of Anti-fouling Systems.

The Guidelines and Related Documents and Issues

- The MEPC noted the concerns of IPPIC and IACS's response regarding the type approval schemes for anti-fouling paint products being carried out by recognised organisations when type approval is not required either under the Convention or its associated guidelines. IACS confirmed that approvals were only being carried out by its members at the request of manufacturers and such approvals were not on behalf of administrations. Furthermore, IACS does not see the AFS Convention as prohibiting such product approvals when desired
- at the 19th session of the IMO Sub-Committee on Flag State Implementation (FSI 19) held from 21st to 25th February 2011, guidelines for inspection of anti-fouling systems on ships were developed being consistent with the survey guidelines for anti-fouling systems adopted at MEPC 61
- the AFS inspection guidelines were forwarded to MEPC 62 in July 2011 for adoption.

Figure 22.1 - Application of anti-fouling sealer

AFS Convention – Annex 1

Anti-fouling system	Control measures	Application	Effective date
Organotin compounds, which act as biocides in anti-fouling systems	Ships shall not apply or re-apply such compounds	All ships	1st January 2003
Organotin compounds, which act as biocides in anti-fouling systems	Ships either: (1) shall not bear such compounds on their hulls or external parts or surfaces; or (2) shall bear a coating that forms a barrier to such compounds leaching from the underlying non-compliant anti-fouling systems	All ships (except fixed and floating platforms, FSUs, and FPSOs that have been constructed prior to 1st January 2003 and that have not been in drydock on or after 1st January 2003)	1st January 2008

Table 22.1 - Controls on anti-fouling systems

BLU Code

Code of Practice for the Safe Loading and Unloading of Bulk Carriers (BLU Code)

BLU Code

The Code of Practice for the Safe Loading and Unloading of Bulk Carriers (BLU Code) was adopted by the IMO in November 1997. It was developed following the increasing number of bulk carrier incidents that resulted in the loss of ships and crew. A whole raft of new safety measures were brought in to address the safety of bulk carriers and the BLU Code is one such measure.

Referred to in SOLAS VI/7 and now included in the supplement of the International Maritime Solid Bulk Cargoes Code (IMSBC), the BLU Code provides the masters of bulk carriers, terminal operators and other parties the necessary information and guidance for the safe handling, loading and unloading of solid bulk cargoes.

The Code provides practical risk management information which includes guidance on ship suitability, ship to shore procedures, cargo transfer and ballast handling.

The Code consists of the following sections:

1. Definitions.
2. Suitability of ships and terminals.
3. Procedures between ship and shore prior to the ship's arrival.
4. Procedures between the ship and the terminal prior to cargo handling.
5. Cargo loading and handling of ballast.
6. Unloading cargo and handling of ballast.

Appendices

1. Recommended contents of port and terminal information books.
2. Loading or unloading plan.
3. Ship/shore safety checklist for loading or unloading dry bulk cargo carriers.

BLU Code

4. Guidelines for completing the ship/shore safety checklist.
5. Form for cargo information for solid bulk cargoes.

BLU Manual

The Manual on Loading and Unloading of Solid Bulk Cargoes for Terminal Representatives, the BLU Manual, is intended primarily for the use of terminal operators, representatives and others who may be involved in training relevant personnel. It provides detailed guidance and information including administrative and technical procedures.

The BLU Manual consists of the following sections:

1. Definitions.
2. Suitability of ships and terminals.
3. Procedures between ship and shore prior to ship's arrival.
4. Procedures between the ship and the terminal, prior to cargo loading/unloading.
5. Cargo loading and handling of ballast.
6. Unloading cargo and handling of ballast.

Annexes

1. Pre-arrival ship/shore exchange of information.
2. Avoidance of damage during cargo handling.
3. Repair of damage incurred during loading and unloading.
4. Training of terminal personnel involved in loading and/or unloading bulk carriers.
5. Hazards.
6. Emergency procedures.

Documentation

Document of Compliance

Bulk carriers of 500 GT or more that carry dangerous goods (other than class 6.2 and 7) must hold a Document of Compliance that lists the cargoes that the ship is considered suitable to carry.

Sometimes referred to as a Bulk Certificate, a Document of Compliance is issued by a Classification Society and is valid for five years.

Stability and Loading Booklet

Ships nominated for loading bulk cargoes must be provided with an approved stability and loading booklet, written in languages understood by the ship's officers. If the language is not English, French or Spanish, a translation into one of these languages must also be included.

Bunkers Convention

International Convention on Civil Liability for Bunker Oil Pollution Damage, 2001 (Bunkers Convention)

The International Convention on Civil Liability for Bunker Oil Pollution Damage, 2001 (Bunkers Convention) is intended to ensure that adequate, prompt and effective compensation is available to persons who suffer damage caused by spills of oil, when carried as fuel in ships' bunkers. The Convention was adopted on 23rd March 2001 and entered into force on 21st November 2008.

The Convention applies to pollution damage in the territory, including the territorial waters and in the exclusive economic zone (EEZ) of a State Party to the Convention.

The registered owner of a ship of more than 1,000 GT is required to maintain compulsory insurance or financial security to cover pollution damage. A certificate attesting that

insurance or other financial security is in place is required to be carried on board each ship. This certificate must include:

a) name of ship, distinctive number or letters and port registry

b) name and principal place of business of the registered owner

Bunkers Convention

c) *IMO ship identification number*

d) *type and duration of security*

e) *name and principal place of business of insurer or other person giving security and, where appropriate, place of business where the insurance or security is established*

f) *period of validity of the certificate which shall not be longer than the period of validity of the insurance or other security.*

Liability

The shipowner at the time of an incident shall be liable for pollution damage caused by any bunker oil on board or originating from the ship, except where:

- *the damage resulted from an act of war, hostilities, civil war, insurrection or a natural phenomenon of an exceptional, inevitable and irresistible character*
- *the damage was wholly caused by an act or omission done with the intent to cause damage by a third party*
- *the damage was wholly caused by the negligence or other wrongful act of any Government or other authority responsible for the maintenance of lights or other navigational aids in the exercise of that function.*

Action against a shipowner or insurer can only be brought in the courts of the State in whose territory the incident occurred. Claims for compensation must be brought within three years of the date of the damage and no action may be taken more than six years from the date of the incident (or the first of a series of incidents).

Problems with Implementation

The collision in August 2010 between the *'MSC Chitra'* and the *'Khalijia 3'* in Jawaharlal Nehru Port, India highlighted the importance of the Bunkers Convention. Without being Party to the Convention, the Indian authorities would have faced a series of challenges, all at a significant financial, economic and environmental cost.

The Bunkers Convention contains clear definitions and helps to simplify the often complex and lengthy litigation process.

Ballast Water Management

Ballast Water Management Regulations

Globally, it has been estimated that, at any time, ships' ballast water is transporting 4,000 different marine organisms. This organic load consists of living organisms and pathogens, such as bacteria and viruses, which are discharged with the ballast water when the ships reach their destination.

International Convention for the Control and Management of Ships' Ballast Water and Sediments (BWM)

The International Convention for the Control and Management of Ships' Ballast Water and Sediments (BWM) is designed to protect the marine environment from the introduction, via ships' ballast water, of non-native (alien) marine species.

Ballast Water Management

The BWM Convention was adopted at MEPC in February 2004. The BWM Convention will enter into force 12 months after the ratification of at least 30 States representing 35% of world merchant shipping tonnage. As of 12th February 2015, the total number of States ratifying the BWM Convention is 44 but the shipping tonnage is just short of the trigger figure at 32.86%. It is anticipated that the Convention will enter into force in 2016.

The BWM Convention shall apply to:

- Ships entitled to fly the flag of a Party
- ships not entitled to fly the flag of a Party but which operate under the authority of a Party.

Note: A Party is defined as a State that has ratified, or is party to, the BWM Convention.

However, the BWM Convention shall not apply to:

- Ships not designed to carry ballast water
- ships of a Party only operating within the jurisdiction of the Party; the Party may decide to include such ships where discharge of ballast water from such ships would cause harm
- ships belonging to a Party under the authorisation of another Party, which only operate within the jurisdiction of the other State, unless discharge from such ships would cause harm to the other Party
- ships that operate in waters under the jurisdiction of one Party and the high seas, except for ships not granted an authorisation, unless discharge of ballast water from such ships would cause harm
- ships with ballast water in sealed tanks that is not subject to discharge
- any ship owned or operated by the State on non-commercial service, warship, naval auxiliary, etc.

Any government that is a signatory of the BWM Convention may require the ships registered with a government that is not a signatory of the Convention to comply with the requirements of the Convention when such a ship is in their waters.

The BWM Convention is divided into 22 Articles and an Annex. The Annex includes technical standards and requirements in the regulations for the control and management of ships' ballast water and sediments. The Annex is divided into five sections, A, B, C, D and E. Section B regulations (see Table 22.2) cover the management and control requirements for ships, including the mandatory Ballast Water Management Plan, the Ballast Water Record book and the implementation timescales (see Table 22.3) following entry into force of the Convention for compliance with the BWM performance standards that are defined in Regulation D-2 (see Table 22.5).

Section	Title
B-1	BW Management Plan
B-2	BW Record Book
B-3	BW Management for Ships
B-4	BW Exchange
B-5	Sediment Management for Ships
B-6	Duties of Officers and Crew

Table 22.2 - Section B regulations

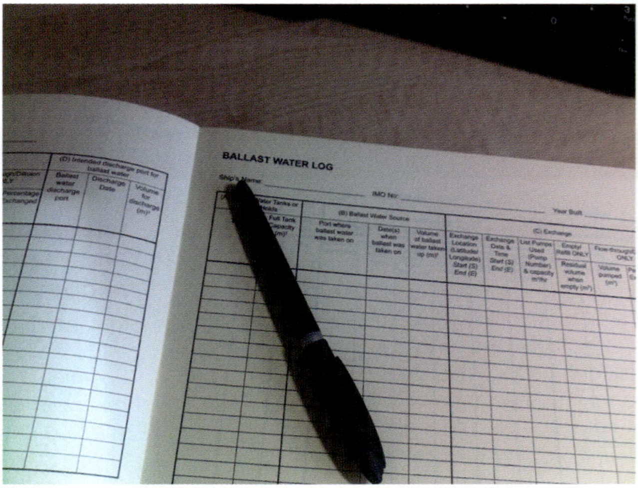

Figure 22.2 - Ballast water record book

Section B-3		
Vessel construction date	**Ballast water capacity (m^3/h)**	**Date of D-2 compliance following entry into force of the Convention**
<2009	≥1,500 and ≤5,000	First renewal survey
<2009	<1,500 and >5,000	Where the Convention enters into force before 31st December 2016: *"First renewal survey following the anniversary date of delivery of the ship in the year of compliance with the standard applicable to the ship"*
		Where the Convention enters into force after 31st December 2016: First renewal survey
≥2009	<5,000	First renewal survey
≥2009 and <2012	≥5,000	Where the Convention enters into force before 31st December 2016: *"First renewal survey following the anniversary date of delivery of the ship in the year of compliance with the standard applicable to the ship"*
		Where the Convention enters into force after 31st December 2016: First renewal survey
≥2012	≥5,000	First renewal survey

Table 22.3 - Regulations in Section B-3 (BW Management for Ships) of the Annex to the BWM Convention corresponding to Resolution A.1088(28)

The BWM Convention will require all ships to:

- Implement a Ballast Water and Sediments Management Plan (Section B-1) which is specific to each ship and approved by the Administration
- carry a Ballast Water Record Book (Section B-2)
- meet BWM (D-1 and D-2) standards (Regulations in Section B-3 and B-4).

Section B-3 outlines the timescales for compliance with the BWM (D-2) Regulations. They were updated in 2013 when Resolution A.1088(28) was adopted at the 28th Assembly of the IMO. This was necessary because the BWM Convention 2004 had taken longer to enter into force than expected and the compliance schedules were outdated.

Compliance with the BWM Convention can be achieved by meeting the Standards outlined in Section D:

- Regulation D-1: the Ballast Water Exchange Standard (BWE)
- Regulation D-2: the Ballast Water Performance Standard (BWM).

Note: According to Resolution A.1088(28), ships are required to comply with either Regulation D-1 (BWE) or Regulation D-2 (BWM) until the D-2 Regulation is enforced.

Section B-4
All ships using ballast water exchange should:
Whenever possible, conduct ballast water exchange at least 200 nautical miles from the nearest land and in water at least 200 metres in depth, taking into account the guidelines developed by the IMO.
In cases where the ship is unable to conduct ballast water exchange as above, it should be conducted as far from the nearest land as possible, and in all cases at least 50 nautical miles from the nearest land and in water at least 200 metres in depth.

Table 22.4 - Regulations in Section B-4 (BW Exchange) of the Annex to the BWM Convention

Ballast Water Management

Regulation D-1 (Ballast Water Exchange Standard)

The ballast water exchange (BWE) Standard (D-1) specifies that ships carrying out BWE should do so with an efficiency of 95% volumetric exchange of ballast water. Ships using a pumping through method will be considered to have met the standard when the volume of each ballast tank has been pumped through three times. If the ship can demonstrate that at least 95% volumetric exchange has been met with less than three times the volume of pumped ballast, the required standard will be considered to have been achieved.

Regulation D-2 (Ballast Water Performance Standard)

Regulation D-2 defines the minimum performance standards that ballast water must achieve after undergoing treatment using a ballast water system. The post-treatment concentrations of organisms, dependent on size and types, are listed in Table 22.5.

Organism Type	IMO Requirements
Organisms ≥50 μm	<10 viable organisms/m³
Organisms ≥10 to 50 μm	<10 viable organisms/ml
Toxicogenic *Vibrio cholerae* (strains 01 and 0139)	<1 cfu/100 ml, or <1 cfu/1 gram (wet weight) (zooplankton sample)
Escherichia coli	<250 cfu/100 ml
Intestinal *Enterococci*	<100 cfu/100 ml

Note: cfu = colony forming unit

Table 22.5 - D-2 Performance standards for BWMS

Regulation D-3 (Approval Requirements for BW Management Systems)

The Regulations in section D-3 require that ballast water management systems must be approved by the Administration in line with IMO guidelines (according to Guideline G8). D-3 also covers the 'Procedure for Approval of Ballast Water Management Systems that make use of Active Substances' (G9) including detailed procedures to ensure the toxicity of treated ballast water is minimised (see Table 22.9).

The United States Federal Ballast Water Discharge Standard

The United States Federal Ballast Water Discharge Standard rulemaking, produced by the United States Coast Guard (USCG), became effective on 21st June 2012. The US Coast Guard Ballast Water Discharge Standard Final Rules are currently aligned with the IMO BW Convention rules for the performance standards (ie the D-2 Standards) but the US Coast Guard plans to revisit the standard. As technologies advance, a review will be carried out, and published no later than 1st January 2016, in order to assess whether a more stringent set of standards is practical.

This legislation has jurisdiction within the waters of the United States, including the territorial sea as extended out to 12 nautical miles from the baseline. It applies to:

- Seagoing vessels
- coastal vessels that do not operate outside the EEZ but are greater than 1,600 GT and transit between COTP Zones, which includes most 'Salties' (vessels that depart the Great Lakes, transit beyond the EEZ, return and pass upstream of Snell Lock).

The USCG Final Rule does not stipulate that installing a ballast water management system on board certain ships is the only way to be compliant. It is a discharge standard that can be met in several ways:

- Install a BWMS that has been approved by the US Coast Guard
- use a supply of public water, such as drinking water
- use a BWMS that has been approved by a foreign Authority. These are called alternate management systems (AMS). It confers a short-term acceptance for a 'grandfather period' of 5 years after a vessel's compliance date, but the manufacturer also has to apply to the USCG for Type Approval in order for ships to continue using the system after the 5-year deadline
- retain ballast on board while in US waters
- discharge ballast water and sediment to a reception facility.

The US BW Discharge Standard has a different implementation schedule to the BW Convention (see Table 22.6).

BW capacity (m^3)	Vessel construction (keel laid) date	Vessel compliance date
All	On or after 1st December 2013	On delivery
<1,500 m³	Before 1st December 2013	First drydocking after 1st January 2016
1,500 to 5,000 m³	Before 1st December 2013	First drydocking after 1st January 2014
>5,000 m³	Before 1st December 2013	First drydocking after 1st January 2016

Table 22.6 - Implementation schedule for the US BW discharge rule

Note: These federal regulations do not prevent independent state action and 25 US states have established their own requirements for ballast water and other discharges.

California State BWM Performance Standards (performance and implementation)

The California BWM performance standards are more stringent than the USCG and IMO BWM Convention standards and also have a different implementation schedule (see Tables 22.7 and 22.8).

Organism size and type	California discharge requirements
Organisms ≥50 µm	No detectable living organisms
Organisms ≥10 to ≤50 µm	<0.01 living organisms/ml
Organisms ≤10 µm	<1,000 living bacteria/100 ml <10,000 living viruses/100 ml
Toxicogenic *Vibrio cholerae* (strains 01 and 0139)	<1 cfu/100 ml, or <1 cfu/1 gram (wet weight) (zooplankton sample)
Escherichia coli	<126 cfu/100 ml
Intestinal *Enterococci*	<33 cfu/100 ml

Note: cfu = colony forming unit

Table 22.7 - California BWM performance standards

Note: The final discharge standard for California is zero detectable living organisms for all organism size classes by 1st January 2020.

These requirements are mandatory at all Californian ports and affect the following ships:

- Vessels arriving in Californian waters from a port or place outside the Pacific coast region
- vessels arriving in Californian waters from a port or place within the Pacific coast region, with ballast water from the Pacific coast region.

Californian legislation accepts several methods for dealing with ballast water on board vessels arriving from outside the Pacific coast region:

- Retain ballast water (no discharge)
- mid-ocean BWE in waters more than 200 nm from the coast and at least 2,000 metres deep
- discharge of ballast water at the same location (within one nautical mile) it was taken on board
- use of an alternative Commission or Coast Guard Approved BWMS (USCG AMS)
- discharge to an approved reception facility (none currently exists)
- ships that have a BWMS on board must meet the California BW discharge standard and complete report forms.

Implementation schedule of California BWM performance standards		
Ballast water capacity of vessel	**Standards apply to new vessels in this size class constructed on or after**	**Standards apply to all other vessels in this size class beginning on**
<1,500 metric tons	1st January 2016	1st January 2018
1,500 to 5,000 metric tons	1st January 2016	1st January 2016
>5,000 metric tons	1st January 2016	1st January 2018

Table 22.8 - implementation schedule for the California BWM performance standards

Ballast Water Management

The Assessment of Ballast Water Management Systems

The IMO BWM Convention Requirements

These guidelines were designed to make sure that, as well as meeting the relevant performance standards (D-2), the technologies had minimal environmental impact, were suitable for use on ships and were robust enough for the job.

There are two sets of procedures for IMO Type Approval of BWM systems depending on the presence of an Active Substance (AS). The Administration decides whether or not a BWM system uses an AS.

G9 Definition:

"Active Substance" means a substance or organism, including a virus or a fungus, that has a general or specific action on or against harmful aquatic organisms and pathogens.

If an AS is not used, the system falls under the G8 Guidelines for Approval of Ballast Water Management Systems (Resolution MEPC.174 (58)). However, if it is decided that an AS is used, the BWM system is subject to the more stringent testing associated with the G9 Procedure for Approval of Ballast Water Management Systems that make use of Active Substances (Resolution MEPC.169(57)).

Type Approval certification must be carried out by the Flag Administration or a recognised organisation and is evidence that:

- The system has been tested according to G8 Guidelines and during the test it met the D-2 Standard
- there is confirmation of other parts of G8, including:
  - environmental testing
  - document review.

The US Ballast Water Discharge Standard Requirements

The US BW discharge rule insists that all vessels operating in US waters must have a BWMS that has either Coast Guard Type Approval or approval as an Alternate Management System (AMS). As of 19th February 2015, there have been 54 BWMS accepted as AMS by the US Coast Guard (ie they have different AMS identification numbers). Most systems are accepted for use in brackish and marine water but nine systems are also accepted for use in fresh water.

In order to operate within the jurisdiction of the Final Discharge Rule, all ballast water management systems must have Coast Guard Type Approval or use an AMS. If a BWMS is granted the temporary AMS designation, this:

- Is not a guarantee that a system will receive USCG Type Approval
- does not contribute directly towards gaining USCG Type Approval
- is not a necessary precursor for USCG Type Approval.

As yet, no BWMS has been granted USCG Type Approval and this approval process is expected to be a 'gold standard' for BWMS testing. The testing is more prescriptive than the current G8 Standards and leaves little scope for interpretation. This will give shippers more confidence that the BWMS will be compliant with the performance standards required. As of 23rd February 2015, there are only two

Type of system	Approval of environmental impact of discharged ballast water (GESAMP BWWG)	Approval of system (by Flag State)		Approval of environmental impact of discharged ballast water (GESAMP BWWG)	Issue of type approval certificate (by Flag State)
Using Active Substances (chemical disinfectants) eg chlorine, ClO_2 ozone	Basic approval	Land-based testing	Shipboard trials	Final approval	Type approval certificate
Not using Active Substances (chemical disinfectants) eg deoxygenation ultrasound		Land-based testing	Shipboard trials		Type approval certificate

Table 22.9 - IMO BWMS approval process

independent laboratories that are approved to test to USCG Type Approval standards: NSF® International (USA) and DNV GL AS (Norway).

Californian BW legislation recognises and accepts the use of a USCG accepted AMS for compliance with the state BW regulations.

BWM Concerns

It is important to note that a Type Approval certificate issued in accordance with the current G8 Guidelines is not a guarantee of performance. The G8 Guidelines for Approval of Ballast Water Management Systems (Resolution MEPC.174(58)) state that *"Approval of a system, however, does not ensure that a given system will work on all vessels or in all situations"*. The certificate:

- Does not provide an assurance that the system will continue to meet D-2
- does not verify safety issues other than sections 7 and 8 of G8
- does not certify compatibility with coatings of ballast tanks
- does not certify that any other standard can be met (for example US California state standards)
- does not certify that Class Society requirements are met
- does not confirm the reliability of the system.

When the Type Approval certificate is issued for a BWMS that does not use an Active Substance, there has been little consistency and rigour between the testing protocols of the Administrations. There has been considerable unease with this lack of robust testing in the G8 test procedures and this has been seen as a barrier for ratification of the BWM Convention. With this in mind, it was agreed at MEPC 67 that a comprehensive review of the Type Approval G8 Guidelines should be carried out with the results reported to MEPC 68.

Note: At MEPC 67, it was agreed that systems already installed on board ships would not be subject to penalisation should the G8 Standard be changed.

There are several elements that will be included in the review of G8 Guidelines (as stated in Resolution MEPC.253(67)):

- Testing being performed using fresh, brackish and marine waters
- testing considering the effect of temperature in cold and tropical waters on operational effectiveness and environmental acceptability

Ballast Water Management

- specification of standard test organisms for use in testing
- challenge levels set with respect to suspended solids in test water
- Type Approval testing discounting test runs in the full-scale testing that do not meet the D-2 Standard and the results of test runs being 'averaged'
- Type Approval testing realistically representing the flow rates the system is approved for
- any differences between Type Approval protocols of Member States
- any items raised by, and any data arising from, the study on the implementation of the ballast water performance standard described in Regulation D-2 of the Convention and any other relevant information provided within the timeline for the review of Guidelines (G8).

CSS Code

The Code of Safe Practice for Cargo Stowage and Securing (CSS Code)

The Code of Safe Practice for Cargo Stowage and Securing (CSS Code) was approved at the Maritime Safety Committee (MSC 54) in 1990, and adopted in 1991 by the IMO Assembly. The Code is regularly reviewed and amended by the MSC, and is referred to in SOLAS.

The Code is intended to provide an international standard that promotes the safe stowage and securing of cargoes to prevent ship casualties, injury and loss of life. To achieve this, the Code provides advice on the need to consider the suitability of ships for cargoes to be carried, securing measures, cargoes known to possess particular difficulties/hazards, carriage of appropriate securing equipment, actions in heavy seas and actions in the event of cargo shifting.

The general principles of stowage and securing of cargoes, described in the CSS Code, include:

- Cargoes are to be stowed and secured so that both the ship and those on board are not put at risk
- stowage and securing should be properly planned, executed and monitored
- personnel carrying out the tasks should be qualified and experienced
- personnel planning and executing the tasks should have sound practical knowledge of the application and content of the ship's Cargo Securing Manual
- improper stowage and securing will be potentially hazardous to other cargoes and the ship

CSS Code

- decisions taken regarding stowage and securing should be based on the most severe weather conditions that could be expected on the voyage
- ship handling decisions taken by the master, particularly in bad weather, should take into account the type and position of the stowage and securing arrangements.

Criteria for estimating the risk of a cargo shift include:

- The dimensional and physical properties of the cargo
- the location of the cargo and its stowage on board
- the suitability of the ship for the cargo
- the suitability of the cargo securing arrangements
- expected seasonal weather and sea conditions
- expected ship behaviour during the voyage
- the stability of the ship
- the geographical area and duration of the voyage.

Information Prior to Loading

It is important that the ship has sufficient information to plan cargo stowage. Section 1.9 of the CSS Code states:

"Prior to shipment the shipper should provide all necessary information about the cargo to enable the shipowner or ship operator to ensure that:

- *the different commodities to be carried are compatible with each other or suitably separated;*
- *the cargo is suitable for the ship;*
- *the ship is suitable for the cargo; and*
- *the cargo can be safely stowed and secured on board the ship and transported under all expected conditions during the intended voyage.*

The master should be provided with adequate information regarding the cargo to be carried so that its stowage may be properly planned for handling and transport".

Cargo Securing Manual

The CSS Code, in line with SOLAS Chapters VI and VII, requires the carriage on board of an approved Cargo Securing Manual. The cargo securing arrangements in this manual should be based on the forces expected to affect the cargo carried by the ship, calculated either in accordance with the methods described in Annex 13 of the CSS Code or an acceptable alternative.

FAL Convention

Convention on Facilitation of International Maritime Traffic, 1965, as amended (FAL Convention)

The FAL Convention was adopted in 1965 at the International Conference on Facilitation of Maritime Travel and Transport. Its main aim is to improve efficiency of maritime transport by limiting red tape and smoothing port/ship transitions.

Customs and immigration protocols vary throughout the world and the FAL Convention establishes clear procedures and an industry-wide standard covering:

- Arrival, stay and departure of the ship
- arrival and departure of persons and cargo
- stowaways
- public health and quarantine.

The FAL Committee developed seven standardised forms covering these procedures, and is a strong proponent of the global electronic data interchange (EDI) system for all ships and ports.

The FAL Convention reaffirms that every ship needs to carry certificates from their flag State that establish the seaworthiness, type of ship and competency of crew. These certificates should be available for inspection as required by Port State Control.

The approved list of necessary certification as of 2011 can be found in Annex 2 of the 2011 Convention.

Ship's Certificates

In the past ships were required to provide different documents at each port. The FAL Convention aims to reduce and harmonise documentation to only nine documents, with

FAL Convention

Courtesy of RH Kreuger

a standardised set of data requirements. Ships are required to carry the following documents, and the Convention provides standard forms for the first seven:

1. IMO General Declaration.
2. Cargo Declaration.
3. Ship's Stores Declaration.
4. Crew's Effects Declaration.
5. Crew List.
6. Passenger List.
7. Dangerous Goods Manifest.
8. The document required under the Universal Postal Convention for mail.
9. Maritime Declaration of Health.

Stowaways

Stowaways pose serious consequences for ships and the shipping industry. Not only are the physical risks very high for the individual stowaway, but their presence on board can lead to lengthy delays and complications for the ship. Annex 1 of the FAL Convention sets out clear procedures for:

- Prevention of stowaways while the ship is in port
- correct treatment of stowaways discovered on board
- disembarkation and return of stowaways.

Amendments

Since 1965, the Convention has undergone many amendments to tackle new problems including drug trafficking, stowaways, modernisation, improvements in communication and new regulations.

The most recent amendments came into force on 15th May 2010. That year also saw a review of the FAL Convention to ensure it meets the emerging needs of the modern shipping industry, particularly with regard to developments in technology.

In September 2010, the FAL Committee finalised and approved the addition of the Explanatory Manual to the Convention. The Manual is intended to help interpretation of the legal text of the Convention and to encourage Member States that are not part of the Convention to join. The Manual covers:

- Definitions and general provisions
- arrival, stay and departure of the ship
- arrival and departure of persons
- stowaways
- arrival, stay and departure of cargo and other articles
- public health and quarantine, including sanitary measures for animals and plants
- miscellaneous provisions.

FSS Code

The International Code for Fire Safety Systems (FSS Code)

The International Code for Fire Safety Systems (FSS Code) provides international standards of engineering specifications for fire safety systems required by SOLAS Chapter II-2, under which the Code is made mandatory.

Figure 22.3 - Fixed foam monitor

Fire safety regulation for shipping had previously been covered under SOLAS, but in December 2000 SOLAS Chapter II-2 was revised, with the subsequent amendments entering into force on 1st July 2002 as the FSS Code. The amendments focused on fire scenario processes rather than specific ship types. The FSS Code expands on many of the original technical provisions that had been transferred from the SOLAS Convention.

The FSS Code underwent major revision in 2010, with amendments adopted at MSC 88. A new Chapter 9 was added, relating to fixed fire detection and fire alarm systems. Chapters 5 and 8 were also amended at this time.

The addition of Chapter 16 entered into force on 1st January 2012, detailing fixed and portable gas detection requirements for new tankers.

The FSS Code provides regulation for:

- International shore connections
- personnel protection
- fire extinguishers
- fixed gas fire-extinguishing systems
- fixed foam fire-extinguishing systems
- fixed pressure water-spraying and water-mist fire-extinguishing systems
- automatic sprinkler, fire detection and fire alarm systems
- fixed fire detection and fire alarm systems
- sample extraction smoke detection systems
- low-location lighting systems
- fixed emergency fire pumps
- arrangement of means of escape
- fixed deck foam systems
- inert gas systems.

Figure 22.4 - Inert gas deck seal

Grain Code

The International Code for the Safe Carriage of Grain in Bulk (Grain Code)

Resolution MSC.23(59) for the introduction of an International Code for the Safe Carriage of Grain in Bulk was adopted on 23rd May 1991. The Code applies to all ships, irrespective of size, involved in the carriage of grain in bulk.

Grain has a tendency to shift and settle while in carriage. This can be very dangerous because stability may be compromised as the grain shifts with the movement vibration and rolling of the vessel.

Grain has a slip angle, or angle of repose, of about 20°. If a ship rolls more than the angle of repose, the grain will shift and may cause the ship to list or even capsize. The Code aims to prevent this from happening by providing detailed instructions on policy and procedures for the safe loading, carriage and discharge of grain from bulk carriers.

The Grain Code identifies grain as covering *"wheat, maize (corn), oats, rye, barley, rice, pulses, seeds and processed forms thereof, whose behaviour is similar to grain in its natural state"*.

Section 6 of the Code is concerned with the Ship's Stability and Grain Loading. It requires that a printed booklet (Grain Loading Manual) is provided, setting out the ship's particulars and stability data, to enable the master to ensure that the ship complies with the Code while on international voyage.

Section 7 of the Code deals with the specific stability requirements that ships carrying grain must adhere to throughout the voyage. The Code states that:

- *the angle of heel due to the shift of grain shall not be greater than 12° or in the case of ships constructed on or after 1 January 1994 the angle at which the deck edge is immersed, whichever is the lesser;*
- *in the statical stability diagram, the net or residual area between the heeling arm curve and the righting arm curve up to the angle of heel of maximum difference between the ordinates of the two curves, or 40° or the angle of flooding (θf), whichever is the least, shall in all conditions of loading be not less than 0.075 metre-radians; and*
- *the initial metacentric height, after correction for the free surface effects of liquids in tanks, shall be not less than 0.30 m.*

Documentation

A Document of Authorisation (DOA) is issued either by the Administration, contracting government or recognised organisation and is evidence that a ship is capable of compliance with the regulations of the Code. The DOA should be incorporated in, or accompany, the ship's Grain Loading Manual.

The Grain Loading Manual should assist the master to meet the stability requirements set out in Section 7. To achieve this, the Grain Loading Manual must reach the standards set out in Section 6.

Methods to Prevent Grain Shift

A ship that does not have on board a DOA issued in accordance with Section 3 of the Grain Code will only be permitted to load bulk grain in accordance with the conditions set out in Section 9 of the Grain Code. Depending on whether the hold is fully or partially filled, the following methods may be employed:

- The use of shifting boards
- saucering
- bundling
- overstowing
- strapping, lashing or securing.

Amendments

Resolution MSC.238(82) extends the BLU Code to ships carrying grain. It came into force on 1st January 2007. In the event of conflict between the BLU Code and the Grain Code, the provisions of the Grain Code will prevail.

HNS Convention

The International Convention on Liability and Compensation for Damage in Connection with the Carriage of Hazardous and Noxious Substances by Sea, 1996 as revised by the protocol of 2010 (2010 HNS Convention)

The purpose of the International Convention on Liability and Compensation for Damage in Connection with the Carriage of Hazardous and Noxious Substances by Sea (HNS), 1996 (and the 2010 Protocol) is to provide adequate,

prompt and effective compensation for loss or damage to persons, property and the environment arising from the carriage of HNS by sea.

The HNS Convention covers:

- Loss of life or personal injury on board or outside the ship carrying the HNS
- economic losses resulting from contamination
- costs of preventive measures, eg clean-up operations
- costs of reasonable measures of reinstatement of the environment.

The HNS Convention does not apply to oil pollution damage from tankers, as defined in the International Convention on Civil Liability for Oil Pollution Damage, nor does it apply to loss or damage as covered by the Bunkers Convention. It also excludes loss or damage caused by radioactive materials.

Hazardous and noxious substances are defined, for the purpose of the HNS Convention, by reference to the lists of substances in MARPOL 73/78 Annex II, Chapter 17 IBC Code, IMDG Code, IGC Code and BC Code.

OPRC-HNS Protocol

The Protocol on Preparedness, Response and Co-operation to Pollution Incidents by Hazardous and Noxious Substances, 2000 (OPRC HNS Protocol) was adopted at IMO on 15th March 2000 and ratified on 14th July 2006. It aims to establish national systems for preparedness and response and to provide a global framework for international cooperation in combating major incidents or threats of marine pollution.

1996 HNS Convention

The International Convention on Liability and Compensation for Damage in Connection with the Carriage of Hazardous and Noxious Substances (1996 HNS Convention) was adopted on 3rd May 1996. It dealt with compensation from HNS spills and has been superseded by the 2010 Convention.

2010 HNS Protocol

The protocol has been open for signature from 1st November 2010 and will come into force 18 months following the date when 12 states have ratified and:

- Four of which must have not less than 2 million units gross tonnage

HNS Convention

- the volume of contributing cargo for the general account must be of at least 40 million tonnes.

Compensation

First Tier

Under the HNS Convention, the shipowner is liable for loss or damage up to a certain amount (first tier). The shipowner is obliged to maintain insurance to cover this liability, which will normally be provided by P&I insurers.

Second Tier

A compensation fund (the HNS Fund) provides additional compensation when the victims do not obtain full compensation from the shipowner or his insurer (second tier). Compensation paid from the HNS Fund is limited to a maximum of 250 million Special Drawing Rights (SDR) inclusive of compensation paid under the first tier.

Necessity of the 2010 Protocol

Failure to implement the Convention has meant there is no international civil liability regime in place to compensate victims for loss or damage as a result of an incident involving HNS. The IMO secretary-general suggested that it is fortunate that no major incident involving ships carrying HNS occurred in the meantime as it would have galvanised public opinion and brought political pressure.

The need to ratify the HNS Convention was highlighted in October 2010 following the collision between the bulk carrier *'Hanjin Rizhao'* and the chemical tanker *'YM Uranus'* off Ushant in northwest France. Fortunately no pollution resulted from the collision, but if there *'had been pollution from the vessel's cargo of pygas (a naphtha-range product with a high aromatics content used either for gasoline blending or as a feedstock), the need for a compensation regime for victims of damage by HNS substances as offered by the failed 1996 HNS Convention would quickly have become clear'*[1].

Contributions to the HNS Fund for Packed Goods

One major issue associated with the 1996 HNS Convention was the requirement to collect data and set up a reporting system on the volumes of packaged HNS that are imported and exported by sea. This requirement was regarded as a great burden, due to the large volume and range of packaged goods transported by sea.

The 2010 Protocol resolved this problem by differentiating between bulk HNS and packaged HNS and by excluding packaged goods from the definition of contributing cargo in the Convention. This means that receivers of packaged HNS goods are exempt from the obligation to contribute to the HNS Fund.

There is also now no need for States to report on the movements of packaged goods, simplifying the administrative process.

Damage by packaged goods, however, remains covered by the compulsory insurance provisions of the Convention (the first tier of liability). Should the shipowner's insurance be insufficient to cover the damage, the HNS Fund will still pay out the excess even though receivers of packaged goods will no longer be providing financial contributions to the HNS Fund.

Liability for Contributions - Accounts

The HNS Fund is divided into four accounts financing the second tier on a market-sector basis:

- Oil
- LPG
- LNG
- General Account, ie other HNS substances including solid bulks and chemicals.

---

1 "*YM Uranus'* collision shows value of HNS Protocol' by Peter Swift, *Lloyd's List*, 13 October 2010.

It was considered disadvantageous for industries in which large volumes of cargo of a particular type are carried by sea to pay into a single account. It was regarded as unfair that these high volume cargoes, while not necessarily more dangerous but simply because of their sheer mass, would be obliged to cross subsidise other hazardous and noxious cargoes carried in much lower volumes.

The effect of having separate accounts is that receivers of oil, LNG and LPG will only become liable to contribute if and when an incident occurs involving oil, LNG or LPG, respectively. In the case of the general account and the oil and LPG accounts, the person responsible for making the initial as well as any subsequent annual contributions is the receiver. The person liable for making contributions to the LNG account is the person who, in the preceding calendar year, held title to an LNG cargo immediately prior to discharge.

This provision was implemented in view of the unique contractual arrangements for the purchase and transport of LNG.

The 2010 Protocol shifts the responsibility for payment to the receiver at the point of discharge, unless there is an agreement for the titleholder to assume responsibility.

Sanctions Against States that do not Fulfil their Obligations

Contracting States are obliged to submit reports on contributing cargo at the time of ratifying the Convention and on an annual basis. These reports are essential for both meeting the entry into force requirements and the management and administration of the HNS Fund.

Failure to submit annual reports after ratification, but before entry into force of the protocol, will result in temporary suspension from being a Contracting State until the reports are submitted.

States that fail to submit reports once the Protocol enters into force will be prohibited, by the Protocol, from claiming compensation until their reports are brought up to date (except in claims for death and personal injury).

IBC Code

International Code for the Construction and Equipment of Ships Carrying Dangerous Chemicals in Bulk (IBC Code)

The IBC Code provides the international standard for the safe carriage of dangerous and noxious liquid chemicals in bulk, by prescribing the design and construction standards of ships and the necessary equipment they should carry.

The IBC Code was adopted by the Maritime Safety Committee (MSC) on 17th June 1983

IBC Code

and, under the provisions of SOLAS Chapter VII, applies to chemical tankers constructed after 1st July 1986.

The IBC Code was extended by the Marine Environment Protection Committee (MEPC) on 5th December 1985 to cover marine pollution under the provisions of MARPOL Annex II.

The Code was amended in October 2004 to keep it consistent with the revised MARPOL Annex II - Regulations for the control of pollution by noxious liquid substances (NLS) in bulk. The amended Code entered into force on 1st January 2007.

The IBC Code applies to all chemical tankers constructed after 1st July 1986, regardless of their size, including ships under 500 GT. It covers liquids with a vapour pressure not exceeding 0.28 MPa absolute at a temperature of 37.8°C, but excludes petroleum or similar flammable products.

Chemical tankers constructed before 1st July 1986 must comply with the *Code for the Construction and Equipment of Ships Carrying Dangerous Chemicals in Bulk* (BCH Code).

IBC Code Ship Types

Chapter 17 of the IBC Code provides a tabulated summary of the minimum requirements for the carriage of identified chemicals and NLS products in bulk by sea, including:

- Pollution category
- hazards
- ship type
- tank type
- tanks vents
- tank environmental control (eg inerting medium)
- fire protection
- emergency equipment.

The IBC Code categorises ships into three types according to the hazard that the cargo poses. Type 1 vessels carry very hazardous noxious liquid chemicals and Type 3 vessels carry low hazard noxious liquid chemicals.

The IBC Code requires that the ship is capable of withstanding damage according to certain assumptions based on type and length.

Type 1 Ship:

> *"A type 1 ship is a chemical tanker intended to transport chapter 17 products with very severe environmental and safety hazards which require maximum preventive measures to preclude an escape of such cargo."*

The vessel will have a double skin and double bottom with a maximum permissible tank size of 1,250 m^3.

Cargo tanks should be located:

- Transversely - the lesser of B/5 or 11.5 m measured at right angles from the ship's side
- Vertically - the lesser of B/15 or 6 m measured at right angles from the ship's bottom plating.

Figure 22.5 - Type 2 chemical tanker deck

Type 2 Ship:

> *"A type 2 ship is a chemical tanker intended to transport chapter 17 products with appreciably severe environmental and safety hazards which require significant preventive measures to preclude an escape of such cargo."*

The vessel will have a double skin and double bottom with a maximum permissible tank size of 3,000 m^3.

Cargo tanks should be located:

- Transversely – not less than 760 mm measured at right angles from the ship's side
- Vertically – the lesser of B/15 or 6 m measured vertically from the ship's bottom plating.

Type 3 Ship:

'A type 3 ship is a chemical tanker intended to transport chapter 17 products with sufficiently severe environmental and safety hazards which require a moderate degree of containment to increase survival capability in a damaged condition.'

These are single skin vessels, constructed with an increased degree of subdivision.

Cargo tanks have no location requirement in the IBC Code.

Figure 22.6 - Inert gas system

Certificate of Fitness

The International Certificate of Fitness for the Carriage of Dangerous Chemicals in Bulk lists the products that the ship is authorised to carry, the conditions of carriage (tanks, segregation, valve settings, etc) and the pollution category.

The certificate must be consulted to determine whether the ship is permitted to load a cargo. The MARPOL Annex II Procedures and Arrangements Manual must be consulted for the carriage requirements.

Marine Pollutants

Substances that present pollution hazards and are assessed or provisionally assessed under MARPOL Annex II Regulation 6.3 may be carried under the requirements of the Code.

Disposal of tank washings is governed by MARPOL Annex II and discharge of NLS into the sea is only permitted if done in full compliance with the provisions. NLS cargoes are divided into four categories; X, Y, Z and Other Substances (OS), based on the severity of the pollution hazard. MARPOL Annex II specifies:

"Category X:

Noxious liquid substances which, if discharged into the sea from tank cleaning or deballasting operations, are deemed to present a major hazard to either marine resources or human health and, therefore, justify the prohibition of the discharge into the marine environment;

Category Y:

Noxious liquid substances which, if discharged into the sea from tank cleaning or deballasting operations, are deemed to present a hazard to either marine resources or human health or cause harm to amenities or other legitimate uses of the sea and

IBC Code

therefore justify a limitation on the quality and quantity of the discharge into the marine environment;

Category Z:

Noxious liquid substances which, if discharged into the sea from tank cleaning or deballasting operations, are deemed to present a minor hazard to either marine resources or human health and therefore justify less stringent restrictions on the quality and quantity of the discharge into the marine environment;

Other substances:

Substances indicated as OS (Other Substances) in the pollution category column of chapter 18 of the International Bulk Chemical Code which have been evaluated and found to fall outside category X, Y or Z as defined in regulation 6.1 of this Annex because they are, at present, considered to present no harm to marine resources, human health, amenities or other legitimate uses of the sea when discharged into the sea from tank cleaning or deballasting operations. The discharge of bilge or ballast water or other residues or mixtures containing only substances referred to as "Other Substances" shall not be subject to any requirements of the Annex."

The 2007 revised Annex II specifies only the Antarctic as a Special Area. However, no discharge of residues containing noxious substances is permitted within 12 miles of the nearest land and more stringent restrictions apply to the Baltic and Black Sea areas.

Procedures and Arrangements Manual

An approved Procedures and Arrangements Manual (P&A Manual) providing ship-specific requirements is required for ships certified to carry substances of category X, Y or Z on board.

Shipboard Marine Pollution Emergency Plan (SMPEP)

An approved shipboard marine pollution emergency plan is required for every ship of 150 gross tonnage and above certified to carry NLS in bulk.

MARPOL Annex II Related Onboard Documentation

Cargo Record Book

All ships to which Annex II applies must carry and maintain a Cargo Record Book. This must be completed on a tank-to-tank basis for all cargo handling, tank washing and ballast operations.

Any discharges into the sea, for whatever reason, must also be recorded. The master and the officer in charge of the operation should sign each entry.

IGC Code

Figure 22.7 - LNG Carrier loading at Hammerfest, Norway

International Code for the Construction and Equipment of Ships Carrying Liquefied Gases in Bulk (IGC Code)

The International Code for the Construction and Equipment of Ships Carrying Liquefied Gases in Bulk was adopted in 1983 and has had several amendments since. While regulation has at times struggled to keep pace with the rate of development in the gas sector, the Code provides guidelines to gas tankers on operational, construction and safety aspects. The main purpose of the Code is to minimise risks to the ships, their crews and the environment.

Areas covered in the IGC Code include:

- Damage limitation to cargo and survival capability in the event of damage
- ship safety arrangements
- cargo containment and cargo handling procedures
- material of construction for containment and carriage facility
- cargo loading and discharging
- fire protection
- pollution control
- use of cargo, vapour or boil-off gas as ship's machinery fuel
- thermal expansion and contraction.

The IGC Code applies to gas carriers constructed on or after 1st July 1986 carrying liquefied gases in bulk having a vapour pressure of more than 2.8 bar at 37.8°C, and other identified products. The revised Code is intended to apply to gas carriers constructed on or after 1st July 2016.

Significant revisions of the Code include:

- Increased separation of cargo tanks from side shell to be between 0.8 m and 2.0 m, as a function of the volume of the individual tank, so as to be consistent with the provisions in MARPOL Annex I for oil tankers. This will affect fully refrigerated LPG carriers
- new requirements for cargo sampling connections, cargo filters, water curtains and the design of high pressure fuel gas system piping for safe handling of all cargo and process liquid and vapour
- new requirement to monitor the quantity of inert gas flowing into individual insulation spaces when the inert gas system is part of the required leak detection system
- a complete re-write of Chapter 10 to incorporate and be consistent with IEC 60092 standards relative to the design of electrical installations to minimise the risk of fire and explosion from flammable products and to ensure availability of electrical generation and distribution systems relating to the safe handling of cargo and its vapour
- separate gas detection systems for primary and secondary insulation spaces in membrane containment systems
- carriage of an approved Cargo Operations Manual addressing the hazards and properties of the cargoes permitted to be carried.

IGC Code

Chapter 19 of the Code summarises the minimum and special requirements for the carriage of identified products.

Certificate of Fitness

A gas carrier engaged on international voyages must hold an International Certificate of Fitness for the Carriage of Liquefied Gases in Bulk. This confirms that the vessel has been surveyed in accordance with Section 5 of the Code and complies with the relevant provisions of the Code. The Certificate identifies the products that the ship can carry and the conditions of loading and carriage. The Certificate remains valid for a period specified by the Administration, and issue of a new Certificate is dependent on further satisfactory survey.

Gas Tanker Types

Gas tankers are designed to carry different products requiring varying degrees of preventative measures. They are built to a standard designated as either Type 1G, 2G, 2PG or 3G, identified in the IGC Code as follows:

.1 *A type 1G ship is a gas carrier intended to transport products indicated in chapter 19 which require maximum preventive measures to preclude the escape of such cargo.*

.2 *A type 2G ship is a gas carrier intended to transport products indicated in chapter 19 which require significant preventive measures to preclude the escape of such cargo.*

.3 *A type 2PG ship is a gas carrier of 150 m in length or less intended to transport products indicated in chapter 19 which require significant preventive measures to preclude escape of such cargo, and where the products are carried in independent type C tanks designed (see 4.2.4.4) for a MARVS of at least 7 bar gauge and a cargo containment system design temperature of -55°C or above. Note that a ship of this description but over 150 m in length is to be considered a type 2C ship.*

.4 *A type 3G ship is a gas carrier intended to carry products indicated in chapter 19 which require moderate preventive measures to preclude the escape of such cargo.*

Revised IGC Code enters into force 1st January 2016

The revised International Code for the Construction and Equipment of Ships Carrying Liquefied Gases in Bulk (the IGC Code) was adopted by the MSC in May 2014. It will enter into force on 1st January 2016, with an implementation/application date of 1st July 2016.

The IGC Code was first adopted in 1983, to provide an international standard for the safe carriage by sea of liquefied gases (and other substances listed in the Code) in bulk, by prescribing the design and construction standards of ships carrying such cargoes, and the equipment they should carry. The IGC Code was made mandatory under the SOLAS Convention for new ships built after 1986. Various amendments have been adopted since then, but the new draft represents the first major revision of the IGC Code.

IMDG Code

The International Maritime Dangerous Goods Code (IMDG Code)

The International Maritime Dangerous Goods (IMDG) Code is an international code for the shipment of dangerous goods by sea. It covers packing, container traffic, stowage and segregation of dangerous goods, and provides recommendations for packing, labelling, handling and emergency response during incidents.

Originally adopted at the IMO Assembly in 1965, it was not until the amendments to SOLAS Chapter VII, adopted by the IMO in Resolution MSC.122 (75) on 24th May 2002, that the IMDG Code became mandatory on 1st January 2004. These amendments are referred to as Amendment 31.

Updating the Code

The Code is constantly evolving and is updated every two years to take into account:

- Any new dangerous goods that should be included
- new technology and methods of working relating to the handling of dangerous goods
- any concerns about safety that have arisen due to a previous experience.

Each new version of the Code is given a sequential Amendment number.

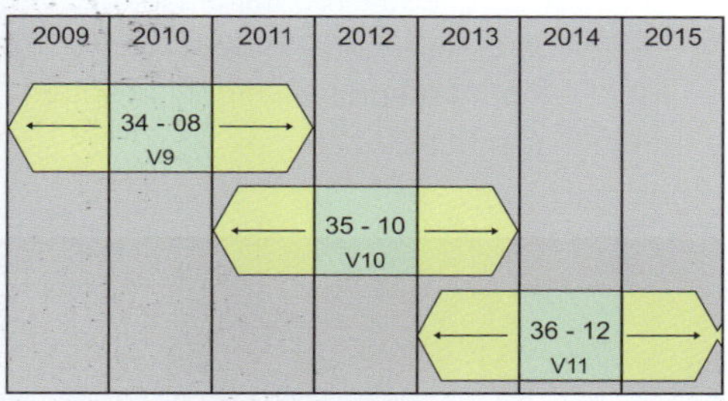

Figure 22.8 - The amendment cycle

As shown in the chart:

- Each amendment is valid for three years
- implementation takes place on alternate years
- the yellow areas show that a new amendment has been published in the January of that year and should be used immediately; this will depend on the timing of the National Competent Authority adoption
- during the yellow period of time, the previous amendment can be used
- during the green years, only the green amendment can be used.

IMDG Code

IMDG Code Structure

The two-volume Code is divided into seven parts:

Volume 1 – Parts 1, 2 and 4-7 of the Code

- General provisions, definitions, training and security provisions
- classification – dangerous goods classes 1 to 9 and marine pollutants
- packing and tank provisions – including the use of intermediate bulk containers (IBCs), portable tanks and bulk containers
- consignment procedures – markings, labelling and documentation
- construction and testing of packaging, IBCs, large packaging portable tanks and road tank vehicles
- transport operations – stowage, segregation, transport of units on ships, packing of units, exemptions, special incident and fire provisions.

Volume 2

- The dangerous goods list presented in tabular format (contains references to the emergency schedules contained in the Supplement, for spillage or fire)
- list of generic and proper shipping names
- limited quantities exceptions
- glossary.

Supplement

The Supplement to the IMDG Code contains the following:

- Emergency Response Procedures for Ships Carrying Dangerous Goods (EmS Guide), containing Emergency schedules for fire and Emergency schedules for spillage
- Medical First Aid Guide for Use in Accidents Involving Dangerous Goods (MFAG). This contains:
  - an emergency action and diagnosis flow chart
  - tables giving brief instructions for various medical emergencies
  - appendices giving more comprehensive medical information, lists of medicines/drugs and a list of chemicals requiring special treatment
  - reporting procedures for accidents and incidents involving dangerous goods
- Reporting procedures
- IMO/ILO/UNECE Guidelines for Packing of Cargo Transport Units (CTUs)
- Recommendations on the safe use of pesticides in ships
- International Code for the Safe Carriage of Packaged Irradiated Nuclear Fuel, Plutonium and High-Level Radioactive Wastes on board Ships (INF Code).

A ship carrying dangerous goods must have a manifest or a detailed stowage plan identifying the positions of all dangerous goods. The class of dangerous goods should be clearly identified.

When loading a cargo of dangerous goods, the shipper should provide a Dangerous Goods Declaration (Dangerous Goods Note) identifying the characteristics and quantity of the cargo referred to.

All ships carrying dangerous goods should have on board a Document of Compliance issued by the flag State certifying the classes of dangerous goods that can be carried, their permissible stowage positions and additional requirements concerning pollution or safety equipment required on board.

IMSBC Code

The International Maritime Solid Bulk Cargoes Code (IMSBC Code)

The International Maritime Solid Bulk Cargoes Code (IMSBC Code) is intended to aid the safe stowage and shipment of solid bulk cargoes through the provision of cargo characteristics and procedural instructions.

On 4th December 2008, the Maritime Safety Committee adopted the IMSBC Code in Resolution MSC.268(85). The Code is developed from the Code of Safe Practice for Solid Bulk Cargoes (BC Code) and is a revised, updated and mandatory regulation for ships with dry bulk cargoes. The Code entered into force on 1st January 2011. Some parts are recommendatory and, as with all IMO instruments, the terminology used denotes this:

- *'Shall'* the provision is *mandatory*
- *'Should'* the provision is *recommendatory*
- *'May'* the provision is *optional.*

Ships carrying solid bulk cargoes may be at risk of:

- Structural damage due to improper cargo distribution
- loss of stability due to liquefaction of cargo
- cargo shift
- cargoes chemically reacting and posing a danger to the ship and crew.

All ships that carry solid bulk cargoes or dangerous solid bulk cargoes, irrespective of their keel-laying date or gross tonnage, must comply with the IMSBC Code.

IMSBC Code

The IMSBC Code categorises cargoes as follows:

- Group A - cargoes that may liquefy if exposed to moisture content in excess of their transportable moisture limit
- Group B - cargoes that pose a chemical hazard that could result in a threat to the ship and crew
- Group C - cargoes that are not liable to liquefy and that do not possess chemical hazards.

Sections 1 to 10 of the IMSBC Code are mandatory and cover, among other things:

- Loading, carriage and unloading precautions
- safety of personnel and ship
- assessment of acceptability of consignments for safe shipment
- trimming procedures
- methods of determining the angle of repose
- cargoes that may liquefy
- chemical hazards of cargoes.

Sections 11 to 13 provide recommendatory information and additional advice on security, stowage factor conversion tables and related IMO instruments.

The Appendices contain individual schedules of solid bulk cargoes, test procedures, and properties of solid bulk cargoes.

Terms of the IMSBC Code

Cargoes listed in the IMSBC Code are given a Bulk Cargo Shipping Name (BCSN). The BCSN is the official name of the cargo and it shall be referred to as such in all sea transport documentation.

Hazardous substances shall also have a UN number - a four digit number that identifies it as hazardous. Sometimes chemicals or products that have similar properties receive a common UN number. The state of the substance or concentration can mean different UN numbers too.

The IMSBC Code contains detailed schedules for each type of cargo. These provide a detailed analysis of the substance, the environmental conditions it should be carried

in and precautions to be taken during loading, stowage, transportation and discharge.

Section 1.3 contains general provisions for carriage of bulk cargo not listed in the IMSBC Code. Shippers are required to provide a description of cargo characteristics to the necessary authorities of the load port, who will assess the acceptability of the cargo for safe shipment.

If the port authority finds that the cargo presents hazards as defined by Group A or B of the Code, it must liaise with the discharge port authority and the ship's flag State to determine suitable conditions.

Supplement

The Supplement to the IMSBC Code contains the following documents:

- BLU Code - Code of Practice for the Safe Loading and Unloading of Bulk Carriers
- BLU Manual - Manual on loading and unloading of solid bulk cargoes for terminal representatives

- uniform method of measurement of the density of bulk cargoes
- lists of solid bulk cargoes for which a fixed gas fire-extinguishing system may be exempted or for which a fixed gas fire-extinguishing system is ineffective
- recommendations for entering enclosed spaces aboard ships
- recommendations on the safe use of pesticides in ships applicable to the fumigation of cargo holds
- guidelines for the submission of information and completion of the format for the properties of cargoes not listed in the IMSBC Code and their conditions of carriage
- guidelines for developing and approving procedures for sampling, testing and controlling the moisture content for solid bulk cargoes which may liquefy
- contact names and addresses of designated national competent authorities responsible for the safe carriage of grain and solid bulk cargoes.

Amendments

On 20th May 2011, the IMO's Maritime Safety Committee adopted Resolution MSC.318(89). The requirements became mandatory on 1st January 2013. To keep pace with developments, it was agreed that the IMSBC Code should be updated bi-annually.

Figure 22.9 - View from the bridge wing of the 'Vale Rio De Janeiro', 400,000 Dwt Rotterdam

Intact Stability

International Code on Intact Stability, 2008

Figure 22.10 - Cargo control room

This Code was adopted on 4th December 2008 at MSC 58 by Resolution MSC.267(85). Its purpose is to ensure the safe operation of ships through the provision of mandatory and recommendatory stability criteria.

The IMO had previously adopted intact stability criteria set out in the Code on Intact Stability for All Types of Ships Covered by IMO Instruments (IS Code) in 1993. This Code covered general precautions against capsizing, weather criterion, effect of free surfaces, icing, watertight integrity and operational aspects.

The International Code on Intact Stability (2008 IS Code) was adopted to take account of developments and to provide mandatory and recommended provisions in a single document.

Part A

Part A contains mandatory criteria on application of the Code, dynamic stability phenomena in waves, righting lever curve properties, severe wind and rolling criterion, and special criteria for certain types of ships.

Figure 22.11 - Ice accretion on deck

Part B

Part B focuses on additional guidelines and recommendations.

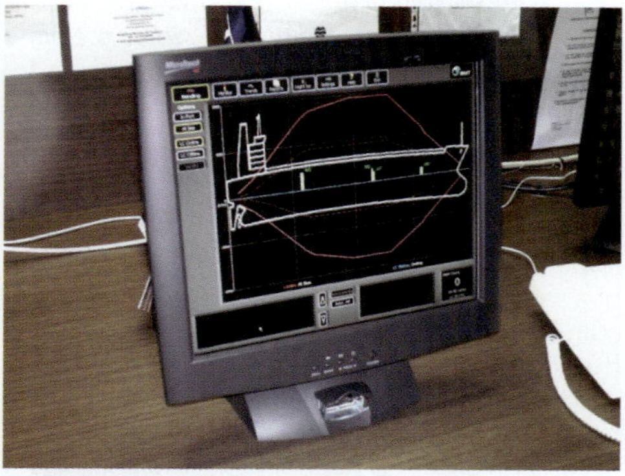

Figure 22.12 - Passive stability computer

Chapter 3 contains information concerning preparation of stability information, focusing on tank calculations, loading conditions and stability curves.

The ship must carry an instrument covering all stability requirements applicable to the ship. However, requirements only encompass passive systems and the off-line operation mode of active systems.

Documentation/Certification

Each ship must be provided with a stability booklet approved by the Administration containing information, set out in Part B, to enable the master to operate in compliance with the Code. Any stability instrument used as a supplement must be approved by the Administration.

A lightweight survey should be carried out on all passenger ships at periodic intervals not exceeding five years to verify any changes in lightship displacement and longitudinal centre of gravity.

Amendments

Resolution MSC.319(89) was adopted on 20th May 2011 as an amendment to Part B. It includes a change relating to Mobile Offshore Drilling Units in light of the 2009 and previous versions of the MODU Code.

Figure 22.13 - Oil tanker hull stress monitor

ISM Code

International Safety Management Code (ISM Code)

During the 1980s, there were a number of serious incidents resulting in pollution and loss of life, including the capsizing of the *'Herald of Free Enterprise'* on 6th March 1987. As a result, in 1989 the IMO at its 16th Assembly adopted Resolution A.647(16) *Guidelines on Management for the Safe Operation of Ships and for Pollution Prevention*. These guidelines were intended to provide the structure to a system where development, assessment and implementation of a culture of safety, pollution prevention and general good practice could be achieved.

With the entry into force on 1st July 1998 of SOLAS Chapter IX, *Management for the Safe Operation of Ships*, the International Safety Management (ISM) Code became mandatory.

A number of Amendments have since entered into force, the latest on 1st July 2010. In addition to amending the requirements for the renewal verification and certification of the Safety Management Certificate (SMC) and the Document of Compliance (DOC), greater emphasis is now placed on companies defining procedures rather than making preparations for the facilitation of them.

Objectives

The objectives of the ISM Code are:

> *"...to ensure safety at sea, prevention of human injury or loss of life, and avoidance of damage to the environment, in particular to the marine environment and to property."*

Through the development and implementation of a safety culture within the shipping industry, the Code seeks to provide an international standard of excellence for safe management and operation of ships and for pollution prevention. By minimising the potential for large scale accidents, the Code aims to eliminate the opportunities for small incidents to occur.

As no two shipping companies or even ships are the same, the Code is expressed in broad principled terms with general objectives to enable the widest application.

The ISM Code concentrates on Safety Management Systems (SMS), which are audited annually to ensure compliance with the Code.

Responsibility

Under the ISM Code, the company is ultimately responsible for the ships it operates. The company may be the shipowner, ship manager or a bare boat charterer. The responsibility for the day-to-day management of the ship thus lies with both those ashore and aboard.

The Code emphasises the importance of a strong, positive relationship between those aboard and ashore to ensure that the company is able to establish a clear structured management system, make practice safer and improve good practice and efficiency. The SMS for those aboard and ashore should establish clearly defined roles and detail all the lines of communication through the company for a good management system.

Designated Person Ashore (DPA)

The ISM Code requires appointment of a Designated Person Ashore (DPA) to provide a clear link from those on board the ship to the highest level of management in the company.

Any member of the ship has the right to contact the DPA if they wish. This allows for direct and open reporting of issues.

The master remains the head of the ship's management and has the power to make decisions, in certain circumstances, that do not necessarily comply with SMS procedures. The master's professional judgement must be respected in such circumstances and the designated person made aware of his decision as quickly as possible.

To implement the ISM Code effectively, the SMS must identify all the safety and environmental hazards that may be faced by the ship. Risk assessment is crucial in this process as an unidentified risk cannot be managed. An effective SMS should include:

- Written procedures
- training and familiarisation programs
- hazard identification
- positive reporting procedures
- monitoring
- regular safety committees
- programs for drills and exercises for emergency actions.

Functional Requirements

The functional requirements (the aspects that need to be achieved) for the application of an SMS include:

.1 a safety and environmental-protection policy;

.2 instructions and procedures to ensure safe operation of ships and protection of the environment in compliance with relevant international and flag State legislation;

.3 defined levels of authority and lines of communication between, and amongst, shore and shipboard personnel;

.4 procedures for reporting accidents and non-conformities with the provisions of this Code;

.5 procedures to prepare for and respond to emergency situations; and

.6 procedures for internal audits and management reviews

Certification

Document of Compliance

A Document of Compliance (DOC) is valid for five years and is subject to an annual external audit, the timing of which is usually arranged by the DPA. If a ship is found to be non-compliant, its certification is invalidated. If a ship entering a port is found to be non-compliant or non-certificated, it can be detained by the port authority or sent back to sea and banned from entering the port.

Safety Management Certificate

A Safety Management Certificate (SMC) is issued to every ship by the Administration or Recognised Organisation after verification that the shipboard management is operated in line with the approved SMS.

Auditing

Auditing is essential in ensuring the SMS is operating correctly and that the requirements of the ISM Code are being upheld.

Auditing will help to establish why a system failure may have occurred and why the applied system did not prevent it.

Auditing of the SMS may be carried out internally, ie by auditors within the company, or externally by a flag State with whom the responsibility for issuing the DOC lies. A flag State can delegate this role to a Recognised Organisation that carries out survey and certification work on the flag State's behalf.

ISM Code

During an audit, the following terms, varying in severity, may be used where a deviation from the SMS has occurred:

Observation - *a statement of fact made during a safety management audit and substantiated by objective evidence.*

Non-conformity - *an observed situation where objective evidence indicates the non-fulfilment of a specified requirement.*

Major non-conformity - *an identifiable deviation that poses a serious threat to the safety of personnel or the ship or a serious risk to the environment that requires immediate corrective action or the lack of effective and systematic implementation of a requirement of this Code.*

ISPS Code

International Ship and Port Facility Security Code (ISPS Code)

The global security threat has been increasing for many years and particular concerns for the shipping industry include terrorism, stowaways, piracy, drug smuggling and human trafficking. These issues required a more effective system of security to be established.

The International Ship and Port Facility Security Code (ISPS Code) was developed by the Maritime Safety Committee and adopted in December 2002 through a new SOLAS Chapter XI-2 on *Special measures to enhance maritime security*. The Code entered into force on 1st July 2004.

The Convention also adopted Resolution 11 on human-element-related aspects and shore leave for seafarers. This Resolution emphasises the importance of the human element, shore leave and the need to afford special protection to seafarers. There must be a balance between human rights, security and the efficient movement of ships and cargoes.

The ISPS Code applies to all passenger ships, cargo ships of 500 GT or more and mobile offshore drilling units.

The Code has two parts, with mandatory requirements in Part A and guidance in Part B.

Under the ISPS Code, Contracting Governments can appoint Designated Authorities to undertake security duties, for example the Maritime Safety Authority in New Zealand.

Objectives of the ISPS Code

The objectives of the ISPS Code are:

- *To establish an international framework involving co-operation between Contracting Governments, Government agencies, local administrations and the shipping and port industries to detect/assess security threats and take preventive measures against security incidents affecting ships or port facilities used in international trade to establish the respective roles and responsibilities of all these parties concerned, at the national and international level, for ensuring maritime security;*

ISPS Code

- *to ensure the early and efficient collection and exchange of security-related information;*
- *to provide a methodology for security assessments so as to have in place plans and procedures to react to changing security levels; and*
- *to ensure confidence that adequate and proportionate maritime security measures are in place.*

Functional Requirements of the ISPS Code

To achieve the objective of providing effective and proportionate maritime security between ship and port, the ISPS Code sets out the following functional requirements:

- Gathering and assessing information with respect to security threats and exchanging such information with appropriate Contracting Governments
- maintenance of communication protocols for ships and port facilities
- prevention of unauthorised access to ships, port facilities and their restricted areas
- prevention of the introduction of unauthorised weapons, incendiary devices or explosives to ships or port facilities
- providing means for raising the alarm in reaction to security threats or security incidents
- requiring ship and port facility security plans based upon security assessments
- requiring training, drills and exercises to ensure familiarity with security plans and procedures.

The Ship's ISPS Plan

In practice, the ship's ISPS plan is an extension of the ship's Safety Management System plans. However, the SMS relates primarily to the voyage, where as the ISPS plan focuses on ports and port authority control areas.

Security Levels

There are three security levels; 1 indicates the lowest threat and 3 the greatest threat:

- ***Level 1, Normal*** – *"the level for which minimum appropriate protective security measures shall be maintained at all times."*
- ***Level 2, Heightened*** – *"the level for which appropriate additional protective security measures shall be maintained for a period of time as a result of heightened risk of a security incident."*

ISPS Code

- ***Level 3, Exceptional*** – *"the level for which further specific protective security measures shall be maintained for a limited period of time when a security incident is probable or imminent, although it may not be possible to identify the specific target".*

Roles

The ISPS Code outlines the different roles, functions and expectations of various people involved in security for ships and port facilities. The Code describes the duties of persons undertaking the following roles:

- Ship Security Officer (SSO) - duties include liaising with the CSO, cooperating with the PFSO, and implementing and upholding the ship security plan
- Company Security Officer (CSO) - duties include ensuring that a Ship Security Assessment (SSA) has been completed for each ship
- Port Facility Security Officer (PFSO)
- shipboard personnel with specific security duties
- port facility personnel with specific security duties.

Certification

International Ship Security Certificate

All ships covered by the Code are subject to periodic verification that their security system and associated security equipment meet the provisions of the Code and the approved Ship Security Plan. If the ship is compliant, it will be issued with an International Ship Security Certificate. Without this, the ship could be subject to serious delays, legal penalties and denial of entry to ports.

Ship Security Plan

Each ship must carry on board a security plan approved by the Administration. The plan must make provision for the three security levels defined in the Code.

Ship Security Assessment

A critical part of the ship security plan is completion of the Ship Security Assessment (SSA), which must include:

- Identification of existing security measures, procedures and operations
- identification and evaluation of key shipboard operations
- identification of threats to key shipboard operations and establishing security measures based on priority and likelihood of occurrence
- identification of weaknesses, including human factors, infrastructure, policies and procedures.

A copy of the SSA must be placed in the company records, protected from unauthorised access or disclosure, and presented if required for a Declaration of Security or other incidence.

Declaration of Security

A Declaration of Security (DOS) demonstrates that an agreement has been reached between the ship and the port facility over the security measures to be undertaken by each party.

Contracting Governments should determine when a DOS is required to be submitted by a ship to a port facility and section A/5 of the ISPS Code details when a ship can request a DOS from a port facility. A ship can request completion of a DOS when:

- The ship is operating at a higher level of security than the port facility or another ship it is interfacing with
- there is an agreement on a DOS between Contracting Governments covering certain international voyages or specific ships on those voyages
- the ship or port has been involved in a security threat or incident

- the ship is at a port which is not required to have and implement an approved port facility security plan
- the ship is conducting ship to ship activities with another ship not required to have and implement an approved ship security plan.

Port Facility Security Plan

Each port is required to develop and maintain a Port Facility Security Plan (PFSP) based on a Port Facility Security Assessment. The PFSP should cover prevention of weapons or other substances or devices being introduced into the port, unauthorised access, response to security threats or breaches, procedures for evacuation, security of cargo and cargo handling equipment, and procedures for facilitating shore leave, crew changes, and access to visitors including seafarer welfare and labour organisations.

Load Lines Convention

International Convention on Load Lines, 1966 and Protocol of 1988, as Amended in 2003

The Load Lines Convention provides regulations for the assignment of a ship's freeboard, depending on the type and structure of the ship, areas that she will trade in and the safety measures assigned to that vessel.

Assigned load lines must be marked amidships on each side of the vessel, together with the deck line. Vessels intended for the carriage of timber deck cargo are granted a smaller freeboard, with the deck cargo regarded as giving a ship a certain additional buoyancy and a greater degree of protection against the sea.

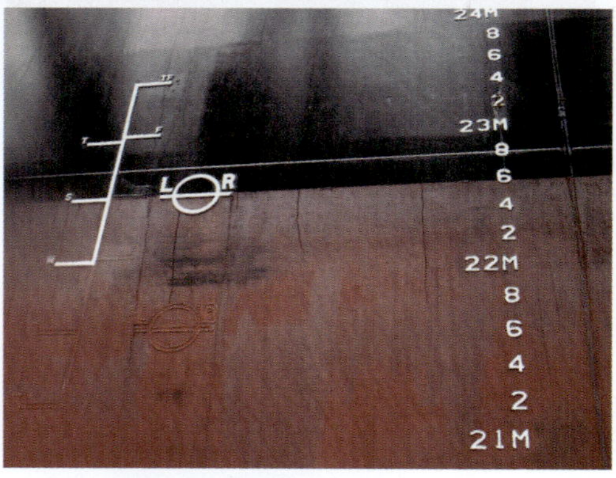

Figure 22.14 - VLCC load lines

Load Lines Convention

To calculate freeboard, ships are categorised as either type 'A' or type 'B'. In simple terms, type 'A' ships are tankers and type 'B' non-tankers. Regulation 27 of the Convention states:

> **Type 'A'** *"...designed to carry only liquid cargoes in bulk, and in which cargo tanks have only small access openings closed by watertight gasketed covers of steel or equivalent material. Such a ship necessarily has the following inherent features:*
>
> *a) high integrity of the exposed deck; and*
>
> *b) high degree of safety against flooding, resulting from the low permeability of loaded cargo spaces and the degree of subdivision usually provided."*

Figure 22.15 - Small inspection hatch on a VLCC

Figure 22.16 - Bulk carrier with steel hatch covers

> **Type 'B'** *"All ships which do not come within the provisions regarding type 'A' ships ... of this regulation shall be considered as type 'B' ships."*

Other factors can reduce the level of freeboard assigned, including compliant hatchways if fitted to type 'B' ships over 100 m in length.

Application

The Convention applies to ships engaged on international voyages except:

- Ships solely navigating the Great Lakes and the River St Lawrence, the Caspian Sea, and the Plate, Parana and Uruguay Rivers
- warships
- ships voyaging between neighbouring ports under sheltered conditions
- vessels with novel features, where application of the Convention might seriously impede research into the development of such features
- ships undertaking single international voyages.

Provisions are made regarding the freeboard of ships by subdivision and damage stability calculations. The technical Annex covers further safety measures such as doors, freeing ports and hatchways with the aim being to ensure the vessel's watertight integrity below the freeboard deck.

Figure 22.17 - RoRo car carriers have large openings in the hull and extensive open cargo spaces. Assigned freeboard is affected by the watertight integrity of the openings and subdivision within the spaces

Development

The first International Convention on Load Lines, adopted in 1930, was based on reserve buoyancy and recognised the need for adequate freeboard.

The 1966 Load Lines Convention focused on improving safety by restricting the draught to which a ship was loaded through freeboards, external weathertightness and watertight integrity.

As part of the Harmonized System on Survey and Certification (HSSC), the Convention's survey and certification requirements were harmonised with both SOLAS and MARPOL in 1988.

The 1998 Load Line Protocol has been modified further by the 2003 Amendments. A number of important amendments were made to the Protocol, covering:

- Strength and intact stability of ships
- superstructure and bulkheads
- hatchways, hatch coamings and hatch covers
- doorways and ventilators
- cargo ports and other similar openings
- spurling pipes and cable lockers
- calculation of freeing ports
- protection of the crew and means of safe passage for crew
- calculation of freeboard
- sheer
- minimum bow height and reserve buoyancy.

Figure 22.18 - Coastal tanker (Type 'A' ships) with a raised focsle and stern area

Figure 22.19 - A raised, protected centreline walkway for the safety of crew on deck

Documentation and Certification

No ship to which the Convention applies is permitted to proceed on an international voyage without an International Load Line Certificate or an International Load Line Exemption Certificate.

The certificate is issued for a period specified by the Administration, but not exceeding five years, with no extension allowed beyond five months. The certificate will no longer be valid if:

- Material alterations are made
- fittings and appliances are not properly maintained
- the certificate has not been endorsed to confirm inspection
- the structural strength of the ship is reduced to such an extent as to render it unsafe
- the vessel is transferred to the flag of another State.

Ships carrying a certificate will be subject to port inspection in order to verify certification.

Surveys

The Convention requires ships to undergo the following surveys:

- Initial Survey - before service
- Renewal Survey - at intervals specified by the Administration
- Annual Survey - to ensure continued compliance.

No change may be made to the structure, equipment, arrangements, material or scantlings covered by the survey, without the sanction of the Administration.

LSA Code

Life-Saving Appliances (LSA) Code

The Life-Saving Appliances (LSA) Code was adopted on 4th June 1996 and has been mandatory under Regulation 34 of SOLAS Chapter III since entering into force on 1st July 1998. The Code provides the international standards for LSA as required by SOLAS Chapter III.

These standards include the general construction requirements of the following equipment:

- Lifebuoys
- lifejackets
- immersion suits
- anti-exposure suits
- thermal protective aids
- rocket parachute flares
- hand flares
- buoyant smoke signals
- line-throwing appliances
- inflatable liferafts
- rigid liferafts
- partially enclosed lifeboats
- totally enclosed lifeboats
- free-fall lifeboats
- lifeboats with a self-contained air support system
- fire-protected lifeboats
- rescue boats
- launching and embarkation appliances
- marine evacuation systems
- general alarm and public address system.

Figure 22.21 - Six-person liferaft located forward on a coastal tanker

Figure 22.20 - Testing lifeboat release systems

The Code also sets out requirements for servicing and maintenance of LSA, and places the responsibility of ensuring the competency of the person performing the repair with the ship company or owner. It is not the responsibility of the Flag Administration to ensure this competency.

The LSA Code requires that LSA should:

- Be constructed with proper workmanship and materials
- not be damaged in stowage throughout the air temperature range of minus 30°C to minus 65°C
- if they are likely to be immersed in seawater during their use, operate throughout the seawater temperature range of minus 1°C to minus 30°C
- where applicable, be rot-proof, corrosion-resistant and not unduly affected by seawater, oil or fungal attack
- where exposed to sunlight, be resistant to deterioration
- be of a highly visible colour on all parts where this will assist detection
- be fitted with retro-reflective material where this will assist detection
- be clearly marked with approval information, including the Administration which approved it, and any operational restrictions
- where applicable, be provided with electrical short circuit protection to prevent damage or injury.

One of the most recent developments in the LSA Code has been amendment to Section 4.4.76 of Chapter IV to incorporate the changed requirements for lifeboat release hooks and retrieval systems introduced by Resolution MSC.317(89) under SOLAS Regulation III/1.5.

The requirements apply to on-load mechanisms installed on all ships (new and existing cargo and passenger ships). The requirements entered into force on 1st July 2014 and compliance must be ensured after the first scheduled drydocking from 1st July 2014, but not later than 1st July 2019.

MARPOL

International Convention for the Prevention of Pollution from Ships (MARPOL)

MARPOL is the primary international convention concerning pollution of the marine environment operationally and accidentally by ships. It was adopted on 2nd November 1973 and absorbed into the 1978 Protocol (as the 73 Convention had not entered into force).

The 1978 Protocol followed a number of tanker accidents in 1976 and 1977. The amended Convention, MARPOL 73/38, entered into force on 2nd October 1983.

The Annex VI Protocol was adopted in 1977 and entered into force on 19th May 2005.

Structure

The Convention contains six technical Annexes which entered into force on different dates and cover different areas of marine pollution.

Annex I - Regulations for the Prevention of Pollution by Oil

Annex I covers the prevention of oil pollution accidentally and operationally.

MARPOL

There have been a number of amendments to Annex I, most notably the introduction of double-hulled oil tankers after the '*Exxon Valdez*' ran aground in Prince William Sound, Alaska, spilling 1,264,155 barrels of crude oil (1989). The subsequent 1992 Amendments for the phasing in of double hulls were later revised, most recently in 2005, adding heavy grade oil as cargo and amending the Condition Assessment Scheme (CAS). CAS is conducted as part of the SOLAS Chapter XI-1 *Enhanced Survey Programme* (ESP) and requires more stringent assessment and survey of single-hull ships of 15 years and older.

In December 1999, the '*Erika*' accelerated the phase-out of single hull tonnage to between 2003 and 2015.

Under the revised Regulation 13G of MARPOL Annex I, the final phase-out dates were brought forward:

- Category 1 tankers (pre-MARPOL tankers) – from 2007 to 2005
- Category 2 and 3 tankers (MARPOL and smaller tankers) – from 2015 to 2010.

MARPOL divides oil tankers into the following categories:

Category 1

- *Oil tankers of 20,000 Dwt and above carrying crude oil, fuel oil, heavy diesel oil or lubricating oil as cargo, and of 30,000 Dwt and above carrying other oils, which do not comply with the requirements for protectively located segregated ballast tanks (commonly known as pre-MARPOL tankers)*

Category 2

- *20,000 Dwt and above carrying crude oil, fuel oil, heavy diesel oil or lubricating oil as cargo*
- *30,000 Dwt and above carrying other oils, which do comply with the protectively located SBT requirements*

Category 3

- *5,000 Dwt and above but less than Category 2*

Operational Discharge of Oil

Restrictions on the discharge of both cargo-related oil and machinery space oil are specified and include oil volume/content, distances from land, and content monitoring/measuring requirements, ie:

- Discharges of operational oil from tankers outside Special Areas:
  - *the tanker is not within a special area;*
  - *the tanker is more than 50 nautical miles from the nearest land;*
  - *the tanker is proceeding en route;*
  - *the instantaneous rate of discharge of oil content does not exceed 30 litres per nautical mile;*
  - *the total quantity of oil discharged into the sea does not exceed for tankers delivered on or before 31 December 1979, as defined in regulation 1.28.1, 1/15,000 of the total quantity of the particular cargo of which the residue formed a part, and for tankers delivered after 31st December 1979, as defined in regulation 1.28.2, 1/30,000 of the total quantity of the particular cargo of which the residue formed a part; and*
  - *the tanker has in operation an oil discharge monitoring and control system and a slop tank arrangement as required by regulations 29 and 31 of this Annex.*
- Discharges of machinery space oil outside Special Areas:
  - *the ship is proceeding en route;*
  - *the oily mixture is processed through an oil filtering equipment meeting the requirements of regulation 14 of this Annex;*

- *the oil content of the effluent without dilution does not exceed 15 ppm;*
- *the oily mixture does not originate from cargo pump room bilges on oil tankers; and*
- *the oily mixture, in case of oil tankers, is not mixed with oil cargo residues.*

- Discharges of machinery space oil outside Special Areas, except the Antarctic, where all discharge is prohibited:
  - *the ship is proceeding en route;*
  - *the oily mixture is processed through an oil filtering equipment meeting the requirements of regulation 14.7 of this Annex;*
  - *the oil content of the effluent without dilution does not exceed 15 ppm;*
  - *the oily mixture does not originate from cargo pump room bilges on oil tankers; and*
  - *the oily mixture, in case of oil tankers, is not mixed with oil cargo residues.*

Figure 22.22 - Oily Water Separator

Annex I Special Areas

The Annex I Special Areas, ie areas with adopted mandatory methods for the prevention of sea pollution by oil, are:

- Antarctic
- Mediterranean Sea
- Black Sea
- Baltic Sea
- North West European Waters
- Red Sea
- The Gulfs (Ras al Hadd to Ras al Fasteh)
- Gulf of Aden
- Oman Area (of the Arabian Sea)
- Southern South African Waters.

Annex II - Regulations for the Control of Pollution by Noxious Liquid Substances in Bulk

Annex II applies to the pollution prevention requirements for ships carrying noxious liquid substances (NLS) in bulk. NLS are divided into four categories; X, Y, Z and Other Substances (OS), depending on the severity of the pollution hazard. Category X cargoes have the most severe pollution hazards and are prohibited from discharge into the sea. Category Z cargoes have the minimum hazards and justify fewer restrictions on discharge to the environment. 'Other Substances' are those not covered by categories X, Y or Z and are considered to have no threat to safety or the environment.

Annex II Discharge Standards

Similar to Annex I, Annex II details the operational discharge criteria of NLS residues, including when mixed with water or other substances. The discharge standards for XYZ or other provisionally assessed substances require that:

MARPOL

- *the ship is proceeding en route at a speed of at least 7 knots in the case of self-propelled ships or at least 4 knots in the case of ships which are not self-propelled;*
- *the discharge is made below the waterline through the underwater discharge outlet(s) not exceeding the maximum rate for which the underwater discharge outlet(s) is (are) designed; and*
- *the discharge is made at a distance of not less than 12 nautical miles from the nearest land in a depth of water of not less than 25 m.*

Where the discharge provisions are not fully adhered to, Annex II substance residues are only permitted to reception facilities. For ships built before 1st January 2007, category Z substance residue standards are not mandatory, and category Z discharge requirements may be waived under the conditions identified in Annex II Regulation 13.2.3. However, irrespective of age or conditions, no discharge of NLS residues is permitted within 12 miles of the nearest land.

The Antarctic area is the only Annex II Special Area.

Procedures and Arrangements Manual

An approved 'Procedures and Arrangements Manual' must be carried on board specifying the arrangements and operational procedures concerning cargo operations, including tank washing, slops and ballast operations.

Certificates

Internationally trading ships carrying NLS in bulk are required to hold:

- *An International Pollution Prevention Certificate for the Carriage of Noxious Liquid Substances in Bulk*
- *a Certificate of Fitness for the Carriage of Dangerous Chemicals in Bulk* (mandatory for tankers constructed before 1st July 1986) or an *International Certificate of Fitness for the Carriage of Dangerous Chemicals in Bulk.*

Annex III - Regulations for the Prevention of Pollution by Harmful Substances Carried by Sea in Packaged Form

Annex III of MARPOL concerns harmful substances in packaged form that are identified as marine pollutants in the IMDG Code, or substances that are identified by any of the three criteria in the Appendix to the Annex.

The Annex regulates the requirements for:

- Packing
- marking and labelling
- documentation
- stowage
- quantity limitations
- exceptions – including where jettisoning is required for the safety of life or the ship.
- PSC requirements.

Annex IV - Regulations for the Prevention of Pollution by Sewage from Ships

Annex IV regulates the control of pollution of the sea by sewage. It defines sewage as:

- *drainage and other wastes from any form of toilets and urinals;*

- *drainage from medical premises (dispensary, sick bay, etc) via wash basins, wash tubs and scuppers located in such premises;*
- *drainage from spaces containing living animals; or*
- *other waste waters when mixed with the drainages defined above.*

Annex III Regulation 11 states that the discharge of sewage into the sea is prohibited, except when:

- *the ship is discharging comminuted and disinfected sewage using a system approved by the Administration in accordance with regulation 9.1.2 of this Annex at a distance of more than 3 nautical miles from the nearest land, or sewage which is not comminuted or disinfected, at a distance of more than 12 nautical miles from the nearest land, provided that, in any case, the sewage that has been stored in holding tanks, or sewage originating from spaces containing living animals, shall not be discharged instantaneously but at a moderate rate when the ship is en route and proceeding at not less than 4 knots; the rate of discharge shall be approved by the Administration based upon standards developed by the Organization; or*
- *the ship has in operation an approved sewage treatment plant which has been certified by the Administration to meet the operational requirements referred to in regulation 9.1.1 of this Annex, and the test results of the plant are laid down in the ship's International Sewage Pollution Prevention Certificate; and*
- *additionally, the effluent shall not produce visible floating solids nor cause discoloration of the surrounding water.*

Certification

An International Sewage Pollution Prevention Certificate is issued by the Administration following satisfactory survey and remains valid for up to five years.

Special Area

On 15th July 2011, MEPC 62 adopted amendments to MARPOL Annex IV introducing the Baltic Sea as an Annex IV Special Area and new discharge requirements for passenger ships transiting Special Areas. These entered into force on 1st January 2013.

Annex V - Regulations for the Prevention of Pollution by Garbage from Ships

This Annex entered into force on 31st December 1988 and concerns all forms of garbage (victual, domestic and operational) created on board ships and requiring disposal ashore, discharge overboard or treatment on board.

Discharge

At MEPC 62 in July 2011, IMO adopted extensive amendments to Annex V which entered into force on 1st January 2013.

The revised Annex V prohibits the discharge of all garbage into the sea, except as provided otherwise, under specific circumstances. Where garbage is of mixed discharge categories, the most stringent requirements are to be complied with.

The disposal of garbage outside Special Areas was amended at MEPC 62 and, from 1st January 2013, is as follows:

1. *Subject to the provisions of regulations 5, 6, and 7 of this Annex, discharge of the following garbage into the sea outside special areas shall only be permitted while the ship is en route and as far as practicable from the nearest land, but in any case not less than:*

   .1 3 nautical miles from the nearest land for food wastes which have been passed through a comminuter or grinder. Such comminuted or ground food wastes shall be capable of passing through a screen with openings no greater than 25 mm.

   .2 12 nautical miles from the nearest land for food wastes that have not been treated in accordance with subparagraph .1 above.

MARPOL

.3 12 nautical miles from the nearest land for cargo residues that cannot be recovered using commonly available methods for unloading. These cargo residues shall not contain any substances classified as harmful to the marine environment, taking into account guidelines developed by the Organization.

.4 For animal carcasses, discharge shall occur as far from the nearest land as possible, taking into account the guidelines developed by the Organization.

2. Cleaning agents or additives contained in cargo hold, deck and external surfaces wash water may be discharged into the sea, but these substances must not be harmful to the marine environment, taking into account guidelines developed by the Organization.

3. When garbage is mixed with or contaminated by other substances prohibited from discharge or having different discharge requirements, the more stringent requirements shall apply.

Disposal inside Special Areas must meet the following criteria:

1. Discharge of the following garbage into the sea within special areas shall only be permitted while the ship is en route and as follows:

.1 Discharge into the sea of food wastes as far as practicable from the nearest land, but not less than 12 nautical miles from the nearest land or the nearest ice shelf. Food wastes shall be comminuted or ground and shall be capable of passing through a screen with openings no greater than 25 mm. Food wastes shall not be contaminated by any other garbage type. Discharge of introduced avian products, including poultry and poultry parts, is not permitted in the Antarctic area unless it has been treated to be made sterile.

.2 Discharge of cargo residues that cannot be recovered using commonly available methods for unloading, where all the following conditions are satisfied:

.1 Cargo residues, cleaning agents or additives, contained in hold washing water do not include any substances classified as harmful to the marine environment, taking into account guidelines developed by the Organization;

.2 Both the port of departure and the next port of destination are within the special area and the ship will not transit outside the special area between those ports;

.3 No adequate reception facilities are available at those ports taking into account guidelines developed by the Organization; and

.4 Where the conditions of subparagraphs 2.1, 2.2 and 2.3 of this paragraph have been fulfilled, discharge of cargo hold washing water containing residues shall be made as far as practicable from the nearest land or the nearest ice shelf and not less than 12 nautical miles from the nearest land or the nearest ice shelf.

2. Cleaning agents or additives contained in deck and external surfaces wash water may be discharged into the sea, but only if these substances are not harmful to the marine environment, taking into account guidelines developed by the Organization.

3. The following rules (in addition to the rules in paragraph 1 of this regulation) apply with respect to the Antarctic area:

.1 Each Party at whose ports ships depart en route to or arrive from the Antarctic area undertakes to ensure that as soon as practicable adequate facilities are provided for the reception of all garbage from all ships, without causing undue delay, and according to the needs of the ships using them.

.2 Each Party shall ensure that all ships entitled to fly its flag, before entering the Antarctic area, have sufficient capacity on board for the retention of all garbage, while operating in the area and have concluded arrangements to discharge such garbage at a reception facility after leaving the area.

Figure 22.23 - Incinerator

Special Areas

Annex V specifies the following Special Areas:

- Antarctic
- Mediterranean Sea
- Black Sea
- Baltic Sea
- North Sea
- Wider Caribbean Region
- Red Sea
- The Gulfs (Ras al Hadd to Ras al Fasteh).

Garbage Management

Applicable ships of 100 GT or above must carry a Garbage Management Plan, providing written procedures for minimising and processing garbage, including the use of onboard equipment. Ships of 400 GT and above must have on board, and maintain, a Garbage Record Book to record all discharges, incinerations and disposals.

Annex VI - Regulations for the Prevention of Air Pollution from Ships

Annex VI was driven by the global focus on climate change and air pollution. It regulates the ship sulphur oxide (SOx), nitrogen oxide (NOx) and particulate matter (PM) content in ship exhaust emissions and prohibits deliberate emissions of ozone-depleting substances.

The levels of PM are not limited to a particular value in IMO regulations, but through the reduction on SOx and NOx emissions the levels of particulates are reduced. Fine particulates, such as black carbon (BC), are also produced on the incomplete combustion of carbon-based fuels. However, facilitating more complete combustion through increasing the oxygen and temperature or using fuel in a different form (ie burning gas rather than a liquid or solid fuel) reduces the levels of BC produced.

Reducing SOx emissions from ships has been achieved through both global and regional caps in fuel oil sulphur limits (expressed in terms of % m/m – by weight). However, these emission control regulations are not a fuel rule but are emissions based, meaning that alternative methods of controlling emissions from ships are permissible for a ship to remain compliant. The requirement is that the emissions produced when using an emissions control method, other than low sulphur fuel, are equivalent to the level they would be if a compliant low sulphur fuel was burned.

The global SOx sulphur in fuel limits set in Regulation 14 of Annex VI are:

- 4.50% m/m prior to 1st January 2012
- 3.50% m/m on and after 1st January 2012
- 0.50% m/m on and after 1st January 2020 (possibly deferred until 2025).

NOx reductions are set at three tiered levels (I, II and III) depending on the RPM of the engine. Tiers I and II are global NOx limits whereas tier III limits are only applicable to ships operating in Emission Control Areas (ECAs). Tier II global limits are in effect for ships with their keels laid on and after 1st January 2011. Before installation on board ship, an engine must undergo a pre-certification survey, usually undertaken at the engine builder's works, to ensure it complies with NOx emissions limits. It is issued with a certificate of compliance for Engine International Air Pollution Prevention (EIAPP).

Emission Control Areas (ECAs)

Stricter limits on SOx and NOx apply in certain areas, ie Emission Control Areas (ECAs), and at all European Union ports (under the EU Sulphur Directive Regulation 2005/33/EC). The current

MARPOL

limit on sulphur content of marine fuels in an ECA dropped from 1.00% m/m sulphur to 0.10% m/m sulphur on 1st January 2015. The current level for sulphur in fuel used in EU ports is also 0.10% m/m.

There are currently four SOx-ECAs and these are all active. Emissions are being monitored and enforcement measures (with penalties for non-compliance) are being increased. This is also the case for EU ports. It is mandatory in these regions to either use a fuel of 0.10% m/m sulphur or make use of an equivalent system to reduce SOx emissions.

The NOx tier III limits come into effect for ships with their keels laid on and after 1st January 2016. These limits are only applicable for vessels operating in NOx-ECA regions and there are currently two of these areas.

The current SOx-ECAs and SOx/NOx-ECAs are:

- The Baltic Sea SOx-ECA
- the North Sea and English Channel SOx-ECA
- the North America SOx/NOx-ECA
- the United States Caribbean Sea SOx/NOx-ECA.

An International Air Pollution Prevention (IAPP) certificate is required for all vessels >400 GT that are party to MARPOL 73/78. Ships must be issued with an IAPP certificate to verify compliance with the prevention of air pollution regulations of Annex VI. Annual, intermediate and renewal surveys must be carried out and passed in order to confirm the validity of the IAPP certificate. Tankers >400 GT carrying crude oil are required to carry and maintain an approved Volatile Organic Compound (VOC) Management Plan.

EEDI and SEEMP

On 15th July 2011, MEPC 62 adopted amendments to MARPOL Annex VI, enacted by MEPC.203(62), which were focused on the reduction of greenhouse gases (GHG), and specifically CO_2. These amendments introduced two new measures that entered into force on 1st January 2013 and are the first globally applicable GHG reducing measures:

- Energy Efficiency Design Index (EEDI)
- Ship Energy Efficiency Management Plan (SEEMP).

EEDI is a technical instrument that sets energy efficiency levels for new ships of >400 GT and some major conversions. It is intended to reduce the amount of CO_2 emissions from ships through non-prescriptive technical and design improvements in energy efficiency. The EEDI regulatory formula is a complex adaptation of:

$$\text{EEDI (Ratio)} = \frac{CO_2 \text{ Emissions}}{\text{Transport Work}}$$

Where: CO_2 emissions = Main Engines + Auxiliary Engines – Innovative Technologies

EEDI works by setting baseline criteria for ship types to be assessed and certified against. It then specifies the amount of energy efficiency that is to be saved (as a percentage comparison). Calculations are made in grams CO_2/tonne-miles.

As a best practice system, SEEMP is an onboard management tool (with reporting requirements) that prescribes improvements in operational energy efficiency on all applicable ships through inclusion and optimisation of:

- Energy efficiency
- speed/power and fuel consumption
- voyage planning
- ship handling
- fleet management
- cargo handling.

SEEMP has applied to all vessels from 1st January 2013 and can form part of the Safety Management System, provided that it is developed in accordance with the IMO guidelines.

MLC

Maritime Labour Convention, 2006 (MLC, 2006)

The Maritime Labour Convention (MLC, 2006) was adopted by a record vote of 314 in favour and none against at the 94th ILO Maritime Session, on 23rd February 2006 in Geneva. This high level of support for the Convention was a result of the lengthy and thorough consultation period (since 2001) between governments, employers and workers to develop the wording of the Convention. The Convention strives to be *"firm on rights and flexible on implementation"*.

The Convention was ratified on 20th August 2012 and entered into force one year later.

The International Labour Organization (ILO) is a specialised United Nations agency that is responsible for drafting and administering international labour standards. The agency's strength is shown through bringing together representatives from governments, employers and workers to shape policies.

Application

The Convention applies to all seafarers on all vessels of ≥500 GT (unless expressly stated otherwise) which are either engaged in international voyages or are operating between ports in a foreign country.

The Convention does not apply to:

- Ships that navigate exclusively in inland waters or waters within, or closely adjacent to, sheltered waters or areas where port regulations apply. In the case of the UK, this is classed as within 60 nautical miles of sheltered waters
- ships engaged in fishing or similar pursuits
- ships of traditional build, eg dhows and junks
- warships or naval auxiliaries.

Purpose

The MLC, 2006 seeks to ensure that there is a worldwide equivalence of employment and social rights for seafarers on ships, as well as to create conditions of fair competition for shipowners. It is often referred to as the "seafarers' bill of rights". The MLC will develop the existing maritime system for enforcing IMO Conventions through Port State Control.

The new Convention combines, simplifies and modernises the 37 existing ILO maritime labour conventions and 31 related recommendations, adopted since 1920, and reflects current conditions on board a 21st century vessel. For example, Regulation 1.1 consolidates the Minimum Age (Sea) Convention, 1920 (No 7), the Minimum Age (Sea) Convention (Revised), 1936 (No 58), and aspects of the Seafarers' Hours of Work and the Manning of Ships Convention, 1996 (No 180).

The Convention provides a more effective enforcement and compliance system than the legislation replaced.

Article XV allows for amendments to the Code to be made through an 'accelerated amendment' procedure rather than 'express ratification'. This was developed to meet the need for more

MLC

efficient updating of the technical details in maritime labour standards, without the need for an entire revision of the Convention. This is a similar approach to the IMO SOLAS Convention. Amendments to the MLC Code enter into force six months after the date of deemed acceptance for all ratifying members.

Many shipowners and flag States provide proper work conditions for seafarers on their vessels. However, they compete on an uneven playing field, where substandard operators can undercut those who take care of their workforce. This problem is addressed under the MLC, ensuring that there will be no favourable treatment for non-ratifying countries. Any country that has ratified the Convention can inspect the ships of any country visiting their ports, whether or not the vessel's flag State is an MLC signatory. Those that do not meet the minimum standards of the Convention may face detention and delays.

Although there will be changes in all areas of the shipping sector as a consequence of the MLC, the many advantages are perceived to outweigh any disadvantages.

Structure

The MLC consists of three different, but connected, sections:

1. The Articles (mandatory)
2. The Regulations (mandatory)
3. The Code
   A. Part A: Standards (mandatory)
   B. Part B: Guidelines (non-mandatory).

The 16 Articles describe the core rights and broad principles, as well as the fundamental responsibilities, of Member States that ratify the MLC.

The Regulations and the Code are amalgamated into five areas called Titles. These five Titles embody the same issues as the 68 maritime labour conventions and regulations. There are some new subjects, eg in the area of occupational health and safety.

Each Title encompasses a group of conditions relating to a particular principle, right or enforcement measure, and the parts of each Title are linked by its number. For example, the second Regulation in Title 3 consists of Regulation 3.2, Standard A3.2 and Guideline B3.2, all relating to food and catering.

Title 1.	**Minimum Requirements for Seafarers to Work on a Ship**
Regulation 1.1	Minimum age
Regulation 1.2	Medical certificate
Regulation 1.3	Training and qualifications
Regulation 1.4	Recruitment and placement
Title 2.	**Conditions of Employment**
Regulation 2.1	Seafarers' employment agreements
Regulation 2.2	Wages
Regulation 2.3	Hours of work and hours of rest
Regulation 2.4	Entitlement to leave
Regulation 2.5	Repatriation
Regulation 2.6	Seafarer compensation for the ship's loss or foundering
Regulation 2.7	Manning levels
Regulation 2.8	Career and skill development and opportunities for seafarers' employment
Title 3.	**Accommodation, Recreational Facilities, Food and Catering**
Regulation 3.1	Accommodation and recreational facilities
Regulation 3.2	Food and catering

Title 4.	**Health Protection, Medical Care, Welfare and Social Security Protection**
Regulation 4.1	Medical care on board ship and ashore
Regulation 4.2	Shipowners' liability
Regulation 4.3	Health and safety protection and accident prevention
Regulation 4.4	Access to shore-based welfare facilities
Regulation 4.5	Social security
Title 5.	**Compliance and Enforcement**
Regulation 5.1	Flag State responsibilities
Regulation 5.2	Port State responsibilities
Regulation 5.3	Labour-supplying responsibilities

Table 22.10 – MLC Titles and Regulations

Certification

There are four appendices to the Convention and these are concerned with Title 5 *Compliance and Enforcement*. They contain two key model documents:

- Maritime Labour Certificate
- Declaration of Maritime Labour Compliance (DMLC).

The Maritime Labour Certificate, along with the attached DMLC, must be retained on board and a copy posted in a prominent place on board. The Maritime Labour Certificate is valid for five years, conditional on continuing inspections by the flag State.

The DMLC must be attached to the Maritime Labour Certificate and has two parts:

1. DMLC Part I is to be completed by the competent authority. It notes the topics for inspection and itemises the relevant pieces of legislation implementing the MLC, 2006 as well as any substantial equivalences and exemptions that have been granted.
2. DMLC Part II is to be completed by the shipowner and verified by the attending surveyor when the first inspection is completed. The measures adopted by the shipowner to ensure ongoing compliance with the national requirements, as well as ensuring there is continuous improvement, are listed in Appendix A5-1. These may be inspected in a foreign port.

Maritime Labour Inspections

Port State Control inspections must be carried out by officers (PSCOs) authorised by the competent authority in the port State and documentary identification is required.

A maritime labour inspection can be divided into two parts:

1. Physical - concerned with the physical items, such as the seafarer accommodation and galley conditions.

MLC

2. Operational - concerned with human and operational issues, such as payment of wages, seafarer employment agreements, minimum age, medical certification and hours of work or rest.

Some areas, such as occupational health and safety, involve both physical aspects (protective equipment/construction) and operational practices on a ship. An inspector will usually employ different methods for a thorough inspection, including:

- Document review
- visual observation
- general discussions with seafarers
- interviews with seafarers in private.

Courtesy of USCG

OSV Code

Code of Safe Practice for the Carriage of Cargoes and Persons by Offshore Supply Vessels (OSV Code)

The Code of Safe Practice for the Carriage of Cargoes and Persons by Offshore Supply Vessels (OSV Code) is a non-mandatory code developed by the IMO. It advises on safe practice for OSVs when in operation, and the management of OSVs when interfacing with offshore installations.

The OSV Code was adopted by Assembly Resolution A.863(20) in 1997.

The Code defines an OSV as "*a vessel which is used for the transportation of stores, materials, equipment or personnel to, from and between offshore installations*".

The Code covers:

- General
  - communications
  - cargo handling and stability
  - pre-planning
  - stowage and securing of cargo
  - bulk cargo
  - PPE
- port operations
- sea transport
- operations at offshore installations
  - mooring requirements
  - communications
  - personnel transfer
  - cargo handling.

The Appendices cover applicability of the Code to different types of offshore installations, hose colour coding, and Resolutions A.863(20) and MSC.237(82).

Non-mandatory requirements for the design and construction of offshore supply vessels are provided in the OSV Guidelines, which were adopted by the IMO Assembly in November 1981.

There is potential for the development of an OSV Chemical Code in response to the increasing volumes and variety of LHNS being carried on OSVs. The Liquid Hazardous Noxious Substance Guidelines were amended in conjunction with the OSV Guidelines.

Salvage

International Convention on Salvage

The International Convention on Salvage was enacted in 1989 following concerns surrounding the increasing size of oil tankers and the increased risk of environmental pollution. Casualties such as the *'Amoco Cadiz'* highlighted the need for a review of the 1910 Convention. In practice, salvors under the 'no cure, no pay' basis were being discouraged to assist ships that states and society wanted to save.

The review was undertaken through the International Conference on Salvage 1989 convened by the IMO.

The Conference recognised the effectiveness of uniform international rules and how beneficial timely salvage operations can be to vessels, crews and the environment. It also took into account the need to ensure adequate incentives for those who undertake such ventures.

The main changes that the Conference created included:

- The adoption of an additional criterion for assessing the salvage reward:

  "The skill and efforts of the salvor in preventing or minimising damage to the environment" (Article 13.1 (b))
- the introduction of 'special compensation' in Article 14 to counter the harshness of 'no cure, no pay'. This enabled the recovery of expenses as a minimum where environmental damage was threatened
- a contract may be annulled/modified if there is undue influence and inequitable terms, or there is excessive payment for services actually rendered
- coastal States retain the right to take action to prevent or minimise environmental damage to their coastline from the threat of pollution.

The Convention endorses the master's authority to conclude contracts for salvage operations on behalf of the owner of the vessel and property on the vessel. It reaffirms that the master must also render assistance (as far as safely possible) to anyone in danger of being lost at sea and that the owner of the vessel will not incur liability for a breach of the duty of the master.

A salvor's reward is fixed in accordance with listed factors and payment shall be proportionate from all parties whose property has been salvaged. The reward is not to exceed the saved value.

The Convention states that no remuneration is due from persons whose lives are saved, but a salvor that has saved a life is entitled to a fair share of the reward with those who have saved property and/or the vessel.

States are to encourage, with the consent of the parties involved, the publication of arbitral awards made in salvage cases.

Amendments

Although the Convention has not been amended to date, Article 14 - Special Compensation was found to be costly and time consuming. The International Group of P&I Clubs therefore developed an alternative method of calculating the Special Compensation, known as the SCOPIC Clause – The Special Compensation P&I Club Clause. The clause came into force in 1999 and the current edition is SCOPIC 2011.

Figure 22.24 - 'MSC Napoli' salvage operation

Ship Recycling Convention

International Convention for the Safe and Environmentally Sound Recycling of Ships, 2009

The International Convention for the Safe and Environmentally Sound Recycling of Ships, 2009 was adopted on 15th May 2009 at an IMO Convention held in Hong Kong (the 'Hong Kong Convention').

The Convention will not enter into force until 24 months after ratification by 15 States, representing 40% of world merchant shipping by gross tonnage.

The Ship Recycling Convention was initiated by the Norwegian Delegation at the Marine Environment Protection Committee (MEPC 41) in November 1998. Concern was raised about the problems associated with ship dismantling and the need for an internationally acceptable solution that would ensure protection of the environment and safety of workers.

The practice of shipbreaking is considered hazardous to health and a threat to both the terrestrial and marine environment. Shipbreaking discharges many kind of pollutants in the form of liquids, metals, gases and solids. Matters of particular concern include:

- Persistent Organic Pollutants (POPs)
- polychlorinated biphenyls (PCBs)
- asbestos
- heavy metals
- oil pollution.

The Hong Kong Convention aimed to:

- Regulate the design, construction, operation and preparation of ships to allow safe and environmentally sound recycling
- ensure that ships being recycled at the end of their operational lives do not pose any unnecessary risk to human health and safety or to the environment
- give guidelines for the safe and environmentally sound operation of ship recycling yards and establish an enforcement mechanism
- ensure ships carry an inventory of hazardous material and have an initial survey to verify the inventory
- monitor these items via periodic surveys and a final survey prior to recycling
- require recycling yards to provide a Ship Recycling Plan
- require Member States to ensure that facilities under their jurisdiction comply with the Convention.

The Convention introduces the concept of a ship's 'Green Passport', which is an inventory of hazardous materials (IHM) present in a ship's structure, systems and equipment that may be hazardous to health or the environment. This is kept up to date for the service life of the ship. Prior to breaking, details of any further hazards and waste material are added, which will help the recycling yard to develop a safer and more environmentally acceptable plan.

Since adoption of the Convention, the following guidelines have been adopted to help introduce the Convention at:

MEPC 62 (July 2011):

- ***2011 Guidelines for the Development of the Inventory of Hazardous Materials (IHM)***

  The guidelines provide recommendations for developing the ship-specific inventory required by the Convention to identify the type, location and quantity of hazardous materials on board. The information will be used by ship recycling facilities to manage hazardous materials to protect health and safety and prevent pollution.
- ***2011 Guidelines for the Development of the Ship Recycling Plan (SRP)***

  Ship recycling facilities are required to develop a ship-specific Ship Recycling Plan (SRP). The SRP should describe the recycling process that the facility will follow including any preparatory work, arrival, management of the hazardous materials, safe working procedures and the dismantling sequence.

MEPC 63 (March 2012):

- ***2012 Guidelines for Safe and Environmentally Sound Ship Recycling***

  These are comprehensive guidelines for the creation of a Ship Recycling Facilities Plan (SRFP). The SRFP will be the main document used to authorise a recycling

Ship Recycling Convention

facility and will include aspects such as facility management, operational processes, health and safety, training, protection of the environment, etc.

- ***2012 Guidelines for the Authorization of Ship Recycling Facilities***

  These Guidelines were developed for use by Competent Authorities and recognised organisations that are required to authorise ship recycling facilities. They cover authorisation application, document verification, site inspection, audits and procedures for the issue, renewal and withdrawal of the *Document of Authorization to conduct Ship Recycling (DASR)*.

MEPC 63 also established a correspondence group to develop *Guidelines for Survey and Certification under the Hong Kong Convention* and *Guidelines for Inspection of Ships*.

Basel Convention

The *Basel Convention on the Control of Transboundary Movements of Hazardous Wastes and their Disposal* entered into force on 5 May 1992.

The main aims of the Convention are:

- *The reduction of hazardous waste generation and the promotion of environmentally sound management of hazardous wastes, wherever the place of disposal;*
- *the restriction of transboundary movements of hazardous wastes except where it is perceived to be in accordance with the principles of environmentally sound management; and*
- *a regulatory system applying to cases where transboundary movements are permissible.*

Source: http://www.basel.int

SAM PANTHAKY/AFP/Getty Images

Figure 22.25 - Ship recycling

SOLAS

International Convention for the Safety of Life at Sea (SOLAS), 1974

The *International Convention for the Safety of Life at Sea* (SOLAS) is considered the most important maritime convention and is primarily concerned with the construction, equipment and operation of ships.

The original version of SOLAS was adopted in 1914 in response to the *'Titanic'* disaster. Three further versions followed in 1929, 1948 and 1960. The latest version was adopted on 1st November 1974 and entered into force on 25th May 1980. Significantly, the 1974 version introduced 'tacit acceptance', enabling amendments to enter into force unless a predetermined number of objections are raised from Parties before a specified date.

The Maritime Safety Committee (MSC) is the highest technical body of the International Maritime Organization (IMO) and one of its main roles is the responsibility for amendments to SOLAS. Amendments adopted by MSC are listed in MSC Resolutions.

A new consolidated edition of SOLAS is scheduled to be published every four years.

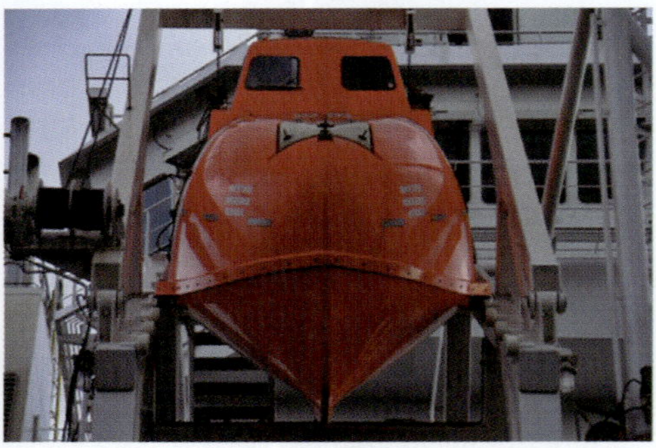

Compliance

SOLAS states that Contracting Governments are obliged to *'promulgate all laws, decrees, orders and regulations and to take all other steps which may be necessary to give the present Convention full and complete effect, so as to ensure that, from the point of view of safety of life, a ship is fit for the service for which it is intended.'*

To achieve this and prove compliance, it is the responsibility of:

- Flag States to ensure their ships comply with the requirements and are issued with the necessary certificates to prove this
- Port States to inspect ships of other Contracting States, ie through Port State Control (PSC).

Structure

The Convention is in two parts. Part 1 contains the Protocols, Articles and text of the Convention and Part 2 contains the Annexes.

Each chapter in Part 1 has links or references to other codes or documents.

Chapter I – General Provisions

- Regulations concerning the survey of ships and the issuing of documents signifying that the ship meets the requirements of the Convention
- provisions for the control of ships in ports of other Contracting Governments.

Chapter II-1 – Construction - Structure, subdivision and stability, machinery and electrical installations

- Subdivision into watertight compartments to ensure the ship remains stable and afloat after assumed degrees of damage
- watertight integrity and bilge pumping arrangements
- stability requirements
- machinery and electrical installations
- "goal-based standards" for oil tankers and bulk carriers.

SOLAS

Chapter II-2 – Construction - Fire protection, fire detection and fire extinction

- Makes the FSS Code mandatory
- detailed fire safety provisions for all ships and specific measures for passenger ships, cargo ships and tankers.

Chapter III – Life-saving appliances and arrangements

- Makes the LSA Code mandatory
- requirements for life-saving appliances and arrangements including lifeboats, rescue boats and lifejackets.

Chapter IV – Radiocommunications

- Incorporating the Global Maritime Distress and Safety System (GMDSS). Ship and shore requirements to carry communication equipment designed to improve the chances of rescue following an accident.

Chapter V – Safety of navigation

- Navigation safety services to be provided by Contracting Governments
- maintenance of meteorological services for ships
- the ice patrol service
- routeing of ships
- search and rescue services.

Chapter VI – Carriage of cargoes

- Cargo other than bulk liquids and gases which may require special precautions
- stowage and securing of cargo or cargo units
- requires cargo ships carrying grain to comply with the Grain Code.

Chapter VII – Carriage of dangerous goods

- Part A - Carriage of dangerous goods in packaged form (makes the IMDG Code mandatory)
- Part A-1 - Carriage of dangerous goods in solid form in bulk
- Part B - Construction and equipment of ships carrying dangerous liquid chemicals in bulk (makes the IBC Code mandatory)
- Part C - Construction and equipment of ships carrying liquefied gases in bulk (makes the IGC Code mandatory)
- Part D - Carriage of packaged irradiated nuclear fuel, plutonium and high-level radioactive wastes (makes the INF Code mandatory).

Chapter VIII – Nuclear ships

- Basic requirements for nuclear-powered ships.

Chapter IX – Management for the Safe Operation of Ships

- Requires a Safety Management System to be established and makes the ISM Code mandatory.

Chapter X – Safety measures for high-speed craft

- Makes the International Code of Safety for High-Speed Craft (HSC Code) mandatory.

Chapter XI-1 – Special measures to enhance maritime safety

- Requirements relating to authorisation of recognised organisations, enhanced surveys and the ship identification number scheme.

Chapter XI-2 – Special measures to enhance maritime security

Establishes:

- The ISPS Code, making Part A of it mandatory
- the role of the master in exercising his professional judgement
- that all ships are to be provided with a ship security alert system
- requirements for port facilities
- information to be provided to IMO
- control of ships in port
- responsibility of companies.

Chapter	Title	Related Code/Document
Chapter I	General Provisions	
Chapter II-1	Construction - Structure, subdivision and stability, machinery and electrical installations	IS, Loadline, IBC, IGC,
Chapter II-2	Construction - Fire protection, fire detection and fire extinction	FSS, FTP, IBC, IGC, IMDG, IMSBC
Chapter III	Life-saving appliances and arrangements	LSA, STCW, IBC, IGC
Chapter IV	Radiocommunications	GMDSS, STCW
Chapter V	Safety of navigation	STCW, Signals, IAMSAR
Chapter VI	Carriage of cargoes	CSS, TDC, IMSBC, BLU, Grain Code
Chapter VII	Carriage of dangerous goods	IMDG, CSS, IBC, IGC, INF
Chapter VIII	Nuclear ships	Code of Safety for Nuclear Merchant Ships
Chapter IX	Management for the safe operation of ships	ISM
Chapter X	Safety measures for high-speed craft	HSC
Chapter XI-1	Special measures to enhance maritime safety	ISM
Chapter XI-2	Special measures to enhance maritime security	ISPS
Chapter XII	Additional safety measures for bulk carriers	BLU, ISM

Chapter XII – Additional safety measures for bulk carriers

- Structural requirements for bulk carriers over 150 metres in length.

An appendix at the end of Part 1 provides a number of forms of certificate, eg Cargo Ship Safety Construction, Passenger Ship Safety, etc.

The two annexes in Part 2 are:

- Annex 1 - Certificates and documents required to be carried on board ships
- Annex 2 - List of resolutions adopted by the SOLAS conferences.

Training Manual

SOLAS requires every ship to carry a Training Manual written in the working language of the ship. Copies are to be kept in each crew mess/ recreation room (or in each cabin). The manual should include:

- Instructions on fire safety, fire-fighting procedures and the use of fire-fighting equipment and systems on board
- details and instructions on PPE carried
- escape systems and appliances
- information regarding survival at sea and hazards of exposure including hypothermia
- instructions and information on the LSA carried on board and their procedures for use
- instructions on launch and recovery of survival craft, ie lifeboats, rescue craft, liferafts, MES, etc
- instructions for emergency repairs of LSA.
- information regarding survival at sea and hazards of exposure including hypothermia
- instructions and information on the LSA carried on board and their procedures for use
- instructions on launch and recovery of survival craft, ie lifeboats, rescue craft, liferafts, MES, etc
- instructions for emergency repairs on LSA.

STCW

International Convention on Standards of Training, Certification and Watchkeeping for Seafarers (STCW)

The International Convention on Standards of Training, Certification and Watchkeeping for Seafarers (STCW) was adopted in 1978. On 1st February 2002, the 1995 Amendments were fully implemented, introducing a new STCW Code divided into two sections, Part A being mandatory and Part B being recommended guidance.

In June 2010, the Manila Amendments were agreed. These were intended to bring the Code up to date and to address perceived weaknesses through the standardisation of practices. Concerns included accidents and casualties, changes in the geographical supply of labour, inconsistent training, and questions related to authenticity and implementation of standards by signatory parties. The changes make the Code more prescriptive and add a strengthened means of enforcement and control.

It is intended that the regulations will be reviewed every 5 years with a full review of the Code every 10 years. The schedule for entry is as follows:

- 1st January 2012 – entered into force. Hours of rest regulations take effect
- 1st July 2013 – approved courses were required to meet and be certified in accordance with new standards. By this date, governments needed to submit compliance documents to remain on the 'white list'
- 1st January 2017 – full implementation, after which all standards, including certificate renewal and revalidation, must be complied with.

The new amendments require an increase in the demonstration of competence using simulator training and the use of modern training methodologies such as eLearning or distance learning. There is greater emphasis on environmental awareness and regulation, leadership, teamwork and management competences, particularly for officers.

ECDIS

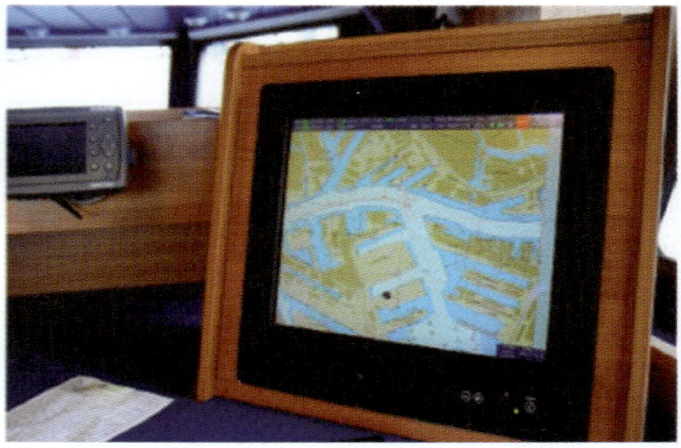

To help prevent the use of fraudulent certificates, signatory Parties are required to maintain an electronic register of ECDIS Certificates that allows controlled access by other parties and companies.

Medical Standards

In-service eyesight standards now relate minimum requirements in the Convention to the category of seafarers affected. The Convention permits Parties to determine the amount of discretion available to medical practitioners on the basis of seafarer duties, except for seafarers who undertake look-out duties in the deck department.

Fitness for Duty/Hours of Rest

The latest amendments draw greater attention to the dangers of fatigue and set new hours of rest that are intended to complement those in the Maritime Labour Convention. The hours of rest stipulate a minimum of 10 hours rest in any 24-hour period, which cannot be divided into more than two periods or separated by more than 14 hours, with at least one period of six hours duration. At least 77 hours rest must be provided in any 7-day period.

Although hours of rest may be disrupted by onboard emergencies and overriding operational conditions, emergency musters and drills should not induce fatigue and their effects on rest periods should be minimised.

Exceptions are stipulated, but must not affect more than two 24-hour periods in any 7 days or continue for more than two consecutive weeks. At least 70 hours rest must still be provided.

Alcohol Limits

The Convention establishes alcohol blood levels of 0.05% and breath limits of 0.25 mg/l for seafarers who perform designated safety, security and marine environmental duties.

Certification

The Convention categorises the standards of competence for the certification of seafarers based on department and role.

Deck Certificates	Categories of Certificate
1) Master	II/2 500 GT or more II/2 3,000 GT or more II/3 less than 500 GT (near coastal)
2) Chief Mate	II/2 500 GT or more II/2 3,000 GT or more II/2 between 500 GT and 3,000 GT
3) Officer of the Watch	II/1 500 GT or more II/3 less than 500 GT (near coastal)
4) Navigational Watch Rating	II/4 500 GT or more
5) Able Seafarer Deck	II/5 500 GT or more
Engineering Certificates	**Categories of Certificate**
1) Chief Engineer	III/2 3,000 kW or more III/3 between 750 and 3,000 kW
2) Second Engineer	III/2 3,000 kW or more III/3 between 750 kW and 3,000 kW
3) Officer of the Watch	III/1 750 kW or more III/3 less than 500 GT (near coastal)
4) Engineer Watch Rating	III/4 over 750 kW
5) Able Seafarer Engine	III/5
Electro-technical Certificates	**Categories of Certificate**
1) Electro-technical Officer (ETO)	III/6 750 kW or more
2) Electro-technical Rating	III/7 750 kW or more

STCW 2010 – Categorisation of certification

The Manila Amendments brought the following changes to seafarer certification.

Rating Certification

The new certification requirements cover the minimum knowledge, understanding and proficiency for ratings. Of particular note is the introduction of new standards of certification for able seafarers and deck, engine and electro-technical ratings.

Engine Officer Certification

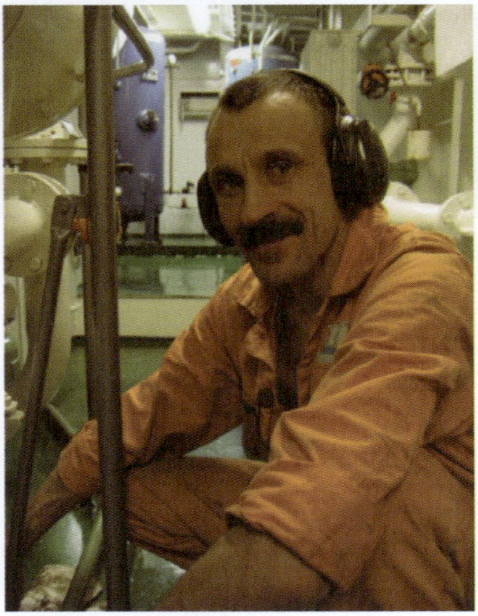

STCW

Substantial changes have been made to the structure and scope of the competencies for engine officer certification, which will affect the training programmes for new trainees particularly the course content and structure.

Significantly, the minimum sea time requirement to attain Engine OOW certification has been increased from 6 to 12 months if a seafarer is completing an approved training programme. Alternatively, if a seafarer is not following such a training programme, 36 months sea time including 30 months in the engine department may be accepted. In either case, at least 6 months must be spent engaged in watchkeeping duties supervised by the chief engineer.

Electro-Technical Officers (ETO) Certification

The minimum qualification requirements have been brought into line with those required for officers in charge of an engineering watch, including the increased minimum sea time requirements.

Special Training for Certain Types of Ships

Tanker Training

The regulations concerning the additional training for seafarers on tankers have been amended to separate the basic (formerly referred to as familiarisation level) tanker training for liquefied gas tankers from that of oil and chemical tankers.

Training for Oil and Chemical Tankers – A-V/1-1

- Basic oil and chemical tanker training - A-V/1-1-1
- Advanced training for oil tanker cargo operations - A-V/1-1-2
- Advanced training for chemical tanker cargo operations - A-V/1-1-3.

Training for Liquefied Gas Tankers – A-V/1-2

The new regulation requires separate certification and training for officers and ratings assigned duties and responsibilities related to cargo or cargo equipment on liquefied gas tankers:

- Basic training for liquefied gas tanker cargo operations - A-V/1-2-1
- Advanced training for liquefied gas tanker cargo operations - A-V/1-2-2.

Sea time and training courses must be completed specific to liquefied gas tankers for both basic and advanced training.

Training for Passenger Ships and RoRo Passenger Ships

The previously separate regulations which existed between RoRo passenger ships (Regulation V/2) and passenger ships (Regulation V/3) have been combined under the new Regulation V/2:

- Crowd management training - A-V/2-1
- Safety training for personnel providing direct service to passengers in passenger spaces - A-V/2-2
- Crisis management and human behaviour training - A-V/2-3.

The only paragraph particular to RoRo passenger vessels relates to cargo and hull integrity.

Security Training

New Regulations VI/5 for security officers and VI/6 for all seafarers have been added to the Convention and the related competencies included in the Code. The training is based on the principles of the ISPS Code and IMO circulars regarding piracy and armed robbery.

Regulation VI/6 distinguishes between security-related training, instruction and familiarisation for all seafarers and security-related awareness training for those with designated security duties.

Standards Regarding Emergency, Occupational Safety, Security, Medical Care and Survival Functions

New requirements added to A-VI require seafarers who hold specific short course certificates to provide evidence of maintaining competence every five years. These include:

- A-VI/1-1 - Personal survival techniques
- A-VI/1-2 - Fire prevention and fire-fighting
- A-VI/1-3 - Elementary first aid
- A-VI/1-4 - Personal safety and social responsibilities
- A-VI/2-1- Survival craft and rescue boats other than fast rescue boats
- A-VI/2-2 - Fast Rescue Boats
- A-VI/3 - Mandatory minimum training in advanced fire-fighting.

TDC Code

Code of Safe Practice for Ships Carrying Timber Deck Cargoes (TDC Code)

Figure 22.26 - 'Ice Prince'

The Code of Safe Practice for Ships Carrying Timber Deck Cargoes (TDC Code) is not mandatory, but applies to all ships of 24 metres or more in length engaged in the carriage of timber deck cargoes. Ships that are provided with and making use of a timber load line must also comply with the Load Line Convention.

The purpose of the TDC Code is to make recommendations on stowage, securing and other operational safety measures designed to ensure the safe transport of timber deck cargoes.

In 1991, the Code was adopted by Resolution A.515(17), with the latest amendments taking effect from 30th November 2011. The Code is referred to in SOLAS Chapter VI – Carriage of Cargoes and updated through the Maritime Safety Committee (MSC).

If timber deck cargo is properly loaded and secured along the entire length of an applicable ship's cargo deck in accordance with the timber conditions of affreightment, it offers additional protection to the ship's hatches and is considered to increase the ship's reserve buoyancy. As a consequence, an increase in draught may be permitted, enabling the ship to increase the weight of cargo carried.

The following definitions are provided within the Code:

- ***Timber*** *is used as a collective expression used for all types of wooden material covered by this Code, including both round and sawn wood but excluding wood pulp and similar cargo*
- ***timber deck cargo*** *means a cargo of timber carried on an uncovered part of a freeboard or superstructure deck*
- ***timber load line*** *means a special load line assigned to ships complying with certain conditions set out in the International Convention on Load Lines.*

Stability

In addition to the increased weight of deck cargo, the Code advises that the following should be taken into account when calculating a ship's stability, and provides appropriate calculation guidance:

- Absorption of water in dried or seasoned timber
- ice accretion
- variations in consumables
- ballast water exchange operations
- free surface moments.

Testing, Examination and Certification

All lashings and components used for securing timber deck cargo should be tested, marked and certified according to national regulations or an appropriate standard of an internationally recognised standards institute. Copies of the appropriate certificate should be kept on board.

Examinations should include a visual examination of lashings and components at intervals not exceeding 12 months. Visual inspections should be performed before loading the timber deck cargo and should include all securing points on the ship, including those on the uprights, if fitted.

Lashing Plans

One or more lashing plans relating to timber deck cargoes are to be provided in the ship's cargo securing manual and maintained on board a ship permitted to carry timber deck cargo.

Stowage and Securing

The Code details the precautions to be taken before timber deck cargo is loaded on deck and the manner in which the cargo should be stowed and secured. On ships provided with, and making use of, a timber load line, specific requirements are prescribed, including the need for solid stowage during all stages of deck loading.

The components and lashings used to secure timber deck cargoes have certain specifications that must be met, eg they should have a breaking strain of not less than 133 kN.

Tightening of Lashings

Vibration and movement can cause the cargo to settle and compact on voyage. Therefore, the Code requires that all lashings are to be carefully examined and tightened at the beginning and at regular intervals during the voyage. Records of these checks are to be kept in the ship's logbook.

Personnel Protection and Safety Devices

The Code describes access and safety requirements for ships with timber deck cargoes, which may include:

- Safe access from the accommodation to all parts used in the necessary working of the ship. This may require guard lines or rails (at least 1 m high) provided on each side of the deck cargo
- a taut lifeline with a tightening device provided as near as practicable to the centreline of the ship
- if cargo is uneven, a safe walking surface of not less than 600 mm in width fitted over the cargo and secured beneath or beside the lifeline
- a lifeline erected above the timber deck cargo so that a crew member equipped with a fall protection system can hook on
- properly constructed ladders, steps or ramps fitted with guard lines or handrails provided from the top of the cargo to the deck.

Tonnage Measurement of Ships

International Convention on Tonnage Measurement of Ships, 1969

The International Convention on Tonnage Measurement of Ships was adopted on 23rd June 1969 and entered into force on 18th July 1982. It was the first successful introduction of a universal tonnage measurement system.

The Convention applies to all ships, except war ships and those navigating in specifically listed waters, built on or after 18th July 1982. Ships built before that date were allowed to retain their existing tonnage for 12 years after entry into force, or until 18th July 1994.

Previously, considerable differences had existed between the various systems used, despite all originating from the same method credited to Admiral George Moorsom of the British Board of Trade in 1854.

The Convention ensured that calculations under the new system did not differ too greatly from the previous ones.

The Convention altered the following terms:

- *Gross register tons* (grt) became *gross tonnage* (GT)
- *Net register tons* (nrt) became *net tonnage* (NT).

Both GT and NT are to be calculated independently:

- Gross tonnage refers to the moulded volume of all enclosed spaces on the ship and is used for manning regulations, safety rules and registration fees. It is calculated by:

Tonnage Measurement of Ships

GT = K × V
where V = Volume (m³)
K = 0.22 to 0.32
(dependent on ship's size)

$$GT = K \times V$$

- Net tonnage refers to the moulded volume of the cargo spaces, sometimes referred to as the earning capacity, and is used primarily in the calculation of port dues (GT is also sometimes used).

Documentation and Certification

An International Tonnage Certificate (1969) shall be issued to every ship by the Administration, or any duly authorised person. However, the Administration remains responsible for the certificate.

A certificate shall cease to be valid if:

- Alterations increase GT or NT
- the ship is transferred to another flag (State), although a period of three months grace is provided while awaiting new certification.

A number of amendments and resolutions have clarified meanings and application, with the most recent being:

Resolution A.791(19) adopted on 23 November 1995 – Application of the International Convention on Tonnage Measurement of Ships 1969 to Existing Ships.

This advises that, where the keel was laid before 18th July 1982, GT is determined in accordance with national tonnage rules that were valid prior to the coming into force of the 1969 Tonnage Convention. In this case, the tonnage certificate need only show the old GT with an appropriate footnote.

NT is the volume of cargo space.

Wreck Removal Convention

Nairobi International Convention on the Removal of Wrecks

The Nairobi International Convention on the Removal of Wrecks (WRC) 2007 was adopted on 18th May 2007 and entered into force on 14th April 2015. It is intended to provide uniform international rules and a legal basis to ensure coastal States remove from their coastlines shipwrecks that pose a hazard to the safety of navigation or to the marine and coastal environments.

The Convention will achieve this by:

- Making the ship's registered owner liable for the costs of locating, marking and removing a wreck
- imposing an insurance or other financial requirement on ships of 300 GT and above to cover the liability
- providing States with a right to take action against insurers.

By providing the first set of uniform international rules for the removal of wrecks beyond their territorial waters, the new Convention also includes an optional clause enabling Parties to apply certain provisions to their territory.

The Convention provides the following definitions:

- "***Wreck***," following a maritime casualty, means:
  - *a) a sunken or stranded ship; or*
  - *b) any part of a sunken or stranded ship, including any object that is or has been on board such a ship; or*
  - *c) any object that is lost at sea from a ship and that is stranded, sunken or adrift at sea; or*
  - *d) a ship that is about, or may reasonably be expected, to sink or to strand, where effective measures to assist the ship or any property in danger are not already being taken.*
- "***Hazard***" means any condition or threat that:
  - *a) poses a danger or impediment to navigation; or*
  - *b) may reasonably be expected to result in major harmful consequences to the marine environment, or damage to the coastline or related interests of one or more States.*

Wreck Removal Convention

- *"**Removal**" means any form of prevention, mitigation or elimination of the hazard created by a wreck. "Remove", "removed" and "removing" shall be construed accordingly.*

The Convention does not apply to:

- *Measures taken under the International Convention relating to Intervention on the High Seas in Cases of Oil Pollution Casualties, 1969, as amended*
- *the Protocol relating to Intervention on the High Seas in Cases of Pollution by Substances other than Oil, 1973, as amended*
- *any warship or other ship owned or operated by a State and used, for the time being, only on Government non-commercial service, unless that State decides otherwise.*

Reporting

Wrecks must be reported by the master and/or the ship's operator to the affected State without delay. The following information must be provided:

a) the precise location of the wreck;

b) the type, size and construction of the wreck;

c) the nature of the damage to, and the condition of, the wreck;

d) the nature and quantity of the cargo, in particular any hazardous and noxious substances; and

e) the amount and types of oil, including bunker oil and lubricating oil, on board.

The Convention sets out the provisions and actions required by the affected State regarding:

- Determining hazards
- locating wrecks
- marking wrecks
- removal of wrecks
- owner's liabilities
- compulsory insurance or other financial liabilities
- time limits
- disputes.

CHAPTER 23

Recent Regulations

EEDI

and it should not be agreed without consensus. On several occasions, requests were called for votes to be taken.

After continued slowing down of progress and a show of cards that served to prove division within the Committee, a roll call was requested and taken. The inevitable result of the roll call, which comprised only of States signatory to Annex VI and so eligible to participate, was 48 for and 2 against the adoption of Chapter 4 to Annex VI.

This perhaps explained the desire of some non-signatory Parties to delay the discussions and demonstrated the foresight of Lloyd's List in this 2010 article:

> *"Without some significant and unexpected compromise from with the UNFCCC, the call on whether EEDI makes it into Marpol Annex VI is likely to come down to a crude tally of numbers of governments for and against."*

Richard Meade, Lloyds List - Thursday 7th October 2010

MEPC 62

The 62nd session of the Marine Environment Protection Committee took place between 11th and 15th July 2011. Debate was dominated by amendments to MARPOL Annex VI concerning the reduction of emissions of greenhouse gases (GHG), specifically CO_2, from new ships. Discussions centred on the intended Energy Efficiency Design Index (EEDI) and Ship Energy Efficiency Management Plan (SEEMP).

The plenary was largely divided between the developed and developing states. The developing countries were under a high degree of pressure from the EU and UN to provide results and strongly back adoption of the amendments. States opposing the adoption argued that it was not in accordance with common but differentiated responsibility (CBDR), the proposals lacked maturity, procedures for submission were unprecedented, technology should be shared among States

What is EEDI?

The Energy Efficiency Design Index (EEDI) is a technical instrument that sets energy efficiency levels for new ships of >400 GT and some major conversions. It is intended to reduce the amount of CO_2 emissions from ships through improvements in energy efficiency.

Improvements are to be achieved through non-prescriptive technical and design measures that encourage innovation and maintain separation from commercial methods – slow steaming, virtual arrival, etc.

EEDI is a measure of the volume of CO_2 produced by a ship per unit of transport provided (capacity), ie the ship's CO_2 efficiency. It is far from a simple regulatory formula:

$$\frac{\left(\prod_{j=1}^{M} fi\right)\left(\sum_{i=1}^{nME} P_{ME(i)} \cdot C_{FME(i)} \cdot SFC_{ME(i)}\right) + (P_{AE} \cdot C_{FAE} \cdot SFC_{AE}{}^{*}) + \left(\left(\prod_{j=1}^{M} f_j \cdot \sum_{i=1}^{nPTI} P_{PTI(i)} - \sum_{i=1}^{neff} f_{eff(i)} \cdot P_{AEeff(i)}\right) C_{FAE} \cdot SFC_{AE}\right) - \left(\sum_{i=1}^{neff} f_{eff(i)} \cdot P_{eff(i)} \cdot C_{FME} \cdot SFC_{ME}\right)}{f_i \cdot Capacity \cdot V_{ref} \cdot f_w}$$

MEPC.1/Circ.681

Simplified, it is the ratio (index) of:

$$\frac{CO_2 \text{ Emissions}}{\text{Transport Work}}$$

Where:

CO_2 emissions = Main Engines + Auxiliary Engines – Innovative technologies

Which Ships Does it Apply to?

EEDI will apply to the following ships:

- Oil and chemical tankers
- gas tankers
- container ships
- bulk carriers
- general cargo ships
- refrigerated ships
- combination carriers.

New ships are considered as either:

- Ships with a building contract submitted on or after 1st January 2013
- ships where the keel is laid (or is at a similar construction stage) on or after 1st July 2013 if there is no building contract
- ships delivered on or after 1st July 2015, irrespective of the building, contract or a keel laying date.

Baselines in discussion ('GHG-WG 2/2/7')

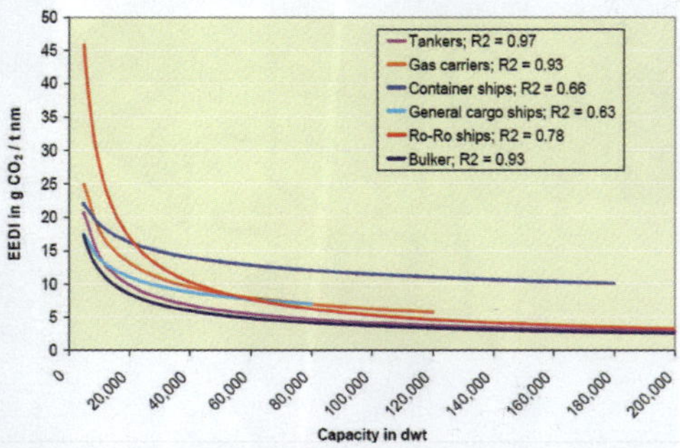

Figure 23.1 - Greenhouse gas emissions from shipping, Germanischer Lloyd, 2009

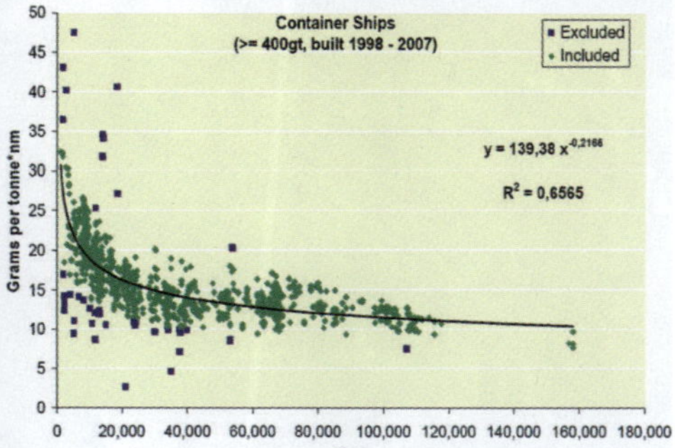

Figure 23.2 - Greenhouse gas emissions from shipping, Germanischer Lloyd, 2009

Some ships will initially be exempt due to engine type, ie turbines, hybrid and diesel electric, and other ships not designed for the transportation of cargo, eg passenger ships, dive support vessels, etc. Where significant difficulty is agreed to exist in calculating EEDI because of propulsion or cargo capacity using present methodology, it will be reviewed at subsequent implementation phases.

Further ship types are anticipated for inclusion when MEPC meets in July 2015.

How Does it Work?

Baselines for the applicable different ship types are set, providing a required EEDI. A ship will then be assessed and certified with an attained EEDI that should not exceed the minimum.

Generally, the capacity is assumed as the deadweight. The curve is produced from a scatter diagram of the EEDIs for each ship within a particular fleet type and a curve is run through the results.

From the baseline, the EEDI will specify minimum efficiency levels that incorporate the incremental 10% reductions (from the original baseline) for each ship measured in grams CO_2/tonne-miles and provide comparison figures between ships of the same type.

Effectively a best practice system, the Ship Energy Efficiency Management Plan (SEEMP) is an onboard ship management tool with reporting requirements that prescribes improvements in operational energy efficiency on all applicable ships through inclusion and optimisation of:

- Energy efficiency
- speed/power and fuel consumption
- voyage planning
- ship handling
- fleet management
- cargo handling.

The SEEMP is permitted to form part of a ship Safety Management System (SMS), provided that it is developed in accordance with the IMO guidelines.

EEDI

What are the Perceived Flaws with EEDI?

A number of concerns have been expressed against the EEDI concept and its introduction. These include:

- The accuracy of the input parameters and the derivation of the baseline curves based on scatter graphs. Faster ships seem to be disadvantaged
- the apparent assumption that ships always operate at the same power. This is considered unlikely as many will only operate at full power during boom periods with high charter rates (world scale 100+). For many ships, this may occur only during a small proportion of the ship's life
- EEDI focuses on CO_2 emissions rather than fuel consumption, meaning that in practical terms it could be considered a mandatory reduction in installed power. However, the amount of installed power used to propel a ship is not linear to the speed, ie a relatively small reduction in speed can result in a disproportionately larger reduction in emissions
- low powered ships are not always more fuel efficient. Higher KW ships may turn larger propellers at lower rpm to achieve the same speed and operate at a lower percentage of installed power. This potentially leaves low powered ships running at a higher percentage of installed power with better EEDI but using more fuel
- the uniform percentage reduction targets for all ship types do not reflect the existing differences between ships and variation in the required remedial measures. Therefore, ships with existing proportionately lower EEDIs may find it more difficult to achieve the reduction target than the traditional big polluters
- specialised and smaller ships will vary considerably in achieving targets, eg RoRos tend to be built to specific trade requirements, so their existing EEDIs will differ and make standardised baselines difficult to apply fairly
- EEDI considers sea power. However, some large geared ships consume almost as much power during cargo operations, which is not perceived as being considered
- EEDI offers no incentive to be more efficient than the EEDI targets
- EEDIs will be based on sea trials and may not reflect realistic non-calm, in-service conditions.

Possible Dangers of EEDI

Many ships are already underpowered, and reducing main power further means engines are likely to be worked harder, which may reduce reliability and increase the likelihood of failure. Consequently, EEDI may increase the prospect of grounding, accidents and pollution by making ships even more susceptible to adverse weather conditions.

EEDI will benefit ships of lighter construction (ie lower lightweight) meaning that greater numbers of ships could be built to the minimum class specifications, so becoming more prone to corrosion and metal fatigue.

Twin-screw propellers are considered safer than singles due to the additional redundancy inherent in having two systems available on board and the improvement it provides in ship handling at slow speed. However, the cost of installation for large ships means the benefits are experienced more for higher power, high speed ships. This will be limited by EEDI.

Do We Need it?

There is a real environmental need and a political will to do something about CO_2 emissions. A 'carbon tax' or 'cap-and-trade' that would effectively promote self-efficiency would require a new convention, whereas EEDI requires only amendments to MARPOL Annex VI. This allowed it to be pushed through quicker.

However, some reports do not see this urgency as entirely necessary because shipping is the least CO_2 intensive form of transportation and, by making it more expensive, cargo may be pushed to other modes of transport. Additionally, rising fuel prices (and reducing charter rates) will continue to reduce consumption and emissions due to slow steaming and increased operational efficiencies.

Entry into Force

The new chapter of Annex VI entered into force on 1st January 2013 and ships with a build contract after this date for delivery not later than 30th June 2015 must meet the required EEDI. Thereafter, EEDI will be implemented in three stages. Each stage reduces the target value by a further 10% from the baseline over a 10-year period, ie ships built between:

- 2015 and 2019 – 10% efficiency improvement
- 2020 and 2024 – 20% efficiency improvement
- after 2024 – 30% efficiency improvement.

A provision was agreed during MEPC 62 that permits administrations to delay their enforcement by up to four years, meaning that EEDI certification would not be required for their ships until 1st January 2017.

"This waiver may not be applied to ships above 400 gross tonnage for which the building contract is placed four years after the entry into force date of chapter 4; the keel of which is laid or which is at a similar stage of construction four years and six months after the entry into force; the delivery of which is after six years and six months after the entry into force; or in cases of the major conversion of a new or existing ship, four years after the entry into force date."

imo.org

During the early stages of phase 1, the status of the technical development and reduction rates will be assessed and the implementation of the later phases reviewed and amended if required.

Conclusion

Aside from the implementation of EEDI, continued rising fuel costs, increasing fleet sizes and competition will result in lower charter rates, meaning managers will look to reduce costs. There is only so far crewing/ operating costs can safely achieve this, so efficiencies will need to be sought elsewhere. Whether these are from slow steaming, virtual arrival or technical/design innovation, they will come regardless of EEDI if companies are to remain competitive. Where markets dictate price, product and service costs are more often than not reduced to remain profitable.

Nevertheless, the achievement of adopting the amendments and the unique agreement for such legally binding global carbon reduction legislation should not be understated. The legislation will continue

EEDI

to be adjusted during the entry into force period and questions regarding the remaining ship types not currently included will be resolved.

Ultimately, EEDI is one part of a wider solution to the emissions reduction issue that focuses on technology, with the SEEMP helping to bring awareness and improvement on operational aspects.

BIMCO released an EEDI calculator in MS Excel format

Download from:
http://tinyurl.com/pux3zzg

EU Fuels Directive

Regulations Controlling Emissions from Shipping

There are mandatory IMO MARPOL Annex VI Regulations for global SOx and NOx emission control as well as several regional limits. The current global SOx limit is 3.50% m/m sulphur. An IMO feasibility study is due to take place before 2018 to confirm whether the next global step-wise reduction to 0.50% m/m sulphur will take place on 1st January 2020 or be deferred until 2025. The EU has already committed to the 2020 date. These more stringent global sulphur level regulations, accompanied by the reduced level now required in Emission Control Areas (see below), are expected to have significant implications for the global refinery network, with necessary upgrading of refineries and increasing the refining capacity.

Note: Sulphur oxide (SOx) refers to all oxides of sulphur. The two major components are sulphur dioxide (SO_2) and sulphur trioxide (SO_3).

The global NOx limits are set at Tier II, whereas the Tier III limits are only applicable to NOx-Emission Control Areas (see Table 23.1).

Emission Control Areas (ECA)

ECAs are regions where specific emissions (SOx and NOx) are subject to stricter limits than the Annex VI Regulations for global emission control. There are four SOx-ECAs that are currently in force, two of which will also become active as NOx-ECAs on 1st January 2016 for ships built after this date.

The four regions with SOx-ECA status all regulate SOx to 0.10% m/m sulphur in fuel (or equivalent):

- The Baltic Sea SOx-ECA (entered into force 19th May 2006) includes the Baltic Sea, the Gulf of Bothnia, the Gulf of Finland and the entrance to the Baltic Sea bounded by the parallel of the Skaw in the Skagerrak at 57°44'8"N
- the North Sea and English Channel SOx-ECA (entered into force 22nd November 2007) has the boundaries:
  - the North Sea southwards of latitude 62°N and eastwards of longitude 4°W
  - the Skagerrak, the southern limit of which is determined east of the Skaw by latitude 57°30'N
  - the English Channel and its approaches eastwards of longitude 5°W and northwards of latitude 48°44'8"N
- the North America SOx/NOx-ECA (entered into force for SOx 1st August 2012). The area is not as easily defined as the European ECA boundaries but extends 200 nm from the coastline of North America. The lists of coordinates for the North American ECA east coast boundary, west coast boundary and Hawaiian island boundary are available in MEPC 60/22 Annex 11
- the United States Caribbean Sea SOx/NOx-ECA (entry into force for SOx 1st January 2014). The US Caribbean ECA extends approximately 50 nm from the territorial sea baselines of the islands included in the ECA. The exact coordinates can be found in MEPC.1/Circ.755.

EU Fuels Directive

Tier	Date of Ship Construction	NOx Limit (g/kWh)		
		Slow Speed Diesel Engines (n < 130)	Medium Speed Diesel Engines (130 ≤ n < 2000)	High Speed Diesel Engines (n ≥ 2000)
Tier 0	1990 to 2000	17.0	$45 \times n^{-0.2}$	9.8
Tier I (Global)	2000 to 2010			
Tier II (Global)	2011 onwards	14.4	$44 \times n^{-0.23}$	7.7
Tier III (*NOx-ECA only)	2016 onwards	3.4	$9 \times n^{-0.2}$	1.96
*Applicable only in NOx Emission Control Areas (Tier II standards apply outside ECAs). n = rated engine speed (rpm)				

Table 23.1 - Global and ECA NOx limits

Figure 23.3 - Diagram illustrating the four existing SOx - ECAs

EU Fuels Directive

After 1st January 2016, NOx will be regulated for new builds (ie vessels with their keel laid on or after this date) operating in both the North American SOx/NOx-ECA and the United States Caribbean Sea SOx/NOx-ECA.

The EU Sulphur Directive 2005/33/EC

In the European Union, ships, as well as other modes of transport, are targeted as contributors to the global problems of climate change and depletion of the ozone layer. A study for the European Commission, which examined all shipping journeys starting or finishing in Europe and calculated the emissions of various pollutants concluded that, by 2010, emissions of sulphur dioxide (SOx) in EU sea areas were likely to equate to 75% of total land-based emissions, including those from all cars, trucks and industrial plants. This knowledge promoted a drive to significantly reduce EU sulphur dioxide emissions and to help the European Community achieve its interim environmental objectives for 2010, as stated in Directive 2001/81/EC, on national emission ceilings for certain atmospheric pollutants. The EU Sulphur Directive applies to ships flying the flag of a European Member State and also those calling at European ports (irrespective of their flag).

From 1st January 2010, this EU Directive required a change to the maximum allowable fuel oil sulphur content of marine fuels used by ships, meaning that ships must use fuel oil with only 0.1% (0.10% by mass (m/m)) sulphur content, or ultra-low sulphur fuel. This applies to all types of combustion machinery, including main and auxiliary boilers on ships at berth in EU ports, and includes ships alongside, at anchor or on a buoy, whether or not they are working cargo. The ships are not required to comply with the 0.1% limit while manoeuvring, but they must comply as soon as possible after arrival in the port, and until as close a time as possible before departure.

It was reported in October 2013 that the global consumption of marine bunkers was approximately 200 million mt/year, with the EU consuming about 25% of that. The reduction in the level of sulphur allowed in fuels to 0.1% for all SOx-ECAs on 1st January 2015 means that the two European ECAs demand the same sulphur in fuel levels (or equivalent) as the EU Sulphur Directive (2005/33/EC) for vessels at EU ports.

There are exemptions to the EU Sulphur Directive:

- Certain 'named ships', and ships that are scheduled to be at berth for less than two hours, will be exempt from these requirements
- vessels may be exempted if they connect to shore power while alongside. This procedure is known as 'cold ironing' or alternative marine power (AMP).

It should be noted that the EU Sulphur in Fuel Directive remains applicable to shipping visiting all EU ports that are outside the SOx-ECA boundaries.

Note: Although Turkey is not a member of the EU, it requires SOx limits at port to the same level as the EU Sulphur Directive.

Emissions Control in California

California has had state emission regulations in place since 1st July 2009 with a phased approach to reduce sulphur in fuel. It has been a fuel rule rather than an emissions rule, and no abatement technologies were allowed as a substitute for MGO and MDO. Since the sulphur emissions limits of the US SOx/NOx-ECA came into effect on 1st January 2015, there has been a sunset review period in California where the effectiveness of the two emissions standards has been reviewed. The ECA rules will eventually supersede the Californian OGV fuel rule and abatement technologies will be acceptable alternatives to using reduced sulphur fuel.

The Port of Long Beach claims that shutting down a single ship's diesel engines at berth for a day achieves the same air quality improvement as taking 33,000 cars off southern California's roads. Californian ports have been keen to develop cold ironing capabilities and now have extensive facilities available. On 1st January 2014, the Port of Los Angeles Harbor Department had a total of 25 berths with an AMP capability. The Port of San Diego completed its shore power project in February 2014 with the AMP system for container and cargo-refrigerated ships. This is in addition to the shore power facilities for cruise ships at the port.

by Dale Frost courtesy the Port of San Diego

Figure 23.4 - The Port of San Diego shore power installation for cargo vessels in February 2014

Controlling Ship Emissions in Practice

Navigating the various low sulphur regulations can be a tricky process. For example, a vessel visiting an EU port that is not within the boundaries of the two European ECAs, for example Glasgow, can use fuel with 3.5% sulphur (the global limit) until berthing, and then it must comply with the EU Sulphur Directive and switch to a fuel with 0.1% sulphur or use an abatement technology to bring its emissions to the equivalent of using 0.1% sulphur fuel. However, if any part of the ship's onward journey involves entering the boundaries of an ECA, the fuel used must be switched from the global limit of 3.5% to a 0.1% sulphur fuel or an abatement technology employed during that passage.

There is a financial consideration to operators in the use of distillates or ULSFO (ultra-low sulphur fuel oil) and these must be weighed up against the cost of a scrubber system cleaning the emissions from using cheaper higher sulphur fuel. Distillate fuels have always been more expensive than residual fuels and it has been estimated that using 0.1% sulphur in fuel could increase the costs of transportation in the Baltic ECA by 20% to 28%. Operators must take into account the operating area of each vessel and compare any return on investment in an abatement technology with the higher cost of compliant fuel.

Low Sulphur Fuels

Low sulphur residual fuel blended with marine distillates can be used to reach the 0.5% sulphur levels required for the reduction in global sulphur in fuels in 2020 in EU waters.

If the global sulphur in fuels level for the rest of the world is delayed until 2025 (the result is subject to a report in 2018) this will add further complexities to remaining SOx emission compliant. The current ECA and EU ports requirement for fuel to be ≤0.1% sulphur means that marine distillates will be used instead of low sulphur residual fuel blends. DNV Petroleum Services (now Veritas Petroleum Services) have indicated that several types of ULSFO, also known as hybrid fuels, were introduced into the market in 2014 by various suppliers in order to meet the demand for 0.1% sulphur in fuel. These new ULSFO fuels have varying technical qualities as well as a complex composition, so each will have different requirements for heating, settling, separation, filtration and sludge. Compatibility issues may arise during changeover between these new fuels and standard distillates or residual fuels.

There are several key parts to an effective ship strategy for compliance:

- Carry out a risk analysis to indicate the issues and risks involved with operating the vessel on low sulphur fuel
- consult engine and boiler manufacturers for advice on operating with each specific type of low sulphur fuel and whether any equipment and system modifications are necessary
- if modifications are required on board, consult the vessel's Classification Society and/or flag State
- when consulting with the engine and boiler manufacturers, prepare a written fuel changeover procedure. Sufficient time must be left to complete the fuel oil changeover prior to crossing the ECA border. Inspections and maintenance schedules must be included
- crew training should emphasise the importance of accurate logbook recordings and the taking and storing of samples
- consult with the fuel suppliers and update the fuel procurement strategy. This is in order to select a low sulphur fuel with properties suitable for the machinery on board and to make sure that the fuel is received well in advance of entering an ECA
- check that the wording of charterparties covers the necessary allocation of responsibilities for the new sulphur regulations.

EU Fuels Directive

It is thought that one of the most likely reasons for non-compliance will be the inability to bunker with the correct fuel before entering the ECA boundaries. The master of a vessel deemed to be non-compliant has to prove that "best endeavours" were made to obtain the correct fuel and that none was available on the voyage of the ship. A key factor in this argument is that vessels are not required to delay or deviate from their passage to purchase compliant fuel.

Monitoring and Enforcing the Use of Low Sulphur Fuels

The monitoring and enforcement of low sulphur emissions regulations within ECAs and at European ports is vital to the effectiveness of the legislation. Without enforcement there is little incentive to comply and, unless the regulations are robustly enforced, operators who are compliant are at a disadvantage compared with those who are not. To promote fair competition, the Trident Alliance was launched in July 2014 to promote and work towards the robust enforcement of maritime sulphur regulations. The rapidly increasing membership of this shipping initiative includes owners and operators such as Maersk Tankers and Maersk Line, Wallenius Wilhelmsen Logistics, DFDS, Hapag-Lloyd, Rickmers-Linie and ARC (American Roll-on Roll-off carrier).

Enforcement relies on accurate monitoring techniques, and checking for compliance has been targeted towards the more high risk ships, ie those vessels that have a higher likelihood of non-compliance through their history and previous inspections. Cooperation and the sharing of information between national competent authorities are imperative in order to focus the limited resources of these bodies and enable more effective monitoring and enforcement.

On 30th December 2014, the Paris MoU issued the *"Guidelines on application of MARPOL Annex VI Regulation 18 in an Emission Control Area (ECA)"*. During the first inspection within an ECA, or the first port after transiting an ECA, the PSCO will look at three key pieces of evidence:

"1. Bunker delivery note showing a sulphur content of not more than 0.10% m/m for fuel oil used onboard (MARPOL Annex VI Regulation 18 (5)).

2. The representative sample of fuel oil with a sulphur content of not more than 0.10% m/m (MARPOL Annex VI Regulation 18 (8.1)).

3. Evidence of a written procedure (note: there is no requirement for this to be in English) and record of changeover to fuel oil with a sulphur content of not more than 0.10% m/m before entering the ECA such that this fuel is being burnt when entering the ECA and the volume of low sulphur fuel oils in each tank as well as the date, time, and position of the ship when any fuel-oil-changeover operation is completed prior to the entry into an ECA or commenced after exit from such an area, shall be recorded in such log-book as prescribed by the Administration. (MARPOL Annex VI Regulation 14 (6))."

Since it is a challenge to check a vessel's fuel sulphur level or SOx emissions whilst at sea and also to the stringent 0.10% limit now mandatory in all ECAs, research is being carried out to develop further monitoring techniques over and above the current methods. Some countries are more proactive than others in this endeavour. The Danish Environmental Protection Agency (EPA) are providing financial backing for the testing of sulphur detection, or 'sniffer', drones (Unmanned Aerial Vehicle (UAV) or Remotely Piloted Aircraft System (RPAS)) to monitor sulphur emissions from shipping. The drone uses a self-guided system that pinpoints ships whilst in transit, measures the sulphur emissions and relays the information in real time. The Danish Shipowners' Association and the Danish Maritime Agency also support the UAV technology. Other examples of emissions compliance monitoring technology being tested include:

- Handheld instruments to measure sulphur levels in the fuel being used in ships
- automated measurement of fuel line temperatures. This is an indicator of the fuel type used, ie HFO or MGO.

SOx sensors have already been fitted to the Great Belt Bridge, Denmark to detect emissions from passing ships. A two year project initiated (from 1st January 2015 to the end of 2016) on the 'Surveillance of sulphur-emissions from ships in Danish waters' is to assess both the monitoring of sulphur emissions from a fixed installation and also airborne monitoring. The results from this project will be reported to the Danish Environment Protection Agency (EPA) no later than March 2017. The Finnish Transport Safety Agency have also been looking at more efficient monitoring and are planning to launch a remote ship emissions monitoring system to cover the northern section of the Baltic Sea.

Continuous Emissions Monitoring Systems (CEMS) will also play an important part in monitoring sulphur emissions from ships. The in-situ, stack-mounted analysers are a robust and mature technology and several readily available systems have been approved according to the MEPC 184 (59) 2009 Guidelines for Exhaust Gas Cleaning Systems. The CEMS can be calibrated to measure up to six exhaust gases such as SO_2, NOx and CO_2. These systems can verify compliance to the very low levels of SOx allowed in ECAs and after acquiring the data can display, log and transmit the information automatically without intervention from the crew. Using a CEMS can be an effective monitoring tool for a vessel to prove compliance, whether a vessel switches from higher to ultra-low sulphur fuel or uses a scrubber.

The US Coast Guard currently checks Bunker Delivery Notes and other records during port State and flag State visits to vessels. The Coast Guard and EPA are also developing plans to board vessels together, and the checks carried out will include fuel oil sampling and on site screening for sulphur levels. The US Coast Guard is enforcing the North American SOx-ECA limits with fines and detentions. The United States EPA published the 'EPA Policy for Violations by Ships of the Sulfur in Fuel Standard and Related Provisions' on 15th January 2015:

Actual Fuel Sulfur Content (%m/m)	First Offence Penalty ($) over the Course of the Violation
	0.10% sulphur ECA limit (per MT of fuel burned while in the US ECAs)
≥ 3.50	$750
3.00	$700
2.50	$650
2.00	$600
1.50	$550
1.25	$500
1.10	$450
1.00	$400
0.80	$350
0.60	$300
0.40	$250
0.20	$200
0.15	$150
0.10	N/A

Table 23.2 - EPA Policy for Violations by Ships of the Sulfur in Fuel Standard and Related Provisions

The first offence penalties for exceeding the sulphur emissions limits are listed in Table 23.2. The penalty for record keeping violations within the US SOx-ECA boundaries ranges from US$2,500 to US$15,000 per violation per day, with first offence violations being towards the lower end of the range.

The US EPS policy states that:

> *"A penalty should remove any significant economic benefit resulting from noncompliance. In addition, the penalty should include an amount beyond recovery of the economic benefit to reflect the seriousness of the violation."*

Penalties for violations of the European Sulphur Directive in European countries have been very different from country to country. For example, the maximum penalty in Germany is US$7,000, in Poland it is US$62,000 and in the UK it is US$83,000. However, in order to align the monitoring and enforcing of the sulphur emissions legislation throughout Europe, new rules are being prepared for more rigorous and standardised monitoring in the EU. These include:

- Member States will check on 10% of vessels calling in relevant member State ports per year to review logs and BNDs
- these checks will then be stepped up from 1st January 2016, when at least 40% of that 10% will be subject to onboard fuel testing for compliance. This will be carried out by inspectors in member States or those fully bordering an ECA. A lower percentage of vessels will be tested in both states partially bordering or not bordering any ECA.

The pre-screening of vessels to target the most likely offenders is an important factor to effective policing of the ECA area.

Scrubber Systems - an Alternative Emission Reduction Measure

Both the SOx-ECAs and EU Directive allow for equivalents and so allow the use of Exhaust Gas Cleaning Systems (EGCS) - also called scrubbers. These systems must achieve the same levels of SOx in the exhaust as if the ship was burning fuel with a sulphur content of less than 0.1%, irrespective of the fuel burnt. The flag Administration of the vessel also has to approve each scrubber as an equivalent.

EU Fuels Directive

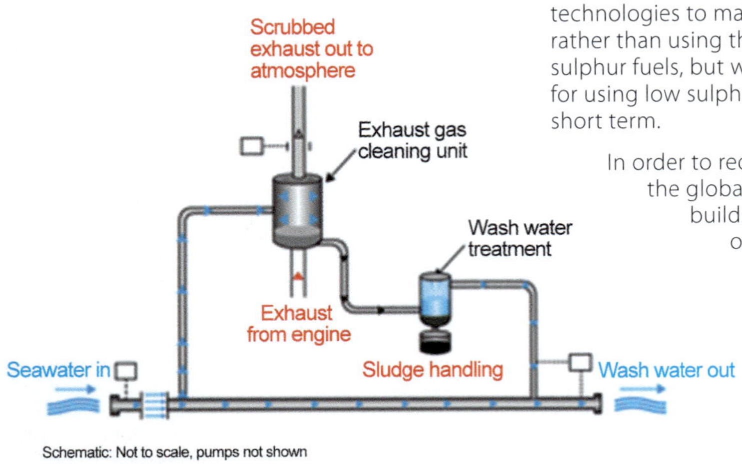

Figure 23.5 - Generalised schematic of an open loop (seawater) scrubber

A number of marine engineering companies have been working on scrubber technology that can reduce SOx emissions from heavier fuel oils to be equivalent to those of a low sulphur graded fuel. In order to remain SOx emission compliant, a ship can invest in the scrubber and use cheaper higher sulphur fuel oil and treat the emissions. This can be an effective compliance strategy for vessels with many operating hours within ECA limits. The installation of a scrubber can range from €3 million to €12 million per ship depending on the vessel size and retrofit issues. The Lloyd's List Sulphur Survey of 2014 found that operators have increased confidence in technologies to maintain compliance rather than using the expensive low sulphur fuels, but will probably opt for using low sulphur distillates in the short term.

In order to reduce NOx emissions to the global levels required in new builds since the beginning of 2011, engines have undergone relatively minor internal modifications which have enabled compliance. However, the 2016 tier III NOx-ECA emissions limits are much more stringent and an upgraded engine will no longer be sufficient. Compliance will require either a primary or secondary strategy:

- A primary strategy would be a change of fuel (such as LNG) which produces less NOx on combustion
- a secondary strategy would involve using an abatement technology to remove NOx once it has been produced during the combustion of a regular fuel.

Using selective catalytic reduction (SCR) is the most efficient abatement technology to reduce NOx emissions from ship's exhaust.

For further information, see *'Marine Fuels and Emissions'* published by Witherbys.

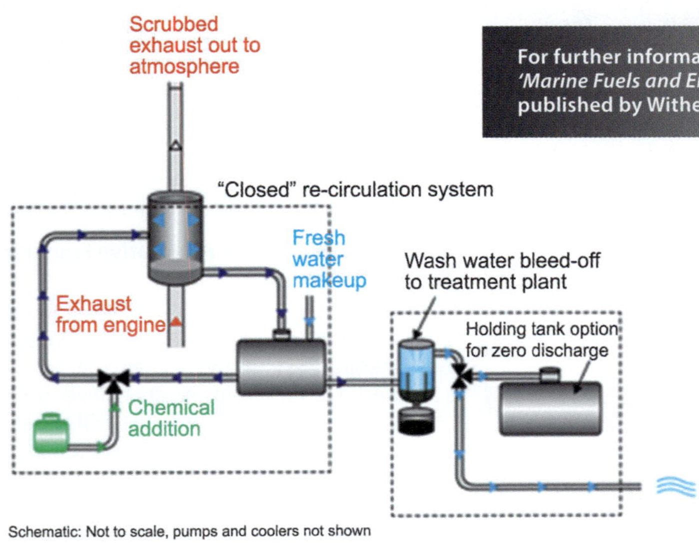

Figure 23.6 - Generalised schematic of a close loop (fresh water) scrubber

New Inspection Regime of the Paris MoU

What Happens After 1st January 2011?

The 32nd Amendment of the Paris MoU introduced the New Inspection Regime (NIR) on Port State Control. It entered into force on 1st January 2011 and replaced the existing target factor with a risk profile for each ship that visits ports in the Paris MoU region, which covers the European coastline and the North Atlantic (as it extends to the east coast of Canada). It classifies ships into three categories and requires certain information from any ship arriving and leaving ports or anchorages in the region.

PSC data is gathered by 'THETIS', the database operated by EMSA that replaces the SIReNaC system.

Key Points of the NIR

- **Ships will be targeted based on a risk profile that considers two elements - Ship Risk Profile and Company Performance**
- **the Ship Risk Profile (SRP) classifies ships into one of three categories: Low Risk Ships, Standard Risk Ships and High Risk Ships. While the SRP assesses type and age of ship, number of previous deficiencies and detentions, performance of the flag of the ship, and the performance of the recognised organisation(s), it also considers a company's performance and takes into account the detention and deficiency history of all ships in a (ISM) company's fleet in the Paris MoU area in the last 36 months**
- **high risk ships will be due inspections every 5-6 months, standard risk ships every 10-12 months and low risk ships every 24-36 months**
- **additional inspections may be carried out between these intervals, for reasons such as reports from pilots, collisions, groundings, etc**
- **the type of inspection will depend on the ship's risk profile; the minimum for a high risk ship will be an expanded inspection**
- **ships requiring an expanded inspection must give 72 hours notice prior to arrival.**

Note: To maintain low risk status, a vessel must have no more than 5 deficiencies during any one inspection and no detention recorded in the preceding 3 years.

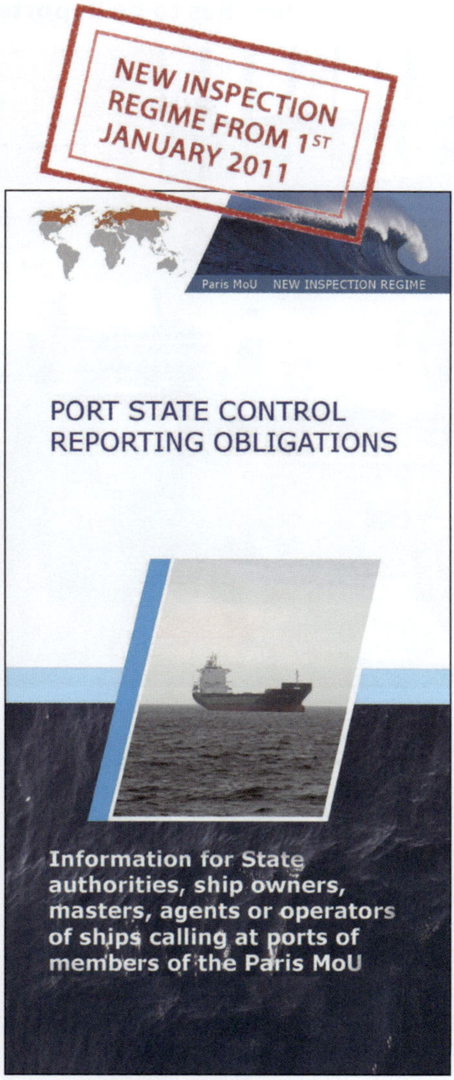

Courtesy of Paris MoU on Port State Control

For more information visit:
http://tinyurl.com/pjdu9ka

NIR heralded a new approach from Port State Control (PSC) to target substandard ships and move away from the 25% inspection regime, where good ships were being targeted as well as poor. The intention is to reward the good operator by increasing the frequency of inspection of 'high risk' ships, while reducing the frequency of inspection of 'low risk'.

New Inspection Regime of the Paris MoU

What Information has to be Reported?

72 Hour ETA Message

The operator, agent or master of a ship that is subject to an expanded inspection shall notify its arrival at least 72 hours before the expected time of arrival in the port or anchorage or before leaving the previous port or anchorage if the voyage is expected to take less than 72 hours.

This provision already exists for certain ships but, as from 1st January 2011, it will be applicable to:

- All ships with a high risk profile, and
- any passenger ship, oil tanker, gas or chemical tanker or bulk carrier, older than 12 years of age.

Information on ships eligible for expanded inspection will be made available online.

At least the following information is to be notified:

- Ship identification (name, call sign, IMO or MMSI number and flag)
- planned duration of the call (ETA/ETD)
- for tankers:
  - hull configuration: single hull, single hull with segregated ballast tanks, double hull;
  - condition of the cargo and ballast tanks: full, empty, inerted;
  - volume and type of cargo
- planned operations at the port or anchorage of destination (loading, unloading, other)
- planned statutory survey inspections and substantial maintenance and repair work to be carried out while in the port of destination
- date of the last expanded inspection in the Paris MoU region.

Ref: (Paris MoU, Annex 12)

24 Hour ETA Notification

The operator, agent or master of the ship shall notify the pre-arrival information (such as ship identification, port of destination, ETA/ETD and total number of persons onboard) to the port authority. The notification shall be done at least 24 hours in advance or at the latest when the ship leaves the previous port if the voyage is less than 24 hours, in line with the requirements of the EU and the Paris MoU.

Ref: (Paris MoU, Annex 12)

Actual time of Arrival and Departure

The actual time of arrival and the actual time of departure of any ship calling at a port or anchorage within the Paris MoU region will be transferred by the relevant Authority to THETIS.

Ref: (Paris MoU, Annex 12)

Useful Points

It is important that senior officers on board are familiar with the PSC process. Companies are urged to ensure that the Safety Management System incorporates procedures to prepare for, and to deal with, PSC inspections and detentions to prevent confusion and unnecessary delay.

Ships should consult the appropriate authorities at their next ports of call to determine local procedures and the means available to report the information required. It may be necessary to implement procedural changes to ensure that the information is transmitted to the relevant authority in due time.

Failures and breakdowns of equipment need not be a cause for detention provided that the flag State and the Recognised Organisation have been advised as soon as the breakdown is experienced and the port State has been alerted prior to arrival. Such reports, however, may be the trigger for PSC Officers (PSCO) to attend on board and so the vessel must be suitably prepared.

The majority of PSC deficiencies, particularly when numerous deficiencies are found that result in a detention, are often ISM related. Proper implementation of the Safety Management System on board can be an effective tool to reduce deficiencies found at PSC and any other inspection. It is important for ships to be aware that, given the nature of the Expanded Inspections, which include a set number of inspection items and operational tests, preparation on board is paramount.

Preparing for Inspection

A number of industry bodies (eg Classification Societies, P&I Clubs, etc) have produced checklists and guidance relating to PSC inspection. Companies may find these useful in ensuring that their vessels are suitably prepared for PSC inspections.

New Inspection Regime of the Paris MoU

Sewage Amendments to MARPOL Annex IV

On 1st August 2010, the Resolution MEPC. 115(51) amendments to MARPOL Annex IV came into force for existing ships. The original legislation entered into force on 1st August 2005 applying only to new ships on international voyages of 400 gross tons and above or certified to carry more than 15 persons.

Under the regulations, ships are prohibited from discharging sewage unless one of the following criteria is complied with:

- Uncomminuted or non-disinfected sewage can only be discharged at a distance more than 12 nautical miles from the nearest land
- comminuted and disinfected sewage can be discharged at a distance more than 3 nautical miles from the nearest land
- a certified sewage treatment plant is in operation meeting Regulation 9.1.1 of Annex 5.

Ships must be equipped with one of the following:

- A type-approved sewage treatment plant
- an approved sewage communiting and disinfecting system
- a sewage holding tank.

When sewage has not passed through an approved sewage treatment plant, it must be discharged at a moderate rate (approved by the Administration) when the vessel is proceeding at a minimum of 4 knots.

In June 2006, MPC 86 clarified that, irrespective of the presence of a sewage treatment plant or holding tank, ships are required to be fitted with a pipeline with a standard discharge connection meeting the following specifications:

Sewage Amendments to MARPOL Annex IV

Description	Dimension
Outside diameter	210 mm
Inner diameter	According to pipe outside diameter
Bolt circle diameter	170 mm
Slots in flange	4 holes 18 mm in diameter equidistantly placed on a bolt circle of the above diameter, slotted to the flange periphery. The slot width to be 18 mm
Flange thickness	16 mm
Bolts and nuts: quantity and diameter	4, each of 16 mm in diameter and of suitable length
The flange is designed to accept pipes up to a maximum internal diameter of 100 mm and shall be of steel or other equivalent material having a flat face. This flange, together with a suitable gasket, shall be suitable for a service pressure of 600 kPa.	

Table 23.3 - MEPC 51/22 Annex 5, Resolution MEPC.115(51) Regulation 10.1

The sewage control equipment below is required to be surveyed in accordance with the ship's International Sewage Pollution Prevention Certificate (ISPPC), which will remain valid for a period specified by the Administration but not longer than five years.

VOCs and VECS

Volatile Organic Compounds and Vapour Emission Control Systems, Revised MARPOL Annex VI, Regulation 15, MEPC 176(58)

On 1st July 2010, the amendments to MARPOL Annex VI, Regulation 15, revised by MEPC 176(58), entered into force.

Regulation 15 applies to the emission of Volatile Organic Compounds (VOCs), the use of Vapour Recovery Systems at load and discharge ports and the use of onboard VOC Management Plans to provide guidance on controlling emissions. It will apply to crude oil tankers, and to gas tankers if their loading and containment system allows for the safe retention of non-methane VOCs on board or their safe return ashore.

The Regulation applies to tankers operating in ports and terminals of signatory States which have been notified to the IMO as being designated for VOC regulation.

In October 2014, there were 76 IMO Signatory Nations representing 95% of the world's tonnage. Operators trading to these countries will have to check whether the port is designated for VOC regulation.

VOCs are organic substances (solids or liquids containing carbon) which release vapour at normal temperature and pressure. VOCs are both hazardous to health and have an adverse environmental effect, in particular contributory effects on global warming and climate change.

To comply with the regulation, applicable tankers should have an approved Vapour Emission Control System (VECS) to be used for relevant cargoes.

VOC Management Plan

A vessel carrying VOC cargoes should carry and implement an Administration approved VOC Management Plan, in accordance with the guidelines in MEPC:1/Circ. 680. The plan should be ship-specific and at least:

- Provide written procedures for minimising VOC emissions during loading, sea passage and discharge of cargo
- give consideration to the additional VOC generated by crude oil washing
- identify a person responsible for implementing the plan.

For ships on international voyages, the plan should be written in the working language of the master and officers and, if this language is not English, French or Spanish, include a translation into one of these languages.

Carriage of Approved Vapour Control Processing Unit

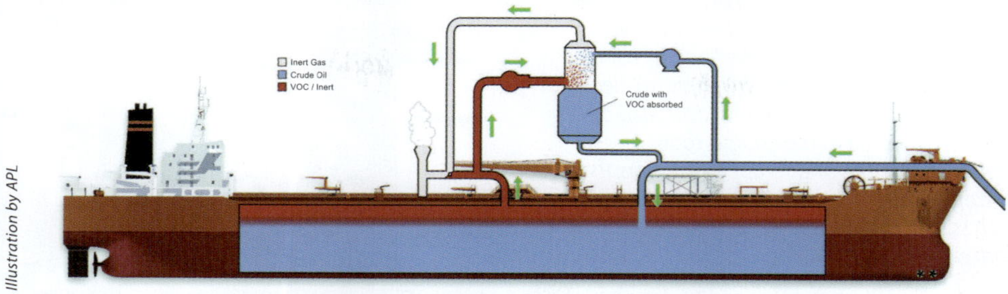

Figure 23.7 - Vapour control processing unit

MSC Circular 585 identifies the construction, operational, training and safety requirements for the VECS, including the need for tankers to carry an approved vapour control processing unit, with permanently installed piping and vapour connections located as close as possible to the loading manifold.

The vapour connection manifold should conform to the industry standard, ie Recommendations for Oil Tanker Manifolds and Associated Equipment section A.5.2.2 (OCIMF).

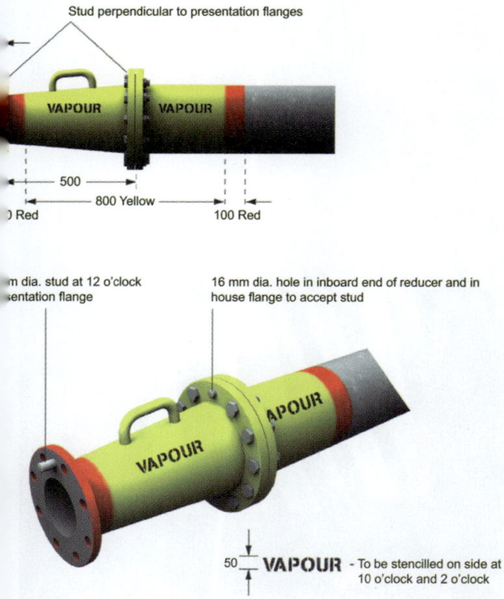

Figure 23.8 - Vapour connection manifold

MSC 585 also requires that:

- Piping should be electrically continuous and bonded to the hull
- hoses should be electrically continuous
- there must be means to separate cargo vapours that react in a hazardous manner, when capable of loading cargo at the same time
- there must be drains or alternate means to eliminate liquid cargo condensate in the system
- it must be possible to isolate vapours from the inert gas supply if utilising the inert gas system piping. The IG main isolation valve may be suitable
- the VECS should not affect the proper operation of the cargo venting system.

Direct Absorption of VOC in the Crude Oil (CVOC System)

MEPC 60 (March 2010) noted an additional technology to reduce the formation and emissions of VOC from crude oil tankers, which was not described in the Annex to MEPC.1/Circ.680, and agreed to issue a separate circular on that technology, as follows:

The CVOC System has been designed to utilize hydrostatic pressure in the cargo tanks to re-absorb emitted VOC back into the Crude Oil. This process allows tank pressure to be reduced without venting to the atmosphere, and thus eliminates all emissions from the cargo during transit – including H_2S. The CVOC system will also reduce VOC emissions from the cargo during loading and cargo transfer operations. The CVOC system is based on direct absorption of VOC in the crude oil. The Swirl Absorber, a combined ejector and mixing unit, are using crude oil from one of the cargo tanks to create a low-pressure area where vapour from the main inert gas line can be mixed with crude oil. The mix of VOC, inert gas and crude oil is then led back into the same cargo tank the crude oil was originally taken from.

VOCs and VECS

VOC is absorbed in the crude oil due to increased pressure in the bottom of the cargo tank, while inert gas rises to the surface without being absorbed. Oil circulation is obtained by using a standard centrifugal pump driven by an electrical motor, and system operation is controlled by a simple PLC located in the engine-room and a number of pressure and temperature sensors. Operation and monitoring is done on two 10" LCD touch screen panels located in the Cargo Control Room and on the Bridge.

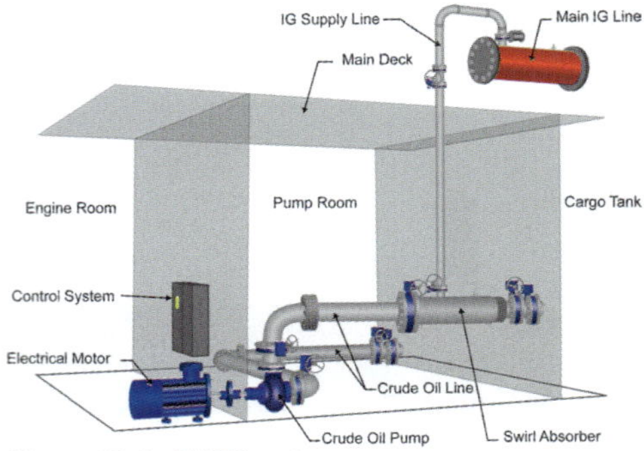

Figure 23.9 - CVOC system

Passenger Ship Musters

At the 92nd Maritime Safety Committee meeting in June 2014, amendments to SOLAS regulations concerning passenger ship safety were approved. They entered into force on 1st January 2015.

The changes to SOLAS Chapter III Regulation 19 2.2 require that a muster shall take place prior to or immediately upon departure for newly-embarked passengers on ships engaged on voyages scheduled to exceed 24 hours. This amends the previous requirement where musters were required to be completed within 24 hours of embarkation. These changes are set out in Annex 14 to document MSC 91/22/Add.1.

'Costa Concordia'

Passenger Ship Musters

Emergency Training and Drills

"2.2 On a ship engaged on a voyage where passengers are scheduled to be on board for more than 24 h, musters of the passengers shall take place within 24 h after their embarkation. Passengers shall be instructed in the use of the lifejackets and the action to take in an emergency.

2.3 Whenever new passengers embark, a passenger safety briefing shall be given immediately before sailing, or immediately after sailing. The briefing shall include the instructions required by regulations 8.2 and 8.4, and shall be made by means of an announcement, in one or more languages likely to be understood by the passengers. The announcement shall be made on the ship's public address system, or by other equivalent means likely to be heard by the passengers who have not yet heard it during the voyage. The briefing may be included in the muster required by paragraph 2.2 if the muster is held immediately upon departure. Information cards or posters or video programmes displayed on ships video displays may be used to supplement the briefing, but may not be used to replace the announcement."

SOLAS Chapter III Regulation 19

The Committee will also review a submission for adoption from the Stability, Load Lines and Fishing Sub-Committee (SLF 55) concerning the development of guidelines on the standard method for evaluating cross-flooding of ships built after the agreed adoption date.

In addition, SLF 55 is continuing the review of subdivision and damage stability regulations contained in SOLAS II-1. The intention is to comprehensively revise and update the provisions for both passenger and cargo ships, including survivability after damage and safe return to port following a casualty. This comes amidst questions over the effectiveness of the existing "safe return to port" concept which, according to the UK submission MSC 91/7/3, does not account for sufficient stability after flooding of a single watertight compartment.

Goal-Based Standards (GBS) for Shipbuilding

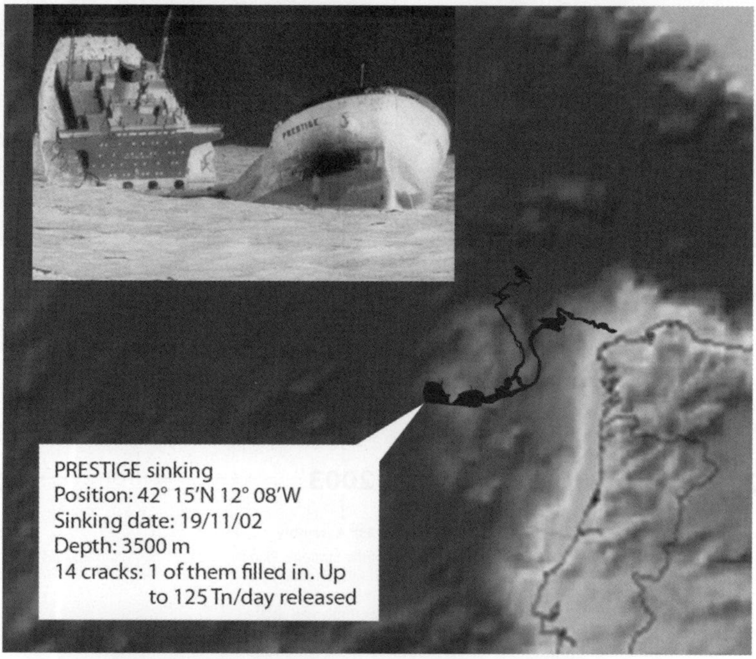

Figure 23.10 - Satellite image showing extent of oil slick from the 'Prestige'

Goal-Based Standards (GBS) for Shipbuilding

The loss of the *'Erika'* in 1999 and the *'Prestige'* in 2002, both of which broke up and sank in heavy weather, led certain marine Administrations to consider that there may be deficiencies in the present scheme of ship construction where ships are designed, constructed, inspected and maintained according to the rules prescribed by the Class Societies approved by the Administrations. Both of these concerned ships that were >25 years old and each cases resulted in a large oil slick and coastal pollution.

Adoption into SOLAS

SOLAS Reg II-1/3-10 'Goal-based ship construction standards for bulk carriers and oil tankers' covers ship types of 150 metres and above in length and requires new ships to be designed with adequate strength, integrity and stability for a specified design life and to be safe and environmentally friendly, in intact and specified damage conditions, throughout their life.

Structure of Goal-Based Standards (GBS)

Tier I	Goals	Includes the high-level objectives that should be met. These goals are defined in SOLAS Regulation II-1/3-10 *(Applicable to all ships)*
Tier II	Functional Requirements	Criteria to be satisfied in order to conform to the goals. *(Applicable to bulk carriers and oil tankers in unrestricted navigation)*
Tier III	Verification of Conformity	Provides the instruments to verify that the rules and regulations for ship design and construction meet the GBS
Tier IV	Rules and Regulations for Ship Design and Construction	Industry standards, codes of practice and safety and quality systems for shipbuilding, ship operation, maintenance, training, manning, etc, which may be incorporated into, or referenced in, the rules and regulations for the design and construction of a ship
Tier V	Industry Practices and Standards	Detailed requirements developed by IMO, national Administrations and/or recognised organisations and applied by national Administrations and/or recognised organisations acting on their behalf to the design and construction of a ship in order to conform to the goals and functional requirements

Introducing the Idea

2002

MSC 76
Greece submits proposal of robust ship concept.

IMO 89th session of the Council
The notion of "goal-based ship construction standards" was introduced through a proposal by the Bahamas and Greece, suggesting that IMO should develop initial ship construction standards that would permit innovation in design but ensure that ships are constructed in such a manner that, if properly maintained, they could remain safe for their entire economic life.

2003

MSC 77
The Bahamas and Greece submitted the proposal of GBS concept to MSC 77, and GBS became new item in agenda for MSC 78.

IMO 23rd Assembly
As part of the Strategic Plan adopted for the Organization for the six-year period 2004 to 2010, it was resolved that "the IMO would establish goal-based standards for the design and construction of new ships" (Resolution A.944(23)).

2004

MSC 78
At MSC 78, the Bahamas, Greece and IACS submitted the proposal of Goal-Based Regulatory Framework.

MSC 79
GBS was continuously discussed in working group.

GBS in Reality

It took seven years for GBS to be approved at the IMO after much debate and general unhappiness from countries with substantial shipbuilding activities.

The agreement, viewed as one of compromise, saw the entry of a diluted and less demanding form of verification that focuses on self-assessment; essentially GBS allows the Class Societies to decide for themselves whether the ships they design meet these new standards.

In an article in June 2009 in Lloyd's List, Douglas Bell, from the Bahamas Maritime Authority, who was the architect of the initial IMO proposal, regarded the revised process as a *"weak measurement"*. He went on to say that:

"What was going to happen was that the group of experts would go through the whole rule and look for compliance with the standards that have been set, and look for the ways the rules had been derived, and for evidence that the standards are being met. Now the classification societies themselves will do that. The auditors in theory can dig as deep as they choose, but they won't be able to look at everything. The theory is that they will look at a bit of each of the standards that have been set and if they have any queries they will go into depth in these particular areas".

Full details of SOLAS Regulation II-1/3-10 and GBS can be found here: http://tinyurl.com/ph4uq5j

2006

MSC 81

The five-tier system for GBS (as shown on the previous page) was agreed.

2010

MSC 87

The SOLAS amendments to make GBS mandatory for ships and the verification guidelines were adopted at MSC 87 in May 2010.

2012

GBS Tiers I to III became mandatory on 1st January 2012.

2013

31st December 2013 was the deadline for receipt of initial verification requests from Class Societies. A total of 13 requests were submitted and the outcome of these audits will be submitted to MSC 96 in May 2016 for approval.

IACS Harmonised Rules for Oil Tankers/Bulk Carriers (CSR-H)

In a report to the IMO's Maritime Safety Committee in May 2010, IACS proposed a deadline of the end of 2013 to submit the harmonised rules to the IMO for verification under the goal-based standards regime. This deadline was accepted.

CSR harmonisation aims to deliver common rules covering oil tankers and bulk carriers. The harmonised CSRs, along with those areas specific to tankers and bunkers, will be produced in three sections, namely:

1) Common parts for both types.

2) Specific part applicable to bulk carriers.

3) Specific part applicable to oil tankers.

A number of items were identified when the CSRs were released for long-term harmonisation:

- Wave loads
- fatigue
- finite element analysis
- buckling
- prescriptive requirements.

The harmonised rules will adapt the Common Structural Rules to include the formal arrangements being set up by the IMO for Goal-Based Standards (GBS).

The original Rules were developed separately for tankers and bulkers and, during their adoption, the IACS Council made a commitment to harmonise them based on a consistent methodology. The following are amongst the principles that will be adhered to during the harmonisation of the Rules:

- The harmonised Rules will be in compliance with the IMO Goal-Based Standards where GBS Functional Requirements fall within the scope of the Rules
- the harmonisation will result in a single set of Rules with sections for oil tankers and bulk carriers
- initial adoption of the harmonised Rules requires a unanimous decision of the Council.

The guiding principle for the development of the harmonised Rules is, as a guideline, that the scantlings will be used as a proxy for the level of structural safety, ie the scantlings required by the harmonised Rules should be the same or higher for a given ship design and structural arrangement than is required to meet the current Rules. Should the harmonised Rules result in lower scantlings than the current Rules, the technical justification is to be provided to the Hull Panel, General Policy Group (GPG) and IACS Council for review.

On 14th December 2005, the Common Structural Rules for Tankers and Bulk Carriers were unanimously adopted by the IACS Council for implementation on 1th April 2006, heralded by Lloyd's List as *"one of the most important initiatives of recent years"*. IACS Common Structural Rules (CSR) are a comprehensive set of minimum requirements for the classification of the hull structures of bulk carriers and double-hull oil tankers. They are applicable to tankers of at least 150 metres in length and bulkers of at least 90 metres.

The IACS CSRs were formulated on a solid technical platform with the ultimate objective of encouraging the design and construction of more robust and safer tankers and bulk carriers. The CSRs mean shipbuilders and designers work with one set of rules, rather than different ones from each society. The CSRs draw on the experience of all the IACS member societies and were developed with an eye towards the International Maritime Organization's goal-based standards philosophy, which is aimed at creating an overarching framework for future standards.

Do the CSRs provide any benefits to the industry?

- Greater transparency of the technical background to the Rules
- all IACS societies will cooperate to maintain a single Rule set
- competition will be focused on service level, ie new building and SiO support
- the net scantling principle, ie the minimum allowable scantlings during the operational lifetime of the vessel is defined as the net scantlings for the new building design
- reduced cost for ship yards by relating to one set of structural Rules only
- the intention of the new Rules is to encourage the design and construction of robust tankers and bulk carriers and to eliminate competition on scantlings
- the minimum fatigue design life is set to a 25-year North Atlantic environment.
- the corrosion additions that have been established take into account the location and the environment to which the structural members' surface is subjected
- stringent and clarified requirements to critical areas.

References:

- Iacs.org.uk
- Lloydslist.com

RO Code Adoption

MSC 92 adopted the Recognized Organizations (RO) Code as a new mandatory instrument. The RO Code provides a standardised, global approach for flag States in delegating tasks and responsibilities to ROs and is designed to improve consistency of assessment, authorisation and ongoing monitoring of ROs.

The Code comprises three parts:

- Parts 1 and 2 will be mandatory and will establish the minimum criteria for assessment of the RO and the requirements of the ROs when acting on behalf of the flag State
- Part 3 will be non-mandatory, but the regulations state that the recommendations should be taken into account to the greatest degree possible in order to ensure uniformity in the implementation of the Code. Part 3 provides advice on establishing an ongoing oversight programme, including surveys, reporting and auditing of ROs.

The Code became mandatory on 1st January 2015, when amendments to SOLAS and the Load Lines Protocol entered into force.

Courtesy of USCG

Tasks normally conducted by the flag State may be delegated to an RO, and the Code will provide criteria to assess the RO

CHAPTER 24

Certification and Endorsements

Endorsement Requirements for Oil,

The STCW Convention was adopted in 1978 to "*establish basic requirements on training, certification and watchkeeping for seafarers on an international level*", and on 1st February 2002 the 1995 amendments were fully implemented. In June 2010, the Manila Amendments were agreed to bring the Code up to date and to address perceived weaknesses. The schedule for entry (relating to training and certification) is as follows:

1st July 2013 – approved courses to meet and be certified in accordance with new standards

1st January 2017 – all standards, including certificate renewal and revalidation, must be complied with.

The STCW 95 regulations concerning the additional training for seafarers on tankers have been amended to separate the basic, formerly referred to as familiarisation level, tanker training for liquefied gas tankers from that of oil and chemical tankers.

Basic oil and chemical tanker training – A-V/1-1-1

hemical or Liquefied Gas Tankers

Required for officers and ratings assigned specific duties and responsibilities related to cargo or cargo equipment on oil or chemical tankers.

To be eligible for certification, the seafarer should meet the standard of competence in section A-V/1-1 and either complete three months approved service on oil or chemical tankers or have completed an approved basic training course for oil and chemical tankers (A-V/1-1-1).

Basic training for liquefied gas tanker cargo operations - A-V/1-2-1

Required for officers and ratings assigned specific duties and responsibilities related to cargo or cargo equipment on liquefied gas tankers.

Similar requirements exist to those in Regulation V/1-1-1, but seatime and training courses must be completed specific to liquefied gas tankers.

Advanced training for oil tanker cargo operations - A-V/1-1-2

Required for masters, chief engineers, chief mates, second engineers and any person with immediate responsibility for loading, discharging, care in transit, handling of cargo, tank cleaning or other cargo-related operations on oil tankers.

To be eligible for certification, the seafarer shall have at least three months approved service on oil tankers while qualified for basic training (A-V/1-1-1) or one month of onboard supernumerary training with a documented training record book, during which three loading and discharge operations were completed. Completion of advanced training for oil tanker cargo operations (A-V/1-1-2) is also required.

Advanced training for chemical tanker cargo operations - A-V/1-1-3

Required for masters, chief engineers, chief mates, second engineers and any person with immediate responsibility for loading, discharging, care in transit, handling of cargo, tank cleaning or other cargo-related operations on chemical tankers.

To be eligible for certification, the seafarer shall have at least three months approved service on chemical tankers while qualified for basic training (A-V/1-1-1) or one month of onboard supernumerary training with a documented training record book, during which three loading and discharge operations were completed. Completion of advanced training for chemical tanker cargo operations (A-V/1-1-2) is also required.

Advanced training for liquefied gas tankers - A-V/1-2-2

Required for masters, chief engineers, chief mates, second engineers and any person with immediate responsibility for loading, discharging, care in transit, handling of cargo, tank cleaning or other cargo-related operations on liquefied gas tankers.

Revalidation of Certificates - A-I/11-3

Revalidation of tanker certificates is established under STCW A-I/11-3, by:

.1 *approved seagoing service, performing duties appropriate to the tanker certificate or endorsement held, for a period of at least three months in total during the preceding five years; or*

.2 *successfully completing an approved relevant training course or courses.*

Training for Passenger Ships and

Under the STCW Convention, as amended in 2010, personnel on board passenger ships, including RoRo passenger ships, are required to complete specific additional training. The 2010 Amendments combined the previously separate regulations that existed between RoRo passenger ships (Regulation V/2) and passenger ships (Regulation V/3) under Regulation V/2.

RoRo Passenger Ships

Crowd management training - A-V/2-1

4 Masters, officers and other personnel designated on muster lists to assist passengers in emergency situations on board passenger ships shall have completed training in crowd management as specified in section A-V/2, paragraph 1 of the STCW Code.

Safety training for personnel providing direct service to passengers in passenger spaces - A-V/2-2

5 Personnel providing direct service to passengers in passenger spaces on board passenger ships shall have completed the safety training specified in section A-V/2, paragraph 2 of the STCW Code.

Crisis management and human behaviour training - A-V/2-3

6 Masters, chief engineer officers, chief mates, second engineer officers and any person designated on muster lists of having responsibility for the safety of passengers in emergency situations on board passenger ships shall have completed approved training in crisis management and human behaviour as specified in section A-V/2, paragraph 3 of the STCW Code.

The only paragraph particular to RoRo passenger vessels is related to cargo and hull integrity (A-V/2 paragraph 4), required by Regulation V/2, ie:

7 Masters, chief engineer officers, chief mates, second engineer officers and every person assigned immediate responsibility for embarking and disembarking passengers, loading, discharging or securing cargo, or closing hull openings on board ro-ro passenger ships shall have completed approved training in passenger safety, cargo safety and hull integrity as specified in section A-V/2, paragraph 4 of the STCW Code.

As with most other safety-related courses, evidence of competence for A-V/2 paragraphs 4, 6 and 7 (not paragraph 5) or refresher training is required at intervals not exceeding five years.

Safety Officials

Introduction

Every person on board has a responsibility for safety.

- *The Company is responsible for ensuring the overall safety of the ship and that safety on board is properly organised and co-ordinated*
- *the master has the day to day responsibility for the safe operation of the ship and the safety of those on board*
- *each employer is responsible for the health and safety of his workers*
- *heads of department are responsible for health and safety in their own department*
- *each officer/manager is responsible for health and safety for those they supervise and others affected*
- *each individual worker is responsible for his own health and safety and that of anyone affected by what he does or fails to do.*

The development of a "safety culture" and the achievement of high standards of safety depend on good organisation and the whole-hearted support of management and all personnel. Those with specific safety responsibilities are more likely to perform well when management is clearly committed to health and safety. It is also important that procedures are in place so that all personnel can co-operate and participate in establishing and maintaining safe working conditions and practices.

Employer Duties

Every employer is required to appoint one or more competent persons to promote health and safety in their undertaking. On board some large ships, where there are personnel working who are employed by several different employers, each employer must appoint (a) competent person(s). They do not have to work on the ship themselves, but to be "competent" for the task they should have a knowledge of the duties undertaken by those for whom they are responsible, and should ensure that any specific risks encountered as a result of that particular working environment are dealt with appropriately - eg by checking that the Company has adequate safety procedures for all on board, and by co-ordinating risk assessments with the Company.

The employer may "appoint" himself where, in a small organisation, there is no one else available to take on this responsibility. Alternatively, he may employ someone from outside his own undertaking to advise on health and safety, provided that person is competent. This requirement applies whether or not a safety officer is appointed for the ship by the Company.

The employer must provide the competent person(s) with all relevant information they need to do their job. This would include a copy of the employer's safety policy and risk assessments, information about the duties of personnel, and any information provided by other employers about risks and safety procedures in shared work-places.

The employer is required to consult workers or their elected representatives on health and safety matters, in particular.

(a) arrangements for the appointment of a competent person;

(b) the findings of the risk assessment;

(c) arrangements for health and safety training; and

(d) the introduction of new technology.

The matters to be discussed might also include selection of work equipment and/or protective clothing and equipment, installation of safety signs and follow-up to accidents and other incidents.

 Source: 'Code of Safe Working Practices for Merchant Seamen'

Workers or their elected representatives must be allowed to make representations to their employer about health and safety matters without disadvantage to themselves. Such representations should be given adequate consideration, perhaps in conjunction with the safety committee, and any agreed measures to improve safety implemented as soon as reasonably practicable.

It is also the employer's responsibility to ensure that workers or their elected representatives have access to relevant information and advice about health and safety matters from inspection agencies and health and safety authorities, and, from their own records, about accidents, serious injuries and dangerous occurrences.

Employers must provide elected representatives adequate time off normal duties, without loss of pay, to enable them to exercise their rights and carry out their function effectively. Workers' safety representatives must not suffer any disadvantage for undertaking this function.

Company Duties

The Regulations

The regulations dealing with safety officials lay duties on the Company for the appointment of ships' safety officers, the appointment of a safety committee and the election of safety representatives with specified powers.

Appointment of Safety Officers

On every sea-going ship on which more than five workers are employed, the Company is required to appoint a safety officer. The master must record the appointment of a safety officer - this should be in the official logbook.

The safety officer is the safety adviser aboard the ship and can provide valuable assistance to the Company and to individual employers in meeting the statutory responsibilities for health and safety. He should have attended a suitable Safety Officer's training course. He should be familiar with the principles and practice of risk assessment, and should be available to advise those preparing and reviewing risk assessments. It is recognised that, where the safety officer also has other responsibilities (eg chief officer) he may well conduct risk assessments himself. However, the general principle is that the safety officer takes an independent view of safety on behalf of the Company.

Although not prohibited by the Regulations the appointment of the master as the safety officer is not generally advisable. This is because the safety officer is required amongst his other duties to make representations and recommendations on health and safety to the master.

If possible, the Company should avoid appointing as safety officer anyone to whom the master has delegated the task of giving medical treatment. This is because one of the duties of the safety officer is to investigate incidents, and he would not be able to give proper attention to this function while providing medical treatment for any casualties.

Election of Safety Representatives

On every ship on which more than five workers are employed, the Company must make arrangements for the election of safety representatives. The regulations specify that no safety representative may have less than 2 years' consecutive sea service since attaining the age of 18, which in the case of a safety representative on board a tanker shall include at least 6 months service on such a ship.

The Company must make rules for the election of safety representatives by the workers on board and cannot disqualify particular persons. It is recommended that the employer should consult with any seafarers' organisation representing his employees when making these rules. The master should organise the election of a safety representative within 3 days of being requested to do so by any two persons entitled to vote.

Safety Officials

The number of safety representatives who should be elected will vary according to the size of a crew. The following ratios are recommended:

6 to 15 crew	*1 elected by officers and ratings together.*
16+ crew	*1 elected by the officers and one elected by the ratings.*
Over 30 ratings	*1 elected by the officers and 3 by the ratings (ie one each from the deck, engine-room and catering departments, general purpose ratings being included in the deck department).*

The master must record the election or appointment of every safety representative in writing - this should be either in the official logbook or in the minutes of safety committee meetings.

When there is a substantial change in those working on board, the master should remind personnel of their right to elect new safety representatives.

Safety Committees

Once safety representatives have been elected, the Company must appoint a safety committee. The committee must be chaired by the master, and members will include, as a minimum, the safety officer and all elected safety representatives. If practical, any competent person appointed by employers other than the Company, should be invited to attend.

It is desirable that there should be a safety committee on every ship with more than five workers, although the statutory requirement only exists on those ships where safety representatives are elected.

The master must record the appointment of a safety committee in writing - this should normally be in the official logbook or minutes of the committee's meetings.

The composition of a safety committee recommended above does not preclude the appointment of other temporary members. However, the committee should be kept compact enough to maintain the interest of members and enable it to function efficiently. Where possible, the relevant shore managers with responsibility for safety on board may attend safety committee meetings on board ship and should in any event see the committee's minutes.

It is preferable to appoint as secretary someone other than a safety official, as officials need to concentrate on the discussion rather than on recording it.

Duties of Safety Officers

General Advice to Safety Officers

It is very important that the safety officer maintains a good working relationship with safety representatives - for example, inviting the relevant safety representatives to join him for the regular inspection of each part of the ship, or while carrying out an investigation, consulting them on safety matters and arrangements, and in particular on any follow-up action proposed.

The safety officer's relationship with the safety committee is rather different since he is both a member of the committee and also to some extent subject to its direction. A committee has the right to inspect any of the records which a safety officer is required by law to keep, and has the power to require the safety officer to carry out any health or safety inspections considered necessary.

Source: 'Code of Safe Working Practices for Merchant Seamen'

Advice on Compliance with Safety Requirements

The safety officer is required by the Regulations to try to ensure compliance with the provisions of this Code and any health and safety guidance and instructions for the ship.

The safety officer's role should be a positive one, seeking to initiate or develop safety measures before an incident occurs rather than afterwards. He should:

- *Be on the lookout for any potential hazards and the means of preventing incidents*
- *try to develop and sustain a high level of safety consciousness among the crew so that individuals work and react instinctively in a safe manner and have full regard to the safety not only of themselves but also of others. The objective is to become the ship's adviser on safety to whom the master, officers and all personnel will naturally turn for advice or help on safe working procedures*
- *where unsafe practice is observed, approach the individual or responsible officer concerned to suggest improvements in his method of working or use the safety committee to discuss examples of dangerous or unsafe practices in a particular area. If this brings no improvement, the safety officer should consider approaching the head of department or, as a last resort, the master to use his influence*
- *ensure that each worker joining the ship is instructed in all relevant health and safety arrangements, and of the importance attached to them before starting work*
- *where possible, ensure that arrangements are made for each new entrant to work with a crew member who is himself thoroughly safety conscious*
- *remind experienced seamen joining the ship for the first time of the importance of a high level of safety consciousness and of setting a good example to less experienced personnel.*

He should also promote safety on board, subject to the agreement of the master, by:

(a) Arranging the distribution of booklets, leaflets and other advisory material on safety matters.

(b) Supervising the display of posters and notices, replacing and renewing them regularly.

(c) Arranging for the showing of films of safety publicity and, where appropriate, organise subsequent discussions on the subjects depicted.

(d) Encouraging members of the crew to submit ideas and suggestions for improving safety and enlist their support for any proposed safety measures which may affect them (the person making a suggestion should always be informed of decisions reached and any action taken).

(e) Effective communication of new requirements or advice in relevant shipping legislation, Marine Notices and Company and ship's rules and instructions relating to safety at work about the ship.

Investigation of Accidents and Dangerous Occurrences

The safety officer has a duty to investigate notifiable accidents or dangerous occurrences affecting persons on board ship or during access, as well as potential hazards to health and safety and any reasonable complaints made by any personnel, and to make recommendations to the master. It is good practice to record and investigate as appropriate all incidents reported by personnel or passengers.

Additional health or safety investigations or inspections may be commissioned by the safety committee.

Safety Inspections

The Regulations require the safety officer to carry out health and safety inspections of each accessible part of the ship at least once every three months, or more frequently if there have been substantial changes in the conditions of work.

"Accessible" should be taken as meaning all those parts of the ship to which any member of the crew has access without prior authority.

Deciding whether "substantial changes in the conditions of work" have taken place is a matter of judgement. Changes are not limited to physical matters such as new machinery but can also include changes in working practices or the presence of possible new hazards. A record should be kept of all inspections.

Source: 'Code of Safe Working Practices for Merchant Seamen'

Safety Officials

It is not necessary to complete an inspection of the whole ship at one time, as long as each accessible part of the ship is inspected every 3 months. It may be easier to get quick and effective action on recommendations arising out of an inspection, if one section is dealt with at a time. When inspecting a section the safety officer should be accompanied by the officer or petty officer responsible for it.

Before beginning any inspection, previous reports of inspections of the particular section should be read, together with the recommendations made and the subsequent action taken. The control measures identified in any relevant risk assessment should also be read, and compliance with them checked during the inspection. Any recurring problems should be noted and, in particular, recommendations for action which have not been put into place. It is important, however, not to allow the findings of previous inspections to prejudice any new recommendations.

Record of Accidents and Dangerous Occurrences

Figure 24.1 - Snap back zone

The safety officer must maintain a record of all accidents and dangerous occurrences. These records must be made available on request to any safety representative, the master or to any person duly authorised by the secretary of State.

Source: 'Code of Safe Working Practices for Merchant Seamen'

Duty to Stop Dangerous Work

The safety officer has a duty to stop any work which he reasonably believes may cause a serious accident and immediately to inform the master (or his deputy) who is responsible for deciding when work can safely be resumed.

Checklist for Safety Officer's Inspection

The following are examples of questions the safety officer should consider. This is not intended to be an exhaustive list, and should be varied according to the particular design or conditions on a particular ship.

Means of Access/Safe Movement

1. *Are means of access, if any, to the area under inspection (particularly ladders and stairs), in a safe condition, well lit and unobstructed?*
2. *If any means of access is in a dangerous condition, for instance when a ladder has been removed, is the danger suitably blocked off and warning notices posted?*
3. *Is access through the area of inspection both for transit and working purposes clearly marked, well lit, unobstructed and safe?*
4. *Are fixtures and fittings over which seamen might trip or which project, particularly overhead, thereby causing potential hazards, suitably painted or marked?*
5. *Is any gear, which has to be stowed within the area, suitably secured?*
6. *Are all guard-rails in place, secure and in good condition?*
7. *Are all openings through which a person could fall, suitably fenced?*
8. *If portable ladders are in use, are they properly secured and at a safe angle?*

Working Environment

Source: 'Code of Safe Working Practices for Merchant Seamen'

Safety Officials

1. *Is the area safe to enter?*
2. *Are lighting levels adequate?*
3. *Is the area clear of rubbish, combustible material, spilled oil, etc?*
4. *Is ventilation adequate?*
5. *Are members of the crew adequately protected from exposure to noise where necessary?*
6. *Are dangerous goods and substances left unnecessarily in the area or stored in a dangerous manner?*
7. *Are loose tools, stores and similar items left lying around unnecessarily?*

Working Conditions

1. *Is machinery adequately guarded where necessary?*
2. *Are any necessary safe operating instructions clearly displayed?*
3. *Are any necessary safety signs clearly displayed?*
4. *Are permits-to-work used when necessary?*
5. *Are crew working in the area wearing any necessary protective clothing and equipment?*
6. *Is that protective clothing and equipment in good condition and being correctly used?*
7. *Is there any evidence of defective plant or equipment and if so what is being done about it?*
8. *Is the level of supervision adequate, particularly for inexperienced crew?*
9. *What practicable safety improvements could be made?*

General

1. *Are all statutory regulations and company safety procedures being complied with?*
2. *Is the safety advice in publications such as this Code, Merchant Shipping Notices etc being followed where possible?*
3. *Have the crew in the area any safety suggestions to make?*
4. *Have any faults identified in previous inspections been rectified?*

Source: 'Code of Safe Working Practices for Merchant Seamen'

Ship Security Officers

From 1st January 2008, the STCW Code has included training requirements for Ship Security Officers (SSOs).

Ship Security Officer

Part A of the STCW Code requires that each ship should have a designated ship security officer (SSO):

A/12.1 A ship security officer shall be designated on each ship.

12.2 In addition to those specified elsewhere in this Part of the Code, the duties and responsibilities of the ship security officer shall include, but are not limited to:

.1 undertaking regular security inspections of the ship to ensure that appropriate security measures are maintained;

.2 maintaining and supervising the implementation of the ship security plan, including any amendments to the plan;

.3 co-ordinating the security aspects of the handling of cargo and ship's stores with other shipboard personnel and with the relevant port facility security officers;

.4 proposing modifications to the ship security plan;

.5 reporting to the company security officer any deficiencies and non-conformities identified during internal audits, periodic reviews, security inspections and verifications of compliance and implementing any corrective actions;

.6 enhancing security awareness and vigilance on board;

.7 ensuring that adequate training has been provided to shipboard personnel, as appropriate;

.8 reporting all security incidents;

.9 co-ordinating implementation of the ship security plan with the company security

Ship Security Officers

officer and the relevant port facility security officer; and

.10 *ensuring that security equipment is properly operated, tested, calibrated and maintained, if any.*

The duties of the SSO listed in the ISPS Code must be included in the ship security plan.

A key requirement of the ISPS Code is for the people with security responsibilities to be appropriately trained to carry out their duties.

STCW Regulations VI/5 for security officers and VI/6 for all seafarers require a specified level of security training depending on the duties to be carried out. They include security awareness and training based on the principles of the ISPS Code and IMO circulars regarding piracy and armed robbery.

Under Regulation VI/5, a ship security officer must meet the following criteria to be eligible for certification:

.1 *have approved seagoing service of not less than 12 months or appropriate seagoing service and knowledge of ship operations; and*

.2 *meet the standard of competence for certification of proficiency as ship security officer, set out in section A-VI/5, paragraphs 1 to 4, of the STCW Code.*

Regulation VI/6 distinguishes between training and instruction for all seafarers and for those with designated security duties. On cargo vessels, it is conceivable that almost all crew will have designated security duties due to the limited number of crew.

All seafarers require security-related familiarisation and security-related awareness training, outlined in Section A-VI/6 paragraphs 1 to 4, and for those with designated security duties the training described in Section A-VI/6 paragraphs 6 to 8.

The competences necessary for all seafarers and those with designated security duties may be demonstrated by previous sea service or as part of their professional qualification. Where this is not included in their qualification, a certificate of proficiency is required.

CHAPTER 25

Business and Chartering

INCO Trade Terms

INCOTERMS (International Commercial Terms) are internationally recognised standard trade terms used in sales contracts. They are published by the International Chamber of Commerce (ICC).

INCOTERMS help traders avoid costly misunderstandings by defining the respective obligations, costs and risks involved in the delivery of goods from the Seller to the Buyer.

INCOTERMS by themselves DO NOT:

- **Constitute a contract**
- **supersede the law governing the contract**
- **define where title transfers**
- **address the price payable, currency or credit terms.**

These items are defined by the express terms in the sales contract and by the governing law.

When a seller and buyer wish to incorporate INCOTERMS into a contract, they must cite the term used, title, and date applicable.

INCOTERMS are divided into two classifications. The first class (Rules for any Mode of Transport) contains seven terms that can be used irrespective of the mode of transport selected and of whether one or more than one mode of transport is employed.

The second class (Sea and Inland Waterway Transport) contains four terms used exclusively for transporting goods by ship. The point of delivery and the place to which the goods are carried to the buyer will both be ports. In the latest amendments to the INCOTERMS, delivery has been defined as when the goods are delivered on board the vessel not to the ship's rail, to better reflect modern shipping practices.

The ICC website for INCOTERMS is: http://www.iccwbo.org/Incoterms/

Definitions

Rules for any Mode of Transport

EXW - Ex Works (... named place of delivery) - The Seller's only responsibility is to make the goods available at the Seller's premises. The Buyer bears full costs and risks of moving the goods from there to destination.

FCA - Free Carrier (... named place of delivery) - The Seller delivers the goods, cleared for export, to the carrier selected by the Buyer. The Seller loads the goods if the carrier pickup is at the Seller's premises. From that point, the Buyer bears the costs and risks of moving the goods to destination.

CPT - Carriage Paid to (... named place of destination) - The Seller pays for moving the goods to destination. From the time the goods are transferred to the first carrier, the Buyer bears the risks of loss or damage.

CIP - Carriage and Insurance Paid to (... named place of destination) - The Seller pays for moving the goods to destination. From the time the goods are transferred to the first carrier, the Buyer bears the risks of loss or damage. The Seller, however, purchases the cargo insurance.

DAT - Delivered at Terminal (... named terminal at port or place of destination) - The Seller delivers when the goods, once unloaded from the arriving means of transport, are placed at the Buyer's disposal at a named terminal at the named port or place of destination. Terminal includes any place, whether covered or not, such as a quay, warehouse, container yard or road, rail or air cargo terminal. The Seller bears all risks involved in bringing the goods to and unloading them at the terminal at the named port or place of destination.

DAP - Delivered at Place (... named place of destination) - The Seller delivers when the goods are placed at the Buyer's disposal on the arriving means of transport ready for unloading at the named place of destination. The Seller bears all risks involved in bringing the goods to the named place.

DDP - Delivered Duty Paid (... named place) - The Seller delivers the goods, cleared for import, to the Buyer at destination. The Seller bears all costs and risks of moving the goods to destination, including the payment of customs duties and taxes.

Rules for Sea and Inland Waterway Transport

FAS - Free Alongside Ship (... named port of shipment) - The Seller delivers the goods to the origin port. From that point, the Buyer bears all costs and risks of loss or damage.

FOB - Free on Board (... named port of shipment) - The Seller delivers the goods on board the ship and clears the goods for export. From that point, the Buyer bears all costs and risks of loss or damage.

CFR - Cost and Freight (... named port of destination) - The Seller clears the goods for export and pays the costs of moving the goods to destination. The Buyer bears all risks of loss or damage.

CIF - Cost Insurance and Freight (... named port of destination) - The Seller clears the goods for export and pays the costs of moving the goods to the port of destination. The Buyer bears all risks of loss or damage. The Seller, however, purchases the cargo insurance.

Types of Chartering on the Tramp and Spot Market

Chartering is the act of hiring a ship for either a specific voyage, a series of voyages or a period of time. The entity employing the ship, provided that it is not also the owner, is the charterer. The charterer may be the importer, exporter or an agent trading between the two.

Charter Types

Voyage Charter

The ship is hired from one port to another and during this period the shipowner retains responsibility for all operational costs.

A voyage charter will commence when the shipowner presents the ship for loading during an agreed period of time (laydays) at an agreed place. The term 'laycan' is often used to identify the final period by which the ship must be presented for loading.

The charter normally ends at the last hose disconnection in the final discharge port. The term 'laytime' refers to an agreed period for the charterer to load and discharge the ship without further cost.

The analogy of hiring a taxi may be used to illustrate a voyage charter.

Consecutive Voyage Charter

This means the hiring on voyage charter terms for a series of successive voyages.

Time Charter

A time charter is the hiring of a specified ship for an identified time period, typically between one and three years. During this period, the shipowner will pay for all operational costs other than fuel, canal and port fees, which will be to the charterer's account.

As the owners remain responsible for maintenance, the charterer may be required to return the ship to the owner for an agreed off-hire period to undertake maintenance. Such a suspension of the hire clause is likely to include other out-of-service periods caused by breakdown, repair, etc.

Commonly, time charters allow the charterers to sublet the ship to another party on a time or voyage charter.

The analogy of a chauffeur-driven limousine may be used.

Bareboat Charter

Under a bareboat charter, the ship is normally hired for a prolonged period during which the charterer is liable for all operational and maintenance costs, with the owners only investing capital. It is typically used by organisations such as banks that do not wish to operate or manage their own ships, but are able to finance ownership.

Types of Chartering on the Tramp and Spot Market

Frequently, a management agreement may be included which requires the shipowner to manage the ship operations on the bareboat charterer's behalf.

The most common form used is BARECON 89 which incorporates BARECON A and BARECON B, designed for short and long period chartering respectively.

The analogy of a long-term car lease may be used and, just like that type of lease, a purchase option may be included at the end of the bareboat charter hire period.

Contract of Affreightment

A contract of affreightment (COA) is not a charter agreement for a specific ship; rather it is a long-term contract between a charterer and owner for a specified volume of cargo to be transported between ports for an identified period of time. However, the agreement can be expected to identify the ship type and size, but leave ship nomination to the discretion of the owners.

The amount of cargo to be loaded on each voyage will be agreed within specific parameters. Loading dates may be nominated and shipping normally spread out evenly during the contracted period.

Freight Rates

The freight rate of a ship is the agreed price for the carriage of the cargo. Normally on a voyage charter the freight invoice is submitted on completion of the voyage with any amendments made, eg change of discharge port, amended cargo quantity or demurrage.

The freight rate is normally identified in one of the following ways:

- Worldscale rate
- lump sum rate
- rate per tonne.

Worldscale Rate

The Worldwide Tanker Nominal Freight Scale (Worldscale) establishes a baseline price per tonnes of cargo that is used when negotiating a charter party. The worldscale system is intended to produce a freight rate that encompasses almost every foreseeable tanker voyage, accounting for port costs, distances, etc, to provide the same income per day irrespective of the voyage performed.

The worldscale rate would reflect a flat rate at 100%, ie WS 100. A lesser rate would be shown as a lower percentage, eg WS 80 would reflect an agreed rate of 80% of the flat rate. Conversely, a better rate is shown in excess of the flat rate, eg WS 150 reflects a rate of 150% of the flat rate.

Worldscale is based on an 'average' ship. Therefore, in addition to market conditions, the agreed rate will reflect a number of factors including:

- Ship size
- ship speed
- fuel consumption.

Worldscale is common in both voyage charters and contracts of affreightment (COA) because of the flexibility.

Lump Sum Rate

An agreed sum is fixed for the delivery of a specified cargo, with the ship's owner/operator paying all operational and voyage costs.

Rate per Tonne

Rate per tonne is most commonly used in chemical tanker charters. It differs from the lump sum rate arrangement in that the charterer will be required to pay voyage and port costs.

Average Freight Rate Assessment

The average freight rate assessment (AFRA) is a system that establishes an average freight rate in the open market over a monthly period for a range of tanker categories based on their deadweight, ie:

GP	General Purpose	16,500 to 24,999	Dwt
MR	Medium Range	25,000 to 44,999	Dwt
LR1	Large Range 1	45,000 to 79,999	Dwt
LR2	Large Range 2	80,000 to 159,000	Dwt
VL	VLCC	160,000 to 319,999	Dwt
UL	ULCC	320,000 to 549,999	Dwt

The AFRA rate is a convenient system used by brokers to agree a freight rate.

Liner Trade

Liner shipping uses a network of regularly scheduled services to transport goods from any place in the world to another. Liner services involve higher fixed costs than tramp shipping not only because of larger administrative overheads, but also because following a fixed schedule creates more stringent capacity requirements. The number of vessels required for a given liner service is determined principally by frequency, distance and speed. For example, a weekly liner service between Rotterdam and New York may require four ships. Some of those vessels may depart the ports only partially full; a tramp service carrying the same amount of cargo between Rotterdam and New York could require fewer ships, because the tramps can wait until they have a full cargo load before departing.

Shipbrokers

A shipbroker may be an individual operating independently or may be a company employing several brokers. Brokers earn commission based on a percentage of the charter rate. The shipowner contacts the broker about the need for a charter. It is the broker's job to find suitable cargo for a charter and to negotiate with the charterer's broker if need be.

Shipbrokers will sometimes provide the service of port agent to their shipowning clients. Port agents attend to owners' and ships' husbandry and port service, and assist the master with operational aspects of cargo loading and discharge. As agents they earn commission.

Spot Market

In spot markets, contracts are executed immediately. The spot market is a real-time commodity market for direct sale and delivery.

In the shipping industry, an example of a spot market would be when ships that are docked in a port enter into a contract to immediately ship crude oil supplied from a nearby company.

Vessels operating in the spot market generate revenues that are less predictable, but companies may be able to increase their profit margins during periods of increasing charter rates.

Shipping Business | Demurrage and Despatch

Demurrage occurs when a ship exceeds the number of laydays for loading and/or discharging as agreed in the charter party. The charterer must pay compensation, called demurrage, to the shipowner for the delay. It is an ancillary cost that represents liquidated damage for delays.

Unlike laydays, demurrage days are not subject to interruption. The phrase 'once on demurrage, always on demurrage' refers to the fact that demurrage is effective 24 hours a day, seven days a week, including holidays, bad weather days and during force majeure. Force majeure is included due to the reasoning that, had the loading/discharging met the agreed laytime, the ship would have left port before the force majeure occurred. Demurrage lasts the entirety of the extra time required to complete loading/discharging operations.

Demurrage (and despatch) is calculated from the statement of facts. The Notice of Readiness (NOR) indicates when the laytime began. Once loading/discharging has been completed, the port agent draws up a Statement of Facts from which a time sheet can be created. The time sheet enables laytime demurrage and despatch to be calculated.

Demurrage can only be interrupted in certain specific scenarios, eg where the fault lies with the shipowner or persons in service of the shipowner.

Shipping Business | Demurrage and Despatch

Statement of Facts (or port log)
Once the vessel has completed its operations in port, the agent will make up the catalogue of all data that is important for the shipowner and the charterer relating to the loading and discharging. This is the Statement of Facts (also known as the port log).

From the Statement of Facts, a time sheet, which must be signed by the master and the shippers/receivers, is drawn up. From the time sheet, the number of laydays is determined and demurrage or despatch money owed calculated.

Demurrage is usually collected daily, usually by the agent. Should the charterer fail to pay demurrage, the shipowner can still exercise his lien on the cargo.

Despatch is the reverse of demurrage. When loading and/or discharge operations are completed sooner than the agreed laydays anticipated by the charter party, the shipowner pays compensation called despatch to the charterer. Despatch is paid on the consecutive time from the end of loading and/or discharging to the end of the laytime – all excluded periods not being counted as laytime, eg bad weather days.

Port Agency

A port agent is a person or a corporate entity who acts on behalf of another party (the principal) and has the authority to bind the principal in matters of contract.

The port agent looks after all the needs of a ship and her personnel while she is arriving at, staying in and departing from the port.

From the outset of the appointment, there should be a clear understanding of what the agent will be required to do on behalf of the shipowner.

Port Agent's Duties

- **To arrange for berthing of vessels and loading and discharging of the cargo, in accordance with local custom and conditions**
- **to supervise and coordinate all activities of the terminal operators, stevedores, tally clerks and all other contractors, in order to ensure the proper performance of the customary requirements for the best possible operation and despatch of the principal's vessel**

Port Agency

- **to arrange for calling forward, reception and loading of outward cargo and discharge and release of inward cargo and to attend to the transshipment of through cargo**
- **to arrange for bunkering, repairs, husbandry, crew changes, passengers, ship's stores, spare parts, technical and nautical assistance and medical assistance as required**
- **to carry out the principal's requirements concerning claims handling, P&I matters, general average and/or insurance, and the appointment of surveyors**
- **to attend to all necessary documentation and to attend to consular requirements if required**
- **to arrange for and attend to the clearance of the vessel and to arrange for all other services appertaining to the vessel's movements through the port**
- **to report to the principal the vessel's position and to prepare a Statement of Facts of the call and/or a port log**
- **to keep the principal regularly and timely informed on port and working conditions likely to affect the despatch of the principal's vessels.**

Role/Duties – Dealing with a Ship

The agent has many responsibilities when dealing with a ship. The owner will have been informed by the ship of necessary repairs or replenishments required on board, which are then communicated to the agent to coordinate once the ship arrives in port. Typical supplies are listed below.

Bunkers. The bunkers a ship requires can range from heavy fuel oil to highly refined gas oil depending on the array of generators and systems on board. The agent must take careful note of the environmental standards the ship is required to operate to, in order that the ship does not violate greenhouse gas emission targets for NOx and SOx. The agent needs to ensure that delivery of the bunkers can be made on time and by a mode allowed by Port State Control, eg some ports may not allow bunkering to take place during unloading. The agent must also communicate the price and purchase options for bunkers to the owner.

Ship spares and repairs. The owner may instruct the agent to source or tender for a repair or replacement part, or they might have the spare delivered to the agent who will then arrange fitting on board.

Stores and provisions. Stores refers to items supplied to the deck and engine departments of the ship and not regarded as fixtures and fittings of the vessel. Deck stores include flags, charts, paints, ropes, cargo securing equipment, etc. Items such as PPE and other safety equipment would be common requirements by both deck and engine departments. Medical equipment may also be required. Provisions refers to foodstuffs for the crew. Larger vessels often fix food costs on a sum per person per day basis. Therefore, it may be necessary to supply the quoted cost for the provisions to the cook in order to stay within budget.

Fresh water. The agent must consider the timeliness of supply as well as the price. The price can fluctuate greatly between ports and the agent should indicate the price when accepting an agency appointment. The master may request a sample to be taken before delivery to check the quality.

Waste removal. Dry waste such as dunnage, galley waste and general rubbish is easily disposed of by conventional means within facilities supplied by the port. Liquid waste poses more of a challenge however, with restrictions and regulation on the disposal of oily wastes. Disposal of such waste is usually carried out by specialist contractors, which can be expensive and is not available in all ports.

A ship requires a large number of certificates in order to engage in trade and commerce. They must be correct and up to date and available for inspection by Port State Control. Some of the different certificates are listed below:

- Load line certificate
- safety construction certificate
- safety equipment certificate
- safety radio certificate
- international oil pollution prevention certificate (IOPP)
- safety management certificate (SMC)
- ship security certificate

Port Agency

- cargo gear certificate
- de-ratting certificate
- safe manning certificate
- grain stability booklet
- cargo securing manual
- hazardous cargo certificate
- the maritime declaration of health certificate.

Dealing with Cargo

Customs

Usually the first official body to be met at any port is Customs. Customs officials are responsible for collecting duties on goods and preventing smuggling. Customs will require full details of the ship's cargo and voyage, and also crew/passenger lists etc. The Facilitation of International Maritime Traffic Convention (FAL) 1965 sets out the basic procedures for reporting and clearing ships through Customs. The basic forms required for inspection under the FAL Convention are:

- General declaration
- cargo declaration
- ship's stores declaration
- crew's effects declaration
- crew list
- passenger list
- the document required under the Universal Postal Convention for mail
- maritime declaration of health.

Different countries and ports will have other reporting requirements in addition to the standardised requirements of the FAL Convention. Therefore, the agent must communicate with the principal and the master to ensure that all additional information is prepared and available for when the ship is due in port.

Ship Documents

A vital document for a ship preparing to load or unload cargo is a Notice of Readiness (NOR).

An NOR is tendered by the vessel, normally through the agent, showing the time and date that the vessel arrived ready to load or unload her cargo. When a business receives an NOR, it needs to make appropriate preparations for loading their cargo once the NOR has been accepted and the agreed laytime begins. The NOR may be a pre-printed or standard form or could even be a hand-written note.

The time at which the NOR becomes valid and begins the vessel's readiness to load or unload cargo is agreed in the charter party.

Tanker charter parties and charter parties for dry cargo vessels have different provisions for when the NOR can be given.

Tanker charter parties commonly allow the NOR to be given on arrival at the pilot station or anchorage with time beginning to count six hours after the arrival at any time of day or night. This is due to oil terminals operating on a non-stop 24 hour a day basis.

Not all terminals that handle dry cargo vessels operate on a 24 hour basis and it is not unusual for the charter party to require NOR to be tendered during normal working hours. This vague wording can lead to ambiguity and dispute between charterer and shipowner as to the exact start/end time and location of the NOR.

Charterers will argue that the vessel cannot be ready unless she is at a working berth. Shipowners will argue that the vessel may be ready even if she cannot berth due to congestion, tidal conditions, or delays in getting customs clearance or official approval to proceed and work within the port.

The tendering of the NOR is the start of the process whereby laytime allowed under the charter party begins to count. It will also help determine whether the ship has exceeded the laytime agreed in the charter party and therefore it is important in the calculation of demurrage.

Cargo Documents

Cargo documents include the bill of lading, delivery orders, cargo manifest and stowage plans.

Bill of Lading

A bill of lading has three functions:

1. **As a receipt for goods.**
2. **As a negotiable document.**
3. **Evidence of a document.**

A bill of lading is a receipt issued by or on behalf of the carrier for goods either received into his custody or shipped on board his vessel. Different types of bill of lading are used for different purposes.

As the cargo is loaded on board, the cargo mate makes out a 'mate's receipt'. The mate's receipt provides details of the number and type of cargo and its condition. The necessary information for the bill of lading is extracted from the mate's receipt. Due to the containerised nature of most break bulk cargo, the mate's receipt is being replaced in some areas by the Standard Shipping Note (SSN).

The mate's receipt is only an acknowledgement of receipt on board and is not a negotiable instrument or a document of title.

The Standard Shipping Note (SSN) enables the shipper to complete one standard document for all consignments irrespective of port or inland depot. The SSN provides the receiving authority with accurate data as well as providing all those with an interest in the consignment with adequate information at each movement stage, until final loading on board the vessel.

The greatest benefit of using the SSN is that receiving authorities receive clear and precise information on how the goods should be handled. The SSN should accompany deliveries from factories or warehouses to inland clearance depots, groupage depots, ports and other cargo terminals.

The SSN must not be used if the delivery includes items classified as hazardous.

An accurate description of the condition of the cargo is recorded on the bill of lading. This is important to the bill's function as a receipt. If the cargo differs from the description provided, the master will enter a remark on the front of the bill concerning the quality or quantity of that cargo. Bills with such a remark are called 'marked' or 'dirty' bills. A bill free of remarks is known as a 'clean' bill. A dirty bill is likely to cause problems in its role as a negotiable document. The cargo owner might accuse the shipowner of not ensuring his cargo was transported properly; a buyer who receives a dirty bill of lading may be reluctant to continue with the purchase if the cargo is in a questionable state.

Bills of lading are not usually issued as a single document. The usual practice is to issue three bills containing three originals and any number of copies. The master must sign all three original bills and hand them back to the shipper or the agent acting on behalf of the shipper. The shipper will then distribute the bills as necessary.

The party claiming the cargo at the port of discharge must produce an original bill of lading to the port agent. The agent is normally obliged to deliver the goods to the party that presents an original bill first. It should be remembered though that there is more than one original bill of lading.

When cargoes on the high seas are sold, they obviously cannot be handed from the seller to the buyer as with ordinary transactions. In the bill of lading's second function, as a negotiable document, it acts like the deeds to a house. When a house is sold, the buyer cannot come and collect the building, rather the seller exchanges deeds with the buyer, thereby transferring ownership of the property. The same is true of a bill of lading, ie the document is passed between the parties. Each time the bill of lading is passed on, the seller endorses the back of the bill.

A bill of lading can be used for letter of credit purposes. A letter of credit is a special arrangement made by banks for assisting and financing international trade. Comparable to a mortgage on property, the cargo owner secures funds against the value of the cargo, represented by the bill of lading.

Cargo Manifest

The cargo manifest is a detailed list of all the cargo carried and a full list of the bills of lading for that cargo. The manifest may also include items of cargo that do not have a bill of lading, such as gifts, ship's spares and items of no commercial value. The manifest format is usually just an abbreviated repetition of the bill of lading details.

Port Agency

Unlike bills of lading, the manifest can be reproduced in unlimited number to be used by owners, agents and port authorities.

Copies of the manifest should be delivered to the different parties as soon as possible. The discharging port agent will need to supply copies to local customs and officials. A copy will also need to be supplied to the stevedores at the port of discharge.

Stowage Plans

Stowage plans are essentially a map of where the cargo is located on the ship and is probably the most important document for stevedores. The stowage plan will be useful to the agent as it will give an indication of how quickly the receiver's cargo will be discharged.

CHAPTER 26

Conflict and Issues Affecting Shipping

Refugees and Migrants

Definition

According to the 1951 UN Convention relating to the Status of Refugees, a refugee is a person who **"owing to a well-founded fear of being persecuted for reasons of race, religion, nationality, membership of a particular social group or political opinion, is outside the country of his nationality, and is unable to or, owing to such fear, is unwilling to avail himself of the protection of that country."**

In simplified terms, a refugee is a person who has been forced to leave their home and seek refuge elsewhere.

Under the Convention:

> "No contracting state shall expel or return a refugee in any manner whatsoever to the frontiers of territories where his life or freedom would be threatened on account of his race, religion, nationality, membership of a particular social group or political opinion."

An asylum seeker is an individual who has applied for international protection and is waiting for a decision as to whether or not they are a refugee.

Not every asylum seeker will ultimately be recognised as a refugee, but every refugee is initially an asylum seeker.

Duty to Render Assistance

Shipmasters have an obligation to render assistance to those in distress at sea without regard to their nationality, status or the circumstances in which they are found. This is a longstanding maritime tradition and the obligation has been enshrined in international and humanitarian law through international conventions.

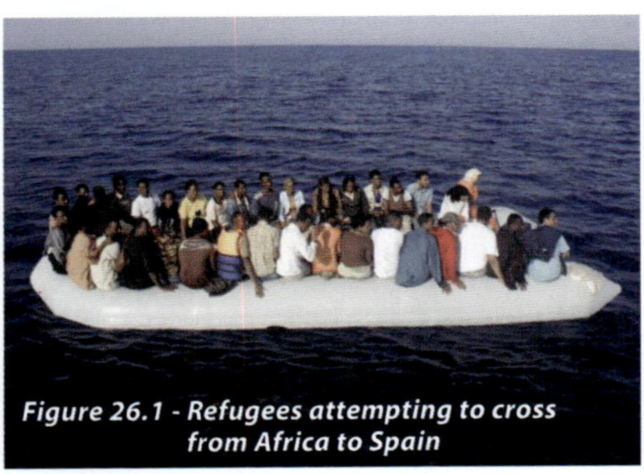

Courtesy of UNHCR/A.Di Loreto

Figure 26.1 - Refugees attempting to cross from Africa to Spain

United Nations Convention on the Law of the Seas (UNCLOS)

Article 98: Duty to render assistance

1. Every State shall require the master of a ship flying its flag, in so far as he can do so without serious danger to the ship, the crew or the passengers:

(a) to render assistance to any person found at sea in danger of being lost;

(b) to proceed with all possible speed to the rescue of persons in distress, if informed of their need of assistance, in so far as such action may reasonably be expected of him;

(c) after a collision, to render assistance to the other ship, its crew and its passengers and, where possible, to inform the other ship of the name of his own ship, its port of registry and the nearest port at which it will call.

1974 International Convention for the Safety of Life at Sea (SOLAS)

Chapter V, Regulation 33(1)

The master of a ship at sea which is in a position to be able to provide assistance on receiving information from any source that persons are in distress at sea, is bound to proceed with all speed to their assistance, if possible informing them or the search and rescue service that the ship is doing so.

Under SOLAS, contracting governments shall coordinate and cooperate to ensure that masters of ships providing assistance by embarking persons in distress at sea are released from their obligations with minimum further deviation from the ships' intended voyage, provided that releasing the master of the ship from the obligations under the current regulation does not further endanger the safety of life at sea.

The International Convention on Maritime Search and Rescue, 1979 (SAR) obliges state parties to *"ensure that assistance be provided to any person in distress at sea … regardless of the nationality or status of such a person or the circumstances in which that person is found"* (Chapter 2.1.10) and to *"provide for their initial medical or other needs, and deliver them to a place of safety"* (Chapter 1.3.2).

A place of safety (as referred to in the Annex to the 1979 SAR Convention, paragraph 1.3.2) is a location where rescue operations are considered to terminate. It is also a place where the survivors' safety of life is no longer threatened and where their basic human needs (such as food, shelter and medical needs) can be met.

An assisting ship should not be considered a place of safety based solely on the fact that the survivors are no longer in immediate danger once aboard the ship. An assisting ship may not have appropriate facilities and equipment to sustain additional persons on board without endangering its own safety or to properly care for the survivors. Even if the ship is capable of safely accommodating the survivors and may serve as a temporary place of safety, it should be relieved of this responsibility as soon as alternative arrangements can be made.

Rescuing Refugees

The master should inform the Company, the nearest Rescue Coordination Centre (RCC) and the P&I insurer of the presence of refugees on board.

If people rescued at sea make known a claim for asylum, key principles as defined in international law need to be upheld.

The master is in no way responsible for determining the status of the people on board but he needs to be aware of these principles.

Ensuring prompt access to fair and efficient asylum procedures is key to ensuring the adequate protection of asylum seekers and refugees amongst those rescued.

While there is a clear duty for ship's masters, their owners and their governments to rescue asylum seekers at sea, there is no obligation under international law for the flag State of a rescuing vessel to grant durable asylum to rescued refugees.

By boarding a vessel, the refugee comes under the jurisdiction of the flag State that is considered to exercise jurisdiction over the ship. There is, however, no valid legal basis for considering that, by boarding a vessel, a refugee has entered the territory of the State that is exercising jurisdiction over the ship.

Steps to be Taken When Rescuing Refugees

Masters should carry out SAR duties in accordance with the provisions of Volume III of the IAMSAR Manual.

Upon receiving a distress signal or being instructed to give assistance from a SAR centre:

- Refer to procedures in the Emergency Contingency Plan and the vessel's SSP when encountering refugees at sea
- contact the nearest and/or responsible Rescue Coordination Centre (RCC), and if necessary nearby ships who may be able to assist
- establish a plan for the rescue prior to its commencement
- consider any PPE to halt any potential spread of disease/infection.

When receiving/bringing refugees on board:

- Assess safety of the crew and passengers should persons brought on board become aggressive or violent
- as each refugee is brought on board, they should be searched and any weapons/dangerous items confiscated
- consider any PPE to halt any potential spread of disease/infection.

Once refugees are on board:

- Obtain as much personal information from each individual as possible
- establish a common language and, if possible, appoint one of the refugees to act as spokesperson and to help manage the group
- consider any PPE to halt any potential spread of disease/infection.

Refugees and Migrants

Health and Safety

The master should do everything possible, within the capabilities and limitations of the vessel, to treat survivors humanely and to meet their immediate needs.

- Consider whether the vessel has sufficient food and provisions on board for the crew and refugees, as well as sufficient medical supplies/equipment
- provide sufficient accommodation. Set aside a protected area for the refugees and provide blankets and beds
- provide for all the basic human needs of the refugees
- establish whether any immediate medical assistance is needed
- if possible, inform the refugees of your intentions and their arrival at a place of safety where the rescue operation is considered to terminate onshore.

Boat People

'Boat people' usually refers to refugees or asylum seekers that emigrate in numbers in boats. The vessels are usually old and/or crudely made, and are often not suitable for navigation on the open seas.

The term boat people emerged in the 1970s after the conclusion of the Vietnam War (November 1955 to April 1975) with the mass departure of refugees from Indochina to escape communist-controlled Vietnam. Despite the unsuitability of the boats, they would aim for the busy international shipping lanes 240 km east of the coast of Vietnam. The hope, realised by a very few, was to be rescued by a freighter and taken to Hong Kong, approximately 2,200 km away.

Boat people are still a contentious issue in the nations they hope to seek refuge in. The recent civil unrest and democratic uprising in the North of Africa has seen an increase in the numbers of refugees fleeing across the Mediterranean Sea to Italy.

Case Study - MV *'Tampa'*

The case of the MV *'Tampa'* highlights the range of diplomatic challenges that can arise by rescuing refugees. This scenario is in no way the norm, but an unfortunate exception.

On 26th August 2011, the Norwegian-flagged container ship *MV 'Tampa'* was en route to Singapore when Australian Search and Rescue (AusSAR) in Canberra requested her to assist and rescue people on board a fishing boat sinking in the Indian Ocean.

The *'Tampa'* rescued 433 persons of Afghan, Iraqi and Pakistani origin. The survivors included 26 women (2 of whom were pregnant) and 43 children (the youngest about 1 year old). One of the male refugees was suspected to have a broken ankle. The *'Tampa'* had no ship's doctor, and limited supplies of medical aid, food, water and blankets.

The rescue took place approximately 158 miles from the Indonesian mainland and 85 miles north of Christmas Island.

After rescuing refugees (or asylum seekers) at sea, it is generally accepted that a ship should proceed to the next port of call for disembarkation. UNHCR Guidelines for Disembarkation of Refugees upholds this approach.

The Master of the *'Tampa'* had strong legal grounds for being entitled to unload the 433 refugees at Christmas Island, an Australian territory in the Indian Ocean close to Indonesia, as it was the closest landfall, coupled with the pressing issue of carrying 383 persons in excess of that licensed under SOLAS.

It was the opinion of the Australian authorities that the rescued refugees should be disembarked at an Indonesian port, as this was not significantly off the *'Tampa's'* original scheduled route, and allegedly where the sinking vessel had originated from. The Australian authorities took the view that it was the responsibility of the Norwegian Government, as flag State, and the Indonesian Government, as the state of embarkation, to process and receive the refugees.

However, the refugees had never been legally present in Indonesia, and there was therefore no basis in international law or any other law for an obligation of any kind to re-admit individuals who had left its shores in such circumstances.

The refugees, who were being provided with shelter in empty containers on board the vessel, responded aggressively when the option of returning to Indonesia was discussed.

In view of the limited supplies on board and the fragile medical state of the refugees, the

Master decided on 27th August to proceed to and attempt to land the refugees on Christmas Island.

The Master was instructed by the Australian Government to remain in the contiguous zone and not enter Australian territorial waters. For two days, the '*Tampa*' remained in the contiguous zone, and on 29th August issued a distress signal. Some of the refugees had made threats to jump overboard, and the male refugees had gone on hunger strike.

With the worsening situation on board, the Master decided to enter Australian territorial waters without permission, stopping approximately four miles off Christmas Island.

In response, the Australian government sent 45 Australian Army SAS personnel to board the vessel. They conducted a medical examination of the refugees and concluded that none was in need of immediate medical attention. The '*Tampa*' was then invited to leave Australian waters with the refugees still on board.

The Master refused on the grounds that the ship exceeded its maximum capacity of 50 persons and that the ship lacked sufficient toilet facilities or safety equipment to make it seaworthy, as required under SOLAS.

Australia as a signatory has a responsibility to detain any vessel that does not meet the safety obligation required by SOLAS.

The '*Tampa*' remained at sea, under the control of the Australian Army SAS, for a further eight days until a diplomatic accord could be reached. Only then were the refugees disembarked but to New Zealand, Nauru and Papua New Guinea, under an agreement between these states.

The whole incident is estimated to have cost the owners of the MV '*Tampa*', Wilhelm Wilhelmsen of Oslo, at least AUS$1 million.

Further Information

With the immigrant crisis in the Mediterranean in 2014-2015, in January 2015 The IMO, UNHCR and ICS published *'Rescue At Sea - A guide to the principles and practice as applied to refugees and migrants'* view this 16pp PDF at: http://tinyurl.com/RescueAtSea

War Zones

Defining a War Zone

Some definitions of war and war zones:

War: a sustained combat involving substantial fatalities.

War: a contention between two or more States through their armed forces, for the purpose of overpowering each other and imposing such conditions of peace as the victor pleases.

War zone: a combat zone where military operations are coordinated (especially a designated area in international waters where the rights of neutrals are not respected by nations at war).

War zone: (during wartime) a combat area in which the rights of neutrals are suspended, such as on the high seas, where ships flying a neutral flag are subjected to attack.

Declaring a War Zone

Maritime areas considered as war zones are declared by a body called the Joint War Committee (JWC). This body is made up of underwriting representatives from both the Lloyd's and the International Underwriting Association of London (IUA) company markets, and normally meets every quarter.

Generally, the belligerents of the conflict declare and define the war zone.

The First World War witnessed the introduction of war zones in which vast areas of the high seas were rendered dangerous to shipping. War zones in WWI were implemented in a haphazard way.

Maritime Exclusion Zones

International law is at a deficiency when it comes to a common language to describe a maritime war zone. In the 20th century, the term

War Zones

'Maritime Exclusion Zone' emerged and, despite small variations, this has been widely adopted for the common description of war zones at sea.

Maritime exclusion zones can be defined as:

An area of water and super-adjacent air space in which a party to an armed conflict purports to exercise control and to which it denies access to ships and aircraft without permission.

Maritime exclusion zones have not been subject to any international treaty, but are widely recognised and accepted.

Due to the establishment of international bodies like the United Nations, the North Atlantic Treaty Organization (NATO) and the European Union, the outbreak of total war has been limited. Coupled also with the foreign and security policies of collective security, ie an attack against one is an attack on all, the scale of combat has been reduced and the theatres of war reduced in size also.

Belligerents in several armed conflicts of the 20th century have established maritime exclusion zones. The term has also been used in peacetime. After the Second World War, the United States (and the UK, France, and the Soviet Union) established 'danger' or 'warning zones' for nuclear weapons testing programmes in the Pacific.

UNCLOS

Article 88 of the 1982 United Nations Convention on the Law of the Sea proclaims:

> *"The high seas shall be reserved for peaceful purposes."*

Under Article 58(2), this clause also applies to the exclusive economic zone.

However, in the San Remo Manual on International Law Applicable to Armed Conflicts at Sea, 1994, an interpretation of Article 88 which would 'prohibit' naval warfare on the high seas is rejected.

Blockades

Historically, belligerent states used blockades of enemy ports or coastlines in order to limit the access of naval forces to the open seas and to restrict the economy by controlling access by neutral vessels.

The introduction of submarines, mines and aircraft to naval warfare in the 20th century enabled belligerents to control vast areas of the ocean. It now became feasible to restrict the flow of neutral trade to an enemy without committing the large naval forces otherwise necessary to institute an effective legal blockade or contraband patrol.

The shift in technology led to a shift in the tactics employed. The blockade was superseded by the maritime exclusion zone (declared war zone).

Iran–Iraq War (1980-1988)

Iraq invaded Iran on 22nd September 1980, triggering an 8-year war.

In 1981, Baghdad had attacked Iranian ports and oil complexes as well as neutral tankers and ships sailing to and from Iran.

By 1982, Iran had regained the territory that was initially lost and pushed across the border into Iraq. Iran rejected a ceasefire proposal.

The Iraqi Government announced the establishment of a maritime exclusion zone around an Iranian oil facility on Kharg Island in August 1982. The main purpose of the zone was to halt Iranian oil exports. It was officially referred to as either a 'naval total exclusion zone' or a 'zone of military operations' and was enforced with fighter aircraft and mines. Neutral powers were adequately informed about geographical limits of the zone. However, the declaration neither designated safe passage routes for merchants nor restricted strikes to warships. Consequently, merchant vessels, predominantly of neutral countries, and tankers loading from Kharg Island were subject to devastating attacks without prior warning.

In March 1984, Iraq initiated sustained naval operations in its self-declared 1,126 km maritime exclusion zone, extending from the mouth of the Shatt al Arab to Iran's port Bashahr, and attacked the Iranian oil terminal on Kharg Island, starting the 'Tanker War'. Both Iran and Iraq attacked oil tankers and merchant ships, including those of neutral nations, in an effort to deprive the opponent of trade. The aim of the Tanker War was also to escalate the conflict to an international level by attacking neutral non-belligerent merchant ships.

One of the Iraqi Government defences for the maritime exclusion zones was that the right to declare a war zone or exclusion zone represented a customary norm of international law.

Iraq expanded the Tanker War by using combat aircraft armed with Exocet missiles. 71 merchant ships were attacked in 1984 alone, compared with 48 in the first three years of the war.

Iran retaliated by attacking a Kuwaiti oil tanker near Bahrain on 13th May 1984 and, five days later, a Saudi tanker in Saudi waters, sending a clear message that, if Iraq continued to harass Iran's shipping, no Gulf State would be safe.

These sustained attacks reduced shipping in the Gulf by 25% and led Lloyd's of London to increase its insurance rates on tankers.

In 1984, Iran and Iraq accepted a UN-sponsored moratorium on the shelling of civilian targets.

Iraq soon forgot the moratorium after it came into effect, and increased and intensified its air raids on tankers serving Iran and Iranian oil-exporting facilities in 1986 and 1987, attacking vessels flagged to conservative Arab states of the Persian Gulf. Iran responded by escalating its attacks on shipping serving Arab ports in the Gulf.

As Kuwaiti vessels made up a large portion of the targets in these retaliatory raids, on 1st November 1986, Kuwait, a non-belligerent, announced it would seek international protection for its ships. On 7th March 1987, the United States offered to re-flag 11 Kuwaiti tankers and to provide US Navy protection.

In early 1988, at least 10 western navies and 8 regional navies were patrolling the area, the site of weekly incidents in which merchant vessels were attached. The Arab Shipbuilding and Repair Yard in Bahrain and its counterpart in Dubai were unable to keep up with the repairs needed to the ships damaged in these attacks.

Lloyd's of London estimated that the Tanker War damaged 546 commercial vessels and killed approximately 430 civilian seafarers.

The vast majority of attacks between 1982 and 1988 happened outside of the war zones declared by both Iran and Iraq.

Falklands War 1982

The Falklands War was fought in 1982 between Argentina and the United Kingdom over the disputed Falkland Islands and South Georgia and the South Sandwich Islands. The Falklands War started on 2nd April 1982, with the Argentine invasion and occupation of the Falkland Islands and South Georgia.

From 12th April 1982, Britain declared a 200 nautical mile maritime exclusion zone from the centre of the Falkland Islands. Any Argentine warships and naval auxiliaries found within this zone were to be treated as hostile and were liable to be attacked by British forces. Neutral merchants and aircraft were not affected by this declaration.

However, on 28th April 1982, Britain declared a total exclusion zone, adopting the same limits previously established by the maritime exclusion zone. The total exclusion zone applied not only to Argentine warships and auxiliaries but also to merchant vessels and aircraft. Any vessel, whether military or civilian, 'operating in support of the illegal occupation of the Falkland Islands by Argentine forces' was to be regarded as hostile and consequently subject to attack without warning. This included vessels or aircraft from any country, belligerent or not.

The Soviet Union objected to the British total exclusion zone, arguing that it hampered full passage on the high seas and therefore violated the 1958 Geneva Convention on the High Seas and the 1982 United Nations Convention on the Law of the Sea.

Throughout the course of the conflict, the then British Prime Minister Margaret Thatcher stressed repeatedly that British measures were taken in self-defence under Article 51 of the United Nations Charter.

The Argentine Government declared on 11th May 1982, without further explanation, that the entire South Atlantic was to be a war zone and that any British vessel found therein could be attacked on sight.

Difficulties of War Zones/Exclusion Zones

The Iran-Iraq war shows how even though a war zone may be declared there is no guarantee that neutral or non-belligerent merchant shipping will be left unharmed.

War Zone Checklists

Biological/Chemical Threat

- ☑ Use low compartments in the ship as shelter for the crew. Ensure there are lavatory facilities, sufficient food and that ventilation and access are secure.
- ☑ Cover the gear on weather decks with absorbent materials, such as linen.
- ☑ Stop all ventilation fans that are not essential for running machinery or, if this is not possible, use canvas cover or adhesive tape to close the openings.
- ☑ Set a continuous water spraying system over the weather decks and the superstructure to prevent contamination settling. If this is not possible, focus on the navigating position, over the top of the shelter positions and above the machinery spaces.
- ☑ If you cannot set such a system, organise working parties at frequent intervals.
- ☑ Reduce the number of the crew who must be on the weather decks or machinery space to the strict minimum required for safe steaming. The rest of the crew should remain in the shelters created in the ship.
- ☑ Ensure the crew remaining in exposed positions wear foul weather clothes, when possible, and all their skin is covered as far as possible.
- ☑ When the number of skilled personnel allows create a rota for the exposed positions in order to spread the radiation dosage. This also applies to the master.
- ☑ On returning to the shelter, ensure that the exposed personnel remove their clothing and wash thoroughly skin that has been exposed, in particular hands, face and neck.
- ☑ Avoid distilling water for drinking in dangerous areas. Instead, use chlorination or boiling for several minutes.

Air/Surface Threat

- ☑ Increase watertight integrity. Hatches and doors shall be kept closed and secured when possible.
- ☑ Increase speed.
- ☑ Personnel should wear fire retardant or non-man-made fibre clothes.
- ☑ Visual lookouts should be continuous, all-around and properly briefed. Pay special attention to the horizon and five degrees above it, in order to detect low flying aircraft.
- ☑ Increase night voyages.
- ☑ Try to identify any vessel approaching and be cautious about small craft. If it is not possible to identify them, carry out evasive manoeuvres.
- ☑ Limit the use of electronic equipment.
- ☑ Turn off all radars.
- ☑ Be ready to issue emergency reports.
- ☑ Ensure there are no inflammable gases in the tanks.
- ☑ Reduce the number of personnel on the weather decks or machinery space to the strict minimum required for safe steaming. The rest of the crew should remain in shelters above the waterline.

Underwater Sabotage Threat

- ☑ Post extra lookouts on the upper deck and ensure they are properly briefed.
- ☑ Deploy your own ship's security patrol.
- ☑ Rotate the propeller continuously or at irregular intervals, when possible.
- ☑ Bow and stern thrusters should be operated at zero thrust.
- ☑ Turn the rudder often.

Mine Threat

- ☑ Avoid waters with less than 200 metres depth.
- ☑ Sail at high water when possible.
- ☑ Keep the minimum steering speed, especially in waters with less than 60 metres depth.
- ☑ Use favourable currents or tidal streams in order to reduce the time spent in a dangerous area but without increasing the speed.
- ☑ Do not throw any objects overboard.
- ☑ Watch for unusual or suspicious activity around you.
- ☑ Reduce the number of personnel below the main deck or the waterline to the strict minimum.
- ☑ Sail directly over the same line as the ship in front of you.
- ☑ Secure non-essential machinery to minimise the acoustic signature of the ship.
- ☑ Avoid course alteration, engines reversing or extreme changes of revolutions.
- ☑ If you sight a mine, order all your crew to wear safety helmets and life vests, to lie down in their bunks when possible or to '*brace for shock*'.

Naval Inspection

"The starting point in high-seas maritime law enforcement is that the principle of the exclusive jurisdiction of the flag State renders a vessel immune from foreign interference, unless there is either a permissive rule of international law allowing the interference or the flag State itself consents to the interdiction. Article 110 of UNCLOS provides that upon the high seas a naval vessel of any State is justified in boarding and inspecting any foreign-flagged vessel where that vessel is suspected of: piracy; unauthorized broadcasting from the high seas; involvement in the slave trade; being stateless; or, through refusing to show its own flag, in fact being of the nationality of the interdicting warship. These are the sole grounds, absent the consent of the flag State, when a State may ignore the exclusive jurisdiction principle."[1]

Various forms of inspection can be carried out by the naval forces of a State on merchant vessels. The first important distinction to make is between naval force's 'right to stop and search' and 'right to visit'. The right to visit on the high seas is detailed in Article 110 of the United Nations Law of the Sea Convention (UNCLOS), whereas the right to stop and search is usually only sanctioned by a UN Security Council Resolution. The right of a merchant vessel to go without interference from any other State on the high seas has always been generally accepted due to the freedom of the seas (*mare liberum*). The right to innocent passage under Article 17 UNCLOS allows foreign flagged vessels to transit the territorial waters of a coastal State without having to stop for inspection by the coastal State authorities.

The area in which the inspection takes place is an important determination of naval inspection. Within the territorial waters of a coastal State, naval inspection is possible where allowed by international law, and under the law and jurisdiction of the coastal State. However, naval inspection on the high seas is a more complicated matter. The exclusive right of jurisdiction of a flag State on a vessel transiting the high seas may only be challenged where expressly sanctioned by international law, like Article 110 UNCLOS or UNSC Resolutions. An unwarranted naval inspection at any other time by a State party could be seen as a challenge to the jurisdiction of the flag State. Power to board may be given by treaty; this method is generally used in the battle against the trade of narcotic drugs and psychotropic substances under the 1988 Vienna Convention against Illicit Traffic in Narcotic Drugs and Psychotropic Substances.

[1] Interdicting Vessels to Enforce the Common Interest: Maritime countermeasures and the use of force pp. 81-82

Naval Inspection

The freedom of the seas is a long-held point in international law. UNCLOS, Articles 87 and 88, state that *"the high seas are open to all States"* and they *"shall be reserved for peaceful purposes."*

UNCLOS is the major international law governing the actions of States and their flagged vessels. It is the primary regulation securing merchant vessels' right to free and innocent passage, codifying the exclusive right of jurisdiction of flag States, and limiting the interference foreign States can have on those rights. UNCLOS, however, is mostly limited to peacetime activities. The San Remo Manual on International Law Applicable to Armed Conflicts at Sea 1994, although non-binding, has the range of applicable international laws and regulation for naval inspection at a time of war.

The UNSC can sanction member States to interdict or coordinate an embargo on particular States in the interest of maintaining international peace and security. This authorises naval forces to stop and search.

Freedom of Navigation and Right of Visit on the High Seas

The freedom of navigation provides vessels of any state with the right to traverse the high seas with minimal interference from any other State (Article 87 UNCLOS). Only in specific situations does a warship have the right to visit a merchant vessel on the high seas. Article 110 UNCLOS states:

Article 110
Right of visit

1. ***Except where acts of interference derive from powers conferred by treaty, a warship which encounters on the high seas a foreign ship, other than a ship entitled to complete immunity in accordance with articles 95 and 96, is not justified in boarding it unless there is reasonable ground for suspecting that:***

   (a) the ship is engaged in piracy;
   (b) the ship is engaged in the slave trade;
   (c) the ship is engaged in unauthorized broadcasting and the flag State of the warship has jurisdiction under article 109;
   (d) the ship is without nationality; or
   (e) though flying a foreign flag or refusing to show its flag, the ship is, in reality, of the same nationality as the warship.

2. ***In the cases provided for in paragraph 1, the warship may proceed to verify the ship's right to fly its flag. To this end, it may send a boat under the command of an officer to the suspected ship. If suspicion remains after the documents have been checked, it may proceed to a further examination on board the ship, which must be carried out with all possible consideration.***

UNCLOS full text:
http://tinyurl.com/7vbg4g7

MV *'So San'*

In December 2002, a North Korean-flagged ship was interdicted by Spanish warships while en route to Yemen from North Korea.

The Spanish warships legally halted the vessel after it failed to fly its flag as required under international law. Suspicions were raised also because no ship called *'So San'* was listed on the North Korean registry.

Upon inspection, 15 Scud missiles were discovered hidden beneath a fake cargo of cement along with 15 conventional explosive warheads, 23 containers of missile fuel oxidisers, and 85 barrels of unidentified chemicals.

The boarding was lawful, but there was no legal basis to confiscate the Scud missiles and the *'So San'* was allowed to complete its journey once nationality was verified.

The 1988 Vienna Convention against Illicit Traffic in Narcotic Drugs and Psychotropic Substances calls on States to cooperate to suppress illicit traffic by sea. The Vienna Convention does not provide a general grant of authority for the right to visit foreign vessels suspected of drug trafficking, but sets a system by which permission can be gained.

Other than where permitted by UNCLOS, warships have very limited authority to interfere with merchant vessels on the high seas. The only time when otherwise unwarranted inspection or interdiction may occur is by United Nations

Security Council resolution. The UNSC will sanction interference by member States where there is a threat to inter- or intra- national peace and stability.

First Persian Gulf War 1990-1991

After Iraq's invasion of Kuwait in 1990, an Arabian Persian Gulf/Red Sea Military Operation was established. In an attempt to bring the invasion and occupation to an end, the United Nations Security Council adopted Resolution 661 on 6th August 1990.

UNSCR 661 prohibited all imports and exports to Iraq and Kuwait except for medical supplies and food stuffs.

UNSCR 665 then called upon member States employing maritime forces in support of the Kuwait Government to halt all inward and outward maritime shipping, in order to inspect and verify their cargoes and destination and to ensure strict implementation of the provisions laid down in Resolution 661.

Naval Inspection, the Right to Innocent Passage, Territorial Waters and the EEZ

Territorial Waters

The territorial waters comprise that area of ocean that is subjected to national jurisdiction by the coastal State and which extends no more than 12 nautical miles to seaward of the baselines that are generally drawn along the low water mark. Beyond the territorial waters, ships of all States enjoy the right to freedom of navigation.

Exclusive Economic Zone

An exclusive economic zone (EEZ) is a sea zone prescribed by UNCLOS over which a State has special rights regarding the exploration and use of marine resources, including energy production from water and wind.

Within the territorial waters and the exclusive economic zone, foreign-flagged merchant vessels have the right to innocent passage so long as *"it is not prejudicial to the peace, good order or security of the coastal State"* (see UNCLOS Articles 17 and 19). Passage through the territorial waters of a coastal State must be continuous and expeditious in order to be consistent with the right to safe passage.

The right of innocent passage exists as a limitation and an exception to absolute coastal State sovereignty in the territorial waters. 'The high seas freedoms coexist with the exclusive rights of the coastal State in this maritime zone, provided that they are not incompatible with the legal regime of the EEZ.'[2]

'Powers Conferred by Treaty' and Proliferation Security Initiative (PSI)

The PSI is a global effort that aims to stop the trafficking of weapons of mass destruction, their delivery systems and related materials to and from States and non-state actors of proliferation concern.

Launched officially by US President George W Bush in May 2003, initially consisting of 11 nations, the PSI has now grown to include 98 nations around the world. This includes four of the five UN Security Council members.

PSI consists of a group of like-minded States committed publicly to aggressively interdict WMDs. 'When a country endorses PSI, it endorses the PSI Statement of Interdiction Principles, which commit participants to establish a more coordinated and effective basis through which to impede and stop WMD' – US Department of State website.

The US has frequently reiterated that the PSI is "an activity, not an organisation." PSI has no exclusive funding or international secretariat; the participant states hold regular high level meetings and exercises to test interdiction techniques.

There are wider concerns that the PSI will give rise to 'new State practices that will weaken and relegate existing international legal norms and institutions mainly relating to the freedom of navigation, right of innocent passage, exclusive right of flag States and ship-boarding provisions enshrined in the UNCLOS.'[3]

PSI Boarding Agreements

'Under these agreements, if a vessel registered in the US or the partner country is suspected of carrying proliferation related cargo, either one of

[2] *The Right of Visit and the 2005 Protocol on The Suppression of Unlawful Acts Against the Safety of Maritime Navigation*, N Klein, p.293

[3] *The Proliferation Security Initiative: Towards Relegation of Navigational Freedoms in UNCLOS? An Indian Perspective*, T Thomas, p.1

Naval Inspection

the parties to this agreement can request of the other to confirm the nationality of the ship in question and, if needed, authorise the boarding, search, and possible detention of the vessel and its cargo' – US Department of State website.

A number of FOC have signed shipboarding agreements with the United States including the Bahamas, Belize, Croatia, Cyprus, Liberia, Malta, the Marshall Islands, Mongolia, Panama, Antigua, Barbuda, Saint Vincent and the Grenadines. FOC boarding agreements ultimately afford the US the opportunity to request a State party to the bilateral agreement to authorise the boarding of a ship belonging to a third party to search and potentially detain the cargo if required. The boarding agreement with Liberia and Panama, the two largest ship registries in the world, gives the US the freedom to board over 30% of the world's cargo vessels.

'If the ship does decline, the United States authorities cannot board. In particular, however, this would be considered an admission that the ship was carrying illicit materials.' – unidir.org

Case study
PSI in action '*BBC China*'

In October 2003, the German-owned '*BBC China*' was diverted to an Italian port while en route to Libya. US and UK intelligence believed that the ship was carrying centrifuge parts necessary for nuclear weapon proliferation.

The German Government – a PSI partner – contacted the German-based owner, BBC Chartering and Logistics GmbH, and asked that the vessel divert to the Italian port of Taranto for inspection.

Upon inspection, thousands of components for uranium enrichment were discovered in a container marked: "Used machine tool parts." The materials were seized by the Italian authorities.

Time of War

At a time of war, naval vessels have more clearly defined rights to inspect merchant vessels. The San Remo Manual on International Law Applicable to Armed Conflicts at Sea, 1994, is the codification of the laws governing naval warfare.

Part V of the Manual covers 'Measures short of attack: interception, visit, search, diversion, and capture'.

114. If the commander of a warship suspects that a merchant vessel flying a neutral flag in fact has enemy character, the commander is entitled to exercise the right of visit and search, including the right of diversion for search under paragraph 121.

118. In exercising their legal rights in an international armed conflict at sea, belligerent warships and military aircraft have a right to visit and search merchant vessels outside neutral waters where there are reasonable grounds for suspecting that they are subject to capture.

119. As an alternative to visit and search, a neutral merchant vessel may, with its consent, be diverted from its declared destination.

120. A neutral merchant vessel is exempt from the exercise of the right of visit and search if it meets the following conditions: (a) it is bound for a neutral port; (b) it is under the convoy of an accompanying neutral warship of the same nationality or a neutral warship of a State with which the flag State of the merchant vessel has concluded an agreement providing for such convoy;
(c) the flag State of the neutral warship warrants that the neutral merchant vessel is not carrying contraband or otherwise engaged in activities inconsistent with its neutral status; and (d) the commander of the neutral warship provides, if requested by the commander of an intercepting belligerent warship or military aircraft, all information as to the character of the merchant vessel and its cargo as could otherwise be obtained by visit and search.

121. If visit and search at sea is impossible or unsafe, a belligerent warship or military aircraft may divert a merchant vessel to an appropriate area or port in order to exercise the right of visit and search.

Summary

Seafarers can be secure in the knowledge that they do not face unwarranted interference from foreign naval vessels. The key beliefs of the international law of the sea and international law aim to uphold and defend the rights to freedom of navigation and passage. However, it should be of slight concern that open-ended language or ambiguity claimed by harsher critics could lead to the unintentional criminalisation of seafarers.

On a larger political level, the international law governing free transit of the world's merchant fleet is focused on the exclusive rights to jurisdiction of the flag State. Yet, it is more often than not innocent seafarers who face the legal consequence for this greater state action. Seafarers, like the crew of the '*BBC China*', could be mistakenly viewed as proactive actors in the carriage of contraband goods. Powers conferred by treaty, such as the PSI, force upon merchant shipping an accusation of criminal collaborator.

State actions conferred by treaty for inspection may be more effective when administered by port State authorities. This would help to intercept suspect cargo before it is loaded onto a merchant vessel rather than criminalising seafarers going about their work on the high seas. However, such shore-based activities brings to mind the controversial US plans for 100% box scanning of all container cargo destined for the United States (for more on US box scanning, see *Shipping Regulations and Guidance,* issue 5).

Drug Smuggling

Drug Trafficking: A Global Market

Drug trafficking is a global illicit trade involving the cultivation, manufacture, distribution and sale of substances that are subject to drug prohibition laws. The trade in illicit drugs is the world's largest illegal market.

A rough estimate of the number of traffickers involved in moving heroin and opiates across countries and regions would likely stand at well above 1 million people. (World Drug Report 2010)

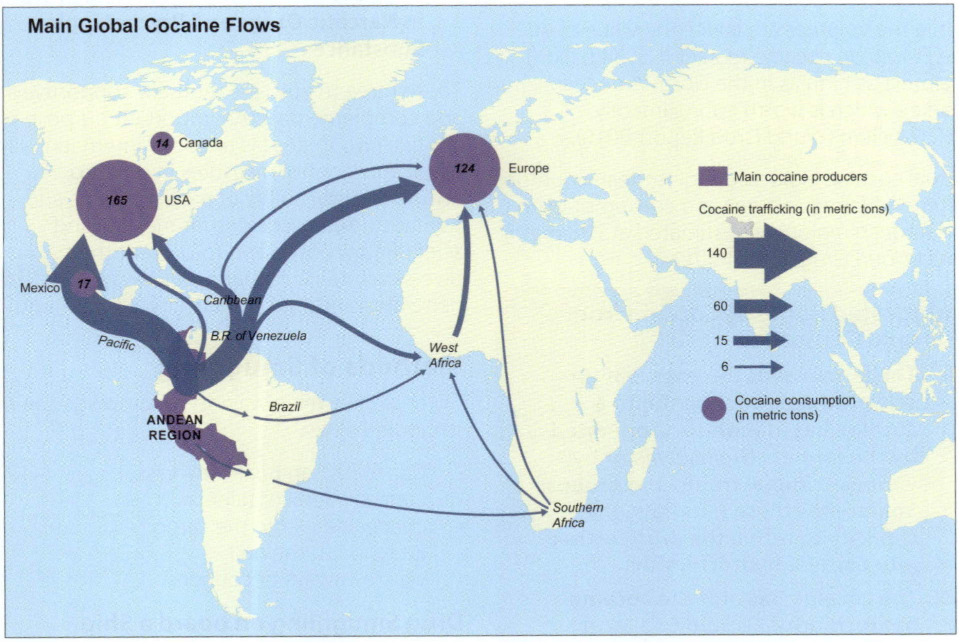

Around 25% of the cocaine moving from South America into Europe (25 to 30 tonnes pa) passes through Belgium. Most of this comes through the port of Antwerp, which has 140,000 employees and 160 km of quayside. Only around 2% of the 8 million containers passing through the port each year are screened. (Source: Guardian, June 2014)

Graphic Source: UNODC, World Drug Report 2009

Drug Smuggling

The transport of drugs by sea falls into the following categories:

(a) drugs shipped on commercial carriers engaged in legitimate (licit) trade, concealed either on the ships themselves or among the cargo

(b) drugs transported clandestinely as the sole cargo, either directly on a private vessel or via operations involving two or more vessels.

In 2010, the US Coast Guard seized just over 90 tons of cocaine destined for US shores, a haul valued at more than US$3.5 billion. The close proximity and relative ease for transporting by water or across land and via the Caribbean make the US an ideal market. Recently, Central and Western Europe has become another important market to drug traffickers. The primary countries of entry for South American cocaine to the European market are Spain and the Netherlands, due to geography and facilitation. Most of the trafficking is conducted via maritime channels. The Netherlands is home to two of the biggest and busiest ports in Europe: Rotterdam and Amsterdam.

While the volumes are lower, the value of the European cocaine market (US$34 billion) is almost as high as in the North American market, which is worth approximately US$37 billion (World Drug Report 2010).

Actual cocaine exports out of Andean countries (after deducting seizures and consumption in the Andean region) are estimated at 788 metric tons (World Drug Report 2011).

Suggested Route of Cocaine from Farm to Consumer:

1. **The farmer sells the coca leaf (or self-produced coca paste) to a cocaine base laboratory, operated by the farmers themselves or by various criminal trafficking groups. Sometimes these labs have the capacity to refine the drug further into cocaine hydrochloride.**
2. **The cocaine base (or the cocaine hydrochloride) is sold to a local trafficking organisation that transports and sells the cocaine to a transnational drug trafficking organisation.**
3. **The drug trafficking organisation contracts yet another group to do the actual shipping.**
4. **The cocaine is shipped to traffickers in Mexico.**
5. **The Mexican traffickers transport the drugs across the US border to wholesalers.**
6. **The wholesalers sell the cocaine to local mid-level dealers or street dealers across the USA.**
7. **The street dealers sell the cocaine to the consumer.**

Anti-Trafficking and Drug Control Legislation

There are three major international drug control treaties:

Single Convention on Narcotic Drugs of 1961 (amended 1972)

Convention of Psychotropic Substances of 1971

1988 UN Convention against Illicit Traffic in Narcotic Drugs and Psychotropic Substances

These three treaties are mutually supportive and complementary. An important purpose of the first two treaties is to codify internationally applicable control measures in order to ensure the availability of narcotic drugs and psychotropic substances for medical and scientific purposes, and to prevent their diversion into illicit channels. They also include general provisions on trafficking.

Methods of Smuggling

There are five main ways in which drugs can be smuggled at sea:

- Concealed on board the vessel
- concealed in containers
- concealed within the cargo
- attached to the hull
- via stowaways or couriers.

Drug Smuggling on board a Ship

Drugs can hidden in a multitude of locations on board a ship, eg the inside of cargo bays, ventilation shafts, crawl spaces, rope and storage lockers, engine room, accommodation, supply closets, lifeboats etc.

The quantities may be smaller than the drug loads that can be smuggled in containers and cargo, but there is an increased risk that, when drugs are seized on board by law enforcement agencies, the vessel will be delayed, detained or a fine imposed by government authorities.

Figure 26.2 - Lazaro Cardenas, Mexico - A view inside the vessel Xoloescuintle's fuel tank filled with cocaine. After a search of the vessel, the boarding team began extracting hundreds of cocaine bales from the tightly-packed confines of the fuel tank voids. In all, 10.5 tons of cocaine were found aboard the vessel.

Drug Smuggling via Containers

Every year more than 420 million maritime containers move around the globe making up some 90 percent of global trade. However, only two percent of containers are inspected.

More than 90,000 merchant and passenger ships docked at US ports in 2004, carrying more than 9 million shipping containers.

Drug smugglers have developed a surprising variety of ways to transport vast quantities of drugs in containers. Common techniques include secret compartments, fabricated inner structures, and the disassembly and reassembly of container structures.

The smugglers utilise a wide range of resources and professions to continue their illegal trade. Thousands of dollars and a range of experts from engineers, chemists and skilled fabricators go into making these seemingly harmless containers.

Drug Smuggling via Cargo

Drugs can be concealed within legitimate cargo or take the place of cargo entirely, fabricated with the merchandise being transported, or concealed within the structure of the packaging/pallet. When drugs are concealed within legitimate cargo consignments, the vessel may well be carrying the drugs unknowingly.

Drug Smuggling via Hull Attachments

Drug traffickers may employ divers to attach containers of drugs to the hull of the vessel beneath the waterline.

Attachment is made in a wide variety of ways. Often the drugs are secured in and around the bow thrusters.

The hull below the waterline is not frequently inspected but in areas where drug smuggling is known to be a problem an inspection could be wise.

Drug Smuggling via Stowaways/Couriers

Drug couriers, whether a stowaway or crew member, can transport a large quantity of drugs with relative ease.

Colombian traffickers are reported to offer seafarers US$20,000 per kilo to smuggle cocaine into Europe from Colombia.

The crew should exercise caution if they discover stowaways on board. Stowaways will try to protect their cargo at all costs and may become violent if confronted.

'Gatun' Ship Drug Seizure

21st March 2007

The cocaine seizure on the Panamanian freighter *'Gatun'*, at nearly 20 tons, was the largest in US maritime history. The US Coast Guard made contact with the ship after it was spotted by a patrol ship in March of 2007. The Coast Guard uncovered more than 42,000 pounds of cocaine with an estimated worth of US$600 million. 14 crew members, all from Mexico and Panama, were arrested. The ship was carrying some legal cargo, but the cocaine was piled up on the top main deck in clear view.

Drugs Found in Cargo

Case study: The Croatian Master of the 1976-built reefership *'Coral Sea',* Kristo Laptalo, together with Lithuanian first mate Konstantin Metelev and Filipino bosun Narciso Carcia, were arrested after 51.6 kilos of cocaine were found stashed in two boxes among more than

Drug Smuggling

27,000 boxes of bananas that were unloaded at the Greek port of Aegion.

The discovery was made during a quality check carried out by the ship's agent, who notified the coast guard and the police.

The Master was sentenced to 14 years in prison; the other two were acquitted. Witnesses for the prosecution stated that they did not believe Laptalo had any involvement with the drugs found on his ship. Even the prosecutor in the appeals process motioned for Laptalo to be acquitted. The Master was eventually cleared of cocaine smuggling on appeal, but spent a total of 16 months in Greek detention.

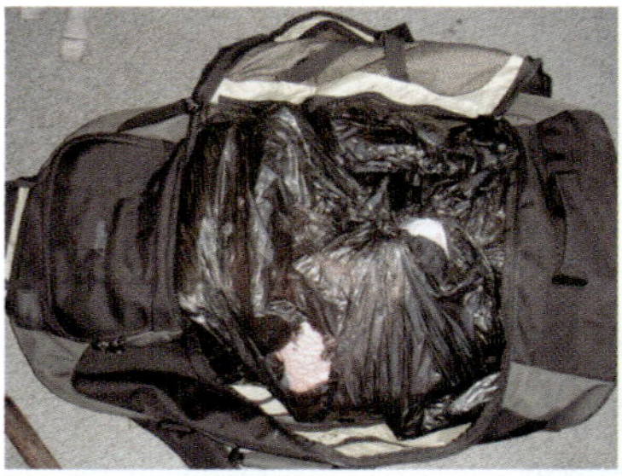

US Coast Guard photo

Figure 26.3 - A duffle bag containing 60,000 tablets of Ecstasy, worth approximately US$720,000, was interdicted by a Coast Guard boarding team from Coast Guard Station Neah Bay, WA, 27th August 2009.

Staff Arrests

"The continued increase in national, regional and international laws and regulations affecting shipping and seafarers threatens to render shipping a less attractive vocation than at any time in the history of the industry. And the trend towards the criminalisation of seafarers - whether for security-related motives or as a result of political pressure to apportion blame in respect of pollution incidents - will discourage conscientious officers from accepting more senior responsibilities."

William O'Neil, Former IMO Secretary-General

Seafarers could be arrested for a range of offences at sea. These include violations relating to marine pollution; maritime security; safety of navigation; crimes against persons on the high seas such as assault or murder; and drugs, arms or people smuggling.

http://www.mastermariners.org.au

Seafarers should be aware that while on board they will always be subject to the jurisdiction of at least one State. The jurisdiction of the flag State continues to be applicable at all times.

The jurisdiction of a sovereign State whose waters are being transited will also be applicable to those on board.

As seafarers transit from port to port, they are subject to the entire range of criminal laws of those port States. They cannot know and they are unlikely to have been warned about local criminal laws, and therefore they are at risk of committing an offence without any awareness or intention to do so. (Seafarers Rights International)

A seafarer is under the jurisdiction of all the State laws that would apply to any person onshore, but seafarers face the added complication of the extensive legislation and regulation that applies to ships, their master and crew.

Each country has its own judicial system, and not all apply procedures with which may be familiar.

There is the potential for seafarers to be arrested for a range of offences at sea. A recent worry throughout the shipping industry has been the 'criminalisation of seafarers', where seafarers have increasingly become the scapegoats for marine accidents or absent shipowners/operators.

Of course, seafarers can be arrested and have been arrested for perfectly justified reasons too.

Seafarers are unlikely to be nationals of the country in which the incident occurs. Consequently, prosecuting authorities may be required – or at least be inclined – to keep seafarers suspected of criminal violations in custody to ensure their availability for prosecution at a later date.

Staff Arrests

It is often difficult to find the owners of a vessel, so arresting and charging the master and officers on duty is an easy solution.

Seafarers' Rights

Sources of protection and rights:

Flag State law – seafarers are entitled to the protection of, and are governed by, the laws of the flag State wherever the ship is and regardless of individual seafarers' nationality.

Port State law – a port State can exercise certain powers over the ship while it is in port.

Seafarers' home state – when abroad, a seafarer's home country should provide support and assistance through its consular offices.

International Law – IMO, ILO, UN human rights, for example.

It is essential that seafarers are treated fairly and that their fundamental rights are respected. These include the right to avoid self-incrimination and the right to be addressed in a language they understand.

IMO Guidelines on the Fair Treatment of Seafarers in the Event of a Maritime Accident (Resolution LEG.3(91), 27th April 2006)

The Resolution and Guidelines apply to all instances where seafarers may be detained by public authorities in the event of a maritime accident. A maritime accident is defined as "any unforeseen occurrence or physical event connected to the navigation, operations, manoeuvring or handling of ships, or the machinery, equipment, material, or cargo on board such ships which may result in the detention of seafarers." Guidance is provided to port and coastal States, flag States, seafarer States, shipowners and seafarers.

Source: http://tinyurl.com/pz9y5sx

UNCLOS Article 292.4 states:

> *"Upon the posting of a bond or other financial security determined by the court or tribunal, the authorities of the detaining State shall comply promptly with the decision of the court or tribunal concerning the release of the vessel or its crew."*

The International Covenant on Civil and Political Rights (1966) provides for equal, non-discriminatory treatment before the law and effective remedy for any persons whose rights or freedoms are violated. Article 9 sets out the right to liberty:

> *1. Everyone has the right to liberty and security of person. No one shall be subjected to arbitrary arrest or detention. No one shall be deprived of his liberty except on such grounds and in accordance with such procedure as are established by law.*
>
> *2. Anyone who is arrested shall be informed, at the time of arrest, of the reasons for his arrest and shall be promptly informed of any charges against him.*
>
> *3. Anyone arrested or detained on a criminal charge shall be brought promptly before a judge or other officer authorized by law to exercise judicial power and shall be entitled to trial within a reasonable time or to release. It shall not be the general rule that persons awaiting trial shall be detained in custody, but release may be subject to guarantees to appear for trial, at any other stage of the judicial proceedings, and, should occasion arise, for execution of the judgment.*
>
> *4. Anyone who is deprived of his liberty by arrest or detention shall be entitled to take proceedings before a court, in order that that court may decide without delay on the lawfulness of his detention and order his release if the detention is not lawful.*
>
> *5. Anyone who has been the victim of unlawful arrest or detention shall have enforceable right to compensation.*

Flag State Protection

The State under which the ship is flagged has the right under international law to institute legal proceedings requesting the immediate release of any seafarers detained following an accident or pollution incident at sea.

Unfortunately, Flags of Convenience (FOC) States are notorious for failing to pursue this right on behalf of crews of ships under their flag.

Source: http://tinyurl.com/qhfr44y

Staff Arrests

IMO Guidelines for the Fair Treatment of Seafarers in the event of a Maritime Accident state that the flag State should:

.4 assist in ensuring that shipowners honour obligations to seafarers involved in a maritime accident or any investigation;

.5 ensure/verify that adequate provisions are in place to provide for the subsistence of each detained seafarer, including, as appropriate, wages, suitable accommodation, food and medical care;

.7 assist seafarers to secure fair treatment, and assist shipowners in the event of an investigation by a port or coastal State;

.8 fund the repatriation of seafarers, where necessary, following the aftermath of a maritime accident in instances where shipowners fail to fulfil their responsibility to repatriate;

.9 assist, as provided for in national law, in the issuance and service of process and the return to a port or coastal State of seafarers subject to its jurisdiction who are needed solely as witnesses in any proceeding following a maritime accident;

.10 take steps to ensure that its consular officers are permitted access to the involved seafarers, irrespective of their nationality;

.11 take all necessary measures to ensure the fair treatment of seafarers who were employed or engaged on a vessel flying its flag. This may ultimately include utilizing international dispute resolution mechanisms, which can secure the prompt release of vessels and crews upon the posting of a reasonable bond or financial security; and

.12 take steps to ensure that no discriminatory or retaliatory measures are taken against seafarers because of their participation during investigations.

Flags of Convenience

'The use of flags of convenience and the establishment of new registers by States with no pre-existing maritime infrastructure is growing. To shipping and fishing interests, the economic attraction of registering a vessel under a flag with lower costs, more relaxed crewing requirements and less vigorous regulation is undeniable. Moreover there can be a competitive disadvantage in registering with more reputable flags. However, the wider consequences should not be underestimated. Without transparency of ownership, without the connection between the beneficial owners of a vessel and the flag State responsible for jurisdiction on board it is not possible to ensure the highest standards in maritime security and safety. For these reasons it is vital for States to address, at the appropriate level and without delay, these important issues of international governance.'

Real and Present Danger: Flag State Failure and Maritime Security, Matthew Gianni http://tinyurl.com/inds3ty

Criminalisation

Seafarers may be prosecuted in a wide range of jurisdictions for a wide range of offences and under a number of laws, which make it virtually impossible for the individual seafarer to have knowledge of the criminal risks associated with a given action.

The focus on security and environmental protection means that seafarers must operate within increasingly complex and stringent regulation. These measures have been accused of being too 'heavy-handed,' resulting in innocent seafarers being treated like serious criminals following events completely out of their control.

A number of highly publicised marine accidents have highlighted the issue of the criminalisation of seafarers. Two such incidents, the '*Erika*' and the '*Prestige*', demonstrate the harsh treatment that seafarers can be subjected to. Both of these incidents resulted in oil pollution caused by accident rather than by negligence of the crew.

The Maltese-flagged Italian-owned oil tanker '*Erika*' broke in two in heavy seas off the coast of France in 1999, spilling 31,000 tonnes of oil into the sea. Due to hurricane-strength gales that followed, the oil was scattered across a large portion of the French coast and adversely affected wildlife. Criminal charges were brought against the owners and operators, and also against the Master. The Master was imprisoned for considerable time by the French

authorities, charged with putting life in danger and causing marine pollution. Although the Master was eventually found not guilty, this result did not occur until 16th January 2008.

In November 2002, the Greek-owned, Bahamas-flagged tanker MV 'Prestige' sank following serious hull failure during a storm off northwest Spain. When the vessel first got into difficulties, the Master sought refuge, but permission was refused by the Spanish, French and Portuguese authorities. The Master was ordered to steer the stricken vessel away from the Spanish coast. The continued exposure to heavy seas caused the vessel to break apart, releasing 70,000 tonnes of heavy fuel oil into the sea. The Master was forcibly removed by the Spanish military and subsequently held in jail for over three months. Bail was set at €3 million. The Master was eventually released from custody, but a lesser bail amount following payment of permission for him to return home to Greece was not granted until two years after the incident. Proceedings were taken against the Master, the Chief Engineer, the first Mate and the Spanish maritime chief who ordered the vessel out to sea. At the trial in 2012, the precise cause of the incident could not be established and so criminal liability could not be determined.

Although serious pollution occurred in both incidents, it was unintentional and both Masters did their utmost to limit the consequences of an incident beyond their control. In addition they had to make judgments while working in extreme weather conditions on structurally flawed vessels. As such, it is of deep concern that they faced criminal charges.

EU Directive 2005/35/EC on ship-source pollution states that ship-source polluting discharges constitute, in principle, a criminal offence. The persons responsible for discharging polluting substances may be subject to criminal penalties if they have acted with intent, recklessly or with serious negligence.

The generally accepted industry standard of liability in the IMO Convention for the Prevention of Pollution from Ships (MARPOL) is based on "intent to cause damage or recklessly and with knowledge that damage would probably result". The European Directive lowers the base to "intent, recklessly or by serious negligence."

UNCLOS Article 230 states that:

> *"Monetary penalties only may be imposed with respect to violations of national laws and regulations or applicable international rules and standards for the prevention, reduction and control of pollution of the marine environment, committed by foreign vessels in the territorial sea, except in the case of a willful and serious act of pollution in the territorial sea."*

Between 1995 and 2005, the US enforced 30 criminal convictions on intentional discharge of oil, netting US$133 million in fines. While all efforts to protect the environment are to be welcomed, an unfortunate side effect within the maritime industry has been a tendency to criminalise seafarers for offences committed unintentionally and/or unavoidably during the course of their professional duties.

http://tinyurl.com/n66htfm

Further Case Studies of Criminalisation

***'Delta Pride'*, 1998**

The owners of the *'Delta Pride'* filed for bankruptcy in March 1998. In May 1998 while in Tampico, Mexico, the ship's Mexican agent confiscated the ship's documents and the crew's passports against a small supply of provisions.

Abandoned by the owners and in a desperate situation, the Master, Captain Maqsood Ahmed, sailed out from Tampico and, on 24th November 1998, anchored three miles off South Padre Island near Brownsville, Texas, hoping for justice in the USA.

However, the ship was not allowed to enter port and was given no assistance. The Master and crew almost starved, relying for several weeks on sea fish and rainwater for their survival. Meanwhile, the court in Brownsville ordered the auction of the vessel, which was sold for the minute sum of US$350,000.

Staff Arrests

The crew's certified claim for wages was US$270,000 and the Master and crew rightly expected that the US court would follow internationally accepted priority from the proceedings of the sale. This did not happen. Instead the crew were taken into custody by immigration authorities and kept in the Brownsville immigration detention centre for six months.

'Nissos Amorgos', 1997

Just before midnight on 28th February 1997, the Greek tanker *'Nissos Amorgos'* struck bottom while being piloted down the Maracaibo Channel (by a local pilot). Her two forward centre tanks were ruptured and 7,000 tonnes of Venezuelan crude oil escaped.

The vessel was one of three tankers to run aground in the waterway within a period of six weeks. The Master claimed that the tanker had struck a submerged object during the pilot-assisted passage. The Venezuelan navy carried out a survey of the Channel and preliminary findings pointed to underwater bank collapses as well as the presence of widespread silting and a number of large metallic objects on the bed of the waterway.

Nevertheless, the Venezuelan authorities kept the ship arrested for nearly five months, and detained the Master for an additional month without charge subsequent to the release of the ship.

The Master was eventually charged and a lengthy series of court proceedings followed. The Master was found guilty of negligence in causing the oil spill, but after a series of appeals, the Criminal Court of Appeal dismissed the conviction on procedural grounds in 2005. No action was taken against the port authorities, who were responsible for the state of the Channel, or the pilots.

Legitimate Arrests

A number of seafarers have received harsh and unfair treatment, but there are also completely legitimate and necessary arrests. The following are some examples.

Drunk Master of Laden Chemical Tanker Sentenced at Court

On 4th November 2008, the Cypriot-registered chemical tanker *'Elousa Trikoukiotisa'* was bound for London from Rostock in Northern Germany under the command of Ukrainian Master Gonchar Volodymyr. The vessel was laden with ammonium nitrate in liquid form and had a crew of 15 on board. When the pilot boarded at the Sunk boarding area, he reported to the Port Authority that the Master appeared drunk.

Metropolitan Police officers boarded the vessel when it berthed at Dagenham Dock and administered a breath test, which proved positive. The Master was arrested and taken to Dagenham Police Station where a later breath test indicated 103 micrograms of alcohol in 100 micrograms of breath. The legal limit for seafarers is 80.

He was charged with breaching the Railways and Transport Safety Act 2003. On passing sentence, Her Honour Judge J Hughes QC took into account Mr Volodymyr's previous good character and record. She noted that he had now lost his job and the effects of the sentence upon his career.

The Judge also noted the nature of the cargo and that the navigation of vessel had been satisfactory, although that was down to the Chief Officer who had taken over. It was also brought up in court that the Master had signed the ship's documents stating there was no alcohol on board, and that he had said that it had been eight hours since his last drink.

Captain Volodymyr was sentenced to two months in prison and deportation on completion of the sentence.

Shipowner Pleads Guilty to Merchant Shipping Act Offences

In the early hours of 27th February 2007, the Antigua and Barbuda-registered coaster *'Jerome H'* was on passage from Dagenham in Essex to Belfast in Northern Ireland when it struck the East Goodwin Light Vessel. The collision seriously damaged the light vessel, which had to be removed from station for repairs. The *'Jerome H'* continued on to Belfast.

Investigations showed that the Mate was alone on the bridge. He had been doing paperwork on an aft-facing desk in the moments leading up to the collision. It was also discovered that the routine on board was for the designated lookout to remain below in the mess room.

Further investigations showed that the vessel did not have adequate charts on board for the voyage between Dagenham and Belfast. It also had inadequate charts for the next voyage.

The shipowner was charged with one breach of Rule 5 of the COLREGS (failure to keep a good lookout) and two breaches of the ISM Code (failing to provide adequate charts and failure to comply with regulations concerning the provision of lookouts at night).

They were fined £3,700 and ordered to pay costs of £13,000.

Master Pleads Guilty to Breach of Rule 10(D)(i) of the International Regulations for Preventing Collisions at Sea 1972

Captain Stanislaw Kurczyn admitted to navigating the 1,394 Dwt cargo ship *'Union Arrow'*, in the English Inshore Traffic Zone (EITZ) on 9th May 2005 while on passage from Littlehampton to Dunkerque, thereby contravening Rule 10(d)(i) of the COLREGS.

Dover Coastguard detected *'Union Arrow'* on their Channel Navigation Information Service (CNIS) radar system and the vessel was questioned over its use of the EITZ. Despite the Officer of the Watch being warned that he appeared to be in contravention of the regulations, the *'Union Arrow'* continued its passage in the EITZ and was subsequently reported to the MCA's Enforcement Branch in Southampton.

Rule 10(d)(i) prohibits any vessel from using the EITZ when it can safely use an appropriate traffic lane within an adjacent Traffic Separation Scheme unless it is under 20 metres in length, a sailing vessel or a vessel engaged in fishing. A vessel may also use the EITZ if it is en route to or from a port or any other place within the EITZ, and if the master of a vessel considers it appropriate to avoid immediate danger. These regulations are there to minimise the amount of vessel traffic navigating close to the UK coastline to reduce the risk of accidents and resultant pollution.

Captain Kurczyn claimed that he had received permission from Dover Coastguard to use the EITZ, but no evidence could be produced to substantiate this. MCA regulations state that no such permission can be granted by the Coastguard.

The Judge, Recorder Mr D Evans, said in his summing up that the International Regulations for the Prevention of Collisions at Sea had a crucial role to play in the safety of shipping.

Mike Toogood, CNIS Manager at Dover Coastguard, said:

"The MCA will continue to prosecute vessels who contravene the shipping regulations and regards full compliance with Rule 10 of the Collision Regulations as a very important and major factor in the improvement of safety in the Dover Strait."

The penalty was a £500 fine and £1,000 costs.

Sailor Faces £400k Smuggling Charge

UK Border Agency officers arrested Siviwe Luma after he arrived at Felixstowe docks as part of the crew on a container ship travelling from Africa in May 2011.

The 34-year-old South African national appeared before magistrates at South East Suffolk Magistrates' Court in Ipswich charged with two counts of importing a class A drug.

UK Border Agency officials confirmed they arrested Luma after three kilos of cocaine were alleged to have been discovered in a rucksack during a search of the ship.

A further three kilos are alleged to have been found on the ship.

The value of the drugs was estimated at £400,000.

Terrorism

The Council for Security Cooperation in the Asia Pacific (CSCAP) Working Group has offered an extensive definition for maritime terrorism:

"...the undertaking of terrorist acts and activities within the maritime environment, using or against vessels or fixed platforms at sea or in port, or against any one of their passengers or personnel, against coastal facilities or settlements, including tourist resorts, port areas and port towns or cities."

This definition, however, does not define what terrorism is and whether it would only include maritime attacks against civilian (merchant) vessels or also attacks against military crafts.[1]

Why is Piracy not Terrorism?

Piracy is committed for 'Private ends' (UNCLOS Article 101), whereas terrorism is an act intended as a platform for political ends. For example, the piracy threat in the Gulf of Aden and Indian Ocean is carried out by organised criminal groups looking to extort money through kidnap and ransom of vessels and crew. They do not direct their attacks exclusively against ships flagged to a particular State or heading to a particular destination. Their motivation is financial not political.

Overview

Since the terrorist attacks of 11th September 2001 in the United States, terrorism and the global effort to combat it have been at the forefront of State foreign policy. The United States and other nations moved quickly to bolster and update their existing anti-terror mechanisms, but also began to call for new legislation both intra- and internationally to reduce the risk of another attack on the same scale.

One of the biggest fears of the US Government was the use of a merchant vessel by terrorists to transport a Chemical, Biological, Radiological or Nuclear (CBRN) Weapon or Weapons of Mass Destruction (WMD) for use against US interests. Shipping is largely seen as a 'soft target.' This fear is in some way understandable. The vast areas transited by merchant vessels leave them open to potential interception and interference by terrorist actors.

Containers also raise many concerns for US officials. It is difficult at times to ascertain the origins of a container and to confirm its true contents while in transit. This leads many officials to believe there is great potential for a terrorist organisation to ship a large CBRN weapon or large quantities of conventional weapons directly into the United States. Oil, LNG and bulk cargo carriers are also believed to have a dangerous potential in the hands of terrorists. It is feared that these ships could be made into floating bombs. The combustible nature of oil and LNG makes tankers an obvious target, while bulk cargo carriers could contain many tons of explosives hidden in the shipment waiting to be detonated at the most opportune moment.

With approximately 90% of world trade travelling by sea, the effect of a large scale terrorist attack against the world shipping fleet or its navigational channels could be devastating to world commerce. An attack on a ship within the Suez or Panama Canal or within the Malacca Straits would have a huge impact on the international flow of goods and oil.

In response to the perceived threat to the global shipping market, a number of new regulations were developed to help strengthen shipping's security. The International Ship and Port Facility Security (ISPS) Code and the 2005 Protocol to the Convention for the Suppression of Unlawful Acts against the Safety of Maritime Navigation, 1988 (SUA Convention) aimed to reduce shipping's vulnerability to infiltration by terrorist groups and make illegal, under international law, attempted or actual acts of terrorism against merchant vessels and their crews.

Individual States have also created legislation to help keep terror threats from their borders, most notably the laws, requirements and programmes created by the United States. Some of these measures, in particular 100% box scanning, met with consternation from other States and industry bodies, who expressed concern about the financial burden these measures place on State authorities, ports and private shipping concerns. Measures suggested and supported by the US Government also

[1] Akiva J. Lorenz, *Al Qaeda's Maritime Threat* (Maritime Terrorism Research Centre, 2007) uploaded: 15/4/2007, accessed: 11/1/2012 p. 3

posed significant logistical challenges to the global shipping market.

ISPS Code 2004

In December 2002, the IMO established the International Ship and Port Security (ISPS) Code to enhance maritime security. The ISPS Code created standards for security, roles and responsibilities, and methodologies for assessing security.

It required that, by 1st July 2004, all 167 IMO Member States must certify compliance. Contracting governments must set security levels, conduct port facility security assessments, approve security plans for both ship and port facilities, identify ports that need port facility security officers, and test approved security plans.

The ISPS Code is implemented through SOLAS Chapter XI-2 – Special measures to enhance maritime security.

In short, the ISPS Code outlines the minimum security procedures that all ships and ports must meet to improve overall maritime security. The ISPS Code requires that all ships:

- Operate an Automated Identification System (AIS)
- clearly display on the hull the IMO Ship Identification Number (SIN)
- have a ship security alarm system
- have a ship security plan and a ship security officer.

In addition, all port facilities must:

- Have a security plan
- have port facility security officers
- monitor and control access
- monitor the activities of people and cargo
- ensure security communications are readily available.

The ISPS Code has been criticised for only being applicable to SOLAS Class vessels. This means the ship security requirements in the ISPS Code are only applicable to ships of ≥500 Dwt.

SUA Convention 1988 and 2005 Protocol

MV *'Achille Lauro'*

On 7th October 1985, the 23,629 Dwt, Italian-flagged cruise ship *'Achille Lauro'* was hijacked off Egypt by four men from the Palestine Liberation Front (PLF).

One passenger, a US citizen, was murdered by the hijackers.

The hijackers demanded the release of 50 Palestinians held by Israel in prison.

After two days of negotiations, the hijackers abandoned the liner in exchange for safe conduct.

Following the hijacking, IMO Resolution 924 called for a review of the existing legal and technical measures to prevent and suppress terrorist acts against ships both at port and at sea.

The original SUA Convention, adopted in 1988, considered the scenario of a merchant ship being hijacked or destroyed. It focused on reactions to a terrorist act rather than its prevention. The 2005 Amendments and Protocol explore the new challenges and dangers posed by terrorist acts. The scenarios now include the carriage of CBRN weapons on board a ship, or the ship being used to carry terrorists. Merchant shipping is no longer exclusively a victim of terrorist acts, but is recognised as having the unintended capacity to be a vector for global terror activities.

The SUA Convention and 2005 Protocol apply to ships navigating waters beyond the outer limit of the territorial waters of a party State, or ships scheduled to navigate to, through or from such waters. The Convention prescribes that each State party must ensure that certain acts will be considered criminal offences by courts within its own jurisdiction (Article 5).

Offences in the 1988 Convention and Protocol are:

- To seize or exercise control of a ship by force or intimidation
- acts of violence on the ship
- destruction of a ship
- placing a dangerous device or substance on board a ship

Terrorism

- damaging maritime or navigational facilities
- communicating false information.

New offences under the 2005 Convention and Protocol are:

- Transporting certain substances (Article 3)
- committing certain acts in order to intimidate a population, organisation, or government or to compel them to undertake or abstain from doing something. All of these acts must be committed 'unlawfully and intentionally.'

Article 8 of the 2005 Protocol establishes a mechanism that allows, having received explicit authorisation from the flag State, the boarding of vessels suspected of engaging in these activities in international waters.

SUA Convention and 2005 Protocol full text: http://tinyurl.com/lz77qv8

Terrorist Attacks Against Ships

USS 'Cole', 12th October 2000

The destroyer *USS 'Cole'* was refuelling in the Yemeni port of Aden when she was rammed by Al Qaeda terrorists using a small boat loaded with approximately 270 kg of explosives.

17 US servicemen were killed and a further 37 wounded.

Damage was estimated at at least US$250 million and repairs took 14 months.

Al Qaeda claimed it cost them less than US$50,000 to execute the attack.

MV *'Limburg'*, 6th October 2002

A small fibre-glass boat loaded with 100 to 200 kg of explosives rammed into the French-flagged VLCC MV *'Limburg'* 400 miles outside the port of Aden killing one crew member and injuring 25 others.

The *'Limburg'* was partially loaded with 400,000 barrels of crude. The double hull structure ruptured and 90,000 barrels spilled into the Gulf of Aden.

The vessel sustained approximately US$45,000 worth of damage.

The incident caused the price of oil to rise US$0.48/barrel due to increased insurance fees for ships calling at Aden.

It also caused the loss of US$3.8 million in monthly port revenue and resulted in almost 3,000 job losses at the port.

Stowaways

Courtesy of US Customs and Border Protection

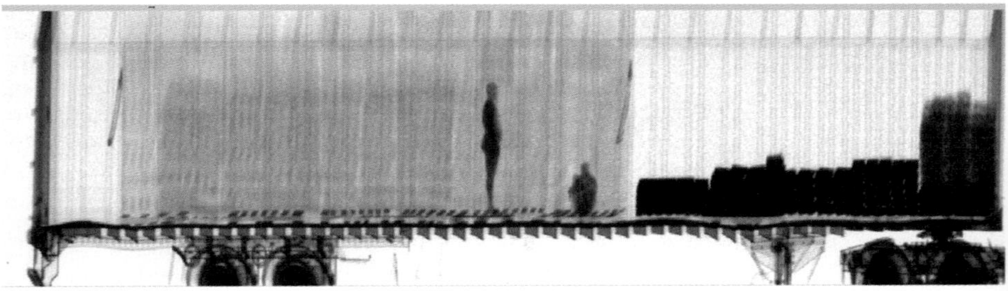

Figure 26.4 - X-ray image of a truck with two stowaways in a container of Styrofoam trays entering the US

Despite implementation of the ISPS Code, the issue of preventing stowaways and dealing with them properly once they have been discovered is still problematic.

A search for stowaways must be conducted and recorded in the ship's log prior to departure from each port. The procedures for conducting such searches should be addressed in the ship's security plan.

Guidelines

Basic Principles

1. Stowaways arriving at or entering a State without the required documents are,

Stowaways

in general, illegal entrants. Decisions on dealing with such situations are the prerogative of the State where such arrival or entry occurs.

2. Stowaway asylum seekers should be treated in accordance with international instruments.
3. Every effort should be made to avoid situations where a stowaway has to be detained on board a ship indefinitely.

Preventative Measures for the Shipowner/Master

1. Stowaways have boarded vessels in a number of ways, including:
   - Climbing up over the side using mooring lines or poles and then hiding in an unlocked locker or void space, an empty drum, a lifeboat or under containers stowed on deck
   - entering soft top containers through the top so that the customs or security seals on the container doors remain intact before the container is loaded on the ship
   - hiding in empty containers
   - hiding in rudder trunks (especially when the ship is in ballast condition)
   - hiding in ventilation trunks (especially in RoRo car carriers)
   - hiding in the ceiling of the tally office.
2. Ships should ensure that adequate security arrangements are in place which, as far as practicable, will prevent stowaways from getting aboard the ship, and, if this fails, as far as practicable, will detect them before the ship leaves port or, at the latest, before it arrives at the next port of call.
3. Advice should be sought from the applicable P&I Club regarding stowaways and smuggling.
4. When calling at ports and during stay in ports where there is a risk of stowaway embarkation, security arrangements should at least contain the following preventative measures:
   - All doors, hatches and means of access to holds or stores that are not used during the ship's stay in port should be locked
   - access points to the ship should be kept to a minimum and adequately secured
   - areas seaward of the ship should be adequately secured
   - adequate deck watch should be kept
   - boardings and disembarkations should, where possible, be tallied by the ship's crew or, after agreement with the master, by others
   - adequate means of communication should be maintained
   - at night, adequate lighting should be maintained both inside and along the hull.
5. When departing from a port, the ship should be searched thoroughly in accordance with a specific plan or schedule, and with priority given to places where stowaways might hide. Search methods that are likely to harm secreted stowaways should not be used.
6. Fumigation or sealing should not be carried out until a thorough search of the areas to be fumigated or sealed has taken place in order to ensure that no stowaways are present.

Responsibilities in Stowaway Cases

The Master

It is the responsibility of the master following discovery of stowaways on board to:

- Ensure the safety and security of the ship and crew as well as the well-being of the stowaways
- search stowaways upon discovery and confiscate any weapons and take custody of any passports, papers and personal belongings
- secure stowaways in a locked cabin
- ensure stowaways are brought to a muster station in the event of a shipboard emergency
- make every effort to determine immediately the port of embarkation of the stowaway
- make every effort to establish the identity, including the nationality/citizenship and the right of residence of the stowaway
- prepare a statement containing all available information relevant to the stowaway for

Stowaways

presentation to the appropriate authorities and the shipowner

- When reporting stowaways, reference should be made to the *Revised Guidelines on the Prevention of Access by Stowaways and the Allocation of Responsibilities to Seek the Successful Resolution of Stowaway Cases* adopted by the International Maritime Organization by Resolutions MSC.312(88) and FAL. 11(37).

- notify the existence of a stowaway and any relevant details to the shipowner and appropriate authorities at the port of embarkation, the next port of call and the flag State, with the understanding that, when a stowaway declares himself/herself to be a refugee, this information should be treated as confidential to the extent necessary for the security of the stowaway
- not to depart from the planned voyage to seek the disembarkation of a stowaway discovered on board the ship after it has left the territorial waters of the State where the stowaways embarked unless permission to disembark the stowaway has been granted by the public authorities of the State to whose port the ship deviates, or repatriation has been arranged elsewhere with sufficient documentation and permission given for disembarkation, or unless there are extenuating safety, security, health or compassionate reasons
- ensure that the stowaway is presented to the appropriate authorities at the next port of call in accordance with their requirements
- take appropriate measures to ensure the security, general health, welfare and safety of the stowaway until disembarkation, including providing him/her with adequate provisioning, accommodation, proper medical attention and sanitary facilities
- ensure that stowaways are not made to work on board the ship, except in emergency situations or in relation to the stowaway's accommodation on board
- ensure that stowaways are treated humanely.

The ship's flag State should be informed whenever stowaways are found on board. These reports should include:

- The date and port where the stowaways embarked the vessel
- when and where they were found on board
- the number, nationality and physical condition of the stowaways
- the planned port of disembarkation (if found at sea or on arrival at a port other than where they embarked).

A follow-up report should be provided when the stowaways are disembarked or in the event that port officials refuse to allow stowaways to be disembarked.

First Port of Call after Discovery of a Stowaway

It is the responsibility of the State of the first port of call after discovery of the stowaway to:

- Accept the stowaway for examination in accordance with the national laws of that State and, where the competent national authority considers that it would facilitate matters, allow the appointed P&I Club correspondent to have access to the stowaway
- favourably consider allowing disembarkation and provide, as necessary and in accordance with national law, secure accommodation, which may be at the expense of the shipowner
- make every effort to cooperate in the identification of the stowaway and the establishment of his/her nationality or right of residence
- make every effort to cooperate in establishing the validity and authenticity of a stowaway's documents and, when a stowaway has inadequate documents, whenever practicable and to an extent compatible with national legislation and security requirements, to issue a covering letter with a photograph of the stowaway and any other important information
- inform the shipowner on whose ship the stowaway was found, as far as practicable, of the level of cost of detention and return of the stowaway, if the shipowner is to cover these costs
- if disembarkation is refused, to notify the flag State of the ship the reasons for refusal.

Subsequent Ports of Call

When the disembarkation of a stowaway has not been possible at the first port of call, it is the responsibility of the State of the subsequent port of call to follow the guidance provided above for the State of the first port of call.

State of Embarkation

It is the responsibility of the State of the original port of embarkation of the stowaway (ie the State where the stowaway first boarded the ship) to:

- Accept any returned stowaway having nationality or right of residence
- apprehend and detain the attempted stowaway, where permitted by national legislation, if the attempted stowaway is discovered before sailing or if the stowaway is discovered while the ship is still in the territorial waters of the State of the port of his/her embarkation.

Container ships are the most vulnerable ship type for stowaway incidents, with 45% of incidents occurring on this type of ship.

This is for a number of reasons:

- **These ships regularly trade between Europe and North America and also between African and European ports, the most desirable routes for stowaways**
- **empty containers present good transportation opportunities for stowaways**
- **container ships provide a wide variety of hiding places, with the port and starboard service tunnels being particularly at risk**
- **container ports are easily accessible to stowaways due to their open plan and low level of security.**

Note: General cargo ships account for less than 10% of the annual stowaway numbers.

Locations on board where stowaways tend to hide include:

- Cargo holds
- containers
- funnel casings
- chain lockers
- storerooms
- cabins
- crane cabs
- mast houses
- engine room bilges
- the rudder shaft space accessed through the rudder trunk.

Precautions to be taken to prevent stowaways boarding while at anchor include:

- Cover and secure hawser pipes on the anchor chains
- raise gangways and accommodation ladders when not in use
- hoist the pilot ladder immediately after the pilot has left
- restrict the size of the rudder housing opening to prevent access
- retrieve rafts used for painting after completion of work
- lock deck stores
- carry out regular and frequent deck patrols with the lookout doubled in poor visibility
- make use of security lighting when available and also rig lighting to shine outboard
- be suspicious of any small vessels approaching, such as fishing or pleasure craft, as they may have potential intruders aboard or even pirates.

The ship should use all available means to prevent a boarding of the ship from such boats. The port authority should be informed immediately of any unauthorised attempt at boarding.

Human Trafficking

Smugglers engaged in human trafficking have little regard for the people they are transporting. There have been a number of cases of smugglers deliberately scuttling the vessel transporting migrants before reaching safe water or any safe distance from the nearest land. Alternatively, they may just leave the vessel and the migrants to drift without full provisions or any means of propulsion.

In the event of being detected, smugglers have been known to deliberately set about destroying the vessel in the full knowledge that the security or coast guard agents that have detected them will be obligated to initiate a rescue.

This poses a challenge to merchant shipping. Under international law, ships have a duty to respond to a distress call and to offer assistance to a rescue where possible. Should a merchant vessel come across a stranded or sinking craft with migrants on board, extreme caution should be exercised.

Upon such a discovery, the local SAR centre or coast guard should be notified immediately.

A number of considerations should be made before engaging with the craft, such as the health risks posed by contact with the migrants and whether own vessel has sufficient space and supplies to safely accommodate the migrants.

At no time is it the responsibility or duty of a ship's officer or crew to consider the legitimacy or immigration status of the migrants in need of rescue.

Masters and officers should refer to MARISEC's advice document *'Rescue at Sea'* for information and guidance on the regulation governing rescuing refugees and persons being trafficked at sea. This document also sets out the procedure a ship should follow when effecting a rescue of migrants/refugees at sea.

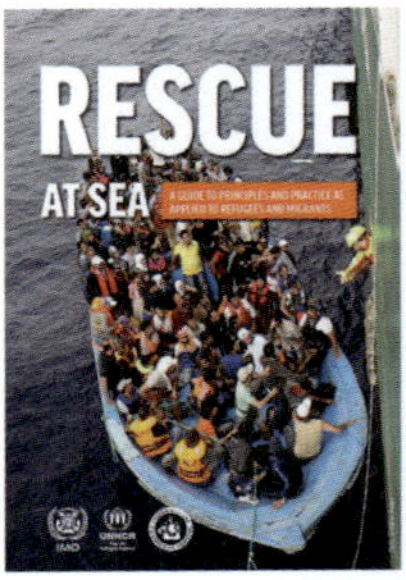

http://tinyurl.com/lbr82gp

CHAPTER 27

Fines for Ships and Ships' Staff

Fines for Ships and Ships' Staff

We live in increasingly litigious times where criminalisation and the seafarer are two words that are seen together far too often. In years gone by, it seemed like fines for ships were part of the cost of doing business and were generally paid with 200 cigarettes and a couple of bottles of whisky.

In the 21st century, your actions can be tracked more than in any time in history. You are a ship's officer of a sophisticated vessel that is transporting goods around the world. Shipping is an industry where there is no room for short-cuts and your conduct, and that of those you work with, has to be impeccable.

This section gives an indication of what port officials are looking out for. In many ports or countries, they will seem to be all too eager to prosecute, particularly if they are seeking a high profile prosecution as a deterrent to others.

You may have heard the saying *"if you think safety is expensive, try the cost of an accident"*.

In a similar manner therefore *"if you think documented procedures and safe systems of work don't always need to be applied, stop and consider the cost of a violation"*.

Baltic States – Fines incurred where a ship violates anti-pollution requirements

a) Discharge against Annex I of MARPOL

- Quantity of illegally discharged oily residues
- Environmental damage caused by the discharge

Minimum fine: US$2,000

b) Violation of the duty to keep the Oil Record Book properly

- No Oil Record Book has been kept on board
- Quantity of sludge not accounted for, based on consumption calculations

Minimum fine: US$1,000

- Oil Record Book is kept on board but entries are missing or wrong, lack of signature
- Quantity of sludge for which entries are missing or wrong
- In the case of bilge water, duration of time during which no entries, or wrong entries, have been made

Minimum fine: US$1,000

c) Discharge against Annex II of MARPOL

- Illegal discharge of noxious liquid substances

Minimum fine: US$2,500

- Violation of the duty to keep the Cargo Record Book properly, lack of signature

Minimum fine: US$250

d) Discharge against Annex IV of MARPOL

- Illegal discharge of sewage

Minimum fine: US$250

e) Discharge against Annex V of MARPOL

- Illegal discharge of garbage

Minimum fine: US$250

UK – Offences that carry a £50,000 fine

Five offences carry an exceptionally high penalty of a maximum fine of £50,000 on summary conviction, or an unlimited fine on conviction on indictment.

These offences are:

(i) Failing to render assistance following a collision.

(ii) Proceeding to sea from a UK port in contravention of a detention order.

(iii) Carrying passengers in excess of the certificated maximum.

(iv) Proceeding against the traffic flow in a traffic separation scheme.

(v) That a ship is unfit to go to sea without serious danger to life.

Failure to Provide Proper Lookout

At 04:40 GMT on 2nd January 2007, the Norwegian-flagged cargo ship *'Sunna'* grounded on the island of Swona in the Pentland Firth. The Chief Officer who was on watch at the time admitted that he had fallen asleep shortly after altering course to transit the Pentland Firth en route to Iceland from Humberside with a cargo of 1,900 tonnes of ferrosilicon.

The ship sustained extensive damage to all double bottom tanks forward of the engine room. The ship was refloated as the tide rose that morning and, with the help of an Orkney harbour tug and the Longhope Lifeboat, it was towed into Lyness.

An investigation by the MCA revealed that, although the ship only had a crew of seven, the Captain had instructed that the seamen were to be used as day workers and not stand a watch.

The STCW Code requires that during the hours of darkness there is a lookout on the bridge with no other duty but to keep a lookout. Had the Master used the crew in this role, this grounding would not have occurred. Sheriff Napier said in his summing up that it is a basic but critical role for seamen to be employed as lookouts especially in such dangerous waters as the Pentland Firth. He continued that he considered this offence to be at the high end of the severity of cases that are brought to the sheriff court. He told Captain Pawlus that he was foolishly misguided to try to impress his owner at the expense of the safety of the ship.

Penalty: Fine £2,500

Fines for Overloading

The German owners of the Antigua and Barbuda-registered cargo vessel *'Katja'* pleaded guilty to the overloading of their vessel, which had arrived in Liverpool laden with rock salt from the St Lawrence Seaway, Canada.

The vessel was loaded to its marks with rock salt and sailed from Goderich to arrive at the Manchester Ship Canal on the 23rd November 2010. Rock salt was in high demand to treat UK highways at this time.

As the vessel entered the River Mersey, the pilot on another passing vessel noticed that the Plimsoll line and load lines were not visible and the vessel appeared very low in the water. When the vessel arrived in the Queen Elizabeth II Dock, it was inspected by MCA Port State Control Officers, who found that the load line that marks the safety limit of the vessel was submerged by 39.5 cm.

In summing up, the Magistrates stated, "we share the Maritime and Coastguard Agency's view of the seriousness of the case, however accept that the overloading was not for gain. We have also considered the early plea of guilty and have reduced the fine of £42,000 accordingly."

Katja Schiffahrtsges Gmbh of Haren, Ems, Germany, owner of the *'Katja'*, was fined £28,015 plus costs of £5,000 awarded to the MCA.

Oil Pollution

In the UK, breaches of the Merchant Shipping (Prevention of Oil Pollution) Regulations of 1996, which implement MARPOL 73/78, incur a maximum fine of £250,000 in the Magistrates' Court. The fine is unlimited in the Crown Court.

Canada – Proposed penalties

Proposed Enhanced Penalties and Information Sharing under the Marine Transportation Security Act.

Failure to File Pre-Arrival Information

On conviction of indictment: A fine not exceeding $75,000 and/or a prison term not exceeding one year.

On summary conviction: A fine not exceeding $50,000 and/or a prison term not exceeding six months.

Fines for Ships and Ships' Staff

Failure to Comply with Ministerial Direction

On conviction of indictment:

Individual: A fine not exceeding $200,000 and/or a prison term not exceeding one year, and for any subsequent offence, to a fine of not more than $500,000 and/or imprisonment for a term of not more than two years.

Corporation: A fine not exceeding $500,000, and for any subsequent offence, a fine of not more than $1,000,000.

On summary conviction:

Individual: A fine up to $100,000 and/or a prison term not exceeding six months, and for any subsequent offence, a fine of up to $200,000 and/or imprisonment for a term of not more than one year.

Corporation: A fine not exceeding $250,000 and for any subsequent offence, a fine of up to $500,000.

Vessel: A fine not exceeding $100,000, and for any subsequent offence, a fine of not more than $200,000.

Providing False or Misleading Information

On conviction of indictment:

Individual: A fine up to $200,000 and/or up to one year in jail and a fine up to $500,000 and/or up to two years in jail for any subsequent offences.

Corporation: A fine up to $500,000 and a fine up to $1,000,000 for any subsequent offences.

On summary conviction:

Individual: A fine up to $100,000 and/or up to six months in jail and a fine up to $200,000 and/or up to one year in jail for any subsequent offences.

Corporation: A fine up to $250,000 and up to $500,000 fine for any subsequent offences.

Liberia – An extract of some fines that can be incurred

Penalty for Non-compliance with Licence Requirement

Failure of an owner of a Liberian vessel to ensure that each officer employed on the vessel is the holder of a valid Liberian licence of competence to fill the position held by him shall subject the owner to a fine of $750 for each officer so employed who is not the holder of such Liberian licence.

Drunkenness; Neglect of Duty

Whoever, being a master, seaman, or other person on any vessel, by willful breach of duty or by reason of drunkenness, does any act tending to the immediate loss or destruction of, or serious damage to, such vessel or her cargo, or tending immediately to endanger the life or limb of any person belonging to or on board such vessel, shall be subject to imprisonment and a fine of not more than $2,500.

Abandonment of Seamen

Whoever, being master or in charge of a Liberian vessel, maliciously and without justifiable cause forces any member of the crew of such vessel on shore in order to leave him behind in any foreign port or place, or refuses to bring to such place as is required under the Articles any member of the crew of such vessel, in condition and willing to proceed when the master is ready to proceed, shall be fined not more than $500.

USA – An extract of some fines that can be incurred

Duty to Provide Assistance at Sea

- A master or individual in charge of a vessel shall render assistance to any individual found at sea in danger of being lost, so far as the master or individual in charge can do so without serious danger to the master's or individual's vessel or individuals on board.
- A master or individual violating this section shall be fined not more than US$1,000, imprisoned for not more than two years, or both.

Penalties for 'magic pipe' offenders

The US Attorney's Office for the District of Maryland ordered a six month sentence for a crew member who obstructed the investigation into a 'magic pipe' case, and a US$2.4 million dollar fine against the shipowner. The "magic pipe" was a bypass hose which permitted waste oil to be dumped directly overboard, the presence of which was concealed by doctored oil logs, which are required by both US law and the International Convention for the Prevention of Pollution from Ships.

Failure to Report Accident

Failure to report steamship grounding brings US$5,000 penalty

A US$5,000 civil penalty was imposed on the owner of a 1959-built Great Lakes steamship for failing to report grounding.

Fines and penalties for operating a vessel while intoxicated

46 USC § 2302(c) provides that an individual who is intoxicated when operating a vessel, as determined under standards prescribed by the Secretary of the department that administers the Coast Guard, shall be liable for a civil penalty of not more than US$100, subject to a fine of not more than US$5,000, and imprisoned for not more than one year, or both.

Fines for dumping oily bilge waste

The Korean owners of the MV *'Keoje Tiger'* and two engineering officers from the ship pleaded guilty in federal court to various environmental crimes. The company pleaded guilty to dumping oily bilge waste in Hawaiian waters, falsifying the vessel's oil record book, and obstruction of justice. The company was sentenced to pay a US$1.15 million criminal penalty. The two engineering officers pleaded guilty to falsifying the oil record book. They were each sentenced to three years' probation, during which time they are banned from entering the United States.

Examples of Penalty Ranges

Specification	Nature of Specification	Maximum Allowed
NAVIGATION SAFETY REGULATIONS		
33 CFR 164.11(a)-(b)	Failure to properly man wheelhouse, or control vessel.	$25,000
33 CFR 164.11(c)-(i), (k)-(n)	Failure to properly navigate vessel as set forth in paragraphs (c)-(n).	$25,000
33 CFR 164.11(j)	Failure to have competent helmsman.	$25,000
33 CFR 164.11(o)	Failure to have anchor ready for letting go.	$25,000
33 CFR 164.11(p)	Failure to direct vessel considering factors set forth in 164.11(p).	$25,000
33 CFR 164.11(q)-(s)	Failure to conduct and log required tests.	$25,000
33 CFR 164.11(t)	Failure to have two steering units online.	$25,000
Navigation Bridge Visibility		
33 CFR 164.15	Failure to provide adequate visibility as specified.	$25,000
Requirements for vessels at anchor		
33 CFR 164.19	Failure to meet anchorage requirements as specified.	$25,000
Test before entering or getting underway		
33 CFR 164.25	Failure to conduct required tests.	$25,000
Charts and Publications		
33 CFR 164.33(a) (1)-(2), (b)	Failure to have current charts on board.	$25,000
33 CFR 164.33(a) (2)-(3)	Failure to have other required publications on board.	$25,000
Navigation Equipment: all vessels		
33 CFR 164.35	Failure to have required navigation equipment on board.	$25,000
.35(a)	- Surface navigation radar	
.35(b)	- magnetic compass	
.35(d)	- gyrocompass	
.35(e)	- gyrocompass repeater	
.35(f)	- rudder angle indicator	
.35(h)	- depth sounder	
33. CFR 164.35	Failure to have required navigation equipment aids.	$25,000
.35(c)	- magnetic deviation table	
.35(g)	- maneuvering info fact sheet	
.35(i)	- continuous record of depth	
.35(j)	- relative motion plotting equip.	
.35(k)-(n)	- steering, engine revolution info.	
Navigation Equipment: Vessels over 10,000 Gross Tons		
33 CFR 164.37(a)	Failure to have independent second radar system as prescribed.	$25,000
33 CFR 164.37(b)	Failure of tanker to have dual radar system as prescribed.	$25,000
Automatic Radar Plotting Aids (ARPA)		
33 CFR 164.38	Failure to have ARPA as specified.	$25,000
33 CFR 164.38(d)	Failure to have ARPA unit properly labeled.	$25,000
Tanker Steering Gear		
33 CFR 164.39	Failure to meet steering gear requirements as specified.	$25,000
Devices to indicate Speed and Distance		
33 CFR 164.40	Failure to have required equipment for measuring speed and distance.	$25,000

Specification	Nature of Specification	Maximum Allowed
Electronic Position Fixing Devices		
33 CFR 164.41	Failure to have required electronic navigation equipment on board.	$25,000
Rate of Turn Indicator		
33 CFR 164.42	Failure to have required rate of turn indicator.	$25,000
Deviation from Rules and Reporting of non-operating equipment		
33 CFR 164.53/55	Failure to report broken equipment, disobey COTP directions.	$25,000
Marine Casualty Reporting and record retention		
33 CFR 164.61	Failure to report marine casualty or maintain records pertaining to casualty.	$25,000
VESSEL TRAFFIC SERVICES REGULATIONS		
Failure to comply with VTC directions		
33 CFR 161		$25,000
Failure to have on board VTS Operating Manual/User Manual		
33 CFR 161		$25,000
Failure to obtain authorization to deviate from VTC rules		
33 CFR 161		$25,000
Failure to comply with Communication Rules		
33 CFR 161		$25,000
Failure to comply with Vessel Movement Report Rules		
33 CFR 161		$25,000
Failure to comply with Traffic Separation Scheme Rules		
33 CFR 161		$25,000
RESTRICTED NAVIGATION AREAS 33 CFR 165		
Failure to comply with regulations as specified in Part 165 (general guidelines).		
No meeting, passing;	Commercial Vessel:	$25,000
No wake zone;	Recreational Vessels:	$25,000
No stopping, anchoring;		
Mooring requirements		
Areas of restricted	Commercial Vessels:	$25,000
Navigation International Regulations for Preventing Collisions at Sea 33 USC 1988 (33 CFR 81)		
Violation of Rule 2 (Good Seamanship) or other Rules not specified below		
33 USC 1602	Operator penalty Commercial Vessels:	$5,000
	Vessel penalty, Commercial Vessels:	$5,000
Failure to comply with Rules 5-8, 11-19 (Sailing Rules)		
33 USC 1602	Operator penalty Commercial Vessels:	$5,000
	Vessel penalty, Commercial Vessels:	$5,000
Failure to comply with Rule 9 (Narrow Channels), Rule 10 (Traffic Separations Schemes)		
33 USC 1602	Operator penalty Commercial Vessels:	$5,000
	Vessel penalty, Commercial Vessels:	$5,000

Oil Spill Penalties

Class I Penalties

Under OPA 90, the USCG can assess a civil penalty on any owner, operator, or person in charge of a vessel, onshore facility, or offshore facility, who fails to notify the appropriate authorities of the discharge of oil or who fails or refuses to comply with regulations issued under the National Response System. The maximum civil penalty for class I penalties is US$10,000 per violation, but not more than US$25,000 per case.

Class II Penalties

For more flagrant violations, the USCG has the option of imposing class II penalties, which may not exceed US$10,000 per day for each day of violation up to a maximum of US$125,000.

Judicial Civil Penalties

The federal government may also, in lieu of USCG penalties, assess larger civil penalties by action in the US district court in any district in which the responsible party is located, resides or is doing business. The owner, operator or person in charge of a vessel illegally discharging oil can also be assessed penalties of up to US$25,000 per day of violation or up to US$1,000 per barrel of oil spilled.

In the case of proven gross negligence or willful misconduct, these penalties may be increased to not less than US$100,000 and not more than US$3,000 per barrel of discharged oil.

US Criminal Fines/Penalties

The federal government can also assess criminal fines of US$25,000 per day of violation and/or one year imprisonment against a party that negligently causes an oil spill. "Knowingly" causing a spill may lead to fines of up to US$50,000 per day of violation and/or up to three years imprisonment. "Knowingly" violating OPA 90 regulations with the knowledge of seriously endangering another person holds penalties of up to US$250,000 in fines and/or up to 15 years imprisonment in the case of an individual and up to US$1 million in fines for a corporate violator. With the second offence, each of these maximum penalties doubles.

Panama

According to Panamanian national law, the Maritime Authority of Panama can fine oil polluters a maximum of 200,000 Panamanian Balboas (US$197,720).

Brazil

In Brazil, state environmental agency authorities can impose fines for oil pollution in marine waters up to a maximum of 50 million Brazilian Reals (US$28 million).

Germany

In Germany, the Penal Code covers breaches of MARPOL 73/78. Under penal law, intentional unauthorised oil pollution of water carries a penalty of imprisonment of up to five years or the imposition of a court fine.

Norway

The Norwegian Pollution Control Act stipulates that serious pollution violations are punishable by prison sentences of up to five years and that "very serious" violations are punishable by prison sentences of up to ten years. In addition, vessel owners can be fined 50,000 to 120,000 Norwegian Krona (US$6,347 to US$15,233). Crew members can be fined about one month's salary.

France

Regulations implementing MARPOL 73/78 in France call for maximum penalties of two years in prison and a fine of approximately US$150,000 for the masters of larger tankers. Penalties for violations from smaller tankers are a one-year prison term and a US$50,000 fine.

Poland

Oil pollution in Polish waters due to dumping of oil is punishable by fines of 1,000,000 Special Drawing Rights, as defined by the International Monetary Fund (currently about US$1,371,289).

Oil pollution violations in Polish waters on the part of the master or other crew member carry fines of up to 20 times the average monthly salary in the national economy for the preceding year.

Russia

Administrative fines for MARPOL 73/78 and other oil pollution violations are calculated in

Oil Spill Penalties

accordance with the minimum monthly salary in the Russian national economy. The maximum fines are 3,000 times the minimum salary. This protocol may be modified in connection with the reform of tax law.

Some Examples of Custom Fines

Customs authorities focus on ship compliance with the Customs Code, paying particular attention to ship's declarations of stores, paints, bunkers and lube oil.

The following examples are recent incidents reported by a P&I correspondent for the UK & Club:

Example 1 – fine: €25,916.33

The fine was imposed on the vessel because of a difference noted between the quantity of lube oil declared by the Master to Customs and the detailed list per grade later requested from the Chief Engineer.

Example 2 – fine: €152,449.02

The fine was imposed on the vessel after Customs personnel visited the engine room and ship's stores to make a complete inventory of all items. Small differences were noted so the boarding officer accused the Master of fraud. The value of the fine imposed represents the combined value of the difference of each gas oil, lube oil and paint, multiplied by four (as allowed by the Customs Code).

Example 3 – fine: €22,867.35

Normal port arrival formalities require the master to provide various documents to Customs and Port Authority departments eg health, immigration, harbour master, etc. The Master accidentally submitted to Customs some documents that were intended for another administration.

The Customs authority noted that the list of paint was not included in the documents they received and notified the Master of the infringement to the Customs Code, despite the fact that the Master provided them with a copy later. According to the authority, all documents must be presented at the first request and the fine was subsequently imposed.

Grey water discharge and pollution fines

Calculation of the fines is based on the vessel's gross tonnage and bears no relation to the extent of the pollution or any alleged environmental damage. A small spill of grey water can result in large fines.

Australia – An extract of some fines that can be incurred

Alien stowaways - Penalties on shipowners

The fines and costs imposed on masters and/or shipowners by the authorities when entering port with a stowaway on board.

Penalties for Deck Washing

Great Barrier Reef – Australia

The Australian Safety Authority and the Great Barrier Reef Marine Park Authority have announced plans to crack down on the illegal disposal of dry bulk cargo residues in the Great Barrier Reef and neighbouring ports.

The authorities have stated that the loading of cargoes such as coal and iron ore frequently results in dust and residues collecting on the ship's deck and superstructure. Consequently, many ships wash their decks soon after leaving port even though the regulations prohibit this within three miles of the outer edge of the Great Barrier Reef.

AMSA and GBRMPA will be conducting increased aerial surveillance and shipboard inspections to enforce these regulations and strict penalties may be imposed on those found in breach.

Australia

In Australia, the national MARPOL legislation, the Marine Pollution Act of 1987, provides for monetary penalties of up to A$200,000 (US$130,907) for the vessel master and up to A$1,000,000 (US$654,537) for the vessel owner. The same penalty applies to all types of MARPOL discharges.

Ukraine – An extract of a typical fine that is reported

Fines for dumping allegedly dirty ballast

A ship was fined for dumping allegedly dirty ballast even though she was more than 12 miles from the coast at the port of Ilyichevsk.

On arrival at the load port, an inspection of the ballast water by local authorities found the ballast unfit for discharge as per maximum particle limits under Ukrainian law. On approval of customs and other local authorities, the ship sailed outside the 12 mile zone for a full ballast exchange. On returning to the port, the ship was fined for polluting the marine economic zone of Ukraine.

The Law of Ukraine Number 162/95 BP (1995), which came into force in 2003, states that Ukraine legislation will apply within a 200 mile exclusive zone. We are advised that this is the first time proceedings have been brought against a ship under this law by any Ukrainian authority.

Fines imposed on ships at Ukrainian ports are most commonly with regard to dirty ballast water, determined by the amount of suspended matter in the sample. In order to avoid polluting ballast taken on board, ballast tanks and systems should be well maintained with particular focus on tank coatings.

Unfortunately the regulations do not consider the level of pollution that may exist in the Black Sea and subsequent ballast samples. We are also advised that the Ukrainian authorities do not publish acceptable levels of suspended matter in ballast samples, and do not accept samples taken or analysed by third-parties.

Ships visiting Ukrainian ports from connecting waters are required to change ballast but should be aware that Ukrainian authorities strictly apply local law and fine heavily for non-compliance. Most fines for dirty ballast are due to the amount of suspended matter in the sample. It may be prudent to dump unnecessary ballast before arriving at Ukrainian ports as the State Ecological Inspection of Environmental Protection of the Black Sea's North-West Region (SIPBS) are particularly interested in ships with 10,000 tonnes or more of ballast on board.

It is also advised that, in advance of the ship's arrival, arrangements be made for a P&I surveyor to be present during sampling. Such precautions will ensure that samples are not taken from the surface of the ballast water or from the tank top.

Magic Pipes

In recent years, 'magic pipes' have received substantial coverage in the marine press.

The term 'magic pipe' describes an illegal bypass pipe used to deliberately discharge pollutants, including oily bilge water, directly to sea, bypassing the oily water separator (OWS). The OWS when working properly separates waste oil for disposal from water being pumped out of machinery space bilges. Magic pipes are most likely to be used when the OWS is not working properly, there is a large volume to be pumped, or operational pressures exist. Reports suggest that reception facilities are not always available:

> *"One of my colleagues has pointed out that 'with good and available facilities, seafarers have nothing to fear if they cannot get the OWS to work. Simply discharge it ashore. Ports claim that they have all kinds of facilities, but there always seemed to be excuses why they are not working or available that particular day'".*

Source: Clay Maitland, 'The Sad Story of the Oily Water Separator'

Pressure exists on many older ships with poor or inadequate waste storage capacity and older monitoring equipment when trying to meet regulations that have become increasingly stringent, ie:

Magic Pipes

Figure 27.1 - Oily water separator

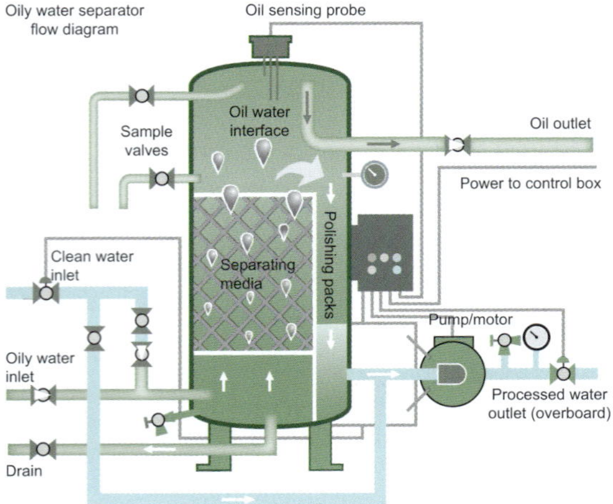

Figure 27.3 - Oily water separator flow diagram

- ***1974 - MARPOL Convention/Resolution A393(X)***
  This made OWS and Oil Record Books (ORB) mandatory and required oil content in the discharge to be less than 100 ppm.
- ***1992 - MARPOL 73/78 Resolution MEPC.60(33)***
  This increased discharge requirements to less than 15 ppm.

Figure 27.2 - OWS Bilge Alarm

- ***2003 - MARPOL 73/78 Resolution MEPC.107(49)***
  This introduced certified bilge alarm requirements or oil content monitors (OCM) to record the alarm conditions. OCMs were to be constructed so they could not be altered and alarms would be activated whenever clean water is used for cleaning or zeroing purposes.

Circumventing monitoring equipment is illegal under the MARPOL Convention and if crew are found guilty it can result in large fines and imprisonment. Port State Control (PSC) officers will almost always want to inspect a ship's Oil Record Book (ORB) and view discharge monitoring equipment.

Where there are signs of damaged paintwork or fresh paint on pipes or valves, PSC inspectors may request that they are dismantled. The presence of flexible hoses and spare pipes may also arouse suspicion that they are being used to bypass monitoring equipment. It is common knowledge both afloat and ashore that in the past clean water was flushed through older equipment in on attempt to match the ORB records to those of the OWS.

The US has brought many prosecutions for the use of magic pipes under their Act to Prevent Pollution from Ships (APPS) and the Act is actively enforced by US PSC. However, criticism has been levied at the US, along with the EU, Canada and Australia, that even accidental oil discharges are being criminalised. Crew should be made aware that in the US they have the right to an attorney and the right to remain silent. Anything that they do state must be completely honest or they could face charges or obstruction or false statement.

Penalties that can be enforced on individuals for a deliberate breach of the MARPOL Regulations can include up to 10 years imprisonment and a US$250,000 fine. Companies may also be fined up to US$500,000 for each charge and senior managers may be held criminally liable. Those aware of such practices and failing to report them could be imprisoned for up to five years.

However, under APPS, personnel who provide information that leads to a conviction may be entitled to a whistleblower award for up to half the imposed fine. This has spawned suspicions that crews, particularly in cases where they, for whatever reason, feel aggrieved towards the company or the ship's staff may make accusations in the hope of significant financial gain.

It is often suggested that seafarers are being criminalised and detained for excessive periods either under investigation or as witnesses. In the US, most prosecutions will hinge on either lying to officials or falsifying documentation, particularly the ORB, as most often the illegal act occurs outside national jurisdiction.

A number of such cases have occurred, including the prosecution of a Chief Engineer and the owners of a ship operated by Casilda Shipping for the falsification of entries and illegal dumping using a magic pipe after photographic evidence was produced by a crew member.

As a result of whistleblowers, the Chief Engineer of the MV *'Atlantic Breeze'* pleaded guilty to making false statements in an ORB and faced between 12 and 18 months imprisonment. Ship managers Wallenius admitted conspiracy to obstruct justice, making false statements and concealing magic pipes. They were ordered to pay a US$6.5m criminal fine.

In 2010, the Chief Engineer of the tanker *'Georgios M'* brought a US$22.8m lawsuit against the ship's owners who had made an agreement to pay a US$1.3m criminal fine and to cooperate with the government case against him. The case had arisen after a tip-off to the authorities. The Chief Engineer was acquitted of any wrongdoing because the illegal actions had occurred before he joined the ship. This did not stop the US authorities from detaining him for 15 months.

Figure 27.4 - Overboard valve tagged and locked shut

Magic Pipes

It is imperative that safeguards are in place to ensure that all onboard practices are strictly in line with MARPOL, eg:

- Safety Management System (SMS) procedures must be regularly reviewed with procedures clearly stated and complied with
- the ORB must be absolutely accurate, fully up to date and printouts/receipts from equipment retained
- superintendents must pay close attention to the systems and documentation during their inspections
- ship staff must be fully certified, regularly trained and completely familiar with procedures and equipment operations on board. During inspections, they must be actively encouraged to give full and honest answers to any questions.
- the OWS must be regularly calibrated and maintained in accordance with the manufacturer's guidelines. All records must be retained.
- valves, such as the overboard discharge valve, that are normally shut should be sealed closed and the serial number recorded in the ORB and engine room logbook
- any painting or maintenance of the discharge system or associated equipment should be recorded
- avoid retaining non-essential spare pipes and particularly flexible hoses on board
- it is advisable to upgrade any older equipment
- only use recommended cleaning agents and, where appropriate, remove any crossover valves or blanks between the bilge and ballast systems.

Criminalisation of Seafarers

Seafarers need to do all they can to avoid causing any pollution whatsoever to the marine environment. However, there will be occasions where commercial pressures from ashore and generally from the ship's charterers place seafarers in an uncomfortable position. The SMS and all the guidance on board the ship will reinforce the need to adhere to the regulations except in the case of immediate danger to life or the ship. Seafarers should conduct themselves professionally at all times and take the necessary time to do each task correctly. Shortcuts should never be taken, particularly when they are deemed to be the only way for a ship to keep to deadlines. In today's litigious society, any action or act of negligence that could result in damage to the environment, whether intentional or by accident, may lead to seafarers being criminally charged.

Varying legal systems

Each country that a ship visits will have its own judicial system, and legal procedures may vary from those in the crew's country of residence or the ship's port of registry. Some examples of legal procedures that may not be available include the right to remain silent, confidentiality of information, safeguards covering arrest and detention, access to legal advice and representation, a fair trial, and processes for extradition between countries.

What should I do if there is an accident?

If your vessel is involved in a maritime accident, there are international guidelines to ensure that you are treated fairly if there is an investigation or if you are detained following the accident.

Be aware that information given in the investigation of a maritime accident could be used against you in a criminal prosecution. So, if you are questioned about an accident involving your vessel, ask for a lawyer if necessary, and contact your union and/or company for advice and assistance.

The State under which your ship is flagged has the right under international law to institute legal proceedings requesting the immediate release of any seafarers detained following an accident or pollution incident at sea. Unfortunately, Flags of Convenience (FOC) States are notorious in failing to pursue this right on behalf of crews of ships under their flag.

Your shipowner and the ship's insurers should provide you with legal support and advice if you are arrested or detained, and support any welfare needs that arise.

ITF states that substandard shipping should be in the dock, not crew members

The International Transport Workers' Federation (ITF) comments that the criminalisation of seafarers is not new. A long line of masters and senior officers have been prosecuted and jailed for pollution incidents, but the increasing emphasis on maritime security since September 2001 and new measures on pollution have added to the list of criminal sanctions.

Seafarers are easy targets in the wake of major incidents, unlike the shipowners themselves, who often hide in a web of Flags of Convenience and brass plate companies. Arrests can be made for marine pollution, breach of maritime security, unsafe navigation, arms or people smuggling, or assault of people on board.

Figure 27.5 - Captain Apostolos Mangouras, the Master of the 'Prestige'

After the Maltese-flagged crude oil tanker *'Tasman Spirit'* ran aground in July 2003 near the harbour mouth at Karachi, the crew were effectively held hostage in Pakistan for nine months. The Master of the *'Prestige'*, Captain Apostolos Mangouras was detained in Spain for two years, following the break-up of the Bahamas-flagged tanker in heavy weather.

Both cases highlighted the risk of unnecessary and unjustified detentions, when seafarers can find themselves at the centre of political battles over compensation and the apportionment of blame.

If you are questioned about a maritime accident involving your vessel:

- If you think it is necessary, ask for a lawyer before answering any questions or making any statements to port, coastal or flag State investigators since these could be used against you in future criminal or other legal proceedings
- contact your Company and/or union for advice and assistance
- make sure you fully understand everything that you are asked
- if there is anything you do not understand:
  - ask the authorities to stop the questioning
  - request the assistance of an interpreter, if necessary.

It is important to ensure that you protect your interests first. Therefore, follow the advice you receive from your company, union or lawyer, and importantly, when advised to provide information, be truthful with investigators.

Ref: itfseafarers.org

CHAPTER 28

In Port and Alongside

Embarkation Arrangements

Positioning of Boarding Equipment

The angle of inclination of a gangway or accommodation ladder should be kept within the limits for which it was designed. Gangways should not be used at an angle of inclination greater than 30° from the horizontal and accommodation ladders should not be used at an angle greater than 55° from the horizontal, unless specifically designed for greater angles.

When the inboard end of the gangway or accommodation ladder rests on or is flush with the top of the bulwark, a bulwark ladder should be provided. Any gap between the bulwark ladder and the gangway or accommodation ladder should be adequately fenced to a height of at least 1 metre.

Gangways and other access equipment should not be rigged on ships' rails unless the rail has been reinforced for that purpose.

The means of access should be checked to ensure that it is safe to use after rigging. There should be further checks to ensure that adjustments are made when necessary due to tidal movements or change of trim and freeboard. Guard ropes, chains, etc should be kept taut at all times and stanchions should be rigidly secured.

Each end of a gangway or accommodation or other ladder should provide safe access to a safe place or to an auxiliary safe access.

The means of access should be sited clear of the cargo working area and so placed that no suspended load passes over it. Where this is not practicable, access should be supervised at all times.

A lifebuoy should be available and ready for use at the point of access aboard the ship.

Lighting and Safety of Movement

In normal circumstances, the boarding equipment and the immediate approaches to it should be effectively illuminated from the ship or the shore. Where the dangers of tripping or falling are greater than usual because of bad weather conditions or where the means of access is obscured, eg by the presence of coal dust, consideration should be given to a higher level of illumination.

The means of boarding and its immediate approaches should be kept free from obstruction and, as far as is reasonably practicable, kept clear of any substance likely to cause a person to slip or fall. Where this is not possible, appropriate warning notices should be posted and if necessary the surfaces suitably treated.

Portable and Rope Ladders

Where, exceptionally, a portable ladder is used for the purpose of access to the ship, it is very important that the ladder is checked regularly by a competent person and that account is taken of vessel movement and tide changes.

When it is necessary to use a portable ladder for access, it should be used at an angle of between 60° and 75° from the horizontal. The ladder should extend at least 1 metre above the upper landing place unless there are other suitable handholds. It should be properly secured against slipping or shifting sideways or falling and be so placed as to afford a clearance of at least 150 mm behind the rungs.

When a portable ladder is resting against a bulwark or rails, suitable safe access to the deck should be provided.

A rope ladder should never be secured to rails or to any other means of support unless the rails or support are so constructed and fixed as to take

Source: 'Code of Safe Working Practices for Merchant Seamen'

the weight of a man and a ladder with an ample margin of safety.

A rope ladder should be left in such a way that it either hangs fully extended from a securing point or is pulled up completely. It should not be left so that any slack will suddenly pay out when the ladder is used.

Where the freeboard is 9 metres or more, a rope ladder should be used in conjunction with an accommodation ladder, leading aft and positioned in such a way as to provide safe and easy access from the rope ladder to the bottom platform.

Safety Nets

A safety net should be mounted whenever possible where a person may fall from boarding equipment or from the ship's deck or quayside. The aim of safety nets is to minimise the risk of injury arising from falling between the ship and the quay or falling onto the quay or deck and as far as is reasonably practicable the whole length of the means of access should be covered. Safety nets should be securely rigged, with use being made of attachment points on the quayside where appropriate.

Maintenance of Equipment for Means of Access

Any equipment used for boarding must be properly maintained and should be inspected by a competent person at appropriate intervals. Any defects affecting the safety of any access equipment, including access provided by a shore authority, should be reported immediately to a responsible person and should be made good before further use.

Aluminium equipment should be examined for corrosion.

Gangways, accommodation ladders and winches used for lifting or access should be tested in the same way as all other lifting appliances and records maintained including any test certificates.

Special Circumstances

In some circumstances it may not be practical to mount proper safe boarding arrangements by conventional means, for example, where there is frequent movement of the ship during cargo operations.

Small boats or tenders used between the shore and the ship should be safe and stable, be suitably powered, correctly operated and properly equipped with the necessary safety equipment and, if not a ship's boat, be approved for that purpose.

Where a vessel is moored alongside another vessel, there should be cooperation between the two vessels to provide suitable and safe boarding arrangements. Access should generally be provided by the ship lying outboard, except that, where there is a great disparity in freeboard, access should be provided by the ship with the higher freeboard.

Care should be taken at all times, but particularly at night, when boarding or leaving a ship, or when moving through the dock area. The edges of the docks, quays, etc should be avoided and any sign prohibiting entry to an area should be strictly observed. Where there are designated routes, they should be followed exactly. This is particularly important in the vicinity of container

Source: 'Code of Safe Working Practices for Merchant Seamen'

Embarkation Arrangements

terminals or other areas where rail traffic, straddle carriers or other mechanical handling equipment is operating, as the operators of such equipment have restricted visibility, placing anyone walking within the working area at risk.

Corrosion of Accommodation Ladders and Gangways

1. *Aluminium alloys are highly susceptible to galvanic corrosion in a marine atmosphere if they are used in association with dissimilar metals. Great care should be exercised when connecting mild steel fittings, whether or not they are galvanised, to accommodation ladders and gangways constructed of aluminium.*
2. *Plugs and joints of neoprene, or other suitable material, should be used between mild steel fittings, washers, etc and aluminium. The plugs or joints should be significantly larger than the fittings or washers.*
3. *Repairs using mild steel doublers or bolts made of mild steel or brass or other unsuitable material should be considered as temporary. Permanent repairs, or the replacement of the means of access, should be undertaken at the earliest opportunity.*
4. *The manufacturer's instructions should give guidance on examination and testing of the equipment. However, close examination of certain parts of accommodation ladders and gangways is difficult due to their fittings and attachments. It is essential, therefore, that the fittings are removed periodically for a thorough examination of the parts most likely to be affected by corrosion. Accommodation ladders and gangways should be turned over to allow for a thorough examination of the underside. Particular attention should be paid to the immediate perimeter of the fittings; this area should be tested for corrosion with a wire probe or scribe. Where the corrosion appears to have reduced the thickness of the parent metal to 3 mm, back plates should be fitted inside the stringers of the accommodation ladder or gangways.*

Source: 'Code of Safe Working Practices for Merchant Seamen'

Standing Orders in Port

General Orders

1. Ensure that the deck watch is maintained strictly in accordance with:
   - All company instructions and regulations
   - all international and local rules and regulations
   - standards for watchkeeping specified in the STCW Code for deck officers in charge of a watch in port.
2. The safety of the ship and all personnel on board is paramount and takes precedence over all other responsibilities. Any additional operational work allocated to the OOW will not relieve him of his immediate cargo watchkeeping duties.
3. When cargo is being worked, the OOW is expected to:
   - Be on deck to supervise all operations
   - make himself available to the foreman/stevedore on duty at all times and identify himself to the new foreman at each change of shift
   - radio check with ABs at intervals not exceeding 30 minutes
   - ensure that the radios are charged and distributed.
4. The chief officer's standing orders include a detailed loading and discharging plan and are to be followed for all cargo operations.

Standing Orders in Port

Any variance to the plan is to be brought to the chief officer's attention immediately.

5. A close watch is to be maintained for any structural damage caused by stevedores during cargo operations and an inspection of the holds should be carried out when discharging is completed. Any damage should be brought to the attention of the chief officer or stevedores' foreman and relevant damage report forms filled and handed over to the responsible parties.
6. An efficient watch guarding against theft is to be maintained at all times when in port.
7. Smoking is only permitted in designated areas.
8. No work should be performed overside without the chief officer's permission and a permit to work.
9. No unauthorised vessel is to approach and, in case of any doubt, the master must be informed immediately.

Gangway Watch

1. The accommodation ladder/gangway must be rigged as per company requirements.
2. A safety net is to be correctly rigged, along with a lifebuoy with a line/safety line available for immediate use.
3. 'No Smoking' and 'No Unauthorised Personnel' signs must be displayed on top of the access.
4. The access area should be well illuminated. The safety lines must be taut, clean and well tended and the steps clean and free of grease, oil, cargo or debris.
5. The bottom roller of the accommodation ladder/gangway should be on an even surface if it is resting on the jetty/quay.
6. Details of the tides should be available to the duty officer in the ship's office and also at the gangway.

Security

1. Gangway and access control requirements must be strictly adhered to.
2. Security rounds should ensure that all restricted areas are secured and the following items are checked:
   - Anchor hawse/spurling pipe covers
   - mooring lines/rat guards
   - confined spaces and hatch coamings
   - illumination on board and overside
   - surveillance of surrounding areas, etc.
3. Only one accommodation door should be used as a means of access and it should be manned at all times. In addition, visitors are to be escorted within the accommodation.
4. Tags and locks on all the other secured/ sealed spaces must be checked while in port and any tampering or breaches reported immediately.
5. Unauthorised vendors must be escorted off the vessel immediately.
6. A close check must be maintained on stores received.
7. Only authorised personnel are to be allowed on board and they must be escorted to their area of interest after the OOW/SSO/CE has been informed.

Standing Orders in Port

8. Any ship personnel going ashore must be logged in the gangway register.
9. Gangway control must be advised of any crew changes expected.
10. Any overside access should be deployed only when necessary and picked up immediately on completion of work.
11. Security rounds should be made at regular intervals, as per the ship's security level.
12. While in port, all outside accommodation doors should be kept locked with the exception of the one required for the daily ship's routine.

Moorings

1. The OOW must advise any crew assigned as watch of a change in tides, allowing them to anticipate any changes to the moorings/gangway.
2. The OOW must ensure that all mooring lines have equal weight on them.
3. Should the vessel surge on her moorings as a result of another ship/craft passing too close, the name of the offending vessel should be noted in the port log, along with the time and the sequence of events.
4. Mooring lines should be checked for signs of chafing. Under no circumstances should they be lubricated with oils or greases of mineral origin.
5. Mooring ropes must not be left on the drum end but are to be secured onto mooring bitts with no less than six figure of eights and a round turn.
6. Before switching on deck hydraulics, permission must be obtained from the engine room and the system is to be primed before use.
7. If the vessel is surging on her moorings or not completely alongside and this cannot be corrected, the chief officer or additional crew must be called.
8. The condition of the anchor cable must be checked if used during berthing.

Cargo Operations

Dry Cargo

1. The OOW must be fully conversant with the loading/discharging plan and operation of ship's cargo gear, ie hatches, cranes and grabs.
2. Crane/grab lashings are to be cleared away before hoisting. The lashings must be stowed securely in mast-houses to prevent theft.
3. Cargo gear is to be checked once every watch.
4. Any leaks of oil from deck cranes must be reported immediately to the duty engineer and the chief officer and containment arrangements made.
5. Any abnormal noise from cargo gear must be reported to the chief officer and investigated immediately.
6. Wire ropes must be intact and the weight of the cargo checked to ensure it does not exceed the SWL of the crane/grab.
7. A log of the crane and the grab running hours must be maintained.

8. The chief officer must be informed immediately of any shore-side request for a deviation from the cargo plan.
9. Draughts are to be checked frequently during loading as per the master's requirements.
10. During discharge, draughts are to be taken in the morning and afternoon and recorded in the mate's log.
11. The cargo must be stowed/trimmed properly and evenly in the hatch square, and not piled in one place or just in the centre.
12. When the shore loader is being used, the clearance between the ship and the loader must be monitored.
13. On completion of loading or discharging a hold, trackways must be cleaned and drain holes checked. The resting pads must be greased and compression bars visually checked for distortion. Similarly, all access hatches, sounding pipes and air pipes are to be secured.
14. Each hold is to be inspected on completion of discharge with particular attention paid to ladders/projections and coamings.
15. It must be ensured that bilge covers are in place (sighted from within the hold), free from any damage and the bilge well clear of cargo.
16. Any loud bang during cargo operations must be investigated. The master should be informed immediately of any serious damage and pictures taken if necessary.

Oil Tankers

The ship/shore safety checklist for tanks from ISGOTT should be completed.

1. Before cargo operations commence, all deck scuppers and, where applicable, open drains on the jetty must be effectively plugged.
2. When a tanker is alongside a berth, fire-fighting equipment is to be ready for immediate use.
3. On double hull tankers, attention should be given to stability during ballast and cargo operations.
4. Care should be taken not to reduce the transverse metacentric height (GM).
5. If leakage occurs from a pipeline, valve, hose or metal arm, operations through that item should be stopped until the cause has been ascertained and the defect has been rectified.
6. If a pipeline, hose or arm bursts or if there is an overflow or other spill, all cargo operations should be stopped immediately and should not be restarted until the fault has been rectified and all hazards from the released oil or chemicals have been eliminated.
7. If there is any possibility of the released oil/chemicals or associated vapours entering an engine room or accommodation space intake, appropriate preventive measures must be taken quickly.
8. Means should be provided for the prompt removal of any spillage on deck. Any oil spill should be reported to the terminal and port authorities and the relevant shore and tanker oil pollution emergency plans should be activated.
9. Harbour authorities and any adjacent tanker or shore installations should be warned of any potential hazard caused by the spill.
10. Accumulations of water should be drained periodically and scupper plugs replaced immediately after the water has been run off.
11. Product-contaminated water should be transferred to a slop tank or other suitable receptacle. The tank pressure should be reduced to facilitate draining, if necessary.
12. A permanently fitted drip tray, provided with suitable means of draining, should be fitted under all manifold connections.

Notices

1. Whenever alongside a terminal, a tanker should display notices on deck, visible on two sides, or at the gangway(s) according to the International Dangerous Goods Regulations.
2. Emergency escape routes from the tanker berth to safe areas ashore should be indicated clearly.

Standing Orders in Port

Manning Requirements

1. A sufficient number of personnel to deal with an emergency should be present on board the tanker and in the shore installation at all times during the tanker's stay at a terminal.
2. All personnel involved with the operations should be familiar with the risks associated with handling products and should be trained to deal with an emergency.

Gas Carriers

1. Any operations that may cause flames, such as welding and fusion cutting, must be avoided on board or around the berth when the tanker is moored at the berth.
2. Radio instruments and radar on tankers should be shut down while operating cargo.

Ballast Operations

1. When ballast pumps are used, hourly soundings must be logged and the pumping rate calculated. The chief officer must be informed if the deballasting operation is deviating from the plan at any time.
2. Do not overflow ballast on deck.
3. During deballasting, the number of pumps to be used will depend on the cargo loading rate.
4. On a bulk carrier, the air draught to the loader must be monitored visually. Deballasting when loading has been stopped for an extended period will result in contact with the loader if it is not checked frequently.

Hatch Cover Operations

1. All hatch cover operations are to be carried out under the supervision of the OOW.
2. Hydraulics must be warmed up 15 minutes prior to operation, particularly in colder climates, and the oil level checked.
3. The hatch cover must be inspected to confirm that all the cleats are off and that there is no equipment/debris on the pontoon.
4. It must be ensured that the hatches are fully open and stoppers are in place. Rams can creep shut and mechanical stoppers are the only secure prevention against inadvertent closure.
5. Any hydraulic line ruptures are to be dealt with immediately and the resultant spill treated as an emergency and contained on board.
6. Sufficient crew must be available when operating hatch covers.

Bunkering

1. The bunkering checklist is to be followed at all times (refer to ISGOTT).
2. 'No smoking' signs must be displayed and regulations strictly enforced. The use of cellular phones on deck while bunkering is also prohibited.
3. No hot work should be in progress during bunkering.
4. The bunker manifold should be manned at all times. If bunkers are supplied by a barge,

its mooring lines should be received and safe access to and from the ship provided.

5. All times relevant to the bunkering operation must be logged.
6. FFA/SOPEP must be in a state of readiness at all stages of the operation.
7. The scuppers should be closed to ensure that no oil goes overboard.
8. If rain water needs to be drained, it must be ensured that there is no oil/oily sheen on the surface. The water should be drained and the scupper replaced after checking overside.
9. An ample amount of sawdust should be kept in sacks on deck to cover any leakage during the bunkering procedure.
10. Handheld radio sets or other means of communication should be established between the ship's crew and the staff at the bunkering installation to avoid misunderstandings.
11. Drip trays should be closed off.
12. The bunkering lines and fuel tank valves should be carefully checked before commencing bunkering.
13. Valves not in operation should be effectively sealed off.
14. A sounding of all the ship's tanks should be carried out before starting the bunkering operation.
15. Port authorities should be contacted immediately in the event of a major oil spill.
16. An undamaged hose of a sufficient length should be available. The couplings should be visually checked for any damage.
17. High level alarms of bunker tanks should be checked before bunkering commences.
18. The SOPEP lockers should be checked to ensure sufficient supplies are available.
19. Oil absorbing apparatus, eg absorbing pads, should be kept at strategic areas to reduce any oil leaks.
20. The bunkering plan should be agreed by all watchkeeping officers on board the ship.
21. Procedures to be undertaken in case of an emergency should be discussed with the bunker supplier.
22. A proper system of signals for communication should be established between the shipboard crew and suppliers.

Repairs/Maintenance

1. When repairs involving hot work by ship/shore staff are being carried out, the work area should be inspected on an hourly basis.
2. The shore supervisor/contractor must be present at the work location at all times.
3. It must be ensured that the permits of both ship and shore are valid, and any work ongoing must be stopped if the permit has expired.
4. Suitable LSA/FFA gear must be ready and at hand for immediate deployment.
5. Before work commences, a check should be made to clear any combustible material that could be ignited by sparks, hot slag/rods, etc.
6. The scaffolding and the working aloft permit should be checked before onboard staff/contractors commence work.

Miscellaneous

1. When garbage is landed ashore, an itemised list signed by the receiver must be obtained.
2. Deck lights must be switched on well in advance of sunset and cargo lights positioned in the holds. Flags/signals must be correctly displayed at all times.
3. The vessel must be kept as close to upright as possible at all times. A 1.5° list is not to be exceeded and the master must be informed immediately if an uncontrollable list begins.
4. It must be ensured that the vessel is alongside and is not suffering contact damage due to insufficient fendering.
5. If there are any barges alongside, it must be ensured that there is sufficient fendering. The moorings should be secured to the vessel's strong points only and under no

Standing Orders in Port

circumstances on pipelines/coamings stays, etc.

6. Overside water discharge from the ship must not land on the quay.
7. While taking fresh water, note the start and stop readings, monitor the hose and taste the water.
8. Garbage bins must have lids covering their openings and should be sprayed with disinfectant if hovering insects are seen.
9. The Company's drug and alcohol policy must be strictly adhered to by the ship/shore staff.
10. Documents must not be signed or stamped without the chief officer's knowledge.
11. A notice regarding the expiry of shore leave should be posted and strictly enforced.
12. The logbook should be completed after each watch and all relevant events recorded.

Deck and Gangway Watch

Deck Watch

General

When in port, the master will arrange for an appropriate deck watch to be maintained, with a deck officer in charge if he considers it necessary. The duration and composition of the watch will depend on the conditions of mooring, type of ship and other duties required of the crew but must ensure:

- The safety of life, the ship, the port and the environment
- the safe operation of all equipment relating to cargo operation
- adherence to international, national and local rules.

Special considerations will be necessary for ships carrying hazardous cargoes.

The chief engineer officer, in consultation with the master, must ensure that engineering watchkeeping arrangements are adequate to maintain a safe engineering watch while in port.

Taking Over the Watch in Port

If any officers in charge of the watch have reason to believe their relieving officer is incapable of carrying out watchkeeping duties effectively, the watch must not be handed over and the master or chief officer notified immediately. Relieving officers must ensure that all members of their watch are fully capable of performing their duties effectively.

If an important operation is being performed at the moment of handing over the deck watch, it is to be concluded by the officer being relieved.

Deck and Gangway Watch

The master will determine the vessel's sailing time and this must be conspicuously posted at the gangway as soon as possible after arrival at a berth.

Prior to taking over the deck watch, the relieving officer must ascertain from the officer in charge:

- The minimum depth of water at the berth or anchorage during the watch and the following two hours, the ship's draught and the level and time of high and low waters
- the securing of the moorings, the arrangement of anchors and the scope of the anchor chain and other mooring features important to the safety of the ship
- the state of main engines and their availability for emergency use
- if the vessel is at anchor, the position of the vessel should be determined by means of visual cross bearing, or by the prudent use of electronic navigational aids including echo sounder if visual bearings are not possible, and compared to the original ship's and anchor position
- all work to be performed on board the ship
- the nature, amount and disposition of cargo loaded or remaining, and any residue on board after unloading the ship
- the level of water in bilges and ballast tanks
- that the correct signals or lights are being exhibited or sounded
- the number of crew members required, which officers are on board and the presence of any other persons on board
- the state of fire-fighting appliances, that safety measures and fire protection regulations are being maintained and the actions to be taken in the event of a fire
- any special port regulations
- the master's standing and special orders
- the weather forecast
- the posted sailing time
- the availability of keys to locked spaces
- the lines of communication available between the ship and shore personnel, including port authorities, in the event of an emergency arising or assistance being required
- any other circumstances of importance to the safety of the ship, its crew, cargo or protection of the environment from pollution
- the procedures for notifying the appropriate authority of any environmental pollution resulting from ship activities.

Performing the Deck Watch

- The officer in charge of the deck watch must make rounds to inspect the ship at appropriate intervals (one per hour)
- particular attention must be paid to:
  - The condition and securing of the gangway, anchor chain and moorings, particularly at the turn of the tide and in berths with a large rise and fall, if necessary taking measures to ensure that they are in normal working condition
  - the draught, underkeel clearance and the general state of the ship, to avoid dangerous listing or trim during cargo handling or ballasting
  - the weather and sea state
  - the observance of all regulations concerning safety and fire protection
  - the water level in bilges and tanks
  - all persons on board and their location, particularly those in remote or enclosed spaces
  - the exhibition and sounding, where appropriate, of lights and signals
- in bad weather, or on receiving a storm warning, all necessary measures to protect the ship, persons on board and cargo must be taken

Deck and Gangway Watch

- every precaution must be taken to prevent pollution of the environment by the ship
- in an emergency that threatens the safety of the ship:
  - The alarm must be raised
  - the master must be informed
  - all possible measures to prevent any damage to the ship, its cargo and persons on board must be taken
  - if necessary, assistance is to be requested from the shore authorities or neighbouring ships
- the ship's stability condition must be known so that, in the event of fire, the shore fire-fighting authority can be advised of the approximate quantity of water that can be pumped on board without endangering the ship
- assistance must be offered to ships or persons in distress
- all necessary precautions must be taken to prevent accidents or damage when the propellers are to be turned
- all important events affecting the ship must be entered in the appropriate logbook, eg:
  - All tests of equipment
  - draughts and deadweight on arrival and departure
  - details of cargo/ballast handled with pertinent details of the operation
  - water salinity on arrival at and prior to departure from a berth
  - weather information
  - cargo segregation, type and loading rate
  - inspection of ship's condition to confirm seaworthiness
  - Notice of Readiness to load
  - tanks (holds) inspection by surveyors
  - any specific instructions concerning the cargo
  - any Notice of Protest issued or received by the vessel
  - precautions taken to minimise the risk of oil spills
  - any information pertinent to the operation of the vessel or its personnel
  - notation of security inspections
  - details of maximum bending moment and shear force on sailing.

Before testing the engines when the vessel is at a berth or at anchor, the engineer officer on watch must obtain the permission of the deck officer on watch. Prior to granting such permission, the deck officer on watch must ensure that all the mooring lines are tight, the gangway is secure and the propeller is clear. During engine testing, a senior officer or the master must be on the bridge and orders to the engine room must be given by him.

Security

General

The possibility that a hijack or sabotage attempt may be made against a vessel cannot be disregarded. The probability of such an attack varies and is largely dependent on the area in which the vessel is trading, current world political activities and the vessel's registry.

Vessel Security

- The master must take all steps necessary, including employing shore-based security guards, to assist vessel personnel in maintaining security
- security guards, when employed, should be from a reputable security organisation and selected with the advice of the local agent
- in the event of an attack on the ship or a hijack attempt, the preservation of the lives of vessel personnel is to be placed above all other considerations.

Stowaways

- The vigilance of the crew can prevent stowaways
- when sailing from ports of high risk, consideration should be given to anchoring

in a convenient position outside the port to make a final search for stowaways after the tugs and pilot depart. Any stowaways found in this final search can be discharged directly to the shore authorities

- agents' warnings regarding the probability of stowaways in their ports must be communicated to the master. Prior to entering such a port, the master should ensure that all doors and hatchways are securely fastened, locked and, if necessary and not needed for regular access, welded shut. Stowaways may join at the anchorage and before the ship is safely on the berth, and plates should be fitted over anchor hawse pipes to prevent this
- accommodation doors should be secured and locked on the inside, leaving only one entrance open. Keys to the locked doors should be placed in convenient positions so that doors can be opened in the event of an accommodation fire
- store rooms and equipment lockers on deck, in the engine room and in the accommodation should remain locked and only opened for access then immediately resecured
- all unoccupied spaces, including the bridge, the radio room and personnel quarters, particularly those containing valuable property, are to be locked in port
- visitors should only be permitted on board in accordance with governmental and terminal regulations, company instructions and with the permission of the master.

Security Patrols

- When the vessel is alongside, the officer of the watch must make a careful inspection of the vessel at least once during each hour and, if unable to do so, another member of the watch is to be assigned to the task
- during the night, watch personnel must make an additional security inspection of unfrequented parts of the vessel, at hourly intervals, to check for any outbreak of fire or other dangerous condition
- on completion of each inspection, an appropriate entry must be made in the deck logbook
- precautions must be taken to prevent unauthorised persons boarding the ship
- only the hatches of holds to be used for the immediate loading of cargo should be opened. On completion of loading of each cargo compartment, the space should be diligently searched then sealed and locked
- the ship's store rooms must be kept locked at all times, only opened when access is required and immediately locked afterwards
- on completion of cargo operations and the disembarkation of all shore-based personnel, the ship must be searched again by crew search teams, led by a responsible officer with intimate knowledge of his search area. The teams should search all areas of the ship simultaneously until they have satisfied themselves that there are no stowaways.

Gangway Watch

To comply with the ISPS Code, many ships will require a member of the crew to be permanently stationed at the gangway for safety purposes, to assist persons transiting the gangway and to be the first point of contact on the vessel for anyone boarding. However, as the gangway watchman often has other duties to carry out, the employment of a shore watchman can be useful. The gangway watch must be maintained in accordance with the Ship Security Plan (SSP).

The officer on watch must ensure that:

- The gangway and gangway nets are properly rigged and illuminated during darkness
- the gangway is adjusted to meet changes in the ship's draught or tidal conditions, it is kept clear of obstructions and a lifebuoy with line and a light is available

Deck and Gangway Watch

- the gangway watchkeeper records the times of all persons boarding or leaving the vessel
- all persons boarding or leaving the vessel do so only via the gangway
- any additional local, port or company regulations are displayed at the gangway.

Fire Wires

Fire Wires

Fire wires are rigged on tankers while they are alongside to provide tugs with a connection point for pulling the tanker from the berth in an emergency situation, without the need for assistance from any of the vessel's crew members.

Two fire wires should be rigged, one near the bow and one near the stern. They are secured to bollards with a minimum of five turns and will be led directly to a Panama lead. The end of the wire overside will have an eye from which a heaving line is attached and led back to the deck. During cargo operations, the heaving line should be periodically adjusted to maintain the eye of the fire wire one to two metres above the water.

In order that enough wire can pay out to enable the emergency tugs to tow effectively, sufficient slack should be retained between the bollard and the Panama lead. To prevent the wire slack from running out, it should be seized with rope yarn or any other method that can be easily released. The diameter of the wire to be used depends on the deadweight of the ship.

See panel on next page - if a marine terminal requires the use of Emergency Towing-Off Pennants ie ETOPS or what are known as 'Fire Wires', it is now recommended that options other than wire rope be considered.

Fire Wires

Fire Wire Incidents Summary

Fire wires can be hazardous and have been the cause of some significant injuries.

2004 A crew member was paying out a fire wire when the wire ran away. The resultant surge caused the bight of the wire to leap off the bitts which then whiplashed and struck the crew member on the lower abdomen. He was hospitalised for swelling, bleeding and severe pain.

2005 An experienced crew member stepped over a fire wire to examine more closely why it was not running out. The fire wire suddenly became free and pinned the crew member's foot and ankle against the bitt, resulting in a broken leg and a lost time injury.

2005 A weak link holding a fire wire broke as a result of a sudden movement during arranging. The wire hit a crew member on his leg and at the same time his leg struck the Panama chock. This caused significant inflammation and a wound requiring five stitches.

2006 A crew member who was guiding the fire wire onto the winch during recovery was injured when a sudden release of a tight bend resulted in the wire lashing him in the mouth.

2008 A Second Officer suffered a partial amputation of his ring finger during the securing of a fire wire.

It is now time to discontinue the use of fire wires

The use of fire wires on board tankers is a historic practice and over 40 years of records detail no occasion where they have actually been used to assist a vessel off the berth, but in fact more than 1,700 personnel have been injured while handling fire wires in that time. This has brought the tanker industry to the conclusion that it is now time to discontinue the routine practice of deploying fire wires.

A Risk Assessment conducted by Lloyd's Register concluded that due to 'the unlikely occurrence of a fire scenario that would necessitate the need for a tow-off and the other alternatives that provide inherently safe means of moving a vessel from a berth, it is recommended that [fire wires] be eliminated from general use and that they should not be generally considered essential equipment for vessel safety'.

The guidance for marine terminals in ISGOTT Section 26.5.5.2 Emergency Towing-off Pennants, Handling states that "*a risk assessment is carried out at the terminal to determine whether or not there should be a routine requirement for ships to rig emergency towing-off pennants.*"

With the publication of '*Lloyd's Register Risk Assessment of Emergency Tow-off Pennant Systems (ETOPS) Onboard Tank Vessels*' by OCIMF in October 2009, the OCIMF position is that ETOPS are not required and have not provided benefit in the past.

If, however, individual marine terminal risk assessments or port authorities still require the use of ETOPS, it is recommended that options other than wire rope be considered.

Reference: ocimf.com/Library/Information-Papers

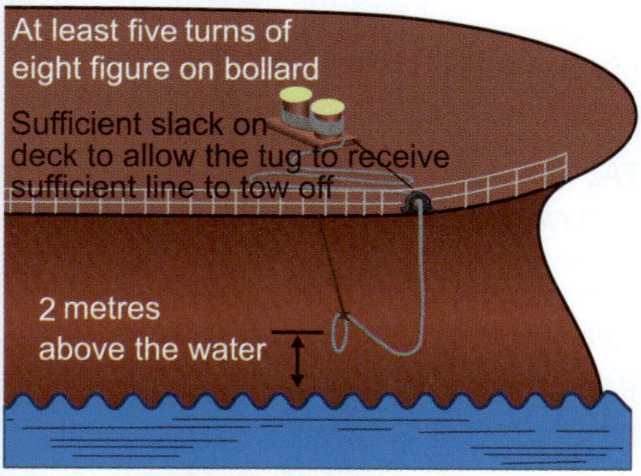

Discharging Port

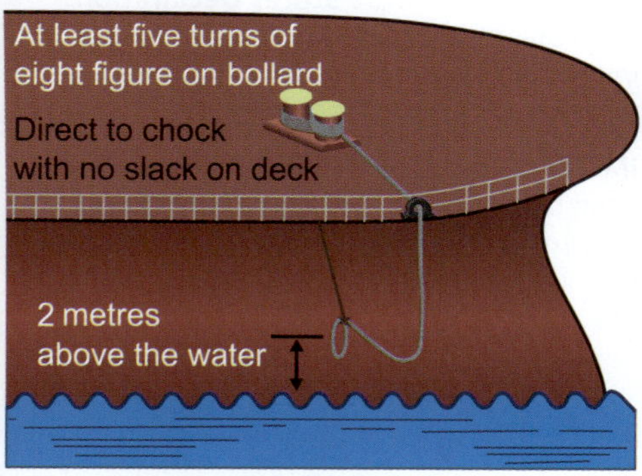

Loading Port

Customs Clearance for Ships

Customs clearance is the official process by which permission is gained to import or export goods. Customs officials will evaluate and inspect both the cargo and cargo documents before agreeing to allow goods to enter or leave the country. Customs clearance also refers to the documentation issued by customs officials proving payment of duty and permitting the further transit of the goods being carried. Customs clearance and control allows for revenue generation, domestic economic interest and national security.

The common practice for obtaining customs clearance is for the master, or a ship's officer assigned by the master, to complete and sign IMO FAL Forms, which are then submitted to the customs office for evaluation. The IMO Convention on Facilitation of International Maritime Traffic, 1965 (FAL Convention) was adopted with the intention of easing and standardising the burden of paperwork associated with international ship movements and trade. The FAL Convention includes a list of documents that public authorities can demand of a ship and recommends the information and number of copies required.

FAL Forms

IMO FAL No 1, General Declaration: Used on arrival and departure to provide the information required by the authorities of a Member State about the ship. (5 copies)

IMO FAL No 2, Cargo Declaration: Information required by public authorities relating to the cargo. Particulars of any dangerous cargo may also have to be provided separately. (4 copies)

IMO FAL No 3, Ship's Stores Declaration: Used on arrival and departure to provide the information required by the authorities of a Member State about the ship's stores. (4 copies)

IMO FAL No 4, Crew's Effects Declaration: Used on arrival to provide the information required by the authorities of a Member State. It is not required on departure. (2 copies)

IMO FAL No 5, Crew List: Used to provide the information required by the authorities of a Member State about the number of crew and the crew's composition on arrival and departure of the ship. (2 copies)

IMO FAL No 6, Passenger List: Used for ships certified to carry up to 12 passengers to provide the authorities of a Member State with information about the passengers on arrival and departure of the ship. (2 copies)

Countries that accept IMO FAL Forms are listed on the reverse of the form. Some countries use their own national form based on the IMO FAL format, with alterations and modifications specific to that Administration. Some Administrations do not require the IMO FAL Form 2, Cargo Declaration as this document is usually replaced by cargo manifests that are valid for commercial purposes and official checks. The ship's agent should advise the master about the local Administration's customs clearance practice.

Some Administrations offer exemption from customs clearance under certain circumstances. For example, in the UK, 'Authorised regular shipping service vessels', ie vessels that only operate between EU ports on regular, previously authorised, scheduled services, can arrive and depart from UK ports without the need to fulfil customs clearance operations.

Port clearance and customs clearance should not be confused as they operate in very separate ways. Customs clearance and customs officers are concerned with issues related to processing customs declarations, collecting duty owed and administering the tax/import policy of the Administration. Customs officers may also be responsible for issuing appropriate import licences, warehouse approvals and other import/export requirements. The port authority is concerned with the physical property and handling of goods as they move from vessels, through the terminal and to the consignee.

Immigration Clearance

Immigration clearance refers to the entry procedures involved to gain entry into a State.

To be granted immigration clearance, a process of vetting and authorisation to legally enter the country may be required. Immigration clearance allows immigration officials of the Administration to inspect an individual's passport, any necessary visa and travel documents to assess the purpose of that individual's visit and to evaluate whether their entry poses a threat to the interests of that State, whether it is for security or economic reasons.

The possession of a valid visa and/or identification documents will usually ensure that immigration clearance is granted, meaning that the individual is permitted to enter the State as per the terms of the visa or travel documents.

Different Administrations will require different types of identification to be provided for immigration clearance. Not all Administrations will accept Seafarers' Identity Documents (SIDs) as defined by ILO Convention C185.

The International Labour Organization C185 Seafarers' Identity Documents Convention (Revised), 2003 updates the previous C108 Seafarers' Identity Documents Convention, 1958. Like the preceding convention, C185 offers a *'rigorous identity regime for seafarers with the aim of developing effective security from terrorism and ensuring that the world's seafarers will be given the freedom of movement necessary for their well-being and for their professional activities and, in general, to facilitate international commerce.'*

– ILO website

Security Alongside

The ISPS Code was adopted in the wake of the terrorist attacks in September 2001. It was adopted through SOLAS Chapter XI-2 – Special measures to enhance maritime security. The ISPS Code is applicable to vessels of ≥500 GT.

The aim of the ISPS Code is to assess and combat commercial shipping's vulnerability to terrorist attack either while in transit or alongside in port. To achieve this, it required contracting governments to set security levels, conduct port facility security assessments, approve security plans for both ships and port facilities, identify ports that need port facility security officers and test approved security plans.

The ISPS Code is comprised of two parts, A and B. Part A details the mandatory security requirements for governments, port authorities and shipping companies. Part B consists of suggested guidelines on the implementation of the ISPS requirements.

The increased portside security measures codified by the ISPS Code help to increase vigilance around shipping terminals. Due to their large area and frequent movement of cargoes and crews, ports and terminals are difficult places to closely monitor persons coming into contact with ships and cargo in the terminal.

The US have adopted a number of homeland security initiatives and programmes aimed at improving the monitoring of cargoes and shippers arriving at US ports and terminals.

The US measures range from pre-screening of risk-assessed cargoes at the port of loading, and pre-screening of shippers to become certified trusted shippers whose cargoes and imports into the US will not be subject to delay through additional screening at the port of arrival.

On a state to state level, the US in agreement with other Administrations has customs and border protection agents stationed at ports across the world to monitor and screen certain container cargoes destined for the US.

The US had proposed mandatory 100% box scanning prior to loading of all cargoes destined for the US, but this met with opposition from both Administrations and the shipping industry. It was seen as the US outsourcing the cost of national security onto other nations, a cost potentially too great for developing nations reliant on US trade. The burden of delay and cost to shippers and carriers was also unpopular. The US dropped the proposed legislation when the European Union discussed requiring a reciprocal screening program for all US cargo destined for European Member States.

Security Alongside

The ISPS Code outlines the minimum security procedures that all ships and ports must meet to improve overall maritime security. The ISPS Code requires that all ships:

- Operate an Automated Identification System (AIS)
- clearly display on the hull the IMO Ship Identification Number (SIN)
- have a ship security alarm system
- have a ship security plan and ship security officer.

In addition all port facilities must:

- Have a security plan
- have port facility security officers
- monitor and control access
- monitor the activities of people and cargo
- ensure security communications are readily available.

The ISPS Code has been criticised for only being applicable to SOLAS Class vessels. This means the ship security requirements in the ISPS Code are only applicable to ships of ≥500 Dwt.

Security Levels

The ISPS Code prescribes three ship security levels. Contracting governments may detail additional requirements to these security levels as they deem appropriate. Level 1 is the state with the least security concern, and level 3 indicates that there is an immediate threat to the safety of the crew and vessel.

Security level 1 - normal, the level at which the ship or port facility normally operates. Security level 1 means the level for which minimum appropriate protective security measures shall be maintained at all times.

Security level 2 - heightened, the level applying for as long as there is a heightened risk of a security incident. Security level 2 means the level for which appropriate additional protective security measures shall be maintained for a period of time as a result of heightened risk of a security incident.

Security level 3 - exceptional, the level applying for the period of time when there is the probable or imminent risk of a security incident. Security level 3 means the level for which further specific protective security measures shall be maintained for a limited period of time when a security incident is probable or imminent, although it may not be possible to identify the specific target.

The ISPS Code also provides the following definitions:

Ship security plan - a plan developed to ensure the application of measures on board the ship designed to protect persons on board, cargo, cargo transport units, ship's stores or the ship from the risks of a security incident.

Ship security officer (SSO) - the person on board the ship, accountable to the master, designated by the Company as responsible for the security of the ship, including implementation and maintenance of the ship security plan and for liaison with the company security officer and port facility security officers.

Company security officer - the person designated by the Company for ensuring that a ship security assessment is carried out; that a ship security plan is developed, submitted for approval, and thereafter implemented and maintained, and for liaison with port facility security officers and the ship security officer.

Port facility security plan - a plan developed to ensure the application of measures designed to protect the port facility and ships, persons, cargo, cargo transport units and ship's stores within the port facility from the risks of a security incident.

Port facility security officer - the person designated as responsible for the development, implementation, revision and maintenance of the port facility security plan and for liaison with the ship security officers and company security officers.

Translation

Common Cargo Instructions in Russian

CARGO INSTRUCTIONS	ИНСТРУКЦИИ ПО ГРУЗОВЫМ ОПЕРАЦИЯМ	IN-STRUK-CI-I PO GRU-ZO-VIM O-PE-RA-CI-JAM
Open the ship's manifold valve	Откройте стояк	Ot-kroy-te sto-jak
Close the ship's manifold valve	Закройте стояк	Za-kroy-te sto-jak
Open the vapour return valve	Откройте клапан возврата газов	Ot-kroy-te kla-pan voz-vra-ta ga-zov
Close the vapour return valve	Закройте клапан возврата газов	Za-kroy-te kla-pan voz-vra-ta ga-zov
Please start loading	Начинайте погрузку пожалуйста	Nachi-nai-te po-gruz-ku po-za-lui-sta
Please start discharge	Начинайте выгрузку пожалуйста	Nachi-nai-te vi-gruz-ku po-za-lui-sta
What is the cargo loading rate?	Какая производительность погрузки?	Ka-ka-ja pro-iz-vo-di-tel-nost po-gruz-ki?
What is the cargo discharge rate?	Какая производительность выгрузки?	Ka-ka-ja pro-iz-vo-di-tel-nost vi-gruz-ki?
What is the maximum loading rate?	Какая максимальная производительность погрузки?	Ka-ka-ja mak-si-mal-na-ja pro-iz-vo-di-tel-nost po-gruz-ki?
What is the maximum discharge rate?	Какая максимальная производительность выгрузки?	Ka-ka-ja mak-si-mal-na-ja pro-iz-vo-di-tel-nost vi-gruz-ki?
What is the manifold pressure?	Какое давление на манифолде?	Ka-ko-e da-vle-ni-e na ma-ni-fol-de?
What is the maximum pressure at the manifold?	Какое максимальное давление на манифолде?	Ka-ko-e ma-kci-mal-no-e da-vle-ni-e na ma-ni-fol-de?
What is the cargo temperature?	Какая температура груза?	Ka-ka-ja tem-pe-ra-tu-ra gru-za?
How much cargo is on board?	Сколько груза на борту?	Skol-ko gru-za na bor-tu?
How much cargo has been loaded in the last hour?	Сколько груза было погружено за последний час?	Skol-ko gru-za bi-lo po-gru-ze-no za po-sled-ni chas?
How much cargo remains until completion?	Сколько груза осталось погрузить?	Skol-ko gru-za o-sta-los po-gru-zit?
What time will cargo finish?	Когда закончим?	Kogda za-kon-chim?

PEOPLE ARRIVING	ПРИБЫТИЕ	PRI-BI-TI-E
At what time will customs and immigration arrive?	Когда прибудут таможенники и иммиграционные власти?	Ko-gda pri-bu-dud ta-mo-zen-ni-ki i i-mi-gra-ci-on-ni-e vla-sti?
At what time will the surveyor arrive?	Когда прибудет сюрвейер?	Ko-gda pri-bu-ded sur-ve-er?
At what time will the pilot arrive?	Когда прибудет лоцман?	Ko-gda pri-bu-ded loc-man?
At what time will the ship's agent arrive?	Когда прибудет судовой агент?	Ko-gda pri-bu-ded su-do-voi a-gent?

TERMINOLOGY	ТЕРМИНОЛОГИЯ	TER-MI-NO-LO-GI-JA
Bow	Нос	Nos
Stern	Корма	Kor-ma
Port	Левый	Le-vi
Starboard	Правый	Pra-vi
Tug boat	Буксир	Buk-sir
Mooring line	Швартовный конец	Shvar-to-vi ko-nec
Temperature	Температура	Tem-pe-ra-tu-ra
Pressure	Давление	Dav-le-ni-e
Sample	Проба	Pro-ba

UNITS	ЕДИНИЦЫ ИЗМЕРЕНИЯ	E-DI-NI-CIIZ-ME-RE-NI-JA
Cubic metres (m^3)	Кубические метры	Ku-bi-ches-ki-e met-ri
Barrels (bbls)	Баррели	Bar-re-li
Tonnes	Тонны	Tonni
Per hour	В час	V chas

NUMBERS	ЧИСЛА	CHIS-LA
1	Один	O-din
2	Два	Dva
3	Три	Tri
4	Четыре	Che-ti-re
5	Пять	Pjat
6	Шесть	Shest
7	Семь	Sem
8	Восемь	Vo-sem
9	Девять	De-vjat
10	Десять	De-sjat
100	Сто	Sto
200	Двести	Dve-sti
250	Двести пятьдесят	Dve-sti pjat-de-sjat
500	Пятьсот	Pjat-sot
1,000	Тысяча	Ti-sja-cha

Translation

NUMBERS	ЧИСЛА	CHIS-LA
1,500	Тысяча пятьсот	Ti-sja-cha pjat-sot
2,000	Две тысячи	Dve ti-sja-chi
5,000	Пять тысяч	Pjat ti-sjach
10,000	Десять тысяч	De-sjat ti-sjach
20,000	Двадцать тысяч	Dvad-tsat ti-sjach
30,000	Тридцать тысяч	Trid-tsat ti-sjach
40,000	Сорок тысяч	So-rok ti-sjach
50,000	Пятьдесят тысяч	Pjat-de-sjat ti-sjach
60,000	Шестьдесят тысяч	Shest-de-sjat ti-sjach
70,000	Семьдесят тысяч	Sem-de-sjat ti-sjach
80,000	Восемьдесят тысяч	Vo-sem-de-sjat ti-sjach
90,000	Девяносто тысяч	De-vja-nos-to ti-sjach
100,000	Сто тысяч	Sto ti-sjach

GREETINGS	ПРИВЕТСТВИЯ	PRI-VET-STVI-JA
Good morning	Доброе утро	Do-bro-e u-tro
Good afternoon	Добрый день	Do-bri den
Good evening	Добрый вечер	Do-bri ve-cher
Good night	Доброй ночи	Do-broi no-chi
Hello	Привет	Pri-vet
Thank you	Спасибо	Spa-si-bo
Yes	Да	Da
No	Нет	Net
No thank you	Спасибо, не нужно	Spa-si-bo ne nuz-no
Please	Пожалуйста	Po-za-lu-sta

TIME	ВРЕМЯ	VRE-MJA
1 o'clock am	Час ночи	Chas no-chi
2 o'clock am	Два часа ночи	Dva cha-sa no-chi
3 o'clock am	Три часа ночи	Tri cha-sa no-chi
4 o'clock am	Четыре часа утра	Che-ti-re cha-sa u-tra
5 o'clock am	Пять часов утра	Pjat cha-sov u-tra
6 o'clock am	Шесть часов утра	Shest cha-sov u-tra
7 o'clock am	Семь часов утра	Sem cha-sov u-tra
8 o'clock am	Восемь часов утра	Vo-sem cha-sov u-tra
9 o'clock am	Девять часов утра	De-vat cha-sov u-tra
10 o'clock am	Десять часов утра	De-sjat cha-sov u-tra
11 o'clock am	Одиннадцать часов утра	Odin-nad-tsat cha-sov u-tra
Midday	Полдень	Pol-den
1 o'clock pm	Час дня	Chas dnja
2 o'clock pm	Два часа дня	Dva cha-sa dnja
3 o'clock pm	Три часа дня	Tri cha-sa dnja
4 o'clock pm	Четыре часа вечера	Che-ti-re cha-sa ve-che-ra
5 o'clock pm	Пять часов вечера	Pjat cha-sov ve-che-ra
6 o'clock pm	Шесть часов вечера	Shest cha-sov ve-che-ra
7 o'clock pm	Семь часов вечера	Sem cha-sov ve-che-ra
8 o'clock pm	Восемь часов вечера	Vo-sem cha-sov ve-che-ra
9 o'clock pm	Девять часов вечера	De-vjat cha-sov ve-che-ra
10 o'clock pm	Десять часов вечера	De-sjat cha-sov ve-che-ra
11 o'clock pm	Одиннадцать часов вечера	Odin-nad-tsat cha-sov ve-che-ra
Midnight	Полночь	Pol-noch
5 minutes	Пять минут	Pjat mi-nut
10 minutes	Десять минут	De-sjat mi-nut
15 minutes	Пятнадцать минут	Pjat-nad-tsat mi-nut
20 minutes	Двадцать минут	Dvad-tsat mi-nut
25 minutes	Двадцать пять минут	Dvad-tsat pjat mi-nut
30 minutes	Тридцать минут	Trid-tsat mi-nut
35 minutes	Тридцать пять минут	Trid-tsat pjat mi-nut
40 minutes	Сорок минут	So-rok mi-nut
45 minutes	Сорок пять минут	So-rok pjat mi-nut
50 minutes	Пятьдесят минут	Pjat-de-sjat mi-nut
55 minutes	Пятьдесят пять минут	Pjat-de-sjat pjat mi-nut
60 minutes	Шестьдесят минут (Час)	Shest-de-sjat mi-nut (Chas)

Common Cargo Instructions in Spanish

CARGO INSTRUCTIONS	INSTRUCCIONES PARA CARGUERO
Open the ship's manifold valve	Abrir la válvula del colector del barco
Close the ship's manifold valve	Cerrar la válvula del colector del barco
Open the vapour return valve	Abrir la válvula de retorno del vapor
Close the vapour return valve	Cerrar la válvula de retorno del vapor
Please start loading	Empiecen a cargar, por favor
Please start discharge	Empiecen a descargar, por favor
What is the cargo loading rate?	Cuál es la tasa de carga del buque?
What is the cargo discharge rate?	Cuál es la tasa de descarga del buque?
What is the maximum loading rate?	Cuál es la tasa máxima de carga?
What is the maximum discharge rate?	Cuál es la tasa máxima de descarga?
What is the manifold pressure?	Cuál es la presión del colector?
What is the maximum pressure at the manifold?	Cuál es la presión máxima en el colector?
What is the cargo temperature?	Cuál es la temperatura de la carga?
How much cargo is on board?	Cuánta carga hay a bordo?
How much cargo has been loaded in the last hour?	Cuánto se ha cargado en la última hora?
How much cargo remains until completion?	Cuánto falta cargar para terminar?
What time will cargo finish?	A qué hora se terminará de cargar?

PEOPLE ARRIVING	RECIBIMIENTO DE GENTE
At what time will customs and immigration arrive?	A qué hora llegan los oficiales de aduana e inmigración?
At what time will the surveyor arrive?	A qué hora llega el agrimensor?
At what time will the pilot arrive?	A qué hora llega el piloto?
At what time will the ship's agent arrive?	A qué hora llega el agente del buque?

TERMINOLOGY	TERMINOLOGIA
Bow	Proa
Stern	Popa
Port	Puerto
Starboard	Estribor
Tug boat	Remolcador
Mooring line	Línea de amarramiento
Temperature	Temperatura
Pressure	Presión
Sample	Muestra

GREETINGS	SALUDOS
Good morning	Buen día
Good afternoon	Buenas tardes
Good evening	Buenas tardes/ Buenas noches
Good night	Buenas noches
Hello	Hola
Thank you	Gracias
Yes	Sí
No	No
No thank you	No gracias
Please	Por favor

NUMBERS	NÚMEROS
1	Uno
2	Dos
3	Tres
4	Cuatro
5	Cinco
6	Seis
7	Siete
8	Ocho
9	Nueve
10	Diez
100	Cien
200	Doscientos
250	Doscientos cincuenta
500	Quinientos

Translation

NUMBERS	NÚMEROS
1,000	Mil
1,500	Mil quinientos
2,000	Dos mil
5,000	Cinco mil
10,000	Diez mil
20,000	Veinte mil
30,000	Treinta mil
40,000	Cuarenta mil
50,000	Cincuenta mil
60,000	Sesenta mil
70,000	Setenta mil
80,000	Ochenta mil
90,000	Noventa mil
100,000	Cien mil

TIME	LA HORA
1 o'clock am	Una de la mañana/madrugada
2 o'clock am	Dos de la mañana/madrugada
3 o'clock am	Tres de la mañana/madrugada
4 o'clock am	Cuatro de la mañana/madrugada
5 o'clock am	Cinco de la mañana/madrugada
6 o'clock am	Seis de la mañana/madrugada
7 o'clock am	Siete de la mañana/madrugada
8 o'clock am	Ocho de la mañana/madrugada
9 o'clock am	Nueve de la mañana/madrugada
10 o'clock am	Diez de la mañana/madrugada
11 o'clock am	Once de la mañana/madrugada
Midday	Mediodía
1 o'clock pm	Una de la tarde
2 o'clock pm	Dos de la tarde
3 o'clock pm	Tres de la tarde
4 o'clock pm	Cuatro de la tarde
5 o'clock pm	Cinco de la tarde
6 o'clock pm	Seis de la tarde
7 o'clock pm	Siete de la tarde
8 o'clock pm	Ocho de la noche
9 o'clock pm	Nueve de la noche
10 o'clock pm	Diez de la noche
11 o'clock pm	Once de la noche
Midnight	Medianoche
5 minutes	Cinco minutos
10 minutes	Diez minutos
15 minutes	Quince minutos
20 minutes	Veinte minutos
25 minutes	Veinticinco minutos
30 minutes	Treinta minutos
35 minutes	Treinta y cinco minutos
40 minutes	Cuarenta minutos
45 minutes	Cuarenta y cinco minutos
50 minutes	Cincuenta minutos
55 minutes	Cincuenta y cinco minutos
60 minutes	Sesenta minutos

UNITS	UNIDADES
Cubic metres (m^3)	Metros cúbicos
Barrels (bbls)	Barriles
Tonnes	Toneladas
Per hour	Por hora

Common Cargo Instructions in French

CARGO INSTRUCTIONS	
Open the ship's manifold valve	Ouvrez la vanne du collecteur du navire
Close the ship's manifold valve	Fermez la vanne du collecteur du navire
Open the vapour return valve	Ouvrez la vanne de retour gaz
Close the vapour return valve	Fermez la vanne de retour gaz
Please start loading	Veuillez commencer le chargement s'il vous plaît.
Please start discharge	Veuillez commencer le déchargement s'il vous plaît.
What is the cargo loading rate?	Quel est le débit de chargement?
What is the cargo discharge rate?	Quel est le débit de déchargement?
What is the maximum loading rate?	Quel est le débit maximum de chargement?
What is the maximum discharge rate?	Quel est le débit maximum de déchargement?
What is the manifold pressure?	Quelle est la pression au collecteur?
What is the maximum pressure at the manifold?	Quelle est la pression maximale au collecteur?
What is the cargo temperature?	Quelle est la température de la cargaison?
How much cargo is on board?	Combien de cargo y-a-t-il à bord?
How much cargo has been loaded in the last hour?	Combien de cargo a-t-on chargé durant cette dernière heure?
How much cargo remains until completion?	Combien de cargo reste-t-il à transférer jusqu'à la fin des opérations?
What time will cargo finish?	Quand le chargement (déchargement) va-t-il finir?

UNITS	
Cubic metres (m^3)	Mètres-cube
Barrels (bbls)	Barils
Tonnes	Tonnes
Per hour	Par heure

PEOPLE ARRIVING	
At what time will customs and immigration arrive?	A quelle heure la douane et le service d'immigration vont-il arriver?
At what time will the surveyor arrive?	A quelle heure l'inspecteur va-t-il arriver?
At what time will the pilot arrive?	A quelle heure le pilote va-t-il arriver?
At what time will the ship's agent arrive?	A quelle heure l'agent du navire va-t-il arriver?

TERMINOLOGY	
Bow	Proue
Stern	Poupe
Port	Bâbord
Starboard	Tribord
Tug boat	Remorqueur
Mooring line	Amarre
Temperature	Température
Pressure	Pression
Sample	Échantillon

NUMBERS	
1	un
2	deux
3	trois
4	quatre
5	cinq
6	six
7	sept
8	huit
9	neuf
10	dix
100	cent
200	deux cents
250	deux cent cinquante
500	cinq cents
1,000	mille
1,500	mille cinq cents
2,000	deux mille
5,000	cinq mille
10,000	dix mille

Translation

NUMBERS	
20,000	vingt mille
30,000	trente mille
40,000	quarante mille
50,000	cinquante mille
60,000	soixante mille
70,000	soixante-dix (septante) mille
80,000	quatre-vingts mille
90,000	quatre-vingt-dix (nonante) mille
100,000	cent mille

GREETINGS	
Good morning/afternoon	Bonjour
Good evening	Bonsoir
Good night	Bonsoir
Hello	Bonjour (Bonsoir)
Thank you	Merci
Yes	Oui
No	Non
No thank you	Non merci
Please	S'il vous plaît

TIME	
1 o'clock am	une heure du matin
2 o'clock am	deux heures du matin
3 o'clock am	trois heures du matin
4 o'clock am	quatre heures du matin
5 o'clock am	cinq heures du matin
6 o'clock am	six heures du matin
7 o'clock am	sept heures du matin
8 o'clock am	huit heures du matin
9 o'clock am	neuf heures du matin
10 o'clock am	dix heures du matin
11 o'clock am	onze heures du matin
Midday	Midi
1 o'clock pm	une heure de l'après-midi (treize heures)
2 o'clock pm	deux heures de l'après-midi (quatorze heures)
3 o'clock pm	trois heures de l'après-midi (quinze heures)
4 o'clock pm	quatre heures de l'après-midi (seize heures)
5 o'clock pm	cinq heures de l'après-midi (dix-sept heures)
6 o'clock pm	six heures du soir (dix-huit heures)
7 o'clock pm	sept heures du soir (dix-neuf heures)
8 o'clock pm	huit heures du soir (vingt heures)
9 o'clock pm	neuf heures du soir (vingt et une heures)
10 o'clock pm	dix heures du soir (vingt-deux heures)
11 o'clock pm	onze heures du soir (vingt-trois heures)
Midnight	Minuit
5 minutes	cinq minutes
10 minutes	dix minutes
15 minutes	quinze minutes
20 minutes	vingt minutes
25 minutes	vingt-cinq minutes
30 minutes	trente minutes
35 minutes	trente-cinq minutes
40 minutes	quarante minutes
45 minutes	quarante-cinq minutes
50 minutes	cinquante minutes
55 minutes	cinquante-cinq minutes
60 minutes	soixante minutes

CHAPTER 29

Shipboard Inspections

Shipboard Inspections

Port State Control (PSC)

Port State Control (PSC) is the inspection of ships that do not fly the flag of the coastal State of the port the ship is visiting. The purpose of a PSC inspection is to verify that the condition of the ship, its equipment, manning and operations comply with international regulations.

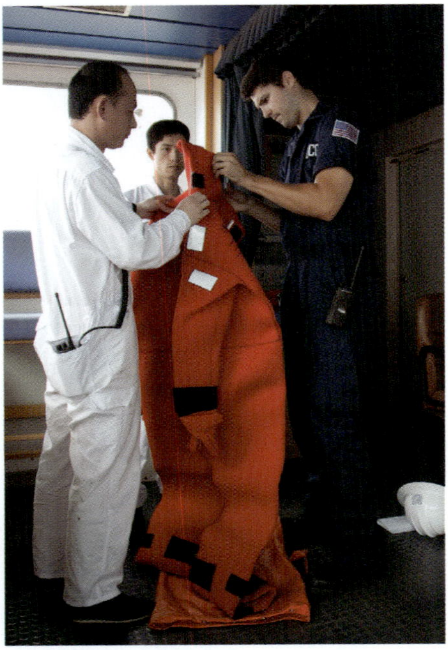

Courtesy of USCG

Figure 29.1 - USCG PSC inspecting an immersion suit

Where deficiencies are found that are considered a hazard to health, safety or the environment, the ship will have action taken against it. This could potentially result in a detention until the deficiencies are rectified.

The IMO has encouraged the establishment of regional Port State Control organisations and implementation of Memoranda of Understanding (MoUs). A Memorandum of Understanding is an official document in which participating maritime authorities agree to follow a harmonised system of port state control. This consistency of approach allows more ships to be inspected to the correct standards and improves sharing of important information.

The MoUs are:

- **Paris MoU** - Belgium, Canada, Croatia, Denmark, Finland, France, Germany, Greece, Ireland, Italy, Netherlands, Norway, Poland, Portugal, Russian Federation, Spain, Sweden and UK
- **Tokyo MoU** - Australia, Canada, China, Fiji, Indonesia, Japan, Republic of Korea, Malaysia, New Zealand, Papua New Guinea, Philippines, Russian Federation, Singapore, Solomon Islands, Thailand, Vanuatu, Vietnam and Hong Kong
- **Acuerdo de Viña del Mar** - Argentina, Bolivia, Brazil, Chile, Colombia, Cuba, Ecuador, Mexico, Panama, Peru, Uruguay and Venezuela
- **Caribbean MoU** - Antigua and Barbuda, Aruba, Bahamas, Barbados, Bermuda, British Virgin Islands, Cayman Islands, Dominica, Grenada, Guyana, Jamaica, Montserrat, Netherlands Antilles, Saint Kitts and Nevis, Saint Lucia, Saint Vincent and the Grenadines, Suriname, Trinidad and Tobago, Turks and Caicos Islands
- **Abuja MoU** - Benin, Cape Verde, Congo, Cote d'Ivoire, Gabon, Gambia, Ghana, Guinea, Liberia, Mauritania, Namibia, Nigeria, Senegal, Sierra Leone, South Africa, Togo
- **Mediterranean MoU** - Algeria, Cyprus, Egypt, Israel, Jordan, Malta, Lebanon, Morocco, Tunisia, Turkey and the Palestine Authority
- **Indian Ocean MoU** - Djibouti, Eritrea, Ethiopia, India, Iran, Kenya, Maldives, Mauritius, Mozambique, Seychelles, South Africa, Sri Lanka, Sudan, Tanzania and Yemen
- **Black Sea MoU** - Bulgaria, Georgia, Romania, Russian Federation, Turkey and Ukraine
- **Riyadh MoU** - Bahrain, Kuwait, Oman, Qatar, Saudi Arabia and United Arab Emirates.

Inspections can be conducted routinely (generally every six months) or where there is doubt over conformity and condition of the ship, operations or crew capability. Certain types of ships, ships flying identified flags and older ships may receive more frequent PSC inspections. Each MoU has a central database that enables appropriate ships to be identified for inspection and, importantly, reduces the likelihood of ships with good PSC records being inspected too frequently. The effectiveness of maintenance will reflect the extent of a PSC inspection

Ships will be considered as priorities for PSC inspections if they are:

- Reported by pilots or port authorities
- carrying dangerous or polluting goods and have failed to report the relevant information to the port and coastal State
- the subject of a report or notification by another authority
- the subject of a report or complaint by the master, crew member or other person/ organisation with a legitimate interest in the safe operation of the ship
- involved in a collision, grounding or stranding en route to the port
- accused of violating the provisions on discharging harmful substances or effluents
- manoeuvred in an erratic or unsafe manner, where routeing measures were not followed
- operated in a dangerous or hazardous way
- suspended/withdrawn from Class for safety reasons in the previous six months.

Courtesy of USCG

The effectiveness of maintenance will reflect the extent of a PSC inspection

When undertaking PSC inspections, ships are not to be unduly detained or delayed, and where this occurs they are entitled to compensation for loss or damage. However, where the ship is detained appropriately, the costs accrued by the port State during the inspection will be charged to the shipowner, and the ship will not be permitted to sail until they are paid or a guarantee of payment is provided.

PSC inspections can be:

- **Initial** - documentation, crew, general condition, machinery spaces and accommodation spaces
- **Detailed** - as a result of missing or invalid documentation or there are clear grounds that the ship fails to meet international standards
- **Expanded** - annually for specific ship types and ages
- **Suspended** - where substandard conditions are found, inspections can be suspended until the ship is brought up to standard. The PSC inspection can then be continued.

A typical initial PSC inspection sequence will involve inspecting:

- Ship's certificates
- ship's condition, equipment and the crew
- prioritised areas of concern that have been identified.

Where a ship is found to be compliant, a 'clean' inspection report will be issued to the master and recorded on the MoU system.

If a ship is found to be deficient, a PSCO will determine the action required, ie:

- Permitting the ship to sail with the noted deficiencies, provided that the deficiencies do not pose a threat to safety, health or the environment, or
- detaining the ship where the deficiencies are considered sufficiently serious to merit returning to the ship before it sails.

There are non-exhaustive lists of detainable deficiencies grouped under the relevant Conventions and Codes. Where deficiencies cannot be rectified at the port, the authorities

Port State Control (PSC)

may permit the vessel to sail subject to specified conditions.

The following provides a typical list of the areas that can be covered during a PSC inspection.

PSC Inspection Checklist

- Name of ship
- IMO number
- official number
- call sign
- gross tonnage
- type of ship
- date keel laid
- date of delivery
- ship dimensions
- ship's Classification Society
- DOC
- SMC
- ISPSC
- management company
- date of inspection
- place of inspection (eg port, country, at sea)
- expected time of arrival off port.

Documentation and Records

- All original copies of trading certificates
- CSR file
- seafarers' national documents, certificates of competency and medical certificates
- approved manuals/documents (eg stability, cargo securing, SOPEP, etc)
- inspection/service records of LSA, FFA, navigation and GMDSS equipment, and survey records
- drill records
- ship's plans.

Life-Saving Appliances

- Lifeboats and rescue boats – condition, equipment and certification
- liferafts and hydrostatic release units (HRUs)
- lifebuoys
- lifejackets and immersion suits
- means of embarkation for lifeboats and liferafts
- emergency lights at survival stations
- donning instructions (lifejackets and immersion suits), launching instructions and IMO symbols are posted
- LSA manufacturer's maintenance instructions and SOLAS training manual.

Fire-Fighting Appliances

- Fire detectors and alarm panels (bridge, E/R and fire control station)
- fire lines, hydrants, equipment and international shore connection
- main and emergency fire pumps
- fixed gas/foam/dry powder/water spray fire-fighting installations

- ventilation and insulation
- portable fire extinguishers
- fire doors, fire dampers/ventilators
- FO/LO quick closing valves, E/R ventilation and FO pump remote stops
- EEBDs, BA sets and fire-fighters' outfits
- escape routes lighted, marked and unobstructed

- training schedule and records.

Charts and nautical publications must be up to date

Navigation Safety and Communication

- Up-to-date and corrected nautical publications and charts
- latest IMO and flag State required publications available
- navigation equipment and inspection and testing records available
- GMDSS installations including testing and records
- voyage plan prepared and approved by ship's master
- compass deviation card
- steering gear changeover procedure posted
- navigational lights, shapes and sound signals
- engine telegraph, engine room and steering gear room communication operational
- pilot ladders/hoist and arrangement for safe boarding
- evidence of proper position plotting and radar plotting.

Machinery and Electrical

- Main and auxiliary engines
- instrumentation
- remote and emergency starting system
- fuel oil and lubricating oil systems
- boilers including the local and remote control of safety devices
- bilge pumping system
- engine control room equipment and switchboards
- emergency generator
- engine room clean and tidy
- quick closing emergency valves
- emergency exits clear of any obstructions
- safety symbols displayed.

Accommodation and ILO Requirements

- Accommodation clean and habitable
- galleys, pantries and food preparation areas are clean and free of any infestation
- hospital and sick bay are clean and free of any infestation, adequate medical equipment, hospital is not used as an extra cabin/store room
- sanitary places are neat and clean
- doors close and lock
- readily available cold and hot water
- proper lighting
- ventilation and heating systems
- sufficient food and fresh water
- refrigerated store room at a suitable temperature
- electrical features are in satisfactory order
- fire-fighting equipment is available in the galley
- medical chest stocked as per WHO standards.

Pollution Prevention

- Oily water separator
- oil discharge monitoring and control system and 15 ppm alarm (if fitted) tested
- oil content meter calibrated
- no illegal bypass piping
- warning placards against prohibited discharges posted

Port State Control (PSC)

- bilge and sludge pumps operational and other arrangements in good order
- standard discharge connection readily available
- garbage reception facilities adequate and categorised
- warning placards against prohibited discharges posted
- oil record book, garbage record book, ODS record book, record book of engine parameters, bunker delivery note, etc up to date and available for inspection.

Load Line and Structures

- Condition of hull, cargo hold/cargo tank structures, deck fittings and equipment and pipelines
- load line marks clearly marked
- hatch covers, coamings and stays
- wooden covers or steel

Structural integrity is essential

- weathertight doors and access
- remote operation of scuppers, inlets and discharges
- guard-rails, catwalks and bulwarks
- ventilators and air pipes, dampers, flaps and closing devices are in order
- approved stability booklet.

Safety Management System

- Safety Management Manual
- working language established
- DPA/shore contact details available
- master and crew familiar with their responsibilities and procedures
- engine room and deck equipment maintenance records
- records/plans/evidence of key shipboard operations
- records of crew familiarisation
- emergency situations identified and drills/training programme established and recorded
- accident, incident and non-conformity reporting procedures
- master's review, internal and external audits
- documents properly controlled.

Ship Security

- Ship Security Plan (SSP) is available and properly protected from unauthorised access
- master's understanding of his responsibility and overriding authority
- ship security officer (SSO) certificate and evidence of understanding
- programmes and records for training, drills and exercises available
- ship security alert system (SSAS) operational and the main and alternative power source properly maintained
- control of access to ship
- stowaway procedures established
- records of security activities maintained.

SOLAS Operational Requirements

- Abandon ship drills and fire drills conducted in accordance with the muster list
- crew familiar with emergency equipment
- effective communication during drills
- evidence of drills.

Flag State Inspections

Flag State is the regulatory authority a country has over commercial ships registered under its flag, including safety and environmental certification and inspection. Inspection programmes are essential to ensure that the owners and ships comply with prescribed national and international regulations.

Some inspections may be conducted by recognised organisations (including Classification Societies) on behalf of the flag State. There are a number of types of inspections:

- Pre-registration – hull, structure, watertight integrity, accommodation, machinery, navigation equipment, safety equipment, cargo and ballast spaces, etc
- Annual Safety – hull and machinery, documents, publications, crew certificates, SMS, training drills, accommodation, safety, LSA and fire-fighting equipment
- Detention Prevention – to detect potential problems and clear previous PSC findings
- Post Detention – to ensure items from detention (and subsequent) reports are cleared
- Post Marine Casualty – investigating officers are assigned the task of assessing the ship after an incident

- ISM additional audits
- ISPS verification audits – audits required by the Code
- Special Safety – unscheduled inspections or where required by the operator.

Expanded inspections are required for ships with previous recent detentions and for bulk carriers, passenger ships and tankers over specified ages.

There are many similarities in the scope of flag State inspections and PSC inspections, and the following lists set out the typical areas that may be covered during a flag State inspection.

Ship Certificates

Certificates that are to be sighted and validity confirmed include:

- Registration
- Safety Management Certificate
- ISM Document of Compliance (copy)
- International Ship Security Certificate.

Documents

Documents that are to be sighted and validity confirmed include:

- Official logbook
- GMDSS/Radio logbook
- Oil Record Book Part I
- SOPEP
- garbage management plan
- garbage record book
- cargo securing manual
- record of security activities
- noise level report (MODU Code rigs and vessels only)
- record of drills
- records of stability calculations.

Publications

The latest versions of the following publications to be sighted:

- Merchant shipping legislation of the flag State
- Ship Captain's Medical Guide or International Medical Guide for Ships

Flag State Inspections

- UK Code of Safe Working Practices for Merchant Seamen or ILO Accident Prevention on Board Ship at Sea and in Port
- If the ship carries dangerous goods (DG):
  - IMO Medical First Aid Guide
  - DG Document of Compliance
  - DG manifest or stowage plan.

Manning and Crew Management

Crew safety awareness and record of onboard training:

- Manning in accordance with the safe manning document
- valid certificates and endorsements
- work schedule and up-to-date record of hours worked
- onboard communication in a common language
- English language used in official logbook, oil record book and muster list
- current copy of the ship's articles up to date.

Navigation and Communication Equipment

To include:

- Compass error logbook
- evidence of navigating equipment checks
- company instruction and procedures
- master's standing orders and night order book
- systematic voyage planning
- nautical charts/publications adequate and up to date
- navigation and communications equipment.

Structure and Accommodation

To include:

- Accommodation
- external hull, weather decks, superstructures, etc
- gangways and other means of access
- deck lighting
- deck piping, valves and electrical conduits/ fittings
- lifting appliances
- cargo compartments, hatches, etc
- mooring equipment
- hull markings.

Life-Saving and Fire Safety

- Safety meeting records
- survival craft
- medical locker
- muster lists and fire control plans updated and displayed
- radar transponders and EPIRB
- signage
- instructions and maintenance records for maintenance of fire-fighting and safety equipment.

Engineering, Machinery Spaces and Equipment

- Maintenance records of main and auxiliary machinery
- engine room logbook
- machinery failure alarms and safety trips
- emergency steering gear
- remote stops
- bunker samples and delivery notes
- chief engineer's emergency procedures and standing orders

- pollution prevention procedures
- company instruction and procedures for engine room management and watchkeeping
- main and auxiliary machinery
- control and alarm functions
- bilge pumps
- oily water separator
- clean engine room, workshop and stores.

Special ship types will require additional areas to be checked, such as crowd management, mustering and evacuation, search and rescue cooperation plan and decision support systems for passenger ships. On tankers, the Oil Record Book Part II, Procedures and Arrangements Manual, SMPEP plan and appropriate certification will be among the documentation assessed (as applicable to the type of tanker).

Classification Societies

In addition to acting on behalf of flag States as recognised organisations (RO) and overseeing the construction, modification and repair of ships, Classification Societies (Class) also complete surveys and inspections of ships to ensure they remain in Class. After a survey, the Class surveyor will report the findings to the society or flag State, advising:

- Compliance and issuance of a Certificate of Class
- issuance of an Interim Certificate of Class that stipulates the period and extent of rectification work required
- withdrawal or suspension of Class.

While not strictly speaking mandatory, a Certificate of Class is very important for a ship to continue to trade, and may be a requirement of:

- Insurance – for cargo, hull and machinery, and P&I
- ship registration – flag States
- ports – PSC and customs.

To be issued with or retain the Certificate of Class, ie to remain in Class, regular inspections are required. These vary in their type and method:

- Open inspections – scheduled inspections that require machinery to be opened up
- Class-approved Planned Maintenance Systems (PMS) – some equipment may be permitted to be inspected by the chief engineer, but inspection and maintenance records are to be inspected by Class regularly
- Condition-based Maintenance Systems – automatic systems to monitor the condition of equipment, the records of which will be evaluated by Class.

Classification Societies

Not all hull inspections and work require drydocking

Class survey programmes normally consist of:

- Annual
- intermediate – during the second or third annual survey
- special - five years
- docking – the frequency depends on maintenance, age and ship type. It normally includes a complete survey of machinery. In-water surveys are sometimes permitted in lieu of some docking surveys
- continuous – not including ships that require SOLAS Chapter XI-1 Enhanced Surveys that apply to bulkers, oil tankers, etc.

Class surveys are extensive, and a number of areas that commonly cause problems are:

- Documentation:
  - Ship certificates and documents, including ship's plans
  - crew certificates and documents
  - ISM and ISPS documentation, records and crew understanding
  - SOPEP documentation
  - stability/loading manual
  - cargo record book, Procedures and Arrangements (P&A) manual, garbage record book, pollution prevention certification
  - muster list, training records, fire control plan, SOLAS training manual, CSR, etc
- deck:
  - Bridge/Navigation - radar, compasses, lights and shapes, GMDSS equipment, charts (including ECDIS) and publications, echo sounder, fire detection systems
  - structural – decks, bulkheads, railings, hatches, doors
  - ventilation
  - mooring arrangements
  - anchoring arrangements
  - cargo tanks/holds and ballast tanks
  - cargo documentation and equipment including oil discharge monitoring equipment
  - lighting and working area safety arrangements
  - loadline freeboard marks
  - means of escape
  - emergency towing arrangements

Figure 29.2 - Emergency deck lighting

- pilot arrangements
- watertight integrity including freeing arrangements

Watertight doors will be tested

- accommodation – sanitation, ventilation, galley, lighting, means of escape and heating
- engine:
  - Main engine and auxiliary machinery
  - cleanliness
  - electrical wiring, breakers, conduits, etc
  - bilge pumping arrangements
  - oil record book and discharge arrangements
  - steering gear and emergency steering operation
  - survey certification for boilers, tailshaft, IGS, refrigeration, automation, etc
- fire safety:
  - Fire-fighting systems and installations, fire doors, detection equipment, extinguishing equipment, dampers, emergency pumps
- LSA:
  - Lifeboats, liferafts, rescue boats and launching arrangements
  - immersion suits, lifejackets and lifebuoys
  - embarkation systems and equipment.

Vetting Inspections

First impressions can provide a positive start

Vetting Inspections

Ship vetting is a careful and detailed examination of a ship to enable a charterer to make decisions regarding selecting ships for chartering. Oil majors may employ company inspectors to vet nominated ships or they may employ the services of a third party. These inspectors will assess the condition, operations and capabilities of the ship to reduce any potential risks to the charterer.

The broad goals of ship vetting are to ensure:

- Compliance with international legislation, industrial standards and national laws
- pollution prevention and protection of the environment
- safety on board and safe management of a company
- that cargo is not carried on substandard ships.

SIRE Inspections

Oil majors and tanker operators normally use the Ship Inspection Report Programme (SIRE). This is a programme developed by the Oil Companies International Marine Forum (OCIMF) as a risk assessment tool to address concerns over substandard shipping, promoting safety and preventing pollution. It comprises of a large, continually updated database of reports that is shared among charterers.

Typically ships can expect two to three inspections each year and some charterers will not accept ships that have not been inspected in the last six months. However, ships on the spot market can experience a number of inspections in a short period, although OCIMF are intending to introduce a rule that prevents ships receiving a second SIRE inspection within 30 days of the last.

The programme uses a uniform inspection format that is based on:

- Vessel Inspection Questionnaire (VIQ) – the base document for the inspection
- Uniform SIRE Inspection Report
- Vessels Particulars Questionnaire (VPQ)
- SIRE Enhanced Report Manager (WebSERM).

In 2004, SIRE was expanded to include barges, by using:

- Barges Inspection Questionnaire (BIQ)
- Barge Particulars Questionnaire (BPQ).

The VIQ covers the following main areas:

- Certification and documentation
- crew management
- navigation

Inert gas systems (IGS) are essential cargo safety systems

- safety management
- pollution prevention
- structural condition
- cargo and ballast systems – petroleum
- mooring
- communications
- engine and steering compartments
- general appearance and condition
- ice operations.

A full version of the VIQ can be found at: www.ocimf.com/SIRE/Introduction

A similar system used for chemical ship and gas tanker inspection is run by the Chemical Distribution Institute (CDI).

P/V valves are commonly found to be a problem or being inappropriately used

Internal Inspections

Internal inspections are required to pre-empt and prepare ships and crews for external inspection, to identify weaknesses and to improve conditions, efficiency, safety, security and environmental protection. Internal auditors/inspectors should have a thorough knowledge of the ship's safety management and other systems, and in theory be better placed to identify shortcomings than an external inspector.

Tools are available to assist companies in assessing their company management systems, including the Tanker Management Self Assessment (TMSA) and the Offshore Vessel Management and Self Assessment (OVMSA). Having completed these assessments, companies file their own assessment online. These provide charterers with a quick initial guide to the suitability of the company, but they will not prevent charterers visiting an office to conduct their own audits. It is at this stage that the information provided by the self-assessment will be verified. If it appears inaccurate, it can prevent the company's ships being hired and damage their reputation.

Irrespective of how well a ship is run and managed, at some point problems will be identified. It is essential that remedial action is undertaken as soon as possible and inspectors advised immediately on completion. However, the best way to prevent excessive observations and non-conformities being issued by external parties is to ensure that internal audits and inspections are carried out diligently and properly followed up.

Internal audits help ensure important internal procedures are followed

CHAPTER 30

Surveys and Classification

Preparing for Classification Surveys

General

The shipowner should be aware of the scope of the forthcoming survey and instruct those responsible, such as the master or the superintendent, to prepare necessary arrangements. If there is any doubt, the Classification Society concerned should be consulted.

Environment in the Space to be Surveyed

The owner must provide the necessary facilities for safe completion of the survey:

- Tanks and spaces are to be safe for access, ie gas freed, ventilated and illuminated
- in preparation for survey and thickness measurements and to allow for a thorough examination, all spaces are to be cleaned including removal from surfaces of all loose accumulated corrosion scale
- spaces are to be sufficiently clean and free from water, scale, dirt, oil residues etc to reveal corrosion, deformation, fractures, damages or other structural deterioration. However, those areas of structure whose renewal has already been decided by the owner need only be cleaned and descaled to the extent necessary to determine the limits of the areas to be renewed
- sufficient illumination is to be provided to reveal corrosion, deformation, fractures, damage or other structural deterioration
- where soft or semi-hard coatings have been applied, safe access is to be provided for the surveyor to verify the effectiveness of the coating and to carry out an assessment of the conditions of internal structures, which may include spot removal of the coating. When safe access cannot be provided, the soft or semi-hard coating is to be removed
- casings, ceilings or linings, and loose insulation, where fitted, are to be removed, as required by the surveyor, for examination of plating and framing. Compositions on plating are to be examined and sounded, but need not be disturbed if found adhering satisfactorily to the plating
- in refrigerated cargo spaces, the condition of the coating behind the insulation is to be examined at representative locations. The examination may be limited to verification that the protective coating remains effective and that there are no visible structural defects. Where poor coating condition is found, the examination is to be extended as deemed necessary by the surveyor. The condition of the coating is to be reported. If indents, scratches, etc are detected during surveys of shell plating from the outside, insulations in way are to be removed, as required by the surveyor, for further examination of the plating and adjacent frames.

Access to Structures

The surveyor must be able to examine the hull structure in a safe and practical way:

For survey in cargo holds and water ballast tanks, one or more of the following means for access, acceptable to the surveyor, is to be provided:

- Permanent staging and passages through structures
- temporary staging and passages through structures
- lifts and movable platforms
- boats or rafts
- other equivalent means.

In addition, particular attention should be paid to the following guidance:

(a) Prior to entering tanks and other enclosed spaces, eg chain lockers and void spaces, the oxygen content must be tested and confirmed as safe. A responsible member of the crew should remain at the entrance to the space and if possible communication links should be established with both the

bridge and the engine room. Adequate lighting should be provided in addition to a handheld torch (flashlight).

(b) In tanks where the structure has been coated and recently deballasted, a thin slippery film may remain on the surfaces.

(c) The removal of scale can be extremely difficult. Removal of scale by hammering may cause sheet scale to fall. If the structure is heavily scaled, it may be necessary to request descaling before conducting a visual examination.

(d) Bulkhead vertical ladders should be examined to ensure that they are in good condition and rungs are not missing or loose. If holds are being entered when the hatch covers are closed, adequate lighting should be arranged.

(e) If a portable ladder is used, it should be in good condition and fitted with adjustable feet to prevent it from slipping. Two crew members should be in attendance to ensure that the base of the ladder is adequately supported during use.

(f) If an extending/articulated ladder (frame walk) is used to enable the examination of upper portions of cargo structure, it should incorporate a hydraulic locking system and a built-in safety harness. Regular maintenance and inspection of the ladder should be confirmed prior to its use.

(g) If a hydraulic arm vehicle ('cherry picker') is used to enable examination of the upper parts of the cargo hold structure, the vehicle should be operated by qualified personnel and there should be evidence that the vehicle has been properly maintained. The standing platform should be fitted with a safety harness. For vehicles with a self-levelling platform, care should be taken that the locking device is engaged after completion of manoeuvring to ensure that the platform is fixed.

(h) Staging should always be correctly supported and fitted with handrails. Planks should be free from splits and lashed down. Staging erected hastily by inexperienced personnel should be avoided.

(i) In double bottom tanks, any build-up of mud on the bottom of the tank should be removed, in particular in way of tank boundaries and suction and sounding pipes, to enable a clear assessment of the structural condition.

Preparing for Classification Surveys

Survey Equipment

The following equipment may be needed by the surveyor:

- Torches approved for use in a flammable atmosphere. A high intensity beam type is recommended for in-tank inspections. Torches are recommended to be fitted with suitable straps so that both hands may be kept free
- a hammer for use inside units, tanks, etc
- an oxygen analyser/multigas detector for verification of acceptable atmosphere prior to tank entry
- safety belts and lines where there is a risk of falling from more than 3 metres.

Survey at Sea or Anchorage

A voyage survey will require assistance from shipboard personnel. Ballasting systems must be secured at all times during tank surveys.

A communication system must be arranged between the survey party in the spaces under examination and the responsible officer on deck.

Documentation on Board

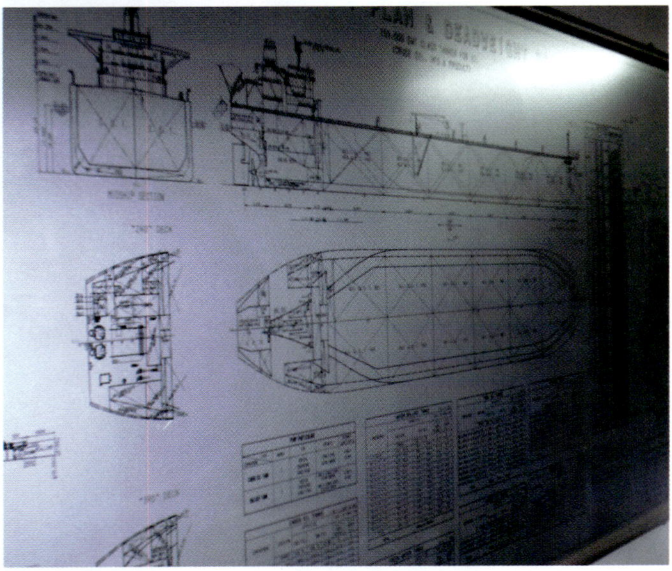

The following documentation should be readily available for the survey:

- Survey Report File: this file includes reports of surveys and thickness measurement reports
- supporting documents:
  - main structural plans of cargo holds and ballast tanks
  - previous repair history
  - cargo and ballast history
  - inspection and action taken by ship's personnel with reference to:
    - (a) structural deterioration in general
    - (b) leakages in bulkheads and piping
    - (c) condition of coating or corrosion protection, if any.

Prior to inspection, it is recommended that the documents on board the vessel be reviewed as a basis for the current survey.

Survey Planning Meeting

Proper preparation and close cooperation between the attending surveyor(s) and the owner's representatives on board prior to and during the survey are an essential part of the safe and efficient conduct of the survey. During the survey, on board safety meetings are to be held regularly.

- Prior to the commencement of any part of the Special and Intermediate Survey, a survey planning meeting is to be held between the attending surveyor(s), the owner's representative in attendance and the thickness measurement (TM) company representative, where involved, and the master of the ship or an appropriately qualified representative appointed by the master or company for the purpose of ascertaining that all the arrangements envisaged in the survey programme are in place.

- The following items should be addressed in the meeting:
  - Schedule of the vessel (ie the voyage, docking and undocking manoeuvres, periods alongside, cargo and ballast operations, etc)
  - provisions and arrangements for thickness measurements (ie access, cleaning/descaling, illumination, ventilation, personal safety)
  - extent of the thickness measurements
  - acceptance criteria (refer to the list of minimum thicknesses)
  - extent of close-up survey and thickness measurement considering the coating condition and suspect areas/areas of substantial corrosion
  - execution of thickness measurements
  - taking representative readings in general and where uneven corrosion/pitting is found
  - mapping of areas of substantial corrosion
  - communication between attending surveyor(s), the thickness measurement company operator(s) and the owner's representative(s) concerning findings.

Preparation for P&I Condition Survey

The inspection will be undertaken using a comprehensive checklist. The surveyor will need to be accompanied by a senior officer throughout the course of the inspection to ensure both his safety and access to all parts of the vessel. The checklist headings, which indicate the scope of the survey, are as follows:

1. Vessel Particulars
2. Ship's Certificates, Documents and Surveys
3. Shipboard Records, Safety and Maintenance Systems/Procedures
4. Publications and Manuals
5. Manning and Crew Competency
6. Navigation and Communication Equipment and Publications
7. Fire-Fighting and Life-Saving Equipment
8. Hull and General (All Vessels)
9. Ballast Tanks including Fore Peak and Aft Peak (All Vessels)
10. Cargo Worthiness – Dry Cargo Vessels
11. Cargo Worthiness – Refrigerated Cargo Vessels
12. Cargo Worthiness – Container Vessels
13. Cargo Worthiness – Tankers and Gas Carriers
14. Engine Room and Machinery
15. Oil Pollution Prevention
16. Accommodation and Galley Area
17. Management and/or ISM.

To minimise disruption and to ensure that the P&I surveyor can complete a full survey, it is essential that the following guidelines are adhered to:

1. Time and place of inspection of cargo spaces
   (a) It is essential that the survey is arranged at a time when the cargo holds and/or cargo tanks are free of cargo and fit for entry.

Preparation for P&I Condition Survey

(b) Adequate time must be made available, with 5 to 6 hours required for smaller vessels (up to 2,500 GT) and up to 10 hours for large bulk carriers and tankers.

(c) Daylight inspections are always preferable so as to facilitate good photography and proper inspection.

(d) Attendance while the vessel is secured alongside or in drydock is always preferable to attending at anchor so as to reduce travelling time and launch costs.

Certification and condition of LSA will be inspected

2. Preparation of access and testing arrangements to ensure cargo worthiness

   (a) At least 50% of all ballast water tanks, including DBs, side tanks, top side tanks, fore peak and aft peak, must be open, well ventilated and ready for inspection.

   (b) All DB and side ballast tanks in way of the cargo holds must be ready and available for hydrostatic pressure testing.

Some tanks will be inspected

   (c) All cargo hold bilge suctions must be clean and ready for testing.

   (d) All hatch covers (including steel pontoon and tarpaulin covers) are to be secured and ready for hose or ultrasonic testing.

3. Standard equipment tests

   The following equipment will be tested/inspected during the survey:

   (a) Bridge equipment including radars and radios, etc.

   (b) General alarm, fire bells and fire detection system.

   (c) Whistle.

   (d) Sidelights.

   (e) Launching and retrieval equipment for survival craft.

   (f) Liferaft hydrostatic releases and weak link securing arrangements.

   (g) Emergency fire pump, general fire main and associated fire-fighting equipment.

   (h) Emergency batteries/generators.

   (i) Quick closing fuel valves.

   (j) Ventilation flaps and remote stops.

   (k) Oily water separator 15 ppm indicator.

   (l) Steering gear, including emergency system and communications system.

   (m) Engine room bilge alarm (if fitted).

4. Document and record book inspection

   The following documentation and records should be up to date/valid and on board the vessel, readily available for the surveyor's inspection:

   (a) Ship's trading certificates issued by flag State authority.

   (b) ISM manuals and records (if applicable).

   (c) Last PSC inspection report.

   (d) Cargo Gear Record of Testing and Inspection.

   (e) Records of stability calculations and Stability Booklet endorsed by Administration.

(f) Medical stores inspection certificate by qualified pharmacist.

(g) Certification/last inspection of Fire-Fighting and Life-Saving Equipment.

(h) Last Class printout and survey report file.

(i) Last report on ultrasonic steel thickness testing.

(j) Minimum Safe Manning Certificate and crew's STCW 95 certification.

(k) Drug and Alcohol Policy.

(l) Magnetic Compass Deviation Card.

(m) Correction records of nautical and radio publications.

(n) Sounding Book.

(o) Master's Night Order Book.

(p) Deck and Engine Room Logbooks and Radio/GMDSS Log.

(q) Oil Record Book and Garbage Record Book.

(r) Compass Error Book and Bell Book.

(s) Safety Officer's Incident Book, Minutes of Safety Committee Meetings and records of accident reporting.

(t) Planned Maintenance Programme.

(u) Engine room and deck maintenance workbooks.

(v) Company Operating and Safety Manuals.

(w) Records of Hot Work Permit System and Entry Permit System for Enclosed Spaces.

5. Engine room equipment records

The following records should be up to date and on board the vessel, readily available for the surveyor's inspection:

(a) Records of change or cleaning of main engine lubricating oil filters.

(b) Records of testing of quick closing valves.

(c) Records of testing of remote stops.

(d) Records of megger test/insulation test of main switch board.

(e) Records of last pressure test of compressed air system.

(f) Records of overhaul of main and auxiliary engines.

(g) Records of lubricating oil analysis for main engine.

(h) Records of main engine crankshaft deflections.

Figure 30.1 - Engine Room Logbook

CHAPTER 31

Systems of Work

Safe Systems of Work

Introduction

This section suggests some control measures that may be taken to protect those who may be put at risk in some key areas on board ship. Such measures should be based on the findings of the risk assessment.

Working Aloft and Outboard

Anyone working and not standing on level ground or at deck level is working at height. Also undertaking work inside a tank, near an opening, such as a hatch, or on a fixed stairway may be regarded as working at height if there is a danger of injury if the worker fell.

Work should only be carried out at height if there is no reasonably practicable alternative to doing so. Where a reasonably practicable alternative does exist it should be adopted. Where work must be carried out at height, the employer must ensure that such work is properly planned, appropriately supervised and carried out in as safe a manner as is reasonably practicable. In this context, planning should include the carrying out of a risk assessment, which might include considering potential risks from falling objects or fragile surfaces.

Personnel working at a height may not be able to give their full attention to the job and at the same time guard themselves against falling. Proper precautions should therefore always be taken to ensure personal safety when work has to be done aloft or when working outboard. It must be remembered that the movement of a ship in a seaway and extreme weather conditions even when alongside, will add to the hazards involved in work of this type. A stage or ladder should also be utilised when work is to be done beyond normal reach.

Personnel under 18 years of age or with less than 12 months experience at sea should not work aloft unless accompanied by an experienced person or otherwise adequately supervised.

Personnel working aloft should wear a safety harness with lifeline or other attesting device at all times. A safety net should be rigged where necessary and appropriate. Additionally, where work is done overside, buoyancy garments should be worn and a lifebuoy with sufficient line attached should be kept ready for immediate use. Personnel should be under observation from a person on deck.

Other than emergency situations personnel should not work overside while the vessel is underway. If such work has to be undertaken, lifeboats or rescue boats should be ready for immediate use. Any such work should be closely monitored/watched by a responsible person.

Before work is commenced near the ship's whistle, the officer responsible should ensure that power is shut off and warning notices posted on the bridge and in the machinery spaces.

Before work is commenced on the funnel, the officer responsible should inform the duty engineer to ensure that steps are taken to reduce as far as practicable the emission of steam, harmful gases and fumes.

Before work is commenced in the vicinity of radio aerials, the officer responsible should inform the radio room or person in charge of radio equipment so that no transmissions are made

Source: 'Code of Safe Working Practices for Merchant Seamen'

while there is risk to personnel. A warning notice should be put up in the radio room.

Where work is to be done near the radar scanner, the officer responsible should inform the officer on watch so that the radar and scanner are isolated. A warning notice should be put on the set until the necessary work has been completed.

On completion of the work of the type described above, the person responsible should, where necessary, inform the appropriate person that the precautions taken are no longer required and that warning notices can be removed.

Work aloft should not be carried out in the vicinity of cargo working, unless it is essential. Care must always be taken to avoid risks to anyone working or moving below. Suitable warning notices should be displayed. Tools and stores should be sent up and lowered by line in suitable containers which should be secured in place for stowage of tools or materials not presently being used.

No one should place tools where they can be accidentally knocked down and may fall on someone below, nor should tools be carried in pockets from which they may easily fall. When working aloft, it is often best to wear a belt designed to hold essential tools securely in loops.

Tools should be handled with extra care when hands are cold and greasy and where the tools themselves are greasy.

Portable Ladders

A portable ladder should only be used where no safer means of access is reasonably practicable. It is very important that the ladder is checked regularly by a competent person.

Wooden ladders should not be painted or treated so as to hide defects and cracks. When not in use, they should be stowed safely in a dry ventilated space away from any heat source.

Portable ladders should be pitched between 60 and 75° from the horizontal, on a firm base, properly secured against slipping or shifting sideways and be so placed as to afford a clearance of at least 150 mm behind the rungs. Where practicable the ladder should extend to at least 1 metre above any upper landing place unless there are other suitable handholds.

When portable extending ladders are in use, there should be sufficient overlap between the extensions.

Personnel negotiating a ladder should use both hands, and not attempt to carry tools or equipment in their hands.

Planks should not be supported on rungs of ladders to be used as staging, nor should ladders be used horizontally for such purposes.

Working from ladders should be avoided as far as possible, but where necessary personnel must use a safety harness with lifeline secured above the work position.

Cradles and Stages

Cradles should be at least 430 mm (17 inches) wide and fitted with guard-rails or stanchions with taut ropes to a height of 1 metre (39 inches) from the floor. Toeboards add safety.

Planks and materials used for the construction of ordinary plank stages must be carefully examined to ensure adequate strength and freedom from defect.

Wooden components of staging should be stowed in a dry, ventilated space and not subjected to heat.

Source: 'Code of Safe Working Practices for Merchant Seamen'

Safe Systems of Work

Ancillary equipment, lizards, blocks and gantlines should be thoroughly examined before use.

When a stage is rigged overside, the two gantlines used in its rigging should be at least long enough to trail into the water to provide additional lifelines should the operator fall. A lifebuoy and line should still be kept ready at a close position.

Gantlines used for working aloft should not be used for any other purpose and should be kept clear of sharp edges when in use.

The anchoring points for lines, blocks and lizards must be of adequate strength and, where practicable, be permanent fixtures to the ship's structure. Integral lugs should be hammer tested. Portable rails or stanchions must not be used as anchoring points. Any anchoring points should be treated as lifting points and should be inspected/ tested.

Stages and staging which are not suspended should always be secured against movement. Hanging stages should be restricted against movement to the extent practicable.

In machinery spaces, staging and its supports should be kept clear of contact with hot surfaces and moving parts of machinery In the engine room, a crane gantry should not be used directly as a platform for cleaning or painting, but can be used as the base for a stable platform if suitable precautions are taken.

Where personnel working from a stage are required to raise or lower themselves, great care must be taken to keep movements of the stage small and closely controlled.

Bosun's Chair

When used with a gantline, the chair should be secured to it with a double sheet bend and the end seized to the standing part with adequate tail.

Hooks should not be used to secure bosun's chairs unless they are of the type which because of their special construction cannot be accidentally dislodged, and have a marked safe working load which is adequate for the purpose.

On each occasion that a bosun's chair is rigged for use, the chair, gantlines and lizards must be thoroughly examined, and renewed if there is any sign of damage, and load tested to at least four times the load they will be required to lift before a person is hoisted.

When a chair is to be used for riding topping lifts or stays, it is essential that the bow of the shackle, and not the pin, rides on the wire. The pin in any case should be seized.

When it is necessary to haul a person aloft in a bosun's chair, it should be done only by hand; a winch should not be used.

If a worker is required to lower himself while using a bosun's chair, he should first frap both parts of the gantline together with a suitable piece of line to secure the chair before making the lowering

Source: 'Code of Safe Working Practices for Merchant Seamen'

hitch. The practice of holding on with one hand and making the lowering hitch with the other is dangerous. It may be prudent to have someone standing by to tend the lines.

Scaffolding

Only scaffolding of an approved design should be used or one rigged in conformity with a generally recognised configuration. If necessary, a calculation of its strength should be carried out and recorded.

Care should be taken when assembling and dismantling the scaffold.

Great care should be taken to ensure the stability of the structure and safe access to it. If it is a mobile structure, it should be securely fixed to ensure it cannot inadvertently move while in use.

Anyone rigging or dismantling scaffolding should have received adequate training.

Measures, such as adequate safety rails etc, should be incorporated to prevent the risk of persons or objects falling off.

Care must be taken to ensure that the safe working load of the structure is not exceeded.

Note: *For further information on 'Scaffolding', refer to Chapter 43.*

Requirements for Ladders

1. *A ladder shall be positioned so as to ensure its stability during use.*
2. *(1) A suspended ladder shall be attached in a manner that*
   - *(a) Is secure;*
   - *(b) ensures it cannot be displaced; and*
   - *(c) prevents it swinging.*

   (2) Paragraphs (b) and (c) of sub-paragraph (1) do not apply to a rope ladder.
3. *(1) Portable ladders shall rest on footing that is stable, firm, of sufficient strength and of suitable size and composition safely to support the ladder so that its rungs or steps remain horizontal.*

   (2) Where, owing to the movement of the ship, it is not reasonably practicable to ensure that the rungs or steps of the portable ladder remain horizontal, all appropriate measures to ensure the stability of the portable ladder shall be taken.
4. *The feet of a portable ladder shall be prevented from slipping during use by:*
   - *(a) Securing the stiles at or near their upper or lower ends; or*
   - *(b) any anti-slip device; or*
   - *(c) any other arrangement of equivalent effectiveness.*
5. *A ladder used for access shall be long enough to protrude sufficiently above the place of landing to which it provides access, unless other measures have been taken to ensure a firm handhold.*
6. *No interlocking or extension ladder shall be used unless its sections are prevented from moving relative to each other while in use.*
7. *A mobile ladder shall be prevented from moving before it is stepped on.*
8. *A ladder shall be used in such a way that:*
   - *(a) A secure handhold and secure support are always available to the user; and*
   - *(b) the user can maintain a safe handhold when carrying a load by hand.*

Source: 'Code of Safe Working Practices for Merchant Seamen'

Safe Systems of Work

Requirements for Scaffolding

1. *Strength and stability calculations for scaffolding shall be carried out unless:*

    (a) *A note of the calculations, covering the structural arrangements contemplated, is available; or*

    (b) *the scaffolding is assembled in conformity with a generally recognised standard configuration.*

2. *Depending on the complexity of the scaffolding chosen, an assembly, use and dismantling plan shall be drawn up by a competent person. This may be in the form of a standard plan, supplemented by items relating to specific details of the scaffolding in question.*

3. *A copy of the plan, including any instructions it may contain, shall be made available for the use of the person supervising and the workers concerned in the assembly, use, dismantling or alteration of the scaffolding.*

4. *The bearing components of the scaffolding shall be prevented from slipping by:*

    (a) *Attachment to the bearing surface;*

    (b) *provision of an anti-slip device; or*

    (c) *any other arrangement of equivalent effectiveness.*

5. *The load-bearing surface of the scaffolding shall be of sufficient capacity.*

6. *The scaffolding shall be positioned to ensure its stability.*

7. *Wheeled scaffolding shall be prevented by appropriate devices from moving accidentally during work at height.*

8. *The dimensions, form and layout of scaffolding decks shall:*

    (a) *Be appropriate to the nature of the work to be performed;*

    (b) *be suitable for the loads to be carried; and*

    (c) *permit work and passage in safety.*

9. *Scaffolding decks shall be assembled in such a way that their components are prevented from moving inadvertently during work at height.*

10. *There shall be no dangerous gaps between the scaffolding deck components and the vertical collective safeguards to prevent falls.*

11. *When any part of a scaffold is not available for use, including during the assembly, dismantling or alteration of scaffolding, it shall be:*

    (a) *Marked with general warning signs in accordance with the Merchant Shipping and Fishing Vessels (Safety Signs and Signals) Regulations, 2001; and*

    (b) *suitably delineated by physical means preventing access to the danger zone.*

Wheeled scaffolding shall be prevented by appropriate devices from moving accidentally during work at height

Source: 'Code of Safe Working Practices for Merchant Seamen'

12. *Scaffolding shall be assembled, dismantled or significantly altered only under the supervision of a competent person and by workers who have received appropriate and specific training which shall include:*
    - (a) *Understanding the plan for the assembly, dismantling or alteration of the scaffolding;*
    - (b) *safety during the assembly, dismantling or alteration of the scaffolding;*
    - (c) *measures to prevent the risk of persons or objects falling;*
    - (d) *safety measures in the event of changing weather conditions which could adversely affect the safety of the scaffolding;*
    - (e) *permissible loads; and*
    - (f) *any other risks which the assembly, dismantling or alteration of the scaffolding may entail.*

Note: For further information on 'Scaffolding', refer to Chapter 43 - 'Hull Monitoring and Inspection'.

Requirements for Rope Access and Positioning Techniques

1. *A rope access or positioning technique shall only be used if:*
    - (a) *It involves a system comprising at least two separately anchored ropes, of which one ("the working rope") is used as a means of access, egress and support and the other is the safety rope;*
    - (b) *the worker is provided with and uses a suitable harness and is connected by it to the working rope and the safety rope;*
    - (c) *the working rope is equipped with safe means of ascent and descent and has a self-locking system to prevent the worker falling should he lose control of his movements;*
    - (d) *the safety rope is equipped with a mobile fall prevention system which is connected to and travels with the worker;*
    - (e) *the tools and other accessories to be used by the worker are secured to the worker's harness or seat or by some other suitable means; and*
    - (f) *appropriate training, including training in rescue procedures, has been provided to the worker or workers concerned.*
2. *A rope access or positioning technique may involve a system comprising a single rope where:*
    - (a) *The risk assessment has demonstrated that the use of a second line would entail higher risk to persons; and*
    - (b) *appropriate measures have been taken to ensure safety.*

Note: For further information on 'Rope Access', refer to Chapter 43 on 'Hull Monitoring and Inspection'.

Source: 'Code of Safe Working Practices for Merchant Seamen'

Safety Management Systems (SMS)

Introduction

A Safety Management System (SMS) is a structured, documented system developed to enhance the safe operation of vessels, prevent human injury or loss of life, and avoid damage to the environment. With an SMS, shipowners and operators are encouraged to resolve safety problems before casualties or incidents occur ("self-regulate"), rather than simply comply with regulations imposed from outside, which usually means waiting for notification of defects before taking corrective action.

The ISM Code contains specific functional requirements for an SMS. It must contain:

- Safety and environmental protection policy
- instructions and procedures to ensure safe operations and environmental protection in compliance with relevant international and flag State legislation
- defined levels of authority and lines of communication between and amongst shore and shipboard personnel
- procedures for reporting accidents and non-conformities with the SMS and the Code
- procedures to prepare for and respond to emergencies; and
- procedures for internal audits and management reviews.

It should be specific to a type of vessel, and may be kept in manual form, a copy of which must be kept aboard each vessel.

Although this is a short list of only six required components, each one represents a significant undertaking by a Company. Some of the components can be drawn from existing documents, such as the vessel's pollution response plan. Other components may require creation of new policies and procedures reflecting the aims of the Code to integrate shore-side and shipboard responsibilities for safety and to systemise procedures for lines of communication and reporting.

Background

International safety management standards were developed in the early 1990s in response to a number of serious marine casualties whose cause was identified as human error or management failure and which occurred despite improvements in engineering and technology designed to prevent them. One of the most serious was the capsize in March 1987 of the passenger/car ferry *'Herald of Free Enterprise'* off the Belgian coast, killing 193 people. The British investigation described the ferry management's failures as *"the disease of sloppiness"*.

In the aftermath of that disaster, the International Maritime Organization (IMO) began developing guidelines for safe ship management, focusing at first on roll-on, roll-off ferries such as the *'Herald of Free Enterprise'*. In May 1991, work began on what became the International Safety Management (ISM) Code, whose stated purpose is to provide an international standard for the safe management and operation of ships and for pollution prevention. In 1993, the IMO decided to make the ISM Code mandatory and, in May 1994, IMO members, including the United States, adopted the ISM Code as Chapter IX of SOLAS. Chapter IX of SOLAS came into force on 1st July 1998. On that date, the ISM Code became mandatory for the following vessels on international voyages: passenger ships, high-speed craft (passenger and cargo) of

500 gross tons or more, tankers, and cargo carriers. For other cargo ships, the Code came into force on 1st July 2002.

Main Elements

A Safety Management System aims to create a "culture of safety" throughout an organisation by:

- Documenting a vessel owner's operational policy, chain of authority, and operational and emergency procedures
- specifying the responsibilities of the owner or operator, managers and masters
- outlining procedures for management review, internal audits and correction of non-conformities (failure to adhere to procedures or regulations).

Procedures are compiled in a safety management manual and a copy is kept on board the vessel. A person or persons is designated in writing to monitor the SMS, and managers conduct regular audits to ensure that employees follow the procedures. Checklists are supplied for critical areas. When deficiencies are noted or an accident or non-conformity occurs, corrective action is taken until the problem is resolved, and the problem is documented from start to finish.

System Safety and SMS

Use of SMS can be generally interpreted as applying a quality management approach to control safety risks. Similar to other management functions, safety management requires planning, organising, communicating and providing direction. A well-structured SMS provides a systematic, explicit and comprehensive process for managing risks. This process includes goal setting, planning, documentation and regular evaluation of performance to ensure that goals are being met. SMS includes several key system safety principles as shown below:

Management commitment to safety - Because the attitudes and actions of management can significantly influence the entire staff, it is critical that these leaders commit to the success of an SMS implementation.

Proactive identification of hazards - Early identification and reporting of hazards can save a significant amount of time and resources in the future.

Actions taken to manage risks - A system must be in place to determine logical approaches to counteract known risks to safe operation.

Evaluation of safety actions - An ongoing evaluation of the impacts of risk management actions is necessary to determine whether further remedial activities are required.

SMS takes a proactive approach to safety management. It goes beyond prescriptive audits and checklist-based inspections to develop procedures and indicators that anticipate safety risks.

SMS spreads responsibility for safe operations throughout all levels and segments of the organisation. This increase in the number of people watching for safety issues makes it less likely that a hazard will go undetected and possibly lead to an accident.

Each SMS implementation will have its own customised set of layers that coordinate to create the safety culture of SMS. Each slice has holes that symbolise the potential for a safety hazard to go unnoticed, because the layer does not deal with that type of hazard or due to human error.

However, when these layers are unified by SMS principles, it becomes less likely that a hazard makes it through all the levels without being identified and mitigated.

Put simply, effective SMS are using risk and quality management methods to achieve the safety goals. In addition, SMS also provides the organisational framework to establish and foster the development of a positive corporate safety culture.

The implementation of an SMS gives the organisation's management a structured set of tools to meet their responsibilities for safety defined by the regulator.

Without doubt, a Company that gives only lip service to the Code will suffer because non-conformities with its SMS will be evident to anyone who inspects the documentation required therein, and it is certain that the

Safety Management Systems (SMS)

SMS will be inspected after a casualty by government investigators, underwriters and courts. On the other hand, the Code is of great value to prudent owners and operators as it provides a single system incorporating all aspects of safety policies and procedures. The internal audit and management review elements of the SMS allow such a Company to inspect, recognise and correct problems before they cause casualties.

Initially, the cost of implementation and training may appear to be high, but should be offset by savings resulting from fewer and less serious casualties. Additionally, the costs of compliance with the SMS will appear small in the event of a casualty, when the Company is able to use reports and audits mandated by its SMS to demonstrate affirmatively that it has taken an aggressive stance with regard to safety.

Certification of Safety Management System

Once the SMS is in place, it must be certified by means of an outside audit by the flag State or those entities as may be delegated this duty, consisting primarily of Classification Societies. In practice, some companies may rely on the societies for development of their SMS, or adaptation of it from a standard form developed by the society. Assuming that the audit is successful, the Company will be issued a Document of Compliance (DOC), valid for 60 months, unless an annually required verification audit or other inspection reveals a major non-conformity. Once the Company has a DOC, each of its vessels receives a 60-month Safety Management Certificate (SMC) upon satisfactory completion of its safety management audit. If the Company's DOC is revoked, its vessels' SMCs will automatically become invalid.

It should be recognised that the certification process takes a significant amount of time. First, a Company-specific SMS must be developed and implemented.

Following implementation, the Company then must be successful in obtaining its DOC following an outside audit by the designated certification authority.

Thereafter, the Company's vessels are expected to operate in accordance with the policies and procedures set forth in the SMS for a period of three months before being permitted to seek individual SMCs. The designated certification authority is expected to ensure by its audits that the requirements of the Code are being met by every vessel under review.

Planned Maintenance Systems (PMS)

Overview

The Planned Maintenance System (PMS) is a system where all the equipment maintenance related job details are recorded, monitored and next due dates are calculated to give the user a better understanding of the equipment maintenance, breakdown details and health of the equipment. All maintenance related KPI are generated through the system. It allows shipowners and/or operators to schedule maintenance according to manufacturers' and Class/Classification Society requirements. The maintenance, primarily supervised by the onboard personnel, is then credited towards inspections required by periodic surveys. The planning and scheduling of the maintenance,

Planned Maintenance Systems (PMS)

as well as its documentation, must be made according to a system that is approved by the Classification Society. This is now mandatory under the ISM Code.

An annual survey is needed to review the status of equipment. A special survey every five years verifies that the PMS programme is functioning. The PMS surveys will be harmonised with other periodic surveys.

Purpose

The purpose of the Planned Maintenance System is:

- To ensure that all maintenance is carried out with adequate intervals, and in accordance with the schedule in the PMS
- to maintain and keep all engines, machinery and technical components in good working order at all times, to avoid stoppages and to maintain charter party speed and consumption requirements
- to avoid interruption and oversights by covering all of the work
- to make clear demarcation between onboard and shore maintenance work.

Requirements for Planned Maintenance Systems

- Inventory content, ie items/systems included in the maintenance programme
- maintenance time intervals, ie time intervals at which the maintenance jobs are to take place
- maintenance instructions, ie maintenance procedures to be followed
- maintenance documentation and history, ie documents specifying maintenance jobs carried out and their results
- reference documentation, ie performance results and measurements taken at certain intervals for trend investigations from delivery stage
- document flow chart, ie chart showing flow and filling of maintenance documents as planning cards, job cards, etc
- signing instructions, ie who signs documents for verification of maintenance work carried out. Documentation on maintenance of the category "Classification Surveys" carried out on items/systems covered by the Rules is to be signed by the chief engineer. With computerised systems, the access to updating the maintenance documentation and the maintenance programme should be possible for the chief engineer only.

The description and documentation of the PMS are to be in the English language. The maintenance instructions and maintenance history on job cards may, however, be in the language most practical and suitable for the maintenance crew. In such cases, the maintenance history and job cards are to be given a summary in English in the maintenance documentation. For ships trading in specific areas, eg ferries, planned maintenance systems using languages other than English may be accepted. This arrangement is automatically cancelled in case of change of trade.

The maintenance system should produce documentation that is useful as a basis for the annual survey of the PMS.

Computerised systems should include backup systems that are updated at regular intervals.

Need of PMS

Managing a fleet of vessels has become even more complex in recent years. Managers need to maximise uptime and ensure good condition of ships while minimising inspection and maintenance efforts, reducing spare parts and repair costs, and complying with all rules and regulations. Experienced ship managers know that good organisation is key: this includes having the right information available when required, keeping track of important processes that have been started, and avoiding spending the whole day only troubleshooting. Modern ship management software increases transparency and productivity, and reduces external costs incurred in ship management and operations.

Planned maintenance software provides a flexible yet solid management system for intelligent scheduling of planned maintenance activities, including:

- Scheduling workloads relating to assets, properties or scheduled services
- reviewing on a daily, weekly, monthly or annual frequency forthcoming activities, including planned maintenance, Occupational Health and Safety (OH&S)

Planned Maintenance Systems (PMS)

schedules, contract renewal and warranty expiry dates

- producing asset reliability and performance reports that provide a comprehensive log for analysis purposes
- automatically highlighting ageing equipment and expiring warranties to allow for maintenance planning
- achieving optimal levels of asset reliability and performance.

How to Use?

The PMS should be monitored and updated by the chief engineer, chief officer and second engineer, with each providing details of all maintenance and inspections completed.

Every month, the completed exports of the PMS should be approved by the chief engineer and the chief officer before being sent to the ship's technical superintendent.

The technical superintendent will ensure that the PMS is performing its role properly and he will respond to any comments from the vessel with appropriate guidance and instructions.

The maintenance interval for every item in the PMS can be adjusted as required. In such cases, the ship should agree each change with the technical superintendent.

How Planned Maintenance Systems Affect Class Surveys

In order to maintain Class, a vessel is required to meet all the conditions imposed by Class. Some of the accepted approaches of satisfying machinery Class inspections are:

- Tear Down Inspection: Scheduled intervals dictate when a machine is to be opened for inspection by the Class Surveyor
- Planned Maintenance Systems: A Class-approved PMS allows a certified chief engineer to carry out inspection on specified pieces of equipment without requiring a surveyor to be present. The records of these activities, along with all maintenance records illustrating that the PMS is being followed correctly and that machinery is operating satisfactorily, are to be evaluated by Class annually
- Condition-Based Maintenance Systems: This approach works as the gathering and trending of various operational parameters and diagnostic results in order to determine the condition of the equipment or the machinery. When the condition of specified pieces of equipment or machinery is shown to have been maintained within designated parameters, credit for survey can be given without requiring the machine to be opened for inspection. The data and records are normally evaluated on a yearly basis.

Maintenance and Ship Management

The primary function of a ship management Company is to provide shipowners with a safely operated ship, while at the same time ensuring optimum cost effective performance. Emphasis will be given to shipboard maintenance by properly trained crew supported by experienced shore-based managers.

Technical costs
Maintenance and repairs cannot be conducted on board without spare parts. The high cost of certain spares is generally viewed as an unnecessary expense, but high freight costs, particularly air freight, can result in even higher costs if a ship is delayed while awaiting spare parts.

Cost of tools
In the same way that maintenance and repairs cannot be carried out without spare parts, completing the work requires the correct tools. On a ship, there is no excuse for lack of availability of low cost tools that are in everyday use, eg hammers or spanners.

The chief engineer can generally only authorise emergency repairs by shore repairers as all other repairs will have to be authorised by the ship's technical manager. Similarly, the chief engineer does not decide the planned maintenance schedule as this is prepared by the shore office.

However, in times of cost savings, a reduction in the amount or frequency of maintenance is the main target area for short-term cost savings.

CHAPTER 32

Permit to Work

Permit to Work

Permit to Work Systems

There are many types of operation on board ship where the routine actions of one person may inadvertently endanger another or when a series of action steps need to be taken to ensure the safety of those engaged in a specific operation. In all instances it is necessary, before the work is done, to identify the hazards and then to ensure that they are eliminated or effectively controlled. Ultimate responsibility rests with the employer to see that this is done.

The permit to work system consists of an organised and predefined safety procedure. A permit to work does not in itself make the job safe, but contributes to measures for safe working.

The particular circumstances of individual ships will determine when permit to work systems should be used. In using a permit to work, the following principles apply:

(a) The permit should be relevant and as accurate as possible. It should state the location and details of the work to be done, the nature and results of any preliminary tests undertaken, the measures undertaken to make the job safe and the safeguards that need to be taken during the operation.

(b) The permit should specify the period of its validity (which should not exceed 24 hours) and any time limits applicable to the work which it authorises.

(c) Only the work specified on the permit should be undertaken.

(d) Before signing the permit, the authorising officer should ensure that all measures specified as necessary have in fact been taken.

(e) The authorising officer retains responsibility for the work until he has either cancelled the permit or formally transferred it to another authorised person who should be made fully conversant with the situation. Anyone who takes over, either as a matter of routine or in an emergency, from the authorising officer, should sign the permit to indicate transfer of full responsibility.

(f) The person responsible for carrying out the specified work should countersign the permit to indicate his understanding of the safety precautions to be observed.

(g) On completion of the work, that person should notify the responsible officer and get the permit cancelled.

(h) The person carrying out the specified work should not be the same person as the authorising officer.

Sanction to Test Systems

A sanction to test shall be issued in an identical manner to a permit to work. A sanction to test shall not be issued on any apparatus on which a permit to work is still in force, or on which another sanction to test is in force.

A sanction to test is to be issued where testing operations require the removal of the circuit main earth.

PTW systems should be clear and simple to understand
Source: 'Code of Safe Working Practices for Merchant Seamen'

Note: *Maintenance and repair cannot be carried out under a sanction to test.*

A permit to work is generally classed under the following categories:

- *Work in Unmanned Machinery Spaces*
- *Entry into Enclosed or Confined Spaces*
- *Machinery or Equipment*
- *Hot Work*
- *Working Aloft/Overside*
- *General Electrical (Under 1000 Volts)*
- *Electrical High Voltage (Over 1,000 Volts).*

Risk Assessment

Introduction

Many routine operations are hazardous and must be risk assessed

Employers are required to ensure the health and safety of workers and other persons so far as possible, by the application of certain principles, including the evaluation of unavoidable risks and the taking of action to reduce them.

Specifically, employers are required to make a suitable and sufficient assessment of the risks to health and safety of workers arising in the normal course of their activities or duties, for the purpose of identifying:

(a) groups of workers at particular risk in the performance of their duties; and

(b) the measures to be taken to comply with the employer's duties under the Regulations;

The assessment should extend to others on board ship who may be affected by the acts or omissions of the employer.

Every employer and every self-employed person on board ship is required to inform the Company of any relevant risks to health and safety arising from the conduct of their business.

Employers must ensure that measures are taken to ensure an improvement in the health and safety of workers and other persons in respect of those risks identified by the assessment.

Employers must review the assessment when there is reason to believe that it is no longer valid, and make any necessary changes.

Workers must be informed of any significant findings of the assessment and measures for their protection, and of any subsequent revisions made.

The Company is also required to ensure that anyone working on the ship, whether or not they are directly employed by the Company, is aware of the findings of the Company's risk assessment and of the measures taken for their protection.

This section explains the principles of risk assessment in relation to occupational health and safety and provides some guidance on how the assessment and control of risks may be approached.

Regulation of occupational health and safety on board ship is of course not new. Existing safety measures may already provide a high level of safety for workers. For example, well-established procedures, inspections by safety officers and the use of "permits to work" which control safety conditions, will contribute to the identification of hazards and measures for safe working.

However, what is new is the explicit requirement in regulation for employers to adopt the risk assessment approach to

Source: 'Code of Safe Working Practices for Merchant Seamen'

Risk Assessment

occupational health and safety. This means that all work activities should be considered from a risk assessment standpoint.

Employers may adapt existing Safety Management Systems to meet the risk assessment principles taking into account the nature of their operations and the type and extent of the hazards and risks to workers.

Key Terms

Key terms used in connection with risk assessment are:

a) A ***hazard*** *is a source of potential harm or damage or a situation with potential for harm or damage;*

b) ***risk*** *has two elements:*

- *the likelihood that a hazard may occur;*
- *the consequences of the hazardous event.*

Principles of Risk Assessment

A "risk assessment" is intended to be a careful examination of what, in the nature of operations, could cause harm, so that decisions can be made as to whether enough precautions have been taken or whether more should be done to prevent harm. The aim is to minimise accidents and ill health on board ship.

The assessment should first establish the hazards that are present at the place of work and then identify the significant risks arising out of the work activity. The assessment should include consideration of the existing precautions to control the risk, such as permits to work, restricted access and use of warning signs or personal protective equipment.

Any risk assessment must address risks to the health and safety of workers. Advice on assessment in relation to the use of personal protective equipment, the use of equipment and manual handling operations are given in Chapters 4, 19 and 20. In addition, specific areas of work involving significant risk, and recommended measures to address that risk, are covered in more detail in Sections 3 and 4 of the Code.

Risk Assessment in Practice

There are no fixed rules about how risk assessment should be undertaken. The assessment will depend on the type of ship, the nature of operations and the type and extent of the hazards and risks. The intention is that the process should be simple, but meaningful. The following sections give advice on good practice.

What should be Assessed?

The assessment should cover the risks arising from the work activities of workers on the ship. The assessment is not expected to cover risks which are not reasonably foreseeable.

Employers are advised to record the significant findings of their risk assessment. Risks which are found to be trivial, and where no further precautions are required, need not be recorded.

Who has to Carry Out the Assessment?

In all cases, individual employers have responsibility for assessing the risks to their workers and other persons who may be affected by their activities. The Company will be responsible for coordinating the risk assessments covering everyone on the ship, including workers directly employed by itself, taking account of the other employers' assessments.

The process of risk assessment should be carried out by suitably experienced personnel, using specialist advice if appropriate.

How thorough should the Assessment be?

A suitable and sufficient assessment should be made of the risks to the health and safety of workers arising in the normal course of their duties. This requirement to assess risk relates only to risks which arise directly from the work activity being undertaken and which have the potential to harm the person(s) actually undertaking that work, or those who may be directly affected by that work. The requirement to assess risk does not extend to any consequential peril to the ship resulting from the particular work activity, nor to any external hazards which may imperil the ship, either of which may cause harm to those on board or to others. These aspects are covered by other regulations.

The assessment of risks must be 'suitable and sufficient'. The process need not be overcomplicated. This means that the amount of effort that is put into an assessment should depend on the level of risks identified and whether those risks are already controlled by satisfactory precautions or procedures to ensure that they are as low as reasonably practicable.

Source: 'Code of Safe Working Practices for Merchant Seamen'

When to Assess?

Risk assessment should be seen as a continuous process. In practice, the risks in the workplace should be assessed before work begins on any task for which no valid risk assessment exists. An assessment must be reviewed and updated as necessary, to ensure that it reflects any significant changes of equipment or procedure.

Elements of Risk Assessment

The main elements of the risk assessment process are:

(a) Classify work activities;

(b) identify hazards and personnel at risk;

(c) identify risk controls;

(d) estimate the risk;

(e) decide the tolerability of the risks;

(f) prepare risk control action plan (if necessary);

(g) review adequacy of action plan;

(h) ensure risk assessment and controls are effective and up to date.

Maintenance

General

Courtesy of Captain HJ Schaefer

No maintenance work or repair which might affect the supply of water to the fire main or sprinkler system should be started without the prior permission of the master and chief engineer.

No alarm system should be isolated without the permission of the master and chief engineer.

Means of access to fire-fighting equipment, emergency escape routes and watertight doors should never be obstructed.

Safety guards on machinery or equipment should only be removed when the machinery is not operating. If removal is essential for maintenance or examination of the equipment, the following precautions should be taken:

- *Removal should be authorised by a responsible person, and only a competent person should carry out the work or examination;*
- *there should be adequate clear space and lighting for the work to be done;*
- *anyone working close to the machinery should be told what the risks are and instructed in safe systems of work and precautions to take;*
- *a warning notice should be conspicuously posted.*

Solvents used for cleaning can be toxic, and should always be used in accordance with the manufacturers' instructions. The area should be well-ventilated, and in confined spaces, smoking should be prohibited.

Floor Plates and Handrails

Lifting handles should be used when a floor plate is removed or replaced. When lifting handles are not provided, the plate should be levered up with a suitable tool and a chock inserted before lifting. On no account should fingers be used to prise up the edges.

Whenever floor plates or handrails are removed, warning notices should be posted, the openings should be effectively fenced or guarded and the area well illuminated.

Maintenance of Machinery

Before machinery is serviced or repaired, measures should be taken to prevent it being turned on or

Source: 'Code of Safe Working Practices for Merchant Seamen'

Maintenance

permitted only in circumstances where no danger exists or where it is impracticable for the machinery to be stopped. Close-fitting clothing should be worn and long hair should be covered. The officer in charge should consider whether it is necessary in the interests of safety for a second person to be in close attendance while the work is being carried out.

Heavy parts of dismantled machinery temporarily put aside should be firmly secured against movement in a seaway and, as far as practicable, be clear of walkways. Sharp projections on them should be covered when reasonably practicable.

started automatically or from a remote control system.

- Electrically-operated machinery should be isolated from the power supply
- steam-operated machinery should have both steam and exhaust valves securely closed and, where possible, the valves locked or tied shut or some other means employed to indicate that the valves should not be opened. The same care is required when dealing with heated water under pressure as is required when working on steam-operated machinery or pipework
- in all cases, warning notices should be posted at or near the controls giving warning that the machinery concerned is not to be used.

Where valves or filter covers have to be removed or similar operations have to be performed on pressurised systems, that part of the system should be isolated by closing the appropriate valves. Drain cocks should be opened to ensure that pressure is off the system.

When joints of pipes, fittings, etc are being broken, the fastenings should not be completely removed until the joint has been broken and it has been established that no pressure remains within.

Before a section of the steam pipe system is opened to the steam supply, all drains should be opened. Steam should be admitted very slowly and the drains kept open until all the water has been expelled.

Maintenance or repairs to, or immediately adjacent to, moving machinery should be

Spare gear, tools and other equipment or material should never be left lying around, especially near to stabiliser or steering gear rams and switchboards.

A marlin spike, steel rod, or other suitable device should be used to align holes in machinery being reassembled or mounted; fingers should never be used.

When guards or other safety devices have been removed from machinery, they should be replaced immediately after the work is completed and before the machinery or equipment is tested.

An approved safety lamp should always be used for illuminating spaces where oil or oil vapour is present. Vapour should be dispersed by ventilation before work is done.

Hydraulic and Pneumatic Equipment

Before repairs to or maintenance of hydraulic and pneumatic equipment are undertaken any load should be removed, or if this is not practical, adequately supported by other means. All pressure in the system should be released. The part being worked upon should be isolated from the power source and a warning notice displayed by the isolating valve, which should be locked.

Precautions should be taken against the possibility of residual pressure being released when unions or joints are broken.

Absolute cleanliness is essential to the proper and safe operation of hydraulic and pneumatic systems; the working area and tools, as well as

Source: 'Code of Safe Working Practices for Merchant Seamen'

the system and its components, should be kept clean during servicing work. Care should also be taken to ensure that replacement units are clean and free from any contamination, especially fluid passages.

Only replacement components which comply with manufacturers' recommendations should be used. Any renewed or replacement item of equipment should be properly inspected or tested before being put into operation within the system.

Since vapours from hydraulic fluid may be flammable, naked lights should be kept away from hydraulic equipment being tested or serviced.

A jet of hydraulic fluid under pressure should never be allowed to spray onto unprotected skin. Any hydraulic fluid spilt on the skin should be thoroughly washed off.

Electrical Equipment

The risks of electric shock are much greater on board ship than they are normally ashore because wetness, high humidity and high temperature (including sweating) reduce the contact resistance of the body. In those conditions, severe and even fatal shocks may be caused at voltages as low as 60V. It should also be borne in mind that cuts and abrasions significantly reduce skin resistance.

A notice of instructions on the treatment of electric shock should be posted in every place containing electrical equipment and switchgear. Immediate on the spot treatment of an unconscious patient is essential.

Before any work is done on electrical equipment, fuses should be removed or circuit breakers opened to ensure that all related circuits are dead. If possible, switches and circuit breakers should be locked open or, alternatively a 'not to be closed' notice attached. Where a fuse has been removed, it should be retained by the person working on the equipment until the job is finished. A check should be made that any interlocks or other safety devices are operative. Additional precautions are necessary to ensure safety when work is to be undertaken on high voltage equipment (designed to operate at a nominal system voltage in excess of IkV). The work should be carried out by or under the direct supervision of, a competent person with sufficient technical knowledge and a 'permit to work' system should be operated.

Some parts of certain types of equipment may remain live even when the equipment is switched off. Power should always be cut off at the mains.

Flammable materials should never be left or stored near switchboards.

Work on or near live equipment should be avoided if possible but when it is essential for the safety of the ship or for testing purposes, the following precautions should be taken:

- *A second person, who should be competent in the treatment of electric shock, should be continually in attendance*
- *the working position adopted should be safe and secure to avoid accidental contact with the live parts. Insulated gloves should be worn where practicable*
- *contact with the deck, particularly if it is wet, should be avoided. Footwear may give inadequate insulation if it is damp or has metal studs or rivets. The use of a dry insulating mat at all times is recommended*
- *contact with bare metal should be avoided. A hand-to-hand shock is especially dangerous. To minimise the risk of a second contact should the working hand accidentally touch a live part, one hand should be kept in a trouser pocket whenever practicable*
- *wrist watches, metal identity bracelets and rings should be removed. They provide low resistance contacts with the skin. Metal fittings on clothing or footwear are also dangerous.*

Meter probes should have only minimum amounts of metal exposed and insulation of both probes should be in good condition. Care should be taken that the probes do not short circuit adjacent connections. When measuring voltages that are greater than 250V, the probe should be attached and removed with the circuit dead.

Source: 'Code of Safe Working Practices for Merchant Seamen'

Personal Protective Equipment

Personal protective equipment must be used only when risks cannot be avoided or reduced to an acceptable level by safe working practices, that cause no health risk to any worker. This is because personal protective equipment does nothing to reduce the hazard, and can only protect the person wearing it, leaving others vulnerable.

It should be noted that the use of personal protective equipment may in itself cause a hazard - for example, through reduced field of vision, loss of dexterity or agility.

Employer Duties

It is the responsibility of the employer to ensure that workers are provided with suitable personal protective equipment where it is needed.

As a general rule, personal protective equipment should be supplied at no cost to the worker.

Employers should assess the equipment required to ensure that it is suitable and effective for the task in question, and meets the appropriate standards of design and manufacture.

Suitable equipment should:

(a) Be appropriate for the risks involved, and the task being performed without itself leading to any significant increased risk.

(b) Fit the worker correctly after any necessary adjustment.

(c) Take account of ergonomic requirements and the worker's state of health.

(d) Be compatible with any other equipment the worker has to use at the same time, so that it continues to be effective against the risk.

The employer is also required to ensure that personal protective equipment is regularly checked and maintained or serviced. Records should be maintained of servicing and any repair required and carried out.

All workers who may be required to use protective equipment must be properly trained in its use.

Defective or ineffective protective equipment provides no defence. It is therefore essential that the correct items of equipment are selected and that they are properly maintained at all times. The manufacturer's instructions should be kept safe with the relevant apparatus and if necessary referred to before use and when maintenance is carried out. Personal protective equipment should be kept clean and should be disinfected as and when necessary for health reasons.

A competent person should inspect each item of protective equipment at regular intervals and in all cases before and after use. All inspections should be recorded. Equipment should always be properly stowed in a safe place after use.

Worker Duties

Workers must wear the protective equipment or clothing supplied when they are carrying out a task for which it is provided, and follow appropriate instructions for use.

Source: 'Code of Safe Working Practices for Merchant Seamen'

Personal protective equipment should always be checked by the wearer each time before use. Workers should comply with the training they have received in the use of protective items, and follow the manufacturer's instructions for use.

Types of Equipment

Overalls, gloves and suitable footwear are the proper working dress for most work about ship but these may not give adequate protection against particular hazards in particular jobs.

Personal protective equipment can be classified as follows:

Type	Examples
Head protection	Safety helmets, bump caps, hair protection
Hearing protection	Ear muffs, ear plugs
Face and eye protection	Goggles and spectacles, facial shields
Respiratory protective equipment	Dust masks, respirators, breathing apparatus
Hand and foot protection	Gloves, safety boots and shoes
Body protection	Safety suits, safety belts, harnesses, aprons, high visibility clothing
Protection against drowning	Lifejackets, buoyancy aids and lifebuoys
Protection against hypothermia	Immersion suits and anti-exposure suits

Hot Work

Introduction

Based on the findings of the risk assessment, appropriate control measures should be put into place to protect those who may be affected. This section highlights some areas which may require attention in respect of hot work.

General

Welding and flame-cutting elsewhere than in the workshop should generally be the subject of a 'permit to work'.

Operators should be competent in the process, familiar with the equipment to be used and instructed where special precautions need to be taken.

Where portable lights are needed to provide adequate illumination, they should be clamped or otherwise secured in position, not handheld, with leads kept clear of the working area.

Harmful fumes can be produced during these operations from galvanising paint and other protective materials. Oxygen in the atmosphere can be depleted when using gas cutting equipment and noxious gases may be produced when welding or cutting. Special care should therefore be taken when welding and flame-cutting in enclosed spaces to provide adequate ventilation. The effectiveness of the ventilation should be checked at intervals while the work is in progress, and if appropriate local exhaust ventilation should be considered. In confined spaces, breathing apparatus may be required.

Personal Protective Equipment

Personal protective equipment complying with the relevant Standard specifications or their equivalent must be worn by the operator and as appropriate by those assisting with the operation to protect them from particles of hot metal and slag, and their eyes and skin from ultra-violet and heat radiation.

The operator should normally wear:

(a) Welding shields or welding goggles with appropriate shade of filter lens to EN 169.

Source: 'Code of Safe Working Practices for Merchant Seamen'

Hot Work

Goggles are only recommended for gas welding and flame cutting;

(a) leather gauntlets;

(b) leather apron (in appropriate circumstances);

(b) long-sleeved natural fibre boiler suit or other approved protective clothing.

Clothing should be free of grease and oil and other flammable substances.

Pre-Use Equipment Check

Welding and flame-cutting equipment should be inspected before use by a competent person to ensure that it is in a serviceable condition.

In cold weather, moisture trapped in the equipment may freeze and, for example, cause valves to malfunction. It is recommended that equipment is thawed out with hot water and cloths, never with naked flames.

Precautions Against Fire and Explosion

Before welding, flame-cutting or other hot work is begun, a check should be made that there are no combustible solids, liquids or gases, at, below or adjacent to the area of work, which might be ignited by heat or sparks from the work. Such work should never be undertaken on surfaces covered with grease, oil or other flammable or combustible materials. Where necessary, combustible materials and dunnage should be moved to a safe distance before commencing operations. Such places should also be free of materials which could release flammable substances, for example if disturbed.

When welding is to be done in the vicinity of open hatches, suitable screens should be erected to prevent sparks dropping down hatchways or hold ventilators.

Port holes and other openings through which sparks may fall should be closed where practicable.

Where work is being done close to or at bulkheads, decks or deckheads, the far side of the divisions should be checked for materials and substances which may ignite, and for cables, pipelines or other services which may be affected by the heat.

Cargo tanks, fuel tanks, cargo holds, pipelines, pumps and other spaces that have contained flammable substances should be certified as being free of flammable gases before any repair work is commenced. The testing should include, as appropriate, the testing of adjacent spaces, double bottoms, cofferdams, etc. Further tests should be carried out at regular intervals and before hot work is recommenced following any suspension of the work. When preparing tankers and similar ships, all tanks, cargo pumps and pipelines should be thoroughly cleaned and particular care taken with the draining and cleaning of pipelines that cannot be directly flushed using the ship pumps.

Welding and flame-cutting operations should be properly supervised and kept under regular observation. Suitable fire extinguishers should be kept at hand ready for use during the operation. A person with a suitable extinguisher should also be stationed to keep watch on areas not visible to the welder which may be affected.

In view of the risk of delayed fires resulting from the use of burning or welding apparatus, frequent checks should be made for at least two hours after the work has stopped.

Electric Welding Equipment

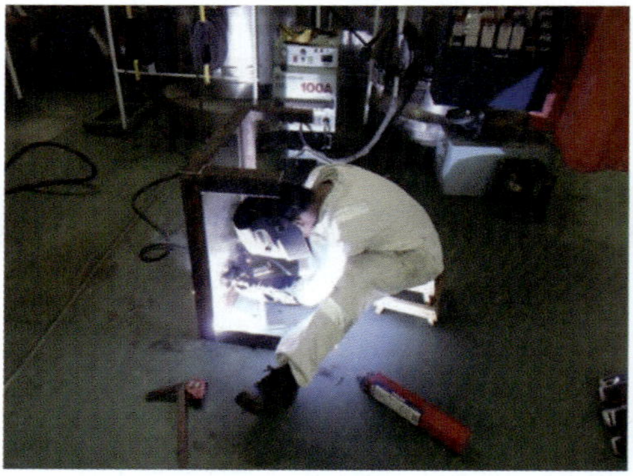

Figure 32.1 - Welding in E/R workshop

In order to minimise personal harm from electric shock, electric welding power sources for shipboard use should have a direct current (DC) output not exceeding 70V with a minimum ripple.

When DC equipment is not available, then AC output power sources may be used providing they have an integral voltage limiting device to ensure that the idling voltage (the voltage between electrode and work piece before an arc is struck between them) does not exceed 25 V rms. The proper function of the device (which may be affected by dust or humidity) should be checked each time a welding set is used. Some voltage limiting devices are affected by their angle of tilt from the vertical, so it is important that they are

Source: 'Code of Safe Working Practices for Merchant Seamen'

mounted and used in the position specified by the manufacturers. This requirement can be affected by adverse sea conditions.

A 'go-and-return' system utilising two cables from the welding set should be adopted; the welding return cable should be firmly clamped to the workpiece.

Earthing of the workpiece is used to provide protection against internal insulation failure of the welding transformer, by keeping the workpiece at or near earth potential until the protective device (eg a fuse) operates to cut off the mains supply. Where the welding circuit is not adequately insulated from the earthed referenced mains supply, the workpiece should be earthed. The 'return' cable of the welding set and each workpiece should be separately earthed to the ship's structure. The use of a single cable with hull return is not recommended. The workpiece earthing conductor should be robust enough to withstand possible mechanical damage and should be connected to the workpiece and a suitable earth terminal by bolted lugs or secure screw clamps.

***Note:** Some manufacturers may recommend earthing as one of their measures to reduce the electrical interference. This is not a safety related measure, but the manufacturer's advice should be followed.*

If an alternative method of protecting against welding transformer insulation failure is used, the hazards caused by stray welding currents can be avoided by not earthing the workpiece or the welding output circuit. Self-contained engine-driven welding sets, and welding power sources which comply with the required standards do not need the workpiece to be earthed. It should be noted, however, that other equipment connected to the workpiece may require earthing for safe operation.

To avoid voltage drop in transmission, the lead and return cables should be of the minimum length practicable for the job and of an appropriate cross-section.

Cables should be inspected before use; if the insulation is impaired or conductivity reduced, they should not be used.

Cable connectors should be fully insulated when connected, and so designed and installed that current carrying parts are adequately recessed when disconnected.

Electrode holders should be fully insulated so that no live part of the holder is exposed to touch, and, where practicable, should be fitted with guards to prevent accidental contact with live electrodes and as protection from sparks and splashes of weld metal.

A local switching arrangement or other suitable means should be provided for rapidly cutting off current from the electrode should the operator get into difficulties and also for isolating the holder when electrodes are changed.

The direct current output from power sources should not exceed 70 volts open circuit. The ripple on the output from the power source should not exceed the values of the table below. The ripple magnitudes are expressed as percentages of the DC, and the ripple peak is that with the same polarity as the DC.

Ripple Frequency Hz	*50/60*	*300*	*1,200*	*2,400*
Max. RMS O/C voltage ripple, (%)	*5*	*6*	*8*	*10*
Max. peak O/C voltage ripple, (%)	*10*	*12*	*16*	*20*

The conditions in the table above are normally met by DC generators incorporating commutators and by rectifier power sources having a 3 phase bridge rectifier operating from a 3 phase 50/60 Hz supply. Rectifier power sources should not be operated from a power supply of less than 50 Hz.

Should it be necessary to use a power source with a DC output having a ripple magnitude in excess of those stated in the table, for example a single phase rectifier power source, then a voltage limiting device should be incorporated in the power source to ensure that the idling voltage does not exceed 42V.

Precautions to be Taken During Electric Arc Welding

In addition to protective clothing, the welding operator should wear non-conducting safety footwear. Clothing should be kept as dry as possible as some protection against electric shock; it is particularly important that gloves should be dry as wet leather is a good conductor.

An assistant should be in continuous attendance during welding operations, who should be alert to the risk of accidental shock to the welder, and ready to cut off power instantly, raise the alarm

Source: 'Code of Safe Working Practices for Merchant Seamen'

Hot Work

and provide artificial respiration without delay. It may be desirable to have a second assistant if the work is to be carried out in difficult conditions.

Where persons other than the operator are likely to be exposed to harmful radiation or sparks from electric arc welding, they should be protected by screens or other effective means.

In restricted spaces, where the operator may be in close contact with the ship's structure or is likely to make contact in the course of ordinary movements, protection should be provided by dry insulating mats or boards.

There are increased risks of electric shock to the operator if welding is done in hot or humid conditions; body sweat and damp clothing greatly reduce body resistance. Under such conditions, the operation should be deferred until such time that an adequate level of safety can be achieved.

In no circumstances should a welder work while standing in water or with any part of their body immersed.

The electrode holder should be isolated from the current supply before a used electrode is removed and before a new electrode is inserted. This precaution is necessary because some electrode coatings have extremely low resistance. Even a flux coating which is normally insulating can become damp from sweating hands and thus potentially dangerous.

When the welding operation is completed or temporarily suspended, the electrode should be removed from the holder.

Hot electrode ends should be ejected into a suitable container; they should not be handled with bare hands.

Spare electrodes should be kept dry in their container until required for use.

Gas Welding and Cutting

While this section deals almost exclusively with oxygen and acetylene, other fuel gases may be used and similar precautions should be taken.

The pressure of oxygen used for welding should always be high enough to prevent acetylene flowing back into the oxygen line.

Acetylene should not be used for welding at a pressure exceeding I atmosphere gauge as it is liable to explode, even in the absence of air, when under excessive pressure.

Non-return valves should be fitted adjacent to the torch in the oxygen and acetylene supply lines.

Flame arrestors should be provided in the oxygen and acetylene supply lines and will usually be

Source: 'Code of Safe Working Practices for Merchant Seamen'

fitted at the low pressure side of regulators, although they may be duplicated at the torch.

Should a backfire occur (ie the flame returns into the blowpipe and continues burning in the neck or mixing chamber) the recommended first action is to close the oxygen valve on the blowpipe - to prevent internal burning - followed immediately by shutting off the fuel gas at the blowpipe valve. When the cause of the backfire has been discovered, the fault rectified and the blowpipe cooled down, the blowpipe may be re-lit.

If there is a flashback into the hose and equipment, or a hose fire or explosion, or a fire at the regulator connections or gas supply outlet points, the first action should be to isolate the oxygen and fuel gas supplies at the cylinder valves or gas supply outlet points - but only if this can be done safely. Further action should follow in accordance with the vessel's fire drill requirements.

A watch should be kept on acetylene cylinders to ensure they are not becoming hot. If they are, this could be sign of acetylene decomposition and there is an increased risk of explosion. The cylinder stop valve should be closed immediately which may limit or reduce the decomposition but is unlikely to stop it. Emergency action, such as evacuating the area and prolonged cooling by immersion or with copious amounts of water will still be required. Consideration should be given to jettisoning the cylinder overboard although movement of the cylinder can promote rapid decomposition, and cooling should continue while it is being moved. Any acetylene cylinder suspected of overheating should be approached with extreme caution because an impact could set off an internal ignition which might cause an explosion.

Only acetylene cylinders of approximately equal pressures should be coupled.

In fixed installations, manifolds should be clearly marked with the gas they contain.

Manifold hose connections including inlet and outlet connections should be such that the hose cannot be interchanged between fuel gases and oxygen manifolds and headers.

Only those hoses specially designed for welding and cutting operations should be used to connect any oxy-acetylene blowpipe to gas outlets.

Any length of hose in which a flashback has occurred should be discarded.

The connections between hose and blowpipe, and between hoses should be securely fixed with fittings which comply with Standard EN 1256.

Hoses should be arranged so that they are not likely to become kinked or tangled or be tripped over, cut or otherwise damaged by moving objects or falling metal slag, sparks, etc; a sudden jerk or pull on the hose is liable to pull the blowpipe out of the operator's hands or cause a cylinder to fall or a hose connection to fail. Hoses in passageways should be covered to avoid them becoming a tripping hazard.

Soapy water should only be used for testing leaks in hoses. If there are leaks which cannot easily be stopped, the gas supply should be isolated and the leaking components taken out of service, replaced or repaired. If the leak is at a cylinder valve or pressure regulator ("bull-nose") connection, the cylinder should be removed to a safe place in the open air. If it is a fuel-gas cylinder, it should be taken well clear of any source of ignition.

Excessive force should never be used on cylinder valve spindles or hexagon nuts of regulator connections in an attempt to stop a leak. Neither are sealing tape nor other jointing materials recommended for use in an attempt to prevent leaks between metal-metal surfaces that are designed to be gastight. With an oxygen cylinder this could result in initiation of a metal-oxygen fire.

Blowpipes should be lit with a special friction igniter, stationary pilot flame or other safe means.

Should a blowpipe-tip opening become clogged, it should be cleaned only with the tools especially designed for that purpose.

When a blowpipe is to be changed the gases should be shut off at the pressure-reducing regulators.

To prevent a build-up of dangerous concentrations of gas or fumes during a temporary stoppage or after completion of the work, supply valves on gas cylinders and gas mains should be securely closed and blowpipes, hoses and moveable pipes should be removed to lockers that open on to the open deck.

Oxygen should never be used to ventilate, cool or blow dust off clothing.

Source: 'Code of Safe Working Practices for Merchant Seamen'

Hot Work

Hot Work: Lighting Up and Shutting Down Procedures

Figure 32.2 - Arc welding

These procedures are appropriate for oxy-fuel gas equipment and, with little modification, also for air-aspirated blowpipes.

Lighting Up

1. *Ensure that the pre-use equipment checks have been made.*
2. *Check that the outlets of adjustable pressure regulators are closed, ie that the pressure-adjusting screw of the regulator is in the fully unwound (anti-clockwise) position.*
3. *Check that the blowpipe valves are closed.*
4. *Slowly open the cylinder valves (or gas supply point isolation valves) - to avoid sudden pressurisation of any equipment.*
5. *Adjust pressure regulators to the correct outlet pressures. Or, check that the pressures in distribution pipework are suitable for the equipment and process.*
6. *Open the oxygen valve at the blowpipe and allow the flow of oxygen to purge* air out of oxygen hose and equipment. If necessary, reset the pressure regulator to ensure correct working oxygen pressure.*
7. *Close the oxygen valve at the blowpipe.*
8. *Open the fuel gas valve at the blowpipe and allow the gas flow to purge* air or oxygen from the fuel gas hose and equipment. If necessary, reset the pressure regulator to ensure correct working fuel gas pressure.*
9. *Light the fuel gas immediately, and preferably with a spark lighter.*
10. *Open the oxygen valve at the blowpipe and adjust it and the fuel gas valve to give the correct flame setting.*

Shutting Down

1. *Close the fuel gas valve at the blowpipe.*
2. *Immediately close the oxygen valve at the blowpipe.*
3. † *Close the cylinder valves or gas supply point isolation valves for both oxygen and fuel gas.*
4. *Close the outlets of adjustable pressure regulators by winding out the pressure-adjusting screws.*
5. *Open both blowpipe valves to vent the pressure in the equipment.*
6. *Close the blowpipe valves.*

* Purging is important. It removes flammable gas mixtures from the hoses and equipment which could result in explosions and fires when the blowpipe is first lit. It should be carried out in a well-ventilated area, and it may take from several seconds to a minute or more depending on the length of the hose and gas flow rates.

† Step 3 is not necessary when the equipment is to be used again in the immediate future.

Source: 'Code of Safe Working Practices for Merchant Seamen'

Earthing of Arc Welding Systems Transformer Casing

Earthed	*Class I Appliance*
Not Earthed	*Class II Appliance*

Transformer Secondary

Earthed

This is an obsolete type of equipment and should be taken out of service. Failure of the weld return connection might not be noticed, and damage to other earthed metallic paths could result.

Isolated

The absence of a weld return conductor will prevent welding being carried out. However, a failure of isolation within the welding set could cause the work item to become live. For this reason, the workpiece should be earthed.

Isolated with double or reinforced insulation

This is the most recent standard to which equipment is being built. Because of the strengthened insulation, the workpiece need not be earthed. Furthermore, to prevent the possibility of stray weld return currents in the supply system earth conductors, it is recommended that the workpiece is not earthed. Such welding power sources may be identified by the additional symbol if made to the relevant parts of BS 638 (ie Parts 1, 2 or 3) and complying with the requirements of British Standard Code of Practice 7418:1991, or they will be marked with the Standards numbers EN 50.060, EN 60.974 or IEC974.

Hot Work: Hoses and Connections/Assemblies

Hoses

Rubber hoses complying with Standard EN 559 are recommended for use in gas welding and cutting processes, which are often carried out in aggressive working environments. Hoses satisfying these standards are reinforced with an outer protective cover designed to be resistant to hot surfaces, molten slag or sparks, and made with linings that resist the action of hydrocarbons (for LPG hose), acetone or dimethyl formamide (for acetylene hoses) and ignition in an atmosphere of oxygen (for all services). Burst pressure is 60 bar g and maximum working pressure 20 bar g.

Hoses meeting the requirements of BS 3212 or equivalent are recommended for LPG vapour-phase applications other than welding or cutting. Hose made of thermoplastics materials is not generally suitable for welding and cutting, because it does not have the same resistance to hot surfaces or hot particles as reinforced rubber hose.

Connections

Hose connections (comprising hose nipples and "bull-nose" hose connections) comply with EN 1256, ISO 3253 or equivalent. Thread sizes specified in these standards are based on Whitworth dimensions which are generally used in this field in many countries. Right-hand threads are used for oxygen and non-combustible gases; left-hand threads are used for fuel gases, with the hexagon nuts on their union connections notched to aid identification.

Hose connections may also be made with a quick-action coupling – a male probe fitted to the end of the hose and a female connector with a self-sealing valve usually fitted to a fixed piece of equipment or gas supply outlet point. The probe is pushed into the female fitting where it locks in position and automatically opens the internal valve. Connections of this type are simple and quick to operate and there is no need to use a spanner to tighten any nuts.

Problems are that the male probe may become damaged (eg from being dragged along the ground or over-use) and cause the coupling to leak, and there is a possibility of connecting the hose to the wrong gas outlet. Both should be avoided if couplings comply with Standard EN 561 or with ISO 7289. These require hard material of construction to be used for the probes, and their design dimensions are intended to prevent interchangeability between oxygen and fuel gas connections.

Hose Assemblies

Hose lengths are usually supplied in the UK as pre-assembled units complete with connection fittings crimped to the ends of the hose. Hose and hose nipple dimensions are matched by the supplier to ensure a good fit. The recommended Standard for hose assemblies is EN 1256, which specifies requirements for leak tightness and resistance to axial loading. Worm drive or similar clips are not recommended for fastening hoses.

Hot Work in Hazardous Areas

Hot work generally refers to the use of open fires and flames, power tools, hot riveting, grinding, welding, soldering, cutting and any work that can involve heat or sparks with the potential for hazards. For the purposes of this section, which is focused on hazardous areas, the most appropriate definition may be found in ISGOTT:

> *"Work involving sources of ignition or temperatures sufficiently high to cause the ignition of a flammable gas mixture. This includes any work requiring the use of welding, burning or soldering equipment, blow torches, some power driven tools, portable electrical equipment which is not intrinsically safe or contained within an approved explosion-proof housing, and internal combustion engines."*

ISGOTT defines hazardous (or dangerous) areas as follows:

> *"Dangerous or hazardous areas are locations on board or within the terminal where an explosive atmosphere could be present...*
>
> *An area on a tanker which, for the purposes of the installation and use of electrical equipment, is regarded as dangerous."*
>
> *Source: ISGOTT 5th Edition*

While this definition is specific to tankers, it applies equally to other vessel types and can be assumed to include any cargo tanks or holds, bunker tanks, fuel lines or those spaces adjacent to or in direct proximity with non-gas safe areas. Such spaces can be expected to include cargo tanks, ballast tanks, void spaces, bunker tanks, double bottoms and pump rooms.

Generally, and explicitly for tankers, any work undertaken outside a space designated for hot work should be strictly controlled under the ship's Safety Management System (SMS) using a permit to work (PTW). Even hot work within a designated space, normally a specified area within the engine room, should be risk assessed and all work permitted must be clearly defined before any work can take place.

It is preferable to remove the equipment to complete any hot work in the designated area.

Most ports will restrict or even prohibit hot work on board when within their limits and will require authorisation to be obtained first. Hot work should never be carried out while at a tanker terminal without explicit approval from the relevant port authority.

The port authorities should be provided with notification of the intended work as early as possible so that they may assess the request and implement any necessary precautions and arrangements. This may include notifying fire authorities, arranging safety inspections of the work area and raising any concerns.

Whenever possible, when work is required on pipelines or other structures, it is recommended that they are removed by cold work and lines blanked before taking the equipment to the designated area. However, if hot work is being considered outside the designated space, it should:

- Be approved, essential and considered justified by either the master or the safety officer
- be fully risk assessed to ensure it can be safely completed
- follow a permit to work system
- follow a written plan agreed by all connected responsible staff
- be conducted under the responsibility of an officer not involved in the work
- be fully prepared and isolated until all risk is removed
- incorporate all necessary fire precautions, including extinguishing equipment and a fire watch for any adjacent spaces
- comply with international guidance, national law and all applicable health and safety regulations.

Under no circumstances should hot work be undertaken in a hazardous area until it has been made safe. Where this includes the potential presence of a flammable atmosphere (hydrocarbon vapours) within that space, adjacent spaces or the atmosphere around the space, the atmosphere must be proven to be safe. All other possible combustible materials, liquid or solid, should be removed and isolated.

On tankers, hot work should only be undertaken in ballast and not while loaded during cargo operations, cleaning or tank atmosphere changes. Dry bulk cargoes such as coal and grain can produce atmospheres that present particular fire risks, so ships must adhere to similarly strict safety regulations.

A safety meeting should be held to carefully review the intended work plan and safety precautions. It should be chaired by the master and include all those with safety responsibilities related to the work. Some sources of reference, eg the ICS Tanker Safety Guides (International Chamber of Shipping) require that a description of the work and proposed safety procedures are sent to the ship's operator for their consent. Where this is required, it should be specified in the SMS and strictly adhered to.

The written statement of work designates work supervision to one officer and the safety precautions to another. This is to be clearly communicated to all those involved.

Before work is started, the area must be prepared and proved to be completely safe. The PTW and written work plan should include a fire watch, which will comprise sufficiently trained crew members to ensure that the following is safely monitored:

- The work being undertaken, including the potential for fumes or oxygen depletion which may adversely affect those undertaking the work
- regular atmosphere testing and recording of the work space and adjacent areas
- potential heat transfer into adjacent areas which may present a hazard for, eg:
  - Hydraulic lines
  - electrical cables
  - cargo and oil residues
  - paint on surfaces.

Any hot work to be undertaken in cargo tanks should follow the guidelines in ISGOTT section 9.4.4.2, notably including the removal of any sediment, sludge or scale that could produce flammable vapour. Inert gas (IG) lines should be purged and cargo lines either similarly inerted or filled with water. Adjacent tanks, including diagonally, should be made safe by either gas freeing, emptying and purging to not more than 2% hydrocarbon by volume, or if necessary and structurally safe, by filling with water.

Hot Work in Hazardous Areas

Equipment used for welding and burning should be carefully inspected before use to ensure that:

- It is in good condition and the cable insulation is completely intact
- all electrical connections are in a gas free space
- the wiring will not overheat through overloading
- it is correctly earthed.

While this section provides general information, it is essential that the ship's SMS is followed and relevant industry guidance adhered to.

Hot Work Habitats

Hot work habitats, or isolation chambers, are more commonly employed in the offshore industry, ie on oil installations and FPSOs, than on board traditional ships. They provide a safe area for hot work (eg welding, cutting, grinding, etc) by creating a temporary shelter and using a constant inflow of breathable atmosphere to produce a positive pressure that is sufficient to stop any ingress of external air. This prevents any explosive gases or hydrocarbons from entering the work area and so reduces the danger of explosion. When used to control the atmosphere for welding, the inflow of air helps purge the habitat of by-products from the work process.

Courtesy of Safehouse Habitats (Scotland) Ltd

Figure 32.3 - Hot work habitat in use on FPSO 'Bonga' offshore Nigeria

Positive pressure inside the chamber is typically around 0.05 kPa above atmospheric pressure, making it virtually undetectable to those inside.

The habitats are generally constructed of lightweight flame-retardant panels, normally joined by zips and/or sealed with velcro. This allows flexibility in their size and shape, enabling use in many different locations. In many cases, the habitats will be supported by a scaffold frame which prevents it collapsing in the event of a break in the air flow from the supply.

Reproduced with permission of Safehouse Habitats (Scotland) Ltd

Access doors are usually of aluminium construction with a window to permit external monitoring of the work.

CHAPTER 33

Enclosed Space Entry

Entry into Enclosed Spaces

An officer will be presented with many dangerous, challenging and nerve-wracking jobs on board ship. None of them can so easily result in fatal consequences as the apparently simple act of entering an enclosed space. Substantial guidance is available on the task of entering an enclosed space, and you will find a summary in this section. However, Olsen & Olsen's book *'Fresh Air'* poses the first and last question you should ask yourself when preparing to enter an enclosed space: "Does the space contain fresh air of 20.9% O_2?"

Careful planning is required for all enclosed space entry operations

Worldwide marine accident and fatality statistics often report that the primary cause of loss of life on board is unsafe enclosed space entry.

Remember: at least 20.9% O_2 is required at all times in enclosed spaces.

What Classifies a Space as an Enclosed Space?

The IMO defines 'enclosed space' as a space that has any of the following characteristics:

- Limited openings for entry and exit
- unfavourable natural ventilation
- not designed for continuous worker occupancy.

On a ship, enclosed spaces include:

Fuel Tanks	Ballast Tanks
Freshwater Tanks	Cargo Tanks
Cargo Holds	Stability Tanks
Chain Lockers	Void Spaces
Cofferdams	Duct Keels
Pump Rooms	Sewage Tanks
Crankcases	Equipment Spaces
Battery Lockers	Ventilation Trunking
Cargo Hold Stairways	Store Rooms/Paint Lockers

Table 33.1 - Enclosed spaces

Why are Enclosed Spaces Entered?

The main reasons include:

- Maintenance and repair work
- cargo cleaning operations
- inspections and surveys.

The type of hazard in an enclosed space will depend on the type of space and the nature of the substances that are or have been present in the space. Hazards include:

- Poor access, poor lighting and obstructions in a confined space
- oxygen-deficient atmosphere
- toxic atmosphere
- flammable atmosphere
- problems effecting a speedy rescue.

Poor Access, Poor Lighting and Obstructions in a Confined Space

Tank manhole covers may be located in easily accessible places on deck, but may be situated in locations that are hard to access, such as under engine room deck plates. Access covers may also be obstructed by pipework or machinery.

Consideration must, therefore, be given to how the access cover will be removed and how it will subsequently be replaced. Personnel entering an enclosed space will need a safe means of access. The options for rescuing an incapacitated crew member must also be planned thoroughly.

If the means of access within an enclosed space is via a fixed vertical ladder, its condition should be checked before use. Corrosion within tanks can cause considerable deterioration at the securing points of ladder mountings and these should be checked.

Cargo residues, oil or rust scale within an enclosed space greatly increase the potential for slips, trips and falls. Attention should be paid to residues on access ladders and internal walkways and platforms.

Depending on the nature of the enclosed space, the work to be conducted may also be considered as work at height.

Intrinsically-safe portable lighting will be needed at the access points and within the enclosed space to ensure that adequate lighting is available in all work areas.

Oxygen-Deficient Atmosphere

Any atmosphere containing less than 20.8% oxygen by volume should not be entered.

An oxygen-deficient atmosphere can occur:

- In an enclosed space, such as a cargo tank or hold, where oxygen-depleting or self-heating cargoes are being carried or have previously been carried
- as a result of the rusting process in tanks, particularly ballast tanks
- in circumstances where work within an enclosed space, such as burning, welding or painting, is being or has recently been performed
- in circumstances where a fire-extinguishing agent, such as CO_2, has been released into a cargo tank, hold or engine room
- where fumigation has been conducted.

Toxic Atmosphere

Toxins are measured in parts per million (ppm). Under no circumstances should anyone enter a confined space exceeding the specified limits.

A toxic atmosphere can pose serious hazards to the health of personnel on board ship. Toxic gases may be inhaled or absorbed through contact with the skin or by ingestion.

A toxic atmosphere may be present:

- In a cargo tank or hold where toxic substances are being or have been carried as cargo. This will be most evident on chemical and oil tankers, but may also be applicable on general cargo ships and bulk carriers carrying cargoes such as grain. Disturbing cargo residues (eg puddles on the tank bottom) may result in the release of toxic gases
- in tanks where toxic substances have previously been carried but where the tanks have remained unused for some time. In such circumstances, the disturbance of rust or scale may release toxic gases
- in tanks that have previously contained crude oil or its products; hydrocarbon gases may be present
- in spaces adjacent to tanks and holds. Special consideration should be given to all pump rooms, cofferdams and void spaces adjacent to or connected to cargo tanks and holds
- in holds or other spaces where hazardous cargoes are carried in packaged form as there may be leakage
- in the presence of water as, while some substances may not be inherently toxic, they may release toxic gases when mixed with water
- where inert gas systems that contain hazardous trace components are used
- after certain types of work within enclosed spaces, including grit blasting, painting, cleaning or hot work. The chemicals used or the interaction between the substances used and the tank coatings or residues within the space may release toxic gases.

Entry into Enclosed Spaces

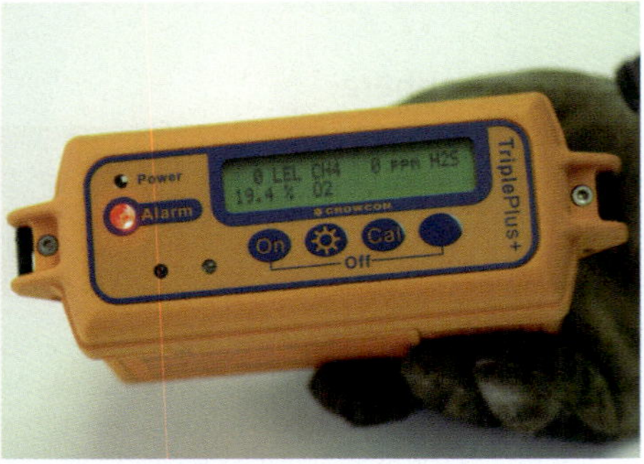

Courtesy of Crowcon

Figure 33.1 - Gas detector showing 0% LEL, 0 ppm H_2S and 19.4% O_2. While there is 0% LEL, the O_2 level is less than 20.8% and it is therefore unsafe to enter. (Note: this O_2 reading was achieved by exhaling on the sensor.)

Flammable Atmosphere

A space with an atmosphere with more than 1% of the 'lower flammable limit' (LFL) or 'lower explosive limit' (LEL) on a combustible gas indicator should not be entered.

Problems Effecting a Speedy Rescue

Confined or enclosed spaces by their nature are spaces that are not easily accessed when wearing the typical PPE required for tank entry. The problems increase in an emergency situation when wearing breathing apparatus and carrying a lifeline and perhaps a stretcher or resuscitator. Careful planning is required and the correct rescue materials must be available at the entrance. Items to consider include:

- Radio reception blind spots
- Means of communication between the tank entry team, standby man and navigation bridge or CCR
- Minimum of two items of rescue equipment consisting of BA sets, lifeline, torches, radio, stretcher, resuscitator and rescue winch
- In the event of an emergency, can time be saved by making a public announcement for the emergency team to proceed straight to the tank entry and coordinate from there, bringing material from the Emergency Headquarters as required.

Note: These difficulties emphasise the need for realistic training exercises covering rescue from an enclosed space.

Training and Drills for Enclosed Space Entry

Crew must be provided with training and drills for confined space rescues, to ensure they are familiar with the actions to be taken and the rescue equipment available (including breathing apparatus) in the event of a confined space emergency.

Masters and officers responsible for the management of enclosed space entry operations must be provided with training in the fundamentals of enclosed spaces, the associated dangers and the precautions to be taken prior to, during and on completion of enclosed space entry. Particular emphasis should be placed on potential hazards such as depleted oxygen, toxic and flammable atmospheres, and the testing equipment that is in use on board.

Drills simulating the rescue of a crew member from an enclosed space should be conducted every two months (amendment to SOLAS 111/19 on 1st January 2015). Such drills should also be used for simulation of tank entry procedures where there is no actual emergency so that personnel become familiarised with the correct methodology and process (see Chapter 39, Shipboard Drills).

Enclosed Space Entry Methodology

The methodology should be clearly defined in the company's SMS and should identify the process for assessing the risks of enclosed space entry control measures available, enclosed space entry precautions and contingency procedures.

The methodology should also emphasise that:

- Enclosed space entry is conducted where there is no other alternative
- all personnel required to enter enclosed spaces or provide assistance in normal or emergency situations are provided with adequate and appropriate levels of training
- all additional requirements and precautions are taken for specific cargoes and vessel types. For example, entry procedures for confined spaces adjacent to loaded tanks on double hull tankers require additional precautions and a two stage entry procedure

- all necessary steps are taken to thoroughly ventilate the enclosed space by all available means
- the atmosphere of the enclosed space is thoroughly tested, at all levels, with appropriate calibrated equipment, to ascertain the oxygen content and potential toxic or flammable atmospheres
- access to enclosed spaces is suitable for safe entry and for safe exit during normal operations and in emergency situations where rescue plans may be put into action
- routine drills are conducted on board for normal enclosed space entry tasks so that personnel are familiar with the equipment, methodology and rescue scenarios.

Isolations

Image courtesy of MCA COSWP

If the confined space to be entered is a cargo tank, fuel oil tank, ballast tank or other compartment where a substance may be inadvertently pumped into the space, appropriate mechanical isolations should be put in place. These may include the securing of pumps and the securing or blanking of valves. In addition, notices should be posted at all relevant control stations (cargo or ballast panels), and the bridge and PTW coordinator should be informed. Any mechanical isolation in place should be clearly noted on the PTW.

It may be necessary to electrically isolate equipment prior to entry into a space. All electrical isolations should be suitably marked and the bridge and PTW coordinator advised. Any electrical isolation should be clearly noted on the PTW.

Isolation of a confined space is a process where the space is removed from service by one or more of the following:

- **Locking out electrical sources, preferably at disconnect switches remote from the equipment**
- **blanking and bleeding pneumatic and hydraulic lines**
- **disconnecting mechanical linkages on shaft-driven equipment where possible, and**
- **securing mechanical moving parts within confined spaces with latches, chains, chocks, blocks or other devices.**

Appropriate notices, which clearly specify the space and the requirements agreed upon for confined space entry, should be displayed in prominent locations such as the bridge, cargo control room, engine control room, etc.

Ventilation

Courtesy of MCA COSWP

Prior to entry into any confined space, suitable natural or mechanical ventilation must take place, the extent of which will depend on the nature of the cargoes, substances and any residues in the space.

Entry into Enclosed Spaces

Ventilation by a blower, eductor or fan may be necessary to remove harmful gases and vapours from a confined space. There are several methods for ventilating a confined space. The method and equipment chosen will depend on the size of the confined space openings, the gases to be diluted (eg are they flammable?), and the source of makeup air.

Under certain conditions where flammable gases or vapours have displaced the oxygen level but are too rich to burn, forced air ventilation may dilute them until they are within the explosive range. If inert gases (eg carbon dioxide, nitrogen) are used in the confined space, the space should be well ventilated and retested before a worker may enter.

A common method of ventilation utilises a large hose, one end attached to a fan and the other lowered into a manhole or opening. For example, a manhole would have the ventilating hose run to the bottom to dilute or displace all harmful gases and vapours. The air intake should be placed in an area that will draw in fresh air only. Ventilation should be continuous where possible, because in many confined spaces the hazardous atmosphere will form again when the flow of air is stopped.

Deballasting a tank does not guarantee a safe atmosphere. Testing and a means of ventilation is still required.

Testing the Atmosphere

Measuring devices for testing toxic, flammable and oxygen-deficient atmospheres should be provided on board all vessels where there is the potential for such hazards to exist.

Figure 33.2 - GX-2009 Multi-Gas Detector

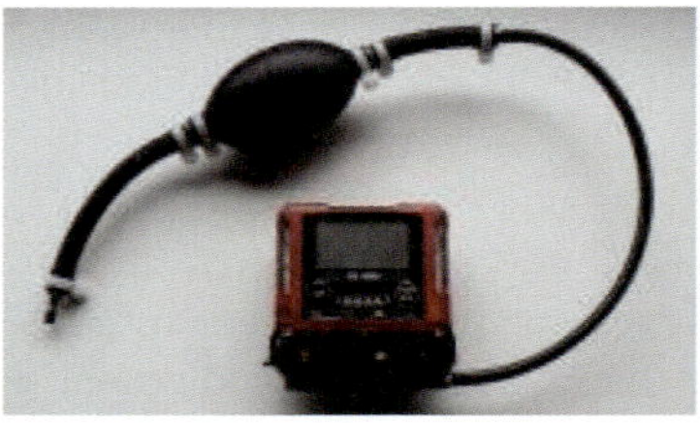

Figure 33.3 - GX-2009 Multi-Gas Detector with hand aspirator

The UK's MCA strongly advises that all ships over 24 metres in length should carry an oxygen meter on board at all times.

- All testing equipment should be in good working order, regularly serviced and calibrated in accordance with the manufacturer's instructions
- understand what conditions your testing equipment is designed to operate in
- personal monitors are not to be used for testing the atmosphere. They are proximity alarms and are not designed for atmospheric testing
- testing of the atmosphere should be conducted at as many levels of the confined space as is practicable. It should be remembered that the gases within the confined space may be heavier or lighter than air and so pockets of gas may be present
- any mechanical ventilation should be stopped during the testing process to ensure that an accurate reading of the confined space atmosphere can be obtained
- testing of the atmosphere should be conducted prior to entry and at regular intervals during the entry. If operations are suspended for any reason, testing should be conducted again before re-entry
- personnel should avoid entering the space to perform testing. If this cannot be avoided, breathing apparatus must be worn and all rescue equipment and personnel must be in place
- if there is deterioration in the atmosphere, all personnel must leave the space immediately

- in circumstances where a confined space has previously been tested and found safe, testing should still be conducted before any re-entry
- no personnel should ever assume that the atmosphere within a confined space is safe
- if safe levels are not recorded, personnel should refrain from entering the confined space until further ventilation and subsequent testing can be conducted.

Oxygen limits for entry should be greater than 20.8%, and less than 1% of the lower flammable limit (LFL). Readings for toxic gases or vapours should be below occupational exposure limits.

Testing should include all areas of the enclosed space

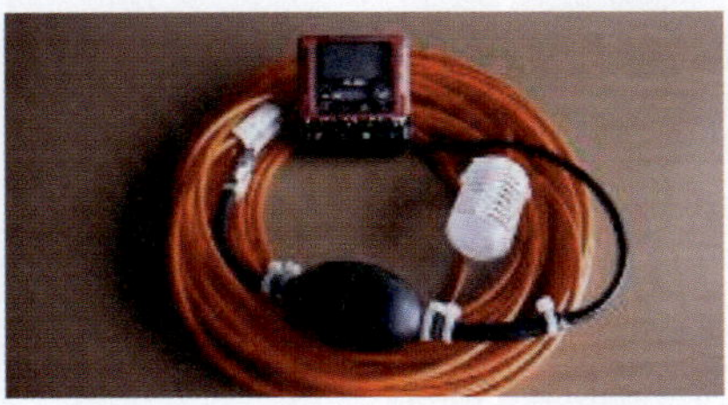

Figure 33.4 - GX-2009 Multi-Gas Detector with hand aspirated sample draw and probe for remote testing

A Classification Surveyor should never be considered to be a competent person even if he is equipped with his own personal testing equipment.

Never trust your senses to determine whether the air in a confined space is safe! You cannot see or smell many toxic gases and vapours, nor can you determine the level of oxygen present.

Testing for Oxygen Deficiency

A combustible gas indicator cannot be used to detect oxygen deficiency.

A steady reading of at least 20.8% oxygen by volume on an oxygen content meter should be obtained before entry is permitted.

Testing for Flammable Gases and Vapours

A combustible gas indicator (sometimes called an explosimeter) detects the amount of flammable gas or vapour in the air. An instrument capable of providing an accurate reading at low concentrations should be used to determine whether the atmosphere is safe for entry.

Combustible gas detectors are calibrated on a standard gas. When testing for other gases and vapours, reference should be made to the calibration curves supplied with the instrument.

In deciding whether the atmosphere is safe to work in, a 'nil' reading on a suitably sensitive combustible gas indicator is desirable but, where the readings have been steady for some time, up to 1% of the lower flammable limit may be accepted, eg for hydrocarbons in conjunction with an oxygen reading of at least 20.8% by volume.

Testing for Toxic Gases

The presence of certain gases and vapours on chemical tankers and gas carriers is detected by fixed or portable gas or vapour detection equipment. The readings obtained by this equipment should be compared with the occupational exposure limits for the contaminant given in international industry safety guides or the latest edition of the Health and Safety Executive *'Guidance Note EH-40 Occupational Exposure Limits'*. These occupational exposure limits provide guidance on the levels of exposure to toxic substances that should not be exceeded if the health of persons is to be protected.

Procedures and Arrangements Before Entry

When opening the entrance to a potentially dangerous space, precautions should be taken in case pressurised or unpressurised vapour or gases are released from the space.

Entry into Enclosed Spaces

The space should be isolated and secured against the ingress of dangerous substances by blanking off pipelines or other openings and by closing valves. Valves should then be lashed or some other means used to indicate that they are not to be opened and notices placed on the relevant controls. The officer on watch should be informed.

Where necessary any sludge or other deposits liable to give off fumes should be cleaned out. This may in itself lead to the release of gases, and precautions should be taken.

The space should be thoroughly ventilated either by natural or mechanical means and then tested to ensure that all harmful gases are removed and no pockets of oxygen-deficient atmosphere remain.

Where necessary, pumping operations or cargo movements should be suspended when entry is being made into a dangerous space.

Access to and within the space should be adequate and well illuminated.

In all cases, rescue and resuscitation equipment should be positioned ready for use at the entrance to the space, ie breathing apparatus together with fully charged spare cylinders of air, lifelines and rescue harnesses, and torches or lamps approved for use in a flammable atmosphere, if appropriate. A means of hoisting an incapacitated person from the confined space may be required.

The number of personnel entering the space should be limited to those who actually need to work in the space. When necessary, a rescue harness should be worn to facilitate recovery in the event of an accident.

At least one crew member should be detailed to remain at the entrance to the space during the entry, as the standby man.

An agreed and tested system of communication should be established between those entering the space and the standby man at the entrance, and between the attendant at the entrance to the space and the officer on watch.

Before entry is permitted, it should be established that entry with breathing apparatus is possible. Any difficulty of movement within any part of the space, or any problems if any incapacitated person had to be removed from the space, as a result of breathing apparatus or lifelines or rescue harnesses being used, should be considered and any risks minimised.

Lifelines should be long enough for the purpose and capable of being firmly attached to the harness, but the wearer should be able to detach them easily should they become tangled.

Standby Man

No person should ever enter a confined space without there being a standby man assigned at the entrance to the space. The standby man should be properly trained and aware that their sole function is to raise the alarm under any circumstances where the safety of personnel within the confined space may be compromised. The standby man must not, therefore, be given any other duties. He must remain at the confined space entry point at all times and must maintain communication lines with the bridge at all times. The standby man must be made aware of the dangers of entering a confined space to effect a rescue and must not, under any circumstances, enter the confined space. The standby man should never leave his post even after help has arrived as he is a key communication link to others on board.

Over 50% of workers who die in confined spaces are attempting to rescue other workers. Rescuers must be trained in and follow established emergency procedures and use appropriate equipment and techniques (lifelines, respiratory protection, standby man, etc). Steps for safe rescue should be included in all confined space entry procedures. Rescue should be well planned and drills should be frequently conducted on emergency procedures. Unplanned rescue, such as when someone instinctively rushes in to help a downed co-worker, often result in a double fatality, or even multiple fatalities if there are more than one would-be rescuers.

REMEMBER: AN UNPLANNED RESCUE WILL PROBABLY BE YOUR LAST!

Procedures and Arrangements During Entry

Courtesy of IACS 'Confined Space Safe Practice'

The number of personnel in the confined space should be limited to only those necessary to conduct the proposed tasks in a safe and controlled manner. Pre-planning of the tasks will also ensure that the time spent within the confined space is limited.

The atmosphere within a confined space can change over a period of time and ventilation should continue during the period that the space is occupied and during temporary breaks. In the event of a failure of the ventilation system, any crew in the space should vacate the space immediately.

The atmosphere should be tested at regular intervals while the space is occupied and personnel should be instructed to leave the space should there be any deterioration of the conditions. Should any personal gas detector go into alarm, all persons in the space should leave immediately.

If unforeseen difficulties or hazards develop, the work in the space should be stopped and the space evacuated so that the situation can be reassessed. Permits should be withdrawn and only reissued, with any appropriate revisions, after the situation has been reassessed.

If any personnel in a space feel in any way adversely affected, they should give the prearranged signal to the standby man at the entrance and immediately leave the space.

Should an emergency occur, the general alarm should be sounded so that backup is immediately available to the rescue team. Under no circumstances should the standby man enter the space before help has arrived and the situation has been evaluated to ensure the safety of those entering the space to undertake the rescue.

In the event of a rescue, once the casualty is reached, giving them an air supply (such as from a resuscitator) must be the first priority.

Unless the casualty is gravely injured, eg a broken back, he should be removed from the space as quickly as possible.

Contingency Arrangements

Contingency Plans

Specific contingency plans for rescue should be in place. They should take into account the type and location of the confined space and the personnel and equipment available to conduct any rescue operation.

Contingency Equipment

Rescue equipment should be available at the point of access

Entry into Enclosed Spaces

Reproduced from 'Onboard Safety'

Emergency escape breathing devices should not be used for entry into enclosed spaces - they are provided for emergency escape

Appropriate rescue and resuscitation equipment should be made available at the access point before any entry is made. All equipment should be checked to ensure it is in a good operational condition.

Equipment should include breathing apparatus together with fully charged spare cylinders, lifelines and rescue harnesses, a recovery stretcher and torches approved for use in a flammable atmosphere. A means of hoisting an incapacitated person from the confined space may be required, depending on the nature of the confined space.

Emergency escape breathing devices should not be worn as rescue equipment.

Due to the fatal errors that have occurred on ships where crew have used a dust respirator believing it to be a breathing device, a number of operators have now removed these from ships.

No one should enter a space where the atmosphere is unsafe or uncertain without wearing breathing apparatus that they are trained to use, even to rescue another person.

Recommendations and Guidance

- The International Safety Guide for Oil Tankers and Terminals (ISGOTT), Chapter 10 'Entry to Enclosed Spaces'
- MNTB Training Course 'Entry into Enclosed Spaces'
- UK MCA MGN 423(M) 'Entry into Dangerous Spaces' http://shippingregs.org/36.re
- IMO Resolution A.864(20) 'Recommendations for Entering Enclosed Spaces Aboard Ships' http://tinyurl.com/odcf2o4
- Code of Safe Working Practices for Merchant Seamen, Chapter 17, 'Entering Enclosed or Confined Spaces'
- 'Onboard Safety' by Gary Ritchie
- IACS 'Confined Space Safe Practice'

Safe Entry Check Card

This should be referred to when considering entry to a confined or enclosed space.
These spaces include but are not limited to: cargo tanks, pump rooms, fuel tanks, cofferdams, duct keels, ballast tanks or similar enclosed spaces.

General Precautions

Do not enter a confined space or enclosed space until all the appropriate safety checks on this card have been considered, any items of concern covered, and the atmosphere has been confirmed to be safe for entry.

The atmosphere in any confined or enclosed space may be incapable of supporting human life. It may be lacking in oxygen content and/or contain flammable or toxic gases. This also applies to tanks that have been inerted.

Remember, the Final Decision for Entry is Yours.

Yes No

Pre-Entry Safety Meeting

☐ ☐ Has a safety meeting been held that covers all areas of the entry, safety measures, risks and work methods?

☐ ☐ Is there a minimum of two people entering the space?

Training

☐ ☐ Have all persons entering the space, including the standby man, been properly trained in confined space entry and rescue?

Instrument Checks

☐ ☐ Are the instruments to be used all properly calibrated, and a record available of these checks?

☐ ☐ Is the person conducting the atmosphere tests a competent person to do so?

Testing of the Atmosphere in the Confined Space

☐ ☐ Has the space been thoroughly ventilated?

☐ ☐ Switch off all ventilation in the space while the atmosphere is checked

☐ ☐ Test the atmosphere of the space at different levels

☐ ☐ Is the oxygen at least 20.8% (and not more than 21.0%)?

☐ ☐ If the space contained hydrocarbons, confirm that the LEL <1%

☐ ☐ Are checks required for other toxic gases?
☐ Hydrogen sulphide ☐ Carbon monoxide
☐ Carbon dioxide ☐ Sulphur dioxide
☐ Others ______________________

☐ ☐ On completion of atmosphere checks, restart all ventilation.

☐ ☐ Are there any doubts as to the adequacy of ventilation/testing before entry? (If so, further checks must be made within the space wearing breathing apparatus.)

Warning

Where it has been determined that the atmosphere in a confined or enclosed space is unsafe, that space should only be entered when it is essential or in an emergency, and then only when all the safety checks on this card have been completed and when wearing breathing apparatus.

Permit to Work

☐ ☐ Has a gas test certificate been issued?

☐ ☐ Has a confined space entry permit been issued?

☐ ☐ Is a cold work permit required?

☐ ☐ Are any other permits required (work aloft, pipelines and vessels, etc)?

☐ ☐ Is the permit up to date and valid for the period of entry?

☐ ☐ Has a toolbox talk been completed with those persons involved in the entry?

Yes No

Isolation

☐ ☐ Has the space been isolated from other systems?

☐ ☐ Has electrical equipment been locked out?

☐ ☐ Have disconnects been used where possible?

☐ ☐ Has mechanical equipment been blocked, chocked and disengaged where necessary?

☐ ☐ Have lines under pressure been blanked and bled?

☐ ☐ Have the necessary notice boards been placed at operational locations and at the confined space entry point?

Ventilation

☐ ☐ Has the space been ventilated before entry?

☐ ☐ Will ventilation be continued during entry and at intervals during breaks?

☐ ☐ Is the air intake for the ventilation system located in an area that is free of combustible dusts and vapours and toxic substances?

☐ ☐ If the atmosphere was found unacceptable and then ventilated, was it retested before entry?

☐ ☐ Will the atmosphere in the space be monitored while work is going on?

Remember – atmospheric changes occur due to the work procedure, the product stored, vessel movements and temperature changes. The atmosphere may change very quickly.

Checks for those Entering the Space

☐ ☐ Have you been given clear instructions?

☐ ☐ Do you know that you must leave the space immediately if the ventilation fails?

☐ ☐ Do you understand the communication arrangements?

Clothing/Equipment

☐ ☐ Is special clothing required (eg boots, chemical suits, glasses, etc)?

☐ ☐ Is special equipment required (eg emergency escape set, communications equipment, etc)?

☐ ☐ Are special tools required (eg intrinsically safe)?

Standby/Rescue

☐ ☐ Is rescue and resuscitation equipment available at the entrance to the space?

☐ ☐ Is there a standby person on the outside in constant contact with the persons within the space?

☐ ☐ Will the standby person be able to see or hear the persons within the space at all times?

This card is based on GCBS Marine Safety Card No. 1, IACS Rec. 2000/Rev.2 2007 and The Code of Safe Working Practice for Merchant Seamen.

How to Gas Free a Tank that has Contained Petroleum Hydrocarbons

This section provides a summary of flammable ranges, the flammable range diagram and the steps to gas free a tank that has just contained a petroleum-based hydrocarbon product.

Flammable Range

The flammable range is the area between the minimum (LFL) and the maximum (UFL) concentration of vapour (% by volume) in air that is capable of forming a flammable mixture.

The upper and lower limits of the flammable range for a substance are usually abbreviated to LFL (Lower Flammable Limit) and UFL (Upper Flammable Limit).

The term 'flammable range' refers to the proportion of flammable gas to air necessary for combustion.

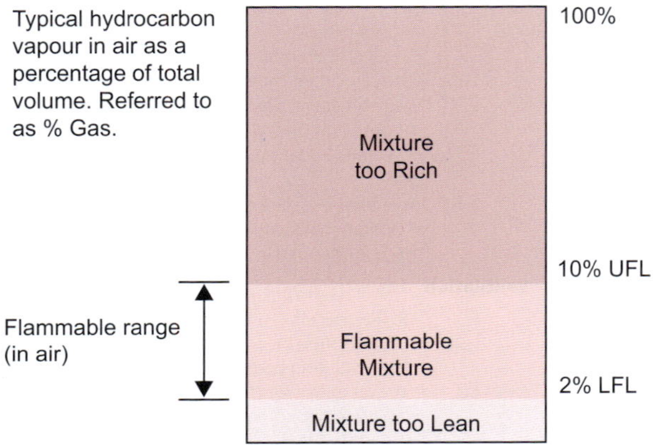

Figure 33.5 - Flammable range

Effect of Reducing the O_2 Content

An atmosphere that is inert (not enough O_2 to support combustion of hydrocarbons) contains less than approximately 12% oxygen.

Figure 33.6 illustrates this for typical petroleum hydrocarbon gases when mixed with air.

Note: Other gases would show slightly different flammable mixture areas depending on their flammable limits and the quantity of oxygen necessary to combust.

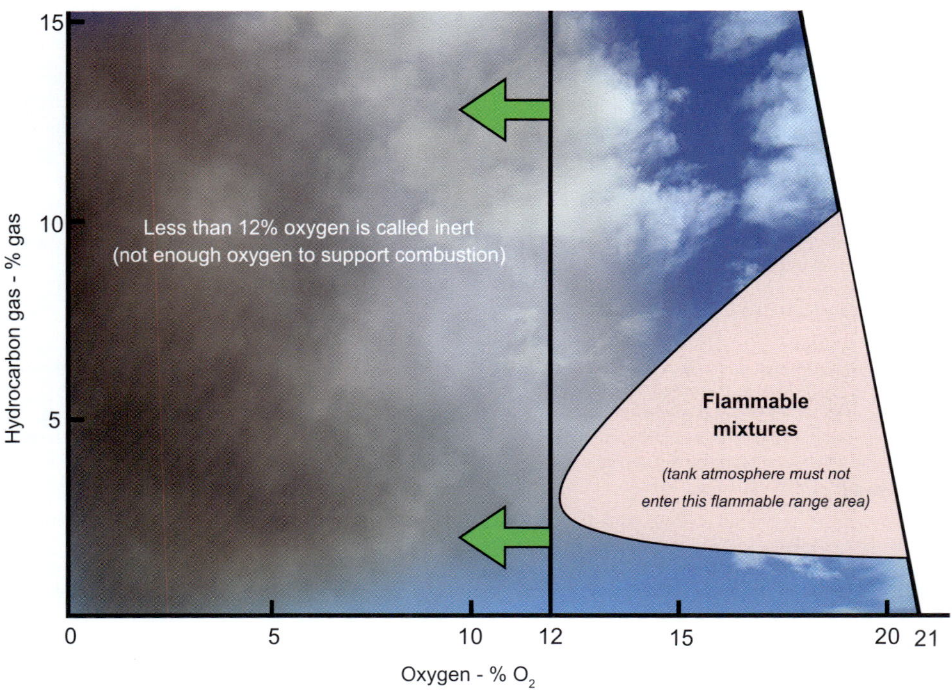

Figure 33.6 - Flammable range diagram, showing the effect of a decrease in oxygen

The flammable range, ie the pink area representing the flammable range between LFL to UFL, reduces as the oxygen content decreases. An O_2 content of less than the left-hand extremity of the flammable envelope (ie 12%) renders the mixture inert.

The O_2 value at which most hydrocarbon gases become inert is between 11 and 12%.

Note: To allow for safety in this area, the ship's inert gas plant will supply no more than 5% O_2 in the header supplying the inert gas to the tanks.

If you look at the flammable area for 20.9% O_2, the LFL = 2% GAS and the UFL = 10% GAS.

Reducing the Hydrocarbon Gas (% Gas) Levels in a Tank (Purging)

If the tank contained hydrocarbons, these must be removed by purging the tank with several volumes of inert gas to progressively reduce (dilute) the % gas/air mixture. This is the 'purge before gas freeing' stage.

After purging, to gas free a tank for entry, once the % gas level is at 2% or less (1.6% if possible) you can open the tank and ventilate it with air. The objective of the gas freeing operation is to ventilate the tank with fresh air until the O_2 level rises to 20.9% volume. Ventilation will be continued after this point to ensure that the O_2 level remains at 20.9%.

Conducting the gas freeing operation in this manner will ensure that the tank atmosphere (throughout the operation) passes as far away as possible from the 'flammable mixture' area, as shown in Figure 33.7.

Summary of Gas Freeing

Introducing air to the tank without having suppressed the hydrocarbon content of the atmosphere (by using inert gas) will cause the mixture to follow path A-Z (see Figure 33.8). This is extremely hazardous. The correct method is to follow line AB and then line BZ.

When presented with a tank of hydrocarbon gas to gas free:

- From starting point 'A', purge inert gas through the tank to the mast riser, reducing the % gas level within the tank.

  Note: The instrument commonly used is the 'tankscope' for '% gas' readings. Use the model of instrument suitable for operation in inert gas.

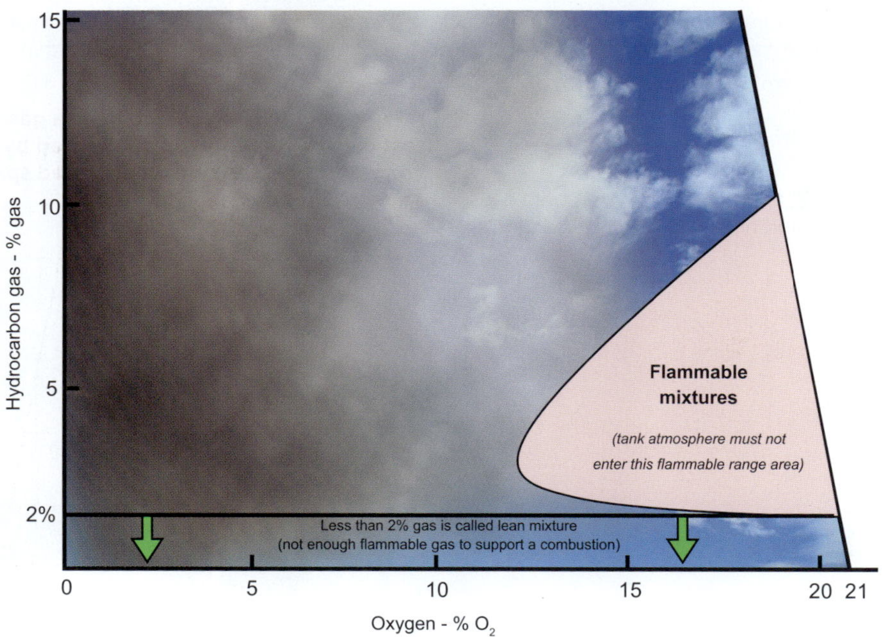

Figure 33.7 - Flammable mixtures

How to Gas Free a Tank that has Contained Petroleum Hydrocarbons

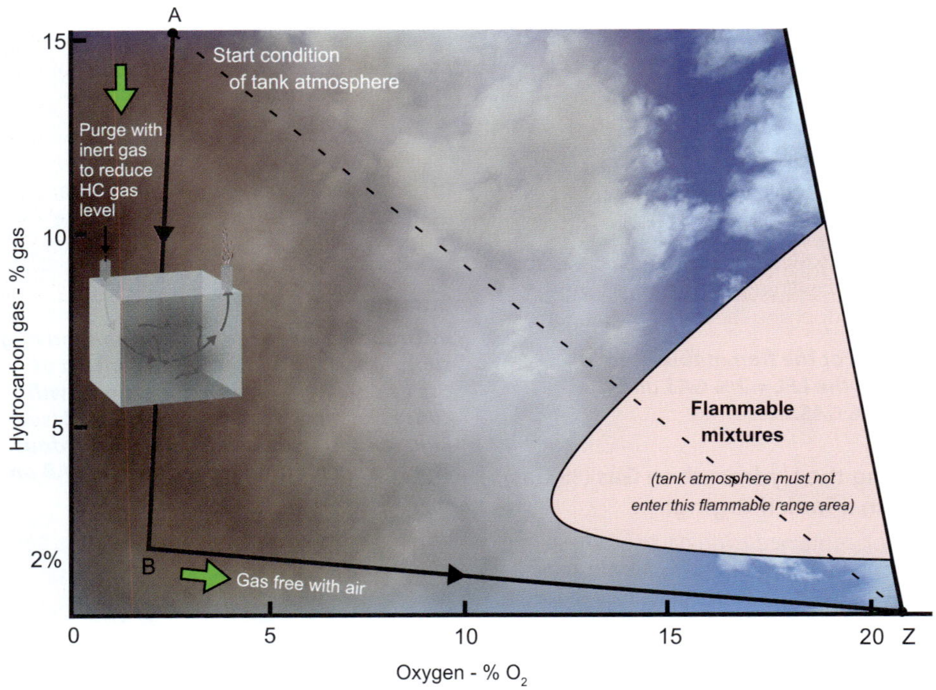

Figure 33.8 - Gas freeing, avoiding the flammable range

- at point 'B', which is 2% gas and equivalent to 100% of the LFL in this case, as read on an explosimeter, open the tank and commence gas freeing with air.

  (***Note:*** *An 'explosimeter' also known as a 'combustible gas indicator' will be used to monitor the % LFL. A meter such as a 'Servomex' will be used to monitor %* O_2*.)*

- at point 'Z', the atmosphere will contain 20.9% O_2 and have 0 to 1% LFL. The tank should be checked for other 'trace' gases using a Dräger tube or similar apparatus. Ventilation of the tank with fresh air should continue throughout the period that the tank is open to the atmosphere.

A tank can only be entered once a gas test certificate has been completed by a competent person and an enclosed space entry permit has been issued.

CHAPTER 34

Health

Health

The Importance of the Human Element in Shipping

For any ship or system to operate safely and effectively it must be designed to support those who will work on it, without being detrimental to their health, safety or performance. This applies particularly to:

- Habitability
- maintainability
- workability
- controllability
- manoeuvrability
- survivability.

Many factors can affect the way a ship operates, eg:

- Badly designed ship or systems
- poor ergonomics
- equipment failure
- fatigue
- stress
- boredom
- commercial pressures
- cultural differences
- different equipment designs
- lack of training.

Fatigue

Types of Fatigue

Physical Fatigue

Physical fatigue is the inability to continue functioning at normal levels of physical activity. People suffering from this type of fatigue will often find everyday tasks difficult, eg climbing stairs or carrying heavy objects.

Mental Fatigue

This can be seen as either someone not being able to stay awake or a general decrease in being able to pay attention.

Causes

Lifestyle Causes of Fatigue

- Too little sleep
- anxiety or stress. Stress can have serious effects on the human body. Suffering from prolonged stress can cause adrenal fatigue, making the sufferer feel run down and worn out
- not taking sufficient exercise
- unhealthy diet
- prescription or over the counter medicines, including antihistamines, some cold and flu remedies, and beta blockers.

A stressful work environment or working long hours can cause mental fatigue. People working on shifts are also prone to suffering from fatigue as the human body is designed to sleep during the night.

Medical Causes

Fatigue can also be caused by the following common medical conditions:

- Insomnia, narcolepsy or sleep apnoea
- chronic pain
- dehydration
- hay fever or asthma
- a poor immune system and chronic infection

- diabetes
- underactive thyroid
- Addison's disease
- anaemia
- illnesses, including heart, liver or kidney disease
- eating disorders
- vitamin and mineral deficiency
- circulation problems
- arthritis
- restless leg syndrome or periodic limb movement
- using alcohol or drugs regularly
- depression
- chronic fatigue syndrome.

Health Effects of Fatigue

- Heart disease and high blood pressure
- stomach problems
- mental changes
- psychological changes.

Effect on Work Performance

Being very tired will reduce performance and productivity and increase the likelihood of accidents and injuries. It will also become more difficult to think clearly.

As work periods increase and the amount of sleep loss increases, performance will drop. Staying awake for 17 hours will have the same effect as having a blood alcohol content of 0.05%; 21 hours will be the same as 0.1%.

The most common effects of fatigue are:

- A desire to sleep
- difficulty in concentrating
- impaired recollection
- irritability
- poor judgement
- inability to communicate
- reduced hand-eye coordination, visual perception and vigilance
- reduced ability to judge risk
- slowed reaction times.

People who are fatigued place themselves and others at risk, for example when:

- Operating machinery
- performing tasks that require a high level of concentration.

Microsleep

A microsleep is a brief nap which lasts four to five seconds. It may occur during normal activities, causing unexplained and unpredictable performance. Concentration failures can occur during normal periods of activity.

Microsleeps can manifest as a failure to recognise hazards or to take appropriate action in an emergency, an inability to make decisions and not being able to concentrate.

Symptoms of Fatigue

- Weakness, lack of energy, tiredness and exhaustion
- fainting or feeling faint
- palpitations
- dizziness
- vertigo
- shortness of breath.

Associated symptoms include:

- Fever
- pain
- nausea

Fatigue

- vomiting
- blood in urine or faeces
- shortness of breath
- chest pain
- constipation
- muscle cramps or aches
- easy bruising
- cough
- changes in thirst or urination
- unable to sleep lying flat
- unable to walk up more than one flight of stairs
- appetite changes
- gaining or losing weight
- swollen legs.

Minimum Hours of Rest (Regulation 5)

4.1 The hours of rest shall be not less than:

a) 10 hours in any 24-hour period; and

b) 77 hours in any 7-day period.

Note: Hours of rest may be divided into no more than 2 periods, one of which should be at least 6 hours long, and the interval in between should not exceed 14 hours.

4.2 It is expected that employers and employees will reach agreement on the arrangements for conducting emergency drills such as musters, fire-fighting and lifeboat drills, in a way which minimises the disturbance to rest periods and provides compensatory rest for seafarers whose normal rest is disturbed by call-outs for drills.

Ref: MSN 1767

Watchkeeping Routines

Historically, deep-sea fleets have followed a three-watch schedule - 4 hours on and 8 hours off. This traditional pattern of watchkeeping makes no apparent contribution to fatigue. However, the reduction in manning levels and shorter ocean crossing time due to increased speed have required watch schedules to be reassessed.

It is recommended that the watchkeeper has 7–8 hours' continuous sleep. However, Sanquist et al in the *Journal of Sleep Research* (1997) state that *'watch keepers on the four on/eight off watch schedule in fact obtained less than four hours sleep in a 24 hour period for just over 22% of their time at sea'.*

According to the data collected during a research study *'Work hours, sleep patterns and fatigue among merchant marine personnel' (Journal of Sleep Research),* the watchkeepers on the 4-on, 8-off schedule show considerable disruption in their sleep. The average sleep duration for all mariners is 6.6 hours; watchkeepers obtain their sleep in fragmented periods that are frequently less than 5 hours in duration. Of particular concern are the watchkeepers on the 04.00 to 08.00 schedules, who sleep less than 4 hours per 24-hour period 22% of the time.

The human body is naturally orientated towards expending energy during daylight hours and resting (restoring energy) during nighttime hours. The amount of energy available over a 24-hour period, therefore, normally peaks in daylight and declines in darkness. Because performance tends to correlate with available energy, the human body tends to function most efficiently in daylight, when the energy level is highest, and least efficiently in darkness, when the energy level is lowest.

Work and watch schedules can be evaluated, and changed if necessary, to help increase endurance and reduce fatigue. In order for these changes to be effective, crew members need to have a thorough understanding of their behavioural choices and lifestyles that contribute to its success. Additional considerations on environmental and operational issues that affect these behavioural choices and lifestyles, as well as risk factors identified, will also play a role in the success or failure of a schedule change.

Watchkeeping Routines

For this reason, a schedule change should not be made until all crew members understand why the schedule needs to be changed and how a new schedule should be chosen.

Criterion for an Effective Watchkeeping Schedule

The following are the fundamental criteria recommended by the United States Coast Guard's Crew Endurance Management System (CEMS) which should be considered for an effective schedule:

Uninterrupted Sleep

- Crew members should have enough time off to obtain 7 to 8 hours of uninterrupted sleep per 24-hour period. *(Sleep research indicates that the average human needs 7 to 8 hours of uninterrupted, quality sleep to recover, both mentally and physically. In the maritime industry it's not possible to get this amount of sleep on a regular basis, if ever, but the goal of a schedule is to allow for as much uninterrupted sleep as possible, ie 5 hours sleep is better than 4 hours sleep, 6 hours sleep is better than 5 hours sleep, etc.)*

Continuity

- Crew members working at night should be able to maintain the same work-rest schedule for at least 2 continuous weeks. *(It takes about one week to acclimate to a new circadian rhythm, and once they are adjusted, it's better not to switch shifts again too soon. If possible, keep on same schedule the entire hitch.)*

Night to Day/Day to Night Avoidance

- Changes in work schedule from day to night, or from night to day, should be minimised in order to avoid a condition similar to jet lag. *(If a person has to do this rapid rotation it's better to change from day to night instead of night to day. If possible, allow 24 hours between this schedule change and at least an opportunity for the individual to take a nap in the afternoon prior to starting the night shift.)*

Length of Work Periods

- Work periods should be no longer than 8 continuous hours, particularly when prolonged exposures to extreme temperature or humidity levels are involved. *(If a crew is working 12-hour shifts, recognise the need for breaks and allowances when necessary due to high workload, weather, etc).*

Light Management

Environmental light management techniques should be used to adapt crew members to night watch:

- Use as much light as possible up to 3 hours before the normal sleep period
- watch out for getting too much light getting off watch.

The Hours of Rest Requirements

Regulation	Work/Rest in 24 hrs	Work/Rest in 7 days	No & Length of Rest Periods	Schedule	Records
STCW	10 hrs rest. This may be reduced to 6 hrs for not more than 2 days	70 hrs rest *(equates to 98 hrs work)*	Not more than two periods of rest, one of which must be at least 6 hrs	Sets out hours of work for watch keepers	
ILO 180 Guidelines	14 hrs of work Or 10 hrs of rest	72 hrs work Or 77 hrs rest	Not more than two periods of rest, one of which to be 6 hrs. Interval between rest periods not to exceed 14 hrs	Specific format table for every position. Actual times for at sea and in port	Daily hours records to be maintained to specific format

Watchkeeping Routines

Evaluation of Watch Schedules

Work and watch schedules have a significant influence on sleep behaviour, and ultimately endurance. Some alternative watchkeeping systems have been proposed, as follows.

Watch Systems based on Three Watches

- Suitable for a minimum crew of three
- the letters A, B and C designate each crew.

Traditional System – Three Four-hour Watches

#	Time	Day 1	Day 2	Day 3	Day 4
1	0000 – 0400	A	A	A	A
2	0400 – 0800	B	B	B	B
3	0800 – 1200	C	C	C	C
4	1200 – 1600	A	A	A	A
5	1600 – 2000	B	B	B	B
6	2000 – 2400	C	C	C	C

This schedule has the same routine or 'watch' hours each day, which some crew find desirable, unless they don't like the hours of their particular watch. The off watches are 8 hours long, allowing adequate time for rest.

Traditional System – Three three-hour watches

#	Time	Day 1	Day 2	Day 3	Day 4
1	0000 – 0300	A	C	B	A
2	0300 – 0600	B	A	C	B
3	0600 – 0900	C	B	A	C
4	0900 – 1200	A	C	B	A
5	1200 – 1500	B	A	C	B
6	1500 – 1800	C	B	A	C
7	1800 – 2100	A	C	B	A
8	2100 – 2400	B	A	C	B

This schedule has shorter shifts and the shifts rotate so that crew are not always working the same time slot day after day. A disadvantage of this schedule is that the 'off-watch' is only 6 hours.

Scandinavian System – Six-four

#	Time	Hours	Day 1	Day 2	Day 3	Day 4
1	0000 – 0400	4	A	C	B	A
2	0400 – 0800	4	B	A	C	B
3	0800 – 1400	6	C	B	A	C
x	Cook duty	x	B	A	C	B
4	1400 – 2000	6	A	C	B	A
5	2000 – 2400	4	B	A	C	B

This schedule has each crew doing a 4-hour night watch, and then splits the 12 daylight hours into two 6-hour watches. The 'off-watch' of the day prepares breakfast and dinner. These long shifts are difficult for single crew to handle and the system works better for crews of six where each watch has two crew members. The schedule rotates so crews work different hours each day.

Scandinavian System – Four-two

#	Time	Hours	Day 1	Day 2	Day 3	Day 4
1	0000 – 0200	2	A	A	A	A
2	0200 – 0400	2	B	B	B	B
3	0400 – 0600	2	C	C	C	C
4	0600 – 1000	4	A	A	A	A
5	1000 – 1400	4	B	B	B	B
6	1400 – 1800	4	C	C	C	C
7	1800 – 2000	2	A	A	A	A
8	2000 – 2200	2	B	B	B	B
9	2200 – 2400	2	C	C	C	C

This schedule is non-rotating, so everyone works the same time slots each day. It has the 4-hour day shift hours as the traditional system but uses shorter 2-hour shifts at night. An advantage of this arrangement is that during the night when it is difficult to stay attentive the crew has shorter shifts to work.

USCG

The Red Zone referred to in the following four schedules is defined by the USCG as 'the daily period when energy and alertness are at their lowest levels, typically spanning from bedtime to sunrise, with the most critical period spanning from 0300 to sunrise:

Square 6 Watch – Traditional Hours (6, 6, 6, 6)

Time	Forward Watch	Aft Watch
2300 – 0500 (6 hours)	* average main sleep period	** getting off watch before daylight
0500 – 1100 (6 hours)	on watch	** average main sleep period
1100 – 1700 (6 hours)	short sleep or nap period	on watch
1700 – 2300 (6 hours)	on watch	short sleep or nap period

* *Good sleep quality because it's in the Red Zone but not enough uninterrupted sleep (average 4.5 – 5 hours).*

** *Getting off watch before daylight and using light management techniques will help the back watch's quality of sleep but still not enough uninterrupted sleep (average 4.5 – 5 hours).*

Square 6 Watch – Alternate Hours (6, 6, 6, 6)

Time	Forward Watch	Aft Watch
2400 – 0600 (6 hours)	* average main sleep period	** getting off watch in daylight
0600 – 1200 (6 hours)	on watch	** average main sleep period
1200 – 1800 (6 hours)	short sleep or nap period	on watch
1800 – 2400 (6 hours)	on watch	short sleep or nap period

* *Good sleep quality because it's in the Red Zone but not enough uninterrupted sleep (average 4.5 – 5 hours).*

** *Getting off watch after daylight will affect the back watch's ability to fall asleep and quality of sleep (average 4.5 – 5 hours).*

Alternate Schedule – (7, 7, 5, 5)

Time	Forward Watch	Aft Watch
2200 – 0500 (7 hours)	* average main sleep period	** getting off watch before daylight
0500 – 1200 (7 hours)	on watch	** average main sleep period
1200 – 1700 (5 hours)	short sleep or nap period	on watch
1700 – 2200 (5 hours)	on watch	short sleep or nap period

* *Good sleep quality because it's in the Red Zone and the opportunity to get 5.5 – 6 hours of uninterrupted sleep.*

** *Getting off watch before daylight and using light management techniques will help the back watch's quality of sleep and the opportunity to get an average of 5.5 – 6 hours of uninterrupted sleep.*

Alternate Schedule – (8, 8, 4, 4)

Time	Forward Watch	Aft Watch
2100 – 0500 (8 hours)	* average main sleep period	** getting off watch before daylight
0500 – 1300 (8 hours)	on watch	** average main sleep period
1300 – 1700 (4 hours)	short sleep or nap period	on watch
1700 – 2100 (4 hours)	on watch	short sleep or nap period

* *Good sleep quality because it's in the Red Zone and the opportunity to get an average of 6.5 – 7 hours of uninterrupted sleep.*

** *Getting off watch before daylight and using light management techniques will help the back watch's quality of sleep and the opportunity to get an average of 6.5 – 7 hours of uninterrupted sleep.*

Operations Ocean Shipholdings, Inc

In 1998, Ocean Shipholdings, Inc established an Alternative Watch System on their five 32,500 Dwt product tankers. This scheme was based on one that had been developed by the West German Ministry for Technology and Research for the operation of single person bridges.

The Alternative Watch System comprises a series of 2-hour and 6-hour watches. Each person stands one 2-hour watch and one

Watchkeeping Routines

The Alternative Watch System												
	2	4	6	8	10	12	14	16	18	20	22	24
Second mate	00-06				08-10							
Chief mate				06-08			12-18					
Third mate						10-12				18-24		

6-hour watch each day. For example, on a '3 Mate' ship, the second mate stands watch from 0001 to 0600 and again from 0800 to 1000 and is off, barring any other onboard operations or overtime work, until 0001 the next day. The chief mate stands 0600 to 0800 and 1200 to 1800, and is off until 0600 the next day, while the third mate stands 1000 to 1200 and 1800 to 2400 and is off until 1000 the following day.

This scheme allows onboard personnel to work 4 hours overtime each day, while fully complying with the requirements of STCW and the US Oil Pollution Act of 1990. It also allows each person to have enough time off to rest, conduct personal business, etc.

The company reported that initially, there was some hesitation, especially from older officers, to start standing these types of watches. This was due, in large part, to the 6-hour watch segment. However, once these individuals actually experienced the benefits of the long, uninterrupted rest period, they quickly adapted to the new system.

The system has been entirely voluntary on the part of the ships' crews. The company doesn't mandate that they work to the Alternative Watch System, but not one ship has changed back to the traditional 4-on-8-off system.

Vessel crews were fully in support of the Alternative Watch System and they report being better rested, have a more 'normal' work experience, and feel that they have enough time off to accomplish their personal tasks without compromising their rest.

Domestic Water Supply Systems

Figure 34.1 - Potable water purification

Pneumatic systems are normally used to supply sanitary and fresh water. Both systems store the water in a tank or reservoir, with inlet and outlet points located at the bottom of the tank. Pumps are used to feed water into the piping system. A pressure switch connected to the tank measures the pressure of the air space

Domestic Water Supply Systems

above the water. As water is discharged, the air pressure drops. This triggers the pressure switch and starts the inlet pump. As the tank refills, the air pressure increases, triggering the pressure switch and turning off the pump. Differential cut-in, cut-out can be adjusted for reasonable running periods while maintaining a satisfactory pressure in sanitary and/or fresh water systems.

Water Purification

Water used for domestic purposes must be slightly alkaline, sterilised, clean, clear and pleasant tasting. To make the water alkaline and to improve the taste, carbonates of calcium and magnesium are used as a filter bed in the neutraliser.

Chlorine is used to sterilise the water, normally in hypochlorite solutions at concentrations of about 100,000:1. To produce clear water, it can be passed through a sandbed filter. To improve taste, a dechlorination process is used. Chlorinated water is passed through an activated carbon filter bed which will absorb excess chloride. The neutraliser, sandbed filter and carbon filter can all have their flows reversed for cleaning purposes.

Water Treatment

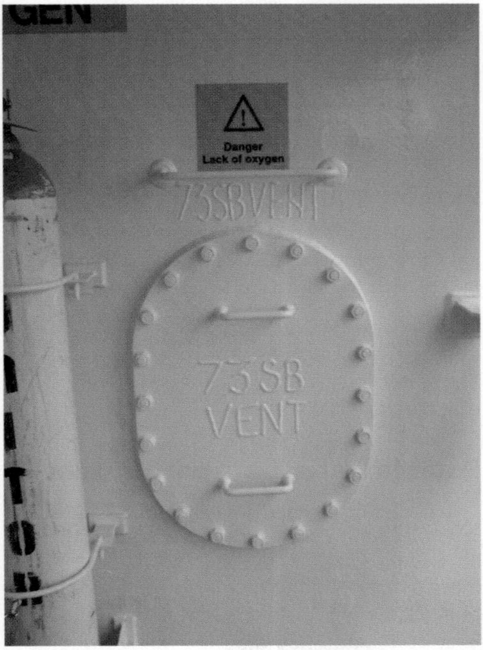

Figure 34.2 - Entry to a potable water tank

Standards and Guidelines

At present, there are no general regulations in place regarding potable water on vessels, although the following guidance is available.

1. US Centers for Disease Control and Prevention (CDC) – information on sanitary issues relating to passenger ship operation and construction.
2. Food and Drug Administration (FDA) – regulations on the source of potable water being used on interstate traffic.
3. Environmental Protection Agency (EPA) – regulations under the Safe Drinking Water Act regarding the standards for safe drinking water and the maximum level of contamination that is allowed in drinking water.
4. US Coast Guard – standards applicable to potable water and waste water systems that are used on systems ashore and afloat.
5. USCG Marine Safety Center – guidelines for reviewing potable water systems when they have been detailed in the construction plan for a ship.
6. US Navy Bureau of Medicine and Surgery – Manual of Naval Preventive Medicine. Information is given about the water supply when afloat, including receiving potable water, storage, distribution and disinfection. One section is devoted to potable water on small vessels, including yard craft, which cannot produce their own potable water. The amount of potable water required for various uses per person per day is also outlined.
7. International Organization for Standardization (ISO) – standards for supplying potable water to ships and marine structures.

Water Treatment

8. The Norwegian Institute for Public Health – checklist for the design of offshore potable water systems. It recommends that there are at least two production units, each one producing 100% of the required water, or three units each producing 50% of the required water. The agency provides information about the criteria for potable water and the recommended analysis programme, addressing issues such as smell, taste, appearance, ph value, conductivity, free chlorine, colour, E coli count, copper, ammonia, benzene and lead.
9. The American Bureau of Shipping (ABS) – guide addressing potable water systems and related issues for crew living on board.
10. Would Health Organization (WHO) – Guidelines for drinking-water quality.

Classification Societies include potable water systems in their rules and regulations for ships that are being built or classified.

Ship owners and operators are responsible for double checking the systems on their vessels.

Health Concerns

A water system that is not correctly managed is an easy route for infectious diseases to be transmitted on board ships.

Most waterborne outbreaks involve ingestion of water containing pathogens from human or animal excreta. There have also been cases of chemicals poisoning water on ships. Contamination can either occur on board or can come from port. Outbreaks have been associated with:

- Contaminated bunker water
- cross connection between potable and non-potable water
- incorrect loading procedures
- poor design and construction of potable storage water tanks
- insufficient disinfection.

It is not uncommon for water potable systems to be close to hazardous substances, for example sewage streams, which increases the risk of cross contamination.

Some of the more common hazards associated with waterborne diseases on ships are listed in the table below:

Pathogens/Toxins	Waterborne Outbreaks 1970-2000 (WHO 2001)
Enterotoxigenic Escherichia coli (ETEC)	5
Norovirus	5
Vibrio spp	2
Salmonella typhi	1
Salmonella spp (non typhi)	1
Shigellaspp	1
Cryptosporidium sp	1
Giardia lamblia	1
Chemical poisoning	1
Unknown agent	4

Potable Water

Potable water is used for drinking, cooking, washing utensils used for cooking and eating, and in the ship's hospital.

Potable water should not contain any pathogenic organisms or harmful chemicals. The water quality should comply with WHO guidelines.

Potable Water Transport System

Port authorities will receive potable water from either a municipal or private supplier. There are usually special arrangements in place for managing the water once it has entered the port. Water will be delivered to ships either by hose connected to a watering point at the dock side or transferred by water boats or barges. Each ship should carry enough hoses to load its potable water and these hoses should be used only for this purpose.

The cleanliness and safety of the ship's filling hose and attachments are the responsibility of a deck officer. He will also be responsible for the dockside connections and the water boat or shipside filling lines.

A ship may have two or three water systems, eg potable, non-potable and water to be used for the fire system. Where possible, there should only be one system on board that supplies potable water. Non-potable water should be loaded using a separate pipe and fittings to prevent contamination.

Filling Hose

To protect water that passes through a hose, the hose should be durable, have a smooth, impervious lining and have fittings, including adapters, that only fit shore potable or non-potable water hydrants.

The hose must be stored in a specific locker marked **'POTABLE WATER HOSE ONLY'**.

Filling Line

Every potable tank must have a dedicated clean filling line that can have a hose attached to it. This line must not be connected to any non-potable water system and should not pass through any non-potable liquid.

To prevent the water from becoming contaminated, the filling line should begin either horizontally or pointing down. The filling line should have a screw cap or plug secured with a chain to an adjacent bulkhead or surface to ensure that the cap does not touch the deck when it is removed from the filling line. Each filling line should be marked **'POTABLE WATER FILLING'**. The filling line should be positioned above the deck and either marked or painted blue.

Water Boats and Barges

Water boats and barges are equipped to receive and provide water for both potable and non-potable systems when it is not practical to carry out direct shore delivery. These boats are fitted with water tanks, hoses and fittings, pumps and independent pipe systems that provide potable water. Receiving, handling, storing and delivering potable water to ships must be completely sanitary. Disinfection must be available and carried out as necessary.

Potable Water Storage

The inside of the water tank must be coated to prevent corrosion of the tank or deterioration of the water quality. Epoxy paints are commonly used. The coating must be approved for contact with drinking water and must not contaminate the water or taint its taste or smell. Each tank should be clearly marked **'POTABLE WATER'.**

To prevent contamination, potable water tanks should not be cross connected to non-potable water tanks through a main air compressor. If a common compressed air system is used for both potable and non-potable water, the air supply should be through a failsafe device, eg press-on air valve and hose which must be manually held on.

Capacity

The number of people on board as well as the length of trip should be considered when calculating the amount of potable water that will be required. Ports en route with approved water sources should also be considered. There must be sufficient storage available to allow water from overboard to be treated effectively and for maintenance work to be carried out.

Less storage may be required if the potable water supply can be supplemented by water that has been purified on board. This is dependent on the purification process being used.

It is not necessary to treat water if it is loaded from approved sources. The volume of stored potable water should never be lower than the baseline allowing for treatment system failures, eg a 2-day supply.

Vents

All potable water storage tanks have a vent located in an area where a contaminating substance cannot get in. A single pipe can be used as an overflow and vent. A potable water tank vent must not be connected to the vent of any other holding tank that is used for non-potable liquids. The external end of the vent should point downwards and be covered with a mesh so that no contaminants can get into the tank. If there is a possibility of the vent being exposed to waves, a back water valve should be fitted to prevent any contamination.

Drains

It must be possible for potable water tanks to be completely drained, eg to remove a contaminant. It is important that the drain is large enough to cope with the volume of water in the tank.

Water Treatment

When drainage is carried out by gravity, the opening can be at the bottom of the tank; this means that drainage will stop either flush with or below the inner surface of the tank's bottom. If a suction line is used to drain a potable water tank, care should be taken to control the contamination. To do this, the drain in the pump discharge line can be located ahead of any branch of the take-off system. A valve can be fitted immediately after the drain line take-off.

Unless a locking type of valve is provided, a plug or cap can be used to stop water being lost due to the valve becoming loose.

System Assessment and Hazard Analysis

Hazards associated with storage tanks include a build-up of sediment at the bottom of the tank, wire mesh being damaged in the vent/overflow, contamination getting in due to damage or during maintenance, leakage, and cross connection with a non-potable water tank or pipe.

Management Plant and Control Measures

Extreme care must be taken to prevent contamination of the storage tank during repair work. An outbreak of typhoid occurred on a ship due to the potable water being contaminated by sewage while the ship was in drydock. This highlights the necessity for good hygiene practice and disinfection once repairs have been completed. Ship builders should provide written instructions on how to clean and disinfect the tanks before the ship is released.

Pneumatic Pumps and Pressure Tanks

Potable water pressure tanks must not be connected to non-potable water tanks through a main air compressor. One of the following can be used:

- A 'snifter' air intake valve used on the potable water pump
- independent compressor
- a main compressed air system, using a press-on valve with a liquid trap in the supply line.

When a common compressed air system supplies pressure to the non-potable and potable water pneumatic tanks, the air supply should be through a press-on type of air valve and hose.

Safe Water Distribution on Ships

Potable water piping should be painted blue and have a light blue strip(s) at the fittings on each side of partitions, decks and bulkheads. The outlets should be labelled **'POTABLE WATER'** or **'FIT FOR DRINKING'**. If the direction of the water flow is important, it should be marked using an arrow pointing in the direction of the flow. It may also indicate whether the water is hot or cold.

Potable water piping must not pass through tanks containing sewage, bilge water or non-potable liquids. Distribution lines must not be connected to piping or storage tanks of any non-potable water system.

Monitoring and Corrective Actions

Hazardous Event	Control Measure	Monitoring Procedures	Corrective Action
Sediment at the bottom of storage tanks	Routine cleaning, eg every 6 months	Routine inspections, documentation	Procedure for cleaning storage tanks
Damage to wire mesh in overflow/vent pipe	Routine inspection, repair and maintenance	Routine sanitary inspections	Repair or replace
Cross connections between potable water storage tank and non-potable water storage tank or pipe	Cross connection control programme	Routine inspections, repair and maintenance	Repair or replace
Defects in potable water storage tanks	Routine sanitary inspection	Routine inspections, repair and maintenance	Repair or replace

When potable water is delivered to a non-potable system under pressure, it is important that the system is protected from backflow by using preventers or air gaps. If the preventers fail, negative pressure can lead to contaminants getting into the system.

Backflow preventers should be located where they can be easily accessed for service and maintenance. Every prevention device should be inspected and serviced in accordance with the manufacturer's instructions to prevent the device failing.

If hot and cold water pipes are to run side by side, appropriate thermal insulation should be used.

System Assessment and Hazard Analysis

Distribution systems on ships are vulnerable to contamination when pressure falls. If the local pressure falls, it could cause contaminated water to be siphoned backwards, unless there are check valves in the water system and the pipes are free of leaks.

Repair work being carried out on a distribution system can contaminate the water supply. The risks will depend on the degree of pollution in the repair site, method of repair, ability to contain contamination and the cleanliness of the personnel, their working practices and materials being used.

Hazards may include external pollution entering the distribution system from repairs to pipes or from pipes being constructed.

Microorganisms, eg biofilms, usually grow in water and on surfaces that are in contact with water. Growth after drinking water has been treated is normally referred to as 'regrowth'.

Elevated HPC levels may occur, particularly in stagnant areas of pipe distribution systems as well as in plumbed devices including softeners, carbon filters and vending machines. Factors influencing regrowth are temperature, available nutrients and a lack of residual disinfectant. At warmer temperatures, Legionella can reach hazardous levels.

Management Plan and Control Measures

Piping should be repaired when necessary and positive pressure maintained. Sanitary inspections should include checking cross connections, defective pipes and backflow preventers.

Temporary patch repairs on fresh water distribution pipes should be avoided; the entire length of pipe should be replaced if there is any damage.

Precautions regarding hygiene should be taken when laying new pipes or carrying out repairs. There should be adequate toilet and washing facilities available for the crew. Anyone who is known to be a carrier of a communicable disease must not come into contact with the potable water supplies.

It is common for a residual disinfectant to be present to control bacteria in the water. This helps to reduce the taste and smell of some types of microbial-influenced corrosion. This residual disinfectant may also kill some pathogens that may be present, but this does not mean that the water is safe to drink. It is important to remember that many viral and parasitic pathogens are resistant to low levels of disinfectant.

Automated disinfection of the potable water system may be more reliable than manual chlorination. Chlorine should be measured in line with the quantity of water that has been bunkered. The chlorine drums should be checked regularly to ensure that the correct disinfectant and dilution are present. Each drum should be checked before, during and after bunkering.

Monitoring and Corrective Actions

Regular checks and tests should be carried out on the backflow prevention devices, possible cross connections, leaks, defective pipes, pressure, and disinfectant residuals.

Water service containers must be kept clean so that microbial growths are controlled. Coolers where there is contact between the ice and the water or where water bottles are inserted neck first into the cooling chamber are not recommended as they are difficult to keep clean.

Water Treatment

Any sea water that is to be treated on board should be taken from an area that is known to be relatively pollution free. Spare parts for the treatment apparatus should be available on board, particularly if they are vital or fragile.

Water Treatment

Halogenation

This is the disinfection of water using halogen disinfectants, eg chlorine, bromine or iodine. Halogen dosing should be reliably controlled, eg by a flow meter or analyser.

The analyser typically measures and indicates the free halogen, eg what is available for disinfection. This should be linked to an audible alarm in a continually manned watch station, eg the engine control room.

A sample cock should be located downstream of the halogen injection point. This allows the halogen doses to be measured and readings from the analyser confirmed.

Chlorine Disinfection

Chlorine requires contact time in order to be effective. If water is regularly treated by chlorination, a baffled holding tank large enough to provide water with sufficient contact with chlorine may be necessary. This period of contact should end before the water moves to the next treatment unit or distribution system. It should be calculated on the basis of the maximum flow rate through the contact tank. When the normal dose of chlorine is used, the contact time is at least 30 minutes. If super chlorination is carried out, the contact time may be less.

Filtration

Tap filters and other terminal filters can often collect and accelerate the growth of bacteria. Storage and manually inserting the replacement filter are both ways for contamination to be introduced. Because of this, using terminal filters is discouraged unless there is an effective way of disinfecting the filtering equipment immediately after it is installed and periodically when it is in use.

Daily Analysis

Potable water on board must be measured and logged daily. The results will indicate whether any adjustments are necessary for the potable water operations.

Smell should not be noticeable. If there is an odour, it may be a sign of contamination. A slight smell of chlorine following the chlorination procedure is normal.

Taste should not be noticeable. An unpleasant taste may be an indicator of contamination.

Appearance – water should be clear with no discolouration. This should be checked using a strong light and a white or black background, depending on the colour of the particles. Discolouration or lack of clarity may indicate contamination.

pH value should be between 6.5 and 9.5. Ideally it should be between 8 and 8.5 to avoid corrosion. Chlorination works best at pH levels below 8. Small deviations in pH value do not cause any health hazard, but if the pH level is above 11 it can cause cauterisation damage particularly to the eyes and skin.

Free chlorine – if chlorination is the only disinfection method used in the potable water system, there should always be a supply of chlorine free water. Free chlorine values should be between 0.05 and 0.5 milligrams per litre. If there is no free chlorine present, the disinfection process has failed.

Total chlorine – this should be below 5 milligrams per litre in water for drinking. If it is higher than this, the water will smell and taste of chlorine.

Monthly Routine Control

Samples of water should be sent to an approved laboratory every month. It is suggested that one sample is taken from the potable tank in use and two samples from the distribution network.

Different points on the distribution network should be used for the samples and should include the galley, hospital and the UV-unit outlet.

Colour smell and taste should be monitored as above.

Turbidity should be below 1 FNU. High turbidity will make the water unclear, normally due to a large number of small particles. Disinfection is less effective and the water will appear less appetising.

Clostridium perfringens should not be present in 100 ml of water. If the limit is exceeded, the entire water system must be investigated to confirm that there is no contamination from other diseases, eg Cryptosporidium or Norovirus.

E Coli should not be present in 100 ml of water. If discovered, the authorities must be

Hazard	Control Measure	Monitoring Procedures	Corrective Action
Cross connections with non-potable water	• Prevent cross connections • procedures for inspection, repair and maintenance • correct identification of pipes and tanks	Routine inspections	Break cross connection
Defective pipes, leaks	Procedures for inspection, repair and maintenance	Routine inspections	Repair pipes
Defective backflow preventers at outlets throughout distribution system	No defects that would allow ingress of contaminated water	Routine inspections • Testing of preventers	Repair or replace
Contamination during repair and maintenance of tanks and pipes	• No defects that would allow ingress into potable water tanks/pipes • procedures for hygienic repair and maintenance • procedures for cleaning and disinfecting.	Inspection of job • Water sampling (microbiological analysis)	Train staff • Written procedures • disinfect fracture area and fitting
Leaking pipes/ tanks	Prevent leakage • System maintenance and renewal	Routine inspections • Pressure and flow monitoring	Repair
Toxic substances in pipe materials	No toxic substances • Specifications for pipe materials	Check specifications for pipes and materials • Check specification certificates	Replace pipes if specification is not correct
Insufficient residual disinfection	Adequate residual disinfection to prevent regrowth, eg <0.2 ppm residual chlorine	On-line monitoring of residual disinfectant, pH and temperature • Routine sampling	Investigate cause and rectify

informed immediately. Human faeces that has a high level of E Coli is the most dangerous microbiological contamination of potable water.

Intestinal enterococci should not be present in 100 ml of water. If it is found, it should be reported immediately to the relevant authorities.

Coliform bacteria should not be present in 100 ml of water. If found without E Coli being present, it is an indication that there is an older contamination present.

Iron the limit value is 0.2 mg/l. If this is exceeded, it is an indication that corrosion is occurring in the potable water system. This is not usually a health issue, but the iron level should be kept as low as possible as iron deposits will affect disinfection. A high iron content will discolour the water, clothes and sanitary installations and will also give the water an unpleasant taste. A high level of iron in the water may be an indication that there are other types of corrosion occurring, eg toxic heavy metal such as lead and cadmium.

Water Treatment

Alternative Means of Disinfecting Freshwater Tanks

By far the greatest risk to the quality of the water within the freshwater tanks is the condition of the tanks themselves. The tanks should be flushed out periodically (6 monthly) and inspected regularly (every 12 months as a minimum). If they are found to have any areas of corrosion, the coatings should be reapplied to avoid corrosion worsening in time. Once inspected and, if necessary, thoroughly cleaned, the tanks should always be disinfected. Traditionally this has been carried out using a solution of sodium hypochlorite to a level of 50 ppm. Although chlorine is effective against planktonic bacteria, its ability to combat biofilming is of concern. A full wet soak of up to 1,000 tonnes is also wasteful of precious fresh water and means downtime for the operation of the vessel. Stronger, more effective chemicals and far more efficient methods are now available and should be used whenever possible.

High pressure spray disinfection equipment may be used to maintain the correct contact times and chemical concentrations within the tank to eradicate biofilming and fully disinfect the tank surfaces. Typically this method can reduce the water quantity used for disinfection from around 2,000 tonnes to as little as 250 litres, representing a tremendous saving in water, downtime and manpower. This method of disinfection is recognised as being effective by many operators now and can save a great deal from already strained maintenance and refit budgets. Once completed, the freshwater tanks can be immediately refilled and dosed with either chlorine or chlorine dioxide to the normal levels of operation. Typically this is equivalent to the 0.2 ppm prescribed for on-line dosing.

Tropical Diseases

Malaria

This infectious disease is caused by a parasite that is transmitted by the bite of an infected female Anopheles mosquito. If left untreated, malaria can be fatal. Malaria is emerging as the number one killer and is the priority tropical disease of the World Health Organization.

- More than 2,400 million people are affected by malaria in over 100 countries, ranging from the South American tropics to the Indian peninsula. The tropics have ideal conditions for the Anopheles mosquito to breed and live
- every year approximately 300 to 500 million people suffer from malaria
- WHO predict that there will be a 16% growth in the number of cases each year
- approximately 1.5 to 3 million people die each year from malaria
- every 20 seconds a child will die of malaria in Africa. There is one death from malaria every 12 seconds worldwide
- it accounts for 2.6% of the total disease burden of the world.

During the 1960s, malaria was almost eradicated due to worldwide campaigns and the World Health Organization's guidance.

Some of the reasons for the increase in malaria include:

- Complacency in anti-malarial campaigns, wars, migrations, deteriorating health systems, poverty
- drug resistance
- insecticide resistance and ban of DDT
- global warming - increased breeding and life span of insects
- shrinking world - spread of malaria from endemic areas to all other parts of the world.

Typical malaria symptoms, which can take between days and years to develop, include:

- Fever
- chills
- flu-like symptoms.

Malaria can also be transmitted by a person coming into contact with infected blood, eg from:

- A blood transfusion
- organ transplant
- sharing needles or syringes.

Malaria can mistakenly be diagnosed as a common cold, flu or another common infection in countries where malaria does not often occur.

Occasionally malaria symptoms may follow a cyclical pattern. In these cases, the symptoms typically last 6 to 10 hours, returning every 2 to 3 days depending on the malaria parasite that has caused the infection.

There may be more severe symptoms, including:

- Kidney failure
- seizures
- mental confusion
- coma
- severe anaemia
- fluid in the lungs
- acute respiratory distress syndrome
- bleeding due to clotting problems
- yellowing of the skin and eyes
- anaemia
- difficulty in moving
- speech difficulties
- deafness
- blindness.

This type of malaria is more likely to affect people who have no immunity to disease or whose immunity is reduced.

Tropical Diseases

Prevention

The type of prevention will be based on:

- The risk of exposure
- prevention from being bitten by mosquitos by using DEET repellent, bed nets and clothing that covers most of the body
- preventive medications.

Medicines do not offer complete protection and medical advice should be sought before travelling.

Some medications commonly used to prevent malaria include:

- Hydroxychloroquine
- Plaquenil
- Chloroquine
- Aralen
- Mefloquine
- Lariam
- Apo-Mefloquine
- Pyrimethamine
- Daraprim
- Sulfadoxine and Pyrimethamine – used mainly to treat Plasmodium falciparum malaria
- Fansidar - used mainly to treat Plasmodium falciparum malaria
- Paludrine.

However, the better precaution method is avoidance by using mosquito nets, bed nets and staying indoors at dusk or during the night.

Typhoid

This is a severe, contagious and life-threatening disease. It is associated with a fever and is most commonly caused by the Salmonella Typhi bacteria, which are passed from a human carrier to food and water where it can then spread to other people.

Since the early 1900s, the number of cases of typhoid has decreased, mainly due to improvements in environmental sanitation. However, in high risk areas, such as India, Pakistan and Egypt, more than 13 million people are affected by typhoid each year, of which approximately half a million die.

Travellers to affected areas should seek medical guidance and vaccination before travelling.

Transmission

There are several ways in which typhoid can be transmitted, but unhygienic conditions are the main cause. The typhoid bacteria are passed by carriers through vomit and faeces. The bacteria are transferred into food, drinks and water by house flies and other insects. When someone eats or drinks the contaminated item, they will be infected with typhoid.

Vegetables grown in sewage-irrigated fields are also a source of infection. The typhoid bacteria can survive in the soil and water for several months, as well as growing quickly in milk and other milk-based products.

Typhoid carriers may have the bacteria for several years.

Symptoms

Symptoms include:

- High temperature, 103 or 104°C
- headaches
- poor appetite
- general aches and pains
- lethargy, weakness and tiredness
- diarrhoea
- rash – this tends to be rose-coloured spots which appear on the lower chest and abdomen.

If left untreated, the patient will suffer from the second stage of typhoid, which will leave them delirious and motionless. The disease can become life-threatening at this stage if medical advice is not sought. Once the patient has received the correct medical care, they should start to improve during the fourth week of the illness and the fever should gradually reduce over 10 days.

Prevention

The best way to prevent typhoid is to use proper sanitation and to have good hygiene. People in areas where the disease is present should avoid drinking any untreated water or eating raw vegetables or fruit. They should only eat foods that have been cooked, as the bacteria cannot withstand heat.

There are two vaccines available which the World Health Organization recommends and they are usually given to people in areas where typhoid is prevalent.

Yellow Fever

This viral disease can be found in the tropical areas of Africa and America. It is transmitted by mosquito and mainly affects humans and monkeys. Outbreaks can be prevented and controlled by vaccination.

The first symptoms will appear 3 to 6 days after infection and include:

- Fever
- muscle pain
- headache
- shivers
- loss of appetite
- nausea and vomiting.

After 3 to 4 days, the patient will start to feel better and the symptoms will go. Some cases may go into the toxic phase, which means that the fever will return and the patient may develop jaundice and bleed. This blood will appear in the vomit. Approximately 50% of patients who enter this phase will die after 10 to 14 days.

There is no specific treatment for yellow fever and it is recommended that travellers are vaccinated before travelling.

Prevention

- Use an insect repellent whenever outdoors, containing DEET, picaridin or oil of lemon eucalyptus
- wear long-sleeved tops, trousers and socks when possible. Mosquitos can bite through thin fabrics so it is important to spray clothing with a repellent
- stay indoors from dusk to dawn as this is the prime time for mosquitos to bite. However, Aedesagypti feeds during the daytime so a repellent should be used during the day as well as during the night
- get a vaccination if it is recommended. A single dose will provide immunity for approximately 10 years, with a booster required every 10 years.

Heat Exhaustion

What is Heat is Exhaustion?

Heat exhaustion is a physical weakness or collapse that occurs when the body becomes too hot and is unable to cool down. The patient may feel sick and suffer from muscle cramps and dizziness.

The hypothalamus is the part of the brain that controls thirst, hunger and the body's core temperature. If the body is exposed to high temperatures for a prolonged period of time without replacing fluids that have been lost by sweating, the system that regulates body temperature will become overwhelmed and the body will produce more heat than can be released. Heat exhaustion is a serious condition and must be treated immediately. Untreated it can develop into heat stroke, which is life-threatening.

Causes of Heat Exhaustion

Causes of heat exhaustion include:

- Over exertion in hot and humid conditions
- dehydration
- drinking alcohol
- overdressing or wearing clothing that does not allow sweat to evaporate easily
- replacing sweat with large volumes of fluids that do not contain enough salt.

Symptoms

Symptoms of heat exhaustion include:

- Heavy sweating
- fatigue
- headache
- red or pale, clammy skin
- thirst
- rapid heartbeat
- dizziness, fainting
- nausea, vomiting
- muscle cramps
- mild rise in temperature
- dilated pupils.

Heat Exhaustion

Complications

If left untreated, heat exhaustion can develop into heat stroke. This occurs when body temperature reaches 140°F or 40°C or higher. Heat stroke requires immediate medical attention to prevent damage to the patient's brain and vital organs or even death.

The following conditions increase susceptibility to heat illnesses:

- Illness or chronic disability
- pregnancy
- cardiovascular disease
- hypertension
- respiratory disease.

First Aid Guide

A combination of the following measures should be used depending on the situation:

- The casualty should rest with their legs slightly raised in a shaded area or a cool, air conditioned room
- clothing should be removed or loosened
- the casualty should drink an electrolyte drink or water. They should not drink anything that contains caffeine or alcohol. A salted drink can be made by adding a teaspoon of salt to one and a half pints of water
- pour water over the casualty or spray with a hose. This should not be done if the casualty is disorientated
- wrap the casualty in a wet cloth and direct a fan at them; their skin will cool as the water evaporates
- apply cold compresses to the neck, armpits and groin.

If possible, take the patient's temperature at the start of the cooling process and again every couple of minutes. Once the casualty's temperature is down to 100°F, the cooling process can be stopped. The casualty's temperature should be checked every 30 minutes for 3 to 4 hours to ensure it is staying down.

Emergency medical treatment should be sought if the casualty does not improve, if the symptoms worsen, or if there are signs of shock, seizure or loss of consciousness.

Heat Index Table

Temp °F	Relative Humidity (%) 40	45	50	55	60	65	70	75	80	85	90	95	100
110	136												
108	130	137											
106	124	130	137										
104	119	124	131	137									
102	114	119	124	130	137								
100	109	114	118	124	129	136							
98	105	109	113	117	123	128	134						
96	101	104	108	112	116	121	126	132					
94	97	100	102	106	110	114	119	124	129	135			
92	94	96	99	101	105	108	112	116	121	126	131		
90	91	93	95	97	100	103	106	109	113	117	122	127	132
88	88	89	91	93	95	98	100	103	106	110	113	117	121
86	85	87	88	89	91	93	95	97	100	102	105	108	112
84	83	84	85	86	88	89	90	92	94	96	98	100	103
82	81	82	83	84	84	85	86	88	89	90	91	93	95
80	80	80	81	81	82	82	83	84	84	85	86	86	87

Source: NOAA's National Weather Service

With Prolonged Exposure and/or Physical Activity:		
	Extreme Danger: Heat Stroke or Sunstroke likely	Danger: Sunstroke, muscle cramps, and/or heat exhaustion likely
	Extreme Caution: Sunstroke, muscle cramps, and/or heat exhaustion possible	Caution: Fatigue possible

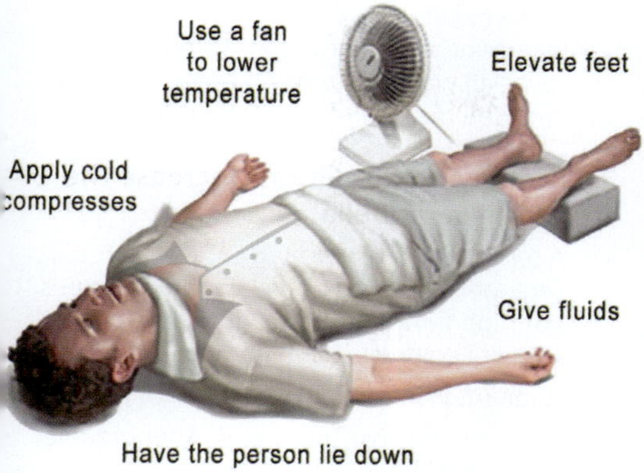

Prevention

When the outside temperature rises, you should:

- Wear loose-fitting, lightweight, light-coloured clothing. Dark or tight clothing will retain heat and hinder sweat evaporation, meaning that your body will not be able to cool properly
- when outdoors, wear a lightweight, wide-brimmed hat or use an umbrella to protect you from the sun. Sunscreen should be applied to any exposed areas because sunburn reduces your body's ability to cool down
- seek a cooler place. Moving into a shaded or air conditioned area for a couple of hours is one of the best ways to prevent heat exhaustion
- drink plenty of fluids. Keeping hydrated will help your body to sweat and maintain its normal temperature
- take precautions with certain types of medicines and seek medical advice if necessary
- avoid hot spots. On a hot day, the temperature inside your car can rise by 20°F in 10 minutes. You should let your car cool down before driving
- let your body adjust to the heat, if you are travelling to somewhere hot or if there is a sudden heat wave, your body can take a long time to adjust to the heat. Even after you have become used to the heat you should still take precautions, but working or exercising in the heat should become easier.

Dermatitis

What is Dermatitis?

Dermatitis is the inflammatory response of the skin following exposure to allergens, irritants or the sun or due to poor circulation or stress. It may also be caused by certain drugs, scratching the skin, varicose veins and fungal infection.

A typical example is atopic eczema, which is an itchy rash with red, blistered and scaling skin.

Most dermatitis is due to skin irritation caused by handling or misusing substances. It is occasionally due to an allergic reaction. The most common irritants are detergents, cleaning powders, solvents, oil and paraffin.

There are several different types of dermatitis but it usually starts with a diffuse reddening of the affected area. Small blisters then appear on this reddened area, usually fairly quickly. The blisters will ultimately burst releasing a yellow liquid, forming a crust on the skin. It is common for the skin to feel very itchy.

You should attempt to identify what is causing the dermatitis. Once identified, every attempt should be made to avoid the irritant. It should be remembered that a substance that the patient has used and been in contact with for a long period of time without any adverse effect may suddenly become an irritant, eg detergent.

Diagnosis is usually based on the symptoms that have been presented and is confirmed by either carrying out a patch test or from skin samples. Any drugs that the patient is taking can assist in identifying the cause, as well as discovering what irritants or infections they have recently been in contact with.

Treatment for dermatitis will depend on what has caused it and the patient's specific symptoms.

Legionnaires' Disease

Legionnaires' disease was named after an outbreak of severe pneumonia that affected a meeting of a chapter of the American Legion in Philadelphia in 1976. It is a potentially fatal form of pneumonia which can affect anybody, although some people are at higher risk than others, including those over 45, smokers and heavy drinkers, those suffering from chronic respiratory or kidney disease, and people whose immune system is impaired.

There have been 50 incidents of Legionnaires' disease, involving over 200 cases, associated with ships in the past 30 years. Surveys of seafarers on cargo ships have also shown that a high proportion have antibodies to Legionella pneumophila, suggesting that those on board ships are at increased risk of legionellosis compared with communities on shore.

Where is it Found?

Legionnaires' disease is caused by the bacterium Legionella pneumophila. This type and related bacteria can be found naturally in environmental water sources. However, on board ship, evaporative coolers, hot water systems and water tanks are suspect areas.

To date, there is no evidence of an outbreak associated with onboard the heating, ventilation or air conditioning systems. However, all water systems on board ship must be considered a potential breeding ground.

The Following Conditions Increase the Risk from Legionella:

- A temperature for growth of 20 to 45°C. Legionella can survive in low temperatures but high temperatures of 60°C and over will kill any Legionella bacteria
- stagnant water in tanks, systems or pipes
- sludge, scale, rust, algae and other organic matter in the tanks or system.

Assessing the Risk

When preparing a risk assessment, the following should be considered:

- Are conditions right for the bacteria to multiply? For example, is the water temperature between 20°C and 45°C?
- are there areas where stagnant water occurs?

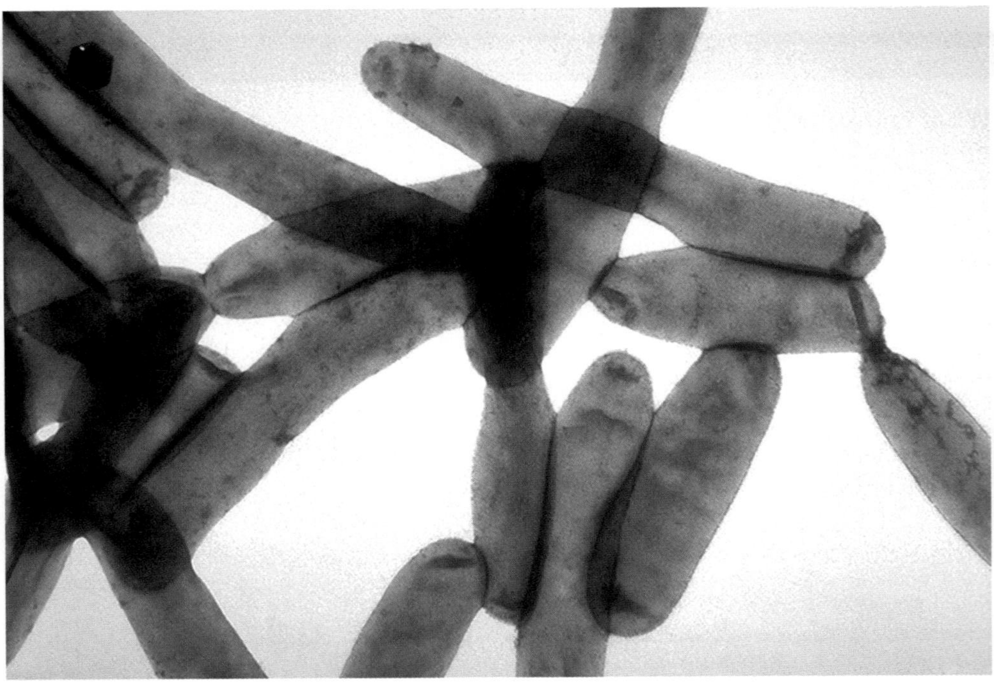

Courtesy of Centers for Disease Control and Prevention

Figure 34.3 - Legionella pneumophila

- are there infrequently used outlets, such as unused cabins with showers or taps?
- is there debris in the system, such as rust, sludge or scale?

The main action to take is to ensure that stagnant water cannot exist in the ship. Unoccupied cabins should have the taps and showers run regularly or the system should be disconnected.

All pipes and storage tanks should be insulated to ensure that water is maintained outside the temperature range 25°C to 50°C.

In cold water distribution systems, temperatures should be maintained at less than 25°C throughout the system to provide effective control.

Heaters should be set to ensure hot water is delivered to all taps at above 50°C.

Periodic maintenance and cleaning of water storage tanks should be carried out at appropriate frequencies and involve draining, physical cleaning and biocide treatment.

Symptoms

Legionnaires' disease is initially difficult to diagnose because the symptoms are similar to flu symptoms. Symptoms first appear between 2 and 10 days after exposure to the bacteria and include:

- High temperature, feverishness and chills
- cough
- muscle pains
- headache

and leading on to

- pneumonia

and very occasionally

- diarrhoea and signs of mental confusion.

Treatment

The illness is treated with erythromycin or a similar antibiotic.

Legionnaires' disease does not spread from person to person.

Contamination of Ships' Air Conditioning Systems by Legionella Bacteria

Recommended Counter Measures

Intakes - The jalousie design and the intake arrangements should be designed to eliminate spray and there should be proper attention to efficient drainage where necessary.

Filters - These should be readily accessible for regular maintenance or replacement. Weekly inspection of filters is recommended, washing or replacing them as necessary. Washable filters should be thoroughly rinsed in a super-chlorinated solution of 50 ppm. The frequency of routine inspection cleaning or replacement may need to be increased when the current rate of fouling caused by polluted ambient air at the intake is high.

Cooler - Careful design of the condensate sump and its drainage is necessary. The sump drains should be regularly inspected and cleaned to ensure that there is no spillage or accumulation of stagnant condensate. It is recommended that the sump is washed through with a super-chlorinated solution of 50 ppm at intervals not exceeding three months.

Adiabatic Spray Type Humidifiers - This type should be installed in new ships unless special measures are taken to reduce the risk. In existing ships, an effective moisture eliminator should be introduced if water carryover into the discharge air stream is found to occur. Regular maintenance and sterilisation of the water spray system is necessary. Modification of humidifier drains and circulating tank pipe suctions and drains should be considered if these are not sited in the bottom face of the unit or tank respectively.

Plenum Insulation - In new ships, a watertight facing should be fitted. In existing ships, the facing of the insulation should be examined at refit periods to ensure that the insulation itself is not becoming saturated.

Norovirus

What is Norovirus and Where Can it be Found?

This virus can cause acute viral gastroenteritis, which is also known as stomach flu. It is extremely contagious and is capable of surviving both extreme heat and cold, as well as in water that has been treated with chlorine.

Outbreaks are particularly common in contained environments, eg cruise ships, schools, hospitals, convalescent homes and nursing homes. The main reason for this is because the virus spreads very easily from one person to another, as well as being able to survive for several days in a contaminated area.

The virus is found in the stool or vomit of those who are infected. The illness can be transmitted in several ways including:

- Eating or drinking anything that has been infected with the virus
- coming into contact with contaminated surfaces or objects and then putting your hands into your mouth
- being in direct contact with anyone who is infected or showing symptoms of the virus, eg caring for someone who already has the illness, or sharing food or cutlery with someone who is ill.

There are many different strains of the virus and it is difficult to develop a long-lasting immunity because individuals can be infected more than once. Anybody can become infected but some people are more prone to being infected and developing more severe forms of this illness than others, eg young children, the elderly, pregnant women and those with a pre-existing illness. It is recently thought that people with blood group O are more at risk from infection than others.

Those who are infected tend to be contagious from the moment they begin to feel ill to approximately three days after recovery. Some have been known to still be contagious two weeks after recovery. It is very important that those who have recently recovered wash their hands regularly thoroughly and follow other hygiene practices to prevent the infection from spreading.

Symptoms

The Norovirus causes gastroenteritis, where the stomach and small intestine become inflamed. The symptoms, which usually last for one or two days, include nausea, vomiting and/or diarrhoea, and stomach cramps. Some people also complain of a headache, fever, chills and muscle aches. During this period, patients may feel very ill. Vomiting may often be violent and without any warning. The symptoms usually begin one to two days after ingesting the virus, although they have been known to appear 12 hours after exposure. There is no evidence to suggest that patients will become long-term carriers of the virus, but the virus may remain in the stool and vomit of the infected person from the day they start to feel unwell to two weeks after they have recovered.

Treatment

There is no specific medicine that kills or a vaccine that protects against the Norovirus. As a result, treatment is aimed at providing supportive care while the body fights the virus. People who have a healthy immune system can usually kill the Norovirus, and after one to two days the symptoms will usually improve.

Special fluids given by mouth, known as rehydration therapy, may be taken to prevent dehydration.

Other treatment suggestions include:

- Allowing the gastrointestinal tract to settle down by not eating anything for a few hours
- sipping small amounts of clear liquids or sucking ice cubes if the patient is still vomiting
- introducing foods gradually, starting with bland and easily digested food, eg toast
- avoiding dairy products, caffeine and alcohol until fully recovered
- taking plenty of rest.

Prevention

The risk of contact with the Norovirus can be reduced by:

- Washing your hands after going to the toilet or changing a nappy, and before eating or preparing food
- washing contaminated clothing or linen immediately in hot soapy water
- disposing of vomit or stools in the toilet, and thoroughly cleaning the surrounding area

- washing fruit and vegetables before consumption. Oysters should be steamed because raw oysters can contain harmful bacteria
- cleaning all surfaces thoroughly with disinfectant.

People who are infected with the Norovirus should not prepare food while they still have the symptoms and for three days after recovery. Any food that may have been contaminated must be thrown out.

Norovirus on Cruise Ships

As cruise ships are effectively a closed community, the Norovirus can rapidly spread around the passengers. As new passengers arrive every couple of days, it is very difficult to eradicate the infection, sometimes resulting in widespread outbreaks. Extreme measures may be required to eradicate the virus, including taking a ship out of service so that it can be thoroughly disinfected.

Case Studies

1. In January 2007, more than 300 people were infected with the Norovirus on board the '*QE2*'. Health officials commented that this was an unusually large outbreak; 17% of those on board were affected. The cleansing regime on board was upgraded and advice was provided to all an board on handwashing and general hygiene. Infected passengers were advised to stay in their cabins until the symptoms subsided.
2. In November 2006, a transatlantic cruise ship had to end its 16-day voyage after 700 people were affected by the Norovirus. Passengers were given injections and anti-diarrhoea medication by the ship's infirmary. Those infected were sent bottled water, soft drinks and rice while they were quarantined in their rooms. The ship was delayed in starting its next voyage until it had been completely disinfected.
3. In June 2006 more, than 100 passengers on the '*Black Prince*' were affected by a highly contagious winter vomiting virus. Passengers who were affected were confined to their cabins. The company stated that they regularly disinfected their ships.
4. In July 2009, one passenger died and four more were hospitalised after more than 150 people were taken ill after a suspected outbreak of Norovirus on Transocean Tours' cruiseship '*Marco Polo*'. The passenger who died was in his 70s and had a pre-existing medical condition. Local politicians were unhappy that passengers and crew were allowed to leave the ship and visit local shops and cafes, potentially bringing the virus on shore.

Medical Oxygen Cylinders

Ships that fall under Column A or B of the Medical First Aid Guide for Use in Accidents Involving Dangerous Goods (MFAG) Appendix 14 – List of Equipment 1 are required to carry a minimum of 44 litres/200 bar oxygen as follows:

- 1 × 40 litre/200 bar medical oxygen cylinder located in the ship's hospital, assembled for direct use, equipped with one flowmeter unit (2 ports) for supplying oxygen for 2 persons simultaneously, and
- 1 × complete portable set, ready for use, with a 2 litre/ 200 bar medical oxygen cylinder and a spare cylinder (also 2 litre/200 bar)
- the single 40 litre/200 bar medical oxygen cylinder may be substituted with either 2 × 20 litre/200 bar cylinders or 4 × 10 litre/200 bar cylinders, provided the equipment/ flowmeter units are arranged to supply oxygen to 2 persons simultaneously
- the cylinders are to be hydrostatically tested every 5 years, or at an interval specified by the manufacturer, whichever occurs sooner
- the contents of the cylinders are to be checked and changed as required according to the manufacturer's requirements, or every 3 years, whichever occurs sooner
- the entire system is to be inspected annually by a competent person in accordance with the manufacturer's instructions.

Medical Drugs in Ships' Safe

Controlled drugs are drugs that are graded according to the harmfulness attributed to the drug when it is misused. For this purpose, there are three drug categories:

- Class A, which includes heroin, morphine, and opium
- Class B, which includes barbiturates and codeine
- Class C, which includes, among other drugs, anabolic steroids.

A ship must not carry excess quantities of Class A or Class C drugs unless authorised by the Administrator.

Controlled Drugs Register

Regulations in some countries require that a record of any treatment given to anybody on board, including the type and quantity of any medicines and drugs supplied, must be entered in the logbook. Additionally, for controlled drugs, the master of the vessel is required to maintain, in a bound book, a two-section register. The two sections of the register should detail why, when and in what quantity the master purchased, impounded, dispensed or disposed of the drugs.

Controlled drugs must be entered into the controlled drugs register on reception by the vessel. The information logged must include the type, quantity and date received.

The following must also be recorded in the Controlled Drugs Register:

- The doses given, including the name of the person ordering the dose, the name of the person giving it and the name of the person receiving it
- date and time when a dose is lost or spoiled (eg broken ampoule, drug prepared but not injected, etc)
- a running count of remaining stocks, updated after each use
- a count, made at least weekly, of remaining ampoules, tablets, etc in store, to be checked against records of use and the running count
- information on disposal, including method, drug type, amount, date, time, receipts and witness documentation, including signatures (eg control signature form)
- stock movements for controlled drugs. This includes the supply, use, disposal, loss or theft of such controlled drugs.

The register of controlled drugs must be kept for a period of two years after the date of last entry.

Security of Controlled Drugs

The Merchant Shipping Regulations require ships to have a lockable medical cabinet for the storage of medicines and drugs. The Regulations also require the cabinet to have an inner cupboard solely for the storage of dangerous drugs (ie the controlled drugs). The inner cupboard should be fitted with a door and a lock that cannot be opened by the key to the medical cabinet. Under the Misuse of Drugs (Safe Custody) Regulations, only the master or a person authorised by him may open the inner cupboard. It is illegal to destroy unwanted Category A and B drugs. They can be disposed of only by giving them to a person who may lawfully supply them, such as a qualified pharmacist or qualified doctor.

It is also possible to dispose of drugs via the police. A receipt should be obtained from the recipient, and kept with, or affixed to, the controlled drugs register.

Carriage of Defibrillators on Ships

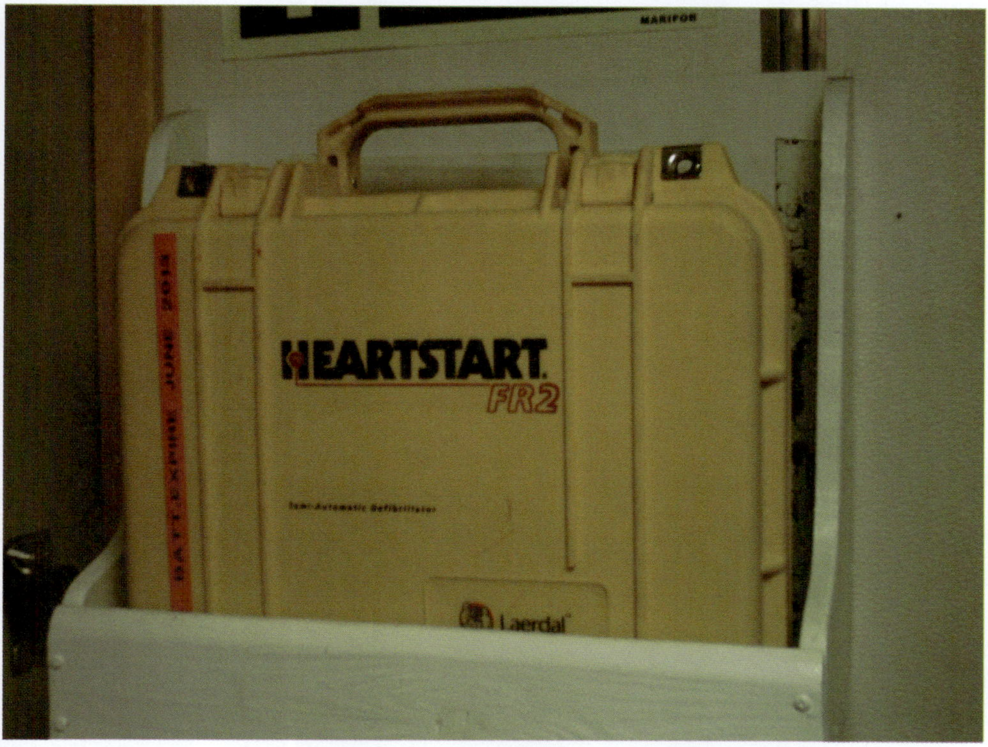

Defibrillators use electric shocks to restore the rhythm of the heart in the event of certain types of cardiac arrest. Technological advances mean that they are straightforward to use, relatively low cost and their use requires only basic training. In particular, automated external defibrillators (AEDs) assess the patient's condition and indicate when the shock should be administered. Since they are now widely available in public places on shore, there may be an expectation that they are similarly available on board ships.

Defibrillators and consumables should be tested in accordance with the manufacturer's recommendations. In addition, first aiders on board ship should receive suitable familiarisation training in the use of AEDs, as well as training in cardio-pulmonary resuscitation. Regular refresher training is also required to ensure that competence is maintained.

All those who may use defibrillators should be aware that their success rate in terms of lives saved is relatively low.

Even where a patient's heart rhythm is restored, the patient will remain very ill and may require continuous assistance and support with breathing and other essential functions until arrival at hospital. The patient will therefore need to be transported to hospital as quickly as possible and the master or vessel operator should wherever possible make suitable arrangements for transport to be available on arrival, as soon as the incident has occurred.

Source: MGN 297

CHAPTER 35

Housekeeping on Board

Marking of Walkways on Board

All deck surfaces used as walkways about the ship shall be kept free from obstructions that could cause a slip or fall. Where appropriate, walkways on decks should be delineated by painted lines and indicated by pictorial signs. Where it is unsafe to walk through an area, it should be cordoned off until it can be cleared or an alternative route made available.

Walkways/transit routes should have slip-resistant surfaces.

Painting Non-slip Walkways

Ready, prepared non-slip paint is available, but it tends to be thick and hard to apply. The easier option is to make non-slip paint by mixing a grit additive into the chosen paint.

Grit additive is available from chandlers and the type of grit chosen depends on where the non-slip paint is to be applied.

Where an area becomes slippery due to snow, ice or water, sand or some other suitable substance should be spread over the area. Spillages of oil or grease etc should be cleaned up as soon as practicable.

Temporary obstructions are dangerous and if they are to remain for any length of time they should be highlighted by appropriate warning signs.

When heavy weather is expected, lifelines should be rigged across areas where access is required.

Safety Signs

Introduction

International standard safety signs should be used to indicate hazards, or control measures to be taken where the hazard cannot be removed.

Signs and Notices

Permanent signs *are used:*

- *To give prohibitions, warnings and mandatory requirements*
- *to mark emergency escape routes*
- *to identify first aid facilities*
- *to show the location of fire-fighting and life-saving equipment.*

Red signs *mean either:*

- *Stop doing something or don't do it (prohibition)*
- *stop/shut down or evacuate.*

They also mark the location and type of fire-fighting equipment.

Signs of prohibition are based on a red circular band with a red diagonal bar and white backing. The symbol for the prohibited action is shown in black behind the red diagonal bar, eg 'No Smoking', with a cigarette depicted.

A sign indicating fire-fighting equipment is a red square or rectangle, with information given in words or by a symbol in white. Alternatively, an IMO sign is a yellow square or rectangle, with information given in words or by a symbol in red.

Yellow signs *are advisory and mean:*

- *Be careful, or take precaution.*

Warning signs are based on a yellow triangle with a black border. The symbol for the hazard is shown in black, eg poisoning risk is represented by a black skull and crossbones on a yellow background.

Blue signs *are mandatory and mean:*

- *Take specific action.*

Mandatory signs are based on a blue disc. The symbol for the precaution to be taken is shown in white, eg 'Goggles to be worn', with a head with goggles depicted. If, no suitable symbol is available, appropriate wording may be used instead, eg 'Keep Clear'.

Green signs *indicate*

- *Emergency escape, or*
- *first aid.*

The sign is a green square or rectangle, with safety information shown by words or a symbol in white, eg a white arrow on a green background points to an emergency exit.

If more information is needed to clarify the meaning of the symbol, a supplementary sign with text only may appear below the sign, eg 'Not Drinking Water'.

The supplementary sign should be oblong or square and either:

(a) White with text in black, or

(b) the same background colour as the safety colour used on the sign it is supplementing, with the text in the relevant contrasting colour.

Shore-based personnel and passengers may not be aware that they are colour blind so colour should not be used as a sole indicator.

Where a language other than English is extensively used on a ship, any text used in conjunction with a sign should also be displayed in that language.

Occasional Signs

Illuminated signs, acoustic signals, hand signals and spoken signals may also be used for temporary hazards or circumstances.

Illuminated signs and acoustic signals must be tested regularly to ensure that they are working. Acoustic signs should comply with the IMO Code on Alarms and Indicators, 1992.

The internationally understood hand signals for use of lifting appliances are given in Annex 21.1 of the Code of Safe Working Practices (COSWP) for Merchant Seamen.

Spoken signals should comply with the IMO Standard for Marine Navigational Vocabulary. This is particularly important when communicating with another ship or with shore-side workers abroad, where English may not be commonly used.

Source: 'Code of Safe Working Practices for Merchant Seamen'

Extract from Annex 1 of COSWP

Safety Signs as required by the MS and FV (Safety Signs and Signals) Regulations 2001 and Merchant Shipping Notice MSN 1763

Part 1 – Prohibitory Signs

Symbol **Meaning**

Prohibition -
Do not do

Examples:

No smoking

Smoking and naked flames forbidden

No access for pedestrians

Do not extinguish with water

Not drinkable

No access for unauthorised persons

No access for industrial vehicles

Do not touch

Source: 'Code of Safe Working Practices for Merchant Seamen'

Additional Useful Prohibition Signs

Do not remove electrical earth

Do not operate

Do not use mobile telephones
or
Turn off mobile telephones

Unauthorised persons

Do not oil or clean

Unauthorised persons

Part 2 – Warning Signs

Symbol **Meaning**

Warning -
Danger

Examples:

Flammable material or high temperature (a)

Explosive material

Toxic material

Corrosive material

Radioactive material

Overhead load

Industrial vehicles

Danger: electricity

General danger

Laser beam

Oxidant material

Non-ionising radiation

---

a) *In the absence of a specific sign for high temperature.*

Safety Signs

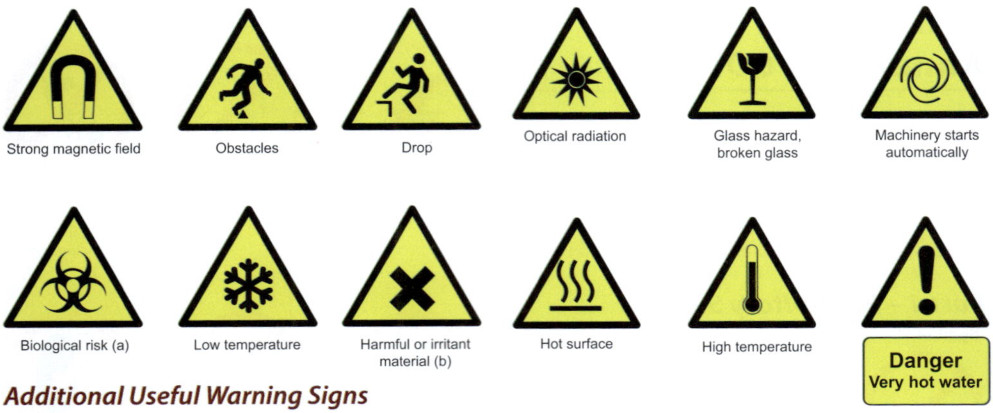

Additional Useful Warning Signs

(a) *Pictogram laid down in Council Directive 90/679/EEC of 26th November 1990 on the protection of workers from the risks related to exposure to biological agents at work (seventh individual Directive within the meaning of article 16(1) of Directive 89/391/EEC) Official Journal No 1,374, 31.12.1990, p1.*

(b) *The background to this sign may exceptionally be amber if justified in order to differentiate it from a similar road safety sign.*

Source: 'Code of Safe Working Practices for Merchant Seamen'

Part 3 – Mandatory Signs Symbol

Symbol | **Meaning**

Mandatory -
Must do

Examples:

Eye protection must be worn

Safety helmet must be worn

Ear protection must be worn

Respiratory equipment must be worn

Safety boots must be worn

Safety gloves must be worn

Safety overalls must be worn

Face protection must be worn

Safety harness must be worn

Pedestrians must use this route

High visibility clothing must be worn

General mandatory sign (to be accompanied where necessary by another sign)

Additional Useful Mandatory Signs

Source: 'Code of Safe Working Practices for Merchant Seamen'

Safety Signs

Part 4 – Emergency Escape, First Aid Signs and Safe Condition

Symbol Meaning

Examples:

Emergency exit/escape route signs

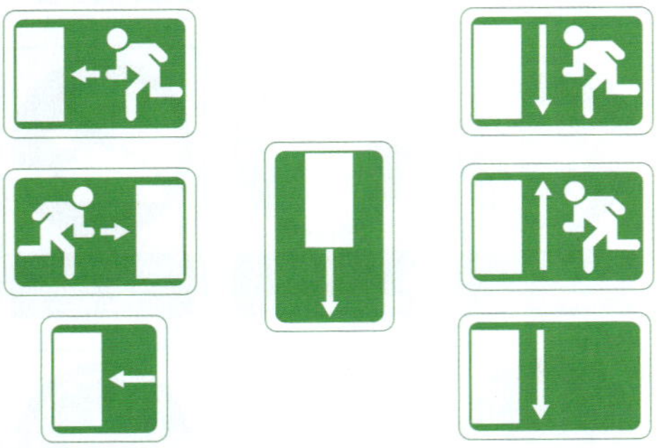

Supplementary information signs

This way

First aid signs

First aid post | Stretcher | Safety shower | Eyewash

Safe condition sign

Emergency telephone for first aid or escape

Emergency stop for machinery

Additional Useful Safe Condition Sign

Part 5 – Fire-Fighting Signs

Symbol Meaning

Examples:

Fire hose | Ladder | Fire extinguisher | Emergency fire telephone

This way
(supplementary information sign)

Fire alarm

Fire extinguisher

Source: 'Code of Safe Working Practices for Merchant Seamen'

Additional Useful Fire Equipment Signs

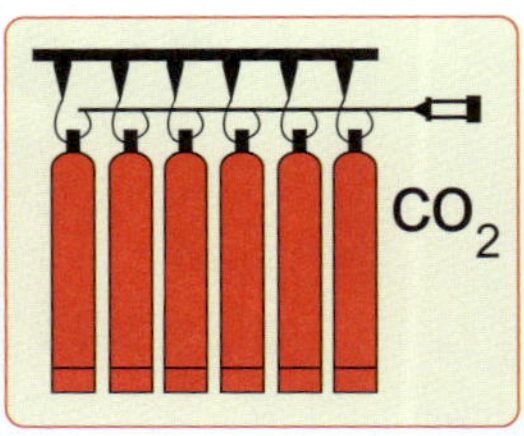

CO_2 fixed installation

FM 200 fixed installation

NOVEC 1230 fixed installation

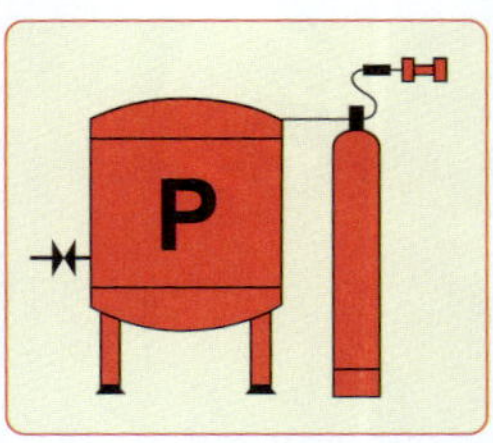

Dry powder fixed installation

Source: 'Code of Safe Working Practices for Merchant Seamen'

Snap-Back Zones

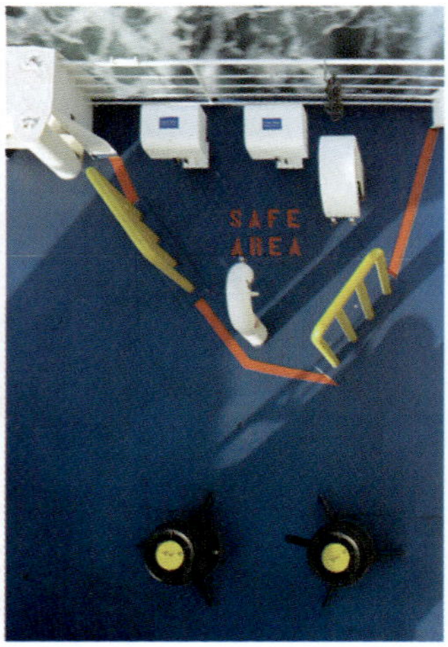

When moorings are under strain, all personnel in the vicinity should remain in positions of safety, ie avoiding all 'snap-back' zones.

It is strongly recommended that a bird's eye view of the mooring deck arrangement is taken to identify danger areas. Immediate action should be taken to reduce the load should any part of the system appear to be under excessive strain. Care is needed so that ropes or wires will not jam when they come under strain and that, if necessary, they can quickly be slackened off.

Where a mooring line is led around a pedestal roller fairlead, the 'snap-back' zone area will change and expand. Where possible, lines should NOT be led around pedestals except during the operation of mooring the ship. Thereafter, lines should be made up on bitts, clear of pedestals if at all possible.

Further information on 'snap-back' zones can be found in section 6.3.5 of the Oil Companies International Marine Forum (OCIMF) publication *'Mooring Equipment Guidelines'*.

Compressed Gas Cylinders

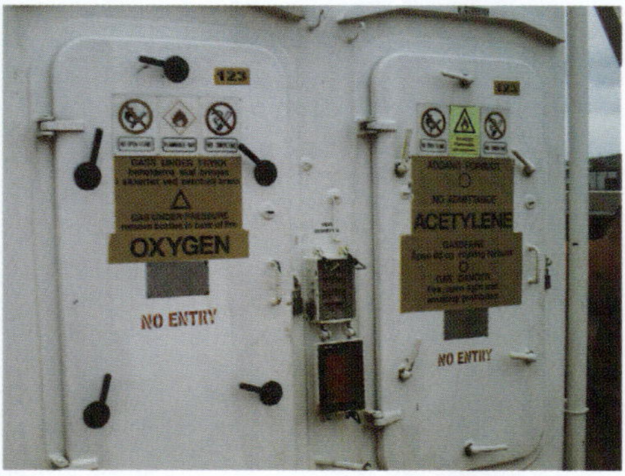

Compressed gas cylinders should always be handled with care, whether full or empty. They should be properly secured and stored in a location appropriate to their intended use and the risks that inadvertent release of gas may present. The cylinders should be secured to be capable of quick and easy release, such as in the case of fire. Where appropriate, cylinder trolleys should be used to transport cylinders from one place to another.

If there are protective caps for the cylinder valve, they should be screwed in place when the cylinders are not in use or are being moved. If there are no protective caps, the valve system should be protected from inadvertent damage. Valves should be closed when the cylinder is empty.

Where the International Maritime Dangerous Goods (IMDG) Code requires cylinders of differing gases to be segregated, they should be stored in separate, well-ventilated compartments that are not subject to extremes of temperature. If gas is flammable, the compartment in which the cylinders are stowed should have no electrical fittings or other sources of ignition and prominent and permanent 'NO SMOKING' signs should be displayed in the entrance and within the space. Empty cylinders should be marked and segregated from full ones. All gas cylinder stores should be marked with safety signs.

- Cylinder valves, controls and associated fittings should be kept free from oil, grease and paint; controls should not be operated with oily hands
- gas should not be taken from cylinders unless the correct pressure reducing regulator has been attached to the cylinder outlet valve
- cylinders found to have leaks that cannot be stopped by closing the outlet valve should be taken to the open deck, away from any sources of heat or ignition, and slowly discharged to the atmosphere.

Gas Cylinder Colour Coding

Gas cylinders should be marked and colour coded according to the relevant internationally recognised standard.

Each cylinder should be clearly marked with the name of the gas and its chemical formula or symbol. The cylinder body should be coloured according to the contents with, where necessary, a secondary colour band painted around the neck of the cylinder to denote the particular hazards of the gas (eg flammability, toxicity, etc).

Name of gas	Chemical formula or symbol	Ground colour of container	Colour of band
Oxygen	O_2	Black	None
Carbon Dioxide	CO_2	Black	None
Compressed Air	None (mixed gases)	French Grey	None
Nitrogen	N_2	French Grey	Black
Acetylene	C_2H_2	Maroon	None
Propane	C_3H_8	Signal Red	None
Butane	C_2H_6	None Specified	Signal Red
Helium	He	Brown	None
Note: Refrigerant gases are not allocated specified ground or band colours under the British Standard Specification.			

Source: British Standard Specifications from the 'Code of Safe Working Practices for Merchant Seamen'

Storage Batteries – General

When a battery is being charged, it 'gases', giving off both hydrogen and oxygen. Because hydrogen is easily ignited in concentrations ranging from 4 to 75% in air, battery containers and compartments will require ventilation to prevent any accumulation of hydrogen.

Smoking and any type of open flame are prohibited in a battery compartment. A conspicuous notice to this effect should be displayed at the entrance to the compartment.

Lighting fittings in battery compartments should be properly maintained, with protective glasses in position and properly tightened. If cracked or broken glasses cannot be replaced immediately, the electric circuit should be isolated until replacements are obtained.

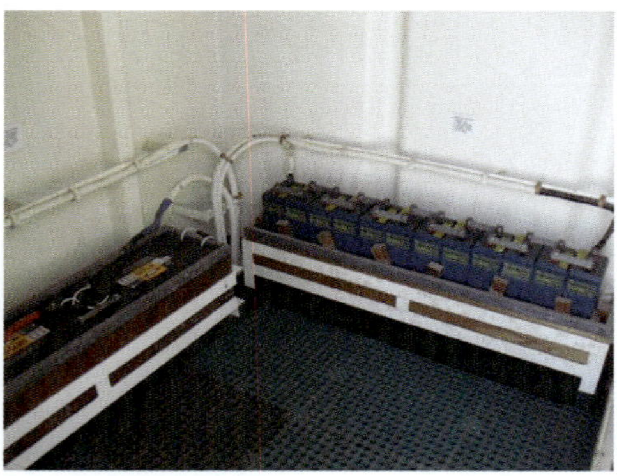

No unauthorised modifications or additions should be made to electrical equipment (including lighting fittings) in battery compartments.

Portable electric lamps and tools, and other portable power tools that might give rise to sparks, should not be used in battery compartments.

The battery compartment should not be used as a store for any other materials or gear.

A short circuit of even one cell may produce an arc or sparks, which may cause an explosion of any hydrogen present. Additionally, the very heavy current that can flow in the short circuiting wire or tool may cause burns due to rapid overheating of the metal.

Insulation and/or guarding of cables in battery compartments should be maintained in good condition.

All battery connections should be kept clean and tight to avoid sparking and overheating. Temporary clip-on connections should never be used as they may be worked loose by vibration, causing a spark or short circuit.

Metal tools, such as wrenches or spanners, should never be placed on top of batteries as they may cause sparks or short circuits. The use of insulated tools is recommended.

Jewellery, watches and rings, etc should be removed when working on batteries. A short circuit through any of these items will heat it rapidly and may cause a severe skin burn. If rings cannot be removed, they should be heavily taped in insulating material.

The battery chargers and all circuits fed by the battery should be switched off when leads are being connected or disconnected. If a battery is in sections, it may be possible to reduce the voltage between cells in the work area, and hence the severity of an accidental short circuit or electric shock, by removing the jumper leads between sections before work is begun. It should be appreciated that, while individual cell voltages may not prevent a shock risk, dangerous voltages can exist when numbers of cells are connected together in series. A lethal shock needs a current of only tens of milliamps and particular care should be exercised when the voltage exceeds 50 V.

Battery cell vent plugs should be screwed tight while connections are being made or broken.

The ventilation tubes of battery boxes should be examined regularly to ensure that they are free from obstruction.

Lids of battery boxes should be fastened while open for servicing and properly secured again when the work is finished.

Batteries should be kept battened into position to prevent shifting in rough weather.

Alkaline and lead-acid batteries should be kept in separate compartments or separated by screens. Where both lead-acid and alkaline batteries are in use, great care should be exercised to keep apart the materials and tools used in servicing each type, as contamination of the electrolyte may cause deterioration of battery performance and mixing of the two electrolytes can produce a vigorous chemical reaction that could be very dangerous.

Both acid and alkaline electrolytes are highly corrosive. Immediate remedial action should be taken to wash off any accidental splashes on the person or on the equipment. Hands should always be washed as soon as the work is finished.

Batteries should always be transported in the upright position to avoid spillage of electrolyte. A sufficient number of men should be employed since the batteries are heavy and painful strains or injury can otherwise easily result.

Storage Batteries – Lead-Acid

When the electrolyte is being prepared, the concentrated sulphuric acid should be added SLOWLY to the water.

If water is added to the acid, the heat generated may cause an explosion of steam, splattering acid over the person handling it.

Goggles, rubber gloves and a protective apron should be worn when acid is handled.

To neutralise acid on skin or clothes, copious quantities of clean fresh water should be used.

An eyewash bottle should be to hand in the compartment for immediate use on the eyes in the case of accident. This bottle should be clearly distinguishable by touch from acid or other containers, so that it may be easily located by a person who is temporarily blinded.

The corrosion products that form round the terminals of batteries are injurious to skin or eyes. They should be removed by brushing, away from the body. Terminals should be protected with petroleum jelly.

An excessive charging rate causes acid mist to be carried out of the vents onto adjacent surfaces. This should be cleaned off with diluted ammonia water or soda solution and affected areas then dried.

Storage Batteries – Alkaline

The general safety precautions with this type of battery are the same as for the lead-acid batteries with the following exceptions.

The electrolyte in these batteries is alkaline but is similarly corrosive. It should not be allowed to come into contact with the skin or clothing. Burns should be treated with boracic powder or a saturated solution of boracic powder. Eyes should be washed out thoroughly with water followed immediately with a solution of boracic powder (at the rate of one teaspoonful to one-half litre or one pint of water). This solution should be always readily accessible when the electrolyte is handled.

Unlike lead-acid batteries, metal cases of alkaline batteries remain live at all times and care should be taken not to touch them or to allow metal tools to come into contact.

Weathertight Doors

The integrity of openings on the freeboard and other decks must be maintained, and weathertight doors are fitted to these openings. These must comply with the requirements of the Load Line Rules and comprise steel doors that may be secured and made tight from either side. Weathertightness is maintained through the compression of a rubber gasket in the frame of the door.

Watertight Doors

The number of openings in watertight bulkheads on passenger ships is to be kept to a minimum in accordance with SOLAS Regulation II-1/13.1 (previous SOLAS Regulation II-1/15.1).

To maintain watertight subdivision, all watertight doors are to be kept closed during navigation except in certain limited circumstances.

SOLAS Regulation II-1/22.3, allows a watertight door to be temporarily opened to permit the passage of passengers or crew, or when work in the immediate vicinity of the door necessitates it being opened. In this case, the door must be immediately closed when transit through the door is complete or the work is finished. SOLAS Regulation II-1/22.4 allows watertight doors to remain open during navigation but only if considered absolutely necessary to the safe and effective operation of the ship's machinery or to permit passengers normally unrestricted access throughout the passenger area.

Watertight doors on deck are heavy safe-like doors with numerous latching dogs around the outer rim. Below the waterline, the doors are generally of the sliding type, either horizontal or vertical.

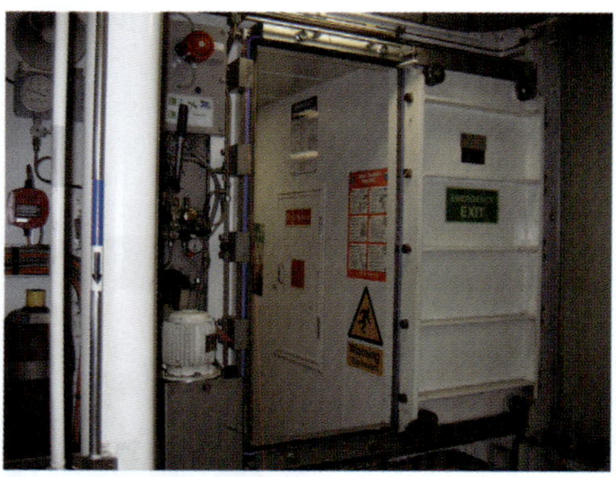

Figure 35.1 - Sliding door

Operation of Watertight Doors

Power-operated watertight doors are designed to be remotely closed in a short period of time with a force sufficient to overcome not only the weight of the door but also water flowing through its opening, and both while a ship is listing 15° in either direction. The operation of watertight doors involves possible danger to persons passing through and injury or loss of life is likely to occur to anyone trapped in the door's path. The audible alarm that sounds for a few seconds before the door starts moving, and continues sounding while the door is in motion, is intended to reduce the risk of persons being trapped.

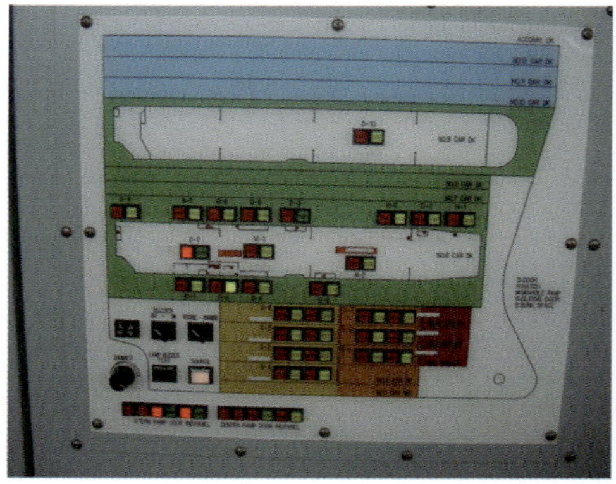

Figure 35.2 - Watertight door indicator panel

SOLAS Regulations regarding Closure of Watertight Doors

1. **Watertight doors shall be power-operated sliding doors capable of being closed simultaneously from the central operating console at the navigation bridge in not more than 60 seconds with the ship in the upright position.**
2. **The door shall have an approximately uniform rate of closure under power. The closure time, from the time the door begins to move to the time it reaches the completely closed position, shall in no case be less than 20 seconds or more than 40 seconds with the ship in upright position.**
3. **The time necessary for the complete closure of the door, when operating by hand gear, shall not exceed 90 seconds with the ship in the upright position.**

Figure 35.3 - Car deck watertight door

Operation of Automatically-Operated Watertight Doors

The various parts of a watertight door are labelled in the diagram and include:

- Hydraulic cylinder, which is necessary for mechanical operation of the door to open and close it
- hand pump, which is necessary in case of failure of the mechanical system. There must always be a manual option for operation of the door
- the necessary monitors and controls in the form of alarm and control valves, which are activated for safety purposes
- a remote switch from where the door can be operated in case of emergency or any other situation where direct access is not possible. There should be an indicator at the remote location that shows whether the door is open or closed.

Depending on the location and situation, the doors may open either through sliding or like normal hinged doors. The material of construction should be strong and durable, such as mild or cast steel. The doors should operate without fail, even when the ship is listed to around 15°.

In the manufacturing yard, testing of the doors is carried out either by applying a high hose pressure of water and checking for water leakage at the other side or by submerging the door under the required pressure of water.

It is also worth noting that, since cutting of the door in the bulkhead leads to reduction of strength, it is important to counter this effect by providing extra stiffeners and frames for reinforcement, otherwise water might rupture the bulkhead itself, which would defeat the purpose of having a watertight door.

Watertight Doors

Safe Use

- All seafarers who may have to use watertight doors should be instructed in their safe use
- power-operated watertight doors can be closed from the bridge and so particular care should be taken when using them. If opened locally when under the control of the bridge, a door will reclose automatically and crush anyone in its path as soon as local control has been released. Both hands are usually required to operate the local controls and, for this reason, no person should attempt to carry any load through the doors while alone. The bridge should be notified whenever the doors are opened and immediately after they are closed
- notices clearly stating the method of operating the local controls of watertight doors should be prominently displayed on both sides of the doors
- no attempt should be made to pass through a watertight door when it is closing or when the warning alarm is sounding
- if it is necessary to leave the area confined by the doors, emergency exits should be used. A warning to that effect should be displayed at the local operating point.

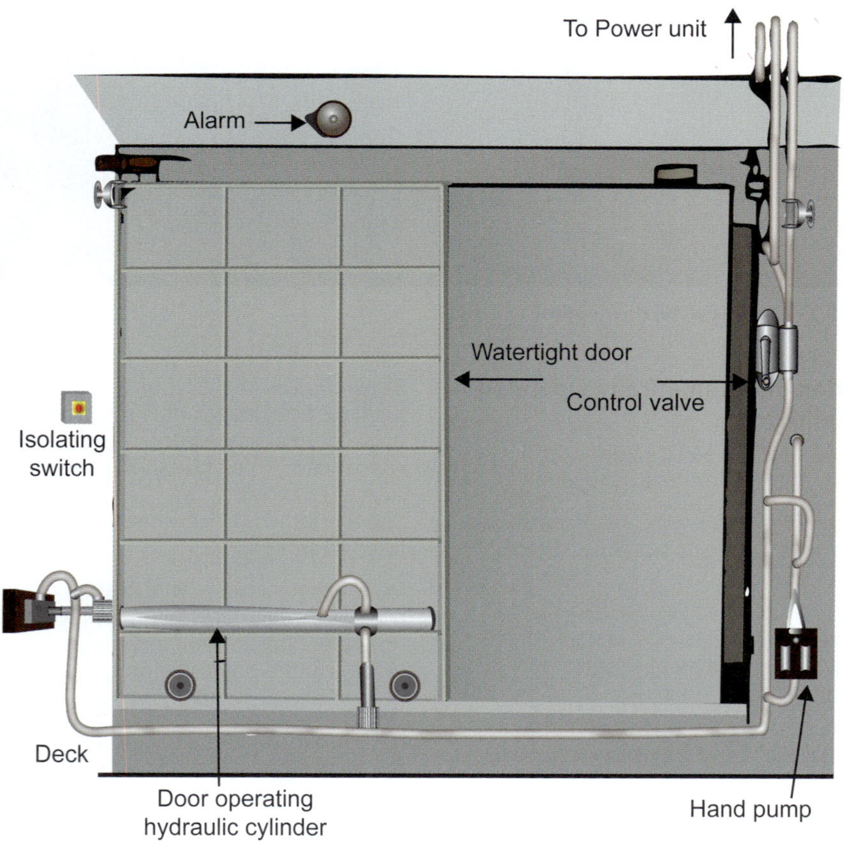

Figure 35.4 - Watertight door mechanism

COSHH Locker

Courtesy of 'Onboard Safety' Publ. 2012

Figure 35.5 - COSHH/chemicals or substances hazardous to health

Many substances found on ships are hazardous to health. They include not only substances displaying hazard warning labels (eg dangerous goods cargoes and ships' stores) but also, for example, a range of dusts, fumes and fungal spores from goods, plant or activities on board.

Whenever crew members work with substances hazardous to health, the master should ensure that any risks from exposure are assessed and appropriate measures taken to prevent or control them. The assessment should include consideration of precautionary measures for other affected groups such as stevedores and maintenance personnel.

Officers should instruct, inform and train crews so that they know and understand the risks arising from their work, the precautions to be taken and the results of any monitoring of exposure.

The health risk from a substance hazardous to health should be assessed by a competent person, who should consider each of the following:

- The identity, concentration, form and possible harmful effects of the hazardous substance
- the likely exposure for the work in hand
- the number of crew who may be exposed.

The risks to crew members and others should be considered separately for each area of the ship and each risk should be assessed individually.

Reference may be made to the International Maritime Dangerous Goods (IMDG) Code.

A record should be kept of the assessment and of any measures taken. When adequate control is not feasible by any other means, personal protective clothing and equipment should be provided and used.

Particular attention must be paid to good housekeeping practices where paints, chemicals or dangerous cargoes are concerned. Spillages from such substances can pose a considerable slip, fire or health hazard. Segregated stowage and adequate securing of paints, chemicals and dangerous cargoes will be part of good housekeeping practice.

Paint Lockers

Inspectors often refer to the initial impression gained from the top of the gangway to the accommodation. However, one of the best indicators of how the crew are treating the ship is the state of the paint locker.

Paint lockers are often the most disorganised areas on board ship and, without due care and attention, they can easily become one of the biggest hazards. Paint lockers should be examined during regular safety inspections, at least every 3 months.

Many paints present a fire hazard because they contain flammable solvents and have a low flash point.

Safety Tips for a Paint Locker

- The locker needs to be organised. If it is in an irretrievable condition, it should be cleared out, cleaned thoroughly and the paint and equipment restowed carefully
- the locker should have an eyewash station that is easily accessible, unobstructed and in good working order. It should have a green sign with white letters denoting 'Eye Wash Station'
- the locker must be adequately ventilated to prevent paint vapours accumulating and creating a toxic and highly flammable atmosphere. If the locker's ventilation is broken, it becomes a critical safety item for repair
- paint must be stowed adequately for sea and must not interfere with the exhaust vent or eyewash station. Paint brushes and stirring sticks should be stored in closed metal containers. Paints should not be stowed together with oxidisers or acids.

Fire-Extinguishing Requirements for Paint Lockers

Every ship >500 tons should protect every paint locker and flammable liquid locker with an approved fire-extinguishing system of the following types:

- A carbon dioxide system, designed to give a minimum volume of free gas equal to 40% of the gross volume of the protected space
- a dry powder system, designed for at least 0.5 kg powder/m^3
- a water spraying or sprinkler system, designed for 5 l/m^2 min. Water spraying systems may be connected to the fire main of the ship.

In each case, the fire-extinguishing system must be capable of being operated from outside the space. A portable fire extinguisher should be fitted immediately outside the entrance to the paint locker.

Gangways and Ladders

Positioning of Gangways

Gangways should not be used at an angle of inclination greater than 30° from the horizontal. Accommodation ladders should not be used at an angle greater than 55° from the horizontal, unless specifically designed for greater angles.

When the inboard end of the gangway or accommodation ladder rests on, or is flush with, the top of the bulwark, a bulwark ladder should be provided. Any gap between the bulwark ladder and the gangway or accommodation ladder should be fenced to a height of at least 1 metre.

Gangways and other access equipment should not be rigged on ships' rails unless the rail has been reinforced for that purpose.

The means of access should be checked to ensure that it is safe to use after rigging. There should be further checks to ensure that adjustments are made when necessary due to tidal movements or change of trim and freeboard. Guard ropes, chains, etc should be kept taut at all times and stanchions should be rigidly secured.

Source: 'Code of Safe Working Practices for Merchant Seamen'

Each end of a gangway or accommodation or other ladder should provide access to a safe place of entry/access on the ship or jetty/quay.

The means of access should be sited clear of the cargo working area and no suspended load should pass over it. Where this is not practical, access should be supervised at all times.

A lifebuoy should be available and ready for use at the point of access aboard the ship.

Gangway Construction

- *Gangways must be carried on ships of 30 metres in length or over and accommodation ladders must be carried on ships of 120 metres in length or over. Access equipment must be of good construction, sound material and adequate strength, free from patent defect and properly maintained*
- *gangways and accommodation ladders must be clearly marked with the manufacturer's name, the model number, the maximum designed angle of use and the maximum safe loading both by numbers of persons and by total weight*
- *gangways must comply with the specifications set out in Standard BS MA 78:1978, or equivalent, and must be fitted with suitable fencing along their entire length*
- *gangways, accommodation ladders and winches used for lifting and/or access should be tested in the same way as all other lifting appliances and records maintained, including any test certificates.*

Accommodation Ladder Construction

Accommodation ladders must comply with the specifications set out in Standard BS MA 89:1980 or after 1st January 2010 should meet applicable international standards such as ISO 5488:1979, Shipbuilding, or an equivalent standard.

Gangways and Ladders

The ladder should be designed so that:

- *It rests firmly against the side of the ship*
- *the angle of slope is no more than 55°. Treads and steps should provide a safe foothold at the angle at which the ladder is used*
- *it is fitted with suitable fencing (preferably rigid handrails) along its entire length, except that fencing at the bottom platform may allow access from the outboard side*
- *the bottom platform is horizontal, and any intermediate platforms are self-levelling*
- *it can easily be inspected and maintained*
- *it is rigged as close to the working area but clear of any cargo operations as possible*
- *it is marked with its safe working load at the top and bottom.*

When a bulwark ladder is to be used it must comply with the specifications set out in the Shipbuilding Industry Standard No SIS 7, or BS MA 39: Part 2, Ships' ladders (steel sloping) or be of an equivalent standard. Adequate fittings must be provided to enable the bulwark ladder to be properly and safely secured.

When an accommodation ladder is being rigged this should be completed with the ladder in the horizontal position so that those working on it can be safely attached with a safety line to the deck and the ladder secured to reduce any unnecessary movement.

Corrosion of Accommodation Ladders and Gangways

- *Aluminium alloys are highly susceptible to galvanic corrosion. Great care should be exercised when connecting mild steel fittings, whether or not they are galvanised, to accommodation ladders and gangways constructed of aluminium*
- *plugs and joints of neoprene, or other suitable material, should be used between mild steel fittings, washers, etc and aluminium. The plugs or joints should be significantly larger than the fittings or washers*
- *repairs using mild steel doublers or bolts made of mild steel or brass or other unsuitable material should be considered as temporary. Permanent repairs, or the replacement of the means of access, should be undertaken at the earliest opportunity*
- *the manufacturer's instructions should give guidance on examination and testing of the equipment. However, close examination of certain parts of accommodation ladders and gangways is difficult due to their fittings and attachments. It is essential, therefore, that the fittings are removed periodically for a thorough examination of the parts most likely to be affected by corrosion. Accommodation ladders and gangways should be turned over to allow for a thorough examination of the underside. Particular attention should be paid to the immediate perimeter of the fittings; this area should be tested for corrosion with a wire probe or scribe. Where the corrosion appears to have reduced the thickness of the parent metal to 3 mm, back plates should be fitted inside the stringers of the accommodation ladder or gangways.*

Safety Nets

A safety net should be mounted, whenever possible, where a person may fall from boarding equipment or from the ship's deck or quayside. Safety nets should be securely rigged, with use made of attachment points on the quayside where possible.

Source: 'Code of Safe Working Practices for Merchant Seamen'

Maintenance of Equipment for Means of Access

Any equipment used for boarding must be properly maintained, and should be inspected by a competent person at appropriate intervals. Any defects affecting the safety of any access equipment, including access provided by a shore authority, should be reported immediately to a responsible person and should be made good before further use.

Gangways, accommodation ladders and winches used for lifting or access should be tested in the same way as all other lifting appliances and records maintained including any test certificates.

Portable and Rope Ladders

Where a portable ladder is used it is very important that it is checked regularly by a competent person and that account is taken of vessel movement and tide changes.

When it is necessary to use a portable ladder for access it should be used at an angle of between 60° and 75° from the horizontal. The ladder should extend at least 1 metre above the upper landing place unless there are other suitable handholds. It should be properly secured against slipping or shifting sideways or falling and placed to afford a clearance of at least 150 mm behind the rungs.

A rope ladder should never be secured to rails or to any other means of support unless the rails or support are constructed and fixed to take the weight of a man and a ladder with an ample margin of safety.

A rope ladder should be left so that it either hangs fully extended from a securing point or is pulled up completely. It should not be left so that any slack will suddenly pay out when it is used.

Rope Ladder Construction

A rope ladder must be of adequate width and length and constructed to be efficiently secured to the ship.

- *The steps must provide a slip-resistant foothold and must be so secured that they are firmly held against twist, turnover or tilt*
- *the steps must be horizontal and equally spaced*
- *the side ropes should be equally spaced*
- *there should be no shackles, knots or splices between rungs.*

Ladders of more than 1.5 metres in length must be fitted with spreaders not less than 1.8 metres long. The lowest spreader must be on the fifth step from the bottom and the interval between spreaders must not exceed nine steps. The spreaders should not be lashed between steps.

Source: 'Code of Safe Working Practices for Merchant Seamen'

Steel-Hinged Inspection/Access Lids

- *Inspection/access hatch lids should be constructed of steel or similar material and hinged so they can be easily and safely opened or closed. Those on weather decks should be seated on watertight rubber gaskets and secured weathertight by dogs, side cleats or equivalent tightening devices*
- *when not secured, inspection/access hatch lids must be able to be easily and safely opened from above and, if practicable, from below*
- *it should be possible to lift inspection/ access hatches by hand without straining or endangering personnel*
- *heavy or inaccessible hatch lids should be fitted with counterweights or a pulley system so that they can easily be opened by one or two persons*
- *open hatch lids should be easily and safely secured against movement or accidental closing.*

Source: 'Code of Safe Working Practices for Merchant Seamen'

CHAPTER 36

Ships' Equipment and Maintenance

Types of Cargo Pump

A variety of different pumps are used on board ship, particularly in the engine room.

This section describes some of the pumps typically seen on various types of tanker.

Reciprocating Pump

Reciprocating pumps are often powered by steam, and are the type of stripping pumps used on older VLCCs.

The self-priming capability of the direct acting reciprocating pump gives it an advantage over the centrifugal pump. Reciprocating pumps are extremely flexible in operation, having an infinitely variable capacity from no load to full load and being suitable for both manual and automatic control.

The simplex type pump has the disadvantage in that its discharge is by a series of fluctuations and not a steady flow. This can result in vibrations and heavy shock loadings, with possible damage to the pump and piping systems if provision is not made to accommodate the pulsations. Such units are normally fitted with air-vessels at the discharge connection of the pump in order to absorb the fluctuations in the discharge pressure.

Duplex direct acting pumps produce a continuous uniform flow of liquid. This is particularly important in such systems as boiler feed water systems. When one plunger has reached the end of its stroke, the other is still moving and so maintaining a smooth flow removing necessity of an air-vessel. The working principle is that the piston of one cylinder operates the steam slide valve of the other cylinder. No dead centre exists as one or the other steam ports is always open and the pump will start as soon as steam is admitted to the cylinder. Figure 36.1 shows a sectional view of a duplex steam pump.

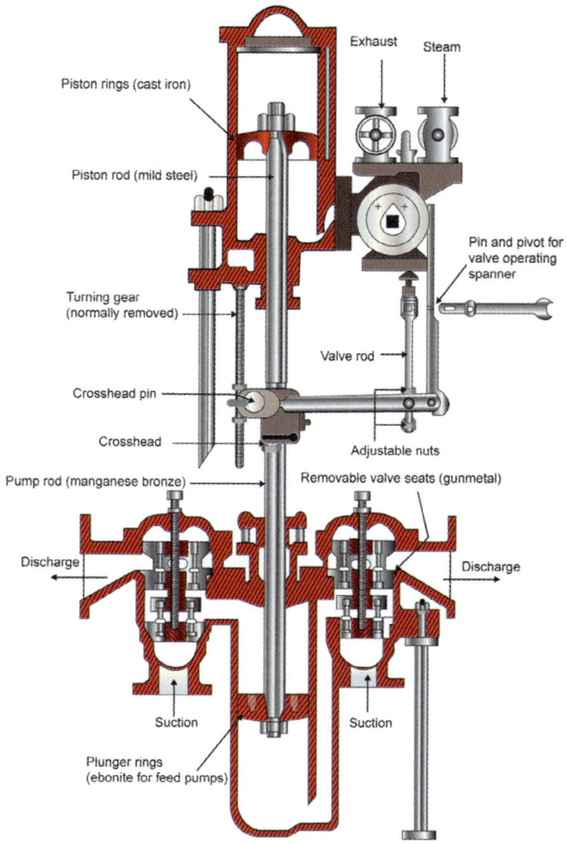

Figure 36.1 - 'Weirs' reciprocating pump, with 'Weirs' shuttle valve

Centrifugal Pumps

Figure 36.2 - VLCC water ballast centrifugal pump

Centrifugal Pumps

Centrifugal pumps are commonly used on board tankers for the transfer of cargo and ballast. The pump consists of a casing (with bearings and seals) and an impeller fixed to a rotating shaft.

A centrifugal pump works by fluid entering the middle of the rotating pump where it is then thrown outwards by an impellor, creating a centrifugal force and entering the volute. Kinetic energy is converted to pressure creating a discharge head. Head refers to the height of the column of fluid that is created by the pump.

The discharge head must overcome the static head, ie the weight of static fluid, in the pipeline to produce sufficient flow rate of ballast or cargo required to transfer the cargo. The pump overcomes the difference between the suction and discharge heads.

Every pump has a volumetric flow rate at which the best efficiency is achieved. This is shown on graphs produced by the pump manufacturer.

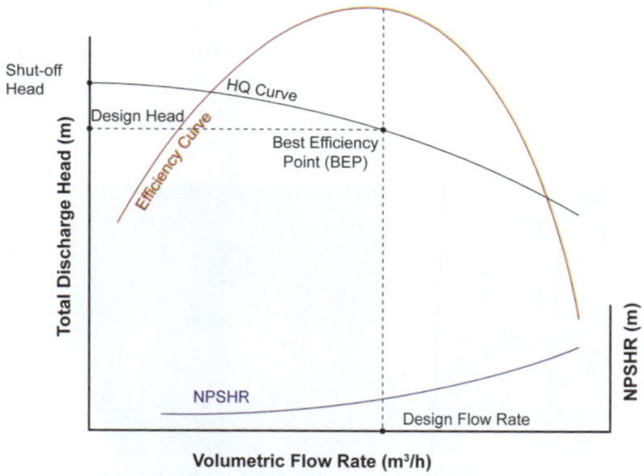

Total Discharge Head – the height (m) of the column of fluid created by the pump discharge.

Volumetric Flow Rate – the volume of fluid that passes one point in one hour.

Shut-off Head – when the maximum head is produced and results in zero flow of fluid.

Design Flow Rate – the optimum designed flow rate for the pump.

Design Head – the optimum designed head for the pump.

NPSHA – Net positive suction head available. This is the effective suction head of the fluid being discharged.

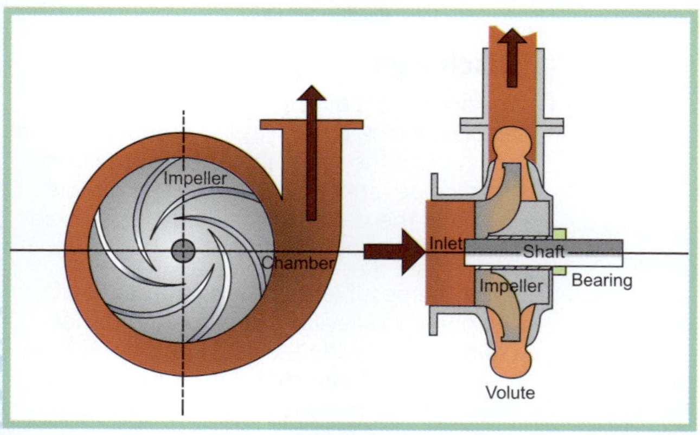

Figure 36.3 - Schematic of a centrifugal pump

Centrifugal Pumps

NPSHR – Net positive suction head requirement. This is the minimum required positive head at the inlet side of the pump.

HQ Curve – shows the relationship between the head (H) and flow rate (Q). It is produced by the manufacturer for a pump operating at its design speed and may also be known as a pump characteristic curve.

Efficiency Curve – illustrates the optimum best efficiency point (BEP) for the operation of the pump.

Where the NPSHR is greater than the NPSHA, the pump will cease to be effective and could lead to pump cavitation, which is where vapour bubbles build and then collapse. Cavitation reduces the flow rate and causes vibration, pitting of the impellor blades and damage to the impellor bearings.

When operating a centrifugal pump, it is important that the manufacturer's instructions are followed and the appropriate pumping conditions are observed.

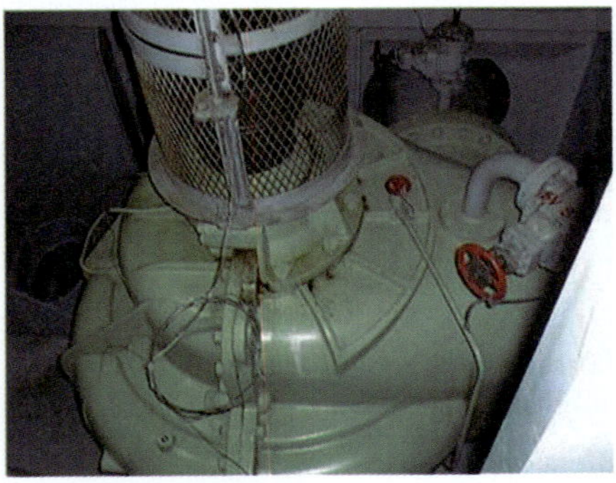

Figure 36.4 - VLCC centrifugal cargo pump

Suction

To maintain positive discharge conditions, the NPSHA must remain above the NPSHR. Suction conditions are affected by a number of factors, including:

- Diameter of the suction pipe
- length of the suction pipe
- directness of the suction pipe (fewer bends in the supply pipe improve fluid flow)
- fluid viscosity
- friction head loss.

Friction head loss is caused when the internal surface of the suction pipe creates frictional resistance due to eddies in the fluid flow. The rougher the internal surface, the greater the effect of friction. The fluid in the centre of the pipe flows quicker than at the walls, creating different layers within the pipe. Higher viscosity fluids generally flow slower and are less affected by friction.

It is important that pump speed is adjusted as the tank discharge nears completion to prevent ingress of gas and subsequent cavitation. Stripping pumps should be used when the appropriate sounding has been reached. As the sounding level reduces and nears the stripping level, it may be necessary to reduce the pump speed and/or partially close the discharge (delivery) valve. Closing the valve enables sufficient fluid to enter and remain in the pump, avoiding cavitation and ensuring enough discharge pressure to exceed the NPSHR.

Figure 36.5 - VLCC remote-operated cargo pump discharge valve

Discharge

The flow rate is directly affected by the resistance factors, such as the number of bends and joins in the shore line, the distance from the storage tanks, the diameter of the shore lines and the static head of fluid in the storage tank that is being discharged to.

It may be possible to increase the speed of the pump to alleviate high shore resistance conditions, provided there is sufficient NPSHA to avoid risk of pump cavitation. Commonly, ships will use two or more pumps working in parallel, which increases the total discharge head and the flow rate. However, the increase is not directly proportional and so does not double when two pumps are employed.

Similarly, depending on shore resistance, the increase in flow rate when using three pumps rather than two may be minimal and not of sufficient merit to use. When using pumps in parallel, they should be operated (either using the speed of the pump or the discharge valve) to ensure they provide the same discharge pressures.

Where low shore resistance is experienced, excessive flow rate can damage lines and equipment, so care must be taken to avoid excess pump speed. To enable the system to work at its optimum level, the discharge valve can be partly closed.

Water hammer is caused when there is a sudden and abrupt change in the speed of the fluid flow rate, often associated with the sudden opening or closing of valves. This can result in damage to components and structure, particularly where the force of the fluid impacts on a bend or restriction in a pipeline or on a suddenly closed valve. To avoid water hammer, opening and closing of valves should be carried out slowly and changes to the flow rate speed should be gradual.

Figure 36.6 - Inspecting a VLCC pump strainer

Centrifugal Pumps Fault Finding

Some common pump problems, operational and design, can include:

- Impellors can be damaged by solid particles or cavitation, the impellor pitch may be incorrect, they can be loose on the shaft or, occasionally, run in reverse. If the impellor clearance is too large, internal circulation problems may be encountered
- pump performance can be affected by being run too slowly or too fast, causing excess heat
- motor under performance can be caused by insufficient steam pressure for steam pumps and, in electric motors, the supply voltage may be too low
- the volute can be damaged by solid particles
- bearings may become worn, damaged or have foreign matter in them
- air can enter the pump from damaged stuffing boxes, seals, gaskets or casing, or from improper priming or bleeding
- the shaft may be damaged, bent or have shifted from operating outside its design parameters
- solids can form when pumping highly viscous or solidifying cargoes (eg low sulphur waxy residue (LSWR), bitumen, etc)which block the impellor, inlet or volute.

General suction problems can be caused by:

- Air entering the suction piping through the valves or flanges, frequently due to damaged gaskets
- the discharge fluid may contain gas, have a high viscosity or have insufficient head due to a low sounding level
- bends in the pipeline close to the pump or a supply pipeline diameter that is too small and restricts flow
- tank readings that are artificially high due to poorly calibrated or stuck gauges.

General discharge problems can be caused by:

- Shore pipelines that are too narrow, long, incorporate too many bends or where shore tanks have too high a static head
- pump discharge pressures that are not matched when used in parallel
- too low a pump speed or when a discharge (delivery) valve needs to be partially closed
- too high an initial flow rate where the discharge outlet is at the bottom of a tank. A low discharge head will initially exist until the appropriate fluid level in the tank is reached
- the casing is not completely filled and contains gas.

Cargo Oil Vacuum Stripping System (Vac Strip)

Centrifugal cargo pumps are the best pumps to use when transferring large capacities of liquid at transfer rates of 8,000 tonnes or more per hour. However, they are unable to deal with mixtures of oil and gaseous or hydrocarbon vapours on their own. This problem was originally resolved by lining up the stripping pump (reciprocating pump) which would cause a partial vacuum in the suction side of the pump and thus lift the liquid from below the level of suction.

An alternative to the stripping pump is the use of an air pump (or vacuum pump) that can be used to maintain a positive suction head above the impeller of the main cargo pump. This also avoids the problem of losing suction when the level of the oil in the cargo tank drops below the level of the pump suction pipe.

If the oil level in the separator rises when there is a partial vacuum, the vacuum retaining valve will close, the vacuum pump will stop and the cargo pump discharge valve will gradually open, maintaining the maximum stripping rate.

To stop the cargo pump from running with insufficient throughput once the tank has been emptied, which would cause damage to the pump and shaft seal etc, a thermostatic sensor is used to detect any abnormal rise in the temperature and to shut down the cargo pump.

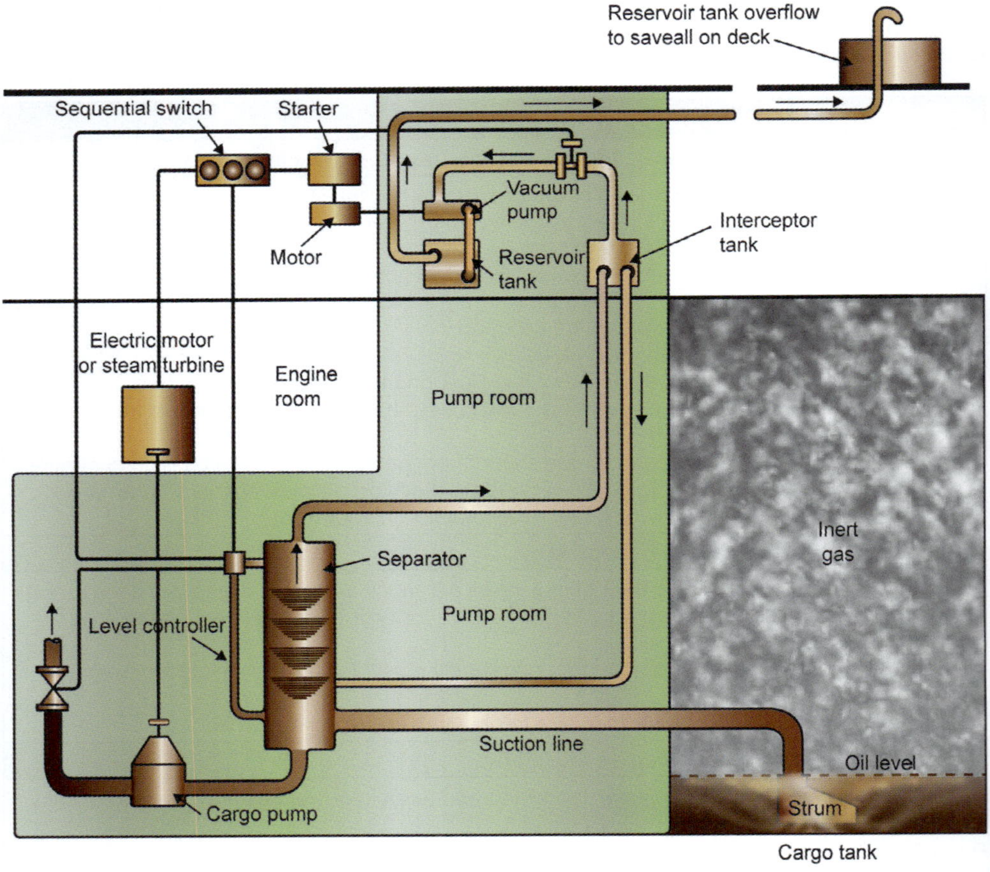

Submerged Pumps

Submerged pumps operate in the same way as normal centrifugal pumps, by drawing fluid into the impellor, forcing it outwards and up a discharge pipe using centrifugal force.

Submerged pumps can be either fixed or portable. The Framo (Frank Mohn AS) brand is often encountered and frequently used as an example of a submerged pump.

Fitted submerged cargo pumps are normally located with their inlet in a 'well' at the bottom of the tank to assist the pump in stripping operations.

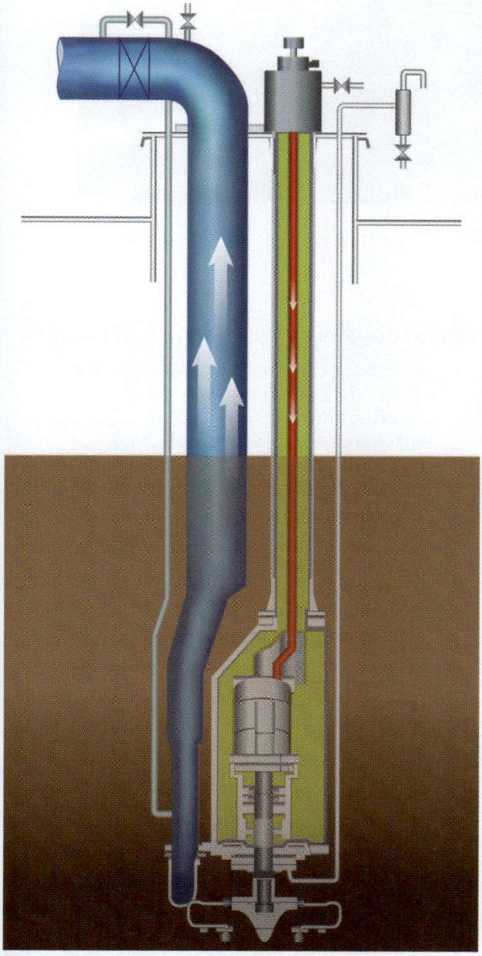

Figure 36.7 - Submerged cargo pump

Centrifugal and submerged pumps are commonly found in smaller tanks, such as in chemical parcel tankers. Larger pumps are also used on gas tankers, where the low temperature cargo helps to cool and lubricate the pump.

When discharging LNG, the NPSH must be kept above the minimum level and the sounding in the tank closely monitored. LNG is carried at its boiling point of minus 162°C, so particular care must be taken to avoid cavitation and to prevent the pump from running dry or it will cause the pump to quickly overheat and damage the impellor bearings. However, during stripping periods, brief instances with dry suction are normally within the design capacity of the pumps.

When using the pumps to strip cargo, the manufacturer's instructions will generally require that the ship is suitably trimmed, one pump is used and the speed reduced.

Submerged Pumps - Fault Finding

Due to their submerged position, these pumps are often more difficult to fix, but there are a number of common faults that may be encountered.

Bearing failures are often caused by pump over-speed or foreign matter entering the casing, in which case it is probable that the bearings will need to be replaced.

If there is any evidence or suspicion of cargo leakage, the cargo pump cofferdam must be tested. Where there is a hydraulic oil leak, it is probable that a replacement seal or a cracked pipe will be required. In the event of hydraulic oil contamination, the filters should be cleaned or changed in accordance with the manufacturer's instructions.

The manufacturer's instructions should also be followed closely when venting the hydraulic system. Indications that there may be gas in the system include:

- Pumps not starting from the remote control station
- abnormal noise or pressure variations
- variations in the hydraulic oil tank level with changes in system pressures
- bubbles present in the hydraulic oil sample or a white appearance
- foaming in the hydraulic oil tank.

Submerged Pumps

Figure 36.8 - LNG Cargo and spray pump arrangement

Common Causes of Faults in Pumps

Lack of or Low Discharge Delivery

- Pump speed is too slow
- insufficient power
- discharge head is too high
- insufficient NPSH
- pump under suction conditions
- pump not fully primed
- gas in the cargo/fluid
- shaft damage
- impellor damage
- incorrect impellor trim
- inlet blocked
- air in the suction line
- air in the pump casing
- air in the impellor inlet
- stuffing box packing worn or blocked
- pressure measurement position
- incorrect pressure gauge reading.

Noisy Pump/Vibration

- Pump cavitation
- damaged shaft
- impellor misaligned or loose
- bearings worn
- damaged impellor
- misaligned drive
- insufficient NPSH
- partially blocked inlet
- pump not operating within design speed parameters
- pipelines may be resonating.

Excessive Power Required to Run Pump

- Pump speed is excessive or incorrect
- flow rate is too high
- bearings are too tight
- discharge head is too low
- gas in the cargo/fluid
- impellor shaft may be damaged
- incorrect impellor trim
- packing insufficiently lubricated
- packing or seal too tight
- abrasives in the cargo/fluid
- misaligned drive
- defective or unsuitable motor.

Leaks from the Stuffing Box

- Packing worn
- packing insufficiently lubricated
- incorrect packing
- damaged shaft.

Pump Works Briefly then Stops

- Stuffing box packing worn or blocked
- insufficient NPSH
- gas in the cargo/fluid
- leakage in the suction line.

Hydraulic System

Hydraulic systems provide a relatively simple way to control and drive much of the machinery on board. The systems work by sucking hydraulic fluid from a reservoir into a pump that pressurises a pipeline system to drive hydraulic cylinders and motors.

The cylinders and motors control and operate machinery including:

- Mooring winches and anchor windlasses
- cranes and other lifting appliances
- cargo handling equipment
- watertight doors
- lifeboat davits
- rudders and steering equipment
- bow thrusters
- liquid cargo control systems.

Hydraulic Fluid

The primary purpose of hydraulic fluid is the transfer of power from a hydraulic pump to the machinery being worked, but it also serves to lubricate and protect components.

Hydraulic fluid is characterised by:

- Viscosity – the thickness of the fluid, affected by temperature
- lubricity – to prevent wear between metals in contact
- oxidation resistance – inhibitors may be added to the fluid to improve resistance to oxidation and prolong fluid usefulness.

In hazardous environments, some hydraulic fluids may also provide resistance to fire.

Care must be taken to follow the manufacturer's instructions in maintaining the hydraulic system by using the correct hydraulic fluid.

Basic Principles

To understand the operation of hydraulics, some of the basic principles need to be understood.

Pascal's Law

Pascal's Law states that 'pressure acting on a confined fluid is transmitted equally and undiminished in all directions'. In this way, a large piston experiences the same force per unit area as a smaller piston. The force exerted on the piston is equal to the product of the pressure and the area, ie:

Force (F) = Pressure (p) x Area (A)

Using this principle, specific ratios can be constructed with hydraulic cylinders where a small torque can create a large force.

The volume of liquid x in Figure 36.9 that has been displaced by the downward movement of the piston is equal to the volume displaced at y, resulting in the lifting of the load by the hydraulic cylinder.

The speed of the load's movement is directly proportional to the volume of fluid fed into the load cylinder.

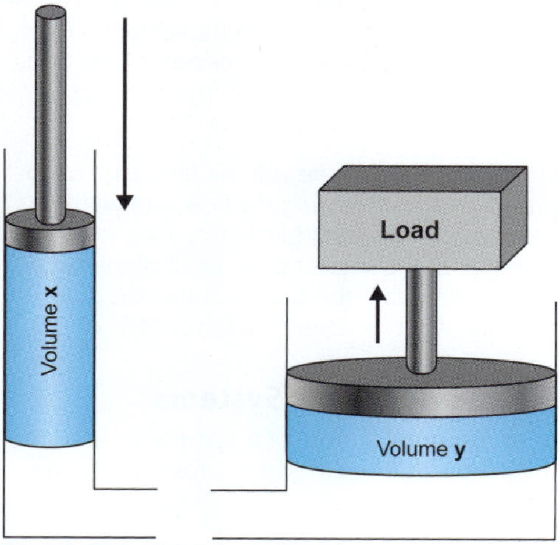

Figure 36.9

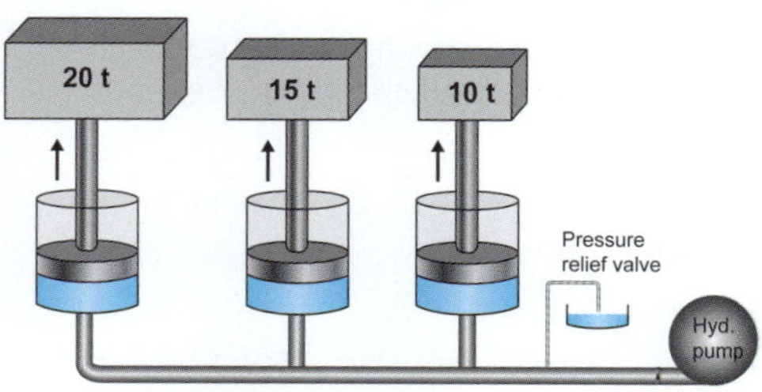

Figure 36.10

Under pressure, the flow of hydraulic oil will occur in the path of least resistance. This is illustrated in Figure 36.10, where the system has been pressurised by the pump causing the 10 t load to be moved first, then the 15 t load and finally the 20 t load. If there are any weak or worn points in the system, leaks are likely.

Hydraulic System

To prevent the system being damaged by initial or subsequent overpressurisation, pressure relief valves are installed. Where the initial pressure is excessive, the valve may not open quickly enough to prevent system overpressurisation and damage.

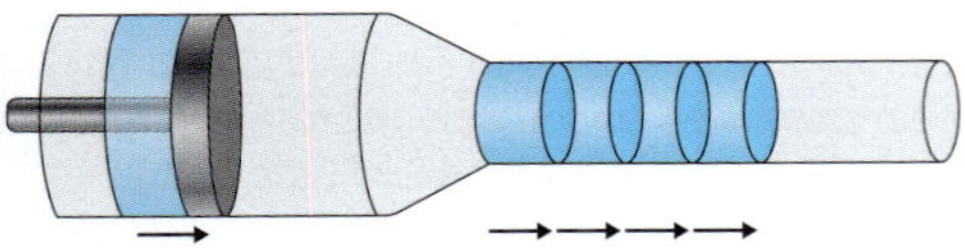

Figure 36.11

Pressure Intensification

When operating hydraulic systems, it is important to understand the effects of pressure intensification. This occurs when a fluid passes into a smaller diameter pipeline as it cannot be compressed. To maintain volume, the rate of flow in the pipe must increase.

Figure 36.11 shows the volume displaced by the piston greatly increasing the flow rate within the smaller diameter pipe. In this instance, the diameter of the smaller pipe is half of the larger. To accommodate the same volume, the fluid flow rate must increase by a factor of four.

Simple Hydraulic Systems

A fundamental feature of a hydraulic system is the simple manner in which a force or torque can be applied and multiplied without the need for gears and levers. A basic hydraulic system comprises:

- A motor (generator) driven hydraulic pump that forces the fluid through the system
- valves, gauges, etc to guide and control the system
- a hydraulic motor or cylinder to drive the machinery.

Open and Closed Loop Hydraulic Systems

In an open loop system, the hydraulic pump takes the oil from a tank (reservoir), pumps it through the system and then returns the exhaust oil to the tank. These pumps tend to be used for low pressure systems and have the advantages of being simple and reliable. However, they are inefficient, use relatively large components and consequently tend to be used for smaller installations.

In closed loop systems, the hydraulic pump is fed directly from the exhaust oil, but does not enter an open tank. Marine equipment normally utilises medium-pressure systems, so open or closed loop systems may be encountered.

Hydraulic Pumps

Hydraulic pumps vary in construction offering different benefits and constraints depending on intended use:

- Gear pumps – internal and external
- axial piston pumps
- radial piston pumps
- vane pumps – unbalanced and balanced.

Hydraulic systems need pressure to operate the machinery and move the loads. It is the resistance to flow, provided by the components, that creates pressure, not the pump, which only produces flow. This can be demonstrated if the system is bypassed and the fluid fed directly from the pump to the reservoir. A pressure gauge would show no increase.

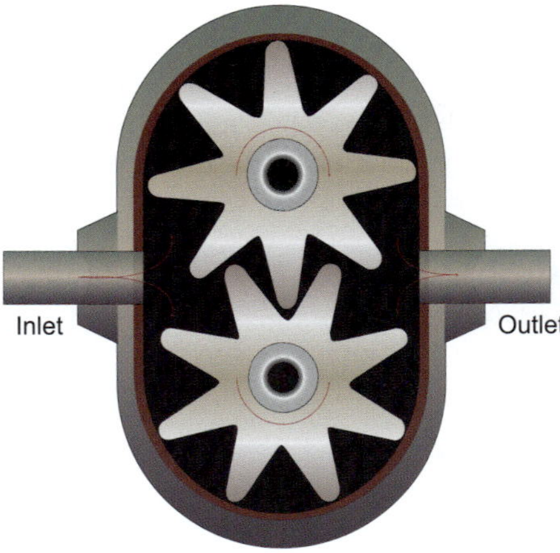

Figure 36.12 - External gear pump

Hydraulic Reservoirs

The reservoir acts as a settling tank for impurities, allows heat to be dissipated, air to be separated and contains sufficient fluid for normal operation and any minor leaks in the hydraulic system. By retaining a small space above the fluid within the tank, it allows the fluid to foam with the air purged via a filtered vent.

The pump suction should be high enough above the bottom of the tank to prevent sediment being drawn in to the system. Sight gauges, filler inlets and inspection covers are required for maintenance, servicing and cleaning.

The correct fluid must always be used.

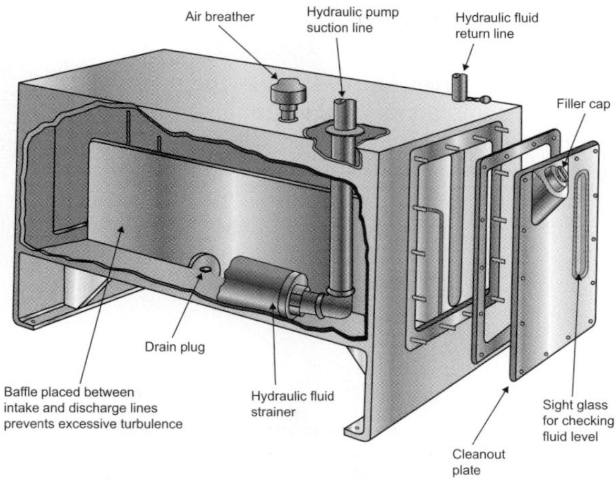

Figure 36.13 - Hydraulic reservoir

Hydraulic Accumulators

To reduce the need for a powerful pump, a hydraulic accumulator may be used. The accumulator stores pressurised hydraulic fluid to ensure sufficient pressure is maintained and to cope with large changes in demand from the system. The system can be pressurised either using a compressed gas or, as in the case of manually starting an emergency generator, a spring-loaded piston.

Directional Control Valves

Control valves determine the route that hydraulic fluid will follow by controlling the actions of the motors or cylinders. Figure 36.14 illustrates a simple method of controlling the direction of flow by moving a three-directional control valve. In this case, the valve determines the extension and retraction of a cylinder, but could also drive the direction and rotation of a motor, eg to drive a winch.

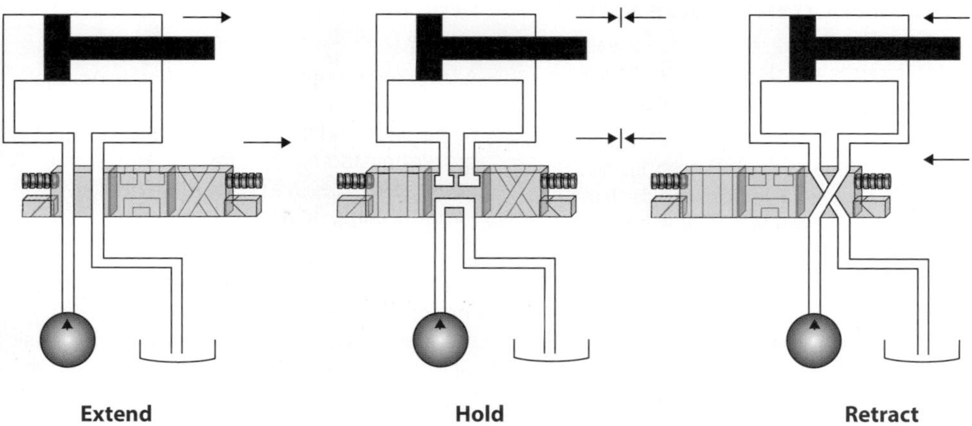

Figure 36.14 - Method for controlling the direction of flow

Hydraulic System

On Board the Ship

Figure 36.15 illustrates a simplified shipboard system for the operation of a winch. The hydraulic pump draws the fluid from the reservoir via an oil strainer to remove any impurities. The oil is then pumped through the system to the control valve which, depending on the setting, dictates the direction of flow of the oil to the hydraulic motor to operate the winch. Once the fluid has been transmitted to the actuators (motors), it is then returned to the reservoir.

It would normally be expected for a hydraulic pump to drive a number of hydraulic cylinders and/or motors as indicated by the winch manifold.

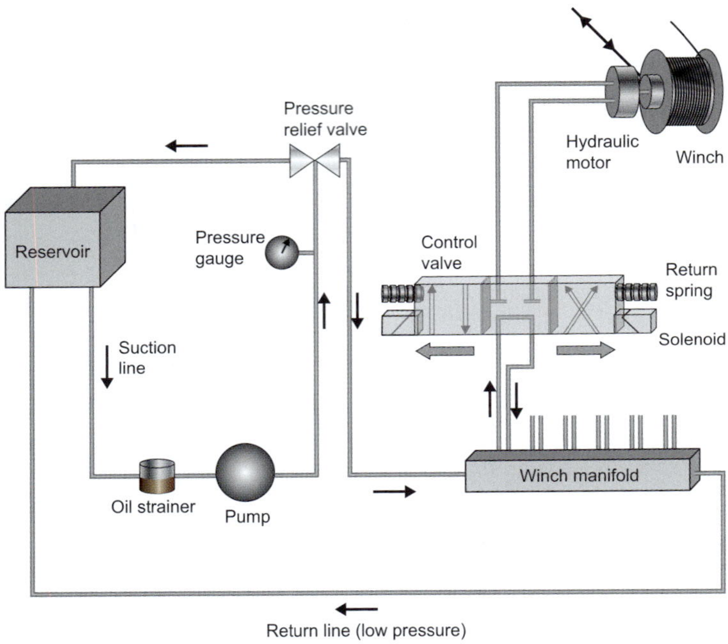

Figure 36.15 - Shipboard system for the operation of a winch

Hydraulic Butterfly Valve System

Figure 36.16 is a representation of a real system used to operate a hydraulic butterfly valve, including valve indicators, pressure reduction and stop valve.

The red pipeline shows the hydraulic flow that directly drives the valve from the deck main pressure line. Activation and flow direction are controlled by the solenoid (control) valve as depicted in Figure 36.14.

When the solenoid valve is opened, the oil pressure activates the throttle valve, which in turn presses oil through the stop valve, activating the turbine and opening the butterfly valve.

Transmitter pressure increases, creating flow to the load indicator (green line), providing a valve position indication in the control room using a potentiometer.

A lever on the butterfly valve spindle gradually closes the stop valve, reducing the hydraulic oil pressure and therefore the rate of turn, preventing sudden closure. This avoids potentially excessive pressure on the valve from the cargo, fuel or ballast.

Low pressure flow from the transmitter to the throttle control reduces the hydraulic flow to the turbine. Pressure on the turbine/auxiliary cylinder is reduced by redirecting the hydraulic oil through the pressure reduction valve to the deck main return line.

Closing the valve works by reversing the directional control valve and reversing the hydraulic flow.

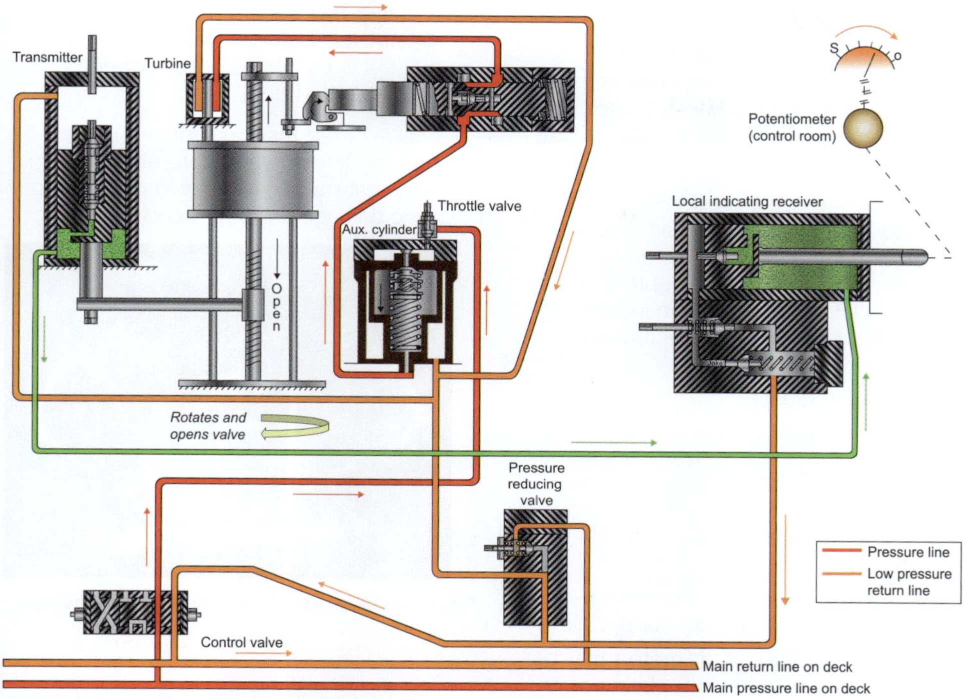

Figure 36.16 - Opening a butterfly valve

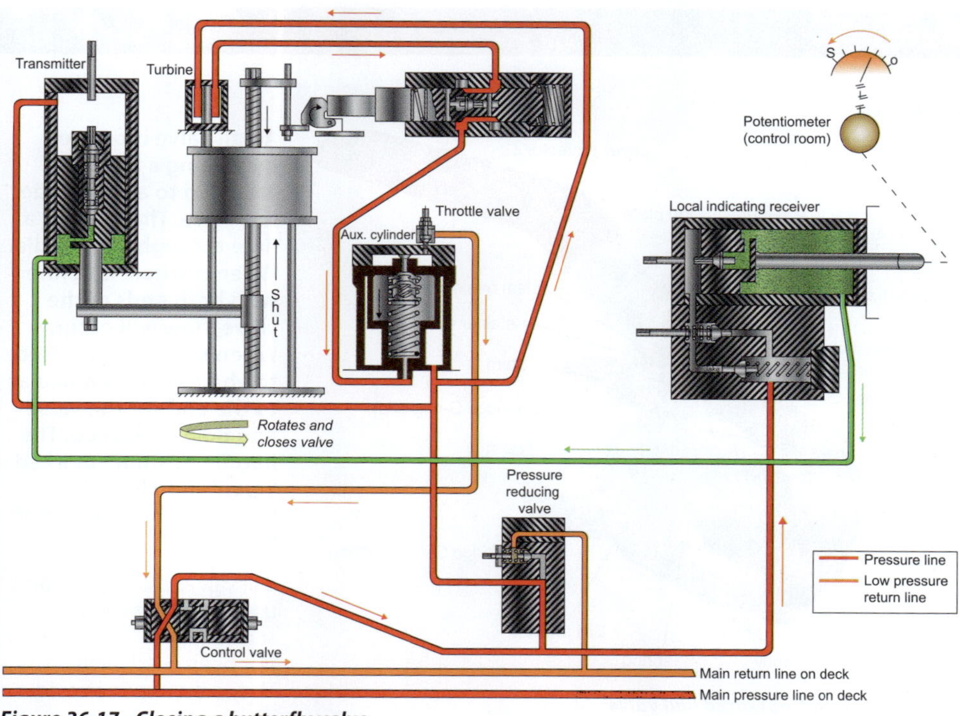

Figure 36.17 - Closing a butterfly valve

Hydraulic System

Troubleshooting

Whenever undertaking maintenance or investigating problems, the equipment instruction manuals should be consulted and all safety precautions observed. Likely causes may include:

- Variation in temperature in the system, particularly cooler areas, could indicate areas of low pressure and often the component with the highest pressure may be at fault. Excessive heat can indicate incorrect pressure settings or internal damage
- unusual operation:
  - Noise or heat from the pumps can be due to cavitation, normally caused by reduced flow in the pump inlet. The restrictions may be due to blocked filters, damaged inlets, aeration in the oil, etc
  - erratic actuators or movement of machinery can indicate trapped air
  - noise from the electric motors may be attributed to worn motor bearings or couplings out of alignment
  - noise from the relief valve is likely to indicate that the valve is not properly closed, possibly due to incorrect pressure settings
- smell – bitter smelling hydraulic oil can indicate deterioration in the additives. It is likely that the oil will need to be replaced to avoid damage to components.

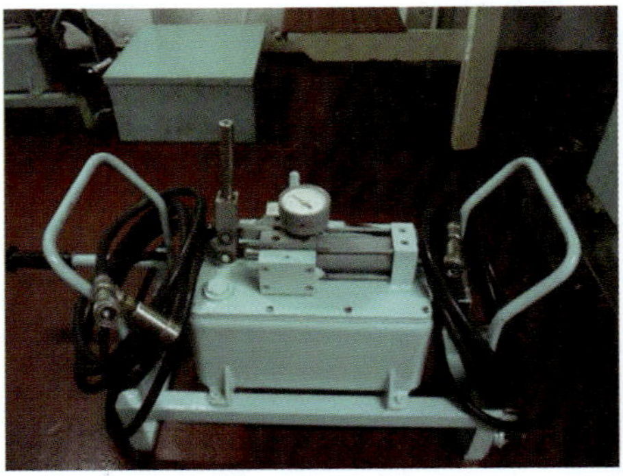

Courtesy of Paul Armitage

Figure 36.18 - Portable manual hydraulic pump

Valves

Ball Valve

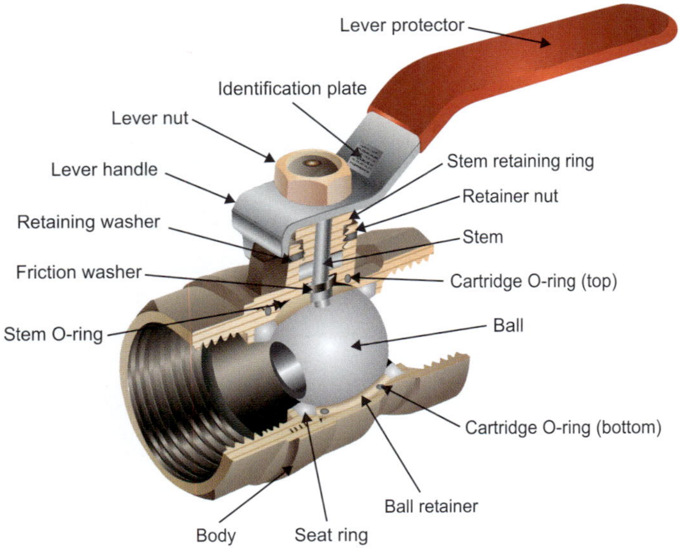

Figure 36.19 - Hand-operated ball valve

A ball valve is opened by turning a handle attached to a ball inside the valve. The ball has a hole through the middle. When the hole is in line with both ends of the valve, flow will occur. When the valve is closed, the hole is perpendicular to the ends of the valve and flow is blocked. The handle position, marked 'open' and 'closed', indicates the position of the valve.

Ball valves are durable and usually achieve perfect shut-off, even if they have not been used for years. They are often preferred

Valves

to globe valves and gate valves. They do not offer the fine control that may be necessary for throttling, although they can be used for this purpose if necessary.

The body of a ball valve may be made of metal, ceramic and/or plastic. The ball may be chrome plated to make it more durable.

Ball valves are popular because of their low resistance to flow liquids. However, there is a danger of static accumulation because the ball is electrically isolated from the body of the valve by non-conducting seals on either side, hampering electrical continuity.

There are three types of ball valve in general use:

Full Port Ball Valve

This valve has an oversized ball so that the hole in the ball is the same size as the pipeline, resulting in lower friction loss. Flow is unrestricted.

Standard Port Ball Valve

This is usually less expensive, but has a smaller ball and a correspondingly smaller port. Flow through this valve is one pipe size smaller than the valve's pipe size, resulting in a slightly restricted flow.

Reduced Port Ball Valve

This is where flow through the valve is two pipe sizes smaller than the valve's pipe size, resulting in restricted flow.

Maintenance and Operating Problems

Operating problems include:

- Operation of handwheel is jerky
- valve stem will not rotate
- opening/closing torque is excessive.

Diagnosis and suggested remedy:

- Line debris is increasing the required closing torque
  - flush or clean valve to remove the debris
- actuator/shaft adaptor misaligned
  - the actuator mounting must be realigned. This is done by loosening the bolting and then repositioning the actuator on the mounting plate
- packing is overtightened
  - loosen packing bolts to hand tight and then reapply torque. Torque values are found in the standard maintenance manuals.

Other problems for motor-operated ball valves may include:

- Where the pneumatic actuator, air supply pressure is inadequate
  - verify either on the submitted drawings what is the required level of air pressure or, if the supply pressure is low, make sure that there are no leak paths in the air supply line
- the shaft key has sheared, disconnecting the stem from actuation
  - to identify this problem, remove the actuator and inspect the drive nut for signs of damage. This problem can usually be solved by installing new components
- the actuator duty cycle was exceeded causing the actuator motor to burn out
  - replace the actuator motor.

If there is a problem with the actuator other than those listed above, the actuator should be inspected by an expert to determine the cause of the problem and the best possible solution.

Gate Valve

A gate valve is opened by lifting a round or rectangular gate out of the path of the fluid. The distinctive feature of a gate valve is that the sealing surfaces between the gate and the seats are planar. The gate faces can form a wedge shape or they can be parallel. Gate valves are sometimes used for regulating flow but many are not suited for that purpose, having been designed to be either fully open or fully closed. When fully open, a typical gate valve has no obstruction in the flow path, resulting in very low friction loss.

All gate valves have either a rising or non-rising stem. Rising stems provide a visual indication of the valve position. Non-rising stems are used where vertical space is limited or if the valve is underground.

Bonnets provide leakproof closure for the valve body. Gate valves may have a screw-in, union or bolted bonnet. A screw-in bonnet is the simplest, offering a durable, pressure-tight seal.

Valves

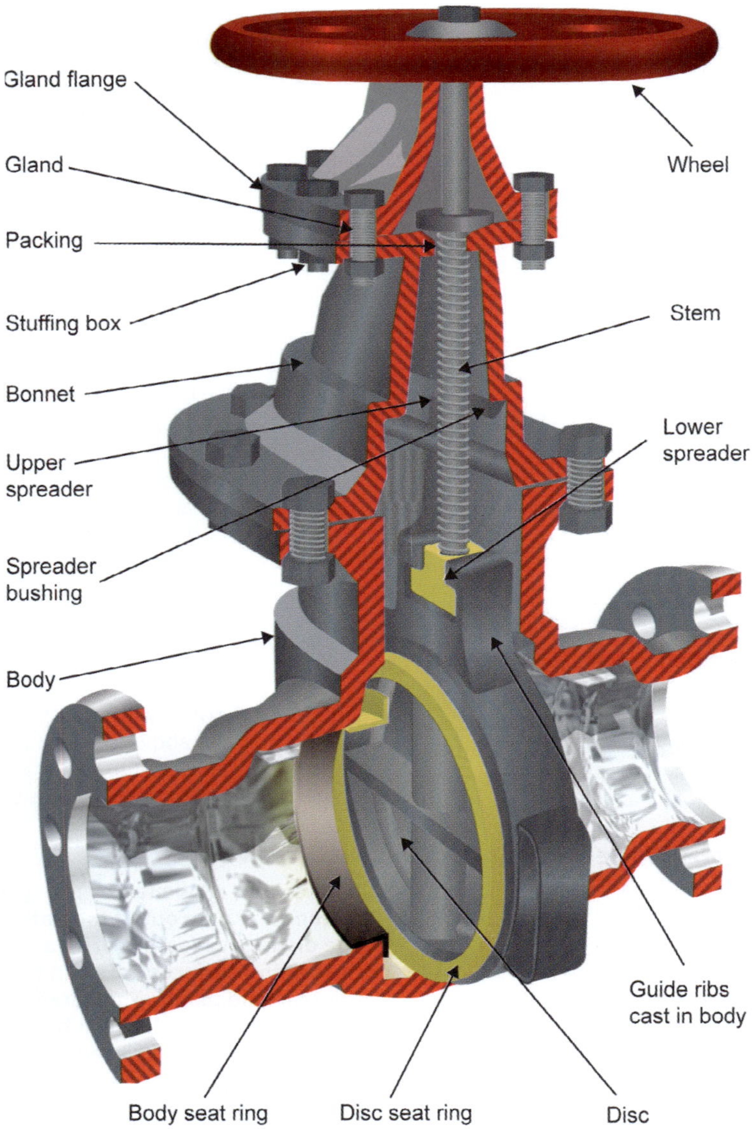

Figure 36.20 - Gate valve

A union bonnet is suitable for applications that require frequent inspection and cleaning. It also gives the body added strength. A bolted bonnet is used for larger valves and higher pressure applications.

Cautions in the Use of Gate Valves

- The valve must be either fully open or fully closed. No intermediate position is allowed
- the valve should not be overtightened as distortion of the gate can occur
- if the valve is sticking, it might be due to deposits of silt and mud in the guides. Slowly opening and closing against the fluid flow will often clear these away
- a gate valve can be used in either direction, which means that the suction and the discharge can be reversed

- a gate valve should not be installed upside down horizontally, as this encourages the deposit of sediment in the guide ways.

Maintenance and Operating Problems

The failure of gate valves to open is likely to be due to overpressurisation or pressure locking.

Overpressurisation is usually caused when liquid trapped between the seats in the valve cavity (valve closed) of a double-seated valve is subsequently heated, causing the trapped fluid to expand.

Pressure locking occurs when the pressure in the body cavity (valve closed) increases or when the line pressure decreases without decrease in the body cavity pressure.

Pressure relief to the body cavity can be achieved by the use of an equalising pipe, connecting the body cavity to one side of the valve. The valve will only seal in one direction, ie high pressure must be on the side of the equalising pipe when the valve is closed.

Another way to provide pressure relief is by connecting the body cavity to the atmosphere. However, the exhaust from a self-activating type relief-valve must be piped to a safe location and caution must be used when opening the drain type relief valve.

If excessive torque is required to operate a valve, the following potential problems and solutions should be considered:

- Valve stem is improperly lubricated or damaged
  - disassemble the valve and inspect the stem. Inspect the threads for any visible signs of damage. Small grooves can be polished with an emery cloth
- foreign debris is trapped on threads and/ or in the packing area. This is a common problem when valves are installed outdoors in sandy areas and not cleaned before operating
  - always inspect threads and packing area for particle obstructions, as even small amounts on the drive can completely stop large valves from cycling. With the line pressure removed from the valve, disconnect the actuator, gear operator or handwheel and inspect the drive nut, stem, bearings and yoke bushing. Contaminated parts should be cleaned with a lint-free cloth using alcohol, Varsol or equivalent. All parts should be relubricated before reassembly. If the valves are installed outdoors in a sandy area, it may be desirable to cover the valves with jackets
- valve components are faulty or damaged
  - if you suspect that a valve component is damaged or faulty, you should ensure it is reported
- the handwheel is too small
  - increasing the size of the handwheel will reduce the amount of torque required to operate the valve. If a larger handwheel is installed, the person operating the valve must be careful not to over-torque the valve when closing it.

Overhauling of Gate Valves

1. Open the wheel nut and remove the handwheel.
2. Open the gland bolts and slacken the gland flange and the gland bush.
3. Open the bonnet bolts and remove the bonnet along with the valve wedge.
4. Unscrew the valve stem from beneath the bonnet.
5. Clean all the parts by buffing and then blowing with compressed air.
6. Examine all the parts for damage and wear. Any marks on the threads must be repaired by dressing the threads.
7. The grooves between the wedge seats must be removed using a scraper, taking care not to damage the seats.
8. If the gate or the seats are damaged and are removable, change them.
9. After cleaning, the same can be reassembled in the reverse order.

Testing

The valve should be filled up with water and then air should be introduced from the other side. The presence of air bubbles indicates a bad sealing and must be rectified.

Valves

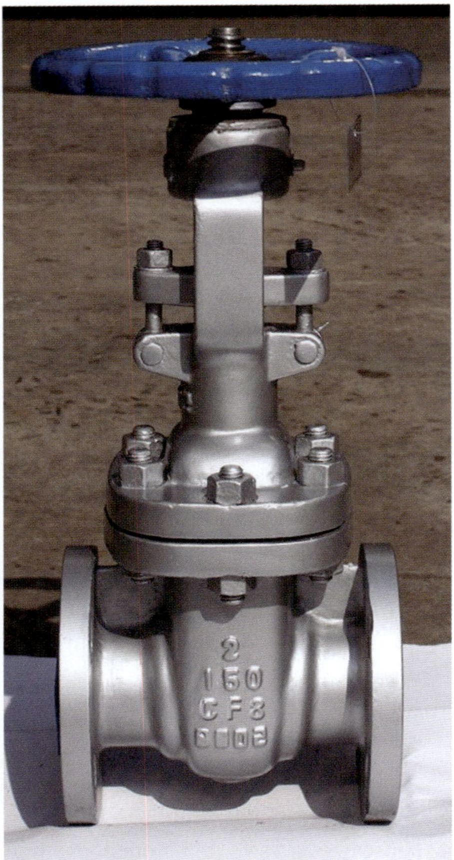

Courtesy of HS

Figure 36.21 - Stainless steel gate valve

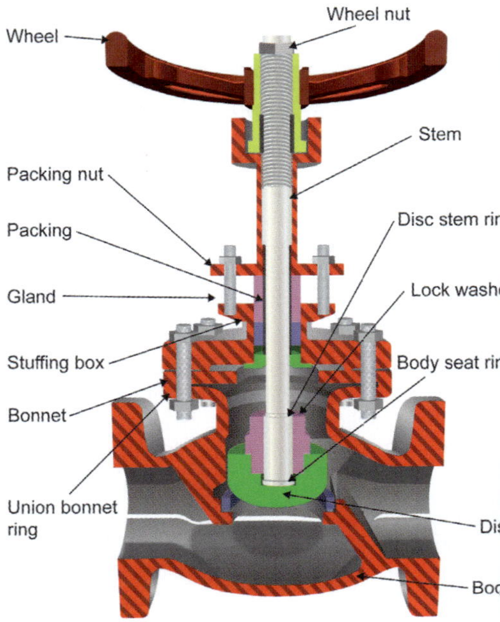

Figure 36.22 - Globe valve

Courtesy of HS

Figure 36.23 - Carbon steel globe valve

Globe Valve

Globe valves have a spherical body shape. The two halves of the valve body are separated by a baffle with a disc in the centre. Globe valves operate by screw action of the handwheel. They are used for applications requiring throttling or frequent operation. Since the baffle restricts flow, they are not suitable where a full, unobstructed flow is required.

A bonnet provides a leakproof closure for the valve body. Globe valves may have a screw-in, union or bolted bonnet. A screw-in bonnet is the simplest, offering a durable, pressure-tight seal. A union bonnet is suitable for applications that require frequent inspection and cleaning. It also gives the body added strength. A bolted bonnet is used for larger valves and higher pressure applications.

Routine Maintenance and Operational Care of Globe Valves

- Valve gland packing must be replaced when deemed necessary. Attempting to forcibly open or close a valve using wheel spanners and pipe extensions can lead to breaking of the spindle or stem
- the valves must be regularly greased at the threads and the yoke nut. The old grease must be removed before applying new grease
- whenever pipes are replaced, care should be taken that the pipes are not pushed into position with the help of crow bars and chain blocks. There should be no residual tension on the valve body as this can lead to failure of the valve body
- the direction of the flow of fluid is marked on the body of the valve. In the event that a marking is not present or visible, it is a rule of thumb that the fluid will flow from below the valve seat/disc. This is especially important in an SDNR valve (screw down non-return valve) because, if the flow is from above the valve disc, it would close the valve by the fluid pressure and flow and act as a check valve
- the screw down non-return valve must be installed horizontally and the direction of fluid flow should always be kept in mind. If the valve is installed vertically, the sediments from the fluid may deposit behind the valve disc and disturb its operation.

Disassembly procedure of globe valve:

1. Remove the wheel nut and the wheel handle.
2. Open the bonnet bolts. The top portion of the valve along with the valve seat, stem, etc will come out. The bottom portion of the valve will be separate.
3. Hold the bonnet in a vice and open the gland bolts. Then loosen the gland flange and the gland bush. The valve stem should then be screwed clockwise and it will come out from below, along with the valve disc.
4. Remove the set screw or other arrangements that secure the valve disc to the stem.
5. Remove the gland flange, gland nut and all the gland packings with a gland packing extractor.

Globe valve overhaul:

1. Clean, buff, and polish all the parts.
2. Check all the threaded parts for damage.
3. Check the stem for straightness.
4. Check the stem for scratches, as these can damage the gland packing. Any scratches must be removed with an emery paper or oil stone.
5. The valve and the valve seat must be inspected and if found to be in fairly good condition, they must be ground together by using a guide for centring and a suitable grade lapping paste.

Assembly procedure:

1. Clean all parts and remove all dust.
2. Put the valve disc on the stem with the set screw or the arrangement provided.
3. Apply grease to the threads and screw in the stem through the yoke nut. Care must be taken to put the gland nut and gland flange in the correct order in between.
4. Put back the wheel handle and the wheel nut and tighten it.
5. Close the valve wheel handle fully, so that the valve stem along with the valve disc extends down to the maximum.
6. Put a correctly sized new gasket on the space provided on the valve body. Stick it with grease or molyslip in case of high temperature applications.
7. Place the valve disc on the valve seat and correctly centre it.
8. Put the nuts and bolts in place but do not tighten them. There should be a gap between the body and the valve bonnet. Check again that the valve is properly centred.
9. Start opening the valve. As you do so, the gap between the bonnet and the body will reduce and they will come together.
10. Fully open the valve and tighten all the bonnet bolts in the correct sequence.
11. Put well-greased gland packings in the stuffing box. Care should be taken that the cut parts are together with no gaps and that the packings are staggered.

Valves

12. Push down the gland nut and the gland flange and put in the gland bolts. The gland bolts must be slightly tightened.
13. Close and open the valve several times and check whether it is free in movement. Check from the opening of the flanges whether it is sitting properly on the valve seat.
14. Complete tightening.

Check Valves (Non-Return Valves)

Check valves, or non-return valves, allow fluid or gas to flow through in only one direction. They can slam shut if the valve disc is not completely parallel to, or fully withdrawn from, the flow when in the open position. This can cause surge pressures.

Excess flow valves are sometimes used instead of remotely-operated rotation valves. The rate of flow of product closes the valve by pressure drop. They are usually selected to have a closing flow rating of at least 50% more than the anticipated normal line flow. Any damage to lines that results in leakage of less than this amount will not bring the valve into operation, meaning lesser leakages can be left undetected. It is better to fit a remote shut-off valve that can be operated, either manually or automatically, from a number of strategically sited locations.

Swing Check Valve

The following procedures should be used to repair a swing check valve:

- Loose disk locknut that is causing water backflow:
  1. Turn off the water supply and remove the cap.
  2. Tighten the locknut.
  3. Replace the cap.
  4. Turn on the water supply and check for leaks and proper operation.
- Hinge not closing completely:
  1. Turn off the water supply and remove the cap.

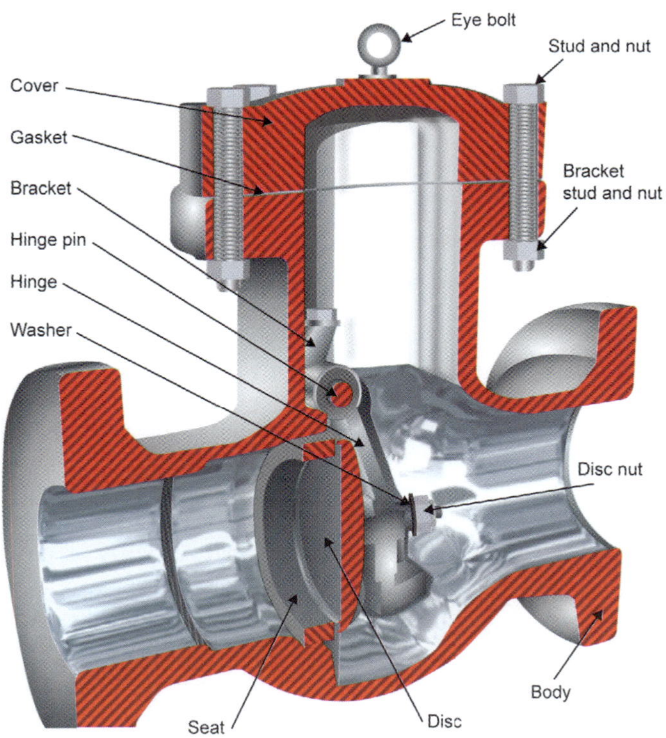

Figure 36.24 - Non-return valve

2. Replace the hinge pin and/or hinge.
3. Replace the cap.
4. Turn on the water supply and check for leaks and proper operation.

- Worn disk face that is causing a leak:
    1. Turn off the water supply and remove the cap.
    2. Remove the locknut and then the disc.
    3. Attach a new disc to the hinge and tighten the locknut.
    4. Replace the cap.
    5. Turn on the water supply and check for leaks and proper operation.

Lift Check Valve

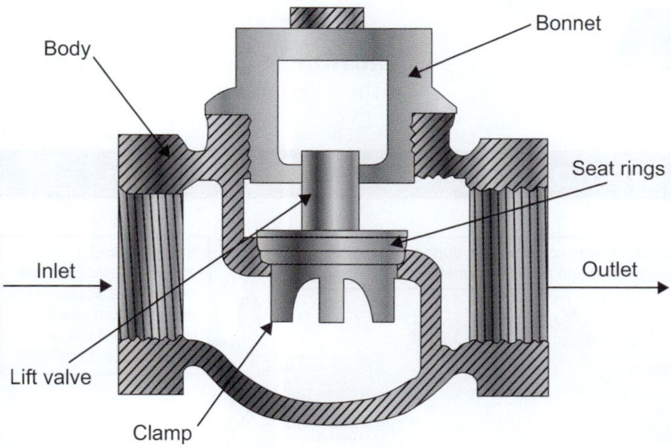

Figure 36.25 - Lift check valve

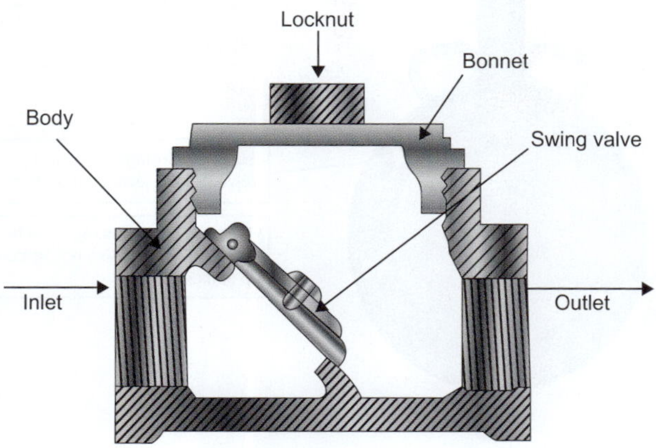

Figure 36.26 - Swing check valve

Note: To avoid repair or replacement of the lift check valve, inspect it once a year.

- Inspect for wear, freedom of motion, and alignment
- inspect the clapper and body seat rings
- remove any dirt or foreign matter lodged in the valve
- if the disc or body seat ring surfaces show signs of wear or corrosion, resurface or replace them.

Butterfly Valves

A butterfly valve can be used for isolating or regulating flow. The closing mechanism takes the form of a disc. Operation is similar to that of a ball valve, which allows for rapid shut-off. Butterfly valves are lower in cost and lighter in weight.

The 'butterfly' is a metal disc mounted on a rod and positioned in the centre of the pipe. The rod is connected to an actuator on the outside of the valve. Rotating the actuator turns the disc either parallel or perpendicular to the flow. Unlike a ball valve, the disc is always present within the flow; therefore, a pressure drop is always induced in the flow, regardless of valve position. The pressure drop can be reduced by providing the valve with a streamlined disc profile. The actuator can be fixed to either an automatic or a remote control mechanism.

When the valve is closed, the disc is turned so that it completely blocks off the passageway. When the valve is fully open, the disc is rotated a quarter turn so that it allows an almost unrestricted passage of the fluid. The valve may also be opened incrementally to throttle flow.

There are different kinds of butterfly valves, each adapted for different pressures and different usage. High

Valves

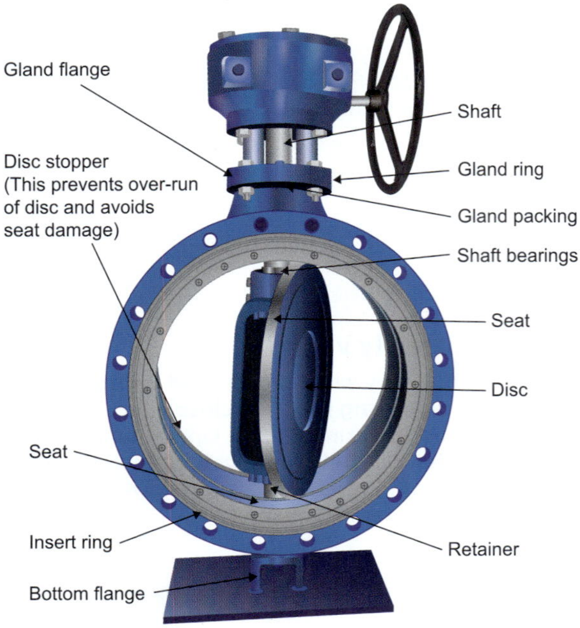

Figure 36.27 - Butterfly valve

performance butterfly valves used in higher pressure systems feature a slight offset in the way the disc is positioned, which increases sealing ability and decreases tendency to wear.

Operating and Maintenance

A butterfly valve may have jerky operation for the following reasons:

- The packing is too tight:
  - Loosen the packing torque until it is only hand tight. Tighten to the required level and then cycle the valve. Retighten, if required.
- The shaft seals are dirty or worn out:
  - Clean or replace components, as per assembly-disassembly procedure.

CAUTION: Always follow safety instructions when working on valves.

Hydraulic Valves – Common Problems

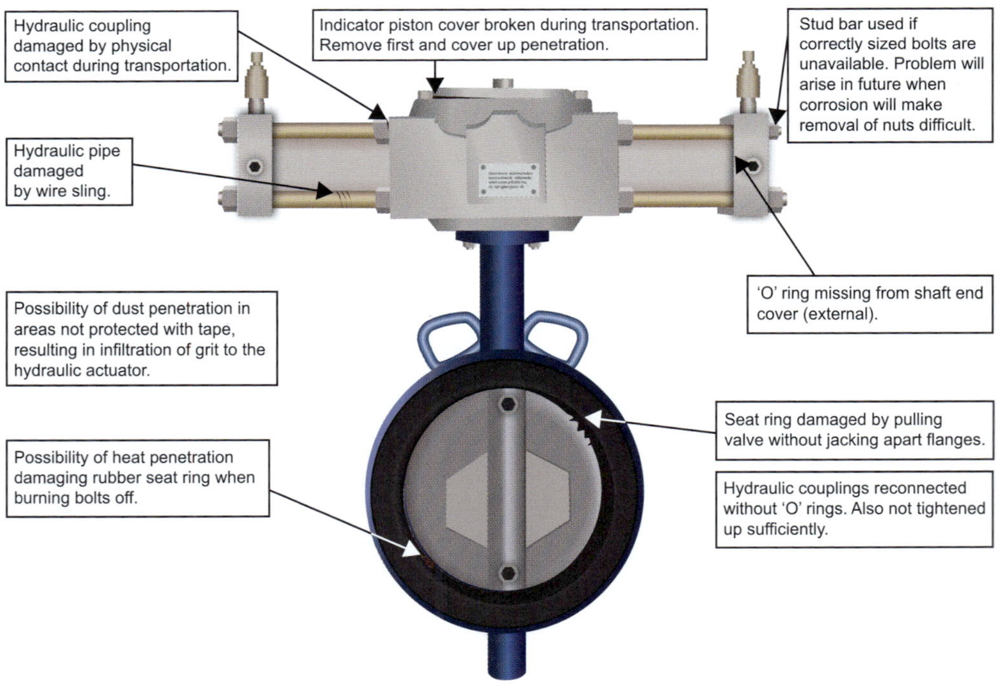

Figure 36.28 - Common problems found with hydraulic valves during repair periods in drydock

Valve Seat Rings

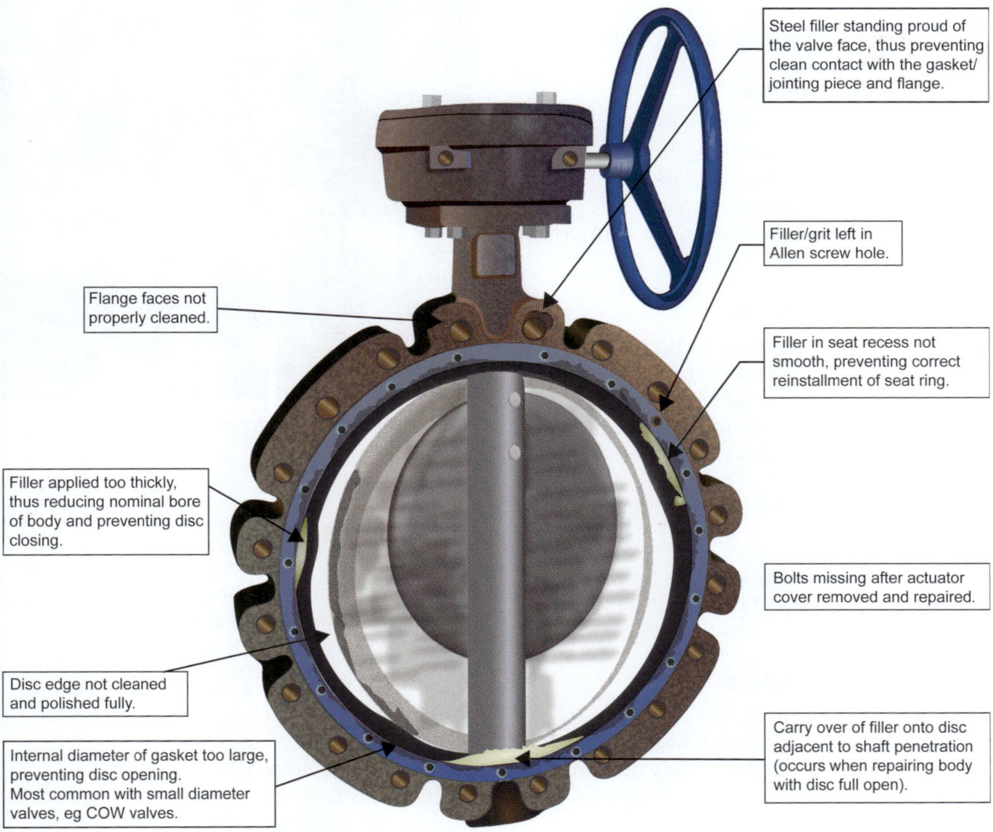

Figure 36.29 - Common faults with valve seat rings

Controllers

Controllers accept the low-power signals from error detectors and present high-power signals to actuators. The high-power signals must be in a physical form. For example, in the case of a hydraulic control system, the output from the controller must be a high pressure oil flow. Generally, a controller does not generate power but regulates power that is generated from an external source. Controllers can be classified as mechanical, electrical, hydraulic and pneumatic.

Mechanical Controllers (Governors)

A mechanical governor can be used in an engine speed control system where the engine speed is monitored by a rotating shaft that in turn rotates the governor fly weights. The movement of the fly weights, due to centrifugal force, actuates a fuel control valve which in turn regulates the engine flow and consequently the engine speed. The main disadvantage of mechanical error detectors and controllers is that the input and the output of a system must be physically close together.

Electrical Controllers

Electrical controllers are frequently in the form of amplifiers. These can be electronic, magnetic or rotary. Electronic amplifiers are generally low power controllers, while magnetic amplifiers and rotary amplifiers are high-power controllers.

Hydraulic Controllers

Hydraulic control systems can be pump-controlled or valve-controlled. In a pump-controlled system, a variable-stroke pump delivers high pressure oil to a fixed-stroke motor. The motor speed is controlled by regulating the flow of oil from the pump. In this case, the controller is the variable-stroke pump.

In a valve-controlled system, the motor speed can be controlled by a fast-operating valve, frequently known as a servo-valve.

Pneumatic Controllers

Air is normally the energy medium used in pneumatic control systems. Low pressure pneumatic systems are frequently used in process control applications and higher pressure systems are frequently used in mechanisation systems such as in mechanical handling and manufacturing. In both of these applications, air is compressed by a compressor, stored in a reservoir and regulated by valves before being exhausted to the atmosphere. Pneumatic valves and actuators are similar in construction to hydraulic valves and actuators. However, air is compressible while oil is frequently assumed to be incompressible, so pneumatic valves need to be pressure-locked in position. The essential difference between pneumatic systems and hydraulic systems is that hydraulic control valves control oil flow while pneumatic control valves control air pressure.

Figure 36.30 - Pneumatic controller

Actuators

Hydraulic Actuators

These actuators can be in the form of hydraulic motors or hydraulic piston devices and are available in a wide range of power capacities, torque capacities and speeds.

Figure 36.33 illustrates a typical double-acting piston and cylinder actuator. Coulomb friction affects the performance of these actuators and pressure differentials as high as 30% of the supply pressure can be necessary in order to overcome this resistance to motion. The mathematical equations that govern the motions of these actuators under steady conditions are:

$$Q = L_p P + A_p v$$

$$F = A_p P$$

where Q is the flow of oil into the cylinder, L_p is the leakage flow coefficient for the piston, A_p is the piston area, v is the piston velocity, F is the force that is generated by the piston and P is the pressure differential across the piston.

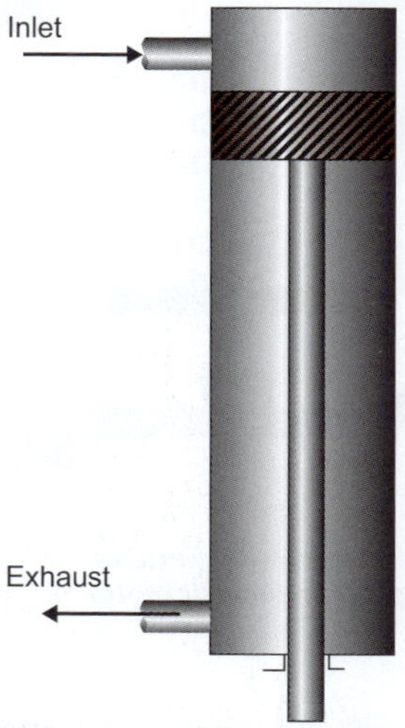

Figure 36.31 - Double-acting piston and cylinder actuator

Figure 36.32 illustrates a typical hydraulic gear motor. In this motor, high pressure oil is forced between the housing and the gears, causing the gears to rotate in opposition. The low pressure oil exhausts through the exhaust port. An output drive shaft is connected to one of the gears. This type of motor is easy to manufacture, efficient in operation and comparatively inexpensive.

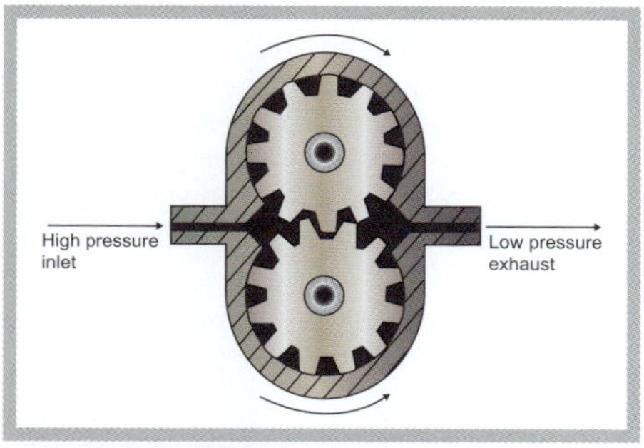

Figure 36.32 - Hydraulic gear motor

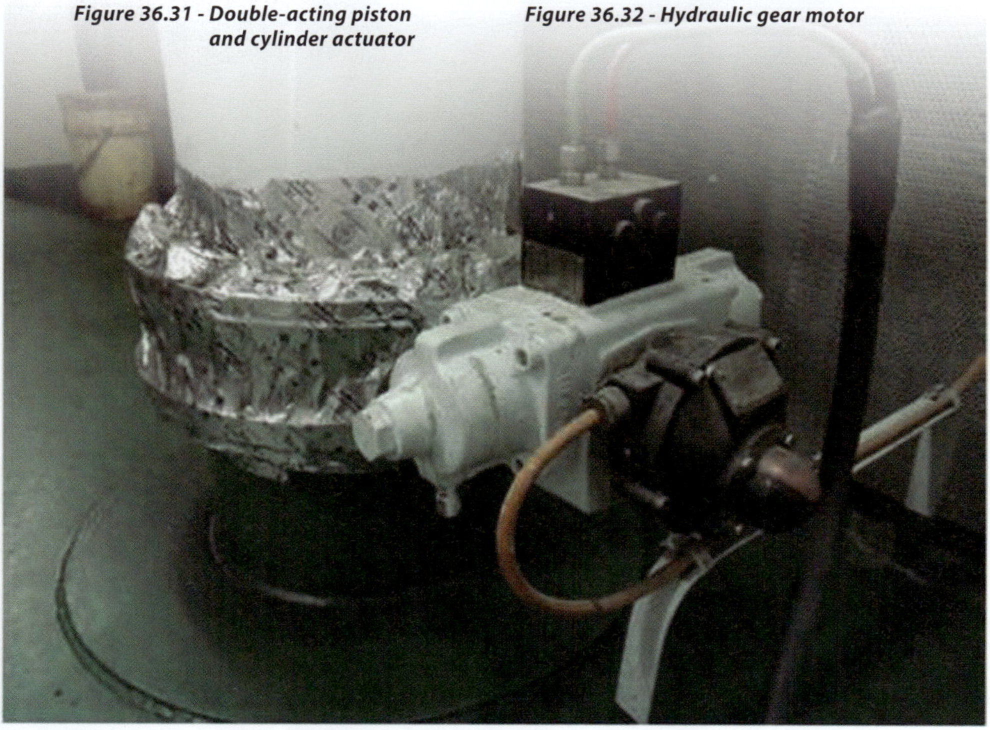

Figure 36.33 - Hydraulic actuator

Controllers

Pneumatic Actuators

Pneumatic actuators can be classified as low pressure or high pressure actuators. High pressure actuators are usually piston-type actuators which are similar in operation to hydraulic piston-type actuators. They are operated usually by spool-type control valves.

Low pressure actuators are frequently known as pneumatic motors and can be used to generate translatory or rotary motions. Figure 36.35 illustrates a typical motor. In this actuator, low pressure air causes the large area diaphragm to deflect, which in turn causes the translatory motion of an output shaft. This type of actuator is used frequently for operating flow control valves. Translatory movements can also be generated by capsules and bellows.

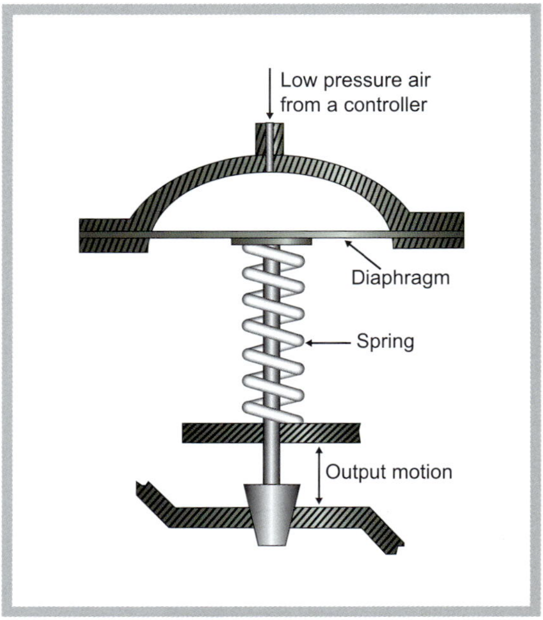

Figure 36.34 - Typical pneumatic motor

Figure 36.35 - Pneumatic actuator

Jointing or Gasket Types

Flanged Joints

Flanged ends of a pipe provide a convenient method of joining two pieces of pipe together. Flanges also provide a convenient method of making a pipeline more easily repairable by breaking into shorter sections.

The size of the flange and the number of bolts depend on the pipe diameter and the internal pressure of the pipe, although temperature may also have to be considered. The larger the pipe diameter and the higher the pressure, the greater number of bolts required to hold the flanges together. Between the flanges, there will be a joint or gasket.

Compressed Asbestos Fibre

Compressed asbestos fibre is used for superheated and saturated steam, gases, alkalis, mild acids, oils, solvents and most chemicals.

Nitrile bound compressed asbestos fibre is used for oils, solvents and petrols.

Wire-reinforced compressed asbestos fibre is usually used with a graphite surface for areas of severe physical conditions, where high temperatures and pressures exist. It is also suitable for diesel exhaust manifolds and cylinder head joints where vibration can be a problem.

Cork/Rubber Jointing

Hard types are used for petroleum fuels, oils and lubricants.

Medium hardness types are used for solvents, greases, oils, refrigerants, coolants, water and air as well as lubricating and mineral oils.

Non-Asbestos Compressed Fibre Jointing

This jointing is used where asbestos in any form is unacceptable. It may be used for sealing against steam, water, oils, gases, dilute acids and alkalis. It can also be provided with a fine steel mesh for applications requiring greater strength.

Figure 36.36 - Miscellaneous joints and gaskets

Instrument Air

Figure 36.37 - Instrument air dryer

This section concerns the air supply for onboard instrumentation equipment, which requires a high degree of solid particle filtration and oil and water removal. Solid particles greater than 5 microns in size can cause blockages and damage diaphragms and 'O' rings.

Oil may be found in droplet, gaseous and vapour forms, and whatever the form it can create problems by blocking orifices and nozzles, closing up dryers and building up layers in the pipelines, eventually blocking them.

Moisture present in the air can cause blockage of orifices and nozzles if in droplet form and cause corrosion, the products of which may cause blockages. Under low temperature conditions, such as a sudden pressure drop, or in low ambient temperatures, it can freeze in the pipelines or actuator mechanisms.

Figure 36.38 shows an air supply system with two compressors. If there is an alternative air supply, one compressor may be dispensed with. The supply pressure should be at 7 bar. Drying and filtering air is expensive, but control air for actuators without positioners and general service air may not need to be treated to such a high degree as instrument air. However, the acceptable water content of the control air will depend on the application and it may have to be dried for use on deck.

Air Drying

This is usually carried out by refrigeration (using chilled water or brine), by absorption driers or by a combination of both, the former being capable of removing about 96% of the moisture and a proportion of the lubricating oil if present. Absorption dryers allow the condensation of water vapour on the surface of a solid desiccant such as silica gel, activated alumina or synthetic zealite. The water capacity of these is low, but the rate of absorption is high.

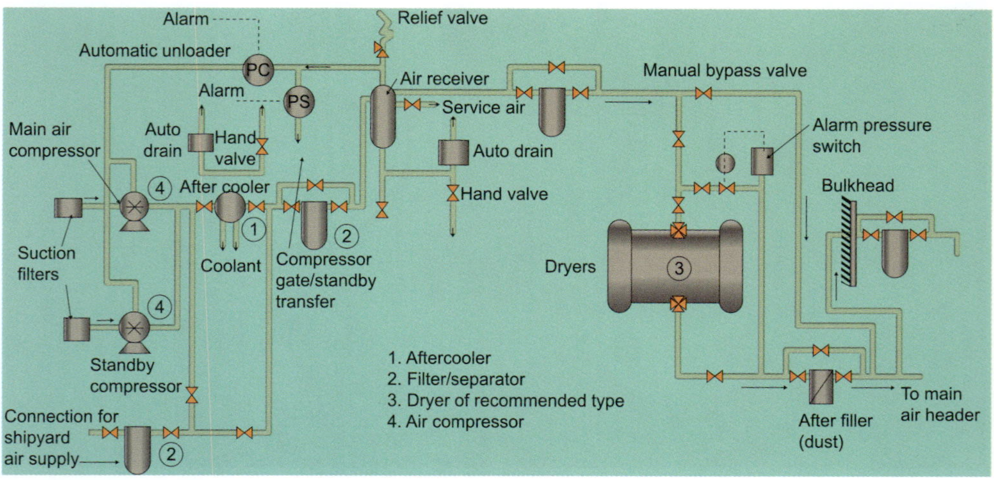

Figure 36.38 - Air supply system with two compressors

Wilden Pumps

Air-Operated Double-Diaphragm Pump

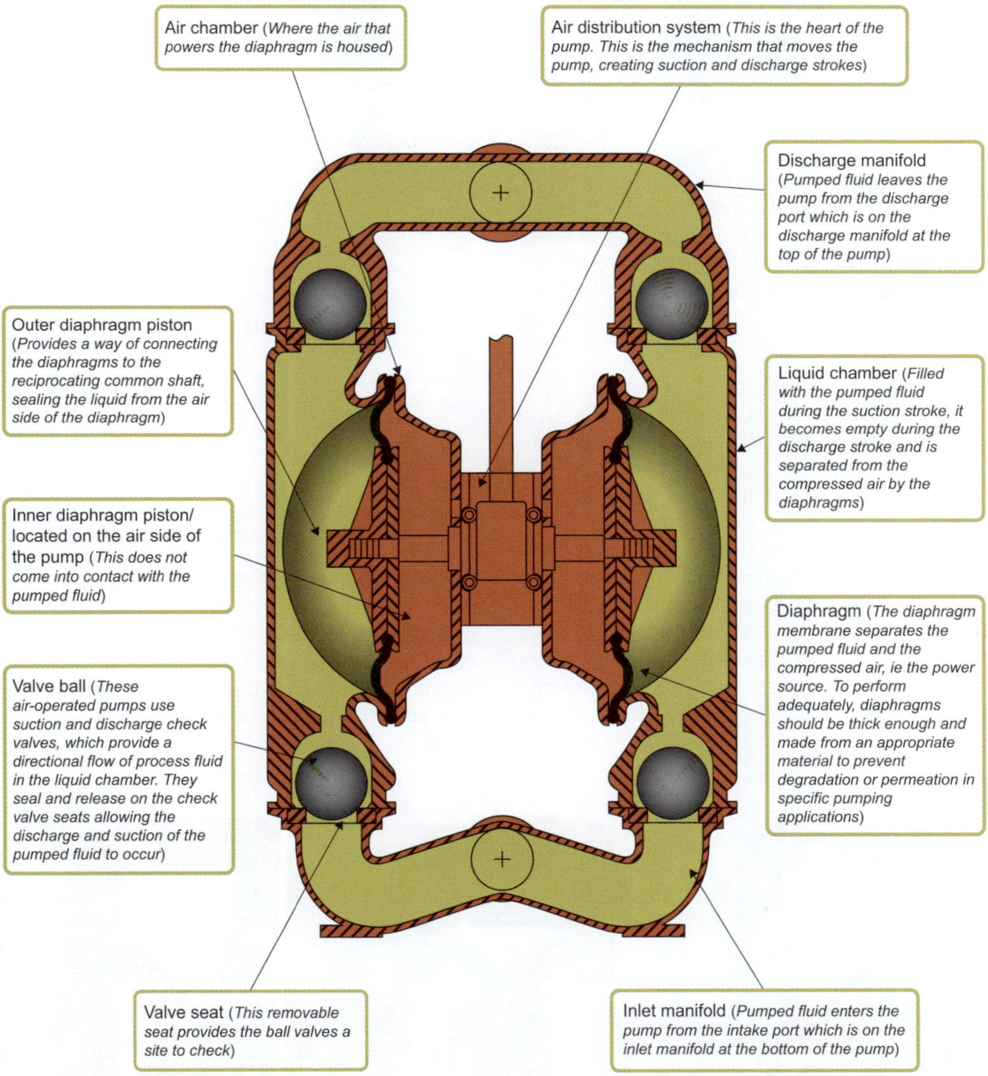

Wilden Pumps

How it Works

This pump is air operated and has a reciprocating double diaphragm. It works by positive displacement. Fluid is displaced from one of the two liquid chambers when each stroke is completed.

There are some wetted parts, which come into contact with the fluid and are known as dynamic. The two diaphragms are connected by a common shaft, the two inlet valve balls and discharge valve balls. The diaphragms act as a separation membrane between the compressed air supply and liquid. If the diaphragm is driven with compressed air rather than the shaft, the load on it is balanced, which will extend the diaphragm's life. The valve balls open and close on the valve seats directing the flow of liquid.

Figure 36.39 The air distribution system directs air to the correct chamber and the back of diaphragm A. The compressed air will move diaphragm A from the centre block towards the liquid chamber. Diaphragm B, which is opposite, is pulled inward by the shaft connected to the pressurised diaphragm A. This means that diaphragm B is now on the suction stroke; the air behind the diaphragm is forced out into the atmosphere through the exhaust port of the pump. Diaphragm A is now working against the atmospheric pressure. Diaphragm B's movement towards the centre block of the pump will create a vacuum in liquid chamber B. Atmospheric pressure will force fluid into the inlet manifold, which will force the inlet valve ball off its seat. Liquid will now be free to move past the inlet valve ball, lower left, filling the liquid chamber.

Figures 36.40 and 36.41 When pressurised diaphragm A reaches the limit of its discharge stroke, the air valve will redirect the compressed air supply to the back side of diaphragm B. The pressurised air will force diaphragm B away from the centre block, while diaphragm A will be pulled towards the centre block by the shaft. The air chamber on side A will expel air into the atmosphere using the exhaust port of the pump. Diaphragm B will now be on its discharge stroke while diaphragm A is on the suction stroke. Diaphragm B forces the inlet valve, on the lower left, onto its seat due to hydraulic forces being created in the pump's liquid chamber and manifold. Diaphragm A's movement to the centre block of the pump will create a vacuum in liquid chamber A. Atmospheric pressure will force fluid into the pump's inlet manifold. The inlet valve ball, lower right, is forced off its seat allowing fluid to enter the right liquid chamber.

When the pump reaches the original starting point, each diaphragm will have gone through one suction and discharge stroke. This constitutes one pumping cycle. The pump will require several cycles before being completely primed, depending on the application variables.

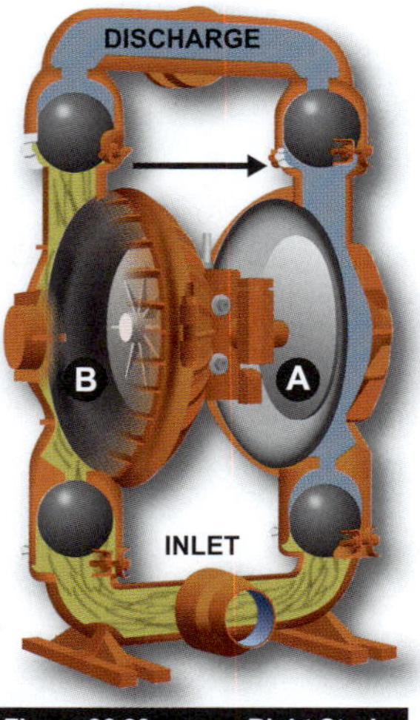

Figure 36.39 Right Stroke

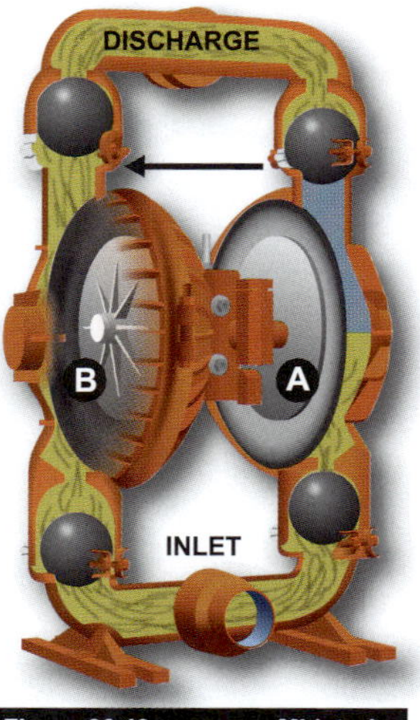

Figure 36.40 Midstroke

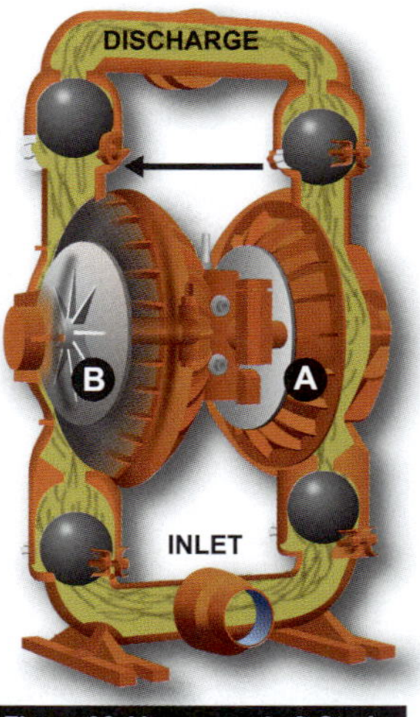

Figure 36.41 Left Stroke

Self-Priming (see right)

A Wilden pump is capable of creating a high vacuum and is designed to allow the pump to run dry with no damage. The pump can create a suction lift of up to 9.5 m of water.

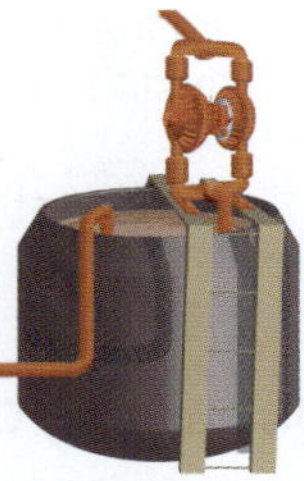

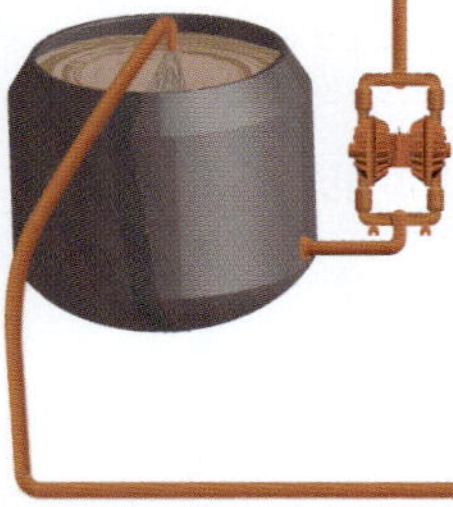

Positive Suction Head (see left)

A Wilden pump is designed so a positive suction head condition is created, for example when it is necessary to draw off the bottom of holding or mixing tanks etc. Wilden pumps are most efficient, and the life of components is maximised when inlet pressure is limited to 0.68 bar (10 psig).

Submerged (see right)

Many Wilden pumps can be completely submerged. The construction material of the pump must be chemically compatible with the process fluid. The air exhaust must be led to atmosphere.

Air Distribution Systems

The air distribution system alternately routes the air supply from one side of the pump to the other, shifting the pump.

Turbo Flo

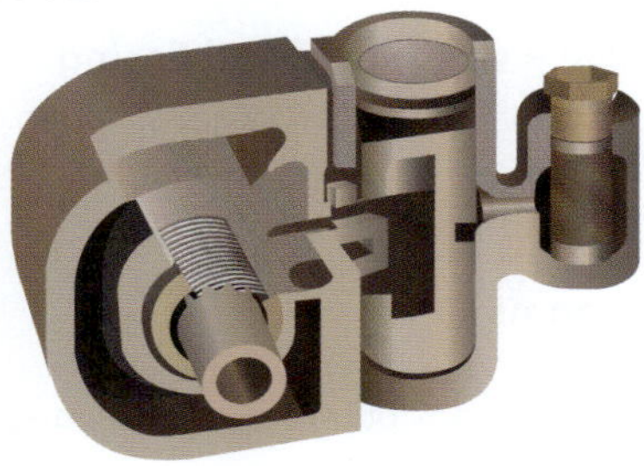

This air distribution system consists of a ported air valve body housing a piston. This piston is the only moving part of the air distribution system. The system uses differential pressure to shift the pump. The air valve is attached to a centre block using matching ports. As air is supplied to the air valve, the differential pressure will cause the piston to move vertically. This vertical movement will alternately supply the power ports with pressurised air. The ports then direct the air to the back side of the diaphragms. Air valve tolerances will allow some moisture and air line particles to be present, at a level that will not compromise free movement of the piston. The turbo flo uses Glyd rings which are PTFE composite seals that provide chemically-resistant centre block seals. The straight shaft used in conjunction with Glyd rings improves the seal and lengthens the pump's life. An anodised hollow aluminium piston provides a clean crisp shift. The air valve components can be inspected without having to take the pump apart.

Figure 36.42 - Wilden pump used for pollution prevention

Wilden Pumps

Inspections

Air Valve Piston/Spool and Casing

- Ensure that the piston/spool is able to move freely
- remove any debris.

Diaphragms

- Make sure that there is no swelling, cracking or any other apparent damage.

Balls/Seats/O-rings

- Ensure there is no swelling, cracking or any other apparent damage
- lubricate shaft if needed.

Replace before Failure

The following Wilden pump parts should be scheduled for replacement as appropriate, before failure due to wear and tear:

- Diaphragms
- valve seats
- valve balls
- o-rings.

Seal Replacement

It is very important that seals are installed correctly as they affect the pump's performance. Care must be taken to ensure that the seals are placed into the proper grooves and are not damaged when they are installed, as an incorrectly installed seal will make the pump inoperable. Damaged seals will reduce performance and result in a shorter seal life.

Maintenance

Disassembly/Reassembly

The following are generic instructions for disassembly/reassembly of a Wilden pump. The manual should always be referred to for detailed instructions for a specific pump.

Before disassembling the pump, you must:

- Put on safety glasses
- shut off the main air supply
- disconnect the air hose from the air valve. This allows the air pressure in the hose to drain
- isolate the pump using isolation valves. This will avoid any spillage from the pipe
- turn the pump upside down to drain all liquid that has been trapped by the valve balls
- mark a line from each liquid chamber to the corresponding air chamber to ensure proper alignment during reassembly.

Disassembly Overview

The following guidance will be of use when disassembling/reassembling a Wilden pump:

- Remove the fasteners that connect the discharge manifold to the liquid chambers. Remove the discharge manifold exposing the valve balls and valve seats
- inspect the ball cage area of the manifold for any excessive wear or damage
- remove the intake and discharge valve balls, seats and o-rings from the discharge manifold and inspect for nicks, gouges, chemical erosion and any signs of abrasive wear. Replace any worn parts
- remove the fasteners that connect the inlet manifold to the liquid chambers
- lift the intake manifold away, exposing the valve balls and seats. Inspect the intake valve ball cage for any excessive wear or damage
- remove the fasteners connecting the liquid chamber to the centre section assembly. Lift the liquid chamber away from the centre section assembly to expose the diaphragm and outer piston. Using an adjustable wrench, remove the diaphragm assembly. Inspect the diaphragm assembly and shaft for any signs of wear or chemical attack. Repeat disassembly instructions for the opposite liquid chamber.

Troubleshooting

Pump Will Not Run or Runs Slowly

- Check the air inlet screen and air filter for any debris
- check for a sticking air valve. Flush the air valve with cleaning fluid
- check for a worn out air valve. Replace if necessary
- check the centre block seals. If they are excessively worn, they will not seal and air will flow through the pump and out the air

exhaust. Use only Wilden seals as they are of special construction

- check for a rotating piston in the air valve
- check the type of lubricant that is being used. A higher viscosity oil than suggested may cause the piston to stick or to run erratically.

Pump Runs but Little or No Product Flows

- Check for pump cavitation. A slow pump speed will allow materials to enter the pumping chambers. The speed should be increased accordingly
- check for sticking ball checks. If the material being pumped is not compatible with pump elastomers, swelling may occur. Replace balls with the correct elastomers
- check to ensure that all suction connections are airtight, particularly manifold connections around intake balls.

Pump Air Valve Freezes

Check for any excessive moisture in the compressed air. A dryer or a hot air generator for compressed air should be installed.

Air Bubbles In Pump Discharge

- Check for a ruptured diaphragm
- check the clamp band's tightness, particularly at the intake manifold.

Product Comes Out of Air Exhaust

- Check to see whether the diaphragm is ruptured
- check the tightness of the large clamp bands
- check the tightness of the piston plates to shaft if applicable.

Pump Rattles

- Use softer balls
- create a false discharge head or suction lift.

Lubrication Oils and Grease

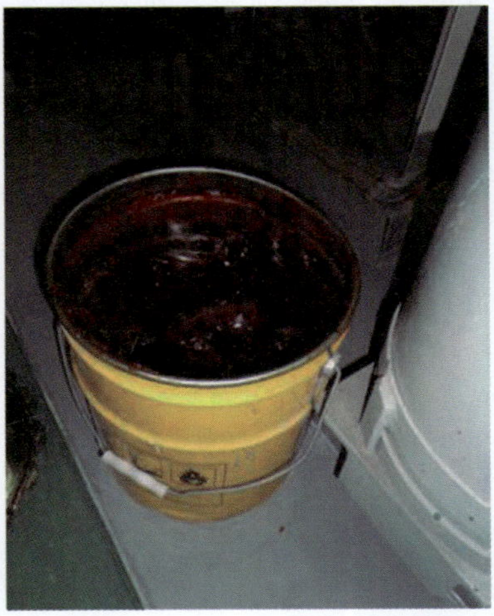

Lubricants are substances used to reduce friction between moving surfaces to improve efficiency, reduce wear and to protect the coated subject from environmental corrosion. They can also be used for distributing heat and dissolving foreign particles.

Engine Oils

The primary roles of engine oil are to reduce friction and prevent corrosion. The secondary role is to dissipate heat and to hold in suspension the micrometre-sized by-products of engine wear such as the metal fines, combustion (soot) and oil degradation products.

Typically, lubricants contain 90% base oil (most often petroleum fractions, called mineral oils) and less than 10% additives. Vegetable oils or synthetic liquids such as esters, silicone, fluorocarbons and many others are sometimes used as base oils. Additives reduce friction and wear and increase viscosity and resistance to corrosion and oxidation.

The Society of Automotive Engineers (SAE) has established a numerical code system for grading motor oils according to their kinematic viscosity. SAE viscosity grading includes the following: 0, 5, 10, 15, 20, 25, 30, 40, 50 and 60. Some of the numbers can be suffixed with the letter W, designating their winter or cold-start viscosity.

Viscosity is graded by measuring the time it takes for a standard amount of oil to flow through a standard orifice at standard temperature. The longer it takes, the higher the viscosity, and the higher the SAE code. A lubricant that is too thick or not thick enough can cause major damage to the moving parts of an engine.

Lubrication Oils and Grease

Note the markings on a carton of typical car engine oil

Cold Weather Conditions

Regular engine oil that may be exposed to cold weather conditions, such as in a lifeboat engine, should be replaced with a multi-grade oil such as 5W-30 or a more appropriate winter grade type.

Synthetic oils reduce friction between all movable parts of a diesel engine and offer more linear viscosity characteristics. A synthetic oil can achieve much easier starting than multi-grade oil, particularly in cold weather.

For extreme arctic conditions, a synthetic SAE 0W-30 has been developed for operating diesel engines. It is also recommended for petrol engines and mobile hydraulic systems operating at very low ambient temperatures. However, guidance on the proper viscosity for lubricating oil should be obtained from the engine manufacturer's manual.

Filters

Lubricant circulation systems have the benefit of carrying away internally-generated debris, and external contaminants that get introduced into the system, to a filter where they can be removed. Lubricants for machines that regularly generate debris or contaminants contain detergent and dispersant additives to assist in debris and contaminant transport to the filter and removal. Over time, the filter will become clogged and require cleaning or replacement. In closed systems, magnets can be used to supplement filters by attracting any iron fines that may be created.

In pressurised systems, these filters can clog with debris or oil that has thickened in cold weather. To avoid damage to equipment, pressure relief valves should be fitted to the filter, especially if the ship is operating exposed machinery in cold conditions.

Hydraulic Fluids

The primary purpose of hydraulic fluid is to convey power. Fluids used include mineral oil, water and synthetic compounds, with the most efficient fluids being those that have a low compressibility.

Increasingly, environmental concerns mean there is a requirement to use biodegradable fluids, especially where there is a risk of oil pollution. This is a particular issue if there are any leakages of deck washing over the side through scuppers during periods of heavy rainfall. The hydraulic oils available are based on vegetable oil and are available as ISO 32, ISO 46 and ISO 68 specification oils.

Grease

Grease consists of a lubricant and a carrier, or base. As grease contains a base oil, it can oxidise. In grease, which does not conduct heat easily, this oxidisation spreads slowly from a hot point causing carbonisation and crust formation. As oxidisation increases, the grease darkens and this has a destructive effect, causing softening and leakage.

The rate of any oxidation of oil-based lubricants depends on temperature. The critical temperature at which a structure breaks down is called the drop point. Once grease is heated above the drop point, it will never regain its consistency and should be replaced.

Grease also has a minimum temperature at which it can be properly used, which is the point at which it will harden.

Additives

Products such as teflon are sometimes added to greases to improve their lubricating properties. Gear greases consist of rosin oil, thickened with lime and mixed with mineral oil, with some percentage of water. Special purpose greases, such as those used in cold weather conditions, contain glycerol and sorbitan esters.

Under high pressure or shock loading, normal grease can be compressed to the extent that the greased parts come into physical contact, causing friction and wear.

Greases for marine use are divided into five main categories:

Mineral oil mixed with solids
These are used in heavy machinery that operates in high load conditions at slow speeds.

Heavy asphaltic-type oils blended with lighter oils
These greases form a heavy protective coating after the application is heated and cooled. A prime use is on open machinery such as windlasses and wire ropes. The lighter oils are blended in to allow the grease to be applied more easily as the flow rate is increased.

Extreme-pressure greases (EP grease)
These greases contain additives that improve the 'film' strength of the lubricant. The film is formed by a chemical reaction of the metal to the additives and it provides resistance to any metal-to-metal contact of the parts to which the grease is applied. The chemical reaction is initiated by pressure being placed on the grease, creating the heat required for the reaction. Different additives are used according to the type, conditions and applications of the equipment.

Soap-thickened mineral oils
This type of grease is the most commonly used. The dropping point of a soap-thickened lubricating grease is the temperature at which it passes from a semi-solid to a liquid state under specific test conditions. It is an indication of the type of thickener used and a measure of the cohesiveness of the oil and thickener of a grease.

The dropping point is used in combination with other testable properties to determine the suitability of greases for specific applications. It is applicable only to greases that contain soap thickeners.

Silicone grease
Silicone grease is a waterproof grease made by combining a silicone oil with a thickener. It is commonly used for lubricating and preserving rubber parts and can be used equally on rubber door seals and on rubber face masks for preservation. It functions well as a corrosion inhibitor and where a thicker lubricant is required. Silicone greases generally have a temperature range of minus 40 to 400°C.

Shipboard Incinerators

Shipboard incinerators are used for incinerating both solid wastes (eg domestic waste, paper, cardboard, etc) and liquid wastes arising from the operation of the ship (eg sludge, cargo-associated waste, maintenance waste, operational waste, cargo residues, etc).

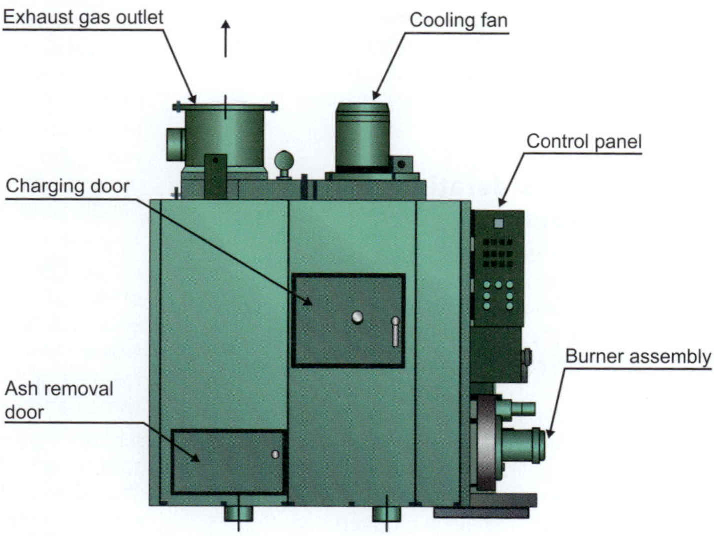

Figure 36.43 - A typical shipboard incinerator

Regulations

To prevent pollution of the marine environment, MARPOL establishes guidelines for solid and liquid waste discharged from ships. The regulations regarding shipboard incinerators are:

Shipboard Incinerators

MARPOL 73/78/97 - MEPC 76(40)	
Object:	Any incinerator loaded on board a ship on or after January 1st, 2000
Summary:	• The prohibition of shipboard incineration of waste materials containing PCBs, heavy metals or similar contaminants • The incinerator must be approved by IMO/MEPC • The incinerator must be designed according to MEPC 76(40) standards
Conditions of operation:	**MARPOL 73/78/97 ANNEX IV, Regulation 16** • Oxygen concentration in the combustion chamber: 6 to 12% • Outlet temperature of the combustion chamber: 850 to 1,200°C • Carbon monoxide concentration in exhaust gas: not to exceed 200 mg/MJ • Smoke concentration in exhaust gas: not to exceed BACHARACH 3 • Weight of unburned material: not to exceed 10% • Temperature of outer wall: not to exceed 60°C • Exhaust gas is to be rapidly cooled to 350°C or less within a space of 2.5 metres in the smokestack • The combustion chamber is normally to be operated in a negative-pressure environment • Requirement for residual heat: 650°C or more (continuous charge incinerator) • It shall be 600°C in at least 5 minutes (batch disposal incinerator)

Working and Disposing

Solid waste is put in properly arranged stacks so that the chances of incomplete combustion are minimised. Oily sludge or waste oil is not put directly into the combustion chamber. A separate tank is made that has its outlet into the combustion chamber. The oily sludge is first heated and once optimum temperature is reached, the oil is passed into the combustion chamber.

The burner then burns the mixture at a thermostatically-controlled temperature to induce complete combustion. The force draught fan provides a continuous supply of air and the rotating shaft creates the required swirling of air. Ash is collected in the ash slide and either disposed to the sea or stored for disposal at the next port.

Special Considerations for Incinerators

Marine incinerator technology is not highly advanced, primarily because the technology has not yet been subject to constraints on air emissions or the types of materials that can be incinerated. Marine incinerators in current use are predominantly designed for intermittent operation and hand stoking and typically do not include any provision for air pollution control. Control of air pollution is required in many ports in the world. Prior to using an incinerator while in port, permission may be required from the relevant port authority. The use of shipboard garbage incinerators in ports in or near urban areas should be discouraged as their use will add to possible air pollution in these areas.

Special considerations for incinerators are:

- Shipboard incinerators must be as compact as practicable and, with operating personnel at a premium, automatic operation is desirable. Most shipboard incinerators are designed for intermittent operation; the waste is charged to the incinerator, firing is started and combustion typically lasts for three to six hours
- marine incinerators vary greatly in size. They have natural or induced draught and are hand fired. It should be noted that incinerator ratings are usually quoted on the basis of heat input rate rather than on a weight-charged basis because of the variability of the heat content in the wastes. Some modern incinerators are designed for continuous firing and can handle simultaneous disposal of nearly all shipboard waste
- incinerators may emit hazardous ash or vapour, have dirty operation or have excessive labour required for charging, stoking and ash removal. They may not meet air pollution regulations imposed in some harbours
- if plastics are to be burnt in a safe manner, to comply with Annex V, the incinerator should be suitable for the purpose, as otherwise the following problems can result:
  - Depending on the type of plastic and conditions of combustion,

some toxic gases can be generated in the exhaust stream, including vaporised hydrochloric acid (HCl) and hydrocyanic (HCN) acid. These and other intermediary products of plastic combustion can be extremely dangerous

- the ash from the combustion of some plastic products may contain heavy metal and other residues which can be toxic and should therefore not be discharged into the sea but be retained on board and discharged at port reception facilities
- the temperatures generated during incineration of primarily plastic wastes are high enough to damage some garbage incinerators
- plastic incineration requires three to ten times more combustion air than average municipal refuse. If a proper level of oxygen is not supplied, a high level of soot will be formed in the exhaust stream.

Incineration options for shipboard generated garbage

Typical examples	Special handling by vessel personnel before incineration	Incineration characteristics				
		Combustibility	Reduction of volume	Residual	Exhaust	Onboard storage space
Paper packaging, food and beverage containers	Minor - easy to feed into hopper	High	Over 95%	Powder ash	Possibly smoky and not hazardous	Minimum
Fibre and paper board	Minor - reduce material to size for feed; minimum manual labour	High	Over 95%	Powder ash	Possibly smoky and not hazardous	Minimum
Plastic packaging, food and beverage containers, etc	Minor - easy to feed into hopper	High	Over 95%	Powder ash	Possibly smoky and hazardous based on incinerator design	Minimum
Plastic sheeting, netting, rope and bulk material	Moderate manual labour time for size reduction	High	Over 95%	Powder ash	Possibly smoky and hazardous based on incinerator design	Minimum
Rubber hoses and bulk pieces	Major manual labour time for size reduction	High	Over 95%	Powder ash	Possibly smoky and hazardous based on incinerator design	Minimum
Metal food and beverage containers	Minor - easy to feed into hopper	Low	Less than 10%	Slag	Possibly smoky and not hazardous	Moderate
Metal cargo, bulky containers, thick metal items	Major manual labour time for size reduction (not easily incinerated)	Very Low	Less than 5%	Large metal fragments and slag	Possibly smoky and not hazardous	Maximum
Glass food and beverage containers, etc	Minor - easy to feed into hopper	Low	Less than 10%	Slag	Possibly smoky and not hazardous	Moderate
Wood, cargo containers and large wood scraps	Moderate manual labour time for size reduction	High	Over 95%	Powder ash	Possibly smoky and not hazardous	Minimum

Tank Gauging

Level Gauging System

Level gauging equipment is used for accurate and consistent measurement of the liquid levels in cargo tanks during loading and discharge. It must be designed and developed specifically for the cargoes carried.

Figure 36.44 - Level gauge head (Whessoe Total Automation Ltd)

The level gauge is float actuated and employs a tensator spring as a counter-balancing mechanism, which maintains a constant tape tension at the float. This ensures that the float maintains the same level of immersion irrespective of the amount and weight of the tape paid out.

The accuracy of a gauging system is dependent on the tank construction and on the operating conditions, but gauge accuracy should remain within 1 cm.

Accurately perforated invar tape transmits float movement to a sprocket wheel, which in turn drives a counter mechanism that provides local mechanical readout that is visible through a window in the counter housing.

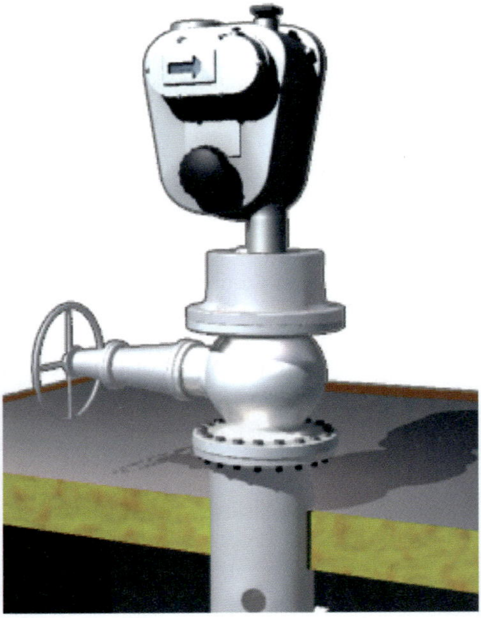

Figure 36.45 - Level gauge head

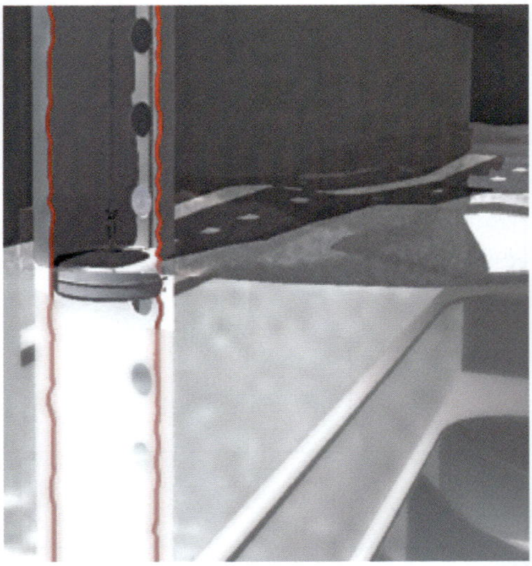

Figure 36.46 - Float immersion

To avoid the risk of tape failure and damage to the gauging mechanism, the level gauge float should be fully stowed at all times except when in use for taking readings. Care should be taken when stowing the float as overtensioning may cause the tape to break.

Level Gauge Assembly

The level gauge comprises the gauge head and the float assembly. The float is clamped to:

- An accurately perforated invar tape
- a viscous damper to control the rate of descent of the float to the cargo level
- a crank for raising the float to the storage position
- a mechanical readout that is observed through the counter window.

A float lockup arrangement provides isolation of the level gauge from the tank when in the stored position. It also provides a gauge datum reference and a means of locking the float in the storage position.

Operating a 'Whessoe' Level Gauge

To obtain the liquid level, the float is released from its stowage position using the release lever located at the base of the gauge head. In the event of a viscous damper failure, the float should be lowered to the liquid surface by hand.

The tank sounding may then be taken, by observation of the local mechanical readouts, to provide level indication.

Whessoe gauges should be checked against the custody transfer system (CTS) during each loading. Cargo tanks must be fitted with primary and secondary level gauging systems. On recent builds, both the primary and secondary gauging systems are radar based.

After use, to return the gauge to its stored position:

1. Turn the crank handle in the 'wind up' position.
2. Raise the float steadily, at a rate of 1.5 m/sec, in an anti-clockwise direction. This is indicated by the arrow on the main cover inspection plate.
3. Watch the readout counter, which will indicate when the float nears the top. At approximately 2 m from the top, slow down the rate to allow the float to pass through the isolating valve.
4. When resistance is felt by the float touching the cushion spring, continue cranking until the plunger is seated, which seals the gauge from the tank, and the automatic float lockup and datum plunger spring fully inward, securing the float.
5. Check that the counter reads exactly the same before and after use.
6. Move the crank handle to its 'storage' position (inboard).

Do not attempt to turn the crank clockwise or interfere with the free-fall of the float as this will severely damage the tape or the tensator spring.

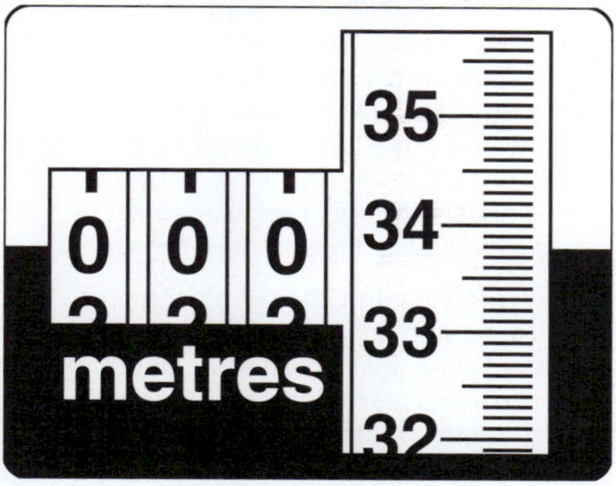

Figure 36.47 - Gauge reading of 33.8 cm

High-High Level Protection Devices

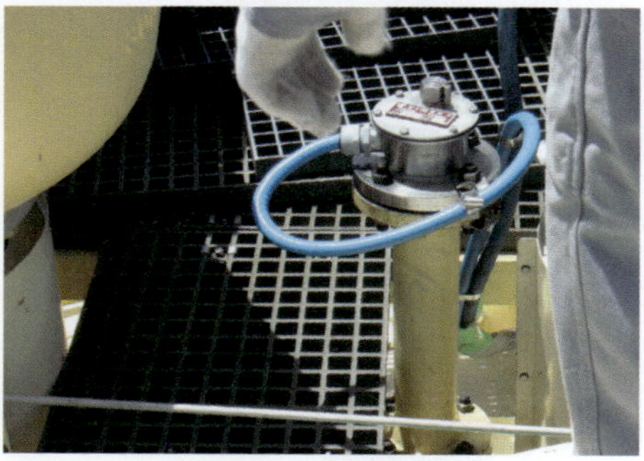

Courtesy of Shell

Figure 36.48 - High level alarm

In addition to the cargo level gauging system, there are other independent devices fitted on the tank domes that provide alarms when the cargo level reaches a certain value.

There are three levels of alarm. In an example based on a filling level of 98%, there will be:

- A high level alarm at 95% of the tank volume (audio-visual warning). This early warning alarm can be activated by the tank level measuring system or by an independent sensor

Tank Gauging

- a high-high level alarm at 98.5% of the tank volume (audio-visual warning that differs in sight but not in sound from the 95% alarm). Isolation of the overfilled tank will automatically take place by shutting the tank loading valve. If the high level warning alarm is activated by the tank level measuring system, the high-high level alarm must be activated by an independent sensor
- an extremely high level alarm at 99% of the tank volume (audio-visual warning that differs in sight from the 95% and 98.5% alarms). The ESDS will be automatically activated. If the high level alarm is activated by the tank level measuring system, the extremely high level alarm must be activated by an independent sensor.

During cargo loading, there is a danger of a significant surge pressure being generated if the valves close against the shore pumping system. For this reason, the closing times of the valves, together with the valve characteristics, must be available to the terminal so that loading rates can be adjusted.

Likely Problems and Maintenance Procedures

The float gauge is a 'closed' gauging device, which means that no cargo vapour is released to the atmosphere during gauging. Float gauges generally fulfil the role of backup gauging devices to the CTS.

Float Type Gauge

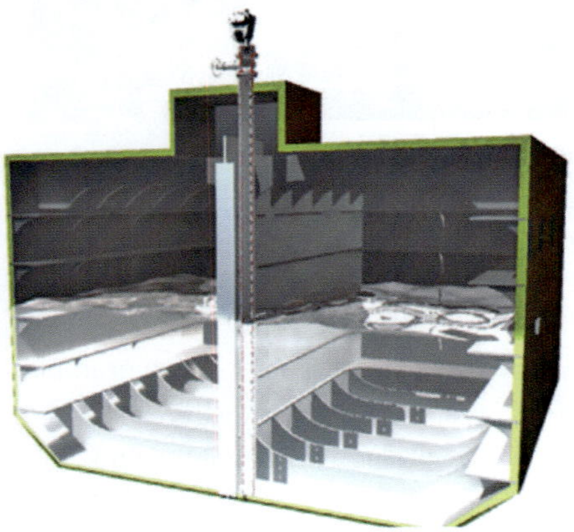

Figure 36.49 - Simulated tank cutaway showing float type gauge and stillwell arrangement

When not in use, float gauges should be housed to protect the tape-tensioning device and to stop the float being parted from the tape.

The 'average level' reading is the mean of five readings from the float gauge at 30 second intervals, with each reading being to the nearest 1 mm.

Isolating Valve and Float Inspection Chamber

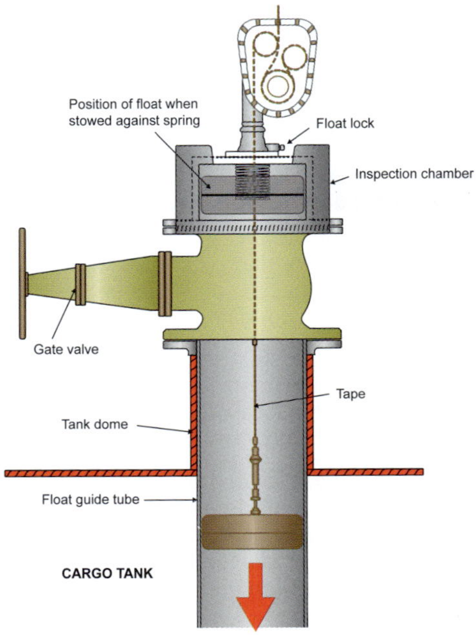

Figure 36.50 - Float level gauge

A gate valve, bolted to the top of the float well, allows the gauge head to be isolated for maintenance.

An inspection chamber constructed of stainless steel will be mounted above the isolating valve to allow access to the float and connection of float recovery tools.

Maintenance

The level gauge system must be operated at regular intervals to ensure that the system is available in the event of any failure of the primary CTS.

The housed reading difference between the level gauge system and the CTS should be recorded at each operation. It is recommended that spare key components are carried.

The gauge head is sealed with locking wire and lead seals by the Classification Society and it is important to avoid damaging them. In the event of the seals being damaged or broken, arrangements should be made for a Class Surveyor to check and re-seal the gauges.

Tape Breakage

In the event of tape breakage, the Company should be notified because if a level gauge is opened a Class Surveyor must be in attendance to oversee the recalibration and then seal the gauge.

Detailed instructions for the recovery and replacement of the float assembly/tape will be included in the operating manual.

Renewal of Tape – Example for a Floatwell Installation

Tape length must always suit the tensator spring range and not the individual tank height measurements.

The springs can be extremely dangerous if they are not kept under control.

Tape can be renewed at any time provided it is permissible to release the small volume of vapour within the gauge head and inspection housing. If the tape has broken and the float is at the tank bottom or at the liquid level, it may be possible to retrieve the float without anyone entering the cargo tank for tape renewal of a Whessoe type system:

1. Close the isolation valve.
2. Remove the covers from the inspection housing and the gauge head.
3. Remove the split pins and washers from the tape and storage drum shafts and then remove both drums together from their shafts. Remove the damaged tape from the drum.
4. Place the two drums on a flat surface with the tape drum uppermost and the tensator spring drums below. Enter the end of the new tape through the rectangular hole in the tread of the tape drum and pass the nearest sprocket hole to the end of the tape over a hook that is under the tread of the tape drum.
5. Rotate the coil of new tape around the tape drum in a clockwise direction so that when the tape is pulled it will rotate the tape drum in a clockwise direction. Continue until all of the tape is wound onto the tape drum and secure the end with some self-adhesive tape.
6. Replace drums onto their shafts, together with the washers and split pins.
7. Turn the tape drum clockwise two full turns and hold (the number of turns of the spring can be seen through viewing holes on the tape drum and on the power drum).
8. Remove the binding from the tape and remove two wraps of approximately 1.3 m (4 ft) of tape from the tape drum.

It is important that you do not rotate the tape drum to remove the two wraps of tape.

9. Pass the tape over the sprocket and under the tape retainer. Pull the tape from the sprocket down through the mounting flange and into the inspection housing.
10. Attach the magnetic float recovery link to the tape. This is a lead weight with three magnets and a tape clamp, usually found in the spares box. The attachment of the magnetic float recovery link is similar to the attachment of the tape to the plunger shaft assembly.
11. Replace the covers on the inspection hatch and gauge head.
12. Using the crank handle, lift the float recovery link off of the closure valve and hold.
13. Open the 10" isolation valve. Carefully let the float recovery link descend into the tank by holding the crank handle to support the weight and to control the rate of descent.
14. When the float recovery link has secured itself to the pick-up plate on the float, the extra weight will be noticeable. Very carefully crank up the float until it is in the inspection housing. Care must be taken to get the float well up into inspection housing to keep the float clear of the isolation valve. Note that the top of the lead weight on the float recovery link will not pass through the gauge head mounting flange.
15. Close the 10" isolation valve and remove the cover from the inspection housing.

Tank Gauging

16. Remove the main cover from the gauge head. Maintain a firm hold of the tape and remove the float recovery link (returning it to the spares box) and then fit the float to the tape with two screws.
17. Raise the float to the stowed position.
18. Adjust the counter as previously described.
19. Adjust the tape retainer so that there is a 0.5/0.75 mm gap between the tape and the retainer.
20. Replace the gauge head main cover and replace the cover on the inspection hatch.

Recap of precautions with float level gauges:

- **Never leave a float level gauge on the liquid when it is not in use**
- **when stowed, check the automatic lock is in place and the stowed reading is as expected**
- **close the gate valve when the level gauge is stowed.**

Radar Type

The electronic box generates and transmits radar waves into the cone antenna. It provides a smooth transition for the waves into the still pipe. Because the still pipe guides the radar waves, very little signal energy is lost, which results in a strong echo from the liquid surface.

The installation of a radar system is very convenient because the only parts inside the tank are the still pipe, cone antenna, thermowell and diffuser plate.

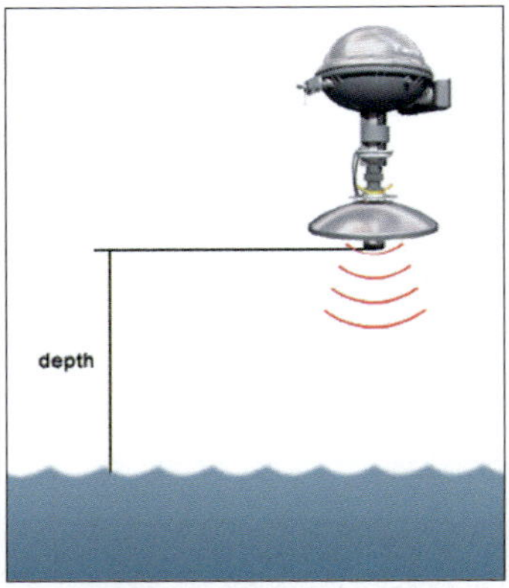

Figure 36.52 - Tank radar, signal out

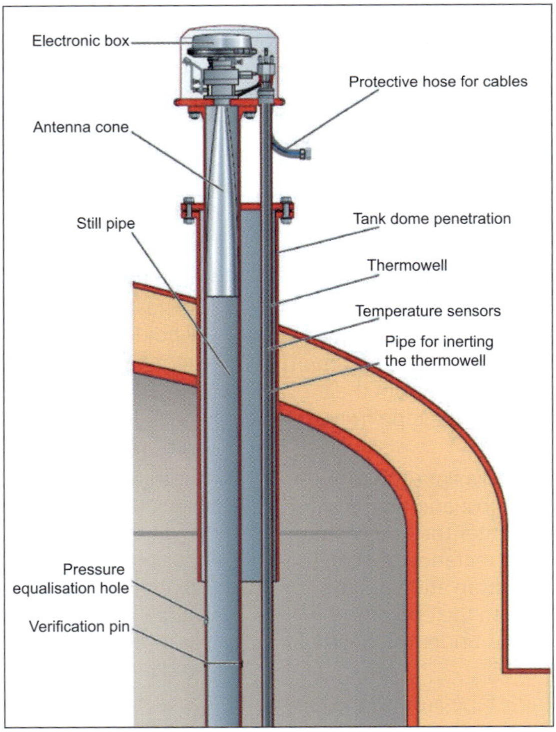

(Saab Rosemount Tank Gauging Ltd)

Figure 36.51 - Layout of Saab TankRadar System, showing still pipe

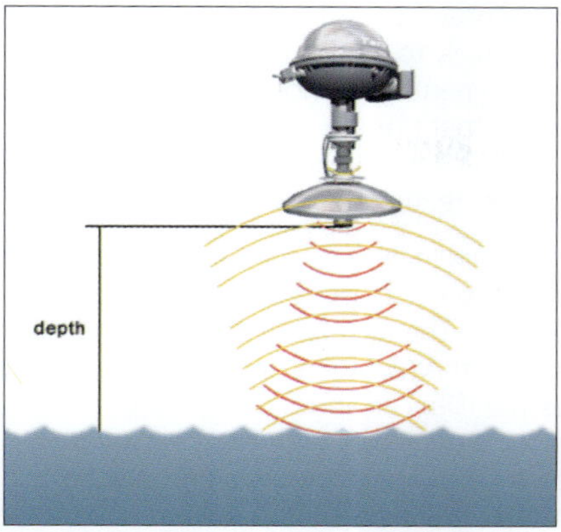

Figure 36.53 - Tank radar, signal return

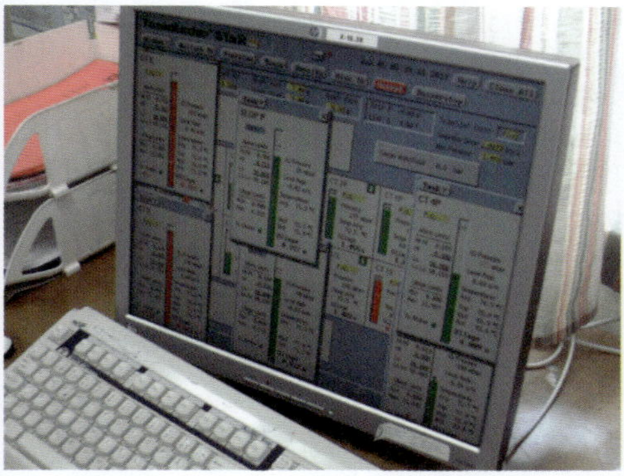

The tank radar system is based on the same principle as the ship radar. If the speed of the radar waves is known, the time needed by the signal to reach the cargo liquid level, bounce back and be picked up by the antenna can be accurately measured.

The distance to the cargo liquid level (ullage) is:

$$\frac{\text{(radar waves speed} \times \text{(measured time)}}{2}$$

(divided by 2 because the signal travels both ways)

Together with the pressure sensor signal and the signals of the various temperature sensors at different levels in the tank, the tank ullage signal is sent to the CCR (Cargo Control Room), via an intrinsically safe circuit, and the cargo volume is calculated.

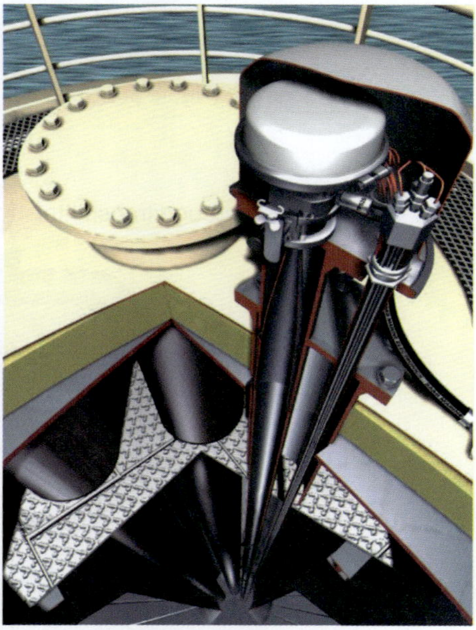

Courtesy of Saab Rosemount Tank Gauging Ltd

Figure 36.54 - Saab TankRadar gauge on top of a still pipe

Bubble Gauges

Bubble gauges (sometimes referred to as pneumatic water level gauges) work by pressurising a tube/small pipe that drops almost the full depth of the tank, normally ballast tanks. They should not be confused with differential pressure systems where the hydrostatic head pressure at the bottom of the tank is measured.

In bubble gauges, compressed gas, normally air (or an inert gas such as nitrogen), is fed into the top of a vertical tube. A regulator ensures sufficient gas is available to produce bubbles from the bottom of the tube and overcome the resisting hydrostatic pressure in the liquid. The resulting back pressure acts on a pressure transducer which is directly connected to a calibrated gauge.

The required gas pressure equals the product of the depth of fluid (surface to the end of the tube) and the fluid density. Consequently, the deeper and more viscous the fluid, the greater the required pressure to produce the flow of bubbles.

As the tank ullage decreases, the back pressure in the tube increases. This increase is reflected on the fluid level gauge (Figure 36.55).

In pressurised closed tanks, a second tube is likely to be used; a minimum level measurement tube and a maximum level measurement tube. Empty tanks, with no hydrostatic pressure in either tube, provide a zero level reading for calibration purposes.

As the fluid level rises, the back pressure in the longer tube increases due to the hydrostatic resistance. The increasing contrast in pressure between the two tubes affects the differential pressure (DP) cell and is transmitted to a remote display. Any difference between the purge gas back pressure and the tank atmosphere needs to be accounted for in the calibration of the DP cell.

Due to the importance of maintaining a steady bubble flow, air flow indicators (eg a rotameter) are often installed in the tube. Where potential exists for sediment to build up, it may be possible to blow out the line, although this requires a line to bypass the regulator.

Where the liquid temperature can vary, calibration should take place at the highest temperature to compensate for expansion and prevent the possibility of overfilling the tank.

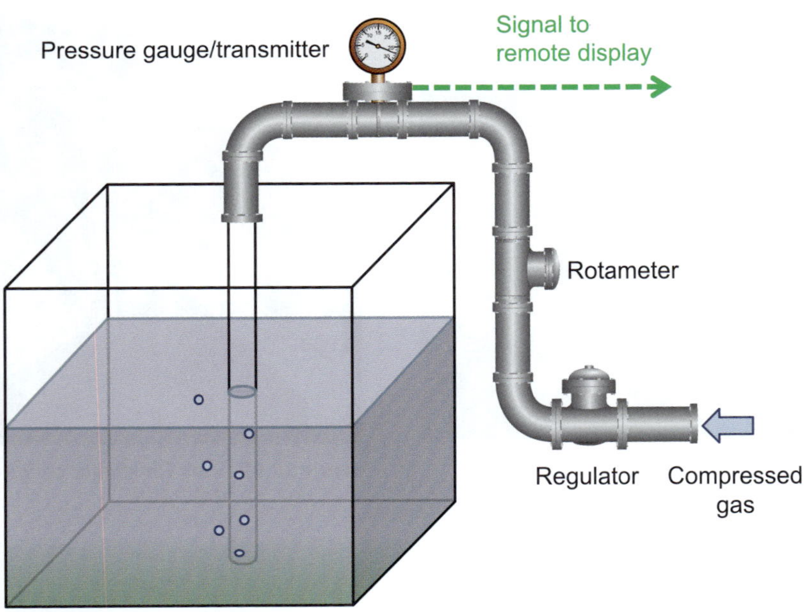

Figure 36.55 - Simple bubble gauge system

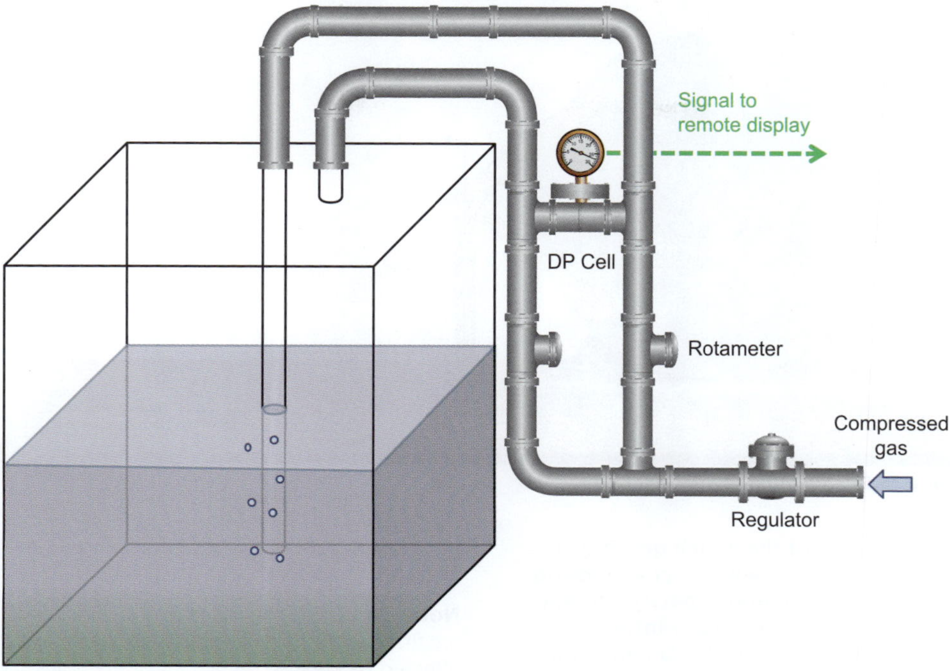

Figure 36.56 - Bubble gauge system incorporating two dip tubes

Bubble gauges provide a relatively simple system where transmitters can be placed at a distance from the tank. Provided the tube is solidly constructed and secured, bubble gauges are unlikely to be damaged by the tank liquid or during cleaning as can occur with float gauges. Short-term variation due to any minimal movement in the tanks (eg wave motion during cargo operation) should have little effect on the indicated pressure. However, significant movement will affect accuracy, particularly at sea.

Where frost is a risk, air lines should be heated. The purge gas must be suitable for the liquid contained and should not react with either the liquid or the tank atmosphere.

Common Problems

The system can be affected by a number of factors including restrictions in the pipe sizes and the volume of purge gas. Similarly, leaks, which may be caused by overpressurising the system during testing or use, will directly affect the pressure reading.

A fluctuating transducer output can be caused by:

- Liquid movement in the tank
- inadequately supported dip tube(s)
- no V-notch at the end of the dip tube.

A shift in the zero level may be caused by:

- Build-up of sediment
- build-up of corrosion
- changes in pressure where there is a long length of tube before the dip tube.

Testing Mooring Winch Brakes

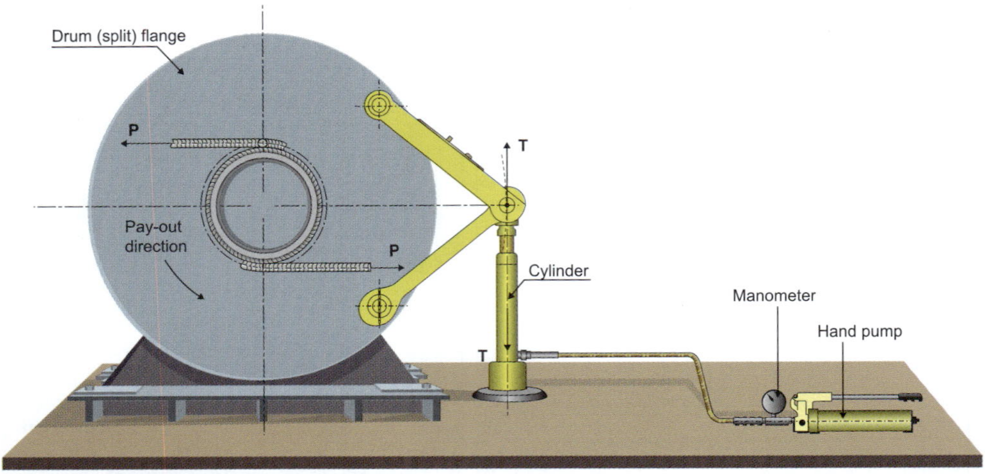

Figure 36.57 - Simplified brake test kit

The condition of the winch gearing and brake shoe linings will affect a mooring winch brake's holding capacity, so they should be tested at regular intervals, not exceeding 12 months. Oil, moisture or heavy rust on the brake linings or drum will also reduce the brake holding capacity.

If there is significant wear of the linings, they must be renewed.

Note: Some self-stowing mooring winches are fitted with disc brakes that are much less affected by wear.

A record of maintenance, inspections and tests should be kept on board.

Testing the Brake

The brake acts as a safety device, if the load in the line becomes excessive, by rendering and allowing the line to shed its load before it breaks (at MBL). For normal operation, the recommended (OCIMF) setting on the brake is 60% of the MBL of the rope, although for new ships it is set at 80% as brake efficiency will reduce with use. All ships should be supplied with a brake testing kit, which simulates the load on the line by means of hydraulic pressure producing a torque on the winch drum.

Example Test

Based on the winch shown, the pressure at 80% MBL can be calculated as follows:

- Winch capacity: 16 T x 15 m/min
- Mooring line MBL: 92 T
- Brake holding force: Po = 73.6 T at first layer (80% of MBL)
- Drum diameter: Dd = 135 cm
- Rope diameter: Dr = 5.0 cm
- Effective area of hydraulic jack: A = 75.0 cm^2
- Test force moment arm: L = 240.0 cm
- Rope PCD: Rpcd = Dd + Dr = 140.0 cm
- Brake torque: Tb = Po x Rpcd/2 = 5,152 T-cm
- Force on hydraulic jack: F = Tb/L = 7.8 T = 21,466 kg
- **Therefore, required pressure: P = F/A = 286.2 kg/cm^2 (at 80% MBL)**

Procedure

The winch testing bracket is connected to the flange of the drum and the winch testing arms are bolted to the flange of the winch drum, with the hydraulic jack positioned under the end of the winch testing arms resting on supports.

If the winches are set manually, a torque wrench should be used and, if hydraulically, the pressure gauge should first be calibrated. The pressure is increased in the hydraulic jack using a manual pump. After the pressure reaches the calculated value (for this example 286.2 kg/cm^2), a marking is made on the brake band. It is held for a minute and the marking is checked to see whether there is any slip. If the brake renders before this value is reached, the rendering force can be calculated, in this case 69T.

Testing Mooring Winch Brakes

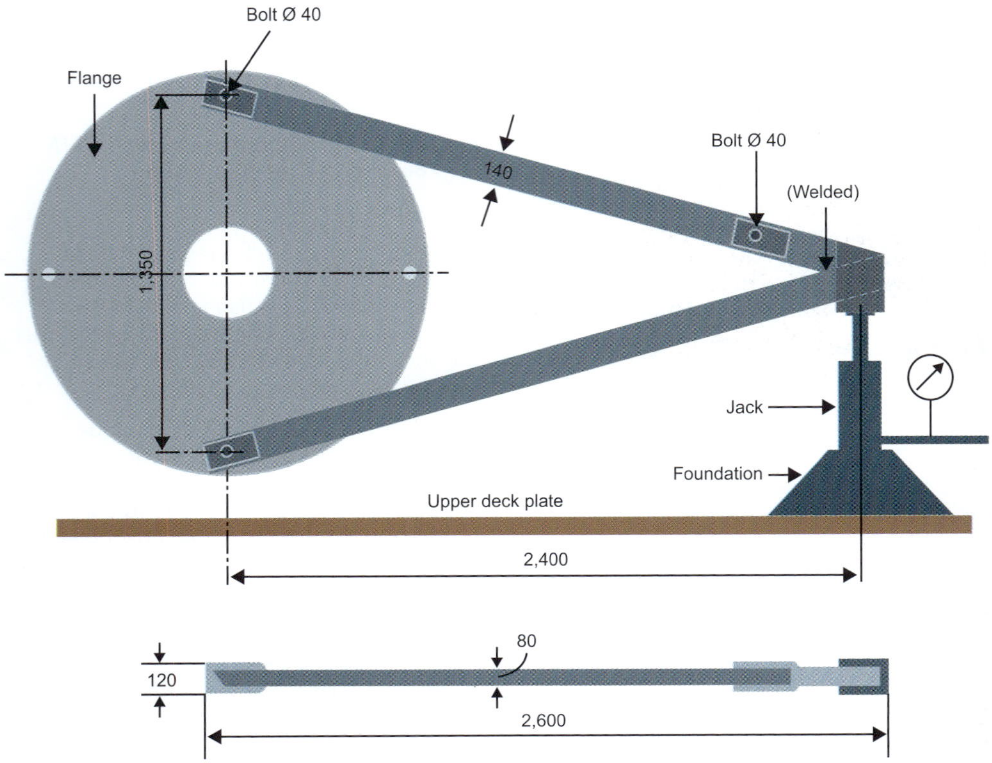

All dimensions are in millimetres

Figure 36.58 - Example test winch

Plumbing

Traditionally, plumbing was the responsibility of the deck department, but with the removal of ships' carpenters and the general reduction in manning, it has moved to the engineering department, which has the appropriate skills for the pipe work involved.

Piping

The piping provides two functions: pressurised water in and gravity water out. Air in the system can lead to a failure to flow and to pipes leaking or bursting under pressure. The gravity water flowing out can also cause leaks, but usually slower as the only pressure is that of the weight of the water at the leak point. Blockages can be due to a build-up of scale or debris in the pipework. Some ships have a pressurised waste system, but most require air ventilation to assist waste clearance.

Piping may be:

- Copper, which is the best system owing to its ability to handle high pressure and its flexibility in use
- galvanised, which might still be found on older ships. It is cheaper but not as flexible or easy to work with as copper

Plumbing

Figure 36.59 - Copper piping

- PVC, which is common for accommodation piping. It is not as flexible or dependable as copper but is easier to work with as no welding is required and piping can easily be cut to size.

Common Fittings for Piping

Elbow

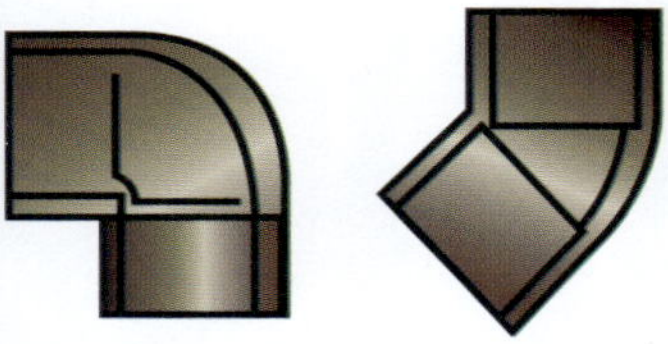

An elbow is installed between two lengths of pipe to allow a change of direction, usually 90° or 45°. The ends may be machined for butt welding or threaded. When the two ends differ in size, it is called a reducing elbow.

Tee

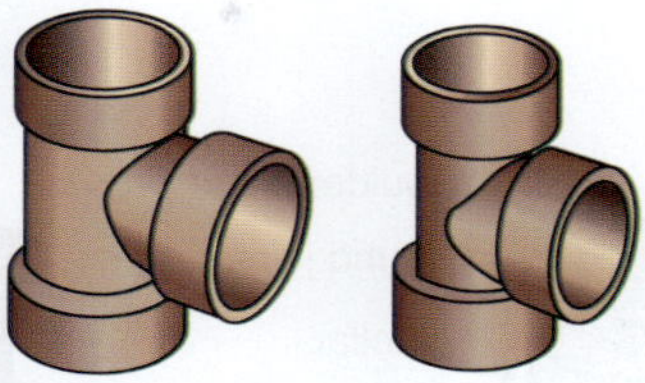

A tee is used to either combine or split water flow. Most common are tees with the same inlet and outlet sizes, but reducing tees are available as well. A cross that divides the water into four segments may also be used.

Plug

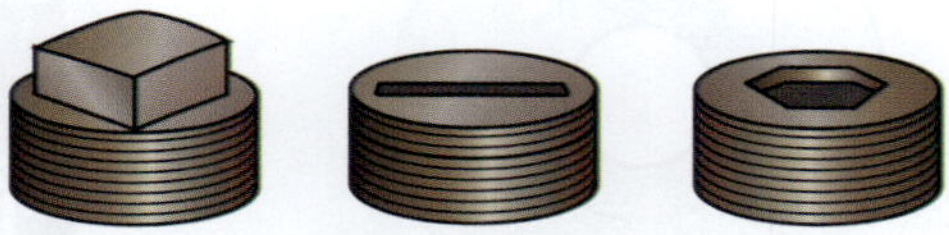

A plug performs the same function as a cap, but fits inside the pipe. These have male threads if fitted into a threaded piping system.

Coupling

A coupling connects two pipes to one another. To connect two pipes of different sizes, a reducing coupler is used.

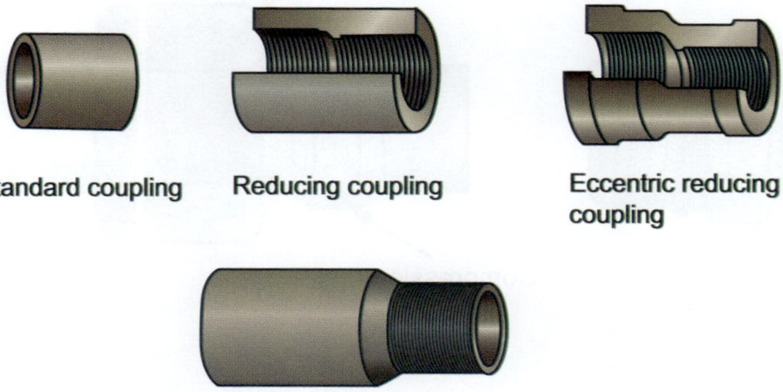

Plumbing

Union

A union works in the same way as a coupling except it is designed for easy use, being a simple screw nut fixing, which also allows for easy removal.

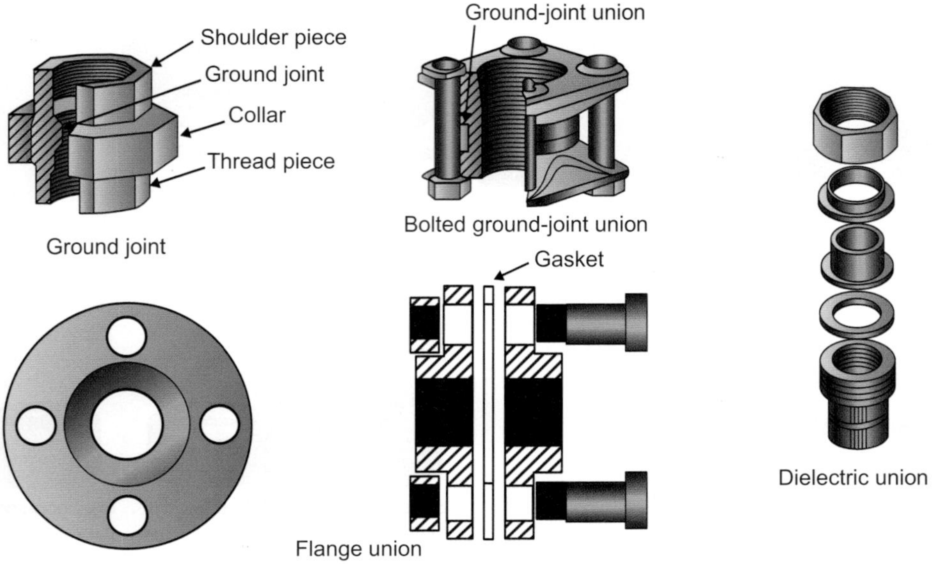

Compression Joints

These joints are more unsightly but are easier to deal with than welded joints. Care should be taken not to overtighten the joint.

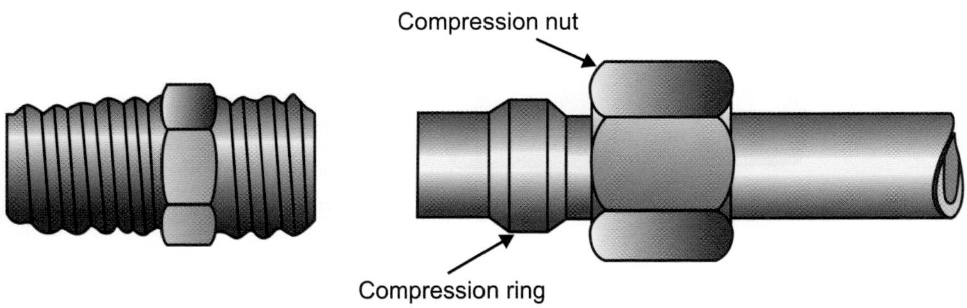

Hot Water

Somewhere between the tanks and the outlet, the hot water has to be heated. The design of the ship dictates how this is done, but there is usually a boiler in the engine room. The normal temperature setting is 60 to 70°C. Where higher temperatures are required, eg in galleys and messrooms, this can be provided by auxiliary boilers or by built-in heaters, eg in dishwashers or laundry machines.

Waste Water

The waste pipe system is subject to more blockages than the incoming system. To assist in managing this, various traps are included in the pipework. Sink traps are fitted below basins, with an easy access bolt at the bottom. Galley sinks and scuppers should all have grease traps.

The combination of traps, vents and piping is referred to as the 'drain-waste-vent' (DWV) system.

Vacuum Waste Water Systems

Vacuum technology is based on differential air pressure. New building is seeing a rise in the number of ships having this system installed. Apart from the lower installation costs, the advantages over gravity systems are:

- Less water required. The average bulk carrier uses 438,000 litres of water per year with a gravity system, while it uses 55,000 litres with a vacuum system. This means that the waste storage tanks and the water tanks can be smaller or have a greater sustainability
- smaller pipes. Gravity systems use 110 mm pipes while vacuum systems use 50 mm. This gives greater flexibility in where the piping is located and allows the installation of heads wherever they are needed. The waste pipes can be of lighter PVC piping
- no ventilation pipes. As the system is enclosed, there is no need to vent.

The disadvantage is that it provides another piece of machinery to maintain.

Piping

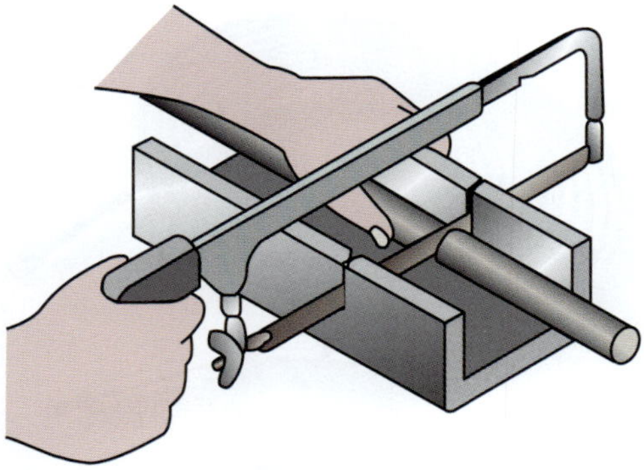

Figure 36.60 - Mitre box

PVC pipe is easy to install and requires little more than a hacksaw, mitre box and solvents to prepare and attach. Before joining, primer should be applied to the ends of the pipe and around the inside of the joining piece. This is to remove any debris and to ensure that the bonding is secure. After the adhesive is applied, the joining pipe should be given a slight twist.

Equipment used when fitting copper piping includes:

- Pipe cutter
- pipe bender
- sealing tape or paste
- plumber's pliers
- adjustable open-ended wrench
- basin wrench. The shape of this tool allows you to work under a basin in confined spaces
- reamer. This removes the residue debris in the pipe at the cut ends and ensures that the pipe end is perfectly shaped
- washers and threads in sizes appropriate for the plumbing fittings on board
- if welding is to be undertaken, flux, solder and a soldering iron will also be required.

Plumbing

Unblocking Drains

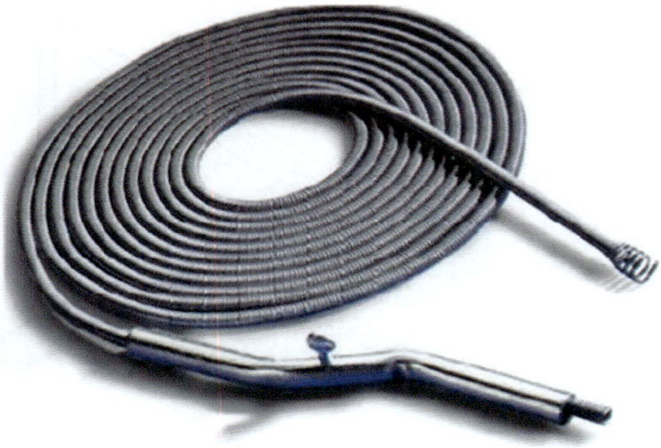

Figure 36.61 - Plumber's snake

Most blockages are caused by a combination of hair, soap and grease. For all metal pipes, the first thing to use is boiling water. Hot tap water will not be hot enough. If this fails to work, use a plunger after ducting over the overflow. If this fails, a plumber's snake, sometimes called a sani-snake, should be used. If the blockage is beyond the waste trap, take off the waste trap, remembering that it is full of water, and use the plumber's snake in the pipe exposed.

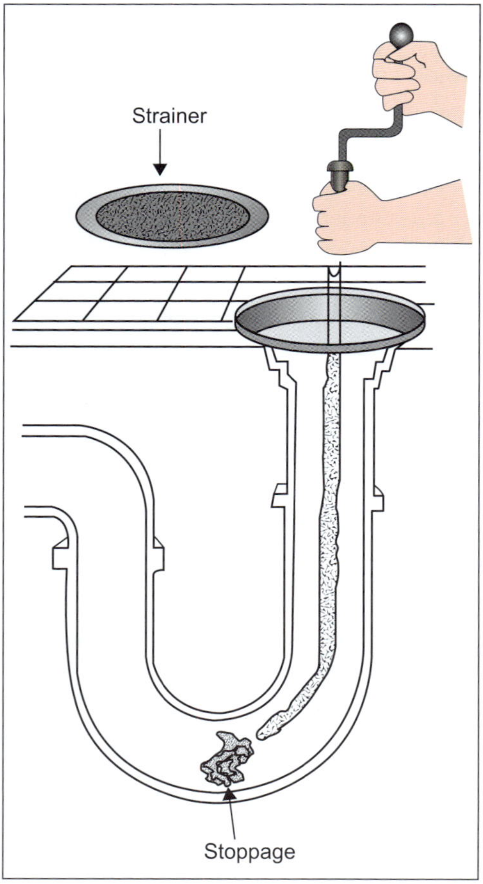

Figure 36.62 - Plumber's snake in use

Drain Cleaners

Chemical

Chemical drain cleaners should be used with caution as they can burn the skin and release irritant gases. Chemical removal methods rely upon the generation of heat and a reaction between the drain cleaner and the blockage material. Chemical cleaners should not be used until all mechanical methods have been tried.

Two main types of chemicals are used. Sulphuric acid immediately begins to dissolve any organic material that it comes into contact with. This means the acid effectively eats away at human waste and hair that may be in a sink, quickly unclogging the drain.

The second type is made of caustic sodium hypochloride (caustic soda). These drain cleaners are cheaper than acidic drain cleaners, but are not as effective. They are however safer as their action time is slower and the user has time to wash any affected area before the reaction occurs.

Biological

The most successful biological products are bacteria or enzyme-based.

Enzymatic drain cleaners utilise chemical reactions to 'metabolise' materials in the blockage. While they are safer to use and more environmentally friendly than chemical cleaners, they are slower in their action and not as effective in dissolving a blockage.

Unblocking Heads

Before using any mechanical tools, a bucket of hot water should be poured into the bowl from standing height. This will often clear a minor blockage.

Next to try is a lavatory plunger and, if this does not work, a plumber's snake. The U bend can be dismantled to deal with any blockage further down the system.

If these fail, a chemical or biological cleaner can be considered.

Leaking Taps

A leaking tap cannot be ignored as, over time, the water wastage will be considerable. In addition, the constant dripping, apart from being annoying, can discolour the coatings on basins. Once discoloured, they cannot be easily cleaned.

Most leaking taps are caused by a damaged washer, which is easy to replace. If there is no spare washer available, the existing washer could be turned over as a temporary measure.

If a tap carries on dripping after the washer has been replaced, the valve seating is probably eroded. This can be repaired using a special grinding tool or a washer and seating set.

Monobloc taps, which are controlled by levers, have ceramic discs. These are very hard wearing and seldom cause problems. If one should leak then a replacement cartridge will be required from the tap manufacturer.

Riding Squads

What is a Riding Squad?

Reproduced from 'Crude Oil Tanker Basics'

A riding squad is a team of workers who are well trained and well experienced in ship voyage repairs, coating protection, and tank and machinery space cleaning.

The riding squad provides specialist technical skills and knowledge not available on board and outside normal operational requirements. As vessels' crews have decreased, vessels have become larger and time in port has been minimised, the riding squad provides additional labour to facilitate workload peaks and repairs that, if time permitted, would be carried out in port or a shipyard. Other benefits of a riding squad include:

- Vessels are maintained to the highest standard
- there is a reduced risk of environmental incidents
- it provides for a safer and cleaner workplace
- it reduces drydocking costs

Riding Squads

- it reduces the length of time that vessels are out of service.

Areas of Work Undertaken by Riding Squads

- Hold cleaning and maintenance
- painting and routine deck maintenance
- repair and routine engine and electrical maintenance
- cargo handling and lashing
- security duties in port and in dangerous areas.

ITF Position on the Use of Riding Squads

The ITF perceives a threat to the employment of seafarers and:

- Condemns the practice of reducing the permanent crew on vessels by the extensive use of riding squads
- supports any amendments to ILO and IMO conventions that clearly define seafarers as any person employed or engaged in any capacity on board a ship
- works with the Classification Societies and others to eradicate the practice of carrying out illegal repairs, particularly where they may endanger the environment and the lives of ships' crew.

ITF Guidelines on Riding Squads

- A riding squad should only be used for one month out of any 12 month period
- persons engaged for security purposes should not undertake other seafaring duties
- Class Societies should be informed of any survey/structural work carried out (Ref: IACS UR Z13)
- riding squads must be covered by agreements giving comparable rates of pay to the crew and minimum conditions and protections as per ILO conventions
- the use of riding squads should not reduce or replace current crew.

CHAPTER 37

Lifeboat Release Mechanisms

Evaluation and Replacement

'Guidelines for Evaluation and Replacement of Lifeboat On-load Release Mechanisms' were adopted by the IMO's Maritime Safety Committee (MSC) in 2011.

The amendments related to the International Life-Saving Appliances (LSA) Code and 'Recommendation on Testing of LSA'.

The Guidelines are the result of work conducted by the IMO's Sub-Committee on Ship Design and Equipment (DE) and the MSC in response to the significant number of injuries and deaths that have occurred during drills and inspections with lifeboats fitted with on-load release gear.

The Requirement for On-Load Release Hooks

In March 1980, Norway's worst offshore accident occurred when the oil platform *'Alexander Kielland'* capsized in the North Sea's Ekofisk field, killing 123 of the 212 persons on board.

PA Images

PA Images

A number of deaths were attributed to the fact that the lifeboats had no means of release when their weight was on the hook and falls. On-load release systems were seen as a solution to this problem.

The 1986 Amendments to SOLAS

In 1986, the mandatory requirement to fit on-load release hooks for lifeboats and rescue boats entered into force under SOLAS in response to the *'Alexander Kielland'* disaster. However, since then an alarming number of deaths and serious injuries have occurred during lifeboat drills and inspections.

IN 2009, THE USE OF WIRE STROPS OR CHAINS AS FPDs WAS BANNED AS THEY DO NOT ABSORB SHOCK LOADS.

Ref: 2009 MSC.1327

MV *'Hoegh Duke'*

20th August 1992

Lifeboat hook slipped - 6 deaths, 6 hospitalised

During a routine lifeboat muster drill while alongside in the port of Surabaya, Indonesia, the starboard lifeboat with 12 persons on board was being lowered into the water when the aft hook released from the lifting ring. The lifeboat swung downwards pivoting about its forward hook, which also released, allowing the lifeboat to fall upside down a distance of 35 feet into the water.

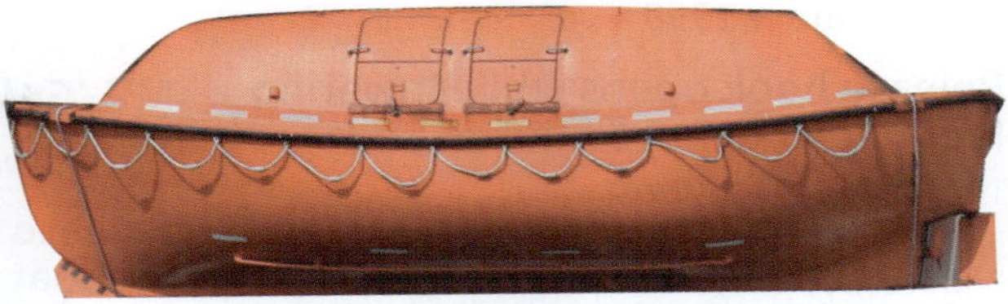

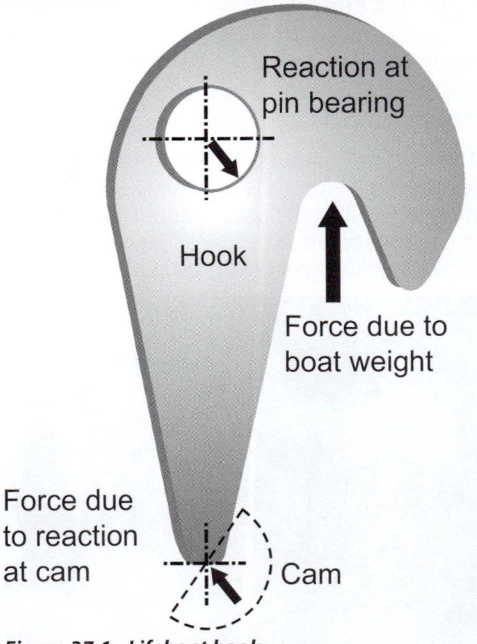

Figure 37.1 - Lifeboat hook

MV *'Kayax'*

9th August 1994

Lifeboat released from davits - 4 injured, 1 severely

The Panamanian-flagged bulk carrier *'Kayax'* was alongside loading in Portland, Victoria.

A surveyor from AMSA boarded the vessel to undertake a grain loading inspection and a Port State Control (PSC) inspection.

As part of the PSC inspection, the port lifeboat was lowered to the boat deck and then recovered to the stowed position. The surveyor asked to see the lifeboat engine operate. After some minutes, with the engine running but the shaft in neutral, the boat suddenly detached from the lifeboat falls and fell to the water, a distance of ~20 metres.

In the lifeboat were the Master, Second Mate and two crew. All four were admitted to hospital with significant injuries, the Second Mate suffering serious head and spinal injuries requiring prolonged hospital care and rehabilitation.

The incident investigation determined that the release mechanism for the lifeboat falls had been armed for instant/on-load release. It was considered likely that a crew member had used the lifeboat falls release lever, believing it to be the gear lever for ahead and astern movements of the engine.

Evaluation and Replacement

MV *'Iolcos Grace'*

9th November 1998

Release hook opens while lowering lifeboat - 1 dead, 5 injured

The bulk carrier *'Iolcos Grace'* was lowering a lifeboat as part of a drill when the forward hook released with the operating lever still in its stowed position. As the keel swung past the vertical, the aft hook also released. The boat fell approximately 7 metres into the water, resulting in five crew injured and one fatality.

MV *'European Highway'*

1st December 2000

4 crew injured as lifeboat falls from RoRo ferry

The *'European Highway'* was berthed in Zeebrugge. During a maintenance inspection, the port lifeboat had been swung out and lowered slightly, with three men on board. The weight of the lifeboat was being taken on 'hanging-off' pendants.

The operating lever of the suspension hook release mechanism was activated and the lifeboat fell into the water. Two crew were trapped underneath the lifeboat, with a third falling into the water alongside. The Second Officer was injured by the rapid rotation of the FRC davit's hand-winding lever.

It was found that the hanging-off pendants had been attached incorrectly.

MV *'Gulser Ana'*

17th October 2001

Release hook opens, suspending lifeboat and throwing crew into the water - 1 unconscious

The Turkish bulk carrier *'Gulser Ana'* underwent a PSC inspection by MCA surveyors on the 16th October 2001. There were 37 deficiencies found, which resulted in the vessel being detained.

On the morning of 17th October 2001, two crew were tasked with freeing up and greasing the releasing hooks on the starboard lifeboat, while it was in the water, as these had been found seized during the inspection the day before. Having freed and greased the forward hook, they then discovered that the aft hook operating rod had sheared. The crew used a lashing to secure the hook in the closed position to allow the lifeboat to be hoisted.

The Chief Engineer and the Chief Officer were called to inspect the operation of the hooks. The Bosun raised the lifeboat to the embarkation deck with two crew members on board. The Chief Officer joined the crew in the lifeboat to inspect the work, shortly after which the forward hook released without warning. The forward end of the boat dropped, leaving it suspended vertically from the aft fall.

The two crew members and the Chief Officer were thrown into the water. The two crew members pulled the unconscious Chief Officer to the surface and kept him afloat until they were all picked up by the pilot launch.

MV *'Galateia'*

26th January 2002

Lifeboat fell 19 metres - 3 crew injured, with 1 serious head injury

A Class surveyor had boarded *'Galateia'* to carry out an ISM safety audit. When the surveyor asked for a lifeboat drill to be conducted, the Master, accompanied by the Chief Officer and four crew, boarded the port lifeboat.

The lifeboat was lowered to the water and taken for a run to test the engine. It was then reconnected and raised to the embarkation deck. Two of the crew disembarked, leaving the others to stow the lifeboat in the davits.

Just as the Chief Officer moved the release gear operating handle into the stow position, both the hooks opened and the lifeboat fell 19 metres, striking the deck as it went. It landed in a partially capsized position with one of the entrance doors underwater. The Chief Officer and an AB suffered bruising, while the other AB had a serious head injury and was unconscious underwater for a time.

The cause of the accident was the crew's lack of knowledge of the lifeboat system, which resulted in failure to engage a locking pin.

MV *'Sea Urchin'*

22nd May 2006

Release hook opens during lifeboat recovery - 1 dead, 4 injured

While at anchor in the Bay of Sept-Îles, Quebec, the bulk carrier *'Sea Urchin'* carried out an abandon ship drill. During recovery of the starboard lifeboat, the aft hook release gear mechanism opened. The forward mechanism, unable to take the full load, also opened. The lifeboat then fell 11 metres, stern first, into the sea.

MV *'Lowlands Grace'*

7th October 2004

Lifeboat hooks released - 2 dead, 3 injured

The *'Lowlands Grace'* arrived at an anchorage off Port Hedland in Western Australia on 6th October 2004. At 15:00 LT on 7th October, the ship's crew mustered at the port lifeboat station for a lifeboat drill.

The port lifeboat was lowered to the boat deck and four of the crew were selected to act as the lifeboat crew under the command of the Third Mate.

After the crew had entered the lifeboat and were seated with their seat belts fastened, the Third Mate operated the remote descent cable from inside the lifeboat. When the boat had descended 2 to 3 metres, he released the cable, bringing the boat to a stop with a jerk. At this point, the crew on deck heard a bang and then saw the lifeboat's stern start to fall, now detached from its fall.

Evaluation and Replacement

The boat continued to swing forward and rotate around the forward hook until it had described an arc of 200 to 220°. The forward hook then released and the lifeboat fell upside down into the sea some 16 metres below.

MV *'Valparaiso Star'*

28th August 2007

Release hooks failed - 2 dead

The Bahamas-registered *'Valparaiso Star'* was docked at Setubal, Portugal where an abandon ship drill was ordered. It began at 07.45. By 08.15, five crew members were aboard the lifeboat.

The Coxswain started lowering from inside the lifeboat. Like many seafarers, he didn't entirely trust the system so he had a crew member on deck controlling the brake.

Two minutes later, the lifeboat davits reached the outboard rest position. There was a loud bang and the stern of the lifeboat dropped as its on-load release hook failed. The boat fell stern first towards the water, with the forward hook fixings being ripped away.

The 2001 MAIB Investigation into Accidents Involving Lifeboats and their Launching Systems

Since its establishment in 1989, the UK's Marine Accident Investigation Branch (MAIB) has received a large number of reports about seafarers being injured or killed in accidents involving lifeboats.

By 2001, MAIB inspectors had become increasingly concerned at the high number of accidents involving ships' lifeboat launching systems. This led them to conclude that there were some fundamental problems with these systems, as the reports suggested that anyone using a lifeboat, whether in a drill or actual abandonment, ran the risk of being injured or even killed.

The MAIB conducted a thorough review of lifeboat accidents to identify where the problems might lie. The MAIB's study set out to achieve five objectives:

- To draw the industry's attention to the number of accidents that had occurred since 1989
- to ensure that lessons are not forgotten
- to identify common factors leading to those accidents
- to review the risks associated with lifeboat launching systems by examining common problems encountered
- to make recommendations that would contribute to improving safety at sea.

The database that the MAIB had accumulated over the 10-year period since it was formed indicated that lifeboats and their launching systems had cost the lives of 12 seafarers, with a further 87 seafarers injured. The accidents all occurred during training exercises or testing, with experienced and qualified seafarers either performing or supervising the operations. They also found that those who use lifeboats are exposed to the greatest risk during embarkation and recovery.

The investigation found that:

- There were some fundamental weaknesses in lifeboat launch systems
- a root cause of many of the accidents was the overcomplicated design of the lifeboat launch system and its component parts

- training, repair and maintenance procedures fell short of what was necessary
- there were extensive problems with manufacture, construction, maintenance and operation of these systems.

To put these accidents in perspective, a search was also made by the MAIB into all other fatal accidents that did not involve lifeboats and their launching systems, over the same 10 year period. The results showed that the lives of 73 seafarers were lost from all accident types on board ship. This search also showed that the same number of lives were lost in accidents involving lifeboats as were lost in the two main causes of death to seafarers, ie entering confined spaces and falls overboard, which resulted in 12 deaths each in the same period.

The MAIB recommended that the IMO should undertake a study of the present value, need and desirability of lifeboats.

A 'Fall Preventer Device' (FPD) can be used to minimise the risk of injury or death by providing a secondary alternate load path in the event of failure of the on-load hook or its release mechanism or of accidental release of the on-load hook. However, FPDs should not be regarded as a substitute for a safe on-load release mechanism.

Evaluation and Replacement

Release Hooks not Meeting the Requirements:

The following are some examples of lifeboat release hooks that may not meet the relevant requirements if they fall out of tolerance due to wear:

Flat to Flat Cam Hooks

Overview

This is the simplest type of flat to flat cam hook where the cam has no offset or undercut. The force from the hook tail creates a turning moment on the cam that holds a tension on the release cable.

Danger

On such systems, the safety lock at the release handle and the strength and stiffness of the cable guiding tube are essential to avoid unintentional release. If there is any slack in the operating system or release cable, or if the guiding tube should fail, the hook opens.

Evaluation

This may easily be tested by dismantling or removing the release cable from the crank arm.

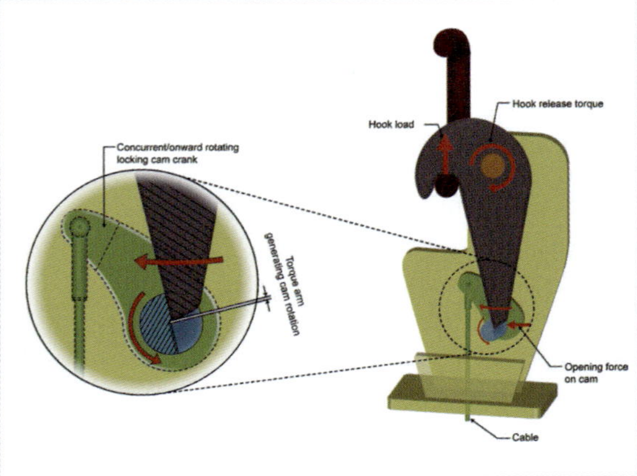

Figure 37.2 - A flat to flat cam hook without any self-locking feature

Forward Rotating Round Cam with a Self-Locking Capability

Overview

This is a concurrent/onward (forward) turning round cam, with a self-locking capability based on a hook segment tail end under the centre of the round forward turning cam.

Danger

As soon as the normal clearances in the hook segment and locking cam bearings are reduced, typically due to wear and tear or corrosion in the bearings, the self-locking arm functionality is lost and the system will open if the operating cable is broken/removed, is too flexible or has any slack.

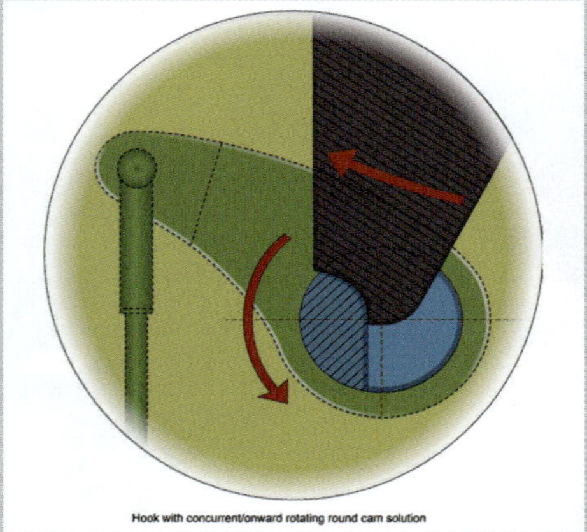

Figure 37.3 - A close-up of a round cam design with some self-locking capability

Flat to Flat Cam with Some Self-Locking Capability

Overview

Some flat to flat cam designs have been modified to give them a kind of self-locking capability. This is achieved through introduction of an undercut or offset in the flat surface of the locking cam surface, allowing the hook tail end to be 0.6 mm longer than the distance between the hook bearing and the locking cam bearing. When new, and under prototype testing, this small distance generates a self-locking factor because the hook tail end point of attack is under the centre of the locking cam centre.

Danger

As soon as the normal clearances in the hook segment and locking cam bearings are reduced below the offset distance (ie 6 mm) typically by wear and tear or corrosion, the self-locking arm disappears and the system opens if the operating cable is broken/removed or is too flexible/has slack.

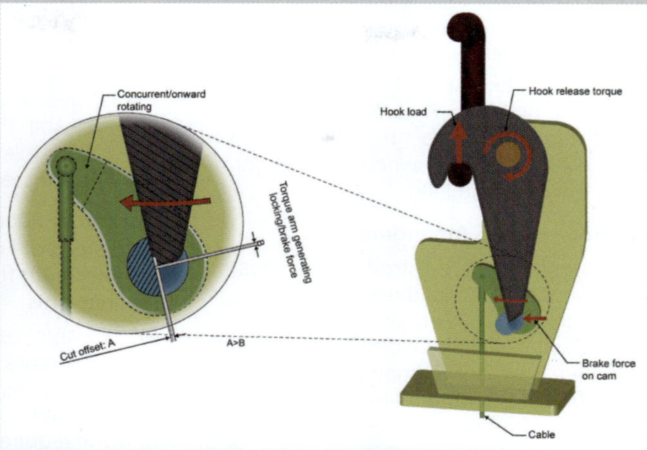

Figure 37.4 - A close-up of a concurrent/onward (forward) turning flat cam, with a self-locking feature based on a hook segment tail end under the centre of the round onwards turning cam

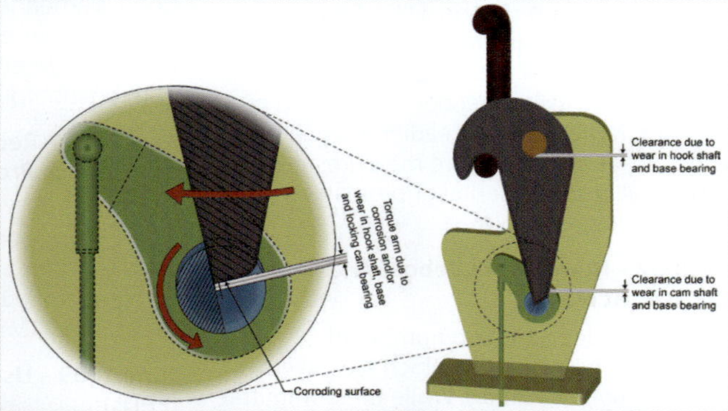

Figure 37.5 - The situation that may arise after use of the hook due to wear and tear

Lifeboat Hooks that Fail to Comply

If a release mechanism does not comply with paragraphs 4.4.7.6.3 to 4.4.7.6.5 of the LSA Code, as amended by the appropriate resolution at MSC.88, all installed release mechanisms of that type should be replaced at the earliest available opportunity, and no later than the next scheduled drydocking after the entry into force date.

Until the release mechanisms are replaced, additional safety measures, including use of fall prevention devices in accordance with MSC.1/Circ.1327, should be employed.

Note: As an alternative to replacement, the hooks may be modified to comply with the requirements of paragraphs 4.4.7.6.3 to 4.4.7.6.5 of the LSA Code, as amended by the appropriate resolution at MSC.88, provided that the modifications are approved by the Administration.

Evaluation and Replacement

Lifeboat Release Hooks at a Glance

March 1980 – Disaster Prompts Need for Release Hook

Norway's worst offshore accident occurs when the oil platform *'Alexander Kielland'* capsizes in the North Sea's Ekofisk field, killing 123 of the 212 persons on board. A number of deaths were attributed to the fact that the lifeboats had no means of release when their weight was on the hook and falls.

July 1986 – SOLAS Amendments

Amendments to SOLAS introduce a mandatory requirement to fit on-load release hooks for lifeboats and rescue boats as a solution to remedy the inability to release a lifeboat when there is weight on the hook and the lifeboat falls. This requirement brought about a situation where manufacturers developed a number of ingenious release mechanisms that resulted in many of the on-load and off-load release hooks becoming overcomplicated.

June 1996 – International LSA Code

Adoption of the International LSA Code by IMO Resolution MSC.48(66). This in turn amended Chapter III of SOLAS by requiring a 'special mechanical protection' to be fitted to new ships, rather than the earlier 'adequate protection', as a preventative measure against the possibility of accidental or premature release of lifeboat hooks.

May 2002 – Number of Lifeboat Accidents Discussed at MSC

MSC 75 considers the high number of accidents with lifeboats in which crew were injured, sometimes fatally. While the Committee considered the problem further, MSC/Circ.1049 was issued to draw the industry's attention to the matter.

May 2004 – Lifeboat Emergency Training

MSC 78 adopts amendments to SOLAS Chapter III Regulation 19 (Emergency training and drills) and Regulation 20 (Operational readiness, maintenance and inspections) concerning the conditions in which lifeboat emergency training and drills should be conducted. Changes to the operational tests to be conducted during weekly and monthly inspections were introduced so as not to require the assigned crew to be on board in all cases (the amendments entered into force on 1st July 2006).

May 2006 – Servicing and Maintenance of On-Load Release Gear

MSC 81 approves guidelines to implement the 2004 SOLAS amendments: Guidelines for periodic servicing and maintenance of lifeboats, launching appliances and on-load release gear and Guidelines on safety during abandon ship drills using lifeboats (MSC.1/Circ.1206; while MSC.1/Circ.1206/Rev.1, issued in 2009, updated the guidelines).

December 2006 – Changes for Launch Provisions of Free-Fall Lifeboats and Requirement for Safer On-Load Release Mechanisms

MSC 82 amends SOLAS Regulation III/19.3.3.4 concerning provisions for the launch of free-fall lifeboats during abandon ship drills, allowing the lifeboat to either be free-fall launched with only the required operating crew on board or lowered into the water using the secondary means of launching without the operating crew on board and then manoeuvred in the water by the operating crew. Also, the LSA Code is amended to require safer design of on-load release mechanisms (hooks) of lifeboats (the amendments to SOLAS and the LSA Code entered into force on 1st July 2008).

May 2008 – Requirements to be Authorised as a Service Provider of On-Load Release Gear

MSC 84 approves interim recommendation on conditions for authorisation of service providers for lifeboats, launching appliances and on-load release gear (MSC.1/Circ.1277).

June 2009 – Use of Fall Preventer Devices (FPDs)

The IMO's Maritime Safety Committee approves Guidelines for the fitting and use of fall preventer devices (FPDs) MSC.1/Circ.1327. It was emphasised that FPDs are only to be considered as an interim risk mitigation measure and are only to be used in connection with existing on-load release hooks, and that wires or chains should not be used as FPDs as they do not absorb shock loads.

February 2010 – Guidelines Agreed to Replace Unsafe Lifeboat Release Mechanisms

The IMO's Sub-Committee on Ship Design and Equipment (DE) agrees guidelines to replace unsafe lifeboat release mechanisms. These 'Guidelines for evaluation and replacement of lifeboat on-load release mechanisms' ensured

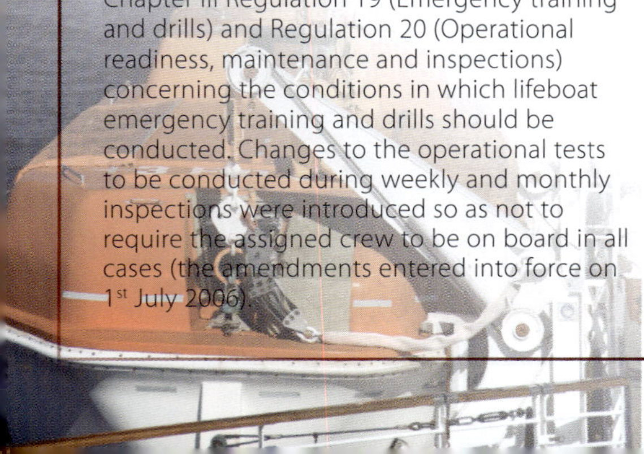

release mechanisms for lifeboats were replaced with those complying with new, stricter safety standards. This included a need for the hook and locking mechanism to remain fully closed under any operational conditions until it is intentionally opened by means of its operating mechanism.

May 2010 – Lifeboat Release Hooks - Adoption of Amendment Postponed to MSC 88

The Committee agreed to postpone (to MSC 88 in November-December 2010) the adoption of an amendment to SOLAS Regulation III/1 in conjunction with the approval of 'Guidelines for evaluation and replacement of lifeboat on-load release mechanisms' and adoption of the related amendments to the International Life-Saving Appliances (LSA) Code.

It was agreed that an intersessional Working Group on Lifeboat Release Hooks would meet in October 2010, to finalise the draft guidelines, review the proposed SOLAS amendment and report to MSC 88.

Fitting of 'Fall Preventer Devices' to Reduce the Danger of Accidental On-Load Hook Release

Design and Operation of FPDs

FPDs (Locking Pins)

The following points should be considered when utilising locking pins as FPDs:

- Existing on-load release hooks fitted to ships must not be modified by drilling to provide a locking pin insertion point as this may significantly reduce the strength of the hook. Any modifications must be agreed with the national Administration
- locking pins should have clear operational instructions located near the insertion point of the locking pin and be colour coded so that it is clear where the pins are to be inserted
- locking pins should be designed so that they cannot be inadvertently inserted in the wrong place
- a strict procedure for removal of the locking pin must be in place to prevent the locking pin being left in the hook before the boat is released in an on-load condition. If the hooks are operated in an on-load condition, with the pins still in, it will not be possible to release the boat until there is no weight on the falls so on-load release capability will be lost
- the removal of the pin should be achievable quickly and easily without posing any risk to the seafarer designated to carry out the task once the lifeboat has reached the water
- if the removal of the pins requires opening of the lifeboat hatch, it should be easily achievable by a person at each device from within the craft.

FPDs (Strops or Slings)

The following points should be considered when synthetic strops or slings are used as FPDs:

- Where FPDs are synthetic strops or slings and no modifications are required to the lifeboat, the on-load release hook or the launching equipment, a functional test should be carried out. The functional test should demonstrate that the equipment performs without interfering with the operation of the lifeboat or the launching equipment. Once the functional test has been conducted to verify that the system works and a snatch load has been applied to the strops, they should be replaced with new strops or slings. Strops or slings should be resilient fibre in construction. Wires or chains are unacceptable as they do not absorb shock loads
- the strops or slings should be issued with an appropriate certificate by a recognised testing establishment. The test certificate should document a SWL. The strops or slings should be inspected in accordance with the Merchant Shipping Lifting Operations and Lifting Equipment Regulations (LOLER Regulations) and replaced every five years. The material of the strop or sling must be rot-proof, corrosion-resistant, not unduly affected by seawater, oil or fungal attack and UV resistant
- it should be verified that any attachment point is sufficiently rated to withstand the dynamic shock that may be imparted during a premature or unintentional

release. The attachment point of the strop or sling to the on-load release hook and the davit falls block must be clearly marked and designed so that any connection device such as shackles cannot be connected to either the wrong part of the block or the wrong part of the on-load release hook

- the release of the strops or slings should be achievable quickly and easily without posing any risk to the seafarer designated to carry out the task once the lifeboat has reached the water. If the release of the strops or slings requires opening of the lifeboat hatch, it should be readily achievable by a person at each device from within the craft. Once detached, the strops or slings must not interfere with the operation of the on-load release gear or the propeller
- once the recovery stage of the operation is underway and the on-load release hooks are connected to the lifeboat, the strops or slings must be reattached to the lifeboat before the boat is hoisted clear of the water. The strops or slings must be designed so that they do not interfere with either the lifting or restowing of the lifeboat into the davits
- a strop or sling used as an FPD should be arranged to allow the transfer of load from the hook mechanism to the strop with minimal movement (drop) of the boat in the event of a release mechanism failure. Should a fall preventer strop or sling be subject to an unintentional dynamic shock loading, the strop or sling should be replaced and the associated attachment points inspected. In such cases, the MCA must be informed as soon as possible and the master should provide a full report of the circumstances of the incident
- fall preventer strops or slings must not be used for any other purpose and should be fitted to the lifeboat at all times or stowed so that they are readily accessible.

Lifeboat and Hook Design to Incorporate FPD

Lifeboat and release gear manufacturers and designers are encouraged to consider the design of both the lifeboat and hook so that FPDs can be released from inside the boat. The possibility of modifying existing boats and hooks so that FPDs can be released from within the boat should be considered. This is particularly relevant to FPDs fitted to oil, gas and chemical tankers. A pragmatic approach should be taken by all stakeholders to allow equipment to be upgraded so that FPDs can be fitted to existing equipment.

Drills, Testing, Inspections and Maintenance of Lifeboats and Launching Appliances

- The ship's master or the officer in charge of any lifeboat lowering or lifting operation should ensure that the lifeboat FPDs are fitted before commencing any drill, testing, inspection or maintenance where persons are in the lifeboat, unless the lifeboat has either an off-load hook system or has been approved to be used without an FPD
- the ship's crew must be fully trained in the operation of the FPD fitted to the lifeboat on their ship. The procedure to be followed should be contained in ISM documentation and the ship's training manual
- it should be taken into account that with certain types of ship such as oil, gas or chemical tankers it may not be possible to use an FPD in an abandon ship situation where the release mechanism of the device is not inside the lifeboat. Those conducting training drills and drafting ISM procedures must consider this. Where a different procedure is followed during routine drills compared with an abandon ship situation, this should be clearly described in the ISM documentation and the training manual
- SOLAS Chapter III Regulation 20.6.3 requires that, at sea, *"lifeboats, except free-fall lifeboats, on cargo ships shall be moved from their stowed position, without any persons on board, to the extent necessary to demonstrate satisfactory operation of the launching appliances, if weather and sea conditions allow"*
- the use of an FPD is currently not mandatory in SOLAS, but this document must be taken into account before a lifeboat is used for training, maintenance or servicing. Reference should also be made to SOLAS Chapter III Regulation 19 and MSC.1/Circ.1206 Annex 2
- if any on-load release hook is subject to a premature or unintentional release, the MCA must be informed as soon as possible and the master should provide a full report of the circumstances of the incident

- the following points should be considered when conducting drills, testing, inspections, or maintenance of lifeboats and launching appliances:
  - the officer in charge of the lowering operations should verify the correct fitting of the FPDs before the lifeboat is boarded and any davit harbour pins or gripes are removed. Where possible, the FPDs should be readily visible by the officer in charge, persons inside the lifeboat and the person at the winch controls
  - it is acceptable to allow lifeboats to be lowered or recovered without the operating crew inside, to reduce the risk of accidents during launching and recovery
  - before removing any securing devices, the on-load release systems should be inspected to ensure that the hooks are properly locked
  - there should be clear visual indication to the coxswain of the lifeboat that the FPD is fitted. This may be achieved by the use of placards at the coxswain's position and/or hook
  - to simulate emergency use, the FPD should be disconnected (strops or slings) or removed (pins) when the lifeboat is just touching the water but with weight still on the falls. The lifeboat should then be lowered until it is fully waterborne and the drill continued by activating the on-load release mechanism in the normal manner
  - on recovery, the lifeboat should be re-connected to the falls and the FPD reconnected. The lifeboat should then be lifted just clear of the water and the on-load release mechanism checked, paying particular attention to ensure that the interlock has reset and the hooks are properly locked. Once confirmed, recovery to the embarkation deck or stowage position can be continued. When the lifeboat is recovered, it should be stowed and checked that all is ready for emergency operation.

Hydrostatic Release Units (HRU) - Stowage and Float Free Arrangements for Inflatable Liferafts

Required Functionally

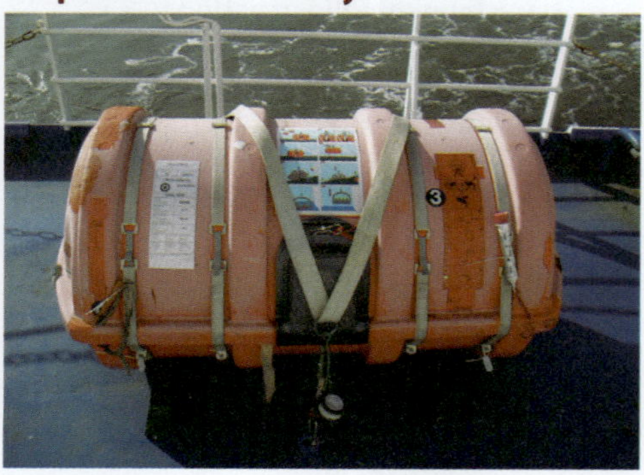

A liferaft is required to do two things:

1. Float free/automatically inflate if the ship sinks
   - This is achieved by fitting a Hydrostatic Release Unit (HRU) which automatically releases when the liferaft is submerged
   - the liferaft then starts to float to the surface because of its internal buoyancy, pulling out the painter which is now only connected by the weak link at the end of the painter to the vessel
   - when the painter is pulled all the way to the end, the gas cylinder is activated and the liferaft inflates
   - at this point, the buoyancy force of the inflated liferaft is sufficient to break the weak link and the liferaft will float to the surface, fully inflated and ready for boarding. For MED approved rafts, the weak link should break at a force of between 1.8 and 2.6 kN. Random pieces of small diameter line are not acceptable for use as weak links
   - some rafts have more than one line coming from the canister. In these cases, the manufacturer's literature must be consulted to establish which line is which. There may be separate firing lines, painter and multiple bowsing lines
2. Be manually released/thrown overboard
   - In a more controlled abandonment, the liferaft retaining strap must be capable of being released quickly and easily, eg by senhouse slip, and the liferaft is physically thrown over the side. The painter is then pulled to inflate the liferaft

Hydrostatic Release Units (HRU) - Stowage and Float Free Arrangements for Inflatable Liferafts

- this system relies critically on the painter being made fast to a strong point
- if the raft is only secured to the ship by the weak link and is thrown over the side, the dynamic shock of being thrown over may break the weak link, instead of pulling out the painter, and therefore the whole liferaft and painter may be lost.

The liferaft and the HRU must be fitted correctly, otherwise one or both of the above functions may not work.

Key Points on the Stowage of Liferafts and HRUs

Servicing

Reusable HRUs must be serviced annually to ensure they will work. Disposable types do not normally need servicing during the working life indicated by the manufacturer. The manufacturer's guidelines must be followed.

Readily Transferable

- **It is the Maritime and Coastguard Agency's view that side to side transfer must be accomplished in less than 5 minutes as follows:**
  - **liferafts of 6 to 15 persons capacity when carried by 2 persons**
  - **liferafts of more than 15 persons capacity when carried by 4 persons**
- **to avoid lifting liferafts over guard-rails or bulwarks, portable rails or hinged openings may be necessary. Suitable protection should be provided to prevent the possibility of persons falling over the side**
- **where doubt exists as to whether the stowage position of a SOLAS liferaft (which can weigh up to 185 kg) allows easy side to side transfer, a practical demonstration must be carried out at the first Safety Equipment Certification survey.**

Davit Launched Liferafts (DLRs)

DLRs must be:

- **At least 9 metres forward of the propeller, if physically possible**
- **at least 2 metres above the waterline at the embarkation position, in fully loaded condition, unfavourable 10° trim and 20° list**
- **capable of being prepared for embarkation and launching by 2 crew in less than 5 minutes per raft.**

Tensioning of HRUs

- **Practical experience has shown that overtensioning can lead to failure of the HRU to operate. Similar problems can occur when there is insufficient load on the HRU. Securing straps should be taut but not overtight.**

Key Points on Stowage of Liferafts and HRUs

Liferafts must:

- **Float free**
- **automatically inflate**
- **have launching instructions displayed**
- **be lit by emergency lighting at the stowage position and launch area**
- **have clear projections and belting when launched**
- **be secured through an approved and compatible HRU**
- **be approved for the stowage height**
- **have adequate length painters for the drop height.**

Do:

- **Consult manufacturer's instructions for HRU fittings**
- **stow clear of propellers and thrusters**
- **stow containers with drain holes at the bottom**
- **stow longitudinally in a horizontally fixed cradle**

- stow to give protection from weather, smoke, soot, oil, flooding and accidental damage
- distribute evenly port and starboard, separated longitudinally to provide redundancy in the event of collision, fire, etc
- carefully identify and remove transport lashings
- inspect frequently for damage to the container. If it is damaged, it should be checked by an approved service station
- ensure the liferaft can be manually released easily in an emergency by operating the senhouse slip or other release mechanism, and does not need tools or a knife.

Do not:

- Lash in cradles
- stow under overhanging decks or awnings
- allow contact with materials containing copper or copper compounds
- hose down
- use bottle screws instead of slips
- concentrate all life-saving appliances in one place.

Consider:

- Whether the liferaft will be able to float free and clear
- interference with other rafts or lifeboats
- effects in icing
- effects on ship's compass
- the ability to transfer liferafts to either side
- height above the waterline – the liferaft should be as near to the waterline as safe and practicable
- that the painter is many metres long and must be deployed to its full length before the liferaft will inflate. Ensure that the risk of the painter snagging on obstructions, which might prevent it from deploying fully, is minimised.

The Most Common Types of Hydrostatic Release Units

Hammar H20

Design

Hammar hydrostatic releases are the most common types used. They cut or release a retaining line/strap that secures the liferaft to its mount. After the retaining line releases, the liferaft floats free from its mount, while its painter line remains attached to the vessel by a weak link. As the vessel sinks, the painter line pays out about 100 feet and activates the raft's CO_2 inflation system. The buoyancy of the inflated liferaft breaks the weak link, allowing the raft to float to the surface.

Common Mistakes

- Attaching the painter line directly to the retaining line pelican hook
- attaching the weak link to the retaining line instead of the painter line
- tying the painter to the cradle without a weak link
- lashing the raft to the vessel and not replacing
- not servicing the hydrostatic release when required.

Improperly Installed Hammar Release

The image below provides an example of a bad installation (note how the painter line is improperly shackled to the retaining line). If this vessel sank, this liferaft would sink with it.

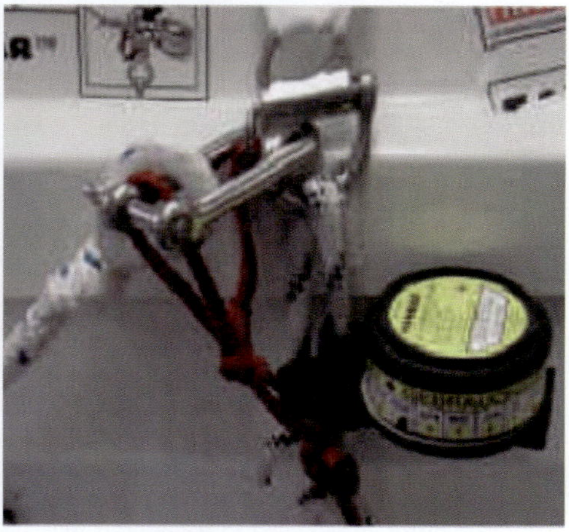

Hydrostatic Release Units (HRU) - Stowage and Float Free Arrangements for Inflatable Liferafts

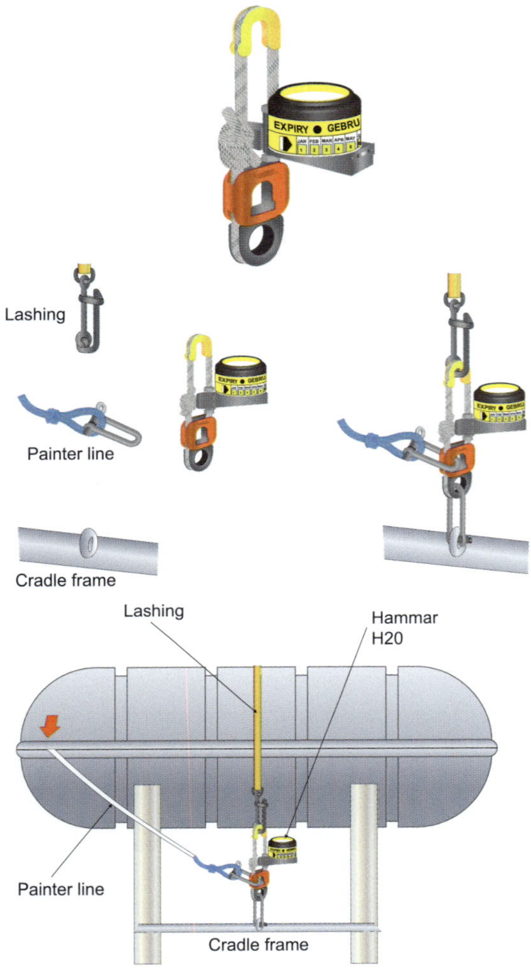

Non-SOLAS Hammar H20

There is a specific non-SOLAS Hammar H20 that is attached in the same way as the Hammar H20 but its body features are green instead of yellow and the lower thimble is green instead of black.

The Hammar H20 Small Rafts Green Top Model Hydrostatic Release Unit (HRU) with Special Weak Line™ has been designed for 4 Person to 12 Person Liferafts which are deemed outside regulations set by the International Convention for the Safety of Life at Sea (SOLAS).

Activated by water pressure, the H20 Small Rafts Green Top HRU will ensure that a liferaft floats free from a sinking vessel when its operation is triggered at a release depth of between approximately 1.4 and 4 metres.

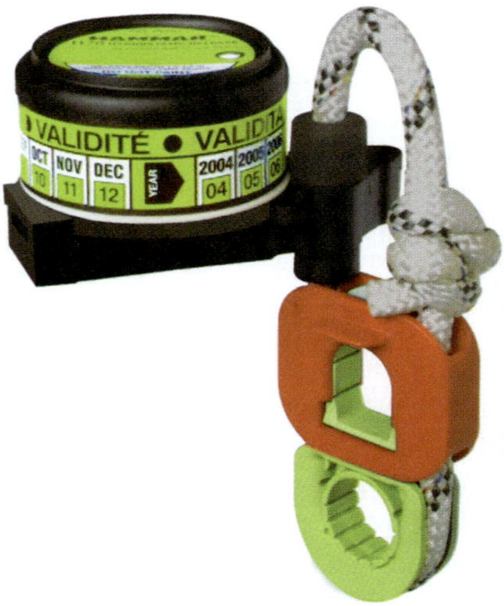

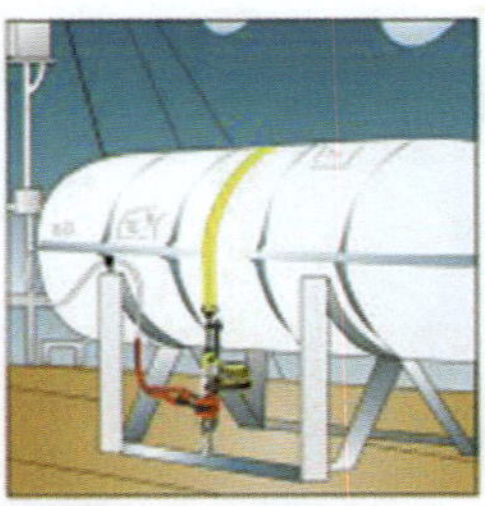

White Hammar H20 strong rope secured to deck or liferaft cradle and attached to liferaft lashing with a sliphook. Liferaft painter line shackled to the red weak link connector.

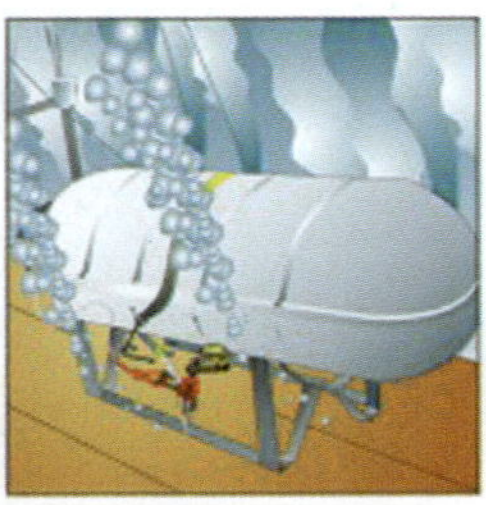

If the ship sinks, the water pressure, within 4 metres, will activate the sharp knife, which cuts the strong rope and the liferaft will float free.

As the ship sinks, the liferaft painter line will be stretched and the liferaft starts to inflate.

The red weak link breaks and survivors can board the inflated liferaft.

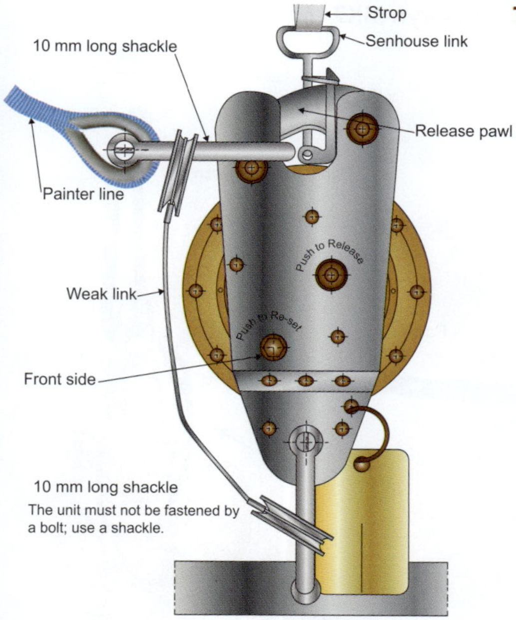

Thanner HRU DK- 2000/2004

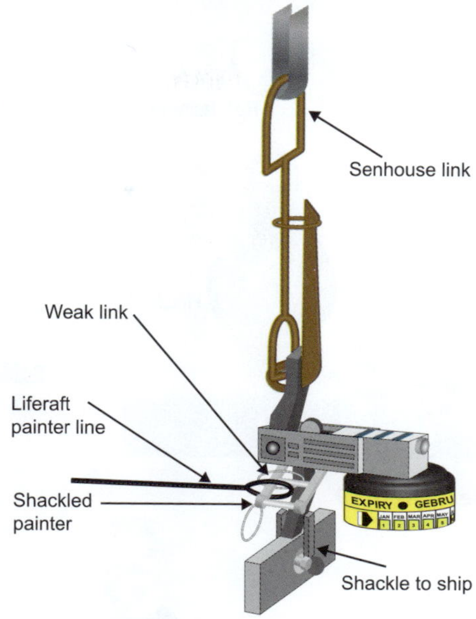

Thanner HRU DK- 84

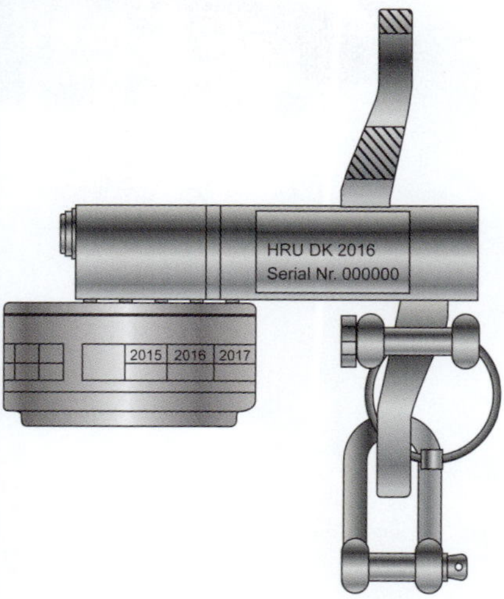

Salcom Servo-Release™ S-R Mk1

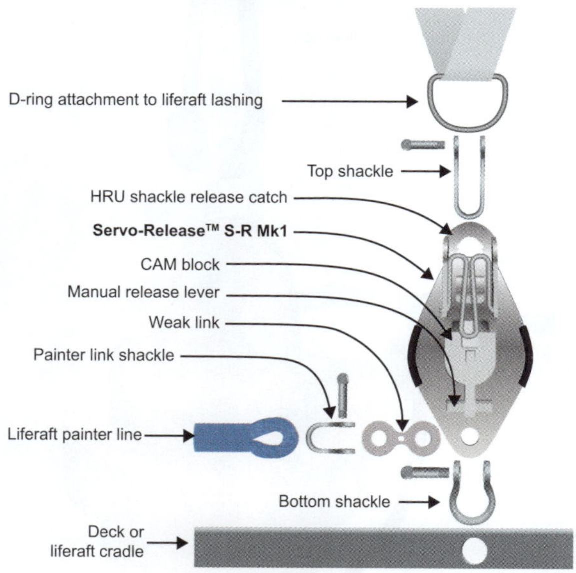

Hydrostatic Release Units (HRU) - Stowage and Float Free Arrangements for Inflatable Liferafts

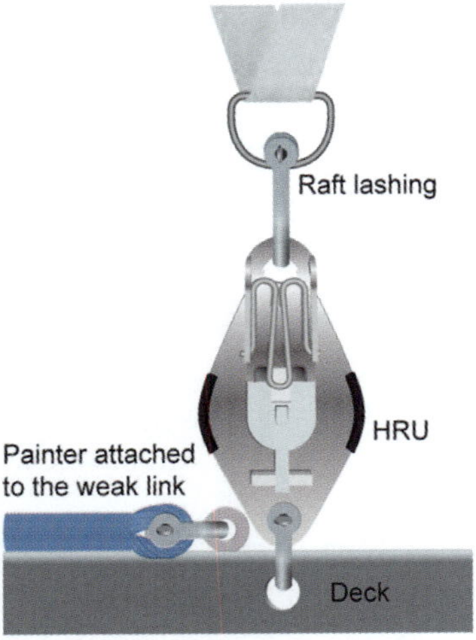

Berwyn MK7

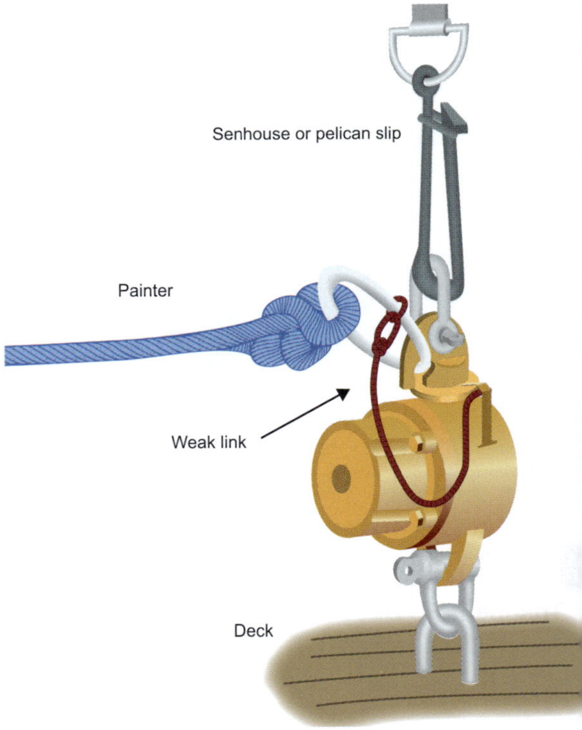

Berwyn MK9

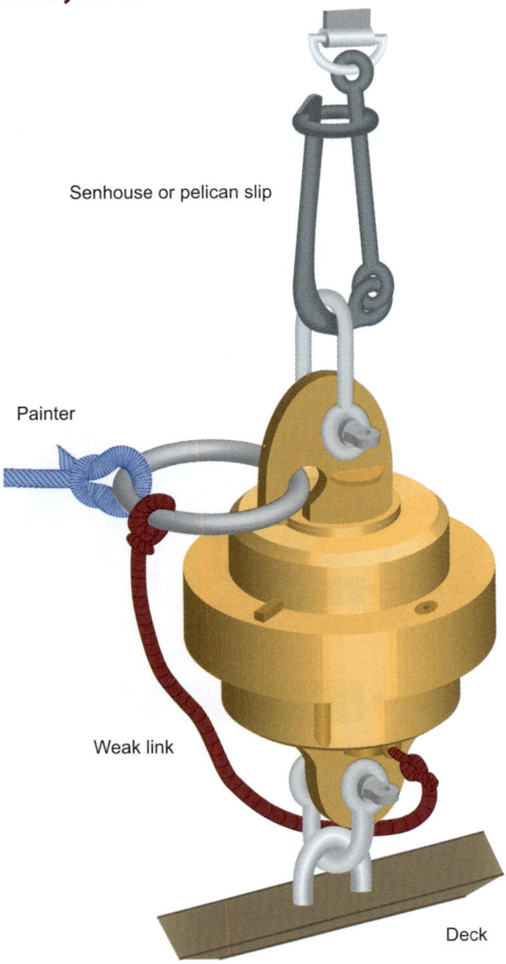

End to End Changing of Lifeboat Falls

The requirement for end to end changing of falls was made redundant with effect from 1st July 2008 by Resolution MSC.216(82) adopted at MSC 82.

The associated IMO resolutions include:

1. Resolution MSC.216(82) adopted at MSC 82: Amended SOLAS III Regulation 20 (by MSC 82)
2. MSC.1/Circ.1206 dated 26th May 2006 covering:
   a) Guidelines for periodic servicing and maintenance of lifeboats, launching appliances and on-load release gear
   b) specific procedures for maintenance and servicing.
3. Resolution MSC.216(82).

Outboard Motors

The Fuel System

Faults with an outboard motor's fuel system are typically ignition or compression related. If all cylinders are firing, it is likely that the problem is fuel related.

Fuel related problems include:

- A weak or faulty fuel pump
- low or no compression on the cylinder supplying a pulse to the fuel pump
- tank not venting
- an anti-syphon valve stuck on the tank
- loose fuel line connections.

Ignition Systems

Faults with ignition systems can be difficult to diagnose as they can present a wide range of symptoms. Outboard ignitions systems differ from the automotive type. Fault diagnosis should include:

- Ensuring that the timing is operating correctly and that there are no broken, damaged or bare wires
- checking that the electrics have not shorted out
- checking there are no rogue arcing sparks around the plug wires.

If the problem is with the ignition component, you will need an engineer/electrician to diagnose and deal with the problem.

Compression

If one or more cylinders are damaged because of incorrect timing settings, lean fuel condition, overheating or stuck rings from a build-up of carbon, the outboard will not work properly.

Outboard Motors

Cooling System

It only takes a few seconds at high RPM for an outboard to overheat and the powerhead to be damaged permanently.

The water pump impeller should be replaced regularly regardless of how many hours the motor has worked. An impeller will suffer from dry rot if not used, which is more likely to be the case than being worn out from overuse.

Common Problems

The following, while a comprehensive list, does not apply to all types of outboard motor:

	Problem	Possible Causes
1	**The engine fails to start**	1. Check level of fuel in tank. 2. Check air vent screw on tank open. 3. Check arrow on primer bulb to ensure fuel line is connected the right way. 4. Check fuel lines connected tightly and bulb primed. 5. Check engine is in neutral and throttle control in START position. 6. Inspect battery and connections (electric start). 7. Check emergency-stop (kill) lock plate connected correctly to switch. 8. Inspect fuel filters (fuel tank, external, internal) and clean if necessary. 9. Check internal fuel filter to ensure filter casing is tightly screwed. 10. Inspect spark plugs and clean if necessary. 11. Check fuel pump to ensure membrane is not torn out. 12. Check carburettor to ensure that draining screw is not opened. If engine starts but stops almost immediately: 1. Check choke has been pushed back in. 2. Checks 1 to 12 above. If engine starts but stops when gear is engaged: 1. Check propeller is not blocked. 2. Inspect spark plugs and clean if necessary. If engine still fails to start, seek mechanical advice.
2	**Manual starter rope pulls out, but pawls do not engage**	1. Friction spring bent or burred. 2. Excess grease on pawls or spring (too heavy a grease used?). 3. Pawls bent or burred.
3	**Starter rope does not return**	1. Recoil spring broken or binding (too heavy a grease used?). 2. Starter housing bent. 3. Loose or missing parts.
4	**Noisy/clattering manual starter**	1. Friction spring bent or burred. 2. Starter housing bent. 3. Excess grease on pawls or spring. 4. Dry starter spindle. 5. Just plumb worn out.
5	**Electric starter fails to operate**	1. Loose or corroded connections or ground. 2. Starting circuit safety switch open, or out of adjustment. 3. Improper capacity or weak battery or corroded battery terminals. 4. Faulty starter solenoid. 5. Moisture in electric starter motor. 6. Broken or worn brushes in starter motor. 7. Faulty fields. 8. Faulty armature. 9. Broken wire in harness or connector. 10. Faulty starter key, push button or safety switch. 11. Worn or frayed insulation.

6	**Electric starter does not engage but solenoid clicks**	1. Loose or corroded connections or ground. 2. Weak battery. 3. Faulty starter solenoid. 4. Broken wire in electric harness. 5. Loose or stripped post on starter motor. 6. Bendix shaft rusted or Bendix clutch broken.
7	**Hard to start or won't start**	1. Empty gas tank. 2. Gas tank air vent not open. 3. Fuel lines kinked or severely pinched. 4. Water or dirt in fuel system. 5. Clogged fuel filter or screens. 6. Motor not being choked to start. 7. Engine not primed -- pump primer system. 8. Carburettor adjustments too lean (not allowing enough fuel to start engine). 9. Timing and synchronising out of adjustment. 10. Manual choke linkage bent -- auto choke out of adjustment. 11. Spark plugs improperly gapped, dirty or broken. 12. Fuel tank primer inoperative (pressurised system). 13. Ignition points improperly gapped, burned or dirty or triggering (CD) system inoperative. 14. Loose or broken wire or frayed insulation in electrical system. 15. Reed valves not seating or stuck shut. 16. Weak coil or condenser. 17. Faulty gaskets. 18. Cracked distributor cap or rotor or shorted rotor. 19. Loose fuel connector. 20. Amplifier (CD) inoperative. 21. Poor engine or ignition ground. 22. Faulty ignition or safety switch. 23. Low cranking speed. 24. Low voltage to ignition, when cranking.
8	**Low speed miss or motor won't idle smoothly and slowly enough**	1. Improper fuel/oil mixture. 2. Timing and synchronising out of adjustment. 3. Carburettor idle adjustment (mixture lean or rich). 4. Ignition points improper (gap, worn or fouled) or triggering (CD) system inoperative. 5. Weak coil or condenser. 6. Loose or broken ignition wires. 7. Loose or worn magneto plate. 8. Spark plugs (improper gap, dirty, or incorrect plug). 9. Head gasket, reed plate gasket (blown or leaking). 10. Reed valve standing open or stuck shut. 11. Plugged crankcase bleeder, check valves, or lines. 12. Leaking crankcase halves. 13. Leaking crankcase seals (top or bottom). 14. Exhaust gases returning through intake manifold (cowling seals missing or damaged). 15. Poor distributor ground (look for a grounding wire or add one). 16. Cracked or shorted distributor cap or rotor. 17. Fuel pump diaphragm punctured (check spark plugs, usually one will be running very rich). 18. Accessory tachometer shorted or not compatible with ignition system. 19. Faulty ignition or safety switch.

Outboard Motors

9	**High speed miss or intermittent spark**	1. Spark plugs improperly gapped or dirty. 2. Loose, leaking or broken ignition wires. 3. Breaker points (improper gap or dirty or worn cam or cam follower) or triggering (CD) system faulty. 4. Weak coil or condenser. 5. Water in fuel. 6. Leaking head gasket or exhaust cover gasket. 7. Incorrect spark plug. 8. Engine improperly timed. 9. Carbon build-up or fouled combustion chambers. 10. Magneto, distributor or CD triggering system poorly grounded. 11. Distributor oiler wick bad. 12. Accessory tachometer shorted or not compatible with ignition system. 13. Faulty ignition or safety switch.
10	**Coughs, spits, slows**	1. Idle or high speed needles set too lean. 2. Carburettor not synchronised. 3. Leaking gaskets in induction system. 4. Obstructed fuel passages. 5. Float level set too low. 6. Improperly seated or broken reeds. 7. Fuel pump pressure line ruptured. 8. Fuel pump (punctured diaphragm), check valves stuck open or closed, fuel lines leak. 9. Poor fuel tank pressure (pressurised system). 10. Worn or leaking fuel connector.
11	**Vibrates excessively or runs rough and smokes**	1. Idle or high speed needles set too rich. 2. Too much oil mixed with gas. 3. Carburettor not synchronised with ignition properly. 4. Choke not opening properly. 5. Float level too high. 6. Air passage to carburettor obstructed. 7. Bleeder valves or passages plugged. 8. Transom bracket clamps loose on transom. 9. Prop out of balance. 10. Broken motor mount. 11. Exhaust gases getting inside motor cover. 12. Poor ignition. 13. Motor too low in water (excessive exhaust back-pressure).
12	**Runs well, idles well for a short period, then slows down and stops**	1. Weeds or other debris on lower unit or propeller. 2. Insufficient cooling water (especially probable with inline). 3. Carburettor, fuel pump filter or screens dirty. 4. Bleeder valves or passages plugged. 5. Lower unit binding (lack of lubrication or bent). 6. Gas tank air vent not open. 7. Not enough oil in gas. 8. Combustion chambers and spark plugs fouled, causing pre-ignition. 9. Spark plug heat range too high or too low. 10. Wrong propeller (pre-ignition). 11. Slow speed adjustment too rich or too lean.
13	**Won't start, kicks back, back fires into lower unit**	1. Spark plug wires reversed. 2. Flywheel key sheared. 3. Distributor belt timing off (magneto or battery ignition). 4. Timing and synchronising out of adjustment. 5. Reed valves not seating or broken. 6. Poor engine or distributor ground. 7. Extremely lean operation.

14	**No acceleration, low top RPM**	1. Improper carburettor adjustments. 2. Improper timing and synchronisation. 3. Spark plugs (improper gap or dirty). 4. Ignition points (improper gap or faulty).Or triggering (CD) system. 5. Faulty coil or condenser. 6. Loose, leaking or broken ignition wires. 7. Reed valves not properly seated or broken. 8. Blown head or exhaust cover gasket. 9. Weeds on lower unit or propeller. 10. Incorrect propeller. 11. Insufficient oil in gas. 12. Insufficient oil in lower unit. 13. Fuel restrictions. 14. Scored cylinder – stuck rings. 15. Marine growth, hooks, rockers or change in load of boat, or flooded bottom. 16. Sticky magneto plate or distributor. 17. Carbon build-up on piston head at deflector. 18. Marginal CD amplifier or pulse pack.
15	**No acceleration, idles well but when put to full power dies down**	1. High or low speed needle set too lean. 2. Dirt or packing behind needles and seats. 3. High speed nozzle obstructed. 4. Float level too low. 5. Choke partly closed. 6. Improper timing and synchronisation. 7. Fuel lines or passages obstructed. 8. Fuel filter obstructed. Fuel pump not supplying enough fuel. 9. Not enough oil in gas. 10. Breaker points improperly gapped or dirty. 11. Bent gearcase or exhaust tube. 12. Marginal CD amplifier or pulse pack. 13. Faulty spark plugs. 14. Incorrect propeller. 15. Roughness or damage on front of gearcase causing ventilation.
16	**Engine runs at high speed only by using hand primer**	1. Carburettor adjustments. 2. Dirt or packing behind needles and seat. 3. Fuel lines or passages obstructed. 4. Fuel line leaks. 5. Fuel pump not supplying enough fuel. 6. Float level too low. 7. Fuel filter obstructed. 8. Fuel tank or connector at fault.
17	**Loss of power under heavy load**	1. Wrong propeller. 2. Weeds or other debris on lower unit or propeller. 3. Breaker points improperly gapped or dirty. 4. Stator plate loose. 5. Ignition timing over advanced or late. 6. Faulty carburetion and/or faulty ignition. 7. Prop hub slips. 8. Scored cylinders or rings stuck. 9. Carbon build-up on piston head at deflector.
18	**Cranks over extremely easy on one or more cylinders**	1. Low compression. 2. Worn or broken rings. 3. Scored cylinder or pistons. 4. Blown head gasket. 5. Loose spark plugs. 6. Loose head bolts. 7. Crankcase halves improperly sealed. 8. Burned piston.

Outboard Motors

19	**Engine won't crank over**	1. Manual start lock improperly adjusted. 2. Pistons rusted to cylinder wall. 3. Lower unit gears prop shaft rusted or broken. 4. Broken connecting rod, crankshaft or driveshaft. 5. Coil heels binding on flywheel. 6. Engine improperly assembled. 7. Water in cylinders.
20	**Motor overheats**	1. Motor not deep enough in water. 2. Not enough oil in gas or improperly mixed. 3. Faulty thermostat. 4. Seals or gaskets (burned, cracked or broken). 5. Impeller key not in place or broken. 6. Plugged water inlet, outlet or cavity. 7. Obstruction in water passages. 8. Broken, pinched or leaking water lines. 9. Improper ignition timing. 10. Motor not assembled properly. 11. Shorted heat light wiring. 12. Faulty water pump impeller, plate, housing or seal.
21	**Motor stops suddenly, freezes up**	1. No oil in gas, or no gas. 2. Insufficient cooling water. 3. No lubricant in gearcase. 4. Rusted cylinder or crankshaft. 5. Bent or broken rod, crankshaft, driveshaft, prop shaft, stuck piston. 6. Faulty water pump or plugged water passages.
22	**Motor knocks excessively**	1. Too much or not enough oil in gas. 2. Worn or loose bearings, pistons, rods or wrist pins. 3. Over advanced ignition timing. 4. Carbon in combustion chambers and exhaust ports. 5. Manual starter not centred. 6. Flywheel nut loose. 7. Flywheel hitting coil heels. 8. Bent shift rod (vibrating against exhaust tube). 9. Loose assemblies, bolts or screws. 10. Broken teeth in gearcase.
23	**Generator or alternator will not charge**	1. Battery condition. 2. Connections loose or dirty. 3. Drive belt loose or broken. 4. Faulty regulator or cutout relay. 5. Field fuse or fusible wire in regulator blown. 6. Generator not polarised (DC generators). 7. Faulty generator or alternator. 8. Worn or sticking brushes and/or slip rings. 9. Faulty rectifier diodes (alternators). 10. Faulty ammeter. 11. CD voltage regulator faulty. 12. Rectifier not grounded. 13. CD safety circuit grounded. 14. Excessive electrical load on system.

24	**Low generator or alternator output and a low battery**	1. High resistance at battery terminals. 2. High resistance in charging circuit. 3. Faulty ammeter. 4. Low regulator setting. 5. Faulty rectifier diodes (alternators). 6. Faulty generator or alternator. 7. Excessive electrical load on system.
25	**Excessive battery charging**	1. Regulator set too high. 2. Regulator contacts stuck. 3. Regulator voltage winding open. 4. Regulator improperly grounded. 5. High resistance in field coil. 6. Regulator improperly mounted. 7. Insufficient battery size (unregulated systems). 8. No water in battery.
26	**Excessive fuel consumption**	1. Hole in fuel pump diaphragm. 2. Deteriorated carburettor gaskets. 3. Altered or incorrect fixed jets. 4. Jets improperly adjusted. 5. Carburettor casting porous. 6. Float level too high. 7. Loose distributor pulley. 8. Incorrect propeller (high rpm). 9. Boat bottom fouled. 10. Lower crankcase seal deteriorated.
27	**Shifter dog jumps**	1. Worn shifter dog or worn gear dogs. 2. Worn or bent linkage. 3. Remote control adjustment. 4. Gearcase loose or sprung. 5. Exhaust housing bent. 6. Linkage out of adjustment. 7. Rear case cover or carrier loose.
28	**Electric shift inoperative or slips**	1. Improper remote control installation. 2. Faulty coils. 3. Faulty springs. 4. Faulty clutch and gear. 5. Faulty bearings. 6. Wrong lubricant. 7. Loose or sprung gearcase. 8. Shorted wiring or poor connections.
29	**Undesirable steering**	1. Improperly set trim tab or corroded trim tab. 2. Improper trim angle setting. 3. Bent steering ram. 4. Internal corrosion in steering cable or support tube. 5. Worn helm gearing. 6. Excessive number of bends or too tight bends in steering cable. 7. Loose mounting at helm or cable output end. 8. Crushed or kinked cable. 9. Friction device at helm overtightened. 10. Leaks, dirt or low fluid level in hydraulic steerers. 11. Binding in swivel connections or motor swivel bracket. 12. Improper tension adjustment on dual cable systems.

Outboard Motors

30	**Engine vibrates**	1. Transom clamps loose. 2. Petroil ratio wrong. 3. Carb maladjusted - too rich. 4. Propeller fouled/broken. 5. Engines mount broken. 6. Ignition faulty. 7. Engine breathing exhaust fumes. 8. Fuel contaminated.
31	**Engine has been submerged**	If outboard motor mounts are not checked regularly, the engine can shake loose and fall overboard. The safety rope or chain should be short enough to prevent the engine going underwater. If these measures are not followed, you will have to deal with an outboard motor that has been fully submerged. Once an outboard has been immersed in sea water, it must be serviced immediately as electrical components and internal parts will begin to corrode. If the engine cannot be serviced immediately, it should be resubmerged in fresh water to prevent corrosion until it can be serviced.

Note: It is important to read the operating instructions as there will be information and advice on troubleshooting relating to the specific motor.

Outboard Motor Submerged in a Salt Water Fix

If the outboard is submerged in sea water, the following should be carried out to stop the motor from ceasing and rusting.

If there is any sand or dirt caught in the motor, it should be professionally serviced.

If the Outboard was Running when it was Submerged

1. Wash the motor completely with fresh water, ensuring that every screw hole, crevice and joint are cleaned.
2. Drain all the fuel, which should then be discarded and replaced with new clean fuel.
3. The spark plugs should be removed and either replaced or washed with clean water and left to dry for 12 to 24 hours before putting them back in the motor.
4. Hand crank the motor while holding it upside down or on its side to allow the water to drain from the motor. If it is difficult to crank, the motor should be serviced professionally.
5. Use alcohol to flush the crank case and cylinder to absorb the water.
6. All the parts that can be removed easily should be washed with warm soapy water, dried and then coated with oil.
7. Try starting the motor.
8. The motor should be run for at least 30 minutes under load to heat it up and to clean out any remaining water and particles.

If the Motor was not Running

1. The entire motor should be washed with fresh water.
2. Start the motor once it has been completely cleaned.
3. Run the motor for at least 30 minutes on load to dry the internal parts of the motor.

Remember

1. The power head must never be lower than the propeller; water can drain back into the crankcase and cylinder.
2. The battery should always be disconnected when the boat is being left for a long period. If there is a leak it may cause electrolytic corrosion or flatten the battery.
3. Oil should never be on the contact breaker points, as this will cause arcing and fouling, resulting in the motor running raggedly. The adjacent oil seals should be checked.
4. Always use the correct fuel/oil mix. An excessive amount of oil will cause the spark plugs to foul and the engine to run ragged or not start. Too little will cause engine wear.

5. The engine should never be run with a damaged propeller. An out of balance propeller will cause engine vibration and substantial wear to the shaft.
6. The highest numbered (hottest) spark plug should be used. Low numbered (cooler) plugs usually foul and affect the motor's operation.
7. The engine should never be run out of water as it will overheat and damage the water pump impeller, which requires water lubrication.
8. The battery should always be disconnected when the electric starter is being worked on. This will stop shocks and the risk of the motor starting accidentally.
9. Detergent-based oils or fuel additives should never be used as these will affect the engine's performance adversely and may invalidate the engine's warranty and guarantee.
10. The earth spark plug must always be disconnected when the manual starter is being worked on. This will stop shocks and the engine from accidentally starting.

Spares

1. Two spark plugs for each cylinder, cleaned and correctly gapped.
2. Can of petroil. The contents should be replaced from time to time.
3. Shear pins or a spare propeller if rubber bushed.
4. Propeller split pins or tab washers.
5. Spare starter cord.
6. Spanners, including special plug spanner.
7. Feeler gauges.
8. Non-linting rag.
9. Plug lead(s).
10. Magneto points.
11. Condenser.
12. Distributor rotor.
13. Distributor cap.
14. Coil.
15. Fuel pump servicing kit and filters.
16. Carb servicing kit including jets and gaskets.
17. Water pump impeller/key.
18. Touch-up paint.
19. De-wetting aerosol.
20. Grease.
21. Oil.
22. Handbook.

Outboard Motor Maintenance

The following checks should be carried out every 6 months or after 50 hours running:

1. Clean and re-gap the spark plugs. Burnt or worn out spark plugs should be replaced according to the manufacturer's instructions. New gaskets and torque plugs should be used where possible. Do not attach the plug leads until the engine is ready to be tested.
2. Tilt the engine slightly forward. Loosen the upper gearcase drain plug, but do not remove it completely. Carefully remove the lower gearcase drain plug and look for any water coming from the gearcase. If there is water or the lube is milky, water has got into the lube; this means that the seal must be repaired. If the lube is not milky, check for metal particles in a sample and also on the magnetic drain plug if there is one. There may be a powdery material on the magnet, but no chunks when this material is rubbed between your fingers. The upper plug should be removed, checking how much has drained out. Check the amount that is required in the manual. It should be remembered that the amount of lube that drains out will depend on how warm it is. If the unit appears to be alright, it should be drained and the gearcase should be flushed with fresh lube. It should be refilled to the correct level according to the manufacturer's instructions.
3. The propeller should be removed and checked that it is at the correct pitch, is not worn or chipped, and does not have badly bent blades. The rubber hub should also be checked for signs of excessive overheating. The forward and reverse thrust washers, the nut and its retainer should be inspected for wear. If there is excessive wear, it is an indication that the prop was loose during operation. Check shaft seal damage from mono-filament fishing line.

Outboard Motors

4. All grease fittings should be lubricated, using the lubricant recommended by the manufacturer. While greasing the motor mount and the swivel area, check the torque of the motor mount bolts.
5. All carburettor and magneto linkages should be lubricated.
6. Check the carburettor and ignition synchronisation following the manufacturer's specifications.
7. Remove and clean the fuel filter. Where possible, replace the fuel bowl element.
8. If necessary, adjust the tension on the magneto and/or drive belts.
9. Clean the battery terminals and coat with grease or another protective compound. Check the fluid level and specific gravity. The battery hold should be checked for signs of wear and corrosion.
10. Check the remote control box, cables and wiring harness for fastening security, wear or binding.
11. Check the condition and connection security of the steering controls. Mechanical steering should be lubricated with an anti-corrosion lubricant.
12. The plug leads should be connected and the engine started. The engine must never run out of water. Check the water pump and thermostat's operation.
13. Using the manufacturer's specifications, check the carburettor.
14. While the motor is running with the cowl removed, check for any signs of leaking fluids or smoke from inside the cowl area. Special attention should be paid to the area under the fly wheel and the power head base where end seal leaks can occur. There should be no leaks under the cowl.

Water Bag Load Testing

Water bags are employed to safely test and inspect lifting equipment. They are much easier to store and operate than solid weights.

Water bags are suitable for load testing:

- Cranes
- derricks
- davits
- winches
- lifeboats
- ramps and lifts.

The bags are easily packed and transported and can be carried into place and water pumped in.

The pumping process allows the total weight of water to be monitored to ensure a safe and replicable testing procedure. Once testing has been completed, the water is pumped out of the bags and they are air dried, either naturally or with an air fan.

It is important to make sure that the water bag system used is compatible with raw water or it could be a burden on the ship's supply of potable water.

It should also be fully compliant with testing regulations as required in SOLAS Chapter III – life-saving appliances and arrangements.

Water Bag Load Testing

Courtesy waterweights.com

Fast Rescue Craft (FRC)

After the *'Estonia'* accident, SOLAS was amended so that all RoRo passenger ferries should have a fast rescue craft deployed on board, as of 1st June 2000. This decision required at least one of the rescue boats on a RoRo passenger ship to be a fast rescue boat approved by the Administration of the flag State. The fast rescue craft must be able to launch and recover in severe weather, of at least force 6 with 3 metres high waves.

The *'Estonia'* was a RoRo ferry, operating in the Baltic, of 15,566 GT and 155 metres in length.

On 28th September 1994, as the ship was crossing the Baltic Sea, en route from Tallinn, Estonia, to Stockholm, she was struck by a large wave on the bow during heavy seas. The continued impact of large waves against the bow doors caused the visor to come away from the ship and the ramp to open. The ship took on a starboard list of 30 to 40° and a large amount of water flooded into the car deck. The ship then rolled to 90° and her four engines stopped working.

Due to the rapid development of the list and intake of water, many passengers could not reach the boat deck. The list also prevented the deployment of some of the liferafts. Of the 989 on board, only 138 survived.

Fast Rescue Craft (FRC)

SOLAS requires that:

- *At least two crews of each fast rescue boat shall be trained and drilled regularly having regard to section A-VI/2, table A-VI/2-2 "Specification of the minimum standard of competence in fast rescue boats" of the Seafarers Training, Certification and Watchkeeping (STCW) Code and the recommendations adopted by the IMO by Resolution A.771 (18), as amended. The training and drills shall include all aspects of rescue, handling, manoeuvring, operating these craft in various conditions, and righting them after capsize.*
- *In the case where the arrangement or size of an existing ro-ro passenger ship is such as to prevent the installation of the fast rescue boat required by paragraph 3.1, the fast rescue boat may be installed in place of an existing lifeboat which is accepted as a rescue boat or boat for use in an emergency, provided that all of the following conditions are met:*
    1. *the fast rescue boat installed is served by a launching appliance complying with the provisions of paragraph.3.2;*
    2. *the capacity of the survival craft lost by the above substitution is compensated by the installation of liferafts capable of carrying at least an equal number of persons served by the lifeboat replaced; and*
    3. *such liferafts are served by the existing launching appliances or marine evacuation systems.*

General Requirements for Fast Rescue Craft in Res. A.656(16) Guidelines for Fast Rescue Craft

1. *Fast rescue boats may be either of rigid, inflated or rigid/inflated construction and should:*
    1. *be of a length adequate for their intended use;*
    2. *be capable of carrying at least five seated persons and a person lying down.*
2. *Fast rescue boats which are a combination of rigid and inflated construction should comply with the appropriate requirements of these guidelines to the satisfaction of the Administration.*
3. *A fast rescue boat should be self-righting or capable of being readily righted by its crew.*
4. *Unless the fast rescue boat has adequate sheer, it should be provided with a bow cover extending for not less than 15% of its length, and be self-bailing or capable of being rapidly cleared of water.*
5. *Fast rescue boats should be capable of manoeuvring, for at least 4 hours, at a speed of at least 20 knots in calm water with a suitably qualified crew of at least 3 persons and at least 8 knots with a full complement of persons and equipment.*

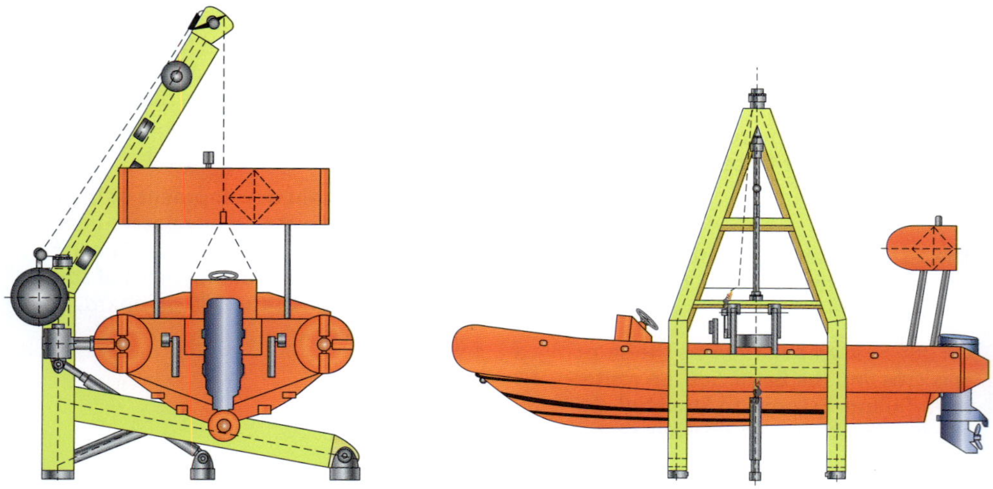

Figure 37.6 - Fast rescue craft and launching appliance

6. *Fast rescue boats should have sufficient mobility and manoeuvrability in a seaway to enable persons to be retrieved from the water, marshal liferafts and tow the largest liferaft carried on the ship when loaded with its full complement of persons and equipment or its equivalent at a speed of at least 2 knots.*
7. *A fast rescue boat should be fitted with an inboard engine or engines or an outboard motor or motors commensurate with its speed, size and displacement. It should be steered by a wheel which is remote from the rudder, water jet or jets and outboard motor or motors and an approved form of emergency steering should be fitted. Notwithstanding the requirements of SOLAS regulation 111/41.6.1, petrol driven outboard motors with approved fuel systems may be fitted in fast rescue boats, but special precautions should be taken to protect the fuel tanks from the effects of an explosion.*
8. *Each engine or motor in a fast rescue boat should stop automatically or be stopped by the helmsman's emergency release switch should the boat capsize. When the boat has righted, each engine or motor should be capable of being restarted, provided the helmsman's emergency release, if fitted, has been reset.*
9. *The fuel and lubricating oil systems should be so designed as to prevent the loss of more than 250 ml of fuel or lubricating oil from the propulsion system should the boat capsize.*
10. *Arrangements for towing should be permanently fitted in fast rescue boats and should be sufficiently strong to marshal or tow life rafts, as required by 6 above.*
11. *Fast rescue boats should be fitted with weathertight stowage for small items of equipment.*
12. *If the fast rescue boat is stowed on a ship, a disengaging gear complying with the requirements of SOLAS regulation 111/41.7.6 or its equivalent should be fitted.*

Fast rescue boat equipment:

- Buoyant oars or paddles attached to the boat
- buoyant bailer
- efficient compass that is luminous or illuminated
- sea anchor with hawser minimum ≥10 m long
- painter attached to release device and placed at the front of the rescue boat
- buoyant line ≥50 m long, strong enough to tow a liferaft
- waterproof electric torch for Morse signalling plus spare batteries and bulb in waterproof container
- whistle or equivalent for sound signal
- first aid kit in waterproof, resealable case
- two buoyant rescue quoits with ≥30 m of buoyant line
- a search light
- radar transponder or efficient radar reflector
- thermal protective aids complying with SOLAS III/34
- boat hook
- bucket
- knife or hatchet
- buoyant knife
- two sponges
- efficient, manually-operated bellows or pump
- repair kit for punctures.

Launching and Releasing FRC

A fast rescue boat should be equipped with an easily operated fixed single-point suspension arrangement or equivalent. Hooks and fastening devices for lowering and hoisting fast rescue boats should be designed to have a safety factor of 6 on the ultimate strength in relation to the loads occurring in a fully loaded condition.

It is important that FRC are stored and maintained correctly. Their usual position on the side of the ship or at the stern means they are subject to the corrosive sea environment. Monitoring this exposure and making sure that the boat and launch equipment remains

Fast Rescue Craft (FRC)

in good working order is vital to ensure the reliability of safety equipment in an emergency.

The crew of the FRC is most at risk during hook-on and release. To improve the safety of the crew and the effectiveness of the release and hook-on procedure, it should be ensured that:

- The FRC provides a stable platform when it is alongside the mother ship during the launch and recovery procedures. This means that the impacts alongside the ship are minimised and the jerking pull on the painter is reduced
- the crew can locate themselves securely in the boat during the launch and recovery procedures
- the release and hook-on procedures are simple, quick and effective and can be operated preferably one-handed so that the crew member has one hand to hold on with
- the painter connection and release systems are simple, quick and effective and can be operated preferably one-handed
- the connection can be made and released without the crew having their hands close to the connection point
- release should only be possible once the hoist wire is slack.

Opinions about training in the use of FRC are mixed. The key to safe and successful training and subsequent use is planning and communication. It is vital that the crew is briefed and prepared before undertaking training exercises.

Further Information

Video | Correct way to launch FRC:
http://tinyurl.com/cmq8p4m

Video | Incorrect way to launch:
http://tinyurl.com/cpzcft8

Video | Correct recovery:
http://tinyurl.com/bqhwsbq

Release

On-Load Release Hooks

On-load release hooks allow the hoist to be disconnected when it is under load and are a requirement for SOLAS approved lifeboats and rescue boats. The demand for this type of release stems from the possibility of a boat being launched without a painter being used, causing the boat to end up being towed by the host ship if it were not possible to disconnect the hoist wire when it was still under load. A safety lock is provided to reduce the chance of inadvertent release. This type of hook requires the hoist wire to be connected manually for lifting. On-load release hooks are fitted with an interlock design that prevents release before the lifeboat enters the water. SOLAS requires that this mechanism can be overridden.

No Load Release Hooks

This type of hook will only release once the load has been taken off the hoist wire and the safety catch has been set for release. Release can often be achieved by remote control via a cable to a lever at the helm of the FRC. To make the connection using this type of hook, the hoist wire ring needs to be inserted manually. The hook is mounted in the boat with a ring on the hoist wire.

Conventional Snap Hook

This is the traditional way to make the connection between the FRC and the hoist. The hook is a standard hook with a spring-loaded clip to close and secure the hook opening once the connection has been made. This makes connecting a relatively straightforward operation, but disconnecting means first opening the tongue before the hook can be slipped. Designs vary but disconnection can usually be effected from outside the hook, enabling the hands to be kept partly away from the connection interface. This type of hook is attached to the hoist wire and may connect with either a fixed ring on the boat or a loose ring attached to flexible slings.

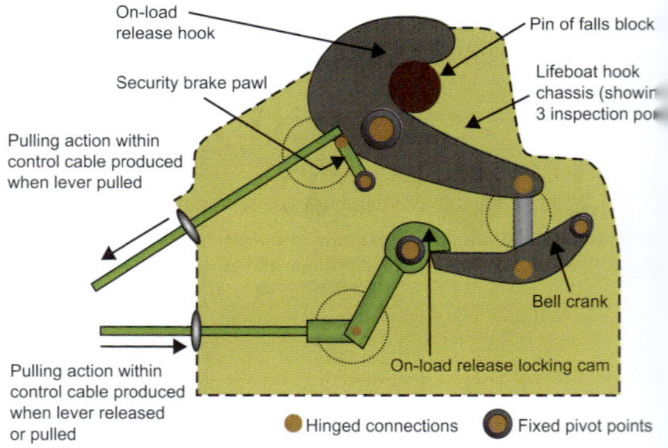

Figure 37.7 - On-load release mechanism

Davits

An FRC can be stored and launched from a range of davits. The most common types are G-type, L-shape pivoting and horizontal slewing. The ship's crane can also be employed for launching and recovering an FRC. However, during lowering and manoeuvring, the FRC can be subject to both rotation and the pendulum effect on the end of the crane hoist. Otherwise, the use of the ship's crane would operate in the same manner as launching from a davit.

Lifeboat Hulls

The marine environment is harsh on deck fixtures and fittings. UV, temperature and sea water/moisture exposure pose a threat, over time, to the integrity of the lifeboat hull finish and structure.

Lifeboat hulls are made from fibreglass, which is a composite of layers of plastic or polymer resins reinforced with fibre cloth. The greater the number of layers, the harder and stronger the structure. The smooth, shiny surface of a fibreglass boat is gained by the application of a gel coat on top of the fibreglass, based on epoxy or unsaturated polyester resin. The gel coat forms a water-resistant barrier between the fibreglass and the external environment. Fibreglass does not corrode but still requires protection.

The ship's crew should note any areas of damage to the gel coat layer during weekly and monthly inspections. Gel coat is relatively simple to repair, requiring some sanding and refilling, usually with an epoxy compound. Repairing minor fractures or damage in the gel coat will help ensure that the fibreglass below will remain sound.

Common areas to check for damage to the gel coat and fibreglass finish are around points of contact. If the lifeboat sits in a frame or similar arrangement when held by the davit, these areas are likely to suffer from abrasion and wear during safety drills, as a result of launching and recovery.

Blisters can form as a result of this water ingress. They can be remedied by draining, sanding the affected area, painting, filling with epoxy and then a final coat of paint. The manufacturer's guidelines and instructions should be consulted before any such repair work is undertaken, or should be delayed until in port for the work to be carried out by or under the supervision of someone accredited by the manufacturer.

It is important to note any areas of discoloration when inspecting lifeboats on the ship and to ensure they are inspected more closely during annual inspection.

IMO requirements for maintenance, under MSC.1/Circ.1206, call for annual and five year inspection and maintenance to be conducted by the lifeboat manufacturer. Any irregularities in the fibreglass structure of the lifeboat hull recorded by the crew during weekly and monthly inspections can be more thoroughly examined during the inspection carried out by the manufacturer. Any remedies or repairs needed to the fibreglass can then be fully completed by the manufacturer.

IMO requirements for the maintenance of lifeboats:

> SOLAS Chapter III – Life-Saving Appliances and Arrangements
>
> Regulation 20 – Operational readiness, maintenance and inspection.

Lifeboat Hulls

Weekly Inspection

The following tests and inspections should be carried out weekly and a report of the inspection entered in the logbook:

1. All survival craft, rescue boats and launching appliances shall be visually inspected to ensure that they are ready for use. The inspection shall include, but is not limited to, the condition of hooks, their attachment to the lifeboat and the on-load release gear being properly and completely reset.
2. All engines in lifeboats and rescue boats shall be run for a total period of not less than 3 minutes, provided the ambient temperature is above the minimum temperature required for starting and running the engine. During this period of time, it should be demonstrated that the gearbox and gearbox train are engaging satisfactorily. If the special characteristics of an outboard motor fitted to a rescue boat would not allow it to be run other than with its propeller submerged for a period of 3 minutes, a suitable water supply may be provided.
3. Lifeboats, except free-fall lifeboats, on cargo ships shall be moved from their stowed position, without any persons on board, to the extent necessary to demonstrate satisfactory operation of launching appliances, if weather and sea conditions so allow.
4. The general emergency alarm shall be tested.

Monthly Inspections

All lifeboats, except free-fall lifeboats, shall be turned out from their stowed position, without any persons on board, if weather and sea conditions so allow.

Inspection of the life-saving appliances, including lifeboat equipment, shall be carried out monthly using the checklist required by Regulation 36.1.

The following items should be examined and checked for satisfactory condition:

- **Lifeboat structure including fixed and loose equipment**
- **engine and propulsion system**
- **sprinkler system, where fitted**
- **air supply system, where fitted**
- **manoeuvring system**
- **power supply system**
- **bailing system.**

Courtesy of Bianchi & Cecchi Service Inc, www.bcserviceinc.com

Servicing Life-Saving Appliances

MSC/Circ.955
The servicing intervals of inflatable liferafts, inflatable lifejackets, marine evacuation systems, inflated rescue boats, hydrostatic release units and satellite EPIRBs required by SOLAS regulations III/20.8, III/20.9 and IV/15.9, respectively, shall not exceed 12 months, which may be extended to 17 months where in any case this is impracticable in exceptional circumstances. In the meantime, according to regulations I/8 and I/9 of the 1988 SOLAS Protocol, the said appliances shall be subjected to an annual or a periodical survey within 3 months before or after each anniversary of the Cargo Ship Safety Equipment Certificate and of the Cargo Ship Safety Radio Certificate, respectively, or the Cargo Ship Safety Certificate, ie maximum 18 months interval.

Most LSA items will require that the annual maintenance is carried out by personnel appointed or approved by the manufacturer.

MSC.1/Circ.1206 Annex 1 paragraph 12
All other inspections, services and repair, other than weekly or monthly, should be conducted by the manufacturer's representative or other person appropriately trained and certified for the work to be done in accordance with MSC.1/Circ.1277.

SOLAS III/20.11.2.2
Lifeboats, rescue boats and free-fall lifeboats are subject to a thorough examination and operational test during the annual surveys by properly trained personnel familiar with the system.

MSC.1/Circ.1977
Terms of validity of certificates

Upon completion of training and competency assessment, a certificate should be issued defining the level of qualification and the scope of the certification. The expiry date should be clearly written on the certificate and should be within three years of issuance of the certificate.

SOLAS Regulation III/20.11
Launching Appliances and On-Load Release Gear

This requires periodic servicing of launching appliances and on-load release gear for LSA on all cargo ships and passenger ships within the safety equipment survey range dates.

Launching appliances for survival craft and rescue boats are required to be examined and tested, by competent persons, annually within the safety equipment survey range dates. The same requirements apply for on-load release gear.

Launching and on-load release gear for LSA on all cargo ships and passenger ships are required to be overhauled and tested every five years. Testing shall be conducted in the presence of a surveyor.

SOLAS III/20.8 and 20.9
Inflatable Liferafts, Lifejackets, Marine Evacuation Systems and Hydrostatic Release Units

These items must be:

- Serviced at intervals not exceeding 12 months, though the Administration may extend this period to 17 months
- serviced at an approved station which is competent to service them, maintains proper servicing facilities and uses only properly trained personnel.

CHAPTER 38

Fire-fighting

Fire Prevention

Fire Prevention

The Fire-Fighting Objectives stated in SOLAS are to:

- *Prevent the occurrence of fire and explosion*
- *reduce the risk to life caused by fire*
- *reduce the risk of damage caused by fire to the ship, its cargo and the environment*
- *contain, control and suppress fire and explosion in the compartment of origin*
- *provide adequate and readily accessible means of escape for passengers and crew.*

The systems and equipment specified in the regulations are the minimum that must be provided and many operators and ships are equipped to a far higher standard.

Fires on ships are quite common but because most fires are small and are put out immediately on discovery they are often unreported. For this reason, a certain complacency can exist about the likelihood of fire on board. If this complacency is allowed to continue, it affects the onboard training and alertness to the possibility of fire occurring.

Ship crews are not trained firefighters. They receive formal basic training in fire-fighting during their initial training and, as they progress their careers, further training for advancement. However, this training is variable, still basic and often many years out of date.

The purpose of fighting a fire on a ship is to save life. Fire-fighting to save the ship from damage or loss, or for environmental concerns, must only be undertaken if those engaged in it are not placed in danger. However, in some situations, saving the ship is necessary to save the lives of those on board.

Fire Type

There are four main classes of fire, categorised according to the kind of material that is burning. For the first three classes of fire, there are two sets of colour-coded icons in common use. Some fires fall into more than one class, eg a fire that involves both burning paper and kitchen grease would be a class AB fire.

Class A

Class A fires are those fuelled by materials that, when they burn, leave a residue in the form of ash, such as paper, wood, cloth, rubber and certain plastics.

Class B

Class B fires involve flammable liquids and gases, such as gasoline, paint thinner, kitchen grease, propane and acetylene.

Class C

Class C fires involve energised electrical wiring or equipment (eg motors, computers and panel boxes). If the electricity to the equipment is cut, a class C fire becomes one of the other three types of fire.

Class D

Class D fires involve exotic metals, such as magnesium, sodium and titanium, and certain organometallic compounds, such as alkyllithium and Grignard reagents.

Fire Risk Assessment

A fire risk assessment should be regularly carried out on the ship, particularly when there has been a change of senior officers or a large number of personnel. The assessment should identify and categorise all possible dangers and risks in all areas of the ship.

Where a risk of fire can be identified, that risk must be eliminated or reduced. This can be achieved by removing the possible source of fire and/or the provision of additional fire prevention, detection and fire-fighting equipment to that area.

A specific fire plan for the risk area can be prepared. This plan should include:

- Monitoring
- access
- availability of equipment
- knowledge of and training on any specialised equipment that might be needed
- the alarm system that should be provided
- any dangers to crew in identified risk areas. This should include their ability to escape from these places.

Onboard fire training and drills can be based on the fire assessment.

Basic Fire Precautions

The majority of fires on ships are caused by some form of human oversight, eg carelessness, lack of maintenance or fatigue. However, with a strict safety regime imposed on the ship, many of the possible conditions that could cause fire can be reduced or eliminated.

Smoking

Smoking is probably the most common cause of cabin fires. Although some countries are bringing in new rules regarding smoking, to comply with their own laws, many flag States leave such rules to individual companies. In the absence of clear guidance from the company, responsibility for enforcement of smoking regulations may lie completely with the master.

Illegal Wiring

This is one of the reasons why a master's inspection of the ship takes place on a regular basis. All at sea are familiar with the prohibition of illegal wiring and the need to inspect all private electrical equipment in the cabins. On these formal inspections, the chief engineer should also check the equipment in the galleys and public rooms.

Oily Rags

These can be a source of fuel for a fire. A strict requirement for disposal can easily be enforced, including keeping oily boilersuits out of cabins and in the work lockers provided.

The Galley

There are a number of standard rules for galley precautions and these should be posted for all to see. It is essential to shut down all equipment at night, remove all cooking implements off the cookers and completely wash down and secure the galley.

One fire blanket should be available in every galley. It must be protected from the elements and available for immediate use. Crew must be trained in its use. Testing should be carried out periodically and after completion the blanket must be checked for damage, eg cracking or crumbling.

Fire Prevention

Night Watch Rounds

This is essential protection for the ship and must be completed every two hours by the duty watch rating during the watch and by the OOW at the end of the watch.

Fire Teams

The format of the teams is entirely dependent on the manning on board. In an ideal situation, with sufficient crew available, the following should be considered as a minimum organisational structure.

Command Team

The bridge, as the command centre, is primarily concerned with communications. The essential communications are with:

- The emergency teams
- the shore organisations
- other vessels in the vicinity.

In addition, it is essential that all others on board, including passengers, are regularly updated as to the situation so they are reassured that they have not been forgotten. The command team comprises:

- Master – in command
- officer – internal communications, bridge management and support
- officer – external communications and navigation
- helmsman.

Main Party

The purpose of the main party will be the location, control and extinguishing of the fire. The second engineer is included in the main party because his knowledge is required of all the machinery spaces outside the engine room. If the fire is in the engine room, he should assume command of the team. There should always be a combination of engine and deck ratings. The main party comprises:

- Chief officer – Fire team lead
- second engineer – second in command
- officer – communications
- electrical officer (if carried)
- bosun
- 2 × ratings - first hose party
- 2 × ratings - second hose party
- 2 × ratings - dressers and safety lines.

Backup Party

The main effort of any backup party will be in boundary cooling, although they must also be seen as a source of spare hands where and when the main party requires them.

If the ship has spare crew members, they should be attached to this team. If the fire is central in the accommodation, the boundary cooling effort will require directing at all sides of the fire and, rather than cooling, might involve the removal of combustible materials from the adjacent compartments. The backup party includes:

- Officer – in charge
- 2 × ratings.

First Aid Party

The ship's doctor is often either the master or another deck officer. However, as all crew should have undergone first aid training, they must be relied on for administering basic medical care for the injured and be trained in this capacity. The first aid party is typically made up of:

- 2 × ratings.

Boat Party

In any serious fire, there must be preparation for abandoning ship. In good weather, the command must have the option of evacuating non-essential crew and passengers from the ship while the fire is dealt with. The boat party consists of:

- Deck officer
- 2 × seafarer ratings.

Equipment

The minimum equipment and standards are given in SOLAS. The capability of such equipment is continually evolving and improving.

Extinguishers

Fires usually start small and, if tackled immediately by the person discovering it, can be easily and quickly dealt with.

There are four types of fire extinguishers, each of which extinguishes a specific type or types of fire.

Newer fire extinguishers are completely red and use a picture or colour labelling system to show the types of fires they are to be used on.

The colour labelling, which must be on no more than 5% of the extinguisher, is coded as follows:

- Red – water
- blue – powder
- black – carbon dioxide (CO_2)
- cream – foam.

Older fire extinguishers are completely coloured, not just the label.

In addition to the colour labelling, some extinguishers have diagrams that show the type of fire they are intended for.

Remember: It is important to establish what is burning. If you don't know what is burning, you don't know what type of extinguisher to use.

If you use the wrong type of fire extinguisher, you can make matters worse. It is therefore very important to understand the differences.

Water Extinguishers (Red Label)

Water extinguishers are suitable for most fires ***except***:

- Flammable liquids. Adding water to a burning liquid will only help to spread the fire
- electrical equipment. There is a risk of electric shock if a water extinguisher is used on an electrical fire.

Dry Powder (Blue Label)

Dry powder is suitable for fires that involve flammable liquids or electrical appliances.

Fire needs three things to keep it going - heat, fuel and oxygen (the fire triangle). The powder smothers the fire and stops it getting the oxygen it needs, which puts it out.

Fire Prevention

Carbon Dioxide CO_2 (Black Label)

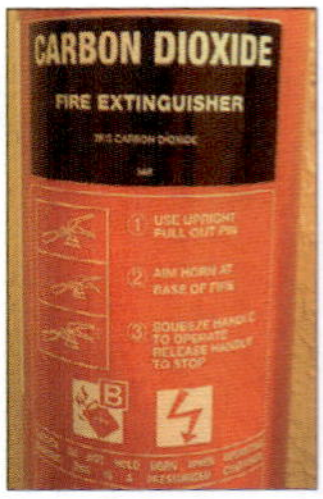

This type of extinguisher is suitable for flammable liquids and electrical equipment.

It also works in the same way as the dry powder extinguisher, by swamping the fire with carbon dioxide (CO_2). This stops the fire getting enough oxygen, so it goes out.

Foam (Cream Label)

This extinguisher is suitable for most fires involving flammable liquids. Again, it works by smothering the fire, rather than cooling down and damping the flames.

It should not be used on electrical fires.

Using a Fire Extinguisher

All fire extinguishers work in a similar way and there is a useful acronym, **PASS**, which will help you to remember the correct procedure:

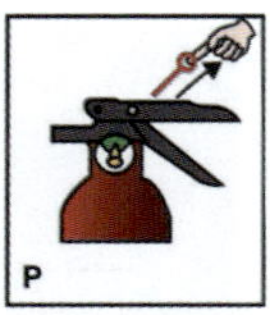

Pull out the pin at the top of the extinguisher. The pin prevents the handle from being pressed accidentally.

Aim the nozzle toward the base of the fire.

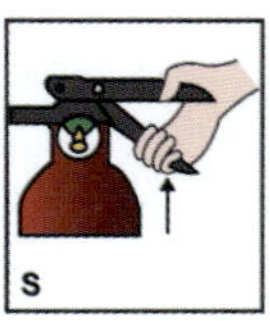

Stand approximately 8 feet away from the fire and **squeeze** the handle to discharge the extinguisher. If you release the handle, the discharge will stop.

Sweep the nozzle back and forth at the base of the fire. After the fire appears to be out, watch it carefully, as it may reignite.

For specific types of extinguisher, it is also useful to remember the following additional tips:

Water Based Extinguishers

You can only use these on solids, such as wood or paper. They must **never** be used on electrical fires or burning fat or oil.

Aim the jet at the base of the flames and move it over the area of the fire.

Dry Powder Based Extinguishers

These are safe to use on most kinds of fire. However, you must be aware that:

- The powder does not cool the fire well
- fires that seem to be out can reignite
- the powder doesn't penetrate small spaces, such as those found inside burning equipment.

Aim the jet at the base of the flames and briskly sweep it from side to side.

Carbon Dioxide (CO_2) Based Extinguishers

These are most effective on liquids and electrical fires.

As the gas disperses quickly, these extinguishers are only effective at distances of 3 to 8 feet.

Care should be taken when using a CO_2 extinguisher in a small space as it will adversely affect the breathable atmosphere.

The CO_2 is very cold as it comes out of the extinguisher. The cooling effect of the CO_2 will often cause ice to form around the 'horn' where the gas is expelled from the extinguisher. Do not hold the horn when operating the extinguisher as your hand could freeze to it.

Since the fire could reignite, continue to apply, even after the fire appears to be out.

Foam Based Extinguishers

These work well on liquids, but they should not be used on electrical fires as the foam could conduct electricity back to you.

For solids, aim the jet at the base of the flames and move it over the area of the fire. For liquids, do not aim the foam straight at the fire. Instead aim it at a vertical surface or, if the fire is in a container, at the inside edge of the container.

When using a foam extinguisher on a liquid fire, initially water is likely to be discharged which can cause a 'flash' before the foam is produced.

Important Things to Remember

Recognise the stage the fire is at. The time to use an extinguisher is in the early stages. If the fire is already spreading quickly, you should leave, ensuring that you close all doors.

If you believe that the fire is beginning to produce toxic smoke, you should stop attempting to fight it and evacuate.

Always position yourself with an exit or other means of escape at your back ***before*** you attempt to use an extinguisher to put out a fire.

To ensure the fire does not reignite, you should seal off the seat of the fire with the extinguishing material. Make sure the boundaries around the fire are kept as cool as possible.

Fire Prevention

Maintenance and Inspection

Fire extinguishers should be regularly serviced and maintained. Records should be kept, with the recent service history clearly marked.

Extinguisher Servicing Intervals

Type of portable extinguisher	Basic service	Extended service (test discharge)
Water, foam and water based	Every year	Every 5 years
Powder	Every year	Every 5 years
Powder – primary sealed	Every year	Every 10 years
CO_2	Every year	Every 5 years

It is the responsible officer's duty to check all extinguishers, but there should be a double check by the safety officer on rounds and rota.

During a routine check, if there is any indication of deterioration, the appliance should be replaced or fixed in accordance with the manufacturer's instructions.

CO_2 extinguishers and gas expellent cartridges of other extinguishers should be recharged or renewed if the loss of gas by weight exceeds 10% of the original charge that is stamped on the bottle or cartridge. The reason for the loss must be investigated.

Spare charges should have the manufacturer's instructions for charging the extinguishers clearly shown and, where the chemicals are liable to deteriorate, the containers should be marked with the date of packing and the date before which renewal is necessary.

Dry powder extinguishers may suffer from compaction when subject to vibration. During routine checks, these extinguishers should be rotated to loosen the powder. At least one should be discharged annually and the retention of contents checked. Where the retention is found to be in excess of 15% of the initial charge, more extinguishers should be discharged and tested.

No attempt to extinguish should be made if there is a large amount of smoke. 7 out of 10 fire-related deaths are due to smoke or gas inhalation.

Positioning of Fire Extinguishers

During the fire assessment, the placement of all extinguishers should be checked. If extinguishers need to be moved, the ship's fire plans will have to be updated to reflect these changes. The Company safety officer or safety department must be advised why such changes are required.

In assessing the placement of fire extinguishers, the following should be considered:

- The extinguisher should not be blocked by equipment that could interfere with their immediate accessibility
- if there is a pressure gauge on the extinguisher, this must be clearly visible to all who pass
- all extinguishers should be placed in a visible position. If they are not, their location must be indicated by a highly visible sign
- extinguishers should not be sited behind doors or in cupboards
- in accommodation and machinery spaces, no crew member should have to travel more than 20 metres from the fire to reach an extinguisher

- extinguishers should be mounted on brackets on a bulkhead no more than 1.5 metres above the deck
- in high risk areas, extinguishers should be placed outside but convenient for use in that area. Anyone using the extinguisher should not be placed in danger while locating and using it
- extinguishers should not be in areas that are affected by extreme heat or cold
- the correct extinguisher(s) should be provided for the risk(s) present in a specific area.

SOLAS requires that two portable fire extinguishers, each having a capacity of not less than 6 kg of dry powder or equivalent, should be provided when dangerous goods are carried on the weather deck, in open RoRo spaces and vehicle spaces, and in cargo spaces as appropriate. Two portable fire extinguishers, each having a suitable capacity, should be provided on the weather deck for tankers.

However, portable fire extinguishers need not be provided in cargo holds of container ships if motor vehicles with fuel in their tanks for their own propulsion are carried in open or closed containers.

Inspection and Maintenance

The SMS will state the maintenance schedule for recharging and pressure testing of fire extinguishers.

Regular maintenance checks on board should include:

- If a pressure gauge is fitted, that the pressure is at the recommended level
- the nozzle is intact and not blocked
- the pin and seal, if fitted, are intact
- the cylinder is not dented
- the extinguisher is free in its bracket
- there is no sign of leakage or corrosion
- any signage or instructions on the extinguisher are clear and readable.

Note: Most manufacturers recommend shaking/rotating dry chemical extinguishers once a month to prevent the powder from settling/packing.

Fire Detection

The combination of engine room, galleys and accommodation into one block and the remoteness of cargo holds means that automated fire detection is a standard requirement.

It is essential that mandatory fire patrols are maintained even on the smallest vessels. These should be completed at the mid-point and the end of each watch.

Smoke Detectors

The simplest smoke detectors are battery powered localised alarms that can guard individual areas such as cabins. The alarm is purely local and only audible to those nearby. When this alarm occurs, the ship's internal fire alarm system must be initiated.

A common type of smoke extraction system used for cargo holds continuously extracts and samples air from the holds or decks. If any sample is found to contain smoke particles, the alarm is sounded and the location of the suspect area is indicated on the control panel, which is usually situated on the bridge.

To cope with the problem of a low smoke fire, the smoke detectors can be combined with an optical detector that senses the deflection by smoke.

Optical detectors are more popular in galleys and other smoke producing workplaces as they are less prone to false alarms.

Fire Doors and Bulkheads

Marine doors are divided into categories A, B and C. Generally, the fire resistance of a bulkhead is expressed as A, B or C followed by a number indicating how long in minutes the division will prevent a specified temperature rise.

Where fire doors are provided, they should be fitted with effective self-closing devices and labelled 'Fire Door - Keep Shut'.

Class 'A'

'A' Class fire door panels consist of mineral wool core or thermax core, covered with electro-galvanised steel sheets.

A door in an 'A' Class bulkhead should provide resistance to fire, as well as to the passage of smoke and flame, for the same length of time as the bulkhead in which it is situated. 'A' Class fire doors should be constructed of steel or other equivalent material.

'A' Class division bulkheads should be insulated so that, on the side opposite to a fire, the average temperature will not rise more than 139°C above the original temperature, nor more than 180°C at any one point.

Class 'A-60' – must prevent the stated temperature rises for at least 60 minutes.

Class 'A-30' – must prevent the stated temperature rises for at least 30 minutes.

Class 'A-15' – must prevent the stated temperature rises for at least 15 minutes.

Class 'A-0' – must prevent the stated temperature rises for at least 0 minutes.

Class 'B'

'B' Class fire door panels consist of mineral wool core, covered with electro-galvanised steel sheets.

The insulation should be such that, on the side opposite to a fire, the average temperature will not rise more than 139°C above the original temperature, nor more than 225°C at any one point.

Class 'B-15' – must prevent the stated temperature rises for at least 15 minutes.

Class 'B-0' – must prevent the stated temperature rises for at least 0 minutes.

Class 'C'

'C' Class doors are required to be fitted in 'C' Class bulkheads.

They do not need to meet the requirements for limiting the passage of smoke and flame nor limitations relative to temperature rise. Combustible veneers are permitted provided they meet other requirements.

Ref: IMO FTP Code

CO_2 Systems

Carbon dioxide systems are very effective at dealing with both flammable liquid and electrical fires. CO_2 is supplied via pipelines from storage cylinders or a tank located away from the protected area at an ambient temperature of ≤60°C. If CO_2 pipelines pass through accommodation areas, they must be thick and pressure tight, only joined by welding and not fitted with openings, eg drains. Pipelines must not pass through refrigerated areas. Fitting through machinery spaces to service cargo holds should be avoided. However, if they have to be routed through machinery spaces, the pipes and the joints must be tested and approved.

The following specifications must be met for CO_2 system components:

- Piping must be constructed of fire resistant material, eg steel
- nozzles that incorporate metal must use stainless steel, copper, copper alloy or galvanised steel
- non-metallic nozzle parts must exhibit consistency over the working life period
- all CO_2 system component materials must be resistant to the different substances they are exposed to as well as the varying temperature extremes.

Controls of the CO_2 system must enable release of CO_2 into the protected area and activate the alarm. Manual control of power to the automatically operated valves should be possible. There must be:

- Two separate controls for the release of CO_2 that operate in the following order:
  1. The valve opening to enable flow of CO_2 to the designated area.
  2. The output of gas from the storage containers.
- a release box containing the two controls which is clearly allocated to a particular area. System operating instructions must be straightforward and clearly displayed. Any associated key to this box must be nearby, obvious and in a breakable container.

Different quantities of CO_2 are specified in the FSS Code for cargo spaces and machinery spaces.

CO_2 Alarm Systems

Carbon dioxide alarm systems are both audible and visible. The audible alarm must sound different to any other alarm, be loud enough to be heard while machinery is operating and be unique to the particular protected space. The alarm must be given automatically before CO_2 is released and the protected area must be evacuated immediately. The alarm should sound for the length of time necessary to evacuate the area, but for not less than 20 seconds. The power supply for the audible alarm should be different from all other alarms and powered from two sources. One of these sources should be the emergency source of electrical power on board.

CO_2 Systems

Protected space on board	Discharge quantity of CO_2	Speed of CO_2 discharge from fixed piping	Using cleaned (minimal O_2, CO, corrosive and combustible elements) gaseous products from fuel combustion
Machinery space	Must provide a minimum volume of free CO_2 that is equal to the larger of either of the following volumes: • 40% of the gross volume of the largest CO_2-protected machinery space excluding a specified part of the casing, but may be reduced to 35% for <2,000 GT cargo vessels when machinery spaces can be considered as one area • 35% of the gross volume of the largest CO_2-protected machinery space including the casing, but may be reduced to 30% for <2,000 GT cargo vessels when machinery spaces can be considered as one area.	85% of the required concentration must be achieved within 2 minutes of operation, and at least 50% within the first minute.	Sufficient quantity of cleaned combustion gases must be available so that every hour ≥25% of the gross volume of the largest protected cargo space is protected and this protection must last for 72 hours.
Cargo space	Must provide a minimum volume of free CO_2 that is equal to 30% of the gross volume of the largest protected cargo space.		These must provide the same protection as a fixed CO_2 system.
Cargo space: vehicle spaces and RoRo space (capable of being sealed)	Must provide a minimum volume of free CO_2 that is equal to 45% of the gross volume of the largest protected cargo space capable of being sealed.	≥66% of the required concentration must be achieved within 10 minutes of operation.	

Table 38.1 - FSS Code CO_2 requirements for cargo and machinery spaces

Tools

Dedicated tools must be allocated for fire party use only and kept with the main party's fire equipment. One problem encountered by the fire team is the limited ability to carry equipment, especially if a hose has to be carried as well. Ideally, one man will enter the fire area, with the hose party carrying any essential tools that may be required.

Master Key

Although it seems obvious, the main fire party rarely has a master key instantly available. It is far easier to open a door than having to try to crowbar or smash it open, especially if it is a fire door.

Axe

An axe is essential when dealing with accommodation fires. It should have a blade at one side and a spike or claw at the other. It should be able to be carried in one hand or in a sheath carried around the waist.

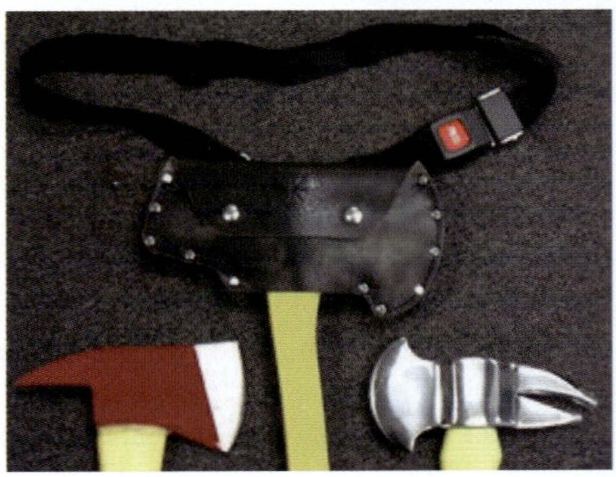

Courtesy of All Hands Fire Equipment

Crow bars

These are useful for breaking into cabins and locked spaces. They may also be used for pulling down bulkheads to reach suspected fire areas.

Tools

Fire Doors

Although heat can travel through the steel divisions of the bulkheads and decks and ignite materials in adjacent compartments, open accesses such as doorways provide a much easier route, especially if ventilation draws the fire.

Ventilation

Fire dampers are fitted throughout the internal ventilation system according to the regulations for the different areas. While the dampers will not stop fires, they can help stop the spread of a fire in two ways. They reduce or stop the supply of air to a fire, which slows the fire's development, and they block the spread of flame, smoke and combustible materials to other compartments or areas. All dampers are designed to be closed manually, but automatically closing dampers are fitted in some areas. When the temperature in a duct reaches a certain limit, usually around 100°C, a fusible link melts and the dampers automatically close.

Closing the dampers and the outside ventilators and shutting down the ventilation machinery are basic precautions in the event of a fire.

Firefighter's Outfit

Revisions to SOLAS, which entered into force in July 2002, set mandatory minimum requirements relating to the type and amount of equipment to be carried on board and how it is to be stored. Firefighter outfits are mandatory on all ships.

Firefighter Outfit Specification

Firefighter outfits must comply with the Fire Safety Systems (FFS) Code. A firefighter's outfit comprises the following:

- Protective clothing
- breathing apparatus
- a strong fireproof lifeline.

Personal Equipment

Personal equipment consists of the following items:

- A protective suit – this should be made of flame and heat proof material and be water resistant. It should be easy to put on and take off, be comfortable and allow for maximum movement of the wearer
- fire-resistant gloves
- safety boots – these should be made of rubber or other electrically non-conducting material
- a rigid helmet, adequate to provide effective protection from impact
- a safety lamp, either handheld or mounted on the helmet. It must be Class 1, intrinsically safe and have a minimum battery life of 3 hours. Electric safety lamps on tankers and those intended to be used in hazardous areas must be of an explosion-proof type
- a fire axe, the handle of which must have high voltage insulation.

Breathing apparatus

Breathing apparatus should be either:

- A self-contained compressed air-operated breathing apparatus, containing at least 1,200 litres of air in the cylinders, or
- other self-contained breathing apparatus which is capable of functioning for at least 30 minutes, for example a supply from a compressed air line from the ship's supply.

Firefighter's Outfit

The apparatus of either type should be capable of working for at least 30 minutes and be provided with one face mask. They should also be fitted with audible pressure drop and minimum levels alarms and an override to the automatic air supply valve.

Breathing apparatus should be clearly marked with details of the maker and year of manufacture. Operating instructions must be available at all times.

Two spare, fully charged air cylinders should be available, providing 2,400 litres of air, and all cylinders for breathing apparatus should be interchangeable.

Lifeline

Day

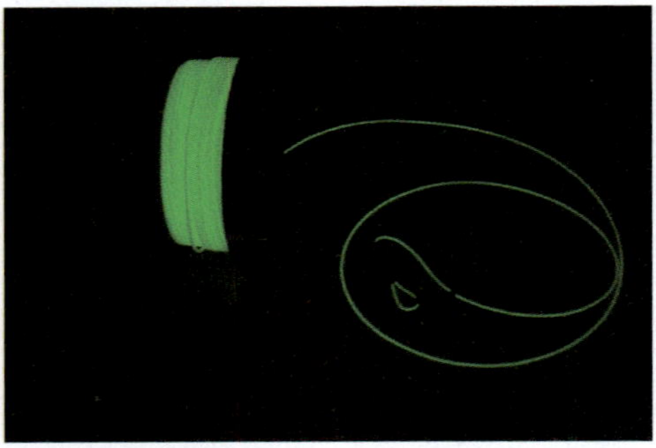

Night

Courtesy of Life Light Solutions Ltd

Extract from IMO FSS Code

> *"For each breathing apparatus a fireproof lifeline of at least 30 m in length shall be provided. The lifeline shall successfully pass an approval test by static load of 3.5 kN for 5 min without failure. The lifeline shall be capable of being attached by means of a snap-hook to the harness of the apparatus or to a separate belt in order to prevent the breathing apparatus becoming detached when the lifeline is operated."*

The problem in using a lifeline is the danger of entanglement, which may occur as the wearer moves about. Its use must be carefully considered and based on where the wearer is being sent. A vertical up and down situation would leave the line clear for use, but in an engine room there is too great a risk of entanglement. Any safety line should be attached to the wearer in a position that can be easily unclipped.

A new type of guide line for use in fire and enclosed space situations contains 100 metres of illuminated fire-retardant line powered by a built-in rechargeable battery. In addition, the line contains a communications system, allowing the user and reel attendees to plug in dedicated communications equipment and keep in constant contact with each other.

Figure 38.1 - Minimum requirements of a firefighter's outfit

SOLAS Requirements for Firefighters' outfits

The amendments to SOLAS which entered into force on 1st July 2002 specify the number and types of firefighters' outfits required.

Types of firefighters' outfits

Firefighters' outfits must comply with the Fire Safety Systems (FSS) Code.

Number of firefighters' outfits required

All ships over 500 tonnes must carry at least two firefighters' outfits.

In addition, on passenger ships there must be two firefighters' outfits per 80 metres length of deck per deck level and two further sets of personal equipment, each set comprising the items stipulated in the FSS Code and summarised in Section 2.1.

On passenger ships carrying over 36 passengers, two additional firefighters' outfits must be provided for each main vertical zone. (For stairway enclosures which constitute individual main vertical zones and for the main vertical zones in the fore and aft end of a ship which do not contain spaces of categories (6), (7), (8) or (12) defined in Regulation 9.2.2.3, no additional firefighters' outfits are required.)

On ships carrying more than 36 passengers, for each pair of breathing apparatus, one water fog applicator must be stored alongside the breathing apparatus.

On tankers, two additional firefighters' outfits must be carried.

The Administration may require additional sets of personal equipment and breathing apparatus, depending on the size and type of ship.

At least two spare charges must be provided for each set of breathing apparatus, except for passenger ships carrying fewer than 36 passengers and cargo ships that are equipped with suitable means for fully recharging the air cylinders with uncontaminated air. In these cases, only one spare charge is needed for each set of breathing apparatus.

Storage of firefighters' outfits

The firefighters' outfits or sets of personal equipment must be kept ready for use at all times. They should be stored in an easily accessible location that is permanently and clearly marked and not likely to be cut off by fire.

Where more than one firefighters' outfit or set of personal equipment is carried, they should be stored in widely separated locations.

On passenger ships, at least two firefighters' outfits and, in addition, one set of personal equipment must be available in any one position. At least two firefighters' outfits must be stored in each main vertical zone.

Harness and lifeline

The adjustable safety belt or harness, together with the snap-hook, should be to BS En 354, 355, 358, 361 and 365 requirements. To ensure that the safety belt or harness is compatible with the breathing apparatus, each type of safety belt or harness supplied should be submitted for the drop test at the same time as the apparatus is submitted for approval.

The point of attachment of the life and signalling line to the safety belt or harness should be such as to be easily removed by the wearer. If a pennant is used for this purpose, it should be such that it cannot easily be removed. Snap-hooks should be of materials resistant to sparking on impact, as far as is possible.

Air Compressors

Where special compressors for the charging of compressed air cylinders are carried on board, they must be of adequate capacity and the air intakes must be carefully positioned to prevent the ingress of water or noxious fumes, even under adverse weather conditions. Also, the vessel's standing orders should contain the manufacturer's detailed instructions for operating and servicing of the compressor and ancillary equipment, eg filters, dryers, etc. At least one member of the crew should be competent in the use of this equipment.

Firefighter's Outfit

Marking

Where any of the breathing apparatus cylinders carried on board have different working pressures, in addition to the normal cylinder markings, the working pressure should be clearly marked on the cylinder in paint.

Training

In addition to the fully charged spare air cylinders required by the Regulations, it is recommended that, where there are no means for recharging cylinders, additional cylinder capacity is provided for training purposes. Training cylinders should be clearly and prominently marked to indicate their intended use, eg by the use of waterproof adhesive labels or tape.

Safety Lamps

Safety lamps may be either the handheld or cap-lamp type. The batteries must be rechargeable. Hand lamps must be fitted with a means of easy attachment to the wearer at about waist level.

Safety lamps for use with firefighters' outfits must be Class 1 standard. These lamps are intended for use in any ship, including those carrying cargoes that are, or may give rise to, flammable gases and vapours. All Class 1 lamps are suitable for use on petroleum tankers but may not be suitable for all flammable cargoes. Special attention should be paid to certification to verify that the equipment is suitable for use with the cargoes of bulk chemical carriers and liquefied gas carriers.

Self-Contained Breathing Apparatus (SCBA)

Breathing Apparatus

The standard SOLAS BA set is worn on the back

An SCBA typically has three main components: a high-pressure tank (eg 2,200 psi to 4,500 psi), a pressure regulator, and an inhalation connection (mouthpiece, mouth mask or face mask), connected together and mounted to a carrying frame.

The typical SCBA set on board ship is an open circuit type that is filled with filtered compressed air. The air flow to the mask is via either a demand valve, which is activated by inhalation by the wearer, or by a continuous positive pressure valve that provides a constant air flow to the mask. Two regulators ensure that the pressure of the air is just above the standard atmospheric pressure.

The cylinders can be of three sizes, rated as lasting for 30, 45 or 60 minutes, although this time can be reduced by up to 50% by the exertions of the wearer. While most cylinders on board ships are made of steel, they can be made of aluminium or, as preferred by firefighters ashore, composite construction, owing to their lightness. This gives them a considerable advantage in reducing fatigue for the wearer, but they are more expensive and have to be hydrostatically tested every 3 years.

Types of SCBA

There are two types of SCBA - open and closed circuit.

Open Circuit, Pressure Demand SCBAs

In this type of SCBA all the breathing gas is carried by the wearer. Exhaled air is expelled through the exhalation valve on the face piece. If there is a small leak in the system or if the face piece seal is dislodged or damaged, there will be sufficient pressure and air volume in the

Self-Contained Breathing Apparatus (SCBA)

cylinder to maintain a positive pressure inside the face piece. This means that, even if there is a large air leak, the device is likely to continue to provide high level protection to the wearer.

In case the regulator malfunctions, the wearer controls a valve which when opened causes air from the cylinder to be delivered to the face piece, bypassing the regulator. This changes the type of operation to constant flow and means that the air in the cylinder will be used up quickly. This emergency bypass is designed to provide enough air to allow the wearer to escape a hazardous environment safely.

Due to their weight, most SCBAs are not suitable for strenuous work. Their bulk also makes them unsuitable for use in confined areas. A limited service life means they should not be used for routine work over a long period of time, although today air line SCBA combination devices resolve this problem. The open circuit device has a relatively short life so the wearer may be limited to areas where they can go from a hazardous to a safe atmosphere to change the tank of air. Extra cylinders are usually required and a way of refilling the tanks is necessary.

The rated duration of use for these devices can be misleading. The National Institute for Occupational Safety and Health (NIOSH) rates these devices as 15, 30 or 60 minute duration using a relatively low breathing rate. The actual use in a stressful situation or when carrying out heavy work may only be half the rated duration. If there is a leakage or if the face piece is compromised, the useful duration will be even shorter. A warning alarm will sound when the device reaches 20% of full capacity, to remind the user to leave the area and replenish the air supply.

Advantages and Limitations of Full Face Piece, Open Circuit, Pressure Demand SCBA:

Advantages:

- Less complicated to operate and maintain than the closed circuit, positive pressure SCBA
- highest APF (Assigned Protection Factors) available (10,000)
- allowed to be used in unassessed areas, fire-fighting, IDLH (Immediately Dangerous to Health and Life)
- allows the wearer comparatively free movement in an unlimited area
- less expensive than closed circuit SCBA
- does not require as much maintenance as closed circuit.

Limitations:

- Expensive
- actual service life may only be half the rated duration
- extra air cylinders are required
- a source of high pressure air is required
- bulk and weight
- unsuitable for routine use over long continuous periods of time
- fairly short service life
- more expensive than supplied air systems.

1. Cylinder and valve assembly
2. Back frame
3. Regulator – controls the flow of air
4. Pressure gauge
5. Chest alarm whistle – warns the user of low air pressure and air depletion
6. Lens
7. Nose cup
8. Head harness

Figure 38.2 - SCBA Unit

Self-Contained Breathing Apparatus (SCBA)

Closed Circuit, Positive Pressure Mode

This type of SCBA operates in the 'closed circuit' mode, which means that exhaled air is retained in the system by a second hose which is attached to the face piece. This second hose takes the exhaled air into the back-mounted apparatus for treatment and recirculation. This is not a true pressure demand device.

Air that has been exhaled by the wearer passes through a catalyst bed in the backpack, where the CO_2 is removed, and is then directed towards a spring-loaded breathing bag that pressurises it. The O_2 in a pressurised cylinder in the backpack bleeds slowly into the breathing bag, the air is re-oxygenated and the pressure in the closed system is increased. As the wearer inhales, the spring-loaded breathing bag provides the pressurised air. The oxygen bleed will quickly increase the O_2 concentration in the breathing gas to more than 30%. This makes these devices useful when working at high altitude, in a low atmospheric pressure environment and in areas where oxygen is deficient.

Unlike open circuit SCBAs, if a closed circuit device is rated for four hours, it will be able to be used for the full four hours. These devices have also been adapted for use underwater.

If there is an air leak in the system or if the seal of the face piece is compromised, the volume of pressurised air in the breathing bag will reach ambient pressure quickly. The O_2 cylinder will start to vent into the breathing bag at a faster rate to try to maintain the system's pressure. If it is a persistent or large leak, the device will revert to its negative mode of operation. An indication that there may be a problem is the low oxygen alarm sounding earlier than anticipated.

This type of device requires more maintenance between each use than the open circuit device. The catalyst bed in the backpack must be replaced after each use, as well as the pressurised oxygen cylinder. It is important that a supply of the catalyst material and several compressed oxygen cylinders are maintained on board.

Advantages and Limitations of Full Face Piece, Closed Circuit, Recirculating Positive Pressure SCBA:

Advantages:

- Very long use times
- highest APF available.

Limitations:

- Breathing air becomes warm during use
- two hoses are attached to the face piece
- weight
- more maintenance is required between each use
- a supply of compressed oxygen cylinders is required
- a source of breathing quality oxygen is required
- a supply of CO_2 absorbent is required.

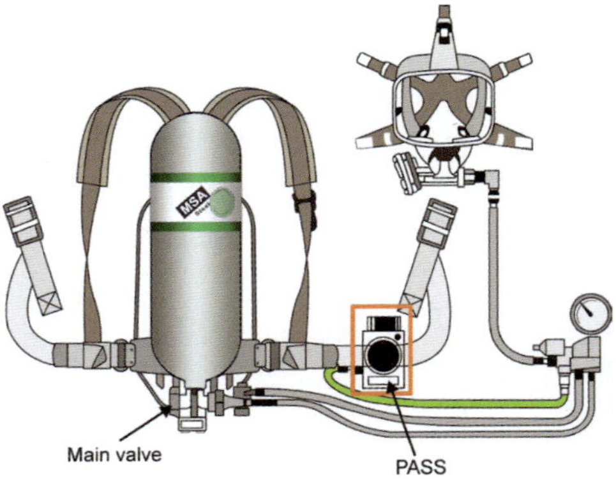

An essential addition to the SCBA is the

Figure 38.3 - Diagram showing a PASS (Personal Alert Safety System) device used by firefighters. If the device does not detect movement within a certain period of time, it will automatically send out a loud audible signal to alert others of the firefighter's distress

Personal Alert Safety System (PASS).

This device emits a high pitched alarm signal that will guide rescuers to a wearer in distress. This signal can be either activated by the wearer or will activate automatically if it does not detect movement from the wearer after a set period of time, usually around 15 to 30 seconds.

Donning Procedure

1. Check that all straps are fully loosened.
2. Ensure that the cylinder valve is off and that the demand valve is correctly fitted to the face mask.
3. Hold the neck strap, demand valve supply hose and right shoulder strap in the left hand. Hold the top of the strap with the

right hand and swing the apparatus onto the back. Place the left hand through the shoulder strap.

4. Fit the neck strap. Adjust the shoulder straps by pulling the loops outward then down towards the waist until the set feels comfortable. Connect and tighten the waist belt buckle.
5. Check that the bypass valve is closed. Depress the first breath mechanism.
6. Turn the cylinder valve fully on. Listen for any leaks.
7. Check the cylinder's contents.

Start-Up Procedure

1. Take a breath and fit the face mask chin first. Adjust the head harness buckles. Ensure that hair does not interfere with the face mask seal. To make this easier, the wearer should lean forward, breathe and inhale sharply to initiate the first breath mechanism.
2. BA wearers should check that their partner's head harness is correctly positioned and that the straps are evenly tensioned.
3. Insert two fingers between your face and mask. There should be an outflow of air which means that the set is operating in positive pressure.
4. After two or three breaths, hold your breath for five seconds. You should not hear any air flow.
5. Check the bypass operation, open then close.
6. Hold your breath, turn off the cylinder, keep your hand on the cylinder valve.
7. Observe the gauge for eight seconds while moving the head around. Extreme movement of the head can cause some leakage. It should stop once the head is in a more central position or movement is less severe.
8. Breathe and watch the gauge, noting when the whistle is activated.
9. Turn the cylinder valve back on and take two or three normal breaths.
10. Hold your breath again and turn off the air supply to the mask. A hand should remain on the cylinder valve.
11. Breathe steadily until the air is exhausted. The gauge will indicate that the cylinder is empty. Inhale making the mask collapse on the face. If the mask is defective or not correctly fitted, a vacuum will not collapse.
12. Hold your breath for a further eight seconds, making sure the mask remains sucked onto the face.
13. If any leaks are identified, the mask should be refitted and retested.
14. Fit the fire hood and check the other team members' hoods.
15. Fit the helmet.
16. Check the gauge reading.

Check the Automatic Distress Signal Unit (ADSU) as the key with tally is removed at Entry Control.

The BA must always be donned and started up in fresh air. The effectiveness of the mask seal must be tested every time the BA is worn.

Doffing Procedure

1. Collect tally and isolate ADSU.
2. Remove helmet and fire hood.
3. Take a breath then reset the first breath mechanism.
4. Loosen the head harness buckles, bottom, middle and top.
5. Remove face mask.
6. Depress the cylinder valve ratchet and turn off the valve.
7. Undo the waist belt.
8. Remove the left arm from the shoulder strap, then remove the neck strap with the left hand.
9. Grasp the right hand shoulder strap with both hands and swing the apparatus round to the front. The apparatus should then be laid on its back plate. It is important that you bend your knees to protect your back from injury.
10. Any remaining air should be drained from the pneumatic system using the bypass valve.
11. The face mask, with the visor on top, should be placed on top of the cylinder.

Duration of Breathing Apparatus

The various types of cylinder, while they may have the same maximum working pressure,

Self-Contained Breathing Apparatus (SCBA)

may have different capacities at this pressure. Duration tables should be used as well as the correct table for cylinder capacity.

The average rate of consumption for compressed air BA sets is assumed at 40 litres per minute, the average rate for someone walking at 4 miles per hour. If heavy work is being carried out, the rate may be higher and as a result the duration will be shorter.

The air consumption rate of an open circuit BA varies over a wide range. This will depend on several factors including the physique and work rate of the person wearing the system, as well as the environmental conditions. Several definitions are used in relation to the duration of BA.

Full Duration:

- The period of time that the BA is expected to provide respiratory protection. This is from the time the cylinder valve is opened until the cylinder is empty.

Working Duration:

- The period of time that the BA is expected to provide protection. This is from when the cylinder valve is opened until the moment when the low pressure warning alarm starts
- the following formula is used to determine the working duration for a CABA:

$$\frac{\text{Contents of Cylinder in Litres}}{40} - 10$$

eg LUXFER LCX (1,800 litres)

$$\text{Working duration} = \frac{1{,}800}{40} - 10 = 35 \text{ minutes}$$

Safety margin (10 minutes or 20%):

- This is when the low pressure warning whistle will operate
- the recommended safety margin for all types of BA system is 10 minutes.

SCBA – Inspections

All SCBA equipment must be inspected periodically to ensure it is ready for use and to find and repair any damage or excessive wear the unit has sustained. The frequency of these inspections is outlined below:

1. After every use, each SCBA should be checked for the following:
    - Cylinders should be cleaned. Any cylinders that are low or empty should be refilled or replaced with fully charged ones
    - components and face pieces must be cleaned, checked for any wear or damage, sanitised and checked that they are working correctly
    - if an SCBA has been used in a contaminated atmosphere, the unit must be decontaminated thoroughly before it is used again.

SCBA – Inspections

2. Monthly Inspection:
   - Every piece of SCBA equipment that is assigned to an apparatus must be inspected monthly by an SCBA officer
   - the inspection must ensure that the SCBA is fully charged, clean, damage free and fully operational
   - cleaning, refilling cylinders and minor repairs should be carried out by personnel who have been trained in using SCBAs
   - any damaged units or faulty units should be removed and a description of the fault should be written on an attached tag. A note of any defects should be handed to the SCBA officer.
3. Annual Inspection:
   - All SCBAs should be inspected annually by an authorised repair facility
   - the inspection and servicing must include:
     - the regulator and other major parts, including the low air alarm and face piece. These must be disassembled and cleaned
     - replacement of any damaged or degraded parts
     - reassembly and testing including a flow test.
4. Hydrostatic Testing of SCBA:

   This should be carried out every five years or as recommended by the manufacturer. The hydrostatic test date must be marked on the bottles. Testing of ultra-lightweight cylinders must be carried out at least every five years, unless there is any mechanical damage or signs of corrosion are identified during other inspections. In these circumstances, the cylinder should be hydrostatically tested before being returned into service.
5. Spare Charges and Recharging Breathing Apparatus Air Cylinders:

   Two spare charges that can be used with the breathing apparatus should be provided for every SCBA, with the following exceptions:
   - If a cargo ship has a suitable way to fully recharge the air cylinders free from contamination, only one spare charge is required for each SCBA
   - on a passenger ship carrying fewer than 36 passengers, only one spare charge is required for each SCBA
   - passenger ships carrying more than 36 passengers must have at least two spare charges for the SCBA.

SCBA – Records

The officer responsible for the SCBA must make sure that the following records are kept:

- A complete inventory of all the SCBA units, cylinders, cascades, fill stations, special tools, spare parts and any other relevant equipment
- an inventory and note of the serial numbers, dates of purchase, vendor, manufacturer, history of any maintenance or repair work carried out, a history of any parts that have been replaced, any upgrades and performance tests carried out
- individual maintenance and repair records for all breathing air compressors and fill stations as well as any equipment that has been used to produce or store breathing air
- all air quality tests carried out.

BA Compressor

Breathing air compressors are used to compress air for human breathing in self-contained breathing apparatus (SCBA) sets. Compressor systems filter atmospheric air, compress it to high pressure and transfer it to the SCBA cylinders. Proper training is required to fill SCBA cylinders. Breathing air compressors require much more maintenance and routine care than other air compressors.

SOLAS II-2 Regulation 10.2.6 and FSS Code Chapter 3 regulate the installation and use of breathing air compressors.

Breathing air compressors on board ships must be driven by a diesel engine separate from the emergency power plant and located in an easily accessible and safe place. The capacity of the compressor shall be at least 75 litres/min.

The means for recharging must be either:

- Breathing air compressors supplied from the main and emergency switchboard, or independently driven, with a minimum capacity of 60 litres/min per required

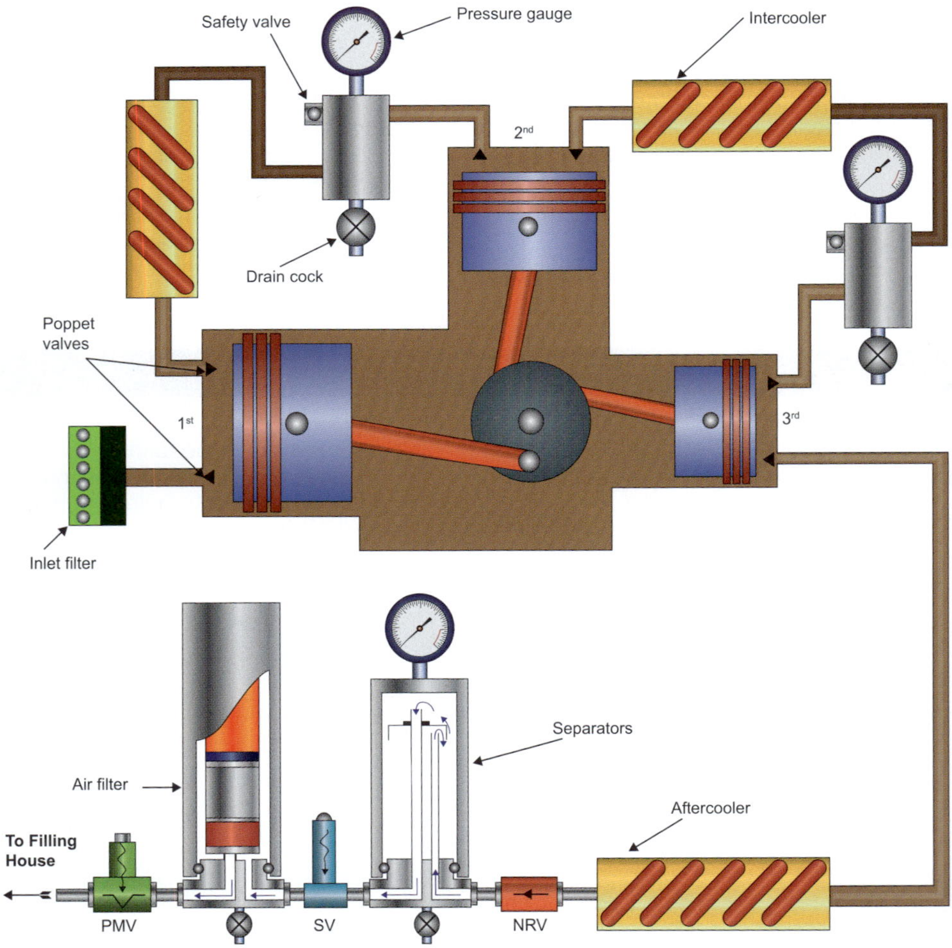

breathing apparatus, not to exceed 420 litres/min; or

- self-contained high-pressure storage systems of suitable pressure to recharge the breathing apparatus used on board, with a capacity of at least 1,200 litres per required breathing apparatus, not to exceed 50,000 litres of free air.

The quality of the air produced by any high-pressure storage system or breathing air compressor should be tested annually by a national accredited laboratory, in accordance with BS EN 12021 - respiratory protective devices - compressed air for breathing apparatus, or an equivalent national standard.

Any breathing air compressor should be installed in an enclosed compartment (dedicated solely for that purpose wherever possible) which should have little or no fire risk and sufficient space on all sides to ensure good ventilation. The area should be as cool as possible but places where freezing may occur should be avoided. The air intake should be located in open air and away from potential contaminant release points.

A maximum charging rate of 27 bar/min will help reduce heat build-up and minimise the need to top up the cylinder after it has cooled down.

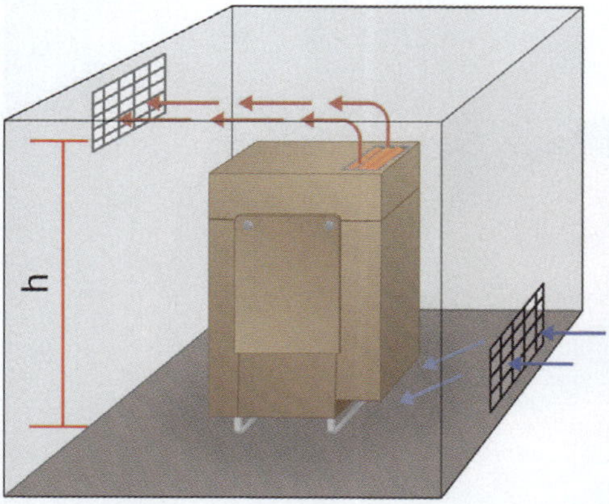

Figure 38.4 - Locating the unit

BA compressors require clean airflow to ensure safe air is pumped into SCBA cylinders. It is important to be certain that the compressor fan can draw clean air, free of contamination, and that the exhaust air is able to be effectively discharged and does not contaminate the fresh air intake.

Compression Process

Compressing air for use in SCBA is a multi-stage process involving cooling, filtering and compression.

Atmospheric air is sucked in via a suction filter that removes dust particles. The filtered air is cooled and compressed. After compression, any excess moisture is separated. The air is then filtered for a second time through the main filter cartridge to remove all impurities. The air is then pumped into the BA cylinder.

Start-up and Shutdown of BA Compressors

Before operating the compressor, read the manufacturer's instruction manual carefully and make sure that all persons involved with the filling process are familiar with the function and controls of the BA compressor.

This section provides general guidelines. The operation and process of the BA compressor that you encounter on board could be very different.

Start-up:

1. Check oil level of motor according to manufacturer's instruction manual.
2. Drain condensate valves on the filters so that the motor starts without load.
3. Once the engine has started, close condensate valves.
4. Run compression unit to final pressure. Check final pressure safety valve and pressure gauge.
5. As soon as final pressure is reached and final pressure safety valve blows off, open condensate drain valves and drain condensate. The compression unit is then ready for filling operation.

Filling:

1. During filling procedure, cylinders will warm up due to recompression. After removing the cylinders, allow them to cool. Once cooled, the cylinders may then be reconnected and topped up to their maximum filling pressure.
2. Never open the filling valve unless a cylinder is connected to the filling line.
3. The filling procedure should not be interrupted for more than 10 minutes to avoid high CO_2 levels in the cylinder.

BA Compressor

4. Upon reaching the final cylinder pressure, close the cylinder valve first then the filling valve. Always secure the filling hose after use.

Shutdown:

1. Close filling valves.
2. Shut down diesel engine. Close fuel shut-off valve.
3. Open condensate drain valves until no more condensate comes out. Close all valves again and leave the unit with residual pressure in the system. This ensures that no moisture can enter the compressor unit.
4. Check the oil level (if applicable) and top up if necessary.

Maintenance

250 operational hours:

- Clean air filters
- check unloader condition
- if belt is provided for driving cooling water pumps, check its tightness.

500 operational hours:

- Change lube and clean sump
- clean lube oil filter
- check and renew suction and discharge valves with overhauled one.

1,000 operational hours:

- Crankcase inspection, main and big end bearing inspection
- relief valve overhaul.

4,000 operational hours:

- piston and big end bearing overhauled, piston ring renewal
- intercooler cleaning
- motor overhauling.

Carriage Requirements for Emergency Escape Breathing Devices

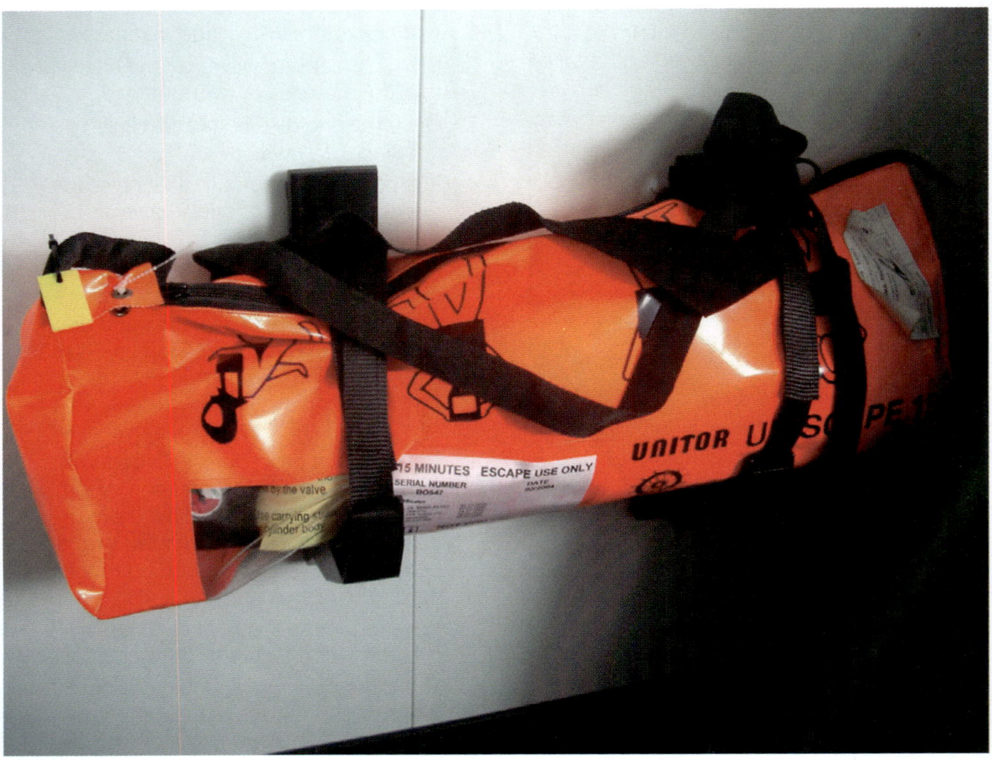

Carriage Requirements for Emergency Escape Breathing Devices

From 1st July 2002, Emergency Escape Breathing Devices (EEBDs) were required to be carried in the accommodation and machinery spaces in both passenger and cargo vessels.

The requirements are as follows:

- EEBDs shall comply with the Fire Safety Systems (FSS) Code
- all ships shall carry at least two EEBDs within accommodation spaces
- spare EEBDs shall be kept on board (for cargo ships, one set spare)
- on all ships, within the machinery spaces, EEBDs shall be situated ready for use at easily visible places that can be reached quickly and easily at any time in the event of fire. The location of EEBDs shall take into account the layout of the machinery space and the number of persons normally working in the spaces.
- the number and location of EEBDs shall be indicated in the fire control plan
- in passenger ships, at least two EEBDs shall be carried in each main vertical zone.

An EEBD includes the following:

- Cylinder containing oxygen
- demand valve and low pressure alarm
- hood/face piece.

Particulars

- The EEBD shall have a service duration of at least 10 minutes
- the EEBD shall include a hood or full face piece, as appropriate, to protect the eyes, nose and mouth during escape. Hoods and face pieces shall be constructed of flame resistant materials and include a clear window for viewing
- an inactivated EEBD shall be capable of being carried hands-free
- an EEBD, when stored, shall be suitably protected from the environment
- brief instructions or diagrams clearly illustrating their use shall be clearly printed on the EEBD. The donning procedures shall be quick and easy to allow for situations where there is little time to seek safety from a hazardous atmosphere.

High Expansion Foam System

Foam Systems

Foam generation is either mechanical or chemical. In mechanically generated foam, the foam concentrate is mixed with water to produce the base solution, and then air is added to produce the bubble effect. In chemically produced foam, a chemical is introduced to water to produce foam bubbles filled with CO_2. The chemical foam has a better blanketing effect and is replacing the older mechanical foam systems. The intention of the foam system is to form a blanket over the fire, but when the concentrate runs out, the tank will continue to produce a water flow that will break down the blanket unless shut off. This means that a watch must be kept over the holding tank where the foam concentrate is mixed.

Foam is available as a fixed installation system or can be in mobile tanks or packs and used with hoses and special foam nozzles that enable the concentrate and water to mix.

There are three types of foam commonly used on ships:

Low-expansion foams with an expansion rate less than 20 times. These are suitable when a large surface area has to be covered.

Medium-expansion foams with an expansion rate between 20 to 200 times. These are used when some depth is required to blanket the fire.

High-expansion foams with an expansion rate over 200. These are used when a high degree of depth is needed.

Foam concentrates have a shelf life ranging between 5 and 10 years depending on the manufacturer.

Foam may be used to fight fires on deck, in the pump room or in the engine spaces. The foam concentrate is held in tanks and, when required, water from the fire pumps will collect the correct amount of foam concentrate through a proportioner. The foam solution moves through the permanent supply lines to the take-off points, fixed foam monitors or, in the case of engine room installations, fixed dispersal nozzles.

High Expansion Foam System

High Expansion Foam System

A 1.5 metre long, 1 metre square generator could produce about 15 m^3/min of foam, which would completely fill the average engine room in about 15 minutes. One litre of synthetic detergent foam concentrate combines with 30 to 60 litres of water (supplied from the sea) to give 30,000 to 60,000 litres of foam.

Advantages:

- Economic
- can be rapidly produced
- could be used with existing ventilation system
- personnel can walk through the foam with little ill effect.

Disadvantages:

- Persistent, could take up to 48 hours to die down in an enclosed compartment
- large trunking required
- must be trunked to the bottom of the compartment to stop convection currents carrying it away.

Portable Foam Applicator Units

Every portable foam applicator should have:

- An induction type of nozzle which can be connected to the fire main by using a fire hose
- a portable tank with at least 20 litres of foam concentrate
- an identical spare tank.

The ship should be supplied with a nozzle at the minimum hydrant pressure. However, regulations require it to be able to produce foam to extinguish an oil fire.

Water Spray Systems

Sprinkler System

An automatic fixed water sprinkler system uses a deflector plate to spread a jet of pressurised water into a spray of water droplets. The water is supplied from a part-filled freshwater tank, with the remaining space filled with pressurised air. When all the fresh water has been used, the source of water is automatically switched to the direct suction of sea water using an electric pump. Control valves are often situated at the pump manifolds in order to separate the system into specific zones and sprinkler heads are located in groups within these areas, each group having an associated alarm. Piping from the water tank transports a jet of water to the protected area and systems can be described as 'wet' (most common) or 'dry' depending on whether water is present in these pipes all the time or only during operation.

The fixed sprinkler system is automatically activated when a threshold temperature at the sprinkler head is reached. This heat activation occurs either by the breakage of a heat-sensitive glass bulb or the fusing of an element in the sprinkler head. Each sprinkler head operates independently of the others, localising the effect of the water spray. There are specific colour codes for sprinkler heads according to the operating temperature so that different sprinkler heads can be used depending on the zone to be protected. In accommodation and service spaces, an operational temperature range of 68°C to 79°C is used, but this can be increased for different areas. Spare sprinkler heads of all types and temperature ratings must be available on board. Activation of a sprinkler head automatically triggers both audio and visual alarms.

Glass bulb sprinkler heads		Fusible element sprinkler heads	
Threshold temperature (°C)	Colour code	Threshold temperature (°C)	Colour code
57	Orange	57 to 77	Uncoloured
68	Red		
79	Yellow		
93 to 100	Green	80 to 107	White

Water Mist and Deluge Systems

A fixed water mist system uses high pressure water in a fine aerosol spray that vaporises due to the heat energy in the air around

Water Spray Systems

the fire. This reduces the temperature of the combustion gases as well as replacing the oxygen near the fire and smothering it. These systems can be automatic (using glass bulbs as with sprinkler systems) or operated manually, and are installed in high-risk areas and considered equivalent to CO_2 systems. A water deluge system produces a concentrated flow of water to flood a particular area, cooling it more effectively than conventional sprinkler systems. The water in a deluge system is applied through an open-type head, meaning that they do not have a bulb that automatically triggers a flow of water when activated and are manually operated.

Fire Pumps

Fire pumps are needed to provide water for fire-extinguishing purposes at the appropriate pressure. The power for these pumps is supplied by a means other than the ship's main engines.

Emergency Fire Pumps

In addition to the standard fire pump arrangement, there is an emergency power source for emergency fire pumps. This is independent of the power system usually used and must be shielded from damage and situated away from the area it protects. Every cargo ship must have the following emergency fire pump arrangements:

- Emergency fire pump capacity must be ≥40% of the total required capacity of the fire pumps
- fire pump capacity for cargo ships of ≥2,000 gross tonnage must be ≥25 m^3/h and for cargo ships <2,000 gross tonnage must be ≥15 m^3/h
- ships must have the regulatory number of fire pumps shown in the tables below:

Size of cargo ship (gross tonnage)	Number of independently-driven fire pumps
≥1,000	At least 2
<1,000	At least 2 power-driven pumps, one of which shall be independently driven

Size of passenger ship (gross tonnage)	Number of independently-driven fire pumps
≥4,000	At least 3
<4,000	At least 2

- the emergency fire pump, its seawater inlet, suction and delivery pipes, and isolating valves must be located outside the machinery space
- any diesel-driven power source for the emergency fire pumps must be capable of a hand crank start in cold conditions (as low as 0°C) and when low temperatures are likely to occur suitable heating arrangements must be provided
- if a cold-start cannot be achieved by hand cranking, alternative arrangements must be made so that the diesel engine is started at least 6 times over a 30 minute period, and at least twice in the first 10 minutes
- there must be sufficient fuel present in the fuel tank of the diesel-driven power source for the emergency pump to run at full load for ≥3 hours. Sufficient reserve fuel must be available for the pump to run under the same conditions for a further 15 hours
- there must be correct ventilation and proper insulation where the power source is based.

Courtesy of Duncan Bruce

Fire Main and Hydrants

Fire mains and hydrants must:

- Either be constructed of heat and corrosion resistant material or be suitably protected
- have associated piping also protected from freezing and corrosion.

Fire Mains

- Five mains on board vessels ≥500 GT must be of sufficient diameter to enable effective distribution of the maximum required water output from two fire pumps operating at the same time, but they need only have a diameter sufficient for the output of 140 m^3/h of water.

Water Spray Systems

Hydrants

Hydrants must be positioned to:

- Allow immediate and easy accessibility, close to the access to the protected space. Access should not be hampered when deck cargo is carried. They should be positioned where they will not be damaged during cargo operations
- ensure that water from two different hydrants (at least two jets of water) can reach any area of the ship that passengers and crew normally access during a voyage or any part of an empty cargo space
- allow easy testing and maintenance, eg applying light grease to the covering cap thread to ensure easy running or replacing leaking hydrant gaskets.

Hydrants should:

- Have only hand-tightened valve wheel and the covering cap
- have interchangeable nozzles and couplings at each hydrant unless there is a fire hose and nozzle provided for each hydrant
- be fitted with screw lift or cock hydrant valves because these allow a fire hose to be isolated and removed while the fire pumps are operating
- have a hydrant pressure during operation of not less than that specified in the tables below (taken from SOLAS, 2009) and be of a level that one crew member can control a hose.

Size of cargo ship (gross tonnage)	Pressure at any hydrant in kPa (psi)
≥6,000	270 (39)
<6,000	250 (36.3)
≥1,000	
<1,000	

Size of passenger ship constructed on or after 1994 (gross tonnage)	Pressure at any hydrant in kPa (psi)
≥4,000	≥400
<4,000	>300

Drainage arrangements are very important to maintain ship stability and must:

- Be able to remove ≥125% of the combined capacity of water spray pumps and number of fire hose nozzles
- have valves that are situated close to extinguishing system controls and operable from outside the protected area.

Fire Hoses

Fire hoses must be made of a material that is resistant to wear and tear in harsh marine conditions, but crew must be alert for signs of deterioration. Extra hoses and nozzles must be available on board ships transporting dangerous goods. All hoses must have approved quick couplings, nozzle and coupling spanner. Fire hoses must be stowed with nozzles attached and be in a readily accessible position close to a hydrant. The number and length of hoses required are shown in the tables below:

Area on board	Length of fire hose (in metres)
Machinery spaces	≥10 m to ≤15 m
Other areas and open decks	≥10 m to ≤20 m
Open decks on vessels with a maximum breadth of >30 m	≥10 m to ≤25 m

Ship type and size	Number of hoses
All passenger ships	There must be at least one fire hose and nozzle per hydrant
Passenger ships with >36 passengers	Hydrants in interior locations must have a fire hose connected to the hydrant at all times
Cargo ships ≥1,000 GT	Must have one hose for every 30 metres of ship length and one spare, but must be ≥5 hoses in total. This total does not include those needed in the machinery spaces and boiler room
Cargo ships <1,000 GT	Must have one hose for every 30 metres of ship length and one spare, but must be ≥3 hoses in total

A major problem with lay-flat hoses, which are the standard type for ships, is the kinking that can occur when they are used around the narrow corners found on ships. This kinking can lead to reduced or complete loss of flow and cause high abrasion in the area of the kink. The best fire hoses are capable of bending around a 45 gallon drum at pressures between 3 and 5 bar without kinking.

Hose should not be subjected to any form of abuse in service and should be handled with reasonable care. It should not be dragged over sharp or abrasive surfaces unless specifically designed for such service. Care should be taken to protect hose from severe end loads for which the hose or hose assembly were not designed.

Hose should be used at or below its rated working pressure. Any changes in pressure should be made gradually so the hose is not subjected to excessive surge pressures.

Maintenance

All hoses should be washed through with fresh water after use. The outer hose can be cleaned with mild detergent solutions unless the makers specify special treatment.

After use, the hoses should be checked for any damage including bulges in the hose wall that indicate an internal weak spot.

The couplings should be checked for damage or any sign that they are bent out of shape. The threads should be cleaned of any debris and the gaskets inspected and changed if cracked or creased.

Care should be taken when storing rubber hose products because they can be affected adversely by temperature, humidity, ozone, sunlight, oils, solvents, corrosive liquids and fumes, insects, rodents and radioactive materials.

The appropriate method for storing hose depends to a great extent on its size (diameter and length), the quantity to be stored, and the way in which it is packaged. Hose should not be piled or stacked to such an extent that the weight of the stack creates distortions on the lengths stored at the bottom.

Where hoses are folded rather than set around a reel, the fold positions should be changed every six months. This is to prevent cracking of the hose liner at the folds.

All hoses should have water run through periodically. A system of rotation should be in use for exercise purposes. Under no circumstances should fire hoses be used for any other purposes, such as washing down, except in fire safety exercises.

All hoses should be air-dried before stowing away.

Nozzles

Dual Purpose

Dual purpose nozzles are common and make it easy to switch between a jet of water with a throw of at least 12 metres, and a curtain spray capable of providing a water barrier of 5 metres diameter at a range of 2 metres. The standard nozzle sizes for dual purpose nozzles are 12 mm, 16 mm or 19 mm but a larger diameter nozzle may be allowed. Accommodation and service spaces should use 12 mm nozzles, but machinery spaces and exterior locations should use a nozzle size that enables maximum output of water from two jets at a specified pressure from the smallest pump.

Smooth Bore Jet

This type still exists on a number of ships. While they are functional as a quick way to deliver a jet of water onto a fire or as cooling, they do not provide heat or flame protection and are fast being replaced in favour of the dual nozzle.

Fog Nozzles

This nozzle breaks up the water into water droplets that have more combined surface area than normal sprays. As these droplets absorb heat they turn to steam, which then smothers the fire by displacing the oxygen.

There are two types of fog nozzle; automatic and manual. The automatic nozzle self-adjusts the stream of droplets to the pressure of the water flow. This ensures that the stream shape is consistent. The manual nozzle has a flow rate adjustment setting and this allows the user to adjust the setting depending on the water pressure and the required rate of output.

The type of spray pattern can also be adjusted from a long reach narrow setting to a broad protective screen.

Water Spray Systems

Fire Main Lines

There are two basic types of fire main systems; a single main system and a looped system. The single main system has a single pipe running fore and aft with branch lines off this. The looped system has two lines running fore and aft connected at the bow and stern to form a continuous loop with branch lines extended from this to the various fire stations. The advantage of this system is that, if there is any damage to the fire main along the loop, the damaged part can be isolated and water continually supplied to other parts of the system.

Fresh water should be flushed through the deck lines every two months to clear the lines of salt build-up and encrustation around the hydrant outlets.

Main deck fire lines are fitted with drain valves that will allow the line to be cleared of water. On approaching freezing conditions, the deck line should be drained down to prevent freezing damage.

Guidelines for the Preparation of Fire Control Plans

No.	Rules SOLAS 74 incl. 2000 amend.	Subject
1.	II-2/15.2.4	**Fire Control Plans** Fire / Plan ***Fire control plan*** (Copies to be provided in the Wheelhouse, at the Mess Rooms and in a weathertight enclosure outside)
2.	II-2/3.9.1	**Fire Alarm Panel** ***Control panel for fire detection and alarm system*** (Located at central control station (e.g. Wheelhouse, E.C.R.))
3.	II-2/3.9.8	**Push Button/Switch for Fire Alarm** ***Push button/switch for general (fire) alarm*** (Located at central control station (e.g. Wheelhouse, E.C.R.))
4.	II-2/7.7	**Manually Operated Call Points** To be provided: – at each exit – in corridors each 40 m ***Manually operated call point***

No.	Rules SOLAS 74 incl. 2000 amend.	Subject
5.	II-2/7.5.1 7.5.5.1 7.5.5.2 7.5.5.3 7.4.1.1 7.4.1.2 II-2/19.3.3	**Fire Detection Systems** Installed in: – all stairways, corridors and escape routes – Method II-C and III-C - all accommodation and service spaces – Periodically unattended machinery spaces – Machinery spaces under remote control – Cargo spaces for dangerous goods in packaged form – RoRo – cargo spaces ***Space or group of spaces monitored by: smoke detector(s)*** ***Space or group of spaces monitored by heat detector(s)*** ***gas detector(s)*** ***flame detector(s)*** (Symbol "space monitored by gas detector" to be used for fixed gas detection systems on tankers only)

Guidelines for the Preparation of Fire Control Plans

No.	Rules SOLAS 74 incl. 2000 amend.	Subject
6.	II-2/10.4, 10.5, 10.6, 10.7, 10.9, 20.6.1.1	**CO_2 Fire Extinguishing System** 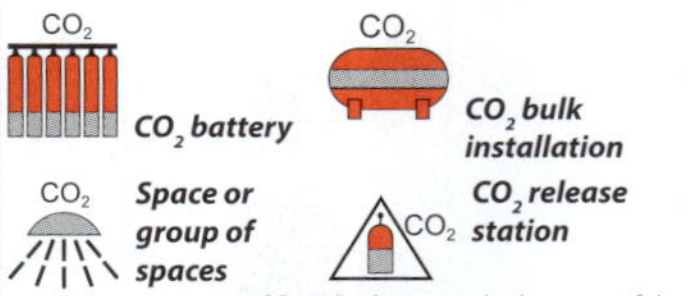 ***CO_2 battery*** ***CO_2 bulk installation*** ***Space or group of spaces protected by CO_2*** ***CO_2 release station*** *(Indicate at the bottom of the symbol the space protected)* (Galley range exhaust duct – it shall be indicated that the system protects the duct only)
7.	II-2/10.4, 10.5, 10.6, 10.7, 10.9	**Halon Fire Extinguishing System** (Permitted on ships with keel laying before 01.10.1994 only. On all ships under EC–flag, halon is prohibited since 01.01.2004) 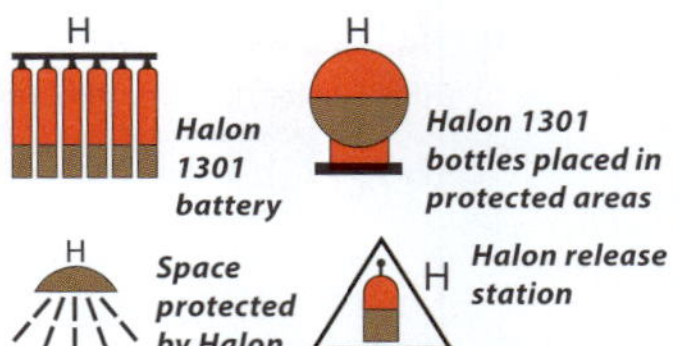 ***Halon 1301 battery*** ***Halon 1301 bottles placed in protected areas*** ***Space protected by Halon 1301*** ***Halon release station*** *(Indicate at the bottom of the symbol the space protected)* The same symbols may be used for fire-extinguishing systems using other gases than halon (e.g. FM200). The indexes **H** and **Halon 1301** are to be replaced accordingly.
8.	II-2/10.4, 10.5, 10.6, 10.7, 10.9, 20.6.1.1	**High-expansion Foam System** 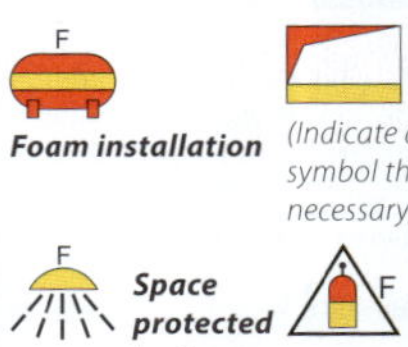 ***Foam installation*** ***High-expansion foam supply trunk*** *(Indicate at the bottom of the symbol the protected space, if necessary)* ***Space protected by foam*** ***Foam release station*** *(Indicate at the bottom of the symbol the space protected)*
9.	IGC Code 11.4	**Dry Chemical Powder Fire-extinguishing System** (Gas Tanker, Chemical Tanker) 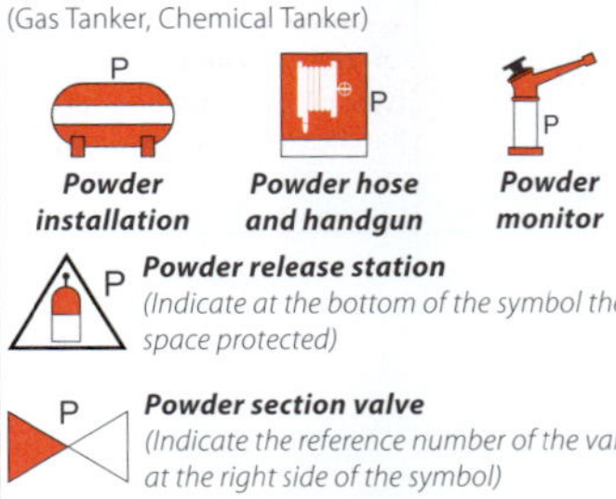 ***Powder installation*** ***Powder hose and handgun*** ***Powder monitor*** ***Powder release station*** *(Indicate at the bottom of the symbol the space protected)* ***Powder section valve*** *(Indicate the reference number of the valve at the right side of the symbol)*

No.	Rules SOLAS 74 incl. 2000 amend.	Subject
10.	II-2/10.5.6, 10.6.4, 10.6, 10.7, 10.8 18.5.1.3 IBC Code 11.3	**Low-Expansion Foam System** (local application, deck system on tanker) 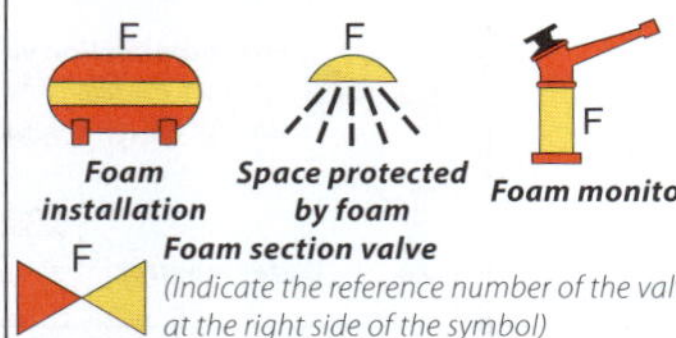 ***Foam installation*** ***Space protected by foam*** ***Foam monitor*** ***Foam section valve*** *(Indicate the reference number of the valve at the right side of the symbol)*
11.	- II-2/10.6.2 - II-2/10.6.3 - IMO Res. MEPC.76(40)	**Automatic Sprinkler System** (Heat released sprinkler nozzles, normally fitted with glass bulbs) Installed in – Method II-C – all accommodation and service spaces – combined incinerator and waste storage space – waste storage space  ***Sprinkler installation*** ***Space or group of spaces protected by sprinkler*** ***Sprinkler section valve*** *(Indicate the reference number of the valve at the right side of the symbol. Valves for automatic dry-pipe sprinkler systems should be indicated in the legend)* The symbols may also be applied to equivalent water-extinguishing systems (water mist systems)
12.	II-2/10.4, 10.5, 10.6, 19.3.9 20.6.1.4 IGC Code 11.3	**Drenching System** (Water-spray system, open nozzle type)  ***Space protected by drenching system*** ***Water spray system valves*** *(Indicate at the bottom of the symbol the protected space, if necessary)* – machinery space total flooding system (e.g. water mist system) – water spraying system for RoRo-cargo spaces – water spraying system for paint store, cargo spaces for carriage of dangerous goods of Class 1; gas tankers: cargo tank deck and boundaries of superstructure.
13.	II-2/10.2, 19.3.1	**Water Supply System** 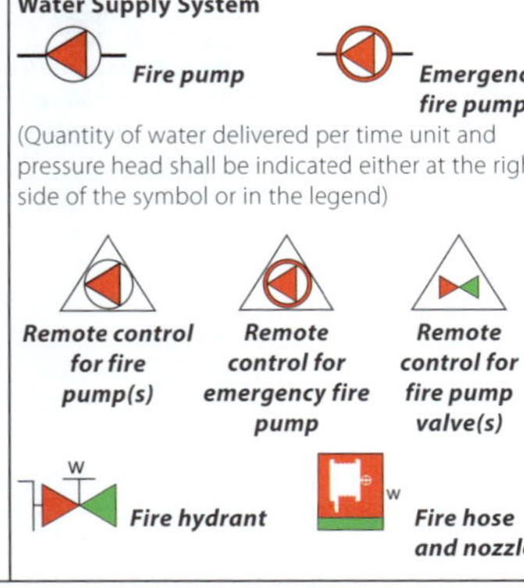 ***Fire pump*** ***Emergency fire pump*** (Quantity of water delivered per time unit and pressure head shall be indicated either at the right side of the symbol or in the legend) ***Remote control for fire pump(s)*** ***Remote control for emergency fire pump*** ***Remote control for fire pump valve(s)*** ***Fire hydrant*** ***Fire hose and nozzle***

Guidelines for the Preparation of Fire Control Plans

No.	Rules SOLAS 74 incl. 2000 amend.	Subject
	10.2.3	(Indicate the hose length at the right side of the symbol; where only one type of hose is used, this information can be shown in the legend) 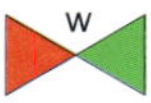 ***Fire main section valve*** *(Indicate the reference number of the valve at the right side of the symbol)*
	10.2.1.7	 ***Water monitor*** 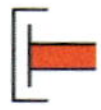 ***International shore connection***
14.	II-2/10.5.6,	**Fixed Water-based Local Application Fire-Fighting System**  ***Fixed water-based local application fire-fighting system, incl. flame detectors for automatic release* and local manual release*** (Required, for ships with keel laying on or after 01.07.2002, in machinery spaces of category A above 500 m^3 on cargo ships of 2,000 GT and above) ** not applicable in manned machinery spaces*
15.	II-2/10.6.4,	**Fixed Fire-Extinguishing System for Deep Fat Cooking Equipment**  ***Fixed fire-extinguishing system for deep fat cooking equipment*** *(The extinguishing media should be colour coded and indicated by a letter)* (required for new installation on all ships on or after 1.07.2002)
16.	II-2/ 10.5.2.2.1 20.6.2.2	**Water Fog – and Foam Applicator**  ***Water fog applicator***  ***Portable foam applicator unit*** *(For ships with keel laying on or after 01.09.1984 only)*
17.	II-2/5.2.2.3/4 II-2/5.2.3.1	**Remote Control of Pumps and Valves** 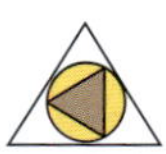 ***Fuel oil pump(s) remote shut-off*** 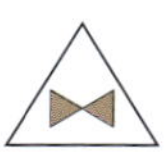 ***Remote control for fuel oil valves*** 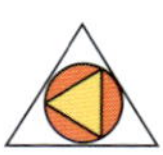 ***Lube oil pump(s) remote shut-off*** 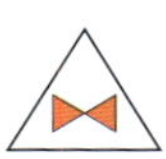 ***Remote control for lube oil valves***  ***Remote control for bilge pump(s)***  ***Remote control for emergency bilge pumps***
18.	II-2/10.3 10.5, 18.5, 19.3.7, 20.6.2 II-2/10.3.3	**Fire Extinguisher** (portable and wheeled)  F 6 L ***Fire extinguisher***  F 50 L ***Wheeled fire extinguisher*** (Indicate type of media and capacity (kg for gas and powder, litres for water and foam) at the right side of the symbol; dry powder and CO_2 extinguisher shall have a minimum capacity of 5 kg (except those in lifeboats with 2 kg min.); foam and water extinguisher shall have a minimum capacity of 9 l, CO_2 extinguishers not to be arranged in corridors of accommodation – spare charge capacities to be indicated in the legend)
19.	II-2/10.10 IGC Code 11.6 II-2/19.3.6 IBC Code 14.1; 14.2 IGC Code 14.2; 14.4.4	**Fire Locker** (Locker containing firefighters' outfits, portable fire-fighting equipment and relevant spare parts)  ***Fire locker*** (Indicate the number of the fire locker at the right side of the symbol. The principal contents of each locker should be indicated in the legend) *Firefighters' outfits* – Cargo ships: at least 2 complete sets – Tanker: at least 4 complete sets *Personal protection* – 4 sets full protective clothing, resistant to chemical attack – 2 sets self-contained breathing apparatus
20.	II-2/13.3.4, 13.4.3 IBC Code 14.2.8 IGC Code 14.4.2	**Emergency Escape Breathing Device (EEBD)**  ***Emergency Escape Breathing Device*** *(EEBD)* (Indicate the quantity of the EEBDs stowed at the right side of the symbol. Training devices shall be indicated with **TRAINING.** Spare devices should be indicated with **SPARE.**)
21.	II-2/13	**Means of Escape**  ***Primary escape route***  ***Secondary escape route*** (Indication at the relevant doors)
22.	II-2/9.2.3, 9.2.4	**A- and B- class Divisions** ***A- class division*** ***B-class division*** (Minimum line point size of 2¼, indication of the fire class e.g. A-60 is not required, only walls to be indicated in the deck-view, decks may be shown in the side view)

No.	Rules SOLAS 74 incl. 2000 amend.	Subject
23.	II-2/9.4.2	**A- and B- class Fire Doors**  ***A-class hinged fire door***  ***A-class hinged self-closing fire door***  ***A-class sliding fire door***  ***A-class self-closing sliding fire door***  ***B-class hinged fire door***  ***B-class hinged self-closing fire door***  ***B-class sliding fire door*** 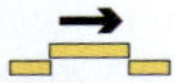 ***B-class self-closing sliding fire door*** (The symbol should be at the door position and should show the actual direction of the door, indication of the fire class e.g. A-60 is not required) Add **WT** to the right side of the symbol in case of a watertight door. Add **SWT** to the right side of the symbol in case of a semi-watertight door. 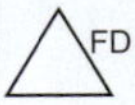 ***Remote control for fire doors or watertight doors*** Add **WT** to the right side of the symbol to indicate remote control for watertight doors or **FD** to indicate remote control for fire doors.
24.	II-2/9.7	**Ventilation Systems** 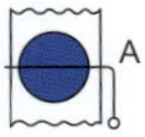 ***Fire damper*** (in ventilation ducts)  ***Closing device for ventilation inlet or outlet*** (for the exterior ventilation openings)  ***Remote control for fire damper(s)***  ***Remote control for closing device(s) for ventilation inlet or outlet***  ***Ventilation remote control or shut-off*** 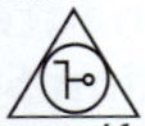 ***Remote control for skylights*** (Colour and/or letter on the right side as follows: **A** = blue – for accommodation and service spaces **M** = green – for machinery spaces **C** = yellow – for cargo spaces)

No.	Rules SOLAS 74 incl. 2000 amend.	Subject
25.	II-2/4.5.5	**Inert Gas System**  ***Inert gas installation***
26.	II-1/43	**Emergency Source of Electrical Power**  ***Emergency source of electrical power (generator)***  ***(battery)***  ***Emergency switch board***
27.		**Air Compressor for Breathing Devices**  ***Air compressor for breathing devices***

Extinguishing media should be colour coded and indicated by a letter as follows:

- carbon dioxide — grey – **CO_2**
- nitrogen — grey – **N**
- gas other than CO_2 or N — brown – **H** (type of gas to be indicated)
- foam — yellow – **F**
- powder — white – **P**
- water — green – **W**
- sprinkler — green – **S**
  (or high pressure water-extinguishing systems)

Fire Testing Requirements of Fire-Fighting Equipment

Hydrants

The fire hydrants, particularly on exposed weather deck and work areas, are susceptible to damage, especially the valve wheel. Both the valve wheel and the covering cap must only be hand-tightened. The outlet covers are secured by a retaining chain which corrodes over time. Occasionally these go missing. The wheel can be broken by excessive force with tools or if it is knocked during cargo operations. Spares should be carried for this eventuality.

Over time hydrants can leak and, when this occurs, the gaskets must be replaced. Wrenches are often used to tighten the control wheel and the outlet caps in an attempt to stop the leak, which means that the hydrant is no longer capable of manual operation.

Testing of hydrants must be carried out monthly. This can be rotated as part of the ship's fire exercise. Before replacing the outlet caps, the thread should be coated with a light grease.

Each hydrant should be considered as a fire station. They must be immediately accessible and ready in all respects to provide water. The hose boxes and their contents must be nearby and ready for use, and all the ship's crew should know their positions around the ship.

Hoses

Hose has a limited life and the user must be alert to signs of impending failure, particularly when the conditions of service include high working pressures and/or the conveyance or containment of hazardous materials. The periodic inspection and testing procedures described here constitute the minimum level of action to detect signs of hose deterioration or loss of performance before conditions leading to malfunction or failure are reached.

An inspection and hydrostatic test should be made at periodic intervals to determine whether a hose is suitable for continued service.

A visual inspection of the hose should be made for loose covers, kinks, bulges or soft spots, which might indicate broken or displaced reinforcement.

The couplings or fittings should be closely examined and, if there is any sign of movement of the hose from the couplings, the hose should be removed from service.

The periodic inspection should include a hydrostatic test for one minute at 150% of the recommended working pressure of the hose.

Fire Main

A ship's fire main is designed for a typical working pressure of about 10 bars. During a ship's initial survey, where the working pressure in the fire main at the pump discharge exceeds 7 bars, the individual lengths of pipe, fittings and valves comprising the fire main should be tested to twice the maximum working pressure to which the system can be subjected when in service. Once these tests have been satisfactorily completed, the fire main need only be subjected to the maximum pressure attainable by the fire pumps under normal service conditions.

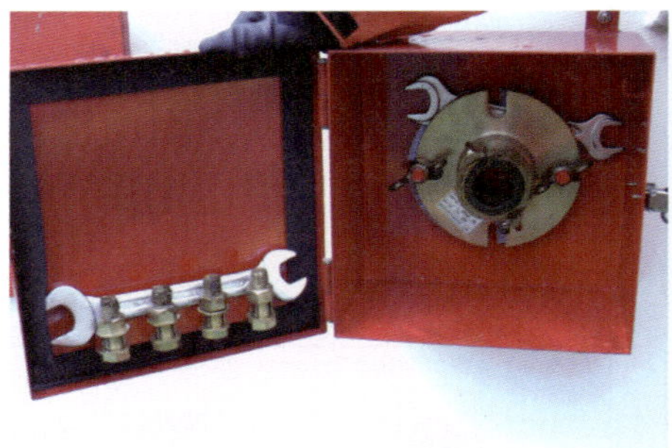

Courtesy Duncan Bruce

Chapter II-2, Regulation 4 of the SOLAS Convention states that during tests the nozzle size shall be such as to obtain the maximum discharge flow possible from two fire hose jets at the pressure mentioned.

Maintenance and Inspection of Fire Protection Systems and Appliances

Maintenance and Testing

On board instructions for maintenance and testing of passive fire protection systems and appliances must be easy to understand and illustrated. These instructions should include:

- Maintenance and repair instructions
- schedule of periodic maintenance
- list of replaceable parts
- a log of the inspections and maintenance carried out.

Weekly Testing and Inspections

These should be carried out to ensure that:

- All public address systems and general alarm systems are working correctly
- there are no leaks in the breathing apparatus.

Monthly Examinations and Inspections

Ships' officers are responsible for carrying out monthly inspections of the fire-fighting equipment. The results of the inspection must be recorded in the ship's logbook. These should be carried out to ensure:

- All firefighters' outfits, fire extinguishers, fire hydrants, hoses and nozzles are in the correct place and in working order
- all fixed fire-fighting system stop valves are in the correct closed or open position
- dry pipe sprinkler systems have the correct pressure
- sprinkler system pressure tanks have the correct level of water
- all fire pumps are operational
- there are no leaks in the fixed fire extinguisher installations that use gas.

Quarterly Inspections and Tests

The ship's officers are responsible for carrying out the quarterly tests and inspections of the fire-fighting system equipment, the results should be recorded in the ship's logbook. These inspections should ensure that:

- All the sprinkler system automatic alarms are tested using the test valves in each section
- the international shore connection is in good condition
- there is an inventory where the fire-fighting equipment is stored and the equipment is in good order
- the fire doors and fire dampers can be operated locally
- all CO_2 bottle connections for cable operating system clips fit tightly on fixed fire-extinguishing systems.

Annual Tests and Inspections

As part of the annual statutory survey for Safety Equipment Certification, the following inspections and tests should be carried out:

- All fire extinguishers are checked for location, charging pressure and condition
- fire detection systems are tested and are operating correctly
- all fire doors and dampers are tested for remote operation
- all foam water and water spray fixed fire-fighting systems are tested and are operating correctly
- all accessible components of fixed fire-fighting systems are visually checked for their condition
- all fire pumps, including sprinkler system pumps, are flow tested for correct pressure and flow
- all hydrants are checked and working
- antifreeze system is checked to ensure it has the correct solution
- sprinkler system connections from the ship's main are operating
- all fire hoses are hydrostatically tested
- air quality for all breathing apparatus air recharging systems is checked
- control valves of the fixed fire-fighting system are inspected
- air is blown through the piping of the extinguishing gas system.

Five-Year Service

The control valves of the fixed fire-fighting system should be inspected internally and tested every five years.

Fire Equipment Location

As per SOLAS Chapter II-2 Regulation 13, fire equipment should be permanently marked with the appropriate symbols in an easily visible place and lit by emergency lighting or a photo-luminescent material. Each portable extinguisher should be marked and their use identified. If various types of fire-fighting equipment is stored in one area, there should be signs stating "Fire Point".

Hydrostatic Pressure Testing of CO_2 and Halon Gas Cylinders

- Monthly inspection should be carried out of the overall system, to include:
  - verification that stop valves are in the closed position

Fire Testing Requirements of Fire-Fighting Equipment

- release controls are in the proper position
- discharge piping and pneumatic tubing are intact
- cylinders are in place and secure
- alarms do not appear damaged

- low pressure CO_2 systems inspections should verify that:
  - the pressure gauge is in the normal range
  - the liquid level indicator is within the proper level
  - the manual storage tank main valve is secured in the open position
  - the vapour supply line valve is secured open
- annual inspection and maintenance is to be carried out in accordance with the system manufacturer's instructions and safety precautions. This should include:
  - visual inspection of the boundaries of the protected space for any modifications that could have created unclosable openings, rendering the system ineffective
  - inspection of all storage containers for any signs of damage
  - inspection for signs of rust or loose mounting hardware
  - hydrostatic testing or replacement of cylinders that are leaking, corroded, dented or bulging
  - visible inspection of system piping to check for damage, loose supports and corrosion
  - inspection of all flexible discharge hoses to ensure that nozzles and fittings are properly tightened.

Minimum maintenance:

- At least biennially (intervals of 2 years ±3 months) in passenger ships or at each intermediate periodical or renewal survey in cargo ships, the following maintenance should be carried out:
  - all high pressure cylinders and pilot cylinders should be weighed and contents verified by reliable means
  - cylinders containing less than 90% of the nominal charge should be refilled
  - liquid level of low level storage tanks should be checked to verify that the required amount of CO_2 to protect against the largest hazard is available
- high pressure cylinders should be subjected to periodical tests at intervals not exceeding 10 years
- every 10 years, at least 10% of the total number of cylinders provided should be subjected to an internal inspection and hydrostatic test
- should one or more cylinders fail, a total of 50% of the onboard cylinders should be tested
- all cylinders should be tested should any more fail.

All cylinders should be hydrostatically tested 20 years after the date of manufacture and every 5 years thereafter. A record of the hydraulic pressure test must be legibly marked on the cylinder.

Any cylinder that has been discharged, or has a reduction in pressure of ≥10 from the original stated pressure, or shows signs of corrosion must be inspected, hydrostatically tested and replaced or recharged.

Specific requirements for halon gas:

- Installation of halon gas systems on new builds is prohibited. The installation of new halon gas systems on existing vessels is also prohibited
- the international community is committed to reducing the use of halon gas and other ozone-depleting gases. This effort and restrictions on halon gas use is found in the Montreal Protocol, IMO Resolution A.655(16) and A.719(17) and in guidance in IMO MSC Circulars 600 and 775
- currently there is no internationally agreed date for the phasing out of halon
- it should be noted that worldwide stocks of halon are diminishing and therefore replacement for the halon gas system should be sought (IMO FP.1/Circ.33).

Portable Fire Extinguishers

FSS Code Chapter 4 | MSC/Circ.850 | IMO | Res.A951(23):

- All fire extinguishers shall be examined annually by a qualified and experienced competent person
- records of the examinations shall be retained on board
- containers for permanently pressurised fire extinguishers, propellant bottles of non-pressurised extinguishers and other extinguishers must be hydraulically pressure tested at intervals of 10 years
- containers of non-pressurised extinguishers shall also be tested at intervals of 10 years
- if the loss of gas or charge from any type of extinguisher exceeds 10% of the original charge, it must be inspected and recharged
- any extinguisher bottle with excessive corrosion must be replaced.

Spare charges:

- The minimum number of spare charges carried on board for portable fire extinguishers shall be in accordance with SOLAS Chapter II-2:
  - 100% for the first 10 extinguishers
  - 50% for the remaining extinguishers up to a maximum of 60
  - additional extinguishers of the same type and capacity shall be carried in lieu of spare charges for any extinguishers that cannot be charged on board the ship.

Additional Survey Requirements

In surveying the safety equipment on a vessel, Recognised Organisations shall verify that:

- All fire-fighting equipment has been inspected and maintained in accordance with the manufacturer's instructions
- the manufacturer's maintenance instructions are on board
- records of inspections, maintenance and pressure tests are maintained
- spare charges are provided in accordance with SOLAS requirements.

Records

Records shall be maintained on board of:

- Annual inspections
- other maintenance and testing
- deficiencies identified and corrective actions performed.

CHAPTER 39

Shipboard Drills

Shipboard Drills

Introduction

Conducting drills at regular intervals is the best way to prepare crew to deal with likely emergency situations that may arise on board. When planning a drill, it is better to have a meaningful one where the crew use the life-saving and fire-fighting systems on board, as this will build confidence that the systems will work effectively in an emergency.

It is the responsibility of each crew member to know where their emergency station is and what their responsibilities are for each drill or emergency. Nobody should be excused from drills unless their attention is required elsewhere for operational or safety reasons, and then only with permission from the master.

Conducting frequent drills provides the crew with the opportunity to practise their roles and gain experience and confidence in the safety equipment in addition to developing as a team.

Frequent crew changes can make it difficult to ensure that all the crew have taken part in drills. It is therefore important that drill scheduling is properly implemented and adhered to. Where possible, any available time in port or while awaiting orders should be used to conduct drills so that the ship's business is not delayed.

In order for drills to have the best benefit, it is important that the skills are exercised regularly. This is why there is a mandate for both statutory and non-statutory drills. Therefore, where possible, drills should be held each week to either meet or exceed the requirements of the flag State and other guidelines.

Each drill should be planned to ensure that, on a rotating basis, all safety equipment is used and training is given in its use. They should never be regarded as an obligatory task that is merely carried out to meet regulatory requirements. Whether they are emergency drills required by SOLAS or additional drills designed to improve crew competence, they should be carried out with the same amount of diligence and seriousness. They should not be rushed; regular practice will improve the efficiency in performing the tasks. Remember, a drill can be paused, so that any difficult elements can be explained. The crew's experience is important in determining how quickly a drill or certain elements of a drill can be carried out.

SOLAS requires drills to be conducted, where possible, as if it were an actual emergency. It is important that drills are carried out in a safe manner, and therefore any elements that may involve unnecessary risk will require special attention or should be removed from the drill.

In an actual emergency situation, crew can become very afraid. However, experience has shown that crew members who regularly train and exercise in safety drills:

- Are less frightened
- do not panic
- respond in a controlled manner
- do exactly what they have been trained to do
- handle a situation much better than they did before the training.

Regular drills will:

- Test and improve emergency plans and procedures
- reveal any weaknesses or omissions in the ship's emergency plans
- highlight any deficiencies in the emergency equipment
- reveal any gaps in resources
- improve communication
- clarify an individual's role and responsibilities
- improve both individual and team performance
- improve the process of managing emergencies
- meet or exceed regulatory requirements.

Conducting an Effective Drill

Before conducting a training exercise, the equipment to be used should be thoroughly examined to ensure that it is safe to use. There have been many tragic accidents, particularly during lifeboat drills, and utmost care must always be exercised.

Training and drills may reveal a need for further training ashore and this should be reported to the Company. Should you consider that additional training materials are required, the Company should be informed.

Consideration should be given to scenarios where a complete walkthrough of the drill may be merited before actually conducting the drill, particularly after a large crew change or if the drill is more complicated in nature.

General Drill Considerations

- Practise different scenarios based on existing risks and the specific cargo that is being carried
- practise different response procedures
- practise drills under varying conditions
- provide advance notice of the drill scenario to those involved in the exercise
- what lessons can be learned from the drill?
- identify weaknesses and the remedial action required.

Drills should be:

- As realistic as possible – this will help reduce fear in the event of an emergency situation
- carried out wearing full emergency equipment, where possible, to familiarise the crew with it
- recorded in the appropriate logbook
- recorded in crew's individual training records.

Exercises should be designed to ensure that they provide crew training that includes, but is not limited to, the following:

- Use of survival craft and rescue boats
- survival techniques
- effects and treatment of hypothermia
- first aid
- use of fire-fighting appliances, refilling of extinguishers
- use of breathing apparatus
- smoke/fume filled atmospheres
- search procedures within spaces
- control of passengers
- donning and use of fire-fighting and chemical suits
- opening of access to spaces
- entry into spaces on fire
- effective fire-fighting techniques
- boundary cooling
- quick closing valves and remote stops.

Any single exercise could incorporate several of the above items.

Preparing a Drills Schedule

The safety officer, directed by the master, should draw up a schedule of emergency drills and exercises, taking into account SOLAS, MARPOL and the requirements of the flag State.

The schedule of drills and exercises (including training as required for statutory drills) includes:

Shipboard Drills

Drill	Every 2 Weeks	Every 2 Months	Every 3 Months
Abandon Ship Drill - Muster	✔		
Fire	✔		
Enclosed Space Rescue Drill*		✔	
Lifeboat launched and manoeuvred in water			✔
Lifeboat (Free-fall)**			✔
Rescue Boat Drill			✔
Emergency Steering			✔
Security Drill as per ISPS			✔

Table 39.1 - Statutory shipboard drills and frequency

* 1st January 2015: An amendment to SOLAS Regulation III/19, on emergency training and drills, makes mandatory the carrying out of enclosed space entry and rescue drills, which will require crew members with enclosed space entry or rescue responsibilities to participate in an enclosed space entry and rescue drill at least once every 2 months.

** Free-fall lifeboats can be launched every 6 months if lowered every 3 months, or extended to 12 months if simulation requirements are met.

Note: Some exercises may require the Company and ship's security officers, port facility security officers and relevant authorities of the Contracted Government to participate. These exercises should be carried out at least once a year but, common to all training and drill regimes, there is a substantial advantage to be gained if crew are trained more frequently than the minimum requirements. These drills specifically test communication, coordination, resource availability and response and, where circumstances permit, such drills should be unannounced.

Some additional safety drills that may be carried out include:

Drill	Monthly	On change of command	Every 3 Months	Every 6 Months	Annually
Oil Spill	✔				
Personal Injury and First Aid	✔				
Anti-Piracy	✔				
First Alert Notification		✔			
Main Engine Control Failure			✔		
Toxic Vapour Release			✔		
Main Engine/Power Failure			✔		
Helicopter				✔	
Grounding/Stranding				✔	
Man Overboard				✔	
Collision				✔	
Break Away From Berth				✔	
Hull Damage/Flooding					✔
Emergency Towing					✔

Table 39.2 - Non-statutory drills and their suggested frequency

Note: The requirement for non-statutory drills will be prescribed in the Safety Management System (SMS) and will reflect the company's requirements.

Debrief After the Drill

A debrief meeting should be held to analyse the drill action and performance.

Items to consider during a drill debrief include:

- Exercise overview
- exercise goals and objectives
- how the drill was carried out
- the key lessons learned from the drill
- whether the teams were able to perform critical tasks appointed to them
- equipment used and any comments
- for specific drill procedures, what can be improved or what should have been done better
- any areas where further training is required.

Benefits of a Debrief:

- **Identifies any areas for improvement**
- **demonstrates proactive response management**
- **provides documentation for any future litigation.**

Note: A debrief should, for the same reasons, also be conducted after any emergency on board.

Port State Control inspections often focus on familiarisation with lifeboat and fire drills. The crew should be well trained in these drills as well as in operating emergency fire generators and pumps. They should also be familiar with emergency procedures concerning:

- Hot work incidents
- galley emergencies
- electrical incidents
- incinerator problems
- oil leaks and spills.

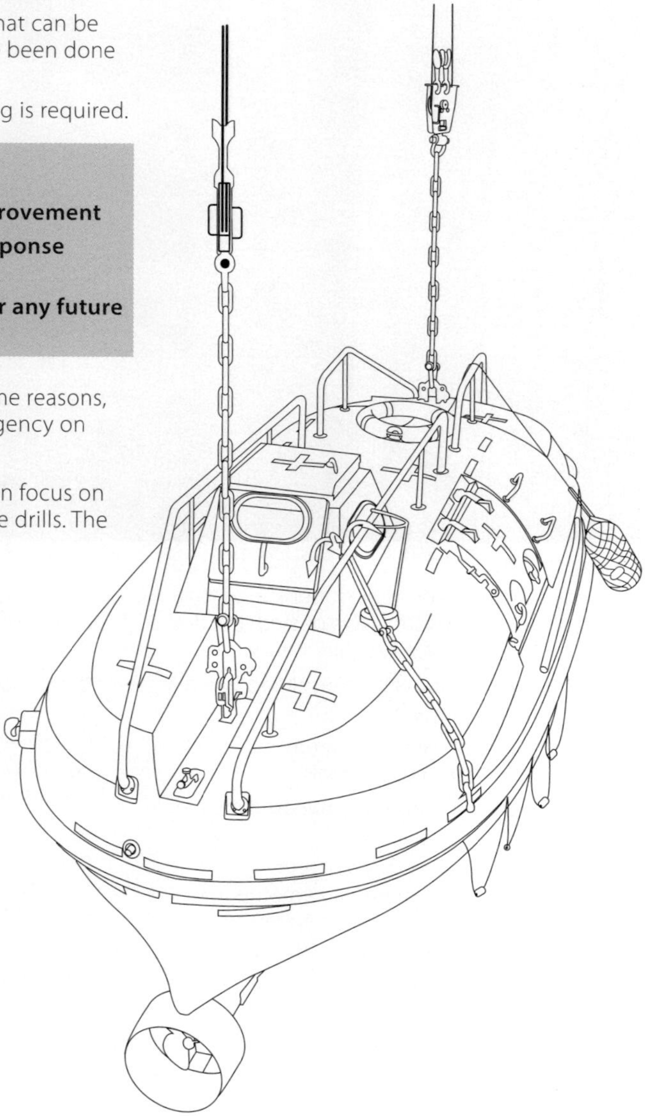

The Muster List

If more than 25% of the crew change, an abandon ship drill and a fire drill should be completed within 24 hours after leaving port. If it is not practical to hold full drills, musters should be held within the 24 hours, with instruction given to the crew on their emergency duties and on abandon ship procedures.

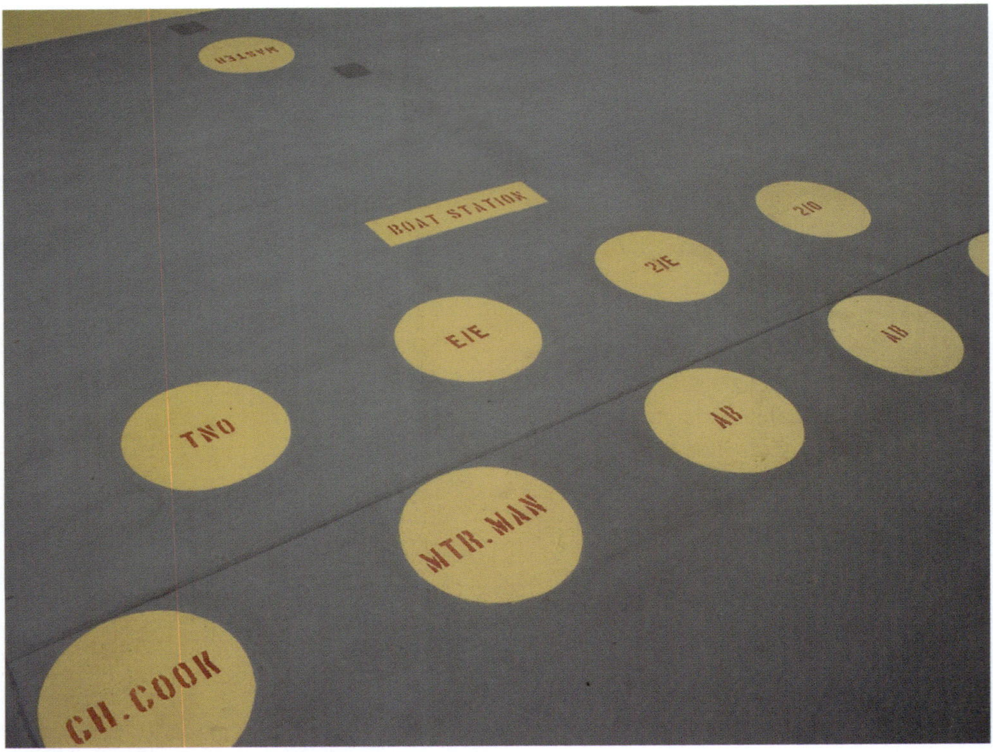

- The master is responsible for ensuring that an up-to-date muster list is posted and that it conforms to SOLAS requirements
- the following should be considered when a muster list is prepared:
  - proximity of each crew member's cabin to their respective lifeboat
  - each crew member's nominated muster station
  - each crew member's role and responsibilities during an emergency. Examples include closing watertight doors, fire doors, valves, scuppers and skylights
- muster lists should be posted on the bridge, emergency HQ, engine room, each accommodation alleyway and at the port and starboard side alleyways on the lifeboat deck
- there should be clear instructions on board in English and, if necessary, also in the official language on board
- crew members' duties on the muster list should not overlap
- each lifeboat should have a deck officer or person in charge who is certified as proficient in survival craft. Lifeboats require a second in command as well as someone who can carry out minor engine repairs
- the person in charge of each lifeboat should have a list of their assigned crew.

Lifeboat Drills

The master must ensure that the person in charge of each lifeboat is notified before the drill, so that any necessary preparations prior to swinging out or lowering the lifeboats can be made. Once the lifeboat drill is complete, the master should record it in the logbook and official logbook and make any other reports as necessary.

Suggested Drill Format

- On hearing the general alarm (and public address), all crew members should go to their lifeboat station and muster
- for an abandon ship drill, all crew should be appropriately dressed and wearing a lifejacket
- those present should be checked and given instruction in accordance with their lifeboat muster duties
- prepare the lifeboat for lowering
- check whether or not the gripes will be thrown clear when the boat is swung out. If not, they should be removed manually
- once the lifeboat is ready, the OIC should inform the master that the lifeboat is ready to launch
- only once the master has instructed should the lifeboats be swung out or lowered to the embarkation deck from their stowed position
- the lifeboat engine should be started
- once the drill is completed, the lifeboat should be returned to its stowed position and, if FPDs were fitted, these should be removed
- ensure the lifeboat is ready for immediate use.

If Lowering to the Water

- Check it is clear overside
- when the lifeboat is lowered into the water, the falls and painter are released
- once in the water, the lifeboat should be tested with some manoeuvres
- prior to lifting the lifeboat out of the water, the hooks should be correctly reset and the locking pin secured
- once the lifeboat is lifted 1 metre clear of the water, check the hooks are secure and that the falls and any other associated equipment are clear and in good order
- the emergency lighting for the muster area should also be checked
- once the drill is completed, a debrief should be carried out with the crew.

Abandon Ship Drill (Additional Considerations)

- Have crew prepare for abandonment:
  - muster check all crew, who should be wearing warm clothing, lifejackets or survival suits where appropriate
  - bring additional equipment to the embarkation deck, eg blankets, first aid kit, torches, distress flares, etc
- simulate activation of EPIRB and SART and bring to the lifeboats
- take voyage data recorder (VDR) cassette if possible
- consider whether embarkation ladders are deployed such that the ship can be reboarded (if necessary)
- consider whether the crew know how they would receive the order to abandon ship?

Considerations for Free-fall Lifeboats

Free-fall Lifeboat Drill

- Drills with free-fall lifeboats should be carried out according to the manufacturer's instructions
- instruct crew on the correct method of embarking the boat
- crew must take their seats in the correct manner
- crew must fasten their seat belts
- crew should be instructed on how to act during launch into the sea
- when the lifeboat is free-fall launched as part of a drill, this should be carried out with the minimum personnel required to manoeuvre the boat in the water and to recover it
- the recovery operation should be carried out with special attention as this operation has a high level of risk.

Guidelines for Simulated Launching of Free-fall Lifeboats

Simulated launching is a means of training the crew in the free-fall release procedure for free-fall lifeboats. It also verifies the satisfactory function of the free-fall release system without allowing the lifeboat to fall into the sea.

Where permitted, simulated launching should be carried out in accordance with the manufacturer's instructions, taking note of available guidance.

Simulated launching should be carried out under the supervision of a responsible person, who should be an officer experienced in such procedures.

Consideration should be given to the correct operation of the on-load release mechanism, the experience of the crew and the use of FPDs.

Typical Simulated Launching Sequence

- Check equipment and documentation to ensure that all components of the lifeboat and launching appliance are in good operational condition
- ensure that the restraining device(s) provided by the manufacturer for simulated launching are installed and secure and that the free-fall release mechanism is fully and correctly engaged
- establish and maintain good communication between the assigned operating crew and the responsible person
- disengage lashings, gripes, etc installed to secure the lifeboat for sea or for maintenance, except those required for simulated free-fall
- participating crew should board the lifeboat and fasten their seat belts under the supervision of the responsible person
- all crew, except the assigned operating crew, should disembark the lifeboat. The assigned operating crew should fully prepare the lifeboat for free-fall launch and secure themselves in their seats for the release operation
- the assigned operating crew should activate the release mechanism when instructed by the responsible person. It should be ensured that the release mechanism operates satisfactorily and, if applicable, that the lifeboat travels down the ramp to the distance specified in the manufacturer's instructions

- the lifeboat should be re-secured to its stowed position using the means provided by the manufacturer. The free-fall release mechanism should be fully and correctly engaged
- the lifeboat should be returned to its normal stowed condition. Any restraining and/or recovery devices used for the simulated launch procedure should be removed.
- the lifeboat should be verified as ready for launching in an emergency.

Ref: MCA Merchant Shipping Notice MSN 1803 (M)

Safety Drill Debrief

This may be conducted in conjunction with an accompanying fire drill debrief. It should be conducted as soon as the drill is completed, while adrenaline levels are still high and memories are fresh.

In no particular order, some of the general points that should be covered are:

- What have we learned?
- what went well?
- what did not go so well?
- did everyone know their role?
- how were communications?
- record of experience, ie how many minutes to bring the lifeboat to the embarkation deck?
- other suggested improvements?
- are the tasks well suited to the assigned crew?

Rescue Boat Drill

The rescue boat crew should fully understand how to lower the rescue boat and use all of the rescue boat's equipment, including the release hook arrangement.

Before lowering the boat, the charging cable should be disconnected and the battery switched on. It is important that the engine is maintained and is ready to start, ie the fuel tank should be fitted, the fuel valve open, batteries charged and the fuel hose connected to the tank with the ventilation screw open if necessary.

Suggested Drill Format

- The launch area should be checked to ensure it is clear of any obstructions. Notify the bridge
- check the painter and ensure that the hoisting arrangement is connected tight with the davit
- the fenders should be checked

Rescue Boat Drill

- the davits and lashings should be prepared for lowering
- the rescue boat crew enter the rescue boat and seat themselves evenly so that the rescue boat will remain balanced
- the rescue boat's lashings should be released and secured so that they do not interfere with launching
- the rescue boat should be lowered into the water according to the manufacturer's instructions
- prepare and then release the hook
  Note: This is a dangerous procedure as the release lever can drop the boat. It is important that this stage is carried out by the coxswain only
- once in the water and free from falls and safety strops, the rescue boat can carry out the rescue drill
- once completed, the boat should be retrieved and stored.

Safety Drill Debrief

This should be conducted as soon as the drill is completed, while adrenaline levels are still high and memories are fresh.

In no particular order, some of the general points that should be covered are:

- What have we learned?
- what went well?
- what did not go so well?
- did everyone know their role?
- how were communications, particularly the launch instruction?
- record of experience, ie how many minutes to launch the rescue boat and retrieve the dummy?
- other suggested improvements?
- are the tasks well suited to the assigned crew?

Fire Drill

A fire drill should be carried out within 24 hours of the ship leaving port if more than 25% of the crew have not taken part in a fire drill within the preceding month, on that particular ship.

Suggested Drill Format

- A fire on board should be simulated
  Note: Locations should be rotated to cover at least: machinery spaces, galley, cargo-related fires, storerooms, workshops or lockers, electrical equipment
- the fire alarm should be sounded and the location of the fire announced on the PA system and handheld radios
- commence taking a log of events, including position
- all crew should muster at their nominated muster stations
- the communication systems with the bridge, emergency HQ and engine room should be checked (engine room advised to simulate standby engines and start second steering motor and fire pump)
- send a fire party, with radio(s), to investigate:
  - location
  - extent
  - type of fire
- close down the vessel as quickly as possible (fans, vents, watertight doors)
- the main fire pumps should be started and, where the scenario permits, the emergency fire pump should be started

Fire Drill

- if the emergency fire pump is used, ensure that it can deliver two charged fire hoses to prove that the system is working correctly
- the emergency and backup party will respond to the fire depending on its location, type and size
- instigate a search for any missing persons (if applicable)
- if breathing apparatus is used, the appropriate entries should be made on the BA board
- isolate electrical supplies
- make an updated PA announcement to crew
- hand steering and both steering motors should both be engaged to simulate the vessel turning (in a real fire these techniques would be used to minimise the effect that the wind will have on the fire).

General Notes

Fire drills should, as far as possible, simulate a real fire on board. The drills should be planned so that there is regular practice in the various emergency scenarios that may occur. The focus during a drill is mainly on fire-fighting, but it should build in procedures for managing crew evacuation and the control of smoke.

- During a fire drill, the crew must carry out the duties that are assigned to them. This includes checking that the fire doors, fire dampers, main ventilation inlets and outlets all work. It should also include closing all fire doors, valves, scuppers, side scuttles, skylight and portholes
- the fire-fighting equipment which is carried on board should be involved in the drill where possible, this equipment includes the firefighters' outfits, personal rescue equipment and sprinkler systems
- the communication equipment, emergency lighting and emergency power system should also be inspected and tested.

Every Fire Drill Should Include

- Reporting to stations and preparing for duties as per the fire muster list
- starting the fire pump, using at least two jets of water to show the system is in correct working order
- checking the firefighters' outfits and personal rescue equipment
- checking the communication equipment
- checking that watertight doors, fire doors and fire dampers are working
- verifying arrangements if a fire cannot be managed and the abandon ship order is given.

Suggestions

- Every crew member should take part in a fire drill each month
- smoke machines have their benefits during fire drills, but should be used with caution. Adhere to any safety notices or guidance regarding their use
- onboard training and instructions on how to use the fire extinguishers and available fire-fighting equipment should be given at the same time as the drills
- any equipment used during a drill should be returned to its fully operational condition immediately. Any faults should be rectified as soon as possible
- crew should be trained to fight fires and deal with a simultaneous abandon ship order. This should include all members of the crew
- fire drills should be carried out as if there is an actual emergency
- fire pumps should be started using sufficient hoses to demonstrate that the system is working correctly
- operate all watertight and fire doors
- all crew members should be aware of:
  - instruction and procedures on extinguishing small fires
    - how a single crew member can put a fire out
    - what is required when extinguishing a fire involving dangerous goods, electrical installations and potential liquid fires
    - how to use the ship's fire-fighting equipment and participate in post drill clean-up and stowage of the equipment
    - dangers from fire-fighting systems, eg CO_2 discharges
    - how to use breathing apparatus, firefighters' outfits and personal equipment

Fire Drill

- instruction on how to escape from any location on the ship and the importance of closing doors once a room has been searched
- first aid techniques.

Record Keeping

- The date and details of fire drills must be recorded in line with SOLAS regulations
- an entry should be made in the log for each drill. The information should include the date, time, how long the drill lasted, the number of fire hoses used, and a statement about the condition of the fire equipment, watertight door mechanisms and valves. If drills do not take place, or only a partial drill is carried out, an entry should also be made in the log
- a record must be kept of crew members who have taken part in drills. New crew members should be assessed before the ship leaves port and the main company office notified of their training status
- the equipment tested in each drill should be recorded by date.

Simulate Communications

- Inform the Coastguard (in port, call the fire brigade) and DPA/Duty Manager. You should advise them of the following information:
  - Position of vessel
  - nature and size of fire (details of cargo)
  - number of crew on board
  - measures currently being taken to fight or contain the fire
  - nature of assistance required.

Actions

- Initiate fire containment and fire-fighting measures
- if fire is getting worse or is out of control, consider using a fixed fire-fighting system.

Actions to Consider at the End of Drill

If the fire is extinguished or well under control:

- Consider temperature/likelihood of re-ignition
- check adjacent compartments to ensure that fire has not spread by heat transfer
- consider restoring ventilation to clear smoke.

Safety Drill Debrief

This should be conducted as soon as the drill is completed, while adrenaline levels are still high and memories are fresh.

In no particular order, some of the general points that should be covered are:

- What have we learned?
- what went well?
- how was the emergency party's response and actions?
  (This should include instructions for fire-fighting, use of fire-extinguishing systems, emergency equipment including breathing apparatus and lifelines, use/control of emergency fuel stops and ventilation)
- what did not go so well?
- how were communications?
- what equipment was used?
- what equipment hindered the effort?
- was fire equipment in the most appropriate location?
- do any items of fire equipment have to be deployed better on board?
- did anyone have to run and get anything?
- are there any changes that should be added to checklists at the EHQ or on the bridge?
- record of experience, ie how many minutes use from SCBA for rescue party?
- other suggested improvements from the team?
- were members of the rescue party in the correct roles to suit their strengths?
- were there enough men in the SCBA rescue party to manage the fire?

Passenger Drills

Passenger/cruise vessels – Evacuation/mustering/abandoning/crowd control

1st January 2015: An amendment to SOLAS III/19 required that passengers undergo safety drills, including mustering at the lifeboat stations, before the ship departs or immediately on departure.

(Note: Prior to this date, the requirement was for the muster of passengers to take place within 24 hours of their embarkation).

Ships that carry passengers in high numbers have the additional difficulty of controlling untrained, confused and frightened people of different ages, nationalities and physical capabilities during emergencies.

The master must ensure that the persons designated to take charge of passenger muster stations, or who have designated responsibilities that relate to the control of passengers, are qualified in crowd management and/or crisis management and human behaviour, as required by STCW and the flag State. The use of decision support systems for the master is required by many flag States and is recommended.

Training in passenger mustering and evacuation is normally conducted simultaneously with, and incorporating other, emergency drills, eg fire. However, separate specific tuition in crowd management and the use of marine evacuation systems (MES) should be encouraged.

Before any drills are commenced, passengers must be advised not to panic at any alarm and, wherever practicable, they should be encouraged to participate. This adds a degree of realism to the drill and improves the confidence of the crew members directly involved.

Suggested Drill Format

- On hearing the general emergency alarm (and public address), all crew members should go to their muster station
- the crew members in charge of the muster stations should report which crew are in attendance and the passenger numbers present. Passengers should be advised about wearing appropriate clothing and kept informed during the drill. It is important that crew members gain confidence through practising communication with and direction of the passengers
- a ship search by designated crew may be undertaken at this time, or after the initial muster
- the bridge or emergency control station should, on receipt of crew passenger numbers, collate the information and report to the master
- a search for missing persons should be completed
- when advised by the master or officer in charge of communications, passengers should be shown and assisted with the donning of lifejackets.

Once satisfied that the muster and/or emergency drill is complete, the abandon ship drill can be commenced. Depending on the number of passengers carried, the abandon ship drill is likely to employ a number of stages.

The appropriate signal should be sounded and a verbal order given by the master. The crew should maintain control, and direct passengers to the designated lifeboat or liferaft stations. Crew should be given instruction in accordance with their duties. Passengers should be checked and instructed as to what would be required of them.

The initial stage normally involves:

- Preparing lifeboats and rescue boat(s) for lowering and reporting the number of crew and passengers embarked to the bridge once ready for launch
- boats should be launched only on the master's command
- nominated crew members should search their designated ship zone to check it is clear and report findings when complete.

After completion of the first stage, each subsequent stage, involving the deployment of the MES, liferaft launching, boarding and

Passenger Drills

towing, should be controlled and ordered by the master. It would be expected that the master, bridge team and senior staff would abandon ship during the final stage.

Additional considerations:

- Crew should wear distinctive clothing to identify them. Jackets are useful but not as easy to see as hardhats when they are also wearing lifejackets
- simulate injuries to crew or passengers and encourage crew to undertake other duties
- have crew or passengers simulate difficult behaviour
- simulate damage to one side of the ship to prepare crew for abandonment using one side only
- the debrief of these drills provides an opportunity to improve performance and to reallocate staff to duties that they may be better suited to.

Emergency Steering Drill

Emergency steering drills provide the necessary training and practice to ensure that, in the event of a steering gear malfunction, the crew are properly trained and can competently gain control of the ship's rudder by engaging the emergency steering system.

- **The deck crew should take part in the exercise to gain experience**
- **emergency steering gear should be tested every three months**
- **SOLAS Ch V, Regulation 26 sets out the requirements for steering gear testing and drills**
- **US Requirement: 33 CFR 164.25 (d) No vessel may enter, or be operated on the navigable waters of the United States, unless the emergency steering drill described in (33 CFR 164.25) is conducted and logged on a regular basis of at least once every three months or has been conducted within 48 hours prior to entry and logged in the vessel logbook.**

Note: If the steering flat is being used as a citadel in the event of pirate attack, consideration should be given to the necessary preparations prior to entering pirate infested waters.

Responsibilities

The master and chief engineer should plan the drill taking into account any possible risks.

- The master is in charge of the drill and should ensure that the vessel has sufficient sea room before proceeding
- the chief officer will brief and give instructions to members of the team and should be present in the steering flat
- the second engineer will brief the team members about the technical/mechanical aspects and will oversee the changeover from bridge control to emergency steering control. He should also be present in the steering flat
- an OOW will accompany the master on the bridge
- members of the deck crew should be available to assist in the steering flat.

Emergency Steering Drill

Recommended Procedures

- Change from manual steering and prepare for emergency steering
- steering motors should be 'on' and bridge steering set to 'hand'
- establish communications between the bridge and the steering flat for passing helm orders
- check the steering position compass with the main gyro compass
- a helmsman must be available for emergency steering in the steering gear flat
- transfer control to the emergency steering position
- carry out orders from the steering compartment. Once complete, return control to the bridge. Confirm that steering is operating by hand from the bridge position.

Emergency Steering Drill Debrief

- How long did it take to engage the emergency steering gear, from the time of the alarm?
- can the time taken to engage the emergency steering be improved?
- what speed was the ship at and how did she respond?
- how were communications with the bridge?
- what practice was conducted in steering the vessel on a specific heading?
- if the steering gear was fitted with a local solenoid override, did this operate correctly? Is the use of a solenoid override understood?
- were the emergency steering changeover instructions clearly understood?
- was all necessary marking and labelling clear in the steering flat?

Enclosed Space Rescue: Training and Drills

Rescue from an enclosed space is one of the drills that should be conducted on board every two months. 1st January 2015: An amendment to SOLAS Regulation III/19, on emergency training and drills, made mandatory the carrying out of enclosed space entry and rescue drills, which will require crew members with enclosed space entry or rescue responsibilities to participate in an enclosed space entry and rescue drill at least once every two months as a minimum. Such drills would also be prudent before a period of tank inspection/survey, ship repair or drydock.

Suggested Drill Format

- Once the general alarm is sounded, an announcement should be made explaining the nature of the emergency
- all personnel on board must proceed to their muster stations
- the standby man at the enclosed space should remain at the point of entry, remaining in communication with the bridge and the emergency team. On mustering at the EHQ, the first two men arriving should immediately don and test their SCBA (this can save valuable minutes)
- each member of the rescue team must be trained to carry out specific duties for the primary roles of the emergency team, for example:
  - rescue of a casualty
  - emergency entry to an enclosed space or smoke filled compartment
  - fire-fighting.

  (Note: other duties will be required, depending on the ship type)
- the officer in charge (OIC) is responsible for assessing the dangers involved in the rescue and for provision of clear instructions to all members of the rescue party
- in each case, the OIC should assess whether the enclosed space rescue is:
  - an injury in an enclosed space?
  - crew member(s) overcome by lack of oxygen in an enclosed space?
- the OIC should determine what rescue equipment is required from the EHQ *(Training helps prepare and identify what equipment is required)*
- the OIC should check what rescue equipment is at the point of entry
- one member of the rescue team should be responsible for first aid, particularly maintaining airways, reducing blood loss and conducting CPR
- it is important that clear and regular communications are maintained throughout

- the pressure gauges on the SCBA air tanks must be checked and their values recorded at the time of entry into the enclosed space, with a note of the time of entry and the time available
- the OIC should remain outside the enclosed area and liaise with the bridge and the rescue team
- a suitably equipped two (or three) person rescue team should enter the area
  (Three persons may be required in certain situations to assist with the resuscitator)
- the rescue team must notify the OIC once casualties have been found. If any first aid is required, the rescue team will carry it out, including placing a resuscitator on the casualty if necessary
- once the casualty is prepared for evacuation, consideration should be given to a stretcher
- if resuscitation was required, casualty response should be checked
- once the drill has been completed, the ship's staff should be debriefed
- SCBA bottles must be recharged immediately after the drill.

General Notes

- The OIC may well have been involved in preparing the permit for entry and therefore will know what equipment is available at the point of entry
- rescue operations should not be carried out until all the rescue equipment is available and the team is ready
- dummies should be used during rescue drills
  (85 kg dummies if possible)
- members of the rescue party should be aware of how many minutes their SCBA set gives them based on the type of exertion they may experience during a rescue
- at least one member of each rescue team must have an up-to-date certificate in basic first aid.

Safety Drill Debrief

This should be conducted as soon as the drill is completed, while adrenaline levels are still high and memories are fresh.

In no particular order, some of the general points that should be covered are:

- What have we learned?
- what went well?
- what did not go so well?
- how were communications?
- what equipment was used?
- what equipment hindered the effort?
- was rescue equipment in the most appropriate location?
- do any items of rescue equipment have to be deployed more efficiently?
- did anyone have to run and get anything?
- any changes that should be added to checklists at the EHQ or on the bridge?
- record of experience, ie how many minutes use from SCBA for rescue party?
- other suggested improvements from the team?
- were members of the rescue party in the correct roles to suit their strengths?
- were there enough men in the SCBA rescue party to manage the casualty?
- was there sufficient time to give medical attention to the casualty?
  (Remember – the priority is to get the oxygen to the casualty, and this will most likely be via the resuscitator. Focus should be given to resuscitating the casualty before any attempt to move him. Think of an ambulance ashore; it does not move until they have done the best for the casualty at the scene).

The debrief creates an opportunity to discuss spaces with entry points that could be made safer by welding handholds in place. Pad eyes to hold a winch could be welded to beams above an entry point that cannot accommodate a tripod. Such feedback provides knowledge of the locations a crew member can be rescued from with the existing equipment on board and, more importantly, the places a man cannot be rescued from.

This emphasises a most important enclosed space rule. Never send anyone into a space that you cannot adequately rescue them from, regardless of the circumstances.

Pirate Attack Drill

The primary consideration is to ensure the safety of the crew.

In addition, a ship should prepare an 'emergency contingency plan' before entering a High Risk Area (HRA) where a pirate attack may occur.

In addition, an emergency communication plan should contain all essential emergency contact numbers with pre-prepared report templates for concerned parties, including the reports that are to be transmitted in the event of an attack.

The ship should have access to the latest edition of the '*Best Management Practices for protection against Somalia Based Piracy* (BMP)'. This provides advice designed to assist ships to avoid, deter or delay piracy attacks in the HRA. Experience, supported by evidence and data collected by naval forces, shows that the application of the recommendations contained within the booklet can and will make a significant difference in preventing a ship becoming a victim of piracy.

Consideration should be given to the location for a safe muster point or citadel. Reference should be made to the appropriate chapter in BMP. Note that BMP advises that establishing a citadel is beyond the capability of ship's staff alone and requires external technical advice and support.

Consideration should also be given to the protection of the crew who may be required to remain on the bridge during a pirate attack, as pirates increasingly fire at the bridge of a vessel to try to force it to stop. Reference should be made to the appropriate chapter in BMP.

If applicable, a copy of BA Chart 66090 'Anti-Piracy Planning Chart – Red Sea, Gulf of Aden and Arabian Sea' should be available.

BMP recommends that ships should proceed at full sea speed. To date, there have been no reported attacks where pirates have boarded a ship that has been proceeding at over 20 knots.

If the vessel is using private maritime security contractors (PMSCs), there should be extensive planning, between them and the ship's management, of training and drills and what their requirements are.

This pre-planning is particularly crucial when a PMSC boards the vessel immediately prior to entry into an HRA. PMSCs can often board a vessel and be within hostile waters within hours.

If it is navigationally safe to do so during the drill, masters are encouraged to practise manoeuvring their ships to establish the series of helm orders that produces the most difficult sea conditions for pirate skiffs trying to attack, without causing a significant reduction in the ship's speed. Substantial amounts of helm are not recommended as these are likely to significantly reduce a vessel's speed.

General Notes

Prior to transiting the HRA, ship operators and masters should carry out a thorough risk assessment to assess the likelihood and consequences of piracy attacks to the vessel, based on the latest available information. Reference should be made to the appropriate chapter in BMP.

Drill Preparation

- Ensure that control of access precautions are in place, in the same manner as would apply when transiting the area
- prepare all fixed counter-measures, such as spray hoses, dummies and razor wire, exactly as you would while in the area.

Drill

- Sounding the ship's alarms/whistle informs the vessel's crew that a piracy attack has commenced. You may wish to continuously sound the ship's foghorn/whistle
- if not already at full speed, increase to maximum. Steer a straight course to maintain a maximum speed. The second steering motor should be started, if not already running
- initiate the ship's pre-prepared emergency contingency plan
  - activate the emergency communication plan
  - sound the emergency alarm and make a 'pirate attack' (PA) announcement, in accordance with the ship's emergency plan
  - report the attack immediately to the appropriate military coordinator (such as UKMTO)
  - activate the ship security alert system (SSAS), which will alert your Company security officer and flag State. Make a 'mayday' call on VHF Ch. 16 (and backup Ch. 08, which is monitored by naval units)
  - send a distress message via the DSC (digital selective calling) system and Inmarsat-C, as applicable
- where possible, alter course away from the approaching skiffs and/or mother ships. When sea conditions allow, consider altering course to increase an approaching skiff's exposure to wind/waves
- members of the crew not required on the bridge or the engine control room should muster in the citadel
- activate water spray and other appropriate self-defensive measures
- ensure that all external doors and, where possible, internal public rooms and cabins are fully secured
- reconfirm that all ship's personnel are in a position of safety
- as the pirates close on the vessel, commence small alterations of helm while maintaining speed to deter skiffs from lying alongside the vessel in preparation for a boarding attempt. These manoeuvres will create additional wash to impede the operation of the skiffs.

Second Stage of the Drill – Pirates Taking Control

- Before the pirates gain access to the bridge, inform UKMTO
- ensure that the SSAS has been activated and that the AIS is switched on
- offer no resistance to the pirates once they reach the bridge. Once on the bridge, the pirates are likely to be aggressive, highly agitated and possibly under the influence of drugs (khat), so remaining calm and cooperating fully will greatly reduce the risk of harm
- if the bridge/engine room is to be evacuated, the main engine should be stopped and all way taken off the vessel if possible (and if navigationally safe to do so). All remaining crew members should proceed to the designated safe muster point with their hands visible.

Third Stage of the Drill – in the Event of Military Action

- In the event that military personnel board the ship, all personnel should keep low to the deck and cover their head with both hands, with hands visible. On no account should personnel make movements that could be misinterpreted as aggressive
- do not use flash photography
- be prepared to be challenged on your identity. Brief and prepare ship's personnel to expect this and to cooperate fully during any military action on board
- be aware that English may not be the working language of naval forces in the region
- simulate the transmission of follow-up reports and post incident reports.

Safety Drill Debrief

- Does everyone know the various types of report to be issued and the methods of raising the alarm?
- discuss the types of attacks that are typical in the area and what the ship knows about them. This could form a small presentation

Pirate Attack Drill

- discuss the vessel's route and the timings of passing areas of concern or entering transit corridors
- discuss the measures that the Company has put in place for the vessel
- discuss watchkeeping arrangement while in the area
- discuss control of access considerations.

This checklist is based on information contained in *'Best Management Practices 4'*.

BMP4 is available free of charge from P&I Clubs, industry organisations such as OCIMF, SIGTTO, ICS, INTERTANKO, INTERCARGO and BIMCO, and from all good chart agents.

The industry organisations engaged in producing BMP endeavour to meet regularly to ensure it is updated as necessary, based upon operational experience and lessons learned.

The latest advice may be found on the MSCHOA, NATO Shipping Centre and MARLO websites. Additionally, the UKMTO may be contacted at any time for updated advice.

ISPS/Security Drill

Drills that are designed to ensure that personnel are proficient in their assigned security duties, and which ensure elements of the ship security plan are tested, are required to be conducted as per the ISPS Code:

> ***13.6 … at least once every 3 months. In addition, in cases where more than 25% of the ship's personnel has been changed, at any one time, with personnel that has not previously participated in any drill on that ship within the last 3 months, a drill should be conducted within one week of the change. These drills should test individual elements of the plan such as those security threats listed in paragraph 8.9.***
>
> ***13.7 Various types of exercises, which may include participation of company security officers, port facility security officers, relevant authorities of Contracting Governments as well as ship security officers, if available, should be carried out at least once each calendar year with no more than 18 months between the exercises. These exercises should test communications, co-ordination, resource availability, and response. These exercises may be:***
>
> ***.1 full-scale or live;***
>
> ***.2 tabletop simulation or seminar; or***
>
> ***.3 combined with other exercises held, such as search and rescue or emergency response exercises.***
>
> ***ISPS Code B/13***

The ISPS Code drills encourage a common sense approach to security that encourages vigilance and an understanding of basic procedures that counter any terrorist or other threat to the ship's security.

The Ship Security Officer (SSO) should be trained and certificated on a course approved by the flag State, and crew with designated responsibilities must complete ship security awareness training.

The SSO should, in consultation with the master and in line with the Ship Security Plan (SSP) and SMS, schedule training to include the following elements:

- **Hijacking/piracy (including attempts to use the ship itself as a weapon)**
- **cargo tampering**

ISPS/Security Drill

- **smuggling (eg firearms)**
- **stowaways**
- **bomb threat.**

Training can and is required annually, to include the cooperation of the Company Security Officer (CSO). Drills may also involve the Port Facilities Security Officer (PFSO) or may be required to be demonstrated by Port State Control.

The SSP will determine the appropriate procedures that must be taken by the ship, depending on each identified threat and scenario.

The following bomb threat scenario, of a ship having left port while operating at security level one, may be useful for guidance.

Drill Preparation

- The ship should be operating at normal navigation levels
- prepare two 'suspect' parcels. One should be easily found on a normal security round, the other in a more challenging location.

Suggested Drill Format

- Simulate a received call from the PFSO that suspected devices have been planted on board immediately prior to departure
- sound the alarm and make an announcement on the PA
- muster crew in the designated area
- initiate and test any alarms required by the SSP
- prepare lifeboats for boarding
- advise the CSO and other external parties involved in the drill and maintain communication
- close down to prevent spread of fire and damage in the event of an explosion, once the device locations are established. This can be amended to direct the blast to minimise the effects. The explosion will take the path of least resistance
- restrictions on the use of VHF/UHF radio must be observed
- commence the security search
- once the first device has been located, continue searching until a search of the entire ship has been completed
- contingency arrangements for a port of refuge or anchorage should be identified.

ISPS/Security Drill

The drill can involve a number of additional scenarios including damage control, fire-fighting, casualties, pollution control and abandoning ship.

Additional Considerations

- Ensure crew maintain communication
- crew should never touch or attempt to move devices
- portable radios should not be used in the vicinity
- consider the effects of key personnel being injured.

Drill Debrief

- Ensure personnel know the actions to be taken and precautions to be observed
- ensure personnel are fully aware of their responsibilities at each security level
- discuss various scenarios, including stowaways and attempted hijacking
- discuss types of weapons and devices, including their effects and probable appearance
- discuss the importance of closing down/ sealing the ship, both at sea and in port, in the event of a suspected incident
- discuss the need to prevent such incidents through observation of behaviour and strict control of access to the ship.

By creating realistic scenarios that test responsibilities and procedures, the drills will ensure crew understand their own duties, take responsibility for security on board and do not assume such responsibility will be taken by others.

Oil Spill Response Drill

An oil spill contingency plan will have very little value if those who are involved do not have adequate training to properly carry out the actions identified in the plan.

Oil spill response drills should vary to take account of the operation, size of the spill and the weather. Consideration should be given to the use of water on deck to simulate oil flow.

Oil Spill Response Drill

Suggested Drill Format

- All operations on board must be stopped. The cargo pumps must be stopped immediately and the ESD activated
- the general alarm should be sounded to indicate to the crew that they should muster at their designated positions
- an announcement should be made on the PA explaining the nature of the spill
- the source of the oil spill should be identified to determine what immediate actions need to be taken
- the toxic nature of the spill and the risk of fire should be assessed and all necessary precautions taken
- the appropriate PPE should be used
- check that the scuppers are closed and, if necessary on oil tankers, isolate and depressurise the slop tanks and open the oil emergency drain
- the oil containment pumps should be appropriately positioned
- if it is likely that there will be a gas leak or a fire, the main and auxiliary air conditioning plants should be changed over to recirculation. It is important that all the vents are shut and that the exhaust fans are isolated
- the crew should clean up the oil, whether by oil containment pumps, draining to the slop tank or mopping up with sawdust/oil absorbent granules
- simulate storage of the recovered oil in a safe location until it can be disposed of safely and correctly.

General Notes

During training, appraise the crew of the following responses in the event of a spill from an oil tanker:

Primary Response

- Sound emergency alarm
- stop all cargo and/or bunkering operations (activate ESD)
- close manifold valves
- switch air conditioning to recirculation or stop air intake to accommodation
- stop non-essential air intake fans to the engine room
- locate source of leakage and stop/reduce oil
- consult SOPEP plan
- consult MSDS/EmS guideline
- assess fire risk
- start fire pump
- commence clean-up procedures using absorbents and permitted solvents
- advise relevant parties (local authorities, coastal State, DPA/company, P&I correspondent, etc).

Secondary Response

- Reduce the oil level in the tank concerned by dropping oil into an empty or slack tank
- reduce the level of oil in tanks in the suspected area
- drain affected line to an empty or slack tank
- reduce inert gas pressure to zero
- if the leakage is at the pump room sea valve, relieve pressure on pipelines
- prepare pumps for transfer of oil to other tanks or to shore or a lightering vessel
- prepare portable pumps if it is possible to transfer spilt oil to an empty tank
- consider pumping water into the leaking tank to create a water cushion and prevent further oil loss
- if the leakage is below the waterline, arrange divers for further investigation
- calculate stresses/stability. If necessary, request shore assistance
- transfer cargo or bunkers to alleviate high stability stresses
- stow residue from the clean-up operation carefully, prior to disposal.

Oil Spilled on Deck

When most of the free oil has been removed and the risk of oil pollution has passed, onboard resources should turn to the clean-up operation. Personnel involved in containment and clean-up operations may be at risk from a variety of hazards. The OIC should ensure that the following precautions are taken:

- The area must be continually checked for the presence of hydrocarbons and toxic gases
- the boundaries of the clean-up site must be clearly indicated

Oil Spill Response Drill

- entry to the clean-up site must be controlled and access allowed only to those with appropriate PPE
- forced ventilation around the accommodation and machinery spaces must be controlled or stopped
- special precautions must be taken to prevent any sources of ignition, including static electricity
- fire-fighting parties and equipment should remain on standby
- surfaces that present a slip hazard must be covered with sawdust or absorbent granules and warning notices posted
- a designated area should be made available for personnel to shower and to change into clean clothing.

Pump Room Spillage

Oil spilled in the pump room from leaking pipelines may not present a pollution hazard to the environment, but it does present a personal health and safety hazard for those entering the pump room. Should a pump room oil spill occur, entry into the pump room must be treated as though it were an enclosed entry into a cargo oil tank, with the pump room entry permit cancelled. Initial actions include:

- Stop cargo operations
- evacuate personnel from the pump room
- withdraw pump room entry permit
- close all remotely operated valves
- monitor percentage LEL using fixed and portable instruments
- prepare the bilge pump, or the pump designated for bilge pumping duty, and set the lines to transfer to a suitable cargo oil tank
- if the pump room bilge alarm has been activated and/or oil is being drawn into the pump room extraction vents, consider changing over to the high extraction vents.

Further action depends on the situation.

Safety Drill Debrief

This should be conducted as soon as the drill is completed, while adrenaline levels are still high and memories are fresh.

In no particular order, some of the general points that should be covered are:

- What have we learned?
- what went well?
- what did not go so well?
- how were communications?
- what equipment was used?
- what equipment hindered the effort?
- was oil spill equipment in the most appropriate location?
- do any items of oil spill equipment on board have to be deployed more efficiently.
- did anyone have to run and get anything?
- are there any changes that should be added to operational procedures?
- are there any impacts on onboard maintenance?
- are there any other suggested improvements?
- was sufficient PPE available to manage a spill?

Hull Damage/Flooding (Damage Control) Drill

Suggested Drill Format

- Sound the emergency signal and make an announcement indicating where on the ship the emergency/damage has occurred
- check the remote tank gauging devices from the control room to get an overview of the situation
- all watertight doors must be closed immediately, with confirmation of closure of each watertight door reported to the bridge/master. After satisfying their operation for the drill, the doors can be reopened
- any doors that were already closed when the drill started must be opened and then closed
- reducing speed or stopping the engines should be simulated
- the extent of the damage/breach must be established and an attempt made to contain the leak or flood

Hull Damage/Flooding (Damage Control) Drill

- if the vessel is listing, a way of reducing the water inflow needs to be considered
- assess the current situation taking into account the weather, location, damage sustained, stability, environmental concerns including pollution, and available support
- a note of the time and the ship's position should be taken. This information should be passed to the officer who is operating the GMDSS station
- a simulation of notifying the coastguard and relevant authorities should be carried out
- the plan should be carried out in consultation with the Company as well as simulating broadcasts to ships in the area
- crew members who have been assigned to sounding duty must immediately sound the tanks and bilges in the section of the ship where the drill is being carried out. A member of the sounding party must communicate with the officer in charge and the chief engineer
- pumps that relate to damage control must be operated by the engine room and connected to the area of the ship where the drill is being carried out
- the bridge must be informed when the pumps are ready for action
- the ship's side doors, valves and similar fittings must be closed (if they are open in port)
- the bridge should be informed once they have been closed
- the lifeboats should be prepared and the possibility of abandoning ship considered
- the accommodation air conditioning may need to be changed to recirculation.

General Notes

Note: Most ship stability books are for intact stability. In cases of damage stability, you should refer to your DPA and/or Classification Society.

Angle of loll is caused by a rise in the height of the centre of gravity (KG) so that it creates a negative metacentric height (GM). There are several reasons why this can develop on a voyage, including:

- **Water absorption in hygroscopic cargoes, eg timber deck cargoes**
- **water trapped on deck, eg within pipes on offshore vessels**
- **ice accretion on deck**
- **cargo shift**
- **flooding.**

Angle of loll should be rectified by reducing the height of the centre of gravity. Care must be taken not to cause the vessel to list too quickly in the opposite direction as this could be sufficient to take the vessel beyond the angle of vanishing stability and capsize it.

- Alter course, putting the ship into the waves and keeping the high side into the wind
- confirm the listed condition is due to the angle of loll:
  - check port and starboard listing moments are equal
  - check for slack tanks
- press up any slack tanks, one at a time and the smallest first, to remove FSE
- discharge any high ballast wing tank
- where three double bottom tanks are available, load ballast into the middle tank first
- where only two double bottom ballast tanks are available, load into the lowest (listed side) first
- if necessary, jettisoning deck cargo can be considered.

It is important that only one tank at a time is worked and it should be remembered that, when loading into low sided tanks or discharging into high sided tanks, the vessel may initially list further. The situation should improve as the height of the centre of gravity reduces.

Helicopter Drill

At the time of the simulated incident, the ship should have the following safety measures in place for conducting a helicopter/ship operation:

The helideck operations party should be wearing:

- **Fire suits and gloves**
- **helmets with visors**
- **safety boots**
- **ear protectors.**

The fire party should be standing by with the following equipment:

- **Fire hoses connected, fire pump on and line pressurised, foam nozzle fitted and foam container standing by**
- **axe**
- **crowbar**
- **hacksaw**
- **boltcutters**
- **ladder**
- **torches (at night).**

Suggested Drill Format

The drill may take the form of a medivac or of a helicopter contact with a vessel's structure during an operational transfer, eg pilot.

- Fire-fighting operations should be simulated as for a fire drill
- the shipboard personnel should gather as instructed in the muster list
- precautions must be taken to ensure that the deck is kept clear of smoke and fire
- crew should only ever approach the helicopter when they are told it is safe to do so by the OIC.

Medivac Drill Considerations

Tankers
A reduction of the inert gas pressure should be simulated in all the cargo and slop tanks. This should be set to a slight positive pressure 30 minutes before the helicopter arrives. P/V valves should be left in the closed position. It is important that all the tank/hatch openings are secured.

- The helicopter pilot should be contacted to arrange the rendezvous point
- the international code pennant or another suitable indicator should be hoisted so that the helicopter pilot can see it clearly
- the master must ensure that the vessel is on a steady course. The relative wind should be 30° on the port bow or as required by the helicopter pilot
- crew must be instructed in how to use a sling correctly.

Cautions

- **Personnel who are directly involved in the operation should be instructed not to touch the winched man, stretcher or winch hook until it is earthed**
- **no lines that have been passed down from the helicopter should be secured**
- **do not shine a light at a helicopter at night**
- **crew must keep clear of the helicopter rotors and exhaust.**

Helicopter Drill Debrief

- Ship's staff should be debriefed once the drill is completed
- it is important that the P/V valves are reset and that the wind indicator is lowered once the drill is finished.

Grounding/Stranding Drill

Suggested Drill Format

- The main engines should simulate being stopped and the emergency alarm should be sounded
- crew should be mustered
- the PA system and handheld radio sets should announce that the vessel is aground
- if necessary, steering should be changed to manual and both the steering motors switched on
- all the watertight doors must be closed and the vessel's position verified
- all tanks and bilges should be sounded for any incoming water
- simulate the transmission of a PAN-PAN message to all stations
- prepare signals for a vessel aground:
  - day: three black balls
  - night: anchor lights plus two all round red lights
- commence appropriate sound signal if in restricted visibility
- update AIS status
- engine room should switch to 'high' sea suction
- investigate vessel damage, including pollution
- simulate soundings all round the vessel (in a real situation, you could consider using a rescue boat)
- confirm the vessel's position and depth of water
- give updates on the PA and simulate update to relevant parties, including SECURITE message.

The following actions should be discussed as part of the training prior to debrief:

- Determine whether the wind or sea is carrying the vessel into further difficulties. If so, consider using the anchors
- before taking further action, consider all relevant information, including:
  - weather and sea state
  - state/height and range of tide
  - nature of seabed
  - depth of water all round the vessel
  - damaged stability condition
- in lightening the vessel, consider the discharge of the following and the resultant change of stability, draught, trim and list:
  - water ballast
  - fresh water
- consider contacting Class or Company, as appropriate, to determine stability in damaged condition
- if unable to float safely by the vessel's own efforts, call for assistance
- log all events in the bridge movement book
- record all details of the incident in the deck logbook, official logbook and on an incident report form.

Records After a Grounding

Discussing and reviewing the following after the drill will contribute to better recordkeeping for future situations where records are requested. These would typically include:

- Date and exact time of the grounding
- position of the grounding
- detailed description of the section of the vessel aground
- nature of the seabed where the grounding has taken place

Grounding/Stranding Drill

- courses at the time of the grounding (charted, steered, gyro and magnetic)
- speed at the time of the grounding (RPM or pitch setting)
- rudder angle at the time of the grounding
- alterations of course and/or speed in the period immediately before the grounding
- orders given
- communications exchanged between ship and shore
- if under pilotage, any communications with the pilot and or tugs prior to the grounding
- detail of positions plotted prior to the grounding
- helm/engine movements before/after the grounding
- weather conditions at the time of the grounding
- tide and current at the time of the grounding
- draught at the time of the grounding
- soundings around the vessel
- soundings of all the ship's tanks from the last record before grounding and the situation after the grounding
- cargo distribution from the last record before grounding and the situation after the grounding.

Navigation and communication equipment in use at the time of the grounding:

- Echo sounder information/range used/printout
- radar/ARPA settings and any adjustments/changes to these settings and the time of such change prior to the incident
- GPS positions
- VHF – location of the radio in use and channels in operation/being monitored
- ECDIS – save data
- any other navigation/comms equipment in use.

Persons Involved

Record the name, rank, duties and location for:

- All persons on the bridge at the time of the grounding
- any further eye witnesses
- engine room personnel
- pilot
- other vessels/traffic in the area at the time of the grounding.

Emergency Towing Drill

Suggested Drill Format

- Confirm that the forward and aft emergency towing arrangements are ready to be used
- the towing plan should be simulated, as should communications with the tug
- the deck party must be ready to simulate deployment of the towline. Instruction should be given to the crew in the safe use of the ship's line throwing apparatus
- the forward emergency towing arrangements typically require that the chain is positioned in the chain stopper and that the towline is connected to the emergency chain
  (The duty officer must instruct the deck party to stand well clear while the towline takes the weight of the emergency chain; the duty officer must simulate confirmation to the master and tug that the towline has taken the weight and that the towing arrangement is holding)
- when ordered to deploy, the eye of the messenger must pass through the centre fairlead before it is shackled up to the towline. The messenger must be connected to the towline
- once the emergency release handles on the box are opened, the messenger line can be released
- simulate that the tug has received the messenger line and that it is ready to accept the emergency towline
- the deck party must stand well clear as you simulate the tug taking the weight on the towline
- once the weight of the towline has been taken by the tug, the OIC should confirm to the master and tug that the arrangement is holding
- once the tug is made fast, the appropriate day or night signals should be displayed and all the relevant parties must be advised.

Once the drill has been completed, the ship's staff should be debriefed.

Emergency Towing Drill

Man Overboard Drill

Suggested Drill Format

- A simulation of the bridge wing smoke/ light lifebuoy being released to indicate man overboard should be carried out. A marker may be released
- the steering should be changed to manual and both steering motors need to be on, wheel placed hard over so that the stern of the vessel is manoeuvred clear of the man overboard
- the emergency alarm (three long blasts) should be sounded and 'man overboard' announced on the ship's PA system and handheld radio sets, indicating on which side
- on the GPS/ECDIS activate the 'man overboard' and record the position
- the MOB position should be plotted and additional lookouts instructed to keep the MOB in sight
- the vessel must carry out the appropriate manoeuvre (Williamson turn, etc) to return to the MOB
- engines should be ready for immediate manoeuvre and thrusters made available
- the daylight signalling lamp and search lights must be ready for use and an additional crew member should be available on the bridge to help with their operation
- the ship's hospital should prepare to treat hypothermia and provide blankets/warm drinks to the main deck/point of rescue
- the authorities and other ships in the area must be alerted. Activate Digital Selective Calling (DSC)
- the lifeboat or rescue boat should be prepared for launching
- the vessel's speed should be reduced
- the gangways, gangway net, heaving lines, and lifebuoys with lines should all be prepared so that they are ready to use

Man Overboard Drill

- once the MOB is recovered, notify the Company.

General Notes

- The MOB should be approached with the ship downwind of his position, with the ship moving upwind
- on passage, this drill will typically take one hour of steaming time. You should be prepared to utilise any opportunities that present themselves when the ship has time in hand and can safely complete an MOB drill and associated manoeuvres.

Blackout/Power Failure – Bridge Response

These procedures may form part of the master's standing orders.

Suggested Drill Format

- Magnetic compass heading should be observed
- change to manual steering and steer using the magnetic compass
- the position of the vessel should be checked for any navigational dangers or hazards
- any equipment that may be affected by a power surge when the power returns should be switched off. This includes radars, ARPA, ECDIS, GMDSS station
- confirm that the emergency generator has started automatically and that designated equipment is actually receiving power
- the remaining steerage way should be optimised so that the vessel can be manoeuvred into a safe position or desired heading, taking into account the wind direction and any resultant drift
- the vessel should simulate the display of NUC light signals/shapes and a warning broadcast made to all other traffic in the area

Blackout/Power Failure – Bridge Response

- the AIS should be set to NUC
- determine what steps are being taken to restore the power
- the local coastguard, VTS and port authorities should be informed of the loss of power. They should also be regularly updated
- if necessary, the general emergency alarm should be sounded. This ensures that all hands are on standby for any possible emergency
- if the vessel is in shallow waters, prepare to carry out emergency anchoring
- the Company should be notified of the power loss and appropriate log entries made of the power loss.

Debrief

This presents an opportunity to train the crew in the use of the emergency generator.

Collision Drill

Suggested Drill Format

- The vessel should be manoeuvred to minimise the effect of a simulated collision
- simulate a reduction in speed, stop or put the engines astern
- sound the general alarm signal, warn the ship's staff by all available means
- all the watertight openings, doors and fire doors should be closed
- the VHF radio must be kept on the emergency channels.

After Simulated Collision

- Make a PA announcement to update all personnel
- complete muster of the crew
- check the remote tank gauging devices from the control room to get an overview of the situation

Collision Drill

- take soundings of the adjacent tanks, bilges and surrounding areas to the point of impact to assess the extent of the damage
- senior crew must assess whether own vessel is in imminent danger of sinking or losing stability
- simulated emergency messages should be prepared
- the vessel's ballast, cargo and GS pumps should be prepared to pump out and transfer any cargo, ballast or flood water
- for the purposes of a drill, one officer should simulate the other vessel
- contact should be established with the other vessel
- if vessels remain embedded together, agreement should be made to remain fixed in this position until action has been taken to restrict flooding. This may require one vessel maintaining ahead propulsion
- switch on deck lighting and simulate NUC signals
- gather information including the correct name of the vessel, Flag, port of registry, the owner, last port, next port, P&I Club, HM underwriters, as well as any other relevant information
- collect information about the incident
- do not discuss who was responsible or accept liability for the incident
- if possible, and without compromising the safety of your crew or vessel, offer to assist the other vessel
- it is important that complete and accurate records are kept
- the position of the vessel should be given to the operator of the GMDSS
- the closest MRCC, vessel traffic system (VTS) and local coastguard must be notified of the incident
- update the Company
- the VDR and ECDIS 'SAVE' button must be pressed
- if the vessel is in danger of sinking, prepare the lifeboats
- update coastguard or RCC. Keep crew and Company updated
- if own ship can safely move, proceed to the nearest safe refuge and moor own vessel safely
- establish whether own vessel is currently a danger to navigation
- log all events in the bridge movement book
- record all details of the incident in the deck logbook, official logbook and on an incident report form.

Additional Measures for Tankers

- Establish whether there is pollution
- change the main and auxiliary accommodation air conditioning plants to recirculation if there is a risk of a gas leak or fire. Shut all natural vents and isolate the exhaust fans
- during the drill, the AC should be put onto recirculation
- make sure that the VHF radio is kept on the emergency channels
- prepare the deck spray system.

Break Away from Berth Drill

Suggested Drill Format

- The terminal should be notified of the drill taking place
- the scenario involving a ship alongside transferring cargo should be simulated
- the general alarm must be sounded and all cargo, bunker and other ongoing operations stopped. The ESD should be activated
- any ship/shore cargo or bunker connections should be disconnected
- instruct the engine room to have the engines on standby as they may be used to relieve the stress on the remaining mooring lines or to manoeuvre so that the vessel remains alongside
- tug boats, mooring boats, linesmen, pilots and other appropriate external assistance should be requested
- letting go an anchor should be considered
- prepare additional or replacement moorings or leave the berth until the situation is resolved.

CHAPTER 40

Accident Investigation

Accident Investigation

The investigation of accidents and incidents plays a very important part in safety. It is by the identification and study of accidents, principally through the MAIB's accident reporting system, that similar events may be prevented in the future.

The statutory requirements regarding accident reporting are set out in the Merchant Shipping (Accident Reporting and Investigation) Regulations 2005, SI 2005 No 881. MGN 289 (M+F) provides guidance on how to comply with them.

The master is responsible for the statutory reporting of accidents and dangerous occurrences covered by the Regulations. Where a safety officer is on board, however, it is his statutory duty to investigate every such incident and it is expected that the master will rely extensively on the results and record of the safety officer's investigation when completing his report. The various stages of the typical investigation might proceed as follows:

1. When an incident occurs, priority must be given to the safety of the injured and of those assisting them, and to the immediate safety of the area. When sufficient help is available, however, the safety officer should, if possible, avoid involvement with the rescue operation and concentrate on establishing the immediate facts concerning the incident.
2. First he should record the names - and addresses in case of non-crew personnel - of all those present in the vicinity of the incident. Not all are likely to be witnesses to the actual incident but this can be ascertained later. He should then note and mark the position of the injured, and the use and condition of any protective clothing or equipment or of any tools

etc likely to have been in use. Possession should be taken of any portable items that might have some relevance to the investigation. Sketches and photographs are often useful.

3. When the injured have been removed, the safety officer should carry out a more detailed examination at the scene of the incident, watching out for any changes that might have occurred since the incident and any remaining hazards.

The points to look out for will depend on the circumstances. For example, after an incident during boarding, the following should be noted:

- Compliance with control measures identified by the risk assessment
- the type of access equipment in use
- the origin of the access equipment, eg ship's own, provided from shore etc
- the condition of the access equipment itself, noting particularly any damage such as a broken guard-rail or rung. The position and extent of any damage should be examined so that it may be compared with witnesses' statements, and it should be noted whether the damage was present before or occurred during or as a result of the incident (if the damage was present before the incident, it might have been potentially dangerous but it may not necessarily have been a factor in the particular incident)
- any effect of external factors on the condition of the equipment, eg ice, water or oil on the surface
- the deployment of the equipment, ie the location of the quayside and shipboard ends of the equipment
- the rigging of the equipment, the method of securing and the approximate angle of inclination
- the use of ancillary equipment (eg safety net, lifebuoy and lifeline, lighting)

Accident Investigation

- the safety of shipboard and quayside approaches to the equipment, eg guard-rails, obstructions and obstacles, etc
- any indication of how the incident might have happened, but remember that subsequent interviews with witnesses must be approached with an open mind
- weather conditions
- distances, where these are likely to be helpful or relevant.

Interviews of witnesses should take place as soon as possible after the incident when memories are still fresh. There may be people who were not actually witnesses but who may nevertheless have valuable contributions to make, for example a crewman who was present when an order was given. These persons should not be overlooked. If it is not possible for some reason to interview a particular person, he should be asked to send the safety officer his own account of the incident.

The actual interview should be carried out in an informal atmosphere designed to put the witness at his ease. To start with, the safety officer should explain the purpose of the interview and obtain some details of the witness's background. It is important to keep any personal bias out of the interview. The witness should be asked to relate the event in his own way with as few interruptions as possible. The accuracy of what is said should be tested. There may, for example, be discrepancies between the account of one witness and those of other witnesses, between different parts of a statement, or with the safety officer's own observations, which he may want to query. Leading questions implying an answer should be avoided, as should simple questions requiring only a yes/no answer which save the witness from thinking about what he is saying. Finally, the safety officer should go over the statement with the witness to ensure that it has been accurately recorded.

Statements for signature by the witness should be prepared as quickly as possible but, if the witness changes his mind about signing a statement, it should be annotated by the safety officer that it has been prepared on the basis of an interview with the witness who had subsequently refused to sign it or comment further. Where the witness asks for extensive alterations to the original statement, a fresh statement may have to be prepared, but the original statement should be annotated by the safety officer and retained.

It is helpful to adopt a standard format for statements by incident witnesses.

It is worth emphasising the importance of distinguishing between facts and opinions. Facts can normally be supported by evidence whereas opinions are personal beliefs. An investigation must depend on the facts gathered, but opinions can be helpful in pursuing a particular line of enquiry and should not be disregarded.

Any record of an incident or dangerous occurrence should contain at least the following information:

- Details of the incident or dangerous occurrence and any investigations, complaints or inspections
- date
- persons involved
- nature of injuries suffered
- all statements made by witness
- any recommendations/representations
- any action taken.

Additionally, it is suggested that the record should contain the following:

- list of witnesses, including addresses, positions and occupations
- whereabouts of original signed statements made by witnesses
- date that the accident/dangerous occurrence report was sent to the MAIB if applicable
- list of items collected, why and where stored
- index.

The record should be kept with the ship since it must be made available on request to the safety representative and safety committee, if any. It is also a necessary item of reference for safety officers on board the ship. If the ship is sold and remains on the UK register, the record should be transferred with the ship. Where the ship becomes a foreign ship, the record should be retained by the original owners.

CHAPTER 41

Stability

Stability

Stability – The ability of an object, such as a ship or aircraft, to maintain equilibrium or resume its original, upright position after displacement, as by the sea or strong winds.

Any ship floating in water will be acted upon by a number of forces. When stationary, the two main forces are the weight acting vertically downwards and the buoyancy acting upwards. Wind will also affect the ship's stability and, when making way or moving in the water, hydrodynamic forces, including centrifugal forces, interaction and wave motion, will all have a bearing on the resultant motion and stability of the ship.

In most practical calculations, officers deal with the ship in a static (stationary) condition to determine the stability and structural forces acting upon the ship. Consideration is given to the ship when underway, particularly in regard to the effects of freeboard and in relation to GZ curves.

Weight is the downward effect of gravity acting on all parts of the ship. The distribution of this weight will determine the draught, angle and positioning of the ship in the water.

Buoyancy is the resultant effect of the pressure distribution on the ship's hull below the waterline and the density of the water the ship is floating in. The draught that the ship will float at is defined by:

- The law of flotation, which states that every floating object displaces its own mass of the fluid in which it floats
- the Archimedes principle, which states that, when a body is wholly or partially immersed in a fluid, it experiences an upthrust equal to the mass of liquid displaced.

In simple terms, this means that a ship will float at a draught where the weight of the volume of the water displaced is the same as the weight of the ship. The volume of this water is calculated as follows:

$$Volume\ (m^3) = mass\ (t)/density\ (t/m^3)$$

When calculating the stability and draught of the ship, the mass is described as the displacement (Δ):

$$Displacement\ (t) = Volume\ (m^3) \times Relative\ Density\ (t/m^3)$$

Density is calculated relative to fresh water (FW), which has a value of 1.000 t/m³, and

Stability

is called relative density (RD). Salt water is considered to have a value of 1.025 t/m³ and dock water (DW) can vary.

As a ship's hull is not a uniform box shape, ie it changes at the stern and bow and with the draught of the ship, it is not possible to accurately calculate displacement or draught without accounting for the change of shape. A ship's shape is described numerically using form coefficients, which are ratios that compare the underwater shape of the ship.

While it is possible to determine small changes of draught using the TPC values (tonnes per centimetre) provided in a ship stability manual, which are calculated at regular intervals of draught, larger changes of draught associated with significant loading or ballasting operations can only be accurately observed by consulting the ship's hydrostatic particulars.

Load lines

With the exception of a few ships (eg warships and small pleasure craft), ships are assigned a minimum freeboard and corresponding set of load lines. Load lines limit the maximum draught that the ship can be loaded to in fresh water and salt water in different ocean regions. These are governed by the International Convention on Load Lines, 1966 (as amended).

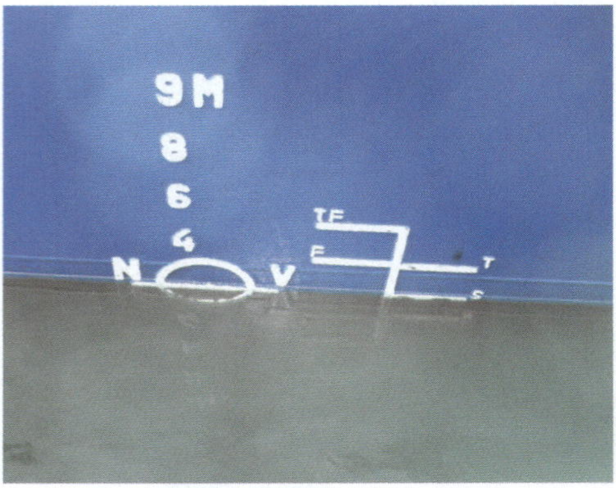

Figure 41.1 - Chemical tanker loaded to her summer marks (load line)

The Convention requires that ships should have the following Plimsoll Line (the line cutting the circle) and corresponding load lines.

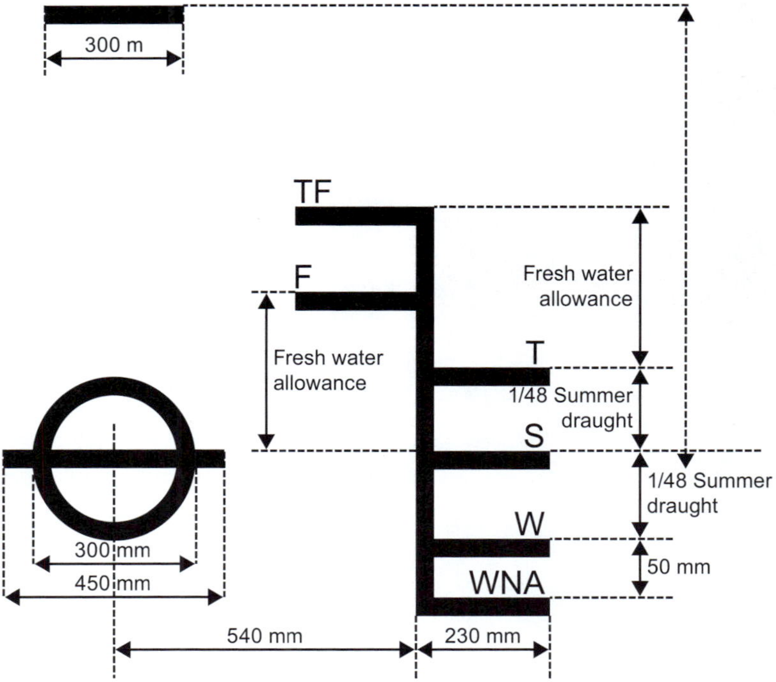

Figure 41.2 - Load line marks (starboard side)

When calculating the quantity of cargo that a ship is to load, it is vital that the draught never exceeds the applicable load line. Consequently, the load line calculation involves the total displacement of the ship including bunkers and water consumed at the appropriate stage of the voyage, including any seasonal changes while on passage.

It is sometimes necessary for the load lines of ships to be amended, eg through legislative changes or onboard structural modifications. The amendments will need to be reflected in the ship's documentation and permanently made on the hull of the ship.

Figure 41.3 - Amended loadlines on the hull of an oil tanker

Simple Trim and Stability

Transverse Stability

When a force, such as from wind or waves, acts upon a ship, it will produce heel. To return a ship from a heeled position after the force is removed requires a 'righting lever'. On a stable ship, the weight force (Wf) acts downwards through the transverse centre of gravity (G) and the buoyancy force (bf) acts upwards through the centre of buoyancy, allowing the lever to return the ship upright, ie:

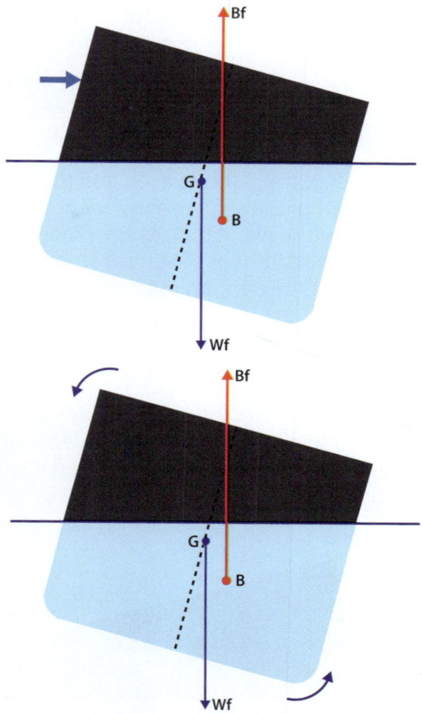

Figure 41.4 - Positive statical stability

This 'righting lever' is the horizontal distance between the centre of gravity and the vertical line acting through the centre of buoyancy. This is shown as GZ and is measured in metres.

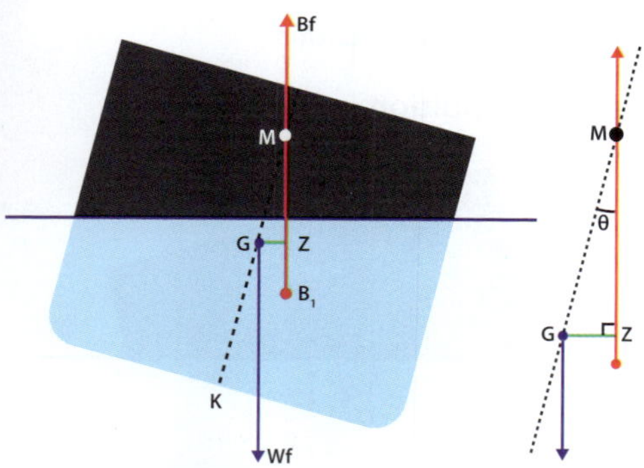

Figure 41.5 - Righting lever

Figure 41.5 illustrates where the force of buoyancy intersects the centreline of the vessel (M). This point is called the metacentre or the initial transverse metacentre. When the ship is heeled beyond small angles (generally beyond 10°), the metacentre will move away from the centreline, as the underwater displacement will

Stability

change, so the centre of buoyancy will move outwards.

The distance from the keel to the metacentre is called KM and the vertical distance GM is the metacentric height.

The product of the righting lever and the displacement of the ship (ie a distance multiplied by the weight) provides a moment, specifically the 'Moment of Statical Stability', also known as the righting moment:

$$\textit{Righting Moment (tm)} = GZ\ (m) \times \Delta\ (t)$$

Stable Condition

Where GM is positive, the ship will have a stable condition, ie it will have positive stability and when the external force is removed it will return upright:

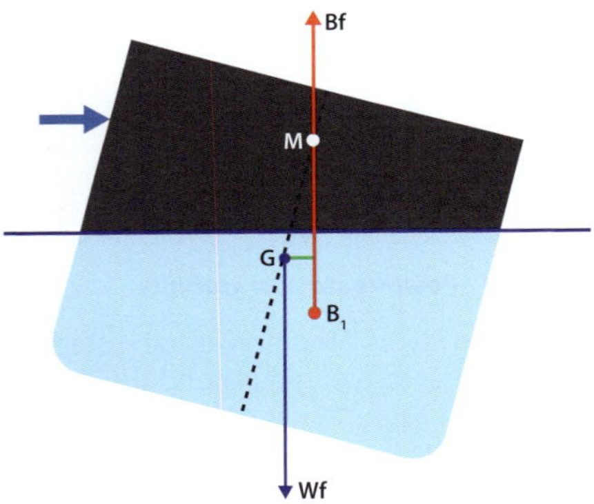

Figure 41.6 - Stable condition

Neutral Condition

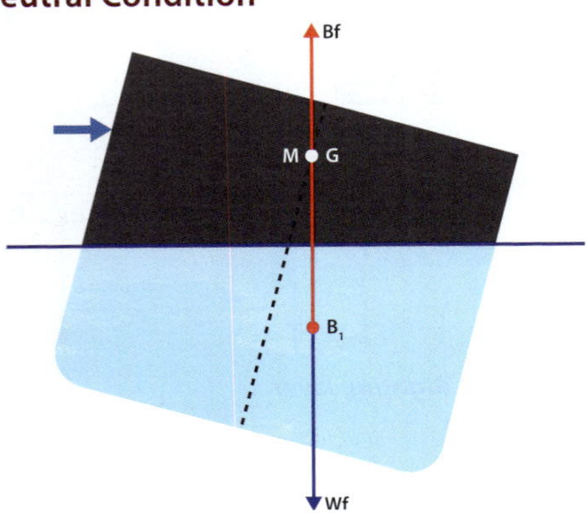

Figure 41.7 - Neutral condition

Where GM is zero (the metacentre is at the same position as the centre of gravity), the ship will have a neutral condition. When the external force is removed, the ship will remain in the heeled position.

Unstable Condition

An unstable condition is where the ship has a negative GM, ie the centre of gravity is above the metacentre. This negative stability means that, when the ship is heeled from the upright, rather than creating a righting lever, a capsizing lever exists that continues to heel the ship further.

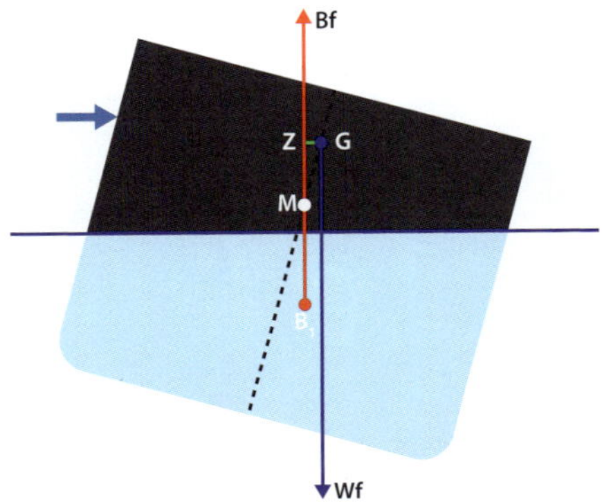

Figure 41.8 - Unstable condition

If the capsizing lever is sufficient, the ship could capsize. However, because the underwater shape changes with the angle of heel, it is possible (provided KG is not too high) that the centre of buoyancy will move out from the centreline below the centre of gravity, holding the ship in the heeled position. This is an 'angle of loll' and is a precarious situation where waves or strong winds could capsize the vessel. There are strict guidelines on how angles of loll should be rectified.

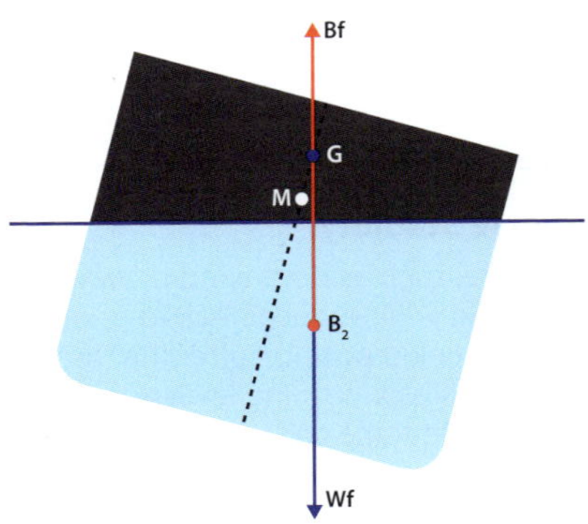

Figure 41.9 - Angle of loll

GZ Curves

The transverse statical stability of a ship is provided on a graphical curve of statical stability, ie a GZ curve. The GZ values are derived from the KN values provided by a shipbuilder at increasing values of heel. The GZ values are plotted against the angles of heel.

In addition to the GZ at specific angles of heel, the initial GM, the approximate angle of deck edge immersion and the moment of statical stability at different angles can be calculated using Simpson's Rules.

Compliance with the IMO intact stability criteria can be established using GZ curves. The criteria are illustrated in Figure 41.12.

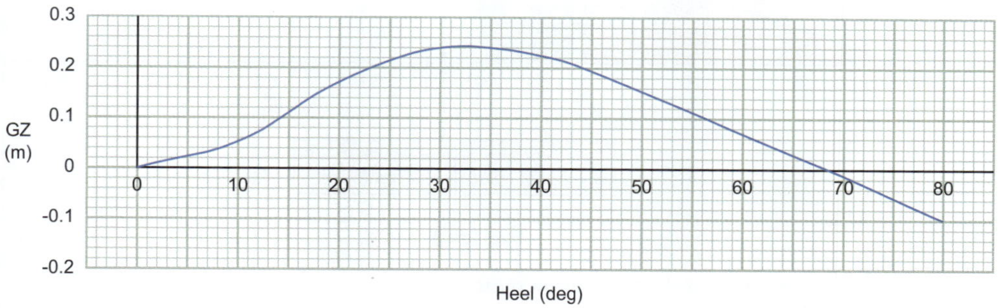

Figure 41.10 - GZ curve

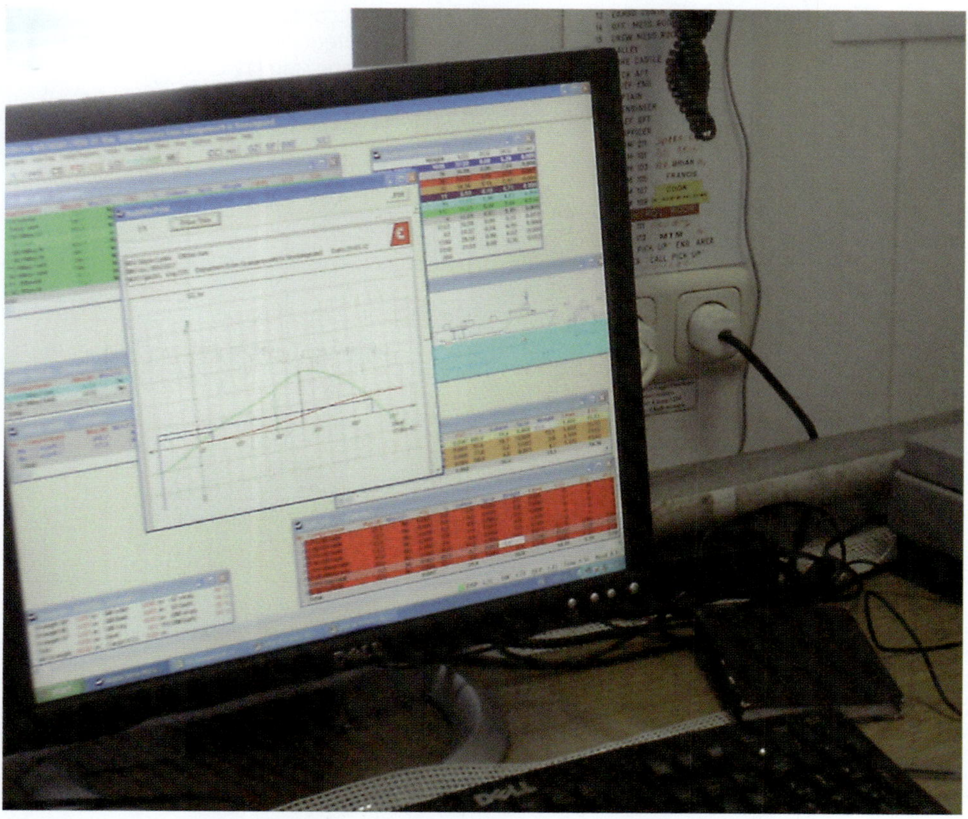

Figure 41.11 - GZ curve loadicator

Stability

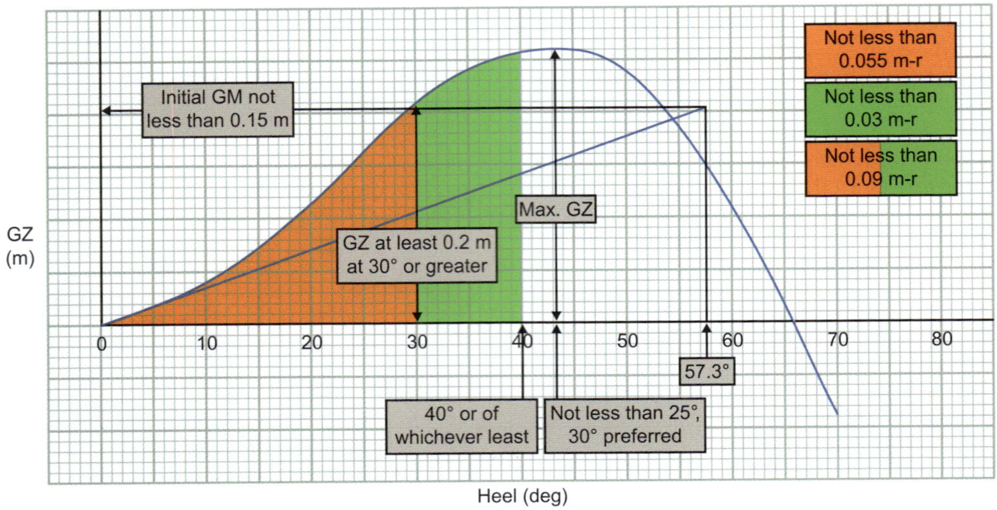

Figure 41.12 - Minimum intact stability for cargo ships

The approximate angle of deck edge immersion (DEI) can be estimated from the point of inflexion on the curve. In Figure 41.12, this is very roughly 25°.

Ships carrying timber can load to a reduced freeboard, provided the cargo is stowed and secured in accordance with the appropriate timber deck regulations and meets the following static stability criteria.

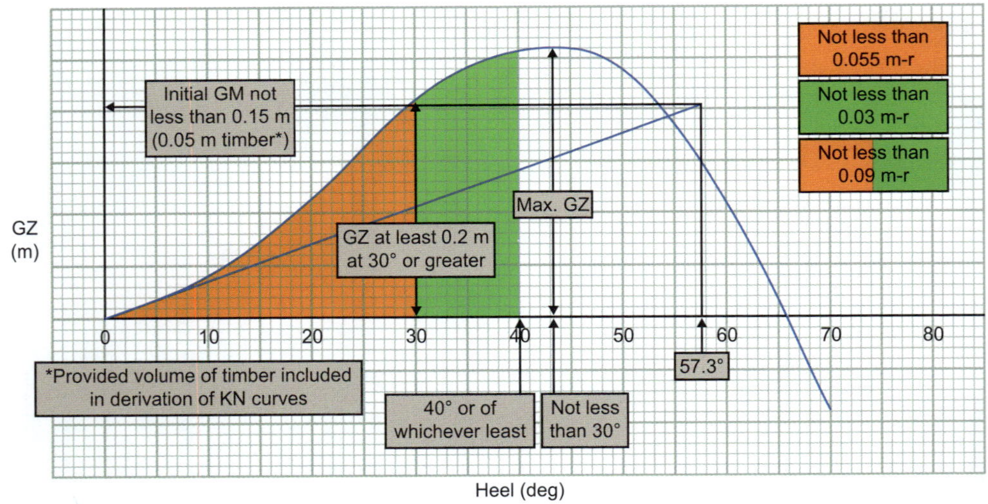

Figure 41.13 - Minimum intact stability for cargo ships carrying timber deck cargo

Metacentric Height (GM)

A ship with a large GM is considered 'stiff'. This is caused by loading excessive weight low in the ship, creating a small KG that gives the ship a very short roll period. In addition to making the ship uncomfortable, it adds to safety concerns for crew movement, possible structural damage, excessive strain on cargo lashings and increased risk of cargo shift. Such a situation can occur on bulk carriers with high density cargo such as iron ore. The use of ballast in hopper tanks can reduce this.

A ship with a small GM is considered 'tender'. This creates a long roll period, where the ship can roll to large angles of heel, reducing stability, retaining strain on lashings for long periods and increasing the risk of cargo shift.

However, it needs to be remembered that the GZ curve only shows statical stability, ie when a ship is momentarily at rest in still seas. The GZ curve has the following limitations:

- Estimates of lightship conditions can introduce errors and variations between the physical ship and the ship's drawings
- it assumes that trim and calculations are correct
- swell and waves cause rolling and pitching which affects the 'area under the curve', reducing the stability of the vessel. When swell and waves pass a ship, the distribution of displaced water volume changes, moving the centre of buoyancy and affecting the position of the transverse and longitudinal centre of buoyancy
- ice accretion, deck cargo water absorption and water shipped on deck can reduce the GM
- water movement on deck will also have a dynamic effect on the GM and list
- swell motion can lift a ship, increasing the vertical position of buoyancy and the magnitude of the force, changing the righting moment.

Most ships are presently unable to monitor or calculate dynamic stability, so it is important that the effects are considered when loading or ballasting a ship to ensure adequate residual stability that at least meets the IMO minimum criteria for statical stability.

GZ Curve Conditions

Stable Ship

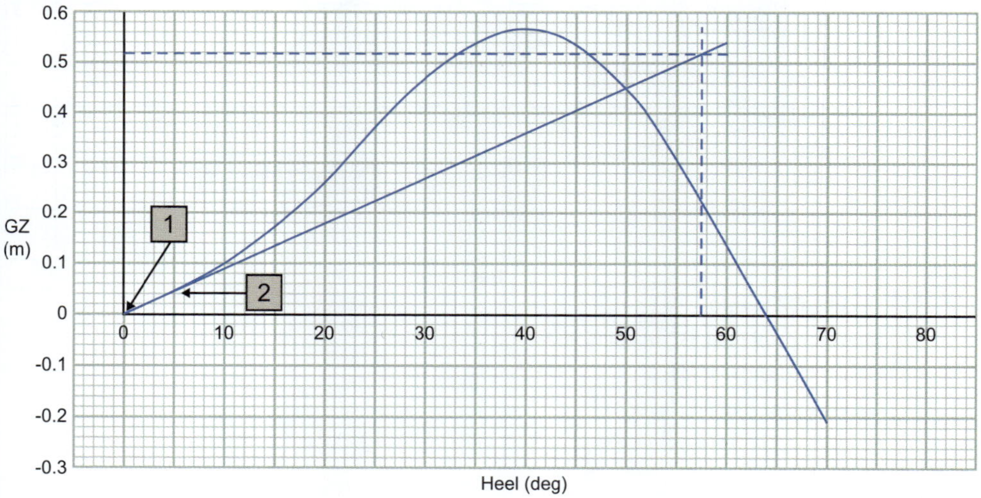

1 Ship upright

2 Small angle of heel, GZ increases, righting lever

Stability

Neutral Ship

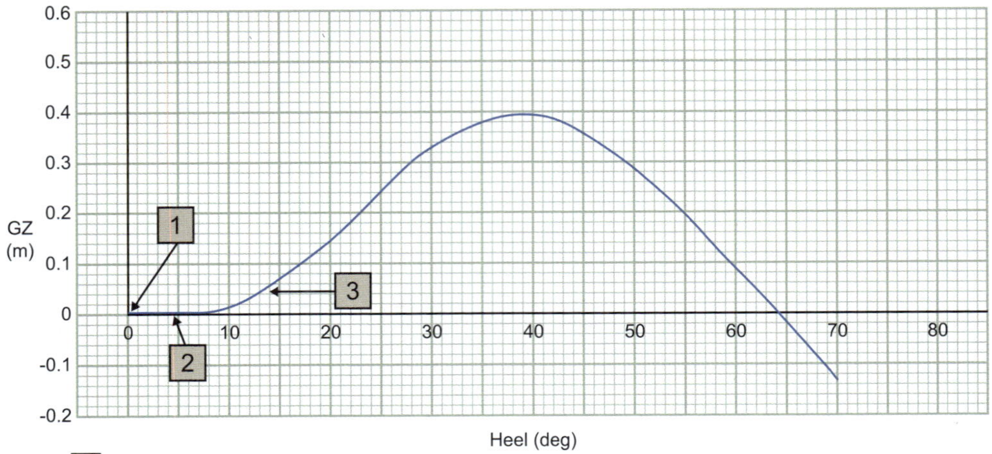

1 Upright, GZ is zero
2 Small angle of heel, GZ remains at 0
3 Heel beyond small angle, GZ increases, righting lever

Angle of Loll

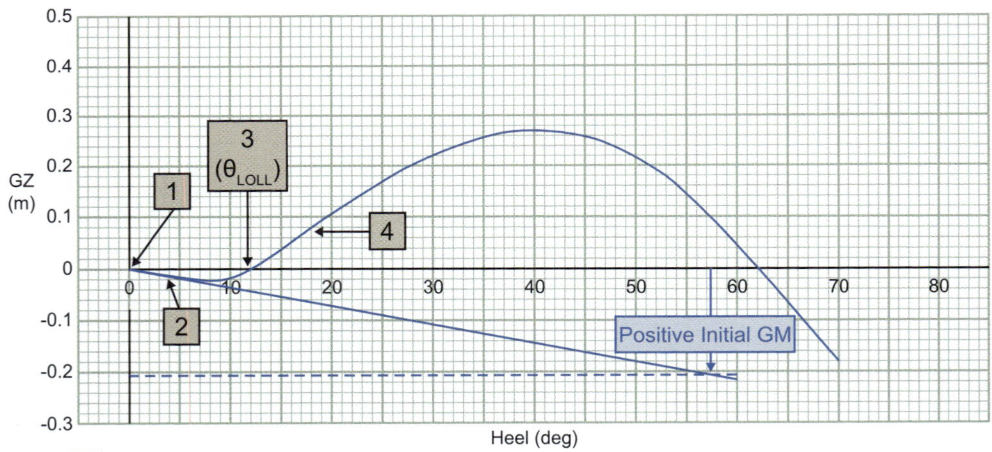

1 Upright, GZ is zero
2 Small angle of heel, GZ remains at 0
3 GZ is zero, angle of loll
4 GZ increases, righting lever

Listed Ship

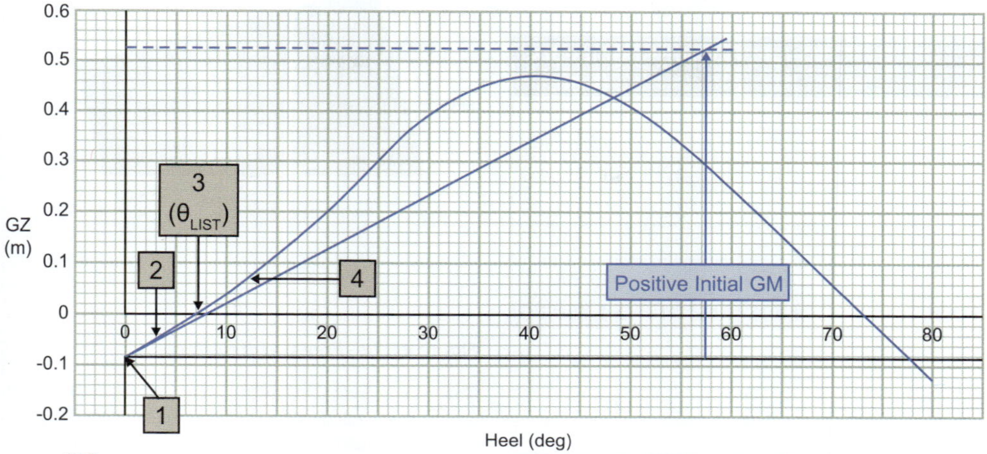

1 Upright, negative GZ, ship will list

2 Negative GZ, ship continues to list

3 GZ equals zero, ship rests at an angle of list

4 GZ increases, righting lever

Final KG and Angle of List

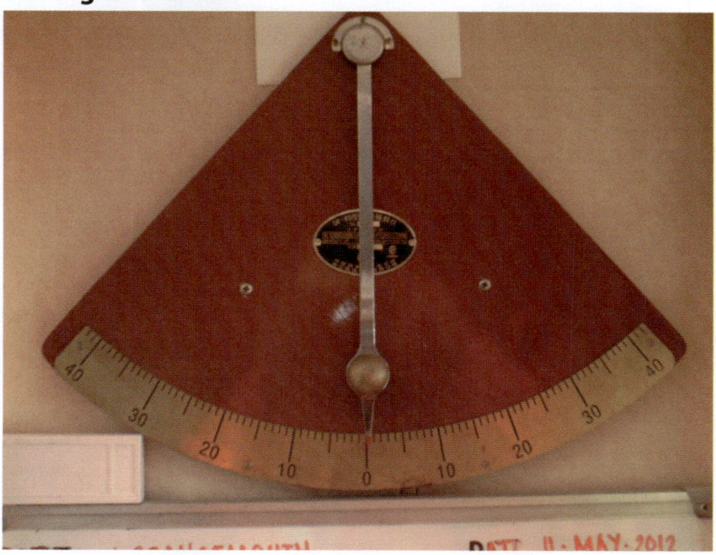

A ship's list can be calculated as follows:

A ship displaces 8,350 tonnes, KG 7.00 m and is initially upright.

The following cargo is worked:

Load	*200 t at Kg 0.8 m, 6.0 m to port of CL* *100 t at Kg 2.3 m, 7.0 m to stbd of CL*
Discharge	*45 t from Kg 4.0 m, 5.0 m to port of CL* *300 t from Kg 13.0 m, 5.2 m to stbd of CL*

The KM for the final displacement from the ship's hydrostatic tables (8,305 t) is 9.1 m.

Stability

The final GM and angle of list on completion of cargo is calculated as follows:

	Weight (t)	KG (m)	Moments (t-m)
Initial Displacement	8,350	7	58,450.00
Load	200	0.8	160.00
Load	100	2.3	230.00
Discharge	-45	4	-180.00
Discharge	-300	13	-3,900.00
Final	**8,305**	**6.594**	**54,760.00**

KM	9.1
KG	6.594
GM	**2.506**

Weight (t)	Distance off Centreline	Port Moments (t-m)	Starboard Moments (t-m)
8,350	0.00	0.00	0.00
200	6	1,200.00	
100	7		700.00
45	5		225.00
300	5.2	1,560.00	
		2,760.00	925.00
	Listing Moment	**1,835.00**	

$$\text{Tan List} = \frac{GG_h}{GM} = \frac{0.221}{2.506} = 5.1° \text{ to port}$$

Free Surface Effect

Free surface effect (FSE) is the effective reduction in GM caused by the movement of fluid in a partially filled tank that negatively affects the transverse statical stability of a ship. This is one of the most common causes of instability in ships and was a particular problem with double hull tankers, due to the width of the double bottom tanks.

The effect is shown in Figure 41.14 where a volume of water has moved to the heeled side. The centre of gravity of the volume of fluid in the tank moves from g to g_1. This fluid movement effectively moves that portion of weight upwards, away from the keel and towards the metacentre. This reduces the GM (solid) to G_VM and is known as the effective or fluid GM.

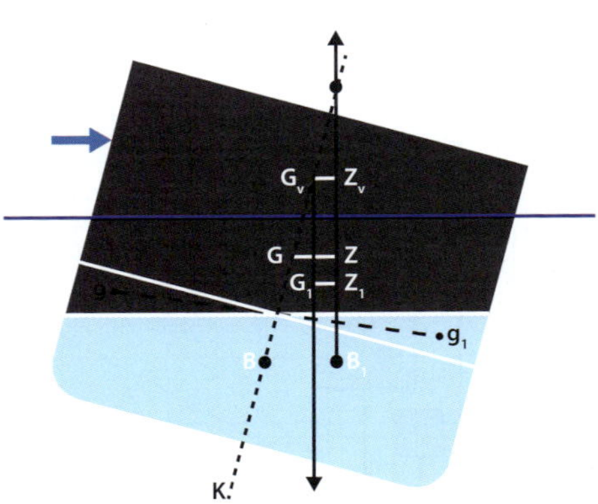

Figure 41.14 - Free surface effect

It is vital when calculating the GM of a ship that all FSEs are accounted for to ensure the final GM is the fluid GM. Free surface effect can be calculated using the formula:

$$GG_V = \frac{lb^3}{12V} \times \frac{dt}{ds}$$

GG_V	*virtual rise of G*
l	*tank length*
b	*tank breadth*
dt	*density of the liquid in the tank*
ds	*density of the water in which the ship floats*
v	*volume of displacement of the ship*

Once calculated, this can be applied to (subtracted from) the solid GM.

Free Surface Moments

It is generally more practical, particularly when dealing with a number of tanks, to use free surface moments (FSM) rather than FSE. The FSM of the fluid in a (rectangular) tank can be calculated by:

$$\text{FSM (t-m)} = \frac{lb^3}{12} \times dt$$

GG_V	*virtual rise of G*
l	*tank length*
b	*tank breadth*
dt	*density of the liquid in the tank*
ds	*density of the water in which the ship floats*

Free surface moments are given at regular sounding intervals for ship tanks in the ship's stability book and can be applied in the same manner as when calculating a final KG.

If the FSM of 630 t from the two loaded tanks (295 t and 335 t) are accounted for and applied to the previous example, this reduces the final (fluid) GM, reducing stability (and increasing the list).

	Weight (t)	KG (m)	Moments (t-m)
Initial Displacement	8,350	7	58,450.00
Load	200	0.8	160.00
Load	100	2.3	230.00
Discharge	-45	4	-180.00
Discharge	-300	13	-3,900.00
FSM			630.00
Final	**8,305**	**6.669**	**55,390.00**

KM	9.1
KG	6.669
GM	**2.431**

Heavy Lifts

When undertaking a heavy lift, special attention needs to be paid to the stability of the vessel, ensuring FSE is minimised, there is adequate fluid GM and the angle of heel is minimised (and monitored).

When involving any suspended weight, the KG of the weight will be transferred to the point from which the weight is suspended, ie the crane or derrick head. When the weight is plumbed over side, the transverse moment will increase to this position too, resulting in an increased angle of list.

A ship displacing 18,000 t, KG 7.00 m and KM 7.9 m, is to load 70 t from a position 16 m to starboard of the ship's centreline on the berth. The crane's head is 40.0 m above the keel. Determine the maximum list and the final list when the weight is loaded 5 m to starboard of the centreline at a height of 12 m above the keel.

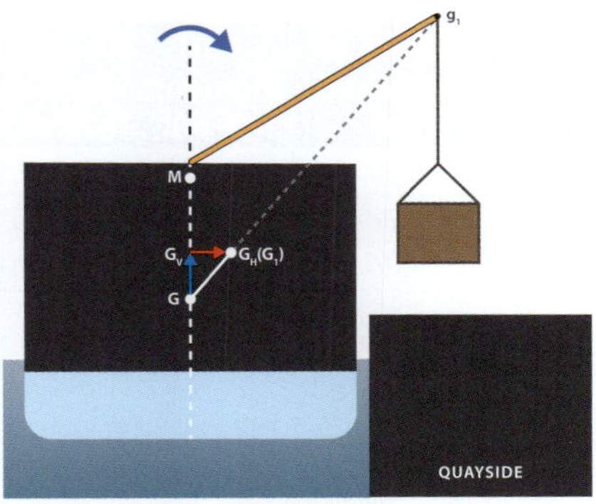

Figure 41.15 - Increased KG and list due to a heavy lift

List when weight suspended:

	Weight (t)	KG (m)	Moments (t-m)
Initial Displacement	18,000	7	126,000.00
Load	70	40	2,800.00
Final	18,070	7.128	128,800.00

KM	7.900
KG	7.128
GM	**0.772**

Weight (t)	Distance off Centreline (m)	Port Moments (t-m)	Stbd Moments (t-m)
18,000	0.00	0.00	0.00
70	15	0.00	1,050.00
		Listing Moment (t-m)	1,050.00

Stability

$$GG_h \frac{\text{List Mom.}}{\text{Final } \Delta} = \frac{1{,}050}{18{,}070} = 0.058$$

$$\text{Tan List} = \frac{GG_h}{GM} = \frac{0.058}{0.772} = 4.3° \text{ to starboard}$$

Final list when loaded:

	Weight (t)	KG (m)	Moments (t-m)
Initial Displacement	18,000	7	126,000.00
Load	70	12	840.00
Final	18,070	7.019	126,840.00

KM	7.900
KG	7.019
GM	**0.881**

Weight (t)	Distance off Centreline (m)	Port Moments (t-m)	Stbd Moments (t-m)
18,000	0.00	0.00	0.00
70	5	0.00	350.00
		Listing Moment (t-m)	350.00

$$GG_h \frac{\text{List Mom.}}{\text{Final } \Delta} = \frac{350}{18{,}070} = 0.019$$

$$\text{Tan List} = \frac{GG_h}{GM} = \frac{0.019}{0.881} = 1.2° \text{ to starboard}$$

Other precautions should include:

- Complete a risk assessment, permit to work and tool box talk prior to commencing the operations
- use additional mast stays
- ensure lifting and running gear is suitable, fully certified, inspected and in good working order
- the working area should be clear and only personnel necessary for the operation should be in the area
- ensure no other cargo or fluid transfers are taking place
- inform the engine room
- crane or winch drivers should be certified and competent
- prepare the deck area for the load. Remove rails if required
- attach guide line to steady the load during the lift if required
- ensure moorings are tight and fenders are in place
- barges should not be fast alongside
- lift the gangway
- clear ice or free water off the decks
- when lifting the load, initially take the weight, inspect the load and equipment and then continue the operation.

Correcting an Angle of Loll

An angle of loll develops where a ship is initially unstable with a negative GM, but then regains a positive GZ at a listed angle. An angle of loll may develop on passage due to the following:

- Bunkers and water, normally located in tanks with low KGs, are consumed
- FSE created by slack fuel or water tanks
- water absorption in deck cargo
- ice accretion on superstructures
- water trapped in cargo pipes
- ingress of water
- flooded compartments when fire-fighting.

Where a ship develops an unexpected list condition, it should be treated as an angle of loll until confirmed otherwise; treating an angle of loll as a list could have severe consequences. To correct an angle of loll, the following should be borne in mind:

- Alter the ship's heading to bring the head into the predominant waves
- confirm the port and starboard listing moments are equal. Ensure it is not a list. Check whether:
  - cargo has shifted
  - fuel has been transferred
  - ballast has not been changed
- confirm any slack tanks
- take action to reduce the KG by:
  - emptying any high ballast tanks one at a time, reducing the high side first
  - pressing up any low ballast tanks
  - transferring bunker fuel
  - ballasting low or DB tanks, one tank at a time to minimise FSE.

When pumping ballast into low tanks, where there are two transverse port and starboard tanks, fill the lowest tank completely first. It is important to avoid the ship lurching upright, and beyond, as it could capsize the vessel. Where there is a third centre tank, fill it first, then fill the low tank and finally fill the high side DB tank.

Also refer to Chapter 42 on Damage Stability.

Longitudinal Stability and Trim

The trim of a ship is the difference in metres between the forward and aft draughts. Generally, ships operate better with a small stern trim to enable better rudder and propeller immersion and general ship handling. However, excessive trim by the stern can cause too much windage forward which will impede handling, cause heavy pitching and could impede visibility from the bridge.

It is rare for a ship to be trimmed by the head as it can reduce propeller immersion, impede handling and can lead to excess water being shipped on the forecastle. As pipe suctions are normally fitted aft, it becomes very difficult to discharge ballast or bilges when necessary.

The following terms relate to the trim of a ship:

Forward Perpendicular (FP)

The vertical line intersecting the summer load waterline at the forward edge of the stem on an even keel.

After Perpendicular (AP)

The vertical line that coincides with the after edge of the stern post or the turning axis of the rudder.

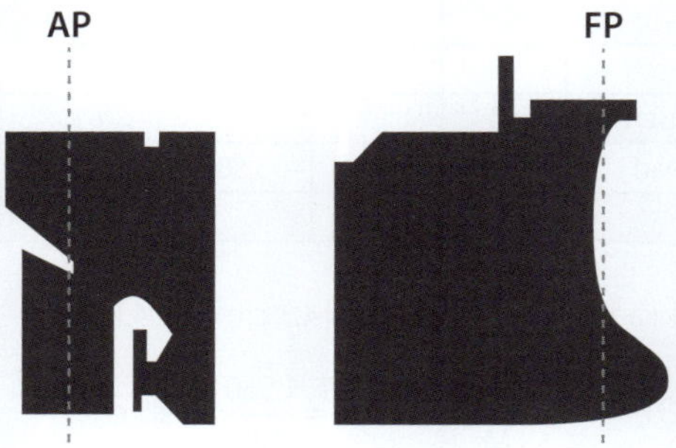

Length Between Perpendiculars (LBP)

The horizontal distance between the FP and the AP.

Length Overall (LOA)

The horizontal distance between the aftermost and foremost parts of the ship.

Amidships

This is the midpoint between perpendiculars.

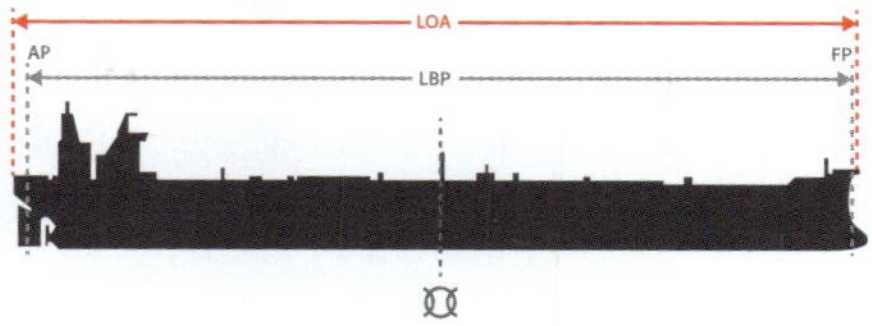

Figure 41.16 - Length between perpendiculars (LBP)

True Mean Draught

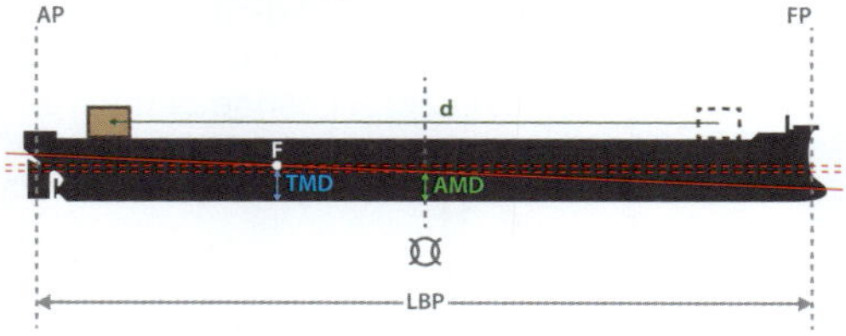

Figure 41.17 - Position of true mean draught (TMD)

The reference point for calculations of LCG, LCB and LCF is normally stated as 'forward of the aft perpendicular' (FOAP).

When the LCF is located amidships ⅊, ie half the length of the LBP, the mean draught of the ship is the arithmetical mean of the forward and after draughts. This is termed the arithmetical mean draught (AMD). However, due to the underwater shape of the ship, the AMD is rarely the actual or true mean draught (TMD) of the ship. The TMD is located at the LCF of the ship and

Figure 41.18 - Draught marks at the after perpendicular

Stability

is required to determine the true displacement of a ship because hydrostatic particulars are produced for a ship floating on an even keel.

TMD can be calculated as follows:

$$\text{TMD} = \text{Draft aft} - \frac{[(\text{Draft aft} - \text{Draft forward}) \times \text{LCF FAOP}]}{\text{LBP}}$$

When using this formula, it should be noted that the relationship Draught aft—Draught forward automatically gives a negative value where the ship is trimmed by the head so provides a correct TMD.

MCTC

Moment to change trim by one centimetre (MCTC) is tabulated in ships particulars and provides the relationship at specific draughts or displacements that enables change of trim to be calculated.

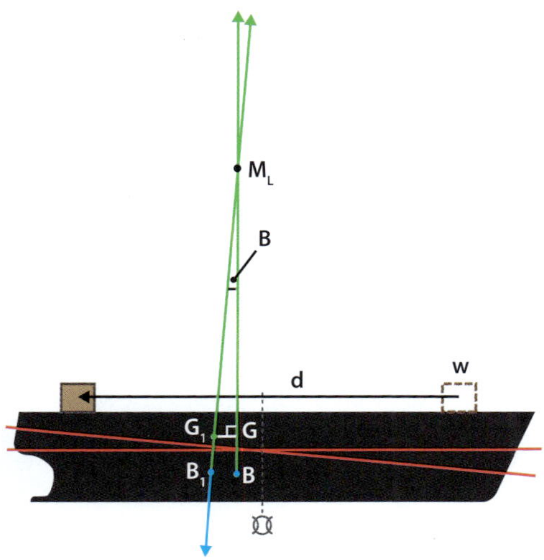

$$\text{MCTC} = \frac{W \times GM_L}{100\ \text{LBP}} \qquad \text{COT (cm)} = \frac{W \times d}{\text{MCTC}}$$

MCTC	*Moment to Change trim by 1 cm*
GM_L	*longitudinal GM*
LBP	*length between perpendiculars*
W	*volume of displacement of the ship*
COT	*change of trim*
w	*transferred weight*
d	*transferred distance*
LCF	*longitudinal centre of flotation*
LCG	*longitudinal centre of gravity*
LCB	*longitudinal centre of buoyancy*
Tf	*change of trim forward*
Ta	*change of trim aft*

Calculating Trim

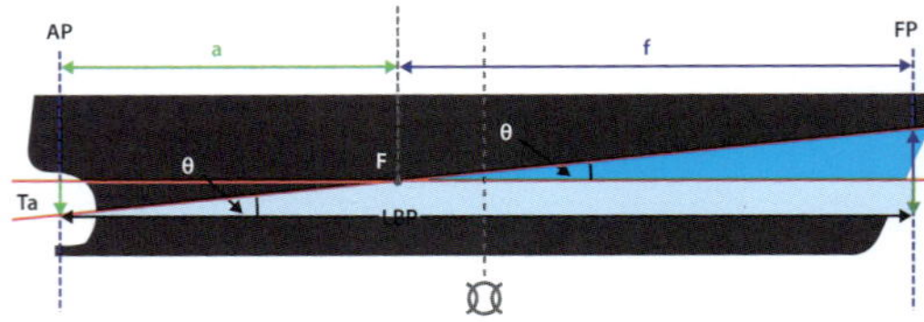

$$\text{Tf} = \frac{f \times \text{COT}}{\text{LBP}} \qquad \text{Ta} = \frac{a \times \text{COT}}{\text{LBP}}$$

NB In this instance 'a' equals the LCF

Figure 41.19 - Calculating trim forward and aft

Small Changes of Draught and Trim

Where there is only a small change in draught, the TPC of the ship can be used to calculate the change of draughts as the underwater volume of the ship is unlikely to change significantly.

A ship with an LBP 122 m and draughts 6.3 m forward and 6.5 m aft loads and discharges a small amount of cargo in the following spaces.

	Weight (t)	LCG FAOP (m)
Load	110	15
Load	55	85
Discharge	45	15
Discharge	55	70

From Hydrostatic Particulars	
LCF	57 m
TPC	13.9
MCTC	125 t-m

This can be calculated as follows:

	Weight (t)	Dist. from LCF (m)	Head Moments (t-m)	Stern Moments (t-m)
Load (+)	105	42		4,410
Load (+)	53	28	1,484	
Disch. (-)	48	42	2,016	
Disch. (-)	50	13		650
Load	60		3,500	5,060
				1,560

$$\text{Sinkage} = \frac{\text{Weight}}{\text{TPC}} = \frac{60\ \text{t}}{13.9} = 4.3\ \text{cm} = 0.043\ \text{m}$$

$$\text{COT} = \frac{\text{Trimming Moment}}{\text{MCTC}} = \frac{1{,}560}{125} = 12.5\ \text{cm}$$

$$\text{Ta} = \frac{\text{LCF} \times \text{COT}}{\text{LBP}} = \frac{57}{122} = 5.8\ \text{cm} = 0.058\ \text{m}$$

Tf = COT ~ Ta = 12.5–5.8 = 6.6 cm = 0.066 m

	Forward	Aft
Initial draughts	*6.300 m*	*6.500 m*
Sinkage	*0.043 m*	*0.043 m*
	6.343 m	*6.543 m*
Trim	*-0.066 m*	*0.058 m*
Final Draughts	***6.277 m***	***6.601 m***

Larger Changes of Draught and Trim (Hydrostatic Tables)

When calculating larger changes to trim, hydrostatic data is more accurate. This works by taking moments about the LCF. In order to do so, the initial TMD is required to establish displacement, MCTC and LCF. The final displacement is then established and the values for MCTC, LCF and TMD are taken.

A ship with an LBP 165 m and draughts 4.0 m forward and 4.2 m aft loads cargo in the following spaces.

	Weight (t)	LCG FAOP (m)
Load	1,500	145
Load	3,000	100
Discharge	2,800	60
Discharge	3,000	45

The AMD, 4.1 m, gives an initial displacement of 12,000 t and LCF 87 m. The initial TMD is then calculated as 4.095 m and from the hydrostatic tables provides the following:

Displacement	12,231 t
LCF	87 m
LCB	88 m
MCTC	310 t-m

The initial LCG is found from:

$$COT = \frac{W \times (LCB \sim LCG)}{MCTC} \qquad LCB \sim LCG = \frac{COT \times MCTC}{W}$$

So, LCG = 87.5 m

The final condition is calculated:

Weight (t)	Weight (t)	LCG (m)	Moments (t-m)
Initial Displacement	12,000	88	1,050,000
Load	1,500	145	217,500
Load	3,000	100	300,000
Load	2,800	60	168,000
Load	3,000	45	135,000
Final Displacement	22,300	**83.88**	1,870,500

From hydrostatic data:

TMD	7.5 m
LCF	84 m
LCB	86 m
MCTC	350 t-m

$$COT = \frac{W \times (LCB \sim LCG)}{MCTC} = 135.1\text{ cm} \quad Ta = \frac{COT \times a}{LBP} = 68.8\text{ cm}$$

Tf = COT – Ta = 66.3 cm

	Fwd	Aft
Final TMD	7.500 m	7.500 m
Trim (stern)	0.663 m	0.688 m
Final Draughts	**6.837 m**	**8.188 m**

Ship Loading Calculation

The following provides a simplified example of loading an older small bulker with 5 holds and 5 tween decks, LBP 142 m. The data in the table is taken from the ship's particulars and cargo loaded and is used to determine the final draughts and fluid metacentric height (GM).

The following would be taken from hydrostatic particulars at the loaded displacement:

TMD	8.16 m	LCB	71.9 m	LCF	71 m
MCTC	221.3 m	KM	8.80 m		

$$KG_{fluid} = \frac{\text{Vert Mom}}{\text{Weight}} = \frac{142{,}168.3}{17{,}894.1} = 7.945\text{ m}$$

$$LCG = \frac{\text{Long Mom}}{\text{Weight}} = \frac{1{,}276{,}271.5}{17{,}894.1} = 71.323\text{ m}$$

$$COT = \frac{W \times (LCB \sim LCG)}{MCTC} = 46.6 = 0.466\text{ m, by the stern}$$

$$Ta = \frac{COT \times a}{LBP} = 0.233\text{ m}$$

Stability

	Capacity (m^3)	Stowage Factor	Weight (t)	KG (m)	Vert Moment (t-m)	FSM (t-m)	LCG (m)	Long Moment (t-m)
Holds (4)	15,986.0	2.03	7,874.9	7.3	57,486.6		79	622,115.3
TD 1	998.0	1.98	504.0	11.2	5,645.3		125	63,005.1
TD 2	1,426.0	2.3	620.0	10.9	6,758.0		95	58,900.0
TD 3	1,350.0	2.72	496.3	10.4	5,161.8		65	32,261.0
TD 4	968.0	1.98	488.9	11.1	5,426.7		35	17,111.1
Consumables			1,700		4,784	3,500		58,736.00
Dwt			11,684.1		85,262.3			852,128.5
Lt Ship			6,210.0	8.6	53,406.0		68.3	424,143.0
Displacement			17,894.1		138,668.3	3,500		1,276,271.5

Tf = COT – Ta = 0.233 m

	Fwd	Aft
Final TMD	8.160 m	8.160 m
Trim (stern)	0.233 m	0.233 m
Final Draughts	**7.927 m**	**8.393 m**

KM	8.800 m
KG_{fluid}	7.945 m
GM_{fluid}	**0.855 m**

Longitudinal and Transverse Forces

Ships experience forces that vary along the length of their hulls due to the effects of uneven weight distribution acting downwards and the buoyancy from the water acting upwards. The most notable and problematic of these are bending moments and shearing forces.

These forces always exist and it is important that they are kept within tolerable parameters to ensure the structural integrity of the vessel, both in harbour and at sea.

Bending Moments and Shearing Forces

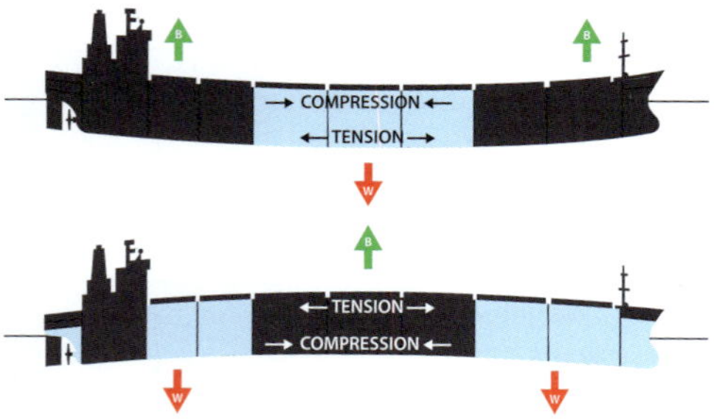

Figure 41.20 - Sagging (top) and Hogging (bottom)

Bending moments refer to moments that act to bend a ship by a force that is applied around a pivot point. Bending moments are created by internal forces (weight) and external forces (buoyancy).

When the bending moments act to bend the mid-section of the ship downwards, it is known as sagging, and when the mid-section bends upwards it is called hogging. Bending moments can occur when loading a ship where excessive volume of cargo is loaded unevenly in holds.

At sea, the situation can be further exacerbated when the ship meets swell with a long period, increasing the forces with potentially catastrophic results.

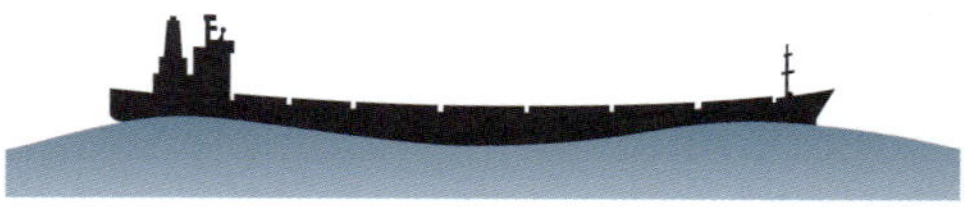

Sagging wave

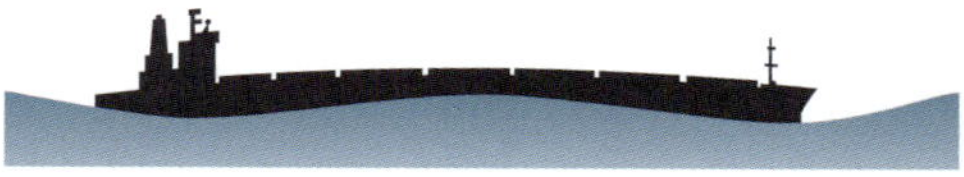

Hogging wave

Shearing forces are created by two forces that act in opposite directions and, if sufficient, may damage (or shear) the structure. These forces commonly occur at transverse bulkheads where forces of weight and buoyancy act in relative opposition to each other.

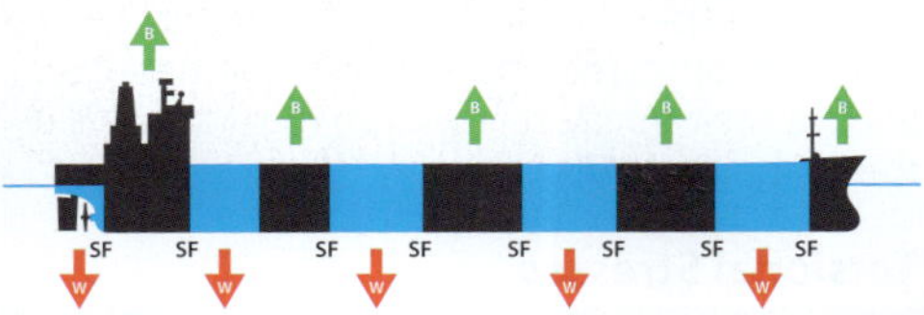

Figure 41.21 - Shearing forces

Both of these forces have resulted in structural failure of ships, with bulk carriers being the most commonly affected ship type due to their construction and often high density cargoes. Where ships with structural limitations are prohibited from carrying solid bulk cargo with a density of 1,780 kg/m^3 and above, SOLAS XII Regulation 8 requires that, in addition to permanent notation in the stability booklet, they should have an appropriate triangle marked on the hull.

Figure 41.22 - Triangle marked on bulk carrier hull

While most ships now have loading computers, it is important that deck officers understand how the forces are calculated in order to fully understand their effects.

Producing SF and BM curves

The following is a simple explanation of a box-shaped vessel.

A ship in fresh water, length 60 m, breadth 10 m, draught 5 m with 3 equal compartments of length 20 m, has loaded 120 t evenly in the middle hold.

The light displacement of the ship is calculated by:

$$Lt\ \Delta = Length \times Breadth \times draught \times density$$

Lt Δ = LBd x Rd = 60 × 10 × 5 × 1.000
= 3,000 t

Lt Δ t/m = 50 t/m

Cargo weight t/m = 6 t/m

Buoyancy force = Lt Δ+ Dwt = 3,120 t

Buoyancy force t/m = 52 t/m

Hold No.	Lt Δ (t/m)	Dwt (t/m)	Total Wf (t/m)	Bf (t/m)	Load (t/m)
1	50	0	50	52	**2**
2	50	6	56	52	**-4**
3	50	0	50	52	**2**

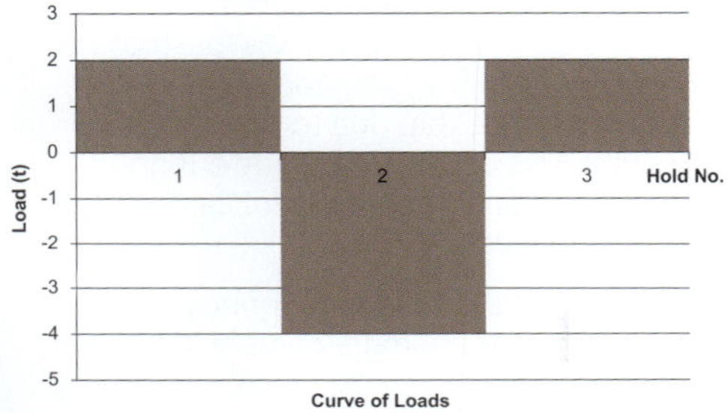

From the curve of loads, the shearing forces can be calculated, by determining the area under the curve from the AP to each point in length. In this case, it is calculated at 5 m intervals.

Length FOAP (m)	0	5	10	15	20	25	30	35	40	45
Shearing Force (t/m)	0	10	20	30	10	-10	-30	-20	-10	0

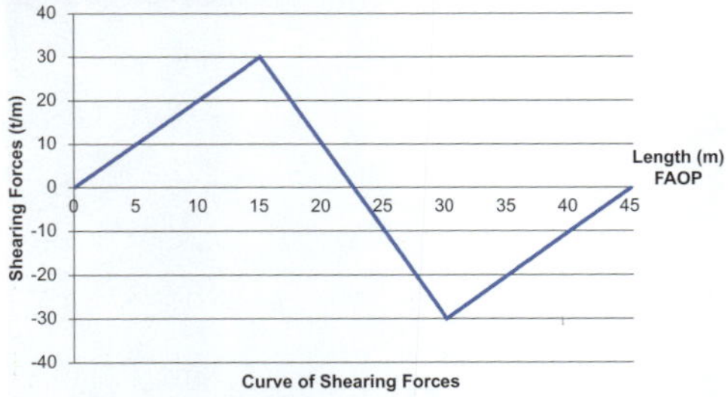

From the curve of shearing forces, the bending moments can be calculated, by determining the area under the curve from the AP to each point in length, again calculated at 5 m intervals.

Length FOAP (m)	0	5	10	15	20	25	30	35	40	45
Bending Moments (t/m)	0	25	100	225	325	325	225	100	25	0

Stability

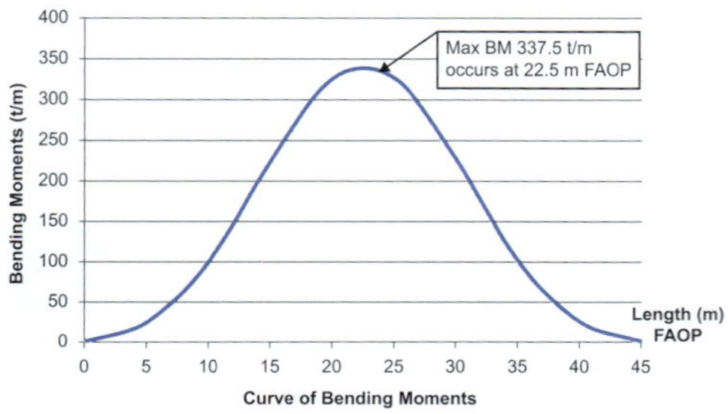

The curve shows a clearly sagged ship, which is as expected with only the amidships hold loaded. It is quite common for ships to experience both hogging and sagging over the length of the ship due to the distribution of weight. This occurs frequently during cargo operations when different cargoes are introduced at various stages.

Although based on the same principles, real ship calculations are more complex as hulls are not box-shaped, cargo spaces vary in size and dimension, and there may be a very large number of holds or tanks involved. By using a ship's loading computer, which should be Class approved, the forces involved can be quickly calculated and the condition assessed. However, the calculations are only as accurate as the data entered by the user, and this data is only as accurate as the measurements taken.

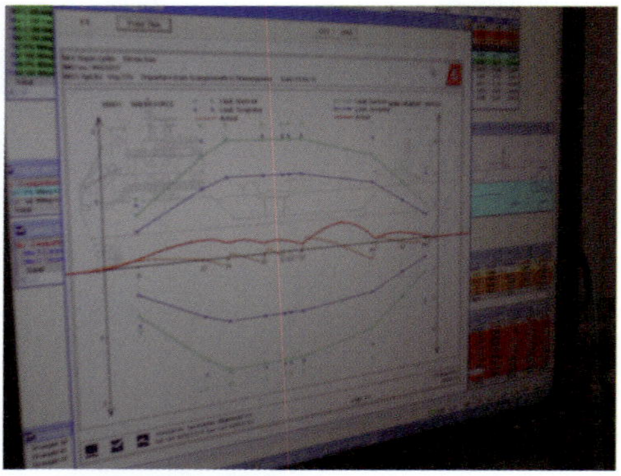

Figure 41.23 - Loading computer SF and BM calculations on a small LPG tanker

When assessing and comparing the results, the harbour (port) maximum permissible values for SFs and BMs will almost always be greater than those given for the seagoing condition. This is due to the dynamic effects of the sea and the potential damage to structures caused by hogging or sagging waves. This enables a greater degree of flexibility for ships to carry out cargo operations while in still water. However, on completion of cargo operations and before departure, the ship must be within the seagoing limits.

Torsional Stresses

Figure 41.24 - Torsional stresses are experienced even on smaller container ships

Torsional stresses occur in vessels where opposing forces are experienced transversely both from internal weight distribution and from the external effects of buoyancy while at sea. The design of container ships, with large open hatches that do not contribute to transverse structural strength, makes them subject to warping and horizontal bending moments, so additional strengthening is required.

When ships are being loaded or ballasted, uneven transverse distribution of weight results in similar forces to those experienced longitudinally.

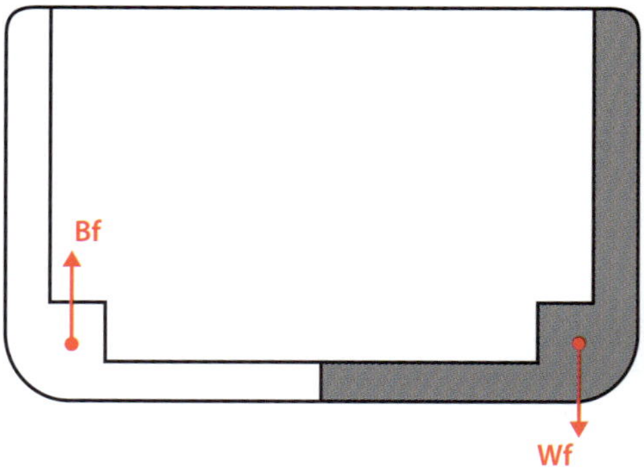

Figure 41.25 - Torsional stress due to internal weight distribution

At sea, a ship can experience similar effects when encountering oblique waves on the shoulder or quarter. The effect of encountering oblique waves at this aspect tends to twist the ship's structure over its length.

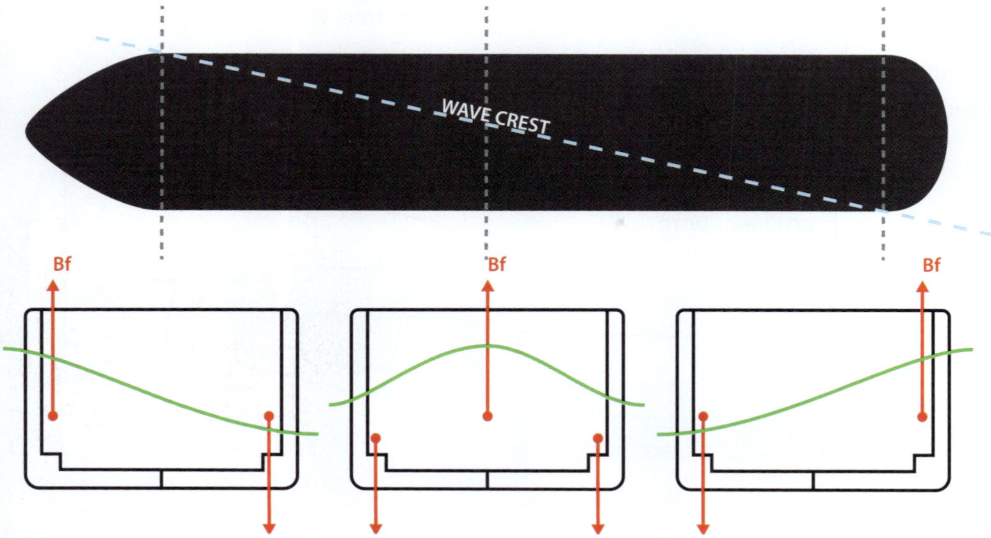

Figure 41.26 - Torsional stress due to oblique wave (viewed from forward)

Ship Stability Formulae

$$\text{FWA (mm)} = \frac{\text{DISPL Summer}}{4\text{TPC}_{\text{SW}}}$$

$$\text{DWA (mm)} = \text{FWA} \times \frac{(1025 - \text{RD Dock Water})}{25}$$

$$GZ = GM \times \sin\theta$$

$$\text{Sinkage (cms)} = \frac{w}{\text{TPC}}$$

Calculating List Caused by a Transverse Shift of Weight

The distance that G moves off the centreline, GGH, is calculated using the formula:

$$GG_H = \frac{w \times d}{W}$$

The angle at the metacentre in the right-angled triangle GGHM is the list (termed q).

$$\tan\theta_{\text{LIST}} = \frac{GG_H}{GM}$$

Change of Trim

$$\textbf{COT (cms)} = \frac{\textbf{Trimming moment}}{\textbf{MCTC}}$$

where the trimming moment is: $w \times d$

'w' being the weight shifted, and

'd' being the distance through which the weight is shifted longitudinally.

Thus: $$\boxed{\text{COT (cms)} = \frac{w \times d}{\text{MCTC}}}$$

The Wall-Sided Formula

$$GZ = (GM + \tfrac{1}{2}BM\tan^2\theta)\sin\theta$$

True Mean Draught

$$\text{TMD} = dA - \left(\frac{(dA - dF)}{\text{LBP}} \times \text{LCF foap}\right)$$

where: ***dA*** is the draught aft
dF is the draught forward
LCF foap is the position of the LCF expressed as being so many metres forward of the aft perpendicular
LBP is the length between perpendiculars.

Stability

Drydocking

Calculate initial TMD

$$TMD = dA - \left(\frac{(dA - dF)}{LBP} \times LCF\ foap\right)$$

Calculate the P force at the critical instant

$$P = \frac{COT\ (cms) \times MCTC}{Dist\ LCF\ foap}$$

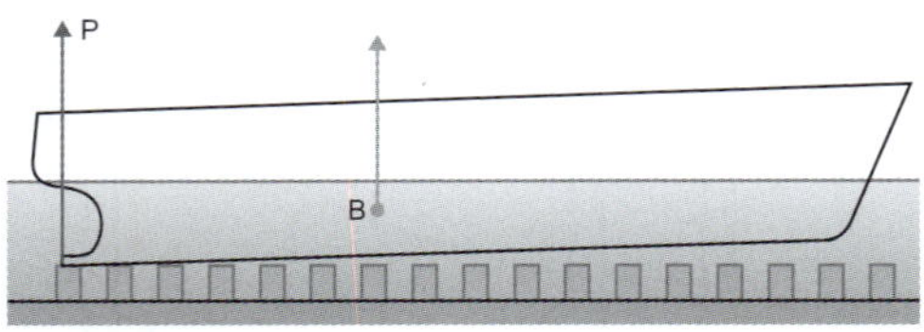

Angle of Heel While Turning

$$Tan\theta = \frac{V^2 \times BG}{g \times R \times GM}$$

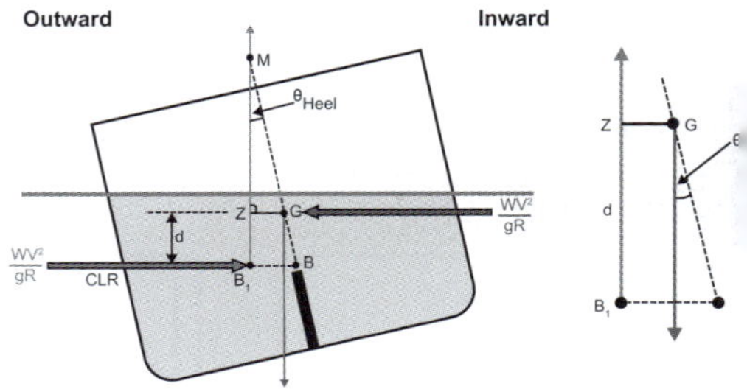

Load Line

Load Line Mark and Accompanying Load Lines

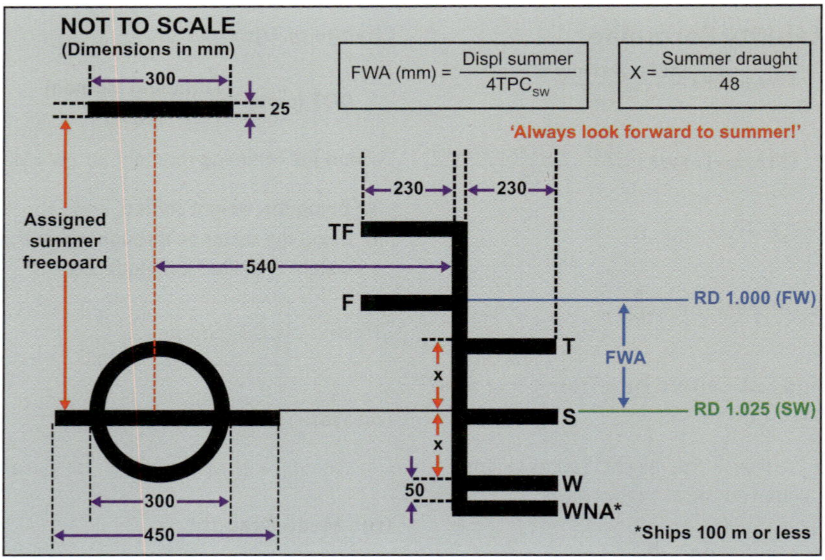

CHAPTER 42

Damage Stability

Damage Stability

A ship will sink or capsize if:

- **The extent of damage is more than the ship was designed to sustain**
- **a small amount of damage spreads within the hull and reaches a dangerous level with watertight integrity compromised**
- **initial stability before damage was not sufficient or the weather conditions were worse than the vessel was built to withstand.**

The fundamental requirement is that a ship can withstand two-compartment damage, as even a very small hole in the hull can flood two compartments if the damage occurs in the way of a watertight bulkhead. Compromising a ship built to withstand three-compartment damage would require damage that is at least as long as the shortest compartment (on a Panamax sized ship, this compartment length would be ~11 m).

Suffering hull damage greater than two compartments is an extreme situation. However, compartments can be lost without breach of the hull, such as in cases where progressive flooding of the hull occurs because watertight doors have been left open or not closed quickly enough.

Damage Stability - Introduction

Damage stability is a ship's ability to cope with damage situations caused by flooding, while ship stability is a ship's performance in still conditions (harbour condition) and in waves (sea condition).

The loss of residual stability generally occurs due to flooding, where water build-up within the hull reduces the centre of gravity and increases the metacentric height. Another case where loss of stability occurs is where an empty tank is breached and filled with water, resulting in a loss of buoyancy of the ship.

While en route from Belgium to Portugal, in January 2007, severe gale force winds and huge waves caused serious damage to the hull of the *'MSC Napoli'*, including a crack in one side and a flooded engine room. *'MSC Napoli'* is shown beached off the south coast of England.

Calculation of damage stability deals with the probability of occurrence and that of survival, ie the damage is combined with consequences to produce a damage stability index number that abides by certain regulations.

Analysis by IMO found that the forward area of ships suffered the most during accidents. This was taken into account to improve the designs of ships and to increase safety.

SOLAS - Stability in Damaged Condition

SOLAS Chapter II-1 specifies the details of Construction – Structure, subdivision and stability.

Part B of Chapter II Regulations 4 to 25 gives details regarding the subdivision and stability requirements for passenger ships and RoRo vessels.

Part B-1 of Chapter II gives the requirements of subdivision and stability for cargo ships.

Damage Stability Calculation According to SOLAS 2009

The latest damage stability calculation regulations were included in MSC.Res.216(82) and incorporated in amendments known as SOLAS 2009.

Courtesy MCA

Damage Stability

Damage stability calculations are more complicated than intact stability calculations.

The loss of stability from flooding may be due in part to the free surface effect. Water accumulating in the hull usually drains to the bilges, lowering the centre of gravity and increasing the metacentric height. This assumes the ship remains completely stationary and upright. However, once the ship is inclined to any degree (a wave strikes it for example), the flood water in the bilge moves to the low side. This results in a list.

Stability is also lost due to flooding when, for example, an empty tank is holed and fills with seawater. The lost buoyancy of the tank results in that section of the ship lowering into the sea slightly, creating a list.

In stability calculations, when a tank is holed, its contents are assumed to be lost and replaced by seawater. If these contents are lighter than seawater (light oil for example), buoyancy is lost and the section lowers slightly in the water accordingly.

Unstable Condition and Angle of Loll

A ship is in an unstable condition if, when heeled by an external force in still water to a small angle, it continues to heel further when the external force is removed.

Consider a ship that is floating upright in still water with G and B as shown. The initial transverse metacentre (M) is below G.

KM – KG = GM, which has a negative value.

The ship now heels to a small angle of inclination.

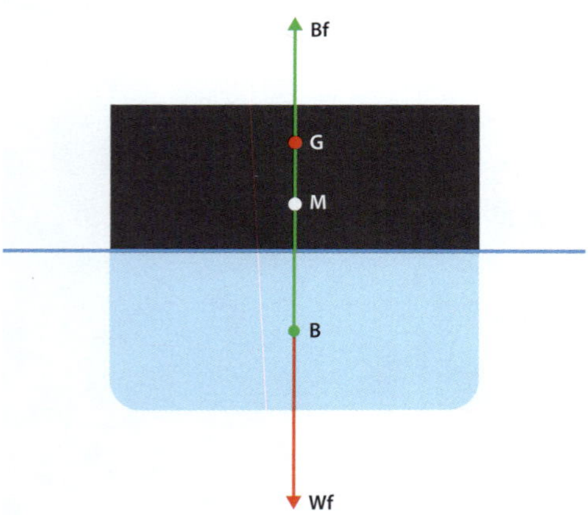

Consider the lines of action of Wf and Bf. They are acting in such a way to cause the ship to heel further over. GZ is a capsizing lever.

As the ship continues to heel, the centre of buoyancy (B) will move outward as the underwater volume of the ship changes shape.

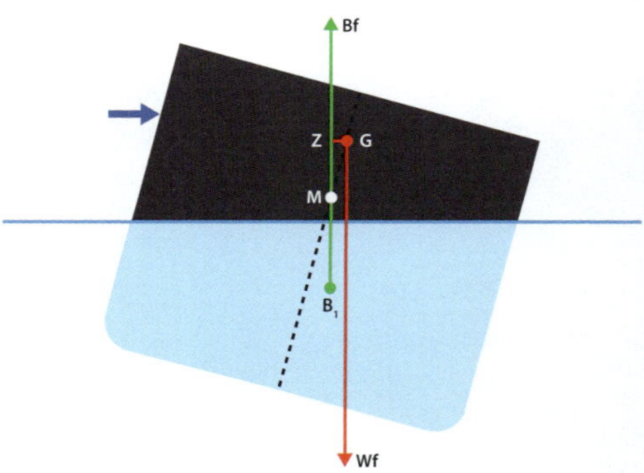

Provided that the centre of buoyancy can move sufficiently outboard to attain a new position vertically below G, the capsizing lever will disappear and the ship will come to rest at an angle of loll. If the centre of gravity were very high, the ship would possibly capsize.

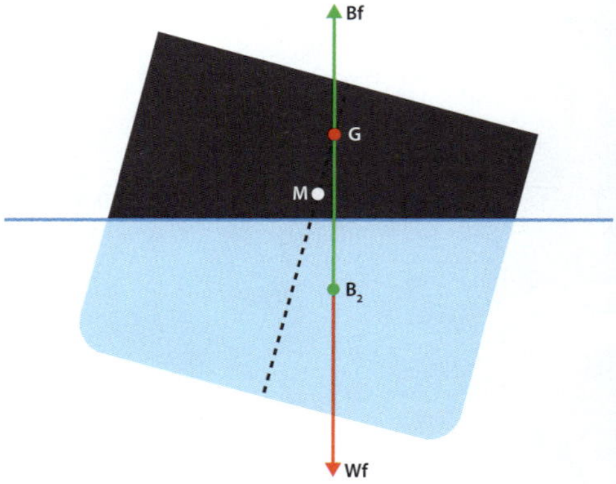

Unstable Condition and Angle of Loll

If the ship is heeled beyond the angle of loll, the centre of buoyancy (B) will move outboard of the centre of gravity (G). This causes a positive righting lever (GZ) that will act to return the ship back to the angle of loll.

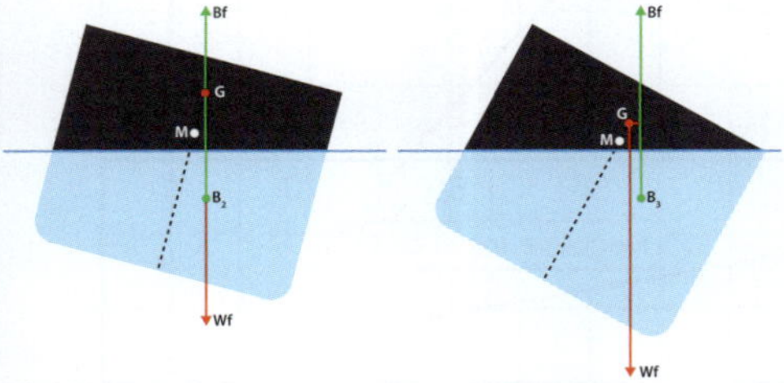

Note: A ship lying at an angle of loll is in a potentially dangerous situation. If wind and/or waves were to cause the ship to roll through the vertical, it would, in theory, come to rest at the same angle of loll on the other side. However, the momentum of the ship as it rolls over may be sufficient to cause it to capsize. In any event, cargo shift would be likely, which would cause the situation to worsen further.

The free surface effect in slack tanks is a principal cause of instability in ships, and is discussed on the following pages.

Curve of Statical Stability for a Ship in an Unstable Condition (Angle of Loll)

A ship is in an unstable condition if, when heeled by an external force in still water to a small angle, it continues to heel further when the external force is removed.

Consider an unstable ship being progressively inclined from the upright. The initial transverse metacentre (M) is below G.

KM – KG = GM, which has a negative value.

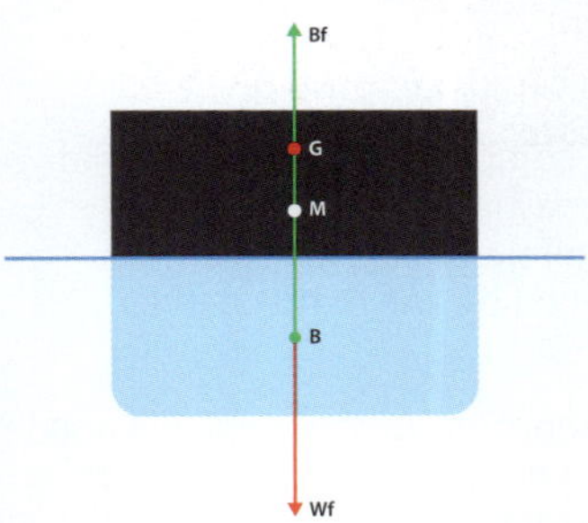

(1) Ship upright – GZ is zero (ship would not remain upright, but would loll to either port or starboard)

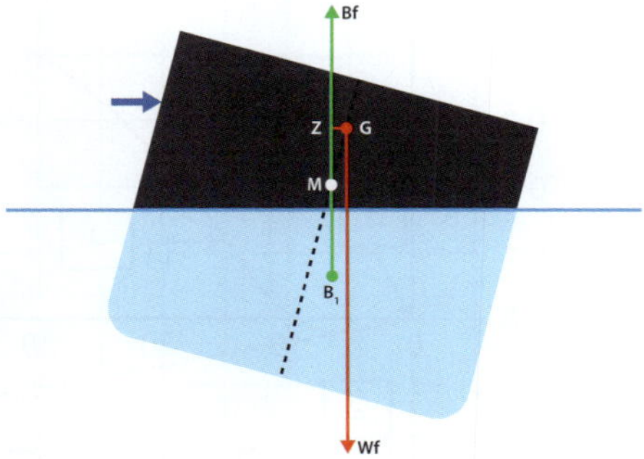

(2) Ship inclined to a small angle – GZ is negative (acting to capsize the ship)

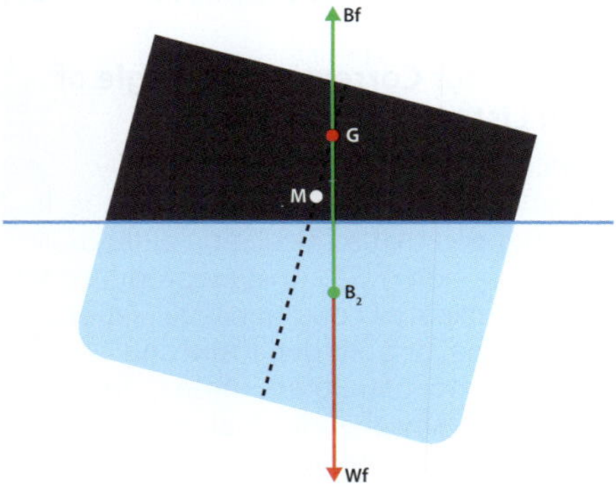

(3) Ship comes to rest at angle of loll – GZ is zero

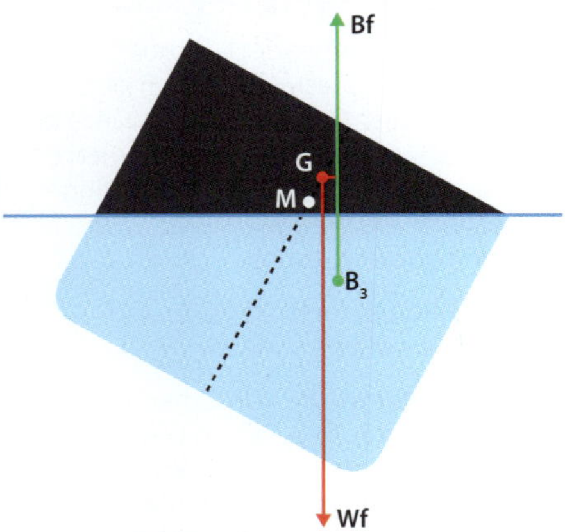

(4) Ship inclined beyond angle of loll – GZ becomes positive

The curve of statical stability for such a ship is depicted in the above diagrams (1), (2), (3) and (4) are related to the curve shown.

Unstable Condition and Angle of Loll

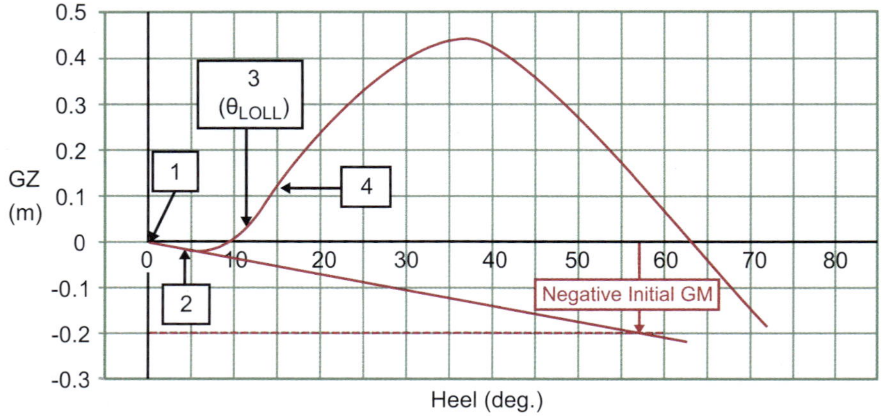

Figure 42.1 - GZ curve showing the previous four ship conditions

Procedures for Correcting an Angle of Loll and List

The stability of the ship should be closely monitored during the course of the voyage. It is recommended that a calculation of fluid GM and a corresponding GZ curve be produced for the worst anticipated condition. Calculations should be done for both departure and anticipated arrival conditions, these being adjusted to suit any changes that may take place as the voyage progresses.

An angle of loll situation can arise for a number of reasons:

1. Ships carrying timber deck cargoes. Timber deck cargoes will absorb moisture, which will cause G to rise. An allowance of 15% of the weight of the timber carried on deck should be made when conducting calculations and determining GZ values for the condition in question.

2. Consumption of fuel and water and introduction of free surfaces.

   Fuel and water will be consumed from low down in the ship, raising G due to the removal of weight from low down in the ship and the introduction of free surfaces in tanks that initially may have been full. Even ballast tanks that are initially full may become slack as a voyage progresses due to the constant rolling and pitching of the ship at sea causing water to escape from tank air pipes on deck. Tanks may need to be topped up occasionally, particularly when stability is considered marginal at any stage during the voyage. Poor cargo and ballast tank management resulting in excessive free surface moments is the most common cause of loll situations, excepting damage scenarios.

3. Heavy lift operations using the ship's lifting gear.

   An instantaneous loss of GM will occur as soon as a weight is lifted either off the deck or from a position over the side. Such large increases in KG must be considered prior to any heavy lift operations, and calculations should be conducted in advance to ensure that:

(a) The ship has adequate stability at all stages during the lift

(b) maximum list is restricted to an acceptable limit.

4. Shift of bulk cargo.

   The vertical component of a shift of solid bulk cargo may reduce GM sufficiently to cause a loll situation, particularly if accompanied by one of the above scenarios.

   The larger horizontal component will also create listing moments, compounding the situation further.

   Unfortunately, things do not always go to plan and mistakes may be made in calculations. Any number of occurrences might take place, such as a collision or a fire where water is introduced into a compartment for fire-fighting purposes. Whatever the cause, a situation might arise whereby the ship is lying at an unexpected angle of inclination.

It is not always possible to ascertain easily whether a ship is listed or lolled and, since the remedial action for each case is very different, it is essential that the cause of the inclination is carefully investigated. The following procedures should be carefully observed:

1. Alter course to put the ship's head into the predominant waves.

   If the ship is in a lolled situation, it is essential that it stays lolled to the same side. Wave action may cause the ship to roll through the vertical to loll on the other side. This is a dangerous situation since the ship will heel from the vertical of its own accord and the momentum it will have in lolling over to the other side may be sufficient to capsize it. In any event, the ship will initially heel beyond the angle of loll before settling at the angle of loll. Cargo shift may result, which will worsen the situation further.

2. Check that port and starboard listing moments are the same.

   By verifying tank soundings and checking for cargo shift, it should be possible to account for any listing moments that may cause the ship to be in a listed situation. If it is calculated that there are no net listing moments, a case of instability may be assumed and the ship will be lying at an angle of loll. Recalculation of the ship's effective KG should also be undertaken to verify the ship's GM.

3. Check for slack tanks.

   In carrying out step 2, it should also be evident whether there are excessive free surface moments causing a loss of GM sufficient to make the ship unstable. In this case, a loll situation may be confirmed.

If a loll situation is confirmed:

4. Take action to lower G (reduce KG).

   It would be impractical at sea to consider shifting weights on board using the ship's lifting equipment. If the ship has high ballast tanks that are full, these may be emptied, discharging ballast from the high side tank first - the greater vertical distance between G of the ship and g of the weight being discharged will ensure that the greatest lowering of G will take place in the first instance. Once the high side tank is empty, the one on the low side may then be emptied.

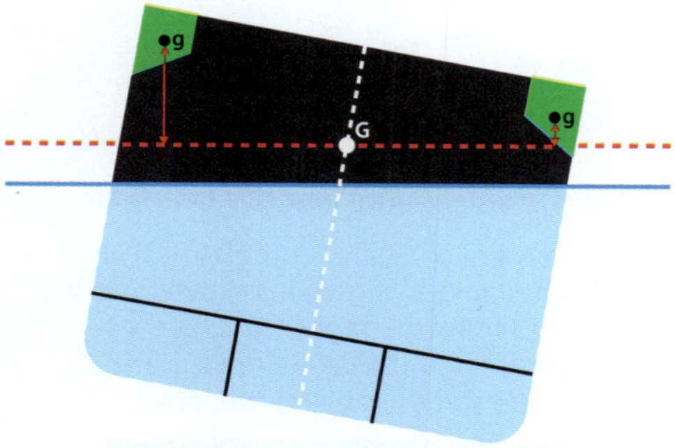

Empty high up ballast tank on the high side first to ensure greatest lowering of G

5. Minimise free surfaces.

   Sounding all the tanks will identity any that are slack. Minimise the loss of GM due to free surface effect by topping up low down ballast tanks and transferring fuel as necessary. This action alone may remedy the situation.

6. Ballast tanks low down in the ship.

   Select a set of suitably subdivided double bottom tanks to ballast. Ideally, start with tanks that have the smallest free surface areas to minimise the effects of free surface while filling. The order of filling is as follows and must be strictly adhered to:

   (a) Start by filling the tank on the low side (No. 1), as shown on the following page. Because of the introduction of more free surfaces while filling the first tank, the situation will initially worsen

   (b) when the first tank is completely full, fill the centre tank (No. 2)

   (c) when the centre tank is full, fill the final tank (No. 3)

   (d) if G is lowered sufficiently, the ship should complete in an upright condition (having initially verified that

Unstable Condition and Angle of Loll

the port and starboard moments were the same).

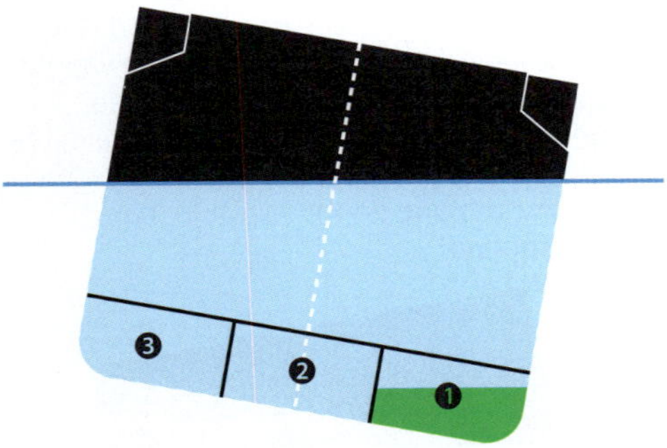

Fill tanks in order shown (low side tank first)

The movement of G after completely filling each of the tanks is shown in below (ignoring the upward movement of G which arises as a result of the introduced free surface at intermediate stages of filling the tanks).

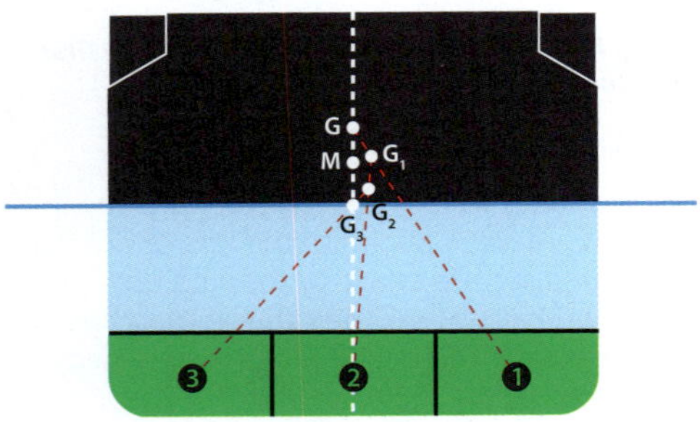

If the situation is not remedied, a second set of tanks must be chosen for filling and the process repeated.

Note: Once a loll situation is confirmed, only ever fill one tank at a time. Always start by filling the **low side** tank first.

The angle of loll may initially worsen because the introduced free surfaces when initially starting to fill the tank may cause a greater rise of G than the fall of G caused by the added bottom weight, hence the importance of filling small tanks first.

If there is any doubt as to whether the ship is lolled or listed, always assume initially that it is a lolled situation and take appropriate action, monitoring the situation carefully.

When correcting a list, it is sufficient to shift a weight to the high side. This may be achieved by shifting weights on deck or by transferring ballast from a listed side tank to a high side tank. Alternatively, excess ballast from the listed side (possibly low down in the ship) may be discharged or a low tank on the high side should be filled.

Calculating the Angle of Loll Using the Wall-Sided Formula

A ship with a negative GM will not remain upright. It will start to capsize, either to port or starboard, until the centre of buoyancy is able to attain a position vertically below the centre of gravity (G) at B2.

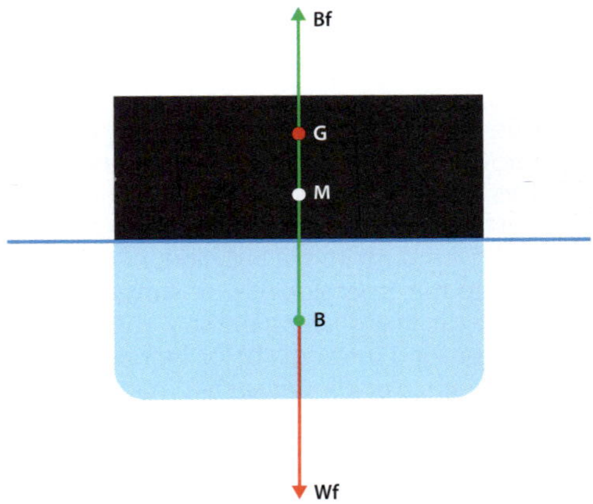

(1) Ship upright with negative GM; G above M.

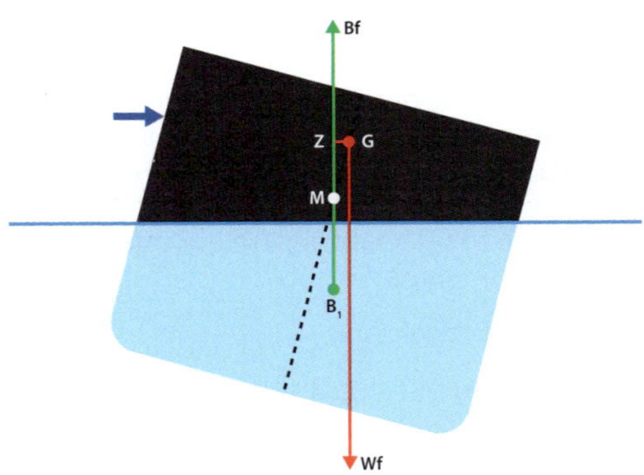

(2) Ship starts to capsize as a result of the negative GM. B moves outward.

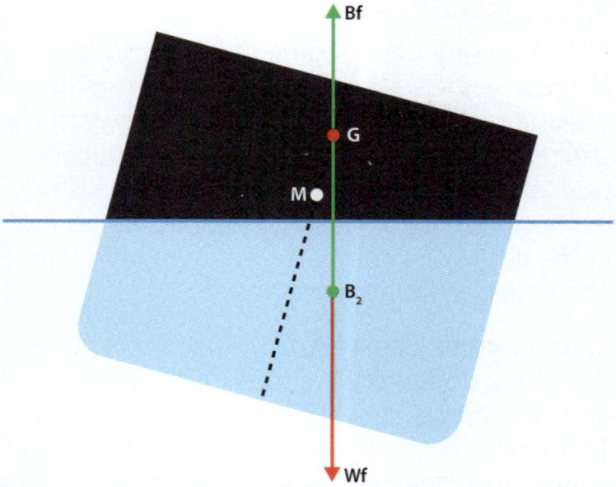

(3) Ship will settle at an angle of loll with B below G. GZ is zero.

At the angle of loll, GZ is zero. The accurate formula for calculating GZ for wall-sided inclinations is:

$$\textbf{GZ} = (\textbf{GM} + \tfrac{1}{2}\textbf{BM}\ \textbf{Tan}^2\ \theta)\ \textbf{Sine}\ \theta$$

A formula for calculating the angle of loll value can be derived from this as follows:

Expanding the above formula gives:

$$GZ = (GM \times \text{Sine}\ \theta) + (\tfrac{1}{2}BM \times \text{Tan}^2\ \theta \times \text{Sine}\ \theta)$$

At the angle of loll, GZ is zero:

$$\therefore\ 0 = (GM \times \text{Sine}\ \theta) + (\tfrac{1}{2}BM \times \text{Tan}^2\ \theta \times \text{Sine}\ \theta)$$

$$\therefore\ -(GM \times \text{Sine}\ \theta) = (\tfrac{1}{2}BM \times \text{Tan}^2\theta \times \text{Sine}\ \theta)$$

Dividing both sides by Sine θ gives:

$$-M = \tfrac{1}{2}BM \times \text{Tan}^2\ \theta \quad \text{or} \quad -GM = \frac{BM \times \text{Tan}^2\ \theta}{2}$$

$$\therefore\ \frac{-2 \times GM}{BM} = \text{Tan}^2\ \theta$$

$$\therefore\ \textbf{Tan}\ \theta_{LOLL} = \sqrt{\frac{\textbf{-2 GM}}{\textbf{BM}}}$$

In this equation, the values of GM and BM used are the original upright values. Because the upright GM is negative, the quantity within the square root becomes positive.

Example 1

In the upright condition, a ship has KB 4.26 m, KG 7.15 m and BM 2.84 m. Calculate the angle of loll.

Solution

KM = KB + BM KM = 4.26 + 2.84 = 7.10 m

GM = KM – KG GM = 7.10 – 7.15 = -0.05 m

$$Tan\ \theta_{LOLL} = \sqrt{\frac{-2 \times GM}{BM}} \qquad Tan\ \theta_{LOLL} = \sqrt{\frac{-2 \times -0.05}{2.84}}$$

$$Tan\ \theta_{LOLL} = \sqrt{\frac{0.10}{2.84}} \qquad = 0.18765$$

θ_{LOLL} = 10.63° (to port or starboard) (Ans)

Calculating the Effective GM at the Angle of Loll

If the ship is heeled beyond the angle of loll, righting levers become positive to act to right the ship back to the angle of loll. It follows that the ship must have acquired a new positive GM for this to happen.

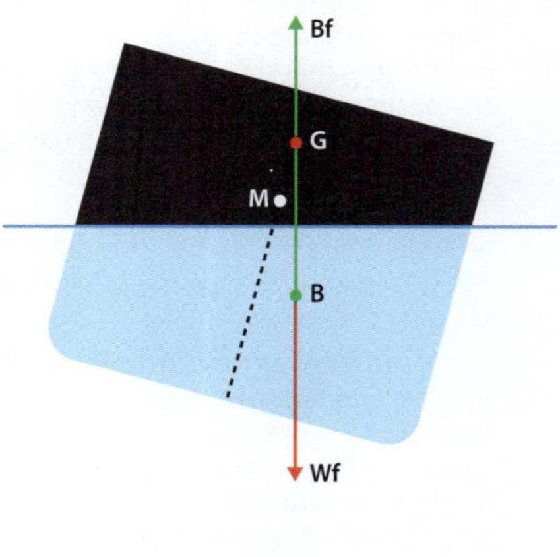

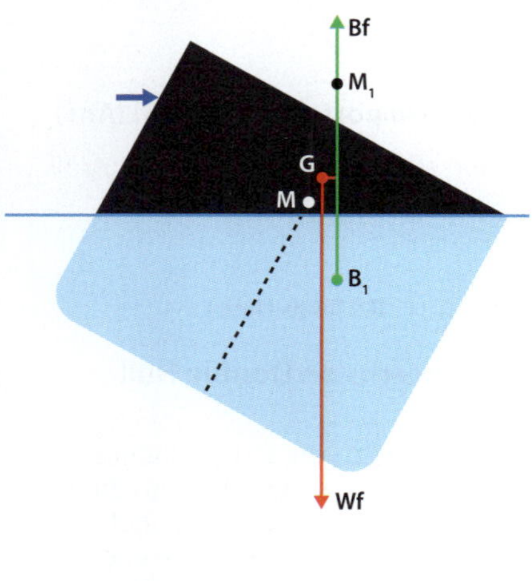

Unstable Condition and Angle of Loll

This new metacentric height is the value shown as GM_1 and is given by the formula:

$$\textbf{GM at the angle of loll} = \frac{-2\ GM}{\cos\theta}$$

where GM is the initial upright GM, which is a negative value, and θ is the angle of loll. It should be noted that the metacentre at this stage (M_1) need not be on the centreline and will constantly move as the ship is heeled further beyond the angle of loll.

Example 2

An upright ship displaces 12,500 t and has KG 7.84 m. 500 t is discharged from a position on the centreline KG 6.00 m. Calculate the resulting angle of loll, given that KB is 3.95 m and KM is 7.85 m in the final condition, and the effective GM at the angle of loll.

Solution

Calculate the KG.

$$GG_V = \frac{w \times d}{W - w} = \frac{500 \times (7.84 - 6.00)}{12{,}500 - 500}$$

$$= 0.077 \text{ m upwards}$$

Final KG = 7.840 + 0.077 = 7.917 m

Final GM = KM – KG

Final GM = 7.850 – 7.917 = -0.067 m

BM = KM – KB

BM = 7.850 – 3.950 = 3.900 m

$$Tan\ \theta_{LOLL} = \sqrt{\frac{-2\ GM}{BM}} \quad Tan\ \theta_{LOLL} = \sqrt{\frac{-2 \times -0.067}{3.900}}$$

$$= 0.18536$$

θ_{LOLL} = 10.50° (to port or starboard) (Ans)

Calculate the effective GM at the angle of loll.

$$\text{GM at the angle of loll} = \frac{-2\ GM}{Cos\ \theta}$$

$$= \frac{-2 \times -0.067}{Cos\ 10.50^\circ} = \textbf{0.136 m (Ans)}$$

Stability Concerns on Double Hull Tankers

The traditional single skin design of tankers, where cargo tanks are subdivided into three by two longitudinal bulkheads and double bottom tanks are fitted in way of the engine room only, was an inherently stable design of ship. Transverse subdivision was sufficient to limit the effects of free surfaces even when three, four or more cargo tanks were slack. The necessary high degree of subdivision of these vessels accompanied by only small, gasketed covers of steel provided a very strong structure despite being single skin. Reduced type 'A' freeboards were assigned to such ships because the risk of sinking was considered low in the event of a compartment containing an oil cargo becoming damaged.

Following the *'Exxon Valdez'* disaster in Prince William Sound and the subsequent spillage of 11 million gallons of heavy crude oil along 1,000 miles of the Alaskan coastline, the United States introduced the requirement that all ships trading in their waters should have complete double hull protection of the oil cargo in an effort to minimise the risk of oil pollution (OPA 1990). The introduction of double hull designs following this increased legislation has caused a number of areas of concern.

Stability Concerns

There are three main areas of concern:

- Double bottoms result in a higher centre of gravity of the cargo and higher ship's KG when loaded.
- The strength characteristics of double hulls permit tank designs with greater free surfaces. Single hull tankers need longitudinal bulkheads which run throughout the length of the ship to provide the necessary longitudinal strength. The transverse spacing of these bulkheads was chosen to give tank sizes of approximate equal capacity and optimum bottom structure loads. The cellular nature of a double hull structure already provides the necessary longitudinal strength, rendering further longitudinal bulkheads unnecessary for structural reasons. This permitted the single tank across arrangement (STA) to be adopted in many designs (recent changes to MARPOL restrict this practice in new ships).
- Increased steel weight of double hull designs and reduced deadweight capacity increased the reluctance of operators to subdivide large centre cargo tanks. The resulting potential for loss of GM due to free surface effects is greatly increased.

These concerns are warranted following the increased tanker lolling incidents that have occurred during load/discharge operations in

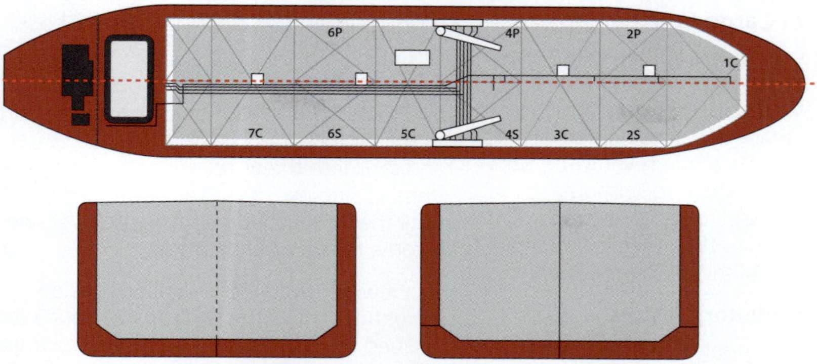

Figure 42.2 - Suezmax tanker (136,055 Dwt) built in 1993 with alternate single tank across (STA) cargo tanks

double hull tankers of STA design in the 35,000 to 150,000 Dwt range. Below this range are mostly product carriers which have greater tank subdivision. Above this range, strength and tank size considerations preclude the use of the STA configuration.

A Suezmax tanker of 136,000 Dwt built in 1993 is shown in Figure 42.2. Cargo tanks 1, 3, 5 and 7 are single tank across (STA) arrangement. Note also the alternate ballast tank arrangements within the double hull structure.

The loss of GM that arises from a single STA cargo tank being slack is of the order of 0.75 m on such a ship. Such large losses in GM have led to the need for operational procedures to be in place to prevent such ships becoming unstable, particularly during simultaneous cargo and ballast handling operations. Such problems did not occur with traditional single hull design ships since these were inherently stable.

Damage Stability Considerations

Compliance with damage stability criteria is not easy. Additional care is required with respect to cargo distribution to ensure that all envisaged damage scenarios as assumed by the regulations result in the ship meeting the required damage stability criteria. If freeboard assignment is considered, the definition of a type 'A' ship includes assumptions with respect to damage and the final condition of equilibrium to be maintained. As a result of the stability problems associated with double hull tankers and the increased damage stability requirements that must be met by type 'A' ships built after June 2000, it is unlikely that any new ships will qualify for the type 'A' tabular freeboard that may have been used in the calculation of the ship's summer freeboard. A type 'A' ship is any ship designed to carry liquid cargoes in bulk, such as tankers, chemical carriers, and LPG and LNG carriers.

If a double hull ship should suffer low impact grounding damage, it is likely that the inner hull envelope containing the cargo will not be breached and oil spillage will not occur. In a smaller tanker, the damaged space might be a 'U'-shaped ballast tank which would allow free flooding right across the structure and up to the level of the waterline outside. The added weight of the floodwater (or lost buoyancy) would be considerable, making it difficult to refloat the vessel. In a single hull tanker, such damage would result in a loss of oil cargo, lightening the ship and making it easier to refloat. Had the damage been caused in a minor impact collision, the loss of freeboard would be considerable in the double hull tanker whereas an increase in freeboard would take place in the single hull ship as oil spilled out.

In the case of a double hull tanker suffering minor impact damage to an 'L'-shaped ballast tank on one side, the ship would list considerably if still free-floating and this would have to be corrected by filling the opposite side tank, with the overall result of substantial loss of freeboard. Another problem is that the introduced stresses might cause the design stress limits to be exceeded.

What is assumed by the regulations with respect to damage is arguably only applicable to low impact collisions or groundings. Many ship collisions in open water are relatively high impact collisions whereby the double hull boundary would be breached and oil loss would inevitably occur.

Case Studies

Liquefaction of Cargo Caused Capsize

A general cargo vessel was loaded with a bulk cargo of 6,000 tonnes of pyrite concentrate. Shortly after leaving port, the cargo liquefied, creating a free surface and causing a severe list (angle of loll). The crew made several attempts to correct the list by ballasting, without success, with the vessel taking a severe list first to one side and then to the other. Eventually it capsized and sank. All the crew were rescued.

Root Cause/Contributory Factors

- The moisture content of the cargo was excessive
- the cargo had been exposed to rain while on the wharf before it was loaded
- no moisture tests were carried out before loading and no information regarding the characteristics of the cargo had been provided to the shipowner or the master
- once agitated by the motion of the ship, the cargo underwent liquefaction
- by ballasting incorrectly to correct the list, the ship's staff made the problem worse.

Capsizing of the MV *'Stellemare'*

Three crew members died when the 289-foot MV *'Stellamare'* rolled onto her side and sank during cargo loading at the port of Albany, New York.

The *'Stellamare's'* crew had loaded a 258-tonne electric generator into the hold using the vessel's two derricks in tandem. The accident occurred as a 340-tonne stator, which was alongside the ship, was lifted on board.

To lift the stator, the ship's ballast tanks had been used to create a 2° list to starboard, which was then shifted to the port tanks to level the ship. After its weight was lifted by the derricks, the stator began moving over the ship but, while it was still outboard of the starboard gunwale and overhanging the pier, a rapid, uncontrolled list to port began.

As the *'Stellamare'* heeled to port, the stator swung inboard toward the ship's centre and, as the list increased, passed over the vessel and sank into the water, still attached to the derricks' rigging. The vessel continued to roll until the list reached approximately 75°, when it came to rest on the bottom.

Six crewmen who were working topside were thrown into the Hudson River and were rescued by a nearby tug, but three crewmen in the hold were trapped by the ingress of water through the open hatches and died.

Error in Calculating Stability Causes Vessel to Sink

A 3,000 GT inter-island cargo vessel capsized and sank alongside as containers were being loaded on her deck. The loss was caused by the Chief Officer failing to make proper allowance for the height of a stow of bagged cement in the lower hold when calculating the vessel's vertical centre of gravity. This produced an over-optimistic prediction of the vessel's stability on completion of loading and unfortunately there was no established procedure for an independent check of the Chief Officer's calculation. It is highly likely that the mistake would have been noticed and the loss of the vessel avoided had one been in place.

Courtesy of Shipowners Club

Poorly Prepared Stow Plan Creates a Dangerous List

A 316 TEU feeder container vessel/bulk carrier started listing 1° to starboard immediately after loading had been completed. Corrective action was taken but, despite this, the list continued to increase and, when it reached approximately 15°, a number of containers fell off the top tier into the water. The vessel then violently rolled to port. The list increased until the waterline had reached the hatch coamings and progressive flooding started. Fortunately, as more containers fell off the top tier, the list reduced and the situation was eventually brought under control by discharging cargo and the vessel returned to an even keel.

Capsizing of *'Gulizar Ana'*

The 3,300 Dwt Turkish general cargo ship *'Gulizar Ana'* capsized in the Romanian port of Galati as a result of its cargo of steel coils and forklifts shifting during loading.

Multraship, the company awarded the salvage contract, brought in its floating sheerlegs vessel *'Cormorant'* and the tug *'Fond'*, along with a salvage team, sludge barge, skimmer vessel and pumps.

The *'Gulizar Ana'* was leaning at an angle of about 60° when the lifting operation got under way. The vessel's engine room and accommodation were pumped out into a sludge barge, bringing the list back to about 28°. Removing one of the vessel's two forklifts further corrected the list to roughly 12°. The vessel was then ballasted and returned to an even keel.

Figure 42.3 - Multraship at work to right the stricken cargo ship 'Gulizar Ana'

Courtesy of Shipowners Club

A poorly prepared stow plan resulted in this vessel having negative stability upon completion of loading. The onboard calculations did not take into account the effects of free surface, masking the true stability condition of the vessel.

Damage Repairs at Sea

Any ship with damage below the waterline, such as a hull crack or damage to the rudder, propeller or sea valves, will require urgent attention from a shipyard with a drydock.

However, as ships are often far from shore when damage or an operational incident occurs, seafarers should be familiar with the following emergency techniques. The goal is to stop or at least reduce the flooding impact of damage, and today this could just as easily be due to corrosion to a seachest or internal ship's piping than a grounding or collision. Responding quickly to such an incident can prevent the level of resultant damage increasing and give the ship time to consider the best means of repair.

Plugging and Patching Holes

Any loss of watertight integrity of the ship's outer hull plating can cause flooding. Therefore, either the holes must be plugged or the area of damage isolated within the ship to prevent more extensive flooding. No temporary patch will be perfectly watertight but, if water ingress can be reduced by only 50%, in many cases it will be possible to control flooding and reduce the risk of sinking.

Wooden Plugs

A simple and effective method of repairing a small hole is to insert a plug made from soft wood as this absorbs water.

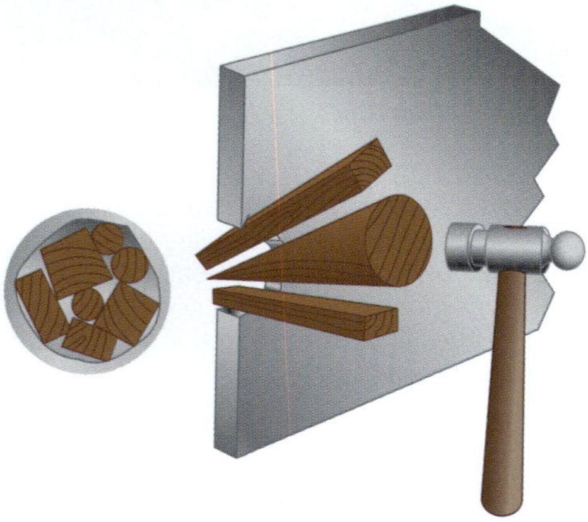

Figure 42.4 - Use combinations of conical and untapered plugs

Wrapping the plugs with lightweight cloth before use will keep them in place and fill some of the gaps. Caulking the remaining area with rags and smaller wedges can help to reduce leaking. However, as there may be metal edges protruding inwards in the damaged area, care should be exercised when inserting the plugs.

Figure 42.5 - Wrap plugs with cloth to keep in place

Pillows, Mattresses and Blankets as Plugs

Pillows, mattresses or blankets, rolled around a wooden plug or a timber to increase their size and offer further rigidity, can be effective for plugging larger holes. While they will have a tendency to be torn out by waves, mattresses have also been used effectively for temporarily reducing large leaks on lines that demand large volumes of water; examples seen include a corroded water supply line to an inert gas system. This serves to prove that prevention of leaks often requires quick thinking and use of all available materials.

Figure 42.6 - A rolled mattress used to plug a large hole

On one occasion, the crew on a damaged vessel were unable to make repairs so constructed their own conical plug. At the core was a piece of heavy line with an eye spliced into each end which was then wrapped with strips of blanket until a cone was built up. The layers of cloth were held together and to the core line by stitching. Lines were secured to the eyes and the plug was lowered over the side and pulled into place as shown in Figure 42.7. It proved very effective as it was flexible, absorbed water and swelled to fit the hole's irregular shape.

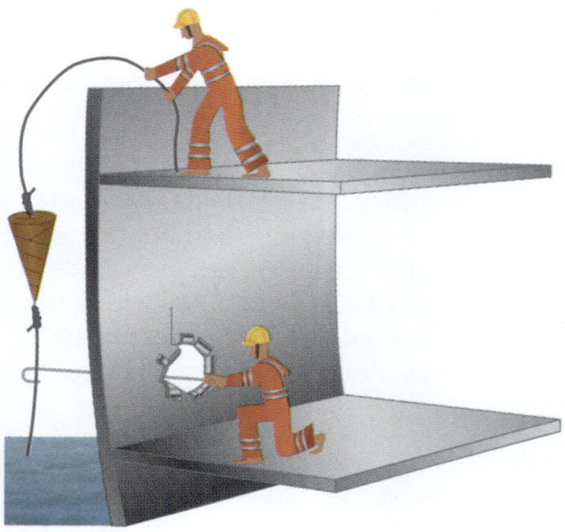

Figure 42.7 - A little ingenuity and using whatever is available can save a vessel

Prefabricated Plate Patches

Prefabricated patches made of a square piece of one-quarter-inch steel plate can be used to cover damage. One side of the plate has a thick gasket with a ring or eyebolt welded in the centre for securing a line to hold it close to the shell of the ship.

The patch is lowered over the side using the handling and supporting line. The centre line is pulled inside the ship through the hole and the patch is pulled tight against the ship's side. The centre line is then made fast to a stanchion.

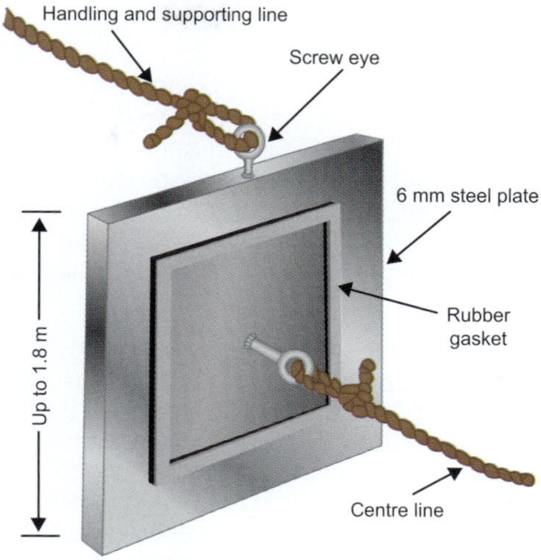

Figure 42.8 - A prefabricated plate patch

In an emergency, one vessel's crew made a similar patch using a floor plate, a mattress and a manila line with an eyebolt welded to the plate to secure the line.

Special Patches

Box Patch

Holes with jagged edges protruding inward can be covered using a steel box up to 45 cm^2 and 15.5 cm deep. The box is open at one end with a rubber gasket running along the facing edges.

The box patch is secured over a shell hole from inside the ship and is held in place with shoring. When the compartment is pumped dry, angle clips can be welded between the box and the hull plating and the timbers can be removed for use elsewhere.

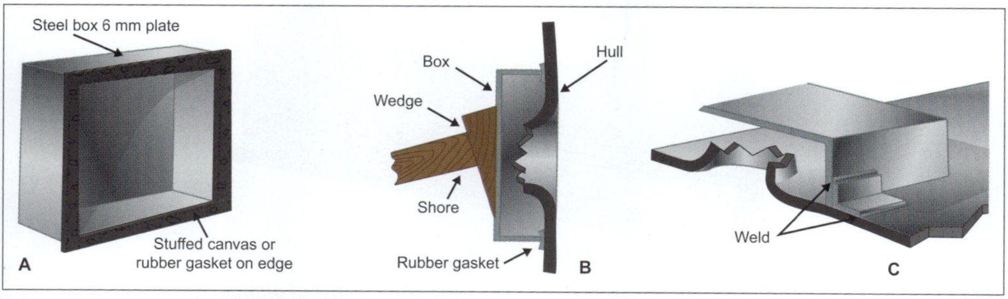

Figure 42.9 - Application of a box patch

Damage Repairs at Sea

Welded Patches

After using one of the temporary patches, large holes in decks and bulkheads can be successfully repaired by welding on steel plates.

Before the plate is welded, all protruding edges must be cut away using an oxyacetylene torch or a pneumatic chisel. Care must be exercised prior to using any flame or spark-producing repair equipment. Always test the air for the presence of explosive fumes, have a carbon dioxide extinguisher at hand and make ready a fire hose.

A steel plate can be held lightly in place by tack welding before being fastened securely with a solid bead to stop all the cracks. If the plate is large, it should be reinforced with welded stiffeners on the back or shoring to prevent excessive motion as the ship moves. These precautions help to prevent the welding cracking. In one case, a vessel failed to follow these precautions and the patch opened wider and acted as a scoop, leaving the vessel in a worse condition than before the plate was installed.

Miscellaneous Leaks

Cracks

Cracks in plating may increase in length as the plating tears. To prevent further damage, 2 cm diameter holes should be drilled at the extreme ends of the crack, as shown in Figure 42.10. The holes should be plugged or, if time permits, should have a plate welded over.

It is not advisable to drive wedges into cracks in thin plating, particularly hardwood wedges, as this tends to open them further. Instead, marline, oakum and rags can often be used as effective caulking materials.

Other Types of Patches

C-clamps and thumb clamps can be used to hold plugs or patches in place. For example, a damaged area of pipe can be covered by a block of soft wood, shaped to fit and held tightly with two thumb clamps. They should be checked regularly as they can work loose under shock or vibration.

A jubilee pipe patch is similar to a commercial hose clip but constructed from heavy sheet metal and secured with nuts and bolts. The flanges at the gap are reinforced with strips of strap iron. Small braces should be welded from the flange to the back of the patch to keep the flange faces more or less parallel under pressure.

The jubilee clamp is sprung open and fitted over a sheet of packing that extends past either side of the hole. When the bolts are tightened, this patch will easily hold a pressure of up to 100 psi.

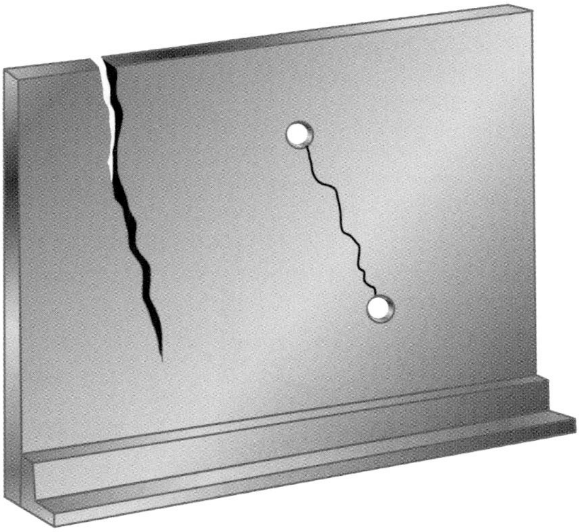

Figure 42.10 - Holes drilled at the ends of a crack and plugged to stop extension

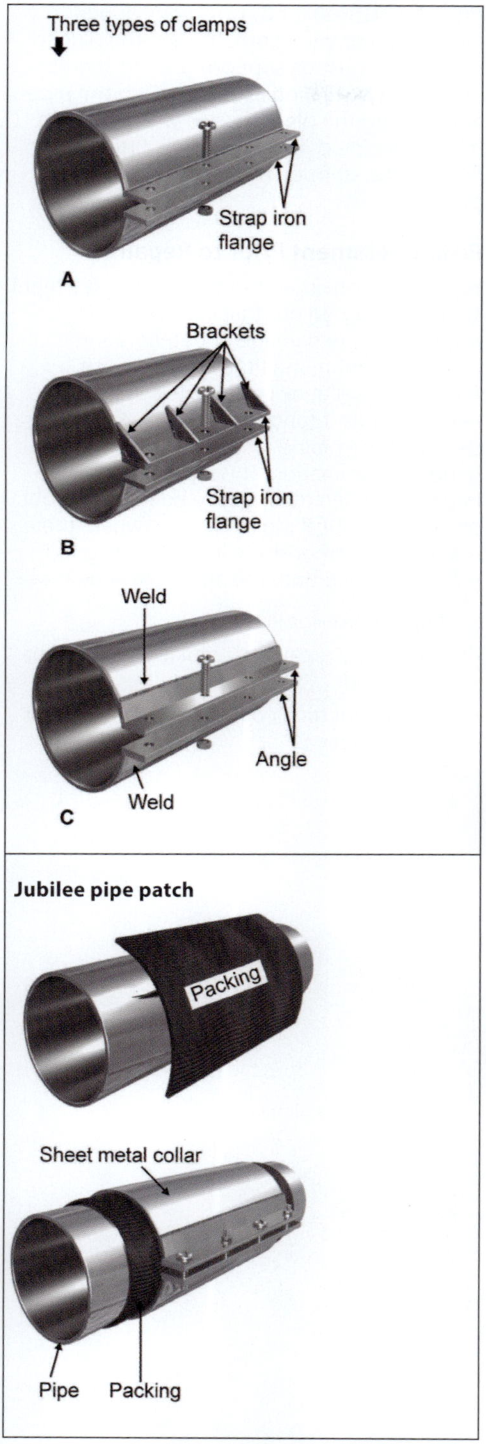

Figure 42.11 - Clamps and jubilee pipe patch

Renewing Pipe Sections

It may be necessary to renew a section of pipe if it is too badly ruptured or holed to patch. Carrying spare sections of the smaller sizes of important pipe on board is advisable but, in an emergency, it may be possible to remove and use a section from a less important system.

If the original pipe was fitted with screw flanges, remove the entire damaged section, cut screw threads on the new piece, refit the flanges and replace it. To renew only the damaged part of a small pipe, cut out the damaged area with hacksaws and cut a fresh piece almost the same length as the gap. Small pipe can be joined by means of a velocity-power pipe bonding press or by cutting screw threads on all exposed ends and making up the joints using pipe unions and couplings. White lead may be used on screw threads to get a tighter joint.

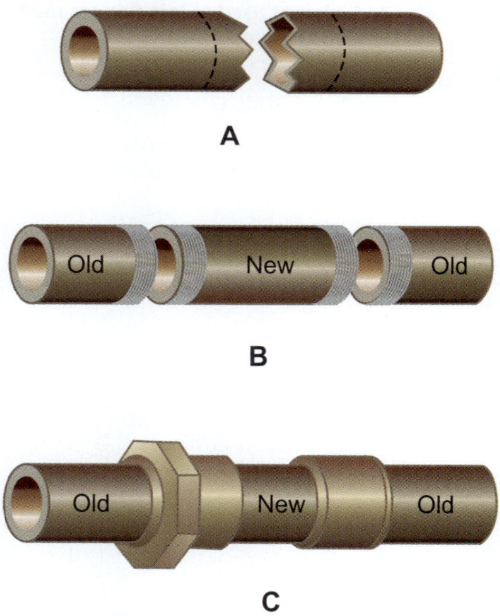

(A) Pipe ends cut off
(B) New section of pipe (threaded) inserted
(C) Union and coupling joins

These methods can be time consuming so unions similar to the soft patches previously described can be used to speed up the process. However, if the joints are not held together, they may be pushed apart by pressure reaction. Therefore, it is advisable to force the joints together using lines, shores or wedges.

Damage Repairs at Sea

Problems can arise when attempting to connect flanges on different sizes of pipe. This can be overcome by inserting a gasket and holding the two flanges together with four heavy C-clamps, as shown in Figure 42.12.

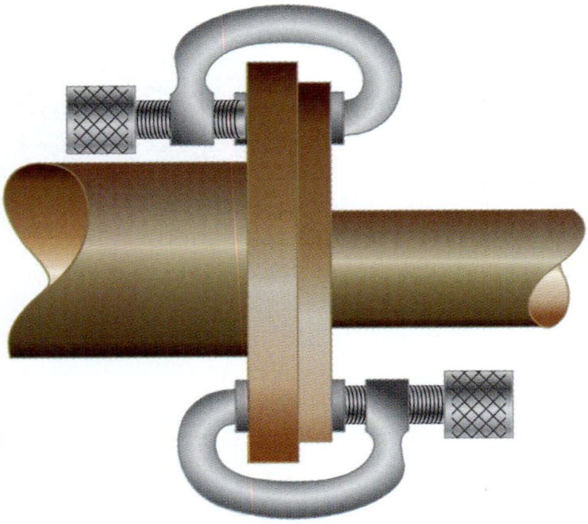

Figure 42.12 - C-clamps used to join flanges that do not mate

Blanking Pipelines

Ruptured pipelines are difficult to isolate while still allowing the system they are part of to function normally. Low pressure pipelines can often be blanked off by driving in wooden plugs covered with cloth. To keep the plug in position, it must be supported using shores or jacks, or by drilling a hole through the pipe and pinning the plug in place with a nail. If a damaged pipe is joined by screw fittings, the flow can be stopped by fitting a pipe cap or plug.

Risk Assessment Prior to Repair

For all pipe repairs, a structured risk assessment should be carried out that considers all potential future damage or deterioration to ensure continuing fitness for purpose. The repair itself may be regarded as being permanent (ie intended to remain in place for the life of the piping system) or may require periodic examination. This is particularly important when repairs have been carried out on a safety-critical piping system, where there is a need to demonstrate it remains in good repair and condition. The approach should be:

- Replace like-for-like
- temporary repair until replacement can be carried out
- permanent repair *only* where replacement is not practical.

CHAPTER 43

Hull Monitoring and Inspection

Hull Stress Monitoring Systems

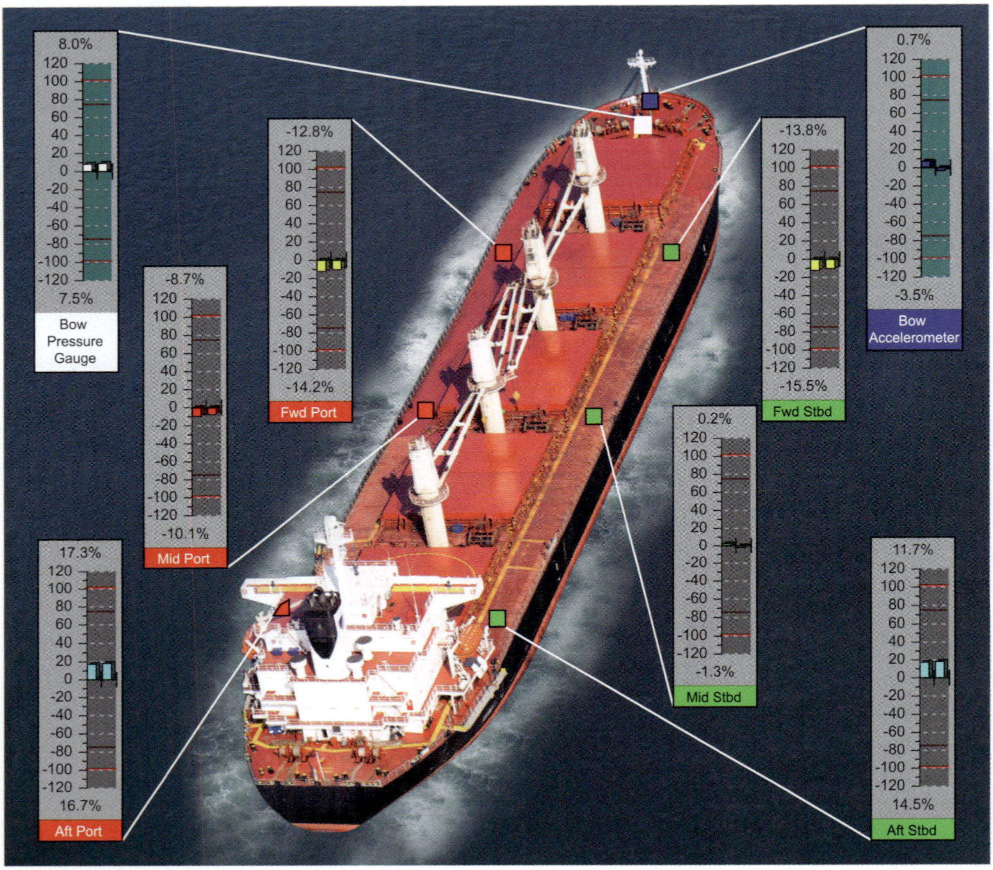

Figure 43.1 - Hull stresses

The IMO recommends the fitting of Hull Stress Monitoring Systems (HSMS) to facilitate the safe operation of ships carrying dry cargo in bulk. Fitting of these systems on other ship types can help reduce hull stresses and damage, such as those that resulted in the loss of the *'MSC Napoli'* in 2007.

The MCA invites owners to fit hull stress monitoring systems on bulk carriers of 20,000 Dwt and above.

Use of an HSMS will provide the master and officers of the ship with real-time information on the motions and global stress the ship experiences while navigating and during loading and unloading operations. The IMO recommendations are published in the Maritime Safety Committee circular MSC/Circ.646.

Owners should ensure that hull stress monitoring equipment is compatible with the VDR fitted and that all monitored data can be transmitted to the VDR.

To monitor the global longitudinal stress and ship motions, the following system components should be used:

- Long-based gauges for strain measurements, located on the main deck at different positions along the ship's length, to detect stresses during loading, unloading and navigation, eg the gauges for strain measurement should be located on the main deck in way of each cargo hold and, if necessary, at the location where the maximum hull girder wave bending stress can be expected during navigation, loading and unloading

- one accelerometer for measuring vertical accelerations at the bow
- two accelerometers for measuring roll and sway, suitably located at the centreline of the ship.

The minimum required number and approximate position of the strain gauges for tankers, bulk carriers and general cargo ships are as follows:

- Two at midships (one port, one starboard on deck)
- one at 25% of the length from the bow (on deck)
- one at 25% of the length from the stern (on deck).

The minimum required number and approximate position of the strain gauges for container ships:

- Four at midships in a ring around the section (two port, two starboard; deck and upper turn of bilge)
- one at 25% of the length from the bow (on deck).

The strain gauges on the main deck, taking due account of temperature effects, are to give information on the stress levels during navigation, loading and unloading. They are to give information on the wave-induced stresses and the mean value of still water stresses. By analysing an offset to a mean value, an indication of water ingress into the holds can also be provided.

The signals from the accelerometers are to describe the vertical and transverse motion of the ship. By analysing the frequency ranges of the signals from the vertical gauge, slamming information can also be provided.

Source: ***MGN 108***

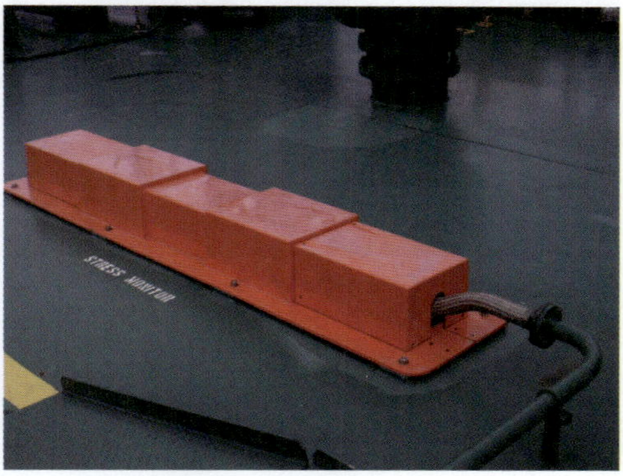

Rafting in a Tank

Introduction

Tank inspection using an inflatable dinghy is known as 'rafting'. This method may be used to inspect cargo tanks, holds and associated spaces that may be filled with water, provided the internal structure layout allows easy escape to deck from any location that is being accessed by the raft.

The raft normally has to be inflated inside the tank and must be deflated each time it is to be moved to another tank.

Rafting Reference

IACS Recommendation No. 39 'Safe Use of Rafts or Boats for Survey'.

General Guidance

- Surveys of tanks or holds using rafts or boats may only be undertaken with the agreement of the attending surveyor(s), who will take into account the safety arrangements provided, including weather forecasting and ship motion in the forecasted sea conditions
- the structural arrangement within the space must allow easy escape to deck from any position being rafted. At least 1 metre clearance above and 0.5 metre clearance beyond the breadth of the raft shall be allowed for the safe passage past any internal obstructions

Rafting in a Tank

Figure 43.2 - Raft inspection of a tank (Note: the raft occupants are not wearing lifejackets)

IACS 'Ship Structure Access Manual' Recommendation No. 90, Oct 2005
http://tinyurl.com/pdq8e9n

- for bulk cargo holds designed for filling of water (eg ballast holds) and where filling up to a height not less than 2 metres below top of side frames is permitted, rafting may be utilised instead of permanent means of access to side frames provided the structural capacity of the hold is sufficient to withstand static loads at all levels of water needed to survey the side shell frames
- only work designated, inflatable rafts or boats shall be used
- the boat or raft should be tethered to the access ladder and an additional crew member stationed down the access ladder with a clear view of the boat or raft
- lifejackets should be worn
- the surface of water in the tank should be calm (under all foreseeable conditions, the expected rise of water within the tank shall not exceed (10 inches) and the water level must be either stationary or falling. The water level should never be rising while the raft is in use
- the tank or hold must contain clean ballast water only
- should a thin sheen of oil be observed on the water, further testing of the atmosphere must be carried out to ensure that the tank or hold continues to remain safe for entry.

Operational Considerations

- Rafting should be stopped if the ship's motion makes the rafting operation difficult or hazardous
- if the tanks or holds share a common venting system or inert gas system, the tank in which the raft is to be used shall be physically isolated from the others to remove the risk of any transfer of gas from the other tanks (or spaces)
- rafting operations in cargo tanks may only be conducted if the tank atmosphere is tested for oxygen content, flammable vapour (<1% LFL/LEL) and concentrations of toxic contaminants and an appropriate permit for entry is prepared
- at least one personal monitor (oxygen monitor or a combination oxygen/ flammability/toxic meter) shall be carried when entering the space
- an EEBD is required if there is any likelihood of a change in the atmosphere within the space
- a system of communication shall be established
- adequate illumination shall be provided
- two persons must be stood by at the tank entrance
- hold a tool box talk prior to entry and re-entry
- do not conduct any ballasting/deballasting or cargo transfer activities (including IG venting) when personnel are in the tank
- make sure that there are no other external shipboard activities occurring (stores transfer, helicopter operations, etc) when rafting
- there must be at least two persons in the raft at any time
- conduct rafting of tanks during daylight hours only.

Rope Access

Introduction

Courtesy of Globex Rope Access NZ Limited

This type of access allows workers to access areas that are difficult to reach, without having to use scaffolding or mobile elevated work platforms.

Workers can ascend, descend and traverse ropes while using a harness or work seat. A support rope is used as well as a backup fall arrest system, involving two ropes, one of which acts as a safety line and the other a working line.

This type of system is commonly used for inspections. It can also be used for welding, cutting and for handling heavy materials. The following precautions must be observed:

- The technician must have a minimum of two ropes attached when working, each with a separate anchor
- every rope must have a failsafe defence mechanism
- tools must be attached using a lanyard on the worker's harness
- there must be at least two trained technicians assigned to each job. All equipment must be inspected and maintained on a regular basis.

Standards and Codes of Practice

IRATA is the leading body in the UK for rope access. There are also European Standards in place for low stretch rope and sit harnesses. SOFT, the Norwegian rope access trade association, is preparing their own code of practice. FISAT in Germany have also produced a code of practice. South Africa has published standards covering worksite procedures, training and certificate procedures. Rope access will be a work item within the International Organization for Standardization (ISO).

Courtesy of Globex Rope Access NZ Limited

Typical Rope Access System

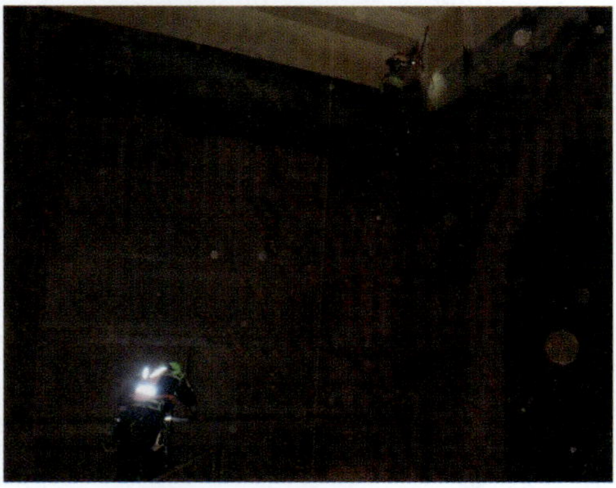

Courtesy of Globex Rope Access NZ Limited

This system consists of a working line and a backup safety line, independently anchored and arranged so there is no abrasion. Specific types of rope, designed for personal protection and meeting the European Standard EN1891, should be used. Low stretch ropes are used as they are more efficient than dynamic ropes. The harness used must have a low central attachment point and meet the requirements of the appropriate standard.

When the work line is ascended, two rope clamps or grabs should be used. Both should be connected to the harness, one directly and one indirectly via a lanyard or foot loop. A chest strap or harness is only used to keep the chest ascender correctly orientated.

The short lanyard connecting the foot ascender to the foot loop provides some safety backup.

Rope Access

When descending or ascending, the operator is connected to the working line and the safety line via a short lanyard and backup device, which is a type of rope clamp. This is not a fall arrest device; it is a prevention device. It moves up and down manually and must always be above the attachment point on the harness. If the working line system fails, a fall will be prevented.

Descending is carried out on the same working line. A descender will stop or allow a slow automatically-controlled descent in the hands-off position. This means the operator will not fall to the ground.

Once the work position is reached, a work seat can be connected to the working line to provide extra comfort and safety. The harness is always the primary attachment point to the working and safety lines.

If the operator wants to climb the structure, a fall arrest system is usually required. The seat harness will be combined with a chest harness so that the high attachment point required for a fall arrest harness is met. Ropes and other types of equipment are also used in order to make a fall as small as possible and to keep the impact forces to a minimum.

It is essential that the attachment point for a fall arrest is at the front of the harness.

Rope Access Technique

Trained rope access technicians may use some of the following safety systems:

- Connect a lanyard directly to the structure or anchor
- vertical safety line using an attended belay or self-belay
- triangulated safety lines
- horizontal safety line
- attended belay for lead climbing.

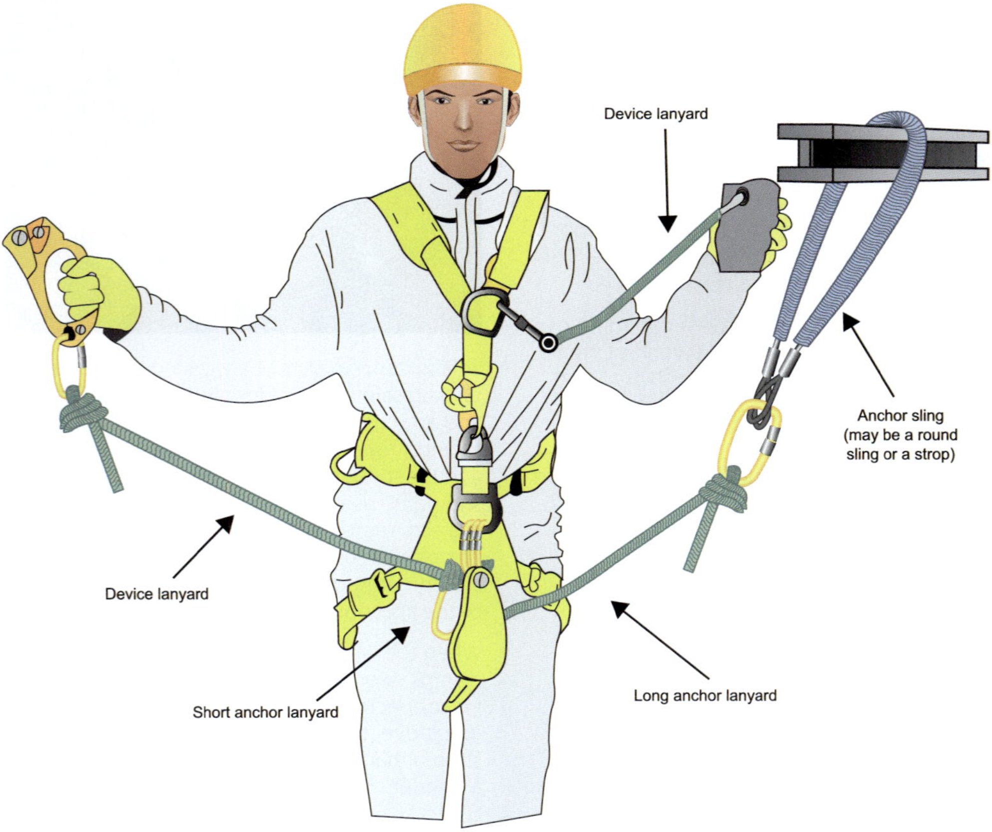

Figure 43.3 - Example of an anchor sling and examples of different types of lanyard based on IRATA International Code of Practice

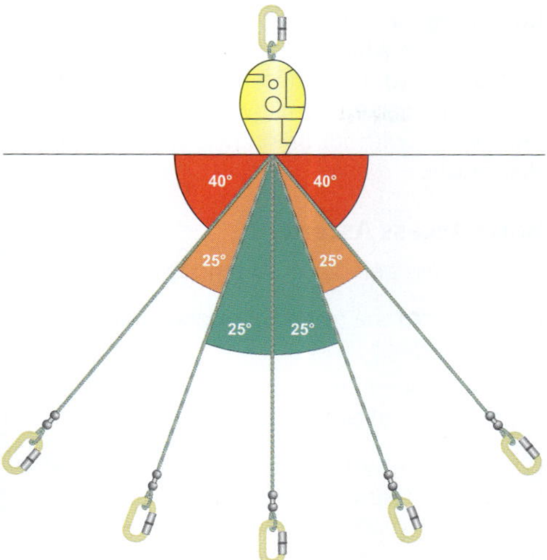

Figure 43.4 - 40° cone of safety with overhead lifelines

Lead Climbing

This can be used to protect a worker while climbing or traversing a structure. It is usually done vertically when the first worker climbs a tower or horizontally by a worker traversing the structure, for example a bridge.

It is suggested that a dynamic kern mantle rope is used. The safety line should be connected to the sternal attachment point. The rope should be tied into the sternal D-ring or a locking connector.

The amount of slack between a climber and the anchor is managed by a trained belayer using a belaying device. The device must be connected to the anchor point and not the belayer.

As the climber progresses, the rope should be clipped into intermediate anchor points using a locking karabiner. To minimise the free-fall distance to 6 feet, intermediate anchors should be placed every 3 feet. Care should be taken to direct ropes around any hazardous edges. This can be done by using anchoring and buffering techniques.

Lead climbing operations do not require two ropes, although they can be useful when the climber is establishing a rope access system for descent or for any future workers. The second rope can be used to retrieve a climber who has fallen. If there is a second rope, the climber must take care not to become tangled in it.

Rope Access Descent

This is usually achieved by using one of two methods:

- Rappelling (travelling brake)
- lowering (fixed brake).

Rope Access

There must be a way to reverse the descent operation if there are any unexpected complications.

Descenders - most of these devices are used for lowering or rappelling. They use friction to control the rate of descent. Systems used in an industrial workplace should have a self-braking mechanism fitted which activates if the operator lets go.

Some devices have an integrated self-braking mechanism and others use a mechanical or rope prusik (friction knot) to create a braking system.

A descender can release a load unexpectedly if a self-braking device is activated when the operator is not holding the control rope.

Rappelling - when used in conjunction with a descent control device, this is the most common and versatile way to descend as the operator is in control of their own descent.

A fixed low stretch rope and backup system attached to two independent anchors is used while rappelling. If the ropes do not reach the ground, they must have a stopper knot to prevent the worker falling off the end.

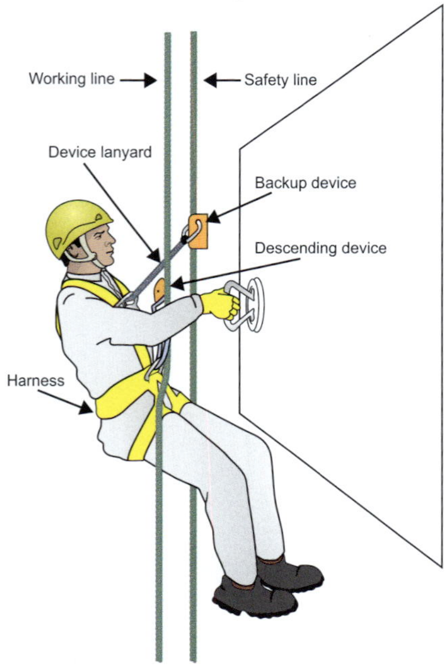

Figure 43.5 - A typical method of working in the descent mode in a rope access system (with descending device locked) based on IRATA International Code of Practice

Lowering - a worker can be lowered by using a fixed brake which is attached to an anchor. This anchored descent device is operated by a second person. This allows the worker to be lowered without being responsible for the descender.

Rope Access Ascent

Rope access personnel can move up by:

- Climbing the rope using mechanical grabs (ascenders)
- a co-worker raising the person using a mechanical advantage system.

Both of these systems require a backup system to be used. Climbing the rope will require mechanical grabs to be used to move up the rope.

Various ascending systems are available. Most require two rope grabs to be used which must be attached directly to the harness.

The most common type of system is the 'frog system'. It uses a chest-mounted ascender attached directly to the harness. A hand ascender connected by a lanyard or 'cow's tail' can also be used. Both of these devices must be securely attached to the harness.

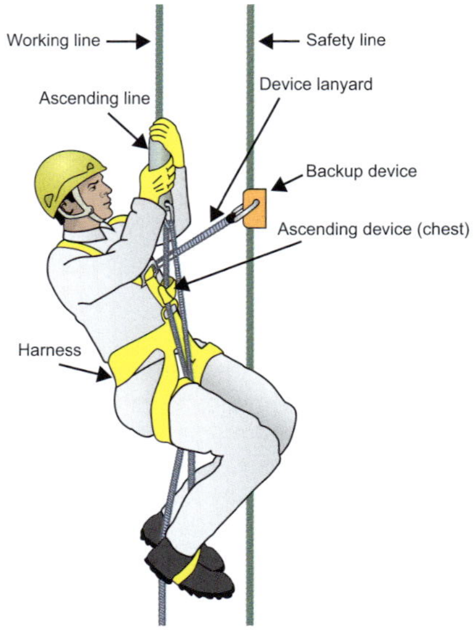

Figure 43.6 - A typical method of ascending in a rope access system based on IRATA International Code of Practice.

The IRATA International Code of Practice can be found at: http://tinyurl.com/corg2gt

Scaffolding

Use of Scaffolding On Board Ship

Tube and Clamp Scaffolding

A tube and clamp scaffolding system is commonly used to form a rigid structure, It employs two-inch diameter tubes clamped together. To be safe, the system must be properly connected and adequately braced.

The system has three basic structural elements: posts, bearers and runners interconnected with double couplers. These elements are repeated in the horizontal and vertical planes to form the desired structure.

Other components include diagonal braces, horizontal and cross bracing, right angle clamps, swivel clamps, base plates, end fitting for each tube, adjustable jack bases and planking.

Scaffolding may be required in the following operations:

- Construction, cleaning and maintenance
- painting of a ship's hull or superstructure
- sand blasting
- repairs and inspection.

General Scaffolding Requirements

The following precautions should be observed when working with scaffolding:

- To be safe, scaffolding must be constructed from specified materials and in an approved manner
- fall protection must be provided for the workers on the scaffold
- protection from falling objects must be provided for workers below the scaffold
- all scaffolds and their supports must be capable of supporting the load they are designed to carry with a safety factor of no less than four
- all lumber used in the construction of scaffolds must be sound, straight and free from defects
- scaffolds must be maintained in a safe and secure condition. Any component of the scaffold that is broken, burned or otherwise defective must be replaced
- unstable objects (such as barrels, boxes, cans or loose bricks) must not be used as working platforms or to support working platforms
- scaffolds must be erected, moved, dismantled or altered under the supervision of scaffold competent persons
- welding, burning, riveting or open flame work must not be performed on any staging suspended by means of fibre rope
- lifting bridles on working platforms suspended from cranes must consist of four legs so that the stability of the platform is assured
- unless the crane hook has a safety latch or is moused, the lifting bridles on working platforms suspended from cranes must be attached by shackles to the lower lifting block, or other positive means must be taken to prevent them from becoming accidentally disengaged from the crane hook.

Potential Hazards

- Failure of the staging components or overloading may result in collapse of the unit in whole or in part, causing workers to fall
- workers falling off the scaffold due to lack of edge guards

Scaffolding

- workers on the scaffold falling to the level below
- items falling off the scaffold and injuring workers below
- surging (for example movement of the work surface) when working on floating scaffolds.

Scaffold or Platform Planking

- Platform planking shall be of not less than 2 × 10-inch lumber
- platforms of staging shall not be less than two 10-inch planks in width except in such cases as the structure of the vessel or the width of the trestle ladders make it impossible to provide such a width

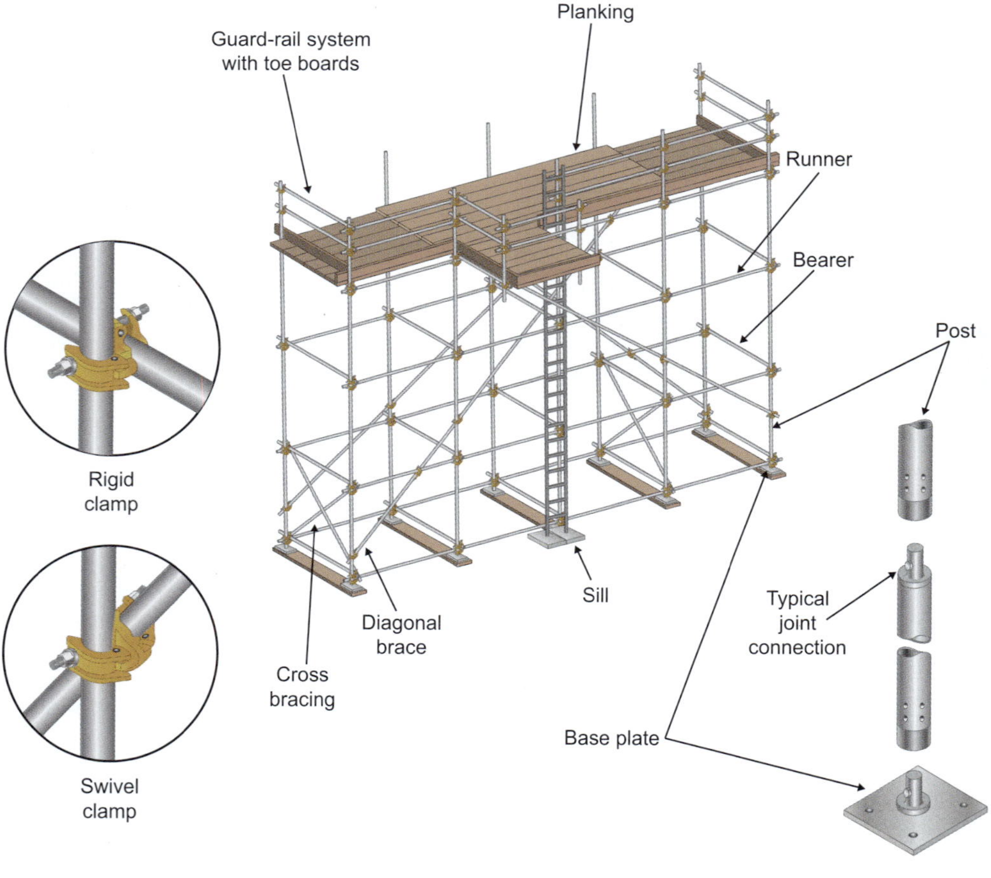

Duty	Load	Max	225 mm boards	Max bay length
Inspection and very light duty	0.75 kN/m²	1 working platform	3 boards	2.7 m
Light duty	1.5	2 working platforms	4	2.4
General purpose	2	2 working platforms + 1 light duty	5	2.1
Heavy duty	2.5	2 working platforms + 1 light duty	5	2

- platform planking shall project beyond the supporting members at either end by at least 6 inches but in no case shall project more than 12 inches unless the planks are fastened to the supporting members
- scaffold planks shall not be overloaded.

Guard-rails and Toeboards

- Scaffolding more than 5 feet above a solid surface, or at any distance above the water, must be provided with a railing that has:
  - a top rail of 42 to 45 inches high
  - a midrail located halfway between the top rail and the platform
- rails must be of 2 × 4 inch lumber, flat bar or pipe:
  - when used with rigid supports, taut wire or fibre rope of adequate strength may be used
  - if the distance between supports is more than 8 feet, rails must be equivalent in strength to 2 × 4 inch lumber
  - rails must be firmly secured
  - where exposed to hot work or chemicals, fibre rope rails must not be used
- rails may be omitted where the structure of the vessel prevents their use:
  - when rails are omitted, employees working more than 5 feet above solid surfaces must be protected by harnesses and lifelines
  - employees working over water must be protected by buoyant work vests
- employees must be protected against falling toward the vessel while working on a swinging or floating scaffold
- when necessary, to prevent tools and materials from falling on workers below, toeboards of not less than 1 × 4 inch lumber must be provided.

Access to Staging

- Staging more than 5 feet high requires appropriate access (eg ladders, ramps, stairways)
- ramps and stairways must be provided with 36-inch handrails with midrails
- ladders must be located so employees do not need to step more than 1 foot from the ladder to any intermediate landing or platform
- staging with built-in ladders meets these requirements
- staging more than 3 feet below the point of access requires a straight, portable or Jacob's ladder.

Fall Protection Devices

A good example of when a temporary platform may not be practicable would be where an item such as a valve that is not routinely operated needs to be accessed. If the valve were 3 metres above deck but not accessible by a movable lift, a scaffold could be built. However, it may take several hours to do so and during this period the scaffold builders would need to work at height and use fall protection devices for much of the time of the build. The time taken for someone to wear a fall protection device and directly operate the valve might only be a few minutes and so, so long as there is no doubt that a secure tie off can be achieved, this should be the method selected.

If a fall protection device is specified for use, you must be able to tie off to an anchorage point with a lanyard and full body harness at all times, including while traversing to and from the work, standing or sitting on a ladder and while performing the actual work.

General Cautions

- All personnel are advised to wear protective headgear when they are below scaffolding or other at height working. Scaffolding should be erected with kick boards to reduce the risk from overhead items being dropped
- the use of safety belts for work involving heights is considered unsafe practice. Research has shown that a person suspended from a properly fitted safety belt will hang upside down, because the upper body tends to be heavier than the lower body. There is also evidence to suggest that safety belts cause damage to internal organs upon impact. Instead a safety harness should be considered
- safety harnesses are full body harnesses which distribute the load generated during a fall over a larger area of the body, thus minimising injury. When used with a 'snap hook' assembly, a person can carry out work at heights in relative safety

Scaffolding

- tools, equipment or materials should never be thrown or dropped from elevated areas without proper safeguards being taken. Examples of such safeguards include slides, chutes and use of a bucket to lower items
- prior to work being performed at height, you should consider whether there is a potential for objects to fall from the overhead area. If this is unavoidable, consideration should be given to one or more of the following safeguards:
  - use of sideboards
  - barricading the area below (with an adequately sized drop zone)
  - enclosure of the scaffolding or work platform with wire mesh.

Suspension Trauma

Suspension trauma can occur when a person is suspended in a full body harness or other fall protection device. It can be fatal, depending on the circumstances and the condition of the suspended individual. Cold and dehydration will quicken the signs and symptoms and in some circumstances death can occur in a surprisingly short period of time.

Suspension trauma is caused primarily by blood pooling in the legs as the leg muscles are then unable to 'pump' it back into the system.

Signs and symptoms can be immediate or have a late onset. Some signs to be observed are:

- Faintness and dizziness
- nausea
- sweating
- paleness
- increased heart rate
- unusually low heart rate or blood pressure
- 'graying' or loss of vision.

Factors that can affect the degree of risk of suspension trauma are:

- Inability to move legs
- fatigue
- injuries during a fall
- dehydration
- hypothermia
- shock
- heart disease
- respiratory disease
- blood loss.

First aid procedures:

- If the suspended person is alert, tell them to keep moving their legs, pushing off a fixed surface if possible
- provide drinks and a warm covering if possible
- release the casualty from the suspended position as quickly as possible
- vertical lifts should be avoided where possible
- the casualty should be closely monitored for symptoms of suspension trauma
- the casualty must not be laid down immediately after being rescued from a suspended position, not even the recovery position
- the casualty should be positioned with the upper body raised – in a seated or crouched position. All restrictive clothing should be unfastened. A doctor should be called immediately
- the casualty should be transported with the upper body raised
- when sat up, squatting or crouched, the blood volume to the heart may be increased carefully. The casualty may be gradually lowered over a 30 minute period, preferably under continuous medical supervision
- the patient should be hospitalised, even if symptoms are minor, as delayed damage is not uncommon.

Ladders

Ladders should be inspected and any that are visibly damaged, dented or loose should be tagged and taken out of service.

- Every portable ladder must, while being used:
  - be placed on a firm footing
  - be secured in such a manner that it cannot be dislodged accidentally from its position
- where the work is to be performed at a height of over 2 metres, a fall protection device and 100% tie-off must be used

- ladders should be cleaned prior to use, taking particular care to remove any grease or oil
- every ladder, whether portable or permanently secured, must be positioned in such a manner that it is not necessary for a person to use the underside of the ladder
- when ascending or descending, you should face the ladder and have free use of both hands and feet to allow three point control at all times
- no tools, equipment or materials should be carried while ascending and descending, except on specifically designed belts
- all portable ladders except stepladders should be tied at the top when in use. During tying and untying, a second party should secure the bottom of the ladder
- where a ladder provides access from one level to another, the ladder must extend, where practicable, at least three rungs above the higher level
- no metal or wire-bound portable ladder should be used where there is a potential for it to come into contact with any live electrical circuit or electrical equipment
- nobody should work from any of the three top rungs of any single or extension portable ladder or from either of the two top steps of any stepladder
- no non-metallic portable ladder shall be painted.

When climbing caged fixed ladders, a ladder safety-climbing device such as rope grabs or a self-retracting lifeline should be used when the distance between platforms is greater than 9 metres (30 feet). When the fixed ladder is not caged, the ladder safety-climbing device must be used when the distance is greater than 6 metres (20 feet).

Case Studies

- A worker fell 9 metres into a cargo hold. The hold did not have barriers in place and the worker was not wearing any fall arrest device. He fell onto the cargo, which cushioned his fall, preventing fatal injuries
- an officer was leaning over the bridge railing to ensure lights positioned under the bridge wing were functional, prior to the vessel's arrival in port. The officer was not using any form of fall arrest device. He lost his footing as the vessel rolled and fell 15 metres to his death
- a crew member fell 13 metres into a cargo hold. He was wearing an improperly buckled safety belt, which came undone, resulting in the fall. He fell onto the cargo, which cushioned his fall, and his injuries were not fatal
- a crew member was involved in hold cleaning duties prior to loading grain. He was wearing a safety belt, which he had attached to a steel protection plate that was welded across a number of frames protecting a pipe. The weld on the protection plate failed and he fell 12 metres to his death
- two men fell about 12 metres to the bottom of an empty cargo hold after a scaffold on which they were working collapsed. One subsequently died of his injuries. An investigation by the Australian Transport Safety Bureau found that:
  - the base of the scaffolding was too narrow for the assembled weight, making the scaffolding inherently unstable
  - the guy ropes were not secured and the castors were not locked
  - the two men had not secured their safety harnesses to the ship's structure
  - the company ISM practices and normal seafarer practice were violated to optimise the work in hand.

Tank Structure and Naming Convention

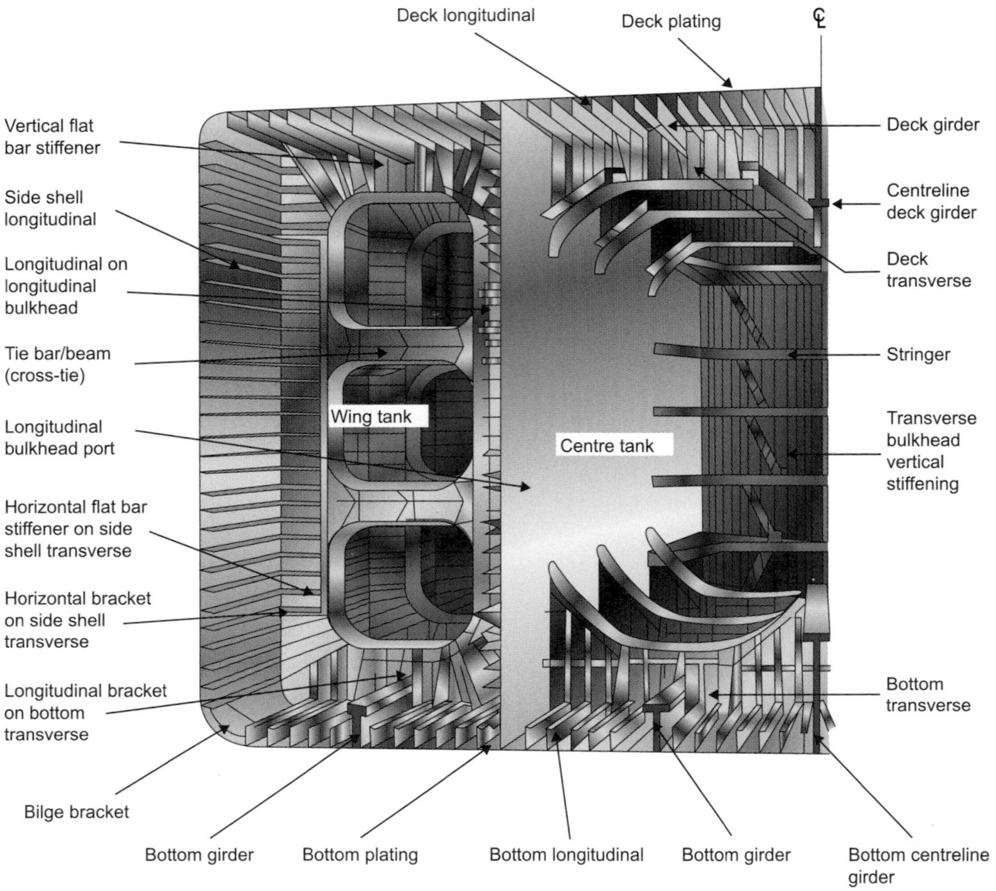

Note: When referring to the structure, you should identify each item with its actual frame number.

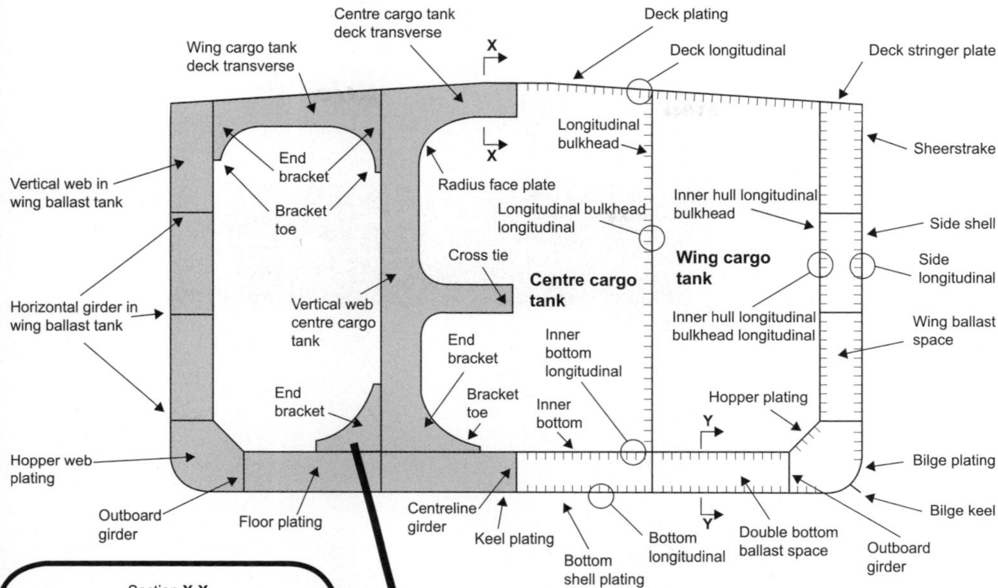

Centre cargo tank deck transverse
Deck plating
Wing cargo tank deck transverse
X
Deck longitudinal
Deck stringer plate
Longitudinal bulkhead
X
Sheerstrake
End bracket
Vertical web in wing ballast tank
Radius face plate
Bracket toe
Inner hull longitudinal bulkhead
Longitudinal bulkhead longitudinal
Side shell
Cross tie
Wing cargo tank
Side longitudinal
Centre cargo tank
Horizontal girder in wing ballast tank
Vertical web centre cargo tank
Inner hull longitudinal bulkhead longitudinal
Wing ballast space
End bracket
Inner bottom longitudinal
Bracket toe
Inner bottom
Hopper plating
End bracket
Y
Hopper web plating
Bilge plating
Bilge keel
Outboard girder
Floor plating
Centreline girder
Keel plating
Y
Bottom longitudinal
Double bottom ballast space
Outboard girder
Bottom shell plating

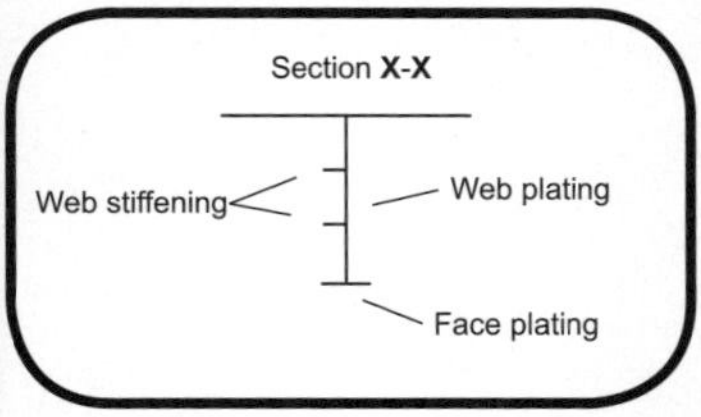

Section X-X
Web stiffening
Web plating
Face plating

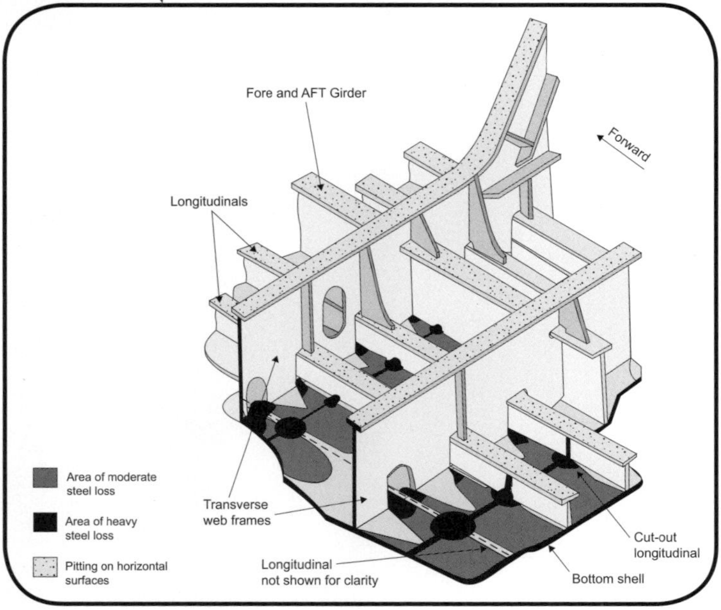

Fore and AFT Girder
Forward
Longitudinals
Area of moderate steel loss
Area of heavy steel loss
Pitting on horizontal surfaces
Transverse web frames
Cut-out longitudinal
Longitudinal not shown for clarity
Bottom shell

CHAPTER 44

Energy Efficiency

Energy Efficiency

The wasteful use of a limited resource is not a prudent or environmentally conscientious approach. Maximising the effectiveness of the hydrocarbons we use will mean that we can utilise them for longer and when fuel prices are high profits can be maximised. The emissions of SOx, NOx and CO_2 produced from burning these reserves are under scrutiny from legislators and regulations are becoming stringent.

Inefficiency in the shipping industry is measured in the bottom line operating profit or, in many cases, the lack of profit.

In a shipping company where half of costs are fuel and profits represent 10% of the turnover, a 10% decrease in fuel consumption would increase profit by 45%.

Despite the fact that the cost of bunker fuel reduced significantly during 2014, the cost of fuel has been only one factor (albeit a large one) in the move towards more efficient shipping. The influence of mandatory regulations in 2011 has been another key factor in the promotion and continuation of energy efficient practices. The Energy Efficiency Design Index (EEDI) is applicable to new ships, and the Ship Energy Efficiency Management Plan (SEEMP) is mandatory for all ships. Similarly, the regulations on ship emissions, specifically SOx, which are tightening both globally and regionally, have a significant effect on promoting efficiency and encouraging the use of alternative fuel sources that are environmentally cleaner, ie the less fossil fuel used, the fewer regulated emissions produced.

Operational Strategies	Vessel Type	Fuel Efficiency Gain (%)	New Build	Retrofit	Operational
Ship speed reduction	● ● ● ● ●	<23%			✓
Overall energy awareness	● ● ● ● ●	<10%			✓
Voyage planning and weather routing	● ● ● ● ●	<10%			✓
Port turn-around time	● ● ● ● ●	<10%	✓	✓	✓
Propeller surface maintenance	● ● ● ● ●	<10%			✓
Automation	● ● ● ● ●	<10%	✓	✓	✓
Condition-based maintenance	● ● ● ● ●	<5%		✓	✓
Optimised vessel ballast and trim	● ● ● ● ●	<5%			✓
Enhanced power management	● ● ● ● ●	<5%	✓		✓
Hull coating	● ● ● ● ●	<5%	✓	✓	✓
Optimised autopilot	● ● ● ● ●	<4%		✓	✓
Hull cleaning	● ● ● ● ●	<3%			✓
Fuel additives	● ● ● ● ●	<2%			✓

● Tankers/Bulkers ● Container ● Ro-Ro ● Ferry/Cruise ● Offshore Supply

(Information from 'Boosting Energy Efficiency' by Wärtsilä, 2008)

Some efficiencies can be put into practice very rapidly and used throughout the shipping industry, whereas some require an increased period of time to develop, are more costly or may only be of benefit to a particular type of vessel. Any efficiency that leads to lower fuel costs, reduced emissions and improved green credentials in the competitive marketplace can only be advantageous.

Operations

Many energy efficiencies can be achieved at the operational level. On existing ships, the easiest way to save energy is:

- Maintaining and operating the ship as per the manufacturer's instructions
- educating and training the crew in how to be more efficient.

Slow Steaming

Slow steaming is an agreement between all parties in the charter chain to manage inherent inefficiencies in the logistics chain, maximise fuel efficiency and minimise port waiting time and, therefore, congestion. It is not a new concept. There are six key factors that can influence the optimum speed for a vessel and whether slow steaming is an economic decision, with freight rate considered the most important:

- Freight rate
- bunker cost
- ship cost
- cargo cost
- interest rate
- environmental cost.

Note: When freight rates are high, the optimal speed increases.

In managing a transport chain, advanced and firm knowledge of a shipment's arrival time is often more important than how long the journey actually takes. Discharge slots at the terminal are pre-booked based on the ship's ETA. When container ships engage in slow steaming (for example cruising at 21 knots rather than 24 knots) the fuel costs and certain emissions can be reduced by between 10 and 30%. It can also help absorb surplus ship capacity since the total CO_2 emissions are less, despite requiring an increase in the overall number of ships necessary in the transport chain.

Note: From full speed at 24 knots:

- **Slow steaming reduces vessel speed to 21 knots**
- **extra slow steaming reduces speed to 18 knots**
- **super slow steaming reduces speed to 15 knots.**

Low fuel prices could be thought an advantage to shippers but there is an interplay of factors involved. If bunker prices remain low, the time is approaching when operating fewer ships at faster speeds could be more cost effective than operating more vessels at slower speeds. However, most new ships being introduced onto the marketplace are designed for slow steaming, so it will not cease in the short and medium term.

It has been calculated that the optimal speed for a vessel would be 25 knots if bunker prices are at $400 per metric tonne (pmt), 21 knots for $600 pmt, 18 knots for $800 pmt and 16 knots for $1,000 pmt.

When considering slow steaming, it is important to remember that operating an engine at a power rating lower than the optimum it was designed for increases the need for maintenance and repairs. The additional cost implication of this may cancel out any fuel savings. When an engine is operated at reduced power, the emission of NOx can vary up or down compared with its certified level. If engine de-rating was proposed, the engine's NOx certification would need to be reassessed.

Figure 44.1 - Container vessel leaving port

There are several possible disadvantages to slow steaming, but mostly these can be countered with simple modifications:

- Possible loss of effectiveness of heat recovery systems
- loss of turbocharger efficiency
- loss of propeller efficiency
- fouling of hull and propellers due to reduced ship speed
- increased use of auxiliary engine fuel to compensate for the reduced heat recovery capability
- increased lubricating oil consumption
- possible increase in vibration levels.

The optimum speed is the speed at which the fuel used per tonne mile is at a minimum level for that voyage – it does not mean minimum speed.

As slow steaming became more popular, engine manufacturers introduced retrofit upgrade slow steaming kits. The modified engines are not permanently de-rated.

Virtual Arrival

Virtual arrival is a concept developed by OCIMF and INTERTANKO to take advantage of existing market inefficiencies. In many cases, ships travel quickly between ports, arrive before their scheduled discharging or loading slot, and then have to wait. This leads to port congestion and increased emissions.

Energy Efficiency

Figure 44.2 - Ships waiting for their time to dock in the bay of Santos

Virtual arrival is not slow steaming since it does not lengthen the total voyage time. The ships will be loaded or the cargo discharged at the original preset time, but the vessel simply times its arrival better. In a similar way to slow steaming, a quality controlled weather-routeing company is used as an independent third party to calculate the revised arrival time depending on the variable journey parameters. The ship operator and charterer use this information to agree a speed reduction en route. The value of the fuel saved and potential CO_2 credits are shared between the operator and the charterer. In addition to reducing fuel costs and lowering emissions, there is less risk of collision or grounding, and less wear on the vessel's engines.

These two examples of improving fleet planning can significantly increase the energy efficiency of the vessels, leading to a company-wide best practice scenario that should be supported by all.

Overall Energy Awareness

The implementation of an Energy Management System (EMS) would ensure that energy efficiencies were integrated into all levels of decision-making. A Ship Energy Efficiency Management Plan (SEEMP) can enable the monitoring of ship and fleet operational efficiency over time, but where possible should present a minimal addition to the onboard administrative burden.

Example 1: Teekay Corporation

The Canadian shipping company Teekay Corporation has been using the CASPER (Computer Analysis of Ship PERformance) performance model on all its vessels since 2009. Data from existing bridge and engine room instruments are recorded at specific intervals and transmitted directly to the Propulsion Dynamics Inc (PDI) office for analysis. The corrected data on wind force and speed, wave height, sea currents and vessel draught and trim enable the CASPER program to calculate the true speed and fuel consumption and any added hull and propeller resistance. The results are sent to both the vessel and Teekay and the information can be assessed to determine improvements - a typical example of which would be determining the ships that require hull and propeller polishing.

In late 2014, Teekay signed up for a two-year extension of CASPER to cover 23 LNG carriers, with a further 7 ships to be included as they come under Teekay management.

Example 2: Maersk

Training the crew is one of the easiest ways to increase energy efficiencies on existing ships. Some owners, including AP Moller-Maersk, have used their fleets of same-class vessels to compare performance to identify areas where savings can be made. Maersk found that, when two identical vessels ran a similar route, the main variable was the crew. The company initiated an ISO 14001 onboard computer-based training course in 2007 and this was distributed to all vessels in 2008. This course must be completed by all seafarers to raise the environmental awareness on the vessels even further. With this training, crews have been made aware of the benefits of fuel saving and to look for ways of achieving it, such as switching off the fuel heating coils in empty or unused bunker tanks.

Example 3: The US Navy

The US Navy Incentivized Energy Conservation (i-ECON) Program was implemented fleet-wide in fiscal year 2000 and the Fleet Readiness Research and Development Program (FRR&DP) began in 2007. The i-ECON training is called 'smart steaming' and encourages maximum fuel efficiency on ships by focusing on engineering procedures and guidelines that do not harm mission objectives, for example:

- Running only those systems and power plants needed to support the mission
- the proper placement of ship's cargo and ballast to ensure balanced weight distribution.

The US Navy surface ships (underway) that lead in fuel conservation receive both special recognition and cash incentives, and these are highly effective motivational forces.

The incentive aspect of i-ENCON can be seen in chapter 1 of SL 101-AA-GYD-010 Shipboard Energy Conservation Guide (revision 4) February 2014.

Voyage Planning and Weather Routeing

Effective voyage planning requires time but software tools are available.

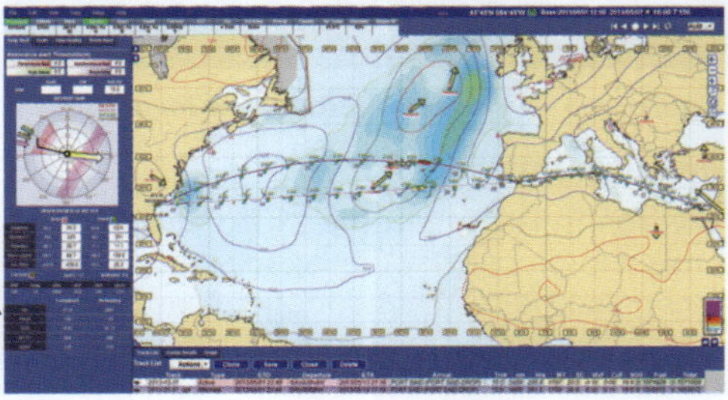

Courtesy of AWT

Figure 44.3 - Bon Voyage system (BVS) created by Applied Weather Technology

IMO Resolution A.893(21) (November 1999) on guidelines for voyage planning provides valuable guidance for ship's crew and voyage planners. The systems employed for weather routeing search for the optimum route for a specific voyage and offer the greatest benefit over longer distances. Shorter routes in rapidly changing weather conditions require a route planning system with a very high level of detail.

Port Turnaround

The efficiency or productivity of a port can be gauged by the ASTA (Average Ship Turnaround) and ASBO (Average Ship Berth Output). World ports are dependent on each other for efficient throughput of cargo. When delays occur such as by labour problems, over-stretching of the port rail network or equipment shortages, they will impact on the other ports in the transport chain. Effective and early communication with the next port can enable a form of virtual arrival to be carried out, where the voyage speed can be adjusted as necessary depending on berth availability.

Adaptive Autopilots

Figure 44.4 - Autopilot

The use of an adaptive autopilot or Integrated Navigation and Command System can achieve major fuel savings by improving course control. This is done on voyage legs in open water, where rigid adherence to the charted course is not necessary and, as opposed to the steering gear continually correcting to maintain heading, it will allow the vessel to ease a few degrees off course before correcting. When operating correctly, this should show as a sinusoidal wave on the course recorder rather than a jagged line.

Propeller Cleaning/Polishing

Regular polishing of the propellers is a valuable energy saving measure. Studies have found that cleaning the propellers alone will result in

Energy Efficiency

recovery of 50% of the recoverable fuel penalty due to fouling since the ship was last cleaned. The majority of the world's major oil companies schedule their vessels for propeller cleaning twice as often as standard hull cleaning as they have long since recognised the cost effectiveness of regular propeller maintenance. It has been estimated that fuel consumption savings of between 3 and 8% are realistic. The US Navy cleans the propellers of its military ships on a quarterly basis, and as frequently as every two months in tropical regions.

Hull Cleaning

There are several key factors that affect the efficiency of a ship's hull:

- The shape of the hull
- the condition of the hull itself
- the coating used on the hull
- the nature and extent of fouling on the hull.

Regular hull cleaning can increase fuel efficiency since a clean hull offers less water resistance. Other benefits include reduced hull corrosion as well as minimal unwanted transfer of marine species from one area to another.

Figure 44.5 - Steam cleaning a ship's hull

Specialist coatings that minimise hull biofouling through their chemical composition and surface characteristics can be applied during routine drydockings. For example, it has been suggested that one of the self-polishing antifouling coating systems from Hempel can offer protection from biofouling from 36 months to 90 months, with reducing fuel consumption by up to 4%.

Biofouling guidelines (Resolution MEPC.207(62)) have been developed by the IMO and these establish the necessary regime for hull cleaning and record keeping. In regions where in-water cleaning is permitted, care must be taken to contain cleaning residues to prevent the transfer of alien marine organisms.

Ballast and Trim Optimisation

Minimising the quantity of ballast carried will reduce the vessel's displacement. This will result in a corresponding reduction in the vessel's water resistance. However, there is an obvious need to have sufficient ballast to immerse the propeller, provide stability and limit slamming. Trim also has a significant effect on a ship's resistance through the water and optimising trim can achieve fuel savings.

Figure 44.6 - A vessel exhibiting non-ideal trim

Design Example 1

The Non-Ballast Water Ship (NOBS) design project (promoted by the Japan Ship Technology Research Association) has been improved with the concept of the minimal ballast water ship (MIBS). The NOBS project created tanker designs that could operate without ballast water, but the design's commercial practicability was limited because of its very wide hull shape. The MIBS design has built on the NOBS' advantages, incorporating these features with a flatter bottom and standard breadth hull. This allows for a considerable reduction in the amount of ballast water needed and maintains the dimensions of a standard VLCC, meaning that a smaller ballast water treatment system is needed and the fuel consumption is reduced. ClassNK granted Approval in Practice (AIP) to the MIBS VLCC design in March 2013.

Design Example 2

Atlantic Container Line (ACL) ordered five new G4 ConRo (Container-RoRo) vessels, with the last due to be in service in 2016, from Hudong-Zhonghua Shipbuilding in China. Each vessel has a container capacity of 3,800 teu, 764 teus of RoRo space and space in the car decks for 1,307 vehicles.

Figure 44.7 - ACL G4 ConRo designed by Knud E Hansen A/S (Knud E Hansen A/S)

These vessels are a redesign and reorganisation of the cargo space (based on cargo weight) and how it is utilised. In a traditional ConRo, the RoRo freight is stored under deck while the container freight is above deck. This typically means that the principal weight is high in a ConRo meaning that large volumes of ballast water are necessary for stability. The designers worked out that, by placing all RoRo cargo midships and loading containers in cells fore and aft of this RoRo section, there was a more efficient utilisation of the space available and it optimised the cargo weight distribution.

Shore Power - 'Cold Ironing' or AMP (Alternative Maritime Power)

Cold ironing, or Alternative Maritime Power (AMP), is a means by which a berthed ship obtains its electricity for cargo handling and hotel requirements from a shore-based source via a high-voltage shore connection (HVSC). This technique has been practised by navies worldwide for many years as their vessels can be alongside for prolonged periods.

While merchant ships are typically berthed for a much shorter time, the reductions in both shipboard emissions and in the risk of pollution have made this technique an attractive option. This method of saving onboard fuel is of particular value to certain types of ship that spend a relatively long time at berth on a regular basis, such as tankers, cruise ships, container ships and reefers, all of which have high in-port power requirements.

Courtesy of the Port of Los Angeles

Figure 44.8 - Alternative maritime power at the Port of Los Angeles

In existing ships, retrofitting of power converters can be carried out on board. It has been estimated that the cost of retrofitting a ship to plug into shore-side power can range from $500,000 to $1.5 million, depending on the vessel type.

The shore-side modification costs vary according to the accessibility of a local power source. The investment costs for the port are high and Government assistance is often crucial.

Example 1

In Juneau, Alaska, the land infrastructure has cost $3.2 million, the vessel modification cost Princess Cruises $500,000 and Holland America Line $1.1 million.

Example 2

At the Port of Oakland, it has cost US$70 million to install 11 berths on six terminals.

Also, many Mediterranean ports are supplied with electricity from coal-fired power stations which, with increased demand, could lead to higher overall emissions. The cost of electricity from shore is also consistently higher than that derived by ship fuel, often by a factor of two or more. This is because shore-side electricity has to cover the costs of the transfer

Energy Efficiency

and distribution infrastructure, the generation capacity required for the ship and a profit for the utility company. LNG is an alternative shore-based power source that is under consideration, although dual-fuel engines would be required in ships and conversions can be expensive.

Many ports worldwide have introduced shore-based power, such as the US ports of Los Angeles, Long Beach, San Francisco, San Diego, Seattle and Juneau, at Vancouver in Canada and at ports in Germany, Sweden, Finland and The Netherlands.

Fuel Additives

Water in Fuel System (WIF)

The formation of nitrogen oxides (NOx) is strongly affected by the temperature of the cylinder liner. By lowering this temperature, the NOx emissions are also reduced. Adding water to the fuel before injection lowers the cylinder temperature, resulting in a reduction of NOx by 30 to 35%. Reducing the combustion temperature leads to an increase in fuel consumption and in particulate matter, and therefore additional measures are necessary. Fuel-water emulsion injection (FWE) combined with variable injection timing is a highly effective method of saving fuel and reducing CO_2, NOx and particulate matter emissions. MAN Diesel & Turbo, for example, provides the emission reduction technology combination of fuel-water emulsions and variable injection timing.

Combustion Additives

During the combustion phase, the presence of fuel oil additives can improve combustion significantly. A combustion improver can be organic or can include an organo-metallic compound, containing iron or other metals. Iron-based additives are used as an oxidation catalyst to accelerate the main combustion and promote the complete combustion of residual fuel oils.

Some additives act by breaking down clusters of fuel molecules leading to improved combustion. This improvement means that significantly less fuel can be used for the same energy output, so saving both fuel and money as well as reducing harmful emissions.

Machinery/Technology

Efficiencies can be made to existing tonnage by retrofitting and to new building projects by the improvement of machinery and propulsion. However, an integrated approach is the most beneficial, since a solitary change is unlikely to provide the maximum return.

Power Sources

Hybrid Machinery

A dual-fuel diesel-electric (DFDE) hybrid achieves propulsion using power from both a diesel engine and a stored energy source. The use of a dual-fuel system allows the diesel fuel to be consumed within the engine's optimum operating range, so minimising pollution. A switch made to electric power during operations would require the diesel engine to operate sub-optimally, such as during part-load operations.

This machinery is of particular benefit when ships have frequent changes in operation, load profiles or speed, such as on offshore support vessels (OSVs), where it can achieve savings of 15 to 35% over conventional main drives when dynamic positioning is a normal aspect of operations. Combined diesel-electric and diesel-mechanical machinery (CODED) can further reduce energy consumption with the electric power plant being used at part load and the mechanical plant at higher load.

Machinery/Technology Strategies	Vessel Type	Fuel Efficiency Gain (%)	New Build	Retrofit
Diesel-electric drives	🔵🟣🔴	5-30%	✓	
Waste heat recovery	🟠🟢🔵🟣	<10%	✓	✓
Engine de-rating	🟠🟢🔵🟣	<3.5%	✓	✓
Enhanced engine tuning and part-load operation	🟠🟢🔵	<4%	✓	✓
Solar power	🟠 🔵🟣	<4%	✓	✓
Combined diesel-electric and diesel-mechanical drives	🟣🔴	<4%	✓	
Variable speed electric power generation	🟣🔴	<3%	✓	
Hybrid auxiliary power generation	🟠🟢🔵🟣🔴	<2%	✓	
Low-loss electric drive	🔵🟣🔴	<2%	✓	
Energy-saving lighting	🟣	<1%	✓	✓
Variable speed pumps	🟠🟢🔵🟣🔴	<1%	✓	✓
Common rail engine	🟠🟢🔵🟣🔴	<1%	✓	✓

🟠 Tankers/Bulkers 🟢 Container 🔵 Ro-Ro 🟣 Ferry/Cruise 🔴 Offshore Supply

(Information from 'Boosting Energy Efficiency' by Wärtsilä, 2008)

Figure 44.9 - The LNG carrier 'Provalys'

Hybrid auxiliary power generation uses a control system that balances the loading of each part of the network: the fuel cell, the diesel gen-set and the batteries. The system can also utilise energy from other sources such as wind or solar power.

The dual-fuel diesel-electric propulsion system uses either oil or gas, depending on the situation. It uses an electric motor like large cruise ships and submarines, not a steam turbine, which is the traditional propulsion system for LNG carriers. The DFDE propulsion system improves fuel efficiency, reacts quickly and provides a smooth voyage.

DFDE Example 1

The world's first operational dual-fuel electric-driven LNGC was the *'Provalys'* which was delivered to her owner, Gaz de France, in November 2006.

DFDE Example 2

BP's Gem class LNG carrier *'British Emerald'* and her three sister ships all use dual-fuel diesel-electric (DFDE) propulsion. It has been found that the *'British Emerald'*, when running at a speed of 20 knots, burns 40 tons less fuel per day than a comparably sized steam turbine propulsion ship.

DFDE technology allows diesel engines to run on the LNG boil-off gases or make the switch to diesel fuel and act as conventional diesel-electric engines. The lower fuel consumption and reduced greenhouse gas emissions these ships offered were critical factors in BP's decision to choose hybrid propulsion technology.

This technology is not new, and has been popular in conventional-sized LNG carriers, but engine manufacturers have continued to develop more efficient, flexible and lower emission engines. For example, the dual-fuel low speed MEGI (M-type, electronically controlled gas injection) engine from MAN Diesel. These engines have significant operational and economic advantages over other low speed propulsion options.

MEGI Example 1

Teekay LNG Partners ordered their 9th MEGI LNG new building from Daewoo Shipbuilding & Marine Engineering Co Ltd in February 2015.

MEGI Example 2

The specification for the Flex LNG order for two new build Panamax LNG carriers from Samsung Heavy Industries was changed in February 2015. The original specification for the use of DFDE propulsion systems was changed to using MEGI main engines. There is a consequential increase in yard price and delivery time. According to Flex LNG, *"For a typical long haul trade, the new and more efficient twin screw LNGC design with MEGI engines will have average daily fuel consumption (gas and fuel oil) of approximately 25% less than the DFDE LNG carrier design recently delivered into the market."*

LNG as a Fuel for Conventional Ships

Using LNG as a fuel for ships cuts CO_2 emissions by about 20% when compared with a diesel engine producing the same power. The NOx emissions are reduced by about 90% and SOx emissions are practically zero since LNG is the cleanest fossil fuel, containing virtually no sulphur compounds.

Using LNG can have a significant impact on reducing emissions and it reduces the demand for energy to separate and heat heavy fuel oil. The hotel load on power can also be reduced when the low temperatures of the LNG are utilised to cool the HVAC. Due to the significant cost of retrofitting, this is a power choice almost exclusively for new builds.

Example

Two Fjord Line ferries *'Bergensfjord'* and *'Stavangerford'* are both powered by four Rolls-Royce BV12PG gas engines. These vessels operate only with LNG and are not dual fuel. In March 2015, they occupied the top two places in the voluntary World Ports Climate Environmental Ship Index (ESI) list. The ESI

Energy Efficiency

measures the amount of NOx and SOx that is released by a ship and includes a reporting scheme on the GHG emission of the ship.

To date, LNG has been used successfully in dual-fuel hybrid engines. Most of these vessels are operating in Europe but numbers are increasing elsewhere as the LNG bunkering infrastructure is improved.

Biofuels

Large, slow-speed two- stroke engines can handle a number of fuel sources, such as HFO, raw vegetable oils, waste oil and tallow, as long as these comply with specific acidity, viscosity and performance characteristics. The use of biodiesel (FAME or fatty acid methyl ester) in marine engines has been trialled in many instances and, on the North American Great Lakes, for example, has been found to be compatible with marine engines – although there may be increased NOx emissions. For vessels running on MDO, blending with biodiesel up to 20% (B20 blend consists of 20% biodiesel and 80% petrodiesel) produces a blend that has more positive characteristics than the original fuels.

The most promising biofuels for use in ships are biodiesel and crude vegetable oil, but other biofuels may prove to be useful alternatives. There are many advantages to using biofuels and blends:

- Biodiesel is biodegradable, meaning that there is less environmental impact should a spill occur
- biofuels are free of sulphur and emissions of particulate matter are greatly reduced
- blending biodiesel with petrodiesel improves the cold operating characteristic of biodiesel
- the blend also has a reduced ability to absorb water compared with pure biodiesel.

Biofuels are more expensive than fossil fuels. Calculations have shown that a typical supply ship for the Norwegian petroleum industry using MDO would almost double its fuel expenses when changing to biodiesel. However, an increase in carbon taxes in the future and the use of cheaper biofuels, such as pyrolysis oils, could make them more competitive by significantly reducing the price gap.

Example

The Channel Islands National Park, off the coast of Southern California, uses B100 in the vessels *'Pacific Ranger'* and *'Sea Ranger II'* as well as in other diesel equipment, including stationary power generators, on the islands. The use of biodiesel and other renewable resources makes the islands petroleum free. Kent Bullard, the maintenance supervisor at Channel Islands National Park has said *"It has been seamless. We haven't had any performance issues; the biodiesel is performing just as well as diesel."*

Wind Energy

Kite Systems

German-based SkySails GmbH has developed a computer-controlled towing-kite system that can be used to supplement the power from a ship's engine. Fuel savings of 10 to 35% are claimed depending on the wind conditions. This technology is most suited to long distance transport routes, for example tankers crossing the Pacific, where the strong winds can be harnessed since the system depends on the strength of winds at an altitude of between 100 to 500 m.

Specialist weather routeing to make the most of the stronger winds at these altitudes would be an additional challenge.

Courtesy of SkySails GmbH

Figure 44.10 - The SkySails towing kite on the MV 'BBC SKYSAILS'

Example

The Wessels Shipping Company's cargo ships *'Theseus'* and *'Michael A'* have this technology installed as a retrofit. It has been found that present crew strengths are sufficient for operating the device.

Flettner Rotors

Flettner rotors are another wind energy concept. These are large, rotating, vertical, metal sailing rotors positioned on deck, which are used to convert wind power into thrust when the wind is at right angles to the direction of ship travel. This provides forward propulsion power in addition to the main engines and reduces fuel consumption.

Example

Four Flettner rotors were fitted to Enercon's *'E-Ship 1'*, which underwent its maiden voyage in 2010. It has been found that the *'E-Ship 1'* can achieve operational fuel savings of more than 15% due to the use of the Flettner rotors, when compared with same-sized conventional freight vessels.

© SteKrueBe

Figure 44.11 - 'E-Ship 1' at Cassens Werft shipyard

Design

It is not only external devices that can utilise wind energy and make energy savings. The shape of the ship itself can be modified to make use of wind power.

Example

The Lade AS design for the Vindskip™ has a hull shaped like a symmetrical aerofoil which acts as a sail-like device, pushing the boat through the ocean. The design can use wind power in the same way as an airplane uses wind power, allowing it to almost sail directly into the wind.

Courtesy of Lade AS

Figure 44.12 - The Vindskip™ concept design by Lade AS

When not using wind, the hybrid merchant concept ship would use LNG and could potentially achieve up to 60% of fuel savings and reduce emissions by up to 80%.

Courtesy of Lade AS

Figure 44.13 - The Vindskip™ concept design by Lade AS

Solar Power

A solar cell converts the energy from sunlight into electricity, and photovoltaic technology is its application for practical use. The electricity produced can be stored for later use. Solar boats are not a new concept. Many small solar-powered passenger craft have been used successfully on European lakes and rivers, with their very quiet operation being appreciated by passengers, crew and wildlife. On a much larger scale:

Example 1

The MV *'Auriga Leader'*, an NYK car carrier launched in July 2009, has 328 integrated solar panels. These can generate up to 10%

Energy Efficiency

of the ship's electrical energy requirement when berthed, which is a very small amount. These panels will be at their most effective, ie produce peak power, in clear sunny daytime conditions with the sun at an ideal angle compared with the solar panels, which may only happen for an hour each day. This was a highly expensive investment, at US$1.6 million, and it will be difficult to recoup this cost with fuel savings, although it is a valuable demonstration to raise awareness of this 'green' technology.

Example 2

Nissan's solar-diesel hybrid RoRo '*Nichioh Maru*' was launched in 2012 with 281 solar panels fitted to the carrier's deck. Nissan has calculated that the energy generated from these panels, along with other efficiency modifications on the vessel such as low friction hull coating and an electronically-controlled diesel engine, will mean that 1,400 tons less fuel will be burned and 4,200 fewer tons of CO_2 per year will be produced compared to the same class of ships.

Fuel Cells

These are electrochemical devices that convert chemically-stored energy, which is present in fuel, directly into electricity through a reaction with oxygen in the air. As long as fuel is supplied to a fuel cell, it will generate electricity. There are several different fuel cell technologies available that make use of different types of fuel. These include hydrogen (with the only by-products being heat and water), natural gas, propane and methanol.

In this case, however, carbon-containing fuels produce up to 50% less CO_2 than those produced by diesel engines running on marine bunker fuel. Fuel cells are characterised by the electrolyte material used in their construction. For example, a solid oxide fuel cell (SOFC) uses a solid oxide material as the electrolyte, while a molten carbonate fuel cell (MCFC) uses an electrolyte composed of a molten mixture of carbonate salts.

The energy efficiency of a fuel cell is about 50% at maximum operating load, which is a similar level to slow-speed diesels. For many years, the power output of fuel cells was so low that they supplied energy only for the onboard electrical devices but not for the propulsion system. This is no longer the case.

An advantage of fuel cell technology is that it is inherently silent and vibration-free, which increases passenger comfort and improves the working conditions for the crew. Far less maintenance is required due to the simpler designs with fewer moving parts. Also, fuel cell technology is modular, enabling systems to be configured for the efficient use of onboard space.

Disadvantages at the moment include:

- High investment costs
- the volume and weight of fuel cell installations
- the expected lifetime of the cell.

Note: There must be a particular emphasis given to the storage of hydrogen on board ships in order to ensure safe operations.

The Fellow SHIP (Fuel Cells for Low Emission Ships) joint industry research project was initiated by DNV to test, and then make commercially viable, the use of fuel cells on board ships. The development of class rules for installation of fuel cells on board vessels was an important part of the project.

Example

As part of the FellowSHIP project, a 330 kW fuel cell was successfully installed on board the offshore supply vessel '*Viking Lady*'. The electric efficiency due to the fuel cell was estimated to be 44.5% and, when heat recovery was enabled, the overall fuel efficiency was increased to 55%. There were no NOx, SOx and PM emissions detected.

Turbines

Steam turbines are now more commonly found in LNG carriers, but until recently were still fitted to a number of older passenger cruise liners and many of the VLCCs built in the 1970s. The thermal efficiency of the conventional main propulsion steam turbine is relatively low compared with diesels. Both Mitsubishi and Kawasaki have introduced more efficient steam turbine designs, promising a 12 to 15% increase in thermal efficiency, which would put the total thermal efficiency of the steam system at about 32%. Gas turbine propulsion systems are popular in both UK and US naval vessels, with the Rolls-Royce MT30 marine gas turbine delivering up to 36 MW of power, excellent thermal efficiency (>40%) and a simple modular design. The Rolls-Royce MT30 engines power the US Zumwalt-class destroyers - see below for example.

All-Electric Ships

In recent years, the US Office of Naval Research and the UK's Royal Navy have been investigating the feasibility and developing the concept of powering all-electric vessels.

Example

The USS *'Zumwalt'* (DDG 1000), launched in 2013, was the first of three planned all-electric US Zumwalt-class warships. The USS *'Zumwalt'* has a 78 megawatt power station supplying electricity to an advanced integrated power system (IPS). This system powers huge induction motors, from GE Power Conversion (a subsidiary of General Electric), which are connected directly to the propeller shafts. The IPS also routes electricity to a large number of sensors, weapons, radar and other essential systems on board.

Mark Dannatt, director for naval business at GE Power Conversion and a retired Royal Navy Captain, has said that, *"by getting rid of the gear box, you can free up as much as 80% of the ship's power that used to be dedicated to propulsion. You can now send it wherever you need it very quickly. By economising on the amount of machinery, you also save a lot of space in the ship."*

Courtesy of US Navy

Figure 44.14 - The USS 'Zumwalt' guided-missile destroyer DDG 1000 is floated out of dry dock in 2013

Nuclear Ships

Nuclear power is particularly useful for vessels that have to remain at sea for long periods of time with infrequent refuelling, such as submarines and icebreakers. Nuclear-powered icebreaking ships have been used successfully in the Arctic for many years. The combination of high power levels needed for icebreaking and limitations for conventional refuelling in the remote Arctic landscape made the nuclear option sensible. Whether this fuel source is feasible for standard merchant vessels remains to be seen.

Machinery and Modifications

Heat Recovery/Electrical Systems - Waste Heat Recovery (WHR) Systems

This is not a novel concept, but the developments in new technologies have the potential of reducing CO_2 emissions by up to 20%. Marine diesel engines are already highly efficient and almost half of the energy in the fuel is converted into shaft power. About 25% of fuel energy is lost through exhaust gas dissipation. It makes sense to utilise this 'waste' thermal energy into valuable electric power. This can be used elsewhere on the ship for auxiliary purposes (such as hotel load or reefer cargo) and to boost the ship's propulsion with an electric motor integrated into the shaft line. Both the fuel consumption and harmful emissions from the vessel are reduced. The WHR systems can be retrofitted or incorporated in new builds.

WHR systems consist of an exhaust gas boiler that supplies steam to a steam turbine. This is connected to a generator that produces electrical energy. For producing optimal amounts of electricity, a dual or even triple steam pressure system may be a possible solution. The system can be extended to employ a gas turbine to use heat in the exhaust gas that is not used by the turbo charger. For a dual steam pressure WHR system, the available electrical power output can be increased to 7% of the shaft power but, in combination with a gas turbine, output can be as much as 11 to 12%. The engine and WHR system must be carefully matched for optimum results. The payback time is shorter when an installed WHR is used in combination with large diesel engines.

Cargo Heating Management System

One system, pioneered by Blue Water Trade Winds, uses software to develop a voyage-specific cargo heating plan using current and previous cargo, ship and climate data.

Energy Efficiency

It is monitored daily, based on heating data sent by the ship, and suggests changes when necessary. The system estimates the optimum boiler load settings and the quantity of fuel oil to be used to maintain the cargo at the temperature required by the charter party.

Example

Blue Water Trade Winds signed a three year contract in 2011 with ST Shipping & Transport to provide cargo heating management services on board its fleet of owned and time-chartered vessels.

Engine De-Rating

While measuring the economics at the new build stage, increased bunker costs can justify the additional investment of an engine with an extra cylinder and the resulting reduction in long-term fuel consumption. Wärtsilä has calculated that using an engine with an extra cylinder than that typically specified could reduce the daily fuel consumption as follows:

- Suezmax tanker or Capesize bulk carrier by 3.4%
- Panamax container ship by 2%
- Post-Panamax container ship by 2.4%.

De-rating can also be carried out to existing ships' engines without adding an extra engine cylinder. For example, if a version of an engine that had increased power and reduced BSFC (Brake Specific Fuel Consumption) was de-rated to the same cylinder power output as the unmodified version, it would have a reduced BSFC at full load. Changing operating conditions, such as slow steaming, may mean that the original engine set-up is not ideal. It might be possible to change the engine rating in consultation with the engine manufacturer and re-assess the NOx certification.

Example

All of Hapag-Lloyd's 8,750 TEU-class vessels have been de-rated since the beginning of December 2009.

Slide Valves

Incorporating this type of fuel valve produces lower emissions of hydrocarbons (around 25%) and particulate matter as well as optimising fuel combustion. The valve gives a more precise operation of camshaft-operated engines and can be retrofitted or purchased as standard components in new engines. By replacing conventional fuel valves, slide valves allow for more complete fuel combustion at lower peak engine temperatures. It is an inexpensive way to reduce emissions significantly.

Integrated Automation System (IAS)

An Integrated Automation System (IAS) maximises the value of the fuel used in part-load operations. It monitors and regulates many ship parameters in operational conditions. There can be a 5 to 10% saving in fuel consumption with the optimisation of engine control, power generation and distribution, thrust control and ballast. These systems can be incorporated into new builds or existing vessels.

Selective Catalytic Reduction (SCR)

SCR technology is a highly effective method of reducing emissions of NOx, typically in the region of 85 to 99%, and hydrocarbons by 70 to 90%. A dose of urea initiates a chemical reaction in the exhaust stream that converts NOx compounds into harmless nitrogen and water. Adjusting the injection rate of the urea leads to a variation in the NOx reduction rate, meaning that different emissions regulations can be met.

Example

The Dansk Teknologi BLUENOX SCR system has been retrofitted on board six Royal Danish Navy patrol vessels (two systems on each vessel). The BLUENOX system uses a multipoint airless urea injection technology that is compact and adaptable for use on any engine running on marine diesel fuel. The system reduces NOx by up to 95%, meaning that the vessels will be IMO Tier III compliant when the regulations enter into force in 2016.

Humid Air Motor (HAM) System

The HAM system is an attractive option for reducing NOx emissions since the system is compact, has a low operating cost and can reduce NOx formation by up to approximately 65%. HAM humidifies the inlet air to the cylinder during combustion, reducing the temperature peaks that cause most NOx generation. The HAM process was designed by Munters Euroform GmbH.

Example

The HAM system has been in full-scale operation on Viking Line's cruiseferry *'Mariella'* since 2001, and emissions of NOx from the ship have been reduced by 68%.

© Ralf Roletschek

Figure 44.15 - The 'Mariella'

Fuel Consumption Monitor

This device monitors, in real time, the fuel consumption measured as distance travelled per ton (or day) of fuel consumed. This information can be correlated with other factors such as variations in weather and sea conditions, wind speed and direction, reducing vessel speed and rudder angle, in order to provide information about fuel efficiency and to aid decision-making during a voyage.

Pump and Cooling Water Optimisation

It is essential that the correct cooler in the seawater cooling system is chosen at the design stage. A bigger cooler has reduced resistance and means that smaller pumps can be installed. Fitting the optimal combination of pump and cooler in a standard bulk carrier saves about 90% of the energy needed to run the pumps. This saving equates to about 10% of the total generated electrical power on board.

Variable speed pumps in the cooling system can optimise energy efficiency. Constant speed pumps operate the cooling system at a higher capacity than may be necessary and the flexibility of variable speed pumps can offer the potential to save energy.

Common Rail (CR)

Common rail technology is well established in the marine market. It is a variant of a direct fuel injection system and can be incorporated at the retrofit or new build stage. The term 'common rail' refers to a pressure accumulator (common fuel rail) where the fuel is stored at high pressure and supplies multiple fuel injectors with high pressure fuel. There is independent and separate control of the injection pressure and timing. The system controls combustion so that fuel consumption can be optimised depending on the ship's operations. This technology leads to smokeless emissions at all loads (particularly important for cruise ships), reduced NOx emissions and low specific fuel oil consumption (SFOC).

Turbochargers

Modern high efficiency turbochargers, which electronically control the quantity of air entering the cylinders to match the amount of fuel injected, lead to more efficient and cleaner combustion.

Turbochargers with variable geometry turbines can be called by different names depending on the manufacturer:

VGT - Variable Geometry Turbocharger (Cummins/Holset)

VNT - Variable Nozzle Turbine (Honeywell/Garrett)

VTG - Variable Turbine Geometry (BorgWarner and ABB)

VG - Variable Geometry turbocharger (MHI)

VGS - Variable Geometry System turbocharger (IHI)

VTA - Variable Turbine Area (MAN Diesel & Turbo).

Compared to a fixed geometry turbine, the variable geometry turbine allows a significant level of flexibility over the pressure ratio/flow relationship across the turbine and, by extension, the engine differential pressure (ΔP). This flexibility can be used for improving low speed torque characteristics, reducing turbocharger lag and, in diesel engines, driving EGR flow.

Scrubber Technology - Freshwater and Seawater Scrubbing

MARPOL and European port legislation is primarily concerned with the actual concentration of SOx emitted from a ship's exhaust, not necessarily that entering the fuel tanks, so exhaust gas SOx scrubbers are allowed as an abatement alternative to using low

Energy Efficiency

sulphur fuel. In California state waters, there has been a fuel rule limiting the fuel allowed to be used since 2009, but this rule entered a sunset review period on 1st January 2015 when the sulphur emissions limits of the US SOx/NOx-ECA came into effect, and the ECA regulations will eventually replace the California rule. This means that abatement technologies are now allowed to reduce SOx emissions in California waters.

Using a scrubber system on a vessel burning HFO, it is possible to reduce the SOx (and also the particulate matter) emission level to a level comparable to that produced using the more expensive low sulphur fuel oil, even for ECA regions where the emissions requirements are much more stringent than the general global requirements. Using a scrubber also eliminates any problems of low sulphur fuel availability.

It is important to note that the sludge removed from scrubber washwater must be retained on board to be disposed of ashore. SOx scrubber manufacturers typically recommend a sludge tank of around 0.5 m^3/MW of scrubbed engine power.

Certification

The IMO Exhaust Gas Cleaning System (EGCS) Guidelines (Resolution MEPC.184(59)) provide the stipulations for testing, survey, certification and verification of scrubber systems. These standards are to ensure that the scrubbers will reduce emissions levels to the equivalent of the fuel sulphur levels allowed in the area of transit.

	Scheme A	Scheme B
Technical and Operating Manual for the scheme including SECP (SOx Emissions Compliance Plan)	Yes	Yes
Initial test of scrubber at manufacturer or on board	Yes	No
Onboard monitoring of SO_2/CO_2	Daily	Continuous
Monitoring of key operating parameters	Continuous	Daily
Monitoring of washwater	Continuous	Continuous

There are two EGCS compliance options and each has specific requirements:

1. Scheme A (also referred to as type approval) describes the thorough testing of the scrubber system, checking the:
   - Unit approval
   - serially manufactured units
   - production range approval.
2. Scheme B compliance is demonstrated in service by continuous emissions monitoring (CEM). The monitoring system should be approved by the Administration and the results of that monitoring made available to the Administration as necessary to demonstrate compliance as required.

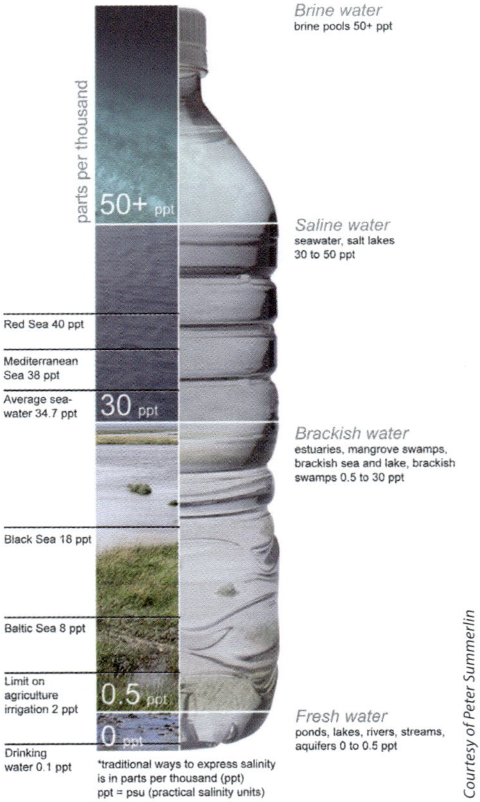

Figure 44.16 - Graphic breakdown of water salinity, defining freshwater, brackish water, saltwater and brine water

Freshwater Scrubber

A freshwater scrubber is based on a closed loop system and requires a supply of freshwater and an alkali, usually sodium hydroxide. The exhaust SOx compounds are neutralised by the alkali into sulphates. Freshwater scrubbers have the advantage that they are self-contained and can operate effectively irrespective of the saltiness or alkalinity of the surrounding water. They are less power hungry than seawater scrubbers and have fewer problems with corrosion.

Seawater (Saltwater) Scrubber

A seawater scrubber is an open loop system where some of the seawater used for engine cooling is used. The SOx compounds react with the alkaline salts (calcium carbonate) in the seawater to produce calcium sulphate and CO. Seawater scrubber design is simple because there is no requirement for freshwater or a neutralising alkali solution. However, the effectiveness of a seawater scrubber can be compromised in brackish and freshwater environments where there are insufficient salts in the water to react with the SOx.

Hybrid Scrubber

A hybrid scrubber uses the salts present in surrounding seawater to neutralise the SOx in emission gases. However, when operating in freshwater or brackish water, the system can be switched to freshwater scrubbing when an alkali solution is added to provide the neutralisation capability. This would be particularly useful when transiting from a seawater environment into less saline environments, for example the Great Lakes or the Baltic Sea. This type of system provides a useful level of flexibility.

Which Scrubber to Choose?

When choosing the type of scrubber system for a particular vessel, as long as it is certified, one type is generally no better or worse than another. The choice is made based on the individual requirements of the vessel and its transiting patterns.

Note: Two key factors in choosing a scrubber are the ship's operating salinity and its route.

As well as the water salinity of the ship's operating area, another factor to consider is the turbidity or sand/sediment content of the water. For example, if the ship routinely operates in shallow or sandy waters, even if it is in a region of high salinity water, a freshwater or hybrid scrubber system could be a better option than a seawater scrubber. This is due to the intake of abrasive sand/sediments along with the scrubbing seawater which will add significantly to maintenance costs. Another key factor could be the amount of power needed to pump large quantities of seawater on board for an open loop system. This is higher in seawater scrubbers than for freshwater systems. However, the freshwater scrubbers require a supply of alkali material for neutralisation, which will cost in both monetary and storage space terms. The complexity of the system will also affect the cost.

Carbon Capture and Storage (CCS)

CCS has three parts:

- Capture of the CO_2
- transport
- storage of the CO_2 emissions.

CCS uses technology to capture CO_2 emissions from stationary sources, like power and industrial plants, and transport it elsewhere for permanent storage.

The results from a maritime CCS research and development project carried out by DNV and Process Systems Enterprise Ltd (PSE) (a global provider of advanced process modelling technology) were released in 2013. The project successfully developed a concept design for onboard CO_2 capture, liquefaction and short-term storage on board until transfer at the next suitable port. The project showed that the concept is technically feasible and could reduce maritime CO_2 emissions by up to 65%.

Example

For a VLCC, this could correspond to capturing more than 70,000 tonnes of CO_2 per year. This would change the CO_2 from a waste emission to marketable product.

Ship Design

There are efficiencies that will take longer to implement and these involve improved ship design for new builds. Structural modifications for existing vessels would be effective immediately.

The Streamline (strategic research for innovative marine propulsion concepts)

Energy Efficiency

international and multi-organisational project funded by the EU was completed in 2014. The research carried out was intended to promote widespread improvements in both vessel and propeller design.

Streamline Project Example

The Walvisstaart pod (WSP) biomechanical fin concept mimics the motion of a whale's tail to generate thrust with up to 30% improved efficiency over a conventional arrangement.

Ship Design Strategies	Vessel Type	Fuel Efficiency Gain (%)	New Build	Retrofit	Operational
Bulbous bow	● Tankers/Bulkers ● Container ● Ro-Ro ● Ferry/Cruise	<20%	✓		
Air lubrication	● Tankers/Bulkers ● Container ● Ro-Ro ● Ferry/Cruise	<15%	✓		
Optimum hull dimensions	● Tankers/Bulkers ● Container ● Ro-Ro ● Ferry/Cruise ● Offshore Supply	<9%	✓		
Lightweight construction	● Tankers/Bulkers ● Container ● Ro-Ro ● Ferry/Cruise ● Offshore Supply	<7%	✓		
Design for reduced ballast operation	● Tankers/Bulkers ● Container ● Ro-Ro ● Ferry/Cruise ● Offshore Supply	<7%	✓	✓	✓
Aft waterline extension	● Container ● Ro-Ro ● Ferry/Cruise	<7%	✓	✓	
Low profile hull openings	● Tankers/Bulkers ● Container ● Ro-Ro ● Ferry/Cruise ● Offshore Supply	<5%	✓	✓	
Efficiency of scale	● Tankers/Bulkers ● Container ● Ro-Ro ● Ferry/Cruise	<4%	✓		
Interceptor trim plates	● Ro-Ro ● Ferry/Cruise	<4%	✓	✓	
Shaft line alignment	● Ro-Ro ● Ferry/Cruise ● Offshore Supply	<2%	✓		
Skeg shape – trailing edge	● Tankers/Bulkers ● Container ● Ro-Ro ● Ferry/Cruise ● Offshore Supply	<2%	✓		

● Tankers/Bulkers ● Container ● Ro-Ro ● Ferry/Cruise ● Offshore Supply

(Information from 'Boosting Energy Efficiency' by Wärtsilä, 2008)

Designs for Improved Hydrodynamics and Reduced Hull Resistance

There are many ways in which the hydrodynamics of a ship's hull can be improved for increased efficiency:

- Designing the shaft line arrangement into a more streamlined shape. This leads to reduced water resistance and less disturbance in the flow to the propeller
- optimising the design of the skeg so that water flows evenly to the propeller. This could produce an improvement of up to 2% in total energy consumption of a container ship
- designing the position and shape of hull openings to minimise water flow disturbance along the hull.

Bulbous Bow

Figure 44.17 - Traditional bulbous bow of dry cargo ship

The advantages of bulbous bows are well known. The presence of a bulbous bow substantially reduces the height of the bow wave and, consequently, the hull drag associated with this wave.

Courtesy of Maersk Maritime Technology

Figure 44.18 - 'Maersk Buffalo' and 'Maersk Baltimore' being fitted with new bulbous bows, 2012

The original shape of a bulbous bow was designed for an optimal vessel speed of about 24 knots. Now that so many vessels slow steam to save on fuel costs, the redesign of the bulbous bow is an interesting energy saving method which, according to Maersk, can save up to 20% of the fuel used. This is a conversion that has been carried out on both Maersk and CMA CGM vessels due to the intention of using these ships at lower speeds.

Air Lubrication

Reducing frictional drag using air lubrication from a layer of bubbles is a complicated problem and has been studied through computational fluid dynamics (CFD) as a method of energy efficiency for several years. The frictional drag experienced by a ship's hull is proportional to the wetted surface, so the idea has been that a layer of air could be used to reduce that area. There are three suggested variations:

- Injection of bubbles
- a film of bubbles
- air cavity ships.

It has been found that the size of the bubbles is critical to the increase in performance of the vessel, ie the smaller the bubbles, the more effectively drag is reduced because of their larger surface area and the greater the savings on fuel. It has also been found that these micro-bubbles are only effective at relatively low speeds. This would tie in nicely with the popular fleet management technique of slow steaming.

It has been suggested that air cavity ships may be more suited to inland waterways, where the water is less turbulent and the air is less likely to escape from the cavities when pitching and rolling. Bunker savings of up to 15% are claimed for using the DK Group technology on low speed vessels like tankers and bulkers, and about 7% for LNG and container ships.

The shape of the ship's underwater hull was thought to be a deciding factor in the effectiveness of the air lubrication technology, with flat bottomed or full hull-form ships thought to benefit the most from this technology. However the MALS technology (see example 3 below) has also proved effective on high speed slender hull-form ships such as the '*Naminoue*'.

Example 1

Retrofit of a mini bulker (2,800 Dwt), the ACS '*Demonstrator*', with the Air-Cavity System from the DK Group (now called Silverstream Technologies) and subsequent trials in 2008 successfully demonstrated the air lubrication concept and cut fuel consumption by 10%. The Norwegian Cruise Line's '*Norwegian Bliss*', which is scheduled for delivery in spring 2017, had the Silverstream Technologies air lubrication system installed in March 2015.

Example 2

Air lubrication technology has been fitted to the '*Quantum of the Seas*', which was launched in November 2014. Royal Caribbean Cruises Ltd (RCCL) has developed an in-house method of producing the micro-bubbles for the energy saving technology. This technology, which only works when the ship is travelling at speed, will provide a net gain in fuel efficiency of 7 to 8%. The micro-bubbles are formed through heating the bubbles to make them smaller and then cooling the micro-bubbles in order to prevent them changing to steam as they hit the seawater. As an added advantage, it has been found that the air bubbles reduce propeller noise considerably.

Example 3

The Mitsubishi Air Lubrication System (MALS), developed by Mitsubishi Heavy Industries (MHI) and supported by ClassNK, reduces frictional resistance between the ship hull and the seawater as the ship cruises. The system has been fitted to, for example, two heavy equipment carrier sister ships the '*Yamatai*' and the '*Yamato*' in 2010, the coal carrier '*Soyo*' in 2012, the A Line RoRo/Passenger Ship '*Naminoue*' in 2012 and the first of three post-Panamax bulk carriers the '*Harvest Frost*' in 2014.

Optimising Hull Dimensions

Optimising the length and hull fullness ratio of a ship must be tailored to the purpose of that vessel and one hull shape does not fit all. The resistance a hull experiences while moving through the water is proportional to the square root of the vessel waterline length. According to Wärtsilä, adding 10 to 15% to the length of a typical product tanker can reduce the power demand by >10%.

Energy Efficiency

Example

(Taken from Hollenbach and Friesch, 2007): A product tanker with main dimensions 135.7 m × 19.6 m × 8.4 m requires an engine output of 3,000 kW to achieve a service speed of 14.5 knots (at sea state 4, wind Beaufort 5). A design with the same cargo carrying capacity, but with limited length (eg due to owner restrictions or to cut the new building price), main dimensions 118.5 m × 21.5 m × 8.5 m, requires an engine output of 3,750 kW for the same service speed. This is an increase of 25%.

Lightweight Construction

Use of lightweight materials such as aluminium in areas that do not contribute to the ship's integral strength, particularly on container ships, is a possible method of reducing weight and fuel costs.

In 2002, SOLAS brought in a new rule that allows the use of materials other than steel, such as composite material, to be used in ship building. This is because technical advances had brought these materials up to the level of steel with regard to fire safety (non-combustibility).

Note: Fire in general represents 10% of all fatalities at sea.

There are several advantages for constructing ships from lighter-weight materials:

- Economical – less dead weight and more paying load; less maintenance and lower fuel costs
- environmental – less fuel is needed to power a lighter vessel
- operational – there is an increase in stability when using a lightweight superstructure.

However, even though the initial cost is higher (a life cycle cost (LCC) analysis would have to be made), the priority must be to ensure fire safety on board.

Research Example

The LASS (Lightweight Construction Applications at Sea) project ran from 2005 until 2009. The project aimed to improve the efficiency and competitiveness of the Swedish shipping industry by both developing and demonstrating the use of lightweight ship construction materials. The target was to design lightweight ships with aluminium and FRP (fibre-reinforced polymer) composites where possible. Aluminium is more acceptable as an alternative to steel in shipbuilding because it is recognised as an 'equivalent material' in SOLAS but composites are not. However, Regulation 17 allows their use if safety can be proven. The LASS research concentrated on demonstrating the fire safety of composites in the construction of, for example, deck, bulkhead, door and window in bulkhead, and deck and bulkhead penetration constructions. As part of the LASS project, over 12 materials were tested and certified.

During the project, it was found that the typical weight reduction of the object (eg the upper decks on a RoRo or the superstructure on a RoPax), when using aluminium or FRP composites, was >50% compared to the conventional steel design (or the original material used). The cost analysis showed that there could be a pay-back time of 5 years or less for the investment in lightweight material.

Ducktail Waterline Extension

A ducktail is an extension to a ship's stern to lengthen a ship's waterline. They are usually between 3 to 6 metres long and can be retrofitted or designed into a new build. Retrofitting a ducktail can improve the stability of older ships and in new builds they improve the propulsion energy efficiency. They are most appropriate for container ships, RoRos and ferries.

Efficiencies of Scale

Larger ships can transport more cargo at the same speed with less energy consumed per unit cargo. However, these economies of scale are restricted by trade factors, the physical port limitations or cargo logistics issues. Therefore, ships tend to be designed to be as large as practical for a given trade.

Example

A 10% increase in ship size will increase transport efficiency by 4 to 5% on a specific route.

Propeller and Rudder Design

The ship's rudder is usually mounted to take advantage of the increased water speed in the propeller race, with the rudder influencing the flow speed and direction passing through the propeller.

Combining propulsion and rudder

There is a proven interaction between propulsion and rudder dynamics and research has indicated that rudder design should be incorporated into propulsion system design.

Commercial Example

In 2008, Wartsila launched their combined propulsion and rudder system Energopac, which was the result of collaboration with rudder experts Becker Marine Systems. The integrated Energopac design created less drag since it reduced the flow separation behind the propeller hub. This reduction in drag was claimed to reduce fuel consumption by 2% and result in power savings of 9%.

Twisted Rudder Design

A twisted rudder design (ie with a twisted leading edge):

- Can reduce the cavitation risk on rudder sections by reducing the effective angle of attack
- can be used to alter the effective thrust/drag of the rudder by recovering rotational energy from the propeller race
- demands an alternative construction technique and so is a clear choice for the use of composites.

Propeller Hub Cap Modifications

Propeller Boss Cap Fins (PBCFs) are small fins that are attached to the hub of the propeller. These fins alter the hub vortex created behind the rotating propeller, cancelling hub cavitation, and can result in up to 5% fuel oil savings. Propeller Cap Turbines (PCT) are also a redesign of hub caps and consist of hydrofoil-shaped blades integrally cast into the hub cap. Both PBCFs and PCTs reduce the size of hub vortices, thereby reducing loss of rotational energy and cavitation, and increasing fuel efficiency.

Improving Flow to the Propeller

Wake Equalisation

Several devices can be fitted to the hull of a ship to improve the water flow to the propeller. Many devices can be retrofitted and it is important to note that different wake equalisation methods may be more effective for different ship types. The two examples below can be fitted to new builds or retrofit and also have the benefit of reducing propeller vibration and cavitation damage and increasing course stability during manoeuvring.

Commercial Example 1: The Mewis Duct® (from Becker Marine Systems)

The Mewis Duct® consists of two components fixed to the vessel ahead of the propeller with an integrated fin system within. The duct both straightens and accelerates the hull wake into the propeller. Power savings of 3% for multi-purpose ships and up to 8% for tankers and bulkers are claimed. Tests on the *AS 'Vincentia'* supramax-bulker indicated a power saving of 5% at a speed of 14.4 knots.

Commercial Example 2: The Schneekluth Wake Equalizing Duct (WED) (from Schneekluth Hydrodynamik)

The WED consists of two half-shell shaped elements attached ahead of the propeller in combination with two flow guidance fins/spoilers attached before the duct (known as Grothues-Spork spoilers) to focus the water flow through the duct. Fuel savings of between 4 and 8% for bulk carriers and tankers are claimed. More than 1,500 vessels have been fitted with the Schneekluth WED system.

Interceptor Trim Plane

The interceptor is a metal plate that is fitted to extend across most of the breadth of the transom. It is positioned at this point to create pressure underneath the hull at the stern. This pressure lifts the hull and changes the running trim of the vessel causing lower wave resistance. It creates a lift similar to a conventional trim wedge but is cheaper to retrofit. It was developed and proven for smaller, faster vessels but has also been used on cruise ships and RoRos.

Contra-Rotating Propellers (CRPs)

This is a well-established idea and consists of a propeller shaft system where the two propellers are arranged in tandem and run in opposite directions. This enables the slipstream rotational energy from the forward propeller to be used by the rear propeller.

Energy Efficiency

Figure 44.19 - An Azipod® propulsion unit with CRP

Commercial Example

The CRP Azipod® system is a hybrid propulsion unit (developed by ABB) and combines an electric pod propulsion unit and a conventional diesel propulsion system. The normal rudder is replaced by a steerable Azipod® downstream of the main propeller and this makes use of rotational energy from the slipstream of the forward CRP propeller as it rotates in the opposite direction. The propulsion system was designed specifically for high-speed, high-power vessels such as ULCCs, LNG carriers and RoPax ferries. The CRP Azipod® units have been fitted to, for example, two high-speed RoPax ferries, the '*Suzuran*' and the '*Suisen*'.

Thrust Fins

Developed by Hyundai Heavy Industries, these devices, like CRPs, recover energy from aft of the propeller. The fins are attached to the rudder behind the propeller and act like wings, producing lift forces from the rotational flow and providing additional thrust. For a right-handed propeller to achieve this thrust, the starboard fin is inclined upwards and the port fin inclined downwards.

Example

In 2008, Hapag-Lloyd's new build container ship '*Kuala Lumpur Express*' was the first vessel to be fitted with a thrust fin. The company subsequently ordered thrust fins for six more ships in their fleet. This is a new build or retrofit device that is claimed to reduce fuel consumption by about 4 to 6%.

Operational Tailoring

Not all vessels emit the same volume of CO_2 per tonne carried per mile, even though they may sail the same distance. It depends on what speed they travel at and the volume of the goods transported per unit of weight. For example, gas tankers emit relatively high levels of CO_2 per transported tonne, as their cargo occupies a lot of space but has a relatively low weight.

Depending on the type of ship, different integrated strategies optimise the use of energy for maximum economy. The biggest savings are gained by concentrating on the biggest energy consumers for a particular ship type. For example, Wärtsilä claim that the combination of diesel-electric machinery and twin steerable thrusters can reduce the annual fuel consumption of a typical supply vessel by up to 35% compared with a conventional vessel.

Tankers and Bulkers

These vessels operate at relatively low speeds over long distances with infrequent ports of call. They would gain significant benefits from reducing frictional drag by optimising the design of the rudder, propeller and main ship dimensions, installing air lubrication and regular hull cleaning. Energy efficiency benefits would also be achieved by engine tuning, weather routeing and using renewable alternative energy sources such as kites, sails or rotors to harness wind energy.

Figure 44.20 - Oil tanker entering the Port of Vancouver, Canada

Container Ships

Significant energy savings can be made by lowering the operating speed of these ships and so reducing the wave resistance. Improving the design of propeller blades, using low friction hull coatings to limit fouling, minimising the resistance of hull openings, having a bulbous bow and lightweight construction would add to these savings. Due to the power-hungry nature of reefers, waste heat recovery from cleaner, low sulphur fuel would be a judicious way to utilise otherwise lost energy from exhaust gases. While alongside, utilising shore-based power would preserve onboard fuel supplies and produce fewer greenhouse gases. Active voyage planning, the use of autopilots and efficiencies of scale would also yield energy saving benefits.

Figure 44.21 - Container Ship

RoRo Vessels

Short sea RoRos have frequent ports of call so improved manoeuvrability and quicker port turnaround would enable a reduction in speed at sea. This would lead to a reduction in the amount of fuel used. Improving propeller efficiency, optimising trim, using the optimal skeg design and reducing water resistance through ballast control would also be efficiencies appropriate for this type of vessel. A combination of power sources would increase efficiency, eg a diesel generator and batteries in a hybrid plant combined with solar panels. Real-time monitoring of the ship's systems and an energy saving attitude by the crew can reduce the ship's energy consumption by a considerable amount.

Figure 44.22 - RoRo Vessel

Ferries

Since ferries usually operate on short routes with frequent ports of call, increasing the efficiency of port turnarounds would mean that speed reductions, and their resultant savings, could be made between ports. This regular service between fixed ports means that bunker logistics would be easier to arrange if LNG fuel were used. The low temperature of the LNG fuel could also be harnessed in air conditioning plants, eliminating the need for conventional heavy fuel heating. Hybrid power plants (such as diesel-electric) provide the best efficiencies for the various ferry operations. The electrical propulsion is highly efficient during manoeuvring and at low speeds, which is of particular benefit to ferries operating in shallow waters with speed restrictions. CRPs are also beneficial while manoeuvring. A lightweight structure and interceptor trim planes also help save energy.

Figure 44.23 - Ferry

Cruise Ships

Reducing the speed of cruise ships has a significant impact on fuel economy. Similarly, running engines on optimal load, correct

Energy Efficiency

ballasting and only using fin stabilisers when necessary are important energy efficiencies. Hotel loads comprise all the onboard equipment and processes that consume power other than that for propulsion, eg HVAC, plant auxiliaries, lighting and galley equipment. On a cruise ship, the air conditioning typically consumes about half of the total hotel load, so the use of cleaner fuel, with lower sulphur content, means that the amount of recoverable heat is increased significantly. The hotel load would also be considerably reduced if absorption chillers were used instead of refrigeration compressors.

Figure 44.24 - Cruise Ship

Offshore Support Vessels (OSVs)

There are many types of OSV but usually they perform multiple tasks and often in rough weather. A single skeg hull offers low operating resistance. High manoeuvrability for dynamic positioning (DP) is often essential so twin steerable, retractable thrusters offer the best alternative in DP mode and the regular single screw propulsion can be used for free running. Proactive power management enables the most energy efficient operation and diesel-electric power plants provide a versatile power source. Improved propeller efficiency can be achieved by optimising its interaction with the ship's hull, and a propeller nozzle increases thrust and saves fuel.

Figure 44.25 - Offshore Support Vessel (OSV)

Reference

U Hollenbach and J Friesch, "Efficient hull forms – What can be gained," 1st Int Conf on Ship Efficiency, Hamburg, 2007.

Source: http://tinyurl.com/osfxwha

CHAPTER 45

Ship Recycling

Ship Recycling

Some History

Before the 1960s, shipbreaking was concentrated in industrialised countries, mainly the United States, United Kingdom, Germany and Italy. From the early 1980s, to maximise profits, shipowners sent their vessels to the scrap yards of India, China, Pakistan, Bangladesh, the Philippines and Vietnam, where the breaking costs were lower and scrap values were, therefore, higher.

In Bangladesh's shipbreaking zone, men work 16-hour days, often with little protection or training. Inside the ships, they face a haze of thick, black smoke from the torches used to cut the metal, unstable gases, asbestos, lead and mercury.

By some estimates, one shipbreaker is killed every day in South Asia's shipbreaking yards. Those who survive typically work for 5 to 6 years before returning to their villages, old before their time and exhausted, facing a high risk of cancer and other illnesses and often too sick to make a living.

In the second part of 2008, as global trade shrank, an increasing number of ships were sent to scrap, leading to the creation of more unsafe yards in different countries. In 2009, land was still being cleared in Bangladesh, with 15,000 mangrove trees across 40 acres cut by 400 men over 3 nights to make way for shipbreaking yards. This increase in business has also pushed up the number of child labourers. Speaking about the fact that 25% of Bangladesh's shipbreaking workforce are under the legal working age of 18, Muhammed Ali Shahin of the Brussels-based NGO Platform on Shipbreaking, was reported in Time magazine as saying, *"The problem is that children are easier to exploit … you can force them to do whatever you want"*.

In September 2009, in Lloyd's List, the China National Shiprecycling Association reported predictions that the economic contraction would lead to 10% of the vessels in the global market being forced into lay-up, that the overcapacity may result in 1,000 vessels being scrapped that year worldwide and that the demolition rate would continue to pick up over the next two years.

Where are Ships Recycled Today?

85 to 90% of the world's shipbreaking and demolition occurs in the yards of India, Pakistan, Bangladesh and China.

Some Global Ship Recycling Statistics

- **It is estimated that over 100,000 workers are employed at shipbreaking yards worldwide**
- **about 700 ships are scrapped every year**
- **about 95% of a ship's mass can be recycled**
- **most ships that are ready to be dismantled were built in the 1970s**
- **recycling values typically hit US$600 to US$800 per ldt up until the economic crisis in September 2008, with all rates in autumn 2009 between US$270 to US$300 per ldt.**

India Ship Recycling Facts

- Employs ~30,000-40,000 workers each year in Alang alone
- Alang is the world's largest ship recycling yard, stretching for 7 miles along the coastline of the Indian state of Gujarat
- Gujarat benefits from the geographical features of the area, including a high tidal range, wide continental shelf, 15° slope and a mud-free coast, which make it suitable for ships to be beached easily during high tide
- the labour employed is mostly illiterate and comes from India's poorest states, such as Orissa, Uttar Pradesh and Bihar
- the wages at the yards vary between Rs 100 to Rs 200 per shift of 8 hours.

Pakistan Ship Recycling Facts

- Employs ~6,000 workers
- the yard is located in Gadani, about 50 kilometres northwest of Karachi
- Pakistani breakers specialise in large sized ships, with the majority scrapped being large oil tankers.

Bangladesh Ship Recycling Facts

- Employs ~30,000 people across 36 breaking yards in Chittagong
- around 150 ships are broken each year
- workers typically work 16-hour shifts
- in 2003, the Bangladesh Supreme Court decreed that all ships arriving for breaking must be cleaned/washed and free of harmful chemicals and toxins or they would be denied entry to Bangladesh. It also closed all yards operating without government environmental clearance, which meant all of them.

China Ship Recycling Facts

- China has approximately 90 breaking yards with about 25,000 workers employed in the breaking yards on the Sitakundu coastline of southeast China
- shipbreaking is carried out in docks and not on beaches, which makes this activity look less dramatic than at the other three locations
- before a number of yard closures in 2004, China dominated the activity of shipbreaking. However, many of these yards reopened in 2009
- in 2009, a total of around 1.5 million ldt was dealt with for breaking in China, which is more than the aggregate of the past 4 years
- many breaking yards are increasing their handling capacity and investing in environmentally acceptable ship recycling methods to gain an edge in an increasingly 'green' world. This activity comes at a time of an expected spike of ships destined for the breakers yard, due to the economic downturn
- in a similar manner to other developing countries, shipbreaking in China is often carried out by poorly paid migrant workers from rural areas.

Note: Chinese yards have invested to improve treatment of pollutants such as oil and asbestos, with asbestos transported to a treatment centre and oils/chemicals disposed of/treated under strict safety controls. Sewage is also being treated.

Although green scrapping is still undeveloped in China, the Chinese believe the environmental awareness of their yards is far ahead of the other three largest shipbreaking countries. A Hong Kong based shipowner, reported in Lloyd's List, concurred with this view, saying that ship demolition in India and Bangladesh is labour intensive. The scrapped vessels are usually dismantled on the beaches, causing serious oil pollution. In the absence of technical support, the demolition process in India, Bangladesh and Pakistan can take much longer than in China.

In October 2009 alone, reports from Bangladesh stated:

- **3 died after an iron plate fell on workers**
- **3 died due to asphyxiation by gas**
- **1 further death in unknown circumstances.**

The Background to the Ship Recycling Convention

The Ship Recycling Convention was initiated by the Norwegian Delegation, at MEPC 41, in November 1998. Concern was raised about the problems associated with ship dismantling and the need for an internationally acceptable solution that would ensure the protection of the environment and the safety of workers.

The debate took account of the capacity of ship recycling facilities against the forecast demand as ships reach the end of their operating life.

The practice of shipbreaking is a threat to both the terrestrial and marine environment and also presents dangers to health. It discharges every kind of pollutant from liquids, metals, gases and various solids.

Matters associated with shipbreaking that have caused concern include:

Persistent Organic Pollutants (POPs)

POPs are chemicals that are highly toxic, remain intact in the environment for long periods, become widely distributed geographically, bioaccumulate through the food web, accumulate in the fatty tissue of living organisms and pose a risk of causing adverse effects to the human population, wildlife and the environment. There has been a realisation

Ship Recycling

that these pollutants, when exposed to the human population, can cause serious health effects that range from increased incidence of cancers to disruption of the hormonal system.

Polychlorinated Biphenyls (PCBs)

PCBs, used in insulation and as oil in transformers, have been banned since 1976.

Asbestos

Asbestos was used in ships built before 1985, after which it was banned. Asbestos was typically used as a heat insulator so it is the older steam turbine and passenger vessels that cause most concern.

As there are often no asbestos disposal procedures in place during scrapping, workers and the surrounding environment are exposed to the asbestos fibres. Exposure to asbestos fibres, even in very low concentrations, particularly through inhalation, may cause cancer and asbestosis. Asbestos handling has also proven to be one of the most lethal practices, as inhaling asbestos fibres can lead to a wide range of pulmonary problems such as asthma and asbestosis and can also be the direct cause of mesothelioma.

On the shipbreaking beaches, asbestos fibres float around in the open air with workers removing asbestos insulation materials with their bare hands.

Heavy Metals

Heavy metals are found in many parts of ships, such as in paints, coatings, anodes and electrical equipment. Exposure can result in cancer of the lungs, skin, intestine, kidney, liver or bladder and can cause damage to blood vessels.

Oil Pollution

As a result of breaking the ships, oil residues and other refuse is spilled, mixed with seawater and left floating along the entire seashore. Oil may cause serious damage in different ways, by reducing the light intensity beneath the water surface to inhibit photosynthesis, for example. Oil films on water reduce the exchange of oxygen and carbon dioxide across the air-sea interface, which is harmful to aquatic life. It also causes damage to the bird population by coating their feathers with oil, which causes loss of buoyancy and insulation. Spilling may also cause widespread mortality amongst the fish, mammals, worms, crabs, molluscs and other water organisms.

The Convention

The International Convention for the Safe and Environmentally Sound Recycling of Ships, 2009 (SR Convention) was adopted, after being ratified by 63 countries, on the 15th May 2009 at an IMO convention held in Hong Kong.

Entry into Force

The SR Convention should come into force 24 months after the following conditions are met:

- Not less than 15 States have ratified the Convention
- the combined merchant fleets of the ratifying States constitute not less than 40% of the gross tonnage of the world's merchant fleet
- the combined maximum annual ship recycling volume of the ratifying States during the preceding 10 years is at least 3% of the gross tonnage of the combined merchant shipping of those ratifying States.

(The value of 3% was based on information provided to the Conference by Japan which indicated that the maximum annual disposal of ships for the last 10 years was 2.98%.)

Then IMO Secretary-General Efthimios Mitropoulos would not be drawn on when the Convention would formally enter into force, stating that IMO conventions historically took 5 years after approval before they were finally ratified, but that the IMO now had a 3-year ratification target. (Lloyd's List, 18th May 2009).

However, the SR Convention could take years to become law. As of March 2015, only three States, Norway, France and the Republic of the Congo, had ratified the Convention.

Who it Applies to

The SR Convention applies to all new and, as far as possible, existing ships (including FSUs, FPSOs, etc) of 500 GT and above, as determined by the International Convention on Tonnage Measurement of Ships, 1969.

Exemptions

The SR Convention does not apply to:

- Warships, naval auxiliary ships or government-owned non-commercial ships
- ships operating throughout their life only in waters subject to the sovereignty or jurisdiction of the State.

How will Ship Recycling Work under the SR Convention?

This is developed in two stages before an International Ready for Recycling Certificate is issued:

First - Provision of the Inventory of Hazardous Materials (IHM)

Second - Development of a Ship Recycling Plan (SRP).

Inventory of Hazardous Materials (IHM)

This inventory consists of three parts:

- Part I comprises a list of hazardous materials (as listed in Appendices 1 and 2 of the SR Convention) contained in the ship's structure or equipment, their location and approximate quantities (compliance with this list can be achieved by the ship having an up-to-date Green Passport). New ships are to be provided with Part I at delivery
- Part II lists operationally-generated wastes on board
- Part III contains an inventory of ship's stores.

Note: For Part I, existing ships are to be provided with this no later than 5 years after the entry into force of the SR Convention. This will require a visual/sampling check plan being prepared by hazardous material experts.

Throughout the operational life of the ship, Part I is to be kept up to date and must reflect any relevant changes in ship structure and equipment on/after the entry into force date of the SR Convention that contain hazardous materials listed in Appendix 2.

The shipowner prepares Parts II and III of the IHM at the time the ship is being prepared for the final survey in accordance with the issuing of an International Ready for Recycling Certificate.

Appendix 1 prohibits the following materials from being used on/after the entry into force date of the SR Convention:

- Ozone-depleting substances
- polychlorinated biphenyls (PCBs)
- asbestos.

Anti-fouling substances are prohibited under the AFS Convention.

Appendix 2 contains a minimum list of hazardous material to be included in the IHM, which includes the substances in Appendix 1 in addition to other hazardous material including cadmium, mercury and lead.

Ship Recycling Plan (SRP)

Once the shipowner has selected an authorised Ship Recycling Facility, a Ship Recycling Plan (SRP) should be developed based on the particulars of the ship and the information that is provided from the shipowner within the IHM.

The SRP includes information concerning:

- The facility
- maintenance
- Permit to Work conditions (enclosed space entry and hot work)
- how the various materials will be managed.

The SRP is then approved by the State of the recycling facility.

Survey and Certification

Initial

An initial survey is carried out to verify that the IHM-Part I corresponds to the ship before either:

- A new ship enters service
- the International Certificate on Inventory of Hazardous Materials is issued.

Ship Recycling

Renewal

A 5-year renewal survey will verify the continued compatibility of the IHM-Part I with the ship.

Additional

An additional survey will be carried out, at the request of the shipowner, to verify that any change, replacement or significant repair complies with the SR Convention, and that IHM-Part I is updated as applicable.

Final Survey

Prior to issuing the 3-month International Ready for Recycling Certificate, a final survey is carried out on board prior to the ship being taken out of service and recycling of the ship commencing.

It is important that the SRP is approved and that Parts II and III of the IHM are completed so that they can be compared with the approved SRP prior to commencing the survey.

Guidelines for Implementation

Six guideline documents are referenced by the SR Convention which detail the obligations of the various parties:

- Development of an inventory of onboard hazardous materials
- survey and certification
- inspection of ships (PSC)
- authorisation of ship recycling facilities
- safe and environmentally sound ship recycling
- development of the Ship Recycling Plan, including guaranteed measures to protect the health and safety of workers.

The documents are being developed to assist in the implementation of this Convention and will be completed at future sessions of the MEPC.

Green Passports

The SR Convention introduces the concept of a ship's 'Green Passport', which is essentially an inventory of materials present in the ship's structure, systems and equipment that may be hazardous to health or the environment. This is kept up to date for the service life of the ship. Prior to breaking, details of any further hazards and waste material are added, which will help the recycling yard to develop a safer and more environmentally acceptable plan.

Green Passports, which are voluntary at present, are typically verified by Classification Societies which now provide an approval and verification service for new buildings and existing ships.

For ISO 14001 certified companies, a Green Passport for each ship assists in demonstrating best practice in managing tonnage in an environmentally responsible manner.

Summary of the Ship Recycling Convention

The Convention aims to:

- Regulate the design, construction, operation and preparation of ships to allow safe and environmentally sound recycling
- ensure that ships, when recycled after reaching the end of their operational lives, do not pose any unnecessary risk to human health and safety or to the environment
- give guidelines for the safe and environmentally sound operation of ship recycling yards and establish an enforcement mechanism
- ensure ships carry an inventory of hazardous materials and have an initial survey to verify the inventory
- monitor these items via periodic surveys and a final survey prior to recycling
- require recycling yards to provide a Ship Recycling Plan
- require Member States to ensure that facilities under their jurisdiction comply with the Convention.

EU Situation

The European Commission wants to create a shipbreaking fund financed by a port levy on ships calling in the European Union. First outlined in a green paper in 2007, and made all the more pressing by the boom in ship dismantling, the fund is designed to help transfer environmentally sound technology to the Indian subcontinent.

This is a convoluted system under which owners and operators, irrespective of nationality, would pay a port levy. The proceeds would then be reimbursed to European owners on condition that they used 'green' scrapping facilities. It is an idea supported by scrapping's most vocal opponents, the non-governmental organisations' 'NGO Platform on Shipbreaking', an alliance of pressure groups.

Both Eurocrats and Euro MPs want something done about the shocking health and safety conditions in breakers yards in India, Pakistan and Bangladesh. Making EU shipowners contribute to improving conditions caused indirectly by their relentless downward pressure on scrapping rates seems justifiable from a Brussels point of view.

The industry argues that the fund is pointless and even counter-productive. The argument is that the fund would actually discourage yard owners from reinvesting profits into improving health and safety, which would accelerate the introduction of cleaner technology and better superstructure.

The EU does need to take this issue in hand because its accelerated phase-out of single-hulled tankers has exacerbated the problem.

US Situation

The US bans overseas scrapping of US ships under the Toxic Substances Control Act of 1976, which prohibits the export of PCB contaminate waste, including entire ships if they carry high enough PCBs, without EPA approval.

There is, however, a loophole if the US Maritime Administration approves a request to change the flag so that sale or scrapping of a ship overseas becomes legally permissible once it departs the US flag.

Inventory of Hazardous Materials

At MEPC 62 on 15th July 2011, the IMO adopted Resolution MEPC.197(62), Guidelines for the Development of the Inventory of Hazardous Materials (IHM). The Guidelines provide recommendations for ships of 500 GT and above for the hazardous waste inventory required for the issue of the International Certificate on Inventory of Hazardous Materials, as required by Regulation 5 of the Hong Kong International Convention.

The Guidelines will remain voluntary until the Convention is ratified and enters into force, making them mandatory. At present, a number of organisations, including Classification Societies, are already providing services for the development of IHM.

Structure of the Guidelines

The IHM is recommended to be structured in three Parts:

- **Part I -** Materials contained in ship structure or equipment
- **Part II -** Operationally-generated wastes
- **Part III -** Stores.

Part I is to be developed during the design and construction stage of new ships. For existing ships, it should follow the five steps recommended in the Guidelines. Part I should be continually updated and belongs to the ship. When the ship changes flag, operator or owner, the continuity and conformity of the inventory must be confirmed.

Parts II and III are to be developed when the ship is to be recycled, but it is expected that the residues of cargo, fuel and waste in Part II are to be minimised before entering the facility.

Materials are to be listed in the Tables A, B, C and D, which are contained within Parts I, II and III as follows.

Figure 45.1 - Removing materials containing asbestos

Part I - Materials contained in ship structure or equipment

Table A includes the following substances and where they may be found on board:

- Asbestos
- polychlorinated biphenyls (PCBs)
- ozone-depleting substances
- anti-fouling systems containing organotin compounds as a biocide.

Table B is primarily aimed at new ships, but encourages existing ships to identify substances to support the recycling process. It provides an indicative list of substances (and compounds), specifically:

- Cadmium
- hexavalent chromium
- mercury
- lead
- polybrominated biphenyls (PBBs)
- polybrominated diphenyl ethers (PBDEs)
- polychlorinated naphthalenes
- radioactive substances
- certain shortchain chlorinated paraffins.

These materials need not be listed when they are used in general construction and are inherent in metals or metal alloys.

Part II - Operationally-generated wastes

Table C lists potentially hazardous solids, liquids and gases including lubricants, hydraulic oils, solvents, refrigerants, antifreeze, propane, oxygen, garbage, incinerator ash, cargo residues, etc. The table identifies whether they should be listed under Part II or Part III (stores).

Part III - Stores

Table D describes regular consumable goods, potentially containing hazardous materials, that are not ship-specific operational equipment, eg electrical goods, office equipment, personal computers, light bulbs, TVs, etc.

Any spare parts containing materials listed in Tables A or B are required to be listed in Part III.

A standard format for Tables A and B is provided in Appendix 2 of the Guidelines, to indicate the material, location and quantity on board, with space for any additional information.

Developing the Guidelines

For new build vessels, owners are encouraged to coordinate with the shipbuilder at the construction stage to identify materials to be included in the inventory.

For existing ships, the Guidelines recommend the following five steps for the creation of Part I:

1. Collection of necessary information.

   Emphasis is placed on the need for the shipowner to identify and collate all reasonably available information, including confirmation from previous owners, builders, Class, etc.

2. Assessment of collected information.
3. Preparation of visual/sampling check plan.
4. Onboard visual/sampling check.
5. Preparation of Part I of the Inventory and related documentation.

Where it is not possible to establish the quantity of anticipated hazardous material in a system due to inaccessibility, it should be classified as potentially containing hazardous material for further investigation or later survey.

Suppliers of Materials

The suppliers of materials and equipment to ships will be required to provide a Materials Declaration that identifies the supplier, the material (including its mass) and whether materials from Tables A or B are present in the product at levels above the specified threshold levels. Chemicals are not considered as part of a finished product, so are not applicable.

Suppliers are required to complete a Supplier's Declaration of Conformity, which identifies the responsible entity and provides assurance that the products in the Materials Declaration have been listed accurately.

Inventory of Hazardous Materials

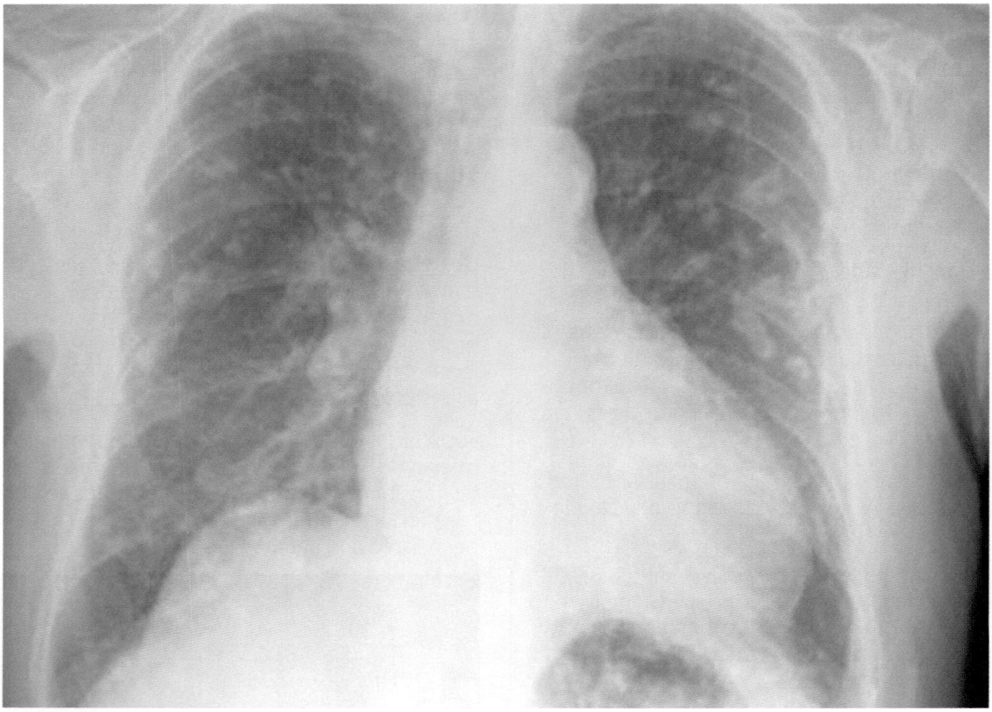

Figure 45.2 - Chest X-ray showing plaques in the lungs caused by asbestos

CHAPTER 46

Traditional Seamanship

Traditional Seamanship

Courtesies

Courtesy of Julie Matyascik

Figure 46.1 - Sailors lower the ensign on 'USS Ponce'

An exchange of greetings between ships at sea by dipping their flags (ie their colours) dates back to the submission of one warship to another or of a merchantman to a warship by the act of lowering topsails.

Historically, various countries have attempted to claim sovereignty over portions of the high seas and required that foreign ships passing through those seas salute the ships and forts of the coastal States by lowering their flags, taking in their sails, and so on. Over the centuries, such claims came to be rejected and the requirements for paying tribute to the coastal State were dropped. Perhaps the only vestige remaining is the custom by which a merchant ship passing near a warship of any country dips its ensign in salute.

The procedure followed is that, as it approaches the warship, the merchant ship lowers its ensign to approximately half-mast position and holds it there. The warship responds by lowering its own ensign at the moment the two ships reach their nearest point of approach, holding it there for an instant, then returning it to the peak of the gaff. The merchant ship then returns its own ensign to the peak or truck.

Cdr Bob Willson RCN (Ret'd) expands on this. *"When Britannia ruled the waves, the RN "demanded" that merchant ships of all countries dip their ensign to a British warship and in certain eras would halt and board a merchant ship that failed to do so. The custom of merchantmen dipping ensigns still persists, although very few merchant ships actually do it anymore."*

"A military vessel never salutes a civil vessel - but if the civil vessel salutes the naval vessel, it always salutes back. At least that's the case in Sweden."

Crossing the Line Ceremony

Roberts

Figure 46.2 - 'USS Triton' crossing the Equator in 1960

History

Line crossing traditions date back to the time of the Vikings.

Early equatorial line crossings were used as a tool to determine whether new crew members were brave enough to endure the hardships of life at sea.

Today, line crossings have a less serious undertone. Sailors are divided up and categorised as either 'shellbacks' (those who have crossed the equator before) or 'pollywogs' (those who are crossing the equator for the first time). For the duration of the crossing, shellbacks assign demeaning tasks to the pollywogs, call them insulting names and force them to compete in talent shows or competitions. This is all done in good fun.

At the end of the ceremony, which in the past often included considerable hazing, they are initiated as *Shellbacks* or *Sons of Neptune* and receive a certificate to that effect.

Line crossing ceremonies, celebrated by seafarers for centuries, build camaraderie among sailors and shipmates, and serve as a rite of passage.

The Ceremony

The actual ceremony revolves around the pretence of 'preparing' the pollywogs for their audience before King Neptune. This preparation involves any number of disgusting, dirty, deprecating and/or difficult actions.

The ceremony begins with King Neptune's procession, which includes his loyal assistant Davy Jones and Her Royal Highness Amphitrite.

Neptune's court is opened and the King addresses the ship's captain and his men. The first new inductee is called for and seated above a pool where angry 'bears' wait.

The inductee is first given a thorough medical by a 'doctor' while the crew watch the spectacle. The medical is a pantomime performance with oversized instruments and crowd involvement, and the outcome is the giving of 'medicine'. The 'medicine' can be a large pill or spoonful of medicine normally made of foul ingredients and given without much care.

Later, the ship's 'barber' gives the inductee a shave. The barber in these ceremonies more resembles a butcher and has fake bloodstains all over his white apron.

He wields a large wooden razor blade and uses barbers foam that is a sticky flour and water mix. The barber shaves off the foam with an oversized razor, while holding the inductee's nose.

The dunking then commences from a chair erected above the pool. Men dressed as bears receive him in the pool. These 'bears' then continue to dunk the inductee until satisfied.

The sailor becomes part of the order of the deep and receives a certificate to prove his new status. Neither commanding nor senior officers can escape the court of King Neptune. The officer's dunkings by the 'bears' are often even more prolonged.

Certificates

Once the ceremony is complete, a pollywog receives a certificate declaring his new status. Another rare status is the Golden Shellback, a person who has crossed the equator at the 180th meridian (International Date Line). When a ship must cross these lines, the ship's captain will usually intentionally plot a course across the Golden X so that the ship's crew can be initiated into the Golden Shellbacks.

Crossing the Line Ceremony

Domain of Neptunus Rex

To all Sailors wherever ye may be –

to all subjects of the Realm of the Raging Main; to all Sharks and Swordfish and other Finny Folk; to all Sea Serpents and Whales; to all Mermaids, Naiads, Sirens and Luring Beauties of the Bays.

Greetings –

Know Ye that on this __________day of ______________________________
on board the Good Ship ____

in Latitude _______ and Longitude ____________ in the___________Ocean
____

attempted without due authorisation or making the customary obeisance, to enter the Royal Domain of His Oceanic Majesty, and was accordingly subjected to the Trial and Inquisition of the Fathomless Deep.

Whereas the said intruder having endured these Ordeals with Courage and Fortitude,____________is now deemed worthy by His Majesty to be numbered as One of his Trusty Shellbacks.

Wherefore we, Davy Jones, Viscount Atlantis, Baron of the Boundless Seas, etc., etc., etc., His Majesty's Principal Scribe, Request and Require in the Name of His Majesty, Neptune, Ruler of the Mighty Oceans, all those whom it may concern to allow the bearer to pass freely without let or hindrance and to afford every assistance and protection to which ___________ is entitled by virtue of this Freedom of the Raging Main.

Davy Jones
Principal Scribe.

Countersigned______________________________
Nautical Assessor to The Ruler of the Raging Main

The rarest Shellback status is that of the Emerald Shellback, which is received after crossing the equator at the prime meridian.

Sailors make these certificates on board and often their quality reflects the available resources of the ship. Some certificates are incredibly intricate works of art, whereas some are small tokens of the day.

Rigging of a Bosun's Chair

Bosun's Chair

In many ways, a bosun's chair is similar to a climbing harness, and it uses the same principles. In both cases, the individual straps in, often with thigh and waist straps to prevent slippage. However, a bosun's chair usually has a rigid seat, which distinguishes it from a climbing harness. A bosun's chair also does not permit the range of movement that a climbing harness does; sailors usually have to be hoisted aloft, for example, because they cannot climb while seated in the bosun's chair.

Like other equipment designed for working at height, a bosun's chair should be carefully maintained to prevent equipment failure. It should always be stored in a cool dry place, and checked frequently for mould, sun damage and other signs of wear. If straps have begun to fray, they should be replaced. The ropes used to raise the bosun's chair into the rigging should also be regularly inspected and cared for.

Rigging a Bosun's Chair

Figure 46.3 shows the typical rigging of the bosun's chair.

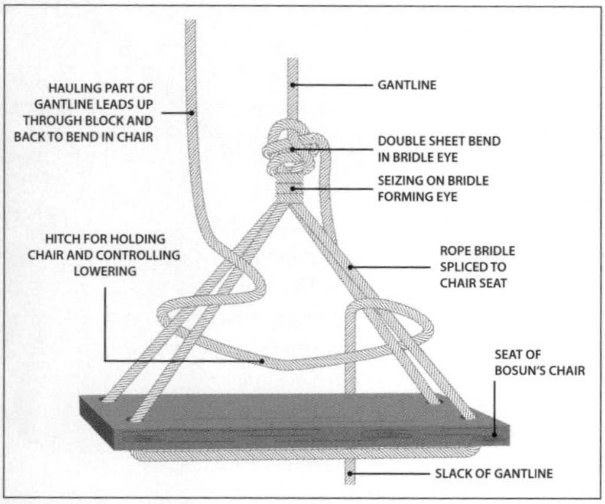

***Figure 46.3 - Rigging a Bosun's Chair** (Note: The standing gantline should be secured by a double sheet bend which will not slip if the person in the chair heaves on the standing part of the gantline to adjust his position. The lowering hitch should be formed by passing a bight of the gantline through the bridle of the chair, over the head of the person, down over the chair and legs of the person and hauled tight below the eye of the bridle).*

Precautions

A thorough inspection should be made of the chair itself and the gantline before use. A safety line and a safety harness must always be worn when working from a bosun's chair. The safety

Rigging of a Bosun's Chair

line should be secured to a separate anchor point.

When using a bosun's chair, the following safety precautions should be observed:

- Always secure the gantline to the chair with a double sheet bend
- always have the chair hoisted manually
- any tools, paint pots, etc should be secured by lanyards to prevent the risk of them falling while working aloft
- when riding a stay, make sure the bolt of the bow shackle is moused
- ensure a permit to work aloft is prepared, together with any appropriate cold work permits.

Rigging of a Stage

A stage is a substantial plank, on which 'horns' are bolted to the underside.

If the stage is to be raised or lowered by the men working upon it, secure tail blocks, stage hooks or lizards in a safe manner and reeve the stage lines through them. Secure the hauling part to the stage with two or three round turns and belay around the horns. Drop a manrope about midway between the stage lines and rig a Jacob's ladder at one end of the stage.

The gantlines on the stage may be rigged by means of a stage hitch. This method is the most reliable because there are two parts of the gantline under the plank instead of one.

Safety precautions when using a stage:

- Check that the stage is clean and is sound in every way
- check that the gantlines are in excellent condition or are brand new
- the gantlines should be of adequate length, and rigged clear of sharp edges, which could cause a bad nip in the rope
- the stage should be load tested to four times the intended load

Rigging of a Stage

- lizards must be in good condition and properly secured
- the stage should not be rigged over a dock or hard surface, only over water
- stages should not be rigged overside for working when the vessel is underway
- a correct stage hitch, together with the lowering turns, must be applied
- ensure a permit to work aloft is prepared, together with any appropriate cold work permits.

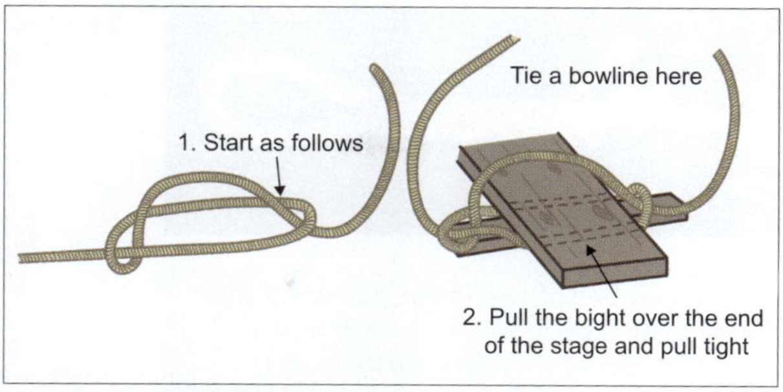

Figure 46.4 - Stage hitch

Rope Splices

Today's seafarer has to acquire certain basic skills fairly quickly in his life at sea and one of these is the ability to make a good splice in rope. The most common splices are as follows:

Short Splice

A short splice is used to join the ends of two ropes together to make one long rope. A short splice increases the diameter of the rope where the join is made by almost double and thus there is a distortion. This must be borne in mind if the rope is to be roved through blocks or narrow openings. The short splice allows the rope to retain up to 95% of its original strength.

This is made by overlaying the opened strands of the two ropes upon one another and then splicing back as you would for an eye splice.

Eye Splice

On a natural fibre rope, as pressure is placed on the eye, the rope is pulled tighter so the spliced strands become more and more compressed and locked in place.

Rope Splices

These can be spliced in the same manner as all other cordage but, owing to the smoothness of the fibre surfaces, it is recommended that for heavy usage five full tucks are required, finishing with one half tuck and one quarter tuck.

Back Splice

This is used on an end of rope to stop the rope from fraying. As this splice is done by doubling back the strands of rope into the end of the rope, it will double the thickness of the spliced area of the rope.

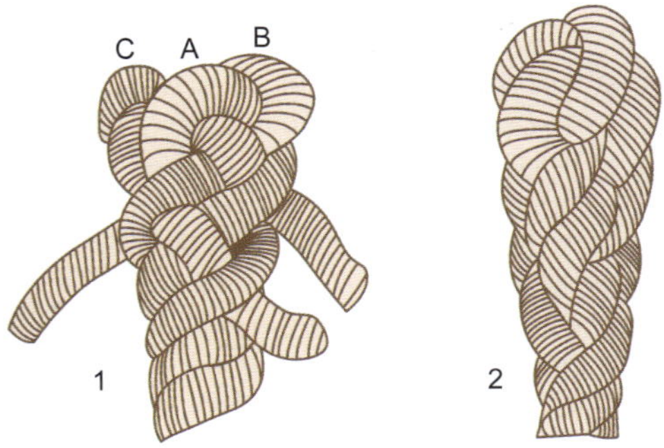

Fabrics

Historically, canvas and fabrics were in common use aboard ship, particularly as this is what the sails were made from.

Even when sailing ships were superseded by motor ships, canvas was still in regular use for hatch covers and awnings. Today, however, the use of fabric on deck has declined, although fabric coverings are often used for weather proofing various deck items, particularly ventilators, air pipes, embarkation ladders and items of safety equipment.

The fabrics used include canvas, coated canvas, polyethylene and polyester. Covers may need to be specifically made on board. Rigid polypropylene fabric is notoriously difficult to manage and often traditional canvas work may be the best option.

Canvas

The best canvas is made from flax. Other canvases can be made from cotton, hemp or jute, although these should not be considered for heavy weather use and, in the case of jute, not for outer deck use.

Canvas is generally supplied as a bolt of canvas that is 24 inches wide.

Canvas, even proofed and waxed, is not waterproof and is subject to shrinkage of around 3%. It is however useful for covering items that might deteriorate due to condensation.

Polyethylene

The strongest polyethylene fabric is lighter than canvas and laminated on both sides with high density polyethylene. It is woven and available in a number of colours.
The advantages of this fabric is that it is lightweight, waterproof, easy to handle, rot proof, shrink proof, UV protected and remains flexible in Arctic temperatures.

Polyester

This is a lighter and more flexible fabric and therefore very easy to handle, but it is not suitable for heavy duty use and is not waterproof.

Vinyl

Vinyl is a product of polyvinyl chloride (PVC). The addition of plasticisers enables it to be used for a wide variety of purposes including upholstery. A top urethane layer is extremely effective at protecting it from scratching, staining, denting and wearing of colour/ patterns.

Increasingly, vinyl is used at sea internally on cabin and public room furniture and for flooring tiles. While it is easy to maintain and clean and is waterproof, it is also subject to tearing and the damage, if not repaired, easily escalates. It is not uncommon on ships to see such furniture temporarily repaired with duct tape, which is not a satisfactory medium for

Fabrics

repair. Flooring tiles tend to lift, especially if wetted during cleaning or if used in way of the accommodation doors. If not immediately repaired, the tiling then cracks and breaks, usually at the corners.

Linoleum

Linoleum is comparatively rare on newer ships, but it can still be found on older vessels. Whereas vinyl is derived from petroleum-based products, linoleum is completely natural, being derived from linseed oil mixed with fine plant material and with a jute backing.

Canvas Work

Of all the materials, canvas is the easiest to repair.

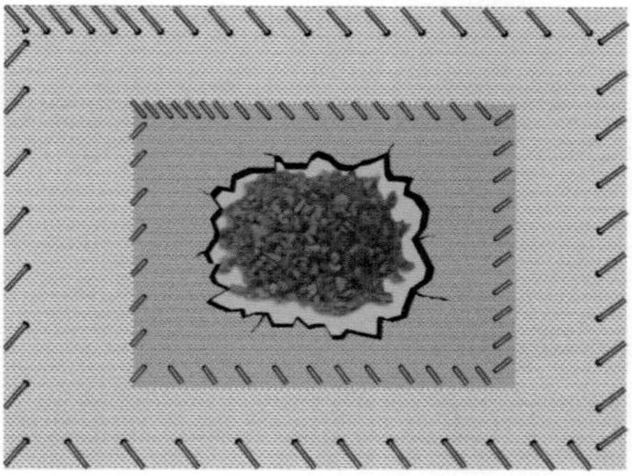

For large repairs, a canvas patch can be made. A patch larger than the damaged section is stitched on to the canvas, turning the edges in on all sides, which is known as tabling, before stitching. The canvas is then turned over and the damaged section's edges are turned over and a further set of stitches are made.

For all canvas stitching, the aim should be five stitches to an inch.

Tools

Sail Needles These are triangular with rounded edges to enable the needle to separate rather than pierce the material as it passes through. Various sizes are required for differing canvases with the heaviest required for roping where the canvas is attached to rope for added strength along an edge. All needles will rust very quickly unless coated in oil or grease.

Palms This is a shield worn over the palm and used to push the needle through the fabric. They are essential to any heavy fabric work and can be left or right handed.

Sail Twine As with needles, this comes in differing sizes and waxed synthetic twine is now common.

Sail Hook This is a hook with a swivel and a 2 metre lanyard which is used to keep the fabric taut while being worked.

Knife A razor sharp knife is essential for fabric work.

Hot Knife A hot knife can be used to cut and seal the edges of damaged synthetic fabric prior to a repair. This prevents further fraying.

Cement Boxes

Cement boxes on board ships are primarily used for short-term repair work to plug leaks, either in piping or plumbing systems or from direct hull damage. Although termed a *cement* box, the cement itself is the binder that, when mixed with water, undergoes a process of hydration causing it to solidify and hold other aggregates together in the mixture to make concrete.

A leak is normally plugged as best able, with a drain system (often a tube) set up to avoid a build-up of any seeping water. This can either be discharged or re-routed to allow work around the damage. A box is then constructed around the damaged area and filled with cement. The box supports the cement as it sets.

The area around the leak should be as dry and clean as possible, with any paintwork roughened to provide a suitable surface.

Cement must be mixed with an aggregate to provide strength. Fine aggregate sand is common and is mixed at

Cement Boxes

an approximate ratio of 2 parts aggregate to 1 part cement. Gravel may be used as a coarse aggregate, often mixed at a ratio of 4 parts aggregate to 1 part cement. A mixture of coarse and fine aggregates can also be used depending on the nature of the work and the drying time required. Reducing the amount of aggregate is likely to reduce the setting time, but is also likely to weaken the concrete.

Fresh water is then mixed with the substance and the concrete then poured into the cement box and left to dry. Once set, the drain tube can either be plugged directly or removed and the remaining hole plugged.

Cement can be mixed at varying consistencies using different materials to provide properties such as longevity, flexibility, temperature resistance, etc. However, ships generally only use cement as temporary repair measures.

Dresser Couplings/Dresser Clamps

Introduction

Some basic information about on board piping:

- The majority of pipes are made from mild steel
- water that circulates round cooling pipes will eventually corrode them
- pipes that pass through tanks that contain liquids are susceptible to corrosion both inside and out
- pipes that carry liquefied gas are unlikely to suffer from internal corrosion
- pipes can be connected by butt welding using either flange connections or mechanical joints. In chemical tankers, the number of flange connections are strictly controlled
- expansion joints, eg dresser joints, can only be used when pipes move due to thermal expansion or contraction or because the ship bends. The Classification Society rules state that they cannot be used to connect pipes on chemical tankers. The most common expansion joints are couplings or slip-on joints
- pipes that carry flammable liquids should have as few joints as possible. These joints should be shielded so that liquids cannot leak onto hot surfaces. These pipes do not normally have mechanical joints.

Cargo Piping – Tankers

This type of piping is usually made from mild steel and is protected from rust by external painting. Large oil tankers tend to have a ring main system. This allows increased operational flexibility but there is less segregation. Tankers that have deepwell pumps in their cargo tanks usually have dedicated piping. Each tank has its own pump, pipe and cargo manifold. Stainless steel piping is usually used with stainless steel tanks. Cargo pipes in chemical tankers must have welded joints. Flanged connections are allowed on oil tankers and chemical tankers for valve connections and for fitting spool pieces. These short lengths of pipe are removable and are used to segregate piping. It is important that cargo pipes are pressure tested regularly, so that any weak points are detected before they fail.

Pipe Repairs

Pipes that fail are usually replaced and not repaired. If they are repaired, the repair must be treated as a temporary measure.

A fundamental aspect in deciding what type of repair to carry out is the condition of the pipe's external surface. If the surface is very badly damaged and an elastomeric seal does not provide a sufficient seal in either the immediate vicinity or surrounding area, the external pipe surface may have to be fixed using a filler material. Recent developments using epoxy-filled steel sleeves have been effective in areas of extensive damage, and there are applications available for a wide range of defects, including corrosion, non-propagating cracks, dents or gouges in axial and circumferential orientation as well as anomalies associated with the girth of the welds.

www.hse.gov.uk

Key Factors:

- **Temporary repairs can be made using binding and rubber, cement blocks, rings and clamps or plastic resin. Wooden plugs with binding are occasionally used to plug a hole**

Dresser Couplings/Dresser Clamps

- **permanent repairs usually involve removing and replacing a length of piping. Welded doublers must not be used as a permanent repair**
- **once repairs have been carried out, a dye penetration test should be carried out as a pressure and non-destructive test**
- **pipe supports and clips should be replaced once a repair is completed. If the pipe vibrates or moves, additional supports should be used**
- **slag can fall into pipes that are joined by welding. This can cause a blockage or clog the valve seats – the pipe should be flushed before use**
- **if lubricating oil or hydraulic pipe repairs are carried out, the manufacturer should be consulted on how the oil and filters should be looked after.**

www.standard-club.com

Repair Couplings and Connectors

Dresser couplings are a type of repair coupling used to splice plumbing pipes.

A dresser coupling is a sleeve designed to slide over particular sizes of pipe. The sleeve is threaded on to both ends externally and comes with two threaded nuts, one at each end. Inside each of these nuts is a moulded rubber compression ring, one end of which is bevelled. The bevelled end must be fitted towards the centre of the sleeve, matching the bevel inside the end of the sleeve. Inside the galvanised dresser coupling nut is a metal friction ring, which must be used when the dresser coupling is assembled during a repair. If not, it is likely the repair will leak.

If there has been extensive damage or deterioration to a section of the pipework, it may not be possible to carry out a repair using clamps or sleeves. Repair clamps are usually available in standard sizes. The lead time and cost associated with producing extra clamps is usually prohibitive, although there may be situations where the cost is acceptable, eg to avoid plant shutdown, assuming that the existing damage has been fully assessed along with the risks involved if the repair is not carried out.

The most economical repair usually involves replacing the damaged section of pipework. This should be straight forward if the existing flange connections are available. The repair may only require a new piece of pipe being welded into place. If the pipework carries hydrocarbons, a welded repair presents problems associated with safe working.

The most economical way to repair pipework that has suffered extensive deterioration or damage is to repair the couplings or connectors as well as replacing the section of pipework.

A dresser coupling should be used as follows:

1. After isolating and clearing the line, cut the pipe where the repair is to be carried out.
2. Slide the nut and rubber compression ring over the pipe end and push them down the pipe to at least the length of the sleeve.
3. Slide the sleeve over the same end of the pipe.
4. Slide the second nut and compression ring on the opposite end of the cut pipe.
5. Centre the sleeve on the cut that was made in the pipe.
6. Move one of the compression rings towards the coupling until it sits inside the sleeve; it must sit squarely and firmly.
7. Slide the nut up in place and hand tighten.
8. Repeat this process for the second compression ring and nut.
9. Once both nuts are hand tightened, use one wrench on the body of the sleeve and a second to tighten both nuts.

www.hubpages.com

Figure 46.5 - Dresser Coupling
www.instructables.com

Dresser Couplings/Dresser Clamps

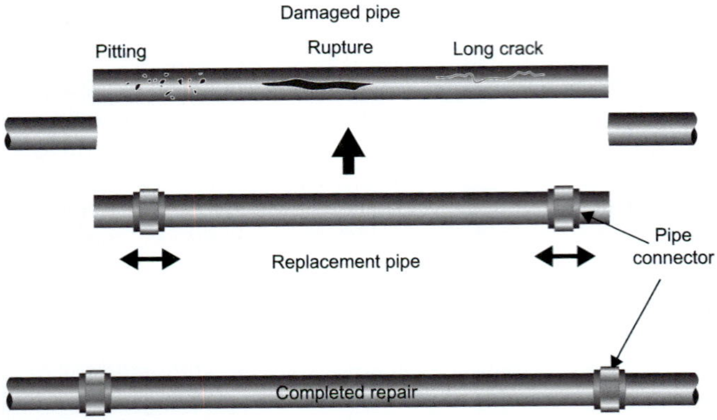

Figure 46.6 - Pipe repair using pipe connectors

Dresser Clamps

A leak repair clamp used for pipe and pipe flanges which will include a frame made up of one piece segments positioned end to end around the pipe. Each segment will include a pair of metal lips which are spaced apart, they are adapted to form a metal to metal seal with a pipe or flange when the frame segments are connected.

Patch Clamp

This metal patch is the simplest form of repair component. It can be used to cover a small non-leaking fault.

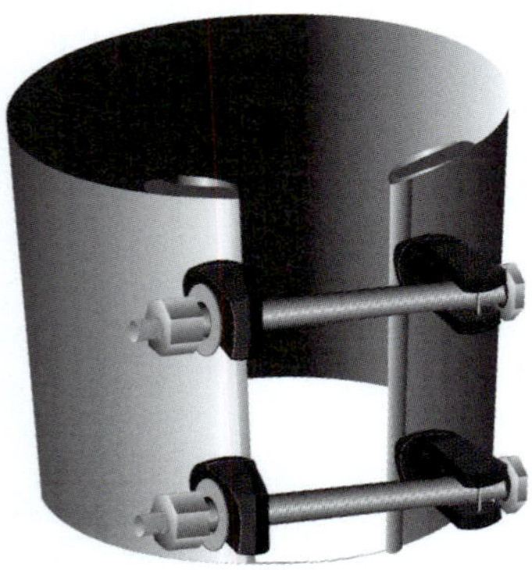

Figure 46.7 - Patch clamp

Pin-Hole Leak Repair Clamp

A small pin-hole leak in a pipe can be repaired using a patch clamp or a pin-hole leak repair clamp. This type of clamp uses a locator pin which guides a pointed cone seal into the hole. Pressure is applied to the cone seal by a force screw. Once the seal is compressed, the pin can be removed, completing the seal.

Figure 46.8 - Pin-hole leak repair clamp

'Stand-Off' Repair Clamp

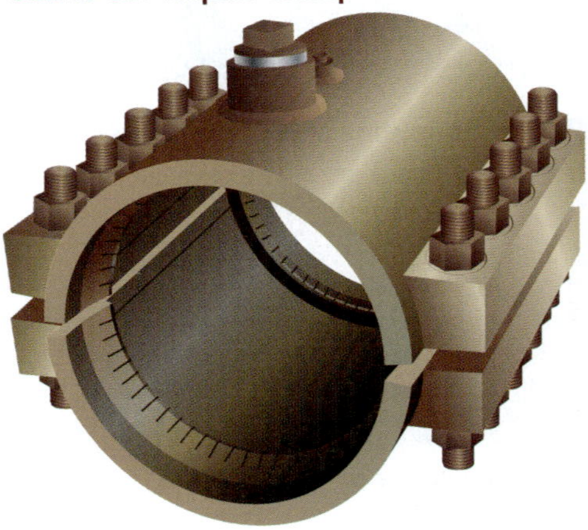

Figure 46.9 - Heavy duty 'stand-off' repair clamp

The most common type of pipe repair is the stand-off repair clamp. They are usually cylindrical in shape and come in two half shells. These clamps are also known as 'enclosures' as they totally enclose the defective area in a sealed pressure containment vessel. The seals can be energised by the compression force caused by tightening the two halves or by a leakage of the pipe contents – acting on a lip-type seal, this is more commonly known as a 'self-seal' arrangement.

Enclosure type repair components can also repair/seal damaged flanges and bends/elbows as illustrated overleaf.

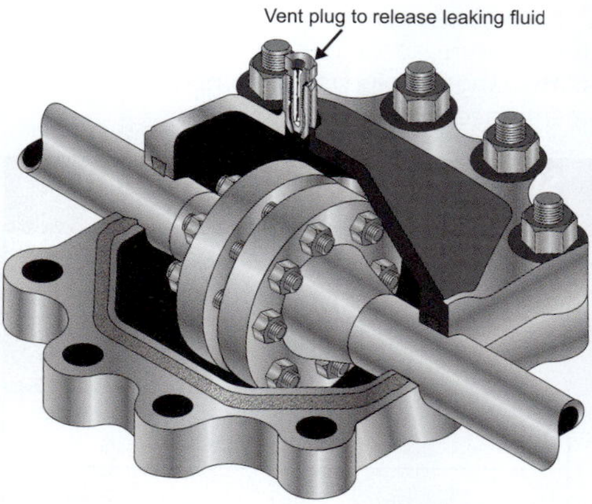

Figure 46.10 - 'Self-seal' type repair enclosure

Pipe Repair Tape

Rapp-it Pipe Repair Bandage

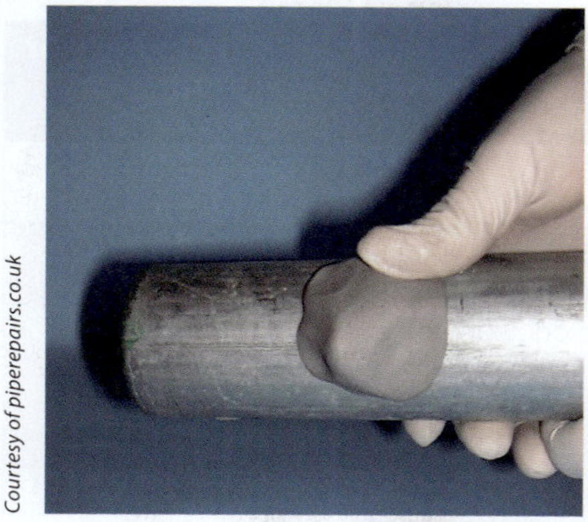

1 - Shut down pipe, apply putty over the hole in the pipe

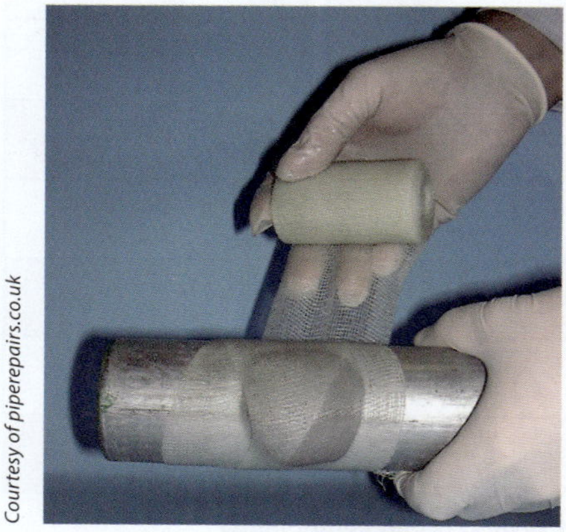

2 - After soaking the Rapp-it tape in water for 10 seconds, wrap it around the pipe, over the putty. Tighten firmly

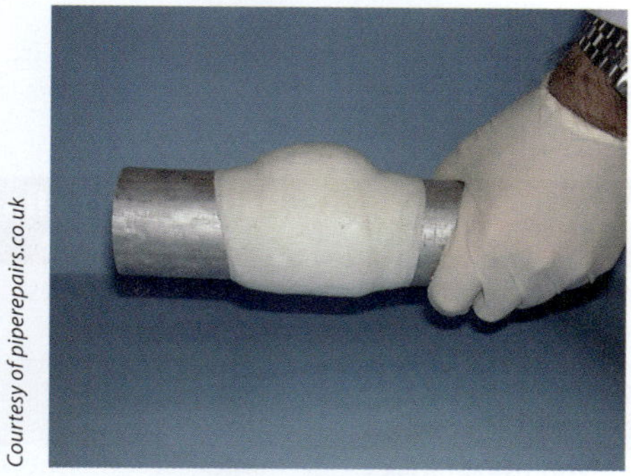

3 - Allow 30 minutes for pipe repair to set rock hard

This type of instant emergency repair system is simple to use. The bandages have a woven fibreglass substrate impregnated with a water-activated polyurethane resin.

Epoxy Putty

This usually comes as a kneadable stick that cures 'steel hard' relatively quickly once it has been mixed. It is tough and durable and adheres to an assortment of surfaces. After an hour, it can be drilled, tapped, sanded, painted, filed or machined. It can be used to bond, seal, plug, mould or rebuild many different surfaces. It can withstand high temperatures and will also harden in water.

For further information on the Rapp-it repair bandage see: http://tinyurl.com/odu5m97

Applicability of Different Repair Components

A large range of repair components are available for common repair scenarios. Each repair solution has advantages and disadvantages, and some may not be suitable or applicable. Table 46.2 provides an overview of individual repair components against a range of repair scenarios. The table concentrates on repairs being carried out on straight sections of pipe. It assumes that further deterioration is avoided and that the remaining pipe wall is able to accommodate the axial loading/stresses.

The remaining wall thickness must be considered when the imposed axial loadings/stresses are being looked at. In cases that involve external metal loss, it is assumed that any repairs carried out will prevent further deterioration. If deterioration cannot be prevented, the suitability of the repair

Dresser Couplings/Dresser Clamps

components should be considered, so that the loadings/stresses can be accommodated if the deterioration continues to affect the pipe's ability to carry these loadings/stresses.

Table 46.2 also gives a summary of the pressure, temperature, size and longevity capabilities of the range of pipe repair components mentioned previously.

Repair scenario	Patch	Encircling sleeve	Stand-off, clamp/ connector	Epoxy-filled sleeve
External metal loss - localised	Yes	Yes	Yes	Yes - consider cost effectiveness
External metal loss - extensive	No	Yes	Yes - c/w new pipe section	Yes
Internal metal loss - localised	Yes	Yes	Yes	Yes - consider cost effectiveness
Internal metal loss - extensive	No	Yes	Yes - c/w new pipe section	Yes
Leak	No	No	Yes - consider seal material suitability	Yes

Table 46.1 - Applicability of repair components to repair scenarios *(straight pipe sections)*

Repair method/ component	Maximum pressure rating	Temperature range	Size (nominal diameter) range	Temporary or permanent repair
Patch clamp	7 bar (100 psi)	Depends on seal material	½" to 42" (13 to 1,000 mm)	Temporary
Pin-hole clamp	140 bar (2,000 psi)	Depends on seal material	½" to 48" (13 to 1,200 mm)	Temporary
Encircling sleeve	Same rating/size as the original piping			Permanent
Complete circle clamp c/w 360° patch gasket	16 bar (230 psi)	Depends on seal material	Up to 30" (800 mm)	Permanent
One-piece stand-off clamp	20 bar (300 psi)	Depends on seal material	2" to 48" (50 to 1,200 mm)	Permanent
Stand-off type (enclosure) clamp	ASA Class 900 lb	Depends on seal material	4" to 48" (100 to 1,200 mm)	Permanent
Flange repair enclosure	ASA Class 600 lb	Depends on seal material	½" to 12" (13 to 300 mm)	Permanent
Outside diameter flange clamp	ASA Class 600 lb	400°C	½" to 24" (13 to 600 mm)	Temporary
One-piece stand-off connector	16 bar (230 psi)	Depends on seal material	Up to 30" (800 mm)	Permanent
Heavy duty connector	ASA Class 2,500 lb	-50°C to +230°C	All diameters	Permanent
Epoxy-filled sleeve	100 bar (1,450 psi)	3°C to 100°C	Same size as the original piping	Permanent
Composite repair	50 bar (725 psi)	-20°C to +60°C	All diameters	Temporary and permanent

Table 46.2 - Temperature, size and longevity capabilities of various repair components

Source: http://tinyurl.com/jwgy7pz

Chain Blocks

Introduction

A chain block is a type of lifting device which consists of two grooved wheels with a chain wound around them in the same fashion as a block and tackle. The chain has a hook at the end, which is attached to the load to be lifted. As the chain is pulled in a certain direction, it winds onto the wheels and the hook begins to rise. A chain block takes the strain out of heavy lifting and allows one operator to perform tasks that would otherwise require several workers to complete. They also help to avoid heavy or cumbersome parts from being damaged during handling.

Chain block capacities for these SWL ranges are typically rove in the following manner:

Chain Blocks

Storage

The following guidelines should be observed when storing chain blocks:

- Store chain blocks in a dry and clean store room or locker, free from chemical influences and vapours
- store chain blocks without any suspended load
- remove dust, damp and impurities from the chain block
- lubricate pulleys, pivots of hook and springs of safety latches of hooks
- suspend the chain block in a dry place.

Safety

Safety Summary

Cautions when using a chain block

- ALWAYS make sure the mounting strong point will provide adequate support for the fully loaded chain block
- ALWAYS let people around know when a lift is about to begin
- NEVER use a chain block for lifting people
- NEVER lift loads over or near people
- NEVER load the chain block more than the SWL shown on the chain block.

Safety Principles

Prior to use

- ALWAYS check the chain block before use
- ALWAYS make sure the length of the chain is long enough for the intended work
- ALWAYS ensure the carrying chain is clean and undamaged
- ALWAYS make sure the carrying chain is firmly fastened to the upper pulley block
- ALWAYS make sure the chain is properly drawn on the grooves in the pulleys
- ALWAYS make sure the pulleys in the upper and lower pulley blocks are free to rotate
- NEVER pull loads firmly imbedded or of unknown weight
- NEVER use a damaged chain block.

When in use

- ALWAYS make sure the load is properly fastened in the hook
- ALWAYS make sure the hook safety latch works correctly
- NEVER use fouled or damaged chain
- NEVER swing the load
- NEVER pull the rope over any edge
- NEVER weld or work on any suspended load.

Maintenance

- Inspect the chain block regularly
- check the carrying chain is clean and undamaged
- check the sliding parts are greased sufficiently.

Daily inspection (performed by the operating staff or the competent person)

Part	Inspection method	Limit/criteria for disposal	Attention required
1. Function of chain block	Visual, listening to determine whether it is operating smoothly	Chain jumps, makes excessive noise	Clean and lubricate the chain. If the trouble is not remedied, replace the chain
2. Fastening parts	Visual check of all bolts, nuts, rivets, etc	Defective or missing parts Loose parts	Remove chain block from use
3. Hooks (1) Appearance (2) Hook rotating (3) Safety latch of hook	Visual 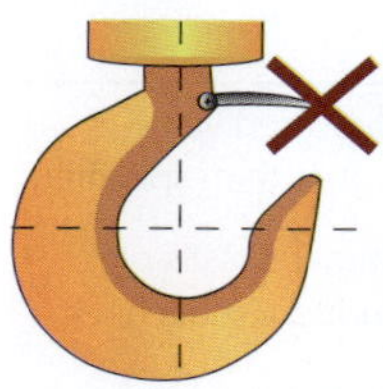 Rotate hook around its axis by manual springing of the safety latch	Safety latch sprung out over the top of the hook Hook does not rotate freely Safety latch does not return after pushing	Professional overhaul of lifting device – exchange of hook and other damaged parts Clean and lubricate Clean, lubricate, repair or exchange
4. Load chain (1) Appearance	Visually check the whole chain	Cracks in the place of welding, deformation, excessive wear, corrosion	Replace chain
Note: The complete wear of the chain cannot be determined by the visual inspection. When sign of wear is found, check the chain according to "Regular inspection"	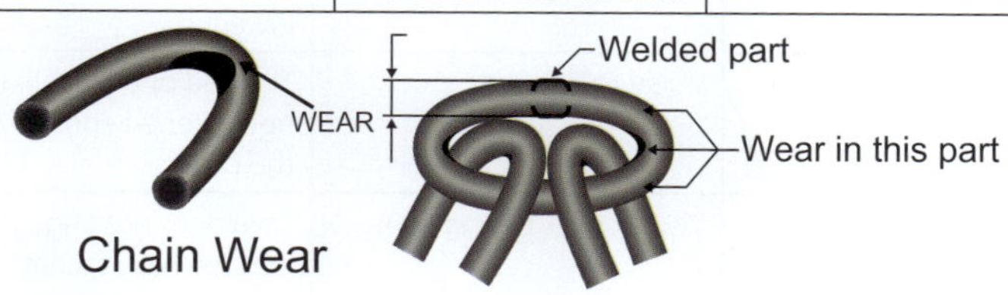		
(2) Lubrication	Visual	Chain is not lubricated	Clean and lubricate the chain
(3) Setting in the chain	Check whether the chain is kinked	The chain is kinked or twisted; welds are not in a row	Straighten the chain and set to normal position
(4) Kinked chain tackle block (only at two loading chain strands)	Visual check	Chain is kinked due to kinked tackle block, welds are not in a row	Straighten the chain by turning back the tackle block
5. Hand chain	Visual	Chain is kinked or twisted Chain is deformed or damaged and does not come correctly to chain wheel	Straighten the chain and set to normal position Exchange chain

Chain Blocks

Regular inspection (performed by the qualified person)

Part	Inspection method	Limit/criteria for disposal	Attention required
1. Fastening parts	Visual check of all bolts, nuts, rivets, etc	Defective or missing parts	Remove chain block
2. All parts	Visual check	Worn or damaged parts Dirty and not lubricated parts	Remove chain block or dismantle, clean, lubricate and assemble again
3. Name plate – marking of lifting capacity on the chain block	Visual check	Illegible lifting capacity	Re-mark the chain block
4. Hooks (1) Deformation of hook (opening) (2) Hook wear	Measure dimension with callipers	Measured value is higher than specified Damage is visible during visual check Do not use the hook, if dimensions are reduced by more than 10%	Remove and replace chain block
5. Brake - function	Suspend the load of weight equal to lifting capacity of the chain block, lift it to min. 250 mm and lower	After interrupting the operation, the brake must keep the load in any position of lifting or lowering	If this does not happen, remove the chain block from use
6. Anchoring the chain	Visual check	The end of the chain is not fastened enough to the body	Fasten the fixing bolt. Replace the chain block
7. Pawl - function	Visual check during lifting	Pawl does not engage into teeth of ratchet wheel	Clean, lubricate or replace the spring
8. Rotating of block sheave	Rotate the block sheave by pulling the chain 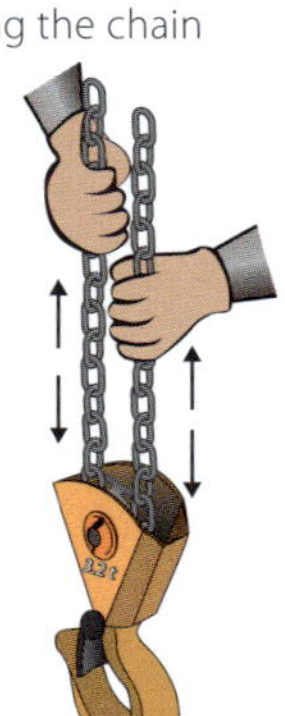	The block sheave does not rotate smoothly	Clean, lubricate or repair

Gangways

Means of Access

All ships require a means of ship-to-shore access that can be safely used by all.

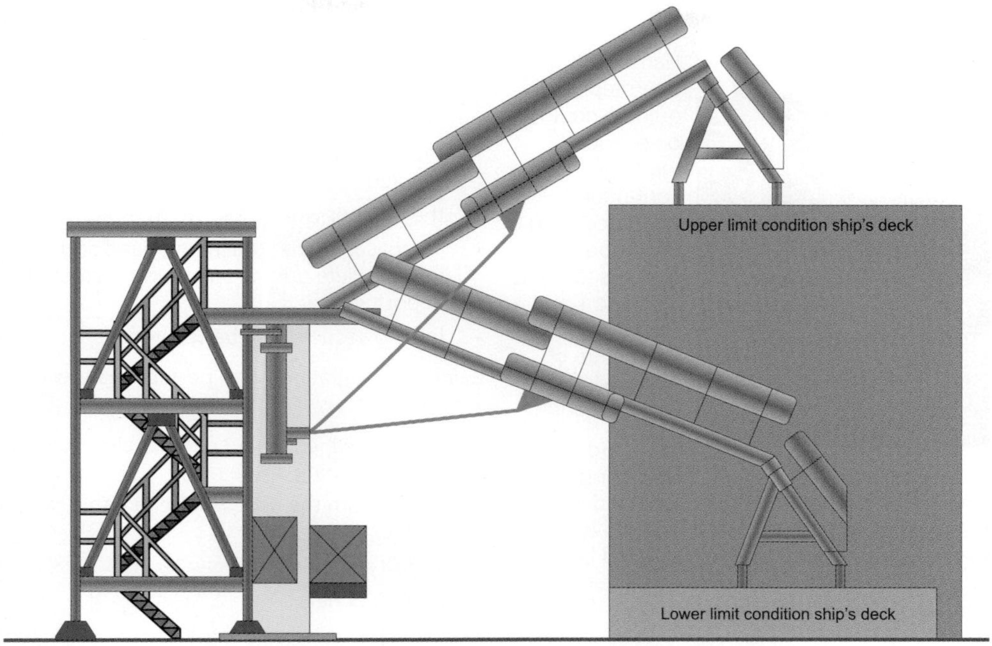

Figure 46.11 - Shore-based rotary type gangway

Shore-Based Gangways

Shore gangways are generally hydraulically operated and may be mounted either on the jetty deck or beside it. They are usually constructed of a steel column supporting a telescopic gangway. Self-levelling steps are provided at the end of the gangway. Movements of the assembly are hydraulically driven and, when the whole system has been put into the "free flow" position, the gangway will automatically follow all of the movements of the ship. Problems with fixed gangways can be caused by:

- Tidal range
- berth space
- size range of vessels
- obstructions on vessels precluding their use.

Ship Gangways

A ship gangway is usually a lightweight aluminium structure that can be used in a horizontal or inclined position, on an angle of up 30º from the horizontal, depending on tidal or freeboard conditions. Special design of the steps allows a more severe angle to be employed.

This type of gangway is covered by BS.MA78 1978, which specifies three designs:

Type A - rigid-decking two handrail gangway

Type B - hinged two handrail gangway

Type C - rigid narrow decking two handrail gangway.

Decking should be made of either continuous flat-topped corrugated sections or individual flat plate surfaces, which may have a non-slip coating. Footsteps are generally constructed from extruded aluminium sections that are secured to the stringers or decking and raised above the decking by a minimum of 30 mm.

Stanchions should be provided at specified heights for types A, B or C and should be vertical with the decking in the horizontal

Gangways

position. Stanchions may either be fixed hinged, with provision made to prevent inadvertent collapse, or portable. They should be secured to prevent accidental displacement from the socket or base support.

Hand and intermediate guides should be provided, made of continuous plastic-covered wire rope, galvanised steel chain or continuous rigid aluminium of either solid or hollow section.

Toeboards should be fitted on each side of the gangway at a height of at least 150 mm above the decking level. Gangways should be permanently marked by a rating plate, which should be prominently displayed. The rating plate should contain the following information:

- Manufacturer's name or trade mark
- type number and serial number
- type of gangway, ie A, B or C
- nominal size
- maximum permitted angle of use
- SWL, which is an indication of the number of persons who can use it at one time.

The gangway should be regularly checked to ensure that:

- There is no distortion of side stringers
- the decking or deck plates are adequately secured
- the roller or wheels revolve freely
- if applicable, the stanchions, hand and intermediate guides can easily be erected in position
- folding sections can be secured.

Safety considerations with portable gangway units include:

- Stability, which is a function of either width or the securing at the rail
- access from the gangway head – ship rail to deck
- stability of pulpits
- rigging of nets
- surveillance/monitoring.

Safety improvements can be achieved by fitting underslung nets. Gangway side nets are also useful additions.

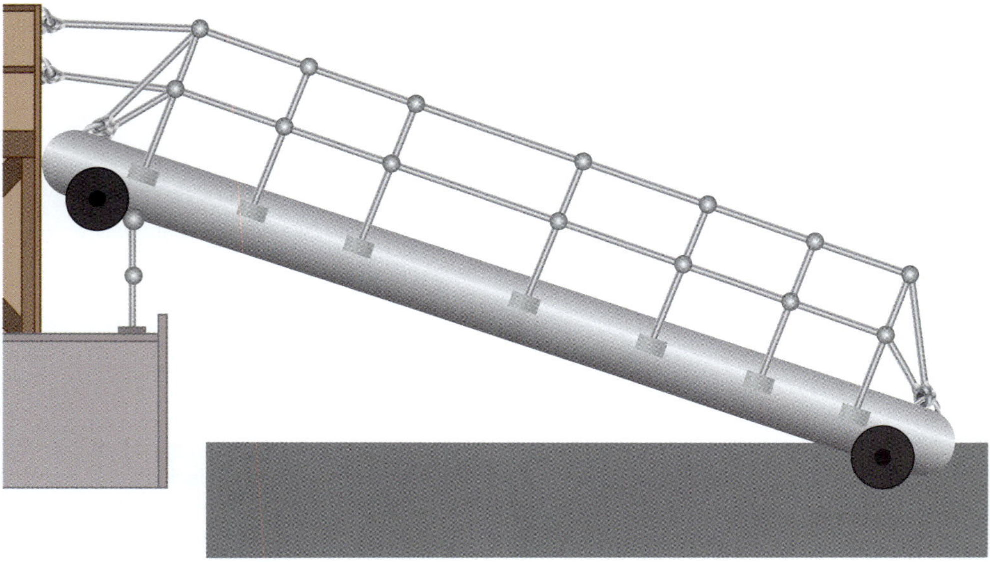

Figure 46.12 - Correctly rigged portable gangway

CHAPTER 47

Wires, Ropes, Chains, Shackles & Slings

Wires

On many ships, the only wire rope on board is used in the various lifting devices. All wire rope must be kept well lubricated to reduce internal friction and prevent corrosion. The lubrication applied must be compatible with the originally applied lubricant and it must not hinder any visual check of the wire. The areas of the wire that are in contact with sheaves or pulleys and exposed to the elements must receive regular lubrication.

A major problem with wires is detecting damage. Unfortunately, visual surface inspection only checks 20% of the rope and so will detect only 20% of the possible damage.

Figure 47.1 - Outside of the wire rope. It appears to be in good condition

Figure 47.2 - Core of the same wire rope. You can see many broken wires and notches

When making a visual inspection of a wire rope, the following should be looked for:

- Broken or cut strands
- distortion, such as kinking, crushed parts, strands coming off, main strand displacement, or core protrusion
- wear
- corrosion
- elongation
- decreased elasticity (look for stiffness and a fine brown powder between the strands).

Shortly after installation, the rope's diameter will decrease slightly. This is normal. This initial decreased diameter should be used as the original rope diameter when making calculations. All wire rope will, over time, stretch and this stretching will also cause the rope to reduce in diameter.

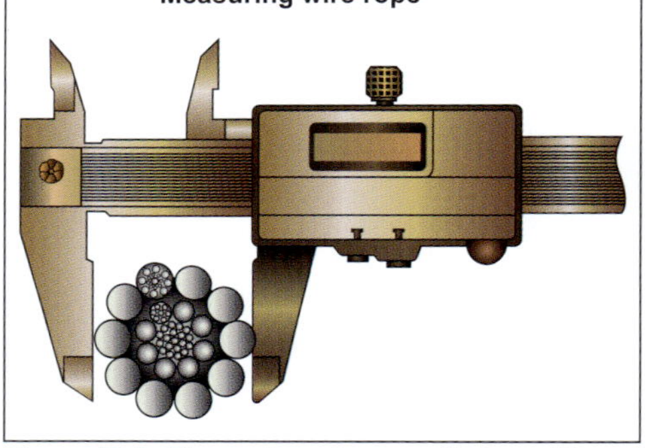

Figure 47.3 - Measuring wire rope. Note position of the callipers

Callipers for the monthly measuring of all load bearing wire ropes should be carried on board.

The following table shows the maximum allowable reduction in wire rope diameter before it should be discarded:

Original diameter	Maximum allowable reduction
5/16 (8 mm) or smaller	1/64 (0.4 mm)
3/8 to 1/2 (13 mm)	1/32 (0.8 mm)
9/16 to 3/4 (19 mm)	3/64 (1.2 mm)
7/8 to 11/8 (29 mm)	1/16 (1.6 mm)
11/4 to 11/2 (38 mm)	3/32 (2.4 mm)

The most common causes of wire rope failure are:

Overloading

Wire fractures can occur over time. An overloaded wire might not fracture or show any sign of deterioration, but the overloading itself will have caused some damage. Further use will continue to add to the fractures of the individual wires in the rope and repeated use will continue to fracture the remaining wires within it, eventually leading to complete fracture.

Mechanical Wear

Mechanical wear in steel wire ropes is the removal of material due to mechanical abrasion. This can be reduced by lubrication.

Bending Fatigue

Rope bending fatigue is caused by running rope over sheaves or on and off single layer drums.

Corrosion Damage

Corrosion is the reaction of metal with oxygen. There are two different types of corrosion; atmospheric corrosion which produces rust, and pitting corrosion which occurs in areas of the wire where the protective coating (galvanised coating) has been damaged. Lubrication, both external and internal, can assist in preventing corrosion.

Steel expands as it corrodes, so any measurable increase in the wire diameter might give an indication of internal corrosion.

Audible Detection

To detect breaks inside a wire rope, hold a length of the rope to your ear and bend it backwards and forwards. If there is a cracking or popping sound, it indicates that there are broken wires inside and that the rope should be replaced immediately.

Wire Rope Single Use and Re-usable

Wire rope has no specific yield limit but elongates steadily until it fails. Experiments with lashing wires have shown that, to keep a wire in good condition and avoid any permanent elongation, it must not be exposed to peak loadings in excess of 55% of the breaking strength. Also, frequent loadings of more than 15% should be avoided. Therefore, if a wire is not exposed to loadings of more than 55% and if loadings of more than 15% are not frequent, the wire will remain in good condition without any deformation of the wires.

Un-Reeling or Un-Coiling Wire Rope

Great care must be taken when removing wire rope from reels or coils.

Looping the rope over the flange of the reel, or pulling the rope off a coil while it is lying on the ground, will create loops in the line. If these loops are pulled tight, kinks will result, permanently damaging the wire rope.

Note: Whenever handling wire rope, take care not to drop reels or coils. This can damage and collapse the reel, making removal of the wire rope extremely difficult, if not impossible.

The method used for opening a coil of vegetable fibre rope, by pulling out the end and running away with it, cannot be used for a wire rope as it will lead to innumerable kinks. Once formed in a wire rope, a kink can never be completely removed. Therefore, the following procedure should be observed.

Remove lashing and covering. Lash the outer end somewhere on deck and unroll the coil, like unrolling a coil of fire hose. An iron rod inserted through the centre of the coil makes the unrolling easier. However, if the size of the rope is large, the coil will be too heavy to roll on deck, in which case the following procedure will have to be adopted.

Make a cross with two battens of wood, about 60 cm longer than the diameter of the coil. Take two lengths of rope about 3 metres long and tie their ends on opposite arms of the cross, about 30 cm away from the centre, to create two similar bridles. Place the coil of rope over this cross and pull out the two bridles through the centre of the coil. The bridles can now be hooked on to a swivelled cargo hook at the end of a derrick runner and the coil hove off the deck. The end of the wire rope can now be pulled out and run along the deck, while two men tend to the turntable.

Wires

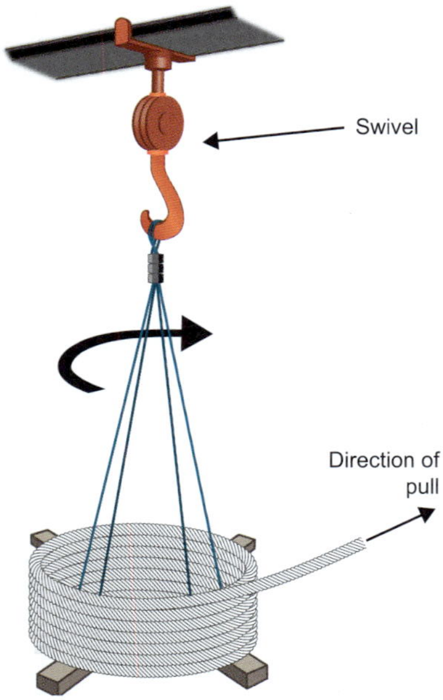

Figure 47.4 - Correct method of uncoiling wire

Figure 47.5 - Correct method of uncoiling wire

Figure 47.6 - Correct method of uncoiling wire

Figure 47.7 - Incorrect method of coiling wire

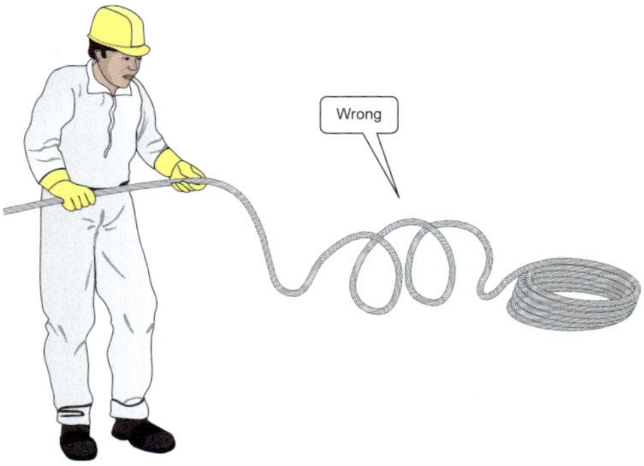

Figure 47.8 - Incorrect method of coiling wire

Care and maintenance:

- Do not open a new coil of wire without using a turntable or similar apparatus to avoid kinking the wire
- handle a wire rope carefully so that no kinks are formed. A kink reduces the strength and permanently damages the rope
- avoid sharp bends and bad nips. Never use a shackle or ring for changing the direction of the rope. If the rope has to pass over a sheave, its diameter should be at least 10 times the diameter of the rope. The diameter of the bitts and warping drum should be at least 13 times. The grooves (score) of the sheaves should conform to the shape of the rope. The rope should not chafe against the sides of the sheave or block
- store the wire rope over gratings to keep it away from seawater. If during use the rope has become wet by seawater, wash off the salt with fresh water and apply oil before storing it away. Wire brush the rope occasionally and coat it with the special wire grease provided on the ship for this purpose

- always inspect the rope before use. A flattening of the rope, rusting of the wires, broken wires, wires breaking when folded and more than 10% broken wires in a length of 8 diameter are all symptoms that indicate that the rope is not to be relied upon.

Re-reeling Wire Rope

When reeling rope from one reel to another, it is important for it to travel from top to top, as illustrated below. Spooling from bottom to bottom is also acceptable, provided the surface over which the wire rope will travel is clean, smooth and dry, to avoid foreign particles becoming embedded in the wire rope.

Note: Spooling from top to bottom or from bottom to top can put a reverse bend into the wire rope. The wire rope should be removed from the reel in the same direction as placed on the drum.

Wire Splice

It is possible, with the right equipment, to make a wire splice in 15 minutes. For larger wires, more time is needed, but even with a 23 cm wire, pulling the tucks through with a winch, this should be completed in a day's work by competent seafarers.

Essential equipment is a fid or marlin spike, a serving mallet, a vice, preferably a wire rope splicing vice or riggers vice, a thimble for eye splices and a wire cutter for finishing off. Bulldog grips are useful for holding the wire in position around the thimble while making the splice.

Eye Splice

The most efficient wire eye splice is made by putting in a 'Liverpool tuck'. This is where the first strand is tucked under three strands, the second strand goes in the same place but only under two strands and the third strand goes in the same opening but only under one strand. The recommended order for finishing the splice is to tuck strands three, two and one, ensuring that each has three tucks in all. Then the splice should be tapered by removing the whipping from each strand, cutting out the heart and half the strands, replacing the whipping and then finishing off with two more tucks.

Once the splice is completed, the finishing consists of:

1. Worming, which is where the lay of the rope or wire is filled with spun yarn to even out the surface of the splice for the parcelling.
2. Parcelling, which is where a broad tape of light canvas, sacking or cloth, about 6 cm in width, is wound around the splice and held in place with a light lashing. If parcelling rigging, always parcel up to allow water to be shed.
3. Serving is a tight lashing made with a serving mallet and a ball of spun yarn.

Tips

When splicing wire, always insert the marline spike against the lay of the wire and make sure not to push it through the core. The core must be on the left-hand side of the spike. Insert the spike obliquely and, if required, tap it lightly with a hammer.

Before unlaying any wire rope, ensure that both the strand ends and the rope itself are properly whipped.

It is essential that all the strands are inserted tightly and beaten down into position, ensuring that there is no slackness in the strand and getting the strand close to protruding at right angles from the wire.

> *"A thimble or loop splice in any wire rope should have at least three tucks with a whole strand of rope and two tucks with one half of the wires cut out of each strand. The strands in all cases should be tucked against the lay of the rope. Any other form of splice which can be shown as efficient as the above can also be used".*

Source: 'Code of Safe Working Practices for Merchant Seamen'

Wires

There are many types of wire eye splices in use but they can all be divided into two groups, namely those that are, after the first tuck, tucked against the lay and those that are, after the first tuck, tucked with the lay. Splices tucked with the lay are liable to open out if the spliced end of a wire is free to rotate. For example, if a load is suspended from a single cargo runner and the sling is spinning for any reason, the splice, if it is tucked with the lay, will open out.

The Factories Act 1931 clearly stipulates that all wire splices used for cargo handling must be tucked against the lay and must have five tucks, namely three tucks with full strands and two tucks with strands halved. When, however, the end of the wire is secured and unable to rotate, there is no objection to a splice tucked with the lay.

The first tuck itself is carried out in many ways but in all of them eventually there is one and only one end protruding out of each crevice. Two types of wire eye splices are described below in brief. Before starting to splice, put a whipping about 30 to 40 cm from the end. Then open out the strands and whip their ends also. Now bend the wire to form the eye and seize the two parts of wire together so that the eye does not shift. These instructions apply to all types of wire splices. In the following description, the opened out ends of the strands are referred to as ends and the unopened strands of the standing part of the wire are referred to as strands.

Liverpool Splice

Keep three ends on the right of the wire and three on the left of the wire. Insert the marline spike and, without damaging the heart, lift three strands on the right side of the wire.

Tuck No. 1 end from left to right under these strands. Now, without withdrawing the spike, just drop one strand and tuck No. 2 end under two strands, also from left to right. Now again drop one more strand and tuck from left to right, No. 3 end under only one strand. It will be seen that the three ends enter at the same place but come out at three different places.

Now lift No. 4 strand and tuck No. 4 end under it from left to right. Similarly, No. 5 end is tucked under No. 5 strand and No. 6 end is tucked under No. 6 strand from left to right. This completes the first round of tucks. For the remaining tucks, each end is wrapped a number of times around the same strand, in a clockwise spiral.

Locking Splice

Lift two strands on the right side of the wire and tuck No. 1 end from left to right under these two strands. No. 2 end also enters the same place as No. 1 end but is tucked under one strand only from left to right. This gives two strands entering the same place but emerging at different places. Now pick up No. 3 strand and tuck under it No. 4 end from left to right and No. 3 end from right to left, forming a cross or a 'lock'. Next, lift two strands on the left side of the wire and tuck No. 6 end from right to left under these two strands. Do not withdraw the spike but just drop one strand and tuck the remaining No. 5 end under only one strand from right to left.

This completes the first tuck. The remaining tucks are done against the lay, over one and under one, like in a rope eye splice.

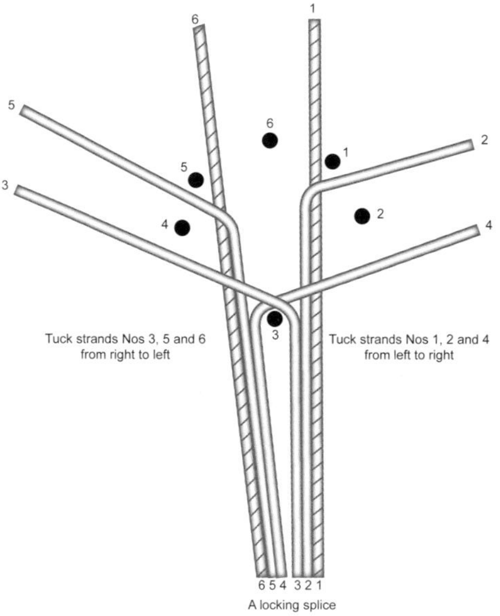

Figure 47.9 - A locking splice

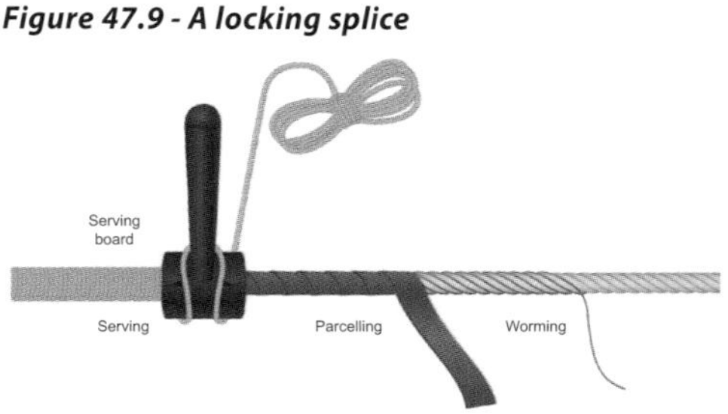

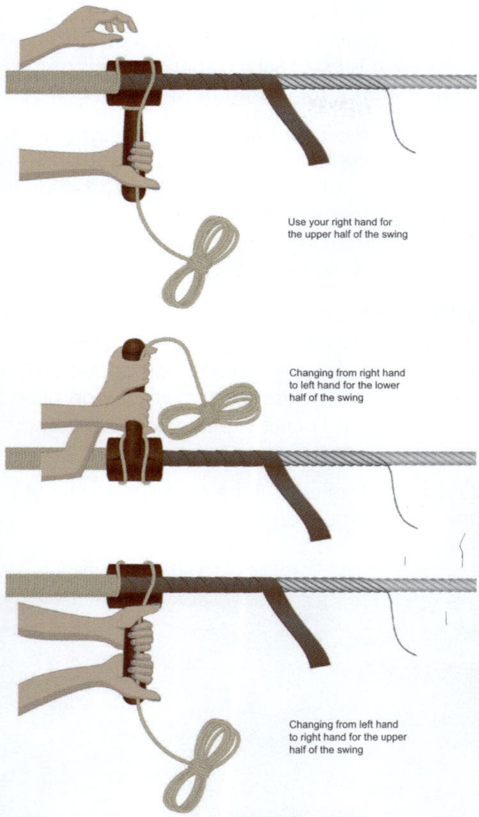

Figure 47.10 - Worming and parcelling of a completed wire splice (worm and parcel with the lay, turn and serve the other way)

Wire Crimps

Most companies have banned the use of wire splices and opt for mechanically-crimped wires.

There are occurrences of new build vessels being delivered with mooring wires that have spliced eyes. The main concern is that the crew parcel/cover the spliced area to make it neat and presentable, the result of which is that this section of the wire does not receive oil/grease during periods of maintenance and is prone to corrosion. Ships with receiving wires like this normally land them at the first opportunity to have a certified crimp fitted.

Making a Wire Rope Eye with Bulldog Grips

- The grips must be the correct size for the diameter of the wire
- the correct number of grips must be used (see table below)

Nominal Diameter of Wire Rope	Minimum Number of Wire Rope Grips
Up to and including 19 mm	3
Over 19 mm, up to and including 24 mm	4

- all grips must be the same way round, with the saddle on the weight-bearing part of the wire
- the first grip must be close to the thimble if one is used
- the other grips must be spaced six rope diameters apart
- the cut end must be whipped or secured in some way. There must be no unlaying of the dead end of the wire and the length of the dead end must be about six rope diameters
- the nuts should be tightened until the U-bolt bites into the wire.

When an eye is made up correctly, the wire will not slip through the grips until the load on the wire is about 70% of its nominal breaking strength.

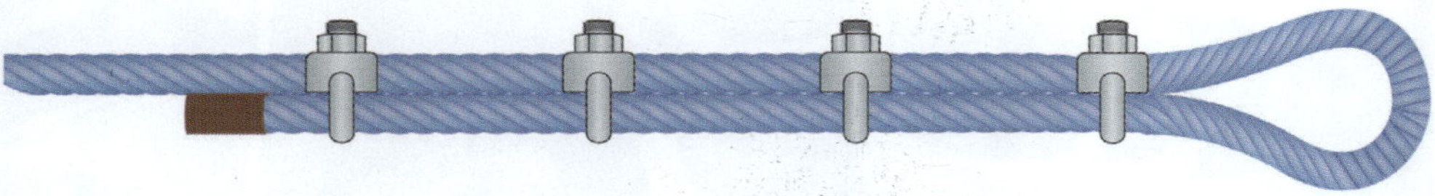

Figure 47.11 - An eye in a wire rope properly made up using four grips

Ropes

Splicing an Eight-Strand Braid Rope

Hollow single braid ropes may be spliced by three methods. The procedures are the same for both eight and twelve-strand construction.

Tucking the Rope Through Itself

Many hollow braids have a long braid pitch, which makes a soft rope that can be opened to allow the rope to be inserted through itself. A number of passes through the rope (tucks) are required.

This splice is easy to make but may not be the most suitable for long-term cyclical loading. It cannot be used on tightly braided ropes.

Burying the Rope in the Hollow Centre

Alternatively, for a rope with a long pitch length (soft braid), the end of the rope may be buried well down into the body. This works well with the slippery nature of HMPE ropes as the bury length can be as long as necessary to hold securely. It is essential to taper the ends of the buried strands for maximum strength.

This is the most common splice for eight-strand hollow braided ropes and is used extensively with twelve-strand hollow braids. It can be a very reliable splice for cyclic loading if the included angle of the eye is small. Lock stitching should be employed.

Tuck Splice

This is an efficient splice and can be used on twelve-strand ropes that are too tightly braided for the methods described above. It works like an eight-strand plaited splice, except that there are six pairs of strands.

End-to-end splices can be made using any of the above procedures.

Splicing a Double Braid Rope

Step 1
Counting and Marking

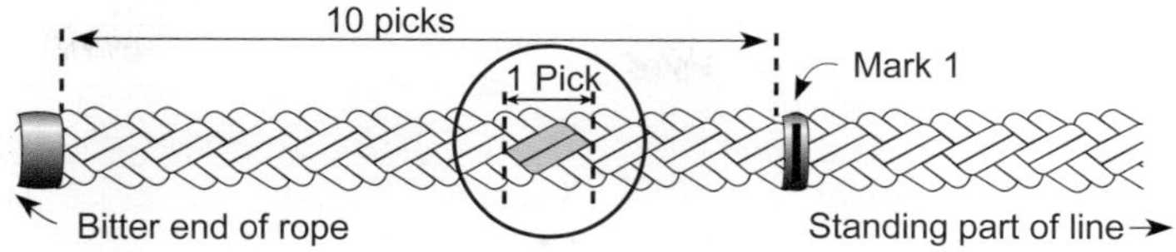

From the end of the rope, count a distance of 10 picks and apply tape securely around the rope immediately after the 10th pick, as shown in the diagram. This is Mark 1. Apply the tape securely enough so that it will not move during the splicing procedure.

Step 2
Making the Eye and Marking the Rope

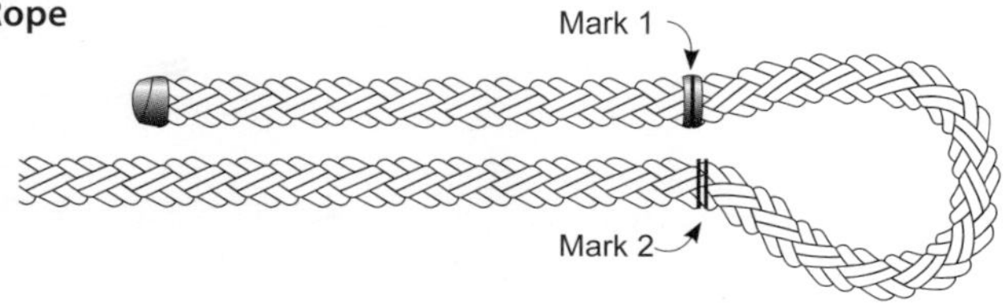

Form the desired size of the eye, being careful not to add twist to the rope. Mark the rope adjacent to the tape. This is Mark 2.

Step 3
Marking the Left-Rotating Strands

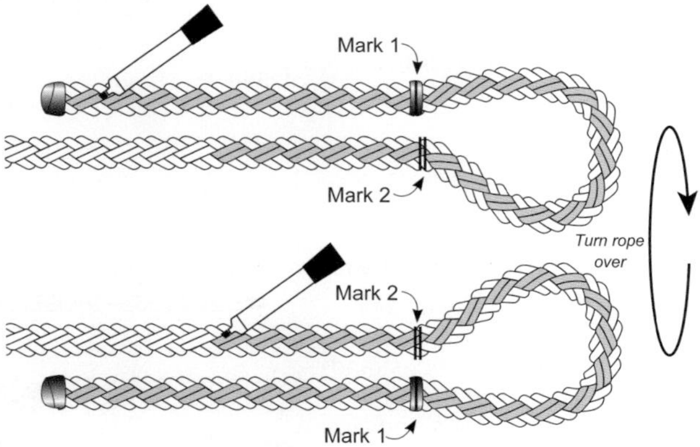

From the end of the rope, mark the first 10 picks up to the tape at Mark 1. Continue marking the length of the eye and at least an additional six picks past Mark 2. Mark all strands that rotate left on both sides of the braided rope.

Note: The strands that rotate left (shaded) are marked for improved visual reference. Eight-strand ropes are composed of four pairs of two strands each. Two of the strand pairs rotate to the left, and two pairs rotate to the right. When marking the left-rotating strands, be sure to turn the rope over and mark the left-rotating strands on the opposite side of the braid.

Step 4
Taping the Ends and Unlaying the Rope

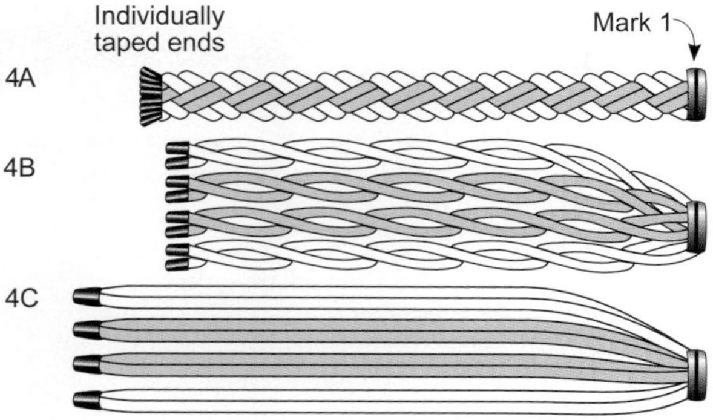

Step 4A Tape the ends of each of the eight strands individually.

Step 4B Unlay the strand pairs all the way back to the tape at Mark 1. Keep the pairs of strands together while unbraiding.

Step 4C When unlayed, the strands in a pair will be twisted around each other. Untwist each strand pair so the two strands lie parallel to each other, rather than twisting around each other. Tape the ends of each pair together.

Ropes

Step 5
Positioning the Strands

Arrange the strand pairs as shown in Figure A. One set of the marked (shaded) strands is on the top, and the other marked strands are on the bottom. The unmarked (white) pair will be on the left and right.

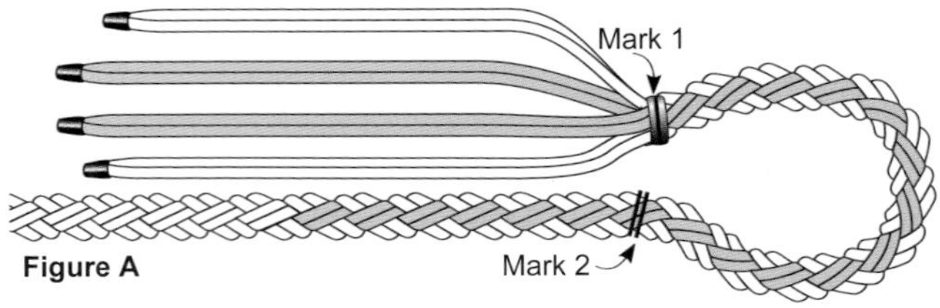

Figure A

Step 6
Forming the Eye

Physically form the eye, making certain there is no twist in the rope. Place the (white) pair that is closest to the standing part of the rope over the rope, at Mark 2, as shown in Figure B, being careful not to add twist to the rope.

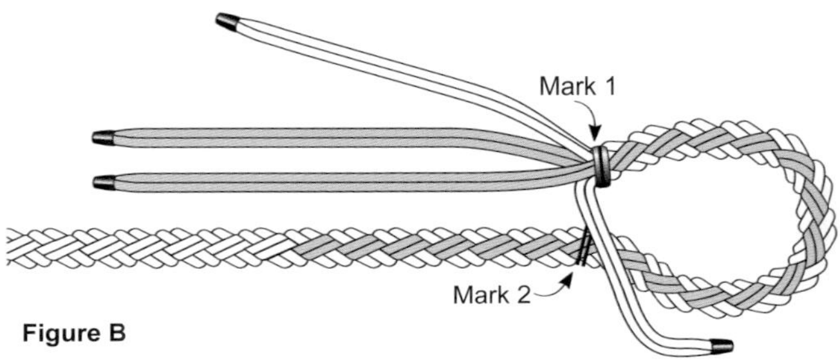

Figure B

Step 7
Route Tucking the Strand Pairs

Note: If necessary, use a fid or marlinspike to loosen the strands. The left-rotating (shaded) strands will be tucked under the right-rotating (white) strands, and vice versa.

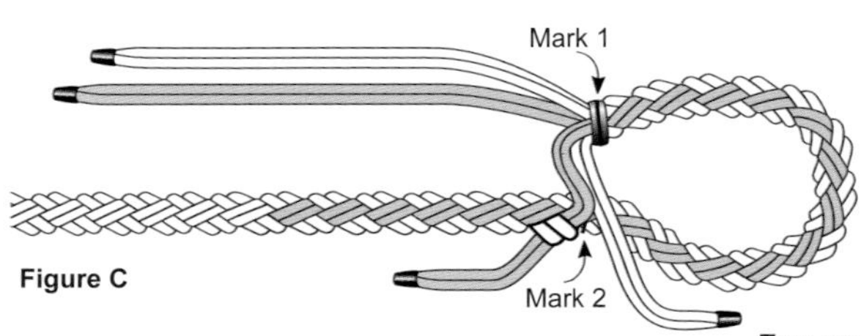

Figure C

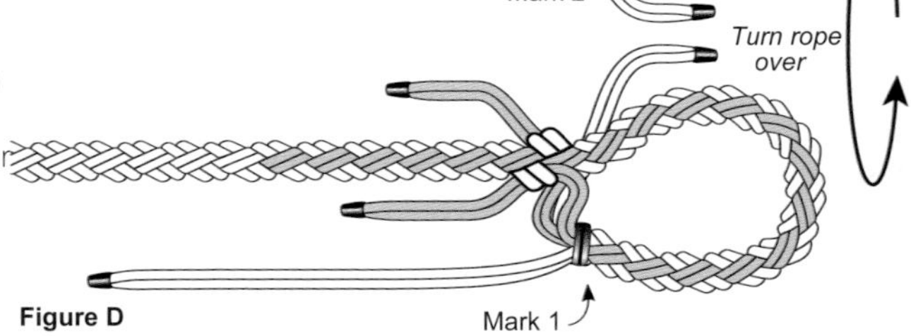

Figure D

Step 7A Beginning with the left-rotating marked (shaded) pair of strands on top, make your first tuck under the right-rotating (white) pair of strands closest to Mark 2. Pull the strands completely through, making sure that the strands don't twist (Figure C).

Step 7B Turn the eye over and tuck the other marked (shaded) pair of strands under the (white) pair of strands directly opposite the previous tuck (Figure D).

Step 7C Tuck the (white) pair of strands under the (shaded) pair of strands closest to the first two tucks. Pull the strands snug, but not tight to avoid distorting the strands in the eye area. Again, make sure there is no twist in the strands (Figure E).

Step 7D Turn the eye over and tuck the remaining (white) pair of strands under the remaining (shaded) pair of strands in the standing part of the rope (Figure F).

Note: A full tuck includes all four pairs of strands.

Step 7E Remove tape and pull all eight strands snug and correct any twist that may have been introduced during the tucking procedure. The first tuck is now complete (Figure G).

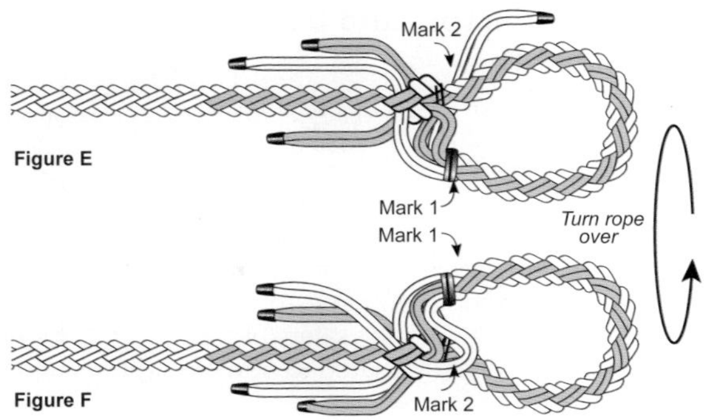

Figure E

Figure F

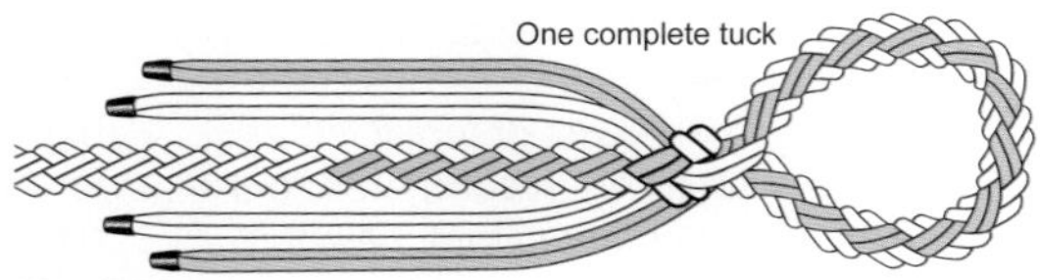

Figure G

Step 8
Completing the Tucks and Finishing the Splice

Step 8A Continue tucking the (shaded) strands under the (white) strands and the (white) strands under the (shaded) strands until at least four full tucks (with all four strand pairs) have been completed.

Step 8B After each round of tucks, pull each strand to make sure they are snug and there is no twist. The splice should look like Figure H.

Step 8C Locate the strand closest to the eye in each strand pair. Tape and cut off, leaving enough of the end protruding so it does not slip back into the rope when loaded. The splice should look like Figure I.

Figure H

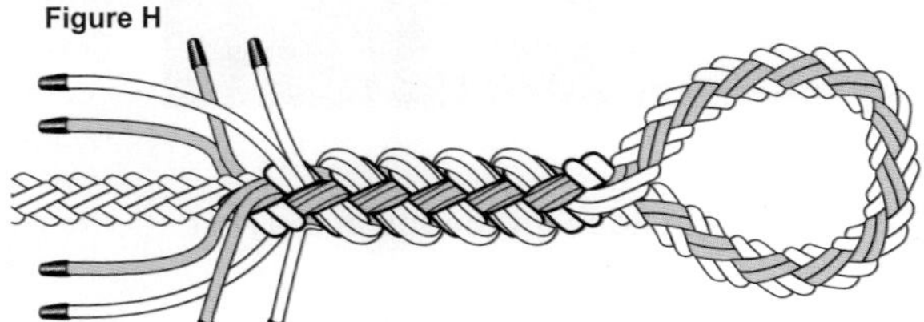

Figure I

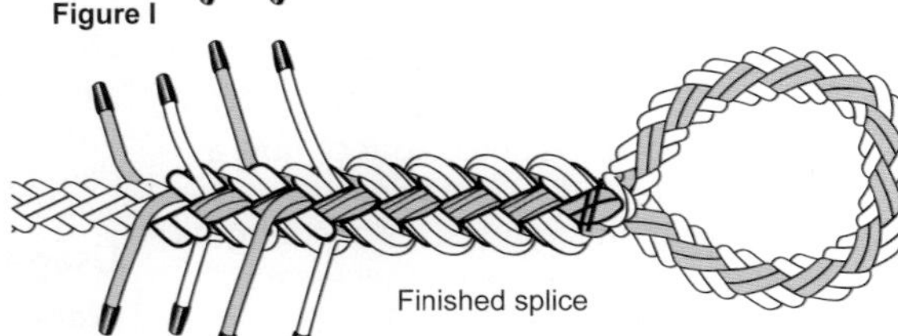

Figure J

Step 8D Continue tucking the remaining strands, with the (shaded) strands under the (white) strands, and vice versa, for two more full tucks.

Step 8E Tape and cut off the remaining strands. The finished splice should look like Figure J.

Note: The eight ends can be heat fused so they don't fray, but be careful not to damage any of the strands.

Ropes

Rope Life Factors and Damage Assessment

The use of rope for any purpose subjects it to friction, bending and tension. All rope hardware, sheaves, rollers, capstans, cleats and knots are, in varying degrees, damaging to the rope. It is important to understand that, even under the most ideal conditions, rope will lose strength during use in any application. Maximising the safety of rope performance is directly related to how strength loss is managed and making sure ropes are retired from service before they can create a dangerous situation. Ropes are serious working tools and used properly will give consistent and reliable service. The cost of replacing a rope is extremely small when compared to the physical damage or personnel injury a worn-out rope can cause.

Selection

Select the Right Rope for the Job in the First Place

Selecting a rope involves evaluating a combination of factors. Some of these are straightforward, such as comparing rope specifications. Others are less qualitative, such as a preference for a specific colour or how a rope feels in your hand. Cutting corners and reducing application factors, sizes or strengths on an initial purchase creates unnecessary replacements and potentially dangerous conditions and increases long-term costs. If fibre and construction are equal, a larger rope will outlast a smaller one because of the greater surface wear distribution, and a stronger rope will outlast a weaker one because it will be used at a lower percentage of its break strength, with less chance of over-stressing.

Strength: When given a choice between ropes, select the strongest of any given size. A load of 200 pounds represents 2% of the strength of a rope with a breaking strength of 10,000 pounds. The same load represents 4% of the strength of a rope that has a breaking strength of 5,000 pounds. The weaker rope is having to work harder and, as a result, will have to be retired sooner.

Elongation: Ropes with lower elongation under load will provide better load control. However, a rope with lower elongation that is shock loaded can fail without warning, even though it appears to be in good shape. Low elongating ropes should be selected with the highest possible strength. Twisted rope has lower strength and more stretch. Braided rope has higher strength and lower stretch.

Firmness: Select ropes that are firm and round and hold their shape during use. Soft ropes will snag easily and abrade quickly, causing accelerated strength loss. A loose or soft rope will almost always have higher break strengths than a similar rope that is firm and holds its shape because the fibres are in a straighter line, which improves strength but compromises durability.

Construction and Abrasion: Rope construction plays an important role in resistance to normal wear and abrasion. Braided ropes have a round, smooth construction that tends to flatten out on a bearing surface. This distributes the wear over a much greater area, as opposed to the crowns of a three-strand or, to a lesser degree, an eight-strand rope. All ropes should be protected against sharp and abrasive surfaces. Wire ropes tend to score and gouge chocks and bitts, creating cutting edges that can damage synthetic ropes. Weld beads on repaired capstans, fairleads, etc are equally damaging unless dressed down smoothly.

Usage

Working Loads: Working loads are the loads that a rope is subjected to in everyday activity. They are normally expressed as a percentage of new rope strength and should not exceed 20%. A point to remember is that a rope may be severely overloaded or shock loaded in use without breaking. However, damage and strength loss may have occurred without any visible indication. The next time the rope is used under normal working loads, the acquired weakness can cause it to break.

Bending: Any sharp bend in a rope under load decreases its strength substantially and may cause premature damage and failure. Sheave diameters on rotating sheave blocks should be ten times the rope diameter for twisted ropes and eight times the rope diameter for braided ropes. The diameter on fixed pin terminations should be at least three times the rope diameter (ie the bending radius for one-half inch ropes should be one to one-half inch).

Knots: A knot reduces strength because of the tight bends that occur within it. With some knots, ropes can lose up to 50% of their strength. It is vital that the reduction in strength by the use of knots is taken into account when determining the size and strength of a rope to be used in an application. To avoid knot strength reduction, it is recommended that a rope is spliced according to the manufacturer's instructions.

Rope Storage: Keep ropes as clean and dry as possible and store them in a coil away from heat sources.

Shock Loads: A shock load is a sudden change in tension from a state of relaxation or low load to one of high load. Any sudden load that exceeds the working load by more than 10% is considered a shock load. The further an object falls, the greater the impact. Synthetic fibres have a memory and retain the effects of being overloaded or shock loaded and can fail at a later time, even though loaded within the working load range.

Retirement

Understanding the Rope Design/ Construction: It is first important to understand the design of the specific rope in use.

Most ropes are designed to have features specifically tailored to their application. These features can lead to misconceptions during visual inspections. When a rope has a braided cover, it is only possible to visually inspect the cover (which, at best, carries only 50% of the load). Rope designs utilising HMPE fibres will show initial rapid abrasion until the rope has a fuzzy appearance – this appearance actually acts as a protective layer.

Determining the Average Condition of the Rope: The average condition of a rope can be an important factor in determining the rope's retirement. To determine the average condition, walk the entire length of the rope and document its overall condition. Many ropes can be classified by the total amount of overall wear and cleanliness.

Ropes

High Modulus PolyEthylene (HMPE) Ropes

The term 'high modulus fibre mooring lines' generally refers to ropes made from high modulus fibres such as aramid and High Modulus Polyethylene (HMPE). These fibres are much stronger and stiffer than conventional synthetic fibres such as polyamide, polyester and polypropylene. This strength ensures that their useful life should be far more than that of other synthetic ropes, provided they are not damaged.

Typical high modulus synthetic fibre ropes are as strong as steel wire ropes, size-for-size, and are lighter, more flexible and easier to handle. They are presented as a possible replacement for wire ropes. However, they are more susceptible to abrasion damage and have a low working temperature.

High modulus lines, which are about twice as elastic as the wire auxiliary lines, are not as greatly affected by the relatively short leads from the bitts to the shore mooring points, but they still have low elastic elongation properties. This provides good control of the ship while alongside but, owing to this low elasticity, the use of tails with a higher elasticity should be considered.

Some vessels now use high modulus fibre rope instead of wire rope as winch-mounted mooring lines. The principal advantage is the lighter weight, which requires a smaller deck crew to handle the lines and also reduces the chances of injuries. Other advantages are that high modulus fibre ropes do not corrode, do not require greasing and generally last longer than wire ropes in typical service. However, the high modulus fibre ropes cost more than conventional fibre ropes and much more than wire ropes of the same strength.

Installation of HMPE Ropes to Mooring Winches and the Use of Split-Drums

During initial installation, the working line should be secured with significant back tension. While spooling the line on to the winch, the line must be closely packed to minimise areas where the rope could bury in to layers of the winch. Each layer should be installed in the valley of the previous layer or crossed over to support each previous layer. Never stack the layers on top of each other.

When the HMPE line is used, 8-10 wraps must always remain on the tension side of the split-drum.

Further information:

Splicing instructions for Samson HMPE ropes: http://tinyurl.com/HMPE-splicing

Vessel mooring system for HMPE ropes: http://tinyurl.com/HMPE-mooring

OCIMF/SIGTTO joint information paper: 'Guide to Purchasing High Modulus Synthetic Fibre Mooring Lines': http://tinyurl.com/pluoj43

Towing

High modulus fibre ropes utilising materials such as kevlar®, vectran® and dyneema® present a cost effective alternative to wire rope for towing purposes. However, it must be noted that, where such ropes have been used as replacements for wire tow ropes, they show wear and tear in line with traditional wire ropes. Nylon rope is much more elastic than wire rope and high modulus fibre rope and, in towing applications, this is a desirable property. However, it is generally undesirable where the motions of the moored or towed vessel must be restricted.

Abrasion

In general, all synthetic rope abrades quite easily, requiring abrasion protection or chafe gear to prevent premature wear. The fitting of such protection, while helping to prevent damage to the synthetic ropes, also has the benefit of helping to avoid injury to personnel as well as protecting the ropes from heat damage. The use of such abrasion protection can double the life of the synthetic rope.

Several options are available, including those made from high modulus fibre rope as follows:

Item: ProMoor	Item: ProGard	Item: Dynalene	Item: DC Gard	Item: Inverted Firehose
Description: Sewn Woven HMPE Application: Working lines body Pros and Cons: Moderate cost. Good durability Fixed to rope or hardware. Install pre-splicing	Description: Velcro Woven HMPE Application: Working lines eye or body Pros and Cons: Moderate cost. Good durability. Easy to install on spliced rope	Description: 32-strand braided chafe sleeve Application: Tug/Mooring eye and body Pros and Cons: Higher cost. Excellent durability Fixed to rope. Install during splicing	Description: 32-strand braided jacket Application: Tug-body up to apex of eyePros and Cons: Highest cost Excellent durability. Fixed to rope or hardware. Install during splicing	Description: Inverted hose-rubber and polyester or nylon fibre Application: Mooring lines body Pros and Cons: Low cost. Fair durability Fix to hardware. Install pre-splicing

Figure 47.12 - Options to prevent abrasion or chaffing of synthetic ropes

Manila Rope, Three-Strand

Features:

- Firm-gripping rope
- knots well and will not slide
- minimal stretching.

Chains

DIA		CIR	Linear density	Linear density	Grade 1 and Grade 2		Grade 3		Design factory
					Tensile strength	Tensile strength	Tensile strength	Tensile strength	
In	mm	In	lbs/100 ft	Kg/30 mt	lbF	kgF	lbF	kgF	Range
3/6	5	9/16	1.37	0.623	405	184	324	184	5 - 12
1/4	6	3/4	1.82	0.827	540	245	432	245	5 - 12
5/16	8	1	2.64	1.200	900	409	702	409	5 - 12
3/8	10	1 1/8	3.79	1.723	1,215	552	972	552	5 - 12
7/16	11	1 1/4	4.87	2.214	1,575	716	1,260	716	5 - 12
1/2	12	1 1/2	6.96	3.164	2,385	1,084	1,908	1,084	5 - 12
9/16	14	1 3/4	9.63	4.377	3,105	1,411	2,484	1,411	5 - 12
5/8	16	2	12.7	5.773	3,960	1,800	3,168	1,800	5 - 12
3/4	18	2 1/4	15.9	7.227	4,860	2,209	3,888	2,209	5 - 12
1 3/16	20	2 1/2	18.6	8.455	5,850	2,659	4,680	2,659	5 - 12
7/8	22	2 3/4	21.4	9.727	6,930	3,150	5,544	3,150	5 - 12
1	24	3	25.7	11.682	8,100	3,682	6,480	3,682	5 - 12
1 1/16	26	3 1/4	29.8	13.545	9,450	4,295	7,560	4,295	5 - 12
1 1/8	28	3 1/2	34.3	15.591	10,800	4,909	8,640	4,909	5 - 12
1 1/4	30	3 3/4	39.7	18.045	12,150	5,523	9,720	5,523	5 - 12
1 5/16	32	4	45.6	20.727	13,500	6,136	10,800	6,136	5 - 12
1 1/2	36	4 1/2	57.0	25.909	16,650	7,568	13,320	7,568	5 - 12
1 5/8	40	5	71.1	31.318	20,250	9,205	16,200	9,205	5 - 12
1 3/4	44	5 1/2	85.0	38.636	23,850	10,841	19,080	10,841	5 - 12
2	48	6	102	46.364	27,900	12,682	22,320	12,682	5 - 12

Table 47.1 - Chain specifications

Chains

Chains are generally used for cargo handling purposes, such as the securing of containers, items of RoRo cargo, heavy lift items and timber deck cargoes.

In many cases, the chain will have been manufactured to the appropriate length, link size and type, and will have end fittings already in place, if appropriate. Chains can be used for securing other types of cargo but they are more difficult to use than wire lashings and do not render when led through or round items of cargo or lashing points. The main advantage of chain is that it does not stretch appreciably under normal loadings and can, therefore, be set tight when being fitted. However, throughout the voyage, the forces acting on the cargo will cause it to move slightly and this may cause the chain lashings to stretch slightly and slacken a little, and may also cause the cargo to settle onto foundations and dunnaging and lead to slackening. Chains, like other lashings, must be checked and re-tightened as necessary at intervals throughout the voyage.

Other uses of chain on board include:

- Anchor chain
- permanent moorings for FPSOs
- chafing chain on SBMs/SPMs
- towing
- buoys
- chain stoppers for wire stoppering off rope
- lifeboat lashings
- deck cargo lashings
- chain blocks and pulleys
- turnbuckle chains
- bridle chains on derricks
- stays, etc.

Annealing

The austenitic stainless steels cannot be hardened by thermal treatments (but they do harden rapidly by cold work). The purpose of annealing is to remove stresses or soften the material for improved machinability or formability, alter the physical or mechanical properties or produce a defined structure. In general, annealing is the opposite of hardening. Annealing consists of heating a metal to a specific temperature, holding it at that temperature for a set length of time and then cooling the metal to room temperature. The cooling method depends on the metal and the properties desired. Some metals are furnace-cooled and others are cooled by burying them in ashes, lime or other insulating materials.

Welding produces areas that have molten metal next to areas that are at room temperature. As the weld cools, internal stresses occur along with hard spots and brittleness. Welding can actually weaken the metal. Annealing is one of the methods used for correcting these problems. Annealing (often referred to as solution treatment) not only recrystallises the work-hardened grains but also takes chromium carbides (precipitated at grain boundaries in sensitised steels) back into solution in the austenite. The treatment also homogenises dendritic weld metal structures and relieves all remnant stresses from cold working. Annealing temperatures are usually above 1,040°C, although some types may be annealed at closely controlled temperatures as low as 1,010°C when fine grain size is important. Time at temperature is often kept short to hold surface scaling to a minimum or to control grain growth, which can lead to 'orange peel' forming.

Safety and Inspection Procedures for Chains and Hooks

- Responsible personnel should inspect chains, including the hooks, at least once a month. Chains that are used for heavy and continuous loading require more frequent inspections. Personnel must pay particular attention to the small radius fillets at the neck of hooks for any deviation from the original inner arc. Each link and hook must be examined for small dents, cracks, sharp nicks or cuts, worn surfaces and distortions. Chains that show any of these weaknesses must be replaced. Apply a light coat of lubricant to prevent rusting and store chains in a dry and well-ventilated place
- when hoisting heavy metal objects using chains for slings, insert padding around the sharp corners of the load to protect the chain links from being cut. The padding may be either planks or heavy fabric. Do not let chains twist or kink when under strain. Do not connect chains with bolts or wire because such connections weaken the chain and limit its safe working capacity
- worn or damaged links should be cut from the chain and replaced with a cold shut link. The cold shut link must be closed and welded to equal the strength of the other links. Small chain links can be cut with a bolt cutter. Large chain links must be cut with a hacksaw or oxyacetylene torch.

Shackles

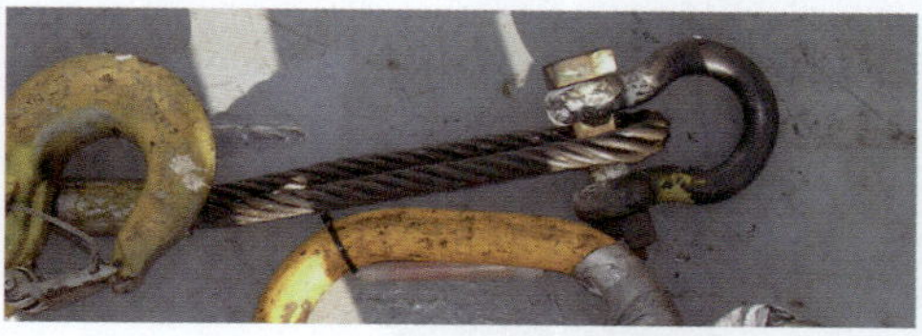

The preferred type of shackles are alloy shackles to US Federal Specification RR-C-27, of the bow or anchor type fitted with a safety pin, ie bolt, nut and split pin. The safe working loads of alloy shackles are set out in the following table.

Anchor shackles with screw pin

Safety anchor shackles bolt type

Chain shackles with screw pin

Safety chain shackles bolt type

DIA bow	DIA pin	Inside width	Inside length		SWL	Width of bow
			Chain type	Anchor type		
mm	mm	mm	mm	mm	mm	mm
13	16	22	43	51	2 t	32
16	19	26	51	64	3.25 t	43
19	22	31	59	76	4.75 t	51
22	26	36	73	83	6.5 t	58
26	28	43	85	95	8.5 t	68
28	32	47	90	108	9.5 t	75
32	35	51	94	115	12 t	83
35	38	57	115	133	13.5 t	92
38	42	60	127	146	17 t	99
45	52	74	149	178	25 t	126
52	58	83	171	197	35 t	146
64	70	105	203	254	55 t	185
76	83	127	230	330	85 t	190
90	96	146	267	381	120 t	238

Minimum breaking strength = 6 x SWL

Table 47.2 - Safe working loads of alloy shackles

It is important to ensure that the correct shackle bolt or pin is fitted as a common problem exists where lost high grade shackle pins are replaced with standard bolts that are not capable of taking the load.

Slings

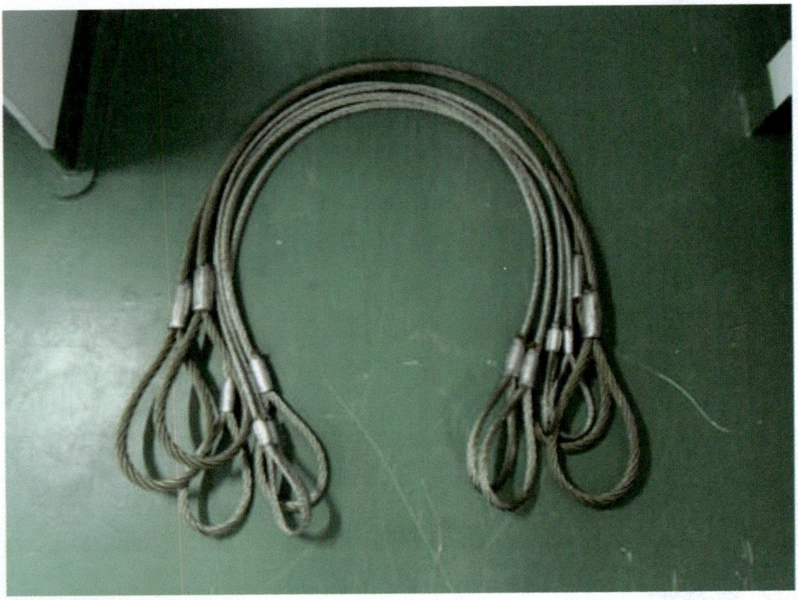

Figure 47.13 - Wire strops

Slings are made from a wide variety of materials including rope, wire rope, wire mesh, synthetic webbing, chain and rope netting. Whatever the material, the following basic rules apply:

- Prior to use, slings must be inspected for damage
- slings should be stowed off the deck, preferably vertical, and in a way that allows them to be easily identified. They should be kept free from abrasion, corrosive action, moisture, extreme heat or kinking
- all slings must be clearly marked with the date of manufacture and the SWL
- sharp edges on loads should be padded
- slings should not be pulled out from under loads. Instead, loads should be settled onto raised blocks to allow their removal.

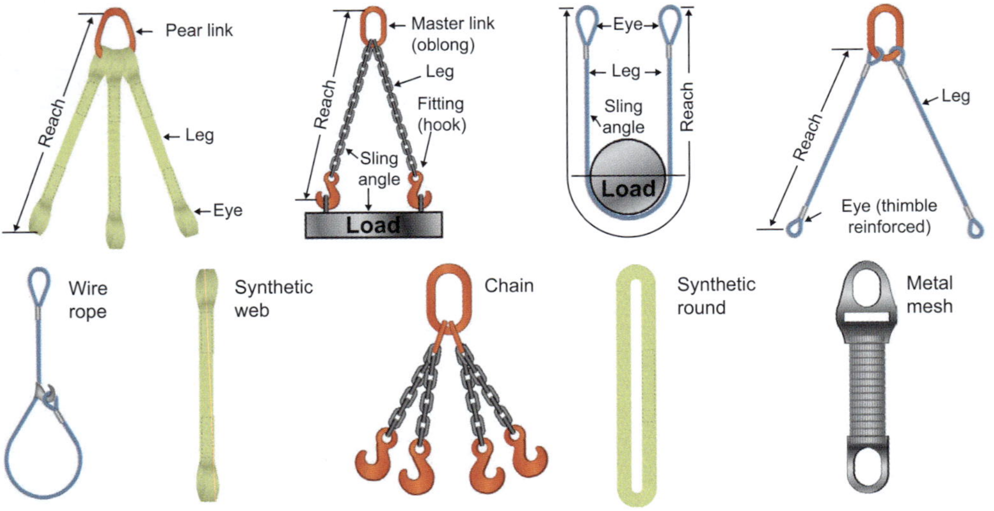

Sling Angles

Sling angles have a direct and sometimes dramatic effect on the working load limit of a sling. This angle, which is measured between a horizontal line and the sling leg or body, may apply to a single leg sling in an angled vertical or basket hitch, or to a multi-legged bridle sling. When pull is exerted at an angle on a leg, the tension or stress on each leg is increased.

To illustrate, each sling leg in a vertical basket hitch absorbs 500 lbs of stress from a 1,000 lb load. The same load, when lifted in a 60° basket hitch, exerts 577 lbs of tension on each leg.

It is critical, therefore, that working load limits are reduced to account for sling angles. Angles less than 45° are not recommended and those below 30° should be avoided whenever possible.

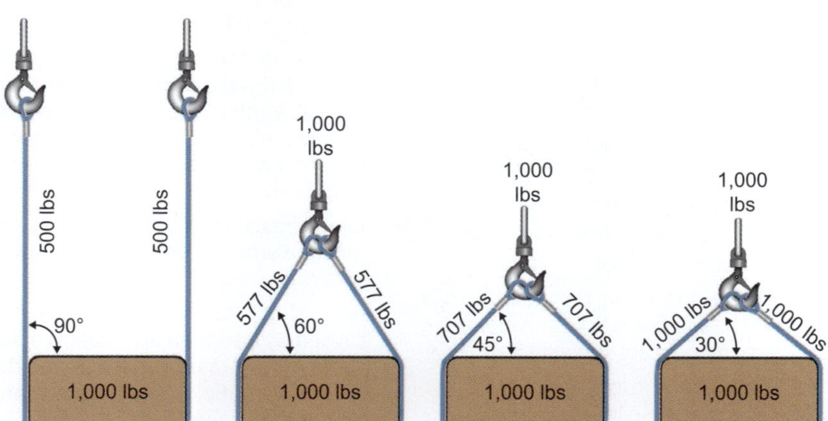

Slings

Care and Use of Chain Slings

Although chain slings are designed for rugged, lasting service, precautions should be taken to extend the product's useful life. Certain hazards are inherent in the operation of chain slings and users must exercise intelligence, care and common sense to ensure a safe working environment:

- Never exceed the working load limit of a chain sling
- all fittings and attachments must have a working load limit (WLL) equal to or greater than that of the chain. If not, the assembly must be rated at the WLL of the weakest component
- do not rest or drop load on chain
- eliminate all twists, knots or kinks before lifting
- do not point load hooks - the load should be seated properly within the throat opening and centred in the bowl of the hook
- balance the load to avoid undue stress on one leg of multi-leg slings
- never bounce, jerk or shock load a sling when lifting or lowering items. Remove slack by slowly applying the load to the chain
- use pads around sharp corners
- never force or hammer hooks or chain into position
- never anneal alloy chain slings
- do not use in acid solutions. Consult the manufacturer for recommendations
- if possible, avoid extreme temperatures (under 20°F or over 350°F)
- temporary and permanent reductions to working load limits occur when chain slings are used at high temperatures
- return slings to the manufacturer to ensure proper repair procedures are followed
- clean chain slings regularly since dirt and grit can cause wear at link bearing points
- protect chain from corrosion
- store chain slings in a clean, dry area, preferably by hanging on racks or A-frames; slings stored on floors are subject to abuse
- institute a continuous inspection programme to maximise life expectancy.

Maintenance of Slings - Chains

Chain slings must be cleaned prior to each inspection, as dirt or oil may hide damage. If a sling has stretched so that it is more than 3% longer than it was when new, it is unsafe and must be discarded.

If a sling has become deformed to the extent that its individual links cannot move within each other freely (termed 'binding'), this is an indication that the sling is unsafe. Generally, wear occurs on the load-bearing inside ends of the links. Pushing links together so that the inside surface becomes clearly visible is the best way to check for this type of wear. Wear may also occur, however, on the outside of links when the chain is dragged along abrasive surfaces or pulled out from under heavy loads. Both types of wear weaken slings and make accidents more likely. Heavy nicks and/or gouges must be filed smooth, measured with calipers, and then compared with the manufacturer's minimum allowable safe dimensions. If in doubt, or in borderline situations, do not use the sling. In addition, never attempt to repair the welded components on a sling. If the sling needs repair of this nature, the supervisor must be notified.

Care and Use of Wire Rope Slings

- The rated capacity of a wire rope sling is based on the nominal or catalogue strength of the wire rope and factors affecting the overall strength. These factors include termination efficiencies (see chart on page 1180), type of hitch, number of rope parts in the sling body, diameter around which the sling is bent and the diameter of the pin or hook over which the sling eye is placed
- never force the eye of a sling onto a hook or pin that has a diameter larger than the natural width of the eye. Avoid placing a sling eye onto a hook or pin whose diameter is less than the diameter of the sling body
- rated capacities of fittings and attachments must be equal to or greater than that of the wire rope sling
- never shock load a sling. The actual force caused by a sudden application of load can easily exceed rated capacities and damage a sling. Abruptly releasing a load can also damage the sling

- protect the sling body against sharp edges and corners of loads, protrusions or abrasive surfaces. Sharp bends can distort wire rope and reduce its strength
- fibre core wire rope slings should never be exposed to temperatures exceeding 200°F. Avoid using IWRC (independent wire rope core) wire rope slings at temperatures above 400°F or below minus 60°F
- slings are susceptible to damage and strength loss when used in chemically active environments
- slings fabricated with a hand-tucked splice can unravel and fail if the sling is allowed to rotate during use
- do not drag slings across floors or pull from underneath loads
- avoid twists, kinks and knots before lifting
- store wire rope slings where they will not be subjected to dirt, moisture, extreme heat, corrosion or mechanical damage.

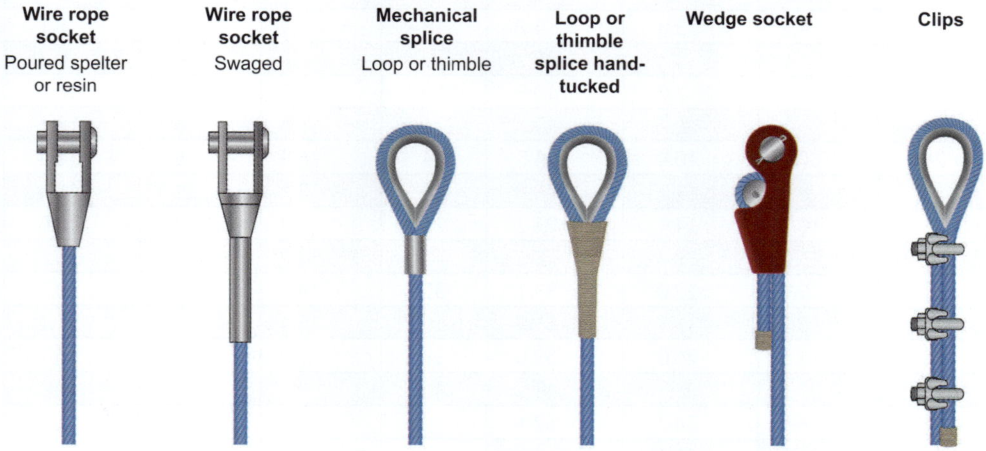

Slings

6 × 196 × 36 Groups steel core				6 × 196 × 36 Groups fibre core			
Safe working load				Safe working load			
Rope DIA	Single leg	Leg angle 0-90° 2 leg	Leg angle 0-90° 3 & 4 leg	Rope DIA	Single leg	Leg angle 0-90° 2 leg	Leg angle 0-90° 3 & 4 leg
mm	tonne	tonne	tonne	mm	tonne	tonne	tonne
10	1.3	1.8	2.7	10	1.2	1.7	2.5
11	1.6	2.1	3.3	11	1.4	2.0	3.0
12	1.8	2.6	3.9	12	1.7	2.4	3.6
13	2.2	3.0	4.5	13	2.0	2.8	4.2
14	2.5	3.5	5.3	14	2.3	3.2	4.9
16	3.3	4.6	6.9	16	3.0	4.3	6.4
18	4.2	5.8	8.7	18	3.9	5.4	8.1
19	4.6	6.5	9.7	19	4.3	6.0	9.0
20	5.1	7.2	10.8	20	4.8	6.7	10.0
22	6.2	8.7	13.1	22	5.8	8.1	12.1
24	7.4	10.4	15.5	24	6.9	9.6	14.4
26	8.7	12.2	18.2	26	8.1	11.3	16.9
28	10.1	14.1	21.2	28	9.3	13.1	19.6
32	13.1	18.4	27.6	32	12.2	17.1	25.6
35	15.7	22.0	33.1	35	14.6	20.4	30.7
36	16.7	23.3	35.0	36	15.4	21.6	31.4
38	18.6	26.0	39.0	38	17.2	24.1	36.1
40	20.6	28.8	43.3	40	19.1	26.7	40.0
44	24.8	34.7	52.1				
48	29.6	41.4	62.2				
52	34.8	48.7	73.1				
54	37.4	52.4	78.5				
56	40.2	56.3	84.4				
60	46.2	64.7	97.0				
64	52.4	73.4	110.0				
70	62.8	87.9	131.0				
76	74.0	103.6	155.0				

Table 47.3 - Safe working loads of wire rope slings based on wire rope with a tensile strength of 180 kgf/mm^2 (1,770 tensile grade) and a safety factor of 5:1. Compiled in compliance with Bs 1290 1983 and Bs 302 Pt.2 1987. Uniform Load Method Calculation used throughout

Maintenance of Slings – Wire Rope

Wire rope slings, like chain slings, must be cleaned prior to each inspection because they are also subject to damage hidden by dirt or oil. In addition, they must be lubricated according to the manufacturer's instructions. Lubrication prevents or reduces corrosion and wear due to friction and abrasion. Before applying any lubricant, however, the sling user should make certain that the sling is dry. Applying lubricant to a wet or damp sling traps moisture against the metal and hastens corrosion. Corrosion deteriorates wire rope. It may be indicated by pitting, but it is sometimes hard to detect. Therefore, if a wire rope sling shows any sign of significant deterioration, that sling must be removed until it can be examined by a person who is qualified to determine the extent of the damage. By following the above guidelines to proper sling use and maintenance, and by the avoidance of kinking, it is possible to greatly extend a wire rope sling's useful service life.

Synthetic Web Slings

Synthetic web slings are generally constructed of nylon or, less frequently, polyester. They are often selected when expensive, highly polished, fragile or delicate loads must be lifted because the softness of the web will not mar, deface or scratch loads, while its flexibility assures a firm, secure grip around the item being lifted. The light weight and flexibility of the material allow the slings to be quickly and safely handled by riggers. Web slings have the ability to elongate, absorbing and minimising the effects of heavy shock loads. Nylon slings may stretch 6 to 8% at rated capacity, while polyester slings limit stretch to approximately 3% under similar circumstances. Long life cycles may be experienced since synthetic web is unaffected by moisture, mildew, rot and certain chemicals. Polyester should be used in the presence of acids and nylon in the presence of alkalis. Synthetic web slings are manufactured from light or heavy duty material that has been surface treated to improve abrasion resistance, seal out moisture, and prevent grit from penetrating the web and causing internal wear. Slings can be fabricated from single or multiple plies and may include accessories such as edgeguard, wear pads or sleeves. They are available in several configurations:

Type 1: Triangle & Choker (TC) - Hardware on each end produces the most effective choker hitch. Can also be used in vertical and basket hitches.

Type 2: Triangle & Triangle (TT) - Hardware on each end for use in basket or vertical hitch.

Type 3: Flat Eye & Eye (EE) - Popular, versatile sling used in vertical, choker and basket hitches. Easy to remove from underneath loads.

Type 4: Twisted Eye & Eye (EE) - Eyes turned at a right angle to sling body. Forms superior choker hitch and allows better fit on crane hook in basket hitch.

Slings

Type 5: Endless (EN) - Economical and adaptable sling with no fixed wear points. Used in all hitches.

Type 6: Reversed Eye (RE) - Extremely strong and durable for continuous and/or abusive applications. Wear pads on both sides of body.

Care and Use of Synthetic Slings

Mechanical Considerations

- Determine weight of the load
- select sling having suitable characteristics for the type of load, hitch and environment
- slings shall not be loaded in excess of the rated capacity. Consideration should be given to sling angles
- slings with fittings used in a choker hitch shall be of sufficient length to assure that the choking action is on the webbing
- slings used in a basket hitch shall have the load balanced to prevent slippage
- slings shall not be dragged on the floor or over an abrasive surface
- slings shall not be twisted or tied into knots, or joined by knotting
- slings shall not be pulled from under loads when the load is resting on the sling
- slings shall always be protected from being cut by sharp corners, sharp edges, protrusions or abrasive surfaces
- do not drop slings equipped with metal fittings
- the opening in fittings shall be the proper shape and size to ensure that the fitting will seat properly in the hook or other attachment.

Environmental Considerations

- Slings should be stored in a cool, dry and dark place, and should not be exposed to ultraviolet light (sunlight)
- chemically active environments can affect the strength of synthetic web slings in varying degrees ranging from none to total degradation. The sling manufacturer should be consulted before using slings in chemically active environments
- nylon is subject to degradation in acids, ranging from none to total degradation. Polyester is resistant to many acids, but is subject to degradation ranging from none to moderate in some acids
- Polyester is subject to degradation in alkalis, ranging from none to total degradation. Nylon is resistant to many alkalis, but is subject to degradation ranging from none to moderate in some alkalis
- nylon and polyester slings shall not be used at temperatures in excess of 194°F (90°C), but they may be used in temperatures as low as minus 40°F (minus 40°C)
- slings incorporating aluminium fittings shall not be used where fumes, vapours, sprays, mists or liquids of alkalis and/or acids are present
- environments in which synthetic web slings are continuously exposed to ultraviolet light (sunlight) can affect the strength of synthetic webbing in varying degrees, ranging from slight to total degradation. The degradation is also cumulative.

Proof Testing of Slings Exposed to Ultraviolet Light

Slings used in environments where they are subject to continuous exposure to ultraviolet light (sunlight) should be proof tested to two times rated capacity semi-annually, or more frequently, depending on the severity of exposure. Testing has confirmed that nylon slings lose 50 to 60% of their strength after 36 months of continuous exposure to sunlight. Polyester loses about 30% over the same period.

Maintenance of Slings – Fibre Ropes and Synthetic Webs

Fibre ropes and synthetic webs are generally discarded rather than serviced or repaired. Operators must always follow the manufacturer's recommendations.

CHAPTER 48

Cranes and Lifting Equipment

General Requirements for Lifting

Equipment

Lifting equipment is required to be:

(a) Of adequate strength and stability for each load, having regard in particular to the stress induced at its mounting or fixing points; and,

(b) securely anchored, or

(c) adequately ballasted or counterbalanced, or

(d) supported by outriggers, as necessary to ensure its stability when lifting.

The maximum Safe Working Load (SWL) and maximum radius of operation of all derricks and lifting appliances are required to be part of the specification on all new constructions with associated ropes, wires and guys, eye-plates, shackles and blocks designed to meet these loads.

In addition to the strength and stability of the lifting equipment, consideration should also be given to the stability, angle of heel and potential down-flooding of any vessel as a result of the use of a crane, derrick or other lifting device fitted on it. This is especially important where a crane is to be fitted on a work boat or other small vessel and it is recommended that advice should be sought from the crane manufacturer in such cases prior to the crane being fitted. Similarly it is recommended that a check of the vessel's stability should be carried out by a suitably qualified person, prior to installation of a crane to ensure that the vessel is capable of operating safely with the crane fitted and in use. Failure to do this could have serious consequences for the safety of the vessel and the workers on it.

If counterbalance weights are moveable, effective precautions should be taken to ensure that the lifting appliance is not used for lifting in an unstable condition. In particular all weights should be correctly installed and positioned.

The operator should check safety devices fitted to lifting appliances before work starts and at regular intervals thereafter to ensure that they are working properly.

Accessories for Lifting etc

Every part of a load that is used in lifting it, as well as anything attached to the load and used for that purpose should be of good construction, of adequate strength for the purpose for which it is to be used and free from defects.

Accessories for lifting should be stored in conditions which will not result in damage or degradation.

Register of Lifting Appliances

All vessels are required to maintain a register of lifting appliances and loose gear in a form based on the model recommended by the International Labour Organization and shown at http://tinyurl.com/l5eex4s

Regular Maintenance

In order to ensure that all parts of lifting equipment and related equipment are kept in good repair and working order, regular preventative maintenance should be carried out. Maintenance should include regular examinations by a competent person. Such examinations should be carried out as required by the Regulations but in any event at least once annually. Checks should look for general material defects such as cracks, distortion, corrosion and wear and tear that could affect safe working load and overall strength.

When there is any suspicion that any appliance or item of equipment may have been subjected to excessive loads, exceeding the Safe Working Load (SWL), or subjected to treatment likely to cause damage, it should be taken out of service until it can be subjected to a thorough examination by a competent person.

Source: 'Code of Safe Working Practices for Merchant Seamen'

General Requirements for Lifting Equipment

Courtesy of Gary Ritchie

Rotating machinery and machinery that could cause a hazard should be guarded

Listed below are some suggested maintenance items:

- *Greasing should be thorough and frequent, as dry bearings impose additional loads that can lead to failure*
- *the condition of all ropes and chains should be checked regularly for wear, damage and corrosion and replaced as necessary*
- *shackles, links and rings should be renewed when wear or damage is evident*
- *structures should be examined frequently for corrosion, cracks, distortion and wear of bearings, securing points, etc.*
- *hollow structures such as gantries or masts should be checked for trapped water inside. If water is found, the structure should be drained, appropriately treated and then sealed*
- *regular function tests of controls, stops, brakes, safety devices for hoisting gear etc, should be carried out preferably before the start of operations.*

The list is illustrative only and additional items may be appropriate dependent upon the equipment fitted to an individual vessel.

Any replacement parts must be in accordance with the manufacturer's instructions and be of an equivalent construction to the original part if instructions are not available. This is because replacement with incorrect parts or parts of inferior quality can seriously affect the safety of the lifting appliance.

After any repairs or alterations are made to any lifting appliance it should undergo a thorough examination and be retested if appropriate. Also if any significant changes are made or noticed to the general condition of the appliance the above applies.

Testing, Thorough Examination and Inspection

Ship's lifting equipment is not to be used unless it has been tested by a competent person within the preceding five years.

Courtesy of Gary Ritchie

Access for maintenance should be considered

Where the safety of lifting equipment depends on the installation conditions, it should be inspected by a competent person before it is used for the first time. Such inspections should be undertaken *on*

Courtesy of Gary Ritchie

The condition of all component parts should be inspected

Source: 'Code of Safe Working Practices for Merchant Seamen'

initial installation or after re-assembly at another location, to ensure that it has been installed correctly in accordance with any manufacturer's instructions, and is safe for workers to operate as well as being able to function safely.

Any lifting equipment or accessory for lifting which is, or has been, exposed to conditions which could cause deterioration in its condition should be:

(a) Thoroughly examined
- *(i) in the case of lifting equipment for lifting persons or an accessory for lifting, at least every 6 months;*
- *(ii) in the case of other lifting equipment, at least every 12 months; or*
- *(iii) in either case, in accordance with an examination scheme; and*
- *(iv) whenever exceptional circumstances which are liable to jeopardise the safety of the lifting equipment have occurred; and*

(b) where appropriate, inspected by a competent person at suitable intervals,

No accessories for lifting should be used unless they have been thoroughly examined within the 12 months immediately prior to such use.

The operating instructions provided by the manufacturer should give the crane operator and maintenance personnel all the information relevant to operating the crane in a safe and efficient manner. These should also highlight all systems that must be isolated prior to conducting any maintenance on the crane. The process for isolating (electrical or mechanical) the crane systems must be provided and the personnel responsible for the maintenance of the crane must be aware of these requirements.

Courtesy of Gary Ritchie

CCTV cameras are an important safety feature

Certificates

Testing a pedestal crane on an OSV using water weights. These are water-filled proof load bags that are designed to provide a test load instead of traditional solid weights. It is a safe, practical and economical method for load testing.

The employer is required to ensure that a certificate is obtained no later than 28 days after the carrying out of any test and thorough examination of any lifting equipment.

Courtesy of Water Weights Ltd

Source: 'Code of Safe Working Practices for Merchant Seamen'

General Requirements for Lifting Equipment

The period of 28 days should however be regarded as the absolute maximum. Whenever possible the certificate, or at least a "provisional certificate", should be provided at the time of test. Absence of a valid certificate could delay operations if a port operator, or a statutory body, requests production of a valid certificate before allowing work, such as unloading, to proceed.

Qualifications

Courtesy of Gary Ritchie

Crane operator familiarisation and training is essential

The qualifications and competence of the crane operator are dependent on the crane being used and on any national standards that may be in place. For example, the national standards for offshore operation of cranes in the UK are based on British Standard (BS) 7121-11 (Offshore Cranes). These standards require all certified crane operators to be assessed every two years by a third party. It should be verified that the operator is competent in the use of the cranes fitted on board the particular vessel.

Controls

Make-shift extensions should not be fitted to controls nor any unauthorised alterations made to them. Foot-operated controls should have slip resistant surfaces.

No lifting device should be used with any locking pawl, safety attachment or device rendered inoperative. If, exceptionally, limit switches need to be isolated in order to lower a crane to its stowage position, the utmost care should be taken to ensure the operation is completed safely.

Safety Measures

A powered appliance should always have a person at the controls while it is in operation; it should never be left to run with a control secured in the "ON" position.

If any powered appliance is to be left unattended with the power on, loads should be taken off and controls put in "NEUTRAL" or "OFF" positions. Where practical, controls should be locked or otherwise inactivated to prevent accidental restarting. When work is completed, power should be shut off.

The person operating any lifting appliance should have no other duties which might interfere with their primary task. They should be in a proper and protected position, facing controls and, so far as is practicable, with a clear view of the whole operation.

Where the operator of the lifting appliance does not have a clear view of the whole of the path of travel of any load carried by that appliance, appropriate precautions should be taken to prevent danger. Generally this requirement should be met by the employment

Source: 'Code of Safe Working Practices for Merchant Seamen'

of a competent and properly trained signaller designated to give instructions to the operator. A signaller includes any person who gives directional instructions to an operator while they are moving a load, whether by manual signals, by radio or otherwise.

The signaller should have a clear view of the path of travel of the load where the operator of the lifting appliance cannot see it.

Courtesy of Gary Ritchie

Crane operators must be familiar with all safety and operational functions

Lifting Operations

Every lifting operation must be:

(a) Properly planned;

(b) appropriately supervised; and

(c) carried out in a safe manner.

All lifting operations must be properly planned, appropriately supervised and carried out to protect the safety of workers. While this applies to all vessels, it is particularly important where cranes are being used on work boats and other small vessels as overloading of the crane, or attempting to lift at the wrong angle could, in some circumstances, result in the vessel sinking.

No person should be lifted except where the equipment is designed or specially adapted and equipped for the purpose or for rescue or in emergencies.

Weather conditions can play a significant part in the carrying out of lifting operations whether in the open air or within the vessel. In the former case high winds or wave action can, for example, cause suspended loads to swing dangerously or cause mobile equipment to topple.

Loads should if possible not be lifted over a person or any access way, and personnel should avoid passing under a load which is being lifted.

All loads should be properly slung and properly attached to lifting gear, and all gear properly attached to appliances.

Figure 48.1 - A tugger winch in use offshore

The use of lifting appliances to drag heavy loads with the fall at an angle to the vertical is inadvisable because of the friction and other factors involved and should only take place in exceptional circumstances where the angle is small, there is ample margin between the loads handled and the safe working load of the appliance, and particular care is taken. In all other cases winches should be used instead. Derricks should never be used in union purchase for such work.

Any lifts by two or more appliances simultaneously can create hazardous situations and should only be carried out where unavoidable. They should be properly conducted under the close supervision of a responsible person, after thorough planning of the operation.

Lifting appliances should not be used in a manner likely to subject them to excessive over-turning moments.

Ropes, chains and slings should not be knotted.

A thimble or loop splice in any wire rope should have at least three tucks with a whole strand of rope and two tucks with one half of the wires cut out of each strand. The strands in all cases should be tucked against the lay of the rope. Any other form of splice which can be shown to be as efficient as the above can also be used.

Wire ropes should be regularly inspected and treated with suitable lubricants. These should be thoroughly applied so as to prevent internal

Source: 'Code of Safe Working Practices for Merchant Seamen'

General Requirements for Lifting Equipment

corrosion as well as corrosion on the outside. The ropes should never be allowed to dry out.

Before any attempt is made to free equipment that has become jammed under load, every effort should first be made to take off the load safely. Precautions should be taken to guard against sudden or unexpected freeing. Others not directly engaged in the operation should keep in safe or protected positions.

When machinery and, in particular, pistons are to be lifted by means of screw-in eye bolts, the eye-bolts should be checked to ensure that they have collars, that the threads are in good condition and that the bolts are screwed hard down on to their collars. Screw holds for lifting bolts in piston heads should be cleaned and the threads checked to see that they are not wasted before the bolts are inserted.

Safe Working Load (SWL)

A load greater than the safe working load should not be lifted unless:

(a) A test is required by regulation; and

(b) the weight of the load is known and is the appropriate proof load; and

(c) the lift is a straight lift by a single appliance; and

(d) the lift is supervised by the competent person who would normally supervise a test and carry out a thorough inspection; and

(e) the competent person specifies in writing that the lift is appropriate in weight and other respects to act as a test of the plant, and agrees to the detailed plan of the lift; and

(f) no person is exposed to danger thereby.

Any grab fitted to a lifting appliance should be of an appropriate size, taking into account the safe working load of the appliance, the additional stresses on the appliance likely to result from the operation, and the material being lifted.

In the case of a single sheave block used in double purchase the working load applied to the wire should be assumed to equal half the load suspended from the block.

The safe working load of a lift truck means its actual lifting capacity, which relates to the load which can be lifted, in the case of a fork lift truck, the distance from the centre of gravity of the load from the heels of the forks. It may also specify lower capacities in certain situations, eg for lifts beyond a certain height.

Use of Winches and Cranes

The drum end of wire runners or falls should be secured to winch barrels or crane drums by proper clamps or U-bolts. The runner or fall should be long enough to leave at least three turns on the barrel or drum at maximum normal extension. Slack turns of wire or rope on a barrel or drum should be avoided as they are likely to pull out suddenly under load.

Ships' cranes should be properly operated and maintained in accordance with manufacturers' instructions. Companies, employers and masters, as appropriate, should ensure that sufficient technical information is available including the following information:

(a) Length, size and safe working load of falls and topping lifts;

(b) Safe working load of all fittings;

(c) Boom limiting angles;

(d) Manufacturers' instructions for replacing wires, topping up hydraulics and other maintenance as appropriate.

Source: 'Code of Safe Working Practices for Merchant Seamen'

Defect Reporting and Testing – Advice to Competent Person

There is a legal requirement for a lifting plant to be tested every five years. This section provides advice to the competent person carrying out the test.

The requirements for testing a lifting plant will be met if before use one of the following appropriate tests is carried out:

(a) Proof loading the plant concerned; or

(b) in appropriate cases by testing a sample to destruction; or

(c) in the case of re-testing after repairs or modifications, such a test that satisfies the competent person who subsequently examines the plant (the re-testing of ships' lifting appliances may be effected by means of a static test, eg by dynamometer where appropriate; or

(d) in the case of a lift truck, the test should be a functional test to verify that the truck is able to perform the task for which it was designed. This test should include a check to ensure that all controls function correctly and that all identification and capacity plates are fitted and contain correct information. A dynamic test should include travelling and manoeuvring, stacking, a lowering speed check and tilt leakage test with the rated load including relevant attachments where appropriate. Following the test the truck should be examined to ensure that it has no defects which would render it unsuitable for use.

Where proof loading is part of a test the test load applied should exceed the safe working load as specified in the relevant Standard, or in other cases by at least the following:

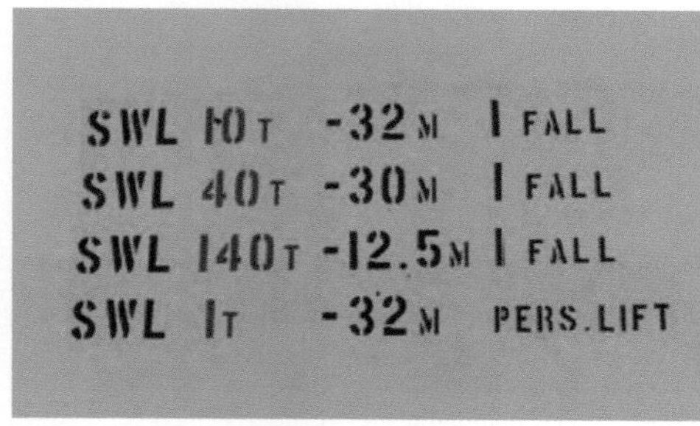

Courtesy of Gary Ritchie

Marked SWLs should be clear and unambiguous

Any defect found in any lifting plant, including plant provided by a shore authority, should be reported immediately to the master or to another responsible person who should take appropriate action.

Proof Load (Tonnes)

SWL (Tonnes)	Lifting Appliances	Single Sheave Cargo and Pulley Blocks	Multi-Sheave Cargo and Pulley Blocks	Lifting Beams and Frames, etc	Other Lifting Gear
0-10	SWL × 1.25	SWL × 4	SWL × 2	SWL × 2	SWL × 2
11-20	SWL × 1.25	SWL × 4	SWL × 2	SWL × 1.04 + 9.6	SWL × 2
21-25	SWL + 5	SWL × 4	SWL × 2	SWL × 1.04 + 9.6	SWL × 2
26-50	SWL + 5	SWL × 4	SWL × 0.933 + 27	SWL × 1.04 + 9.6	SWL × 1.22 + 20
51-160	SWL × 1.1	SWL × 4	SWL × 0.933 + 27	SWL × 1.04 + 9.6	SWL × 1.22 + 20
161+	SWL × 1.1	SWL × 4	SWL × 1.1	SWL × 1.1	SWL × 1.22 + 20

Note: *Where a lifting appliance is normally used with a specific removable attachment and the weight of that attachment is not included in the marked safe working load, then for the purposes of using the above table the safe working load of that appliance should be taken as being the marked safe working load plus the weight of the attachment.*

Source: 'Code of Safe Working Practices for Merchant Seamen'

General Requirements for Lifting Equipment

Similar principles apply to cargo securing devices as to lifting equipment. The crew and persons employed for the securing of cargoes should be instructed in the correct application and use of the cargo securing gear on board the ship. For guidance on the securing of cargoes and handling of security devices refer to the ship's approved Cargo Securing Manual.

Signals to be Used

*The following sets of coded signals are examples of those implemented by the EU Directive 92/58/EEC, but where there are accepted national signals in common use (as indicated *) these too are acceptable. Visit the HSE website to see these signs demonstrated in a video clip: http://tinyurl.com/cmlogt*

Meaning	Description	Illustration
	A. General Hand Signals	
START Attention Start of Command	both arms are extended horizontally with the palms facing forward.	
Taking the Strain or Inching the Load	the right arm points upwards with the palm facing forwards. The fingers clenched and then unclenched.	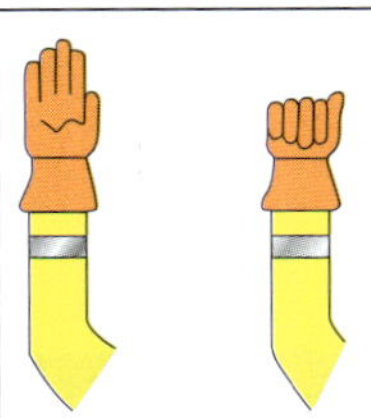 *
STOP Interruption End of movement	the right arm points upwards with the palm facing forwards.	
END of the operation (operations cease)	both hands are clasped at chest height.	
	OR	
	both arms extended at 45° down-wards and lower arms crossed back and forth sharply across torso.	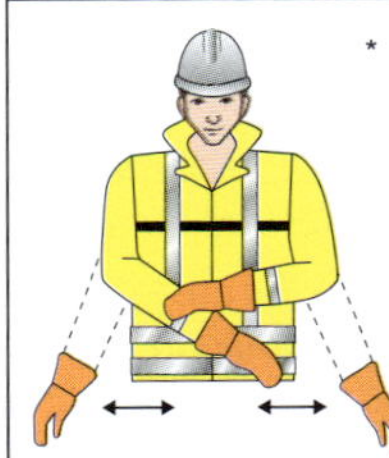 *
	B. Vertical Movements	
RAISE	the right arm points upwards with the palm facing forward and slowly makes a circle.	
LOWER	the right arm points downwards with the palm facing inwards and slowly makes a circle.	
DERRICKING THE JIB	signal with one hand. Other hand on head.	 *
		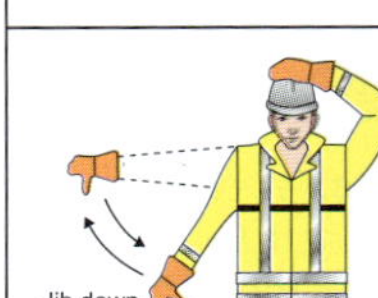 *

Source: 'Code of Safe Working Practices for Merchant Seamen'

Meaning	Description	Illustration
TELESCOPING THE JIB	*signal with one hand. Other hand on head.*	 
VERTICAL DISTANCE	*the hands indicate the relevant distance.*	
C. Horizontal Movements		
MOVE FORWARDS (Travel to me)	*both arms are bent with the palms facing upwards and the forearms make slow movements towards the body.*	
MOVE BACKWARDS (Travel from me)	*both arms are bent with the palms facing downwards and the forearms make slow movements away from the body.*	
RIGHT to the signalman's (in the direction indicated)	*the right arm is extended more or less horizontally with the palm facing downwards and slowly makes small movements to the right.*	

Meaning	Description	Illustration
LEFT to the signalman's (in the direction indicated)	*the left arm is extended more or less horizontally with the palm facing downwards and slowly makes small movements to the left.*	
HORIZONTAL DISTANCE	*the hands indicate the relevant distance.*	
SLEWING (In direction indicated)	*both arms close to side extending one arm 90° from elbow.*	 

General Requirements for Lifting Equipment

Meaning	Description	Illustration
	D. Danger	
DANGER EMERGENCY STOP	*both arms point upwards with the palms facing forwards.*	
	E. Other	
SECURE Secure the Load	*both arms are crossed closely to the chest with hands clenched.*	 *
TWISTLOCKS Twistlocks on/off	*the left arm points upwards. Rotate wrist of left hand clockwise signalling twist on, and anti-clockwise for signalling twist off.*	 *
	F. Operating Instructions	
QUICK	*all movements faster.*	
SLOW	*all movements slower.*	

Source: 'Code of Safe Working Practices for Merchant Seamen'

A crane operator must obey STOP signals no matter who gives it.

Construction and Typical Damage to Crane Wires

The most common construction for wire ropes on ship's cranes or lifting appliances is the 'single layer' wire rope corresponding, as the name suggests, to a single layer of strands helically wound around a core. Other types are manufactured such as 'rotation resistant' or 'multi-strand' in which a number of layers of strands are contra-helically wound to reduce the rotational tendency and torque in the rope under tension. These ropes can also have 'compacted' strands in which the individual wires are not round but shaped to provide a greater surface area of contact with a sheave and thus reduce the contact pressure.

International Standard ISO 4309 provides a comprehensive listing and photographs showing a number of defects that can occur on crane or lifting appliance wire ropes. Obvious defects such as kinks and basket deformation in which the external shape of the wire rope changes should be able to be identified relatively quickly. External corrosion should also be obvious during inspection.

Wire ropes should be frequently checked closely for other damage and defects, such as indications of wear (flattening of wires) and broken wires in the strands. The extent of broken wires in a given length and the grouping of wire breaks are all factors that need to be considered when judging criteria for allowing the rope to continue in service. Tables in standards set out the relevant criteria, although there are differences in this respect between the various reference documents and standards.

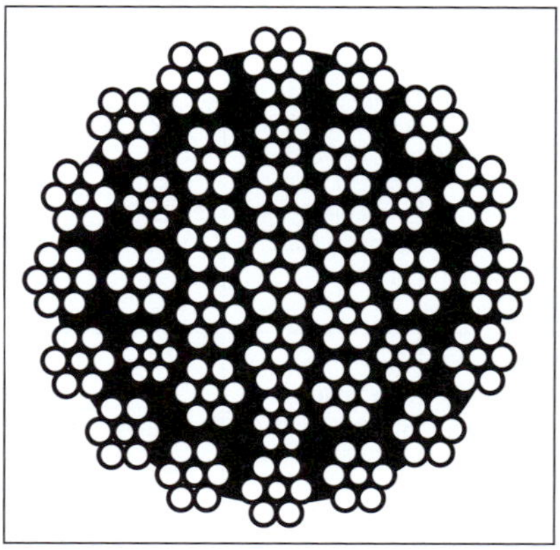

Courtesy of Certex

Figure 48.2 - Cross section of 34 × 7 WRC low rotation hoist wire

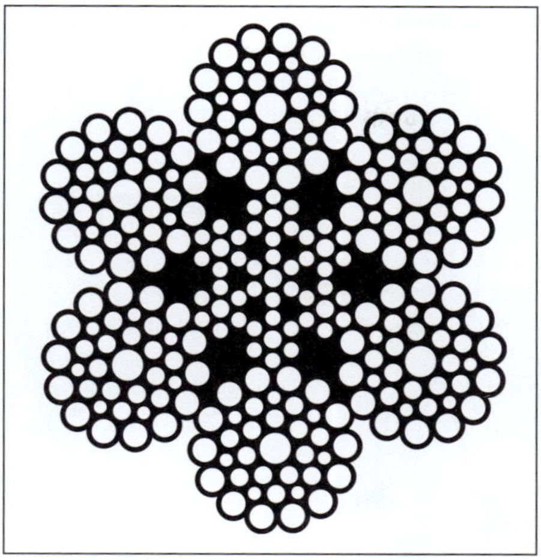

Courtesy of Certex

Figure 48.3 - Cross section of 6 × 36 WRC crane boom wire showing compacted outer strands

Probably the most common defect on wire ropes, which cursory examination of a greased rope can often overlook, is wear. This is shown by flattening of the round wire elements. Wear can be accelerated by defective (non-rotating) sheaves with the rope abrading around it or if the wire rope diameter is larger than, and not matched to, the sheaves. Too small diameter sheaves can also result in excessive bending of the rope.

Eventually, flattening of the wires reduces the load-bearing cross-section of individual wires, which can lead to wire fractures. Wear can also initiate fatigue. From a maintenance and safety perspective, regular inspection and lubrication of sheaves in accordance with the manufacturer's instructions should be followed.

There is no set period for the expected lifetime of ropes. However, in practice, a survey cycle period of five years would be a typical maximum lifetime for crane or lifting appliance wire ropes.

Crane ropes should be removed if they show any of the following criteria:

- A strand has broken
- a wire breakage cluster has appeared
- the number of visible broken wires exceeds the permissible limits
- corkscrew-type deformation which exceeds one-third of the rope diameter (Figure 48.1)
- basket-type deformation (Figure 48.5)
- hair-pin type extrusion of wires or clusters of wires from the rope (Figure 48.6)
- structure of rope is loose (Figure 48.7)
- reduction of rope diameter by 15%, or 10% below the nominal diameter accompanied by corrosion and/or wear (Figure 48.8)
- necking (Figure 48.8)
- rope is bent or flattened (Figures 48.10 and 48.8)
- kinks or residual deformations (Figure 48.11).

Where particular damage to the rope is detected, ascertain the cause and remedy the problem before installing a new rope!

According to ISO 4309, a 7% reduction in nominal rope diameter warrants discard of the rope even if no wire breaks are visible.

Figure 48.4 - Wire rope with corkscrew-type deformation

Figure 48.5 - Wire rope with basket-type deformation

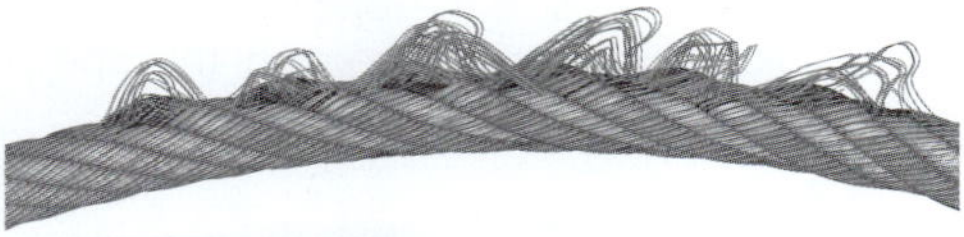

Figure 48.6 - Wire rope with loops formed

Figure 48.7 - Wire rope with individual wires loosened by corrosion and abrasion

Figure 48.8 - Wire rope with local decrease in diameter

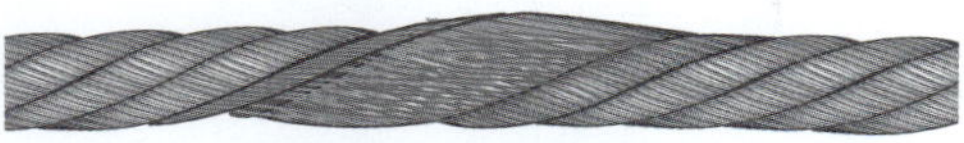

Figure 48.9 - Wire rope with flat caused by being run over

General Requirements for Lifting Equipment

Figure 48.10 - Wire rope with kink caused by pulling a loop

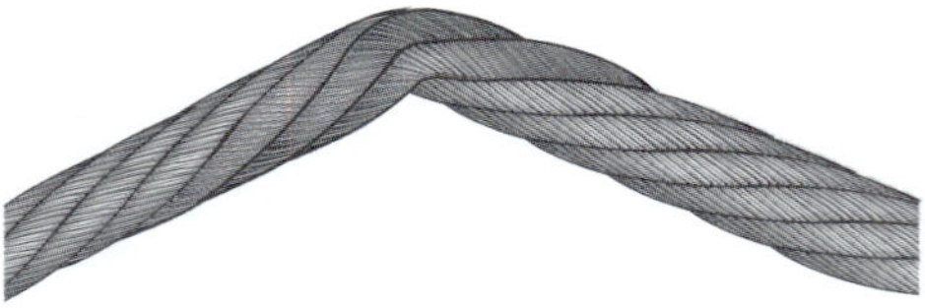

Figure 48.11 - Wire rope with bend caused by mechanical effect

Replacing a Crane Wire

1. Unload the rope properly and relieve any twists. Pull the rope off the shipping reel or unroll it from a shipping coil as shown. (If done improperly, you may kink the rope, which will result in permanent damage to the rope). Then lay the rope on the ground in a direct line with the boom. This helps release any twist in the rope.
2. Attach the end of the rope to the drum. Pull the rope over the point sheave and attach the end to the drum. Before making any end attachment, be sure the rope strands are free to adjust (ie make sure the end of the rope is not welded together).
3. Wind rope onto drum slowly and carefully. At this point, it is not necessary to provide additional load other than the weight of the rope being pulled across the ground.

Unreel rope from a shaft supported by two jacks. Uncoil rope by rolling it along the ground like a hoop.

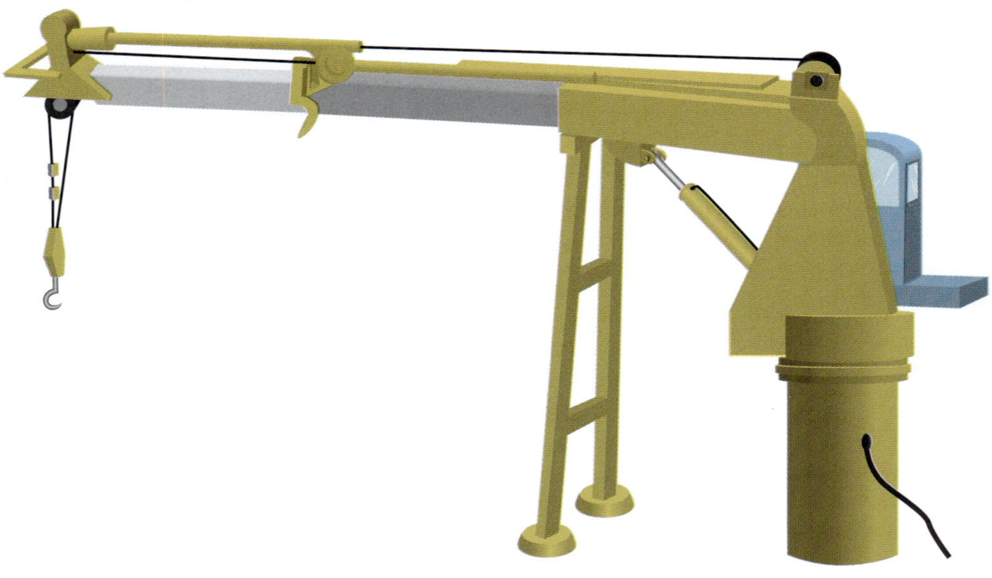

4. Spool first layer tightly. It is essential on smooth-faced drums that the first layer is spooled with wraps tight and close together since the first layer forms the foundation for succeeding layers. If need be, use a rubber, lead or brass mallet (but never a steel hammer) to tap the rope in place.

Make sure the foundation layer is spooled tightly

5. Spool multiple layers with sufficient tension. It is very important to apply a tensioning load to the ropes during the rope breaking-in process. (If not, the lower layers may be loose enough that the upper layers become wedged into the lower layers under load, which can seriously damage the rope).

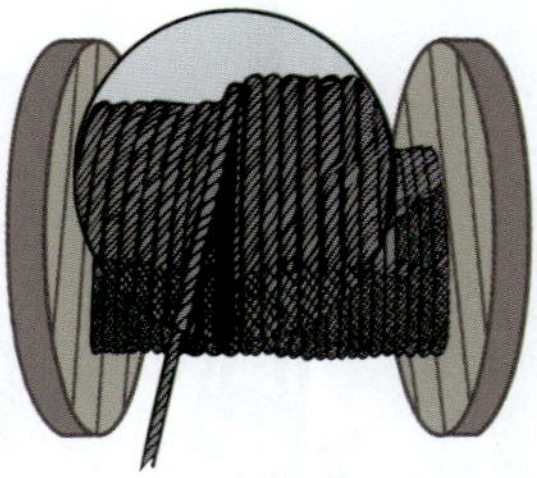

The result of improper tensioning is a "pulling in" of the rope

The tensioning load should range from 2 to 3% of the rope's minimum breaking force.

6. For ropes in multi-part systems, reeve the travelling block and boom tip sheaves so the rope spacing is maximised and the travelling (hook) block hangs straight and level to help assure block stability. Avoid dead ending the rope at the travelling block if possible.

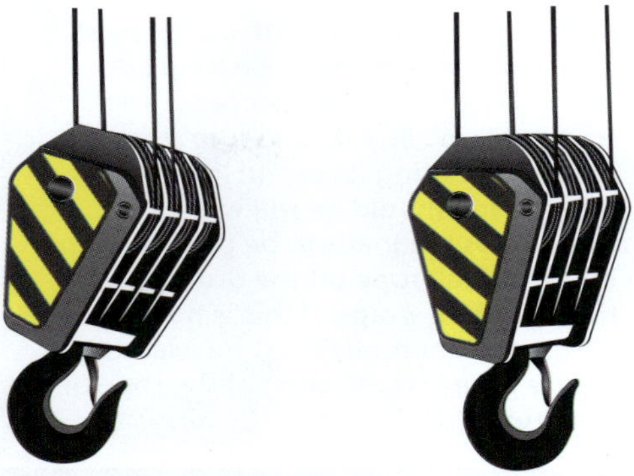

Incorrect ***Correct***

7. Check rope for twist. With the rope slack, pull enough rope out to allow it to hang in a loop. If the rope hangs without twisting together (right), there is no twist in the rope. If the rope twists together (left), the rope has twist in it.

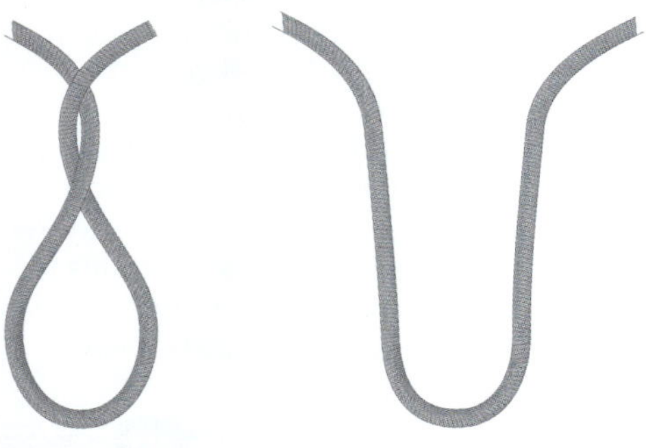

Twist in rope ***No Twist***

Breaking in New Wire Rope

After installation, new wire rope should be properly broken in to allow the rope's component parts to adjust to the operating conditions.

With the boom fully raised – and fully extended if using a hydraulic boom – attach a light load at the hook and raise it a few inches off the ground. Allow to stand for several minutes. Then cycle the load between the full up and down positions several times. Stand back and watch the drum winding and rope travel for any potential problems.

General Requirements for Lifting Equipment

After making the lifts with a light load, increase the load and cycle it up and down a few times. This procedure will train the rope and help assure smooth operation during its useful life. Ideally, these loads should be run with reeving that allows the loads to be placed on the block with all rope off the drum except the last three wraps. If this is not possible, alternative methods must be used to assure proper tensioning of the rope on the drum.

Always leave three wraps on drum.

Although ASME B30.5 states that two wraps must remain on the drum when the hook is in the extreme low position, it is common practice to leave at least three turns on the drum.

If there is insufficient space to lay new rope out on the ground before rigging, it should be pulled directly from the reel using the following procedure. Mount the reel on a shaft through flange holes and on jack stands, making sure you spool as illustrated below. While unspooling, do not allow the reel to "free wheel." Brake the reel by applying pressure to a flange. Never apply braking pressure to the rope on the reel or pass the rope between blocks of wood or other material.

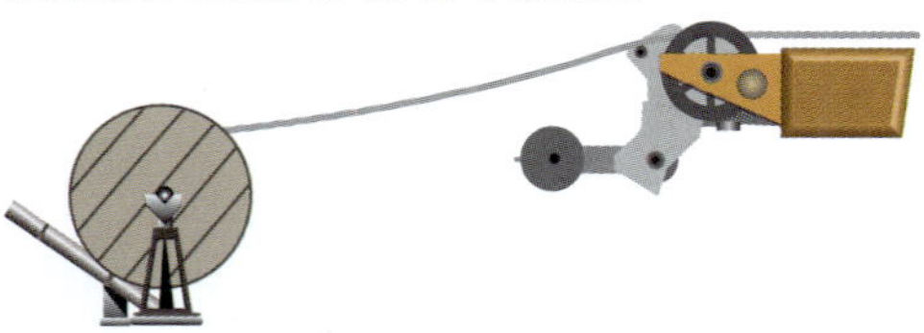

Install from reel top over the point sheave

How to determine the proper direction of drum winding:

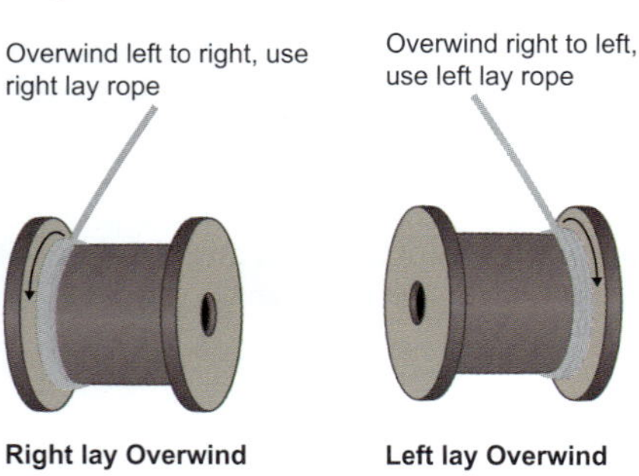

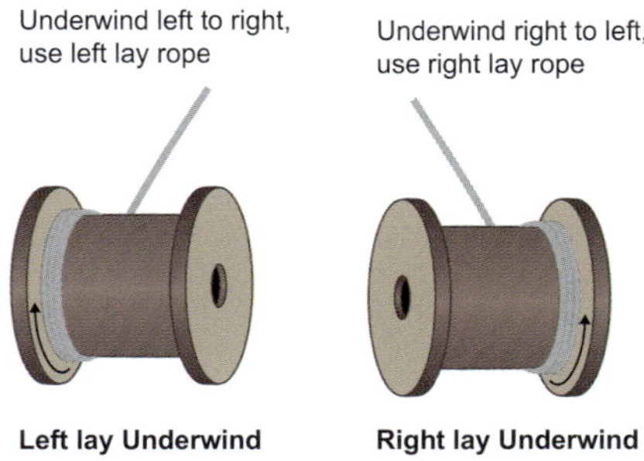

Relieving Twist

To relieve twist that may be trapped in a rope spooled directly off a reel to the drum, raise the boom to its highest position while letting out the rope until it almost touches the ground. Let the rope hang free without added load while standing clear. When twist is fully relieved, proceed with rigging the crane.

Block Rotation

Block rotation occurs when multi-part reeving twists together at a certain height, entangling the parts of rope between the travelling block and the boom tip. It can happen with little warning and makes it virtually impossible to lift or lower a suspended load. Twisted hoist lines can bring an operation to a sudden halt, resulting in downtime.

Block rotation can be minimised through proper installation and handling, as well as by taking corrective measures.

Lubricating Wire Rope

Regular lubrication reduces friction between the rope's components as well as the friction between the rope and sheaves or drums.

Rope receives internal lubricant during manufacture but it is insufficient to last the rope's entire life due to the constant bending over sheaves and drums. The need to keep ropes properly lubricated cannot be overemphasised.

Excess dirt, grit or other materials should be cleaned off the rope before lubricating as these will prevent lubricants from properly penetrating into the rope.

Lubricant may be applied manually by painting or spraying. Alternatively, an automatic lubrication system may be used to drip or spray lube onto the rope as it passes over a sheave at preselected intervals.

Procedure of Changing Crane Cargo Runner Cable

1. Lower the hook and secure the block.
2. Bridge the slack rope device.
3. Disconnect the limit switch for runner drum (mark the exact position of drum and turn on the drum to established exact position at later connection).
4. Disconnect the thimble at the crane house and lower this end of the wire to the deck.
5. Make a whipping behind the thimble and cut the thimble off.
6. Connect the new wire to the old wire using a snake wire.
7. Heave up carefully.
8. Stop heaving when the turn of the wire is on the drum inside the crane house.
9. Set a stopper inside the crane house (2 or even 3 stoppers).
10. Slack the wire a little in the crane house and disconnect the old wire from the new wire.
11. Slack down the old wire on deck until 2 turns are on the drum.
12. Disconnect the old wire from the drum and lower the rest of the wire slowly with a rope on deck. Lowering from inside the crane house is much easier.
13. Connect the new wire to the drum.
14. Continue heaving up slowly. Break the drum on deck to avoid slack in the new wire.
15. When 10 turns are left on the drum disconnect the new thimble from the drum and lay the wire in long ways on deck.
16. Pull the thimble up and reconnect thimble to crane house.
17. Continue heaving the wire to the position marked in step 3.
18. Reconnect the limit switches.
19. Disconnect the slack rope device.
20. Check all limits.
21. Finally heave and slack the wire 3 to 4 times to lay the wire.

Safety during Crane Operations

If you must lift at an angle, do not exceed 10° from the vertical. If you do exceed a 10° angle from the vertical, the crane or hoist will be off centre and the load can start swinging from side to side when lifted.

Never run the crane or hoist all the way up or down. This can damage the guide pins, alignment plates and/or the chain or wire rope.

Always lift the load in the centre of the hook. Lifting from any other location is unsafe.

The centre of gravity of an object is a point around which the entire weight may be concentrated. To make a level lift, the crane hook or point of suspension must be directly above this point. While slight variations are usually permissible, if the crane hook is too far to one side of the centre of gravity, unequal stresses will result.

Overloading must be avoided.

Sudden dynamic loading by jerking a load can cause a momentary overload sufficient to break or damage the crane wire or the sling. The weight of the load should be taken gradually and smoothly. This also reduces any immediate load swing.

Hydraulic Cranes

Before each Operation

- Have a thorough walk-around inspection of the crane
- check that the hydraulic oil level is between the upper and lower marks on the hydraulic oil reservoir
- check the hydraulic oil reservoir cap is tight. If loose, this could result in the loss of hydraulic oil
- check each part of the crane is operating smoothly
- check any limit switches and alarms
- visually inspect the condition of the wire rope.

Periodic Greasing

- Where the crane is being used frequently, this should be done weekly
- grease nipples should be clean before lubricating
- when greasing a bushing, ensure that the grease gun forces the old grease out of the bushing.

Other Maintenance Checks on Hydraulic Cranes

Check the manufacturer's guidelines for details of:

- When to change oil filters
- changing the hydraulic oil
- checking the hydraulic oil system pressure, temperature and flow
- checking condensation in the supply tank
- annual lubrication schedule
- visual checks required as part of the crane's thorough examination.

Cranes as Cargo Lifting Devices

These can be either crane or gantry systems. Normally, they are used by shore personnel who board the ship on arrival in port. Rarely do shore personnel make anything more than a superficial check and they depend on the ship's personnel to have made all the appropriate checks.

Apart from the standard period maintenance checks that are made, before any storing crane, cargo crane or gantry is used, the following checks should be made where appropriate:

- Perform a walk-around visual examination of the crane boom and support structure to ensure that no damage exists
- check all bolts, rivets, nuts and pins are present and secure
- check all control mechanisms for maladjustment, excessive wear and contamination by lubricants or other foreign matter that could interfere with proper operation
- visually check wire rope for deterioration, damage or improper reeving
- check for damage to the hook. If the hook is bent out of the throat opening by more than 15°, it must be replaced

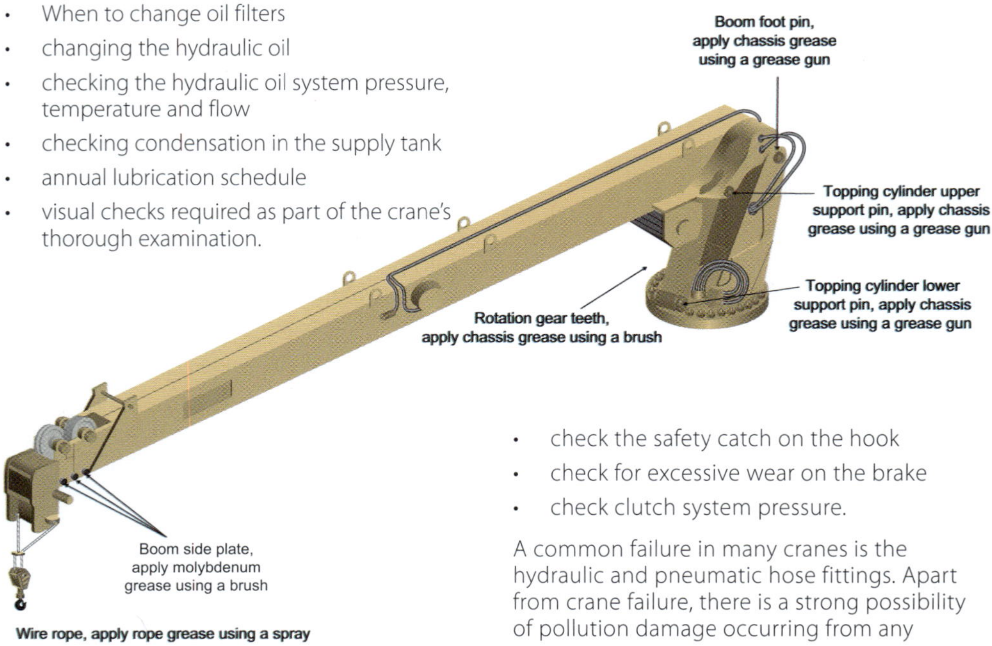

- check the safety catch on the hook
- check for excessive wear on the brake
- check clutch system pressure.

A common failure in many cranes is the hydraulic and pneumatic hose fittings. Apart from crane failure, there is a strong possibility of pollution damage occurring from any hydraulic oil spillage. The crane should be checked periodically for:

- Any sign of leakage on the surface of the flexible hoses
- any sign of blistering on the surface of the hoses
- leakage at threaded or clamped joints
- any sign of rubbing or wear on the surface of the hoses.

Gantry Cranes

The gantry system allows one or two gantry cranes to service all the hatches of a ship by their ability to travel on trackways along the length of the main deck cargo area. In addition, they can be stowed aft after use, leaving the decks clear forward of their stowed position.

A further advantage is that the operator sits in a travelling cab that allows him to be positioned over the shore pickup point and over the stowage position in the ship, giving better and safer control over the loading or discharging operation.

The gantries also have the ability of lifting the hatchtops, which means that a ship's main deck area can be free of machinery and hydraulic pipework.

While the gantry system offers obvious advantages, the trackway on the main deck hampers movement and requires frequent greasing to prevent corrosion. The gantries are also heavy and add considerable top weight to the ship. Covered gantries, which protect cargowork during rain, can also be a problem during extreme winds at sea.

Shipboard Gantry Cranes

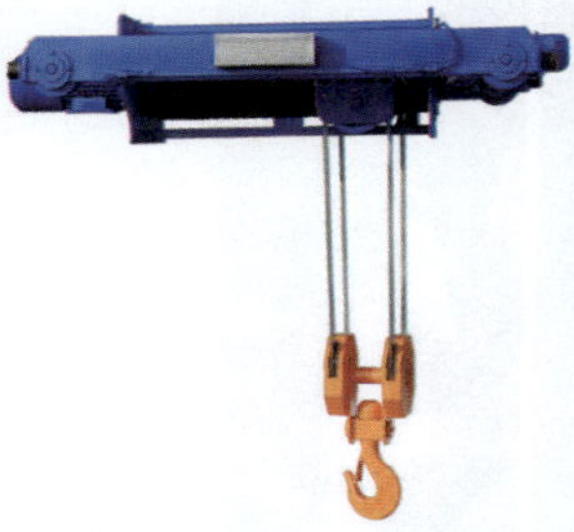

Engine room cranes are also of the gantry type

Gantry cranes have steel girders across the beam of a vessel, supported by legs and travelling on rails mounted on the ship's decks. The gantry houses the operator's cabin as well as the lifting mechanism, and it can travel athwartships on the bridge girders. The whole gantry can travel fore and aft on wheels mounted at the base. Hydraulic buffers at the ends of the rails prevent the crane from overrunning the rails.

A shelter may be used to cover this type of crane so that cargo operations may be carried out during light rain. These are usually fitted onto ships that handle weather-critical cargo, such as plywood or paper products. Prior to bringing the crane into operation, hinged outriggers are swung out, allowing the discharge or loading of products over the ship's side. The outriggers are usually hydraulically operated and have a mechanism to lock them in place. Prior to sailing, the outriggers are folded in and locked onto the side of the girders.

The other type of gantry crane is the jib type crane. The main difference is that the jib is mounted on the bridge girders. In some types, the jib can travel athwartships along the bridge girders, while on other models the jib is fixed in the centre. In both cases, the jib swings from port to starboard and the operator's cabin is mounted on the jib. This type of gantry crane is used on small feeder container ships as the container spreader at the end of the jib can be used to load and discharge cargo from a very stable base.

Advantages of gantry cranes:

- Mobile over the length of the deck
- unobstructed view for the operator
- shelters may be fitted to protect cargo during handling operations
- reduced possibility of load rotation due to box-shaped girders
- fast operation possible with experienced operators.

Safety Features

- Klaxon and light when moving along the deck
- maximum safe trim cut-out
- emergency stop switch at deck level
- hydraulic buffer at the end of deck rails
- two block limit switch
- slack wire limit switch
- maximum SWL limit switch
- outrigger cut-outs if not locked in place
- 'cow-catcher' safety guards on the wheels, which cut the power if they hit an obstruction.

Hydraulic Cranes

Stores Cranes

Figure 48.12 - Stores Crane

If stores cranes are to be used to launch rescue craft, it must be remembered that these are not gravity cranes and are dependent on mains power for their operation.

Control

Stores cranes can be cab operated, remote wire, or even wireless operated. All these have their various problems. The cab-operated type tend to limit the operator's view of the loading operations on the shore and he is reliant on good communications with whoever is directing the operation. If there is no personal communications link, the driver is reliant on watching for hand signals.

Remote control by extended control box, known as a pendant, allows the operation to be undertaken by one less person and gives the operator a clear view throughout the operation. However, it makes the operator remote from the crane and thus unaware of any safety issues that arise during the operation, such as personnel inadvertently entering the crane radius. In addition, the trailing power lead is on the deck and this can be accidently cut or tripped over.

The wireless control system is relatively new and is dependent on electronic signals being passed from a leadless remote to the crane. The obvious possible problem with this, in addition to the issues described above, is any interference with the signal between the control and the crane.

Pedestal Cranes

Shipboard pedestal cranes rotate on a pedestal and are permanently mounted. The main housing normally consists of the operator's cabin, winches and the jib, which projects from the pedestal. The crane is either electrically or hydraulically operated and the housing rotates on the pedestal. There are usually two winches inside the housing, one for the topping of the jib and the other for the hoist. Both are controlled from inside the cabin, using a joystick.

Advantages

- 360° rotation
- good spot loading
- fast operation
- low maintenance
- the SWL of two cranes may be combined when used together
- grabs, container spreaders, etc can be fitted to the cargo hook.

Safety Features

- Limit switches for topping and hoisting
- jib angle indicator, which indicates the angle of the jib that corresponds to the SWL
- two block limit switch, which prevents inadvertent contact of the floating runner block and the jib-mounted runner block
- slack wire cut-off
- SWL cut-off prevents a weight in excess of the SWL from being lifted
- topping and hoisting winch cut-off, which cuts the power when less than 3 turns remain on the winches or if the wires become fouled
- a flashing light placed at the end of the jib to prevent accidental contact with shore cranes.

Figure 48.13 - Pedestal crane on an offshore installation

Other Crane/Derrick Types

Stülcken Heavy Lift Derrick

The Stülcken derrick is a heavy lift derrick that can lift up to 300 tonnes. Unlike conventional heavy lift derricks, a Stülcken does not require a large amount of space and it can be made ready in a few minutes. The Stülcken is operated by four winches and is mounted between two V-shaped Samson-posts. This allows the Stülcken derrick to swing between the Samson-posts to reach another hatch.

Hallen Derrick

The boom of the Hallen derrick is connected with the Y-shaped mast and allows operation as a single swinging derrick. On the cross trees, two guys are fastened using swivel outriggers which are stayed vertically and horizontally. Three winches control the operation of the Hallen derrick; two for the guys and one for the purchase wire.

Only one winchman is needed and within a few minutes the Hallen can be brought into use. The SWL range of the Hallen is between 10 and 80 tonnes.

Other Crane/Derrick Types

Velle Ship Crane

The Velle derrick is a similar design to the Hallen but without use of outriggers. At the top of the boom, the guys serve for both topping and lowering the boom. The topping and lowering guys are secured to half-barrels on one winch. This means that the boom moves at the same speed as the winch pays out or hauls on the boom. The slewing guys are wound onto another half-barrel, and operate on the same principle. For hoisting/lowering the cargo hook, there is a third winch dedicated for this purpose.

CHAPTER 49

Checklists

Safety Items

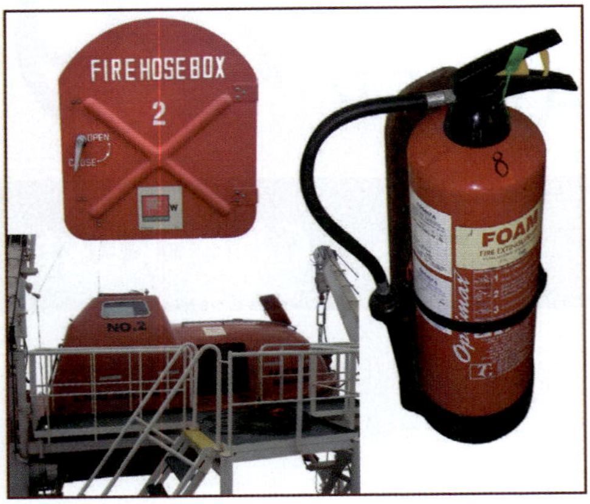

Safety items are always at the top of the list when surveys and inspections are carried out. The ship, while realising the importance of these items, will generally be conducting such surveys in port and will be focused on cargo work. Therefore, it is important that robust procedures are in place that cover the care of safety items. In addition to the obvious dangers, too often it is the failure to take such care that causes delay to a vessel through the need to make corrections before the ship can sail.

A proper procedure should cover exactly which department is responsible for what, the Safety Officer's responsibilities and the documentation and maintenance of all equipment.

Departmental Responsibilities

- The Shipboard Safety Officer's responsibilities are as designated in the Safety Management System
- the Electrical Officer tests should be reported to the Engine Department management team and deficiencies to the Safety Officer.

Safety Equipment on Deck

Action Officer: Third Officer/Deck Officer of the 8 to 12 watch

Maintenance

- All deck equipment must be maintained using a planned maintenance system
- a logbook must be kept and all maintenance must be recorded. This log should be signed weekly by the Chief Officer and monthly by the Master
- the Chief Officer should arrange to have available any crew that are required by the Safety Officer for maintenance purposes.

Defects

If shipboard repairs are required:

- ❑ The Chief Officer must be notified
- ❑ a repair request should be made to the head of the department that is required to make the repair
- ❑ once the repair is completed, it must be logged in the departmental Safety Logbook
- ❑ the Chief Officer must advise the management team of all safety repairs in that week.

If shore repair or assistance is required:

- ❑ Shore repairs are decided by the Chief Officer
- ❑ the Chief Officer/Chief Engineer should make out the appropriate landing form
- ❑ if necessary, the Company should be advised
- ❑ any shore technician should be accompanied by the Safety Officer and departmental Safety Representative
- ❑ the Safety Officer must advise the departmental head, Master and Safety Committee once the repair has been carried out to his satisfaction
- ❑ the completion of the repair must be logged in the Safety Logbook
- ❑ the Safety Officer must advise the Company through the Master that the repair has been completed.

Safety Equipment in the Engine Room

Action Officers: Fourth Engineer/Officer keeping the 8 to 12 watch and the designated Safety Officer

Maintenance

- All engine space equipment must be maintained under a planned maintenance system

- a logbook must be kept and all safety maintenance work must be recorded. This should be signed weekly by the Second Engineer
- the Second Engineer must arrange to have available any crew that are required by the departmental Safety Officer for maintenance purposes.

Defects

If shipboard repairs are required:

- ❑ The Safety Officer must be notified
- ❑ a repair request must be issued to the head of the department that will make the repair
- ❑ the repair must be noted as a priority and treated as such
- ❑ the Safety Officer must be informed when the repair is completed
- ❑ the repair should be entered in the departmental Safety Logbook.

If shore repair or assistance is required:

- ❑ Any shore repair must be agreed by the Safety Officer
- ❑ the Second Engineer must make out the appropriate landing form
- ❑ the Second Engineer must advise the Master and the Chief Engineer
- ❑ the Safety Officer must advise the Company
- ❑ the Safety Officer should accompany any shore technician attending
- ❑ the Second Engineer must confirm to the Safety Officer that the repair has been carried out to his satisfaction
- ❑ the Second Engineer should sign the work sheet stating that he is signing only for the work that has been done
- ❑ the repair should be logged in the departmental Safety Log
- ❑ the Safety Officer must notify the Master, Chief Engineer and the Company that the repair has been completed.

Safety Stores/Safety Spares

Action Officer: Safety Officer

- The Safety Officer is responsible for the care and issue of all safety stores
- requisitions for new stores and spares must be made through the Chief Officer or Chief Engineer (as appropriate)
- the engine department should initially requisition stores from the Safety Officer. If these are not on board, he must then requisition them through the Chief Officer or Chief Engineer (as appropriate)
- the Safety Officer must keep a list of safety stores and spares on board.

Safety Surveys

A safety survey fulfils two objectives. The first is to ensure that all of the equipment is in good order. The second is an indirect inspection of the management of the safety aspects of the vessel.

Action Officers: Chief Engineer, Chief Officer and Safety Officer

- ❑ The Company's head office/the ship manager is responsible for arranging safety surveys
- ❑ after receiving notification, the Chief Officer should advise the Chief Engineer and Safety Officer of the survey
- ❑ the Safety Officer must check and prepare the equipment according to the safety survey checklist. Once everything is in order, the Safety Officer should be informed that the department is ready for inspection
- ❑ the Safety Officer should notify the Master when the ship is ready to be surveyed, or must give reasons why it is not
- ❑ the surveyor should always be accompanied on the survey by the appropriate Department Head and Safety Officer
- ❑ when the survey is completed, the Safety Officer should accompany the surveyor to the Master
- ❑ the Master and the Safety Officer should discuss the survey with the surveyor. Repair of any defects noted must be put in hand and, where necessary, equipment should be ordered
- ❑ the Company should be notified of the results of the survey.

Safety Items

Shipboard Safety Meetings

Action Officers: Safety Officer and Departmental Safety Representatives

- ❑ Safety meetings should be held monthly
- ❑ The Master will normally chair the meeting and introduce the agenda, which should include the following:
  - near misses and any accidents on board
  - near misses and accidents in the fleet
  - important safety messages from the Company
  - any outstanding safety non-conformities
  - any recent changes in the industry.
- ❑ all Safety Committee members must attend the meeting
- ❑ a copy of the safety meeting minutes should be given to the Master, Chief Engineer and Chief Officer, placed in the Safety Meeting file in both the officer and crew recreation rooms and posted on notice boards.

Drills and Exercises

If you are to have a drill, it is better to have a meaningful one. For example, the regular lowering of boats gets crew into a routine that becomes familiar and normal.

Action Officers: Chief Officer and Safety Officer

Where possible, you should use any available time in port or while awaiting orders to conduct drills so that the ship's business is not delayed. Each drill should be planned to ensure that, on a rotating basis, all safety equipment is used and training is given in its use.

- Drills should be held each week to either meet or exceed the requirements of the flag State and other guidelines
- during these drills, the boats should be lowered, weather permitting, to the boat deck
- normally, an exercise is held as part of the drill routine.

Exercises should cover the following drills:

Statutory Drill Type	Intervals Not Exceeding
Abandon Ship	1 month
Fire	1 month
Enclosed Space Entry	2 months
Lifeboat Launched and Manoeuvred in Water*	3 months
Rescue Boat Drill	3 months
Emergency Steering	3 months
ISPS Security Drill	3 months
Davit Launch Liferaft	4 months

* Free-fall lifeboats can be launched every 6 months if lowered every 3 months, or extended to 12 months if simulation requirements are met.

If more than 25% of crew change, an abandon ship drill and a fire drill should be completed within 24 hours after leaving port. If it is not practical to hold full drills, musters should be held within the 24 hours with instruction given to the crew on their emergency duties and on abandon ship.

Non-Statutory Drills	Suggested Interval
Personal Injury/First Aid	6 weeks
Anti-Piracy	6 weeks
Oil Spill/Pollution	6 weeks
Main Engine Failure	3 months
Toxic Vapour Release	3 months
Power Failure	3 months
Man Overboard	6 months
Helicopter Evacuation	6 months
Grounding/Stranding	6 months
Collision	6 months
Break Away from Berth	6 months
Hull Damage/Flooding	12 months
Emergency Towing	12 months
First Alert Notification	Change of Command

Drill Debriefing

Once the exercise has been completed, the officer in charge of the emergency party should conduct the debrief. This should cover:

- ❑ How the drill was carried out
- ❑ how to improve specific drill procedures
- ❑ any areas where more training is required
- ❑ equipment used, including any defects or necessary maintenance.

The purpose of any drill is to prepare for emergencies and this should be borne in mind when they are being organised. Drills should be conducted as if there is an actual emergency and should be varied to cover a range of situations. The Master should ensure that they are not allowed to degenerate into a periodic chore with no semblance of reality.

Crew should be trained to carry out their own emergency duties efficiently and to know as much as is reasonably possible about other people's emergency duties. Drills should ensure that the crew reacts correctly to the particular circumstances devised for the exercise.

So far as weather conditions and time allow, exercises should be organised to incorporate as much realism as is safe and practical. Exercises should simulate a wide variety of hypothetical emergencies and contingencies, including:

- ❑ Fire(s) in:
  - machinery spaces
  - galley
  - vehicle decks
  - storerooms, workshops or lockers
  - electrical equipment, wheelhouse or switchboards
- ❑ 'hampered' operations:
  - loss of electrical power
  - machinery failure
  - loss of normal steering
  - bridge or engine room out of action
  - one side of the vessel inoperable/ inaccessible
  - senior officer/key personnel casualties
- ❑ damage control:
  - collision
  - hull holed after contact with quay, etc
  - internal flooding following burst piping
- ❑ dangerous goods spillage
- ❑ entry into/rescue from dangerous spaces
- ❑ man overboard
- ❑ accident on board:
  - injury
  - serious illness/death
- ❑ abandon ship.

Exercises should be designed to ensure that they provide crew training that includes, but is not limited to, the following:

- ❑ Use of survival craft and rescue boats in heavy weather
- ❑ survival techniques; effects and treatment of hypothermia
- ❑ first aid
- ❑ use of fire-fighting appliances, refilling of extinguishers
- ❑ use of breathing apparatus
- ❑ smoke/fume-filled atmospheres
- ❑ search procedures within spaces
- ❑ control of passengers
- ❑ donning and use of fire-fighting and chemical suits
- ❑ entry into spaces on fire, opening of access to spaces
- ❑ effective fire-fighting techniques
- ❑ boundary cooling
- ❑ quick closing valves and remote stops.

Any single exercise could incorporate several of the above items. Consideration should be given to a pre-drill discussion on the purposes of the drill. Each drill should be followed by a debriefing session to analyse and reinforce particular points, provide explanations and consider suggestions for improved procedures. Every effort should be made to encourage a positive response to the exercises.

Training

Action Officer: Safety Officer

- The Safety Officer is responsible for producing the ship's training programme
- formal safety training should take place each week after emergency drills
- the Master should stand the navigational watch during this period
- all officers should be involved in this training

Safety Items

- the programme should provide a mixture of practical, video and classroom instruction
- the Safety Officer must keep a record of all instructions in a training record book.

Regular and realistic training is essential for the development and maintenance of emergency preparedness on board, helping to foster a safety culture.

In an actual emergency situation, crew can become very afraid. However, experience has shown that crew members who regularly train and exercise in safety drills:

- Are less frightened
- do not panic
- respond in a controlled manner
- do exactly what they have been trained to do
- handle the situation much better than before the training.

If you wish your crew to perform competently in an emergency situation, you must remember that:

- There is no substitute for regular hands-on training and drills
- everybody on board must be familiar with the response procedures in the event of an emergency
- emergency procedures for specific events will need to be followed
- a well-trained crew with an ability to manage emergencies will prove invaluable should it be needed.

You must

- ❑ Adhere strictly to the frequency of lifeboat, abandon ship, fire, ship security and other drills as prescribed by international laws and conventions
- ❑ use every opportunity to improve the routines of such drills
- ❑ conduct training as frequently as possible
- ❑ ensure that everybody attends any training provided
- ❑ have the training conducted and supervised by experienced officers, to show commitment from the highest level.

All drills should be followed by a debrief/wash-up session. Here important lessons can be learnt and implemented for the future.

Drills should be

- ❑ As realistic as possible - this will help reduce fear in the event of an emergency situation
- ❑ carried out wearing full emergency equipment, where possible, to familiarise the crew with it
- ❑ recorded in the appropriate logbook
- ❑ recorded in crew's individual training records (if applicable).

Safe Training

Before conducting a training exercise, the equipment to be used should be thoroughly examined to ensure that it is safe to use. There have been many tragic accidents, particularly during lifeboat drills, and the utmost care must be exercised.

Training and drills may reveal a need for further training ashore and this should be reported to the Company. Should you consider that additional training materials are required, the Company should be informed.

Do not be too concerned if mistakes and errors are made during onboard training exercises and drills as this presents the best opportunity for the crew to learn from their mistakes and improve their skills.

Port State Control inspections often focus on familiarisation with lifeboat and fire drills. You should ensure that the crew are not only well trained in these drills, but also well trained in operating emergency fire generators and pumps and are familiar with emergency procedures concerning:

- Hot work incidents
- galley emergencies
- electrical incidents
- incinerator problems
- oil leaks and spills.

Port State Control and Other Safety Inspections

Action Officer: Safety Officer

- ❑ When any official safety inspector or coastguard arrives on board, the Master and Chief Officer must be informed
- ❑ they should be shown to the ship's reception room, where the trading certificates must be presented

- ❑ all safety record books and checklists should be brought to the reception room for their inspection
- ❑ during any inspection, the inspectors must be accompanied by the Safety Officer. If he is not available, the senior Department Officer present must delegate another officer to accompany them
- ❑ once the inspection is completed, the Master and the Chief Officer must be informed. A meeting will then be held in the ship's conference room/meeting room to discuss the inspection and any deficiencies found
- ❑ the Master must advise the Company of the findings of the inspection.

Accident Prevention and New Crew Safety Induction

There are three reasons why new personnel must be inducted into the safety procedures of the ship:

- It is an SMS requirement
- to protect the ship and the Company should the inductee have an accident
- a ship is a complicated and dangerous workplace and it is a sensible use of time for a new joining crew member to spend time familiarising himself with the ship, paying particular attention to key safety and operational items that he may need to rely on in the event of an emergency or operationally in his first few days on board.

Action Officers: Safety Officer, Chief Officer and 2nd Engineer Officer

- The Chief Officer and the Second Engineer Officer are responsible for reviewing their individual department working practices and for ensuring that the safety induction is completed for joining crew
- they are responsible to the Safety Officer for ensuring that the safety familiarisation checklist is completed. The Second Engineer Officer is responsible for all the engine department personnel and the Chief Officer is responsible for all the deck and catering department personnel
- they are responsible for maintaining sufficient PPE (Personal Protective Equipment) in stock for their departments
- they are responsible for issuing and ensuring that crew members wear the correct PPE for the work being undertaken.

Accidents

In the event of any accident on board, the following procedure should be adopted.

Action Officers: Safety Officer, OOW and Medical Officer

- ❑ Depending on the type of accident, the casualty will either be escorted to the ship's hospital or the ship's Medical Officer and stretcher party will be called to the scene. Any treatment given must be entered in the Medical Logbook
- ❑ if the casualty is suffering from any back or head injury, they should not be moved
- ❑ the Master must be informed
- ❑ the departmental Safety Officer for the area in which the accident occurred should start the accident investigation
- ❑ the OOW should maintain a log of all events and times throughout
- ❑ if the accident takes place in port:
  - where a terminal worker is involved, the stevedore's office must be informed
  - if the seriousness of the casualty warrants, contact the port emergency services with details of the accident and request medical services
  - if the casualty is a member of the ship's company and requires shore medical treatment, this should be arranged immediately
- ❑ if the accident takes place at sea and is of a serious nature, prepare to contact the following:
  - the Rescue Coordination Centre, Stavanger. INMARSAT A
  - the International Medical Centre, Rome. SATCOM
- ❑ the Navigation Officer will lay courses for the nearest port or facility
- ❑ Safety Officers must complete the accident report for their areas of responsibility. This report must be completed as soon as possible after the accident
- ❑ a shipboard inquiry should be held by the Master, assisted by the Chief Engineer

Safety Items

- ❑ the Company must be notified, using a method appropriate to the seriousness of the accident. The accident report should be faxed to the Company
- ❑ on UK-flagged ships or on ships in UK waters, an MAIB report must be completed.

Slips, trips and falls are the major cause of personal injury on board. The following precautions should be taken:

- ❑ Obstacles such as steps, sills, low overhead spaces, protruding handles, etc must be clearly marked
- ❑ the decks and alleyways of the vessel must be kept clean and free from any slippery substances
- ❑ hydraulic pipes on deck must be checked regularly to prevent leaking oil dripping onto the deck
- ❑ in colder climates, special attention must be paid to access areas to prevent slipping on ice
- ❑ debris should be cleared from the deck
- ❑ defective anti-slip paint must be renewed
- ❑ sufficient lighting should always be provided
- ❑ handrails and grips must be in good condition
- ❑ appropriate warning signs should be provided where needed.

Pollution

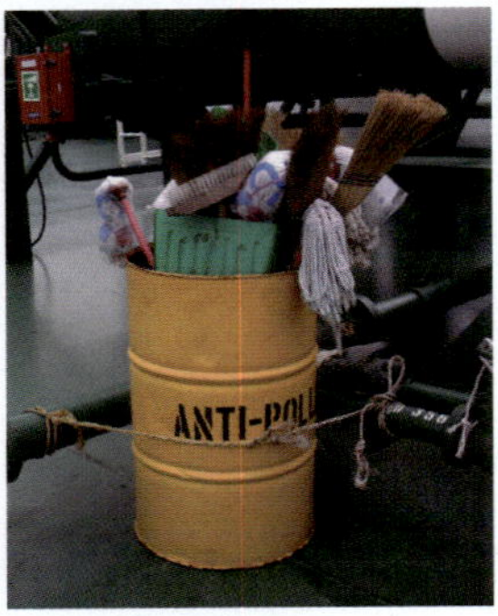

As far as the port or flag State whose waters you are in are concerned, pollution is a most serious issue. Arrest and detention, of both ship and personnel, can follow and you can certainly expect delay to your vessel if an incident occurs in port. Pollution does not only come from oil. Even the smallest amount of garbage from your vessel can be perceived as pollution and heavy fines can be levied.

It is imperative that you can show that all procedures have been followed correctly and that your ship has done everything possible to minimise pollution.

One major problem for a ship is that, once oil has gone into the water, there is little the ship can do except rely on the shore clean-up facilities. The longer the shore takes to deal with the spill, the further it spreads.

Responsibilities

- The Chief Officer is responsible for all anti-pollution measures
- the Chief Officer is responsible for all anti-pollution equipment and stores
- the Chief Engineer is responsible for all bunkering procedures
- the Chief Engineer is team leader for the pollution clean-up team.

Garbage

Action Officers: Deck Officer keeping the 12 to 4 watch and designated Waste Disposal Officer (WDO)

Responsibilities

- The WDO must keep all departments advised about the nature of the garbage disposal zone the ship is in
- he must keep the Garbage Disposal Logbook
- he should advise the Master, prior to arrival, about any garbage that will need to be disposed of by port facilities.

Garbage Disposal

- ❑ When biodegradable garbage is ready for overboard disposal, the OOW on the bridge must be contacted for his authority
- ❑ the OOW must check that, in the area the ship is in, such disposal is permissible
- ❑ when garbage is thrown overboard, the OOW must enter the event's date, time and position in the Garbage Disposal Logbook
- ❑ non-biodegradable items must be placed in plastic bins
- ❑ prior to arrival in port, the WDO must advise the Master if any waste is to be disposed of ashore

Pollution

- ❑ the Master should arrange for waste to be disposed of once in port. The WDO should obtain a receipt for this disposal, which will be filed by the Chief Officer.

Pollution from Garbage

The disposal of ship's garbage, which is prohibited under MARPOL Annex V, is a criminal offence viewed in many countries in a similar manner to an act of oil pollution.

In ports with garbage disposal facilities, you should dispose of garbage in accordance with the vessel's Garbage Management Plan.

Bunkering

Master's Standing Orders: Port

Action Officers: Chief Engineer, Chief Officer and OOW

- Prior to arrival in the bunkering port, the Chief Engineer must complete the Company checklist and the oil spill contingency plan
- the Chief Officer must ensure that the Chief Engineer has a copy of the emergency contact list
- the Chief Engineer must check that all pollution precautions have been taken
- the Chief Engineer must ensure that all shipboard communications are in working order. He is responsible for communications with the shore or barge
- the Chief Officer must ensure that there is fire-fighting equipment in the vicinity of the bunkering position and that it is ready for use
- the Chief Officer must take all deck anti-pollution measures, such as blocking scuppers and preparing the pollution control equipment
- the deck department are responsible for making any bunkering barge fast alongside. They must assist with hoisting the bunkering pipe on board and are responsible for the ladder to the barge
- the deck department must put up no smoking signs and rope off the bunkering position from shore workers
- the Chief Engineer must take fuel samples
- the Chief Engineer must agree and sign a receipt for fuel oil received and advise the OOW when bunkering is complete
- the Chief Engineer must advise the Chief Officer of the amount received and the tanks that were filled.

Bunkering Checklist (before transfer)

A precursor to a successful bunkering operation is the exchange of information prior to the operation. This should contain at least the following:

- ❑ Location, date and time of supply
- ❑ position where the bunkering is to occur
- ❑ acceptable weather and sea state conditions
- ❑ exact specification and amount of bunkers required
- ❑ is the bunker barge moored adequately?
- ❑ is there safe access from the ship to the bunker barge?
- ❑ are there new gaskets available for the bunker hose?
- ❑ is the connecting flange fitted with well-tightened bolts?
- ❑ is there a suitable webbing strop for the bunker hose?
- ❑ is the bunker hose(s) properly rigged?
- ❑ is there an effective watch in attendance on the ship/barge?
- ❑ are all pressure gauges, sampling devices and thermometers fitted securely?
- ❑ are save-alls available under each bunker hose? With plugs fitted?
- ❑ are all unused bunker connections properly blanked?
- ❑ are all scuppers effectively plugged?
- ❑ are vent flame screens on each bunker tank clear?
- ❑ is fire-fighting equipment available for immediate use?
- ❑ is oil spill equipment available for immediate use?
- ❑ is there an agreed communication system between own ship and the bunker barge?
- ❑ has an emergency stop procedure been agreed?
- ❑ are no smoking regulations in force on own ship and the bunker barge?
- ❑ has a bunker plan been agreed between own ship and the bunker barge?

Pollution

- ❑ have all unused bunker valves been checked to confirm they are closed and means introduced to prevent accidental operation?
- ❑ have the tanks to be bunkered been gauged prior to the bunker transfer commencing?
- ❑ is there sufficient capacity in the bunker tanks on own vessel to receive the requested quantity without any bunker tank being filled beyond 95% capacity?
- ❑ are the sampling requirements and procedures for representative sampling before the commencement and during the bunkering operation agreed?

Oil Pollution from an Oil Tanker

Immediate Action

- ❑ Sound emergency alarm.

Initial response

- ❑ Stop all cargo and/or bunkering operations
- ❑ close manifold valves
- ❑ switch air conditioning to recirculation or stop air intake to accommodation
- ❑ stop non-essential air intake fans to the engine room
- ❑ locate source of leakage and stop/reduce oil
- ❑ consult SOPEP plan
- ❑ consult MSDS/EMS guideline
- ❑ assess fire risk from release of flammable substances
- ❑ start fire pump
- ❑ commence clean-up procedures using absorbents and permitted solvents
- ❑ advise relevant parties (local authorities, coastal State, DPA/Company, P&I correspondent, etc).

Secondary response

- ❑ Reduce the oil level in the tank concerned by dropping oil into an empty or slack tank
- ❑ reduce the level of oil in tanks in the suspected area
- ❑ drain affected line to empty or slack tank
- ❑ reduce inert gas pressure to zero
- ❑ if the leakage is at the pump room sea valve, relieve pressure on pipelines
- ❑ prepare pumps for transfer of oil to other tanks or to shore or lightering vessel
- ❑ prepare portable pumps if it is possible to transfer spilt oil to an empty tank
- ❑ consider pumping water into the leaking tank to create a water cushion and prevent further oil loss
- ❑ if the leakage is below the waterline, arrange divers for further investigation
- ❑ calculate stresses/stability. If necessary, request shore assistance
- ❑ transfer cargo or bunkers to alleviate high stability stresses
- ❑ stow residue from the clean-up operation carefully, prior to disposal.

Oil Spilled on Deck

When most of the free oil has been removed and the risk of oil pollution has passed, onboard resources should turn to the clean-up operation.

Personnel involved in containment and clean-up operations may be at risk from a variety of hazards. The officer in charge of the operation should arrange for the following precautions to be taken to ensure that a safe working environment is maintained:

- ❑ The area must be continually checked for the presence of hydrocarbon and other suspected toxic gases (the MSDS will provide information regarding concentrations of specific toxic gases in a particular cargo)
- ❑ the boundaries of the clean-up site must be clearly indicated
- ❑ entry to the clean-up site must be controlled and access allowed only to those with appropriate PPE

- ❑ forced ventilation around the accommodation and machinery spaces must be controlled or stopped
- ❑ special precautions must be taken to prevent any sources of ignition, including static electricity
- ❑ fire-fighting parties and equipment should remain on standby
- ❑ surfaces that present a slipping hazard must be covered with sawdust or absorbent granules and hazard signs should be posted
- ❑ a designated area should be made available for personnel to shower and to change into clean clothing.

Pump Room Spillage

Oil that is spilled in the pump room from leaking pipelines may not present a pollution hazard, but it does present a personal health and safety hazard for those entering the pump room. When a spill is suspected, entry into the pump room must be treated as though it were an enclosed entry into a cargo oil tank. The pump room entry permit must be cancelled.

The initial strategy should be as follows:

- ❑ Stop cargo operations
- ❑ evacuate personnel from the pump room
- ❑ withdraw pump room entry permit
- ❑ close all remotely operated valves
- ❑ monitor percentage LEL using fixed and portable instruments (in the case of portable instruments, no metal probes should be used)
- ❑ prepare the bilge pump or the pump designated for bilge pumping duty and set the lines to transfer to a suitable cargo oil tank
- ❑ if the pump room bilge alarm has been activated and/or oil is being drawn into the pump room extraction vents, consider changing over to the high extraction vents.

Further action depends on the situation.

Oil Pollution of Unknown Origin

If oil is detected in the water near the vessel and it is not due to a collision or grounding, steps must be taken to determine the source by:

- ❑ Taking surface samples, using a purpose designed surface sampler or a wipe or clean rag attached to a sounding rod, to determine the type of oil for comparison. At least two samples should be taken, clearly labelled with the position they were taken from with respect to the tanker, the geographical position, date and time
- ❑ taking a set of ullages and soundings of fuel and cargo tanks and comparing them with the last daily record of soundings and ullages
- ❑ sequentially shutting down all possible systems that discharge overboard.

Other Sources of Pollution

You should familiarise yourself with items of pollution documented in your Company's SMS and with the provisions of MARPOL 73/78 (plus latest amendments).

Sewage

Strict regulations to prevent pollution of the sea by sewage have been implemented. MARPOL 73/78 Annex IV details the regulations for the Prevention of Pollution by Sewage from Ships.

Ballast Water

Ballast water is one of the major sources of the spread of harmful aquatic organisms and pathogens to new areas.

The 'Guidelines for the Control and Management of Ship's Ballast Water to Minimize the Transfer of Harmful Aquatic Organisms and Pathogens' (IMO Resolution 868) were adopted by the IMO in December 1997.

To control the invasion of aquatic organisms and pathogens, the United States Federal Ballast Water Discharge Standard rulemaking became effective in June 2012. This legislation was produced by the US Coast Guardbut does not pre-empt any state BW regulations. Therefore, when the implementation schedule for the California rules becomes effective for a particular ship type, the stricter California BW standards must be met in California waters.

The USCG federal rules do not stipulate that installing a ballast water management systemis the only way to be compliant. It is a discharge standard that can be met in several ways:

- Install a BWMS that has been approved by the US Coast Guard
- use a supply of public water, such as drinking water

Pollution

- use a BWMS that has been approved by a foreign Authority. These are called alternate management systems (AMS). It confers a short-term acceptance for a 'grandfather period' of 5 years after a vessel's compliance date, but the manufacturer also has to apply to the USCG for Type Approval in order for ships to continue using the system after the 5-year deadline
- retain ballast on board while in US waters
- discharge ballast water and sediment to a reception facility.

If trading to the US or other countries where ballast water regulations are in force, you should:

- Ask the agent before entering the Exclusive Economic Zone (200 nautical miles) how you best comply with the country'sballast water requirements
- ensure you are familiar with all relevant local and international requirements in force.

You should be aware that certain countries have imposed significant fines on vessels discharging ballast water in their jurisdictions without the correct procedures in place. The monitoring and enforcement of the BW regulations has become more commonplace as the entry into force of the IMO BWM Convention comes closer.

Air Pollution

In April 1999, the European Union issued Directive 1999/32, which came into force on 1st July 2002, stating that a sulphur cap is in place on inland use of middle distillate fuels, with a similar cap placed on the marine use of such products. This Directive placed a sulphur limit on all grades of fuel and now includes a sulphur cap of 1.5% by mass on marine diesel oil (MDO), placing restrictions on its use, particularly for transit between EU ports.

Exhaust gases from any combustion engine, including ships' engines, contribute to these emissions and can be reduced, improving the efficiency of the combustion of fuel oils.

Visible air pollution by soot from the ship's funnel may still occur and the consequences are often far reaching. Soot can be carried for miles on the wind and result in damage to property. Annex VI of MARPOL covers air pollution and came into force in May 2005.

Evidence to be Collected in the Event of a Pollution Incident

In addition to maintaining a continuous record of all events, the following evidence must be collected.

Description of the incident

- ❑ Date and time of pollution
- ❑ nature of the pollution
- ❑ ongoing operation at the time the pollution occurred
- ❑ estimation of the amount spilled
- ❑ ship's position
- ❑ weather conditions (particularly wind direction and force)
- ❑ tide and current
- ❑ draught of the vessel.

If pollution occurred at sea

- ❑ Courses on charts
- ❑ speed and engine setting
- ❑ position log and distances to the nearest coastline.

Description of the ongoing operation at the time of the pollution

- ❑ Type of operation
- ❑ time the operation commenced and pertinent facts
- ❑ details of the persons involved (and responsibilities) on the ship and/or bunker barge.

Details of other companies involved in the pollution

- ❑ Name and contact details
- ❑ names, details and duties of their personnel involved in the operation
- ❑ name of bunker barge
- ❑ if the pollution occurred during bunkering:
  - whether procedures had been agreed, in particular regarding commencement, rate of flow and interruptions
  - how communications were maintained
- ❑ any difficulties in communicating or conducting the operation.

Damage caused by the pollution

- ❑ Description of the pollution
- ❑ location and extent of the pollution.

Medical

Responsibilities

Responsible Officer: Master

Action Officer: Deck Officer keeping the 12 to 4 watch, designated ship's Medical Officer

- The ship's Medical Officer is responsible for the onboard medical treatment of all the ship's company. He is also responsible for maintaining their medical files
- he is responsible for the care and maintenance of all medical equipment, such as the respirator. He must ensure that any crew who are to use this equipment are instructed on how to do so
- he is responsible for the maintenance of the first aid lockers in the galley, engine room, deck office and on the bridge. He will ensure that the emergency first aid party pack is complete
- the cleanliness and preparedness of the hospital and dispensary are the Medical Officer's responsibility, and they should never be used as a store or cabin
- the Medical Officer will maintain the Medical Logbook, which must be available in the hospital for inspection by the Master
- the dangerous drugs list is compiled by the Medical Officer
- all medical stores and supplies are his responsibility
- while on passage, if a medicine expires, it will need to be declared as such in any customs declaration. Any surplus medicines not recorded in the medical stores list may arouse suspicions with authorities and may have serious consequences
- access to the medicine locker should be restricted to authorised personnel only, in accordance with the Company's or the flag State's rules
- no crew member should be allowed to possess private medicines without the Master being notified. The crew should be requested to compile a list of any private medicines carried on board. Possession of undeclared private medicines may in some countries constitute a breach of customs or other regulations, with the possibility of a fine being imposed on the Master and the individual crew member. If a crew member has been prescribed medication, the original or a certified copy of the prescription should be carried, together with the medicine
- the presence of any serious infection may lead you to request the Company to arrange for repatriation of the crew member concerned.

Treatment

Action Officers: Ship's Medical Officer and Heads of Department

The procedure for treatment should be as follows:

- [ ] The dispensary must be opened for treatment by contacting the Medical Officer
- [ ] any treatment given should be logged. This will evidence proper medical care and will demonstrate to any authorities how medicine abuse is being prevented
- [ ] should the Medical Officer have any doubt about a diagnosis or the treatment to give, the Master should be consulted
- [ ] if the Medical Officer decides that shore treatment is required, the appropriate medical treatment form must be completed
- [ ] the Medical Officer should advise the Chief Engineer or the Chief Officer if a member of their department needs to be sent ashore for medical treatment. If possible, a convenient time should be arranged for the patient to attend the doctor
- [ ] the Medical Officer must advise the Master of any shore treatment that is required so that the Master can arrange this through the agents
- [ ] on the patient's return to the ship, the medical form must be collected and a copy sent to the Company

Medical

- ❑ if any patient is placed off duty, either by the ship's Medical Officer or by the shore medical authorities, the Head of the Department and the Master must be advised immediately
- ❑ any patient who is off duty must be checked daily by the Medical Officer, who will then report daily to the Master
- ❑ if hospitalisation or repatriation is recommended by the shore medical authorities, the Master, agent and Company must be advised immediately
- ❑ the Head of Department will arrange the patient's personal effects to be landed
- ❑ the Administration Officer (Master) should arrange for the patient's documents to be landed
- ❑ the Master must arrange for the patient's payoff
- ❑ should the Medical Officer be unavailable, a Head of Department may place a crew member temporarily off duty until the Medical Officer becomes available
- ❑ any injury or illness that prevents a seafarer from working for more than three days should be reported to the MAIB if on a UK vessel or on any vessel in UK waters.

Injury, Illness or Death

Injury

In the event of an accident causing personal injury, your P&I Club should be contacted at the earliest opportunity.

Action to be taken

- ❑ Refer to any Emergency Action Plans/SMS
- ❑ provide medical care using the most skilled medic on board
- ❑ where risk of internal injury may occur, do not move the casualty until an experienced medic is in attendance
- ❑ obtain medical advice from ashore
- ❑ at sea, consider deviating for medical assistance
- ❑ in port, call an ambulance and the local P&I correspondent
- ❑ notify the Company and your P&I Club
- ❑ maintain a record of all communications
- ❑ submit an MAIB report as appropriate.

If a crew member is hospitalised and is unable to return to the vessel, you should:

Collection of evidence

- ❑ Ensure the area is not disturbed until photographs and videos have been taken as evidence
- ❑ note the date/time that each photograph/video was taken
- ❑ if no camera is available, make drawings/sketches showing the location/position in which the person was found
- ❑ record all communications concerning the event
- ❑ retain wires, shackles or tools that may have caused the injury. Mark or label as appropriate and store in a safe place.

Further evidence to be collected

- ❑ Name, sex and duties of the person concerned
- ❑ date and time (ship's and UTC) when the accident occurred
- ❑ ship's position
- ❑ weather conditions
- ❑ vessel movement
- ❑ illumination levels at the time, eg daylight, darkness, artificial light
- ❑ exact location on the vessel and the conditions in that area
- ❑ work activity the person was engaged in and the time it began
- ❑ hours of work and rest records, any indications of fatigue
- ❑ permit to work/risk assessment for the task
- ❑ PPE in use at the time
- ❑ witness details
- ❑ details of hospital/doctor who administered treatment
- ❑ medical treatment given
- ❑ any indications of intoxication or drug abuse
- ❑ detailed statements.

Illness

In the event of illness of a crew member or passenger, the procedure should be as set out below. Adherence to agreed Company procedures will limit the possibility of a subsequent claim for negligence being issued by a passenger who was taken ill.

Action to be taken

- ❑ Provide medical care using the most skilled medic on board
- ❑ obtain medical advice from ashore
- ❑ at sea, consider deviating for medical assistance
- ❑ in port, call an ambulance and the local P&I correspondent
- ❑ notify the Company and your P&I Club
- ❑ maintain a record of all communications
- ❑ submit an MAIB report as appropriate.

If a crew member is hospitalised and is unable to return to the vessel, you should:

- ❑ Make a record of and pack all the personal effects of the crew member, preferably with two officers as witnesses. The effects should be delivered to the care of the ship's agent to arrange for transfer to the hospital
- ❑ ask the P&I correspondent to notify the local consulate of the crew member
- ❑ request a replacement for the crew member.

Death

In the event of a death on board, there will not generally be a doctor available to examine the deceased and determine the likely cause of death. In the event of accidental death or death by unnatural causes, a post-mortem will almost certainly be required by the local/national police authorities once the body is landed ashore.

Action to be taken

- ❑ Seek medical advice to establish with certainty that the person is dead. Refer to the Ship Captain's Medical Guide
- ❑ determine how best to preserve the corpse. There may be body bags in the medical stores. The corpse should be kept cool by keeping it in the refrigerated stores
- ❑ if a means of preserving the corpse is not available, seek guidance from your Company and P&I Club regarding the ship deviating to land the body ashore (if deviating, notify the Company and P&I Club as this will allow them to assist and notify the appropriate authorities)
- ❑ if in port, request both a doctor and the local P&I correspondent immediately. This will allow them to assist in notification to the appropriate authorities
- ❑ all medical-related messages should be recorded
- ❑ ensure that the next of kin are notified
- ❑ make a record of and pack all the personal effects of the deceased, preferably with two officers as witnesses. The personal items should be delivered to the care of the ship's agent who will arrange for return to the next of kin
- ❑ ask the P&I correspondent to notify the local consulate of the deceased
- ❑ request a replacement crew member.

Collection of evidence

- ❑ Ensure the area is not disturbed until photographs and/or videos have been taken as evidence
- ❑ note the date/time that each photograph/video was taken
- ❑ if no camera is available, make drawings/sketches showing the location and position in which the person was found
- ❑ record all communications concerning the event
- ❑ evidence such as wires, shackles and tools that may have caused the death should be collected, marked, labelled and retained in a safe place.

Further evidence to be collected

- ❑ Name, sex and duties of the deceased
- ❑ date and time (ship's and UTC) when the death occurred
- ❑ ship's position
- ❑ weather conditions
- ❑ vessel movement
- ❑ illumination levels at the time, eg daylight, darkness, artificial light
- ❑ exact location on the vessel and the conditions in that area
- ❑ work activity the deceased was engaged in and the time it began
- ❑ hours of work and rest records, any indications of fatigue
- ❑ permit to work/risk assessment for the task
- ❑ PPE in use at the time of death

Medical

- ❑ witness details
- ❑ details of hospital/doctor who attended the deceased
- ❑ medical treatment given
- ❑ any indications of intoxication or drug abuse
- ❑ detailed statements from any witnesses to the event.

Drugs and Alcohol

You should ensure that the Company's drugs and alcohol policy is strictly enforced. Any deviations may have serious consequences for the safety and security of the crew, vessel and operations.

General

Comprehensive information should be provided to the crew on:

- The drugs and alcohol policy of the Company
- the possibility that the vessel could be used for smuggling drugs and the consequences of any of the ship's crew giving support to drug dealers
- the consequences should a crew member be found with drugs for personal use (ie criminal prosecution).

Drug Use On Board

You should make it very clear to the crew that the possession or use of drugs has an impact on the safety and security of the vessel and crew and is likely to lead to instant dismissal, with all associated costs of repatriation and replacement deducted from the individual's salary.

Measures to Prevent Drug Smuggling

The cover provided by your P&I Club may be void if the vessel is found to be smuggling drugs.

The following basic measures, which can be taken in port or in an anchorage, will assist:

- ❑ Prepare a detailed search list for drugs
- ❑ regular searches, based on this list, should be completed prior to and upon sailing from any port with a reputation for drug smuggling
- ❑ at night, illuminate the exterior of the vessel and the adjacent pier and water areas
- ❑ all doors to the accommodation and storerooms should be locked and those that are not required during the stay should be sealed
- ❑ any compartments that could be used for smuggling or concealment of drugs should be secured and sealed
- ❑ any areas of the ship that cannot be sealed should be accessible to authorised personnel only
- ❑ employ a gangway security system 24 hours a day
- ❑ any empty containers should be locked and sealed and the serial number of the seal noted.

If Drugs are Found

The Company and the P&I insurer should be contacted immediately. Actions should be taken and evidence collected to protect the Company and the crew.

Before the authorities arrive:

- ❑ The drugs must not be touched
- ❑ photograph/video the location where the drugs were found
- ❑ ensure the area is left untouched
- ❑ seal off the area to prevent any unauthorised access.

If any broken seals are discovered, they should be recorded in the logbook and on the bill of lading, noting the seal numbers.

Alcohol

You should make it clear to the crew that any deviation from the Company's alcohol policy will have serious personal consequences, including possible instant dismissal.

While moderate consumption of alcohol is considered a social activity, excessive amounts can seriously affect the safety and security of the vessel and the crew.

Your rights to carry out breath or blood tests will be subject to the regulations of the flag State and the terms of the crew contracts of employment.

Navigation

The Navigation Officer should know what the Master expects of him and what his sphere of responsibility is. However, all Masters are different and they must advise the deck officer how he expects the navigation of the ship to be carried out.

Responsibilities

Responsible Officer: Master

Action Officers: Officer keeping the 12 to 4 watch and designated ship's Navigation Officer

The Navigation Officer is responsible for:

- The upkeep of all navigation and bridge publications
- all charts and their corrections
- charterer's and owner's log abstracts
- passage planning
- routine navigational messages
- correct functioning of all bridge equipment
- all the ship's stationery requirements
- all noon and owner's/charterer's position reports
- maintenance of all bridge equipment
- all ETAs to port/pilot and agents.

Passage Planning

When the ship is advised of its next employment, the Navigation Officer must:

- Check that all the necessary charts are on board and corrected with the latest available information
- check the port of destination for draught and navigational dangers and consult with the Master if he has any doubt as to the safety of the port or passage into the port
- consult with the Master to discuss the voyage and obtain the Master's general guidance and preferences for the passage. At this time, the Navigating Officer can share his general observations for the passage. After this passage planning discussion, he will prepare the passage, advising the Master once it is completed
- once the course is charted (or plotted on the ECDIS), the Navigation Officer must prepare a list of courses and distances and a detailed voyage plan
- if required, prior to arrival, request the pilots at the destination port to email the port approach plan to the ship.

Communications

The Navigation Officer will issue, as required, the following navigational messages:

- AMVER position reports
- national ship reporting system messages
- routine charter position reports
- routine Company position reports.

GMDSS Logbook Entries

The following is a summary of what should be recorded in the GMDSS Logbook:

- ❑ A summary of any distress, urgency or safety communications received
- ❑ ship's position, at least once per day
- ❑ condition of the radio equipment
- ❑ details of personnel assigned the responsibility for sending distress alerts
- ❑ training on the use of the radio equipment to relevant crew members
- ❑ pre-sailing checks to ensure that the GMDSS station is in working order
- ❑ results of the testing of the DSC distress and safety radio equipment at least once a week. This should be by means of a test call
- ❑ monthly testing of SART, EPIRB and GMDSS VHF radios
- ❑ results of the testing of the distress and safety radio equipment at least once a day (by means of a test without radiating any signal)
- ❑ daily test of the batteries (on-load and off-load)
- ❑ weekly hydrometer test of the batteries

Navigation

- ❑ results of the monthly integrity check of each battery and its connections
- ❑ the Master is to sign the GMDSS Logbook once per day.

Equipment Maintenance

- ❑ If there is any malfunction of bridge equipment, the Navigation Officer should issue a repair chit to the department or officer concerned with the repair
- ❑ he must advise the Master of any equipment malfunction
- ❑ once the repair has been carried out, he should let the Master know
- ❑ should shore assistance be required, he should advise the Master, who will consult with the officer responsible for the maintenance of the equipment
- ❑ the Company should be kept informed as necessary.

Flags

Action Officers: Deck Officer keeping the 8 to 12 watch and OOW

- ❑ Once the ship has been advised of its next intended voyage, the flags required for this voyage must be checked and new ones ordered if necessary
- ❑ all flags and halyards should be kept in a good state of repair. The Chief Officer will arrange crew as required by the Action Officers for this
- ❑ prior to arrival in port, the required flags should be labelled and put out ready for use.

Helicopter Transfer - Planned Operation

Helicopter operations are commonplace on many vessels and are used for a variety of tasks, such as pilot transfer, delivery of stores, emergency medical evacuation and crew transfer. As with all frequent operations, as they become routine, the various precautions tend to decline. It is only when an accident happens that the essential need for these precautions becomes apparent.

Helicopter operations have the potential of being one of the most dangerous operations taking place on a ship, with the possibility of an accident always present. If an accident occurs, the precautions taken by the ship and the readiness of the deck party for emergency response will determine the outcome.

The Helicopter Landing Officer is in charge of the landing operation at all times, from when the helicopter makes its final approach until it has taken off and is clear of the ship. He must at all times be in direct contact with the bridge and be able to direct the helicopter by light signals and/or communications throughout the operation. If at any time he is not satisfied as to the safety of the operation, he has the authority to abort the operation and wave off the helicopter. He should have a signal torch that can show red for wave off and green for safe approach.

It is imperative that all the deck party remain upwind of the operations area and a good distance away. Those not immediately involved with the operation should, if possible, be sheltered. A helicopter accident can scatter pieces of rotor blade and burning debris over a wide area.

The ship's emergency party should be regularly drilled in dealing with such an emergency.

Prior to Helicopter Operations

The following information should be provided to the helicopter operators or the agent:

- ❑ ETA
- ❑ ship's speed and course
- ❑ present weather conditions, including visibility
- ❑ present pitches, roll and heave
- ❑ diameter of landing zone or winch area
- ❑ VHF frequencies to be used
- ❑ any locating aids, such as non-directional beacons.

On Helicopter Approach

- ❑ Establish VHF contact
- ❑ confirm the vessel's speed and course
- ❑ confirm pitch, roll and heave
- ❑ confirm wind direction, force and visibility
- ❑ if safe, set course and speed as requested by the helicopter
- ❑ confirm the landing area is clear for landing or winch area is clear for operations
- ❑ advise the pilot if the landing area is wet and taking water (in exceptional circumstances, to avoid skidding, netting

can be laid on the landing area. This should only be done after discussion with the pilot).

Deck Preparation

- ❑ A windsock should be hoisted where the approaching helicopter will have a clear view. At night, this should be illuminated
- ❑ ensure the area of operations is clear of loose equipment and debris. Cargo residue should be washed down
- ❑ ensure that all rigging in the area is secure and clear of the operations area
- ❑ the whole area should initially be illuminated, especially masts, aerials and rigging in the vicinity. Any lighting that could interfere with the helicopter pilot's vision should be shielded
- ❑ the bridge should ensure that personnel are standing by to control the lighting when required to do so by the helicopter
- ❑ the fire party should be standing by with the following equipment:
  - fire hoses connected, fire pump on and line pressurised, foam nozzle fitted and foam container standing by
  - axe
  - crowbar
  - hacksaw
  - boltcutters
  - ladder
  - torches (at night).

PPE

The helideck operations party should wear the following:

- ❑ Flame-retardant overalls and gloves (hose party fire suits)
- ❑ helmets with visors
- ❑ safety boots
- ❑ ear protectors.

Other Considerations

Unsafe Port – Unsafe Berth

You should be attentive to the possibility that a port or berth may become unsafe during your visit. If you are concerned that your vessel may become damaged, eg due to prevailing weather conditions or the condition of the berth, you should take appropriate action immediately.

Before approaching any berth or terminal where you have any suspicion that there could be a problem with the berth, you should consider taking a number of photographs before berthing as evidence of the condition of the berth.

Sailing on a Critical RPM for a Prolonged Period of Time

Should you be instructed or required to proceed over a period of time within the critical RPM range, you should notify the engine room to prevent any damage to the vessel's propulsion system.

Tug Assistance

The main cause of damage to locks, berths and the vessel itself is insufficient tug assistance, particularly in areas of prevailing strong tides and/or winds.

Proper consideration should be given to the level of tug assistance required to enable your vessel to arrive and depart safely from a port or berth.

A standard towage contract will allocate any liability to the vessel being towed, even if there is no fault or negligence on their part. It is generally difficult to prove any fault or negligence on the part of the tug as most towage contracts are based on the fact that the tug is the servant of the tow, even where the navigation is conducted by the tug. Therefore, your owners and ultimately your P&I Club may be held liable if a tug is damaged or causes any damage during any berthing or unberthing operation.

Any damage to your own vessel will affect your hull and machinery insurance cover, as the tug's liability is generally excluded under most towage contracts.

When working with tugs, you should:

- Be alert when any manoeuvres are carried out by your own vessel or the tug(s)
- always be aware as to the position of any tugs
- always monitor your own vessel's speed to avoid overrunning the tug
- cooperate with the pilot and the tug master.

Navigation

The names of the tugs and the time they were made fast/released should be recorded in the bridge movement book.

Parametric/Synchronous Rolling

It is important to continually monitor any changes in the vessel's trim and/or rolling period to avoid excessive rolling (referred to as parametric or synchronous rolling). A ship can quickly generate large angles of roll together with violent pitch and yaw motions when the following conditions occur:

- The vessel is in head or near head seas (head-on seas result in lower ship's speed, which results in larger roll motions)
- the length of the waves, crest to crest, is of a similar length to your own vessel
- the height of the waves is greater than the height that allows the natural pitch/roll cycle of the vessel to harmonise with the period of oncoming waves.

Cargo

The cargo is the responsibility of the Chief Officer.

Responsibilities

The Chief Officer is responsible for

- The planning and loading of all cargo
- preparing the cargo handling equipment
- the safe stability of the vessel at all times
- monitoring the cargo on board
- efficient cargo watch in port.

Voyage Orders

The Chief Officer must ascertain:

Dry Cargo Carriers

- ❑ The voyage number
- ❑ the ETA at load or discharge port
- ❑ draught at load or discharge port
- ❑ the name of the terminal
- ❑ the quantity and type of cargo to load/discharge
- ❑ laydays
- ❑ the ship's speed en route - maximum, chartered speed or economic
- ❑ safe port/safe berth
- ❑ name and communications addresses of agents
- ❑ communications schedules
- ❑ notices of ETA
- ❑ any pertinent charter party clauses
- ❑ bunkering port.

Special requirements

- ❑ Any stowage requirements
- ❑ any special hold preparation requirements
- ❑ hold and cargo surveys
- ❑ instructions for cargo work in rain
- ❑ ventilation requirements
- ❑ routeing requirements.

Prior to arrival, from the agent

- ❑ Confirmation of receipt of ETA
- ❑ confirmation of pilot ordered or anchor instructions
- ❑ which side alongside
- ❑ number of loaders or discharge grabs
- ❑ loading rate
- ❑ berth number, length and draught
- ❑ ship or shore gangway
- ❑ confirmation of acceptance of load or discharge plan
- ❑ port forms required and number of copies
- ❑ bunkers/stores/fresh water advice

Cargo

- ❑ time of attendance and granting of port clearance.

On arrival

- ❑ Confirmation of receipt and acceptance of notice of readiness (NOR).

Tankers

- ❑ The voyage number
- ❑ the ETA at the load port(s)
- ❑ terminal name
- ❑ loading date range
- ❑ quantity and grade of cargo(es) to load
- ❑ identification of cargo inspector
- ❑ cargo sampling instructions
- ❑ port clearance information
- ❑ cargo supplier
- ❑ consignor
- ❑ B/L number
- ❑ the ship's speed en route and/or required ETA at discharge port
- ❑ cargo instructions, including:
  - cargo tank preparations for the next cargo
  - any cargo heating requirements
  - cargo and vapour segregation requirements
  - vapour recovery (where applicable)
  - load-on-top instructions
  - any other relevant information (ship/consignor's agent, etc)
- ❑ information about the discharge port, which may include:
  - port name
  - terminal/berth
  - discharge date
  - identification of cargo inspector
  - cargo sampling instructions
  - port clearance information
  - consignee
  - cargo instructions, including:
    - vapour balance
    - discharge temperature
    - any other relevant information (ship/receiver's agent, etc).

Cargo Records

Oil Tankers

The following papers must be retained for each cargo:

- ❑ Cargo nomination email (or telex)
- ❑ NOR
- ❑ cargo plan
- ❑ ship/shore safety checklist
- ❑ cargo log sheet (including pumping log)
- ❑ certificate of discharge
- ❑ also, where issued:
  - receipt for any ballast/slops discharged
  - letter(s) of protest
  - request for water plug
  - B/L.

Bulk and General Cargo Ships

- ❑ Cargo orders
- ❑ stowage plan
- ❑ discharge plan
- ❑ ballast replacement plan
- ❑ ballast discharge and load plan
- ❑ all communications regarding cargo, including copies of emails
- ❑ NOR
- ❑ notes of protest
- ❑ letters of protest
- ❑ hold survey certificates
- ❑ cargo chemical analysis and hazard data sheets
- ❑ any dangerous goods declarations
- ❑ moisture content certificate
- ❑ draught surveys - initial, intermediate and final
- ❑ cargo survey certificate
- ❑ rain indemnity
- ❑ master's receipts
- ❑ arrival draught calculations
- ❑ discharge programme
- ❑ damage report
- ❑ timesheets
- ❑ off-hire report
- ❑ cargo log.

Cargo

The Cargo Log

- ❑ How you want the cargo stowed or loaded
- ❑ lashing and dunnaging if a dry cargo
- ❑ the cargo plan
- ❑ recording of damage to cargo
- ❑ the ballasting programme
- ❑ topping-off of tanks
- ❑ soundings
- ❑ overboard discharge
- ❑ stoppages
- ❑ when to be called
- ❑ handover
- ❑ cargo disputes.

Cargo Loading

- ❑ Prior to loading a cargo, the Chief Officer must ensure that the ship is ready to receive it
- ❑ he should prepare an initial loading plan based on the charterer's requirements. This plan must then be sent to the charterer
- ❑ once the plan is accepted and the cargo is confirmed, a detailed loading plan must be prepared and sent to the load port
- ❑ throughout these operations, the Master should be consulted about the stresses, draught and trim
- ❑ the Chief Officer must ensure that, prior to arrival, all deck officers are fully conversant with the cargo loading plan
- ❑ he must ensure that all local port regulations are complied with
- ❑ the ship/shore safety checklist or port compliance form should be given to the terminal for signature
- ❑ the Chief Officer must complete the deadweight report
- ❑ on completion, the Chief Officer must ensure that the ship is secured and make a logbook entry to that effect.

Discharge

- ❑ The Chief Officer must make a discharge plan and forward it to the agents at the discharge port
- ❑ he must ensure all deck officers are fully conversant with the plan
- ❑ on completion, he must ensure that the ship is ballasted and ready for sea
- ❑ he should ensure that the ship is secured and make a log entry to this effect.

Cargo Checklists – Oil Tankers

Arrival at a Terminal Using a Vapour Emission Control System (VECS)

Before arriving at a loading port where a VECS is used, it is essential that the following preparations are carried out:

- ❑ Contact the terminal to determine:
  - diameter of the vapour line to be used (so the appropriate vapour line reducer can be fitted)
  - maximum liquid transfer rate
  - requirements for additional processing (purging) of vapour in cargo oil tanks (the facility may impose limits on oxygen, hydrocarbon and hydrogen sulphide content)
- ❑ purge the tanks to reduce the oxygen content to less than 8% by volume and the hydrogen sulphide content to 10 ppm or less

- ❑ check the operation of the fixed closed tank gauging system
- ❑ check the operation of the portable closed gauging system
- ❑ set high level alarms to no greater than 95% of the tank volume and test the visible and audible alarms
- ❑ test overfill alarms for each tank
- ❑ isolate the inert gas system from the deck main
- ❑ check function and pressure settings of each tank P/V valve or high velocity vent
- ❑ check the function and setting of any P/V relief valve on the inert gas distribution pipeline
- ❑ check that the liquid level in the deck seal is correct
- ❑ ensure that the cargo transfer plan is consistent with the VECS manual required under the IMO Standards for Vapour Emission Control Systems, MSC/Circ.585 and MARPOL Annex VI, Regulation 15 and USCG 46 CFR 39, as appropriate
- ❑ briefly open the drain line to clear the system of any condensate
- ❑ check the electrical conductivity, ensuring that the vapour piping is correctly grounded to the hull with a maximum resistance of no more than 10 KΩ
- ❑ check the function and settings of the audible and visual high and low pressure alarms for the inert gas distribution piping system
- ❑ check the integrity of the manifold valve
- ❑ reduce the tank pressure to 10 mb (100 mmWG or 1 kPa).

Cargo Valve Failure

If the cargo valve control system fails during cargo operations, the following actions should be taken:

- ❑ If the cargo valve hydraulic system leaks, sections of the pipeline system should be isolated, ensuring that the maximum number of valves can be hydraulically operated
- ❑ arrange for crew members to be available to operate valves manually
- ❑ place portable units in positions where they will be most effective and require minimum effort to move
- ❑ valves with an auto/manual changeover set-up should be switched to manual operation. A prominent notice should be posted at the valve control position, making it clear which valves have been switched to manual control
- ❑ regularly check critical isolation valves that cannot be manually operated, ensuring they remain closed
- ❑ arrangements should be made to ensure that critical isolation valves that have been switched to manual control are not inadvertently opened
- ❑ when loading cargo, the transfer rate should be reassessed because of the extra time required to operate valves manually
- ❑ personnel involved in the operation should be briefed and given familiarisation training in the use of portable hydraulic units.

Failure of Inert Gas System (IGS)

When a serious failure of the IGS occurs during cargo operations, the following should be carried out:

- ❑ Stop cargo operations and close all valves
- ❑ advise the port authority, if necessary
- ❑ make the necessary notifications required by the operator's procedures
- ❑ advise the facility representative
- ❑ check for any leaks on the venting system and confirm that the cargo openings are tightly closed. Any leaks found must be managed without opening cargo oil tanks
- ❑ institute control measures to prevent the opening of any tank vents, valves or tank openings
- ❑ monitor tank pressures if possible
- ❑ prepare for the possibility of continuing operations with an external inert gas supply.

Oil Discharge Monitoring Equipment (ODME) Failure

When an ODME failure occurs and discharge control can only be carried out manually, overboard discharge must be stopped and an entry made in the Oil Record Book Part II, Cargo/Ballast Operations (Oil Tankers), operational code M, alongside items 70, 71 and 72. The recorded times of when the system failed, was repaired and was made operational should be consistent with the ODME printouts.

Cargo

The record of the failure should be factual and supported by a technician's report.

If the unit cannot be repaired on board, the tanker's operator must be advised and arrangements made for a technician to attend or for the spare parts to be delivered at the next port of call.

MARPOL Annex 1 Regulation 31, Oil discharge monitoring and control system, states that:

"A failure of the monitoring and control system shall stop the discharge. In the event of failure of the oil discharge monitoring and control system a manually operated alternative method may be used. The defective unit must be made operable as soon as possible. With the permission of the flag State authority, a tanker with a defective oil discharge monitoring and control system may undertake one ballast voyage before proceeding to a repair port."

If a failure occurs during the ballast passage, ballast or slops from cargo oil tanks can be discharged under permitted conditions with the ODME operated in manual mode. The following must be carried out:

- ❑ The Master's authorisation should be sought before operating the ODME in manual mode
- ❑ the tanker operator's procedure for manual operation of ODME should be implemented
- ❑ the manufacturer's approved instructions for manual operation must be followed strictly
- ❑ when monitoring of the effluent discharge can only be carried out visually, it must be carried out during daylight hours only
- ❑ during discharge, the oil/water interface must be continually checked using an approved oil/water interface detector
- ❑ when dirty ballast is discharged, a small amount should be left in each tank being deballasted. This should be transferred to a designated slop tank for decanting.

If the ODME is unable to provide data automatically, the following methods can be used to determine the required information:

- If the oil content cannot be determined automatically due to the oil content or sampling system failing, it can be estimated using a visual observation of the sea surface in the area of the overboard discharge, in combination with the oil/water interface level measurements taken from tanks that are being deballasted
- if the flow meter fails, the flow rate can be approximated by referring to the pump characteristic curve under the actual discharge conditions, or it can be determined by the calculation of changes in ballast volume using cargo oil tank calibration tables
- when a failure renders speed indication unavailable, speed can be calculated using rpm, propeller diameter, pitch and predicted slip
- when failure renders geographical position information unavailable, a position can be obtained from other position fixing instruments on board.

If a processor fails, the instantaneous rate of discharge and total oil content can be calculated using the following formulae:

$$\text{Instantaneous rate of discharge} = \frac{\text{estimated oil content (ppm)} \times \text{flow rate (m}^3\text{/h)}}{1{,}000 \times \text{speed (knots)}} \text{ l/nm}$$

$$\text{Oil discharged} = \frac{\text{flow rate (m}^3\text{/h)} \times \text{oil content (ppm)} \times \text{time (mins)*}}{60{,}000} \text{ litres}$$

* The oil discharged in the second equation refers to the time interval in minutes, when the oil content of the effluent is considered to be constant.

The total oil discharged, which must be no greater than 1/30,000 of the volume of the previous cargo, is the aggregate or running total of the oil discharged calculations.

For example, a tanker travelling at 15 knots, discharging dirty ballast with an oil content of 60 ppm at 1,000 m^3/h for 8 minutes, then ballast with an oil content of 80 ppm at 900 m^3/h for 6 minutes:

$$\text{The instantaneous rate of discharge is constant} = \frac{60 \times 1{,}000}{1{,}000 \times 15} = 4 \text{ litres/nm}$$

$$\text{The oil discharged} = \frac{1{,}000 \times 60 \times 8}{60{,}000} = 8 \text{ litres}$$

$$\text{The instantaneous rate of discharge is constant} = \frac{80 \times 900}{1{,}000 \times 15} = \frac{72{,}000}{15{,}000} = 4.8 \text{ litres/nm}$$

$$\text{The oil discharged} = \frac{900 \times 80 \times 6}{60{,}000} = \frac{72{,}000}{10{,}000} = 7.2 \text{ litres}$$

Total oil discharged = 8 + 7.2 = 15.2 litres

Pump speed and discharge valve operation should be controlled manually, ensuring that the flow rate of the discharge overboard is such that the instantaneous rate of discharge of oil does not exceed 30 litres per nautical mile.

Signing Bills of Lading (B/L) - Letters of Indemnity

The difficulties and liabilities arising from issuing and signing B/Ls is an area that your P&I Club should have published guidance on. The information contained here is for rapid reference only.

General

A bill of lading is a valuable legal document with three very important functions:

- It is a document of title
- it is evidence of the contract of carriage between the Company and the cargo interests
- it is a receipt for the goods loaded.

When signing the B/L, it is important that you ensure the information is accurate. If it is inaccurate or false, there will be serious consequences for your Company or charterer, including exposure to possible claims from other cargo interests. This is particularly the case if the B/L has been endorsed to a third party consignee.

If the B/L is traded while the vessel is en route to the discharge port, an innocent buyer will not be aware of the actual condition or quantity of the cargo. The details in the B/L are therefore considered to be conclusive evidence of the condition and quantity of the goods when shipped. The Company will be unable to defend any claim if the actual condition or quantity of the cargo is not in accordance with that stated in the B/L.

Your P&I cover may be affected as P&I rules tend to exclude cover for claims in certain circumstances where the information in the B/L is found to be incorrect.

Particular attention should be paid to the following details:

- Description of the condition and quantity of the cargo
- date of issue of the B/L.

If the cargo is seriously damaged, or you are unsure as to the extent of the damage, especially in the case of steel cargoes, the Master should contact the P&I correspondent to arrange for a survey.

If there appears to be no damage to the cargo, you should write on the B/L that the cargo was received 'in apparent good order and condition'.

The B/L must also record the correct quantity of cargo loaded. Alternatively, it should be claused 'weight and quantity unknown' or 'said to weigh'. You should note on the face of the B/L if the vessel's figures differ from the shore figures.

Date of issue

A 'shipped on board' B/L confirms that the cargo was loaded onto the vessel on a particular date. The date of shipment often has important implications, eg in the contract of sale between the shipper and the receiver. If the date is incorrect, the Company or charterer may face claims from the receiver. The B/L must therefore be signed and dated to record accurately the date when the cargo was actually loaded. You must not sign a post-dated B/L.

Authority on behalf of the Master to sign B/L

When charterers or agents are authorised to sign the B/L on your behalf, you should ensure that all the details you would have inserted into the B/L with regard to quantity, condition and date are inserted into the Mate's receipt. You should ensure that the charterers and/or agents are instructed to sign the B/L only in accordance with the Mate's receipt. If charterers and/or agents refuse to do so, you must issue a letter of protest and inform the Company immediately. Your P&I correspondent may also be able to assist.

Letters of indemnity

It is common practice for the shipper to offer a letter of indemnity in exchange for a clean B/L or a B/L that is postdated. Such letters of indemnity are unenforceable in most jurisdictions because the courts consider the carrier a party, with the shippers, to a fraud, ie the B/L is issued in the knowledge that it contains information on which the receivers will rely, but which is known to be incorrect.

Cargo

A letter of indemnity is therefore not legally binding and will offer the Company no protection if the shipper goes back on his promise. There will be no P&I cover available either as the P&I rules exclude cover for claims arising from the issue of a postdated B/L or claims arising from the issue of a B/L known to contain an incorrect description of the cargo, its quantity or condition.

Whenever you are requested to issue a clean or incorrectly dated B/L in return for a letter of indemnity, you should:

- Refuse, despite threats to delay the vessel or other pressures
- immediately contact the Company and/ or the P&I correspondent for advice and assistance.

Meetings

Meetings are important and useful, such as planning meetings for port arrival, drydocking, safety, cargo planning or repairs. Although most meetings on board tend to be informal, the following are some useful guidelines for planning and conducting them efficiently. These considerations apply equally to ships with large crew numbers with various specialised departments and to smaller crews, particularly for weekly management and regular Safety Committee meetings.

Safety Committee Meetings

The Code of Safe Working Practices for Merchant Seamen recommends that Safety Committee meetings take place at intervals of 4 to 6 weeks, although it recognises the need for flexibility. It is very prescriptive in format, structure and who should attend, ie at least the Master, Safety Officer and Safety Representatives.

It states that the Master should act as Chairman, and it is improbable in all but departmental meetings that any other member of the crew would take this role.

General Guidelines

All meetings must have a clear objective, which should be advised to all participants in advance or at the start of the meeting.

The Chairman plays an important role in controlling the meeting and steering it towards its intended objective. If appropriate, meetings can be structured with an agenda and, wherever possible, this should be circulated well in advance of the meeting.

The first duty of the Chairman is to start the meeting on time, welcoming the participants, stating the objective/s and reviewing the previous minutes. This establishes the Chairman's authority, sets the appropriate level of formality and focuses the group mind.

The Chairman should not:

- Use the position to demonstrate his knowledge
- allow familiarity to obscure the importance of the meeting

Meetings

- give too much direction or introduction to each item
- become too involved in debate
- make cynical, oppressive or demeaning retorts
- interfere with the outcome of the final decision.

An effective Chairman will:

- Remain calm, alert and attentive
- make swift and equitable decisions
- maintain good order
- remain impartial but take action when necessary
- encourage and ensure all participants have the opportunity to speak
- limit the number of interruptions in the meeting by protecting the person speaking
- act as facilitator, managing the meeting
- ensure progress is made in line with the items on the agenda
- keep discussions to the point and prevent unrelated subjects taking over
- not interfere with the direction or final decisions.

It may sometimes be appropriate for the Chief Engineer or Chief Officer to take the lead in discussions, for example on technical matters, and this can enable the Master to gain a better understanding of the matter under discussion. By taking a step back, he can also observe the personalities and dynamics of the crew.

For formal meetings (such as Safety Committee meetings), minutes should be taken and circulated as soon as possible after the meeting to maintain momentum. The minutes should record concisely the matters discussed, decisions reached, further actions to be taken and the identity of the person/s responsible for undertaking each action.

It is the Chairman's duty to formally close the meeting, and closing remarks should be kept brief and positive. He must not allow the meeting just to peter out because part of the group believes it is over as this can detract from the perceived importance of the meeting.

At the end of each meeting, an appropriate date for the next meeting should be set.

Communications

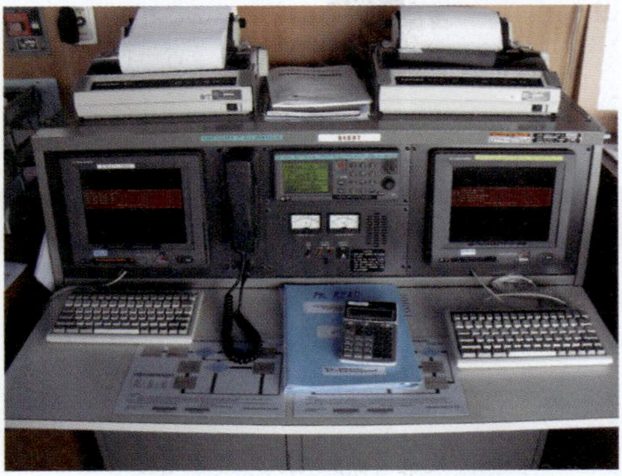

Responsible Officer: Second Officer

Responsibilities

- Maintenance of all communication equipment
- maintenance of all electronic bridge equipment
- instruction of the ship's company in safety communications
- requisition and maintenance of all spares and stores required
- correction of the Admiralty Lists of Radio Signals (ALRS)
- preparation of all radio and telephone accounts
- requisition and maintenance of all ship's stationery requirements
- requisition and maintenance of all flags
- maintenance of the GMDSS Logbook.

Repairs and Surveys

- ❑ When any fault is found with the ship's communication system (GMDSS) or with any electronic bridge equipment, a repair chit should be made out to the officer responsible for communications
- ❑ he will look at the equipment and advise the Head of Department of any repair that is required
- ❑ should shore technical assistance be required, the company should be advised

Communications

- ❑ the Second Officer is responsible for signing the work sheet and completion papers for the attendance of any shore technician
- ❑ he is also responsible for safety radio surveys and attending to the surveyor.

Administration

A number of the administrative functions will be carried out by the Master, but certain items will be delegated to others on board.

Responsible Officer: Master

Responsibilities

- ❑ Preparation of the monthly food stock accounts
- ❑ control of the ship's administration office
- ❑ reception of port officials and visitors
- ❑ preparation of port papers, including:
  - customs declaration
  - stores lists
  - crew lists
  - port health
  - list of narcotics
  - list of arms and ammunition
  - passenger declaration
  - emergency contact list
- ❑ issue of, and accounting for, the bond
- ❑ preparation and issue of cash advances
- ❑ advance weekly cash requirements
- ❑ the ship's postal services
- ❑ preparation of the Company mail envelopes and listing of contents
- ❑ care of the official documents and personnel files of the officers and crew
- ❑ filing and correction of all the Company fleet instructions.

Administrative Functions

- ❑ Administrative matters of the ship may be dealt with by the administration officer designated by the Master
- ❑ all personnel with questions on pay or the ship's administration should, in the first instance, refer their questions directly to the administration officer
- ❑ prior to arrival in port, the administration officer should prepare the port entry papers as detailed in the 'Guide to Port Entry'
- ❑ on arrival in port, he should receive the port officials on the gangway and conduct them to the port reception room and, in the absence of the Master, begin the ship's clearance
- ❑ in the absence of the Master, he should deal with the agent on ship matters
- ❑ he should receive all visitors to the ship in the port reception room and arrange the attendance of relevant ship's personnel when required
- ❑ on departure, he should collect mail from the ship's mail box and give this, together with the official mail, to the agent.

Accommodation

Hotel Services

On many ships, a Chief Steward is not carried and the Chief Cook carries out the duties of Chief Steward. He may not have the experience required to assume the traditional duties of the catering department and, in this case, the following guidelines are suggested to assist the efficiency of this department.

Do consider the needs of this department, which is expected to work seven days a week, continually judged and to continue with the same work regardless of weather or conditions on board.

It is important to ensure that the crew is responsible for their part of the ship and that the same standard of cleanliness is maintained in all areas.

Accommodation

Regardless of the size of ship, the weekly inspection should be a formal occasion with effort made to prepare the ship for it. It is an occasion for praise and reprimand, and for noting deficiencies that should be dealt with before the next inspection.

Responsible Officer: Master

Action Officers: Chief Officer, Chief Steward or Chief Cook

Working Hours and Overtime

- Working hours and overtime records are the responsibility of the Chief Steward or Chief Cook
- at the end of the month, he should submit the overtime figures of the catering department to the Chief Officer.

Cleanliness

The officers' quarters are serviced as follows:

Steward 1 is responsible for:

- ❑ Service in the officers' saloon
- ❑ cleanliness of the officers' pantry, duty mess, saloon and smoke room
- ❑ cleanliness and maintenance of all officers' cutlery and crockery
- ❑ cleanliness of the hospital (and passenger cabins if any)
- ❑ cleanliness of the accommodation deck, alleyways, stairs and bulkheads
- ❑ distribution of laundry, bath soap and cleaning materials to the crew
- ❑ cleaning officers' cabins as designated
- ❑ officers' laundry.

Steward 2 is responsible for:

- ❑ Serving officers' lunch in the duty mess
- ❑ assisting with the washing and maintenance of the officers' cutlery and crockery
- ❑ cleanliness of the accommodation deck, alleyways, stairs and bulkheads
- ❑ cleaning officers' cabins as designated
- ❑ assisting the Chief Cook in cleaning and general duties
- ❑ assisting Steward 1
- ❑ officers' laundry.

Ratings' Quarters

- ❑ Ratings' cabins are cleaned by the occupants
- ❑ ratings' quarters and public areas are cleaned by all departmental ratings, as designated by the Bosun.

Inspections

- ❑ All the accommodation should be inspected every week by the Master and heads of department
- ❑ the Bosun should accompany the inspection party for all crew areas
- ❑ all food storage rooms and refrigeration chambers must be inspected
- ❑ the Chief Officer should make a note of all defects and report them to the various departments for action
- ❑ all cabins should be vacated for inspection unless special exemption has been granted. Normal watchkeeping is not exempted
- ❑ keep a keen eye for any suspicious articles or strange conditions on board.

Accommodation inspections have to go beyond just checking everything is present and correct and in a clean condition. They should in particular look for deficiencies in any of the following areas:

- ❑ Spare gear lockers
- ❑ cabins
- ❑ messrooms
- ❑ galley
- ❑ storerooms
- ❑ refrigeration spaces
- ❑ toilets.

Many things can be wrong with the ship but if the food is good, the galley clean and the catering well managed, much will be forgiven. Get these wrong and problems will surely follow.

If you have no Chief Steward, you must ensure that the crew are consulted in decisions regarding their food.

Bedding is a neglected area on many ships. Bedding should be clean and, if the cleaning cannot be done by the ship's laundry, it should be sent ashore. If the condition of mattresses is poor, new ones should be provided.

Accommodation

An unhygienic environment could lead to outbreaks of food poisoning on board, which could seriously affect the health of the crew and ultimately the safety of the ship. Clean and well-kept galleys, storerooms and crew accommodation will help ensure the health of the crew.

Storerooms (including fridges and freezers) should be checked regularly and expiry dates for foodstuffs observed. Frozen food should be carefully checked for any signs of 'freezer burn' and any affected meat must be disposed of.

The entire water system must be regularly checked and cleaned. Careful maintenance of the entire water piping system, including the air conditioning unit, must take place at scheduled intervals to prevent the outbreak of bacterial infections such as Legionnaires' disease, especially when trading in areas with mild temperatures.

If fresh water is used in swimming pools, regular water quality tests (bromine, hardness, pH, etc) must be carried out and recorded.

You should be aware that there are various ILO and flag State regulations to be complied with and Port State Control may well inspect the accommodation, galleys and storerooms and take action if necessary.

Victualling

The following may be the procedure if a Chief Steward is not carried.

Responsible Officer: Master

Action Officer: Chief Cook

- ❑ The Chief Cook is responsible for the preparation of all the food
- ❑ the Chief Cook is responsible for the cleanliness and maintenance of all the galley, pantry and food store rooms
- ❑ the Chief Cook is responsible for menu preparation. He will prepare the menu book and present it to the Master each week
- ❑ the Chief Cook is responsible for the preparation of the list of food stores in good time before arrival at port
- ❑ a victualling committee is one approach to achieve balance of the stores on board. This could consist of:
  - the Master
  - deck officer representative
  - engineer officer representative
  - deck crew representative
  - engine crew representative
- ❑ the victualling committee should meet before each order is submitted to the chandler
- ❑ payment of bills should be authorised by the Master. The bills must be filed and available for inspection, clearly showing the rate of exchange and any discount allowed
- ❑ at the end of the month, the victualling accounts should be posted for the officers and crew
- ❑ any complaints regarding food, cooking or quality should initially be directed to the complainant's representative.

Laundry

- ❑ Ratings are responsible for the laundry of their own sheets, pillowcases and towels, apart from the clean items issued on joining
- ❑ officers' sheets, duvet covers, pillowcases and towels are changed for laundering every week
- ❑ dirty blankets or duvets are to be dry-cleaned only, and should be sent ashore in selected ports.

Stores

Action Officer: Chief Cook

- ❑ Soap and soap powder must be issued to each cabin on the last day of the month
- ❑ the Chief Cook should keep a check of cabin stores and advise the Chief Officer of any requirements
- ❑ the Chief Cook should make a list of required items for the 6 months' requisition and hand this to the Chief Officer.

Personnel

New personnel joining a ship should have a clean cabin with fresh laundry available on arrival, as well as all required safety equipment, correctly sized and checked as part of their safety induction.

Joining Procedure

Action Officers: Chief Officer, 1st Engineer Officer and Chief Steward/Chief Cook

- ❑ Prior to personnel joining, the cabin they are to occupy must be cleaned
- ❑ the Chief Steward/Chief Cook must ensure that fresh linen, towels and blankets are issued for all newly joined personnel
- ❑ the Chief Steward/Chief Cook must ensure that joining information and checklists are placed in the cabins of new arrivals
- ❑ on their arrival, newly joined personnel should be accompanied by their superior to the Master's office to hand over their documents. They will then sign the ship's articles of agreement
- ❑ as soon as possible after joining, the Chief Officer and 1st Engineer Officer should arrange a guided tour of the ship. The Chief Officer is responsible for the catering department personnel
- ❑ it is important that heads of department meet their new personnel as soon as possible, and check that the joining procedure has been followed
- ❑ in the case of large crew changes (where more than 25% changes), a general emergency drill and boat stations muster should be held as soon as possible after sailing.

New Joiner Induction

These are to meet the requirements of the Safety Management System, STCW 95 and ISM Code.

Deck Officers

As many of the following items should be completed during the handover period and as much time as possible made available to the joining and leaving officers.

If insufficient time is available for the handover, the Chief Officer will be responsible for completing the familiarisation of the equipment and procedures concerning the deck department.

- ❑ Bridge equipment, including:
  - voyage plan
  - autopilot/steering console
  - electronic navigation aids
  - GMDSS
  - electronic charts
  - ARPA/RADAR/ECDIS
  - deck stress monitoring system
  - location of manuals
- ❑ alarms:
  - general emergency
  - lifeboat stations
  - CO_2 release
- ❑ main engine controls:
  - bridge
  - emergency steering gear
- ❑ IGS
- ❑ cargo system:
  - cargo pump room (including entry procedures)
- ❑ Crude Oil Washing (COW) system
- ❑ mooring patterns:
  - mooring winch controls
  - anchoring procedures
- ❑ safety induction of the vessel to include:
  - muster stations – lifeboat and emergency
  - fixed fire-fighting equipment (FFE)
  - CO_2 smothering
  - portable FFE
  - life-saving equipment
  - emergency escape routes
  - remote stops and trips
  - PPE
- ❑ briefing prior to taking up duties on:
  - man overboard
  - casualty in enclosed space
  - closing of fire and watertight doors
  - explanation of safety symbols
- ❑ current security level/CSO and SSO designations:
  - where security information is detailed
  - gangway/visitors log/pass system and procedures

Personnel

- basic lockdown and sealing procedures, as required
- restricted areas/procedures

- ❑ Master's standing orders read and understood
- ❑ Company standing orders
- ❑ handover notes read and understood (copy placed in ISM office file).

Crew Qualifications and Documentation

Crew Qualifications

You should ensure that all new crew who are assigned to the vessel are qualified and certificated appropriately for the voyage and that they meet the requirements of:

- ❑ The vessel's flag State
- ❑ STCW 95.

Crew Documentation

Crew documentation includes:

- Certificates of competency
- flag State certification and endorsements
- correct seafarer's identification book
- vaccination certificates
- training record book
- medical certificate.

Crew Competency

Each member of the crew should have the appropriate training and experience to perform their allocated duties. For newly joined crew members, you should satisfy yourself that they:

- Have a valid and genuine certificate of competency and the appropriate flag State endorsements (eg dangerous cargo endorsement)
- are properly familiarised with their duties on board, particularly those involved with watchkeeping duties
- are fit and healthy.

Any deficiency should be reported to the Company and a replacement requested.

You can achieve a general impression of the qualifications of new crew members from their ISF Personal Training and Record Book, or any other similar documents, which should contain all the relevant information on their professional qualifications, training and service.

Crew Fitness

You are required to monitor the fitness and health of your crew during the voyage, including:

- Alcohol consumption
- any signs of drug or medication abuse
- fatigue.

Should you observe any of the above, you should take appropriate corrective action without delay.

Particular attention should be paid to mandatory resting times prior to watches, as required by STCW 95, if applicable.

Crew Fatigue

You should watch for any indications of fatigue or psychological unfitness and should, if necessary:

- Review working hours/workloads of the individuals concerned
- initiate a medical examination
- inform the Company and request a substitution
- ensure ILO hours of work and rest requirements are adhered to and recorded correctly.

Leaving Procedure

Action Officers: Chief Officer, 1st Engineer Officer, Administration Officer and Chief Cook

- Prior to departure, all departing personnel must ensure that their cabins are clean
- ratings should hand all used linen and blankets to the Chief Cook. Stewards must replace the linen and blankets in the officers' cabins
- all personnel should hand in their ship-issued PPE to the Bosun and Fitter and have their PPE checklist signed. This list is not to be signed without presentation of the cabin key
- leaving personnel must collect their documents and payoff papers from the Master and, on presentation of the signed PPE checklist, sign off the ship's articles.

Discipline

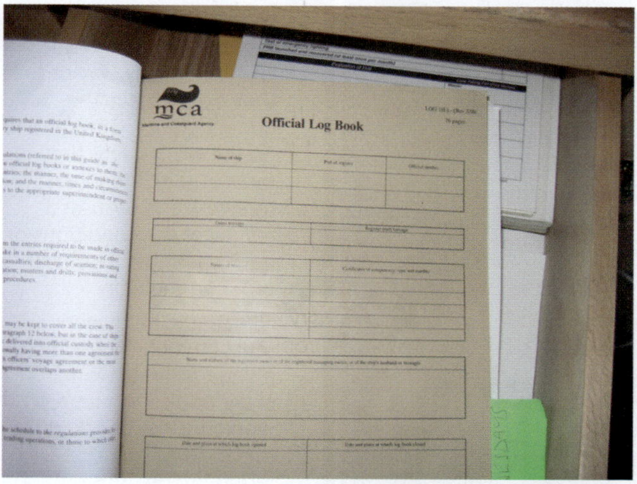

At sea, we have to live and work in an environment that requires conformity. This requires rules that govern behaviour while on the ship.

Without discipline, no ship can properly function. Effective discipline coupled with a well-managed ship that has a system in place for all grievances to be heard and addressed provides the background for a pleasant and fair environment for all.

Discipline begins with the presentation and appearance of each crew member, and includes wearing of the correct safety clothing/ PPE as required. In port, each crew member should display identification for officials and other visitors to see.

Discipline is best achieved out of respect. You must earn the respect of your officers and crew through the example of your leadership and management skills.

Ratings

- ❑ If any rating has a problem, relating either to his department or another aspect of shipboard management, he must first see his CPO
- ❑ if the CPO cannot deal satisfactorily with the problem, the CPO must advise the Chief Steward, Chief Officer or the 1st Engineer Officer of the situation
- ❑ the Chief Officer or 1st Engineer Officer should arrange a time to interview the rating concerned
- ❑ if the 1st Engineer Officer cannot resolve the problem, he should take the matter to the Chief Engineer
- ❑ if the Chief Steward cannot resolve the problem, he should take the matter to the Chief Officer
- ❑ if the Chief Engineer or Chief Officer cannot resolve the problem, they should refer the matter to the Master
- ❑ if the Master cannot resolve the problem to the rating's satisfaction, the matter should be referred to the Company.

Officers

- ❑ Any complaint a CPO or junior officer may have regarding a rating or any other shipboard matter must go directly to the Chief Officer or 1st Engineer Officer
- ❑ should the 1st Engineer Officer be unable to resolve the matter, he should refer it to the Chief Engineer
- ❑ if the Chief Officer or Chief Engineer cannot resolve the problem, the matter should be referred to the Master who will, if unable to resolve the problem, pass it to the Company.

Disciplinary Procedure

- ❑ Any discipline proceedings that involve crew members must initially be dealt with by the Chief Officer or 1st Engineer Officer, in the presence of the rating's CPO. Should the 1st Engineer Officer consider that the case is serious, he should take it before the Chief Engineer
- ❑ regardless of the way in which the situation is handled, the Master should be advised of the matter
- ❑ if the offence is of a serious nature and is likely to involve officially recorded warnings or punishment, the case should be brought to the Master, who might then order a hearing
- ❑ a suitable time for a hearing will be arranged. The case will be heard in the presence of the Head of Department, the CPO of the department, the rating involved and any witnesses.

ISM and ISPS Codes

Compliance with the International Safety Management (ISM) Code is a requirement for shipping.

Responsibilities

- Personnel involved in safety and environmental protection are responsible to the ship's Safety Officer
- CPOs are directly responsible for ensuring that those working under them are properly equipped for the work in hand
- the Safety Officer is responsible for ensuring that all safety equipment is in good order
- officers are responsible for ensuring that a safe environment exists within their department work areas
- the Safety Officer is responsible for ensuring that the correct equipment is available for the designated work
- department officers are responsible for ensuring that all PPE has been issued, is available and is used.

ISM Management

- ❑ The company SMS procedures must be adhered to and regularly reviewed
- ❑ any order given that involves any form of unsafe practice, puts a crew member in any form of danger or commits a crew member to work without the proper safety equipment is an illegal order
- ❑ CPOs must also ensure that the work is being carried out in a safe manner. If they feel that the work they are ordered to do is unsafe in any way or they do not have the correct equipment to do the work safely, they must immediately cease the work and request a review of the conditions or equipment by the officer ordering the work
- ❑ all departmental work must be recorded in a departmental work order book. Each item of work must be checked for conformity with ISM requirements. This notation must be signed by the officer giving the work order and the officer or crew member directly in charge of completing the work
- ❑ you must ensure that a common working language, understood by all on board, is used
- ❑ all risk assessment requirements must be adhered to and followed.

ISPS Code Checklists

The International Ship and Port Facility Security (ISPS) Code requires both ship and port to adopt security measures conforming to the level of security risk deemed to exist either by the ship or by the port. There are three levels of security and each level requires the ship to be prepared to take certain actions as required. Such actions must be in accordance with the Ship Security Plan (SSP) and would include the following.

Ship's Security Level 1

- ❑ Check the identity and business of all persons wishing to board the ship
- ❑ in liaison with the port, establish designated secure areas for the searching of persons, personal effects, baggage, and vehicles and their contents
- ❑ in liaison with the port, vehicles being loaded should be searched prior to loading with the frequency designated in the Ship's Security Plan

- ❑ all checked personnel and their personal effects are to be separated from unchecked persons and their effects
- ❑ embarking and disembarking passengers are to be segregated
- ❑ access points to be secured or guarded should be identified
- ❑ unattended spaces adjoining areas to which visitors or passengers have access should be secured
- ❑ brief all ship's company on the threat and the procedures for reporting suspicious persons, activities and objects.

Ship's Security Level 2

In addition to the above:

- ❑ Assign additional personnel to patrol deck areas during the silent hours
- ❑ limit the number of access points to the ship
- ❑ in liaison with the port, deter waterside access to the ship
- ❑ in liaison with the port, establish a restricted area on the shore side of the ship
- ❑ increase the frequency of searches of persons, effects and vehicles being embarked or loaded onto the ship
- ❑ escort visitors on the ship
- ❑ provide additional specific briefings on the security threat to the ship's company
- ❑ carry out a full or partial search of the ship.

Ship's Security Level 3

In addition to the above:

- ❑ Limit access to a single controlled point
- ❑ allow access only to those responding to a security incident or threat
- ❑ stop all embarkation and disembarkation
- ❑ stop all cargo and stores handling
- ❑ if required, prepare for:
    - evacuation of the ship
    - movement of the ship
- ❑ prepare for a full or partial search of the ship.

Note that, at security level 3, the ship should comply with the instructions of those responding to the incident or threat.

Checklist to Prevent Intruders (Stowaways)

History and experience demonstrate that skilled intruders are, once on board, extremely hard to find, even on a ship with efficient search procedures.

You should develop formalised plans for conducting thorough and extensive searches of the ship for any intruders.

The following precautions should be among those taken while in port:

- ❑ Anchor watch maintained
- ❑ main deck and gangway well illuminated and manned
- ❑ forecastle and all storerooms locked
- ❑ hawse/spurling pipe covers fixed in position
- ❑ lifeboat properly secured
- ❑ mooring lines well tended and fitted with large rat guards
- ❑ no pilot ladders etc to be left hanging over the ship's side
- ❑ visitors challenged and identified at the gangway
- ❑ high profile deck watch
- ❑ careful checking of containerised, palletised and other unitised cargoes
- ❑ access doors to the accommodation locked and sealed where possible, without compromising a safe means of escape.

In ports where a pass system is not viable, it will be helpful to maintain:

- ❑ A log with each visitor's name, duties, name and rank of the person visited, and times of boarding and disembarking
- ❑ a running total of the persons boarding and leaving.

The following measures for deterring intruders should be taken prior to departure:

- ❑ A thorough search of all areas of the vessel should be conducted to discover any stowaways who may be on board. This must be carried out in accordance with the vessel's own search list
- ❑ where available, professional shore-based companies with dogs should be engaged

ISM and ISPS Codes

- ❑ notices should be displayed at the gangway stating that 'Cargo holds will be treated with gas prior to departure'. This may well act as a deterrent for stowaways who can read and, on departure, compressed air could be injected to give the impression of injecting gas into the holds
- ❑ the vessel's next port of call should not be displayed unless it is suitably unattractive for a stowaway.

After departure following berthing at certain problematic countries, it is beneficial to stop the vessel within port limits and carry out a further search, including the stores and, if possible, the cargo holds. This is because it is easier to land stowaways before the vessel has left territorial waters.

All measures taken should be logged as evidence to immigration authorities that all proper precautions were taken.

Note: *In certain ports, there are significant risks of explosive devices being placed on board. However, it is considered that an efficient stowaway search should be sufficient to detect any such devices.*

Crew Identity

Before beginning the voyage, you must be satisfied that each crew member has full and proper identification that reflects the requirements of the ISPS Code.

Improper or incomprehensible seafarer identification may arouse suspicion of national immigration authorities and could result in the ship being refused entry to a port or the immediate repatriation of the crew member concerned.

Should you have any concerns, you should contact the Company for direction.

Steering Gear and Engine Tests

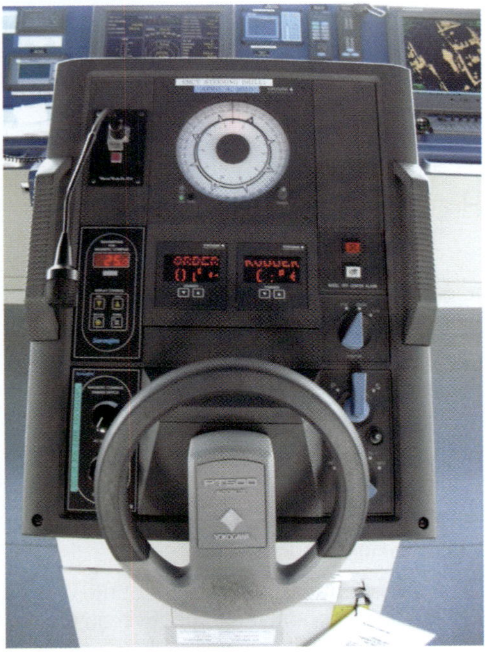

Responsibilities

- The Master is responsible for choosing a time for steering gear and engine tests to be made prior to arrival at port and prior to the engines being put on standby for any particular passage. Tests should be carried out in consultation with the Chief Engineer
- tests will normally be conducted within 24 hours of arrival and, in the case of the USA, 12 hours prior to entering the EEZ.

Steering Test at Sea

- ❑ At the time and place designated, the engines should be stopped to test the steering gear, provided that the traffic and weather conditions permit
- ❑ the OOW and the duty Engineer Officer should complete the tests as instructed in the Company checklist
- ❑ on completion of the checklist, it should be signed by the OOW and the duty Engineer Officer and placed in the bridge steering checklist file
- ❑ should any defect be noted, the Master and Chief Engineer should be advised immediately.

Steering Test in Port

- ❑ In port and prior to sailing, a steering test will take place as part of the gear test
- ❑ because the testing of gear is normally done once cargo operations are completed, and owing to time restrictions, the steering test

Steering Gear and Engine Tests

can be carried out as a separate test within 12 hours of the anticipated sailing time

- ❑ the time of testing should be arranged between the OOW and the duty Engineer Officer
- ❑ the steering checklist must be completed and filed
- ❑ regardless of whether or not this test is completed, the steering will again be tested in hand steering by the bridge during the normal gear test, once cargo operations are completed.

Engine Tests at Sea

- Engine testing should be carried out at the same time as the steering gear tests
- engine tests consist of astern and ahead movements in bridge control mode and under engine room control
- the Chief Engineer may ask for other engine tests to be carried out, such as from the emergency control position
- engine tests must be logged and the engine room movement record from the bridge must be kept.

Engine Tests in Port

- All engine tests in port must be coordinated between the deck and engine departments
- engine tests should, when possible, be arranged with the shore cargo supervisor
- before any engine test, all lines must be tight, cargo equipment clear of any ship obstruction, security of the gangway checked and the propeller clear
- the bridge controls should be manned and should control the test. The OOW on deck must be in constant communication with the bridge during the test and is authorised to halt the test at any time
- the shore cargo supervisor must be advised when the test is completed.

Ballast Water Management

Ballast water management is a matter of international concern and you are advised to obtain detailed information for all ports or countries of call on passage to ensure compliance with their national legislation (for more specialist information, see *Ballast Water Management* published by Witherby Publishing Group).

Non-compliance with any such legislation is likely to result in fines and/or delays, with claims possibly being made by the charterers against the ship. Recommendations are contained in the IMO's Resolution 868 from the 20th Assembly (A20) on 'Guidelines for the Control and Management of Ship's Ballast Water to Minimize the Transfer of Harmful Aquatic Organisms and Pathogens'. There are no mandatory IMO international regulations yet, but they are predicted to enter into effect in 2016. There are, however, a large number of national and regional ballast water measures that have been passed and the requirements for these include:

- Ballast water exchange prior to arrival
- clear and documented ballast water exchange procedures
- production of a ballast water exchange report upon arrival.

Any failure to comply with such requirements will often result in a fine. Any ballast water exchange must be closely monitored, with contingency procedures in place to deal with any eventualities that may arise.

Any ballast water transfer or operation at sea will require:

- A plan before commencing any such operations, detailing all stages and confirming the stability of the vessel at each stage

Ballast Water Management

- effective communication between all personnel involved
- procedures to be prepared by the Company.

You should adhere to the procedures and safety precautions on ballast water exchanges provided in your SMS. These may include:

- Prevention of over/under pressurisation of ballast tanks
- the effect of free surface on stability
- maintenance of adequate intact stability
- permissible seagoing strength limits of shear forces, bending moments and torsional forces
- maximum permitted draughts
- prohibiting weather conditions.

In freezing weather conditions, such operations should be avoided as tank ventilation pipes or the valve on the ballast system could freeze, compromising the safety of the vessel.

For further information, see *'Ballast Water Management'* published by Witherbys.

Standing Orders

Courtesy of Stena Bulk

During the course of a voyage, whether entering port, leaving port, anchoring or during the many other procedures that we carry out, all of us at some time or another forget something, sometimes with considerable consequence.

All Masters are required to write their standing orders and rarely are they the same. They are, or should be, the accumulation of the experience of the Master in situations where he has observed fault or problems that could have been avoided by well laid down orders. Checklists for emergencies have not been included in this section, but will be found, where relevant, throughout this book.

Standing Orders (Sea)

Responsibilities

- The Chief Officer is head of the deck department and is responsible to the Master for all matters of deck crew, watchkeeping duties and bridge maintenance. He is responsible for maintaining the Deck Logbook and it is essential that this is completed correctly. The basis is that, if you are in doubt, enter your remarks
- the Second Officer is the navigation officer and is responsible for all aspects of navigation. He should prepare the passage plan and charts for the forthcoming voyage in good time and advise the Master if there is any additional chart or publication required. He is required to draw the Master's attention to any area on the chart that the ship will pass that might require particular attention. In addition, he must bring to the Master's attention any navigation warning that might affect the ship
- he should advise the times of high and low water throughout the ship's stay in port
- he is responsible for the readiness and good order of the bridge equipment
- prior to arrival in port, he must advise the bridge of any special national or port requirements

Standing Orders

- the Third Officer is responsible for all signalling equipment and flags. He must ensure that the required flags are ready for use prior to port entry
- he will assist the navigation officer as required
- he must prepare routine port and sea messages
- he is responsible for the maintenance of all portable communications equipment
- he should act as the ship's meteorological (met) officer and ensure that all weather reports are received in a timely fashion and that the ship's position is plotted on the weather charts.

Standing Orders

- For the purpose of these orders, the following will apply:

  Good visibility: above 5 miles
  Restricted visibility: 2 to 5 miles
  Poor visibility: 1 to 2 miles
  Fog: below 1 mile

- these orders are not comprehensive. They are intended to complement existing professional understanding and the Company instructions and guidelines. All officers are expected to use their initiative in following them. They are to be read and acted upon in conjunction with the following:
  - International Regulations for Preventing Collisions at Sea, 1972 (2003 edition)
  - Bridge Procedures Guide, fourth edition, 2007
  - Company standing orders
  - Company SMS
  - the Ship Security Plan
- the Master's attention should be brought to any perceived conflict between his orders and any of the above
- all bridge equipment and controls are there to be used if the circumstances require. All officers are expected to read the instrument manuals provided and have an understanding of the operation and limitation of the instruments
- all navigational equipment and controls are to be tested at least 2 hours prior to departure and the test list completed. As part of this check, the gyro compass and all repeaters, including radar, are to be aligned. Engine room and bridge clocks must be synchronised. The steering gear must be tested in main and secondary modes
- the Master must be advised of the following:
  - any decrease in visibility
  - any malfunction of bridge equipment
  - any doubt whatsoever regarding the safe navigation of the vessel
  - if at any time his presence or advice are required
  - any adverse weather reports
- the Master should expect the OOW to act with common sense regarding the RPM of the vessel. Should the vessel start to pound, the RPM should be reduced as required, at the same time advising the Master
- when making large course alterations, the Master may wish the ship to be put into hand steering. The wheel is not to be handed over during any such alteration until the vessel is steady on the new course. When in traffic that requires a number of alterations, the Master will expect the helmsman to be on the wheel
- when altering course for other vessels, early action must be taken and the alteration substantial, so that there can be no confusion on the other vessel about your intentions. Under normal circumstances, alterations should take place not less than 'x' miles away and ships should not be passed less than 'y' miles away
- no other duties are to interfere with keeping of a responsible lookout. If, at any time, essential work is to be completed by the OOW, he must tell the Chief Officer, who will ensure that adequate lookouts are provided for that work period. Under no circumstance is work to be undertaken by the OOW in regular shipping waters
- the Master's presence on the bridge does not relieve the OOW from his charge. The Master will verbally take the con. If there is any uncertainty about who has command, the OOW must ask the Master for clarification
- irrespective of the Master taking command, the OOW must check the Master's actions, continue with plotting the vessel's position and call the Master's attention to the

movement of other vessels or any unsafe navigational procedures he might be taking

- the OOW's prime responsibility is for the safety of the ship and he must take any action required to ensure this. If, at any time, he feels that the ship is standing into danger or he is unsure of the situation, he must call the Master if time allows. Otherwise, he should, without hesitation, take any action required to put the vessel into safety. These actions might include use of helm and engines, change or reversal of course, or stopping the ship until the situation can be resolved
- in the event of an emergency stop at sea, if there is power to the rudder, the ship is to be put onto a course away from any immediate danger. Generally, this should be to steer the ship away from any land or ship in the area
- the OOW is not to take the watch until he is completely satisfied about the ship's position and the safety of the present course. Should there be any dispute about either the position or safety of the ship, the Master is to be called immediately
- in taking any immediate action, if there are other ships in the vicinity and if time permits, they should be alerted through the use of sound signals and/or VHF
- any defect or malfunction of equipment must be entered into the bridge defect book, with the date and time, and sent to the appropriate person or head of department for signature
- if, due to deteriorating weather conditions, the OOW feels that it is unsafe on deck, he must place the decks out of bounds by broadcast and by informing the heads of department. If any personnel are on deck at the time, they are to be ordered into the accommodation
- the Deck Logbook is an important legal document and the OOW must ensure that all entries are properly made, particularly in respect of weather conditions. When the ship is rolling, he should enter the degree of roll together with remarks about any pitching or taking water on deck
- the OOW is responsible for displaying the correct flag and light signals. The ensign must be hoisted at the gaff when the ship is under way and at the stern when the ship is alongside or at anchor
- prior to arrival in port, the OOW must test communications, both bridge and portable. He must also synchronise the clocks between the bridge and the engine room. He is responsible for ensuring that the pilot ladder is rigged in good time and that the crew are called to stations ready for arrival.

Under Pilotage

- When the pilot is on the bridge, he is to be treated with the same courtesy as if he has the rank of Master. The pilot is adviser to the Master for the direction of the ship. His presence on the bridge does not relieve the OOW of any of his responsibilities for the safe navigation of the ship and he must continue with his duties, advising the pilot of any navigation or shipping hazards he feels might endanger the ship
- should the pilot at any time give an order that does not directly concern the navigation of the ship, give any cause for concern, or if he has any complaint regarding any aspect of the ship, the Master is to be informed immediately.

Standing Orders (Port)

Quite often, while the standing orders for sea are comprehensively covered, the same is not true for port. In actual fact, these should be the responsibility of the Chief Officer, under the guidance of the Master. Even if they are written by the Chief Officer, they should be subject to the Master's satisfaction before they are distributed.

These orders are intended to complement those of the Chief Officer. The OOW, in addition to cargo duties, is responsible for the safety and security of the ship and those on board. To assist in this, the following will apply:

- The OOW must ensure that the ship is held fast alongside and that the mooring lines are adjusted with the rise and fall of the ship
- in the event of the weather deteriorating, the OOW should not hesitate to order additional moorings to be put out to ensure the ship is secure. If required, the outboard anchor may be walked out to the bottom. If there is danger of the ship coming off the berth, the VHF should be

used to contact the port and tugs should be ordered to keep the vessel alongside

- the OOW must ensure that the gangway is kept at the correct height to avoid damage, with particular regard for passing vessels, and that the gangway is safe, well lit and secure at all times
- when ships are passing, it is important to ensure that all the mooring lines are tight. Should any damage to the ship or lines occur when a vessel passes, the time and name of the ship should be entered immediately in the deck log and the port authorities advised of the occurrence by VHF. A damage report should then be filed
- safety equipment must be worn by all personnel, both ship and shore, when on the decks
- in the event of any oil spill, the ship's emergency response plan must be followed
- it is important that any oil in the water near the ship is immediately investigated. The engine room should be checked and any pumping that is taking place stopped until the source of the oil is established. If the oil is from the ship, the emergency response plan must be followed and the harbour authorities immediately advised. If it is not from the ship, the terminal operators must be advised and the agents notified. An immediate entry must be made in the deck log, together with the names of those notified
- any deposits of oil or grease on the decks must be cleared immediately and the area secured until safe for use
- during the hours of darkness, all gangway and deck lights must be switched on and working
- should an accident occur on board, it is imperative that, if required, shore assistance is obtained as soon as possible. If there is no immediate contact or telephone available, the port authorities should be contacted on the VHF. The following information should be given:
  - ❑ name of ship
  - ❑ position in the port
  - ❑ nature of the problem and the services required.

  An officer should be stationed at the gangway to ensure that, on arrival of the requested services, they can be directed immediately to the accident area
- in the event of any injury to any person, shore or crew, it is essential that the facts of the accident are recorded as soon as possible. The following details are required:
  - ❑ nature of injury
  - ❑ treatment given, if any
  - ❑ place and time
  - ❑ lighting conditions
  - ❑ safety equipment worn by the injured person
  - ❑ any suspicion of drug or alcohol use
  - ❑ statements and names of witnesses.

  In addition, the Company accident form must be completed
- in the event of any damage occurring to the ship or equipment, a damage report must be filed, signed by the appropriate personnel and an entry made in the deck log
- no shore worker should enter the accommodation except on official business. Any shore worker found in the accommodation must be challenged and either taken to the person they wish to see or requested to leave
- if, at any time, the OOW observes a shore worker behaving in an erratic manner or suspects that they might be under the influence of alcohol or drugs, or that they are working in such a manner that they might cause injury or damage to others or to the ship, their supervisor must be informed. This must be entered in the deck log. Should their behaviour continue to cause concern, the OOW must request their removal from the ship
- each morning, the deck area in the way of the gangway and accommodation entrance must be washed down and the main deck alleyway cleaned
- flags should be hoisted at 08:00 and lowered at sunset
- the bridge equipment checklist must be completed when testing gear prior to departure
- the bridge wings and coamings must be washed down prior to departure, and the bridge windows cleaned

Standing Orders

- should the OOW at any time have difficulties, if any accident occurs or there are difficulties with shore personnel, the OOW must consult with his head of department and the Master if on board. The Master is to be advised immediately of any accident, damage or pollution incident. In dealing with any member of the ship's company or shore personnel, the OOW is acting on the Master's behalf and with his authority and, provided that he has acted in a responsible manner, will always have the Master's support. All visitors to the ship must be dealt with in a courteous manner, regardless of who or what they are
- the gangway board must state clearly the date and time of departure and the time the crew must be on board. This must be put on the board at least 24 hours prior to the ship's ETD
- no smoking signs must be displayed and enforced where relevant
- no alcohol is to be brought onto the ship by any crew member or shore worker
- during bunkering, the pollution prevention equipment must be placed out on deck at the bunkering position ready for immediate use and the appropriate signal is to be hoisted. The bunkering checklist must be completed prior to bunkering operations
- the Ship Security Plan must be complied with in line with the requirement of the security level the vessel is at. Any persons on board who are not identified as bona fide workers must be challenged and identified
- each morning while in port, the OOW will obtain the weather forecast and bring any change in the weather conditions to the attention of the Chief Officer and the Master.

Preparation for Port Arrival

If your ship is regularly running between the same ports, preparation becomes automatic and many problems are avoided. Equally, when ships are frequently calling at major ports, completing procedures can be less important because anything missed in one port can be completed in the next. It is when a ship is entering port infrequently, or is entering a port from which it will depart for a prolonged voyage, that port preparation is important, especially if the stay is to be short.

Port Arrival

- ❑ The Navigation Officer must ensure that all relevant navigational warnings are up to date for the port
- ❑ he must ensure that all relevant navigational messages are sent
- ❑ the navigational map of the port must be put into a file on the ARPA computer
- ❑ a tidal table for the duration of the port stay must be made
- ❑ currents in the area of the port approach must be listed and plotted on charts that are suitable for this purpose
- ❑ the Master must note on the chart the positions of '1 hour's notice' to the engine room and stand by
- ❑ the OOW must complete the arrival checklist and ensure that the pilot data cards are up to date

Preparation for Port Arrival

- ❑ the OOW must ensure that the correct flags/signals are displayed
- ❑ the intended port approach plan should be laid on the chart
- ❑ where applicable, a security declaration should be sent in advance.

Shipboard Preparation

- ❑ Anchors cleared away
- ❑ flags hoisted if it is the day of arrival
- ❑ if bunkering, scuppers must be blocked and anti-pollution equipment should be checked and readied
- ❑ store's crane checked
- ❑ covers taken off ropes and windlasses
- ❑ mooring lines and stoppers readied, windlasses tested
- ❑ if advised that the berth is clear, swing gangway out
- ❑ clear decks of lifelines
- ❑ secure fireboxes and stow away lifebuoys
- ❑ secure lifeboats
- ❑ check deck lighting
- ❑ test engines, steering systems and sound signal
- ❑ check communications, fore and aft
- ❑ if the weather is cold, switch on the hydraulics to allow for warm-up time
- ❑ lock non-immediate use hatches and lockers.

If Anchoring

- ❑ Check anchor lights
- ❑ if required, set a security watch
- ❑ after anchoring, put covers on the hawse pipe
- ❑ tender NOR
- ❑ set engine notice.

Information to Pass to the Agent

- ❑ Your requirements regarding presentation of manifests, etc prior to discharge
- ❑ personnel leaving or joining
- ❑ personnel who require medical or dental treatment
- ❑ fresh water requirements
- ❑ any technical assistance required or technicians that have been requested to attend. It is essential that the equipment is specified, together with the suspected problem or area of concern
- ❑ surveyors requested and what the surveys are
- ❑ what cash is required, together with the denomination of the notes and exchange rates
- ❑ any stores or spares that have been sent to the port, preferably with the shipment number
- ❑ if you have a single crane and will be storing, tell the agent which side the crane is on and request that side alongside in the port
- ❑ request for delivery of charts. If you do not have an appropriate chart for entering the port, arrange through the agent for the pilot to bring it to the ship. The same applies to courtesy ensigns. Order any charts required for the next port, if known
- ❑ bunkers that have been ordered, together with the required time of delivery
- ❑ any special ship peculiarities, such as unusual mooring arrangements or malfunction of navigational equipment
- ❑ for your port emergency listings, you will require the names and telephone numbers of the pollution agencies. At the same time, find out what pollution protection, if any, the port provides
- ❑ quantity of waste for disposal and whether any of it is special or hazardous waste
- ❑ whether the lowering of lifeboats is required
- ❑ what the port regulations are on engine immobilisation
- ❑ ship security state
- ❑ whether the agency representative is attending on arrival
- ❑ when cargo is to commence and which hatches start first.

Berth Check

- ❑ Is there room for the ship? Ensure the ship's length is known
- ❑ is there any overhang of the ship? Can good leads be given for the mooring lines?
- ❑ what is the locally declared depth on the berth? Is it a safe berth for the ship, ie always afloat
- ❑ cranes and loaders must be clear

Preparation for Port Arrival

- ❑ what fendering is at the berth
- ❑ whether fresh water connections are available
- ❑ whether garbage bins are available
- ❑ what the gangway arrangements are. Shore or ship gangway? Can the safety net be secured ashore?
- ❑ whether the berth is clear of previous cargo residue
- ❑ on approach, note and log whether any oil is in the water in way of the berth (it is advisable to draw this to the attention of the port)
- ❑ what the berth security arrangements and requirements are.

Port Documentation

- ❑ Last port clearance
- ❑ crew lists
- ❑ passenger lists (if supernumeraries are on board, check with the agent whether they can be listed as crew or have to appear on a separate passenger list)
- ❑ customs forms
- ❑ health forms
- ❑ vaccination lists (many ports do not require this - check with the agents)
- ❑ list of arms or ammunition
- ❑ general stores declaration
- ❑ list of previous ports
- ❑ dangerous drug list
- ❑ stores or spares to be landed
- ❑ security declaration.

The above are the general forms that are required for a port. There could well be local forms required for a specific port and these should be notified to the ship by the agents.

Documentation

Before arrival in port, check that the following are up to date and signed:

- ❑ Oil Record Book
- ❑ Garbage Disposal Logbook
- ❑ GMDSS Logbook. Remember this has to be signed daily, not just each page
- ❑ pilot card
- ❑ logbooks
- ❑ port passage plan
- ❑ hours of work records
- ❑ work permits ready
- ❑ Medical Logbook
- ❑ Ship security record.

Port Departure

- ❑ Under normal circumstances, bridge equipment should be tested at least one hour before the ship is due to sail. This will normally be after cargo operations have been completed
- ❑ if there is any malfunction, the officer responsible for the maintenance of the equipment must be called immediately to the bridge and the Master informed
- ❑ the relevant port chart must be ready for use, the port departure plan laid and all navigation instruments ready
- ❑ currents in the port area must be listed and plotted on charts that are suitable for this purpose.

Preparing for Port Departure

It is surprising just how quickly the last few hours of a ship's stay in port can descend into chaos. Regardless of how well you manage the ship at sea, you do not have much control over all the outside influences in port. A checklist of items to do and reports to receive on your desk can be most useful at such a time:

- ❑ All crew on board
- ❑ navigation equipment and engines tested
- ❑ all cargo stowed and secured and ship secured for sea
- ❑ ship's certificates returned
- ❑ crew and ship mail posted
- ❑ local currency cash remaining returned
- ❑ ETA given for the next port
- ❑ departure plan prepared
- ❑ pilotage card completed
- ❑ shore hoses disconnected
- ❑ shore loaders/cranes, etc moved from way of the ship
- ❑ garbage landed
- ❑ port clearance given
- ❑ weather report checked
- ❑ tugs and pilot ordered
- ❑ stowaway search completed.

Insurance and P&I Clubs

The extent of insurance coverage for your ship depends on the scope of cover taken out by your Company. A copy of this coverage should be available on board.

Hull and machinery (H&M) insurance is insurance of the vessel as the primary asset, covering damages to the vessel, structure, machinery and fittings, and liabilities to third parties arising out of a collision or damage to fixed and floating objects, where not otherwise covered under the P&I coverage. This will be defined by the insurer's cover note, and any applicable clauses attached.

P&I Insurance

This covers a shipowner's liability toward third parties. The main areas of the coverage include:

- Liabilities to third parties arising from collision/damage to fixed and floating objects (generally covering those items not covered under the hull and machinery insurance cover)
- personal injury, illness or death
- damage to the marine environment
- cargo damage
- damage to third party property.

The two types of insurance, ie H&M and P&I, interact in the areas of liability in the event of collision or contact damage to third party property.

Under the standard English hull and machinery insurance terms (ITC Hulls – Institute Time Clauses Hulls), collision liability cover has, historically, been limited to three-fourths of the own ship's liability towards the other vessel in a collision.

Some shipowners have placed full (four-fourths) collision liability with their P&I insurer. This cover would be the most comprehensive liability cover available, as all third party liabilities arising out of the collision would be covered in principle. In such cases, however, the shipowner would still need H&M cover to deal with the loss of or damage to the vessel.

Apart from concern about the damage or injuries that result from an accident, you can be sure that paperwork and blame will also be high on the list. Even if you had nothing to do with the accident or you perceive that it is not the ship's fault, there will be someone trying to prove it is. That is why it is essential that, in any incident that takes place on the ship or involves the ship, if it results in damage to ship, cargo or personnel, the utmost should be done to accurately record all the events, together with any additional information that might help show a complete picture of what happened.

In the event of an incident or allegation that gives, or may give, rise to a third party claim, there are certain actions you should always take and certain actions you should never take.

Always:

- ❑ Call your owner or operator
- ❑ investigate every allegation of injury or damage
- ❑ collect evidence or documentation relating to the incident, including any defective equipment. Store it in a safe place and label the pieces of evidence. Throw nothing away
- ❑ take photographs of any damage or circumstances relating to the incident
- ❑ instruct witnesses to write a review of what they saw and heard and to draw a diagram if possible. This should be done as soon as possible after the incident. Write personal notes about the incident yourself.

Never:

- ❑ Allow a surveyor or lawyer to board the ship or to interview crew members unless he has identified himself and produced appropriate authorisation to satisfy you that he is acting for your owner or your P&I Club
- ❑ allow surveyors or lawyers acting for the opposing parties on board unless you have authorisation to do so
- ❑ give written material or physical evidence to opposing lawyers and surveyors. If in doubt, do not give anything to anyone or let anyone examine anything
- ❑ give a personal opinion about who or what was responsible. Keep to the facts. If in doubt, say nothing
- ❑ allow crew members to express opinions
- ❑ admit liability, either verbally or in writing
- ❑ sign a document that you know contains incorrect information. This includes making false entries in logbooks
- ❑ think that the problem will go away if you do nothing.

Insurance and P&I Clubs

In preparation for the attendance of the P&I Club surveyor, the following could be required:

- ❑ Witness statements
- ❑ witnesses standing by for interview
- ❑ initial assessment of damage
- ❑ logbook entries:
  - date and time
  - nature of damage or injury
  - weather
  - any initial action taken
  - position of the vessel
  - required signatures
- ❑ copy of the above entries prepared
- ❑ list of casualties (if any)
- ❑ details of any medical treatment given
- ❑ Medical Logbook entry
- ❑ all relevant ISM procedures and pertinent records
- ❑ any letters of protest
- ❑ maintenance schedules, if relevant
- ❑ all ship's certificates
- ❑ all officer and crew certificates
- ❑ copy of the standing orders.

If there is pollution:

- ❑ Quantity of the pollutant
- ❑ Oil Record Book
- ❑ video images/photographs of the extent of the spill (if possible)
- ❑ all relevant correspondence, emails, etc
- ❑ samples of the spilled oil, or of any oil collected near own ship, and samples of on board fuel and oil cargo

  ***Note:** This evidence collection is not applicable for liquefied gas carriers*

- ❑ accounts of the incident from all crew members involved
- ❑ evidence of any previously sighted oil pollution in berth or port area
- ❑ details of the procedure followed during transfer of cargo or bunkers within the vessel
- ❑ rates and ullages of loading and/or discharging operations at the time of the spill
- ❑ a copy of the terminal's cargo or bunker instructions relating to the acceptable loading rate
- ❑ the name of the crew member in charge of transfer operations
- ❑ times and results of inspections of equipment used in cargo and bunkering operations
- ❑ instructions from the owner and/or the charterer
- ❑ methods of activating emergency stops
- ❑ procedures in place at the time governing the use of equipment such as scupper plugs and drip trays
- ❑ any broken equipment whose failure contributed to the spill
- ❑ whether vessel's ropes/wires are involved
- ❑ certificates of ropes/wires
- ❑ records of dates or renewals
- ❑ register of lifting equipment
- ❑ list of relevant contacts and communications made
- ❑ list of actions taken by other parties
- ❑ any statements made by other parties
- ❑ any photographs of the incident and scene of incident
- ❑ lighting conditions at the time of incident.

Letter of Undertaking

You may have to ask that your P&I Club issues a Letter of Undertaking (LOU) to prevent your vessel being arrested.

Such a situation will typically arise when:

- Persons other than the crew are injured while on board
- cargo has been damaged during the voyage
- there has been a pollution incident
- your vessel has been involved in a collision.

Claimants may threaten to arrest the vessel to seek security for their alleged claim.

To prevent any delay to the vessel, the P&I Club usually provides an LOU if certain conditions are met, such as the claim is within the scope of the P&I cover provided, the P&I premiums are paid up to date, etc. However, you should be aware that your P&I Club is not obliged to issue an LOU.

Generally, a claimant will accept an LOU rather than insisting on a bank guarantee as an LOU can be provided within a short period of time, while preparing a bank guarantee can be time consuming.

In the case of a collision, your hull and machinery underwriters will cover 3/4ths of the liability. However, your P&I Club may be requested to provide an LOU to cover liability that will be allotted to your hull and machinery underwriters.

Fines

It will often feel like fines are issued when the port notices even the slightest discrepancy.

Fines may be presented to you for a range of violations, typically including:

- Contravening the international collision regulations or local traffic regulations
- contravening a traffic instruction that was given to the vessel
- out-of-date certificates
- any irregularities concerning customs forms, manifests or crew lists
- any irregularities concerning declared ship's stores, medical stores (including out-of-date medicines on board) or the crew's personal effects
- pollution of the marine environment
- any perceived breach of MARPOL regulations
- arriving with stowaways on board.

Non-Standard Items

War Zones

A war zone can be declared by a government, an insurance grouping such as the Lloyd's Market Association, which is a group representing the underwriters at Lloyd's, or a shipping group such as the IBF (International Bargaining Forum).

A war zone can be an area in which danger of warlike acts exists or an area in which terrorist or piracy threat has reached such a scale that a war zone designation is warranted.

War zones can range from an area encompassing thousands of square miles of seas in which general war operations are being conducted, to a localised area considered by shipping and/or insurance groups to be at high risk from piracy.

To determine the precautions required, it is sensible to carry out a threat analysis. This would be based on intelligence regarding any aggressive action that poses a threat to the ship.

The threat can be broken down into four main categories, each with their own subdivisions:

Surface

- Gunfire
- missile attack
- FPB (fast patrol boats)
- small arms
- boarding.

Air

- Missile attack
- gunfire
- helicopter
- bomb
- boarding.

Subsurface

- Submarine attack
- mines
- underwater obstacles.

Internal

- Explosives
- piracy
- sabotage.

For many of these threats, the merchant ship is entirely reliant on external support and protection and whatever initiatives and equipment is decided on by their government. There are, however, certain elementary precautions that ships can take when in such areas, and the scale of these precautions should be in proportion to the threat evaluation. Prior

Non-Standard Items

to entry into the area, contact other vessels in the vicinity. For a low threat evaluation, such as piracy, an informal convoy system might prove a deterrent.

War Zone Checklist

- ❑ Boat lowered to the embarkation deck and prepared for immediate launch
- ❑ double up the watches
- ❑ lookouts placed on both bridge wings
- ❑ close all watertight and weather doors
- ❑ close down all deadlights, no visible lights other than navigation lights
- ❑ fire hoses run out in the most vulnerable areas
- ❑ distribution of safety equipment around the vessel
- ❑ crew cleared from most vulnerable areas. Places in the ship with tiles or glass should be considered highly dangerous if the threat is from explosives
- ❑ consider engine room manning
- ❑ two steering motors running
- ❑ consider lighting. This will range from blackout for air attack to high visibility as an anti-piracy precaution
- ❑ first aid items placed at strategic points throughout the accommodation
- ❑ muster point established in the safest area of the ship
- ❑ is additional safety equipment required, such as chemical gas masks?
- ❑ pre-entry meeting with crew to discuss the threat and the procedures.

Piracy

There is an increase in violent attacks in certain parts of the world notably:

- East Africa
- West Africa
- South East Asia
- East Coast of South America
- Caribbean Sea (certain areas).

Somalia

Pirates off the Somali coast launch their attacks from so-called mother ships, using small speedboats. The pirates are armed with assault rifles and rocket-propelled grenades (RPGs), which are capable of penetrating the ship's hull. The pirates will approach the target in darkness by speedboat, or even in broad daylight, and will then threaten the ship with their RPGs, come alongside and board using grappling hooks, scramble onto the deck with their automatic weapons and take the crew hostage.

After boarding, which is usually effected in international waters, they will normally bring the ship into Somali waters to one of several ports that are essentially pirate safe havens, with Eyl in the Puntland area of Somalia being the most popular. At this point, through intermediaries, they will commence negotiations with the ship's insurers and owners for a ransom payment, which until late 2008 had typically been US$1 million although more high profile captures of larger vessels, including VLCCs, have seen this ransom demand increase to tens of millions of dollars. In exchange for this payment, they will release the ship and the captive crew. Reports indicate that the Somalis are running this operation as a commercial business and are not harming the crews that they capture, maintaining a commercial interest in 'looking after the goods'.

There are no reports of successful pirate attacks on ships with speeds of over 16 knots.

The small craft that the pirates are using limit their operations to relatively calm weather and it is perceived to be difficult to operate these craft when the sea is above sea state 3. The drowning of 5 attackers, when escaping with US$3 million from a hijacked VLCC in January 2009, was put down to the sea state.

The likelihood of an attack increases in the period immediately after the release of a hijacked vessel.

Shipowner considerations for ships that are transiting or visiting a port in an attack prone area

- ❑ Provide suitable surveillance and detection equipment to assist crews and to help protect the ship
- ❑ eliminate or reduce the need to carry large amounts of cash on board the ship

- ❑ where possible, route ships away from attack risk areas and avoid geographical bottlenecks
- ❑ transit high risk areas in daylight, if possible
- ❑ enhance security watches in anchorages where ships are deemed to have a high risk of attack
- ❑ provide low-light/night vision binoculars for officers and lookouts
- ❑ fix a yacht radar astern to provide valuable radar cover that is able to detect small craft approaching from that direction
- ❑ provide kevlar jackets and blankets to protect both the crew and sensitive equipment such as oxyacetylene bottles
- ❑ protect the bridge windows by fixing security glass film
- ❑ on vessels that regularly visit attack prone areas, purchase CCTV and physical deterrent devices, such as barbed wire. In certain circumstances, non-lethal weapons may also be appropriate. Infrared detection and alerting equipment may also be utilised

  Note: Where CCTV is implemented, this should record the main access points to the ship's secure areas and the corridors approaching the entrances to key areas and the bridge
- ❑ construct barriers of barbed or razor wire
- ❑ coat the gunwhales and rounded sheerstrake areas with anti-climb paint
- ❑ fit a dedicated enhanced group calling system (EGC) receiver for maritime safety information broadcasts. This would provide a receiver that is not used for commercial purposes to ensure no urgent broadcasts are missed.

General onboard considerations before transiting an attack prone area

- ❑ Place dummies at strategic lookout positions around the vessel to help give the impression of a well-guarded ship
- ❑ make constant visible patrols around the vessel, preferably by no less than 2 crew, equipped with powerful hand lamps and portable radios
- ❑ ensure you have a ship security plan specifically for a piracy/armed robbery attack. The plan should cover:
  - improving surveillance and the use of lighting and detection equipment
  - crew response to a potential or actual attack
  - the radio alarm procedures to be followed
  - the reports to be made after an attack or an attempted attack.

Armed raiders have traditionally targeted valuables, such as:

- Contents of the ship's safe
- personal cash from the crew
- cameras, laptops, MP3 players, etc.

However, recent attack activity, particularly off Somalia, has seen high profile hijacking of merchant tonnage for ransom. In this case, it was organised crime as opposed to the previously experienced acts of petty theft.

- ❑ early detection of a likely attack is the most effective deterrent, and a clear demonstration to attackers that the ship has a vigilant and well-trained crew will help deter them from attacking the ship. This is the stage at which the security forces of the nearest littoral or coastal State must be informed through the rescue coordination centre (RCC). The ship's crew should be warned and, if not already in their defensive positions, they should move to them and employ evasive manoeuvres. An aggressive response to an attack can increase the risk to the ship and crew
- ❑ action to prevent the attackers making it on board the vessel is the second line of defence. Attackers will generally try to board the vessel at the lowest accessible point above the waterline – generally the poop deck
- ❑ if the GMDSS station does not automatically update the position, update it at regular intervals manually
- ❑ decide whether AIS is to be switched off or left on
- ❑ use sandbags to protect sensitive equipment located outside of the accommodation
- ❑ all access doors to the bridge, engine room, steering gear compartments, officers' cabins and crew accommodation should be secured and regularly inspected

Non-Standard Items

- windows and portholes that could offer access should be closed tight and deadlights sealed
- internal accommodation doors within secure areas, which give access to vital areas such as the bridge, engine room and Master's cabin, should be reinforced/strengthened and have additional control systems and automatic alarms
- muster areas should be nominated, preferably a central citadel that is equipped with food and water supplies and external means of communication, where the crew can muster in the event of an attack and communicate their position and head count to the bridge and outside world,
- to prevent crew members being seized and threatened by attackers:
  - all crew members not engaged in essential outside duties should remain within a secure area during the hours of darkness
  - crew members who need to patrol/work outside of the secure area at night should be in constant contact with the bridge and should have trained in using an alternative route to return to the secure area should an attack occur or have a place where they can take temporary refuge
- use the maximum permissible lighting available, provided this does not interfere with the safe navigation of the vessel:
  - forecastle and lights over the ship's side should be switched on, so long as these do not endanger navigation

    Note: ships should not have their deck lights on when underway, as this could lead other ships to presume that they are at anchor
  - astern of the ship, wide beam floodlights can be used
  - steaming with the ship's lights blacked out except for navigation lights is a further option. While this may affect the attackers' orientation on approaching the ship, suddenly switching on the ship's lights to dazzle the attackers and alert them to your awareness of their approach may also place the crew at a disadvantage as they will experience a temporary loss of night vision at the most critical time. It is, however, difficult to maintain a total blackout on the typical merchant ship and this will be influenced by external factors such as the level of moonlight
- fire hoses have been found to deter boarders as the attacker has to cope with a powerful jet of water (typically 80 psi). The water may swamp their attack craft and possibly damage/stall the engines/electrical systems. Recent success has involved the fitting of a splash plate a short distance from the fire or tank washing hose nozzle mounted on the ship's side bulwark/railing, creating a fanned downward spray/deluge that has discouraged attackers
- when attackers are on board, your actions should focus on:
  - securing the greatest level of safety for those on board the ship
  - seeking to ensure that the crew remain in control of the navigation of the ship
  - securing the earliest possible departure of the attackers from the ship

  The options available to the Master and crew depend on the level of control the attackers have achieved. For example, gaining control of the bridge or engine room or holding crew members hostage means the hijackers can coerce the Master into complying with their wishes.
- there have been accounts of entire crews being locked up, so consideration should be given to hiding equipment within the likely areas on board that are capable of holding all of the crew
- if you can confirm that your crew are safe within a secure area and the attackers are outside of the secure area and do not place the ship at any imminent risk, you may consider conducting heavy manoeuvres to encourage the attackers to return to their craft
- carrying and use of firearms is strongly discouraged. Carriage of arms on board ship may escalate an already dangerous situation. The use of firearms requires special training and aptitudes. In certain ports, killing a national may expose you or the crew to imprisonment or execution. This will also increase the risk that the

pirates themselves will use firearms, with the possibility that a crew member may be killed or injured

- ❑ you should ask the local agents or P&I correspondent for:
  - any advice on security issues in that particular port or area and the reliability of official security authorities and private firms
  - contact details for the dock, police or security authorities.

Additional considerations if your ship is visiting a port/anchorage in an attack prone area

- ❑ If approaching an anchorage where attacks have taken place, you should consider delaying anchoring by slow steaming or taking a longer route to keep well off shore and reduce the period of risk
- ❑ if you have crew going ashore in ports in attack prone areas, they should be advised not to discuss the ship, her voyage or cargo details with anyone ashore
- ❑ as attackers may select their targets based on the cargo stipulated on the manifest, you should limit the circulation of cargo plans and associated documents providing information on the cargoes on board
- ❑ security guards employed in a port or anchorage should be in contact with their colleagues on different ships and the port authorities. You should only use security firms that have themselves been vetted by the appropriate authorities.

Action Points On Board

Implementing the ship's security plan

- ❑ Before entering an attack prone area, train and drill the crew on the alarm signals, procedures and actions in the ship's security plan
- ❑ all doors allowing access to the bridge, engine room, steering gear and crew accommodation/cabins should be secured and controlled in attack prone areas and should be regularly inspected. On accommodation doors that do not have a key, the lock should be changed. Doors can be temporarily secured by fixing a 3″×3″ joist of wood between the deck level and the door handle to secure and prevent opening of the door from outside
- ❑ secure all lockers to help prevent the attackers gaining access to tools and equipment on board
- ❑ train with any surveillance/detection equipment provided on board.

Watchkeeping in the area

Maintaining a vigilant lookout is essential. There are frequent reports that the first indication of an attack was when the attackers appeared on the bridge or in the Master's cabin. Being vigilant and able to pre-warn of a likely attack gives opportunity to:

- ❑ Sound the alarm
- ❑ alert other ships and coastal authorities
- ❑ illuminate the approaching craft
- ❑ initiate an evasive manoeuvre.

Clear signs that demonstrate the ship is aware it is being approached have proven to deter attackers.

Give plenty of searoom to small objects, particularly when they show no lights.

Increase the lookout:

- ❑ Bridge watch increased
- ❑ additional lookouts covering the stern or radar blind spots should be considered
- ❑ radar should be constantly manned, although it may be difficult to detect low profile fast moving craft on ship's radars.

Communications:

- ❑ Verbal instructions must be clear
- ❑ use caution when passing information by VHF regarding cargo, valuables or the crew nationality in areas where attacks occur
- ❑ ensure an officer responsible for communications is on duty at all times when the ship is in an attack prone area:
  - maintain a constant listening watch with the appropriate shore or naval authorities when in attack prone areas
  - monitor all maritime safety information broadcasts for the area as INMARSAT's enhanced group calling system (EGC) will normally be issued via the SafetyNET service.

Be alert for small craft matching your speed. Small craft that appear to be matching the speed of the ship on a parallel or following

Non-Standard Items

course should always be treated with suspicion as they could close in rapidly to mount an attack.

Where a suspicious craft has been observed, it is important that an effective watch is maintained in case this craft is a distraction with the attackers' intent to approach from a second attack craft rather than the decoy.

Suspected Attack

- If suspicious movements are identified that could indicate an imminent attack, you should contact the appropriate rescue coordination centre (RCC) or radio station that is recommended for that area. A danger message should be transmitted on VHF Channel 70 using the 'safety' priority, with further announcements on a working channel
- if AIS has been switched off, it should be switched on
- signal projector and beam lights can be used to check suspect craft
- when it is apparent that the safety of the ship is threatened:
  - the Master should contact the RCC/ Coast Radio Station
  - if appropriate, broadcast an 'All Stations' 'Urgency Message' (PAN-PAN) on VHF Channel 16 or any other radio communications service considered appropriate such as INMARSAT. This should be supplemented by DSC calls on VHF Channel 70 (and/or 2,187.5 kHz) using the 'all ships urgency' category
  - if the urgency signal has been used and an attack does not develop, the ship should cancel the message as soon as it knows that action is no longer necessary, again addressing 'all stations'
- navigation permitting, heavy wheel movements made as the attackers approach may deter them or make it difficult for them to attach poles or grappling irons to the ship. Attackers' confidence may diminish when faced with a vessel that is making rapid wheel movements.

Confirmed Attack

- Should an attack occur placing the ship and crew in danger and requiring urgent assistance, immediately broadcast a distress message (MAYDAY) using all available radio communications systems. To reduce any delays, if using a ship earth station, you should ensure the CES associated with the RCC is used
- alarm signals, including the ship's whistle, should be sounded on the approach of attackers. Announcements or a specific alarm signal that can indicate where the attackers are boarding will assist crew in exposed locations as they determine the best route to a secure area
- distress flares should only be used where you consider that the actions of the attackers are putting the ship into imminent danger. Radio transmissions, rather than distress flares, should be used to alert nearby shipping of the risk of attack
- from a secure location on board, the ship may be able to covertly send a message to an RCC. You must be aware that, with the attackers on board, when the RCC relays the message or attempts to establish communication with the ship, the attackers could become aware that a piracy/attack alert has been transmitted. This may further endanger the lives of the crew on board.

If the attackers gain control and take hostage(s)

- Remain calm
- leave the CCTV recording equipment running
- if the attackers are willing to negotiate, your objectives should be:
  - achieving the safe return of any hostages
  - ensuring your crew retain control over the safe navigation of the ship
  - helping the attackers make the decision to leave the ship. This can be assisted by assuring them that they have been given everything they demand and that nothing has been hidden
    (There will, however, be occasions where compliance with the attackers' demands is the only safe option and resistance or obstruction of any kind is patently dangerous)
- if you can confirm that the attackers do not have firearms, rushing at them, in the form of a sortie by a trained crew has, in the past,

forced the attackers to leave a ship. A sortie attack by the crew should:

- only be carried out if there is minimal risk to the crew. The sortie party should always stay together
- only be carried out if the sortie party significantly outnumbers the attackers
- have its chance of success improved by use of water hoses.

Do not:

- Come between the attackers and their craft
- seek to capture attackers. However, if you do apprehend an attacker, he should be placed in secure confinement and cared for as you would a stowaway, notifying the coastal State at the first opportunity.

Attackers Leave the Ship

If the crew are in a secure position, it is unwise to leave the safety of this position until it is verified that the attackers have left the ship. A signal known to the crew on the ship's whistles and alarm bell can be used to signify the 'all clear'.

Piracy Reporting Centre (PRC)

If you are attacked, you should report the attack to the PRC of the International Maritime Bureau (IMB) in Kuala Lumpur, Malaysia. The Centre can be contacted on a 24-hour basis.

Tel: + 60 3 2078 5763
Fax: + 60 3 2078 5769
Telex: MA34199 IMBPCI
Email: imbkl@icc-ccs.org or piracy@icc-ccs.org
24-Hour Anti-Piracy Helpline Tel: + 60 3 2031 0014

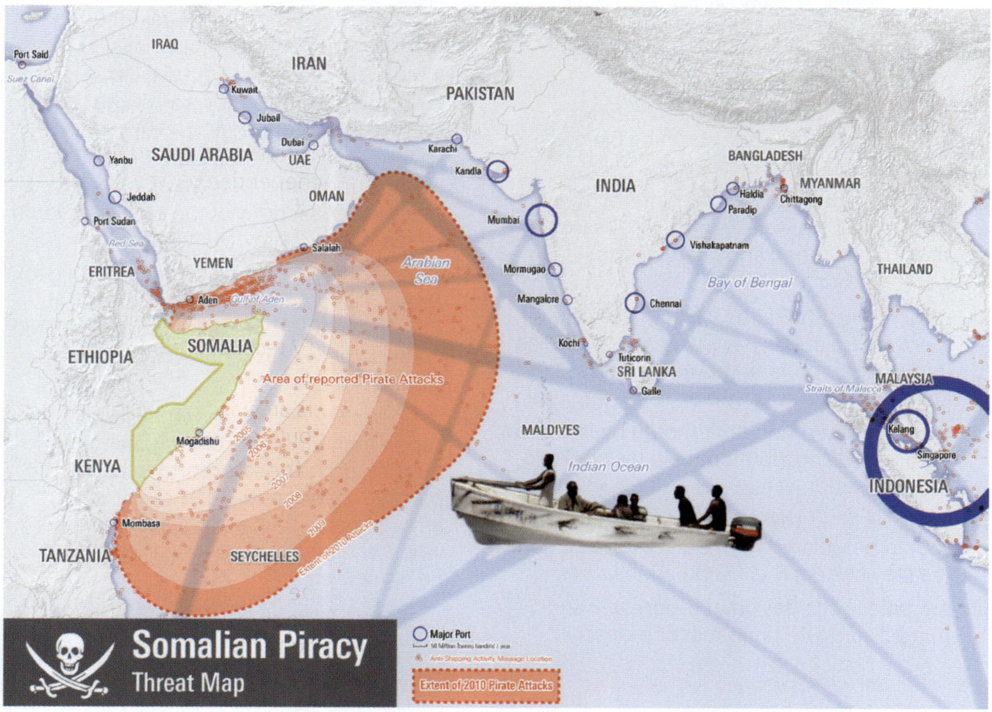

Non-Standard Items

Hot Work in Cargo Oil Tanks

Before hot work is carried out, a formal risk assessment must be conducted by those who will be involved.

Precautions to be taken before carrying out hot work in cargo oil tanks should include the following:

- Cargo oil tanks where hot work is to be carried out must be water washed and gas freed and any flammable material must be removed
- adjacent or surrounding tanks must be water washed and gas freed and any flammable material must be removed or moved away from the bulkheads and structures adjacent to cargo oil tanks where the hot work is to be carried out
- apart from the designated slop tank that contains residual pipeline and tank washings, all other cargo oil tanks on the tanker should be either purged or water washed and gas freed
- cargo oil tanks that have been water washed and gas freed should be blanked from the IGS distribution main
- cargo suction pipelines that interconnect gas free and non-gas free cargo oil tanks should be washed and charged with clean water
- cargo valves should be set so that cargo oil tanks are isolated by at least two valves. The designated slop tank should be isolated by as many valves as possible
- the designated slop tank should be isolated from the IGS distribution main by closing the IG isolation valve
- cargo oil tanks that have been purged should be isolated from the IGS distribution main by closing their IG isolation valves
- pressure in the designated slop tank and purged cargo oil tanks must be closely monitored, and should be maintained at about 200 mmWG (20 mb or 2 KPa)
- heating coils should be blown through with compressed air and positively isolated by blanking
- hydraulic pipelines in a tank, as part of the cargo valve control or pumping system, should be depressurised and, in the area of the hot work, they should be protected with heat-retardant coverings. Isolation valves should be closed. Hydraulic pumps or power packs should be isolated and an electrical isolation certificate issued. If hot work is to be carried out near to the hydraulic pipelines, a risk assessment must be made to identify the control measures necessary to prevent ignition of hydraulic oil
- the mast riser vent valve should be kept open so that the accumulation of hydrocarbon gas in the IGS distribution main is avoided
- if there are no slops on board, when all the tanks have been water washed and gas freed and all sections of the cargo pipeline system have been thoroughly water washed and either drained or left full of clean water, sections of the pipeline should be left open to allow ventilation
- when hot work is to be carried out on deck above a cargo oil tank or on the vertical side of the hull, that tank must be prepared in the same way as if hot work was to be carried out in it
- the permit issued for hot work should be supplemented with a plan showing the location of the hot work and detailing the precautionary, control and monitoring arrangements that are in place. Conditions where the permit is no longer valid should be made clear.

Heavy Weather (Port)

It is sometimes surprising how, with all our attention to weather at sea, we can let ourselves be lulled into a relaxation of this attentiveness just because we are alongside. A ship is often more vulnerable in port than at sea and it is better to prepare for that vulnerability, even if it does not happen:

- ❑ All lines should be out and doubled up where possible
- ❑ all lines should be tight, with crew standing by to slacken as required
- ❑ when appropriate, stop cargo operations and close the hatches or disconnect the hoses
- ❑ have any shore cargo loaders or cranes moved from the vicinity of the ship
- ❑ ensure that all loose gear on the decks is cleared away and stowed, including cargo residue
- ❑ stop all shore leave
- ❑ if required, request a standby tug
- ❑ put the engines on standby
- ❑ if you are a light ship, and there is enough draught, ballast down as much as possible
- ❑ if the bottom is clear and shallow enough, consideration can be given, depending on the severity of the approaching weather, to ballasting down sufficient to place the ship on the bottom
- ❑ if you are a smaller vessel, consider putting the inboard cable ashore around a bollard
- ❑ lower the outboard anchor to the bottom
- ❑ check whether the port has any available storm lines
- ❑ take down flags and ensigns
- ❑ if necessary, hoist the gangway clear of the berth
- ❑ when all precautions have been taken, this should be logged.

Heavy Weather (Sea)

Crew and passengers have, on occasion, been lost overboard in heavy weather conditions.

You should, on entering heavy weather:

- ❑ Prevent crew or passengers from accessing the deck and exposed areas
- ❑ prohibit working on deck except for essential safety operations
- ❑ make a tannoy announcement covering these items to crew and passengers.

Apart from exceptional cases, you are warned about what is coming and have time to prepare your ship and crew:

- ❑ Check that the windlass and anchors are well secured
- ❑ ensure that all forward mooring lines are stowed below or lashed and covered securely on their drums
- ❑ if, after mooring, lines cannot be stowed below, they should be lashed securely to the ship's structure and covered
- ❑ any forecastle hatch openings must be secured tight and a rope web lashing put over the cleats
- ❑ all hatch tops and entry points must be checked and the retaining cleats tightened
- ❑ remove lifebuoys and liferafts from open deck positions forward and stow away
- ❑ check the lashings of all deck cargo
- ❑ ensure that all the vents are covered and well lashed down
- ❑ all weather doors in exposed areas are to be battened down
- ❑ tighten and secure all halyards
- ❑ check the mast stays
- ❑ remove all loose gear from the decks
- ❑ if intending to run before the seas, ensure that the poop deck is clear
- ❑ rig lifelines if they are not already rigged
- ❑ check all deck lights are ready for use
- ❑ warn all departments in ample time to ensure they secure their stores and work places
- ❑ ensure that all furniture in public rooms is secured
- ❑ have engines on standby in ample time
- ❑ if close to land, consider finding a lee

Non-Standard Items

- ❑ if on a weather shore, stand clear of the land as much as possible before the onset of the weather
- ❑ if at anchor, heave it and ride out the weather at sea. Your anchor is not designed to be used in extreme weather conditions
- ❑ do full engine and steering checks prior to the onset of heavy weather
- ❑ be prepared to go to hand steering at any time required
- ❑ place all external decks out of bounds, except in an emergency
- ❑ check windscreen washers, wipers and clear view screens
- ❑ have searchlights trained forward to enable you to see the seas over the bow and the fore part of the ship
- ❑ adjust speed and course for the best way of the ship
- ❑ ensure that all vessels in the immediate vicinity are kept advised of your intentions
- ❑ rearrange crew to ensure adequate bridge team cover to meet hours of rest requirements.

Cold Weather/Freezing Conditions

You don't have to go into icebound areas with ice class ships to encounter freezing conditions, nor does the sea have to be frozen to freeze your freshwater pipes and tanks. Freezing conditions can occur in severe winter weather in many places around the world such as Korea, China, the North Sea and the Barents Sea. If you do not take precautions in such areas, severe damage can result.

When developing plans and ship-specific checklists for entering cold weather or areas of ice, the following objectives should be considered:

- ❑ Obtaining available weather and ice reports prior to entering the area
- ❑ notifying the departments on board of the approaching conditions and likely hazards
- ❑ maintaining the sea suctions, rudder and propeller immersed
- ❑ limiting the vessel's trim
- ❑ reducing ice flows when manoeuvring and berthing
- ❑ preventing hull plate damage (by reducing speed)
- ❑ preventing rudder and propeller damage by avoiding astern engine movements
- ❑ avoiding anchoring
- ❑ verifying the hull integrity (from the soundings of all tanks and spaces)
- ❑ maintaining clear walkways (using scrapers and salt or sand)
- ❑ ensuring there is suitable PPE for all crew
- ❑ making the crew aware of the dangers of exposure
- ❑ ensuring that all unused piping is properly drained
- ❑ ensuring that any unused steam winches are disengaged, turning slowly and lubricated as necessary
- ❑ ensuring that all heating coils are suitably drained and blown through when not in use.

If you are going into an area where there is a chance of encountering freezing conditions, there are certain precautions that you must consider taking, depending on the severity of the expected conditions.

Checklist for the Deck Department

The following represents a list of items to be checked prior to entering ice or carrying out ice operations:

General

- ❑ Check the inventory of cold weather gear on board and replenish any deficiencies
- ❑ if the ship is not fitted with double glazing, perspex or cling film placed over windows can help insulate the accommodation
- ❑ examine towing fittings on the forecastle and ensure that a suitable messenger is available to pick up a bridle or towline
- ❑ ensure regular monitoring of the water level in all spaces and compartments. This could be as frequently as hourly in areas of heavy ice concentrations. This should also be instigated after a strong ice impact
- ❑ searchlights fitted and tested
- ❑ pilot ladders should not be lowered too early as ice can accumulate from spray
- ❑ ship's hydraulic systems filled with a fluid suitable for cold weather operations. Ships fitted with tunnel thrusters should not use these as they are liable to damage from ingested ice.

Deck Service Lines

Isolate and drain the following lines, leaving the drains open:

- ❑ Fire mains. Valves must be left cracked open
- ❑ general service line and freshwater line to all deck outside taps
- ❑ deck air line
- ❑ chain locker eductor
- ❑ anchor wash lines
- ❑ winch cooling lines
- ❑ all external taps
- ❑ bridge window wash systems unless antifreeze has been added
- ❑ be alert for the formation of ice at any overboard discharges and the resultant impact.

Whistles

- ❑ Drain main and forward whistles and close drain cocks.

Safety Gear

- ❑ Stow forward liferaft and LSA gear
- ❑ stow deck foam and water fire extinguishers in heated areas
- ❑ stow lifebuoys.

Lifeboats

- ❑ Drain freshwater tanks
- ❑ ensure portable freshwater tanks are full and located in a warm room nearby
- ❑ fit lifeboat drain plugs.

Consider the addition of:

- ❑ Sets of sub-zero temperature insulated clothing (S, M and L sizes) including hooded jackets, trousers, gloves and boots
- ❑ sets of thermal underwear and socks
- ❑ sets of face masks and goggles
- ❑ sleeping bags (down filled)
- ❑ Arctic type igloo-shaped survival tents
- ❑ additional high energy food supplies such as chocolate bars.

Grease

Grease should be applied liberally to all the moving parts on the decks including:

- ❑ Windlasses
- ❑ mooring winches
- ❑ cargo winches
- ❑ engaging clutches
- ❑ pins
- ❑ operating handles
- ❑ brake clamping bolt threads
- ❑ all nipple points
- ❑ sounding pipe cap threads
- ❑ hatch dogs
- ❑ davits
- ❑ cranes.

Note: A little antifreeze is effective when mixed into the grease.

Halyards and Stays

- ❑ If halyards are left up, they should be slacked down.

Protection

- ❑ Covers off all searchlights
- ❑ covers on hatch control boxes

Non-Standard Items

- ❑ covers on all fire hydrants
- ❑ covers on all fire hose boxes
- ❑ covers on all mooring lines on drums, leaving lashings clear before making fast to enable release
- ❑ covers on bunkering sounding pipes
- ❑ grease and burlap (hessian) hatch drive motors and gypsies.

Heaters

- ❑ Forecastle fan and space heaters switched on
- ❑ winch hydraulic header tank and hatch hydraulic heaters switched on
- ❑ anti-condensation heaters on hydraulic systems switched on
- ❑ winch, hatch pump and exhaust fan motor heaters switched on
- ❑ any deckhouse space heaters switched on
- ❑ fire pump and davit heaters switched on
- ❑ space heaters in emergency headquarters switched on.

Additional Items for Tankers

- ❑ Decontamination showers and eyewash stations to be accessible to crew in all weather conditions
- ❑ drain foam lines
- ❑ cargo heating coils either to be empty or steam to be circulated
- ❑ aft peak tank to be heated, if ballasted
- ❑ pressure vacuum (P/V) breaker to have the correct amount of antifreeze (glycol)
- ❑ steam to be opened to deck water seal and cargo oil pump separators
- ❑ crude oil wash (COW) lines and COW machine stand pipes to be drained
- ❑ P/V valves to be operated to ensure free movement
- ❑ insulate lines from cold with a trace heating system. Care should be taken that thermostats are functional and have enough power to run through cables to provide effective trace heating.

Tankers – Cargo Heating Systems

If the cargo heating system is not required:

- ❑ Drain/blow through inlet/exhaust lines to remove all presence of water.

If cargo heating is required:

- ❑ Introduce steam to the cargo heating system before encountering freezing temperatures
- ❑ consider fitting a small diameter line (jumper line) between the supply and return manifolds on the forward tanks to prevent freezing of the exhaust returns
- ❑ test all steam and exhaust valves for tightness so as to prevent leakage into 'dry lines'
- ❑ maintain heating until ship reaches warmer climates
- ❑ blow through all coils/lines with air immediately after turning off the steam.

Additional Items for Gas Carriers

- ❑ Drain both deck water spray/sprinkler lines and safety relief valve drains
- ❑ Drain both safety relief valves and vent masts
- ❑ cargo heaters and cargo condenser fresh water cooling systems to be kept on continuous circulation. Suitable antifreeze is to be added
- ❑ emergency eye wash and decontamination shower lines and tanks to be drained
- ❑ attach and post a pipeline drawing of the number and location of the drains and indicate which drains are to be blanked and drained. The same is to be clearly marked at their location
- ❑ isolation valves of lines to be posted and clearly marked at their location
- ❑ if space heaters are not provided, cluster-lights may be safely rigged close to the machinery and electrical panels and kept on.

Note for Dry Cargo Ships

Ships regularly trading in ice should carry a long-handled blow torch fired by propane, and a sufficient stock of cylinders should be maintained on board.

Checklist for the Engine Department

The engine room should not be left unattended in ice-covered waters.

General

- ❑ Ensure there is sufficient fuel and fresh water for at least 7 days extended manoeuvring when approaching Canadian waters
- ❑ can trace heating lines be utilised?
- ❑ are combustion air preheating systems operational for diesel engine jacket water heaters and other systems as applicable?
- ❑ compartment space heater switched on
- ❑ change over to ballast seawater recirculating tank (if fitted)
- ❑ oil tank heaters on (keep steam valve cracked open to prevent bursting of pipe)
- ❑ keep all steam tracing lines active
- ❑ heat up diesel oil settling and service tank to 30°C
- ❑ clean diesel oil filters daily to prevent wax accumulation
- ❑ lube oil and heavy oil purifiers to be run continuously
- ❑ keep sterntube cooling water tank slack (after peak)
- ❑ oily water separator to be drained of all water if exposed
- ❑ regular check of the stern glands to determine whether water is passing through.

Domestic/sanitary system

- ❑ Monitor domestic freshwater pumps, since continuous running is an indication of ruptured piping
- ❑ watch the freshwater tank levels
- ❑ crack the steam on freshwater tank coils
- ❑ circulate fresh water continuously to eliminate any possibility of freezing
- ❑ maintain a small flow of water through the sanitary system and soil drains
- ❑ if the ambient space temperature falls below 5°C (41°F), apply heating to the sanitary holding tank and the overboard line. If time permits, purge air or steam through all wash water outlets that do not drain to a level well below the waterline. If necessary, either add a small amount of antifreeze (environmentally safe) or salt to unused drain traps and toilets, or insert rubber hoses for ease of future removal.

Ventilation

- ❑ Reduce ventilation and/or provide shields to avoid any direct cold airflow against control and gauging equipment and also small diameter piping systems
- ❑ with a diesel-driven ship, the closing of dampers and a reduction in the ventilation will not create a higher than normal vacuum to build up inside engine room spaces

  Recirculation of air in the engine room should be avoided as this will result in a build-up of aromatic hydrocarbon and noxious gases.
- ❑ close funnel flaps as required
- ❑ stop engine room vent fans and/or close distribution flaps as conditions dictate
- ❑ leave the funnel skylights open to maintain funnel circulation (ensure funnel temperature is kept above freezing)
- ❑ use engine room fan heaters as required.

Auxiliary boiler

- ❑ Run on backup if steam demand makes it necessary.

Main engine seawater system

- ❑ Maintain seawater temperature at inverter (45°F or 7.2°C)
- ❑ activate seawater recirculation system by recirculating to low seachest and/or pump suction as required
- ❑ monitor suction and discharge pressures of seawater pumps and carry out steam injection if any signs of ice formation are noticed in the seachests. This is determined by pressure/flow fluctuations. Steam injection hoses to be kept ready. Open steam to seachests and the overboard discharge valve, if required.

Hydraulic pump rooms

- ❑ Ship's hydraulic systems should be filled with fluid intended for cold weather operation
- ❑ space heater switched on
- ❑ oil tank heater switched on
- ❑ close compartment vent or use a shield
- ❑ use 70% isopropyl alcohol to remove moisture in hydraulic oil and assist movement of the controls.

Non-Standard Items

Steering gear flat compartment

- ❑ Space heater switched on
- ❑ if no space heater is available, run hydraulic pumps continuously and use oil suitable for low temperatures
- ❑ oil tank heater switched on
- ❑ close compartment vent or use a shield.

All under-deck passages and duct keel

- ❑ Space heater switched on
- ❑ close compartment vent or use a shield.

Bow thruster room

- ❑ Space heater switched on
- ❑ oil tank heater switched on
- ❑ close compartment vent or use a shield.

Emergency Generator Room

- ❑ Fuel: use winter grade oil

  SOLAS II-1, Reg 44 states: "Emergency generating sets should be capable of being readily started in their cold condition at a temperature of 0°C. If this is impracticable, or if lower temperatures are likely to be encountered, provision acceptable to the Administration should be made for the maintenance of heating arrangements, to ensure ready starting of the generating sets."
- ❑ add antifreeze (suitable to minus 40°C) to generator and compressor
- ❑ close the external vents
- ❑ any freshwater lines to be blanked off
- ❑ radiator vents must be open for recirculation
- ❑ space heater switched on.

Double bottom tanks

- ❑ Transfer maximum heavy fuel oil up to the wing tanks
- ❑ isolate unused heating coils and blow through with air or leave steam on and ensure returns maintained warm
- ❑ turn on bilge tank heating coil, unless tank is empty.

Fire main

- ❑ Put the pump suction on a low seachest
- ❑ drain the fire main down to sea level
- ❑ leave the fire pump suction and discharge valves open.

Deck air

- ❑ Isolate deck service air at the engine room valve and drain the line
- ❑ ensure that air to control air and whistle is moisture free.

Sea inlets

- ❑ Reduce quantity of seawater pumped into cooling system to reduce blockage by ice
- ❑ monitor pressure of seawater at inlet and clean strainer as necessary.

Ice Accretion

Despite the best precautions, ice accretion may occur, leading to dangerous situations such as list, negative metacentric height (GM) and angle of loll. Accretion can occur through any of the following freezing on the ship's structure:

- ❑ Rain
- ❑ sea spray, with sea temperature less than minus 1°C
- ❑ shipping seas
- ❑ water leakages from burst pipes or tanks
- ❑ freezing fog.

It is important that all possible precautions are taken, including:

- ❑ Ensuring full compliance with ice accretion allowance stability requirements
- ❑ maintaining a close watch on weather forecasts
- ❑ increasing the frequency of meteorological observations
- ❑ monitoring the icing effects and build-up
- ❑ reviewing the voyage plan to consider more sheltered areas.

Should the level of ice build-up cause concern, the following actions will help alleviate the situation:

- ❑ Reduce speed
- ❑ adjust course to run with wind, reducing relative wind speed
- ❑ head to warmer areas
- ❑ seek a lee from land to reduce wind spray
- ❑ report any unforecasted ice or freezing conditions
- ❑ inform all vessels in the area.

Refugees and Migrants

If you pick up refugees, your P&I Club should be contacted.

The refugees may have been at sea for a number of weeks and could be suffering from any or a combination of the following:

- Exposure
- hunger
- dehydration
- seasickness
- fatigue.

The United Nations High Commission for Refugees (UNHCR) has issued 'Guidelines for the Disembarkation of Refugees', which detail a scheme for the reimbursement of certain costs involved in the landing of refugees. However, this scheme may not cover a deviation for the purpose of landing the refugees. You should therefore consult with your Company, provided time allows, if you are considering deviating the vessel.

Action to be Taken

In addition to any other guidance on board, when refugees are picked up by your vessel:

- ❑ Obtain medical advice from ashore if required (administer rehydration salts and possibly suncreams)
- ❑ prepare provisions for the refugees
- ❑ prepare accommodation on board, including blankets and beds
- ❑ notify your Company and P&I Club
- ❑ the Company Security Officer (CSO) will inform the appropriate authorities
- ❑ once a decision is made to land the refugees, inform the Company's agent and P&I correspondent.

The following information should be provided to the Company and the P&I Club:

- ❑ Date, time and position where the refugees were picked up
- ❑ ETA at next port of call
- ❑ ETA at nearest suitable port if the vessel deviates to land the refugees
- ❑ personal details of the refugees
- ❑ medical condition of the refugees and any medical assistance required.

Non-Standard Items

The following evidence is required in connection with a deviation to land refugees:

- Date, time and position where the refugees were picked up
- date, time and position where the vessel deviated from her scheduled course
- fuel ROB at the time of deviation
- fuel used for the deviation
- record of all communication expenses
- copies of all relevant logbooks.

Asylum Seekers

If rescued persons appear to indicate that they are asylum-seekers or that they fear persecution or ill-treatment if disembarked at a particular place, the Master should inform the rescued persons concerned that the Master has no authority to hear, consider or determine an asylum request.

Care should therefore be taken to ensure that:

- Arrangements for the disembarkation of rescued persons do not result in their return to a place where they risk persecution or ill-treatment; and
- personal information regarding possible asylum-seekers or refugees is not shared with the authorities of their country of origin or any country from which they have fled and in which they claim a risk of harm, or with persons who may convey this information to the authorities of those countries.
- UNHCR should be contacted if there are difficulties reaching agreement regarding arrangements for the treatment or disembarkation of rescued people who may be asylum-seekers or refugees.
- Asylum-seekers and refugees have a right to contact UNHCR. This would usually take place as soon as possible after disembarkation.

Ref: 'Rescue at Sea - A Guide to the Principles and Practice as Applied to Refugees and Migrants' released by The IMO, UNHCR and ICS in 2015. http://tinyurl.com/lbr82gp

Reference should also be made to pages 702 and 728.

Stowaways

Where stowaways are found on board, your P&I Club should be notified. They will prepare for identification and repatriation of the stowaways.

Initial Actions

- ❑ The stowaway should be treated humanely and not threatened with any violence whatsoever
- ❑ place the stowaway in a locked cabin (he should not be allowed to wander about the vessel)
- ❑ if more than one stowaway has been discovered, they should, where possible, be accommodated separately
- ❑ the place where the stowaway was discovered should be searched for further stowaways and any documents/personal effects/drugs
- ❑ the place where the stowaway was discovered should be photographed or video recorded
- ❑ the stowaway should be asked/searched for identity papers (such papers must be confiscated as stowaways often try to hide their identity or destroy their papers)
- ❑ the stowaway should be thoroughly searched for drugs
- ❑ the stowaway should be questioned at length as to where and when he boarded
- ❑ if there is more than one stowaway, question them individually to determine whether they knew each other prior to boarding
- ❑ question them as to the circumstances under which voluntary return may be possible
- ❑ explain that, if economic/monetary reasons are behind the stowing away, no country will accept him and his repatriation will be inevitable
- ❑ if you cannot communicate with the stowaway, an interpreter should be engaged.

Evidence to be Collected

- ❑ Date, time and port where the stowaway came on board
- ❑ date, time and position where the stowaway was discovered
- ❑ location where the stowaway was discovered
- ❑ period that the stowaway was hidden

- ❑ medical/physical condition of the stowaway
- ❑ security/gangway watch in place at the port where the stowaway boarded
- ❑ details of those on watch when the stowaway boarded
- ❑ whether shore guards were employed at the port where the stowaway boarded and, if so, details of the company
- ❑ details of the stowaway search conducted prior to departure and details of any stowaways found during that search and where they were delivered ashore
- ❑ records of the care/treatment given to the stowaway (frequency/type of meals, accommodation, sanitary provisions and times allowed for exercise).

Handover Arriving/Leaving

Too often when a new Master joins, the Master being relieved leaves himself with insufficient time to pack his bags and properly handover, due to being involved in the approach into the port and dealing with the port officials.

It is not surprising that things are left behind, work is not completed and some important handover advice not given. Even safe keys have had to be posted back to the ship! Just a little preparation a few days before can avoid this last minute rush:

- ❑ Final portage account completed
- ❑ cash required drawn and remaining cash itemised
- ❑ safe keys and combination handed over
- ❑ ship's trading documents listed detailing validity, expiry date, renewals and extensions
- ❑ continuous synopsis record up to date
- ❑ list of documents with the agent
- ❑ bond listed and, if possible, checked and agreed
- ❑ list of drugs
- ❑ any ship's weapons and stowage.

Sign the Following

- ❑ Logbooks
- ❑ ISM documents
- ❑ GMDSS
- ❑ Oil Record Book(s)
- ❑ Garbage Disposal Logbook
- ❑ sign off members of crew who are also leaving
- ❑ your documents collected
- ❑ discharge books
- ❑ certificates
- ❑ entry of handover made in Logbook and signed.

Handover Notes for Incoming Master

Prepared, including:

- ❑ Cargo charter party information
- ❑ bunker fuel and water state
- ❑ fuel and water consumption
- ❑ budget status
- ❑ equipment out of order or needing attention
- ❑ repairs ordered or needed
- ❑ crew joining/leaving
- ❑ personnel status
- ❑ exchange rates in use
- ❑ victualling accounts if no Chief Steward
- ❑ charts in order or ordered, plus other related items such as digital chart correction service or digital charts, ie Admiralty Vector Chart Service
- ❑ next port advice
- ❑ inspection and surveys
- ❑ any survey deficiencies still uncorrected
- ❑ critical equipment status for:
- ❑ engines/propulsion
- ❑ cargo/equipment
- ❑ navigation equipment
- ❑ fire-fighting equipment
- ❑ life-saving equipment
- ❑ mooring/anchoring equipment
- ❑ agent contact address for next port
- ❑ cabin keys handed over
- ❑ leave a full refrigerator!

Handover Arriving/Leaving

Transferring Command

The Master signing off retains command until he is ready to disembark.

Up until this time, the relieving Master will be ensuring that the vessel is in a seaworthy condition and that there are sufficient bunkers, stores, provisions, water, etc on board for the forthcoming voyage, plus an allowance for a safety margin. The relieving Master will also ensure that all navigational equipment, machinery, mooring equipment and LSA/FFE equipment is in good working order before sailing.

Each Master will complete all flag State required logbook entries and associated documentation, where applicable. When the Master signs the logbook, command is officially transferred. In practice, this is done as close as possible to the time the Master signing off disembarks from the vessel.

Certificates/Documents Required to be Carried On Board Ships

On all Ships

- ❑ Certificate of Registry
- ❑ International Tonnage Certificate
- ❑ International Load Line Certificate
- ❑ International Load Line Exemption Certificate
- ❑ ship stability booklet/damage control plans
- ❑ safe manning document
- ❑ certificates of competency for Masters, officers and ratings, including relevant endorsements
- ❑ medical certificates
- ❑ records of seafarers' hours of work/rest and a schedule of shipboard working arrangements
- ❑ International Oil Pollution Prevention Certificate
- ❑ Oil Record Book
- ❑ Shipboard Oil Pollution Emergency Plan (SOPEP)
- ❑ International Sewage Pollution Prevention Certificate
- ❑ International Air Pollution Prevention (IAPP) Certificate
- ❑ fire control plans/wallet/operational booklet
- ❑ record of onboard training and drills
- ❑ garbage management plan
- ❑ Garbage Disposal Logbook
- ❑ voyage data recorder, compliance certificate
- ❑ cargo securing manual
- ❑ copy of Company ISM Document of Compliance
- ❑ Safety Management Certificate
- ❑ International Ship Security Certificate (ISSC) or interim certificate
- ❑ Ship Security Plan and associated records
- ❑ Continuous Synopsis Record (CSR)
- ❑ Declaration of Security (DOS)
- ❑ record of ship security levels.

Passenger Ships

In addition to the certificates listed for 'all ships', passenger ships shall carry:

- ❑ Passenger Ship Safety Certificate
- ❑ Exemption Certificate
- ❑ Special Trade Passenger Ship Safety Certificate
- ❑ Special Trade Passenger Ship Space Certificate
- ❑ search and rescue cooperation plan
- ❑ list of operational limitations
- ❑ decision support system.

Cargo Ships

In addition to the certificates listed for 'all ships', cargo ships shall carry:

- ❑ Cargo Ship Safety Construction Certificate
- ❑ Cargo Ship Safety Equipment Certificate
- ❑ Cargo Ship Safety Radio Certificate
- ❑ Cargo Ship Safety Certificate
- ❑ Exemption Certificate
- ❑ document of authorisation for the carriage of grain
- ❑ certificate of insurance or other financial security in respect of civil liability for oil pollution damage
- ❑ enhanced survey report file
- ❑ record of oil discharge monitoring and control system for the last ballast voyage
- ❑ cargo information
- ❑ bulk carrier booklet.

Ships Carrying Noxious Liquid Chemical Substances in Bulk

In addition to the certificates required for 'all ships' and 'cargo ships', where appropriate, any ship carrying noxious liquid chemical substances in bulk shall carry:

- ❑ International Pollution Prevention Certificate for the Carriage of Noxious Liquid Substances in Bulk

- ❑ survey report file
- ❑ ship structure access manual
- ❑ cargo record book
- ❑ Procedures and Arrangements Manual (P&A Manual)
- ❑ Shipboard Marine Pollution Emergency Plan for Noxious Liquid Substances.

Chemical Tanker

In addition to the certificates required for 'all ships' and 'cargo ships', where appropriate, any chemical tanker shall carry:

- ❑ Certificate of Fitness for the Carriage of Dangerous Chemicals in Bulk
- ❑ International Certificate of Fitness for the Carriage of Dangerous Chemicals in Bulk.

Liquefied Gas Carriers

In addition to the certificates required for 'all ships' and 'cargo ships', where appropriate, any gas carrier shall carry:

- ❑ Certificate of Fitness for the Carriage of Liquefied Gases in Bulk
- ❑ International Certificate of Fitness for the Carriage of Liquefied Gases in Bulk.

High-speed Craft

In addition to the certificates required for 'all ships', 'passenger ships' and 'cargo ships', where applicable, any high-speed craft shall carry:

- ❑ High-Speed Craft Safety Certificate
- ❑ Permit to Operate High-Speed Craft.

Ships Carrying Dangerous Goods

In addition to the certificates required for 'all ships' and 'cargo ships', where applicable, any ship carrying dangerous goods shall carry:

- ❑ Document of compliance with the special requirements for ships carrying dangerous goods.

Ships Carrying Dangerous Goods in Packaged Form

In addition to the certificates required for 'all ships' and 'cargo ships', where applicable, any ship carrying dangerous goods in packaged form shall carry:

- ❑ Dangerous goods manifest or stowage plan.

There are other certificates/documents whose carriage is not mandatory. These include:

- ❑ Special Purpose Ship Safety Certificate
- ❑ Certificate of Fitness for Offshore Support Vessels
- ❑ Diving System Safety Certificate
- ❑ Dynamically Supported Craft Construction and Equipment Certificate
- ❑ Mobile Offshore Drilling Unit Safety Certificate
- ❑ Wing-in-ground Craft Safety Certificate
- ❑ Permit to Operate WIG Craft
- ❑ Noise Survey Report.

On Taking Over

On taking over, the incoming Master should obtain as much information as possible from the Master signing off. This should include:

- ❑ Knowledge of your duties
- ❑ understanding the vessel
- ❑ understanding the Company's systems and procedures.

Questions to ask the outgoing Master:

- ❑ Portage account. Run through it with him and see his final account for handover
- ❑ consumables, fuel and water for the next voyage
- ❑ his assessment of Officers and key ratings, especially the Chief Officer, Chief Engineer, watchkeepers and Cook
- ❑ probe him about the Company, the way they like things done and how you might find the superintendents that you will come across
- ❑ any bridge and engine room equipment problems and any peculiarities
- ❑ any hull or structural damage and next scheduled drydocking
- ❑ is ship fully stored?
- ❑ if you are unfamiliar with the port and the next scheduled port, ask about these and any problems with navigation, port facilities or officials
- ❑ if you can, check the bond, although it is probably sealed. At least see the final bond statement
- ❑ check the cash and make sure you have the safe keys and the combination
- ❑ communications with the Company. Run through the email system or any other system being used.

Ship's certificates and status. Check these against the checklist and also verify:

- ❑ Validity

Handover Arriving/Leaving

- ❑ expiry dates
- ❑ any renewals or extensions required to cover the forthcoming voyage
- ❑ that they are complete.

These include the ship's certificate of registration issued by the flag State and the statutory certificates that may be issued by a Classification Society. If any of the certificates are ashore with the agent, make sure you have the receipt.

The Master should be fully familiar with:

- ❑ The Company's documented SMS
- ❑ the lines of communication and responsibilities
- ❑ any peculiarities of the vessel's SMS
- ❑ the documented Ship Security Plan (SSP)
- ❑ the lines of communication under the SSP
- ❑ any other standing instructions prior to assuming full command.

Any non-conformity regarding an item of maintenance or a section of the SMS should be reported and corrective action taken.

Charter and cargo. The Master should:

- ❑ Be made aware of the charterer and their contact details
- ❑ be made aware of the terms and conditions of the charter party
- ❑ seek input where required from the Chief Officer and Chief Engineer as to the performance ability of the vessel
- ❑ clarify with the Company any item of the charter party that he has any doubts about or the vessel's ability to perform the charterer's requirements.

On a general inspection of the vessel, you should pay particular attention to the condition of:

- ❑ Anchors and their arrangements
- ❑ mooring arrangements/condition of the mooring lines
- ❑ watertight doors
- ❑ ventilation heads
- ❑ hatch covers including dogs and clamps
- ❑ hatch access covers including dogs and clamps
- ❑ scuppers and their plugs
- ❑ rubber gaskets.

Fire and safety equipment. Ensure that:

- ❑ Life-saving equipment is in order
- ❑ fire protection, detection and extinguishing systems are available
- ❑ a copy of the fire control plan is stored in a prominent location
- ❑ fire equipment lockers, including breathing apparatus sets, are in order
- ❑ fire dampers operate
- ❑ any watertight doors and fire doors operate
- ❑ other fire-fighting equipment is operational and in order.

General. Before the commencement of the voyage, check:

- ❑ All medicines required to be in the medicine stores are actually on board and are within their expiry dates, with any out-of-date medication replaced immediately
- ❑ check the charts and courses laid off.

You should satisfy yourself that the vessel is in a seaworthy condition and that the crew are qualified and certificated for the voyage and cover any requirements of the flag State. If you find any shortcomings in this regard, which you believe could affect the safety and/or seaworthiness of the vessel, you must immediately report these to the Company, even if the situation suggests there is insufficient time to rectify these deficiencies before commencing the voyage. There will be instances where the Class Society and/or flag State administration may require these deficiencies to be rectified before commencing the voyage.

The procedure of taking over command should be properly documented in the vessel's SMS records and acknowledged in writing by both the relieving and the relieved Master.

The outgoing Master should show the new Master round the bridge. This presents an opportunity for him to explain the basic operation of unfamiliar bridge equipment.

The new Master should ask about the handling of the ship. What is the power of the thrusters, if fitted? Right hand or left hand propellers? If variable pitch, which way does the bow sheer when going astern? If it is a standard motor ship, how many starts can be made before the air bottles need to be recharged and then how long before the ship can make the next movement? The new Master will have many more questions to consider before the leaving Master is down the gangway, at which point he will be on his own. And make sure that you have received your cabin keys!

Emergency Checklist

Emergency - Collision

Initial

- ❑ Manoeuvre own vessel to minimise the effects of collision
- ❑ sound general alarm/ship's whistle
- ❑ muster crew and passengers (with lifejackets)
- ❑ close all watertight doors and fire doors
- ❑ issue distress/urgency message to all stations.

Actions on Impact

- ❑ Switch on deck lighting and exhibit NUC signals
- ❑ if vessels remain embedded together, agreement should be made to remain fixed in this position until action has been taken to restrict flooding. This may require one vessel maintaining ahead propulsion
- ❑ investigate damage and initiate control measures, including pollution:
  - determine the vessel's position and the available depth of water
  - sound tanks/ship spaces
- ❑ offer assistance to, or request assistance from, the other vessel involved if required
- ❑ consider the loss of stability, taking into account free surface effect of any flooded compartments
- ❑ consider salvage assistance
- ❑ consider beaching if own vessel is sinking
- ❑ establish communications with the other vessel and exchange the following information:
  - name
  - port of registry
  - port of departure
  - port of destination
- ❑ update Coastguard or RCC
- ❑ keep crew informed
- ❑ inform Company
- ❑ if own ship can safely move, proceed to the nearest safe refuge and moor your vessel securely. Your own vessel may currently be a danger to navigation
- ❑ log all events in the Bridge Movement Book
- ❑ record all details of the incident in the Deck Logbook, Official Logbook and on an incident report form.

After the Event

- ❑ You should not discuss the collision with anyone unless the correspondent or lawyer appointed by the Company, hull and machinery insurer or P&I insurer is present

  (If there is pollution caused by the escape of oil from the other vessel, the insurance cover provided by the hull and machinery insurer may be involved. In such cases, the hull and machinery insurer or their correspondents must be contacted).
- ❑ it is advisable to lodge a note of protest in some jurisdictions to protect the right to claim against the other vessel. You should seek advice from your P&I correspondent or lawyer
- ❑ after taking the necessary preventative measures, ensure all witnesses make a record of their recollection of events and the run-up to the collision. You should counsel any witnesses to give an honest account of the incident as they saw it, even if they believe that this is to the detriment of the vessel. Any photographs or video footage captured by the crew should be gathered. A suitable incentive could be offered to any member of the crew who has collected such evidence
- ❑ any VHF correspondence between the vessels involved (or with the shore/port/VTS) in the run-up to the collision should be recorded in writing to show what exchange of information/warnings were conveyed
- ❑ if your ship has ECDIS, the data for the relevant period should be stored as soon as possible.

You should liaise with your P&I correspondent/lawyer to confirm the other details they require, but copies of the following documents, together with the vessel's trading documents, will need to be retained:

- ❑ Chart used (paper or electronic) – do not tamper with or erase any marks/data
- ❑ Deck Logbook
- ❑ Bridge Movement Book
- ❑ any scrap logs
- ❑ Engine Logbook
- ❑ Engine Movement Book
- ❑ course recorder printouts
- ❑ records of working and rest hours of the Master, officers and crew on duty.

Emergency Checklist

Emergency - Grounding

- ❑ Stop engines
- ❑ sound general alarm/ship's whistle
- ❑ muster crew and passengers (with lifejackets)
- ❑ close all watertight doors and fire doors
- ❑ if assistance is required urgently, send a PAN-PAN message to all stations. Otherwise, inform the Coastguard by VHF
- ❑ exhibit signals for vessel aground:
  - day – three black balls
  - night – anchor lights plus two all round red lights
- ❑ commence appropriate sound signal if in restricted visibility
- ❑ update AIS status
- ❑ ensure 'high' sea suction in use
- ❑ investigate vessel damage, including pollution, and initiate control measures:
  - sound all tanks and ship spaces
  - sound all round vessel; consider using rescue boat
  - confirm vessel's position and depth of water, including direction of navigable water
- ❑ determine whether the wind or sea is carrying the vessel into further difficulties. If so, consider using the anchors
- ❑ keep all ship's departments and passengers informed
- ❑ inform the DPA/Company, and keep updated
- ❑ before taking further action, consider all relevant information including:
  - weather and sea state
  - state/height and range of tide
  - nature of seabed
  - depth of water all round the vessel
  - damaged stability condition
- ❑ in lightening the vessel, consider the discharge of the following and the resultant change of stability, draught, trim and list:
  - water ballast
  - fresh water
  - survival craft and passengers
  - stores
- ❑ consider contacting Class or Company, as appropriate, to determine stability in damaged condition
- ❑ if unable to float safely by the vessel's own efforts, call for assistance
- ❑ log all events in the Bridge Movement Book
- ❑ record all details of the incident in the Deck Logbook, Official Logbook and on an incident report form.

Records after a Grounding

Evidence to be gathered following a grounding:

- ❑ Date and exact time of the grounding
- ❑ position of the grounding
- ❑ detailed description of the section of the vessel aground
- ❑ nature of the seabed where the grounding has taken place
- ❑ courses at the time of the grounding (charted, steered, gyro and magnetic)
- ❑ speed at the time of the grounding (RPM or pitch setting)
- ❑ rudder angle at the time of the grounding
- ❑ alterations of course and/or speed in the period immediately before the grounding
- ❑ orders given
- ❑ communications exchanged between ship and shore
- ❑ if under pilotage, any communications with the pilot and/or tugs prior to the grounding
- ❑ detail of positions plotted prior to the grounding
- ❑ helm/engine movements before/after the grounding
- ❑ weather conditions at the time of the grounding
- ❑ tide and current at the time of the grounding
- ❑ draught at the time of the grounding
- ❑ soundings around the vessel
- ❑ soundings of all the ship's tanks from the last record before grounding, and the situation after the grounding
- ❑ cargo distribution from the last record before grounding and the situation after the grounding
- ❑ navigation and communication equipment in use at the time of the grounding:
  - echo sounder information/range used/printout
  - radar/ARPA settings and any adjustments/changes to these settings

and the time of such change prior to the incident
- GPS positions
- VHF – location of the radio in use and channels in operation/being monitored
- ECDIS – chart used and last update
- any other navigation/comms equipment in use.

Persons Involved

Record the name, rank, duties and location for:

- ❑ All persons on the bridge at the time of the grounding
- ❑ any further eye witnesses
- ❑ engine room personnel
- ❑ pilot's details
- ❑ other vessels/traffic in the area at the time of the grounding.

You should liaise with your P&I correspondent/ lawyer to confirm whether they require any other details, but copies of the following documents, together with the vessel's trading documents, will need to be retained:

- ❑ Chart used (paper or electronic) – do not tamper with or erase any marks/data
- ❑ Deck Logbook
- ❑ Bridge Movement Book
- ❑ any scrap logs
- ❑ Engine Logbook
- ❑ Engine Movement Book
- ❑ course recorder printouts
- ❑ records of working and rest hours of the Master, officers and crew on duty.

Emergency Checklist

Emergency - Man Overboard

Initial Actions

- ❑ Let go quick release buoy
- ❑ turn ship/hand steering/commence recovery manoeuvre
- ❑ initiate position fix on satnav/GPS/ECDIS
- ❑ sound alarm/3 long blasts
- ❑ maintain visual contact/post lookout
- ❑ Master to bridge.

Subsequent Actions

- ❑ Engines on standby
- ❑ inform engine room
- ❑ distress/urgency broadcast
- ❑ muster crew/communications established
- ❑ prepare rescue boat/medical party stand by
- ❑ flag signal 'O'
- ❑ deck preparations for recovery:
  - deck lights
  - pilot ladder
  - cargo net/equipment
  - heaving line
  - line throwing apparatus.

Notes

In turning the ship:

- ❑ If the MOB is visible, turn the ship in the direction of the MOB
- ❑ if in visual contact with the MOB, turn vessel to maintain contact
- ❑ do not initially stop the ship. Turning the ship will slow it down and speed can be reduced thereafter.

Where someone has fallen overboard or is found to be missing, the cover provided by the P&I Club is involved. You should contact your Company and your P&I Club or their local correspondent.

Emergency - Fire

Initial

- ❑ Determine location of fire
- ❑ acknowledge the alarm
- ❑ send fire party, with radio(s), to investigate:
    - location
    - extent
    - type of fire
- ❑ close down the vessel as quickly as possible (fans, vents, watertight doors).

Actions

- ❑ Sound fire alarm
- ❑ start fire pumps
- ❑ exhibit NUC signals/shapes
- ❑ update AIS.

Bridge

- ❑ Alter course and speed to minimise any effects of fire/smoke
- ❑ confirm vessel's position
- ❑ apprise yourself of the location of any hazards
- ❑ muster crew and passengers
- ❑ close fire doors
- ❑ instigate a search for any missing persons (if applicable).

Actions

- ❑ Close down manual fire dampers and vent flaps
- ❑ isolate electrical supplies
- ❑ commence taking a log of events, including position
- ❑ make appropriate PA announcement to passengers/crew.

Communications

- ❑ Inform the Coastguard (in port, call the fire brigade) and DPA/Duty Manager. You should advise them of the following information:
    - position of vessel
    - nature and size of fire (details of cargo)
    - number of passengers and crew on board
    - measures currently being taken to fight or contain the fire
    - nature of assistance required.

Actions

- ❑ Initiate fire containment and fire-fighting measures
- ❑ consider effects on stability, including free surface.

If fire is getting worse or is out of control:

- ❑ Consider using fixed fire-fighting system
- ❑ consider anchoring vessel
- ❑ update fire brigade/Coastguard
- ❑ consider abandoning ship.

If fire is extinguished or well under control:

- ❑ Consider temperature/likelihood of re-ignition
- ❑ check adjacent compartments to ensure fire has not spread through heat transfer
- ❑ consider restoring ventilation to clear smoke
- ❑ update fire brigade/Coastguard
- ❑ record details of incident in Deck Logbook, Official Logbook and on an incident report form.

Emergency Checklist

Emergency - Dangerous Goods Incident

- ❑ Sound general alarm/ship's whistle
- ❑ muster crew in a safe area upwind of the hazard
- ❑ close watertight and automatic fire doors
- ❑ shut down fans and mechanical ventilation
- ❑ start fire pumps
- ❑ put additional electrical generators in ready state
- ❑ confirm vessel's position and proximity of hazards
- ❑ issue distress or urgency signal (as appropriate) to all stations
- ❑ exhibit NUC signal
- ❑ determine which dangerous good(s) are involved
- ❑ consult EMS Guide (Emergency Procedures) within IMDG supplement to determine:
  - actions in event of spillage
  - actions in event of fire
- ❑ first aid equipment ready; consult MFAG (Medical First Aid Guide)
- ❑ assess risks and whether it is safe for crew to enter the affected area to investigate cause/extent of incident, using the appropriate PPE
- ❑ fight fire and control/remove any spillage in accordance with EMS guidelines
- ❑ if crew can be sent safely to the affected area:
  - close all watertight/weathertight openings
  - secure the cargo using all available means
  - determine any leakage of fuel or dangerous goods
- ❑ consider jettisoning of cargo
- ❑ can the voyage be safely resumed? If not, determine the nearest safe port or anchorage
- ❑ keep ship's departments and passengers updated
- ❑ notify the Company/DPA
- ❑ update Coastguard or RCC
- ❑ record details of the incident in Deck Logbook, Official Logbook and on an incident report form.

Emergency - Cargo Shift

- ❑ Sound general alarm/ship's whistle
- ❑ muster crew and passengers (with lifejackets), preferably on the high side of the vessel if listed
- ❑ close watertight doors
- ❑ exhibit NUC signal
- ❑ confirm vessel's position and proximity of hazards
- ❑ reduce speed and manoeuvre the vessel to minimise motion
- ❑ if there is danger of capsizing or flooding, issue distress or urgency signal (as appropriate) to all stations and prepare for abandonment
- ❑ assess risks and investigate cause/extent of shift
- ❑ assess stability and confirm angle of loll
- ❑ if crew can be safely sent to the affected area:
    - close all watertight/weathertight openings
    - secure the cargo using all available means
    - determine any leakage of fuel or dangerous goods
- ❑ is it safe and prudent to use water ballast to correct list or trim?
- ❑ consider jettisoning of cargo
- ❑ can the voyage be safely resumed? If not, determine the nearest safe port or anchorage
- ❑ keep personnel updated
- ❑ notify the Company/DPA
- ❑ update Coastguard or RCC
- ❑ record details of the incident in Deck Logbook and Official Logbook.

Emergency Checklist

Emergency - Salvage/Search and Rescue (SAR)

- ❑ Establish communication with the casualty and the Coastguard
- ❑ implement rescue boat drill to gather resources and crew to prepare for the situation
- ❑ advise the passengers of the situation. Consider seeking any medical practitioners on board if necessary
- ❑ advise the following of the ship's ETA at the casualty:
    - Coastguard station coordinating the search and rescue
    - coordinator of the surface search (CSS) – if applicable
    - on scene commander (OSC) – if applicable
- ❑ where practical, use radar to identify and plot the casualty and other ships proceeding to the scene
- ❑ keep a full log of events and a full log of communications
- ❑ increase the bridge team as required (post extra lookouts)
- ❑ advise the CSS, OSC or casualty of the following resources that the ship has available:
    - life-saving equipment
    - medical equipment
    - fire-fighting equipment
    - fast rescue boat
    - reception and catering facilities
- ❑ while proceeding to the scene, order adequate preparation to be made for recovery and reception of survivors, including preparation for helicopter operations
- ❑ once on the scene, if the casualty has not been located, initiate the surface search (refer to the IAMSAR Manual)
- ❑ when the casualty is located, follow the directions of the CSS. If there is no CSS, consider the most appropriate action to recover survivors (refer to the IAMSAR Manual)
- ❑ agree rescue boat operating and communication procedure with the bridge
- ❑ rig guest warp, overside ladders and additional painters
- ❑ rig additional overside lighting for the rescue boat
- ❑ inform the Duty Manager
- ❑ record details of incident in Deck Logbook, Official Logbook and on an incident report form.

Records when Salvor is in Attendance

Salvage costs concern the hull and machinery and cargo insurers. You should therefore immediately contact your Company and the hull and machinery insurer, enabling them to decide what actions to take.

Whenever a salvor is in attendance, you should keep a detailed chronological record of the following items:

- ❑ Weather, wind, sea and tidal conditions from commencement of the refloating operation
- ❑ names and positions of tugs in attendance
- ❑ times that tugs commenced the refloating operation
- ❑ each activity undertaken and the result achieved
- ❑ materials used by the salvor
- ❑ personnel involved
- ❑ any damage to the salvor's equipment
- ❑ communication with the salvors.

During a refloating operation, you should keep a detailed record of the vessel's expenses and excess costs incurred in respect of:

- ❑ Crew involvement (name, time and activity involved)
- ❑ fuel used (heavy fuel, diesel and lubrication oil)
- ❑ vessel's equipment used and damaged.

Emergency - Medical

- ❑ Administer first aid:
  - ensure own safety
  - get assistance – if possible, establish whether there are any medical practitioners on board
  - administer immediate treatment – airway, breathing and circulation
  - check whether casualty is conscious/unconscious
  - assess blood loss/clinical shock
- ❑ provide medical care and make the patient as comfortable as possible.

Signs and Symptoms

- ❑ Signs and symptoms to check include:
  - respiration/breathing
  - pulse rate
  - blood pressure
  - temperature
  - injuries/bruising/wounds/bleeding
  - faeces/urine/sputum/vomit
- ❑ consult the Ship Master's Medical Guide
- ❑ obtain as much of the following information/history as possible:
  - name and nationality
  - age and sex
  - address
  - medical history
  - medication taken/required
  - what countries the patient has recently visited
- ❑ establish the ship's position/ETA of nearest port
- ❑ if in mid-ocean, consult ALRS for radio advice, eg CIRM Rome
- ❑ if sufficiently close to port, arrange ambulance/medical services for arrival
- ❑ if coastal, call Coastguard/RCC using urgency message requesting medical assistance
- ❑ where medivac is requested, prepare for helicopter or ship to ship transfer
- ❑ inform the DPA/Duty Manager
- ❑ record details of incident in Deck Logbook, Official Logbook, Medical Logbook and on an incident report form.

Emergency - Pollution Incident (Oil Tanker)

Emergency Checklist

Emergency - Pollution Incident (Oil Tanker)

Immediate Action

- ❑ Sound emergency alarm.

Initial Response

- ❑ Stop all cargo and/or bunkering operations
- ❑ close manifold valves
- ❑ switch air conditioning to recirculation or stop air intake to accommodation
- ❑ stop non-essential air intake fans to the engine room
- ❑ locate source of leakage and stop/reduce oil
- ❑ consult SOPEP plan
- ❑ consult MSDS/EmS guideline
- ❑ assess fire risk from release of flammable substances
- ❑ start fire pump
- ❑ commence clean-up procedures using absorbents and permitted solvents
- ❑ advise relevant parties (local authorities, coastal State, DPA/Company, P&I correspondent, etc).

Secondary Response

- ❑ Reduce the oil level in the tank concerned by transferring oil into an empty or slack tank
- ❑ reduce level of oil in tanks in the suspected area
- ❑ drain affected line to empty or slack tank
- ❑ reduce inert gas pressure to zero
- ❑ if the leakage is at the pump room sea valve, relieve pressure on pipelines
- ❑ prepare pumps for transfer of oil to other tanks or to shore or lightering vessel
- ❑ prepare portable pumps if it is possible to transfer spilt oil to an empty tank
- ❑ consider pumping water into the leaking tank to create a water cushion and prevent further oil loss. If leakage is below the waterline, arrange divers for further investigation
- ❑ calculate stresses/stability. If necessary, request shore assistance
- ❑ transfer cargo or bunkers to alleviate high stability stresses
- ❑ carefully stow residue from the clean-up operation prior to disposal.

Emergency - Abandon Ship

- ❑ Issue distress/mayday
- ❑ sound general emergency alarm
- ❑ close watertight and remote fire doors
- ❑ have crew prepare for abandonment:
    - muster check all crew and passengers, who should be wearing warm clothing, lifejackets or survival suits where appropriate
    - bring additional equipment to the embarkation deck, eg blankets, first aid kit, torches, distress flares, etc
- ❑ lower lifeboats to embarkation deck and rig painters
- ❑ activate EPIRB and SART and bring to the lifeboats
- ❑ take VDR (Voyage Data Recorder) cassette if possible
- ❑ can the vessel be reboarded (if necessary)?
- ❑ update mayday
- ❑ when ready, give the order to abandon ship.

Once clear of vessel:

- ❑ Ensure that all crew are accounted for in survival craft
- ❑ ensure that all survival craft are secured together and restrained from drifting away from the vessel separately
- ❑ issue seasickness tablets.

Emergency Checklist

Emergency - Angle of Loll

Angle of loll is caused by a rise in the height of the centre of gravity (KG) so that it creates a negative metacentric height (GM). There are several reasons why this can develop on a voyage, including:

- Burning of fuel or consumption of water, lowering G and introducing free surface effect (FSE)
- water absorption in hygroscopic cargoes, eg timber deck cargoes
- water trapped on deck, eg within pipes on offshore vessels
- ice accretion on deck
- cargo shift
- flooding.

Angle of loll should be rectified by reducing the height of the centre of gravity. Care must be taken not to cause the vessel to list quickly in the opposite direction as this could be sufficient to take the vessel beyond the angle of vanishing stability and capsize it.

- [ ] Alter course, putting the ship into the waves and keeping the high side into the wind
- [ ] confirm the listed condition is due to the angle of loll:
    - check port and starboard listing moments are equal
    - check for slack tanks
- [ ] press up any slack tanks, one at a time and the smallest first to remove FSE
- [ ] discharge any high ballast wing tank
- [ ] where three double bottom tanks are available, load ballast into the middle tank first
- [ ] when only two double bottom ballast tanks are available, load into the lowest (listed side) double bottom tanks first
- [ ] if necessary, jettisoning deck cargo can be considered.

It is important that only one tank at a time is worked. It should be remembered that, when loading into low sided tanks or discharging into high sided tanks, the vessel may initially list further. The situation should improve as the height of the centre of gravity reduces.

CHAPTER 50

Tsunamis and Marine Phenomena

Tsunamis

Tsunami is a Japanese word that is formed from the words 'tsu' meaning 'harbour' and 'nami' meaning 'wave'.

Approximately 60% of tsunamis occur in the Pacific Ocean, but they can occur in any region of the world. They tend to be generated along tectonic plate boundaries.

The earth's crust is divided into different sized segments called tectonic plates. These move relative to each other leading to volcanic activity along their edges.

Generation of Tsunamis

A tsunami is a series of ocean waves that can be generated by a number of events, both natural and man-made, the most common causes being earthquakes and underwater landslides. These waves are very different from wind-generated ocean waves.

Earthquakes

Although not all earthquakes generate tsunamis, those that are large (with a magnitude of at least 7.5 on the Richter scale) and shallow (<30 km depth in the earth) with an epicentre near or on the ocean floor can potentially cause very destructive tsunamis. These mostly occur along tectonic plate boundaries where sudden movement of large areas (from a few km to over 1,000 km) of the ocean floor can generate tsunami waves. The source of the tsunami is usually where the earthquake rupture breaks the ocean floor; this is not necessarily the earthquake's epicentre. The Great 1960 Chilean tsunami was produced by a magnitude 9.5 earthquake that had a rupture zone of over 1,000 km. Its waves spread destruction from Chile to Hawaii and Japan.

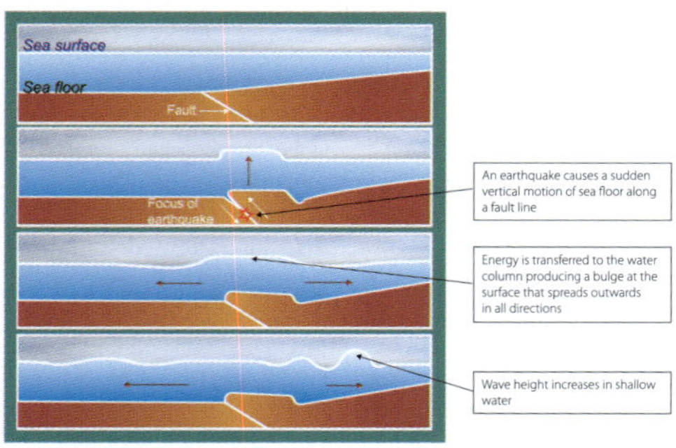

Figure 50.1 - Generation of tsunami waves by earthquake

Figure 50.2 - A fishing boat carried ashore by the tsunami wave caused by the earthquake on 27th March 1964 in the Gulf of Alaska

Volcanic Eruptions

Tsunamis generated by volcanic activity are relatively uncommon, but have been known to have destructive waves. They are caused by water suddenly being displaced by a volcanic slope failure or, more likely, an explosion caused by the magma coming into contact with cold ocean water. These tsunamis are localised to the area around the volcano. One of the largest and most destructive tsunamis recorded was caused by the collapse of the volcano Krakatoa in Indonesia in 1883. The explosion created waves reaching 41 m (135 ft), devastating coastal towns and causing around 36,417 fatalities.

Landslides

Tsunamis generated by icefalls, rock falls and underwater landslides can occur following an earthquake. Generally, energy from tsunami waves caused by landslides tends to be localised, dissipates rapidly and causes less damage than that caused by the uplift of large areas of the ocean floor during an earthquake. The largest tsunami ever seen was caused by an earthquake-triggered rock fall at the head of Lituya Bay Alaska in July 1958. The resulting wave reached 520 m (1,720 ft) but dissipated rapidly when it reached the open ocean.

Human Activities

Tsunamis can be generated by human activities that cause landslides or underwater disturbances. For example, in the 1980s, an airport runway being constructed in southern France caused an underwater landslide leading to localised tsunami waves in Thebes harbour.

Characteristics of a Tsunami

	Wind-Generated Waves	Tsunami Waves
Wave length (crest to crest) in deep water	<100 m (300 ft)	>200 km (125 mi)
Wave period	30 seconds or less	Several minutes to one hour
Height in deep water	2 m (6.6 ft)	1 m (3.3 ft)
Speed	<100 km/hr (62 mph)	>800 km/hr (500 mph)

Table 50.1 - Comparison of the characteristics of wind-generated waves and tsunamis

Tsunamis are very different when compared to wind-generated waves. They have longer wave lengths and travel at far greater speeds. Tsunami waves often have a height of about 1 m in deep water, and generally they are unnoticed by ships unless it is a particularly calm day.

Figure 50.3 - A strong tsunami wave surge of turbulent water

On approaching a coastline, the tsunami wave is compressed in the shallower waters and its speed reduces to below 80 km/hr (50 mph). The first part of the tsunami wave to reach the coast is the long trough. The sea will look as though it is retreating very rapidly from the shore; this is a critical natural warning sign.

When a tsunami wave is compressed by shallow water, the huge wavelength creates problems, and the wave height can reach 30 m (100 ft) or more. It should be noted that most tsunamis do not have very high breaking waves but hit the shore as a very powerful surge of water. The state of the tide also affects how much damage a tsunami wave will do, and more damage will occur during high tide.

A tsunami is a series of waves and the pattern becomes more complicated as the waves reach the shore, with reflected and scattered wave energy producing many hits by tsunami waves at a particular point on the coast. The first tsunami wave is often not the largest and these waves can still be dangerous many hours after the initial hit.

Figure 50.4 - Countries affected by the Indian Ocean Earthquake, 2004

In December 2004, a magnitude 9.0 earthquake with an epicentre off the west coast of Sumatra triggered a devastating series of tsunamis along the coasts of most land masses bordering the Indian Ocean. The death toll exceeded 220,000, with survivors being picked up in various parts of the Indian Ocean clinging to flotsam weeks after the event.

Courtesy of US Dept of Defense

Figure 50.5 - Tsunami damage to Ofunato, Japan, 15th March 2011

On 11th March 2011, a tsunami 72 km off Japan's north east coastline resulted in a death toll exceeding 10,000 and extensive damage to ports and infrastructure.

Tsunamis

Forecasting Tsunamis

It is impossible to predict when a tsunami will occur. However, when a tsunamigenic earthquake is detected, an integrated approach of real time measurements and mathematical modelling can provide reliable estimates of the:

- Tsunami amplitude
- flow velocity
- arrival time off shore and at the coast
- inundation area.

Tsunami Warning Centres (TWC) are internationally coordinated early warning centres that provide information to the emergency services and the public when appropriate. Local and global real time seismological measurements are assessed to detect earthquakes that could generate tsunamis. They are not able to detect tsunamis that are generated by landslides and volcanoes.

Figure 50.6 - Geophysicists working at the Pacific Tsunami Warning Centre

Waterspouts

Waterspouts are of two types; 'fair weather' and 'tornadic'.

Figure 50.7 - Fair weather waterspout

Fair weather (non-tornadic) waterspouts generally form along the base of cumuliform clouds in light winds and tend to be almost stationary. They develop on the surface of the water and work upward, with wind speeds only around 30 ms^{-1}. They are not normally persistent (lasting less than 20 minutes) and dissipate quickly when moving overland. The visible spout is comprised of water droplets formed by condensation, rather than water lifted from the surface.

Tornadic waterspouts are less frequent and are associated with thunderstorms. They can form either over water or land, moving onto the sea. They retain similar characteristics to land tornados and may be accompanied by high seas, strong winds and lightning. They are formed in the clouds and develop downward.

Courtesy of NOAA, USA

Figure 50.8 - Tornadic waterspouts can form over land before moving over water

Waterspouts are found in many areas of the world and are considered a hazard to shipping due to the damage they can cause. Meteorological warnings should be monitored in areas that are prone to tornadic waterspouts.

Deep Sea Bioluminescence

Some marine organisms, including fish and invertebrates, have developed the ability to emit light using chemicals within their bodies. It most commonly appears as a blue-green colour and is called bioluminescence.

The reaction is created in special organs called photopores and typically uses two chemicals; a luciferin, which creates the light, and a luciferase, which acts as the catalyst. Where oxygen is present they will react, creating light and oxyluciferen (an inert substance).

Some organisms emit light continuously while others produce it at specific times. The light is used by the organisms for various reasons, eg communication, warnings, luring prey and attracting mates.

Figure 50.9 - Bioluminescent dinoflagellates (Lingulodinium polyedrum) lighting a breaking wave at night

Bioluminescence can be expected in most parts of the ocean at almost any time, but it is most commonly observed when the bow wave and the wake of a ship disturb (mechanical excitation) single cell organisms and dinoflagellates, such as algae. It can also be caused by the movement of fish or whales through the water.

Figure 50.10 - Bioluminescent jelly fish

In the Indian Ocean, bioluminescent bacteria can occasionally produce stunning areas of soft glowing seas that last for several hours. This is sometimes referred to as *milky seas*.

Mainly in the Indian Ocean, Persian Gulf and the South China Sea, bioluminescence can produce large circles and spiral effects, known as 'marine phosphorescent wheels' or 'oceanic light wheels'.

There are differing thoughts on the cause. One theory is that underwater seismic activity can cause sufficient disruption to create rising luminous balls of light. The apparent circular or spiral patterns associated with the wheels may be created by perspective distortion due to the lens effect of waves. Other theories suggest the patterns may be the result of local geomagnetic fields or disturbances caused by the vibration of the ship.

The Red Tide

The 'red tide' is a common name for large concentrations of aquatic microorganisms, referred to as algal blooms. In high concentrations, they can discolour large areas of water.

The algal blooms are not always red, but can vary in colour and are not always associated with tidal changes.

Some blooms are considered as harmful algal blooms, as they may be caused by oxygen depletion or natural toxins in the water. These may be associated with mass mortalities of marine and coastal species of fish and animals. Connections have been suggested between the El Nino climatological effects, which are

believed to have led to red tides in areas as far afield as Hong Kong.

Green Flash

Figure 50.11 - Green Flash at Sunset

A green flash, which may be seen at sunrise or sunset, appears to turn the very top part of the sun green. The flash generally only lasts one to two seconds, although it can last longer at higher latitudes. It is caused by refraction of light.

As light travels from the sun when it is just visible on the horizon, the atmosphere acts like a prism, separating the light into parts of the visible electromagnetic spectrum.

Rays of light nearest the surface are refracted the least through the densest atmosphere and are separated from red, through orange to yellow. The light furthest from the surface is refracted more and appears as violet, blue and green. Due to the violet and blue rays being scattered more widely, it is the green light that is most prevalent and appears as the flash.

The flash is normally seen with some form of magnification, but varying climatic effects involving significantly differing surface and air temperatures can create complex refraction, resulting in a more visible green flash.

Superior Mirage

A superior mirage is the apparent increase in the size of objects caused by refraction of light through the atmosphere. This includes the increased apparent size of the sun, moon, stars and planets created by light rays bending (refracting) as they enter the atmosphere. The lower the altitude of the celestial object, the greater the effect.

Atmospheric density (which is directly affected by temperature) and the variation between layers at different heights, greatly affects the extent of refraction.

The superior mirage effect on terrestrial objects is caused by a temperature inversion in the atmosphere, ie a warmer air mass above a relatively cooler air mass. This bends the rays of light downward, giving the appearance of increased height.

This is a common effect in areas with comparatively cool surface temperatures, such as in high latitude and polar regions during the summer months.

Figure 50.12 - Diagram of the superior mirage phenomenon

22° Ice Halo

A common phenomenon is the appearance of a halo around the moon (or sun) caused by the refraction of light through the ice crystals that make up cirrus clouds. As the light passes through the crystals, it forms a coloured rainbow-like ring.

The halo forms at approximately 22° around the moon due to the hexagonal formation of ice crystals. The extent of the bending, which occurs as the light enters and then exits the crystals, is dependent on their diameters, ie less than 25 μm (25×10^{-6}m).

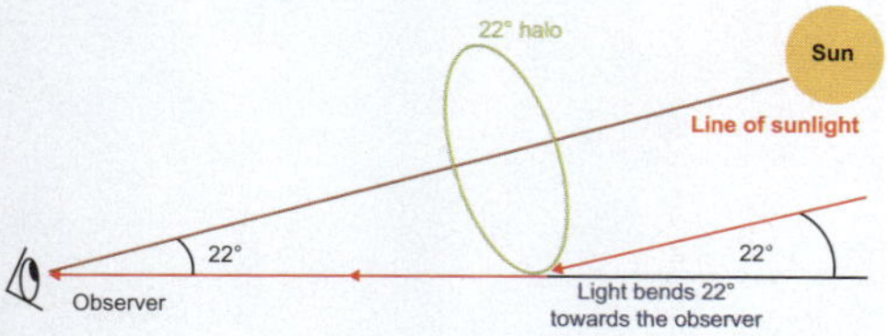

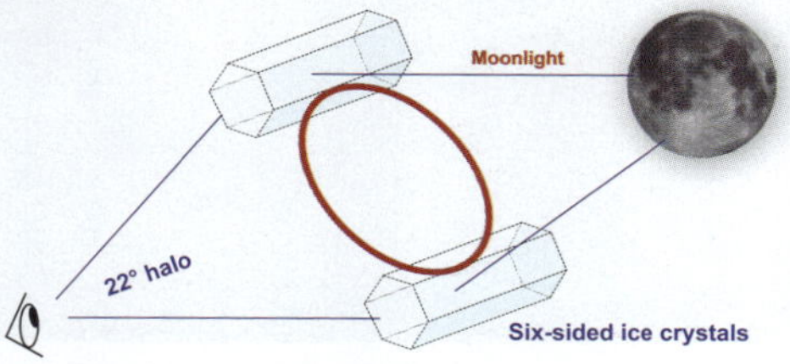

Where the sky has only partial cloud cover, the halo can appear fragmented.

Solar and Lunar Coronas

Figure 50.13 - Solar corona

Solar and lunar coronas resemble halos but are due to diffraction of light around water droplets rather than the refraction of light through ice crystals.

They can be distinguished from halos as they are much smaller, almost fringing the body, and the colour sequence is reversed with red comprising the outermost ring, rather than the inner ring in a halo.

The diameter of the corona is dependent on the size of the water droplets in the atmosphere, and the larger the droplets, the smaller the ring.

Aurora Borealis

The Aurora Borealis (Northern Lights) and the Aurora Australis (Southern Lights) is a spectacular natural phenomenon caused by charged electrons from the sun interacting with the earth's magnetic fields in the polar regions.

These highly charged electrons or solar winds, which stream from the sun and take around 40 hours to reach the earth, follow the magnetic and electrically charged force lines of the magnetosphere.

The colours of the aurora are created when the electrons meet with nitrogen and oxygen atoms. The altitude of the collision and atoms encountered determine the colour of the aurora, ie:

- Nitrogen:
  - Up to 60 miles - blue
  - over 60 miles - violet/purple
- Oxygen:
  - Up to 150 miles - green
  - over 150 miles - red.

The visible movement or dancing is caused by the continuous reaction between the various forces involved. Although normally situated in the Arctic and Antarctic circles, auroras form as ovals around the magnetic poles and can sometimes be seen further south, particularly during peak sunspot activity when solar winds increase.

St Elmo's Fire

St Elmo's Fire is the name given to a brush discharge or corona discharge of electricity from an object to the atmosphere. The phenomenon appears as a glow around metal objects, typically ships' masts. It is caused by a large difference in electrical charge between the object and the air that surrounds it.

During thunderstorms when the air is ionised and becomes a more effective conductor of electricity, the object can build up charge at a rate greater than it is dissipated. When the voltage is sufficiently large, the build-up is discharged to the surrounding air as a glow, which, due to the presence of nitrogen and oxygen in air, is normally blue or violet.

The glowing may last for several minutes and indicates that lightning could strike the object, so observers should keep well clear.

The name St Elmo's Fire is derived from St Elmo, the patron saint of seafarers, as many sailors thought it was a sign of his appearance. It was mainly considered a good sign, as it is generally experienced at the peak of a thunderstorm signifying that weather will start to improve.

Index

Index

Index

Index

Index

Index

Index

Index

Index

Index

Index